B A T M A N

KNIGHTFALL

volume three

KNIGHTSEND

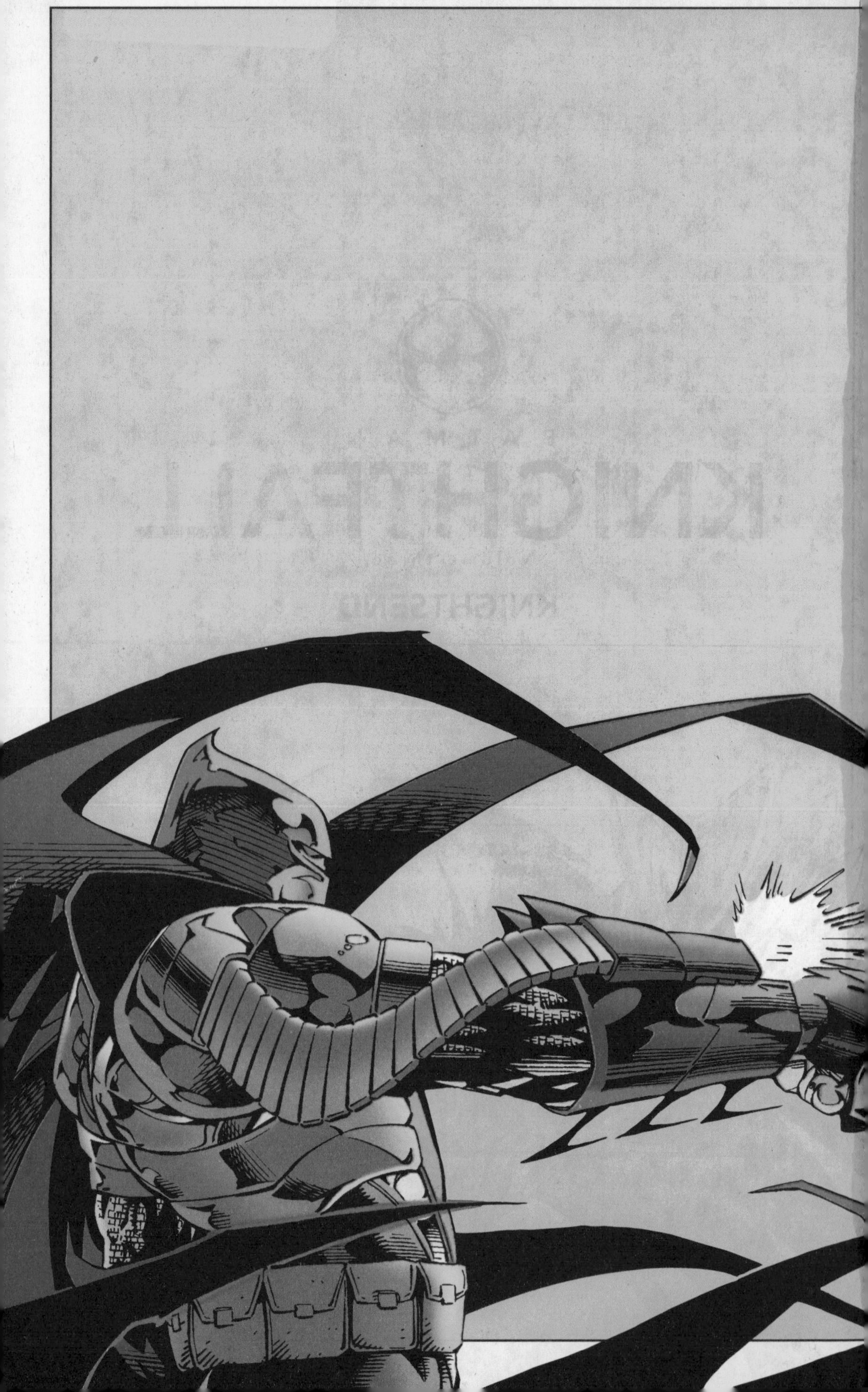

BATMAN

volume three

KNIGHTSEND

DOUG **MOENCH** ALAN **GRANT**
CHUCK **DIXON** JO **DUFFY**
DENNY **O'NEIL**
writers

MIKE **MANLEY** BRET **BLEVINS**
GRAHAM **NOLAN** RON **WAGNER**
TOM **GRUMMETT** JIM **BALENT**
JOE **RUBINSTEIN** BARRY **KITSON**
MIKE **VOSBURG** MIKE **GUSTOVICH**
ROMEO **TANGHAL** LEE **WEEKS**
PHIL **JIMENEZ** MD **BRIGHT**
JOHN **CLEARY**
pencillers

DICK **GIORDANO** BRET **BLEVINS**
BOB **SMITH** SCOTT **HANNA**
RON **McCAIN** RAY **KRYSSING**
RICK **BURCHETT** MIKE **MANLEY**
JOE **RUBINSTEIN** MIKE **GUSTOVICH**
ROMEO **TANGHAL** JOHN **STOKES**
KLAUS **JANSON** PHIL **JIMENEZ**
inkers

ADRIENNE **ROY** DIGITAL **CHAMELEON**
BUZZ **SETZER** DAVID **HORNUNG**
colorists

KEN **BRUZENAK** TODD **KLEIN**
JOHN **COSTANZA** WILLIE **SCHUBERT**
ALBERT **DE GUZMAN** BOB **PINAHA**
letterers

KELLEY **JONES** WITH ALLEN **PASSALAQUA**
collection cover artists

Batman created by
BOB **KANE** with **BILL FINGER**

Denny O'Neil Scott Peterson Archie Goodwin Jim Spivey Neal Pozner Editors – Original Series
Jim Spivey Associate Editor – Original Series
Jordan Gorfinkel Darren Vincenzo Chuck Kim Assistant Editors – Original Series
Jeb Woodard Group Editor – Collected Editions
Rowena Yow Editor – Collected Edition
Steve Cook Design Director – Books
Robbie Biederman Publication Design

Bob Harras Senior VP – Editor-in-Chief, DC Comics

Diane Nelson President
Dan DiDio and Jim Lee Co-Publishers
Geoff Johns Chief Creative Officer
Amit Desai Senior VP – Marketing & Global Franchise Management
Nairi Gardiner Senior VP – Finance
Sam Ades VP – Digital Marketing
Bobbie Chase VP – Talent Development
Mark Chiarello Senior VP – Art, Design & Collected Editions
John Cunningham VP – Content Strategy
Anne DePies VP – Strategy Planning & Reporting
Don Falletti VP – Manufacturing Operations
Lawrence Ganem VP – Editorial Administration & Talent Relations
Alison Gill Senior VP – Manufacturing & Operations
Hank Kanalz Senior VP – Editorial Strategy & Administration
Jay Kogan VP – Legal Affairs
Derek Maddalena Senior VP – Sales & Business Development
Jack Mahan VP – Business Affairs
Dan Miron VP – Sales Planning & Trade Development
Nick Napolitano VP – Manufacturing Administration
Carol Roeder VP – Marketing
Eddie Scannell VP – Mass Account & Digital Sales
Courtney Simmons Senior VP – Publicity & Communications
Jim (Ski) Sokolowski VP – Comic Book Specialty & Newsstand Sales
Sandy Yi Senior VP – Global Franchise Management

BATMAN: KNIGHTFALL VOLUME 3
KNIGHTSEND

DC Comics, 2900 W. Alameda Avenue, Burbank, CA 91505
Printed by Transcontinental Interglobe Beauceville, Canada. 3/25/16. Fifth Printing.
ISBN: 978-1-4012-3721-9

Library of Congress Cataloging-in-Publication Data

Batman : Knightfall volume 3 : Knightsend.
    p. cm.
"Originally published in single magazine form in BATMAN 509, 510, 512-514, BATMAN: SHADOW OF
THE BAT 29, 30, 32-34, DETECTIVE COMICS 676, 677, 679-681, BATMAN: LEGENDS OF THE DARK
KNIGHT 62, 63, ROBIN 8, 9, 11-13, CATWOMAN 12, 13."
  ISBN 978-1-4012-3721-9 (alk. paper)
1. Graphic novels. I. Title: Knightfall. Volume 3. II. Title: Knightsend.
PN6728.B36B4169 2012
741.5'0973—dc23
                              2012019507

PEFC Certified
Printed on paper from
sustainably managed
forests and controlled
sources
PEFC/01-31-106   www.pefc.org

THE STORY SO FAR...

Batman has lost his once mighty grip on Gotham thanks to a seemingly never-ending slew of menacing villains. Pushed to the physical and mental limit, he is finally defeated by Bane in an epic showdown and he retreats to heal. Worried for the state of Gotham, Batman appoints Jean Paul Valley (aka Azrael) to temporarily take his place.

Lacking Bruce Wayne's sense of integrity and infused with a violent, vengeful spirit, Azrael swiftly gets out of hand, alienating both Robin and Commissioner Gordon in the process. He seals off the Batcave from Wayne Manor and grows increasingly disturbed and turbulent. Against Bruce's orders, he defeats Bane, wearing enhanced armor he designed. He allows the crazed mass murderer Abattoir and his hostages to fall to their deaths, and feels no remorse.

At first, Bruce is impressed with Azrael's results, but when a beleaguered Robin tells Wayne of Abattoir's death, he resolves to reclaim the Batman mantle.

Cover art by KELLEY JONES and JOHN BEATTY

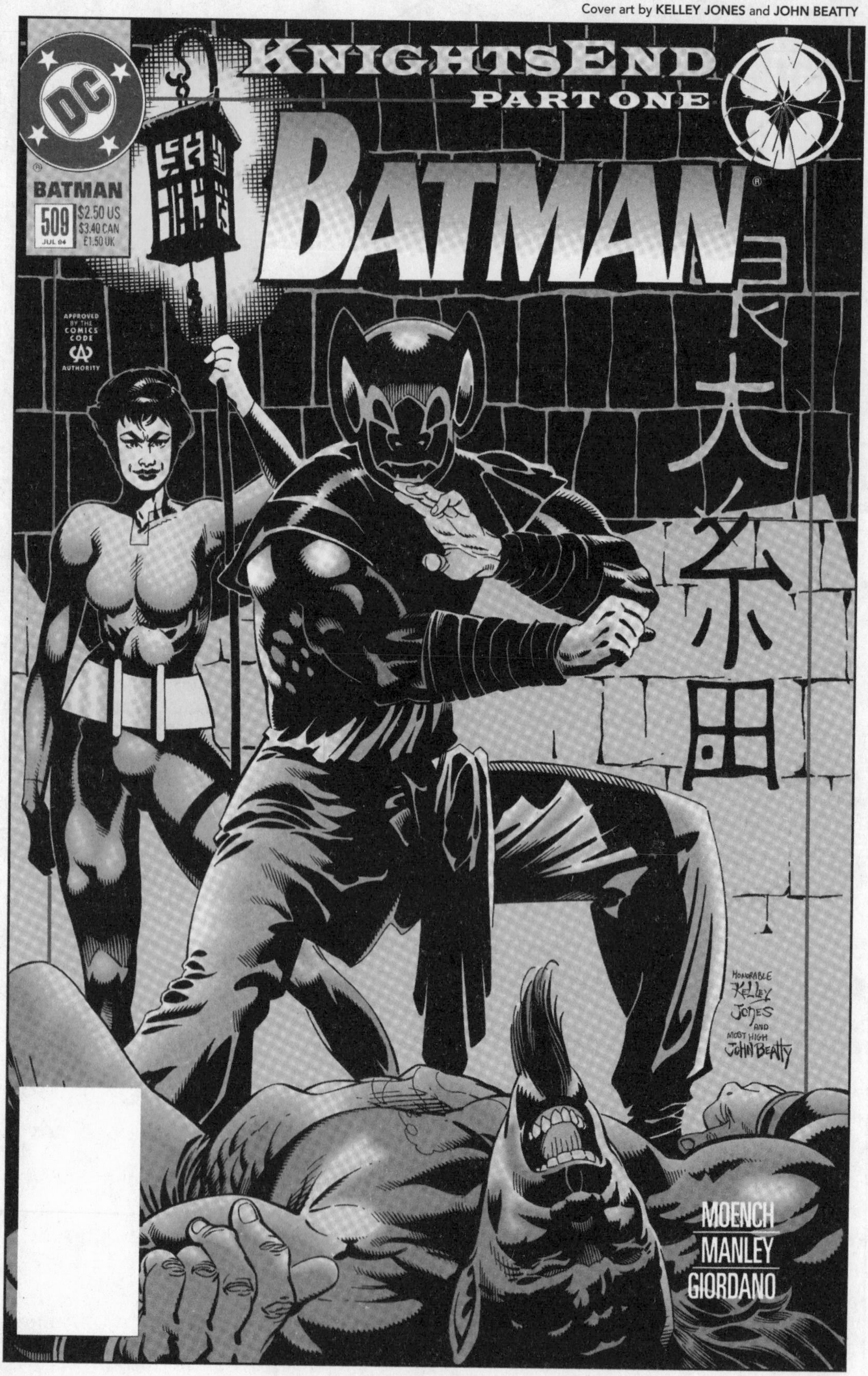
KNIGHTSEND
PART ONE
BATMAN
BATMAN
509
$2.50 US
$3.40 CAN
£1.50 UK
JUL 94
APPROVED BY THE COMICS CODE AUTHORITY
HONORABLE KELLEY JONES AND MOST HIGH JOHN BEATTY
MOENCH
MANLEY
GIORDANO

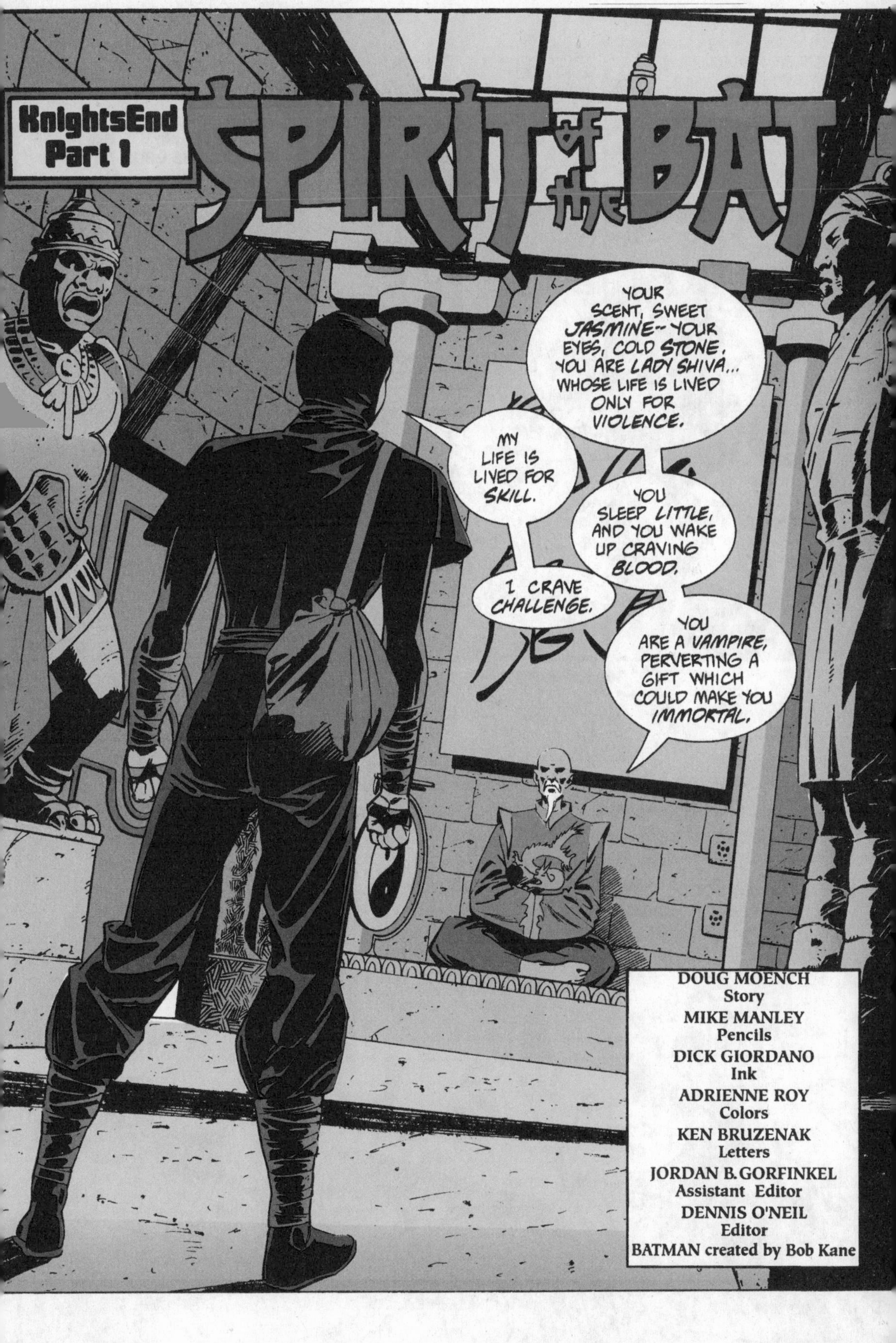

KnightsEnd Part 1
SPIRIT of the BAT
YOUR SCENT, SWEET JASMINE-- YOUR EYES, COLD STONE. YOU ARE LADY SHIVA... WHOSE LIFE IS LIVED ONLY FOR VIOLENCE.
MY LIFE IS LIVED FOR SKILL.
YOU SLEEP LITTLE, AND YOU WAKE UP CRAVING BLOOD.
I CRAVE CHALLENGE.
YOU ARE A VAMPIRE, PERVERTING A GIFT WHICH COULD MAKE YOU IMMORTAL.
DOUG MOENCH Story
MIKE MANLEY Pencils
DICK GIORDANO Ink
ADRIENNE ROY Colors
KEN BRUZENAK Letters
JORDAN B. GORFINKEL Assistant Editor
DENNIS O'NEIL Editor
BATMAN created by Bob Kane

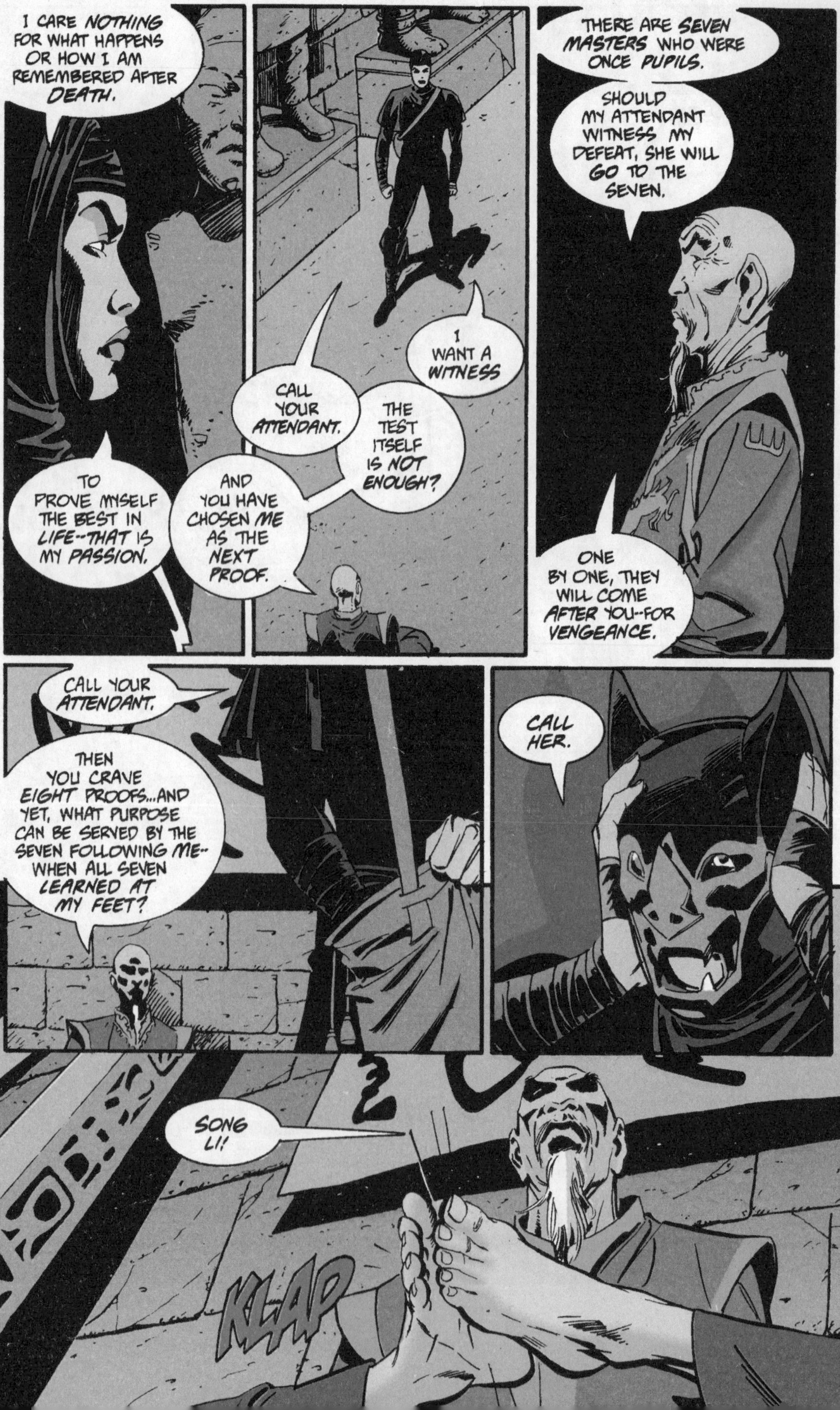
I CARE NOTHING FOR WHAT HAPPENS OR HOW I AM REMEMBERED AFTER DEATH.
TO PROVE MYSELF THE BEST IN LIFE--THAT IS MY PASSION.
I WANT A WITNESS
CALL YOUR ATTENDANT.
THE TEST ITSELF IS NOT ENOUGH?
AND YOU HAVE CHOSEN ME AS THE NEXT PROOF.
THERE ARE SEVEN MASTERS WHO WERE ONCE PUPILS.
SHOULD MY ATTENDANT WITNESS MY DEFEAT, SHE WILL GO TO THE SEVEN.
ONE BY ONE, THEY WILL COME AFTER YOU--FOR VENGEANCE.
CALL YOUR ATTENDANT.
THEN YOU CRAVE EIGHT PROOFS...AND YET, WHAT PURPOSE CAN BE SERVED BY THE SEVEN FOLLOWING ME-- WHEN ALL SEVEN LEARNED AT MY FEET?
CALL HER.
SONG LI!
KLAP

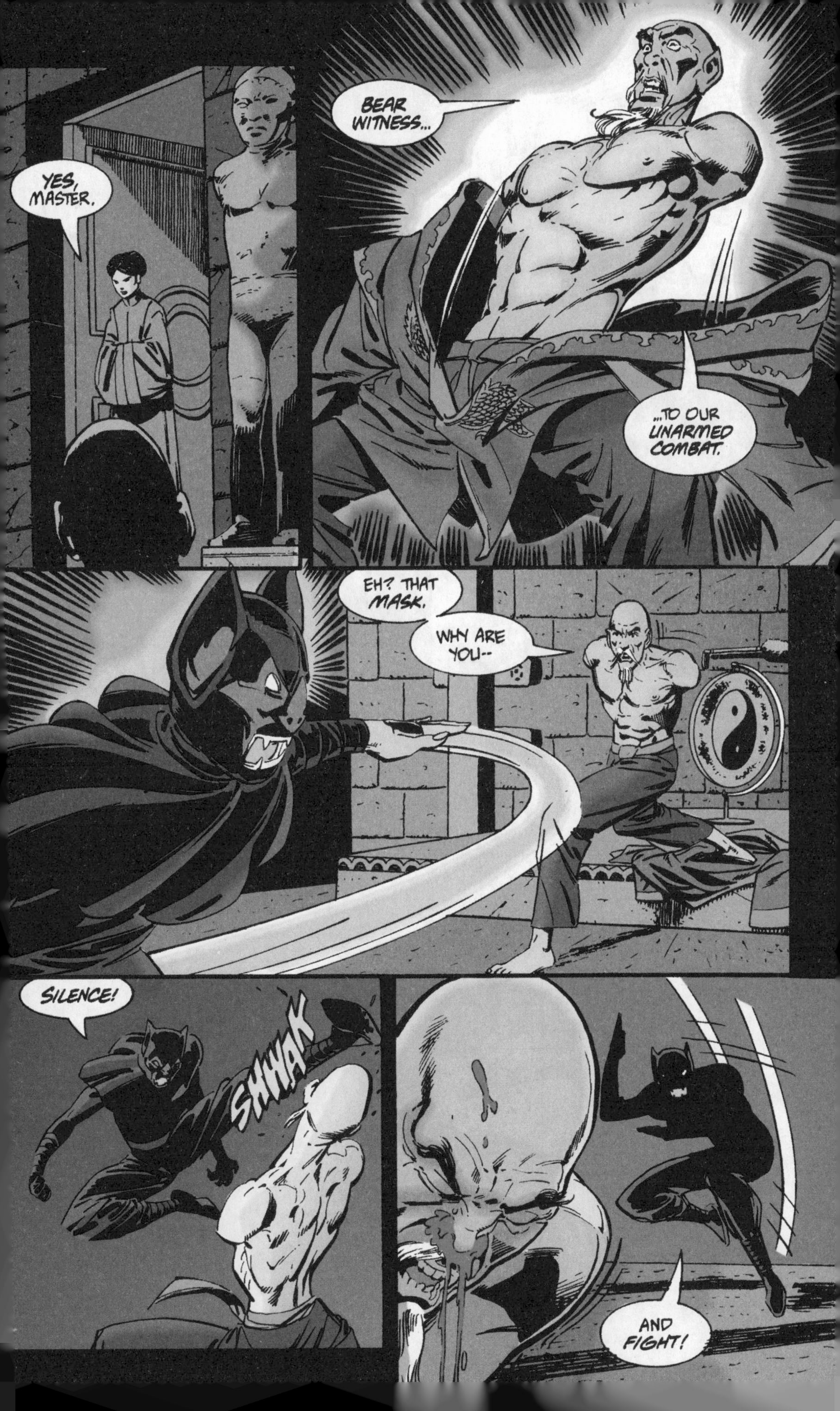
YES, MASTER.
BEAR WITNESS...
...TO OUR UNARMED COMBAT.
EH? THAT MASK.
WHY ARE YOU--
SILENCE!
SHHAK
AND FIGHT!

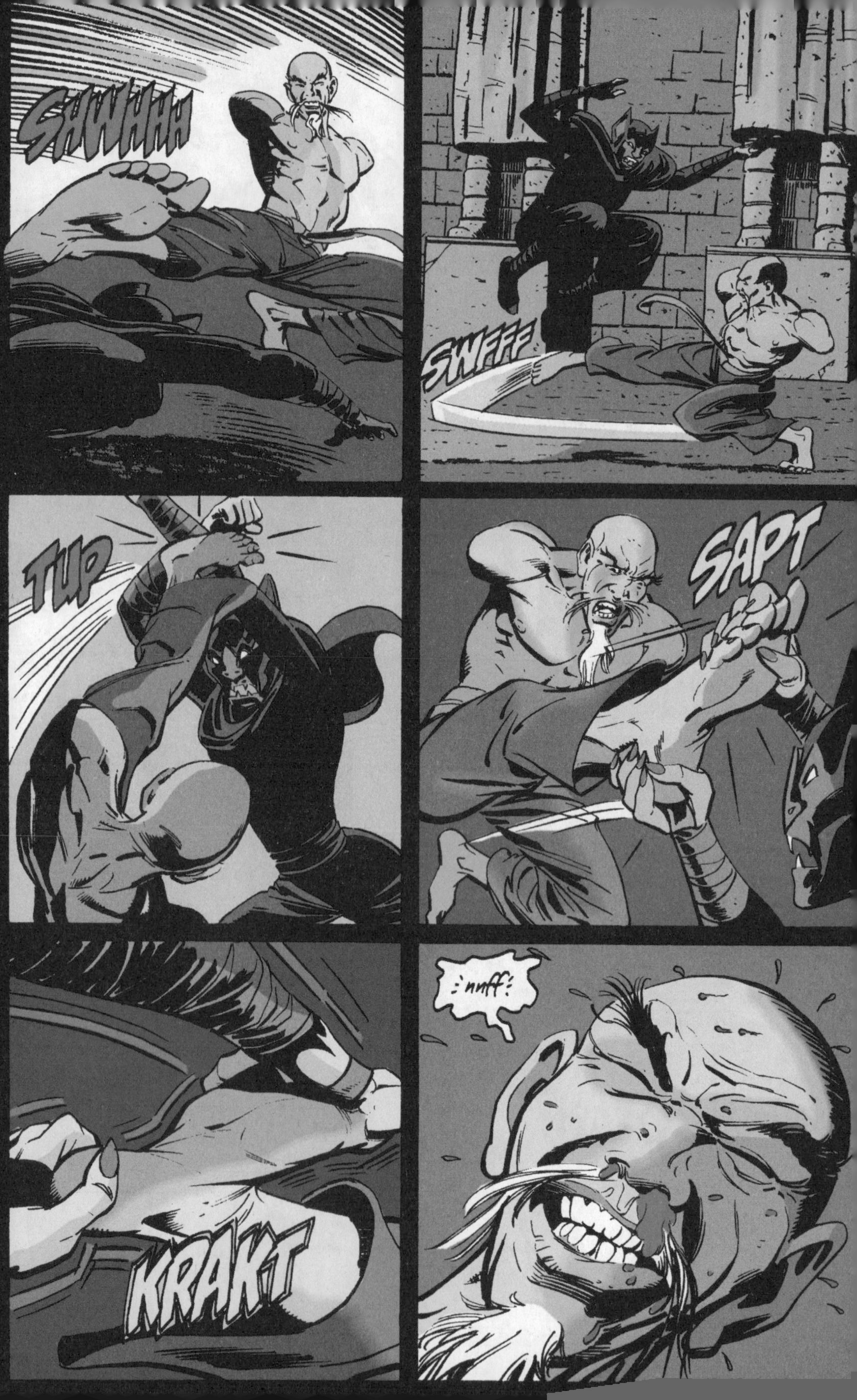
SHWHHH
SWFFF
TUP
SAPT
KRAKT
nnff

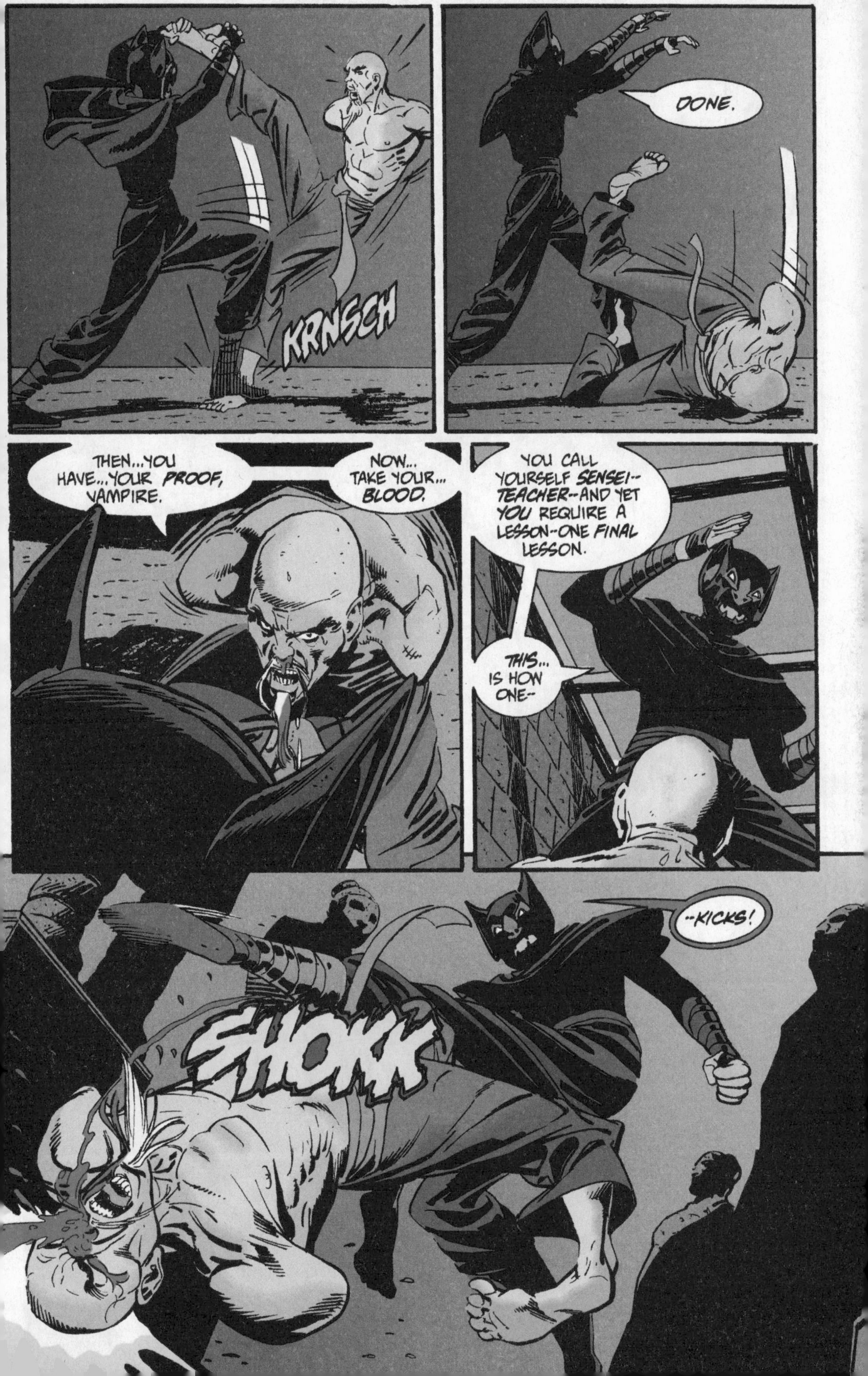
KRNSCH
DONE.
THEN...YOU HAVE...YOUR PROOF, VAMPIRE.
NOW... TAKE YOUR... BLOOD.
YOU CALL YOURSELF SENSEI-- TEACHER--AND YET YOU REQUIRE A LESSON--ONE FINAL LESSON.
THIS... IS HOW ONE--
--KICKS!
SHOKK

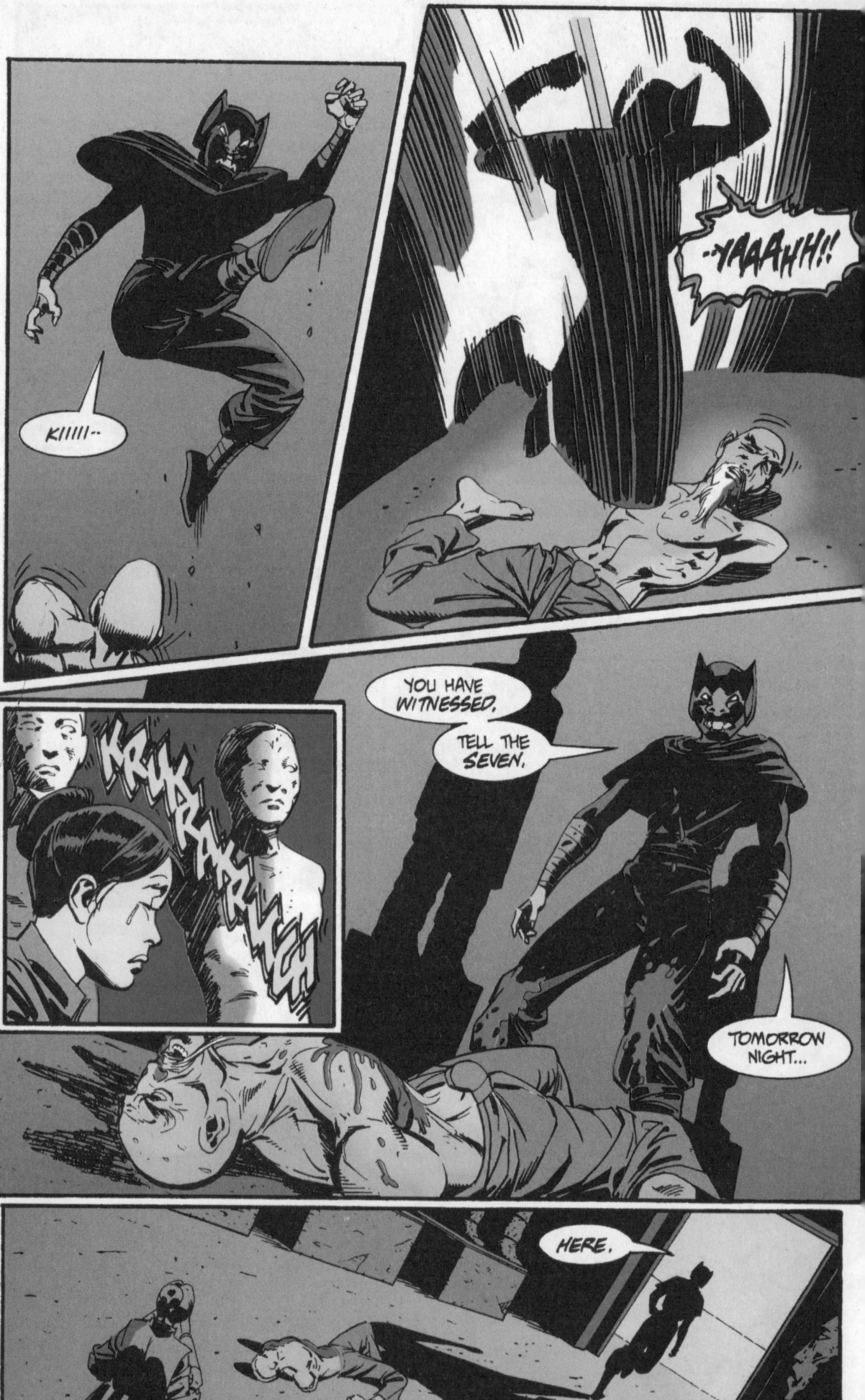
KIIIII--
--YAAAHH!!
KRUKRAKRUCH
YOU HAVE WITNESSED.
TELL THE SEVEN.
TOMORROW NIGHT...
HERE.

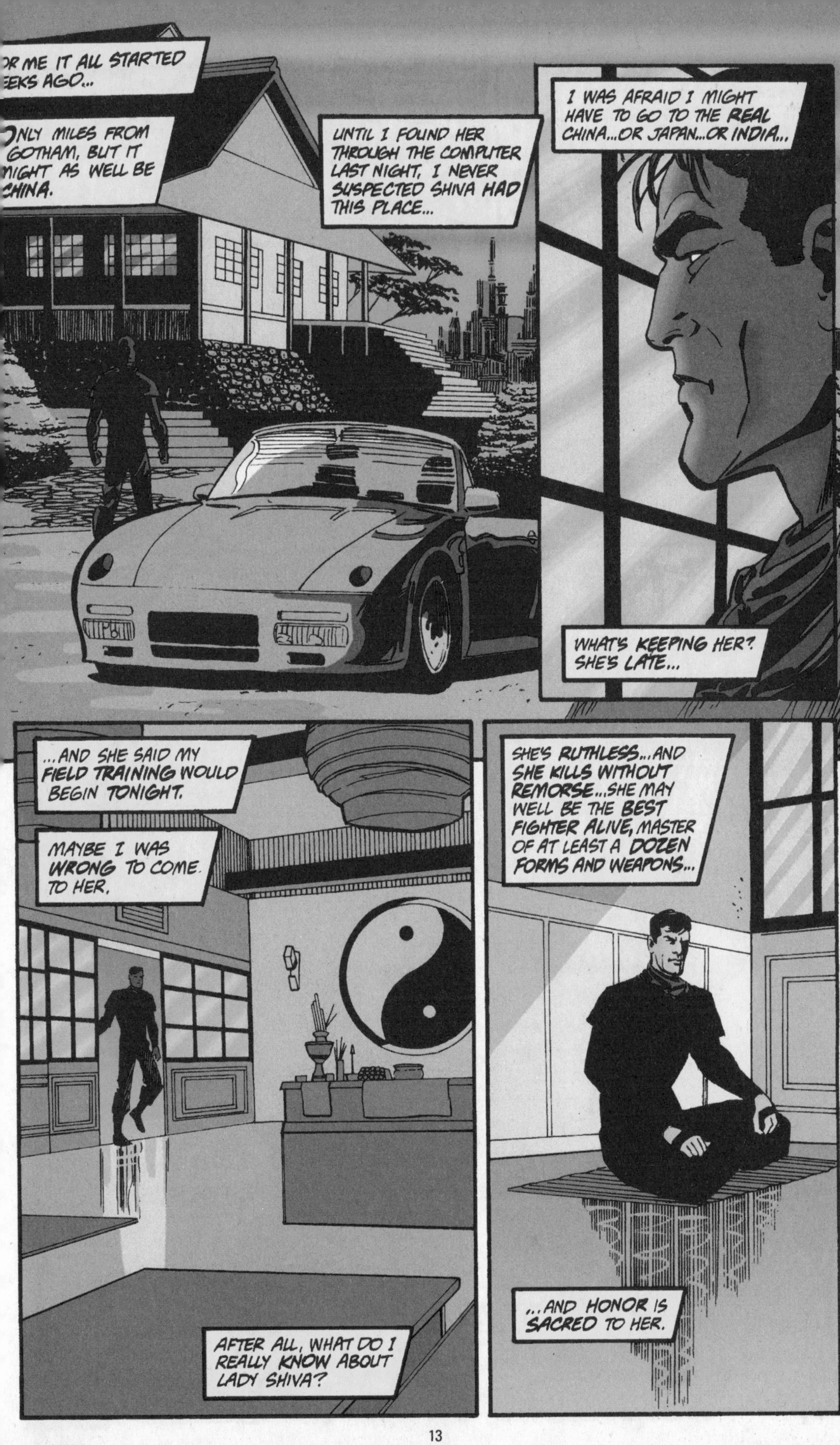
...OR ME IT ALL STARTED
...EEKS AGO...
ONLY MILES FROM GOTHAM, BUT IT MIGHT AS WELL BE CHINA.
UNTIL I FOUND HER THROUGH THE COMPUTER LAST NIGHT, I NEVER SUSPECTED SHIVA HAD THIS PLACE...
I WAS AFRAID I MIGHT HAVE TO GO TO THE REAL CHINA...OR JAPAN...OR INDIA...
WHAT'S KEEPING HER? SHE'S LATE...
...AND SHE SAID MY FIELD TRAINING WOULD BEGIN TONIGHT.
MAYBE I WAS WRONG TO COME TO HER.
AFTER ALL, WHAT DO I REALLY KNOW ABOUT LADY SHIVA?
SHE'S RUTHLESS...AND SHE KILLS WITHOUT REMORSE...SHE MAY WELL BE THE BEST FIGHTER ALIVE, MASTER OF AT LEAST A DOZEN FORMS AND WEAPONS...
...AND HONOR IS SACRED TO HER.

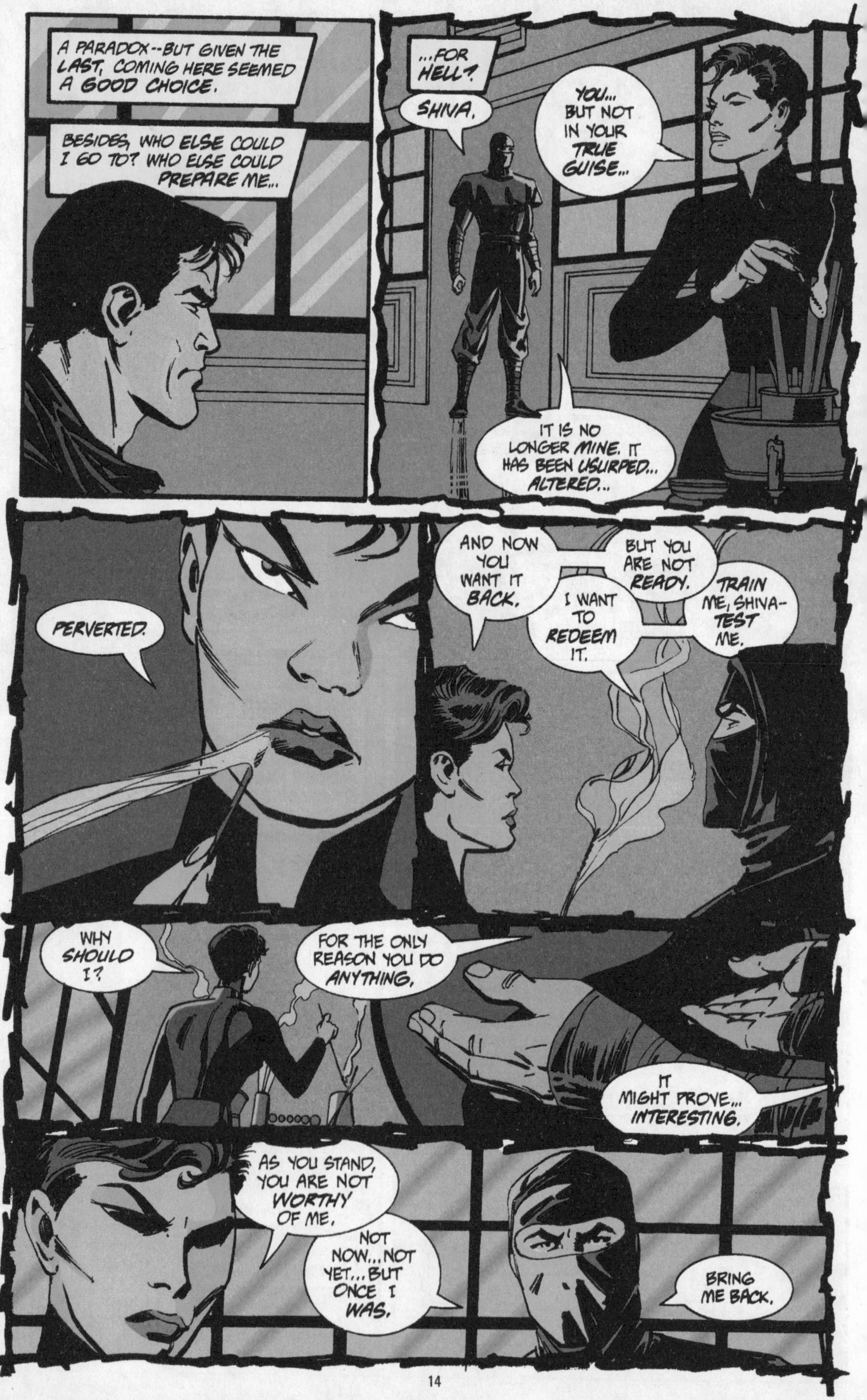
A PARADOX--BUT GIVEN THE LAST, COMING HERE SEEMED A GOOD CHOICE.
BESIDES, WHO ELSE COULD I GO TO? WHO ELSE COULD PREPARE ME...
...FOR HELL?
SHIVA.
YOU... BUT NOT IN YOUR TRUE GUISE...
IT IS NO LONGER MINE. IT HAS BEEN USURPED... ALTERED...
PERVERTED.
AND NOW YOU WANT IT BACK.
BUT YOU ARE NOT READY.
I WANT TO REDEEM IT.
TRAIN ME, SHIVA-TEST ME.
WHY SHOULD I?
FOR THE ONLY REASON YOU DO ANYTHING.
IT MIGHT PROVE... INTERESTING.
AS YOU STAND, YOU ARE NOT WORTHY OF ME.
NOT NOW... NOT YET... BUT ONCE I WAS.
BRING ME BACK.

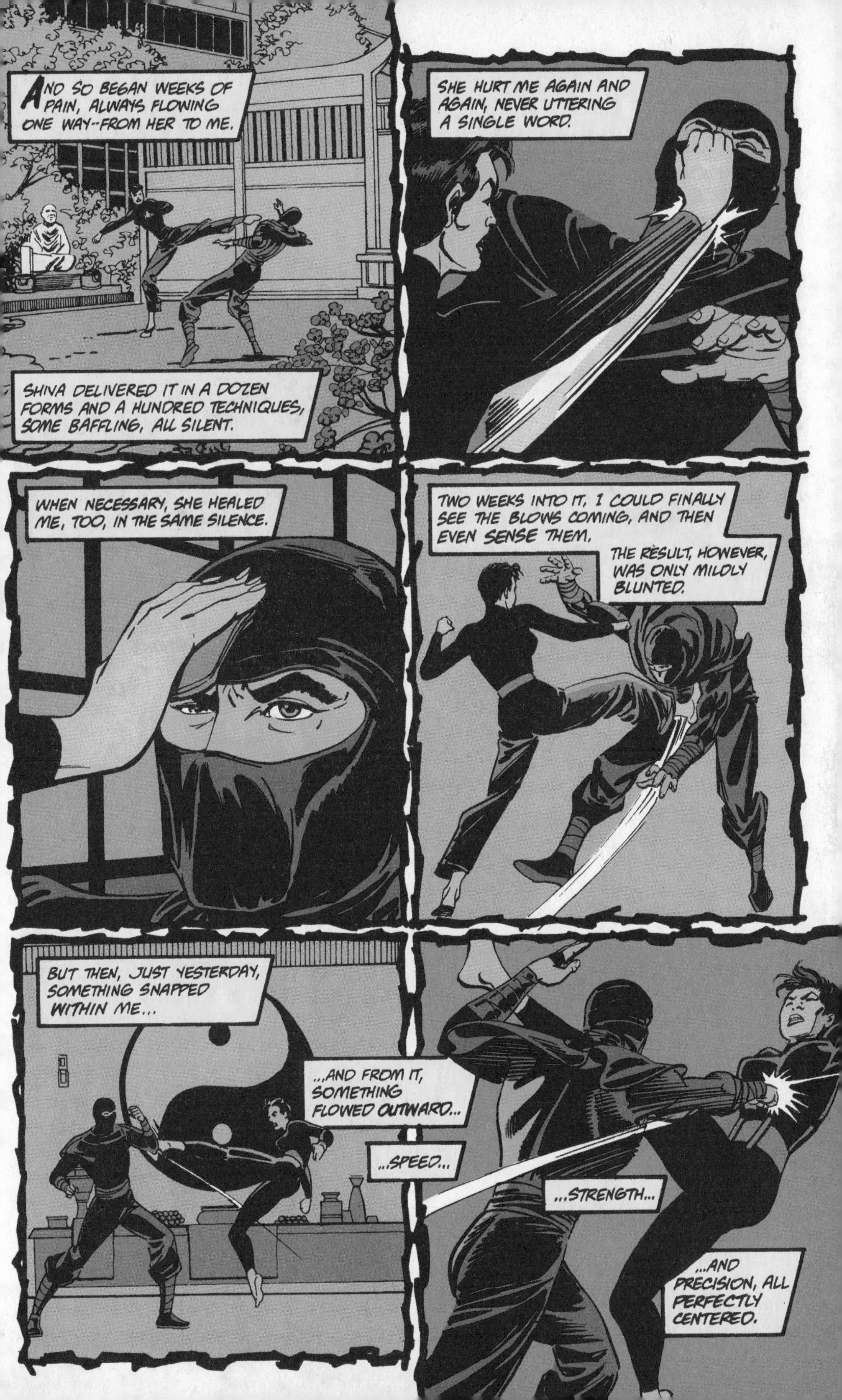
AND SO BEGAN WEEKS OF PAIN, ALWAYS FLOWING ONE WAY--FROM HER TO ME.
SHIVA DELIVERED IT IN A DOZEN FORMS AND A HUNDRED TECHNIQUES, SOME BAFFLING, ALL SILENT.
SHE HURT ME AGAIN AND AGAIN, NEVER UTTERING A SINGLE WORD.
WHEN NECESSARY, SHE HEALED ME, TOO, IN THE SAME SILENCE.
TWO WEEKS INTO IT, I COULD FINALLY SEE THE BLOWS COMING, AND THEN EVEN SENSE THEM.
THE RESULT, HOWEVER, WAS ONLY MILDLY BLUNTED.
BUT THEN, JUST YESTERDAY, SOMETHING SNAPPED WITHIN ME...
...AND FROM IT, SOMETHING FLOWED OUTWARD...
...SPEED...
...STRENGTH...
...AND PRECISION, ALL PERFECTLY CENTERED.

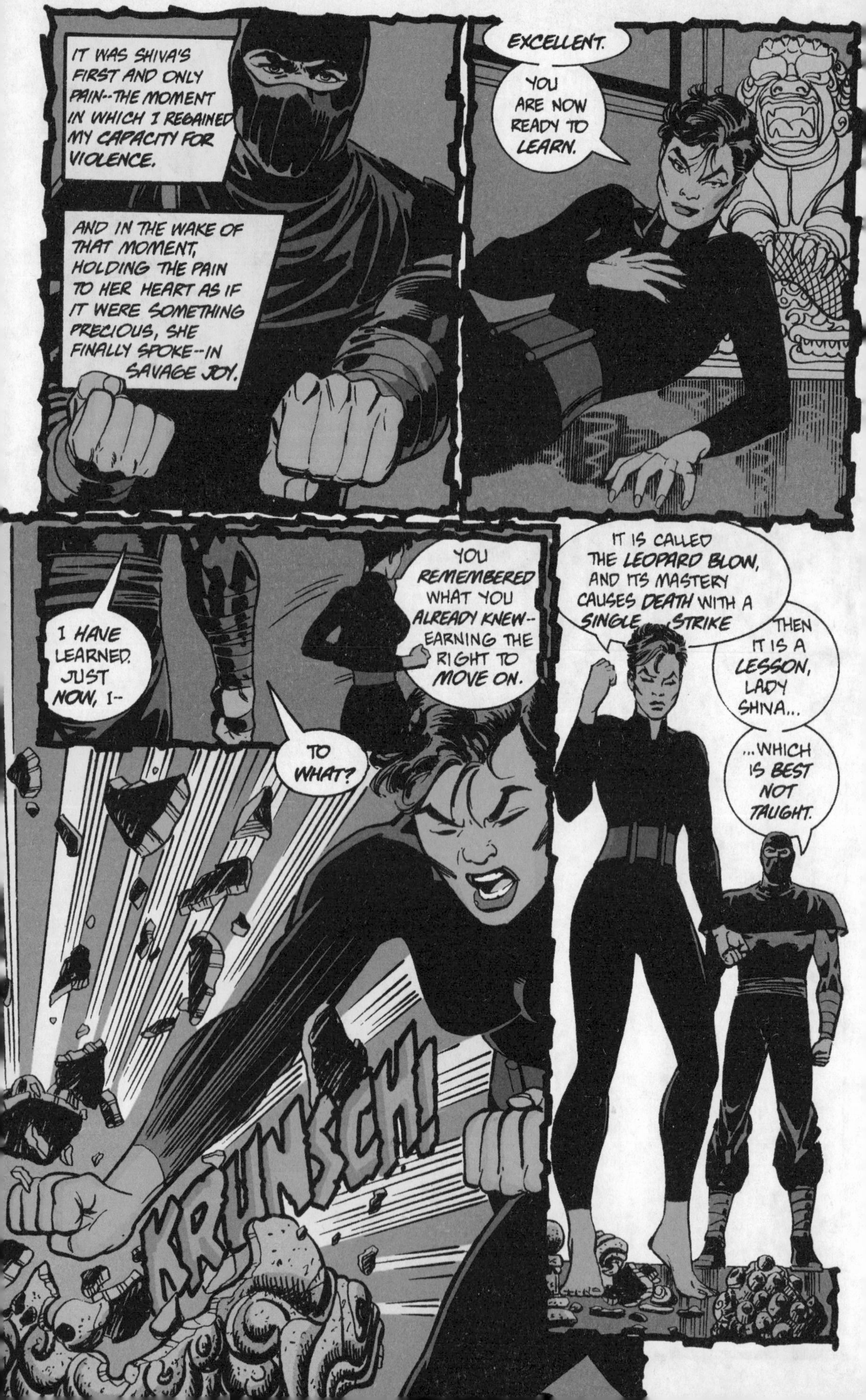
IT WAS SHIVA'S FIRST AND ONLY PAIN--THE MOMENT IN WHICH I REGAINED MY CAPACITY FOR VIOLENCE.
AND IN THE WAKE OF THAT MOMENT, HOLDING THE PAIN TO HER HEART AS IF IT WERE SOMETHING PRECIOUS, SHE FINALLY SPOKE--IN SAVAGE JOY.
EXCELLENT.
YOU ARE NOW READY TO LEARN.
I HAVE LEARNED. JUST NOW, I--
YOU REMEMBERED WHAT YOU ALREADY KNEW--EARNING THE RIGHT TO MOVE ON.
TO WHAT?
KRUNSCH!
IT IS CALLED THE LEOPARD BLOW, AND ITS MASTERY CAUSES DEATH WITH A SINGLE STRIKE
THEN IT IS A LESSON, LADY SHIVA...
...WHICH IS BEST NOT TAUGHT.

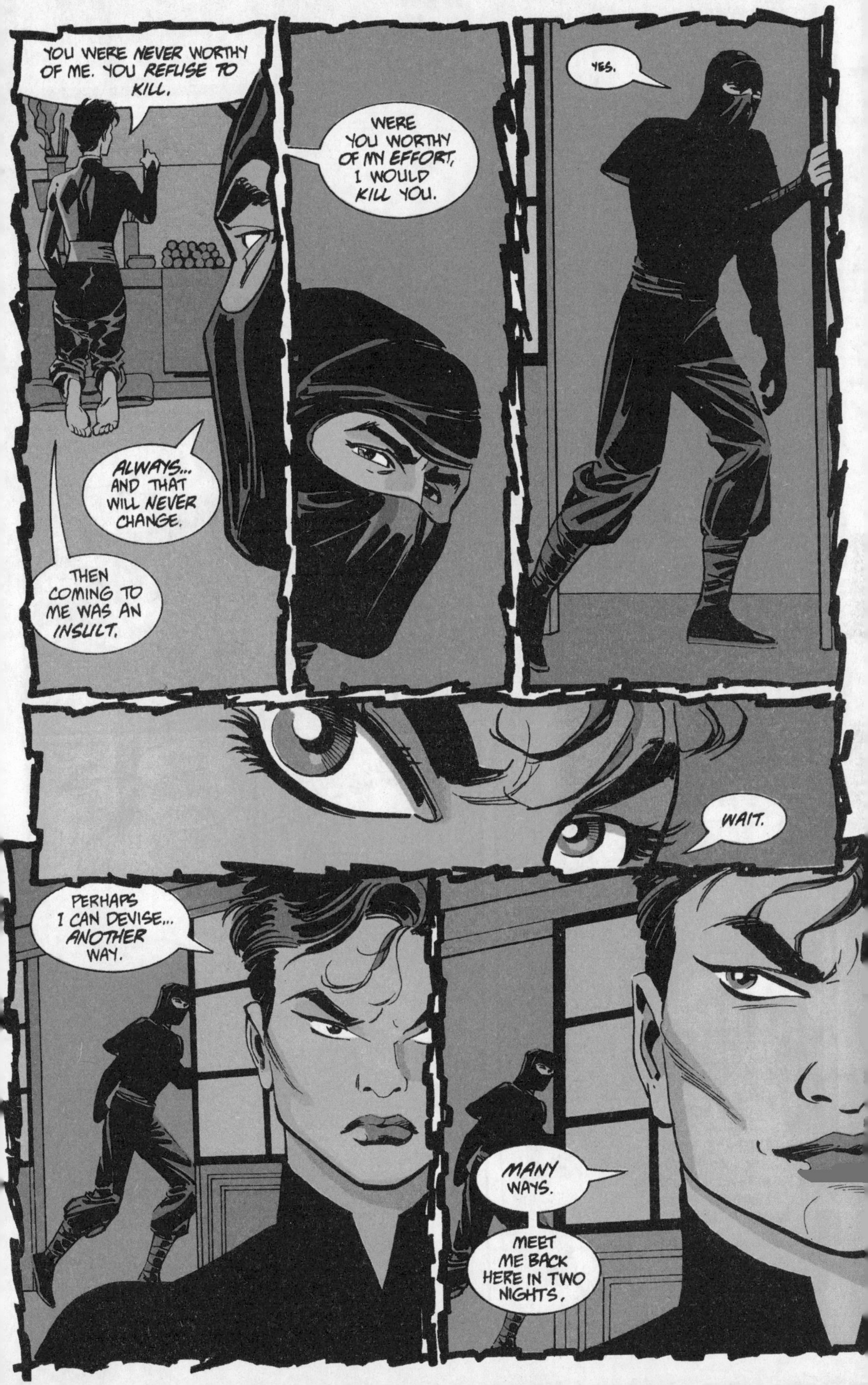
YOU WERE NEVER WORTHY OF ME. YOU REFUSE TO KILL.
WERE YOU WORTHY OF MY EFFORT, I WOULD KILL YOU.
ALWAYS... AND THAT WILL NEVER CHANGE.
THEN COMING TO ME WAS AN INSULT.
YES.
WAIT.
PERHAPS I CAN DEVISE... ANOTHER WAY.
MANY WAYS.
MEET ME BACK HERE IN TWO NIGHTS.

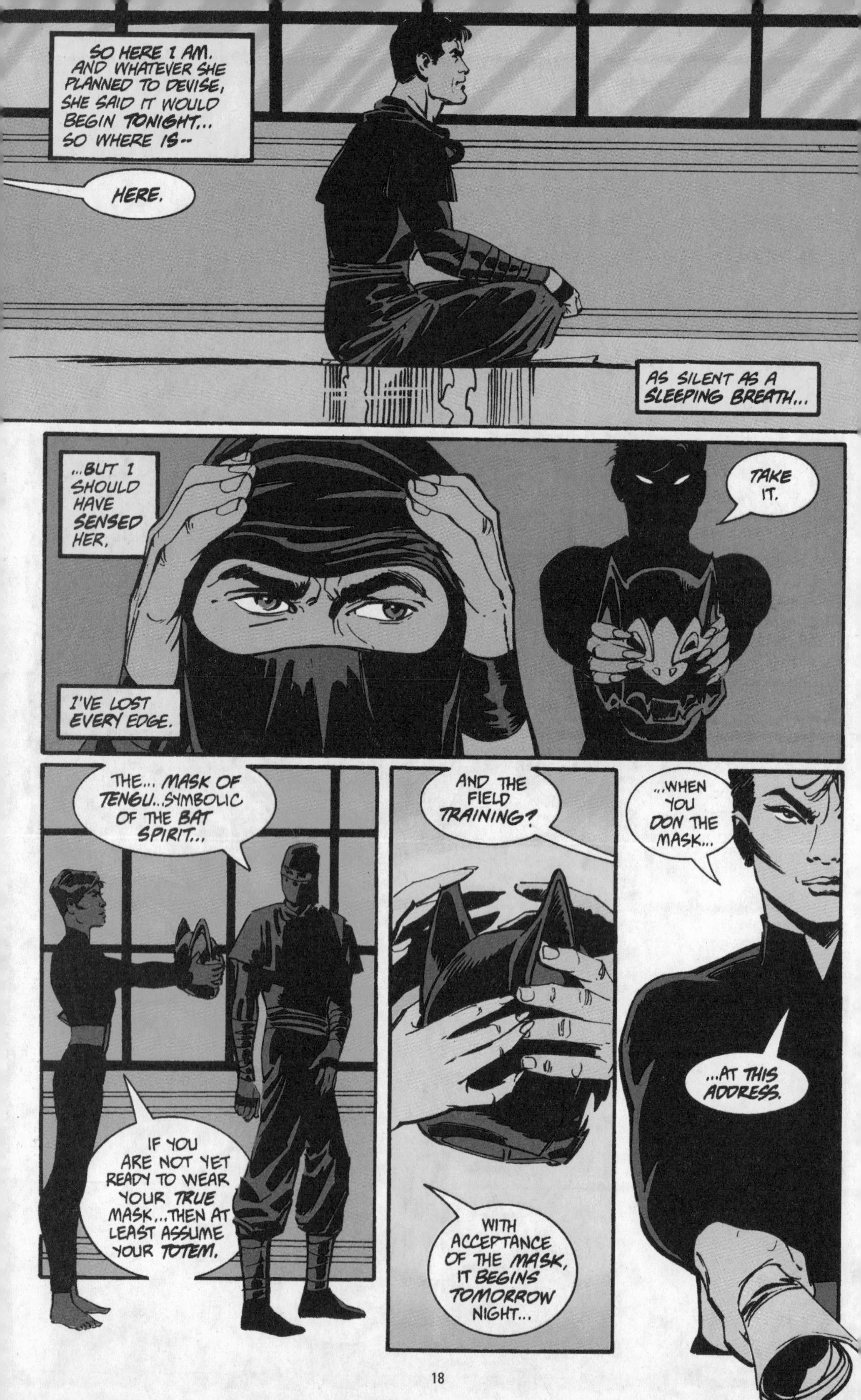
SO HERE I AM. AND WHATEVER SHE PLANNED TO DEVISE, SHE SAID IT WOULD BEGIN TONIGHT... SO WHERE IS--
HERE.
AS SILENT AS A SLEEPING BREATH...
...BUT I SHOULD HAVE SENSED HER.
TAKE IT.
I'VE LOST EVERY EDGE.
THE... MASK OF TENGU...SYMBOLIC OF THE BAT SPIRIT...
IF YOU ARE NOT YET READY TO WEAR YOUR TRUE MASK...THEN AT LEAST ASSUME YOUR TOTEM.
AND THE FIELD TRAINING?
WITH ACCEPTANCE OF THE MASK, IT BEGINS TOMORROW NIGHT...
...WHEN YOU DON THE MASK...
...AT THIS ADDRESS.

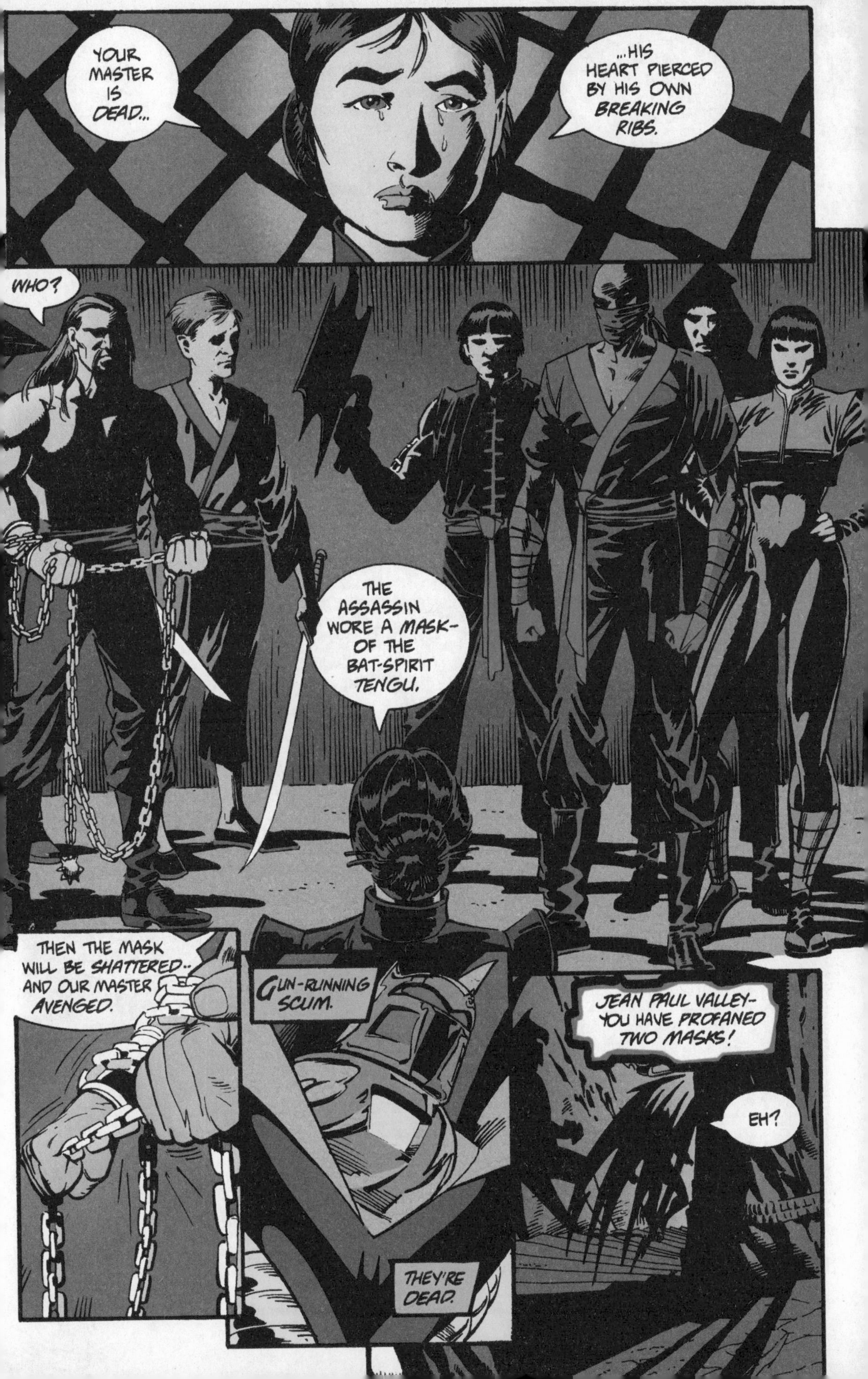
YOUR MASTER IS DEAD...
...HIS HEART PIERCED BY HIS OWN BREAKING RIBS.
WHO?
THE ASSASSIN WORE A MASK- OF THE BAT-SPIRIT TENGU.
THEN THE MASK WILL BE SHATTERED.. AND OUR MASTER AVENGED.
GUN-RUNNING SCUM.
THEY'RE DEAD.
JEAN PAUL VALLEY- YOU HAVE PROFANED TWO MASKS!
EH?

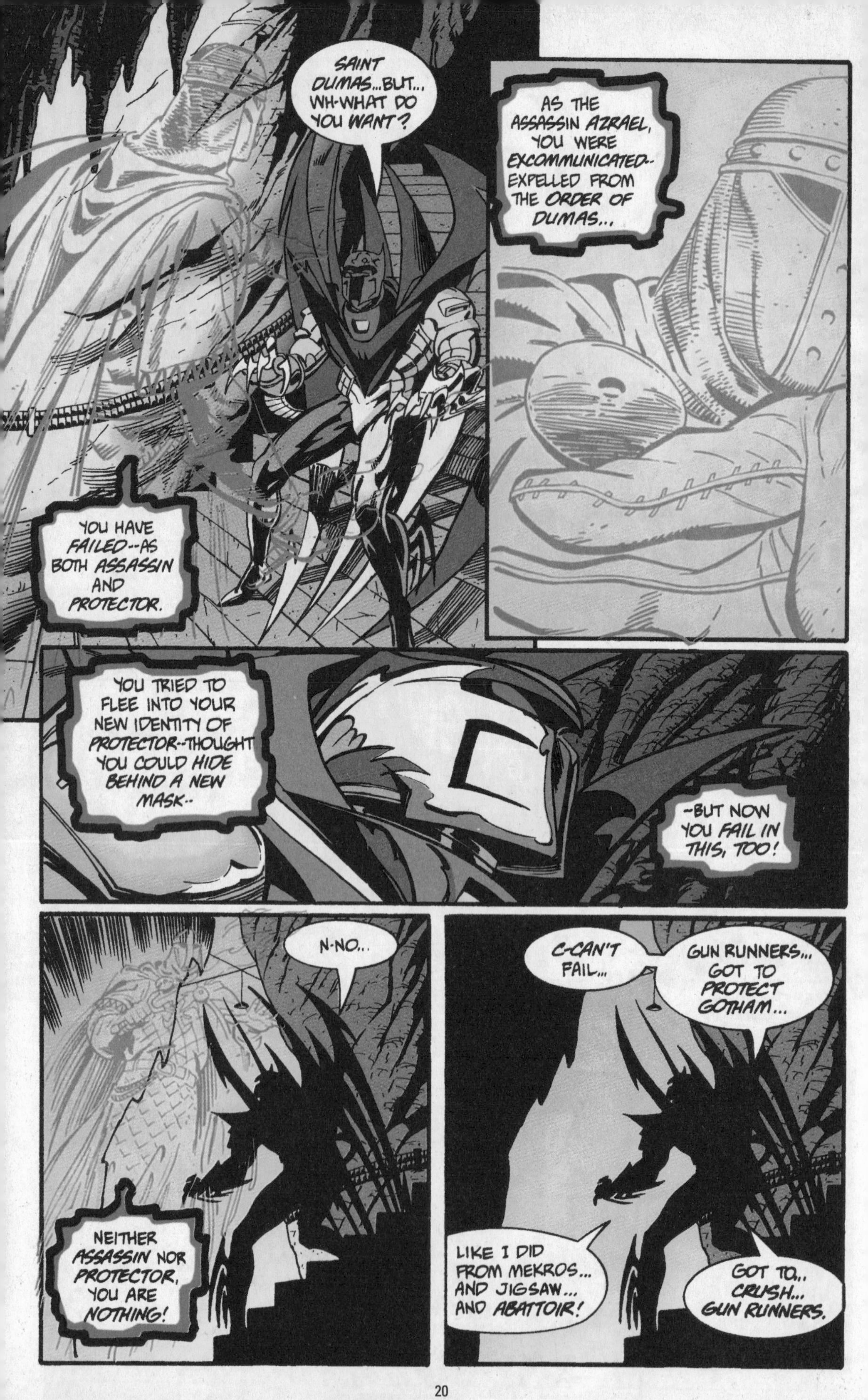
SAINT DUMAS...BUT... WH-WHAT DO YOU WANT?
AS THE ASSASSIN AZRAEL, YOU WERE EXCOMMUNICATED-- EXPELLED FROM THE ORDER OF DUMAS...
YOU HAVE FAILED--AS BOTH ASSASSIN AND PROTECTOR.
YOU TRIED TO FLEE INTO YOUR NEW IDENTITY OF PROTECTOR--THOUGHT YOU COULD HIDE BEHIND A NEW MASK--
--BUT NOW YOU FAIL IN THIS, TOO!
N-NO...
NEITHER ASSASSIN NOR PROTECTOR, YOU ARE NOTHING!
C-CAN'T FAIL...
GUN RUNNERS... GOT TO PROTECT GOTHAM...
LIKE I DID FROM MEKROS... AND JIGSAW... AND ABATTOIR!
GOT TO... CRUSH... GUN RUNNERS.

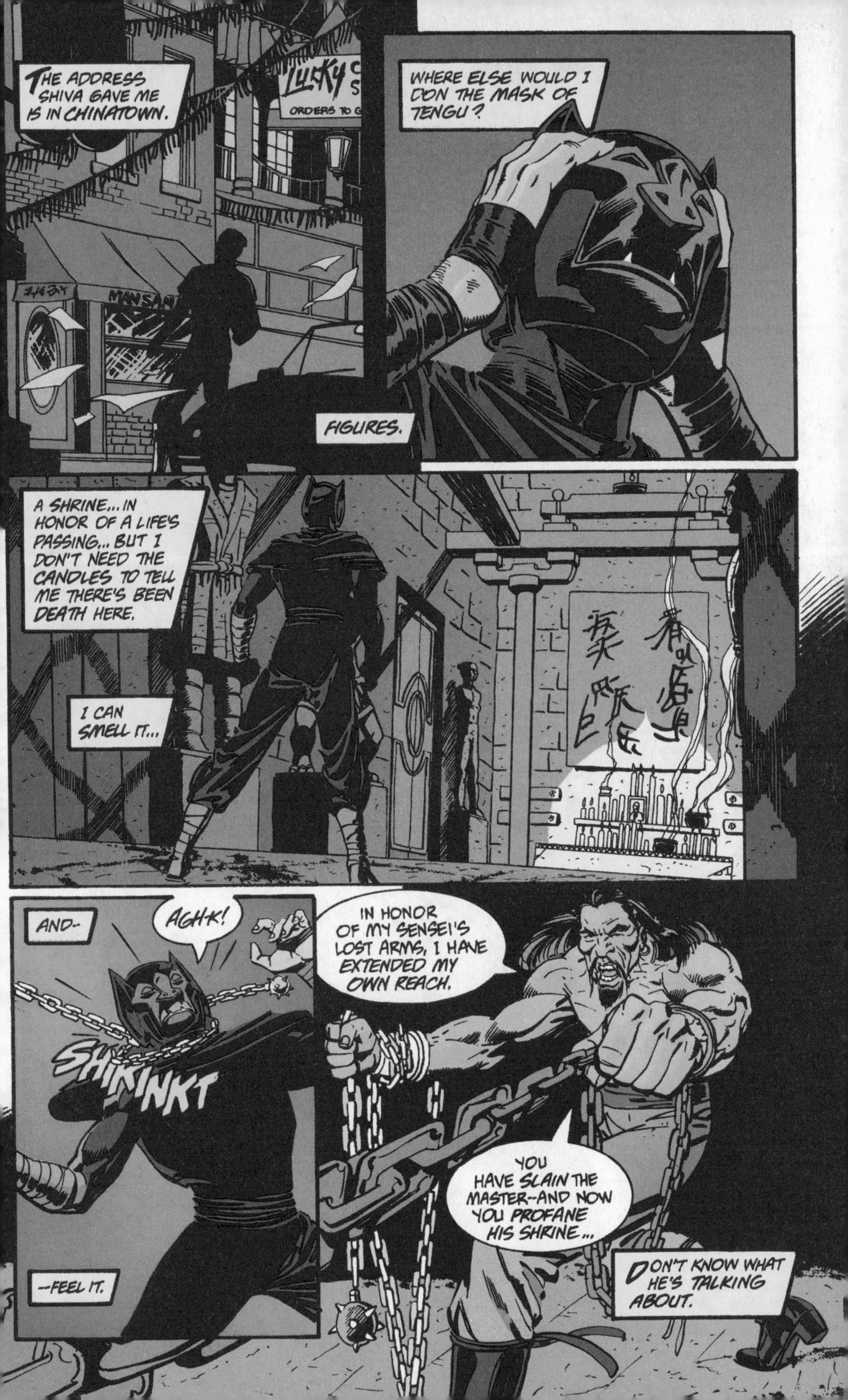
THE ADDRESS SHIVA GAVE ME IS IN CHINATOWN.
LUCKY
ORDERS TO G
MANSAN
WHERE ELSE WOULD I DON THE MASK OF TENGU?
FIGURES.
A SHRINE... IN HONOR OF A LIFE'S PASSING... BUT I DON'T NEED THE CANDLES TO TELL ME THERE'S BEEN DEATH HERE.
I CAN SMELL IT...
AND--
AGH-K!
SHIKINKT
--FEEL IT.
IN HONOR OF MY SENSEI'S LOST ARMS, I HAVE EXTENDED MY OWN REACH.
YOU HAVE SLAIN THE MASTER--AND NOW YOU PROFANE HIS SHRINE...
DON'T KNOW WHAT HE'S TALKING ABOUT.

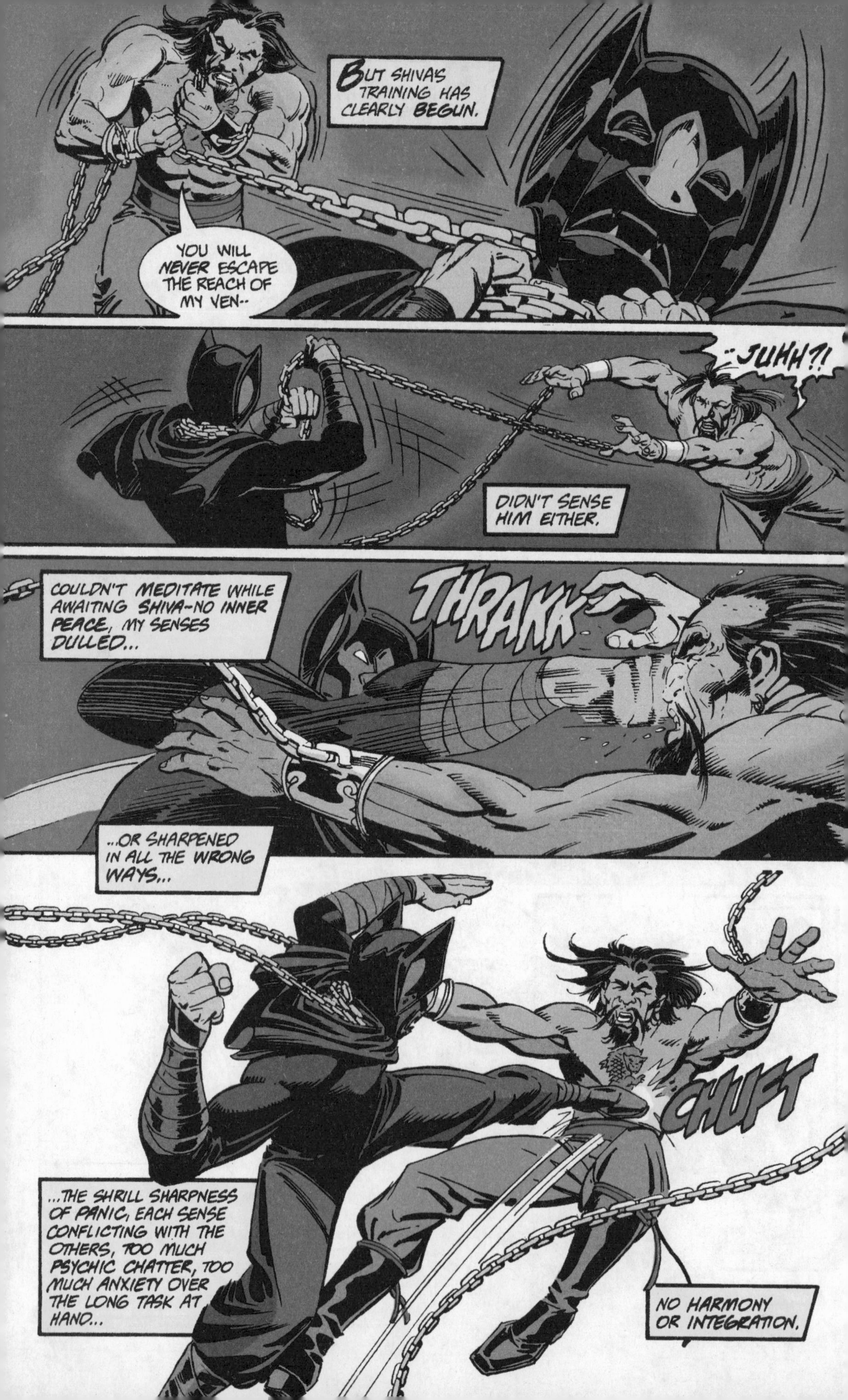

BUT SHIVA'S TRAINING HAS CLEARLY BEGUN.
YOU WILL NEVER ESCAPE THE REACH OF MY VEN--
--JUHH?!
DIDN'T SENSE HIM EITHER.
COULDN'T MEDITATE WHILE AWAITING SHIVA--NO INNER PEACE, MY SENSES DULLED...
THRAKK
...OR SHARPENED IN ALL THE WRONG WAYS...
...THE SHRILL SHARPNESS OF PANIC, EACH SENSE CONFLICTING WITH THE OTHERS, TOO MUCH PSYCHIC CHATTER, TOO MUCH ANXIETY OVER THE LONG TASK AT HAND...
CHUFT
NO HARMONY OR INTEGRATION.

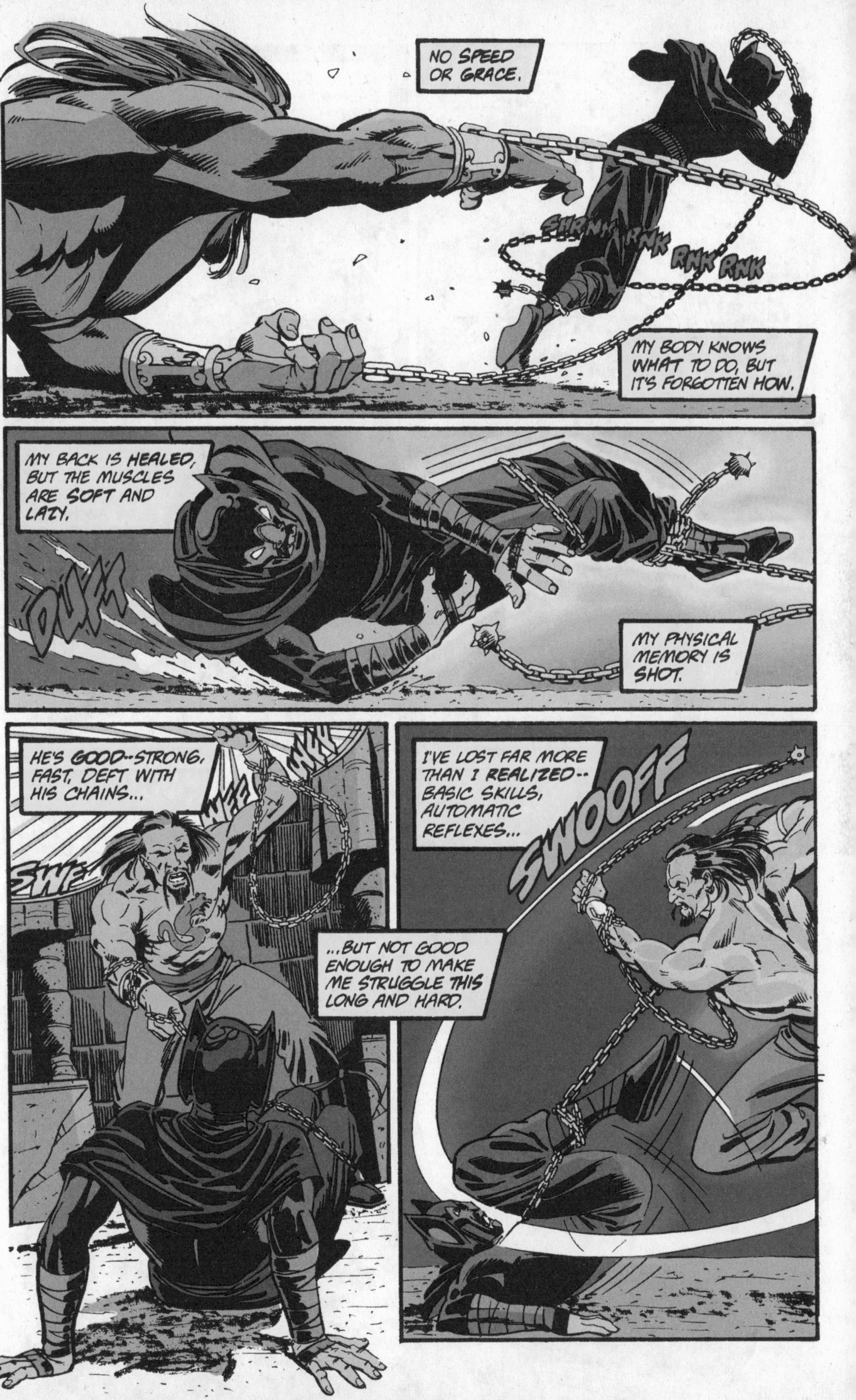
NO SPEED OR GRACE.
SHRNK RNK RNK RNK
MY BODY KNOWS WHAT TO DO, BUT IT'S FORGOTTEN HOW.
MY BACK IS HEALED, BUT THE MUSCLES ARE SOFT AND LAZY.
DUFF
MY PHYSICAL MEMORY IS SHOT.
HE'S GOOD--STRONG, FAST, DEFT WITH HIS CHAINS...
...BUT NOT GOOD ENOUGH TO MAKE ME STRUGGLE THIS LONG AND HARD.
I'VE LOST FAR MORE THAN I REALIZED-- BASIC SKILLS, AUTOMATIC REFLEXES...
SWOOFF

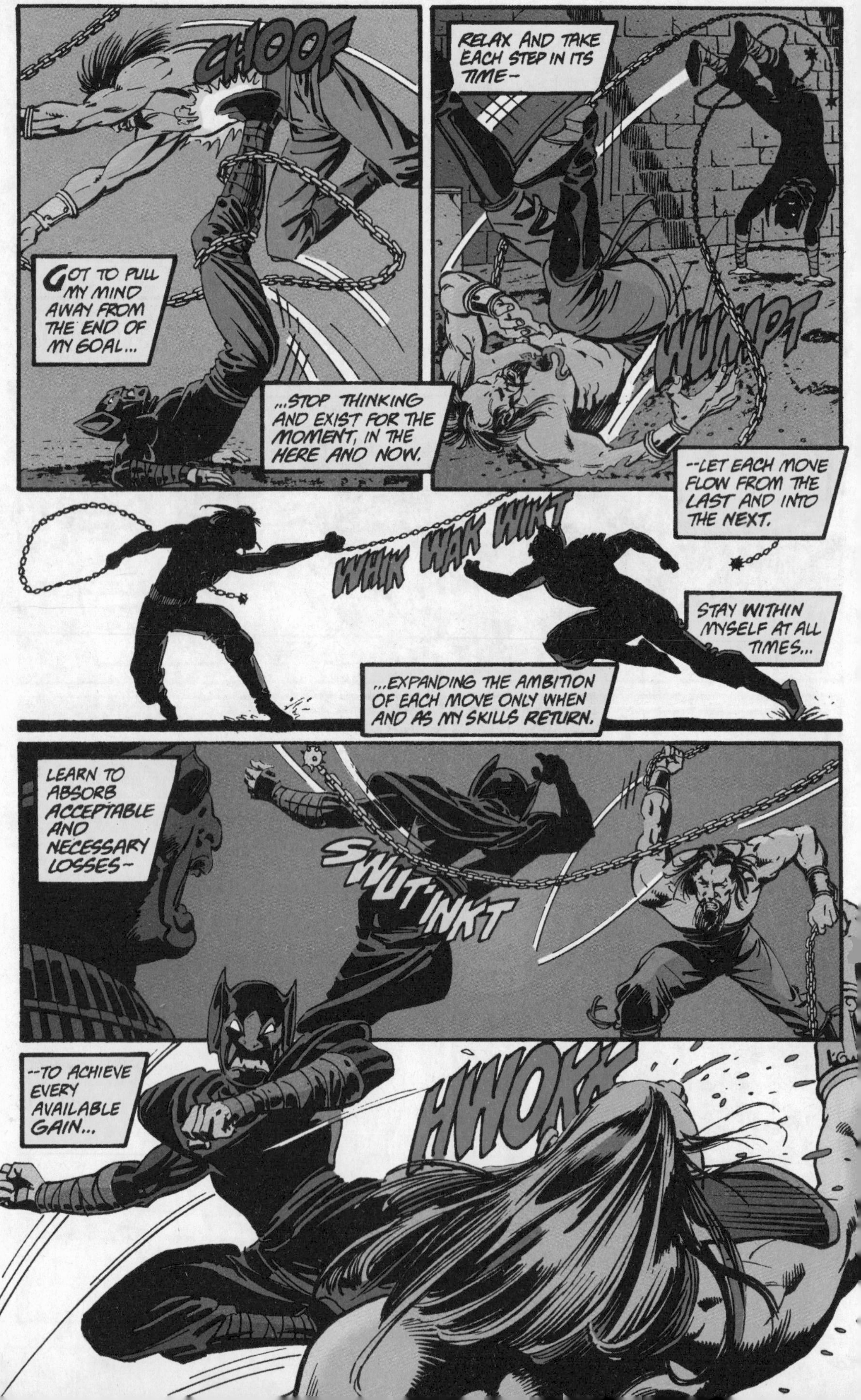
CHOOF
GOT TO PULL MY MIND AWAY FROM THE END OF MY GOAL...
...STOP THINKING AND EXIST FOR THE MOMENT, IN THE HERE AND NOW.
RELAX AND TAKE EACH STEP IN ITS TIME--
WUMPT
--LET EACH MOVE FLOW FROM THE LAST AND INTO THE NEXT.
WHIK WAK WIKT
STAY WITHIN MYSELF AT ALL TIMES...
...EXPANDING THE AMBITION OF EACH MOVE ONLY WHEN AND AS MY SKILLS RETURN.
LEARN TO ABSORB ACCEPTABLE AND NECESSARY LOSSES--
SWUT'INKT
--TO ACHIEVE EVERY AVAILABLE GAIN...
HWOKK

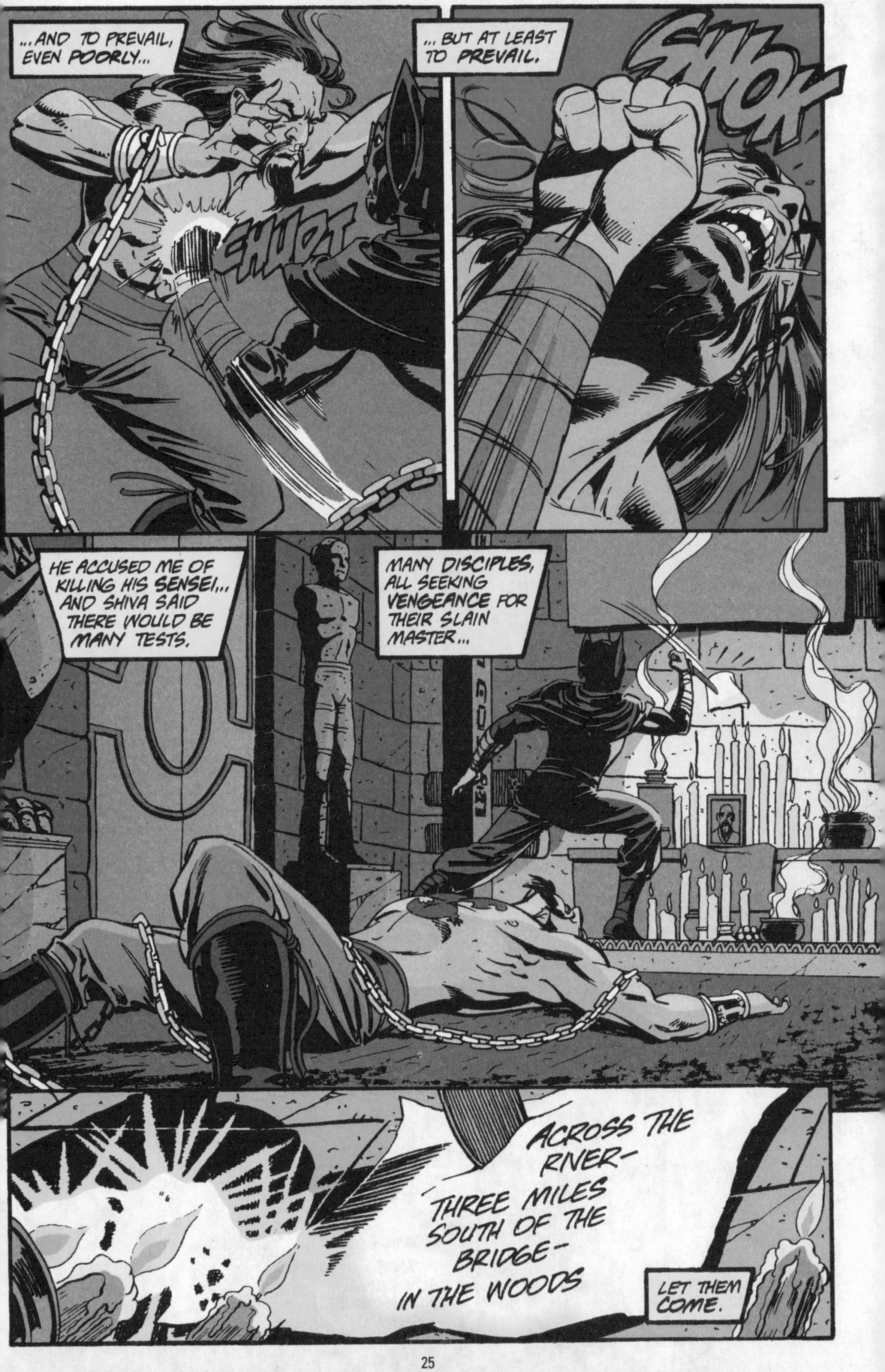
...AND TO PREVAIL, EVEN POORLY...
CHUDT
...BUT AT LEAST TO PREVAIL.
SMOK
HE ACCUSED ME OF KILLING HIS SENSEI... AND SHIVA SAID THERE WOULD BE MANY TESTS.
MANY DISCIPLES, ALL SEEKING VENGEANCE FOR THEIR SLAIN MASTER...
ACROSS THE RIVER-
THREE MILES SOUTH OF THE BRIDGE-
IN THE WOODS
LET THEM COME.

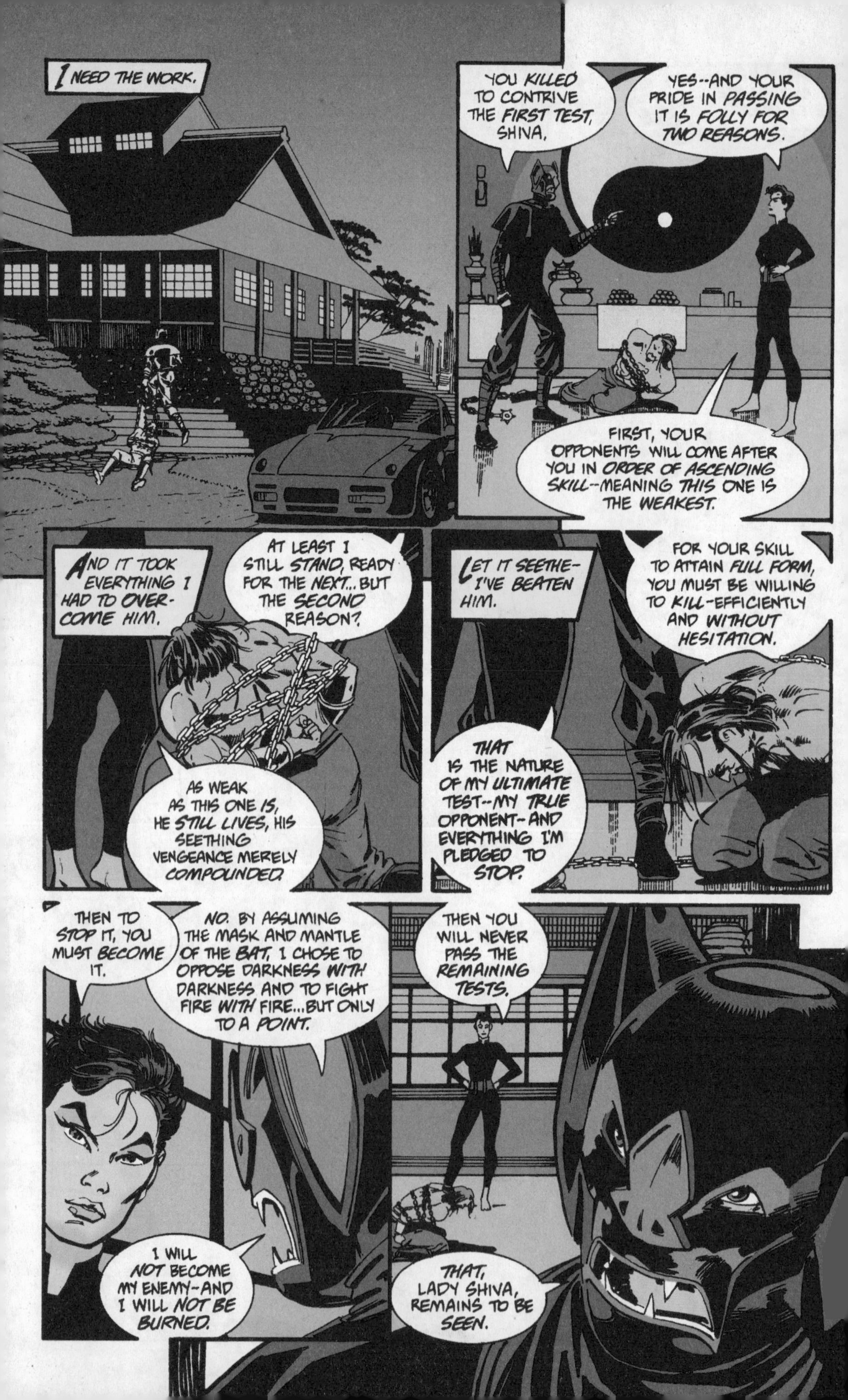
I NEED THE WORK.
YOU KILLED TO CONTRIVE THE FIRST TEST, SHIVA.
YES--AND YOUR PRIDE IN PASSING IT IS FOLLY FOR TWO REASONS.
FIRST, YOUR OPPONENTS WILL COME AFTER YOU IN ORDER OF ASCENDING SKILL--MEANING THIS ONE IS THE WEAKEST.
AND IT TOOK EVERYTHING I HAD TO OVERCOME HIM.
AT LEAST I STILL STAND, READY FOR THE NEXT... BUT THE SECOND REASON?
AS WEAK AS THIS ONE IS, HE STILL LIVES, HIS SEETHING VENGEANCE MERELY COMPOUNDED.
LET IT SEETHE- I'VE BEATEN HIM.
FOR YOUR SKILL TO ATTAIN FULL FORM, YOU MUST BE WILLING TO KILL-EFFICIENTLY AND WITHOUT HESITATION.
THAT IS THE NATURE OF MY ULTIMATE TEST--MY TRUE OPPONENT--AND EVERYTHING I'M PLEDGED TO STOP.
THEN TO STOP IT, YOU MUST BECOME IT.
NO. BY ASSUMING THE MASK AND MANTLE OF THE BAT, I CHOSE TO OPPOSE DARKNESS WITH DARKNESS AND TO FIGHT FIRE WITH FIRE... BUT ONLY TO A POINT.
I WILL NOT BECOME MY ENEMY--AND I WILL NOT BE BURNED.
THEN YOU WILL NEVER PASS THE REMAINING TESTS.
THAT, LADY SHIVA, REMAINS TO BE SEEN.

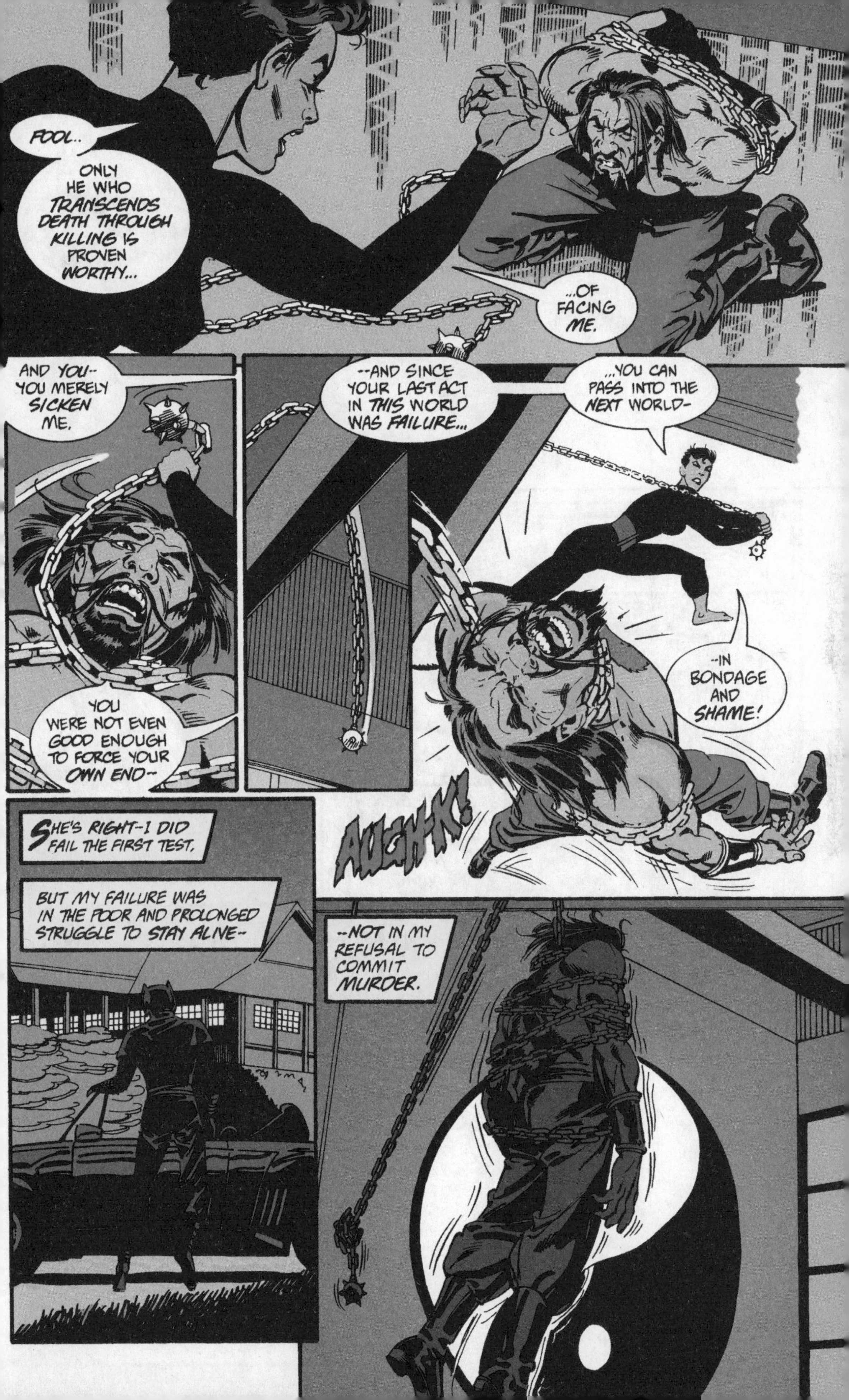
FOOL..
ONLY HE WHO TRANSCENDS DEATH THROUGH KILLING IS PROVEN WORTHY...
...OF FACING ME.
AND YOU-- YOU MERELY SICKEN ME.
YOU WERE NOT EVEN GOOD ENOUGH TO FORCE YOUR OWN END--
--AND SINCE YOUR LAST ACT IN THIS WORLD WAS FAILURE...
...YOU CAN PASS INTO THE NEXT WORLD-
--IN BONDAGE AND SHAME!
AUGH-K!
SHE'S RIGHT--I DID FAIL THE FIRST TEST.
BUT MY FAILURE WAS IN THE POOR AND PROLONGED STRUGGLE TO STAY ALIVE--
--NOT IN MY REFUSAL TO COMMIT MURDER.

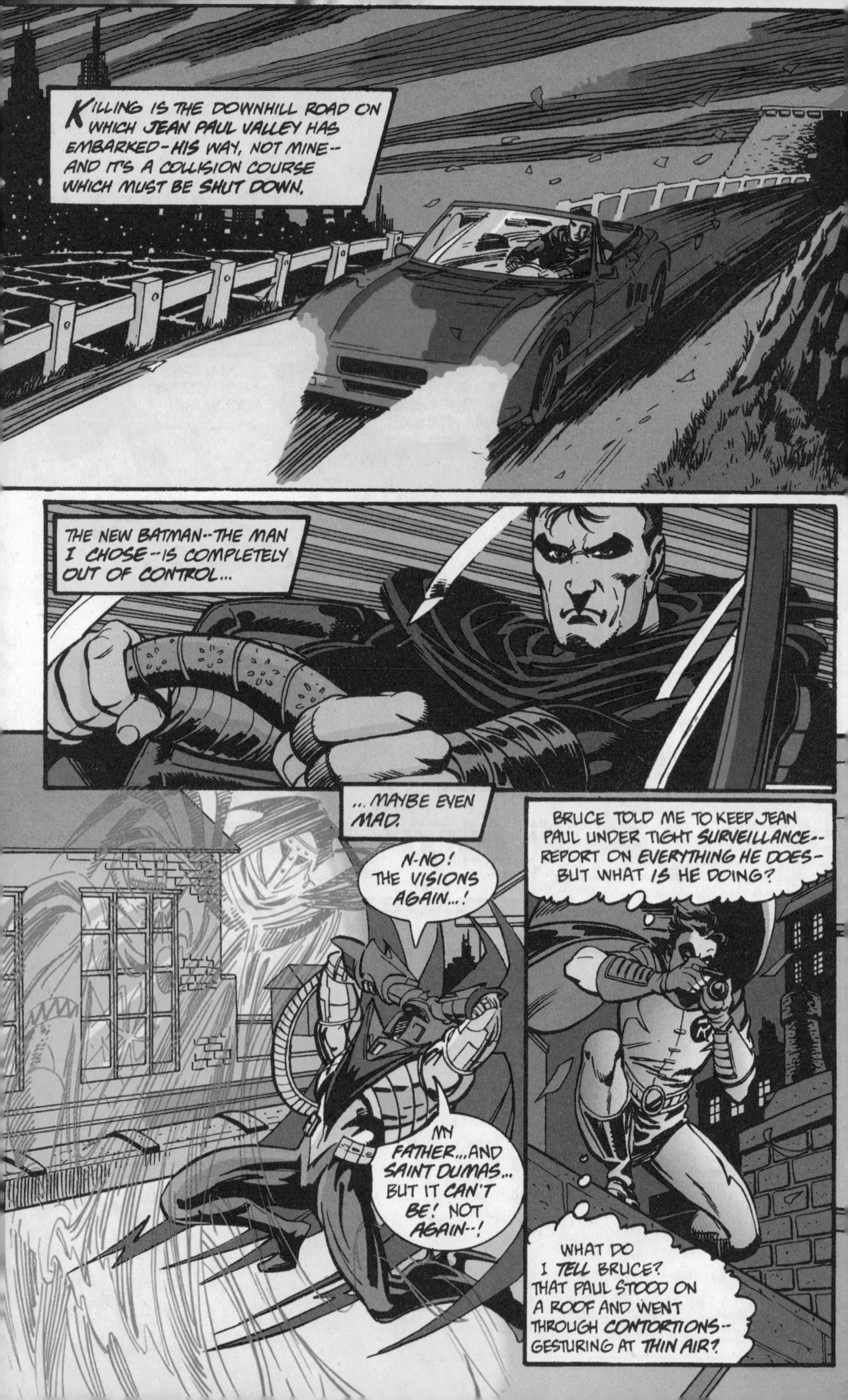
KILLING IS THE DOWNHILL ROAD ON WHICH JEAN PAUL VALLEY HAS EMBARKED--HIS WAY, NOT MINE--AND IT'S A COLLISION COURSE WHICH MUST BE SHUT DOWN.
THE NEW BATMAN--THE MAN I CHOSE--IS COMPLETELY OUT OF CONTROL...
...MAYBE EVEN MAD.
N-NO! THE VISIONS AGAIN...!
MY FATHER...AND SAINT DUMAS... BUT IT CAN'T BE! NOT AGAIN--!
BRUCE TOLD ME TO KEEP JEAN PAUL UNDER TIGHT SURVEILLANCE--REPORT ON EVERYTHING HE DOES-BUT WHAT IS HE DOING?
WHAT DO I TELL BRUCE? THAT PAUL STOOD ON A ROOF AND WENT THROUGH CONTORTIONS--GESTURING AT THIN AIR?

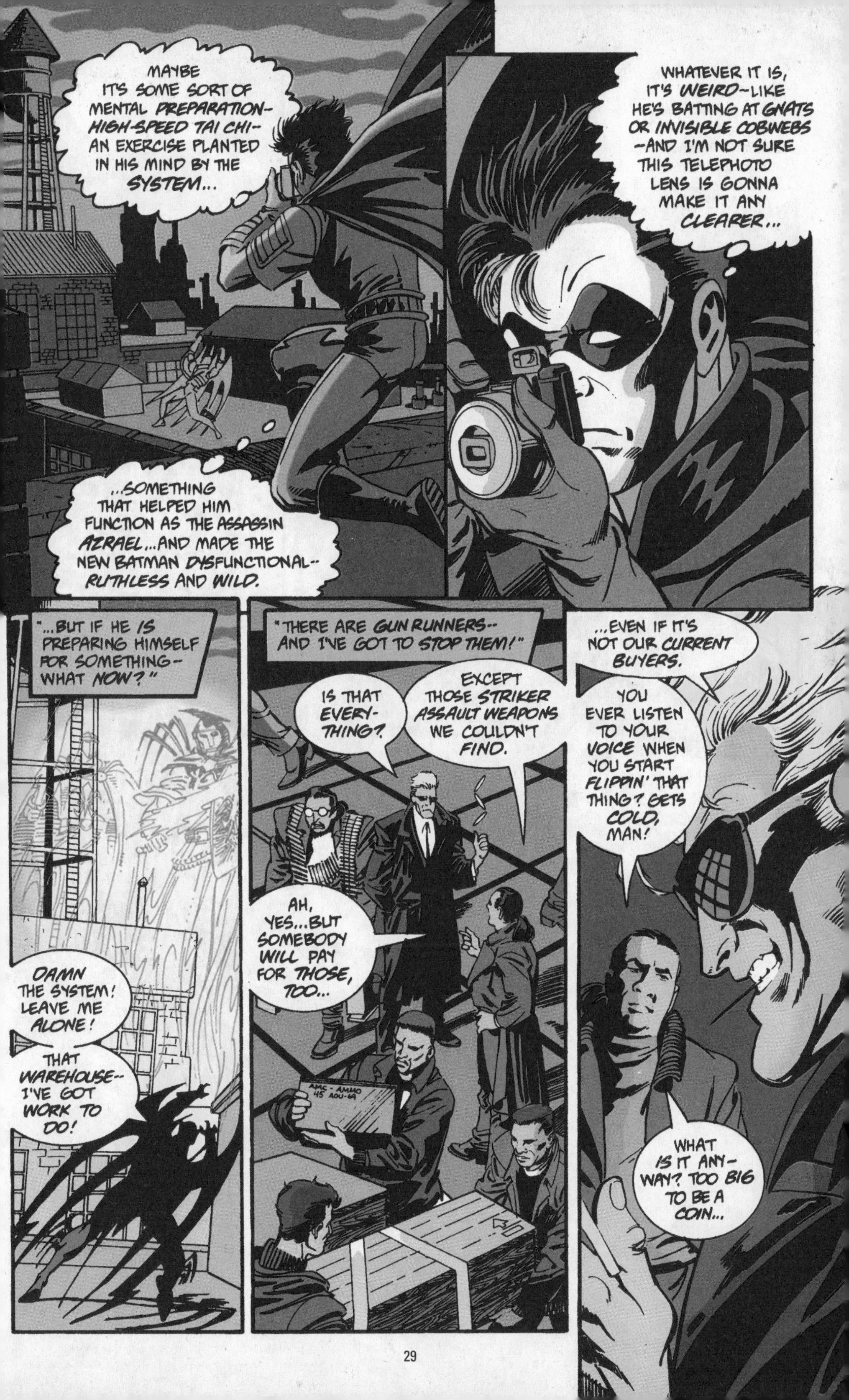
MAYBE IT'S SOME SORT OF MENTAL PREPARATION-HIGH-SPEED TAI CHI-AN EXERCISE PLANTED IN HIS MIND BY THE SYSTEM...
...SOMETHING THAT HELPED HIM FUNCTION AS THE ASSASSIN AZRAEL...AND MADE THE NEW BATMAN DYSFUNCTIONAL--RUTHLESS AND WILD.
WHATEVER IT IS, IT'S WEIRD--LIKE HE'S BATTING AT GNATS OR INVISIBLE COBWEBS --AND I'M NOT SURE THIS TELEPHOTO LENS IS GONNA MAKE IT ANY CLEARER...
"...BUT IF HE IS PREPARING HIMSELF FOR SOMETHING--WHAT NOW?"
DAMN THE SYSTEM! LEAVE ME ALONE!
THAT WAREHOUSE--I'VE GOT WORK TO DO!
"THERE ARE GUN RUNNERS--AND I'VE GOT TO STOP THEM!"
IS THAT EVERY-THING?
EXCEPT THOSE STRIKER ASSAULT WEAPONS WE COULDN'T FIND.
AH, YES...BUT SOMEBODY WILL PAY FOR THOSE, TOO...
AMC - AMMO 45 AOU-69
...EVEN IF IT'S NOT OUR CURRENT BUYERS.
YOU EVER LISTEN TO YOUR VOICE WHEN YOU START FLIPPIN' THAT THING? GETS COLD, MAN!
WHAT IS IT ANY-WAY? TOO BIG TO BE A COIN...

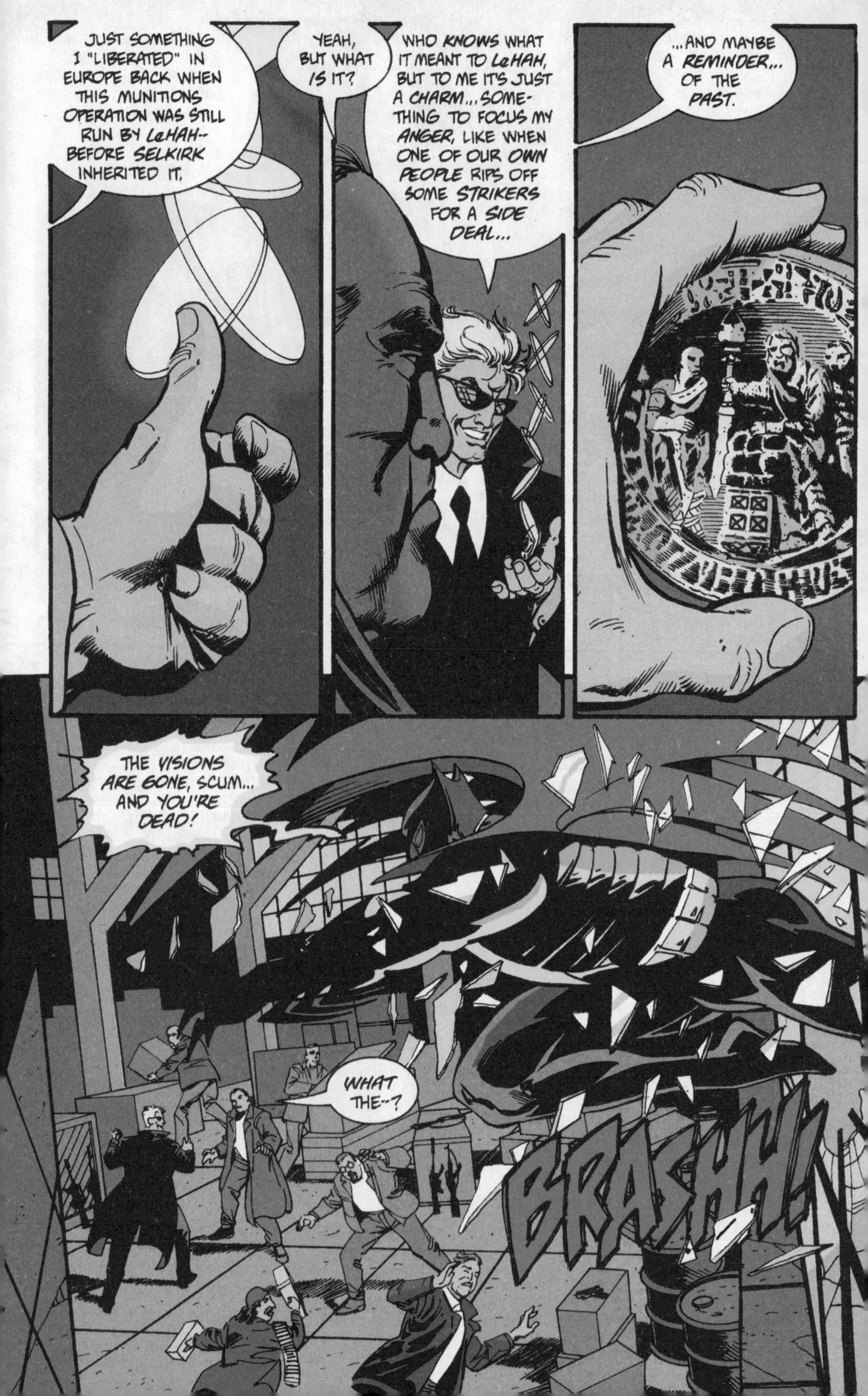
JUST SOMETHING I "LIBERATED" IN EUROPE BACK WHEN THIS MUNITIONS OPERATION WAS STILL RUN BY LaHAH-- BEFORE SELKIRK INHERITED IT.
YEAH, BUT WHAT IS IT?
WHO KNOWS WHAT IT MEANT TO LaHAH, BUT TO ME IT'S JUST A CHARM... SOME-THING TO FOCUS MY ANGER, LIKE WHEN ONE OF OUR OWN PEOPLE RIPS OFF SOME STRIKERS FOR A SIDE DEAL...
...AND MAYBE A REMINDER... OF THE PAST.
THE VISIONS ARE GONE, SCUM... AND YOU'RE DEAD!
WHAT THE--?
BRASHH!

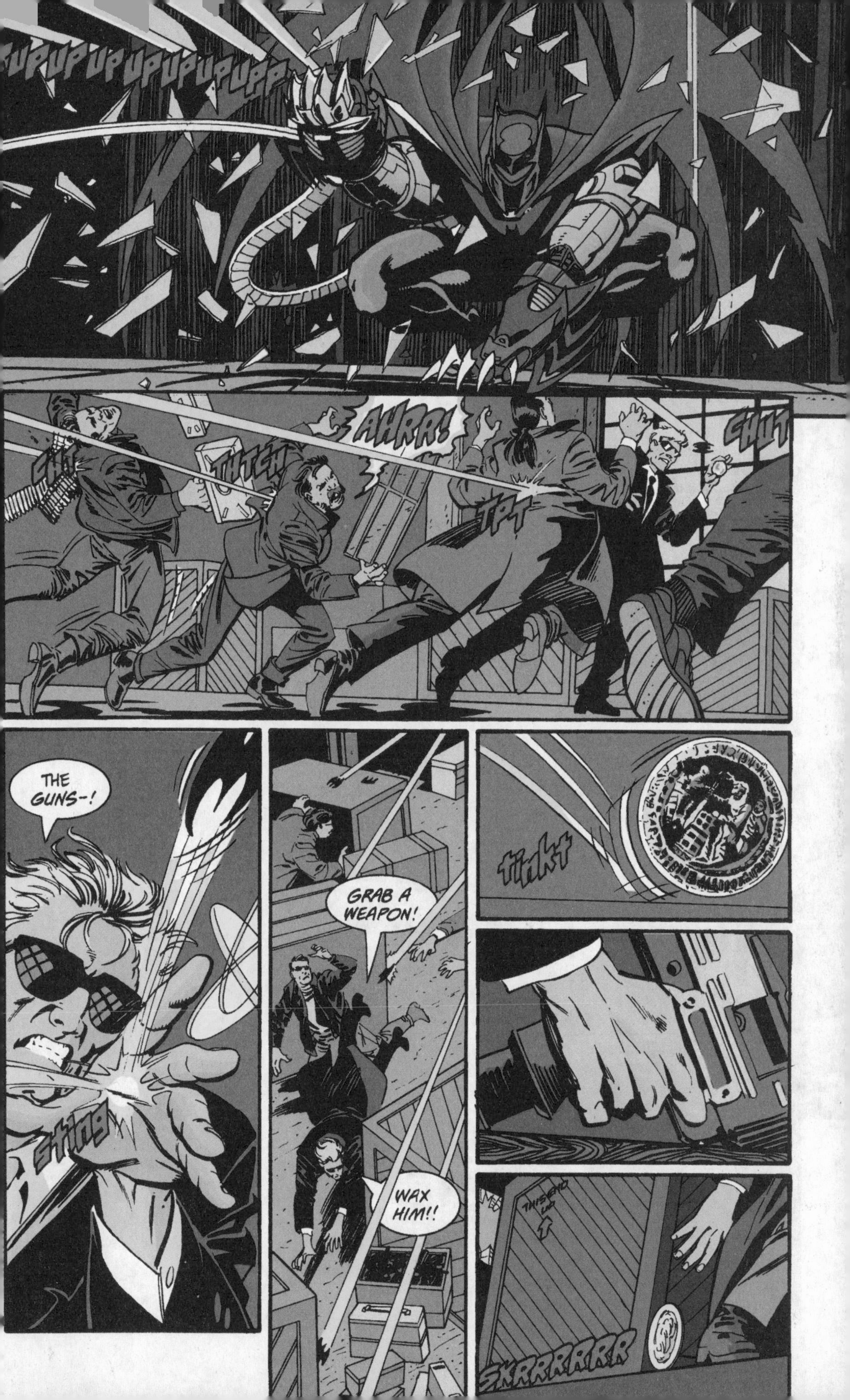
UPUPUP UP UPUPUPUPP
AHRR!
CHUT
THTCH
TPT
CHUT
THE GUNS-!
sting
GRAB A WEAPON!
WAX HIM!!
tinkt
THIS END UP
SKRRRRRR

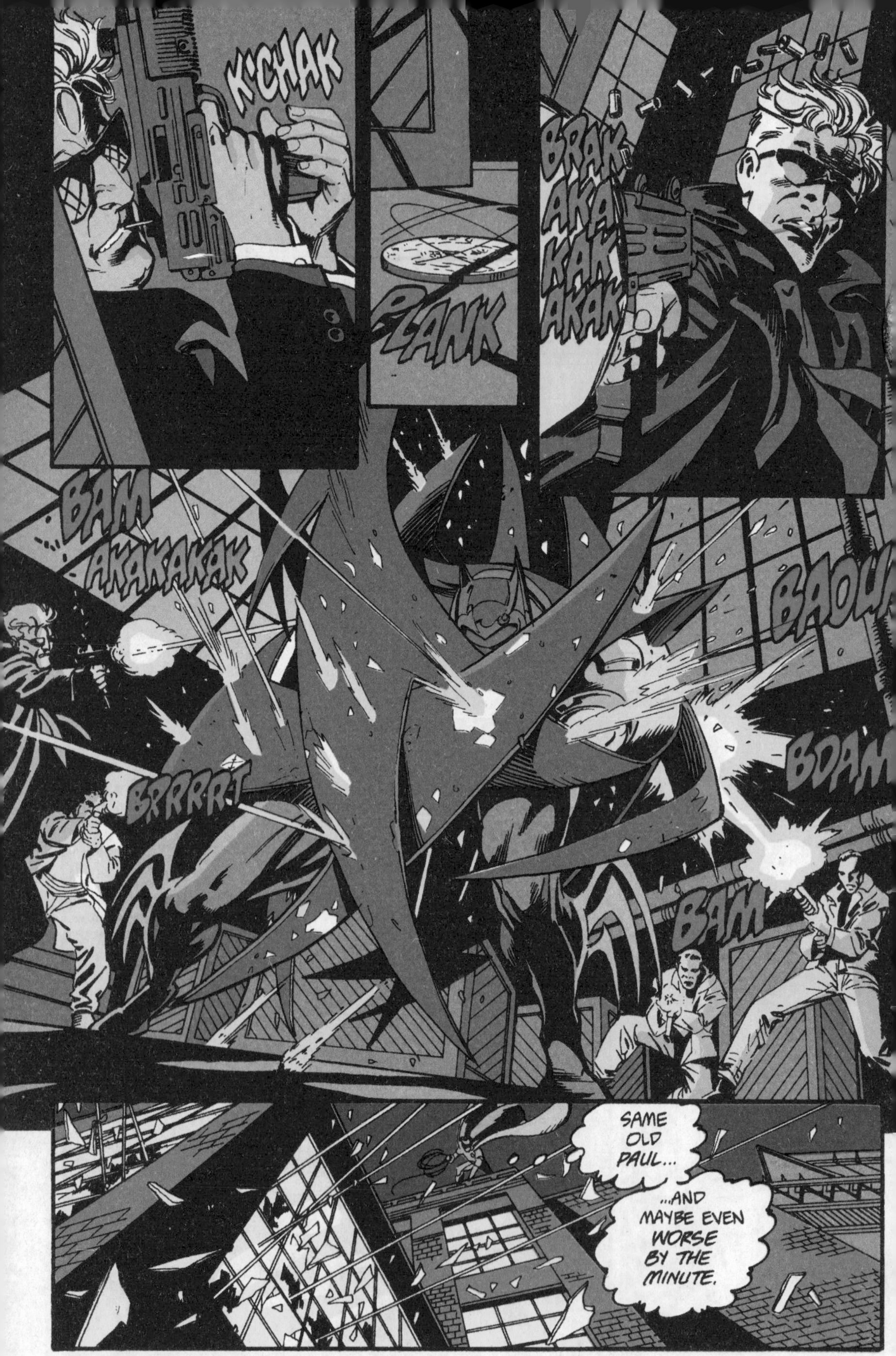
K'CHAK
PLANK
BRAK
AKA
KAK
AKAK
BAM
AKAKAKAK
BAOW
BRRRRT
BDAM
BAM
SAME OLD PAUL...
...AND MAYBE EVEN WORSE BY THE MINUTE.

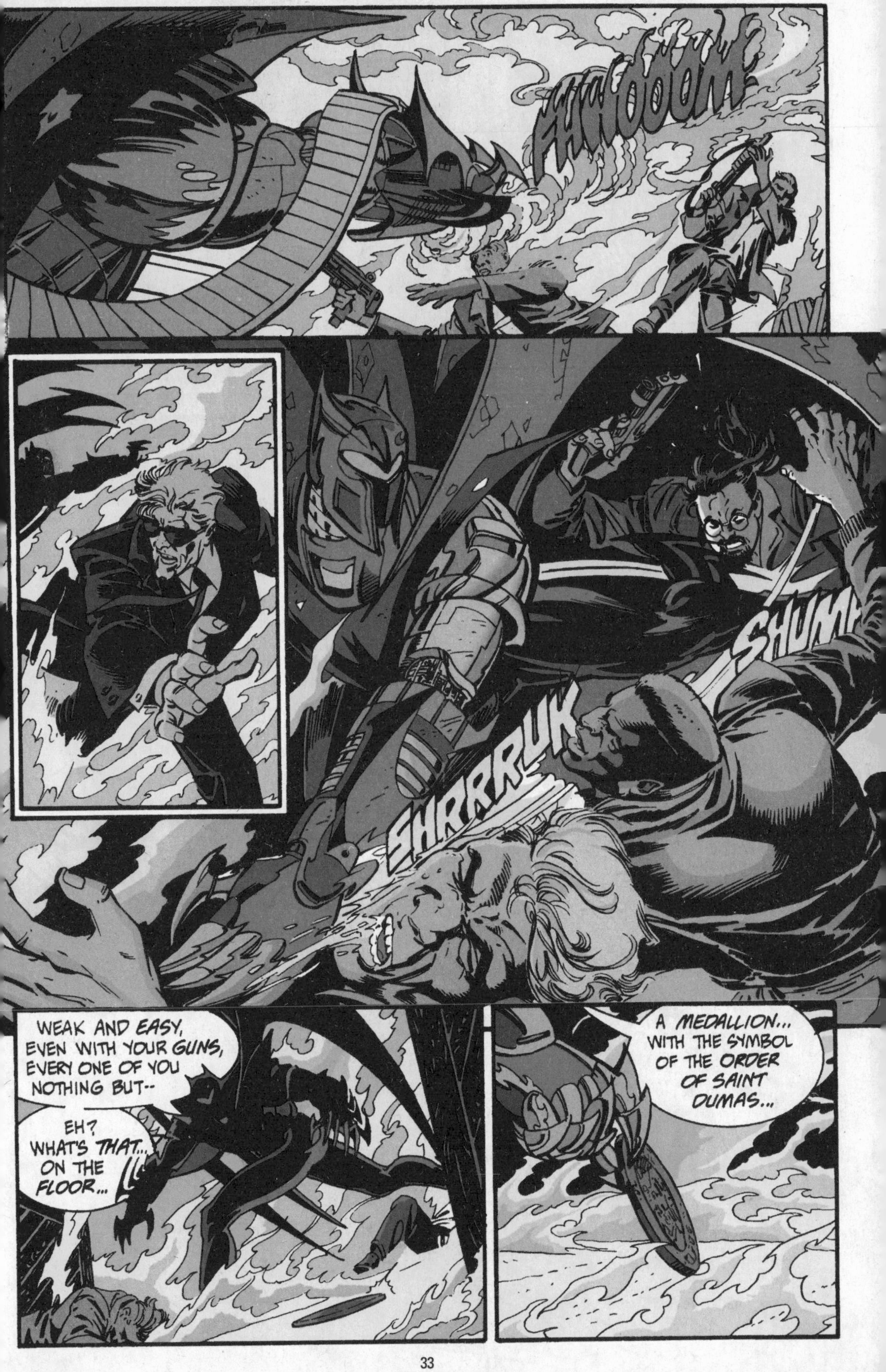
FWOOOM
SHUM
SHRRRUK
WEAK AND EASY, EVEN WITH YOUR GUNS, EVERY ONE OF YOU NOTHING BUT--
EH? WHAT'S THAT... ON THE FLOOR...
A MEDALLION... WITH THE SYMBOL OF THE ORDER OF SAINT DUMAS...

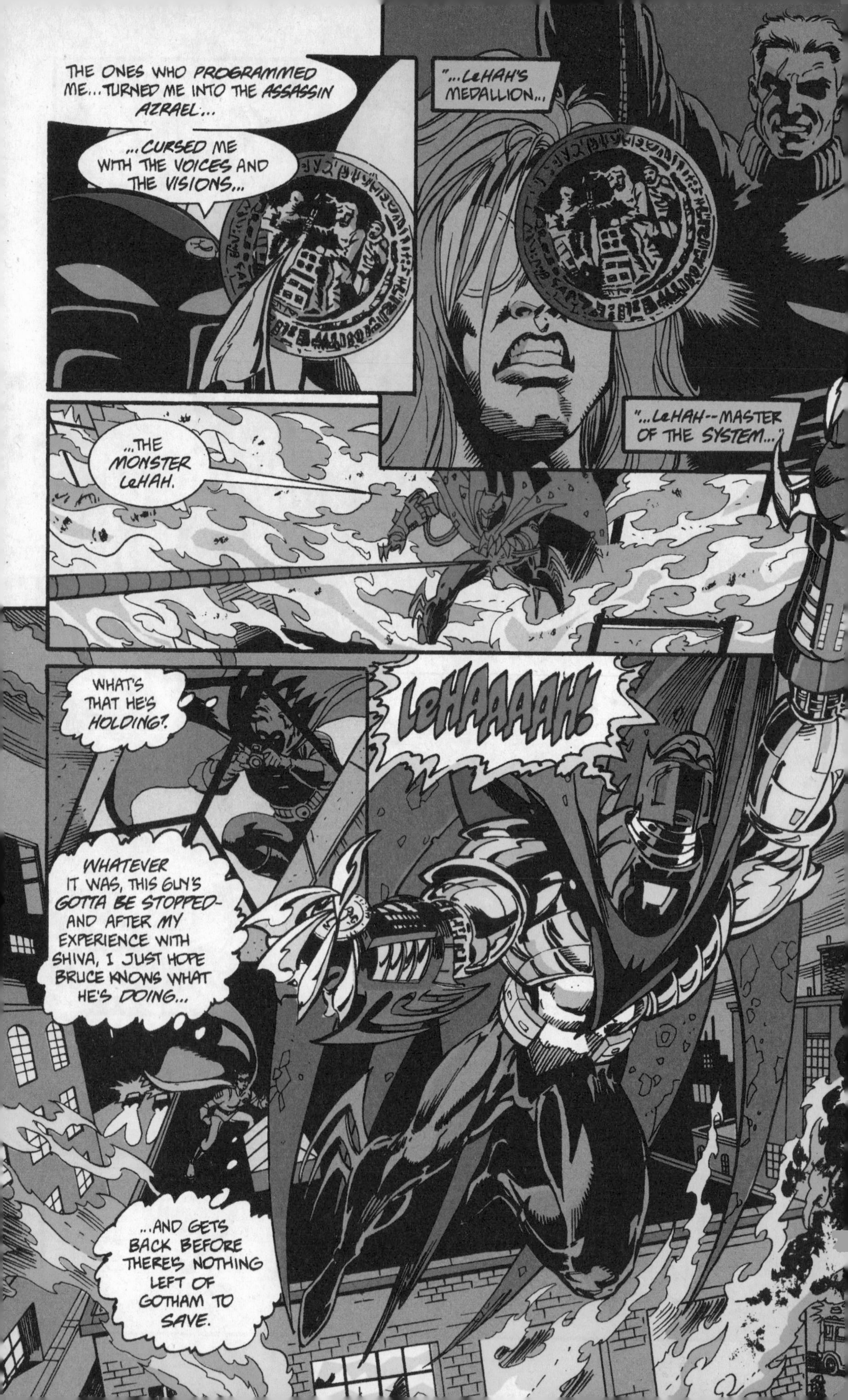
THE ONES WHO PROGRAMMED ME...TURNED ME INTO THE ASSASSIN AZRAEL...
...CURSED ME WITH THE VOICES AND THE VISIONS...
"...LeHAH'S MEDALLION..."
...THE MONSTER LeHAH.
"...LeHAH--MASTER OF THE SYSTEM..."
WHAT'S THAT HE'S HOLDING?
LeHAAAAH!
WHATEVER IT WAS, THIS GUY'S GOTTA BE STOPPED-- AND AFTER MY EXPERIENCE WITH SHIVA, I JUST HOPE BRUCE KNOWS WHAT HE'S DOING...
...AND GETS BACK BEFORE THERE'S NOTHING LEFT OF GOTHAM TO SAVE.

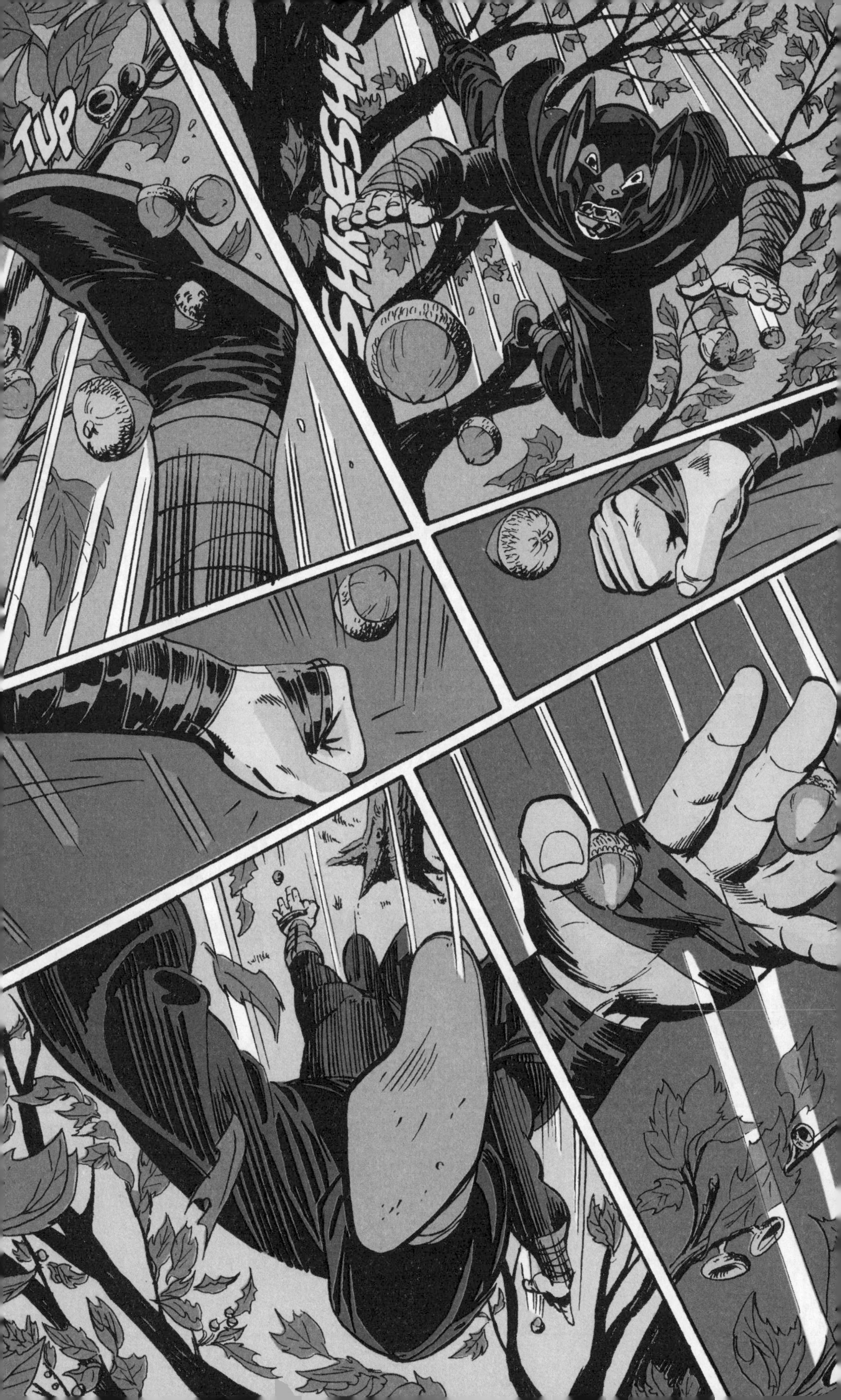
TUP
SHHESH

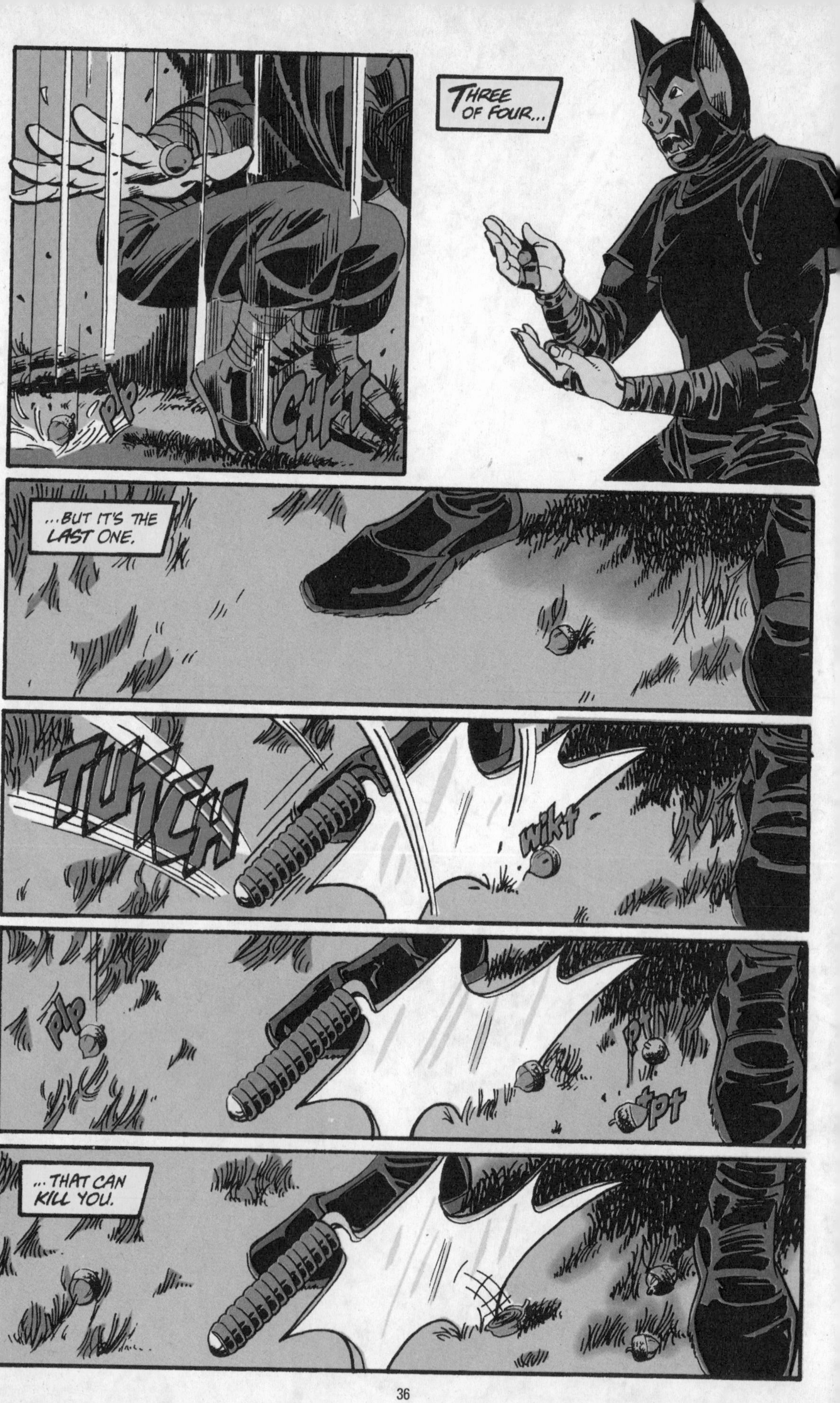

THREE OF FOUR...
plp
CHFT
...BUT IT'S THE LAST ONE.
TUTCH
wikt
plp
pt
pt
...THAT CAN KILL YOU.

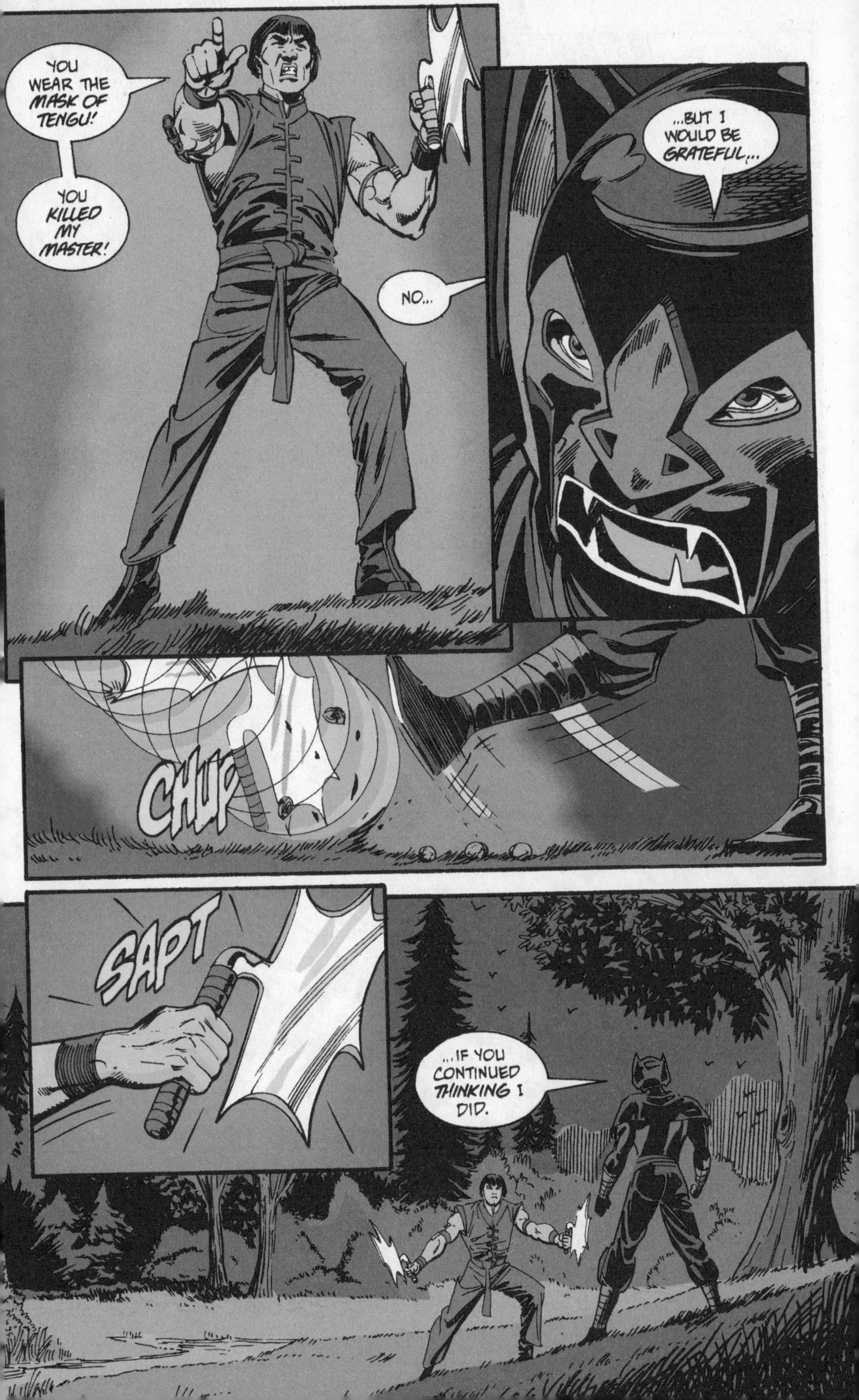
YOU WEAR THE MASK OF TENGU!
YOU KILLED MY MASTER!
NO...
...BUT I WOULD BE GRATEFUL...
CHUP
SAPT
...IF YOU CONTINUED THINKING I DID.

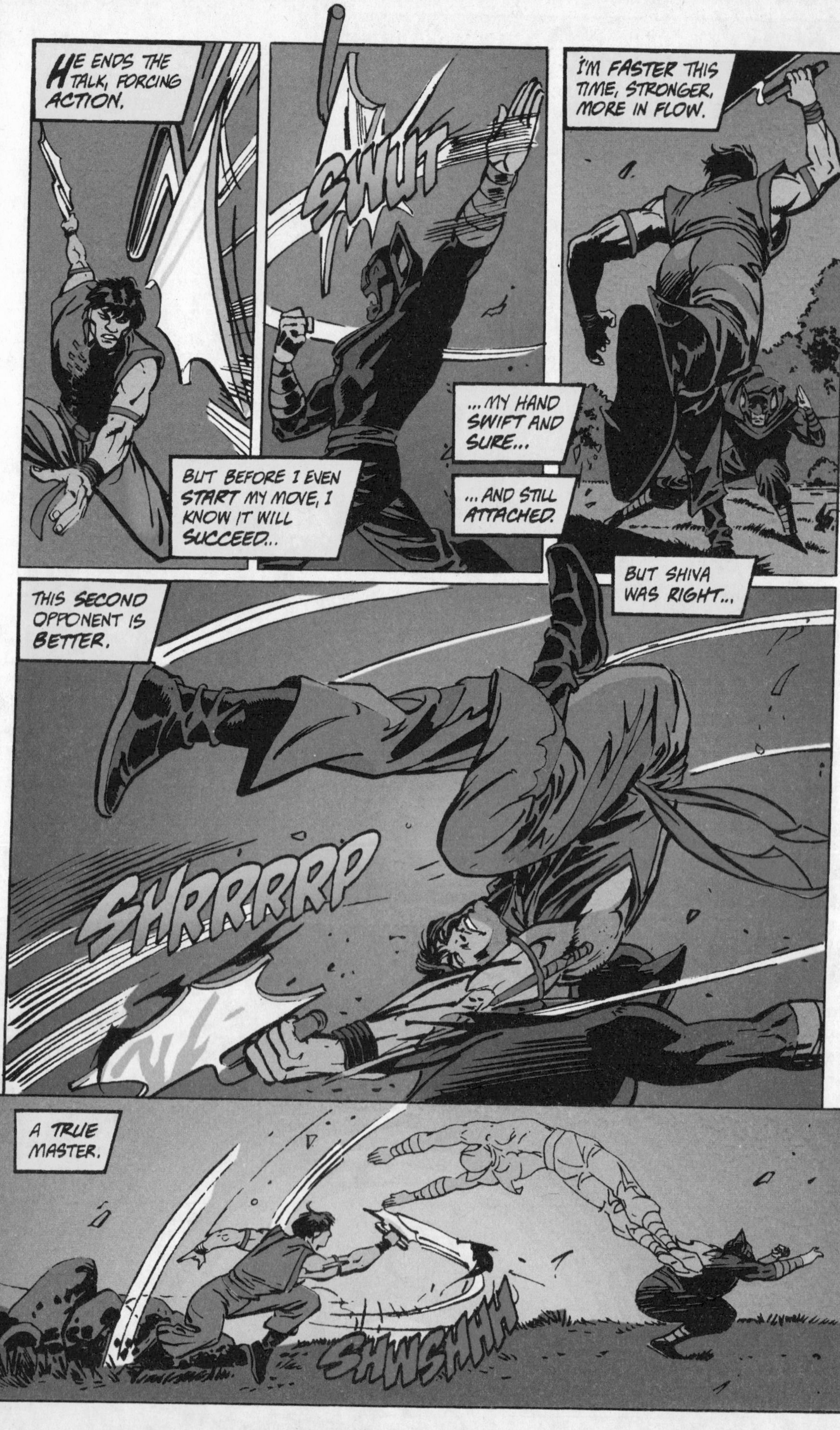
HE ENDS THE TALK, FORCING ACTION.
SWUT
I'M FASTER THIS TIME, STRONGER, MORE IN FLOW.
BUT BEFORE I EVEN START MY MOVE, I KNOW IT WILL SUCCEED...
...MY HAND SWIFT AND SURE...
...AND STILL ATTACHED.
THIS SECOND OPPONENT IS BETTER.
BUT SHIVA WAS RIGHT...
SHRRRRP
A TRUE MASTER.
SHWSHHH

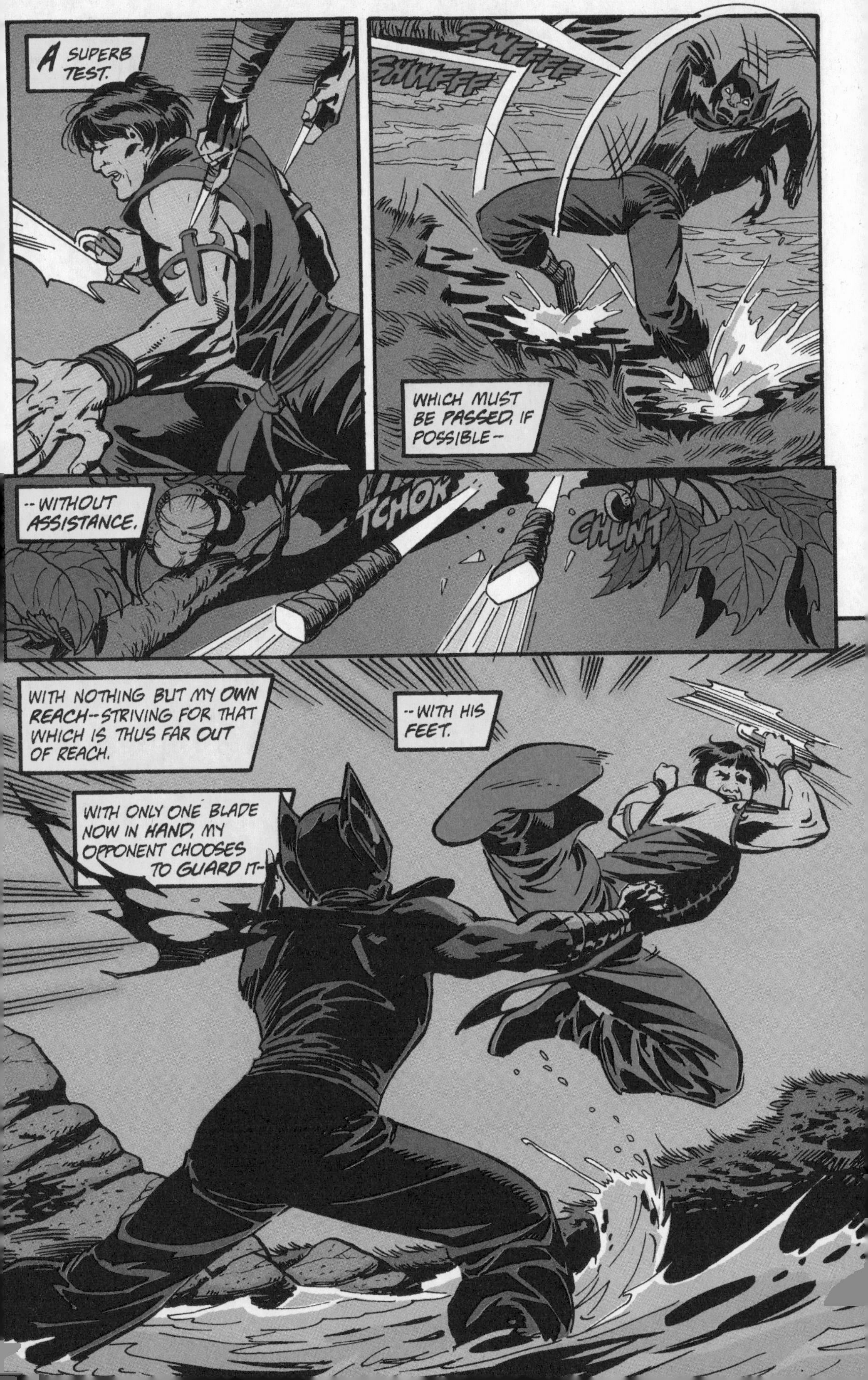
A SUPERB TEST.
SHWFFF
SHWFFF
WHICH MUST BE PASSED, IF POSSIBLE--
--WITHOUT ASSISTANCE.
TCHOK
CHUNT
WITH NOTHING BUT MY OWN REACH--STRIVING FOR THAT WHICH IS THUS FAR OUT OF REACH.
--WITH HIS FEET.
WITH ONLY ONE BLADE NOW IN HAND, MY OPPONENT CHOOSES TO GUARD IT-

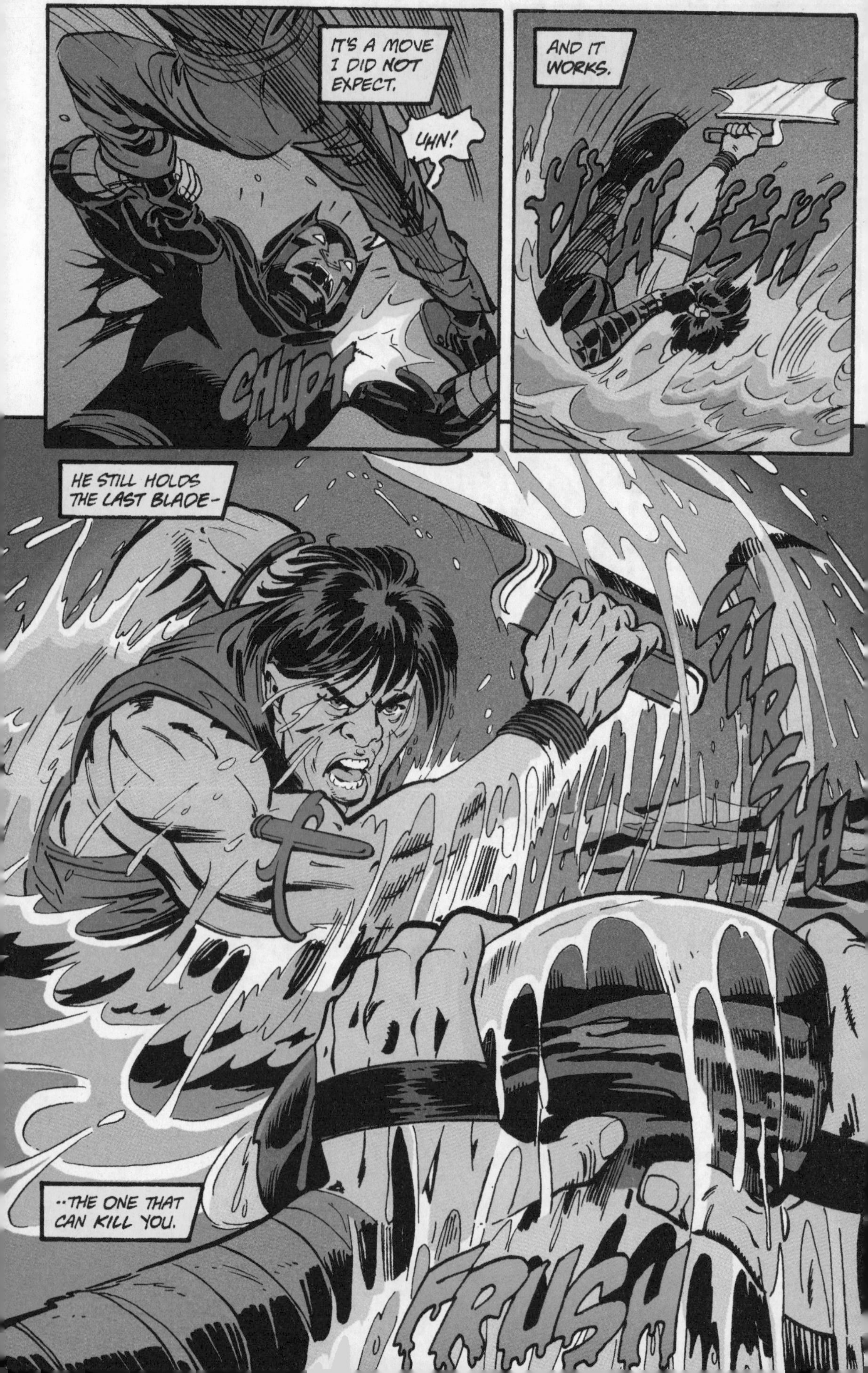
IT'S A MOVE I DID NOT EXPECT.
UHN!
CHUPT
AND IT WORKS.
PLAASH
HE STILL HOLDS THE LAST BLADE-
SHRSHH
..THE ONE THAT CAN KILL YOU.
FRUSA

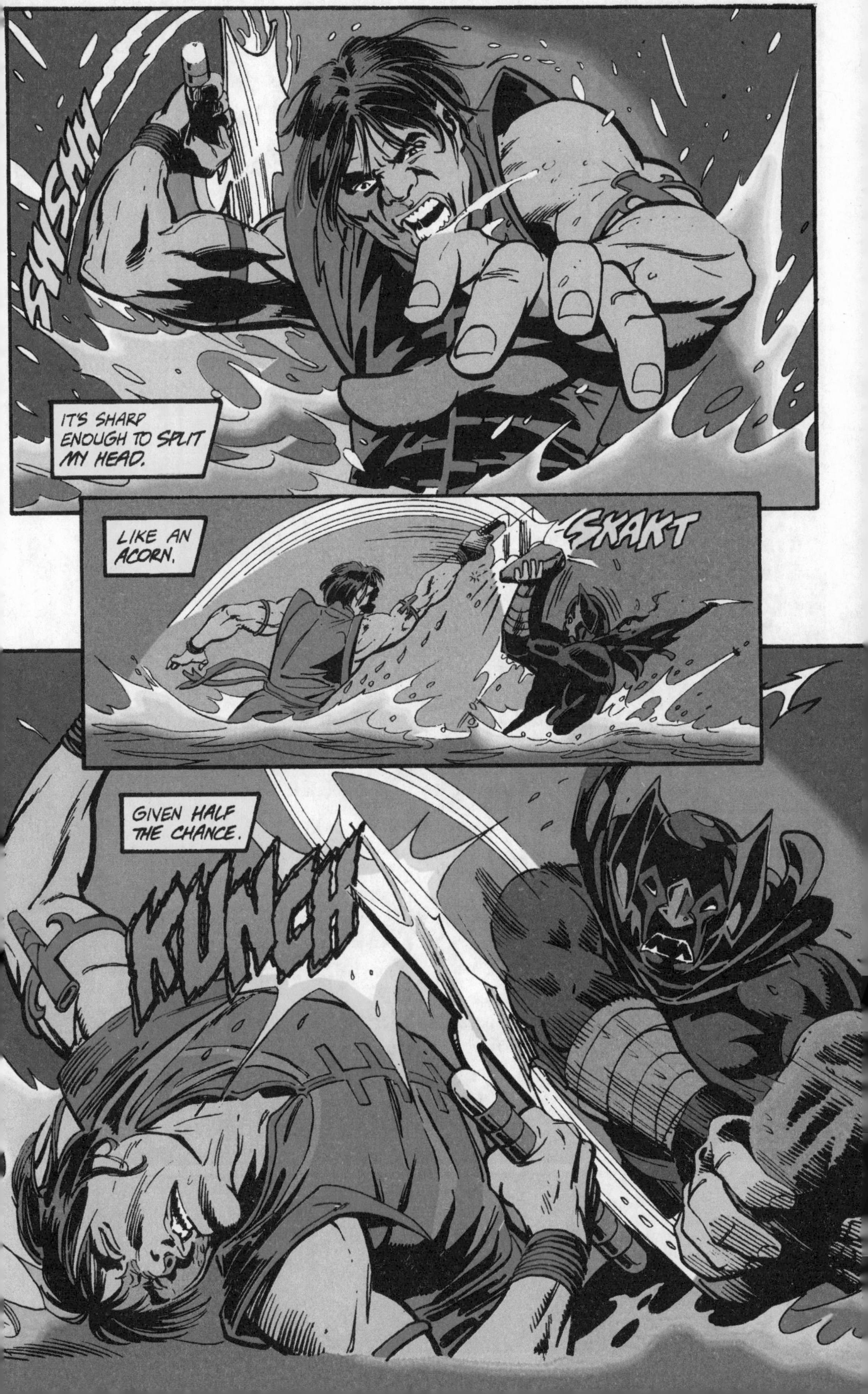
SHSHH
IT'S SHARP ENOUGH TO SPLIT MY HEAD.
LIKE AN ACORN.
SKAKT
GIVEN HALF THE CHANCE.
KUNCH

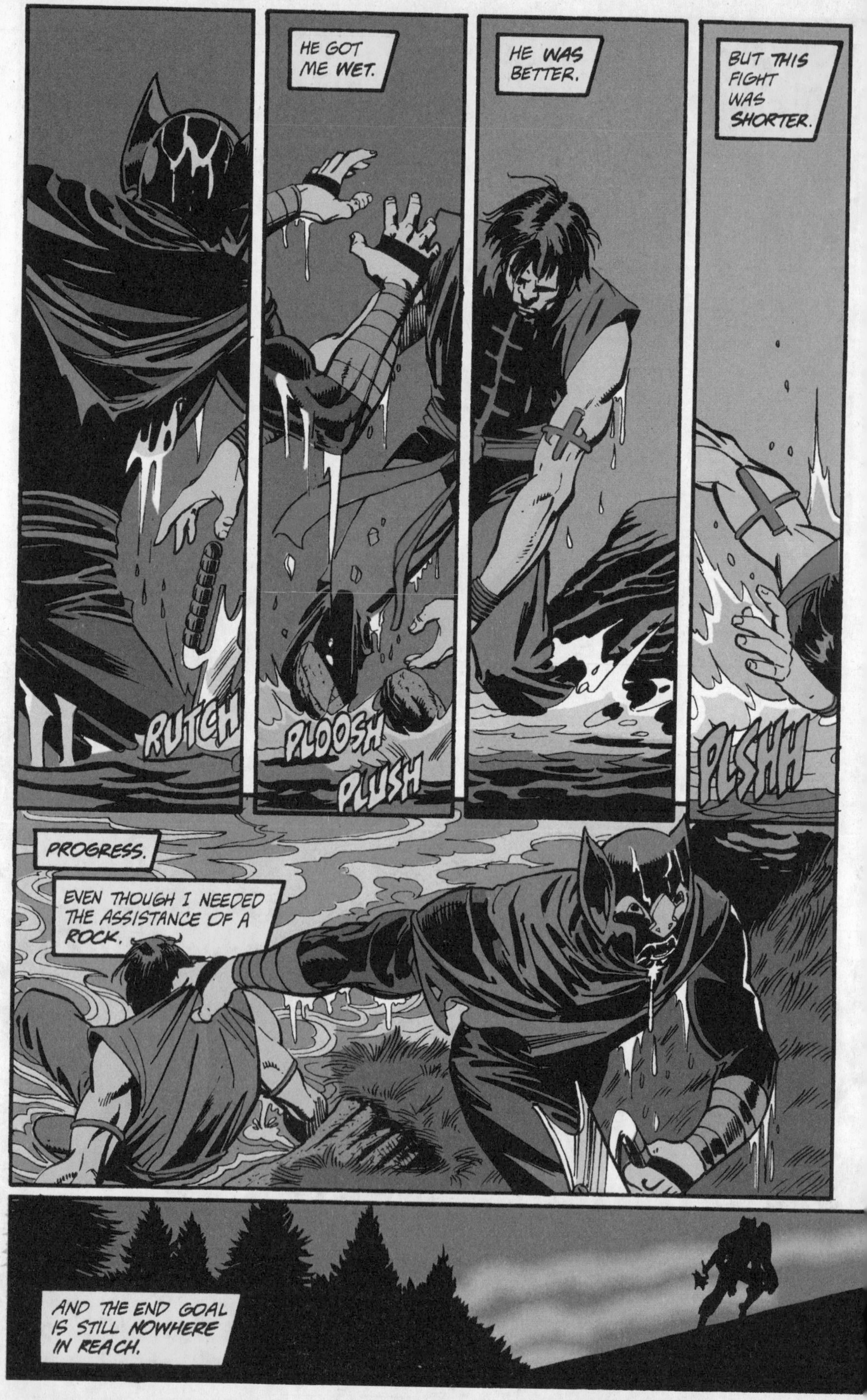
RUTCH
HE GOT ME WET.
PLOOSH
PLUSH
HE WAS BETTER.
BUT THIS FIGHT WAS SHORTER.
PLSHH
PROGRESS.
EVEN THOUGH I NEEDED THE ASSISTANCE OF A ROCK.
AND THE END GOAL IS STILL NOWHERE IN REACH.

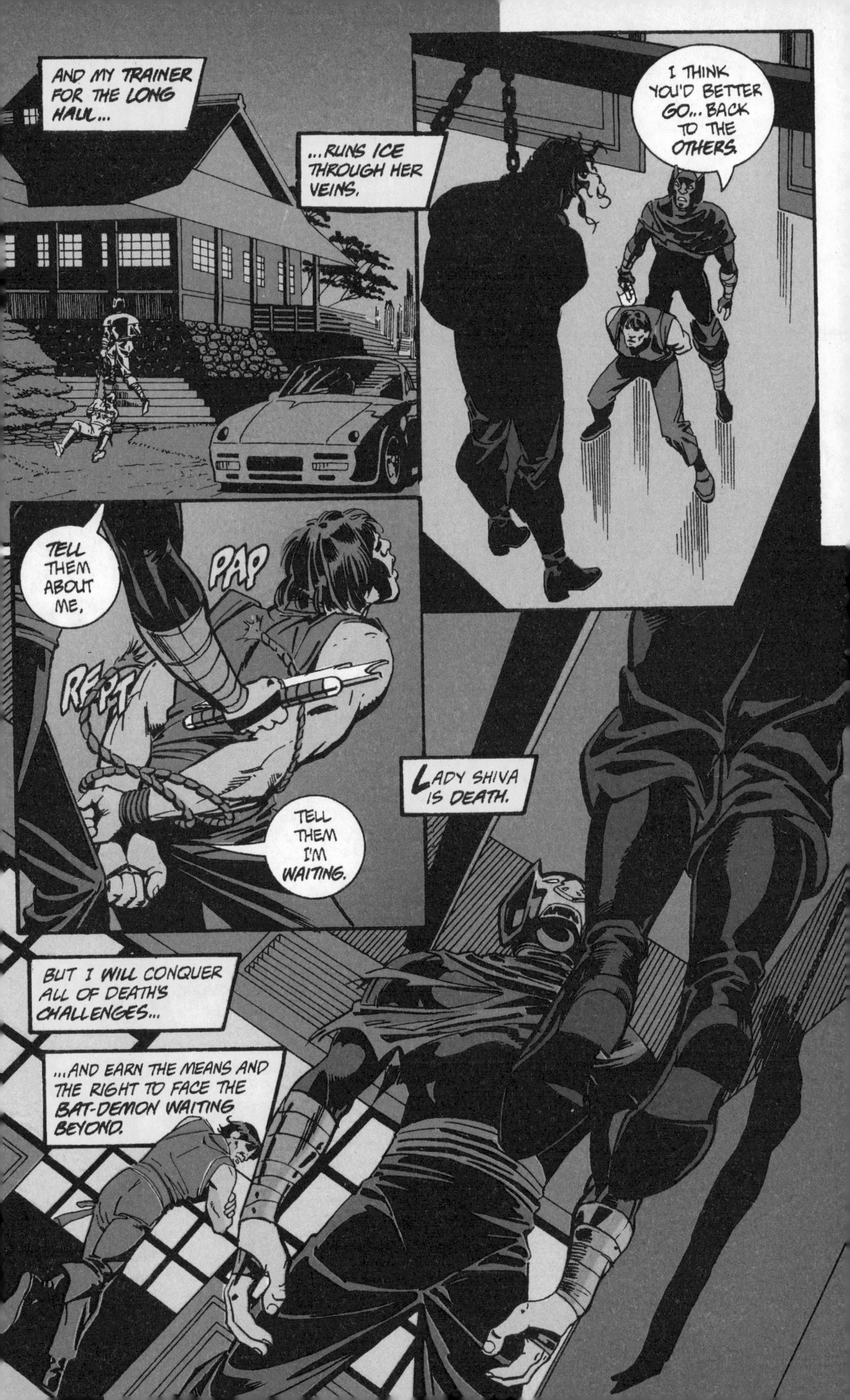
AND MY TRAINER FOR THE LONG HAUL...
...RUNS ICE THROUGH HER VEINS.
I THINK YOU'D BETTER GO... BACK TO THE OTHERS.
TELL THEM ABOUT ME.
PAP
REPT
TELL THEM I'M WAITING.
LADY SHIVA IS DEATH.
BUT I WILL CONQUER ALL OF DEATH'S CHALLENGES...
...AND EARN THE MEANS AND THE RIGHT TO FACE THE BAT-DEMON WAITING BEYOND.

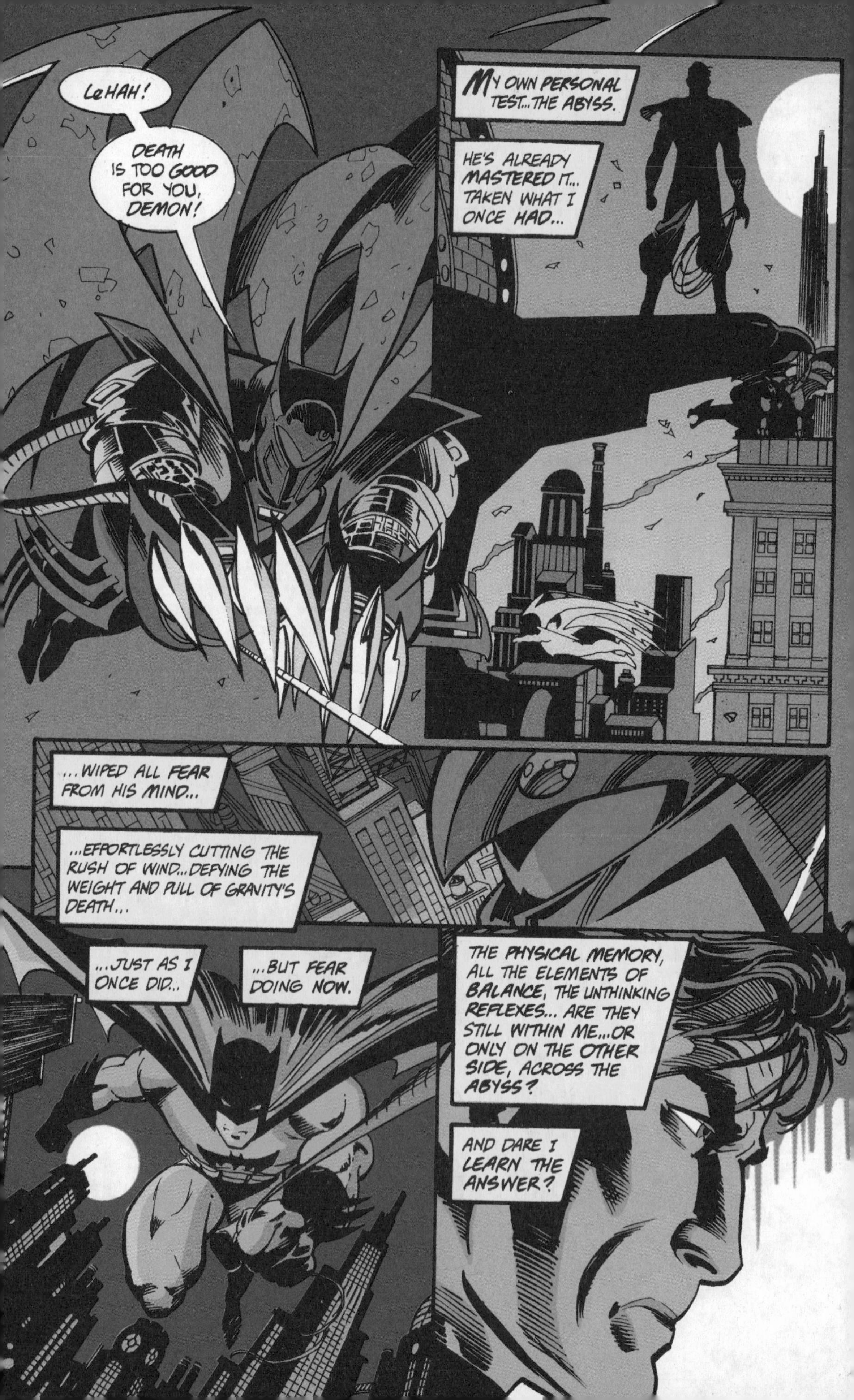
LeHAH!
DEATH IS TOO GOOD FOR YOU, DEMON!
MY OWN PERSONAL TEST... THE ABYSS.
HE'S ALREADY MASTERED IT... TAKEN WHAT I ONCE HAD...
...WIPED ALL FEAR FROM HIS MIND...
...EFFORTLESSLY CUTTING THE RUSH OF WIND...DEFYING THE WEIGHT AND PULL OF GRAVITY'S DEATH...
...JUST AS I ONCE DID...
...BUT FEAR DOING NOW.
THE PHYSICAL MEMORY, ALL THE ELEMENTS OF BALANCE, THE UNTHINKING REFLEXES... ARE THEY STILL WITHIN ME...OR ONLY ON THE OTHER SIDE, ACROSS THE ABYSS?
AND DARE I LEARN THE ANSWER?

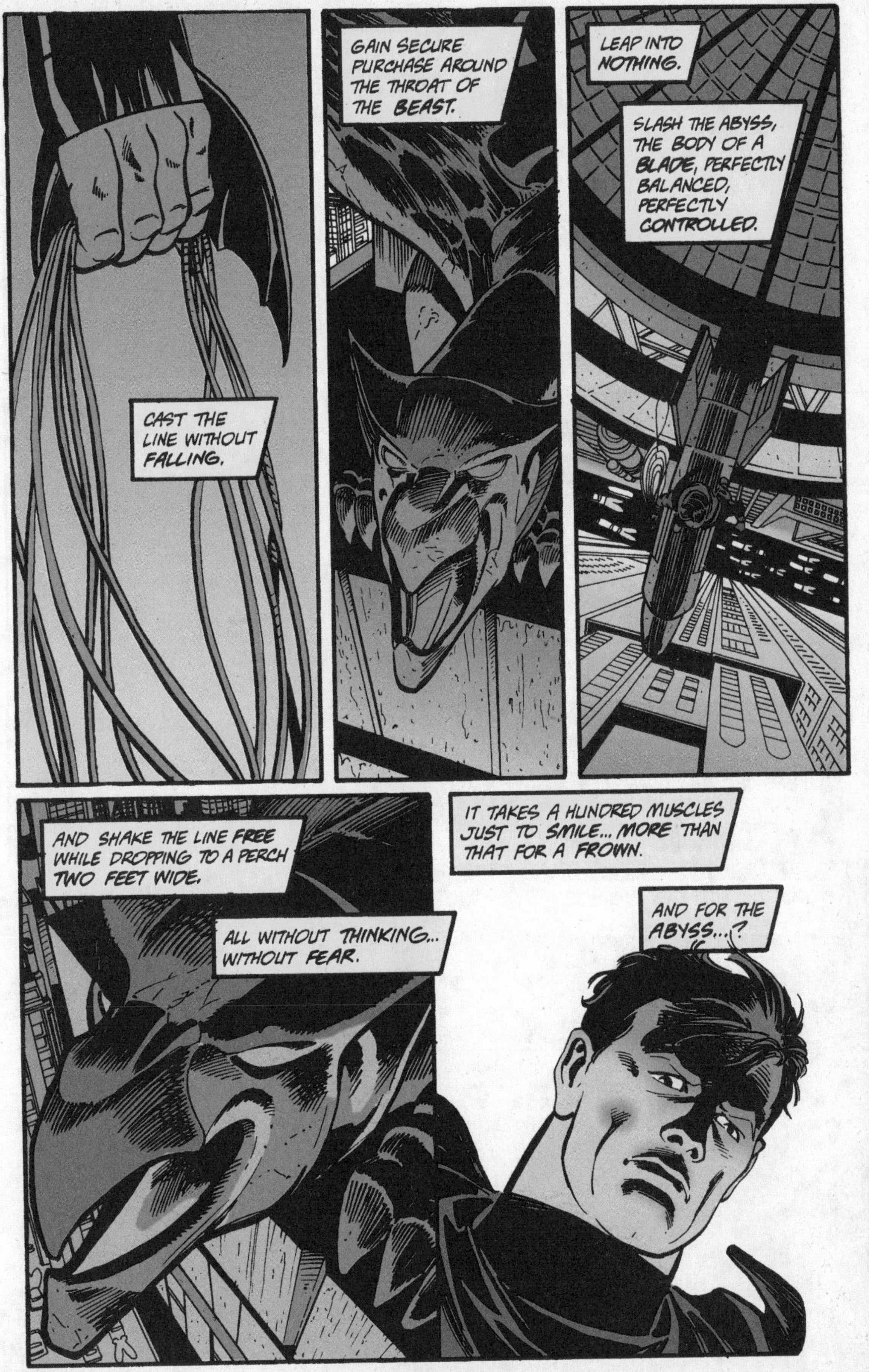

CAST THE LINE WITHOUT FALLING.
GAIN SECURE PURCHASE AROUND THE THROAT OF THE BEAST.
LEAP INTO NOTHING.
SLASH THE ABYSS, THE BODY OF A BLADE, PERFECTLY BALANCED, PERFECTLY CONTROLLED.
AND SHAKE THE LINE FREE WHILE DROPPING TO A PERCH TWO FEET WIDE.
ALL WITHOUT THINKING... WITHOUT FEAR.
IT TAKES A HUNDRED MUSCLES JUST TO SMILE... MORE THAN THAT FOR A FROWN.
AND FOR THE ABYSS...?

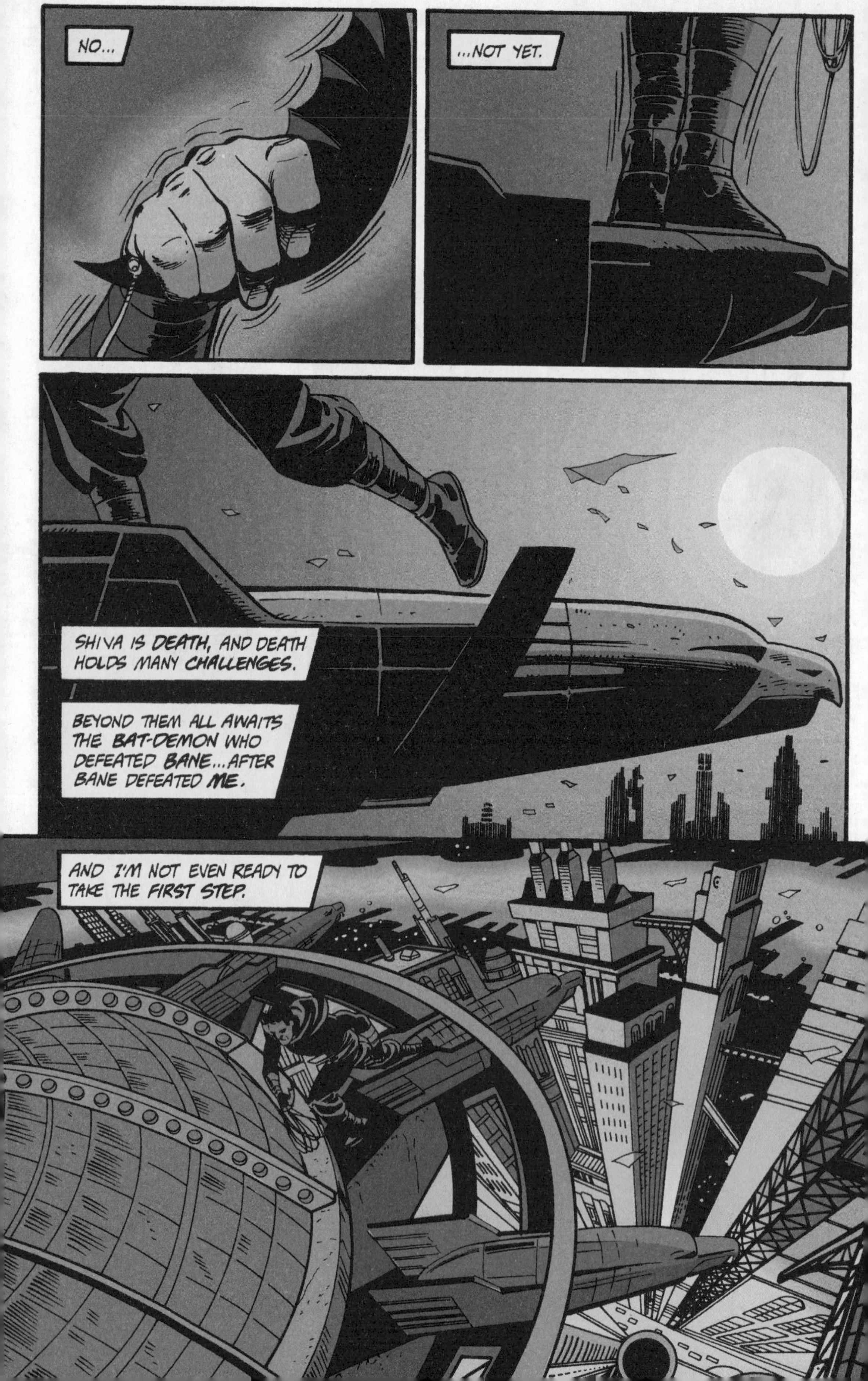
NO...
...NOT YET.
SHIVA IS DEATH, AND DEATH HOLDS MANY CHALLENGES.
BEYOND THEM ALL AWAITS THE BAT-DEMON WHO DEFEATED BANE...AFTER BANE DEFEATED ME.
AND I'M NOT EVEN READY TO TAKE THE FIRST STEP.

Cover art by **BRIAN STELFREEZE**

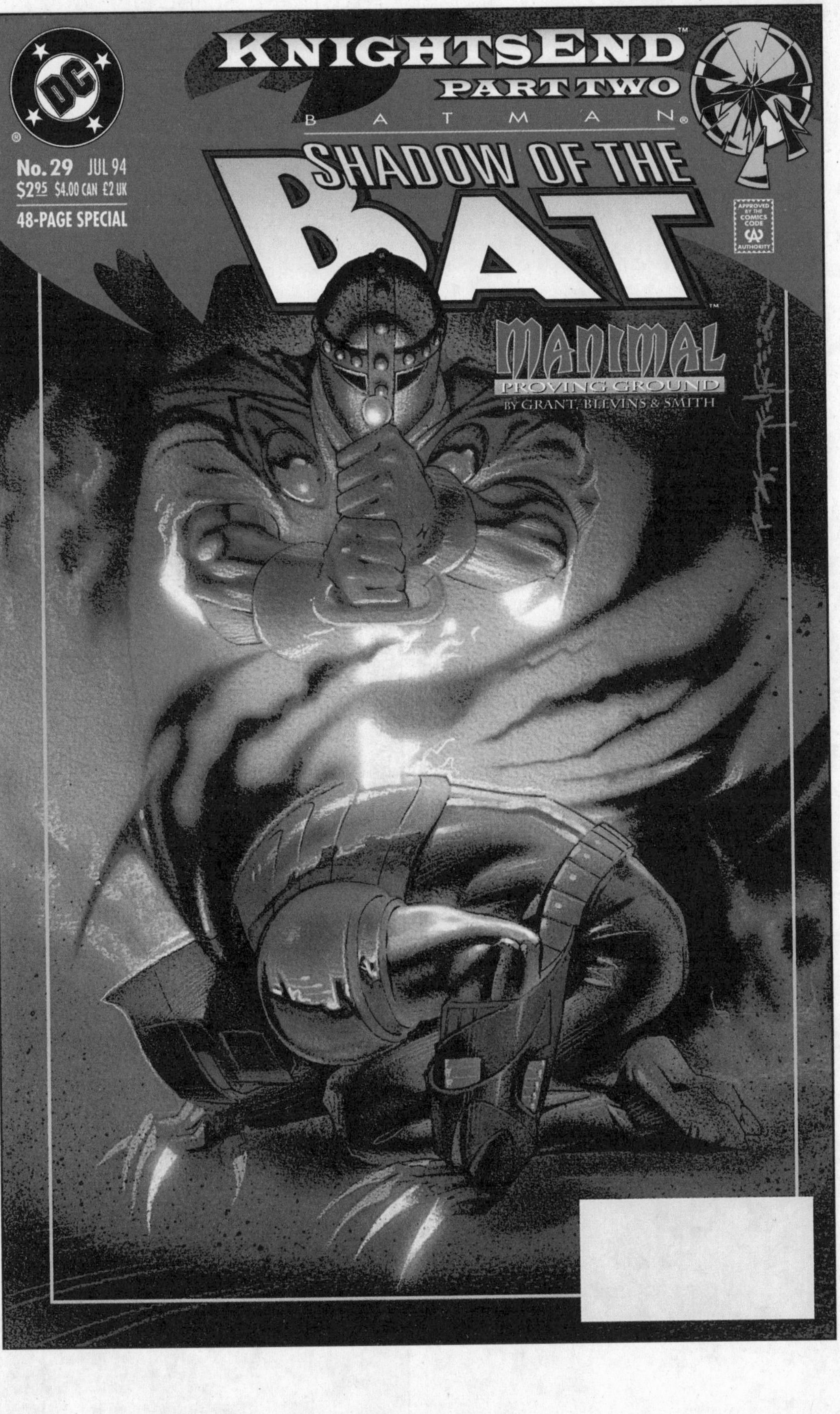
DC
KNIGHTSEND
PART TWO
BATMAN
No. 29 JUL 94
$2.95 $4.00 CAN £2 UK
48-PAGE SPECIAL
SHADOW OF THE BAT
APPROVED BY THE COMICS CODE AUTHORITY
MANIMAL
PROVING GROUND
BY GRANT, BLEVINS & SMITH

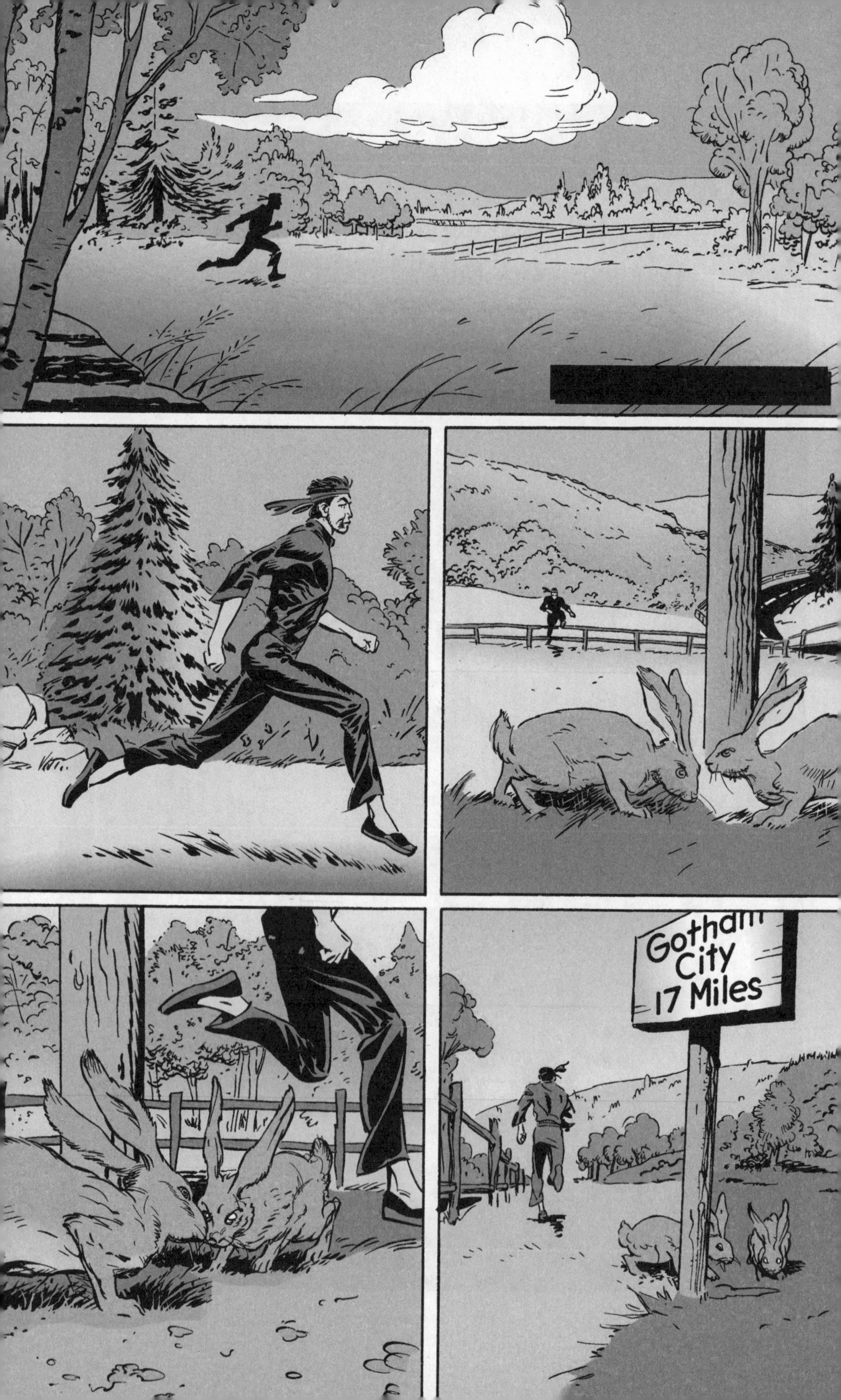
[redacted]
Gotham City 17 Miles

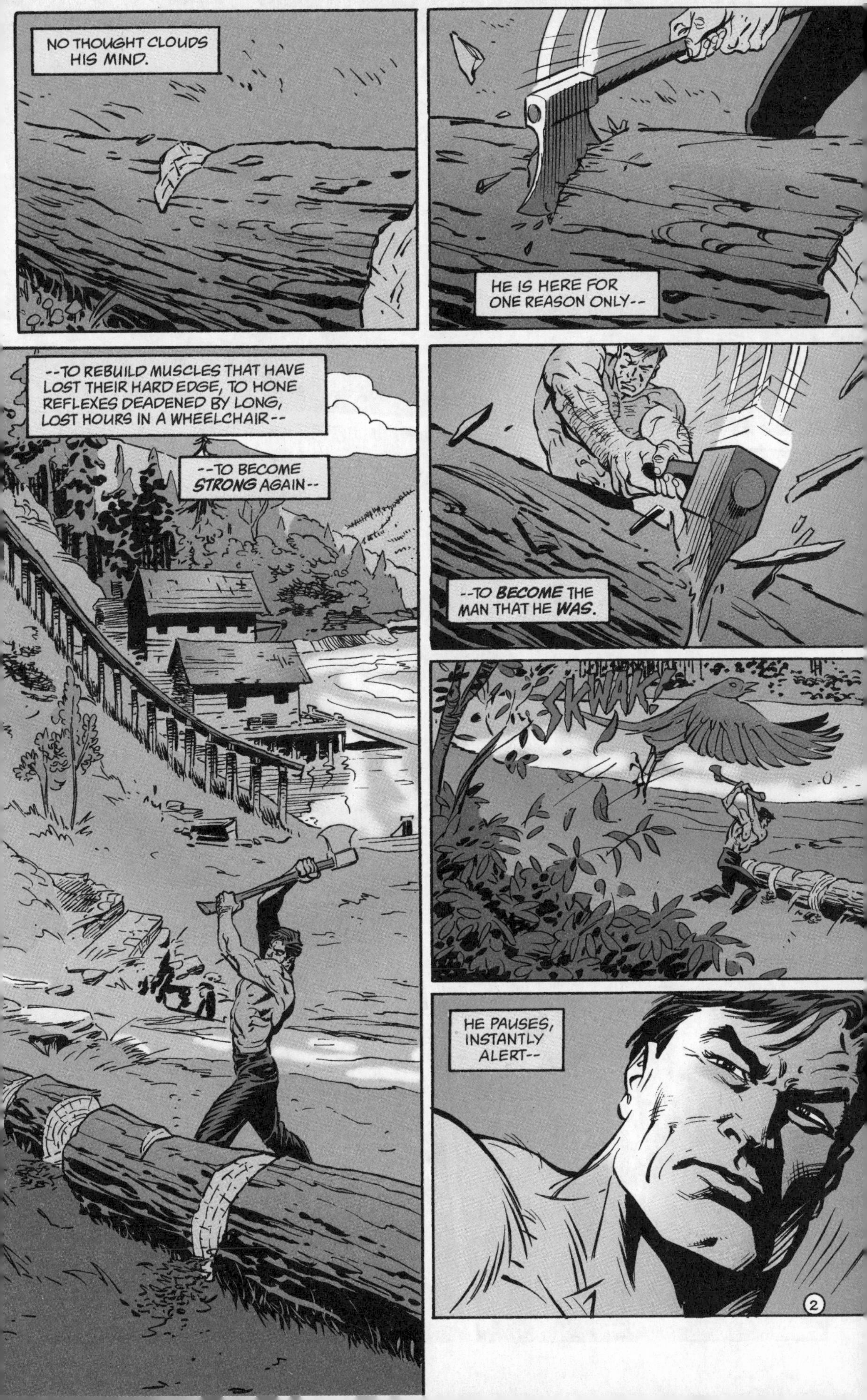
NO THOUGHT CLOUDS HIS MIND.
HE IS HERE FOR ONE REASON ONLY--
--TO REBUILD MUSCLES THAT HAVE LOST THEIR HARD EDGE, TO HONE REFLEXES DEADENED BY LONG, LOST HOURS IN A WHEELCHAIR--
--TO BECOME STRONG AGAIN--
--TO BECOME THE MAN THAT HE WAS.
SKWAK!
HE PAUSES, INSTANTLY ALERT--
2

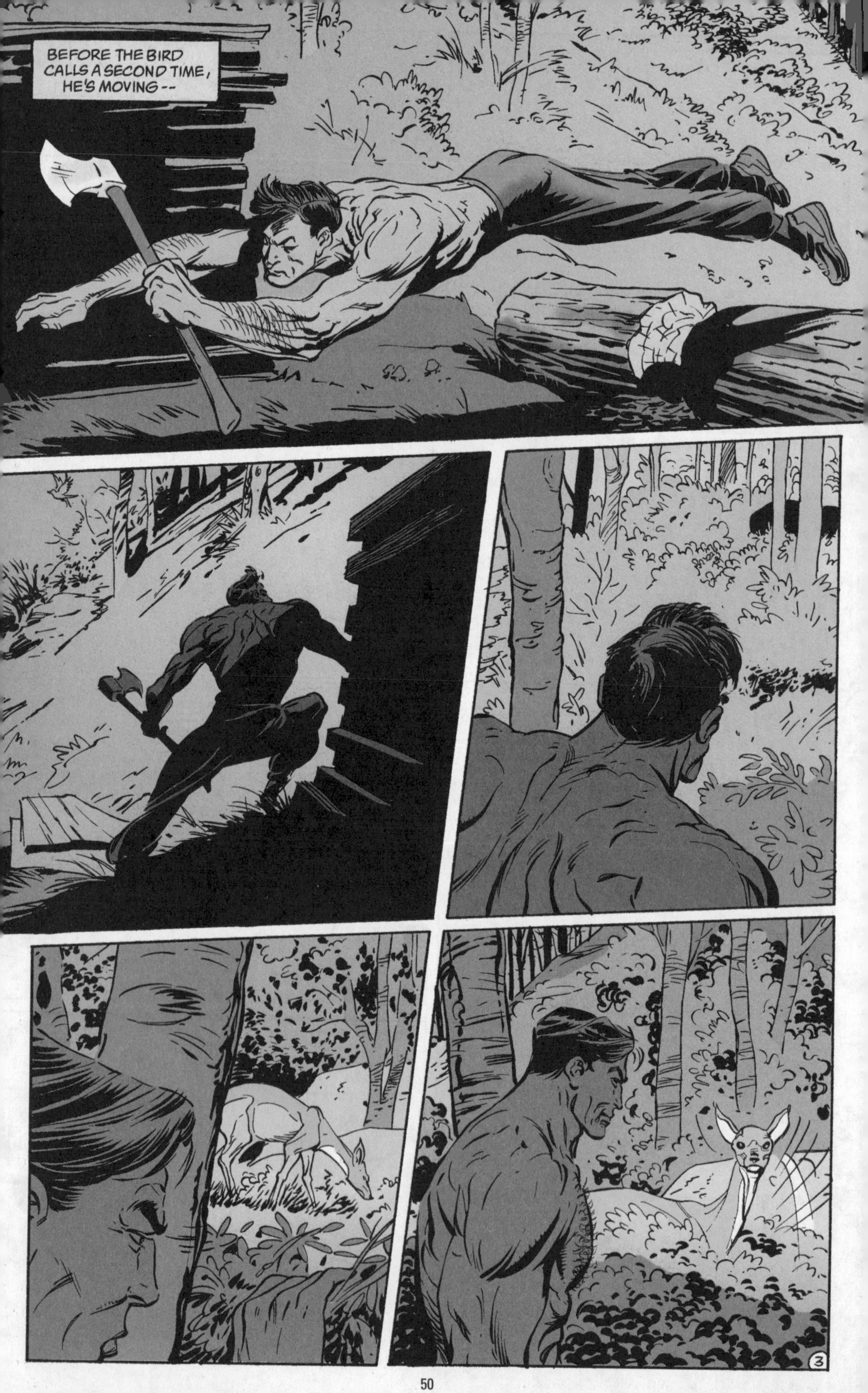
BEFORE THE BIRD CALLS A SECOND TIME, HE'S MOVING --
3

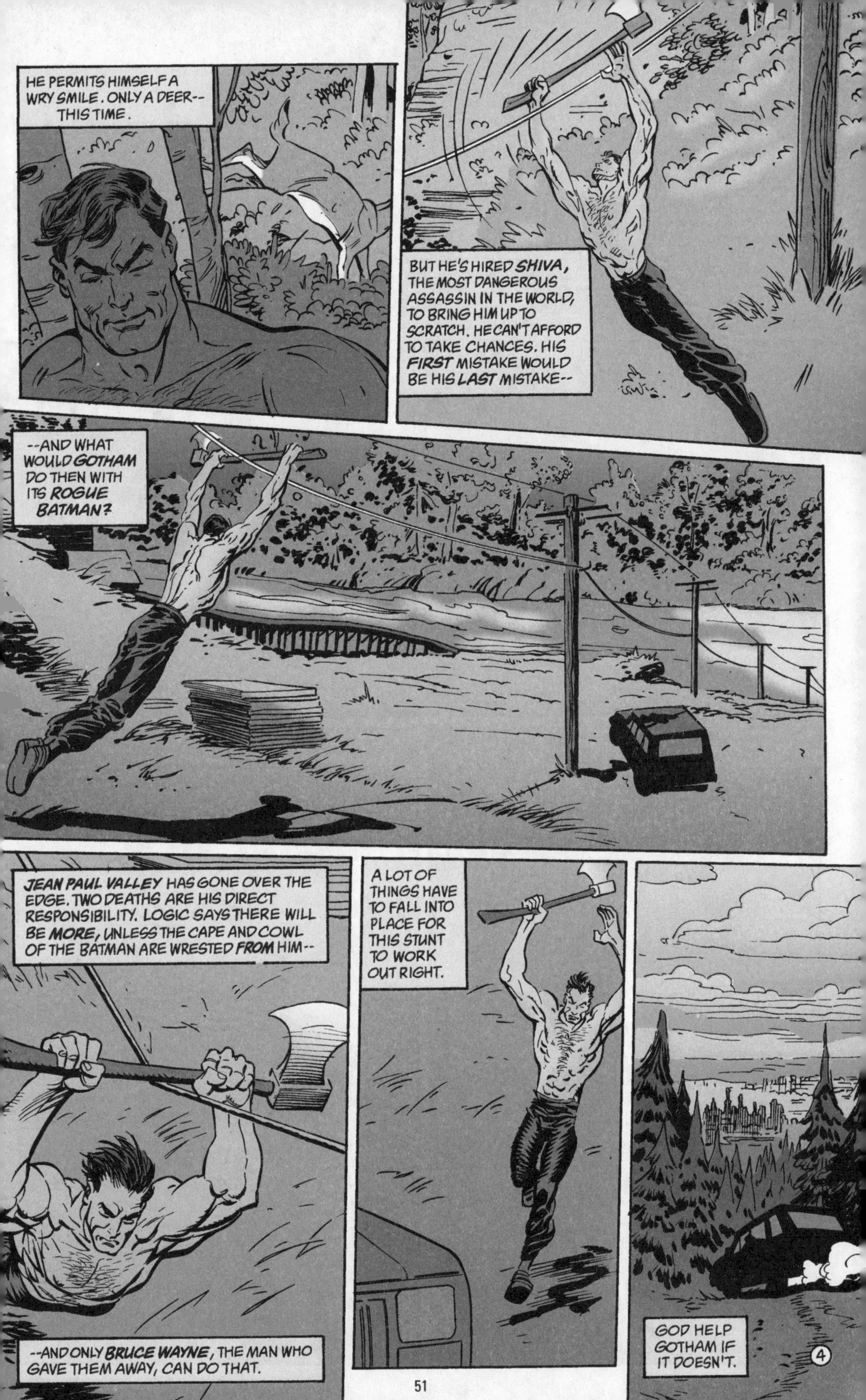
HE PERMITS HIMSELF A WRY SMILE. ONLY A DEER-- THIS TIME.
BUT HE'S HIRED SHIVA, THE MOST DANGEROUS ASSASSIN IN THE WORLD, TO BRING HIM UP TO SCRATCH. HE CAN'T AFFORD TO TAKE CHANCES. HIS FIRST MISTAKE WOULD BE HIS LAST MISTAKE--
--AND WHAT WOULD GOTHAM DO THEN WITH ITS ROGUE BATMAN?
JEAN PAUL VALLEY HAS GONE OVER THE EDGE. TWO DEATHS ARE HIS DIRECT RESPONSIBILITY. LOGIC SAYS THERE WILL BE MORE, UNLESS THE CAPE AND COWL OF THE BATMAN ARE WRESTED FROM HIM--
--AND ONLY BRUCE WAYNE, THE MAN WHO GAVE THEM AWAY, CAN DO THAT.
A LOT OF THINGS HAVE TO FALL INTO PLACE FOR THIS STUNT TO WORK OUT RIGHT.
GOD HELP GOTHAM IF IT DOESN'T.
4

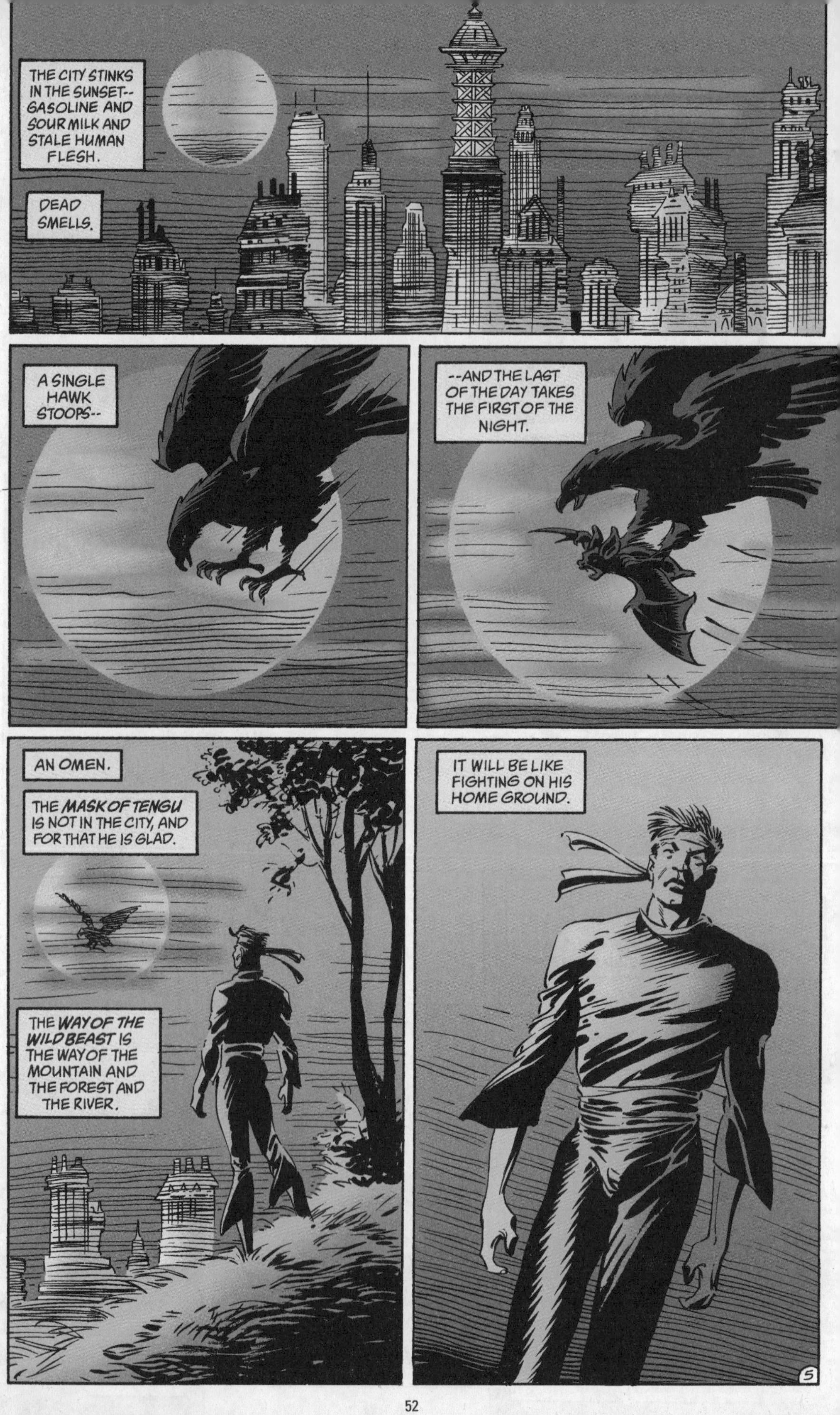
THE CITY STINKS IN THE SUNSET-- GASOLINE AND SOUR MILK AND STALE HUMAN FLESH.
DEAD SMELLS.
A SINGLE HAWK STOOPS--
--AND THE LAST OF THE DAY TAKES THE FIRST OF THE NIGHT.
AN OMEN.
THE MASK OF TENGU IS NOT IN THE CITY, AND FOR THAT HE IS GLAD.
THE WAY OF THE WILD BEAST IS THE WAY OF THE MOUNTAIN AND THE FOREST AND THE RIVER.
IT WILL BE LIKE FIGHTING ON HIS HOME GROUND.
5

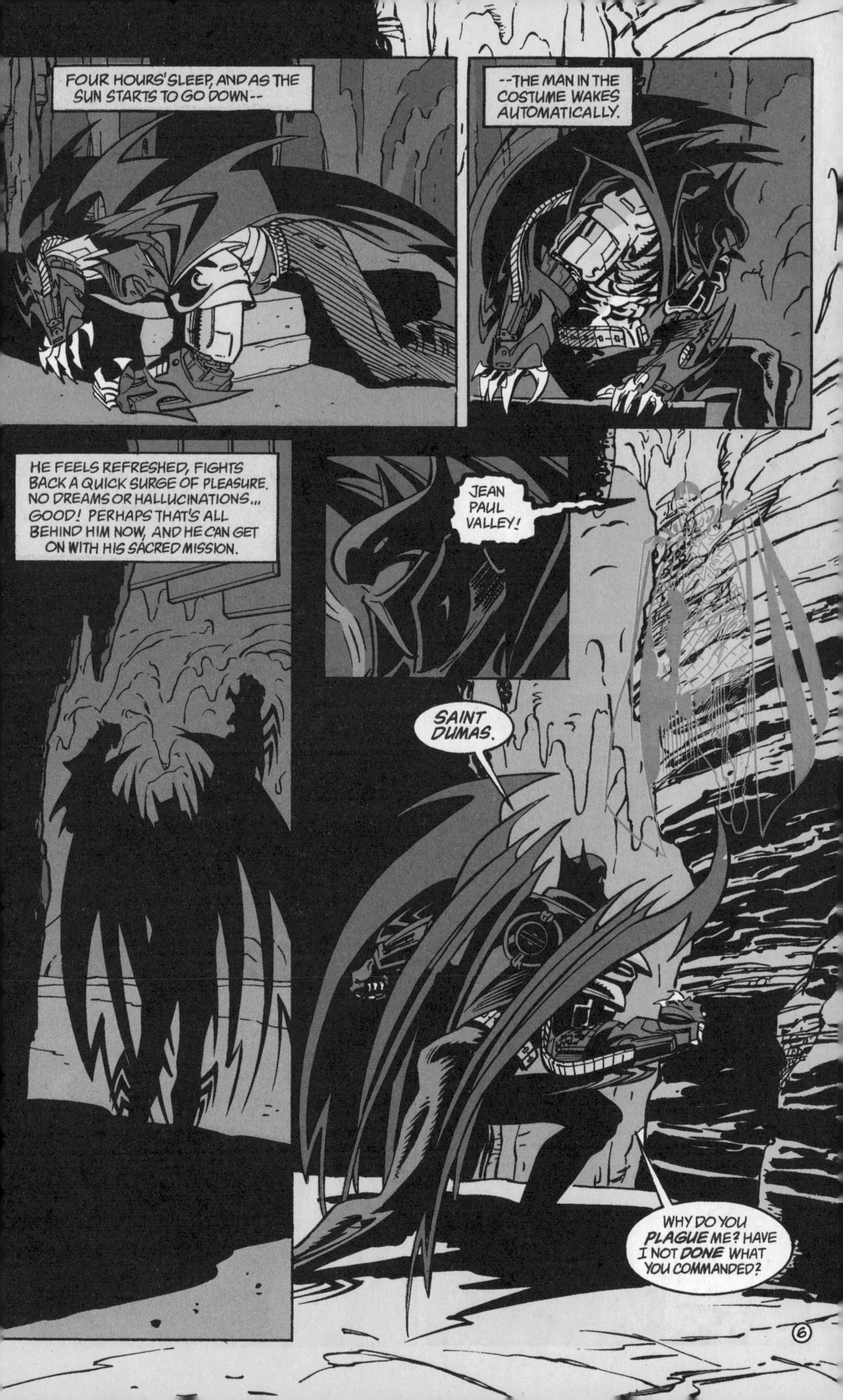

FOUR HOURS' SLEEP, AND AS THE SUN STARTS TO GO DOWN--
--THE MAN IN THE COSTUME WAKES AUTOMATICALLY.
HE FEELS REFRESHED, FIGHTS BACK A QUICK SURGE OF PLEASURE. NO DREAMS OR HALLUCINATIONS... GOOD! PERHAPS THAT'S ALL BEHIND HIM NOW, AND HE CAN GET ON WITH HIS SACRED MISSION.
JEAN PAUL VALLEY!
SAINT DUMAS.
WHY DO YOU PLAGUE ME? HAVE I NOT DONE WHAT YOU COMMANDED?

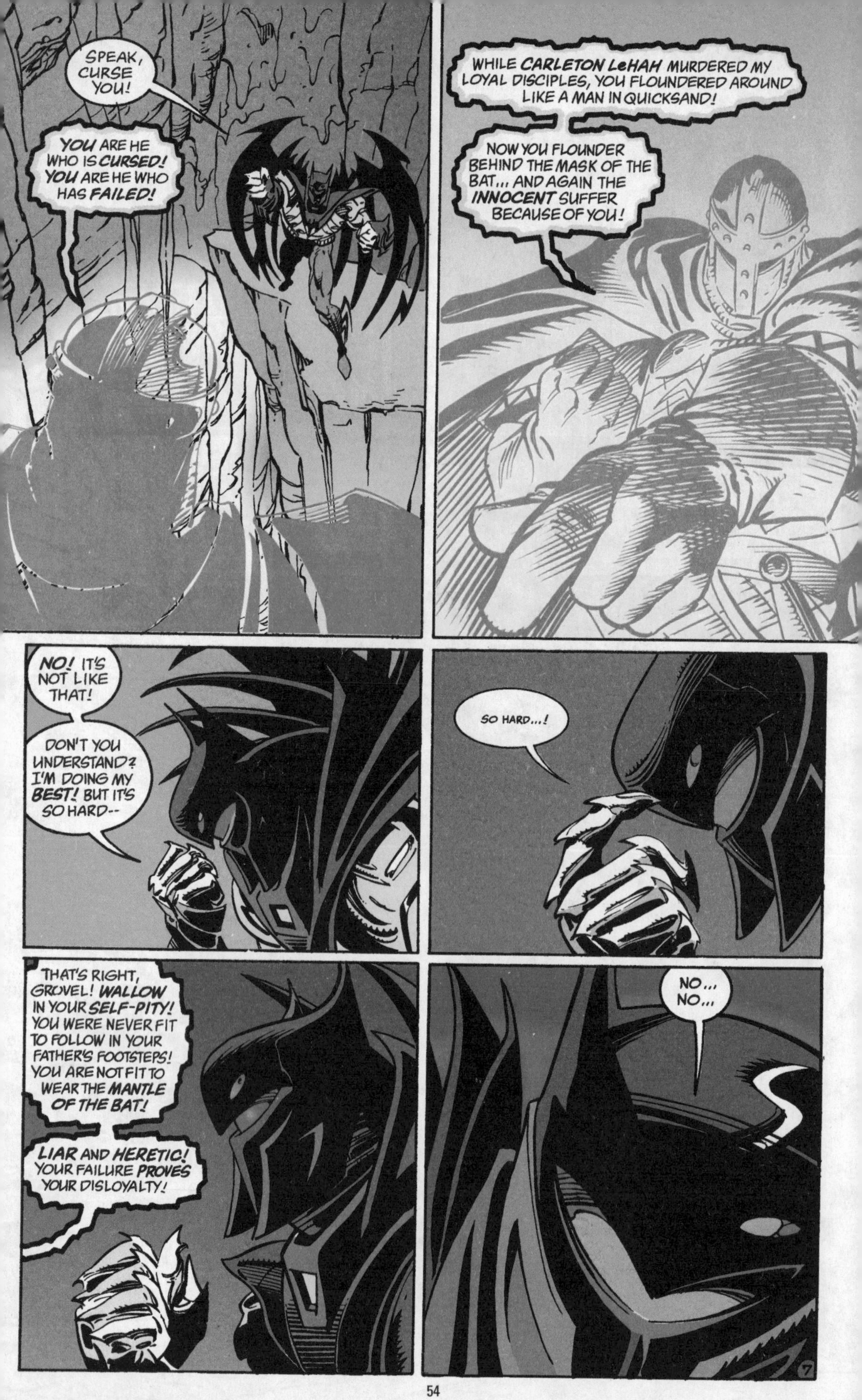
SPEAK, CURSE YOU!
YOU ARE HE WHO IS CURSED! YOU ARE HE WHO HAS FAILED!
WHILE CARLETON LeHAH MURDERED MY LOYAL DISCIPLES, YOU FLOUNDERED AROUND LIKE A MAN IN QUICKSAND!
NOW YOU FLOUNDER BEHIND THE MASK OF THE BAT... AND AGAIN THE INNOCENT SUFFER BECAUSE OF YOU!
NO! IT'S NOT LIKE THAT!
DON'T YOU UNDERSTAND? I'M DOING MY BEST! BUT IT'S SO HARD--
SO HARD...!
THAT'S RIGHT, GROVEL! WALLOW IN YOUR SELF-PITY! YOU WERE NEVER FIT TO FOLLOW IN YOUR FATHER'S FOOTSTEPS! YOU ARE NOT FIT TO WEAR THE MANTLE OF THE BAT!
LIAR AND HERETIC! YOUR FAILURE PROVES YOUR DISLOYALTY!
NO... NO...
7

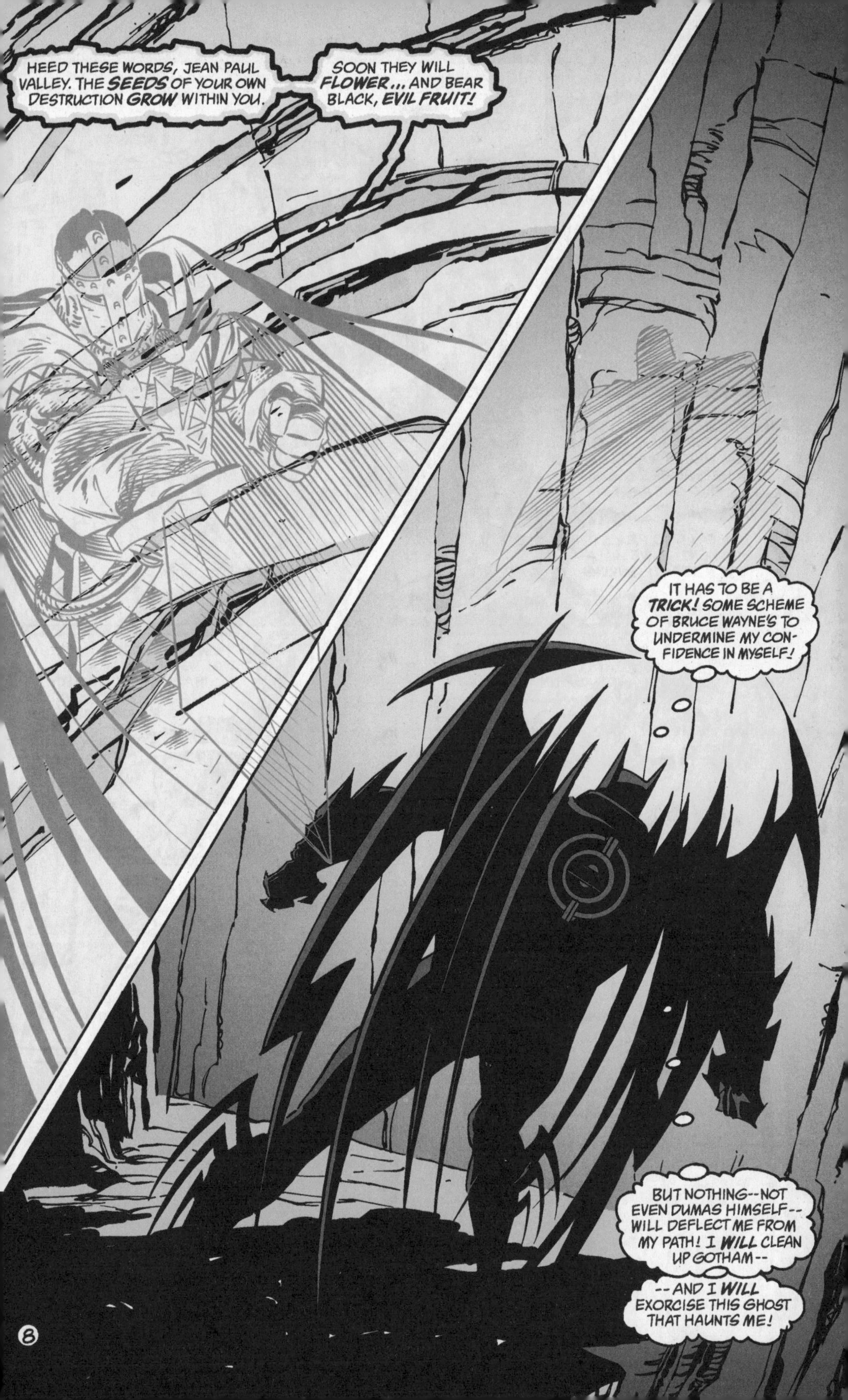
HEED THESE WORDS, JEAN PAUL VALLEY. THE SEEDS OF YOUR OWN DESTRUCTION GROW WITHIN YOU.
SOON THEY WILL FLOWER... AND BEAR BLACK, EVIL FRUIT!
IT HAS TO BE A TRICK! SOME SCHEME OF BRUCE WAYNE'S TO UNDERMINE MY CONFIDENCE IN MYSELF!
BUT NOTHING--NOT EVEN DUMAS HIMSELF--WILL DEFLECT ME FROM MY PATH! I WILL CLEAN UP GOTHAM--
--AND I WILL EXORCISE THIS GHOST THAT HAUNTS ME!

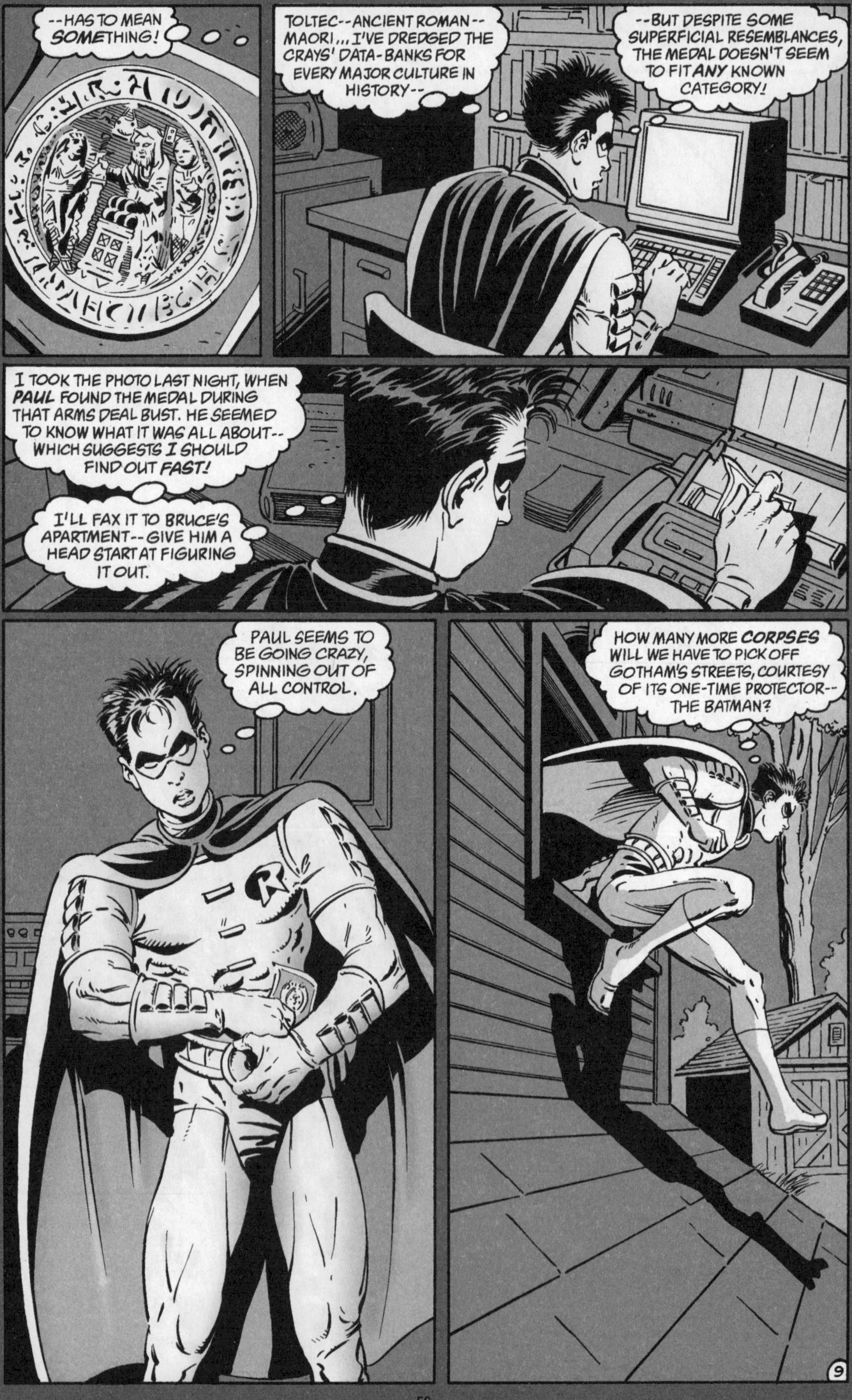
--HAS TO MEAN SOMETHING!
TOLTEC--ANCIENT ROMAN--MAORI... I'VE DREDGED THE CRAYS' DATA-BANKS FOR EVERY MAJOR CULTURE IN HISTORY--
--BUT DESPITE SOME SUPERFICIAL RESEMBLANCES, THE MEDAL DOESN'T SEEM TO FIT ANY KNOWN CATEGORY!
I TOOK THE PHOTO LAST NIGHT, WHEN PAUL FOUND THE MEDAL DURING THAT ARMS DEAL BUST. HE SEEMED TO KNOW WHAT IT WAS ALL ABOUT--WHICH SUGGESTS I SHOULD FIND OUT FAST!
I'LL FAX IT TO BRUCE'S APARTMENT--GIVE HIM A HEAD START AT FIGURING IT OUT.
PAUL SEEMS TO BE GOING CRAZY, SPINNING OUT OF ALL CONTROL.
HOW MANY MORE CORPSES WILL WE HAVE TO PICK OFF GOTHAM'S STREETS, COURTESY OF ITS ONE-TIME PROTECTOR--THE BATMAN?
9

I'VE GOT A GUT FEELING THAT THE QUICKER WE SOLVE THIS ONE, THE BETTER! BUT I'M GETTING NO-WHERE FAST.

MAYBE A *WISER* HEAD THAN MINE'LL KNOW...!

.... ONE NINETY-THREE....

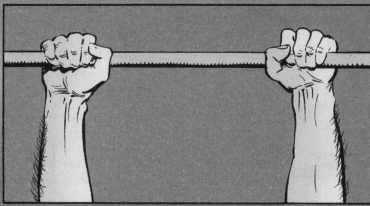

.... ONE NINETY-FOUR....

RAP RAP!

⑩

EXPECTING TROUBLE?

ALWAYS -- AT LEAST, WHEN *SHIVA'S* IN THE GAME!

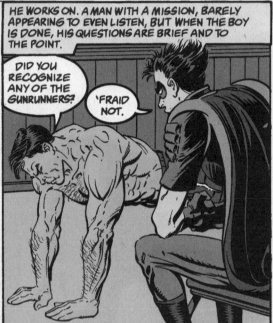

HE WORKS ON. A MAN WITH A MISSION, BARELY APPEARING TO EVEN LISTEN, BUT WHEN THE BOY IS DONE, HIS QUESTIONS ARE BRIEF AND TO THE POINT.

DID YOU RECOGNIZE ANY OF THE GUNRUNNERS?

'FRAID NOT.

CARLETON LeHAH?

I THOUGHT HE WAS DEAD...?

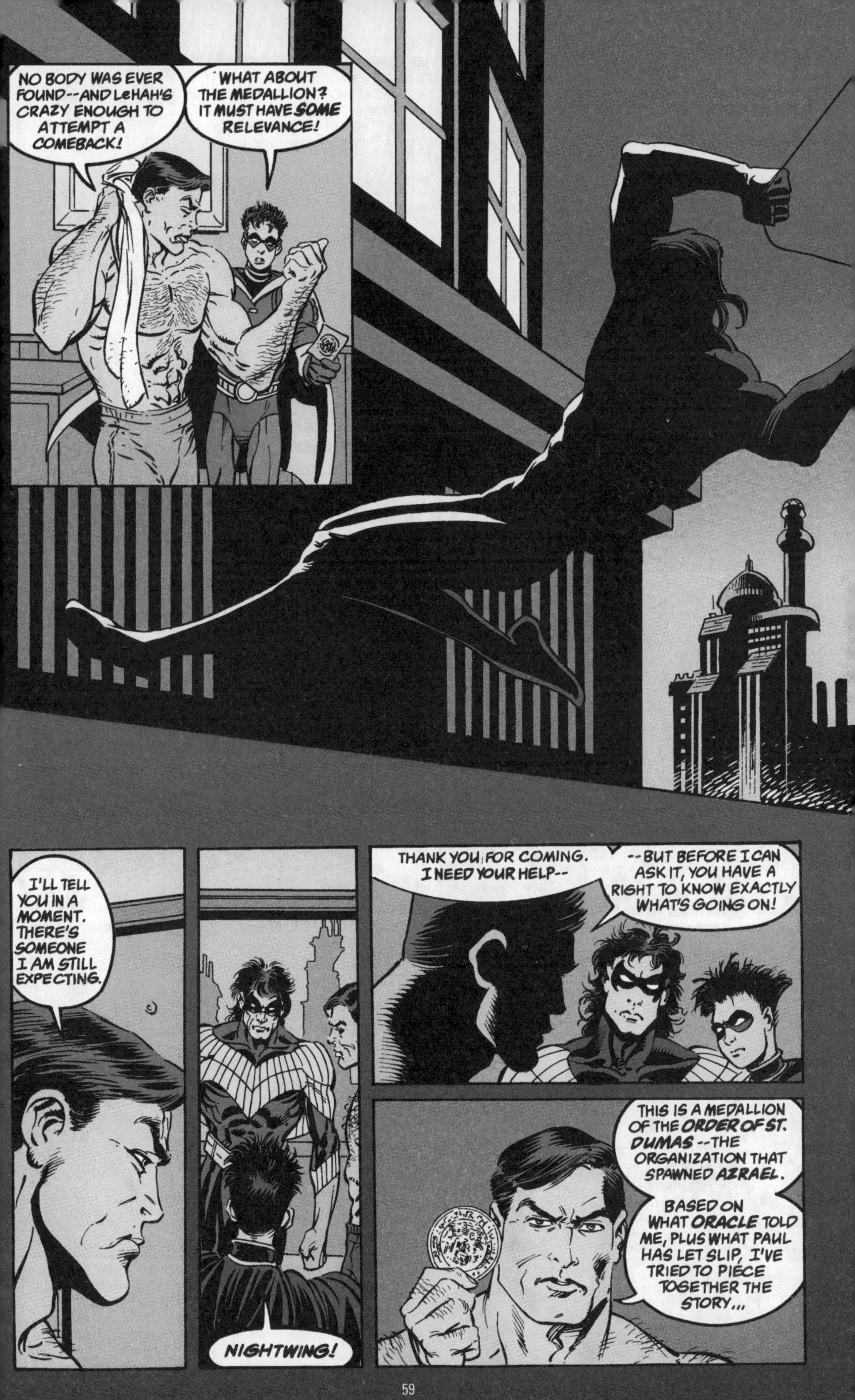

NO BODY WAS EVER FOUND--AND LeHAH'S CRAZY ENOUGH TO ATTEMPT A COMEBACK!
WHAT ABOUT THE MEDALLION? IT MUST HAVE SOME RELEVANCE!
I'LL TELL YOU IN A MOMENT. THERE'S SOMEONE I AM STILL EXPECTING.
NIGHTWING!
THANK YOU FOR COMING. I NEED YOUR HELP--
--BUT BEFORE I CAN ASK IT, YOU HAVE A RIGHT TO KNOW EXACTLY WHAT'S GOING ON!
THIS IS A MEDALLION OF THE ORDER OF ST. DUMAS --THE ORGANIZATION THAT SPAWNED AZRAEL.
BASED ON WHAT ORACLE TOLD ME, PLUS WHAT PAUL HAS LET SLIP, I'VE TRIED TO PIECE TOGETHER THE STORY...

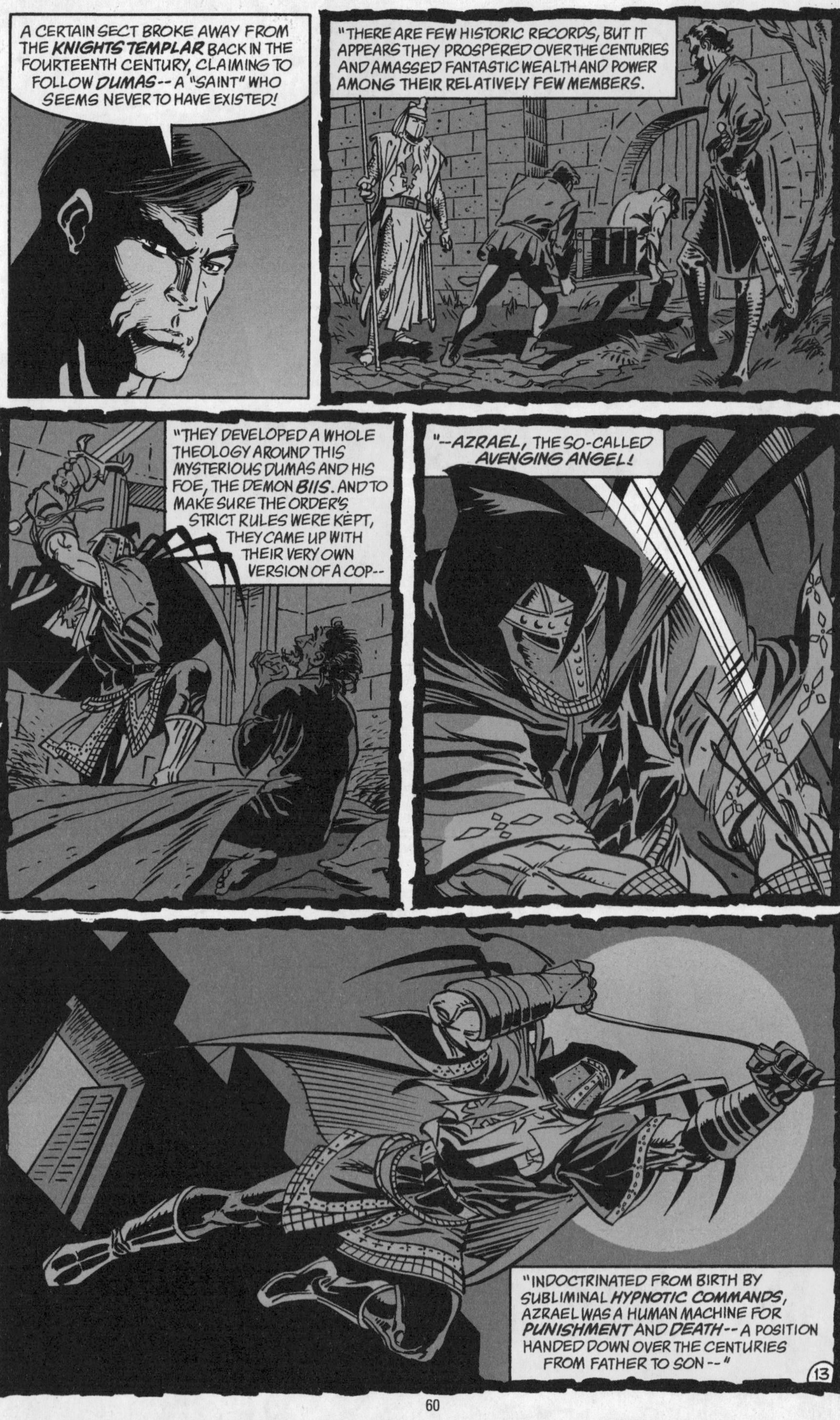
A CERTAIN SECT BROKE AWAY FROM THE KNIGHTS TEMPLAR BACK IN THE FOURTEENTH CENTURY, CLAIMING TO FOLLOW DUMAS-- A "SAINT" WHO SEEMS NEVER TO HAVE EXISTED!
"THERE ARE FEW HISTORIC RECORDS, BUT IT APPEARS THEY PROSPERED OVER THE CENTURIES AND AMASSED FANTASTIC WEALTH AND POWER AMONG THEIR RELATIVELY FEW MEMBERS.
"THEY DEVELOPED A WHOLE THEOLOGY AROUND THIS MYSTERIOUS DUMAS AND HIS FOE, THE DEMON BIIS. AND TO MAKE SURE THE ORDER'S STRICT RULES WERE KEPT, THEY CAME UP WITH THEIR VERY OWN VERSION OF A COP--
"--AZRAEL, THE SO-CALLED AVENGING ANGEL!
"INDOCTRINATED FROM BIRTH BY SUBLIMINAL HYPNOTIC COMMANDS, AZRAEL WAS A HUMAN MACHINE FOR PUNISHMENT AND DEATH-- A POSITION HANDED DOWN OVER THE CENTURIES FROM FATHER TO SON--"
13

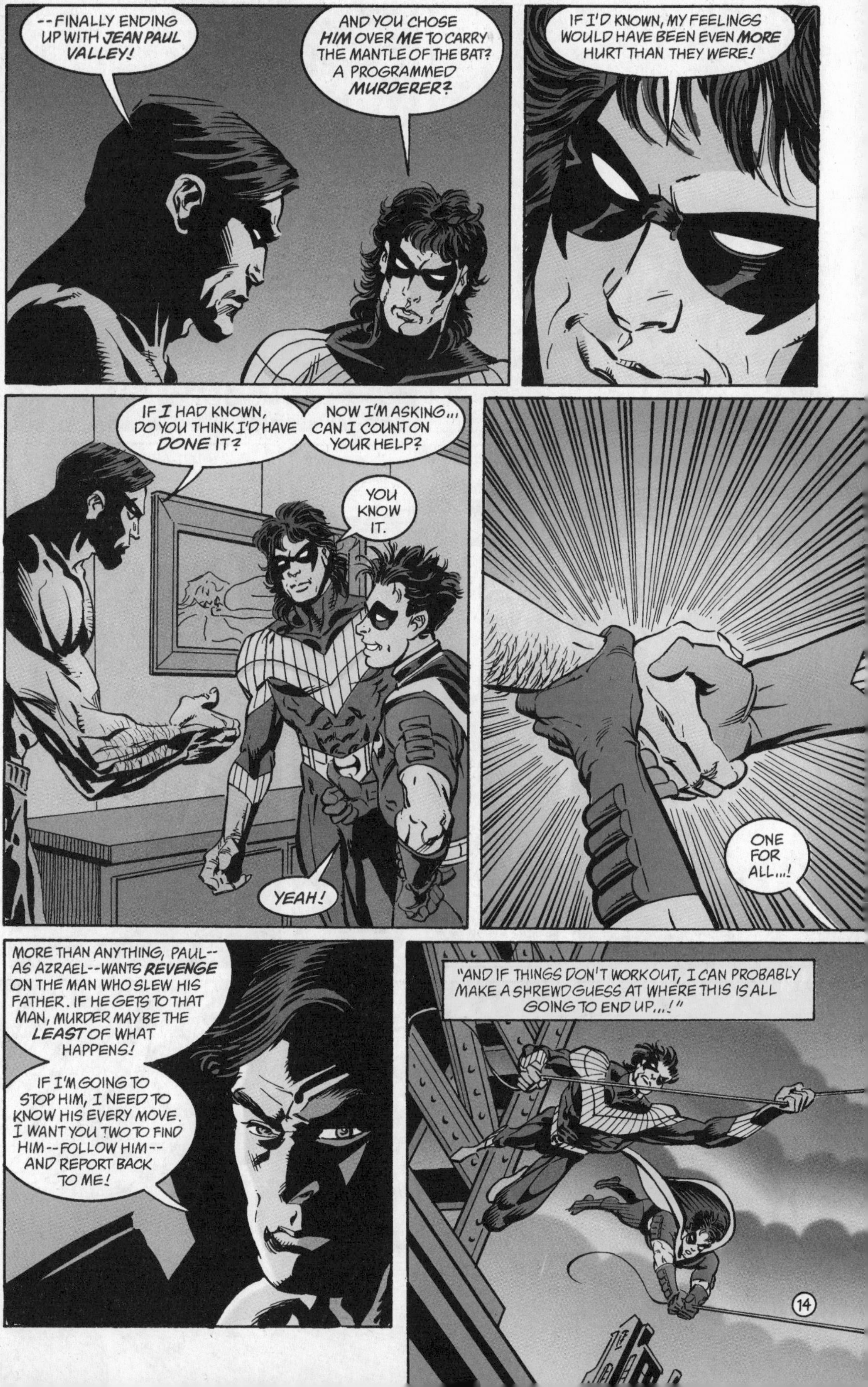
--FINALLY ENDING UP WITH JEAN PAUL VALLEY!
AND YOU CHOSE HIM OVER ME TO CARRY THE MANTLE OF THE BAT? A PROGRAMMED MURDERER?
IF I'D KNOWN, MY FEELINGS WOULD HAVE BEEN EVEN MORE HURT THAN THEY WERE!
IF I HAD KNOWN, DO YOU THINK I'D HAVE DONE IT?
NOW I'M ASKING... CAN I COUNT ON YOUR HELP?
YOU KNOW IT.
YEAH!
ONE FOR ALL...!
MORE THAN ANYTHING, PAUL--AS AZRAEL--WANTS REVENGE ON THE MAN WHO SLEW HIS FATHER. IF HE GETS TO THAT MAN, MURDER MAY BE THE LEAST OF WHAT HAPPENS!
IF I'M GOING TO STOP HIM, I NEED TO KNOW HIS EVERY MOVE. I WANT YOU TWO TO FIND HIM--FOLLOW HIM--AND REPORT BACK TO ME!
"AND IF THINGS DON'T WORK OUT, I CAN PROBABLY MAKE A SHREWD GUESS AT WHERE THIS IS ALL GOING TO END UP...!"
14

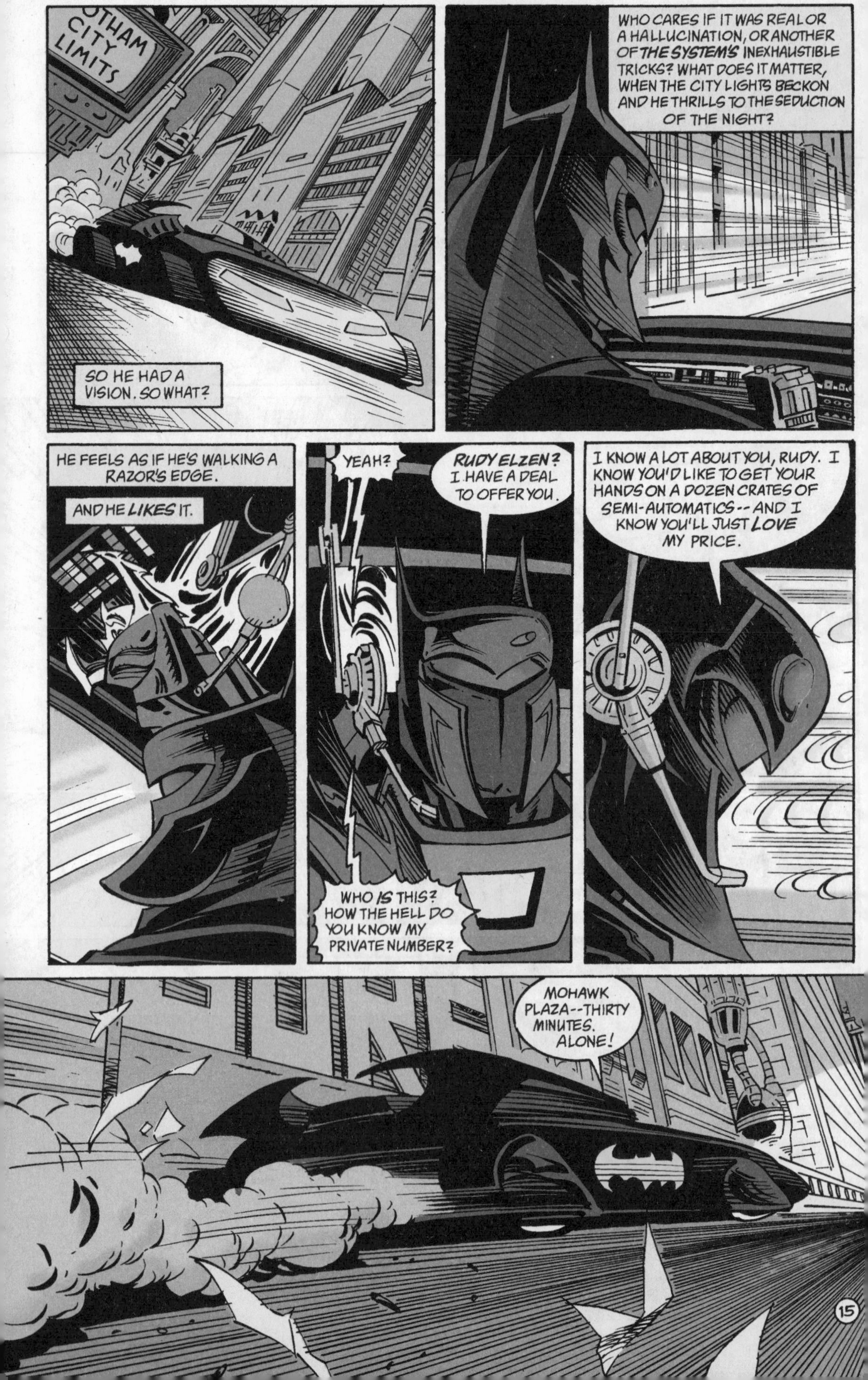
OTHAM CITY LIMITS
SO HE HAD A VISION. SO WHAT?
WHO CARES IF IT WAS REAL OR A HALLUCINATION, OR ANOTHER OF THE SYSTEM'S INEXHAUSTIBLE TRICKS? WHAT DOES IT MATTER, WHEN THE CITY LIGHTS BECKON AND HE THRILLS TO THE SEDUCTION OF THE NIGHT?
HE FEELS AS IF HE'S WALKING A RAZOR'S EDGE.
AND HE LIKES IT.
YEAH?
RUDY ELZEN? I HAVE A DEAL TO OFFER YOU.
WHO IS THIS? HOW THE HELL DO YOU KNOW MY PRIVATE NUMBER?
I KNOW A LOT ABOUT YOU, RUDY. I KNOW YOU'D LIKE TO GET YOUR HANDS ON A DOZEN CRATES OF SEMI-AUTOMATICS -- AND I KNOW YOU'LL JUST LOVE MY PRICE.
MOHAWK PLAZA--THIRTY MINUTES. ALONE!

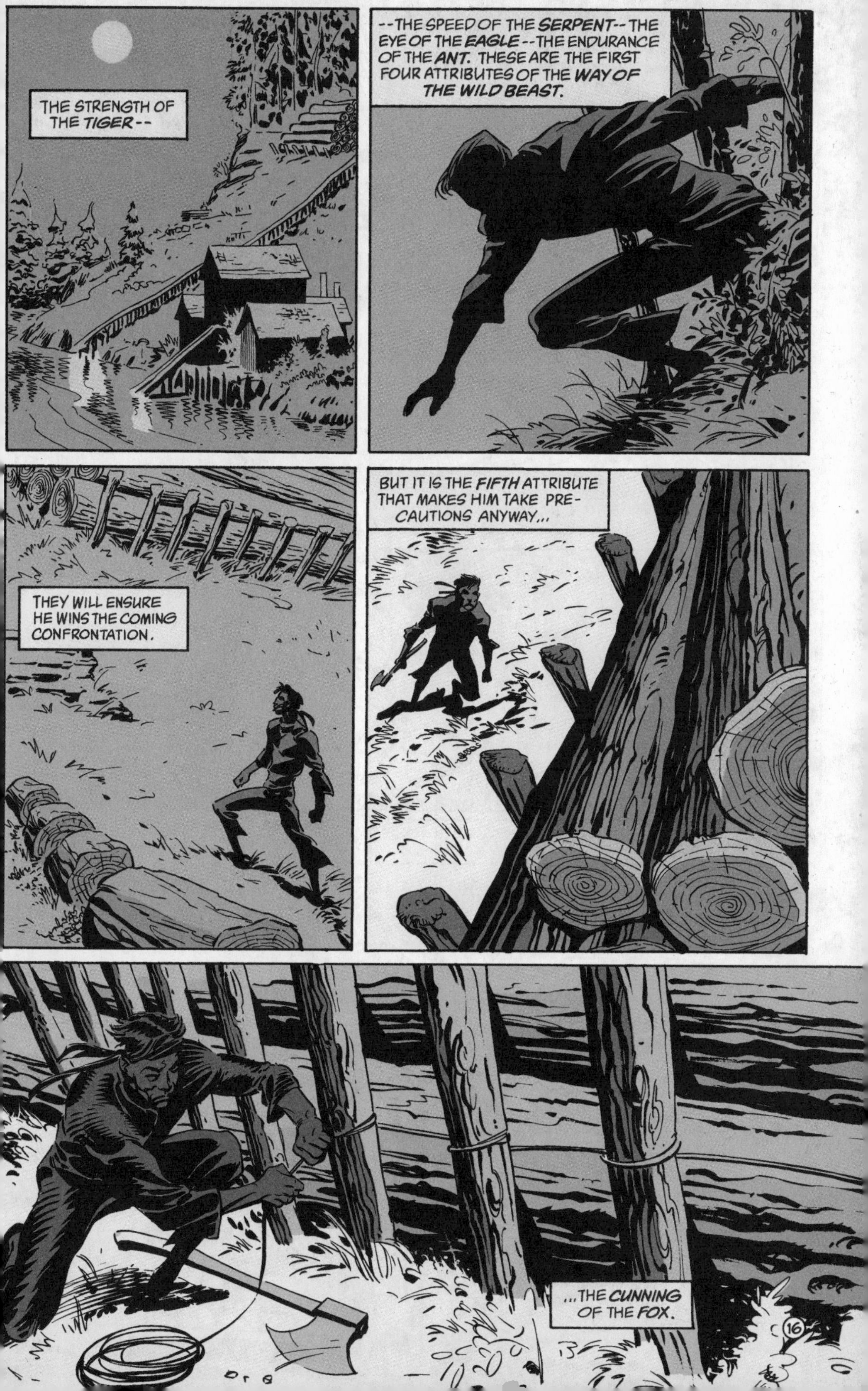

THE STRENGTH OF THE TIGER--
--THE SPEED OF THE SERPENT--THE EYE OF THE EAGLE--THE ENDURANCE OF THE ANT. THESE ARE THE FIRST FOUR ATTRIBUTES OF THE WAY OF THE WILD BEAST.
THEY WILL ENSURE HE WINS THE COMING CONFRONTATION.
BUT IT IS THE FIFTH ATTRIBUTE THAT MAKES HIM TAKE PRE-CAUTIONS ANYWAY...
...THE CUNNING OF THE FOX.

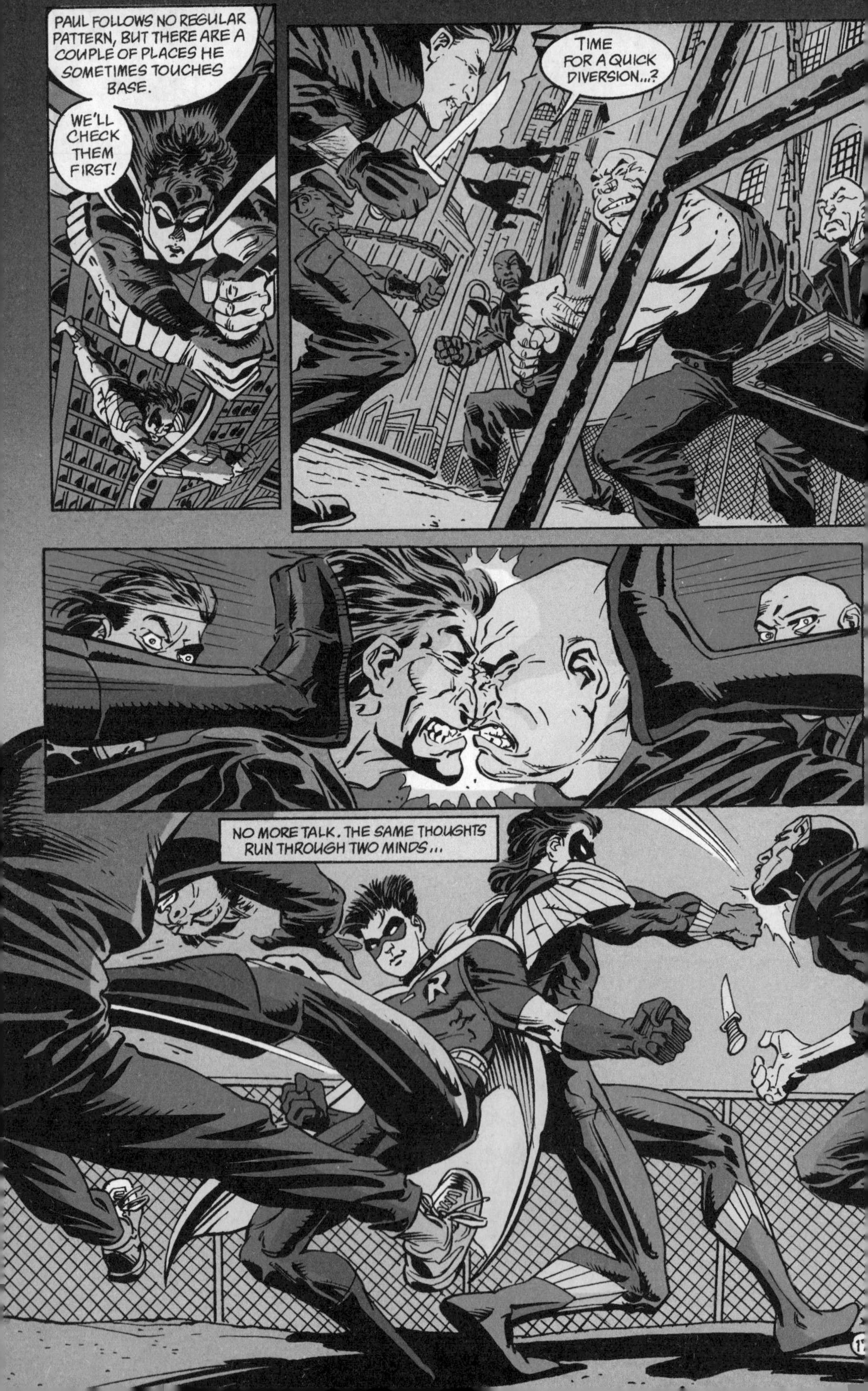

PAUL FOLLOWS NO REGULAR PATTERN, BUT THERE ARE A COUPLE OF PLACES HE SOMETIMES TOUCHES BASE.
WE'LL CHECK THEM FIRST!
TIME FOR A QUICK DIVERSION...?
NO MORE TALK. THE SAME THOUGHTS RUN THROUGH TWO MINDS...

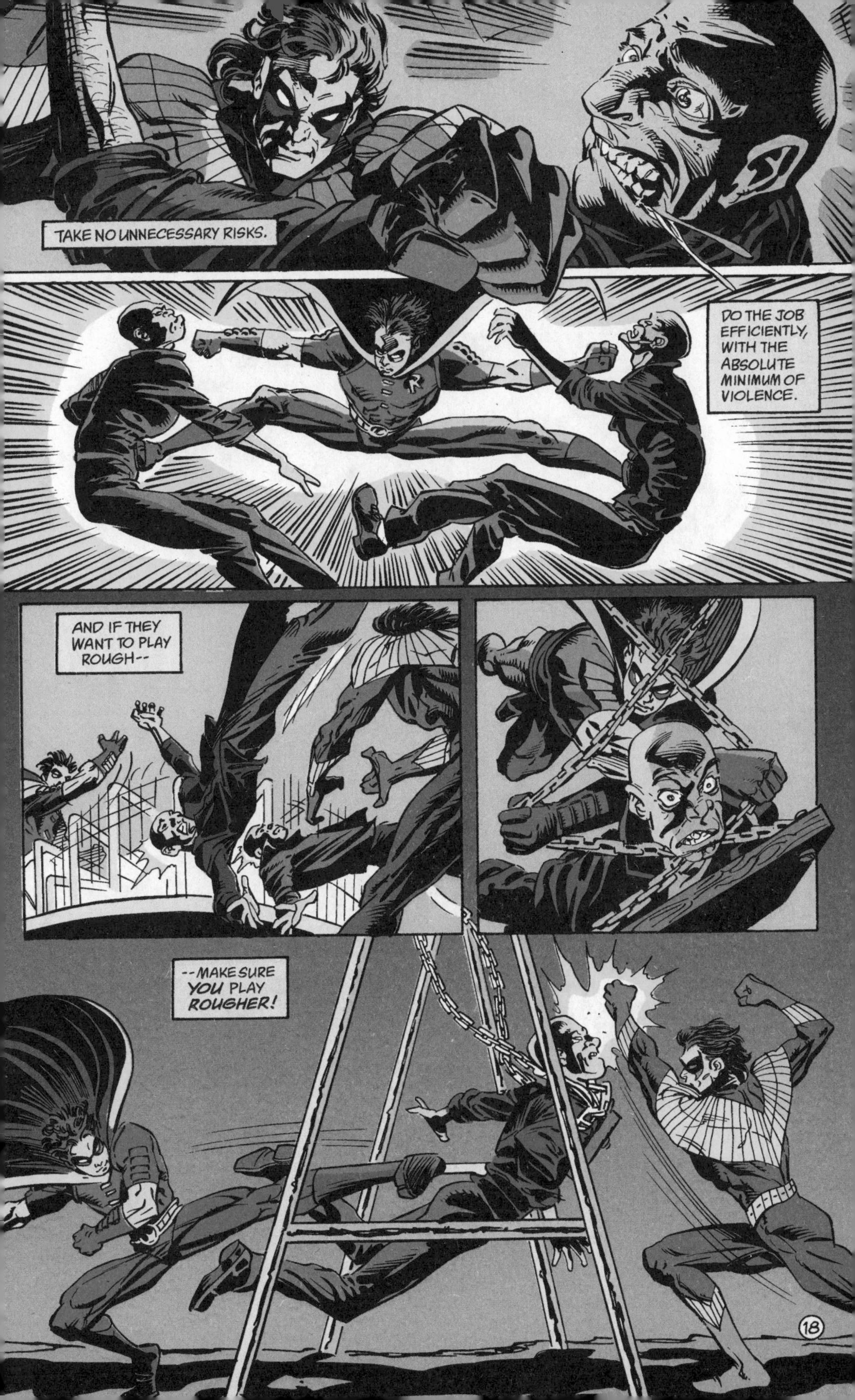
TAKE NO UNNECESSARY RISKS.
DO THE JOB EFFICIENTLY, WITH THE ABSOLUTE MINIMUM OF VIOLENCE.
AND IF THEY WANT TO PLAY ROUGH--
--MAKE SURE YOU PLAY ROUGHER!
18

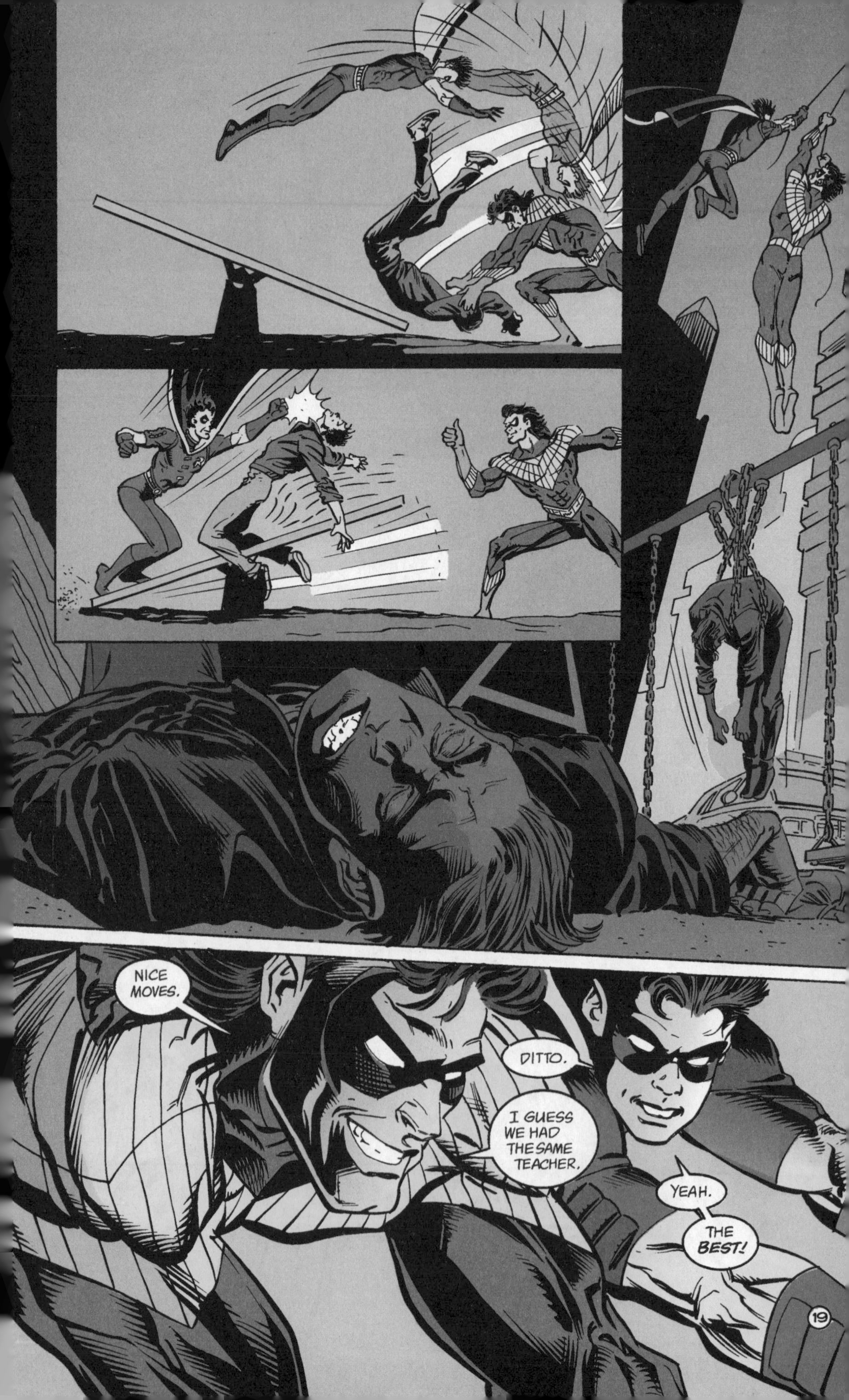
NICE MOVES.
DITTO.
I GUESS WE HAD THE SAME TEACHER.
YEAH.
THE BEST!

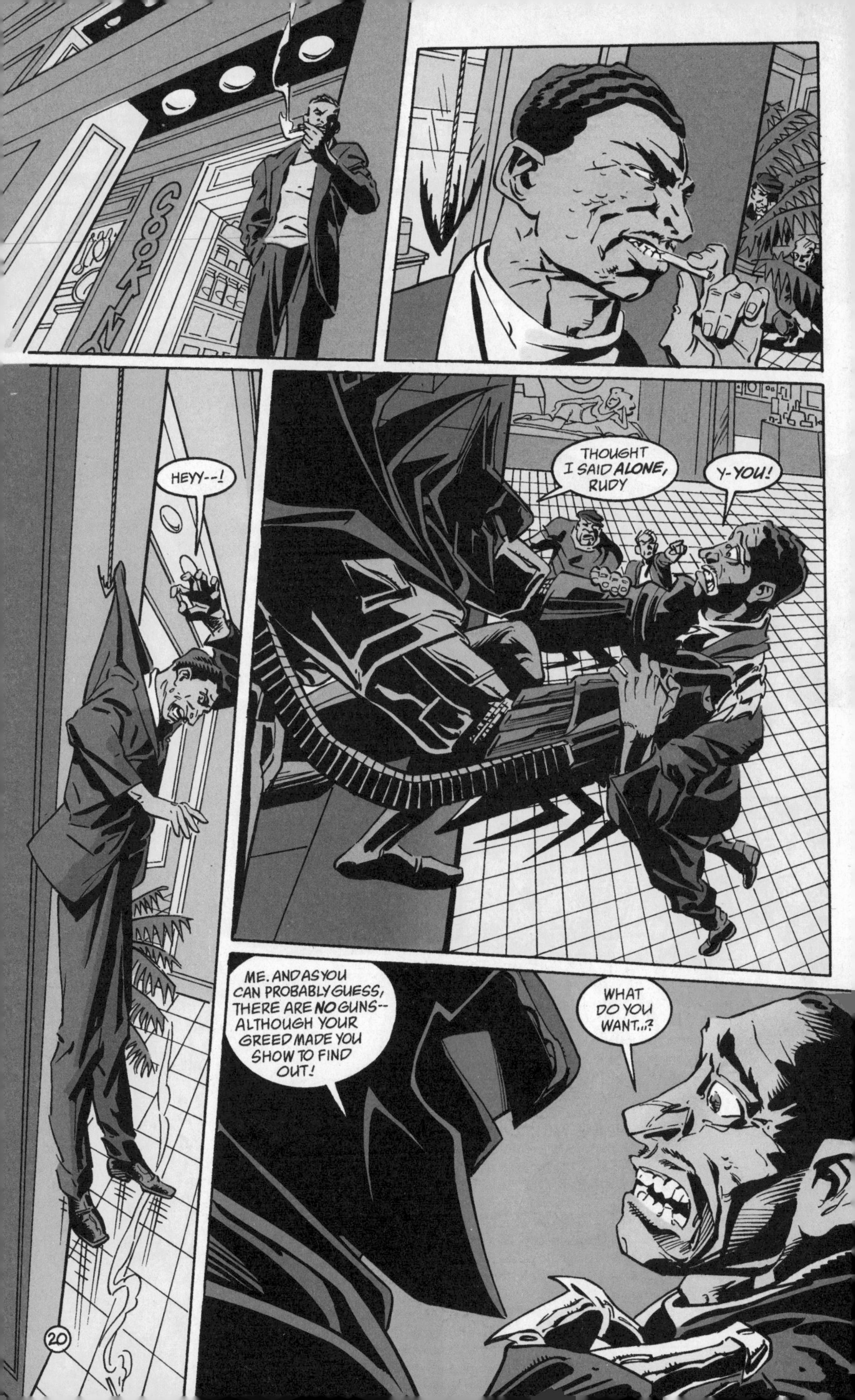
HEYY--!
THOUGHT I SAID **ALONE**, RUDY
Y-**YOU**!
ME. AND AS YOU CAN PROBABLY GUESS, THERE ARE **NO** GUNS-- ALTHOUGH YOUR GREED MADE YOU SHOW TO FIND OUT!
WHAT DO YOU WANT...?

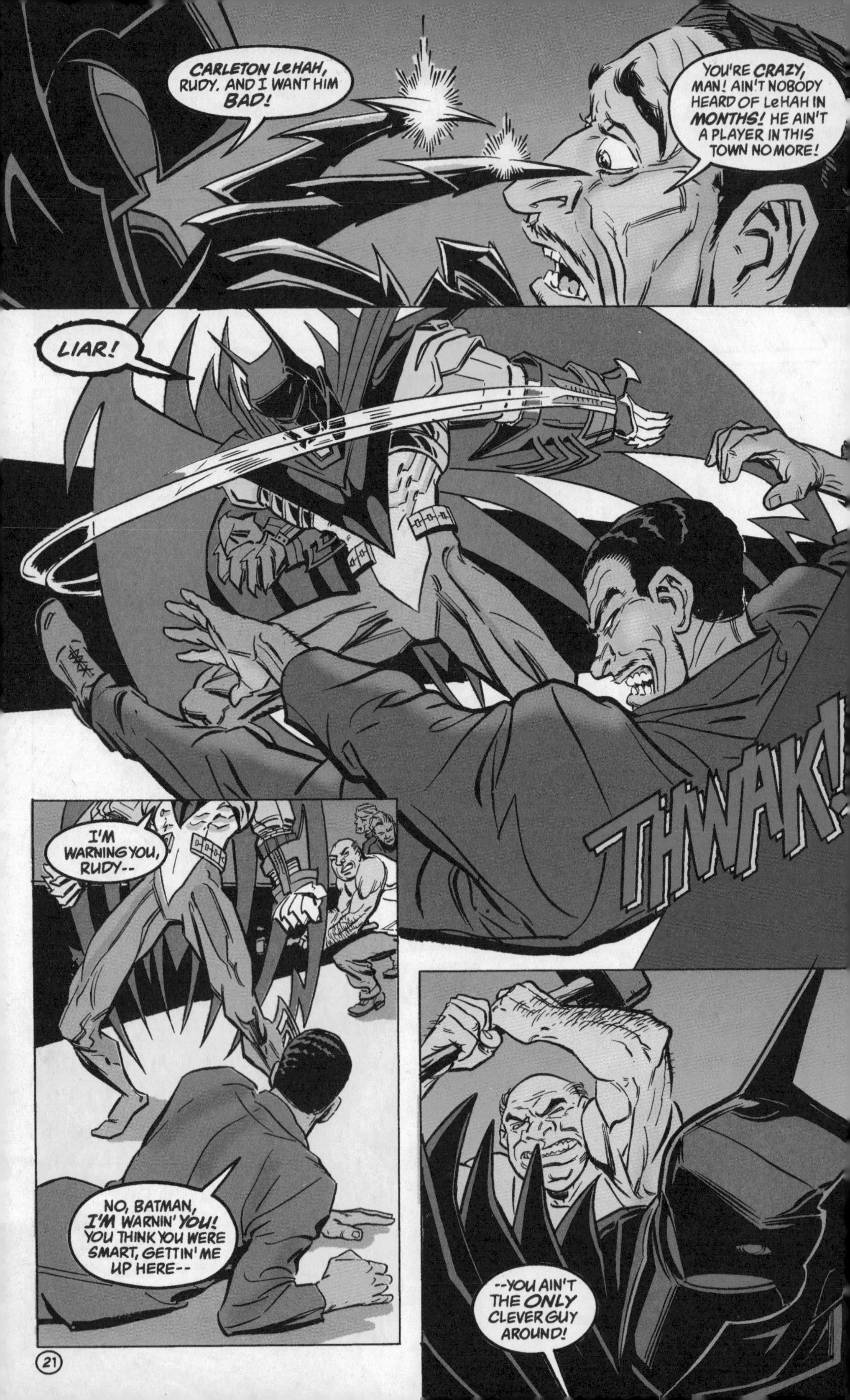

CARLETON LeHAH, RUDY. AND I WANT HIM BAD!
YOU'RE CRAZY, MAN! AIN'T NOBODY HEARD OF LeHAH IN MONTHS! HE AIN'T A PLAYER IN THIS TOWN NO MORE!
LIAR!
THWAK!
I'M WARNING YOU, RUDY--
NO, BATMAN, I'M WARNIN' YOU! YOU THINK YOU WERE SMART, GETTIN' ME UP HERE--
--YOU AIN'T THE ONLY CLEVER GUY AROUND!

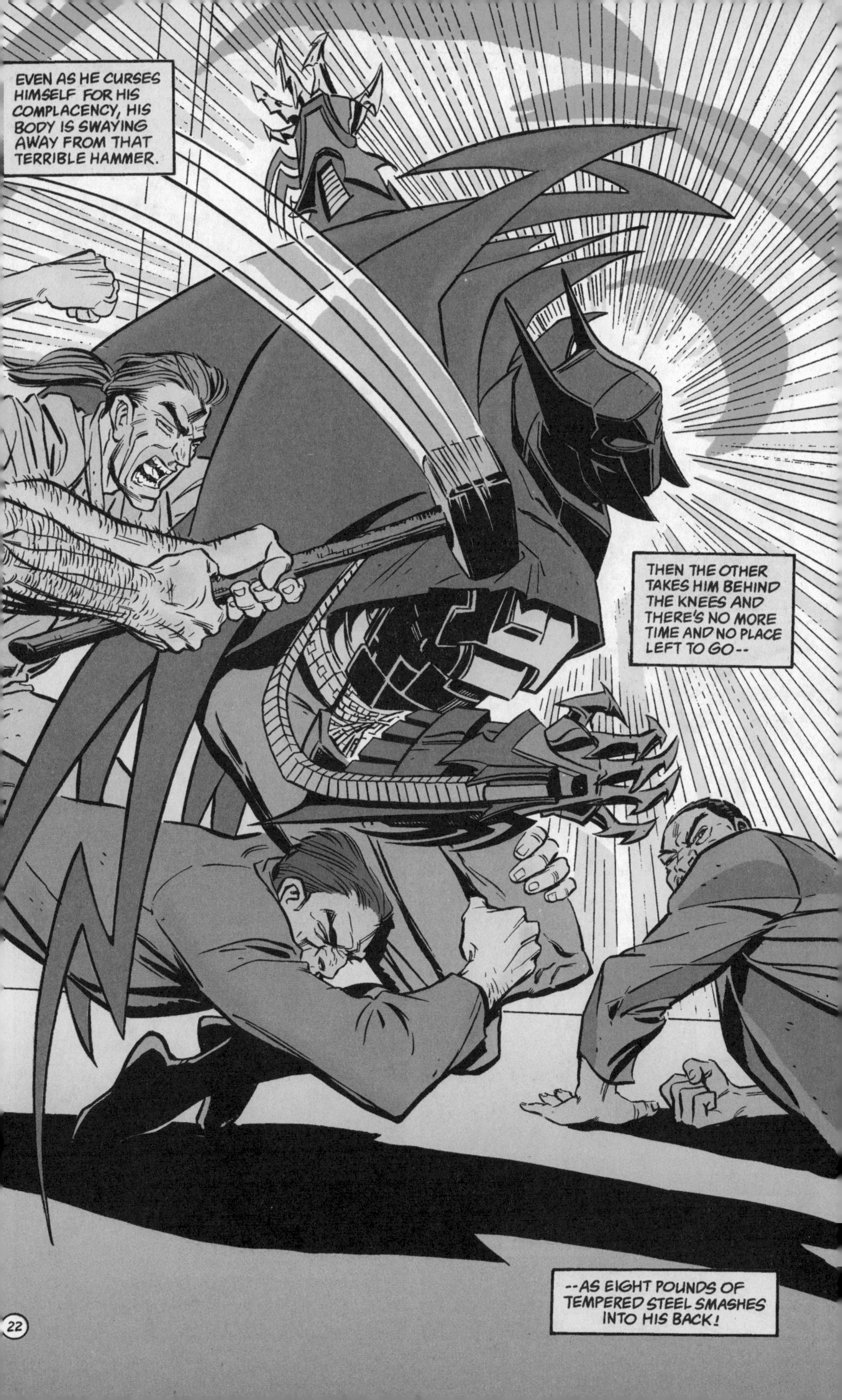
EVEN AS HE CURSES HIMSELF FOR HIS COMPLACENCY, HIS BODY IS SWAYING AWAY FROM THAT TERRIBLE HAMMER.
THEN THE OTHER TAKES HIM BEHIND THE KNEES AND THERE'S NO MORE TIME AND NO PLACE LEFT TO GO--
--AS EIGHT POUNDS OF TEMPERED STEEL SMASHES INTO HIS BACK!

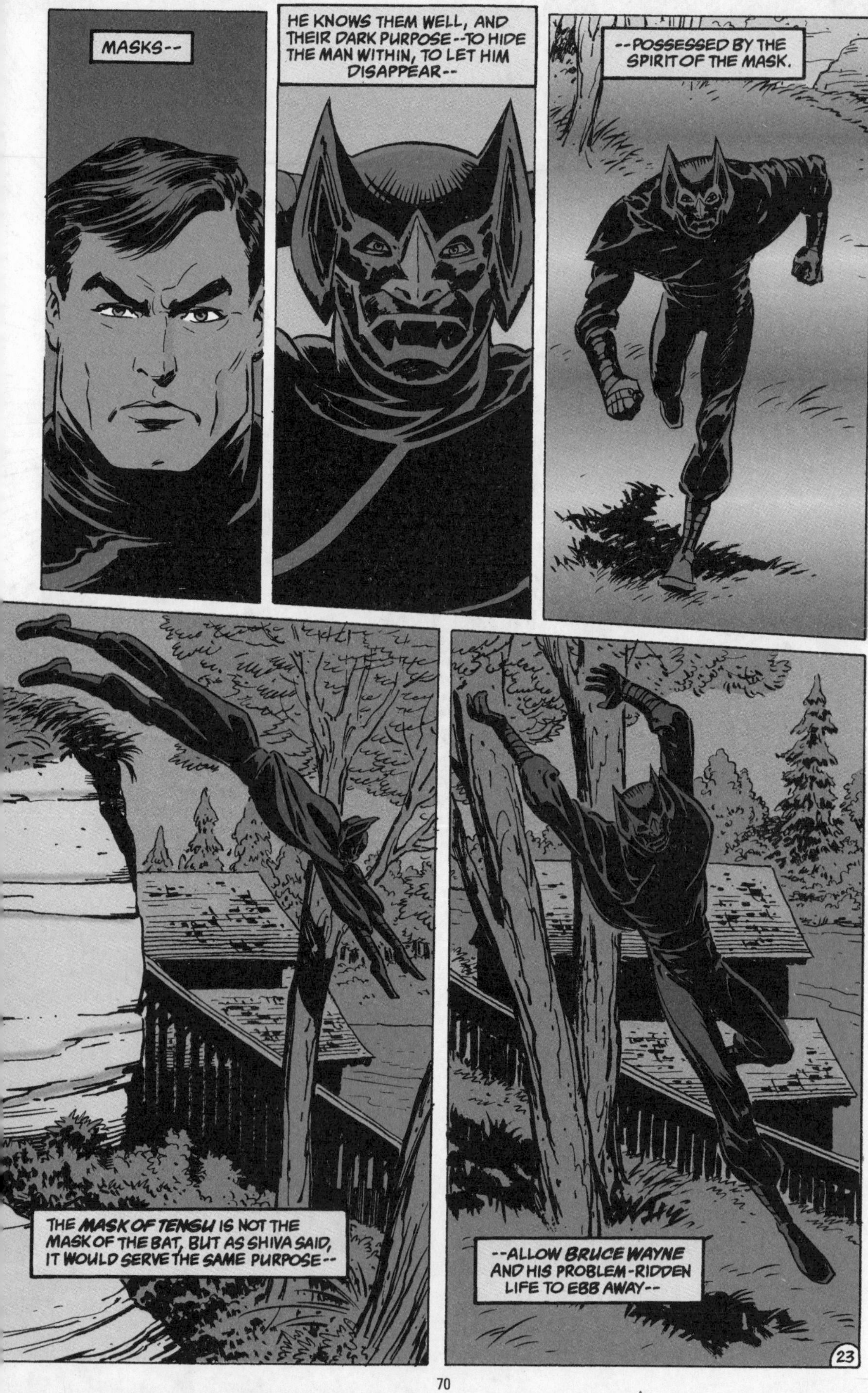
MASKS--
HE KNOWS THEM WELL, AND THEIR DARK PURPOSE--TO HIDE THE MAN WITHIN, TO LET HIM DISAPPEAR--
--POSSESSED BY THE SPIRIT OF THE MASK.
THE MASK OF TENGU IS NOT THE MASK OF THE BAT, BUT AS SHIVA SAID, IT WOULD SERVE THE SAME PURPOSE--
--ALLOW BRUCE WAYNE AND HIS PROBLEM-RIDDEN LIFE TO EBB AWAY--
23

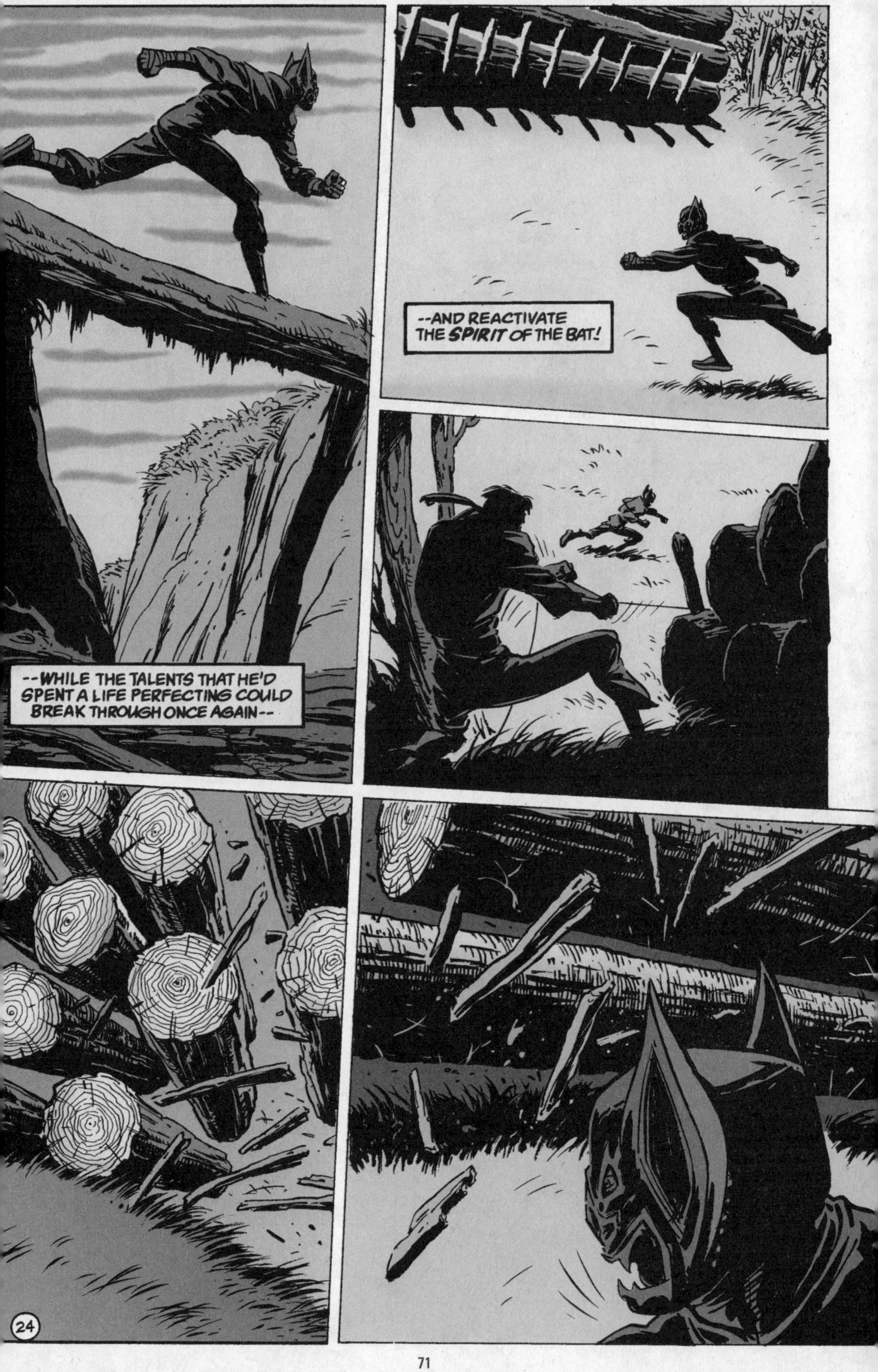
--AND REACTIVATE THE SPIRIT OF THE BAT!
--WHILE THE TALENTS THAT HE'D SPENT A LIFE PERFECTING COULD BREAK THROUGH ONCE AGAIN--
24

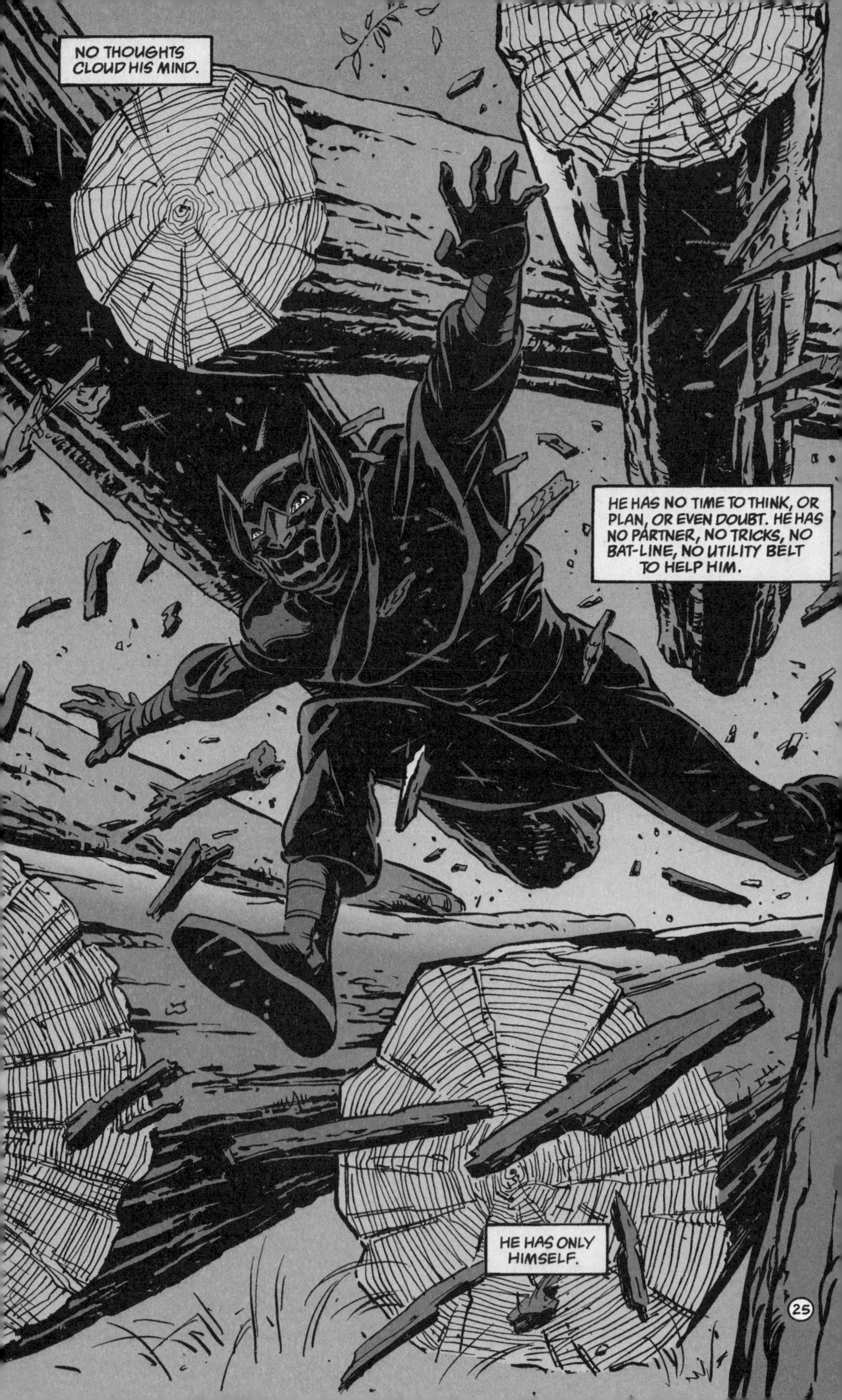
NO THOUGHTS CLOUD HIS MIND.
HE HAS NO TIME TO THINK, OR PLAN, OR EVEN DOUBT. HE HAS NO PARTNER, NO TRICKS, NO BAT-LINE, NO UTILITY BELT TO HELP HIM.
HE HAS ONLY HIMSELF.
25

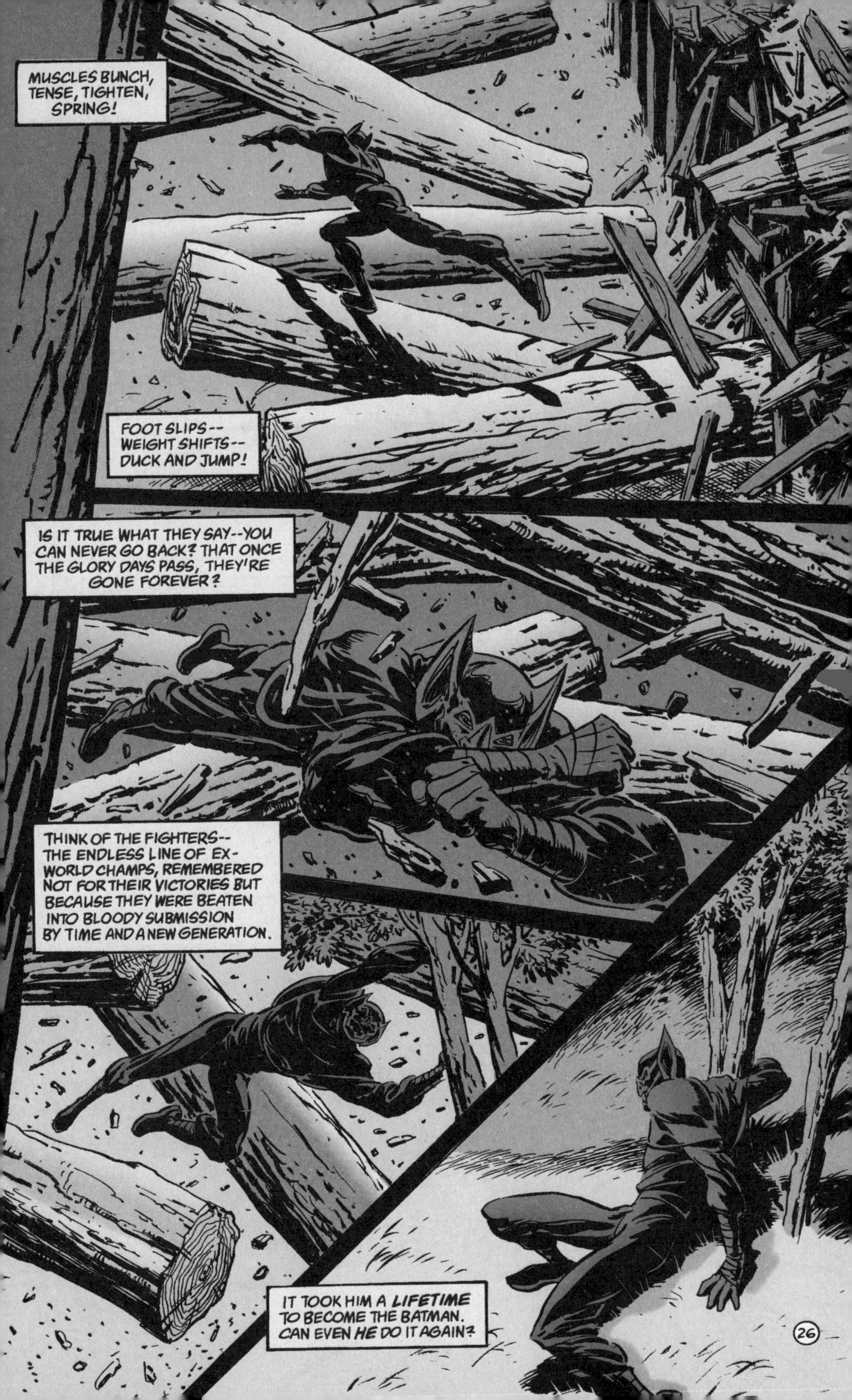
MUSCLES BUNCH, TENSE, TIGHTEN, SPRING!
FOOT SLIPS-- WEIGHT SHIFTS-- DUCK AND JUMP!
IS IT TRUE WHAT THEY SAY--YOU CAN NEVER GO BACK? THAT ONCE THE GLORY DAYS PASS, THEY'RE GONE FOREVER?
THINK OF THE FIGHTERS-- THE ENDLESS LINE OF EX-WORLD CHAMPS, REMEMBERED NOT FOR THEIR VICTORIES BUT BECAUSE THEY WERE BEATEN INTO BLOODY SUBMISSION BY TIME AND A NEW GENERATION.
IT TOOK HIM A LIFETIME TO BECOME THE BATMAN. CAN EVEN HE DO IT AGAIN?
26

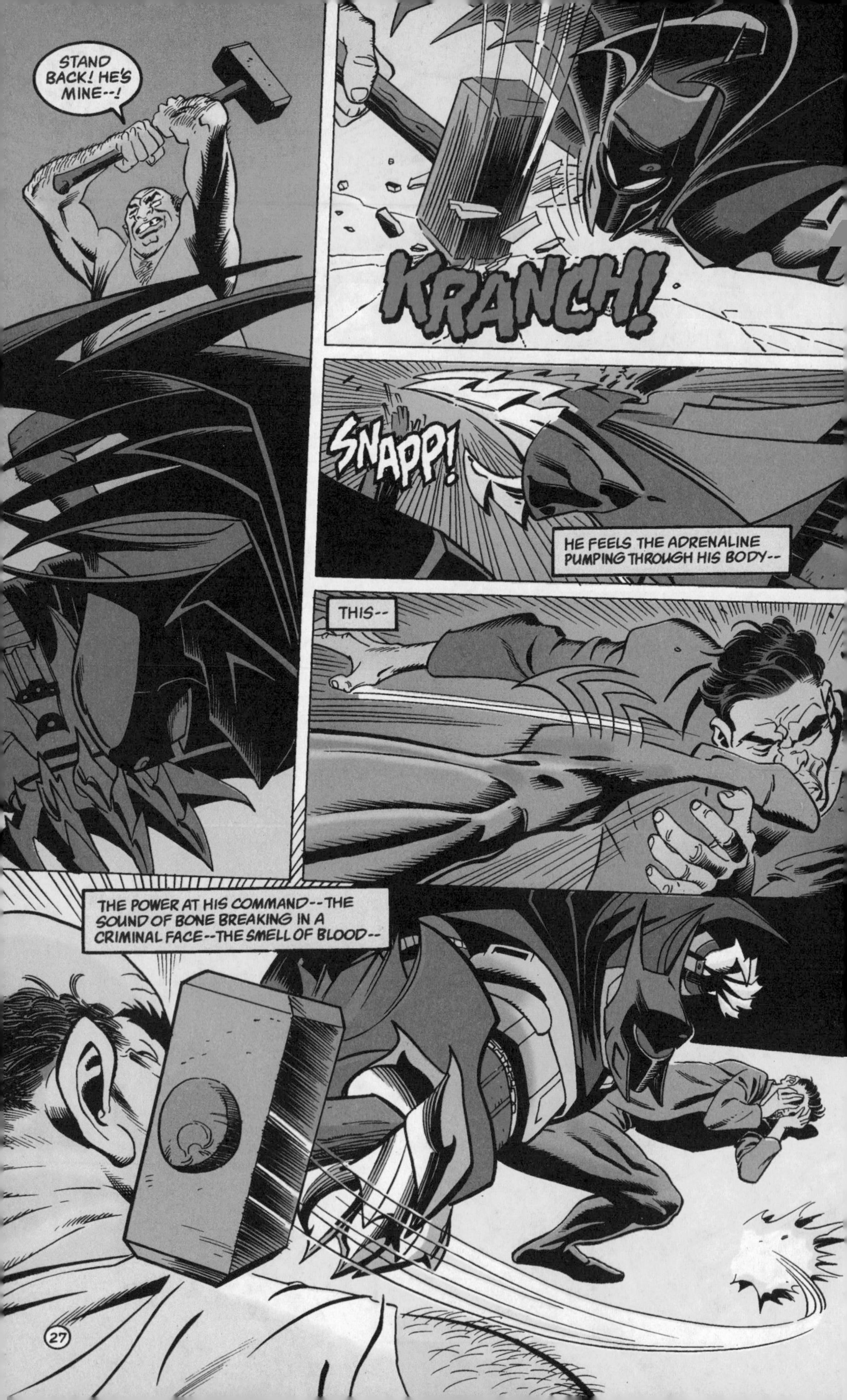
STAND BACK! HE'S MINE--!
KRANCH!
SNAPP!
HE FEELS THE ADRENALINE PUMPING THROUGH HIS BODY--
THIS--
THE POWER AT HIS COMMAND--THE SOUND OF BONE BREAKING IN A CRIMINAL FACE--THE SMELL OF BLOOD--

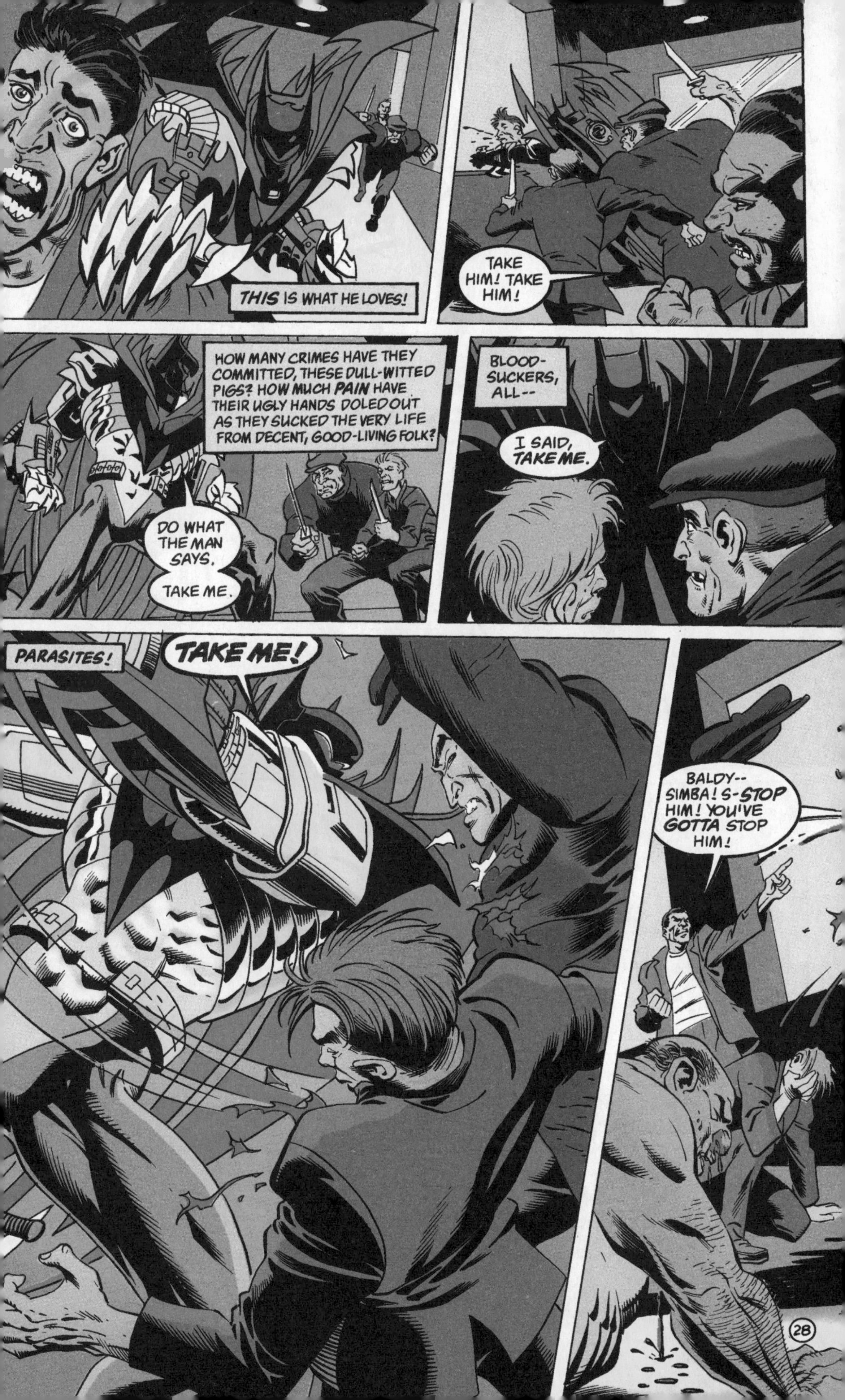
THIS IS WHAT HE LOVES!
TAKE HIM! TAKE HIM!
HOW MANY CRIMES HAVE THEY COMMITTED, THESE DULL-WITTED PIGS? HOW MUCH PAIN HAVE THEIR UGLY HANDS DOLED OUT AS THEY SUCKED THE VERY LIFE FROM DECENT, GOOD-LIVING FOLK?
DO WHAT THE MAN SAYS.
TAKE ME.
BLOOD-SUCKERS, ALL--
I SAID, TAKE ME.
PARASITES!
TAKE ME!
BALDY-- SIMBA! S-STOP HIM! YOU'VE GOTTA STOP HIM!
28

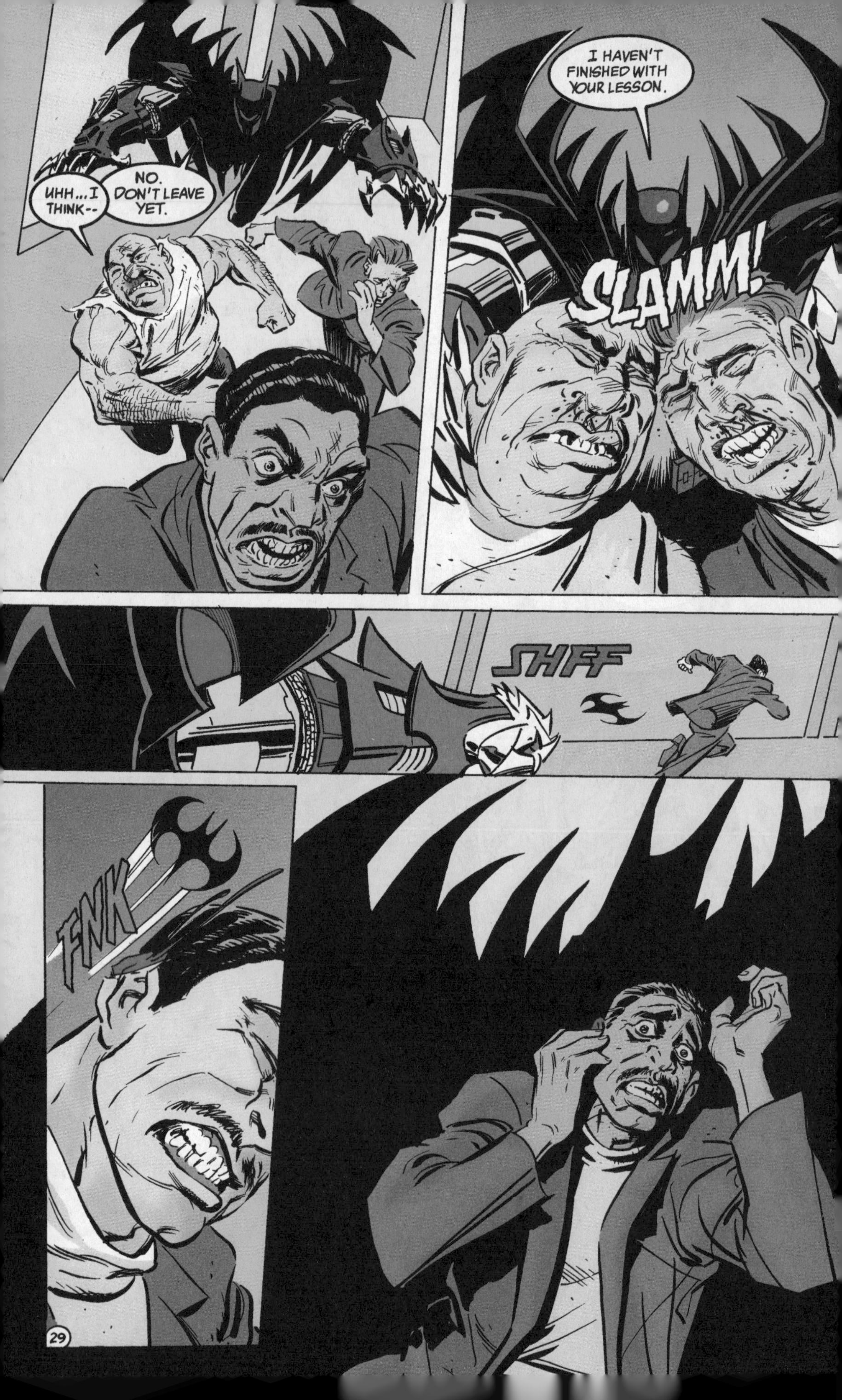
UHH...I THINK--
NO. DON'T LEAVE YET.
I HAVEN'T FINISHED WITH YOUR LESSON.
SLAMM!
SHFF
FNK
29

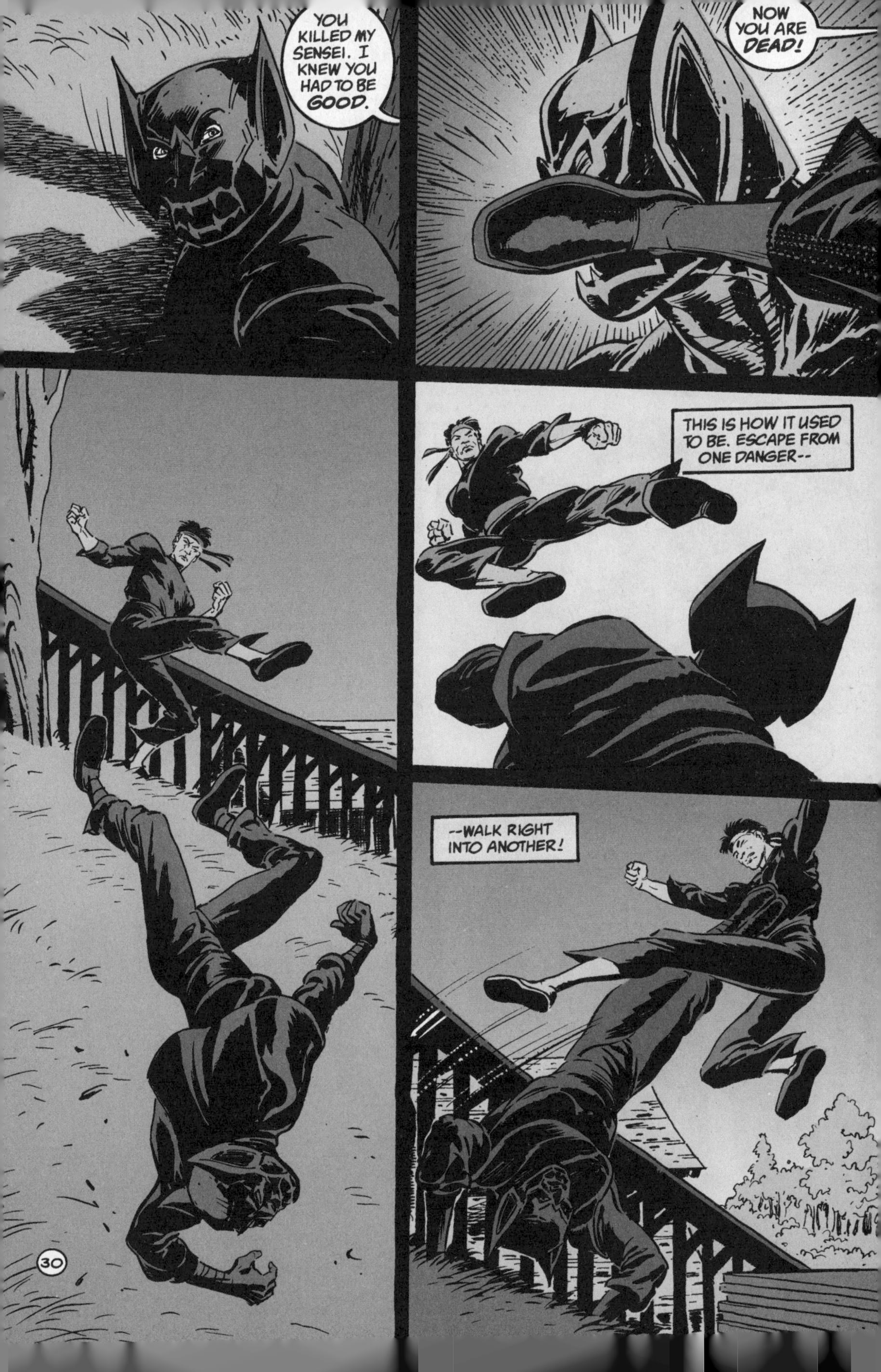
YOU KILLED MY SENSEI. I KNEW YOU HAD TO BE GOOD.
NOW YOU ARE DEAD!
THIS IS HOW IT USED TO BE. ESCAPE FROM ONE DANGER--
--WALK RIGHT INTO ANOTHER!
30

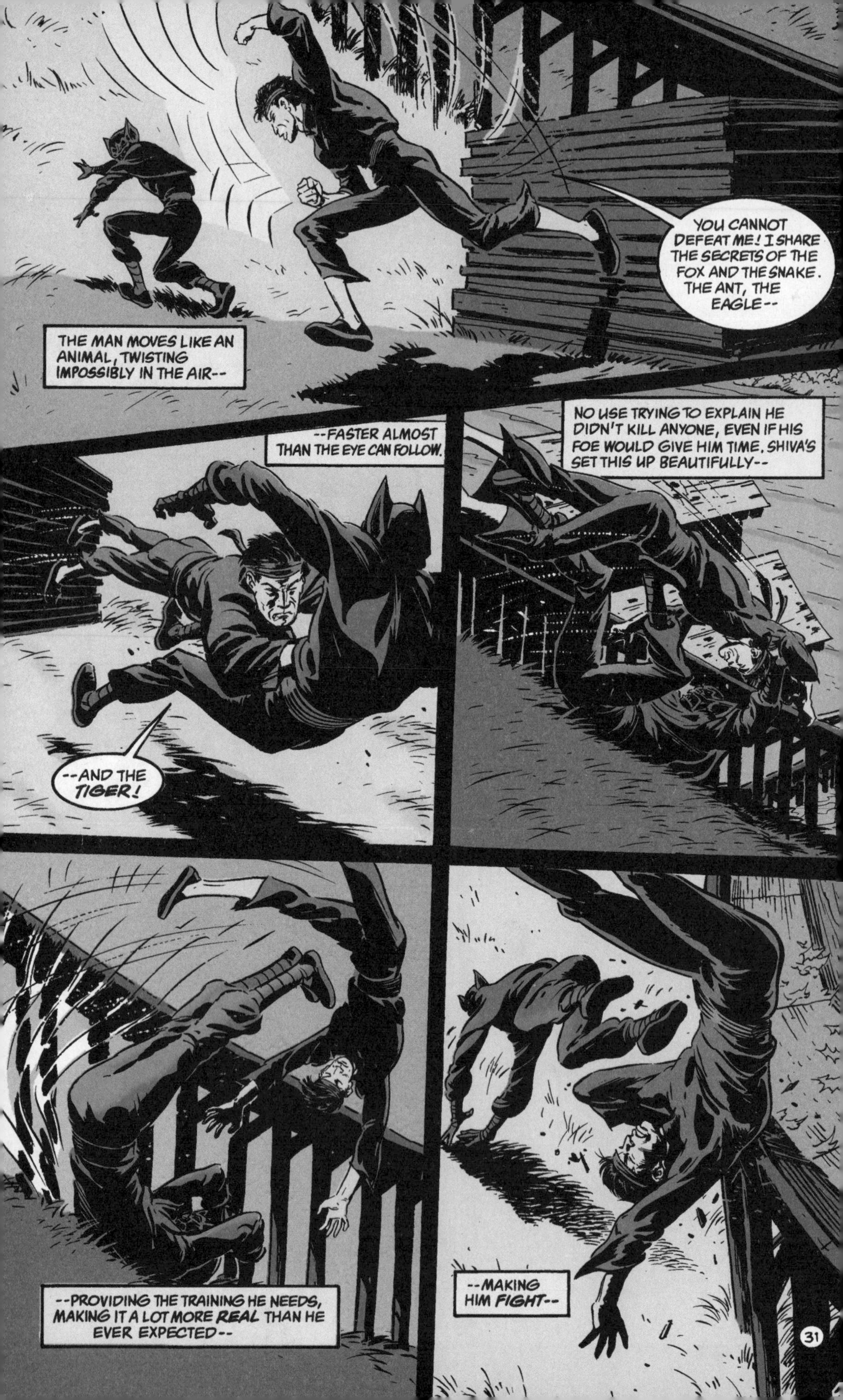
THE MAN MOVES LIKE AN ANIMAL, TWISTING IMPOSSIBLY IN THE AIR--
YOU CANNOT DEFEAT ME! I SHARE THE SECRETS OF THE FOX AND THE SNAKE. THE ANT, THE EAGLE--
--FASTER ALMOST THAN THE EYE CAN FOLLOW.
--AND THE TIGER!
NO USE TRYING TO EXPLAIN HE DIDN'T KILL ANYONE, EVEN IF HIS FOE WOULD GIVE HIM TIME. SHIVA'S SET THIS UP BEAUTIFULLY--
--PROVIDING THE TRAINING HE NEEDS, MAKING IT A LOT MORE REAL THAN HE EVER EXPECTED--
--MAKING HIM FIGHT--

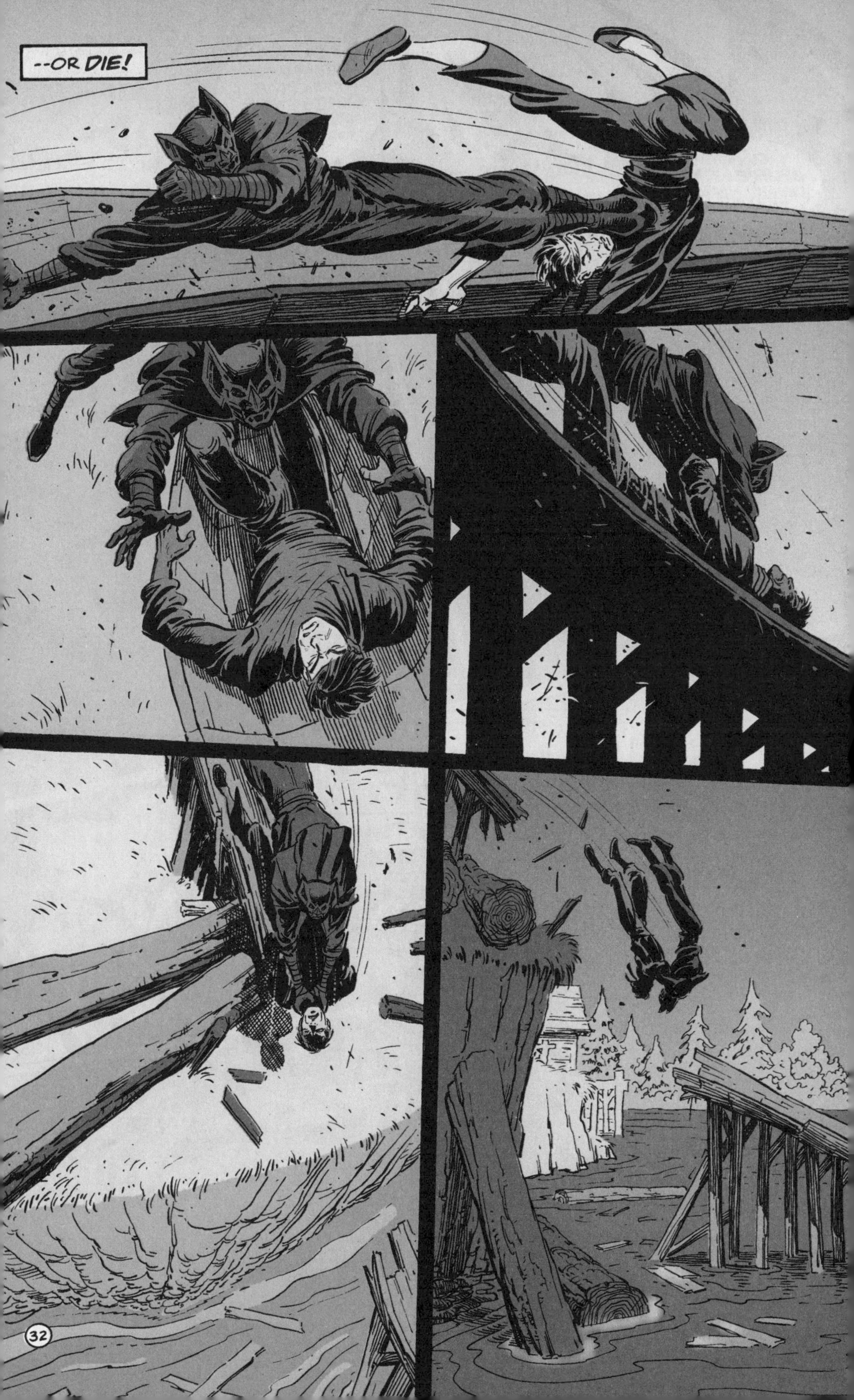
--OR DIE!

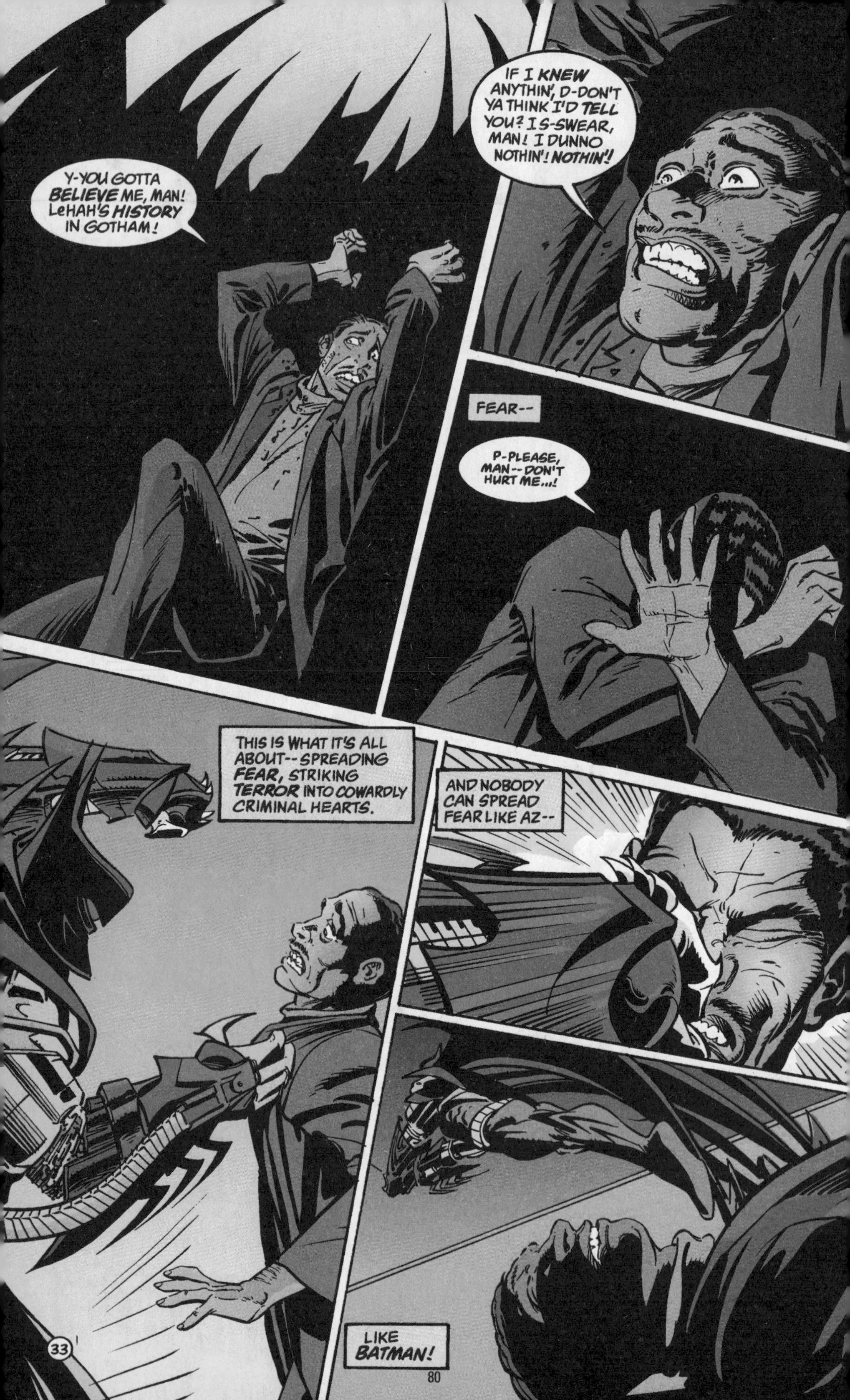

Y-YOU GOTTA BELIEVE ME, MAN! LeHAH'S HISTORY IN GOTHAM!
IF I KNEW ANYTHIN', D-DON'T YA THINK I'D TELL YOU? I S-SWEAR, MAN! I DUNNO NOTHIN'! NOTHIN'!
FEAR--
P-PLEASE, MAN--DON'T HURT ME...!
THIS IS WHAT IT'S ALL ABOUT--SPREADING FEAR, STRIKING TERROR INTO COWARDLY CRIMINAL HEARTS.
AND NOBODY CAN SPREAD FEAR LIKE AZ--
LIKE BATMAN!
33

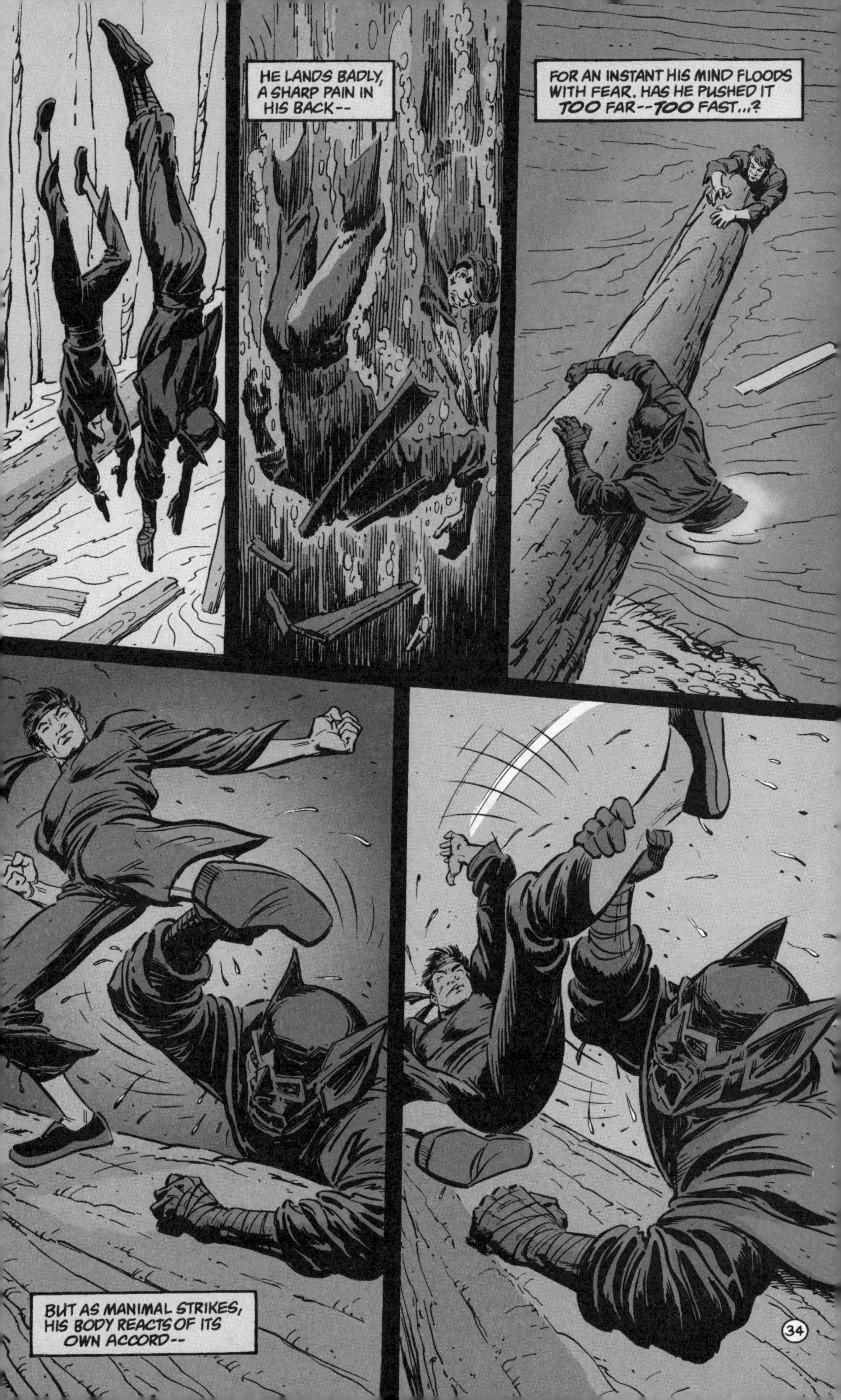
HE LANDS BADLY, A SHARP PAIN IN HIS BACK--
FOR AN INSTANT HIS MIND FLOODS WITH FEAR. HAS HE PUSHED IT TOO FAR--TOO FAST...?
BUT AS MANIMAL STRIKES, HIS BODY REACTS OF ITS OWN ACCORD--
34

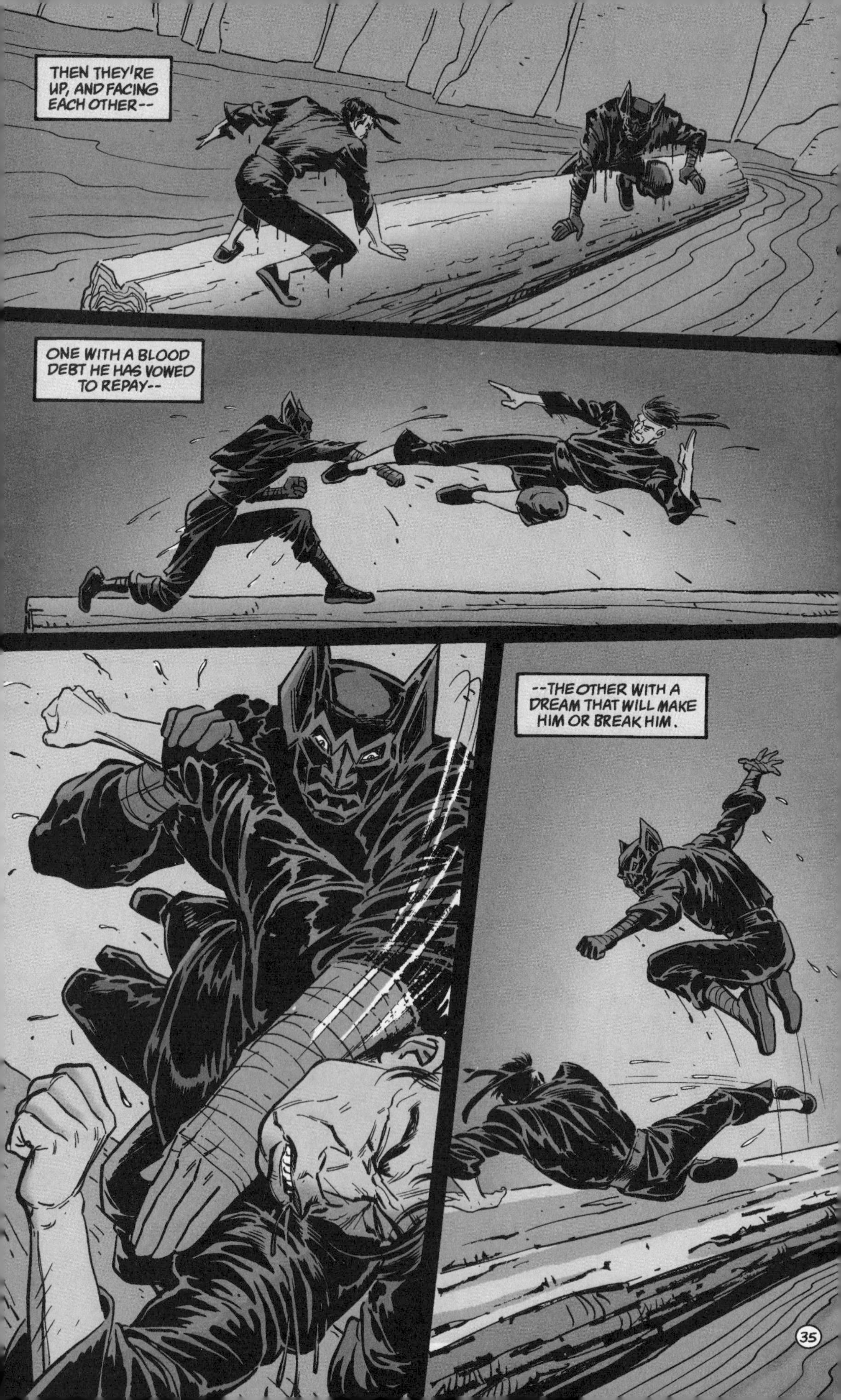
THEN THEY'RE UP, AND FACING EACH OTHER--
ONE WITH A BLOOD DEBT HE HAS VOWED TO REPAY--
--THE OTHER WITH A DREAM THAT WILL MAKE HIM OR BREAK HIM.

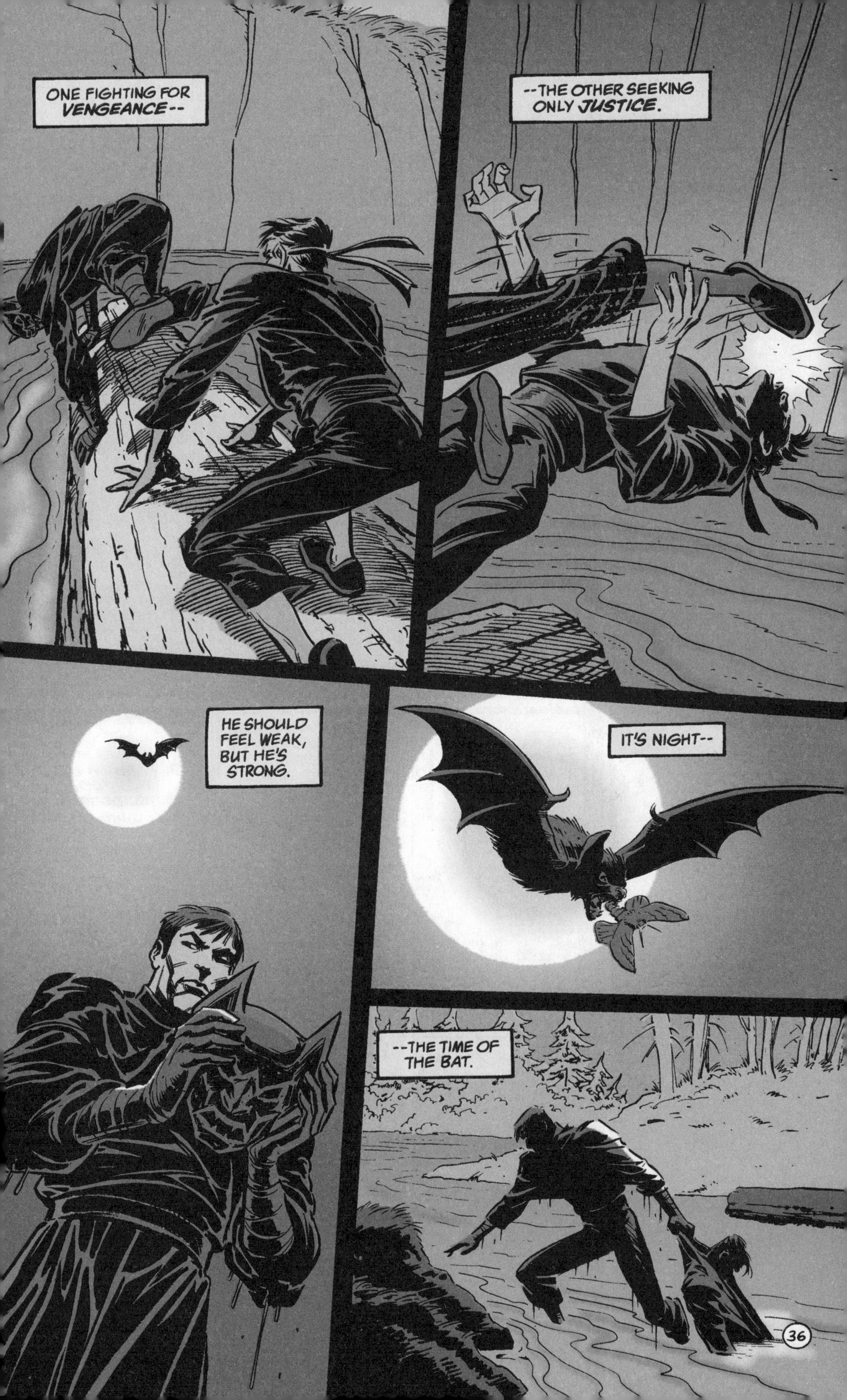
ONE FIGHTING FOR VENGEANCE--
--THE OTHER SEEKING ONLY JUSTICE.
HE SHOULD FEEL WEAK, BUT HE'S STRONG.
IT'S NIGHT--
--THE TIME OF THE BAT.
36

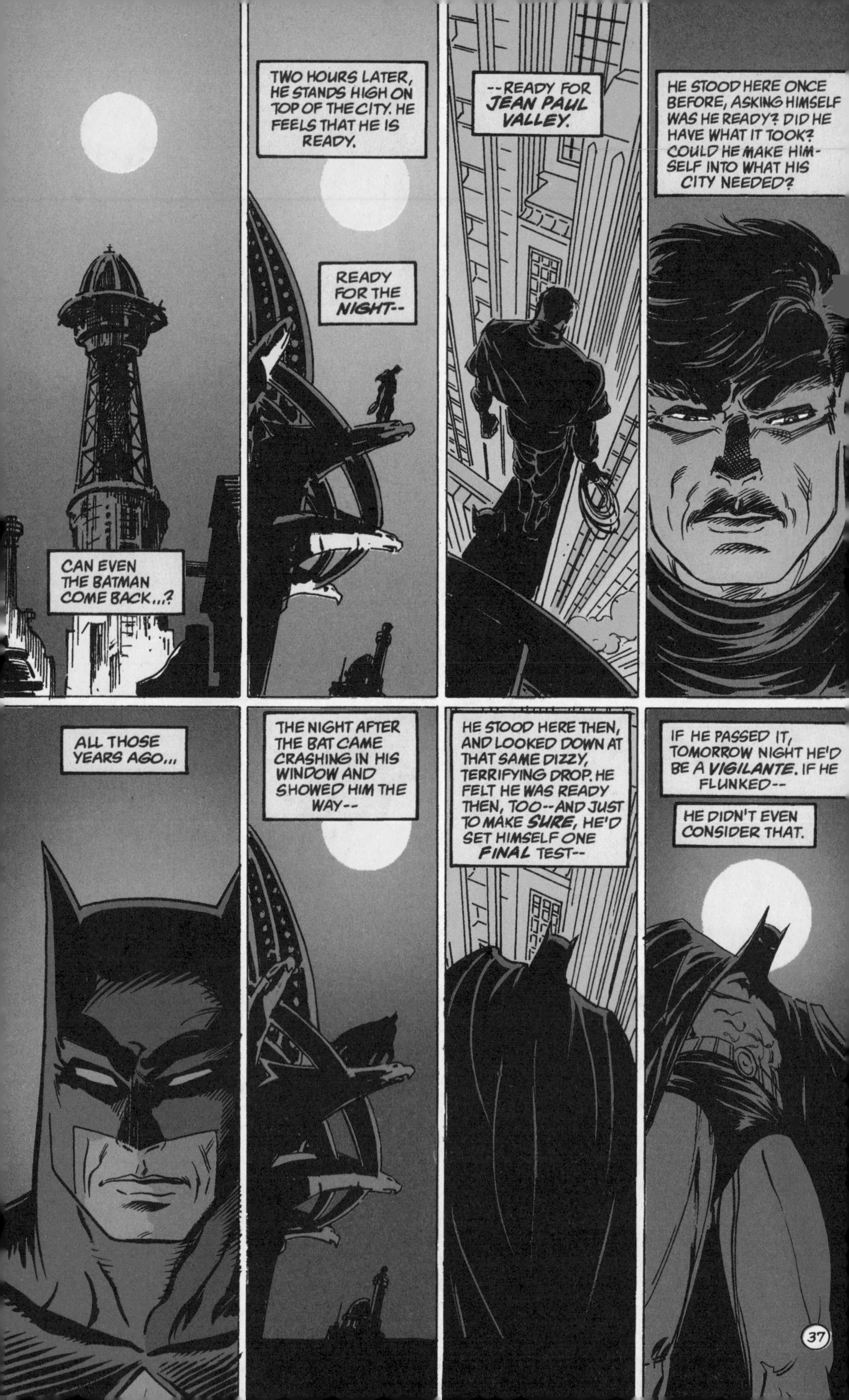
CAN EVEN THE BATMAN COME BACK...?
TWO HOURS LATER, HE STANDS HIGH ON TOP OF THE CITY. HE FEELS THAT HE IS READY.
READY FOR THE NIGHT--
--READY FOR JEAN PAUL VALLEY.
HE STOOD HERE ONCE BEFORE, ASKING HIMSELF WAS HE READY? DID HE HAVE WHAT IT TOOK? COULD HE MAKE HIMSELF INTO WHAT HIS CITY NEEDED?
ALL THOSE YEARS AGO...
THE NIGHT AFTER THE BAT CAME CRASHING IN HIS WINDOW AND SHOWED HIM THE WAY--
HE STOOD HERE THEN, AND LOOKED DOWN AT THAT SAME DIZZY, TERRIFYING DROP. HE FELT HE WAS READY THEN, TOO--AND JUST TO MAKE SURE, HE'D SET HIMSELF ONE FINAL TEST--
IF HE PASSED IT, TOMORROW NIGHT HE'D BE A VIGILANTE. IF HE FLUNKED--
HE DIDN'T EVEN CONSIDER THAT.

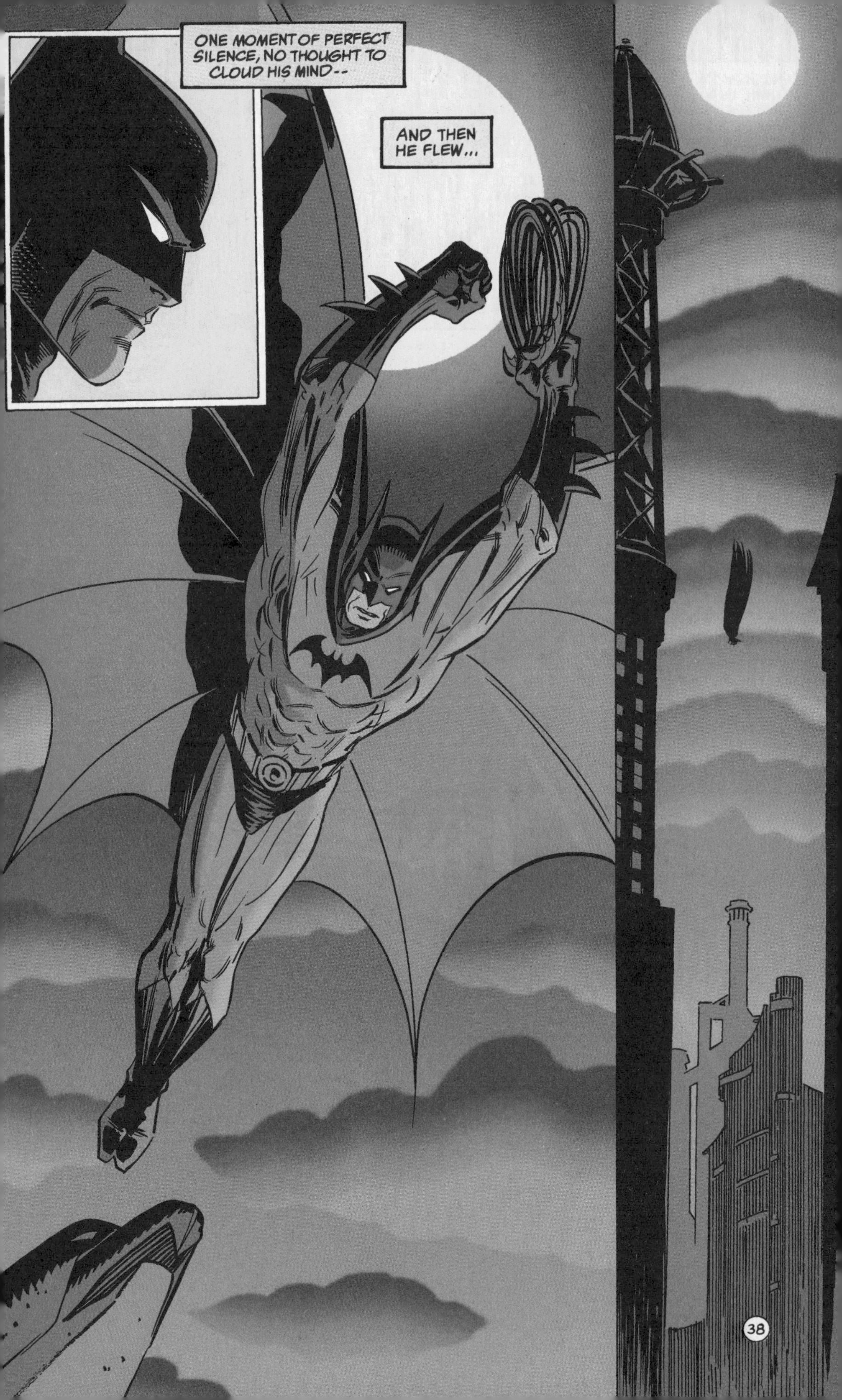
ONE MOMENT OF PERFECT SILENCE, NO THOUGHT TO CLOUD HIS MIND--
AND THEN HE FLEW...

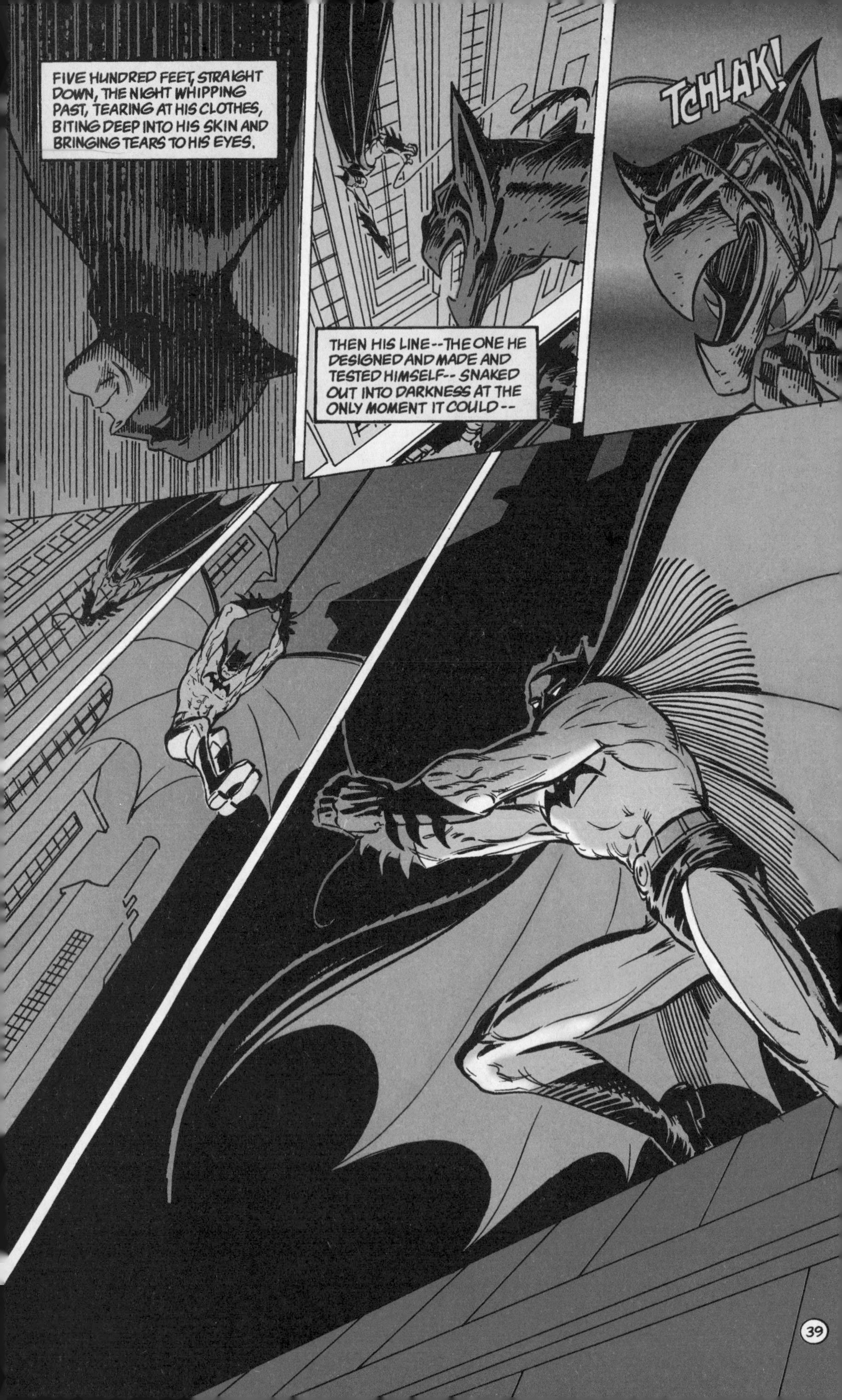
FIVE HUNDRED FEET, STRAIGHT DOWN, THE NIGHT WHIPPING PAST, TEARING AT HIS CLOTHES, BITING DEEP INTO HIS SKIN AND BRINGING TEARS TO HIS EYES.
THEN HIS LINE--THE ONE HE DESIGNED AND MADE AND TESTED HIMSELF-- SNAKED OUT INTO DARKNESS AT THE ONLY MOMENT IT COULD--
TCHLAK!

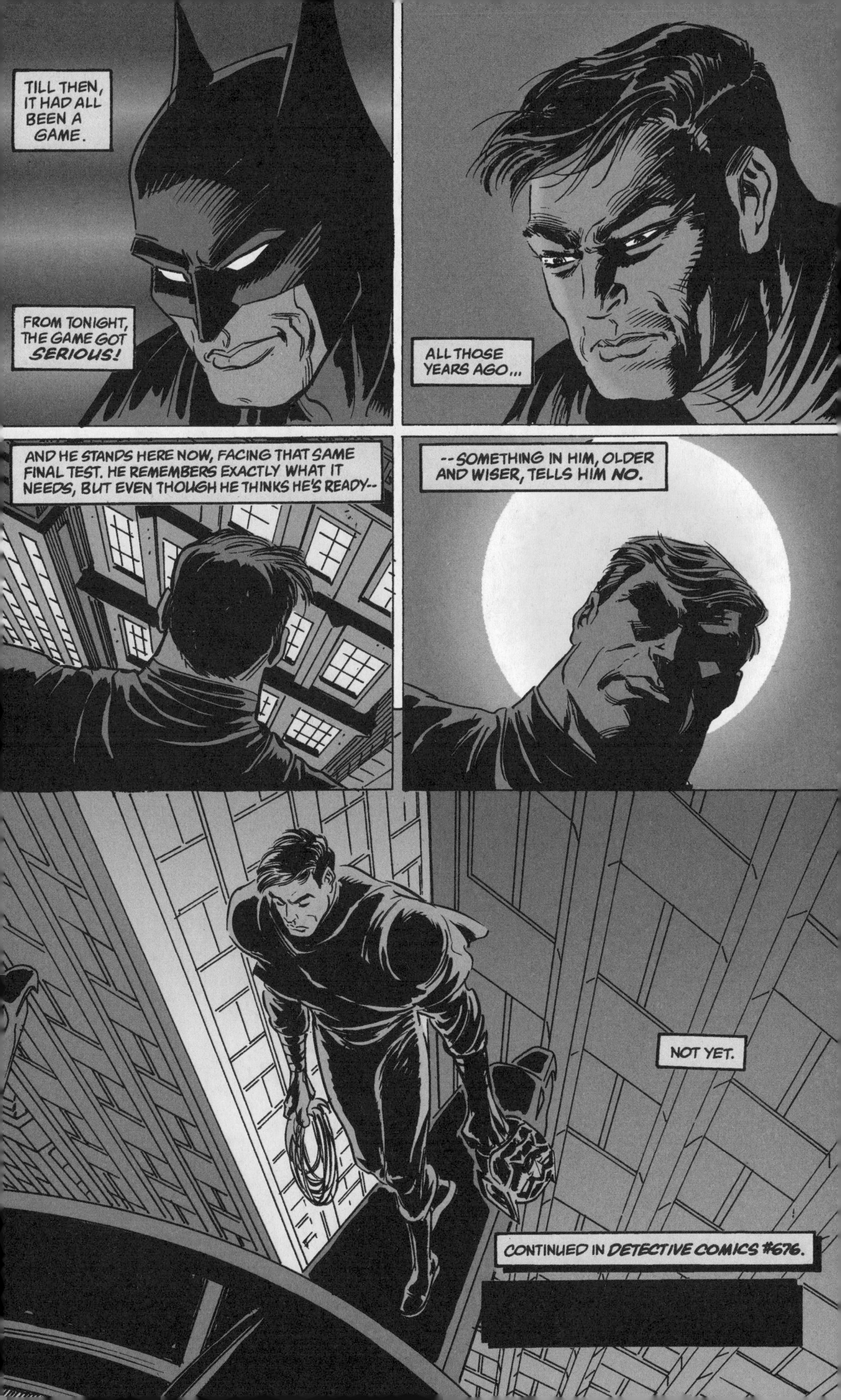
TILL THEN, IT HAD ALL BEEN A GAME.
FROM TONIGHT, THE GAME GOT SERIOUS!
ALL THOSE YEARS AGO...
AND HE STANDS HERE NOW, FACING THAT SAME FINAL TEST. HE REMEMBERS EXACTLY WHAT IT NEEDS, BUT EVEN THOUGH HE THINKS HE'S READY--
--SOMETHING IN HIM, OLDER AND WISER, TELLS HIM NO.
NOT YET.
CONTINUED IN DETECTIVE COMICS #676.
[redacted]

Cover art by **KELLEY JONES** and **JOHN BEATTY**

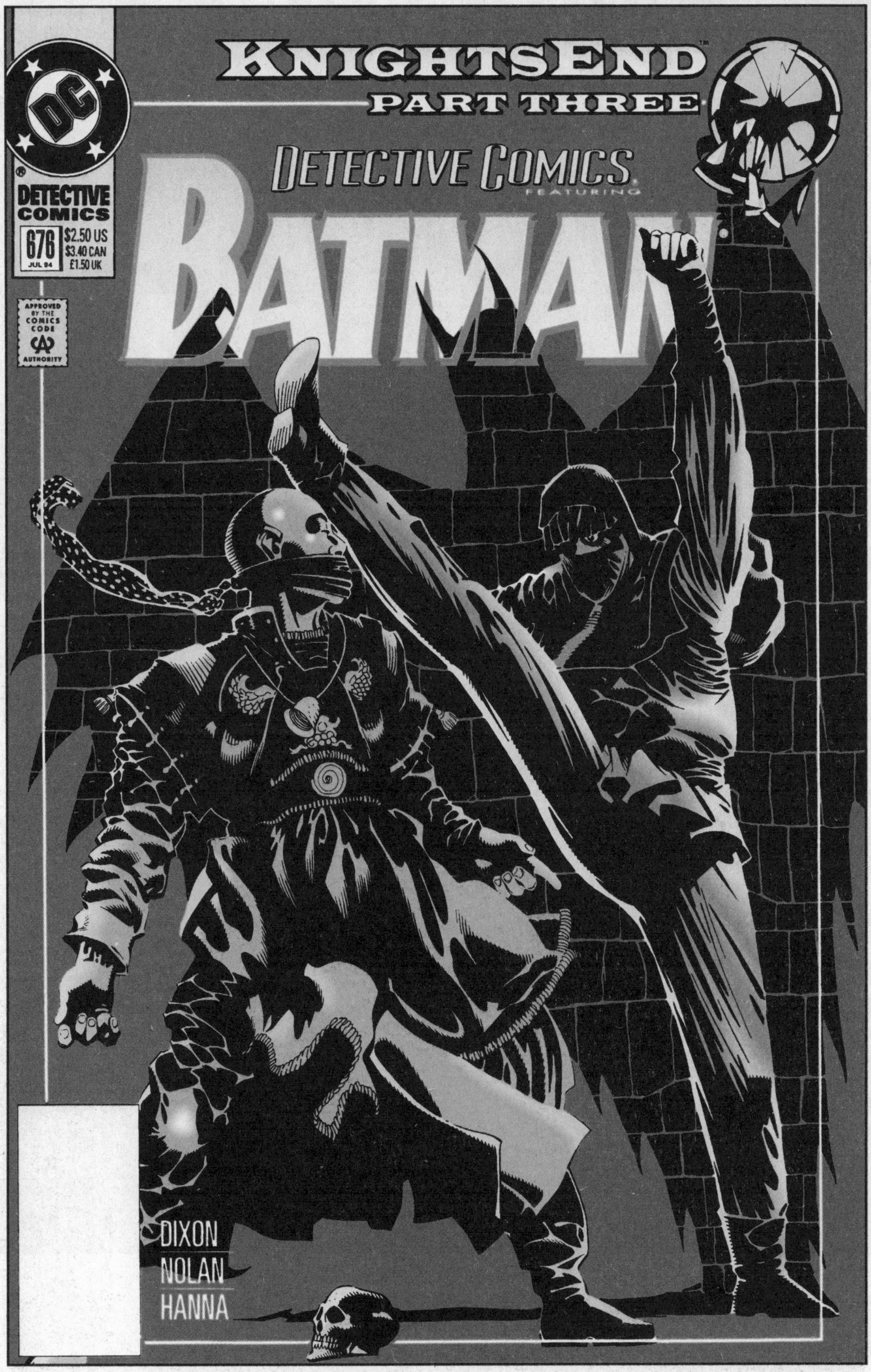

KNIGHTSEND
PART THREE
DC
DETECTIVE COMICS
676
JUL 94
$2.50 US
$3.40 CAN
£1.50 UK
APPROVED BY THE COMICS CODE AUTHORITY
DETECTIVE COMICS
FEATURING
BATMAN
DIXON
NOLAN
HANNA

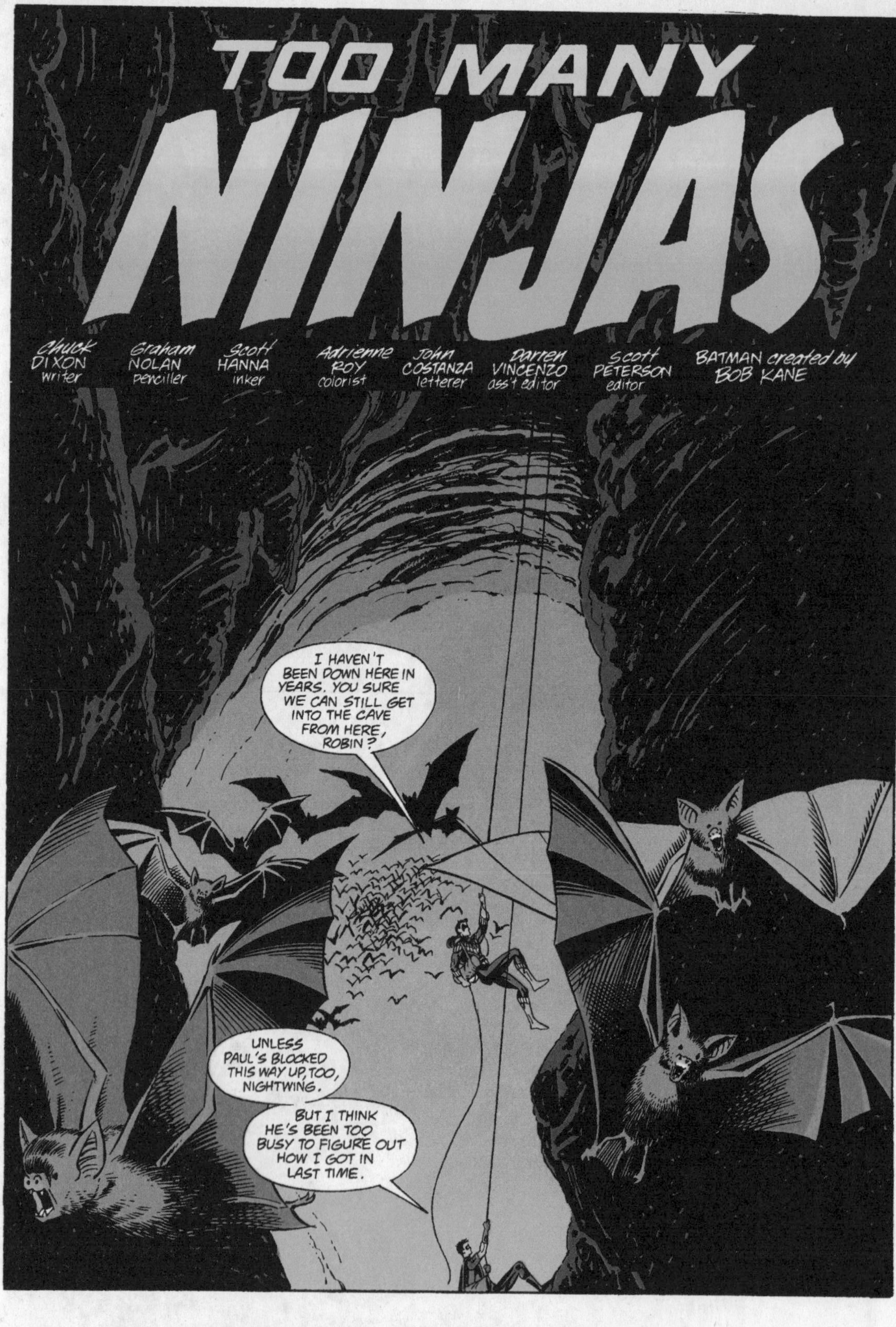

TOO MANY NINJAS
Chuck DIXON writer
Graham NOLAN penciller
Scott HANNA inker
Adrienne ROY colorist
John COSTANZA letterer
Darren VINCENZO ass't editor
Scott PETERSON editor
BATMAN created by BOB KANE
I HAVEN'T BEEN DOWN HERE IN YEARS. YOU SURE WE CAN STILL GET INTO THE CAVE FROM HERE, ROBIN?
UNLESS PAUL'S BLOCKED THIS WAY UP, TOO, NIGHTWING.
BUT I THINK HE'S BEEN TOO BUSY TO FIGURE OUT HOW I GOT IN LAST TIME.

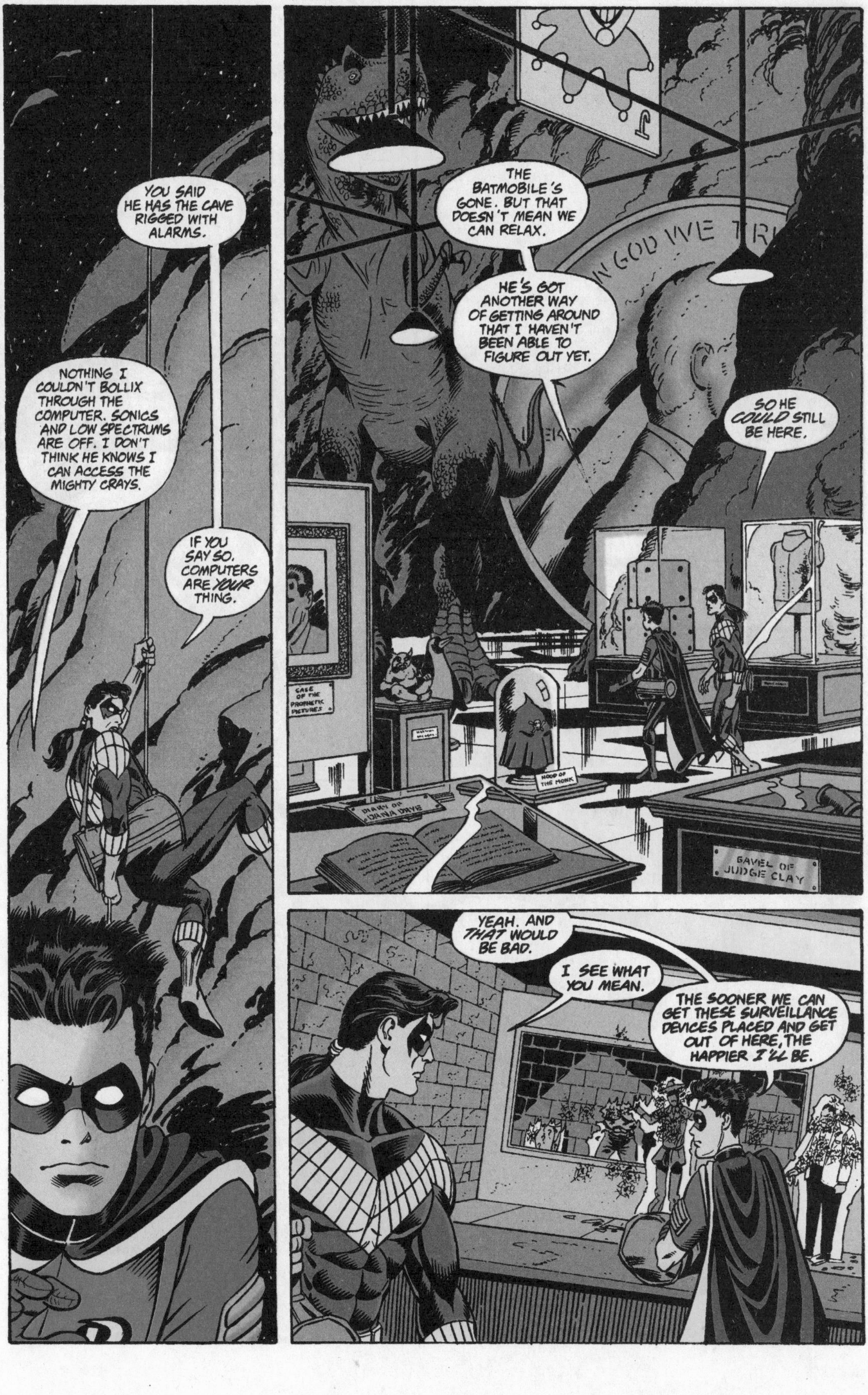

YOU SAID HE HAS THE CAVE RIGGED WITH ALARMS.
NOTHING I COULDN'T BOLLIX THROUGH THE COMPUTER. SONICS AND LOW SPECTRUMS ARE OFF. I DON'T THINK HE KNOWS I CAN ACCESS THE MIGHTY CRAYS.
IF YOU SAY SO. COMPUTERS ARE *YOUR* THING.
THE BATMOBILE'S GONE. BUT THAT DOESN'T MEAN WE CAN RELAX.
HE'S GOT ANOTHER WAY OF GETTING AROUND THAT I HAVEN'T BEEN ABLE TO FIGURE OUT YET.
SO HE *COULD* STILL BE HERE.
CASE OF THE PROPHETIC PICTURES
DIARY OF DANA DRYE
HOOD OF THE MONK
GAVEL OF JUDGE CLAY
YEAH. AND *THAT* WOULD BE BAD.
I SEE WHAT YOU MEAN.
THE SOONER WE CAN GET THESE SURVEILLANCE DEVICES PLACED AND GET OUT OF HERE, THE HAPPIER I'LL BE.

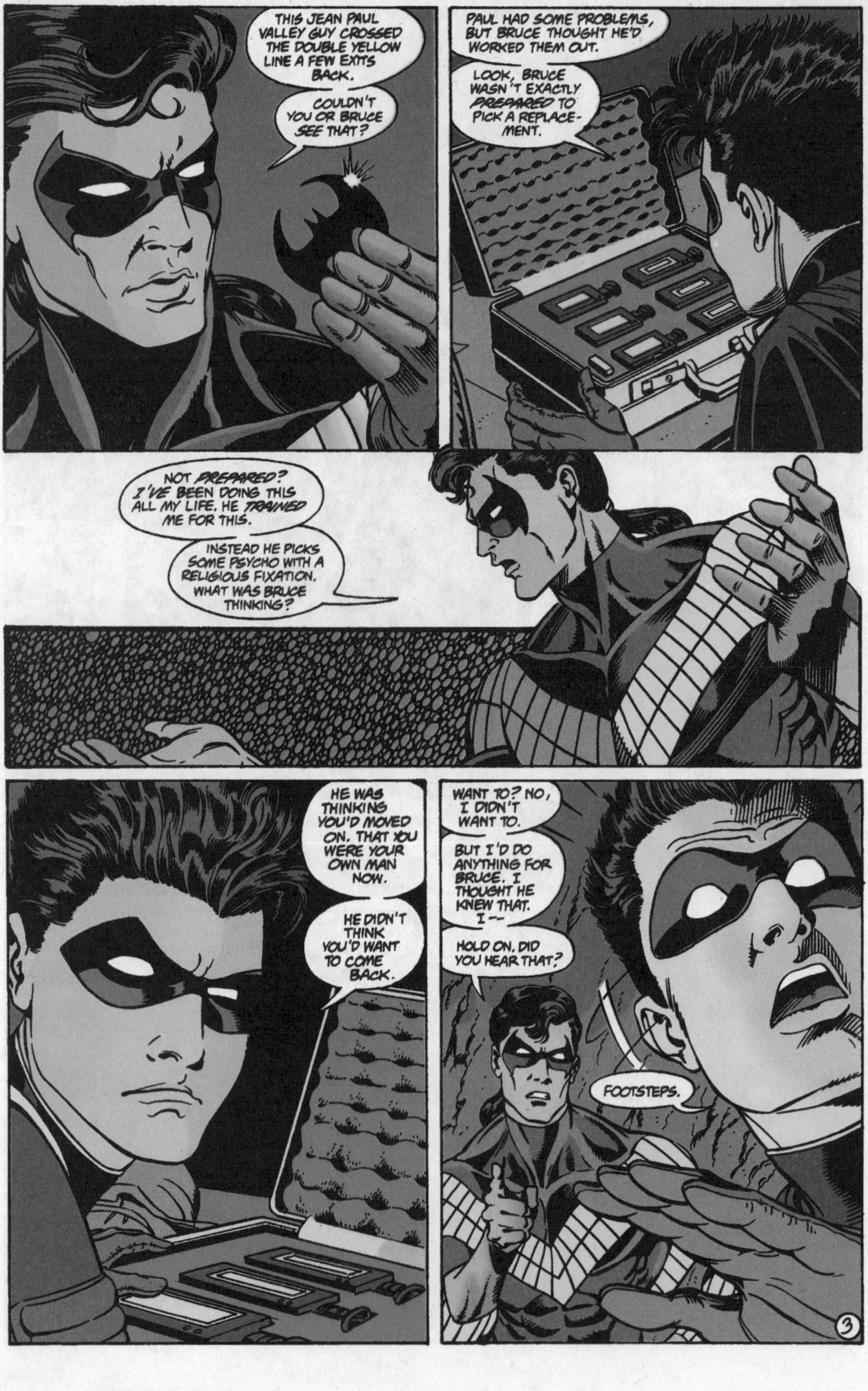
THIS JEAN PAUL VALLEY GUY CROSSED THE DOUBLE YELLOW LINE A FEW EXITS BACK.
COULDN'T YOU OR BRUCE SEE THAT?
PAUL HAD SOME PROBLEMS, BUT BRUCE THOUGHT HE'D WORKED THEM OUT.
LOOK, BRUCE WASN'T EXACTLY PREPARED TO PICK A REPLACE-MENT.
NOT PREPARED? I'VE BEEN DOING THIS ALL MY LIFE. HE TRAINED ME FOR THIS.
INSTEAD HE PICKS SOME PSYCHO WITH A RELIGIOUS FIXATION. WHAT WAS BRUCE THINKING?
HE WAS THINKING YOU'D MOVED ON. THAT YOU WERE YOUR OWN MAN NOW.
HE DIDN'T THINK YOU'D WANT TO COME BACK.
WANT TO? NO, I DIDN'T WANT TO.
BUT I'D DO ANYTHING FOR BRUCE. I THOUGHT HE KNEW THAT. I--
HOLD ON. DID YOU HEAR THAT?
FOOTSTEPS.
3

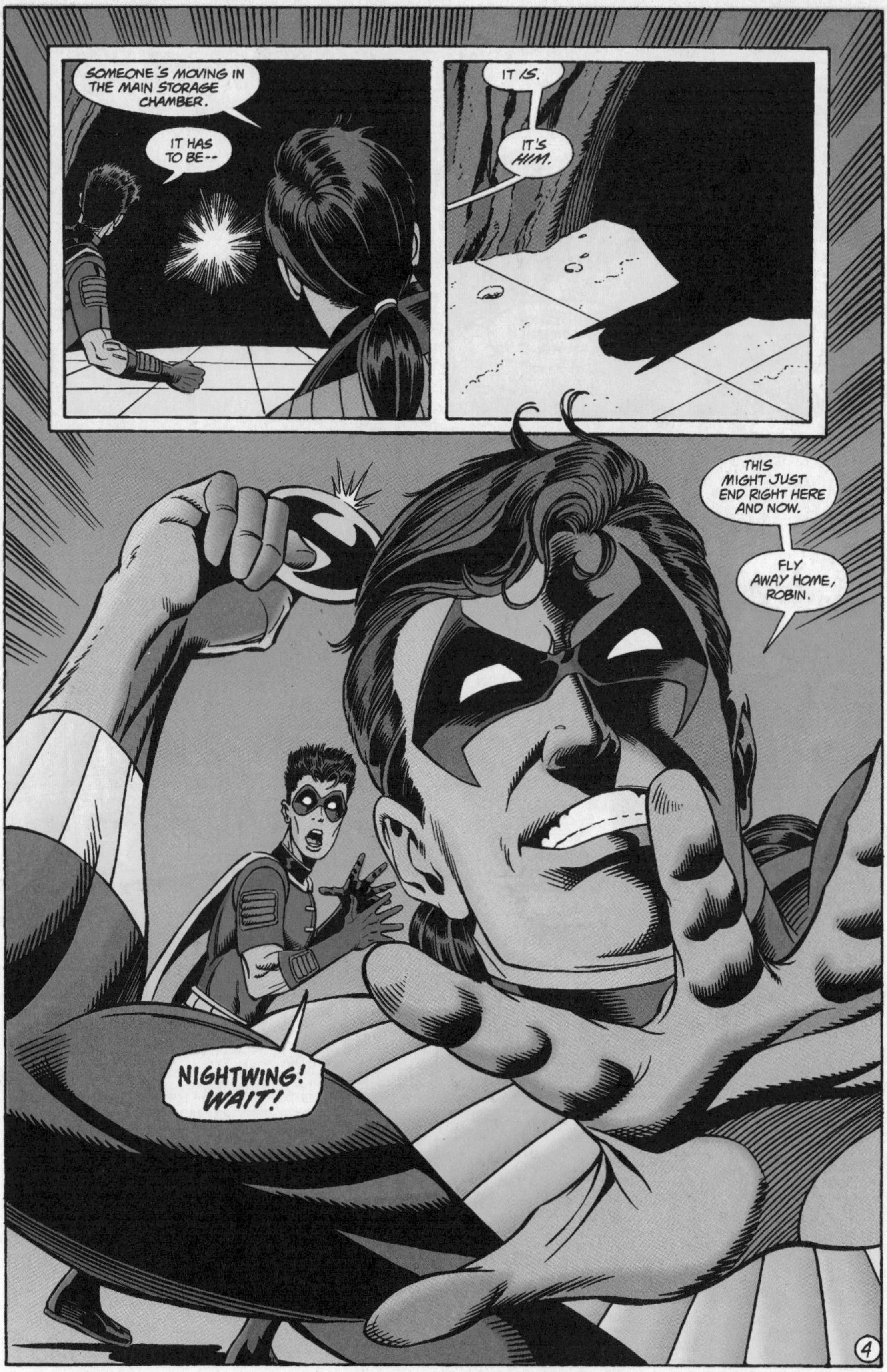
SOMEONE'S MOVING IN THE MAIN STORAGE CHAMBER.
IT HAS TO BE--
IT IS.
IT'S HIM.
THIS MIGHT JUST END RIGHT HERE AND NOW.
FLY AWAY HOME, ROBIN.
NIGHTWING! WAIT!
4

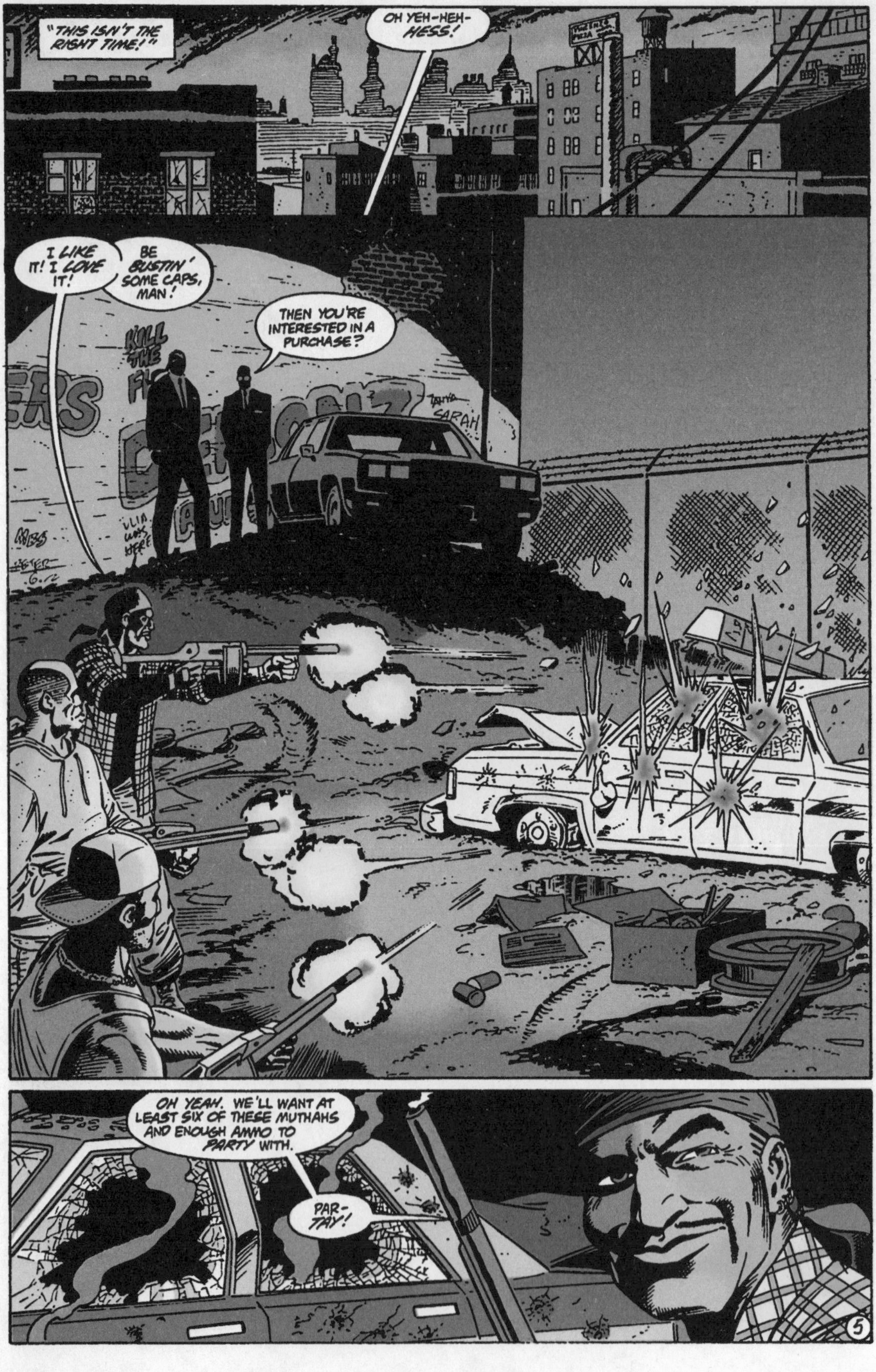
"THIS ISN'T THE RIGHT TIME!"
OH YEH-HEH-HESS!
I LIKE IT! I LOVE IT!
BE BUSTIN' SOME CAPS, MAN!
THEN YOU'RE INTERESTED IN A PURCHASE?
OH YEAH. WE'LL WANT AT LEAST SIX OF THESE MUTHAHS AND ENOUGH AMMO TO PARTY WITH.
PAR-TAY!
5

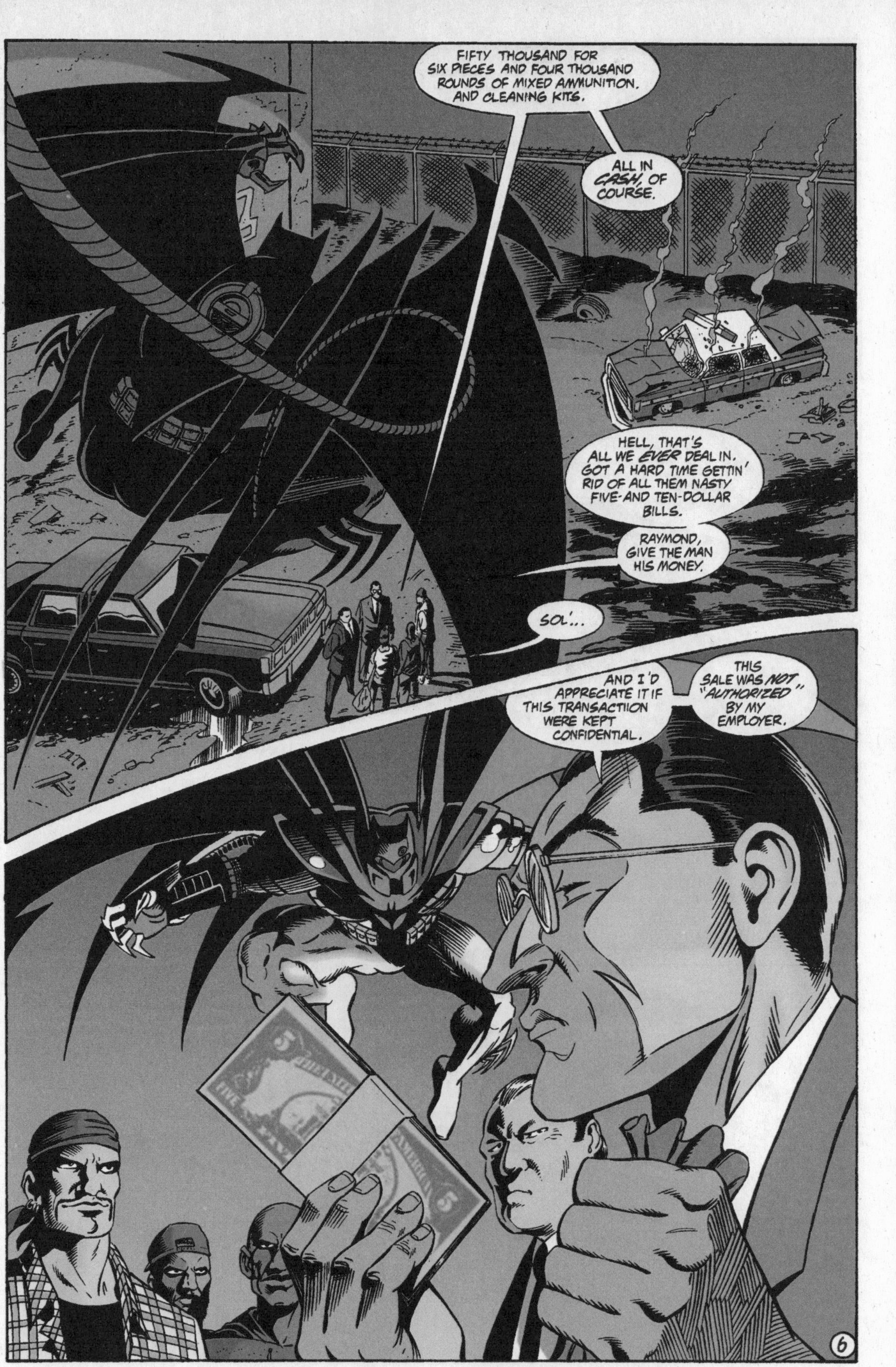
FIFTY THOUSAND FOR SIX PIECES AND FOUR THOUSAND ROUNDS OF MIXED AMMUNITION. AND CLEANING KITS.
ALL IN CASH, OF COURSE.
HELL, THAT'S ALL WE EVER DEAL IN. GOT A HARD TIME GETTIN' RID OF ALL THEM NASTY FIVE-AND TEN-DOLLAR BILLS.
RAYMOND, GIVE THE MAN HIS MONEY.
SO!...
THIS SALE WAS NOT "AUTHORIZED" BY MY EMPLOYER.
AND I'D APPRECIATE IT IF THIS TRANSACTIION WERE KEPT CONFIDENTIAL.
6

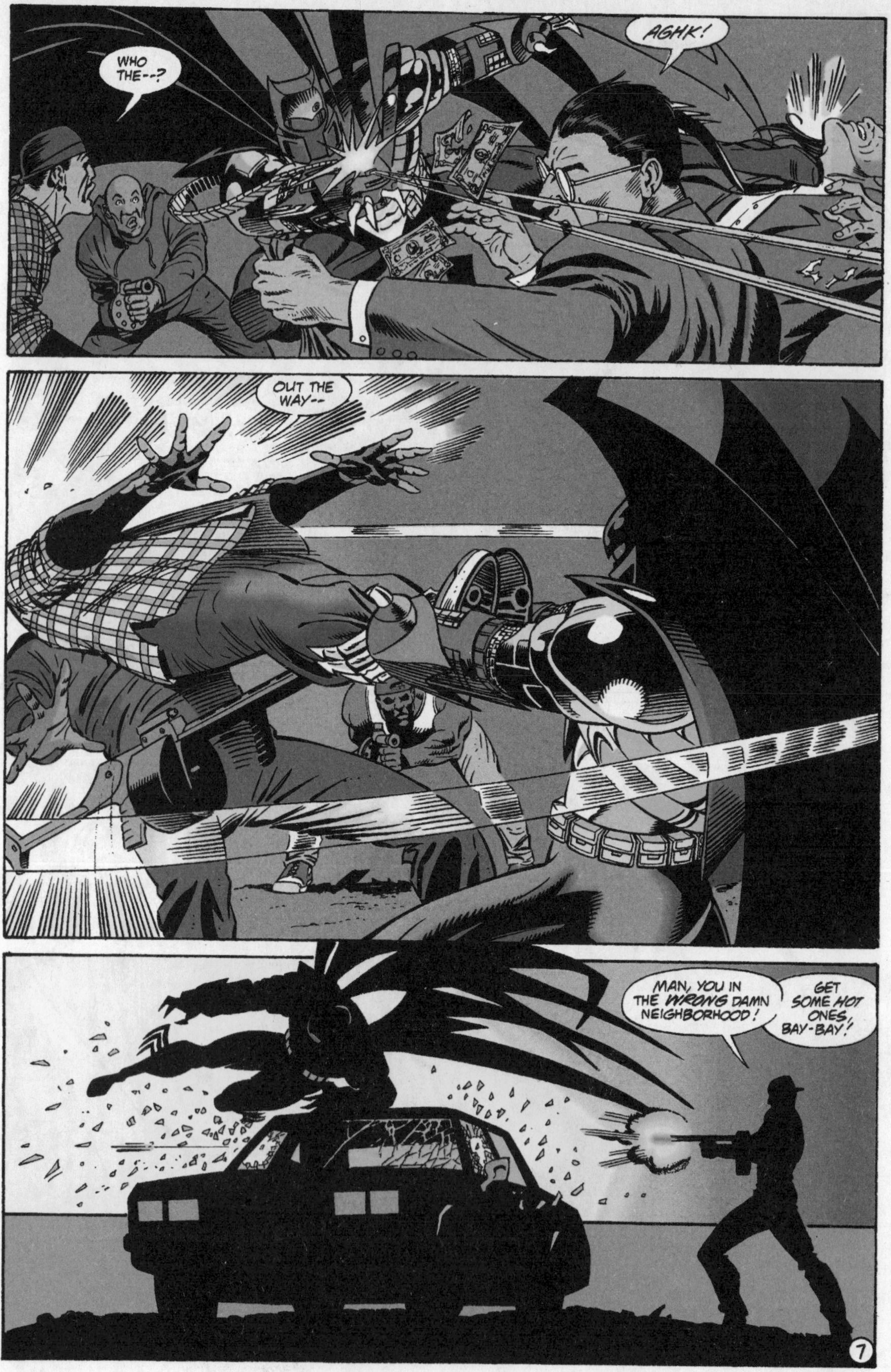
WHO THE--?
AGHK!
OUT THE WAY--
MAN, YOU IN THE WRONG DAMN NEIGHBORHOOD!
GET SOME HOT ONES, BAY-BAY!
7

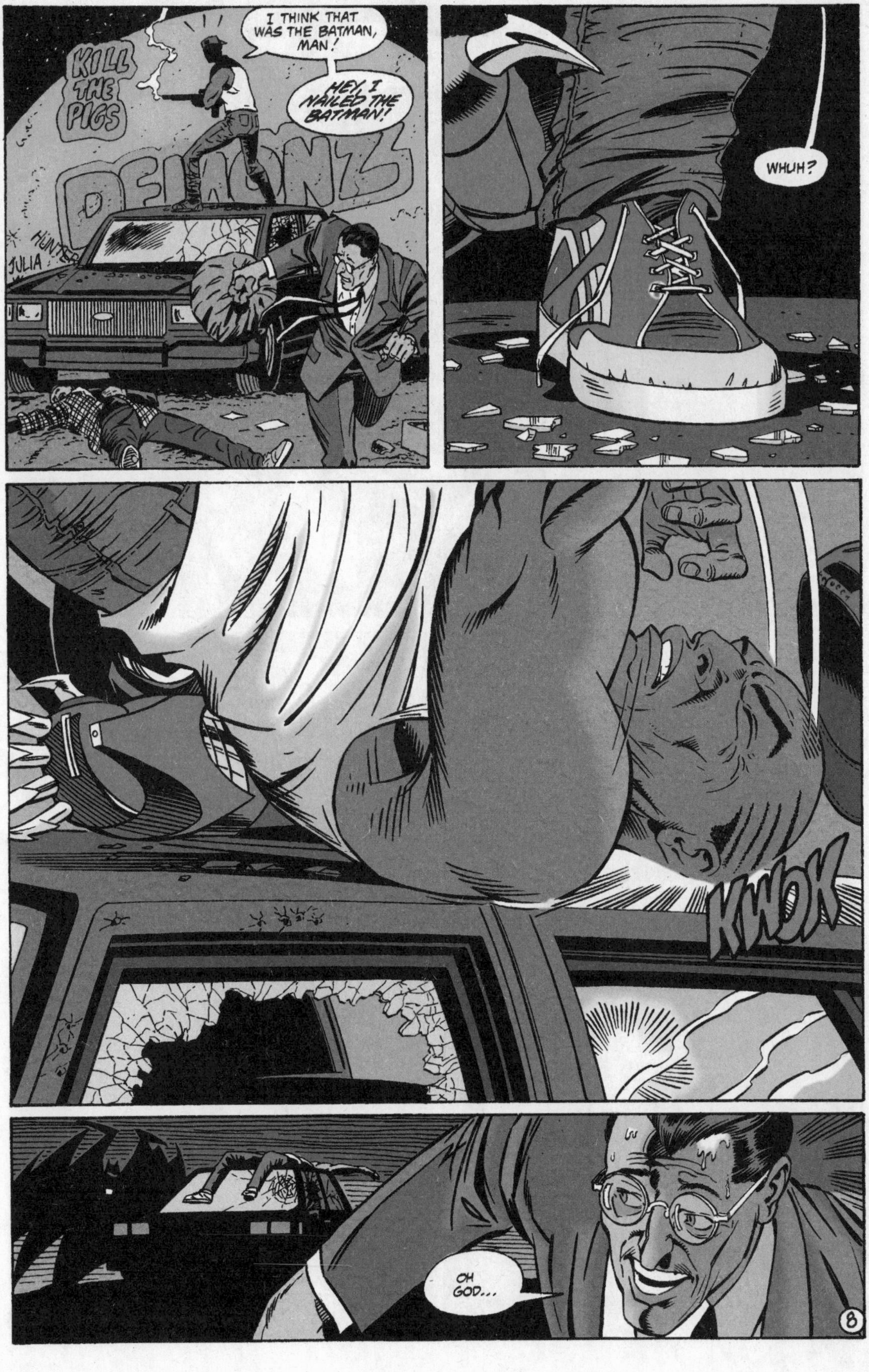

KILL THE PIGS
DEMONZ
HUNTER
JULIA
I THINK THAT WAS THE BATMAN, MAN!
HEY, I NAILED THE BATMAN!
WHUH?
KWOK
OH GOD...
8

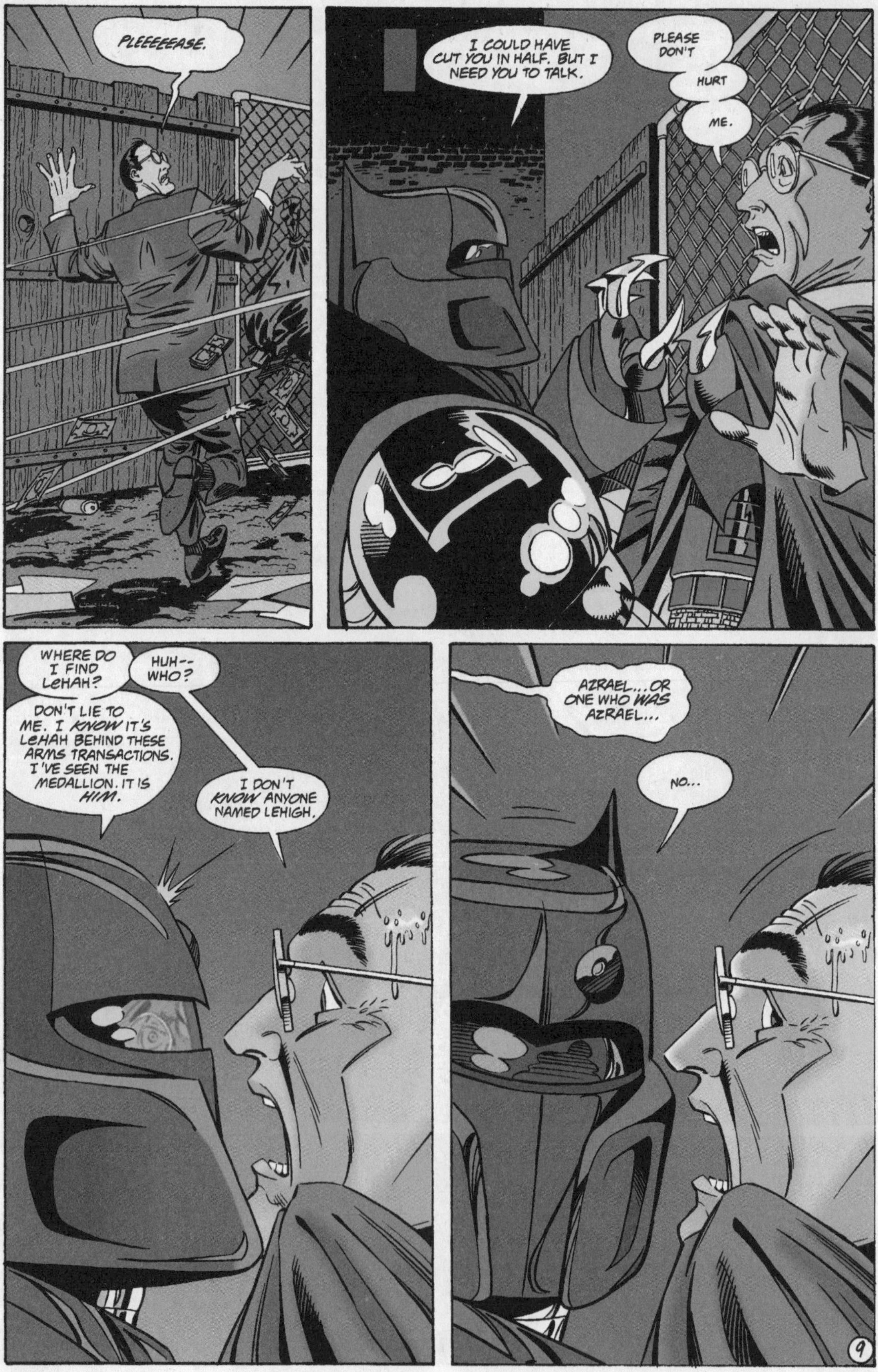
PLEEEEEASE.
I COULD HAVE CUT YOU IN HALF. BUT I NEED YOU TO TALK.
PLEASE DON'T
HURT
ME.
WHERE DO I FIND LeHAH?
HUH-- WHO?
DON'T LIE TO ME. I KNOW IT'S LeHAH BEHIND THESE ARMS TRANSACTIONS. I'VE SEEN THE MEDALLION. IT IS HIM.
I DON'T KNOW ANYONE NAMED LEHIGH.
AZRAEL... OR ONE WHO WAS AZRAEL...
NO...
9

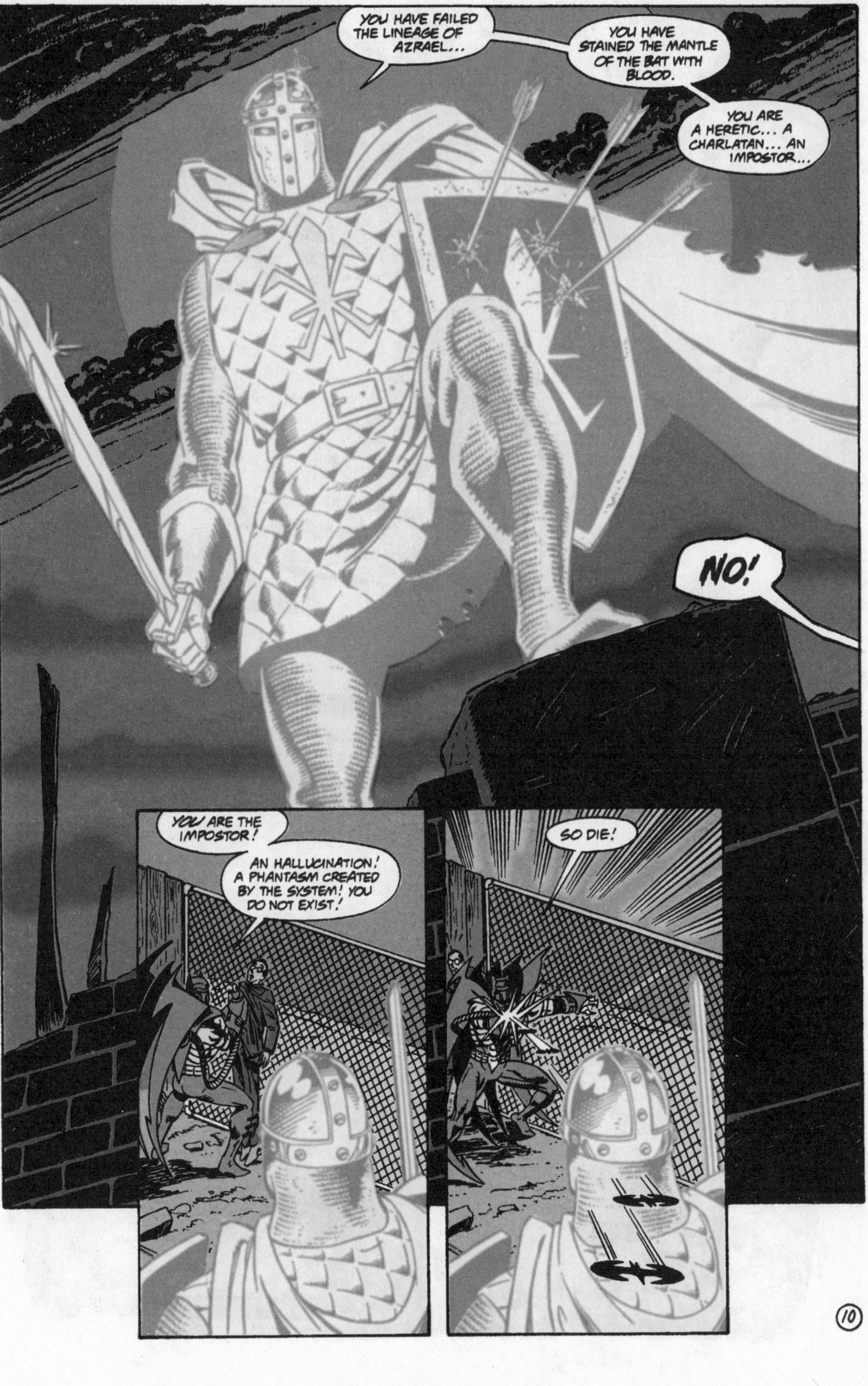
YOU HAVE FAILED THE LINEAGE OF AZRAEL...
YOU HAVE STAINED THE MANTLE OF THE BAT WITH BLOOD.
YOU ARE A HERETIC... A CHARLATAN... AN IMPOSTOR...
NO!
YOU ARE THE IMPOSTOR!
AN HALLUCINATION! A PHANTASM CREATED BY THE SYSTEM! YOU DO NOT EXIST!
SO DIE!
10

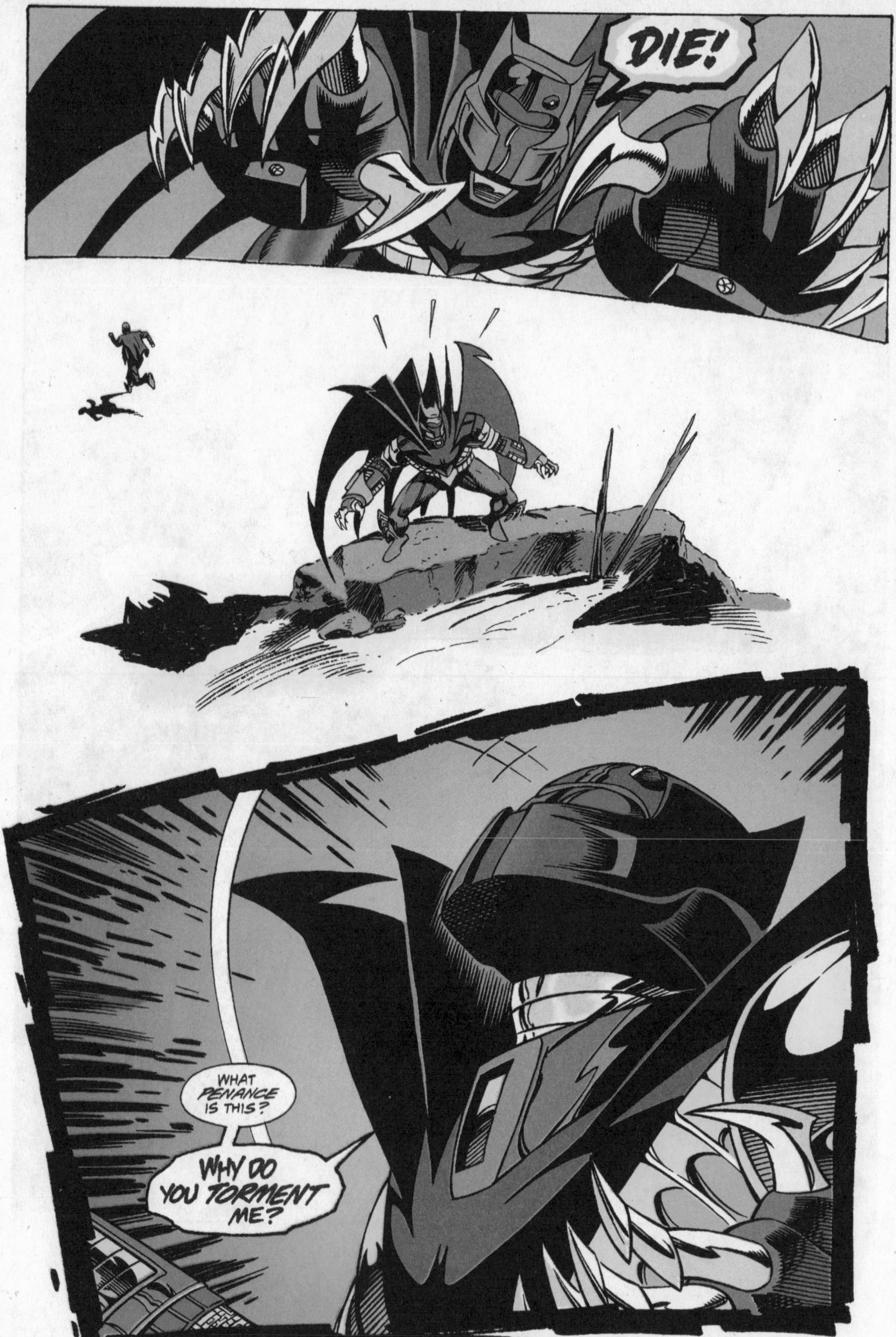
DIE!
WHAT PENANCE IS THIS?
WHY DO YOU TORMENT ME?

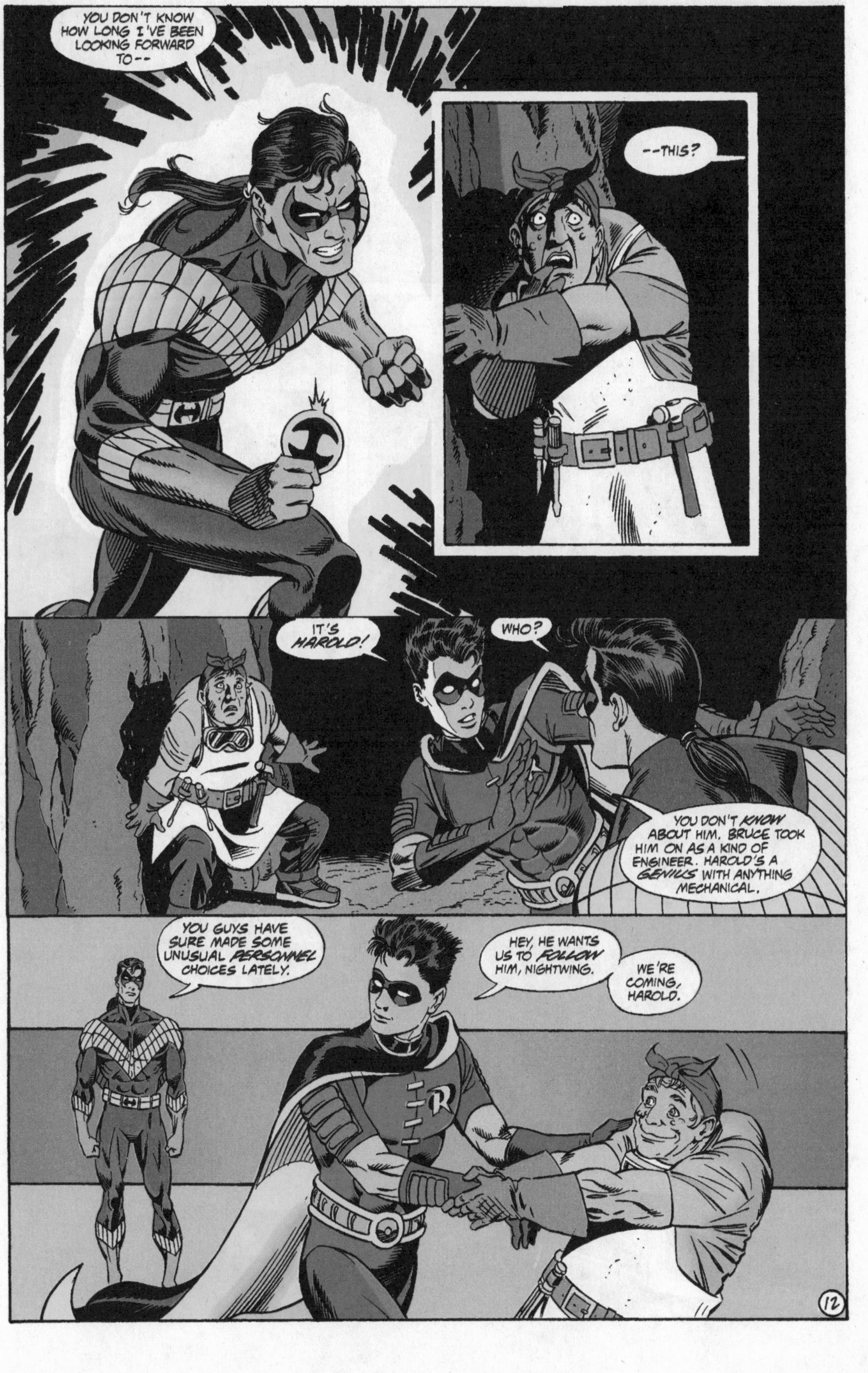
YOU DON'T KNOW HOW LONG I'VE BEEN LOOKING FORWARD TO--
--THIS?
IT'S HAROLD!
WHO?
YOU DON'T KNOW ABOUT HIM. BRUCE TOOK HIM ON AS A KIND OF ENGINEER. HAROLD'S A GENIUS WITH ANYTHING MECHANICAL.
YOU GUYS HAVE SURE MADE SOME UNUSUAL PERSONNEL CHOICES LATELY.
HEY, HE WANTS US TO FOLLOW HIM, NIGHTWING.
WE'RE COMING, HAROLD.
12

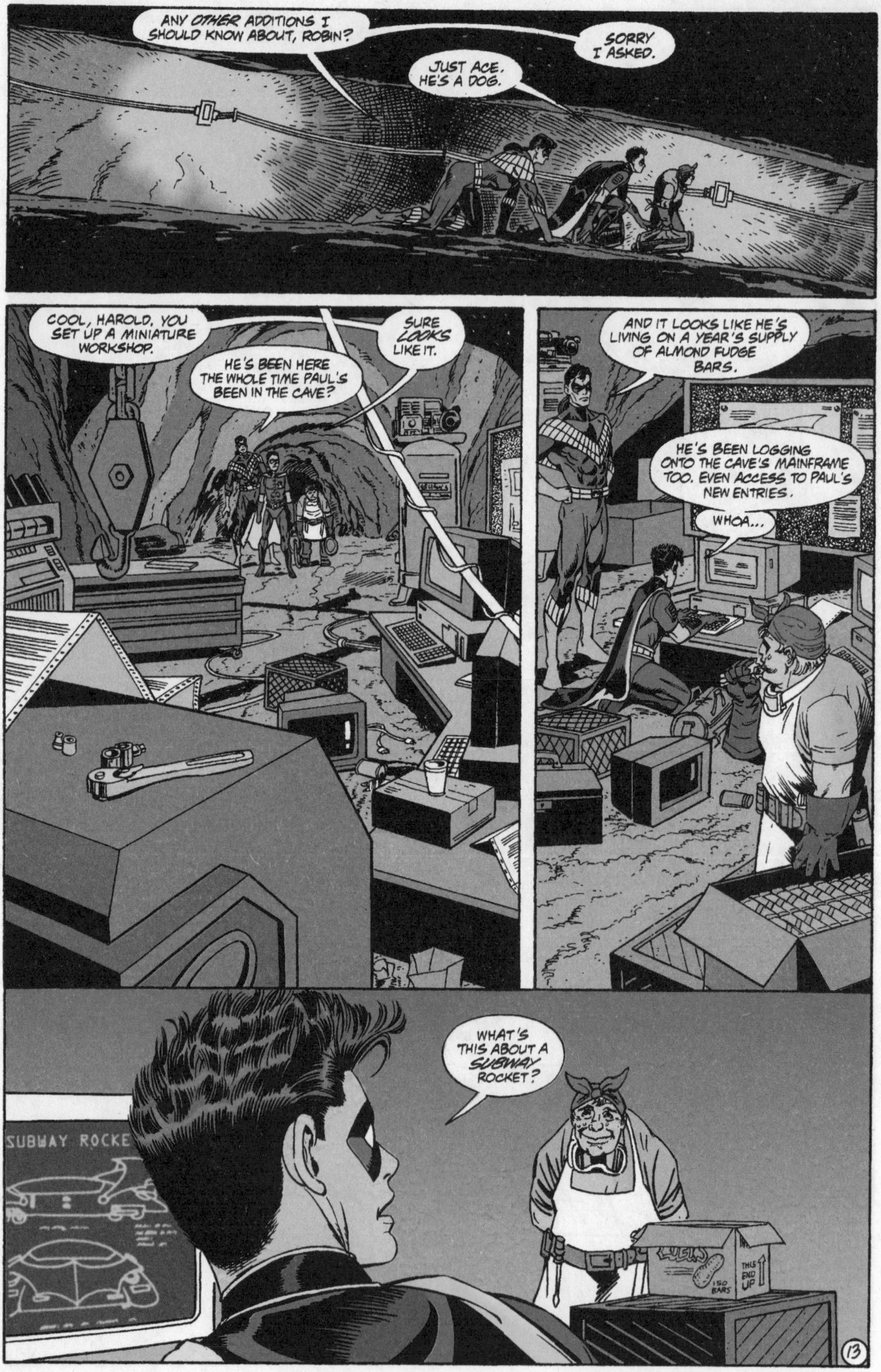
ANY OTHER ADDITIONS I SHOULD KNOW ABOUT, ROBIN?
JUST ACE. HE'S A DOG.
SORRY I ASKED.
COOL, HAROLD, YOU SET UP A MINIATURE WORKSHOP.
HE'S BEEN HERE THE WHOLE TIME PAUL'S BEEN IN THE CAVE?
SURE LOOKS LIKE IT.
AND IT LOOKS LIKE HE'S LIVING ON A YEAR'S SUPPLY OF ALMOND FUDGE BARS.
HE'S BEEN LOGGING ONTO THE CAVE'S MAINFRAME TOO. EVEN ACCESS TO PAUL'S NEW ENTRIES.
WHOA...
WHAT'S THIS ABOUT A SUBWAY ROCKET?
SUBWAY ROCKE
THIS END UP
150 BARS
13

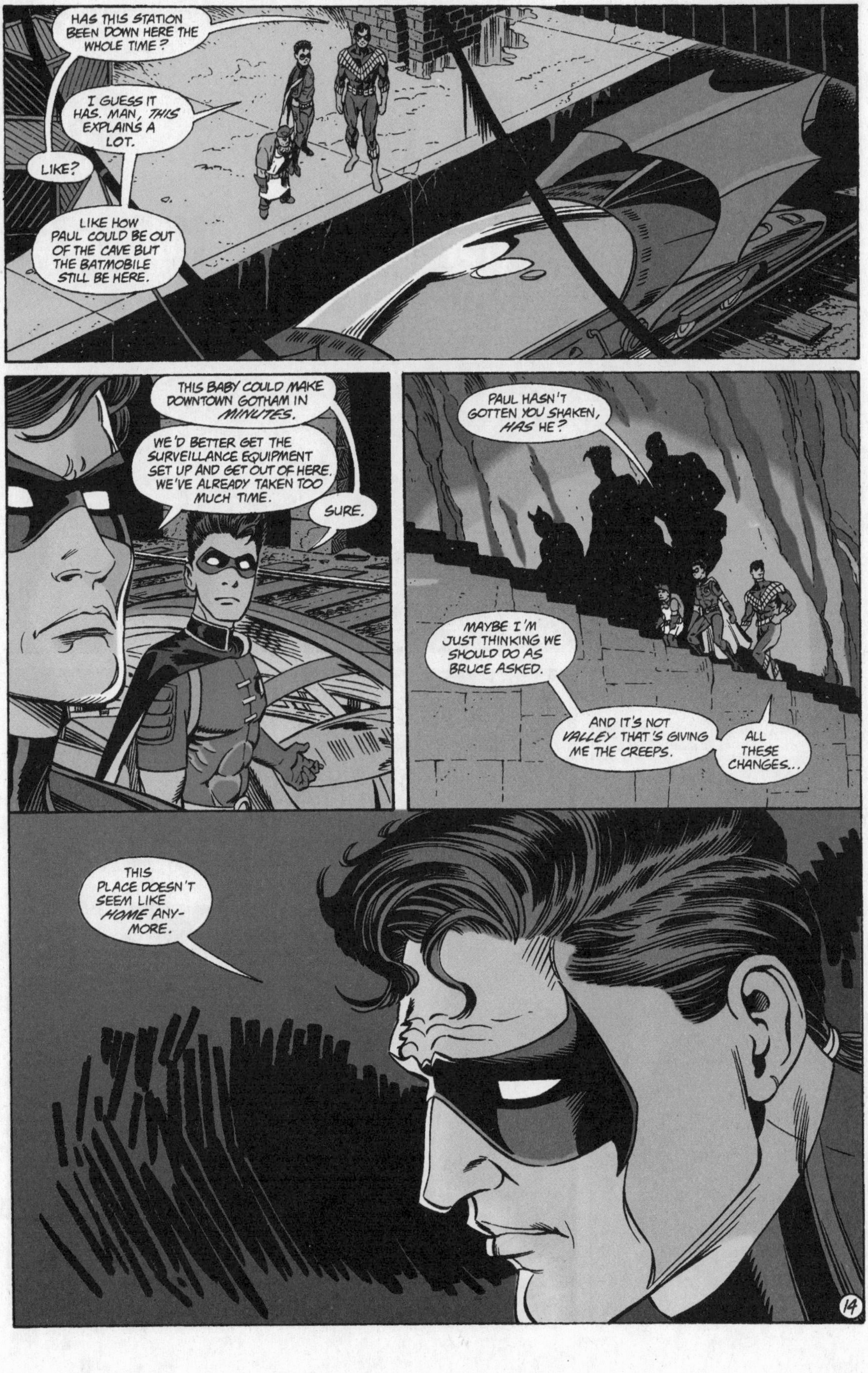

HAS THIS STATION BEEN DOWN HERE THE WHOLE TIME?
I GUESS IT HAS. MAN, THIS EXPLAINS A LOT.
LIKE?
LIKE HOW PAUL COULD BE OUT OF THE CAVE BUT THE BATMOBILE STILL BE HERE.
THIS BABY COULD MAKE DOWNTOWN GOTHAM IN MINUTES.
WE'D BETTER GET THE SURVEILLANCE EQUIPMENT SET UP AND GET OUT OF HERE. WE'VE ALREADY TAKEN TOO MUCH TIME.
SURE.
PAUL HASN'T GOTTEN YOU SHAKEN, HAS HE?
MAYBE I'M JUST THINKING WE SHOULD DO AS BRUCE ASKED.
AND IT'S NOT VALLEY THAT'S GIVING ME THE CREEPS.
ALL THESE CHANGES...
THIS PLACE DOESN'T SEEM LIKE HOME ANY-MORE.
14

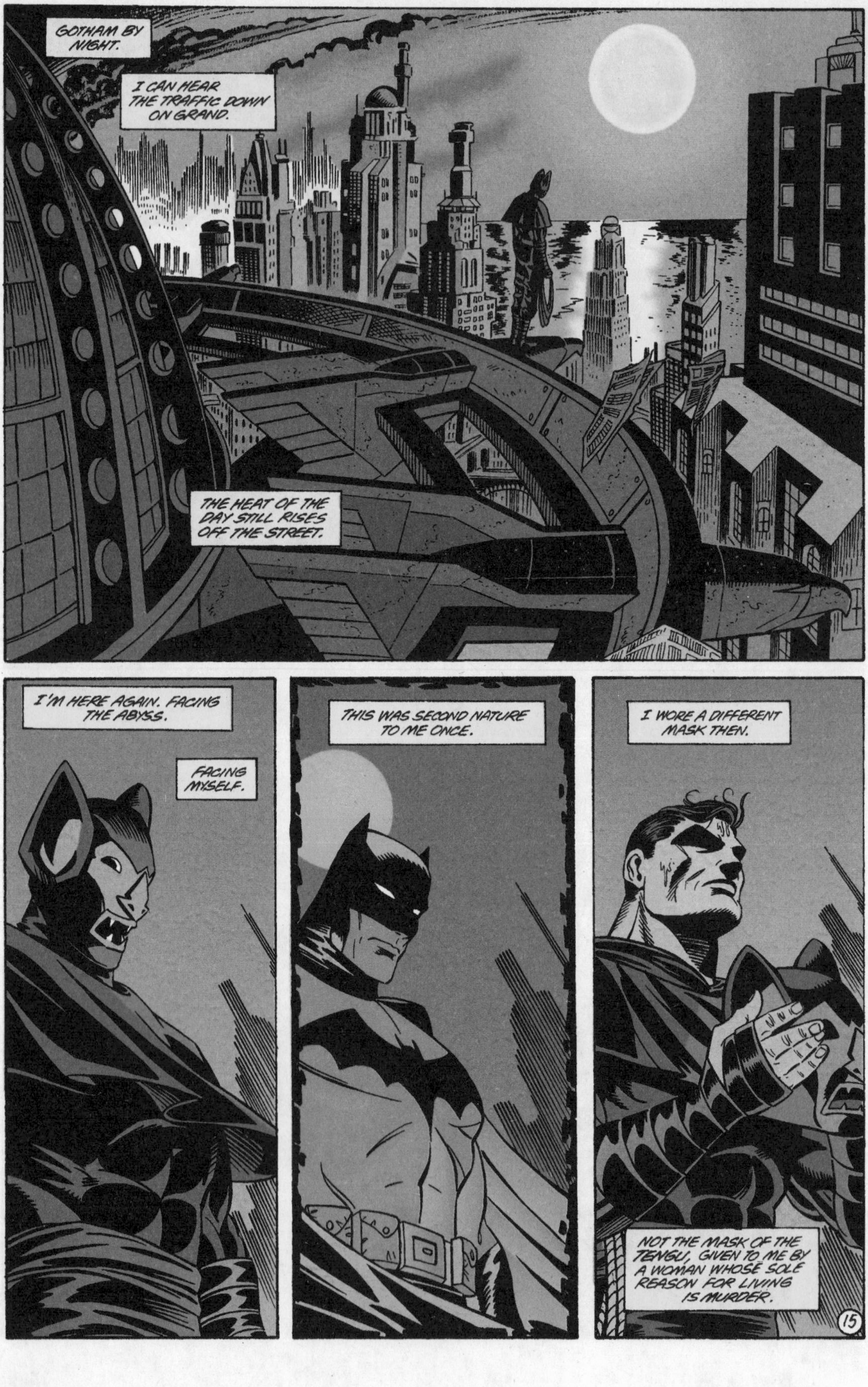
GOTHAM BY NIGHT.
I CAN HEAR THE TRAFFIC DOWN ON GRAND.
THE HEAT OF THE DAY STILL RISES OFF THE STREET.
I'M HERE AGAIN. FACING THE ABYSS.
FACING MYSELF.
THIS WAS SECOND NATURE TO ME ONCE.
I WORE A DIFFERENT MASK THEN.
NOT THE MASK OF THE TENGU, GIVEN TO ME BY A WOMAN WHOSE SOLE REASON FOR LIVING IS MURDER.
15

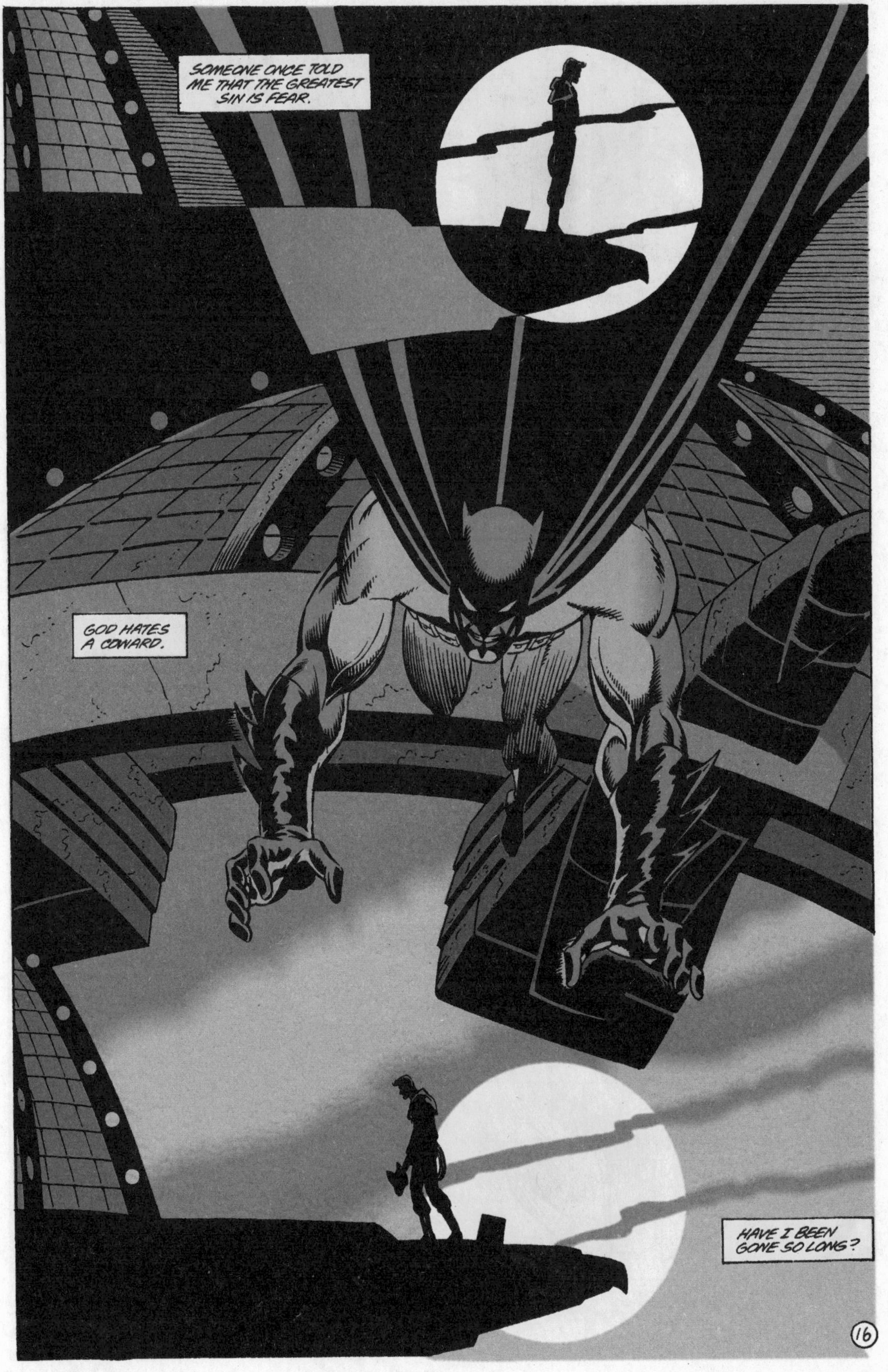
SOMEONE ONCE TOLD ME THAT THE GREATEST SIN IS FEAR.
GOD HATES A COWARD.
HAVE I BEEN GONE SO LONG?
16

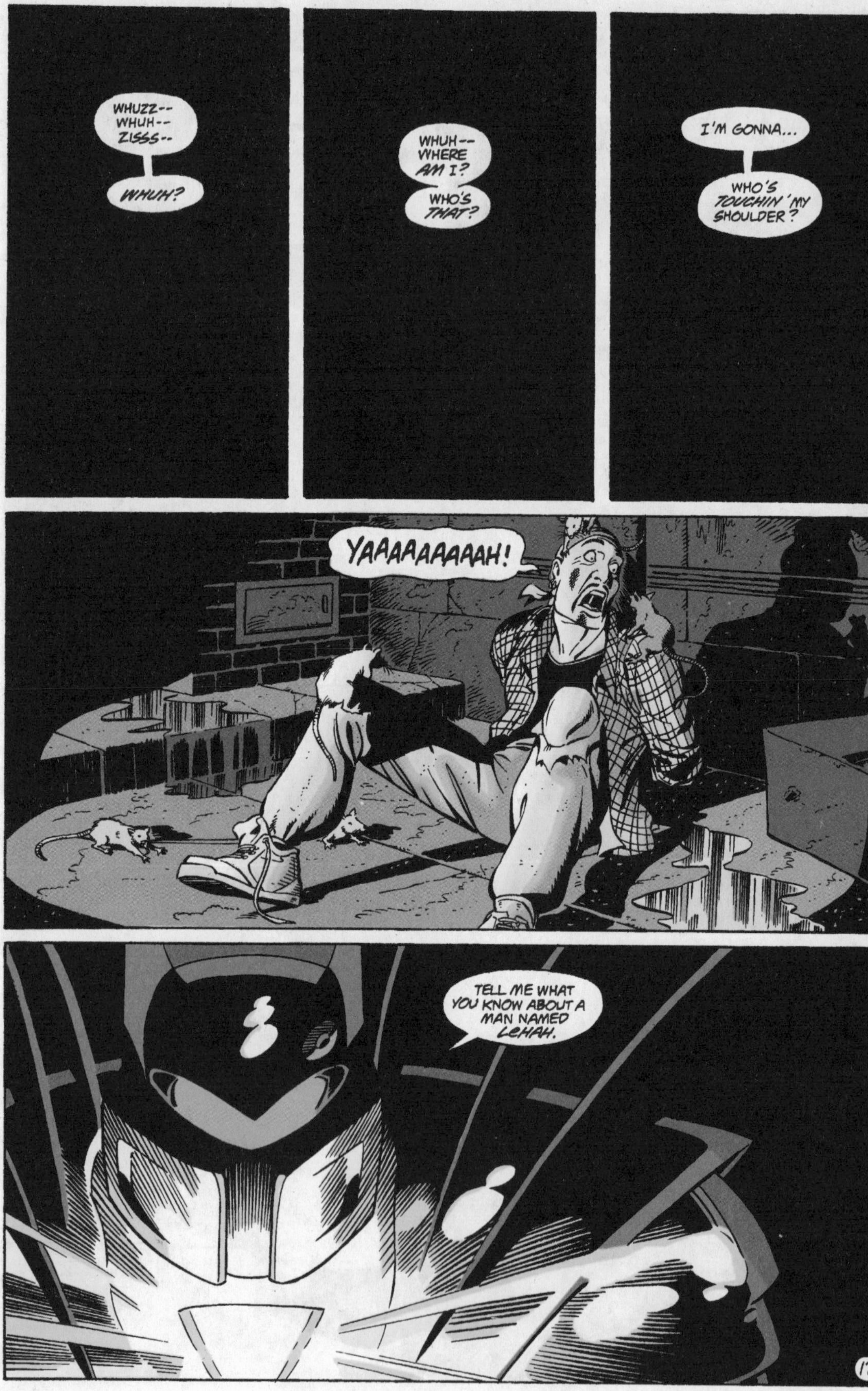

WHUZZ-- WHUH-- ZISSS--
WHUH?
WHUH-- WHERE AM I?
WHO'S THAT?
I'M GONNA...
WHO'S TOUCHIN' MY SHOULDER?
YAAAAAAAAAH!
TELL ME WHAT YOU KNOW ABOUT A MAN NAMED LEHAH.
17

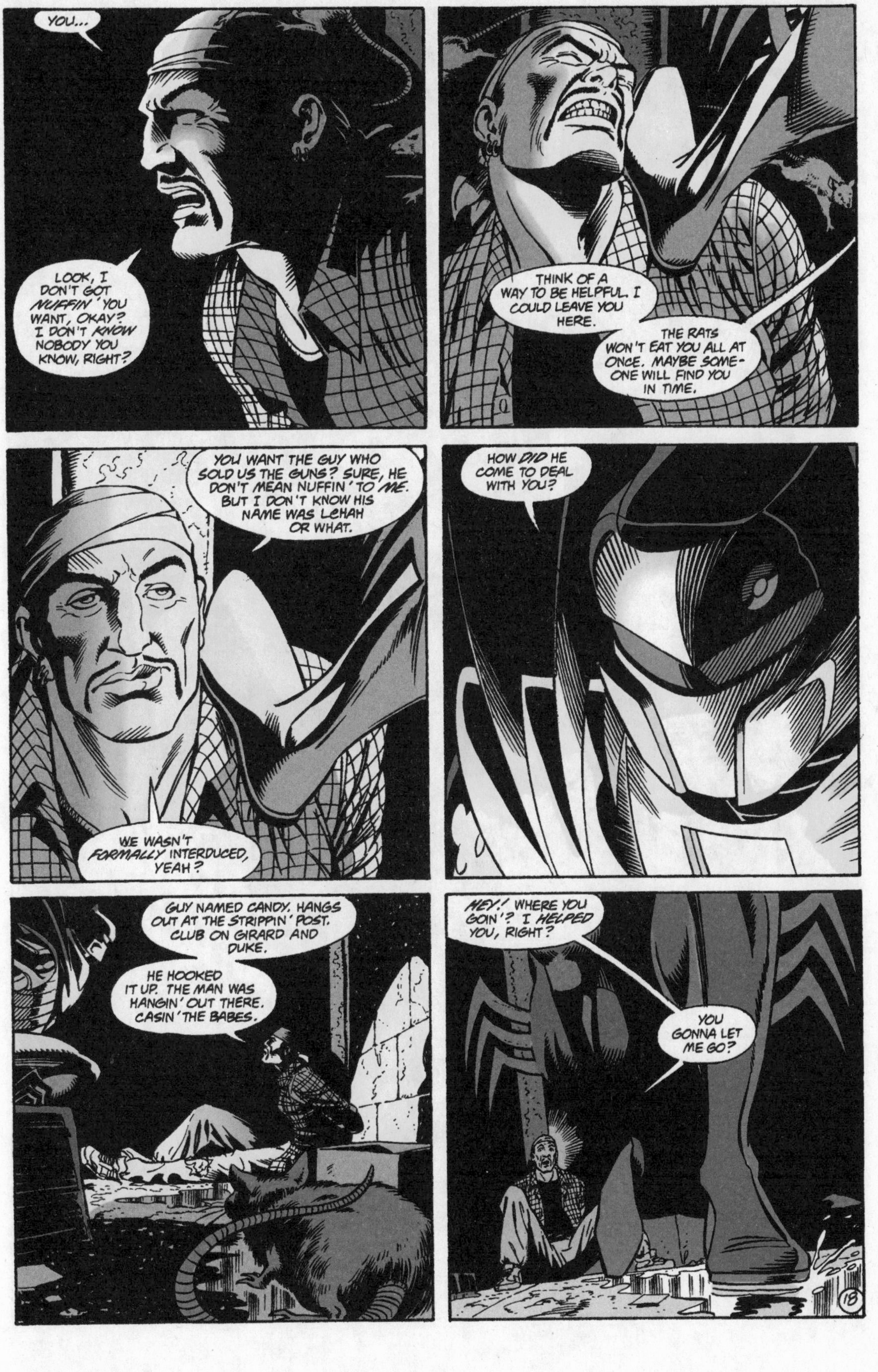
YOU...
LOOK, I DON'T GOT NUFFIN' YOU WANT, OKAY? I DON'T KNOW NOBODY YOU KNOW, RIGHT?
THINK OF A WAY TO BE HELPFUL. I COULD LEAVE YOU HERE.
THE RATS WON'T EAT YOU ALL AT ONCE. MAYBE SOME-ONE WILL FIND YOU IN TIME.
YOU WANT THE GUY WHO SOLD US THE GUNS? SURE, HE DON'T MEAN NUFFIN' TO ME. BUT I DON'T KNOW HIS NAME WAS LEHAH OR WHAT.
WE WASN'T FORMALLY INTERDUCED, YEAH?
HOW DID HE COME TO DEAL WITH YOU?
GUY NAMED CANDY. HANGS OUT AT THE STRIPPIN' POST. CLUB ON GIRARD AND DUKE.
HE HOOKED IT UP. THE MAN WAS HANGIN' OUT THERE. CASIN' THE BABES.
HEY! WHERE YOU GOIN'? I HELPED YOU, RIGHT?
YOU GONNA LET ME GO?
18

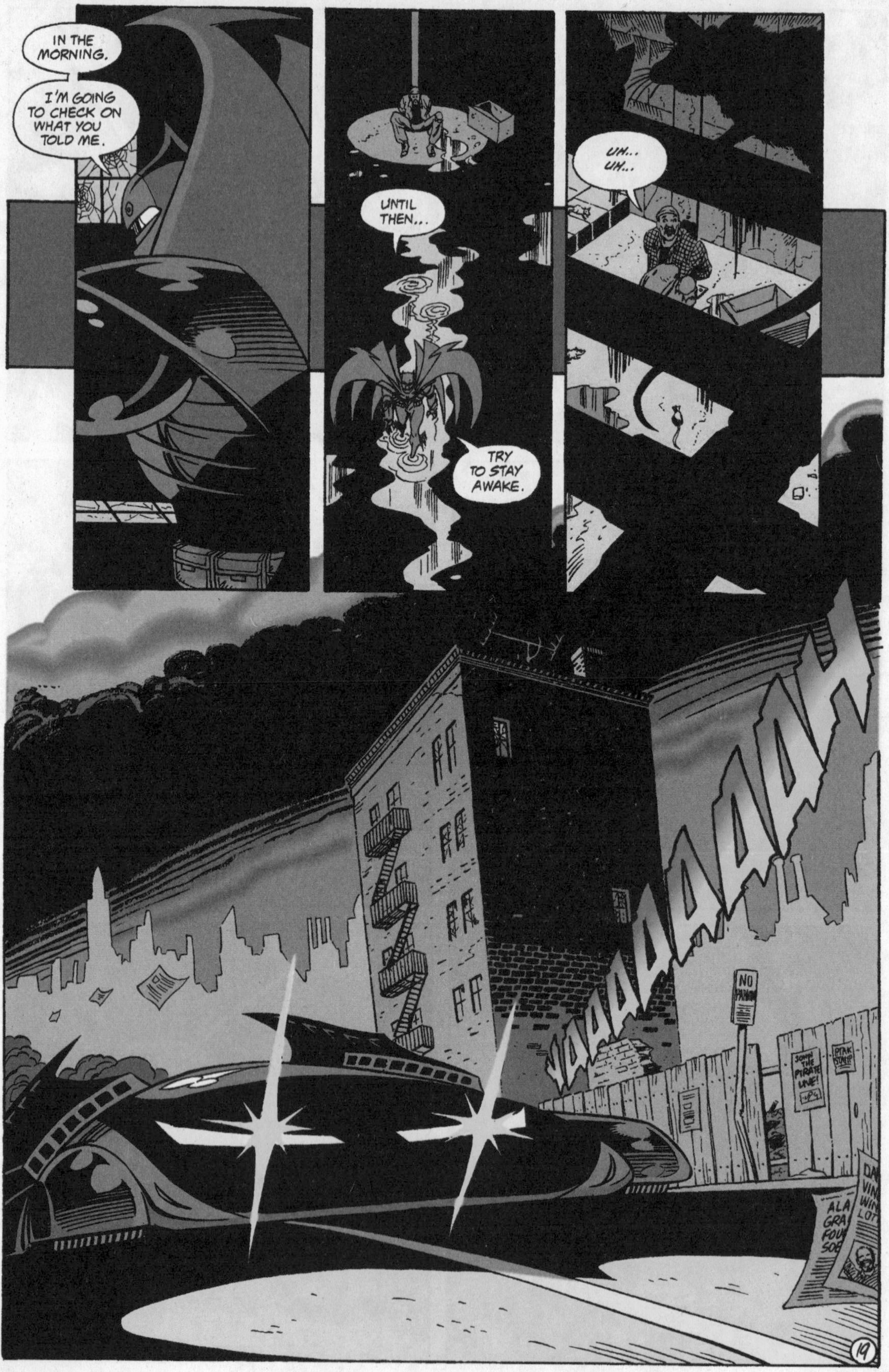

IN THE MORNING.
I'M GOING TO CHECK ON WHAT YOU TOLD ME.
UNTIL THEN...
TRY TO STAY AWAKE.
UH... UH...
19

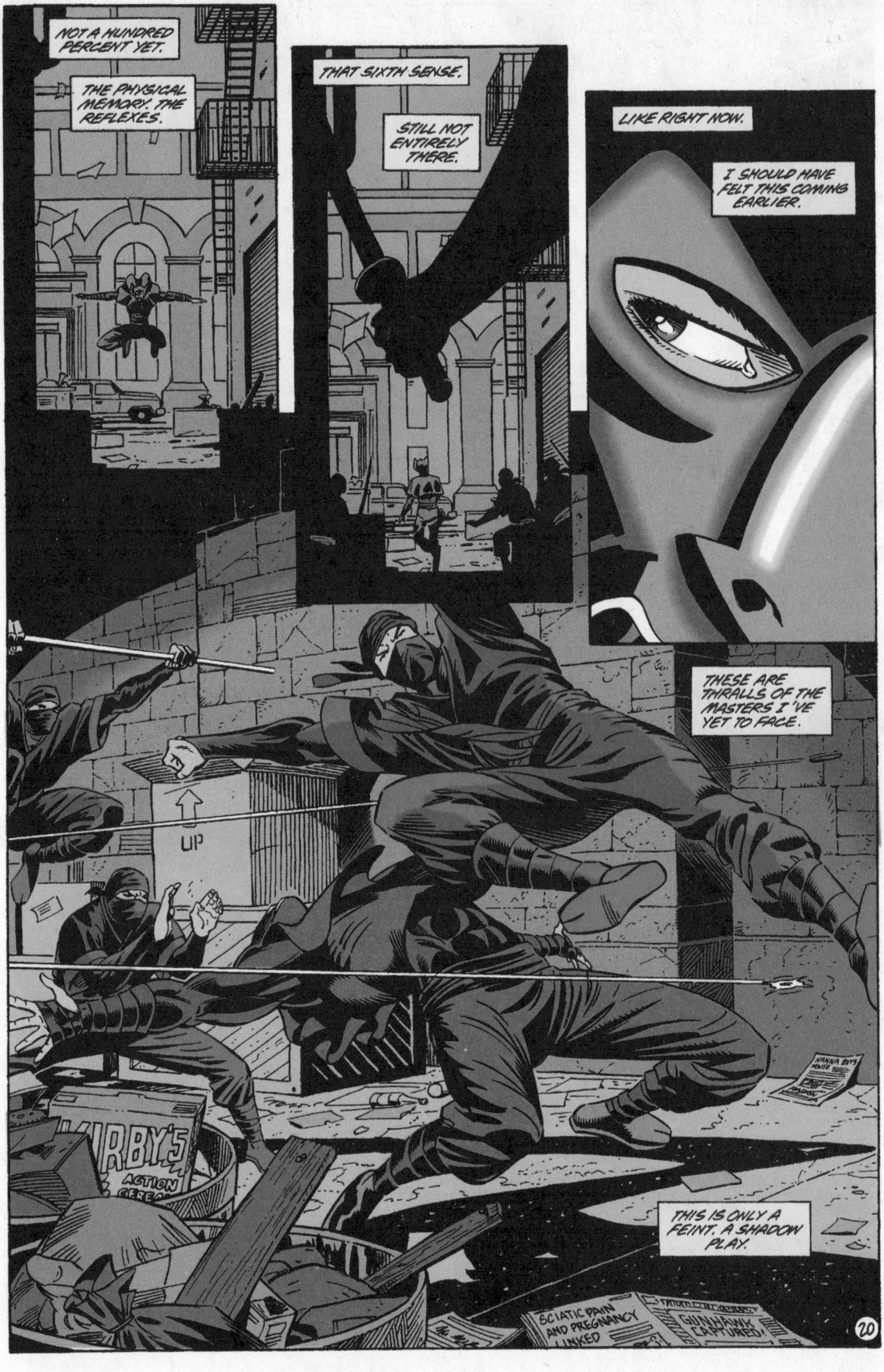
NOT A HUNDRED PERCENT YET.
THE PHYSICAL MEMORY. THE REFLEXES.
THAT SIXTH SENSE.
STILL NOT ENTIRELY THERE.
LIKE RIGHT NOW.
I SHOULD HAVE FELT THIS COMING EARLIER.
THESE ARE THRALLS OF THE MASTERS I'VE YET TO FACE.
UP
THIS IS ONLY A FEINT. A SHADOW PLAY.
SCIATIC PAIN AND PREGNANCY LINKED
GUNHAWK CAPTURED!
20

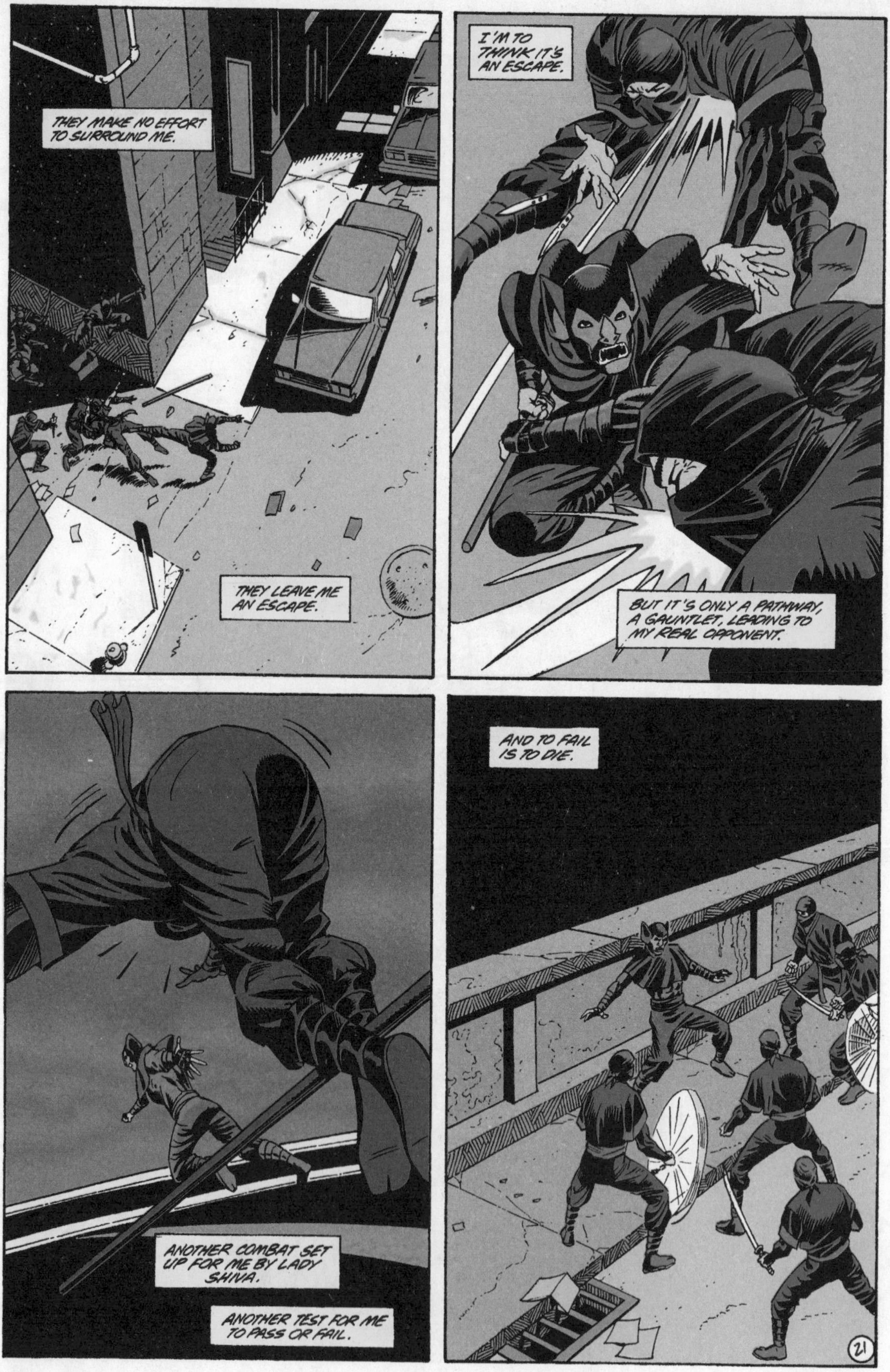
THEY MAKE NO EFFORT TO SURROUND ME.
THEY LEAVE ME AN ESCAPE.
I'M TO THINK IT'S AN ESCAPE.
BUT IT'S ONLY A PATHWAY, A GAUNTLET, LEADING TO MY REAL OPPONENT.
ANOTHER COMBAT SET UP FOR ME BY LADY SHIVA.
ANOTHER TEST FOR ME TO PASS OR FAIL.
AND TO FAIL IS TO DIE.
21

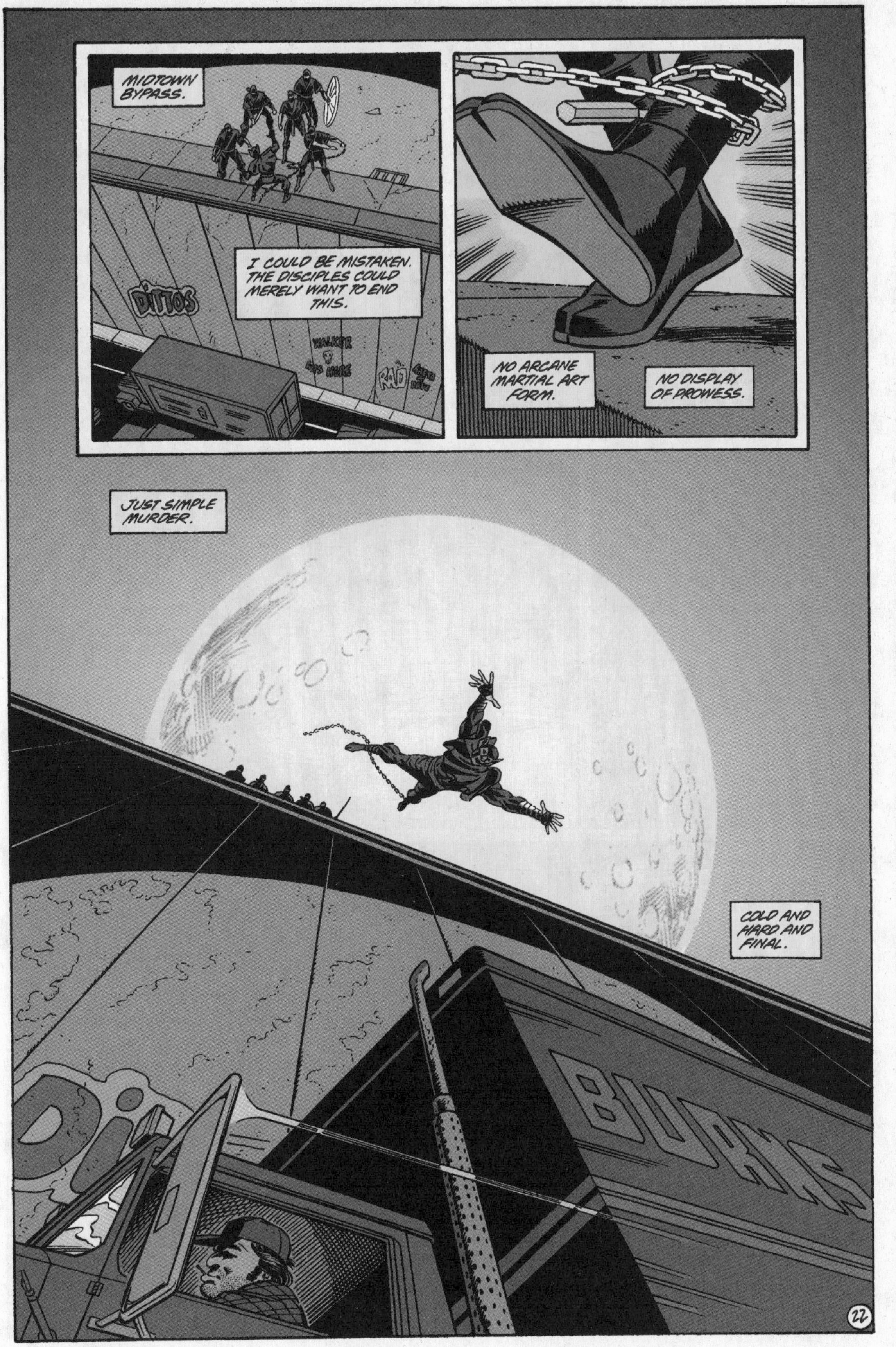
MIDTOWN BYPASS.
I COULD BE MISTAKEN. THE DISCIPLES COULD MERELY WANT TO END THIS.
DITTOS
WALKER
NO ARCANE MARTIAL ART FORM.
NO DISPLAY OF PROWESS.
JUST SIMPLE MURDER.
COLD AND HARD AND FINAL.
22

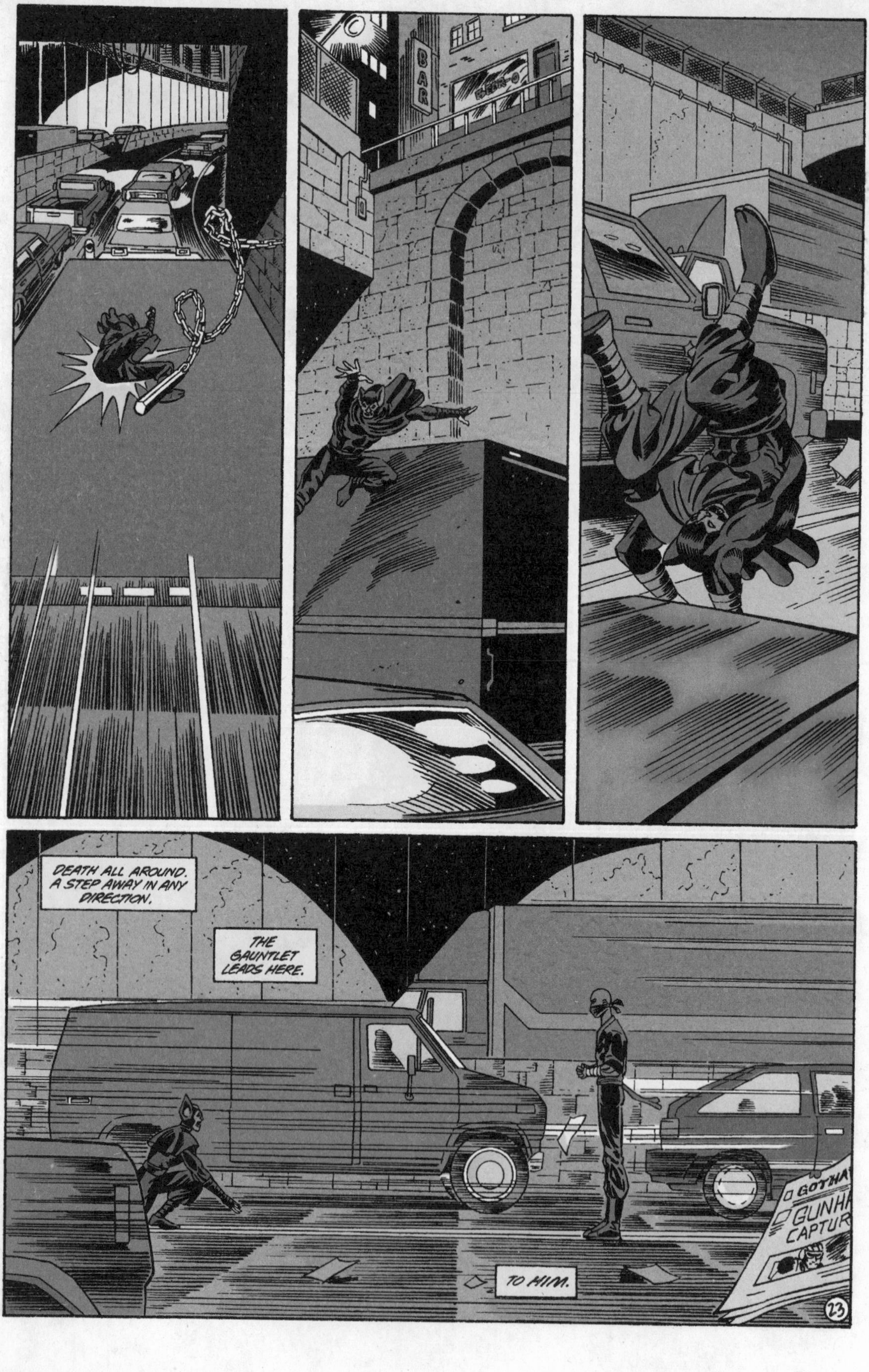
BAR
DEATH ALL AROUND. A STEP AWAY IN ANY DIRECTION.
THE GAUNTLET LEADS HERE.
TO HIM.
23

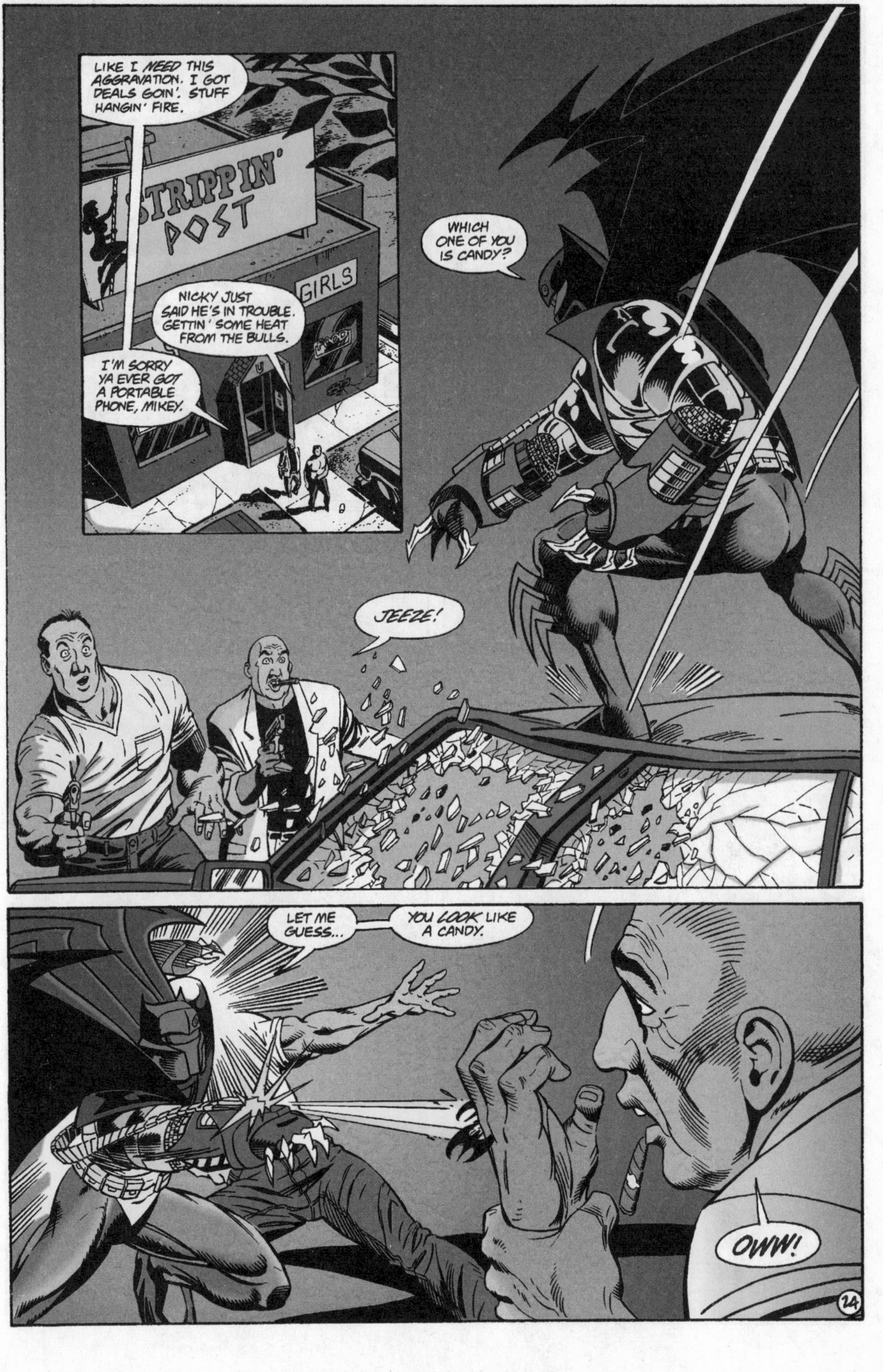
LIKE I NEED THIS AGGRAVATION. I GOT DEALS GOIN'. STUFF HANGIN' FIRE.
STRIPPIN' POST
GIRLS
NICKY JUST SAID HE'S IN TROUBLE. GETTIN' SOME HEAT FROM THE BULLS.
I'M SORRY YA EVER GOT A PORTABLE PHONE, MIKEY.
WHICH ONE OF YOU IS CANDY?
JEEZE!
LET ME GUESS...
YOU LOOK LIKE A CANDY.
OWW!
24

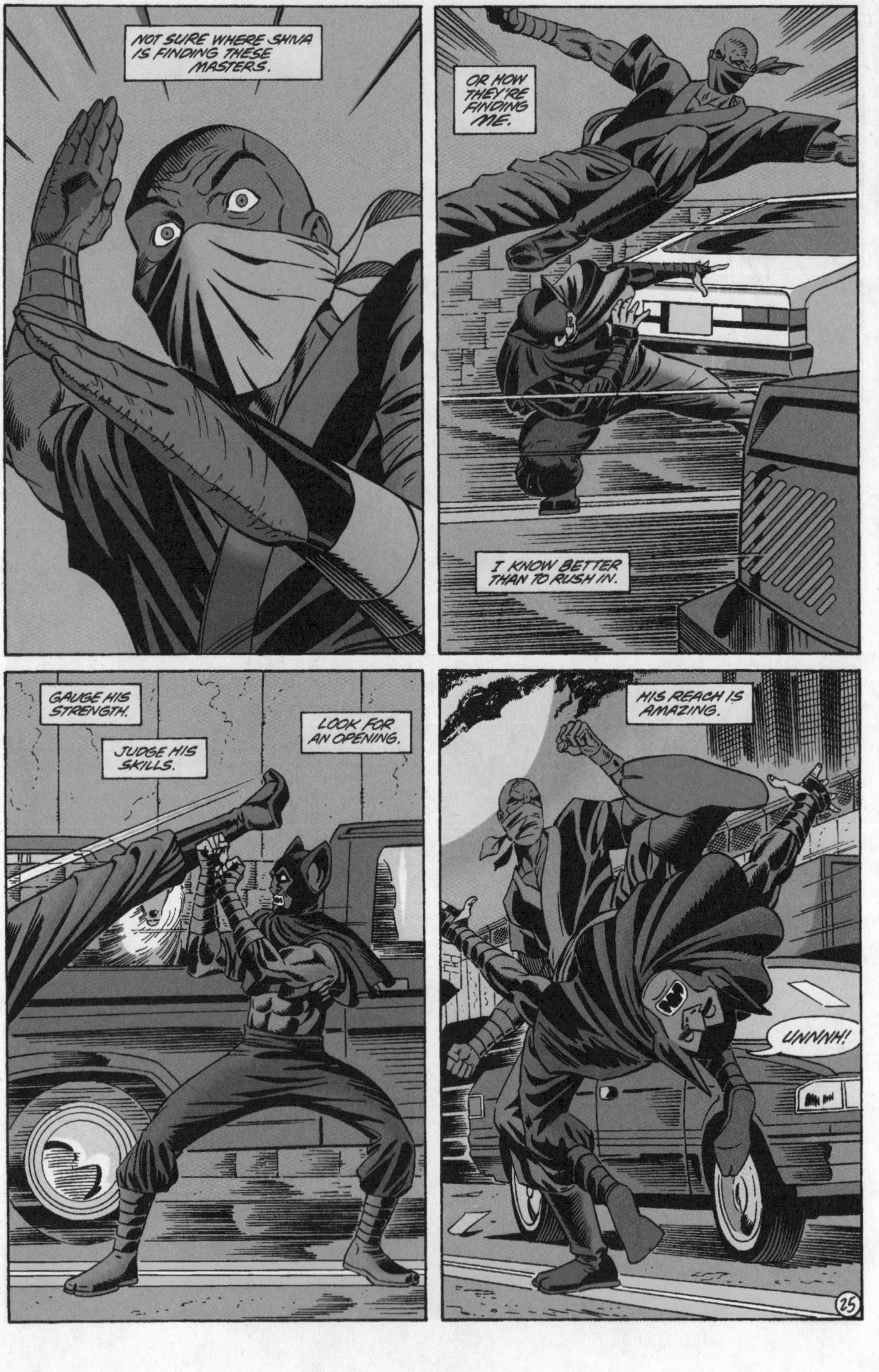
NOT SURE WHERE SHIVA IS FINDING THESE MASTERS.
OR HOW THEY'RE FINDING ME.
I KNOW BETTER THAN TO RUSH IN.
GAUGE HIS STRENGTH.
JUDGE HIS SKILLS.
LOOK FOR AN OPENING.
HIS REACH IS AMAZING.
UNNNH!
25

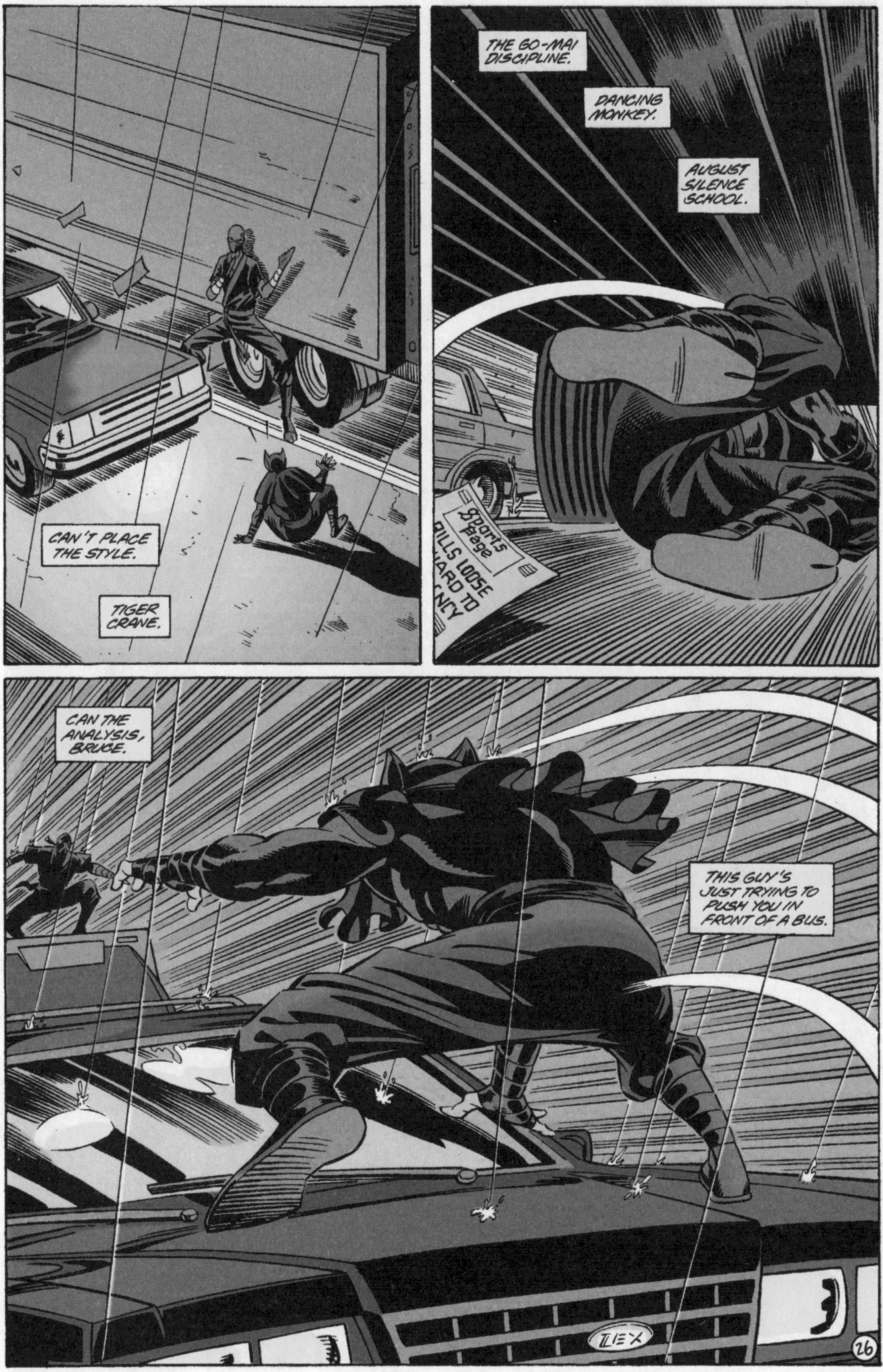
CAN'T PLACE THE STYLE.
TIGER CRANE.
THE GO-MAI DISCIPLINE.
DANCING MONKEY.
AUGUST SILENCE SCHOOL.
Sports Page
BILLS LOOSE
CAN THE ANALYSIS, BRUCE.
THIS GUY'S JUST TRYING TO PUSH YOU IN FRONT OF A BUS.
26

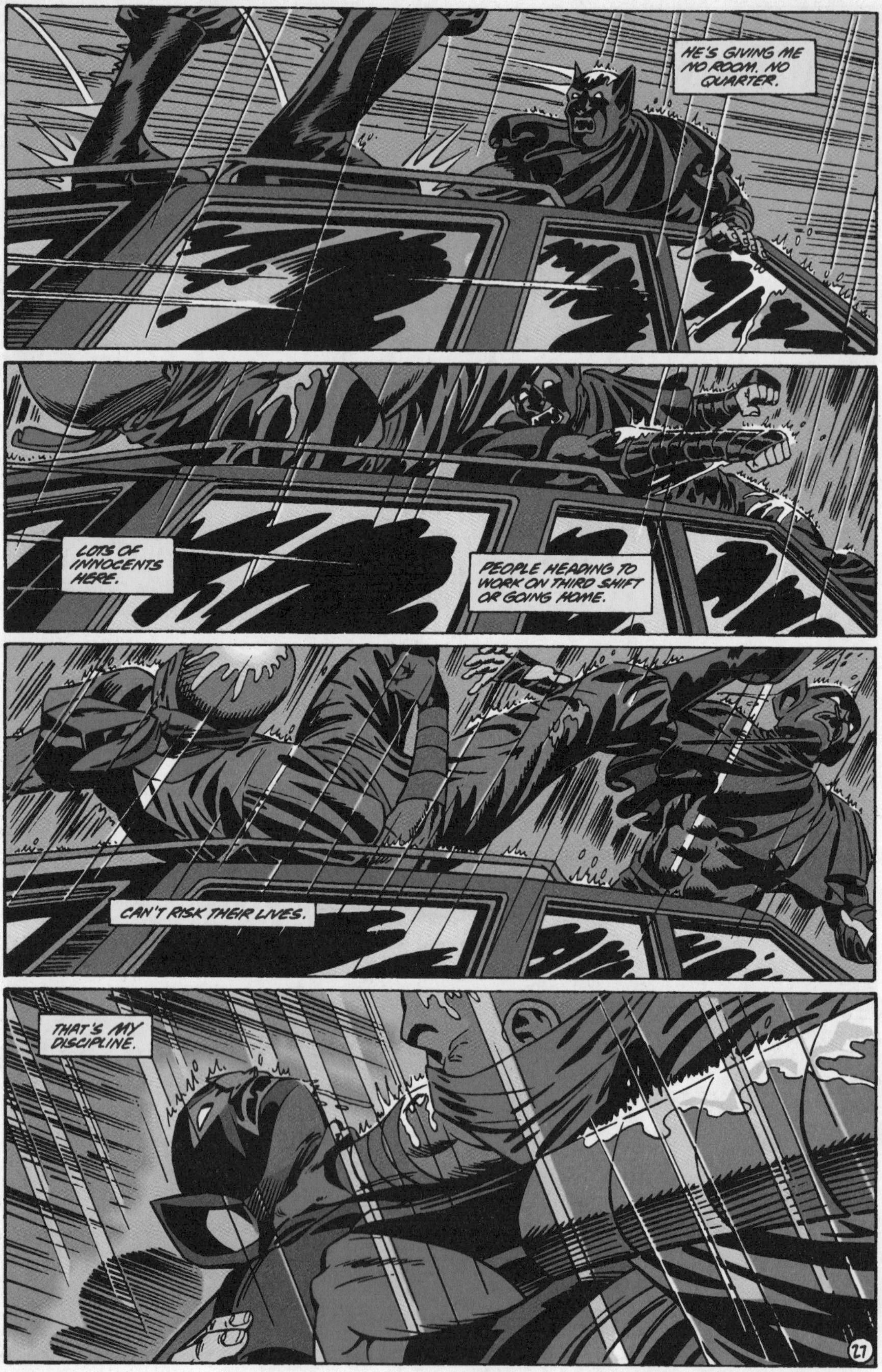
HE'S GIVING ME NO ROOM. NO QUARTER.
LOTS OF INNOCENTS HERE.
PEOPLE HEADING TO WORK ON THIRD SHIFT OR GOING HOME.
CAN'T RISK THEIR LIVES.
THAT'S MY DISCIPLINE.
27

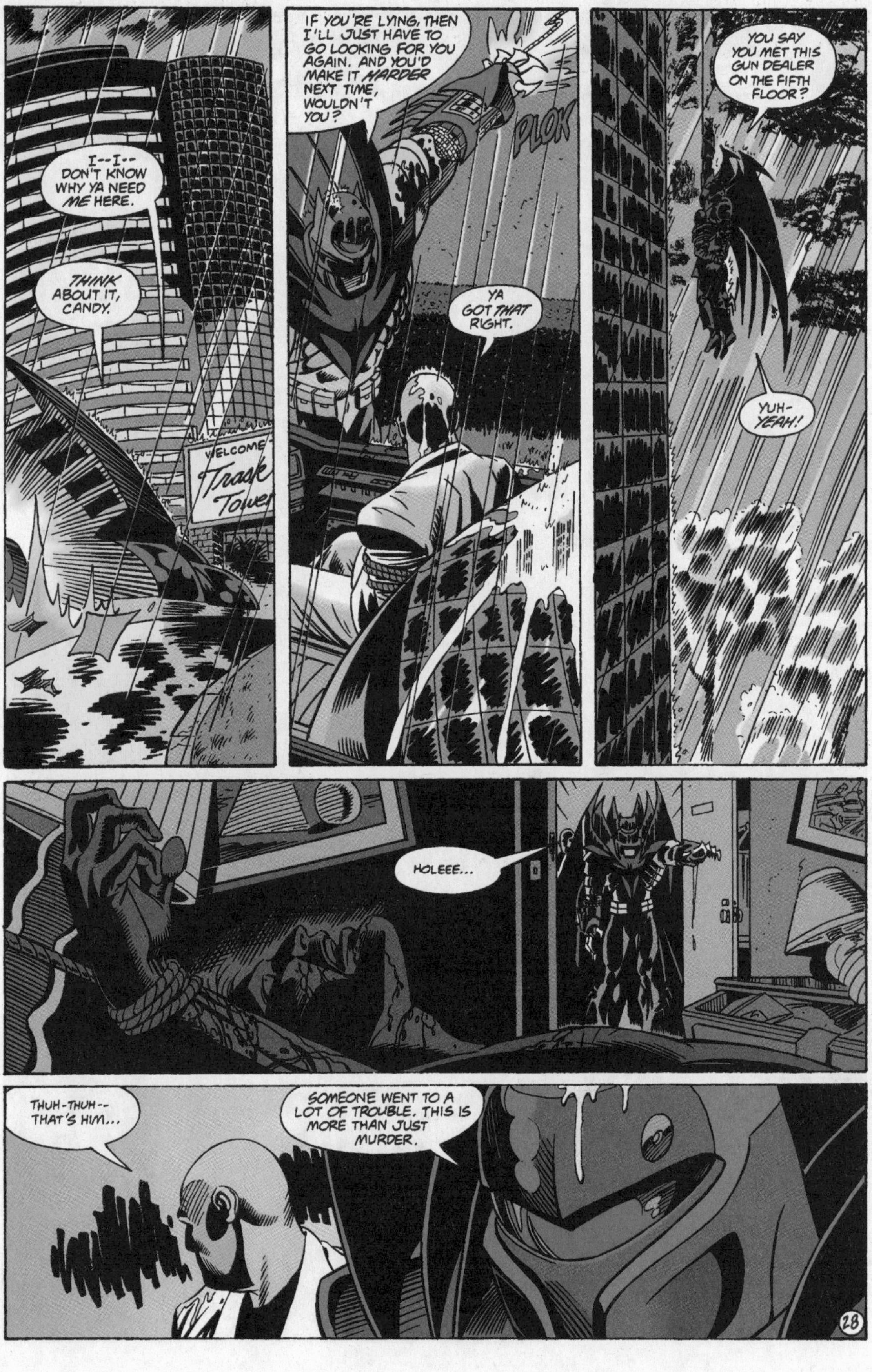
I--I--
DON'T KNOW
WHY YA NEED
ME HERE.
THINK
ABOUT IT,
CANDY.
WELCOME
Track Tower
IF YOU'RE LYING, THEN
I'LL JUST HAVE TO
GO LOOKING FOR YOU
AGAIN. AND YOU'D
MAKE IT HARDER
NEXT TIME,
WOULDN'T
YOU?
PLOK
YA
GOT THAT
RIGHT.
YOU SAY
YOU MET THIS
GUN DEALER
ON THE FIFTH
FLOOR?
YUH-
YEAH!
HOLEEE...
THUH-THUH--
THAT'S HIM...
SOMEONE WENT TO A
LOT OF TROUBLE. THIS IS
MORE THAN JUST
MURDER.
28

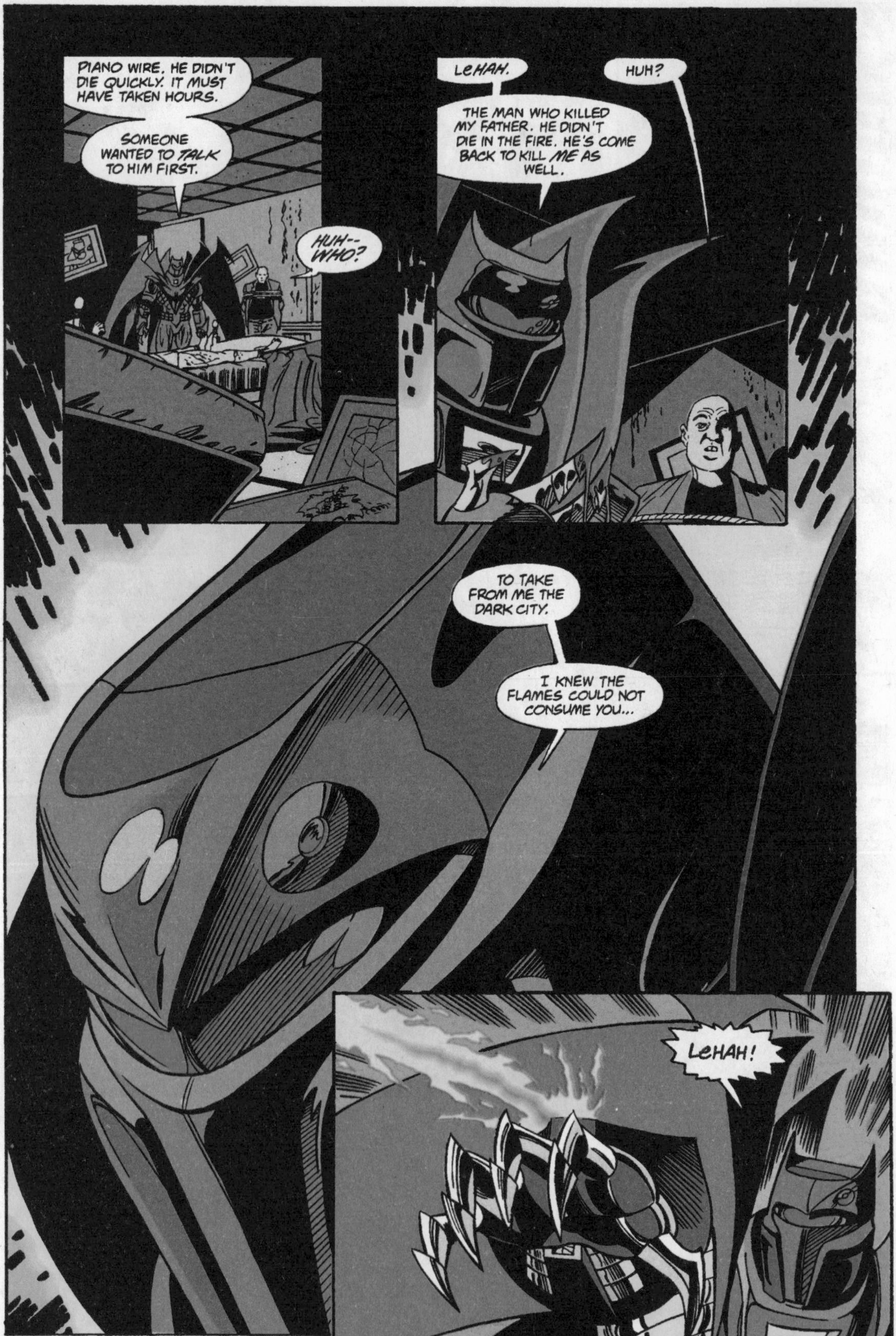
PIANO WIRE. HE DIDN'T DIE QUICKLY. IT MUST HAVE TAKEN HOURS.
SOMEONE WANTED TO TALK TO HIM FIRST.
HUH-- WHO?
LeHAH.
THE MAN WHO KILLED MY FATHER. HE DIDN'T DIE IN THE FIRE. HE'S COME BACK TO KILL ME AS WELL.
HUH?
TO TAKE FROM ME THE DARK CITY.
I KNEW THE FLAMES COULD NOT CONSUME YOU...
LeHAH!
29

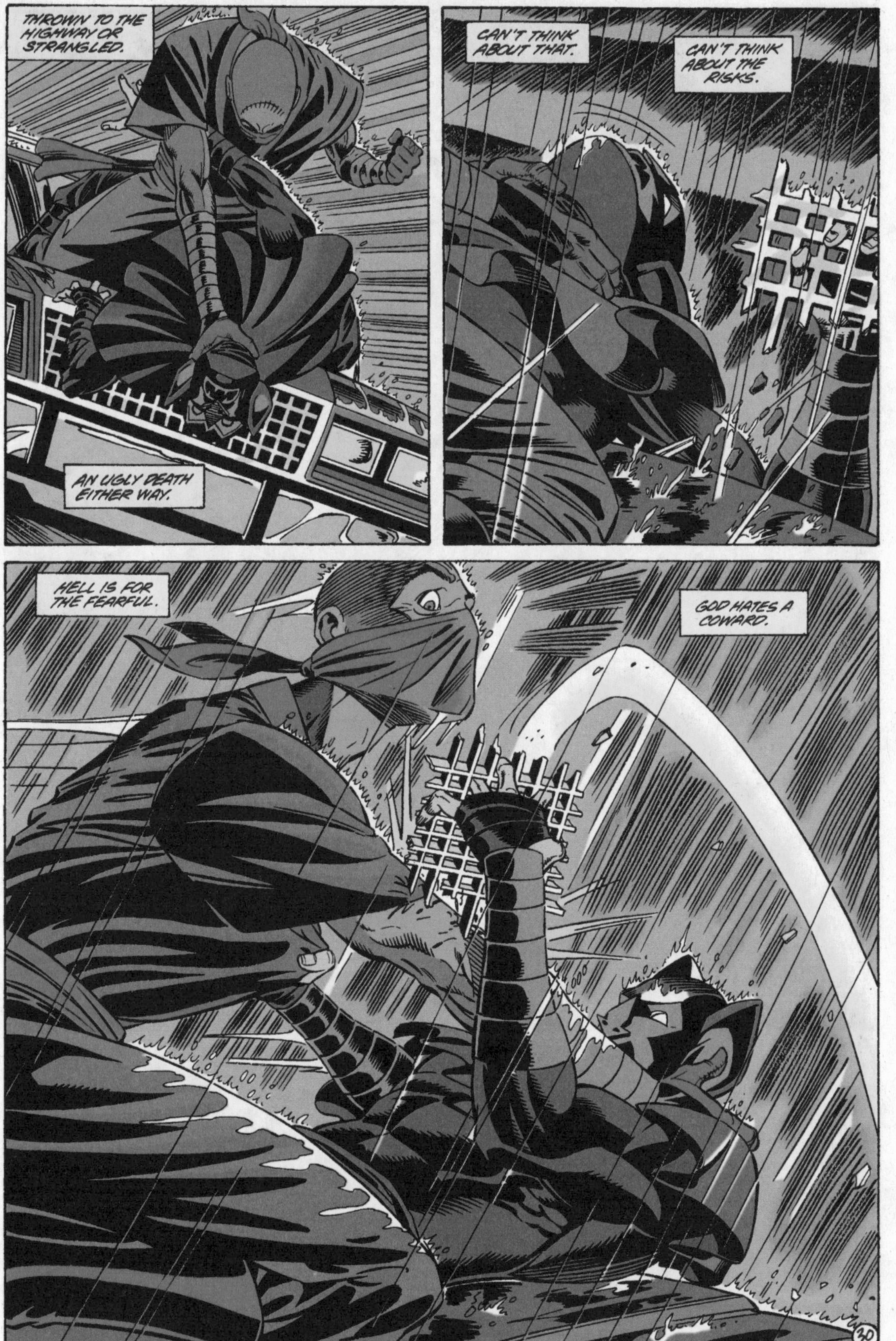

THROWN TO THE HIGHWAY OR STRANGLED.
AN UGLY DEATH EITHER WAY.
CAN'T THINK ABOUT THAT.
CAN'T THINK ABOUT THE RISKS.
HELL IS FOR THE FEARFUL.
GOD HATES A COWARD.
30

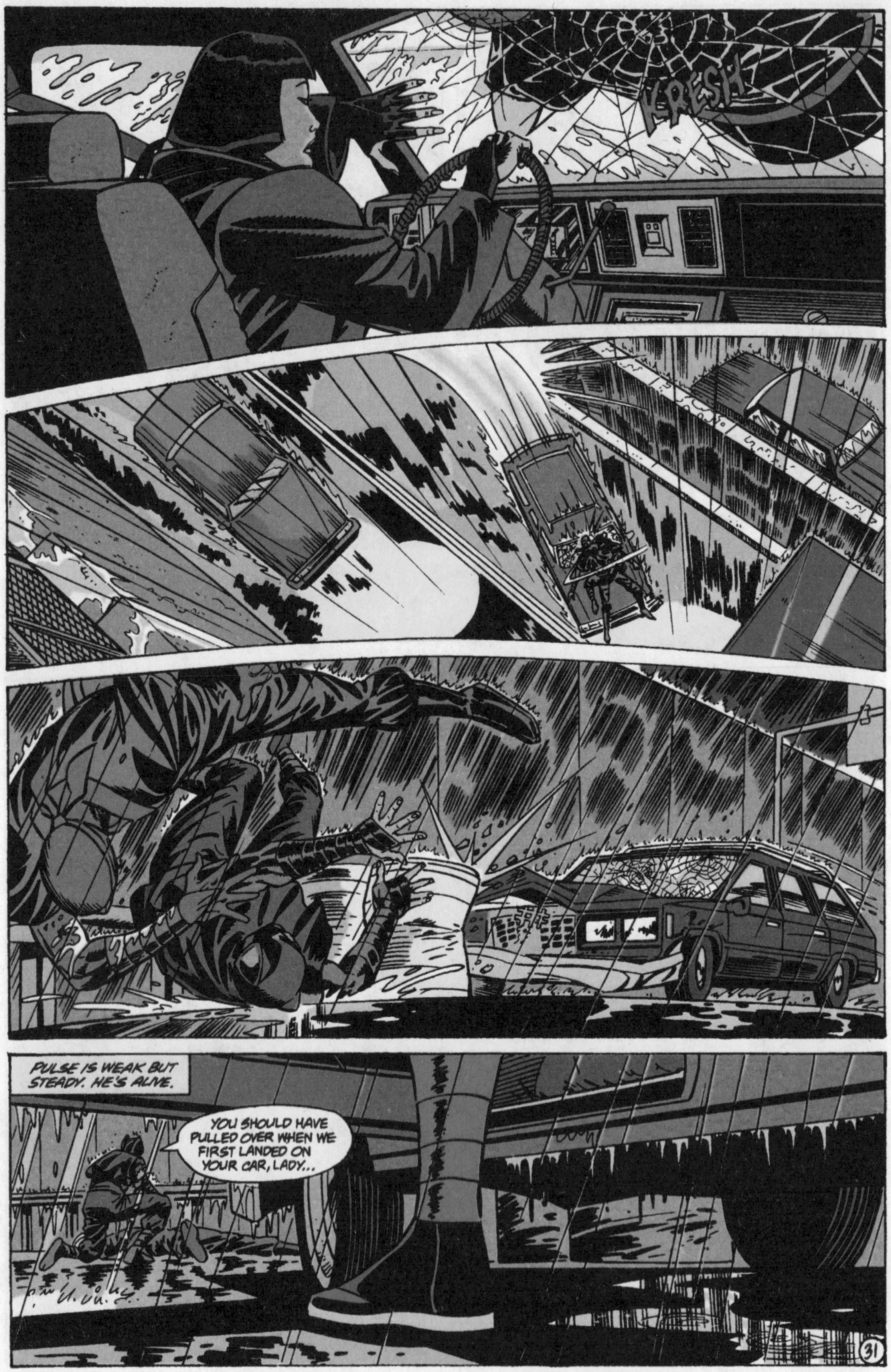
KRESH
PULSE IS WEAK BUT STEADY. HE'S ALIVE.
YOU SHOULD HAVE PULLED OVER WHEN WE FIRST LANDED ON YOUR CAR, LADY...
31

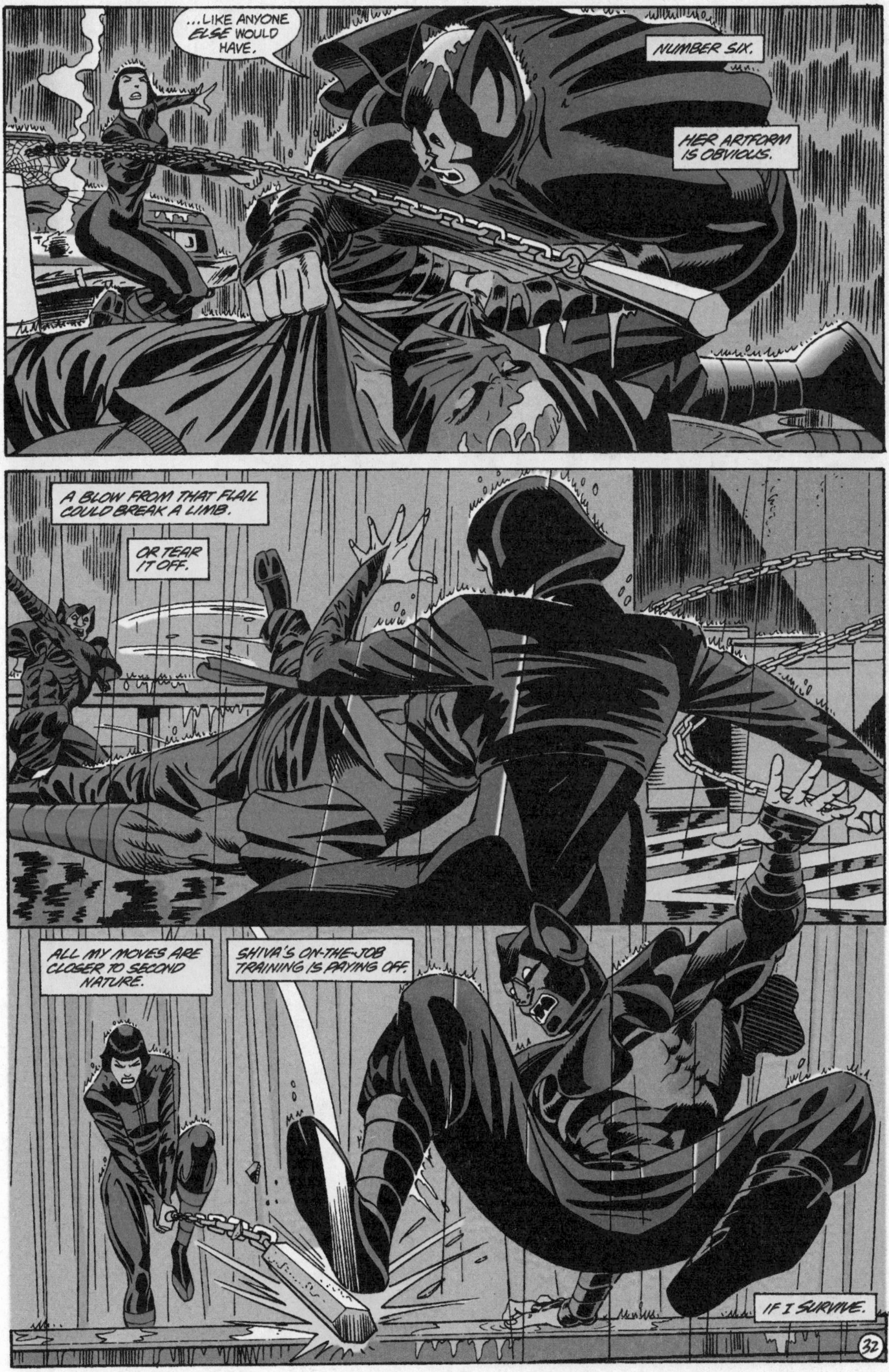

...LIKE ANYONE ELSE WOULD HAVE.
NUMBER SIX.
HER ARTFORM IS OBVIOUS.
A BLOW FROM THAT FLAIL COULD BREAK A LIMB.
OR TEAR IT OFF.
ALL MY MOVES ARE CLOSER TO SECOND NATURE.
SHIVA'S ON-THE-JOB TRAINING IS PAYING OFF.
IF I SURVIVE.
32

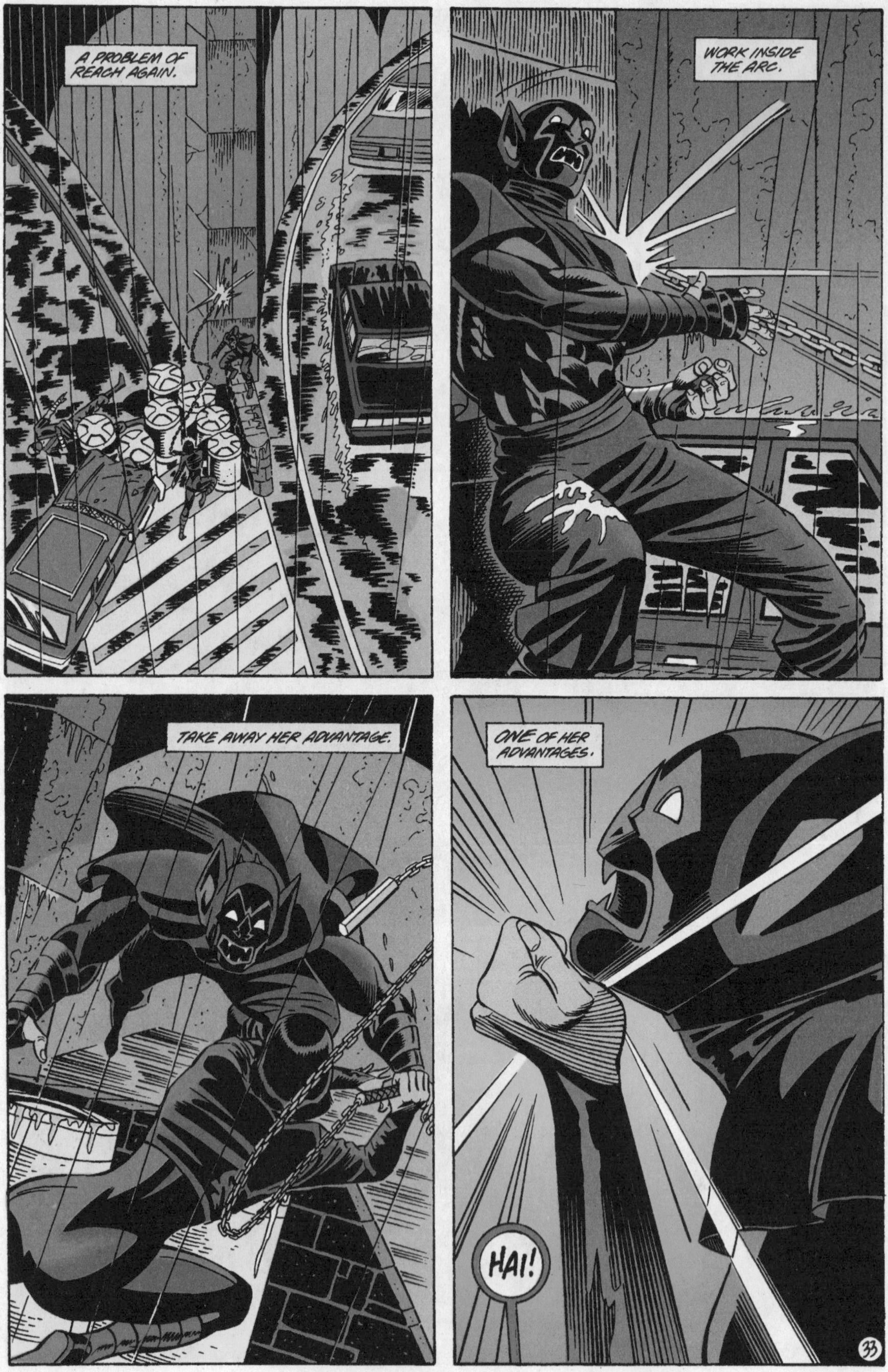
A PROBLEM OF REACH AGAIN.
WORK INSIDE THE ARC.
TAKE AWAY HER ADVANTAGE.
ONE OF HER ADVANTAGES.
HAI!
33

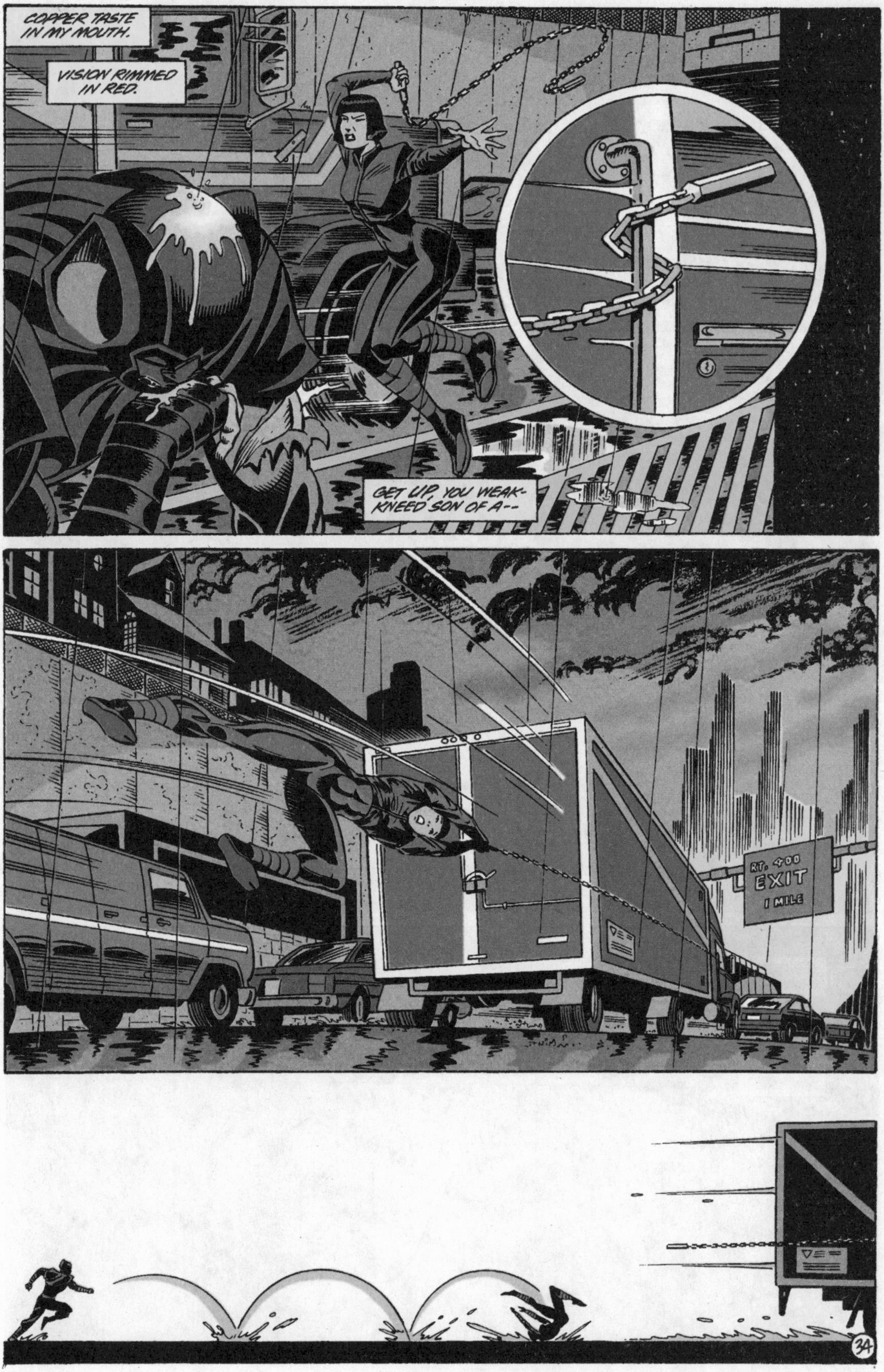
COPPER TASTE IN MY MOUTH.
VISION RIMMED IN RED.
GET UP, YOU WEAK-KNEED SON OF A--
RT. 400
EXIT
1 MILE
34

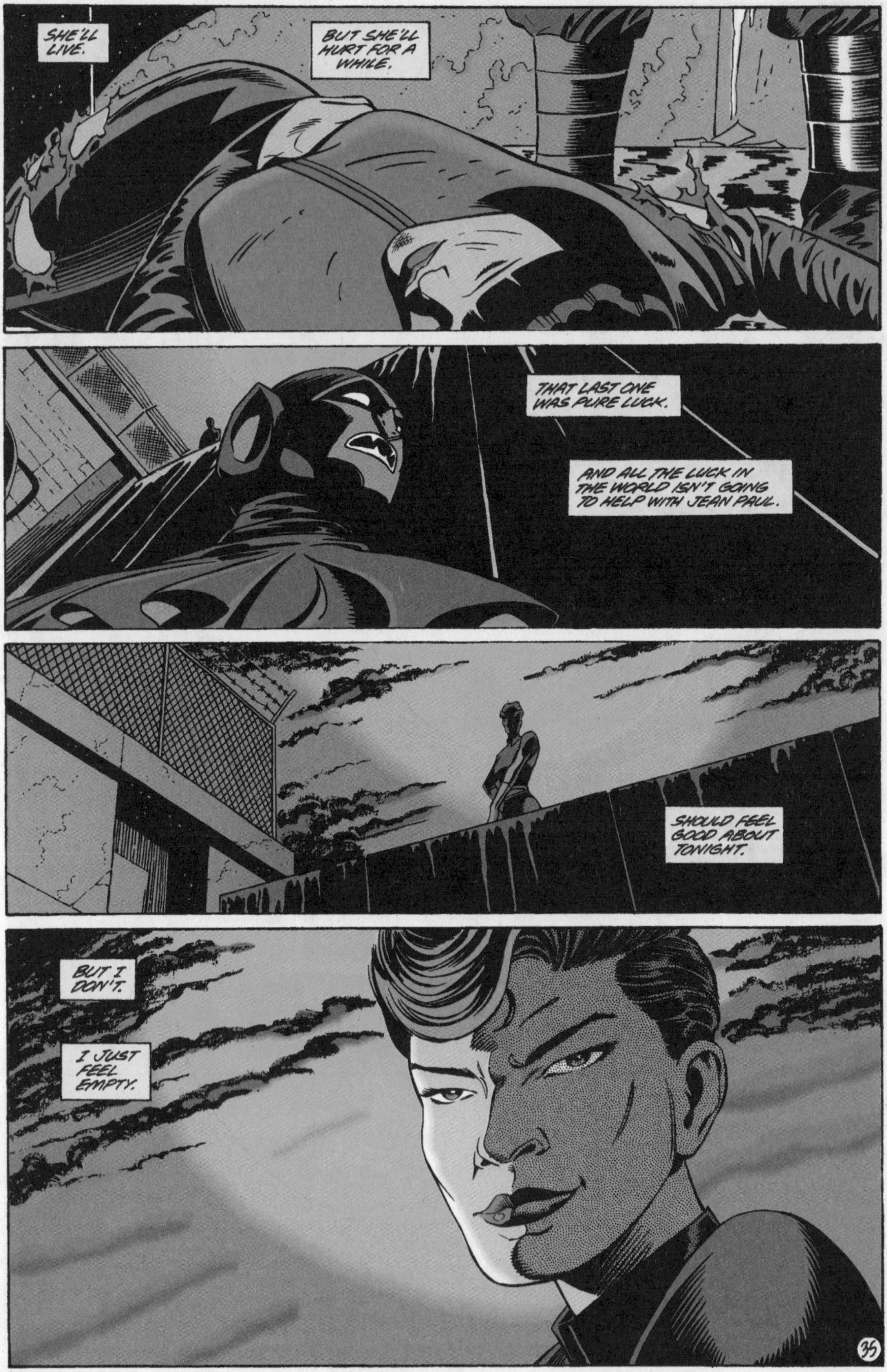
SHE'LL LIVE.
BUT SHE'LL HURT FOR A WHILE.
THAT LAST ONE WAS PURE LUCK.
AND ALL THE LUCK IN THE WORLD ISN'T GOING TO HELP WITH JEAN PAUL.
SHOULD FEEL GOOD ABOUT TONIGHT.
BUT I DON'T.
I JUST FEEL EMPTY.
35

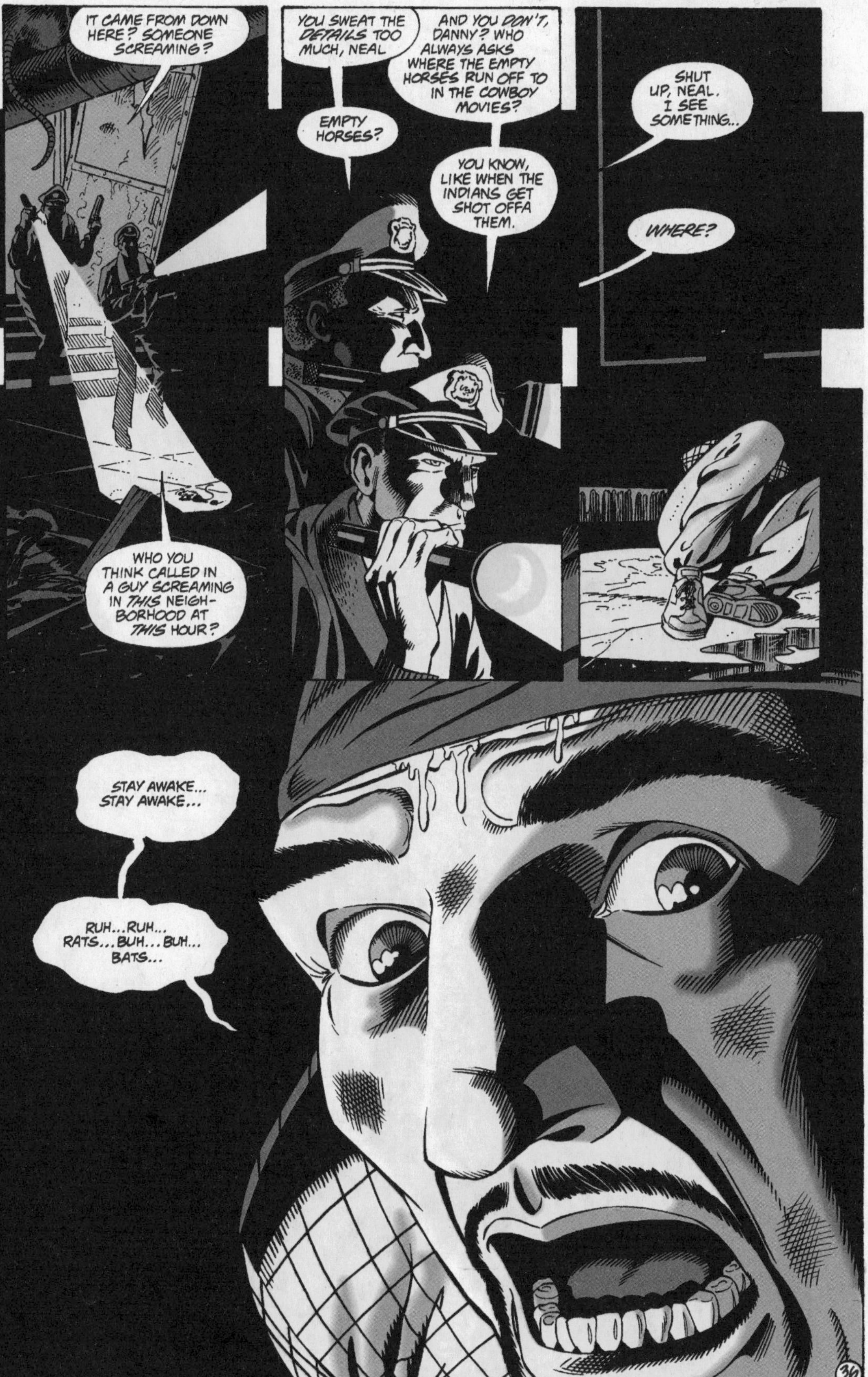
IT CAME FROM DOWN HERE? SOMEONE SCREAMING?
WHO YOU THINK CALLED IN A GUY SCREAMING IN THIS NEIGHBORHOOD AT THIS HOUR?
YOU SWEAT THE DETAILS TOO MUCH, NEAL
AND YOU DON'T, DANNY? WHO ALWAYS ASKS WHERE THE EMPTY HORSES RUN OFF TO IN THE COWBOY MOVIES?
EMPTY HORSES?
YOU KNOW, LIKE WHEN THE INDIANS GET SHOT OFFA THEM.
SHUT UP, NEAL. I SEE SOMETHING...
WHERE?
STAY AWAKE... STAY AWAKE...
RUH...RUH... RATS...BUH...BUH... BATS...
36

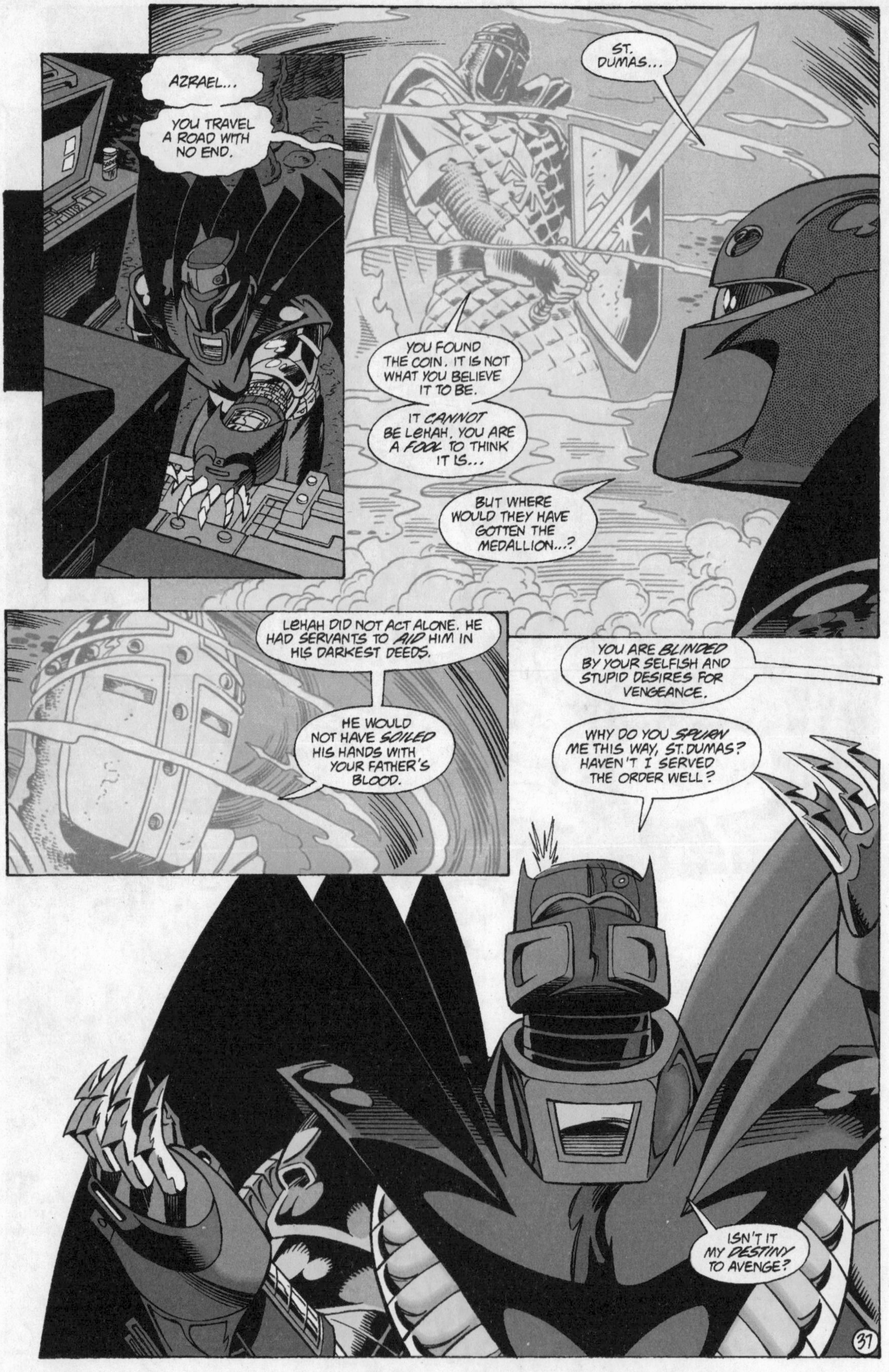
AZRAEL...
YOU TRAVEL A ROAD WITH NO END.
ST. DUMAS...
YOU FOUND THE COIN. IT IS NOT WHAT YOU BELIEVE IT TO BE.
IT CANNOT BE LEHAH. YOU ARE A FOOL TO THINK IT IS...
BUT WHERE WOULD THEY HAVE GOTTEN THE MEDALLION...?
LEHAH DID NOT ACT ALONE. HE HAD SERVANTS TO AID HIM IN HIS DARKEST DEEDS.
HE WOULD NOT HAVE SOILED HIS HANDS WITH YOUR FATHER'S BLOOD.
YOU ARE BLINDED BY YOUR SELFISH AND STUPID DESIRES FOR VENGEANCE.
WHY DO YOU SPURN ME THIS WAY, ST. DUMAS? HAVEN'T I SERVED THE ORDER WELL?
ISN'T IT MY DESTINY TO AVENGE?
37

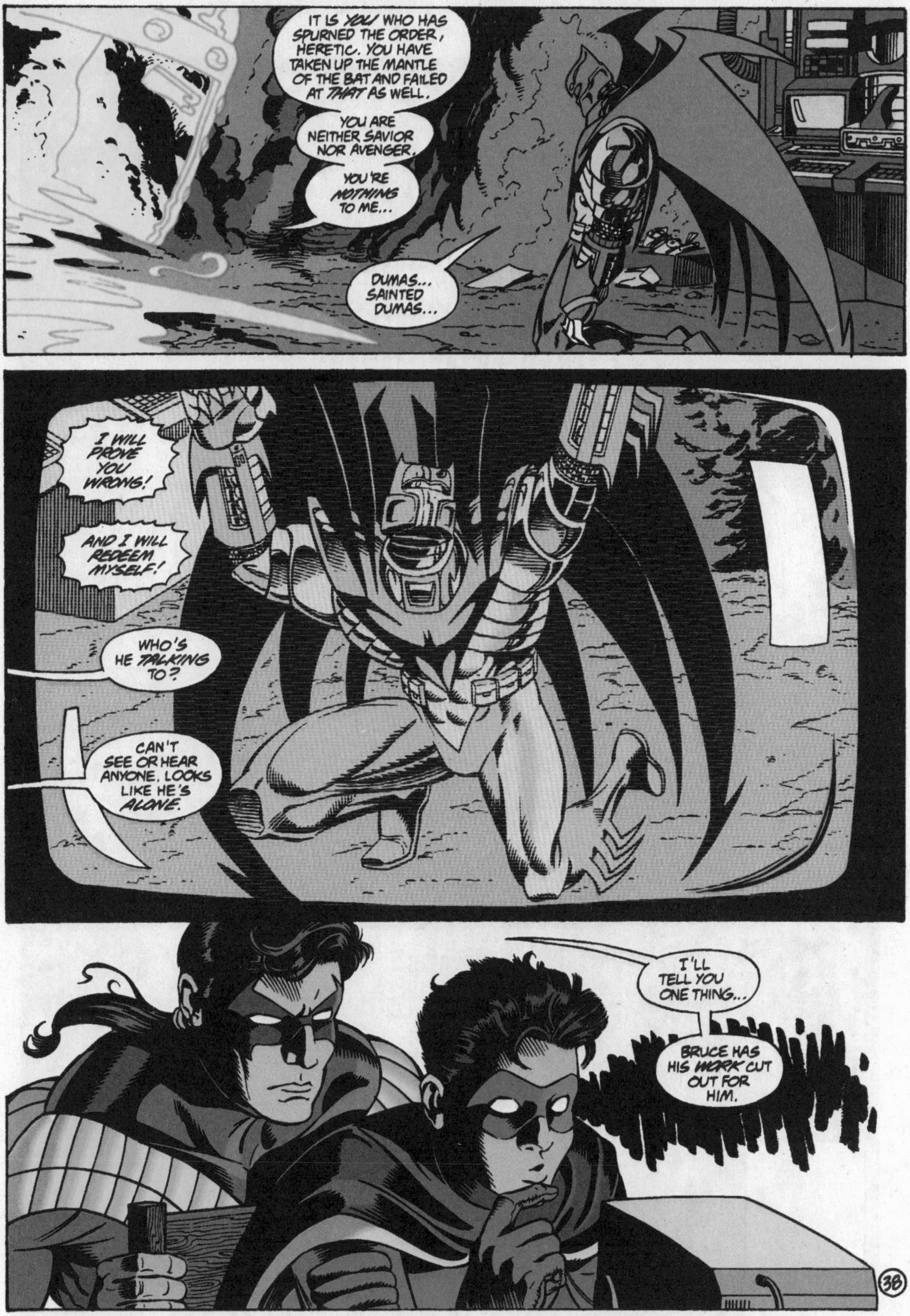
IT IS YOU WHO HAS SPURNED THE ORDER, HERETIC. YOU HAVE TAKEN UP THE MANTLE OF THE BAT AND FAILED AT THAT AS WELL.
YOU ARE NEITHER SAVIOR NOR AVENGER.
YOU'RE NOTHING TO ME...
DUMAS... SAINTED DUMAS...
I WILL PROVE YOU WRONG!
AND I WILL REDEEM MYSELF!
WHO'S HE TALKING TO?
CAN'T SEE OR HEAR ANYONE. LOOKS LIKE HE'S ALONE.
I'LL TELL YOU ONE THING...
BRUCE HAS HIS WORK CUT OUT FOR HIM.
38

Cover art by MIKE MIGNOLA

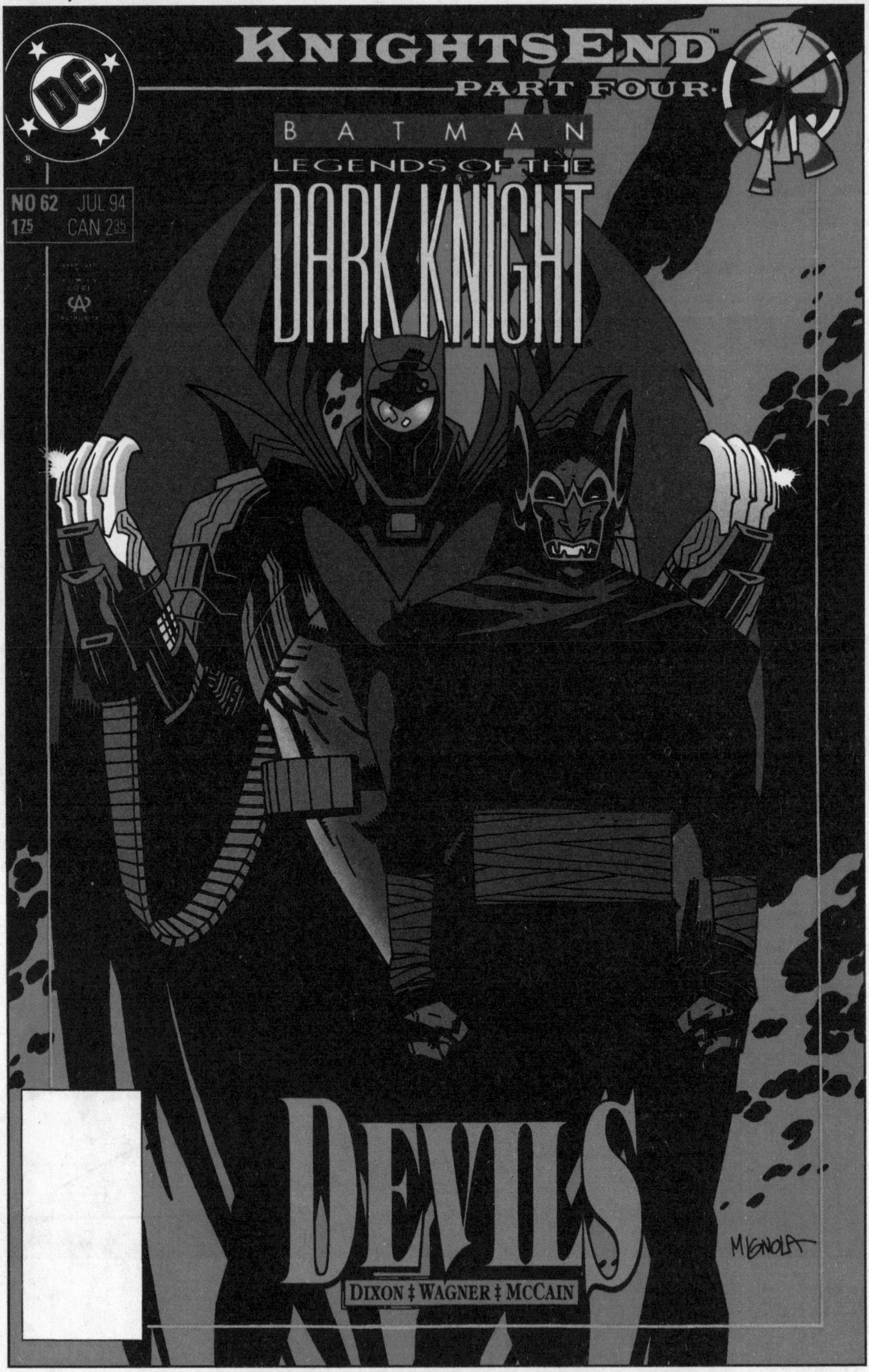
KNIGHTSEND
PART FOUR
BATMAN
LEGENDS OF THE
DARK KNIGHT
NO 62 JUL 94
1.75 CAN 2.35
DEVILS
DIXON ‡ WAGNER ‡ McCAIN
MIGNOLA

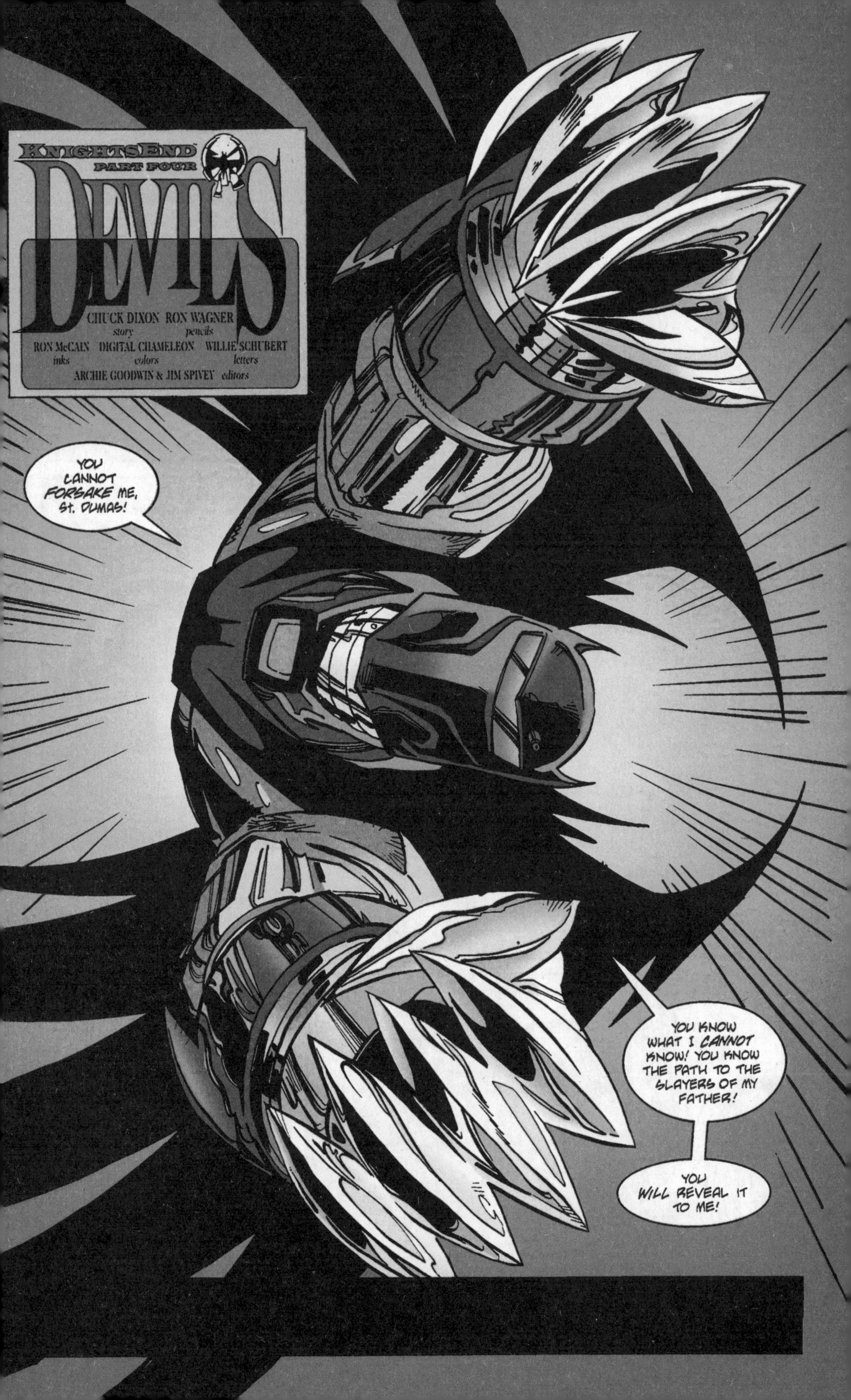
KNIGHTSEND
PART FOUR
DEVILS
CHUCK DIXON story RON WAGNER pencils
RON McCAIN inks DIGITAL CHAMELEON colors WILLIE SCHUBERT letters
ARCHIE GOODWIN & JIM SPIVEY editors
YOU CANNOT FORSAKE ME, ST. DUMAS!
YOU KNOW WHAT I CANNOT KNOW! YOU KNOW THE PATH TO THE SLAYERS OF MY FATHER!
YOU WILL REVEAL IT TO ME!

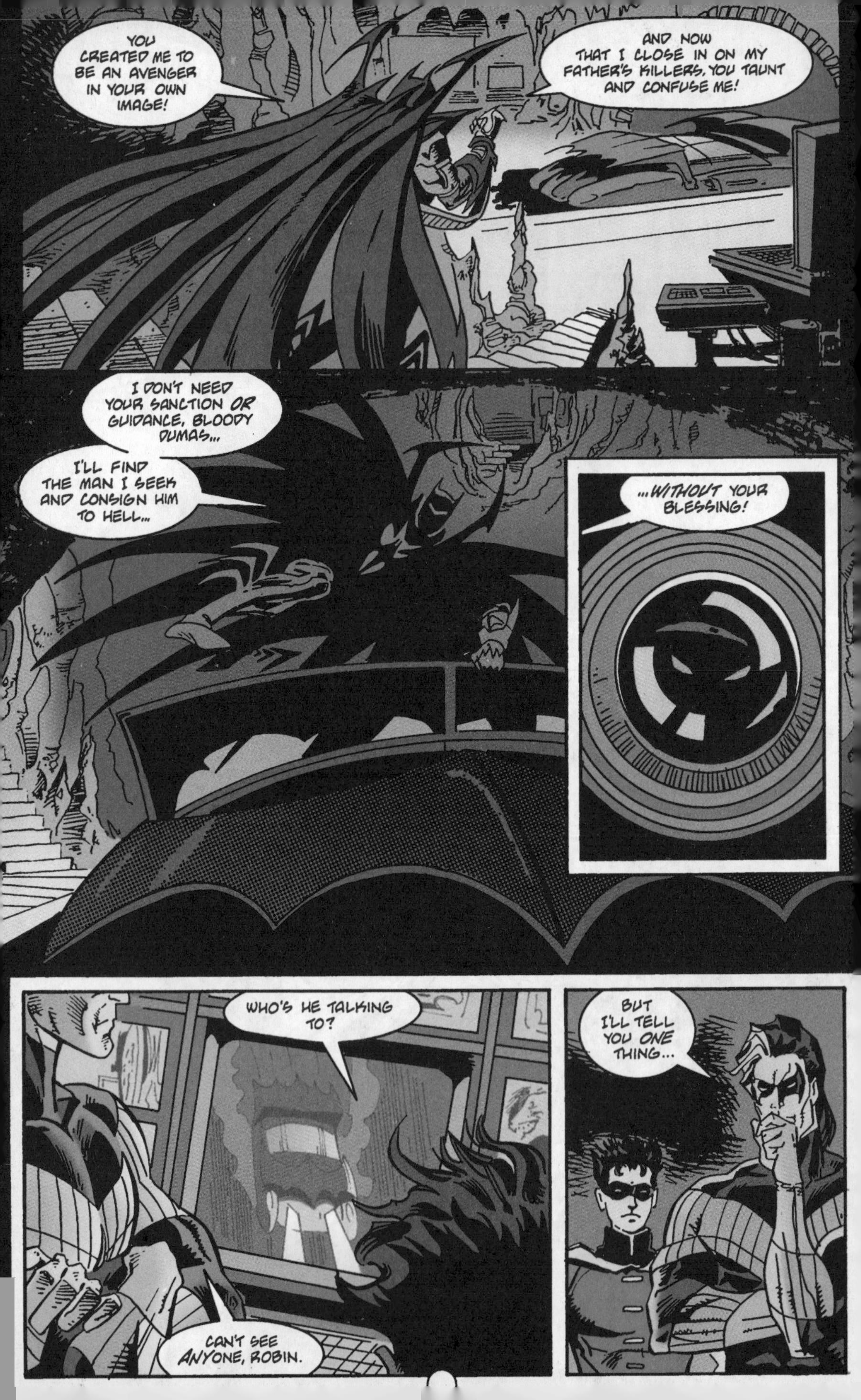
YOU CREATED ME TO BE AN AVENGER IN YOUR OWN IMAGE!
AND NOW THAT I CLOSE IN ON MY FATHER'S KILLERS, YOU TAUNT AND CONFUSE ME!
I DON'T NEED YOUR SANCTION OR GUIDANCE, BLOODY DUMAS...
I'LL FIND THE MAN I SEEK AND CONSIGN HIM TO HELL...
...WITHOUT YOUR BLESSING!
WHO'S HE TALKING TO?
CAN'T SEE ANYONE, ROBIN.
BUT I'LL TELL YOU ONE THING...

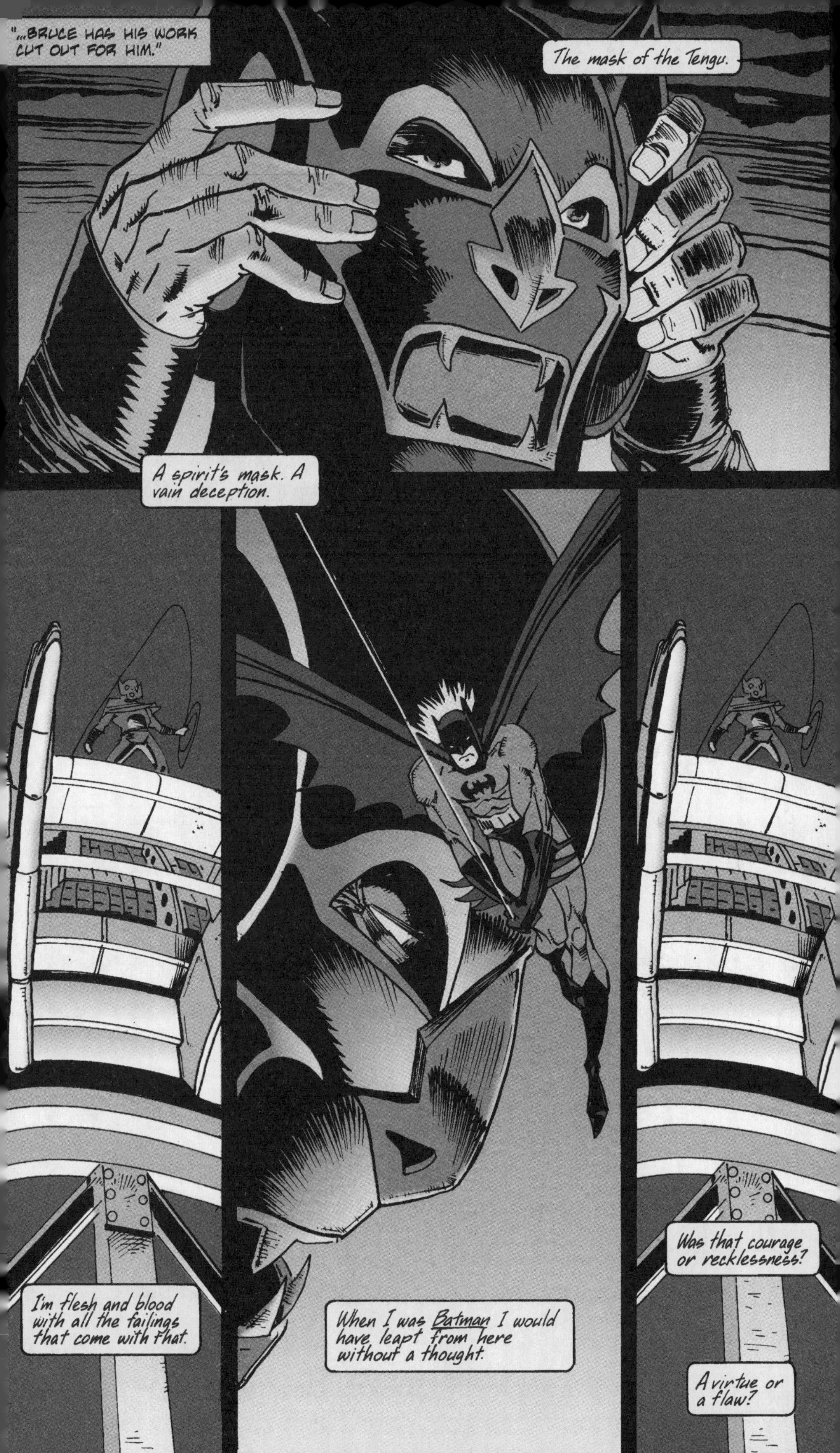
"...BRUCE HAS HIS WORK CUT OUT FOR HIM."
The mask of the Tengu.
A spirit's mask. A vain deception.
I'm flesh and blood with all the failings that come with that.
When I was Batman I would have leapt from here without a thought.
Was that courage or recklessness?
A virtue or a flaw?

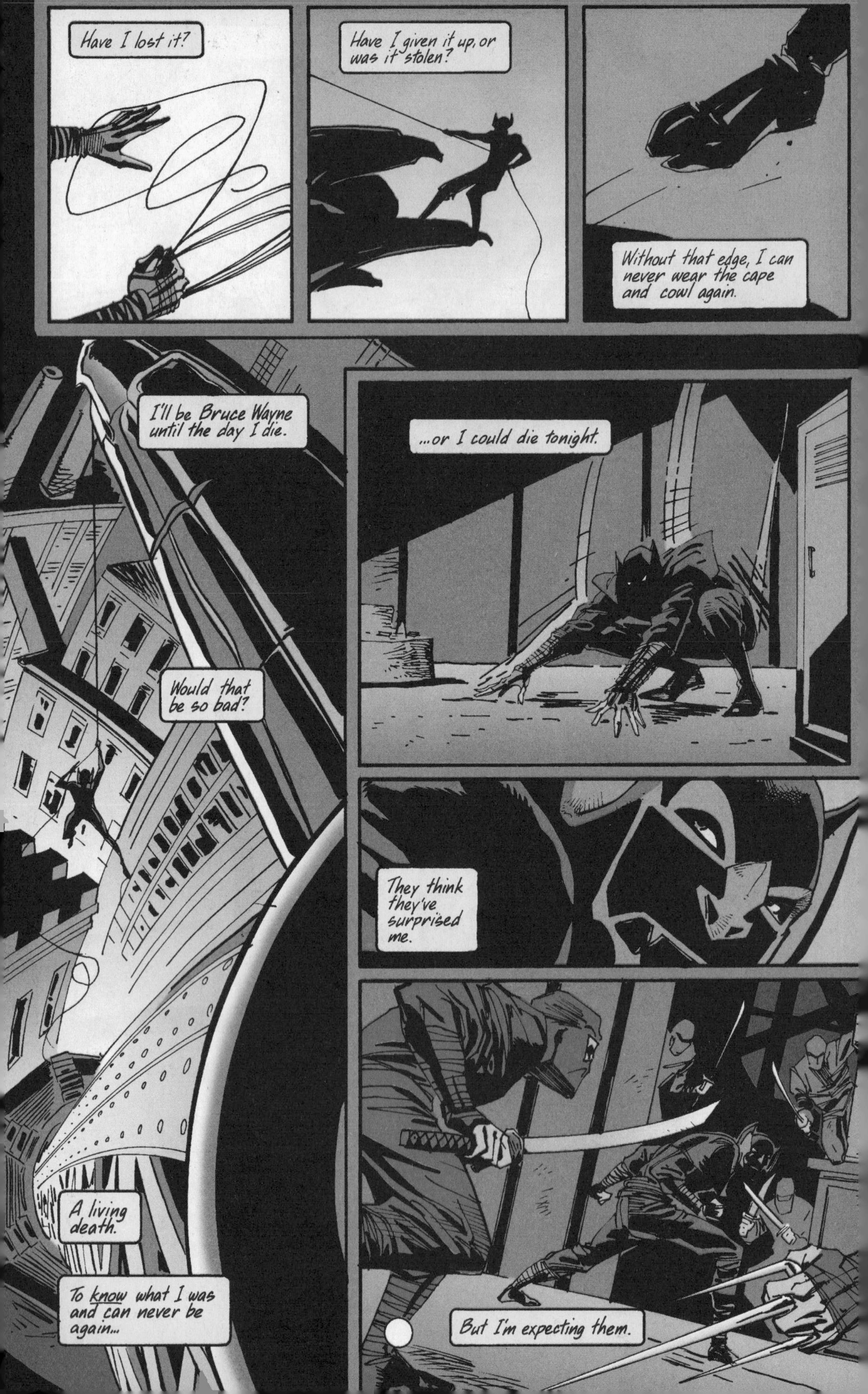
Have I lost it?
Have I given it up, or was it stolen?
Without that edge, I can never wear the cape and cowl again.
I'll be Bruce Wayne until the day I die.
...or I could die tonight.
Would that be so bad?
They think they've surprised me.
A living death.
To know what I was and can never be again...
But I'm expecting them.

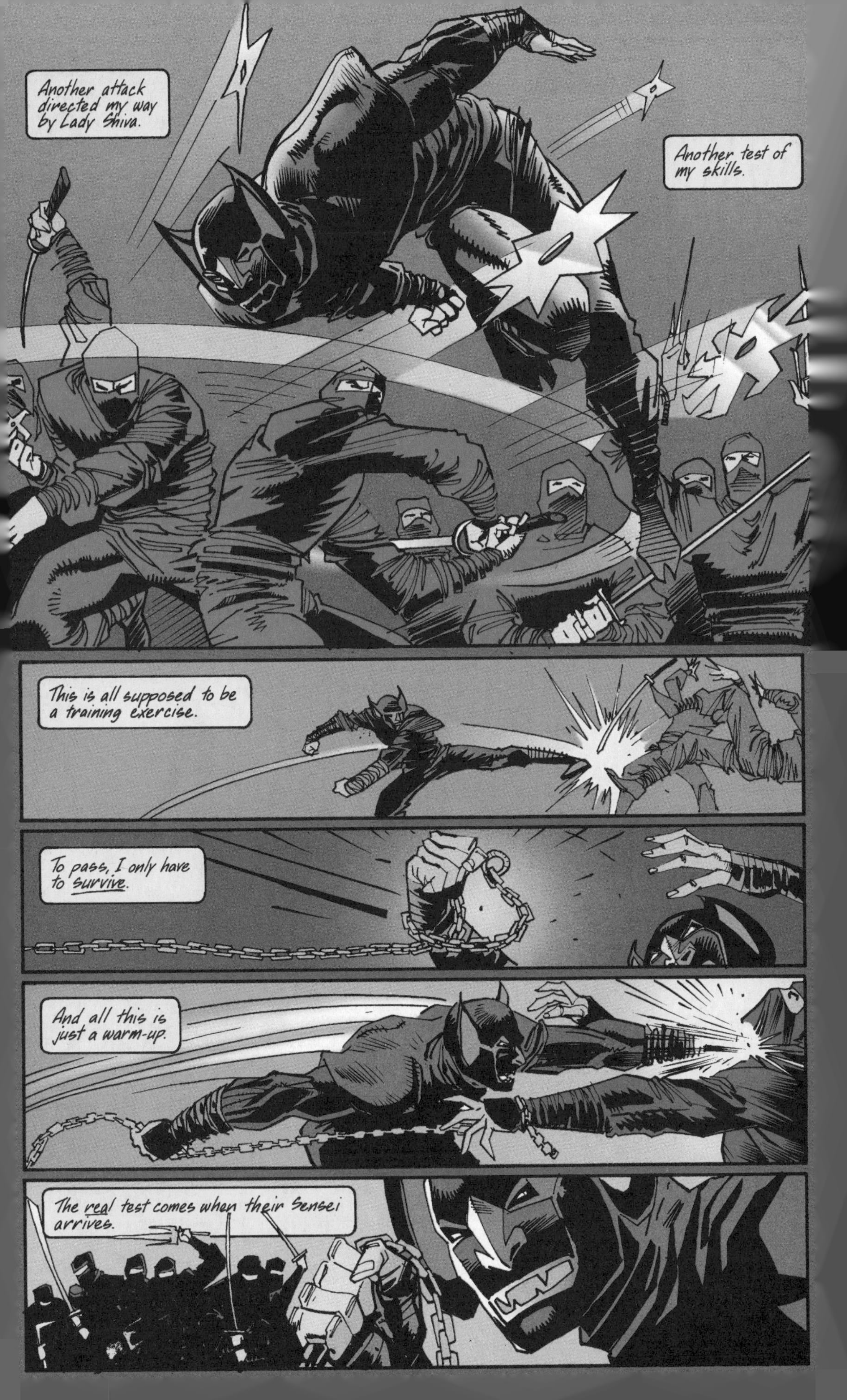
Another attack directed my way by Lady Shiva.
Another test of my skills.
This is all supposed to be a training exercise.
To pass, I only have to survive.
And all this is just a warm-up.
The real test comes when their Sensei arrives.

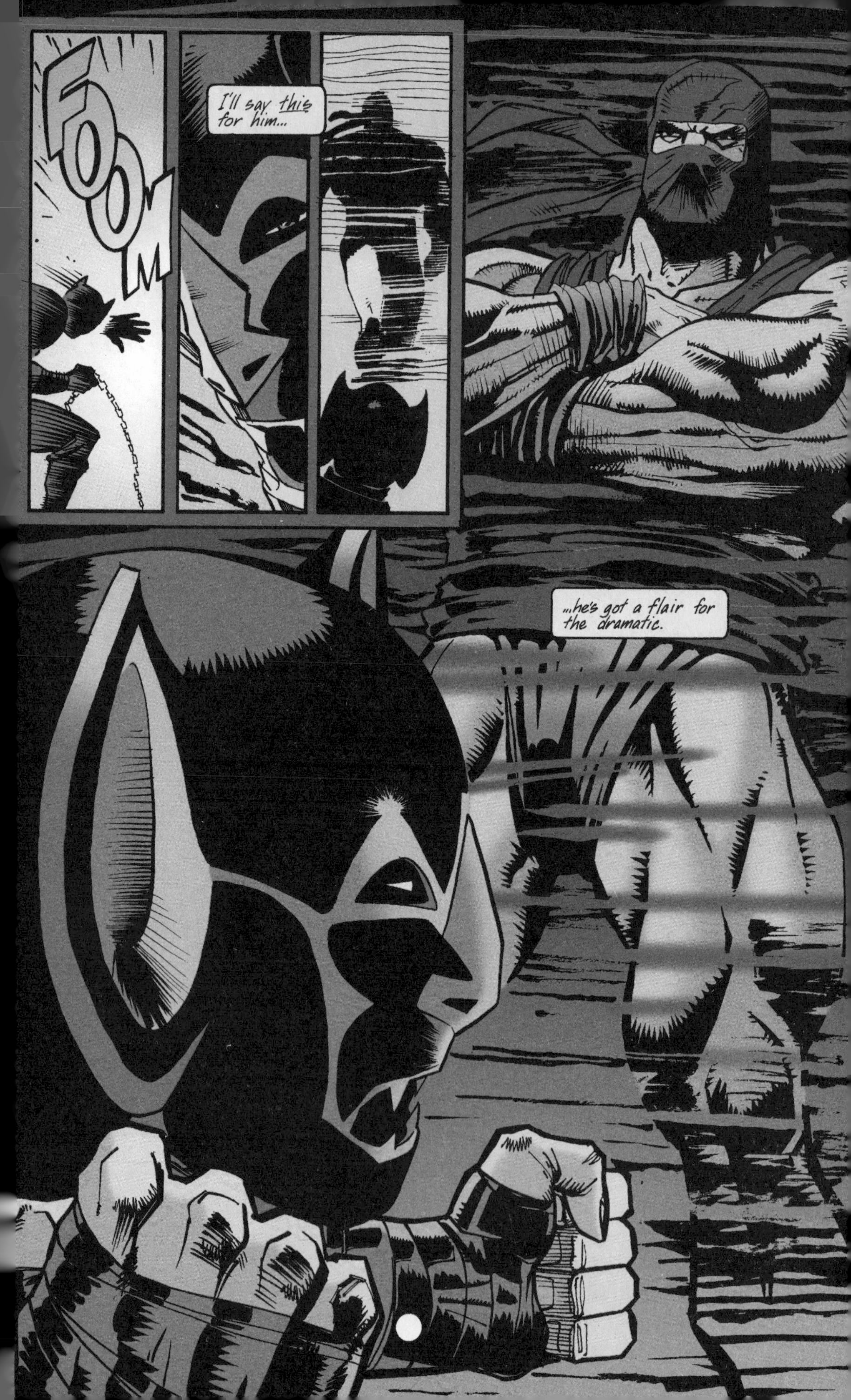
FOOOM
I'll say this for him...
...he's got a flair for the dramatic.

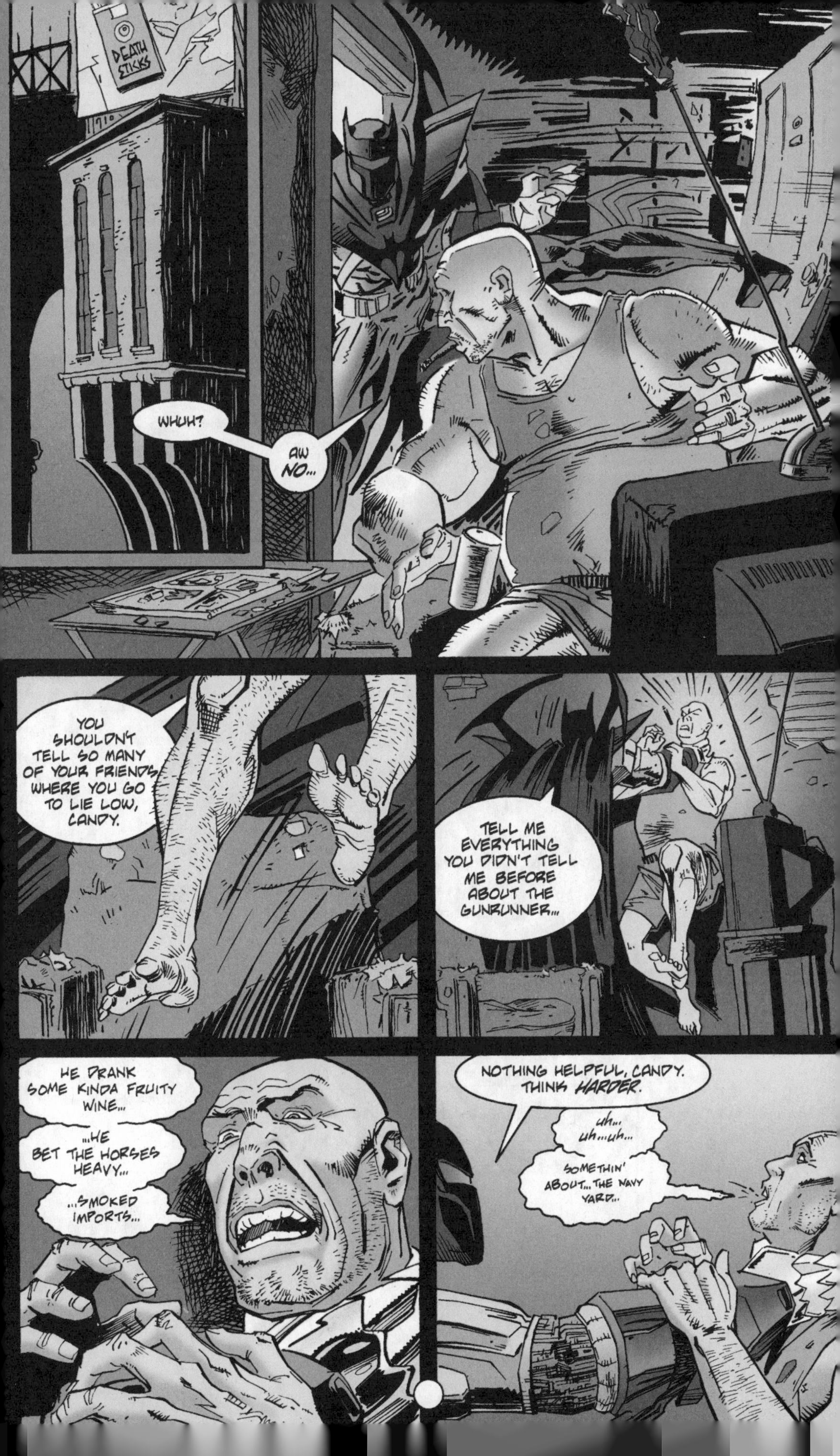
DEATH STICKS
WHUH?
AW NO...
YOU SHOULDN'T TELL SO MANY OF YOUR FRIENDS WHERE YOU GO TO LIE LOW, CANDY.
TELL ME EVERYTHING YOU DIDN'T TELL ME BEFORE ABOUT THE GUNRUNNER...
HE DRANK SOME KINDA FRUITY WINE...
...HE BET THE HORSES HEAVY...
...SMOKED IMPORTS...
NOTHING HELPFUL, CANDY. THINK *HARDER*.
uh... uh...uh...
SOMETHIN' ABOUT... THE NAVY YARD...

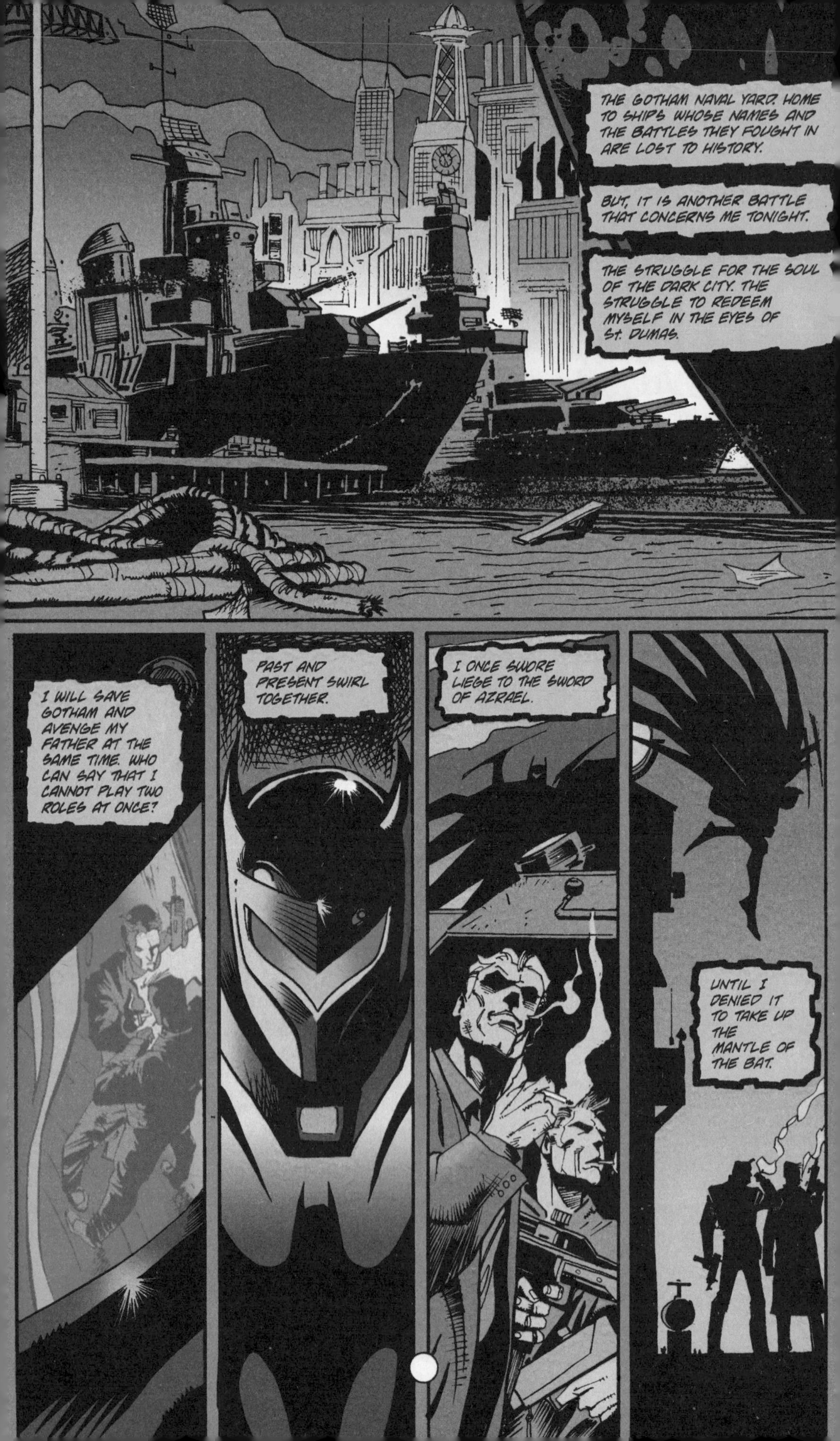
THE GOTHAM NAVAL YARD. HOME TO SHIPS WHOSE NAMES AND THE BATTLES THEY FOUGHT IN ARE LOST TO HISTORY.
BUT, IT IS ANOTHER BATTLE THAT CONCERNS ME TONIGHT.
THE STRUGGLE FOR THE SOUL OF THE DARK CITY. THE STRUGGLE TO REDEEM MYSELF IN THE EYES OF St. DUMAS.
I WILL SAVE GOTHAM AND AVENGE MY FATHER AT THE SAME TIME. WHO CAN SAY THAT I CANNOT PLAY TWO ROLES AT ONCE?
PAST AND PRESENT SWIRL TOGETHER.
I ONCE SWORE LIEGE TO THE SWORD OF AZRAEL.
UNTIL I DENIED IT TO TAKE UP THE MANTLE OF THE BAT.

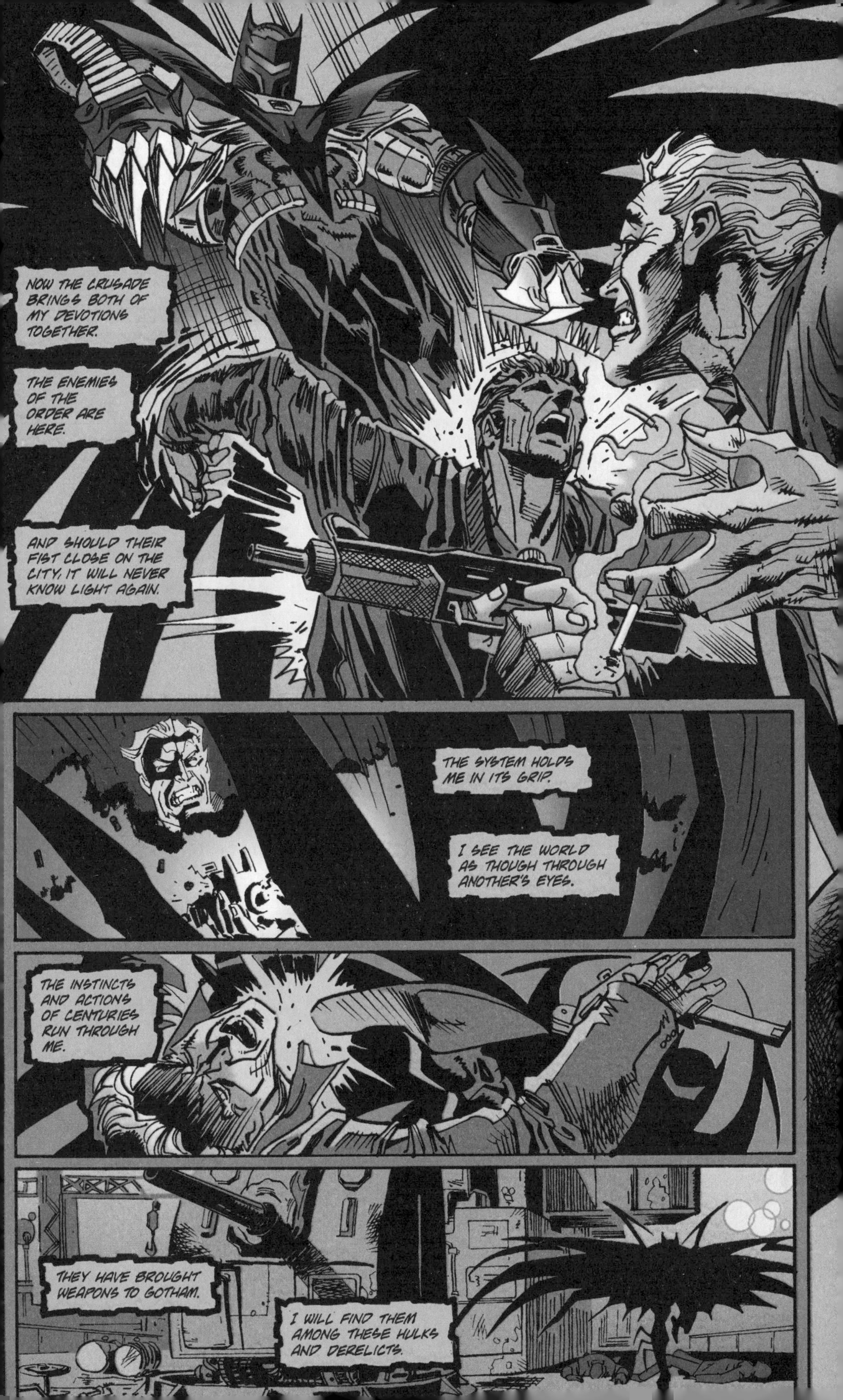
NOW THE CRUSADE BRINGS BOTH OF MY DEVOTIONS TOGETHER.
THE ENEMIES OF THE ORDER ARE HERE.
AND SHOULD THEIR FIST CLOSE ON THE CITY, IT WILL NEVER KNOW LIGHT AGAIN.
THE SYSTEM HOLDS ME IN ITS GRIP.
I SEE THE WORLD AS THOUGH THROUGH ANOTHER'S EYES.
THE INSTINCTS AND ACTIONS OF CENTURIES RUN THROUGH ME.
THEY HAVE BROUGHT WEAPONS TO GOTHAM.
I WILL FIND THEM AMONG THESE HULKS AND DERELICTS.

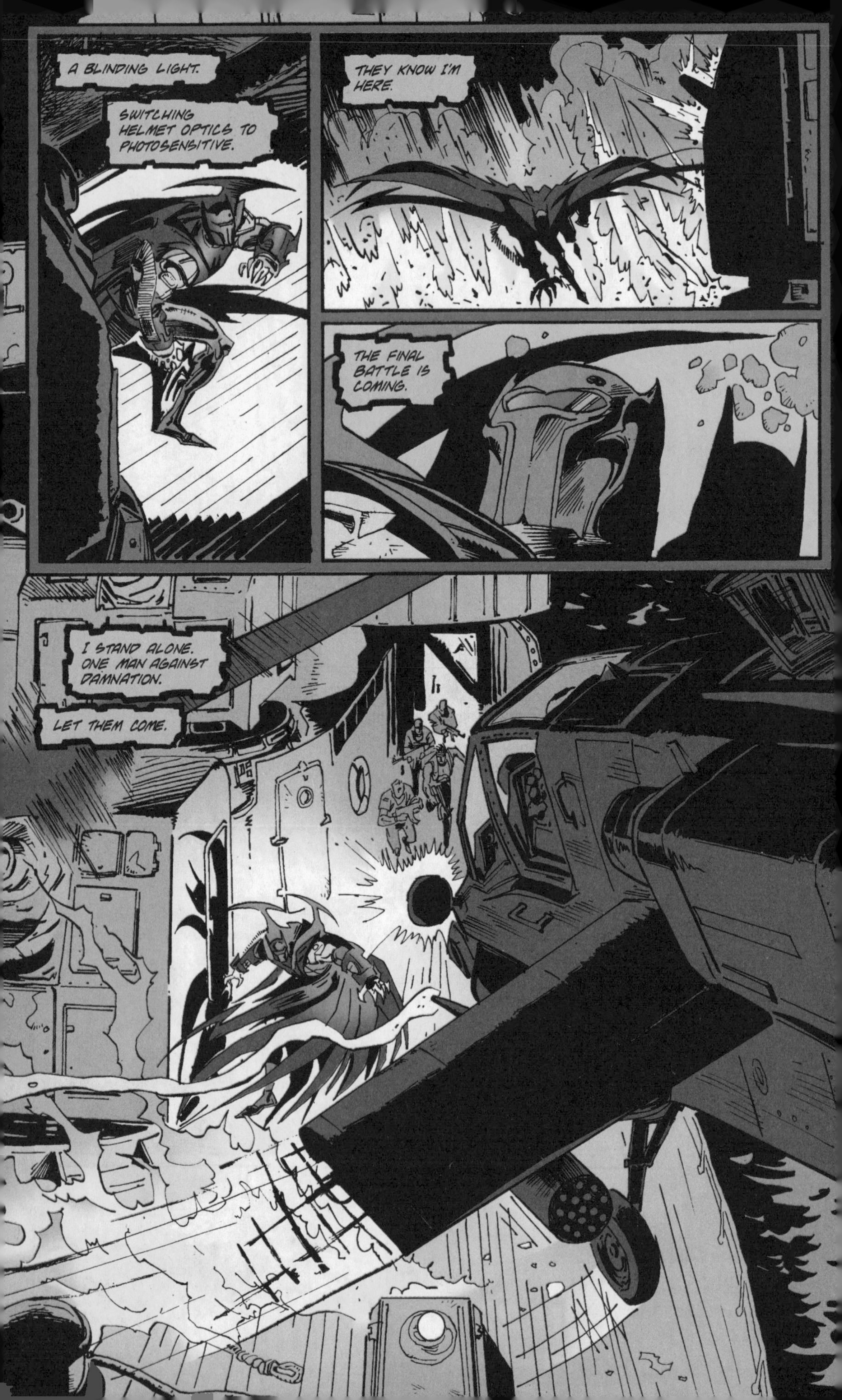

A BLINDING LIGHT.
SWITCHING HELMET OPTICS TO PHOTOSENSITIVE.
THEY KNOW I'M HERE.
THE FINAL BATTLE IS COMING.
I STAND ALONE. ONE MAN AGAINST DAMNATION.
LET THEM COME.

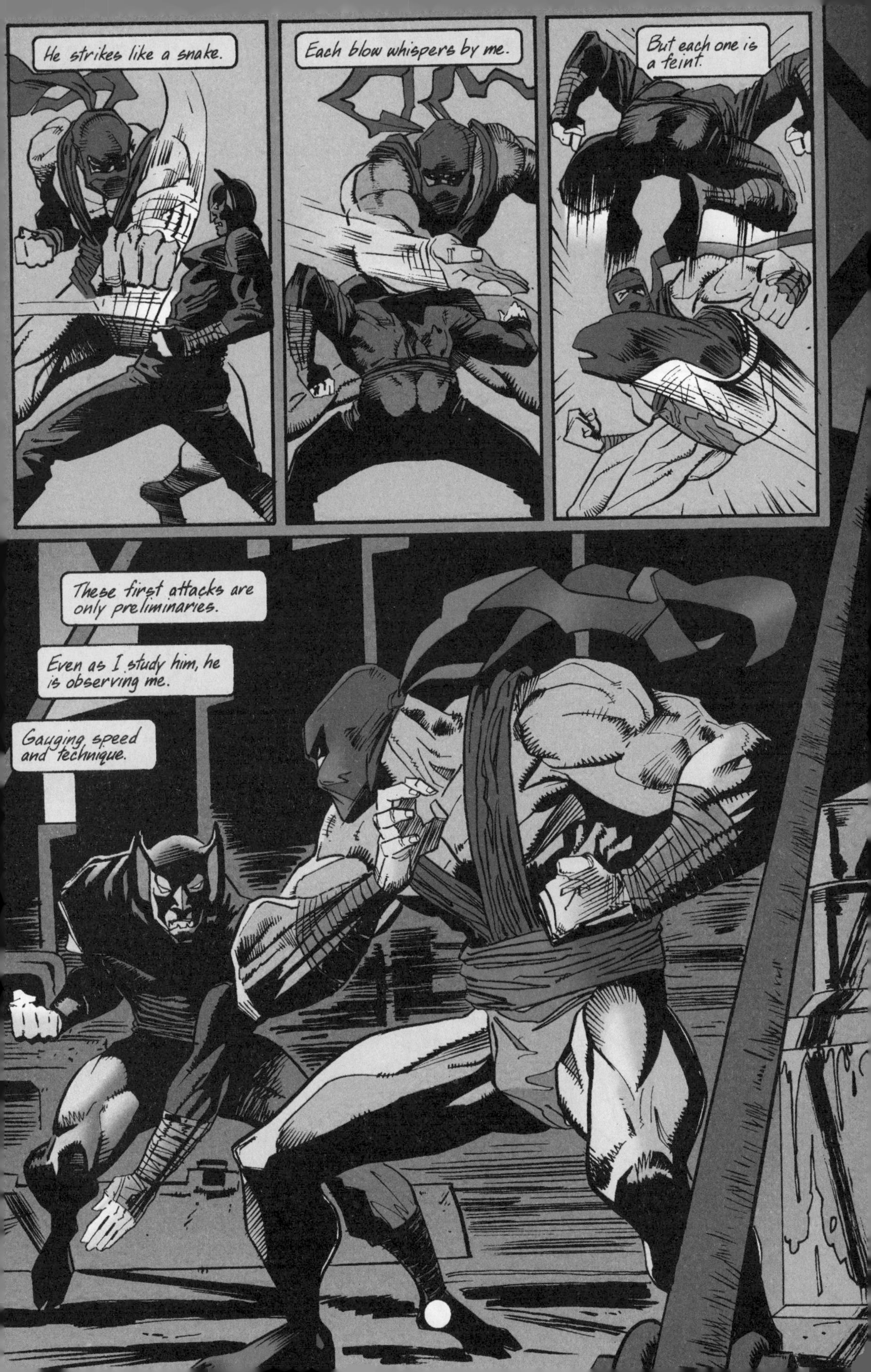
He strikes like a snake.
Each blow whispers by me.
But each one is a feint.
These first attacks are only preliminaries.
Even as I study him, he is observing me.
Gauging speed and technique.

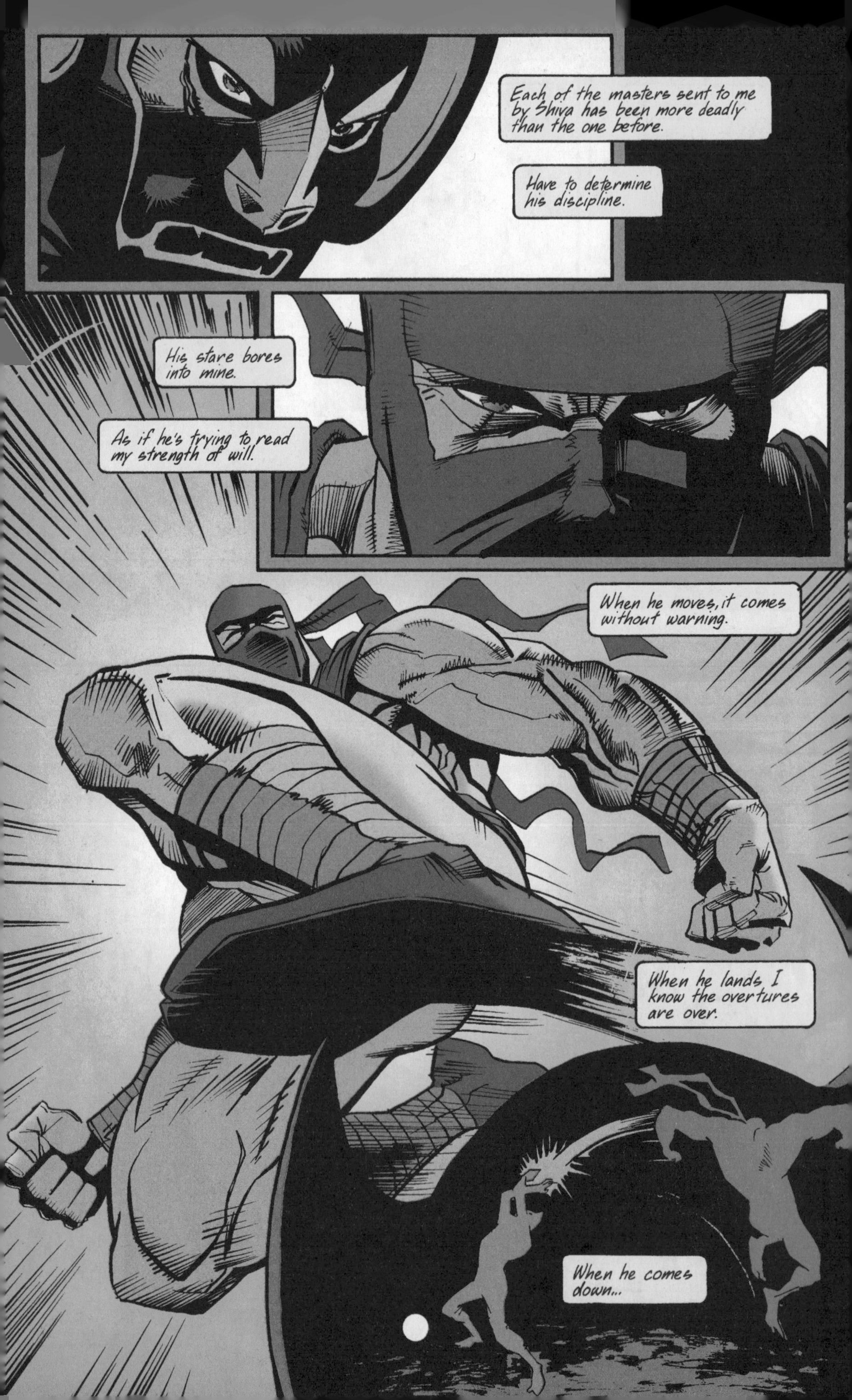
Each of the masters sent to me by Shiva has been more deadly than the one before.
Have to determine his discipline.
His stare bores into mine.
As if he's trying to read my strength of will.
When he moves, it comes without warning.
When he lands I know the overtures are over.
When he comes down...

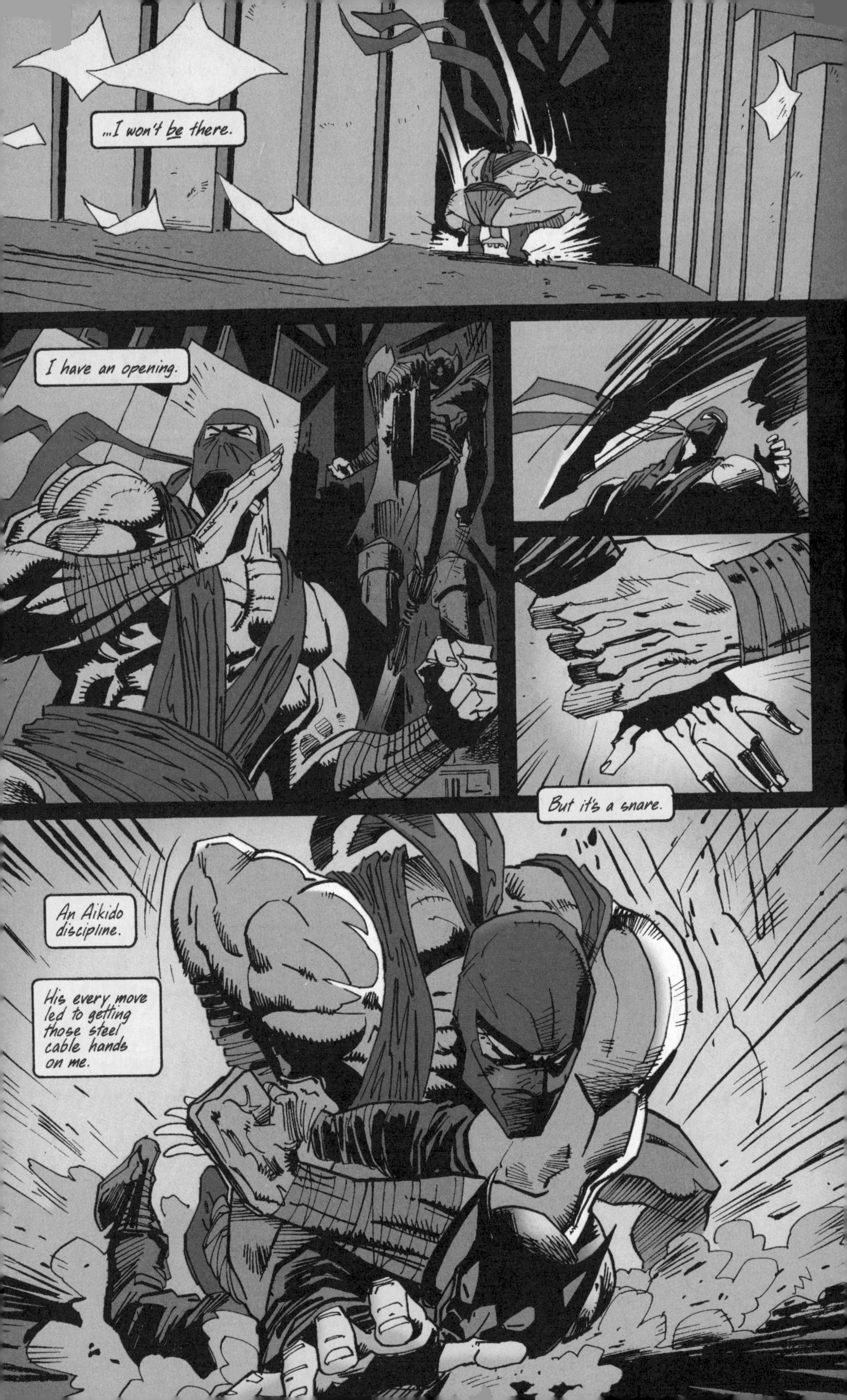

...I won't be there.
I have an opening.
But it's a snare.
An Aikido discipline.
His every move led to getting those steel cable hands on me.

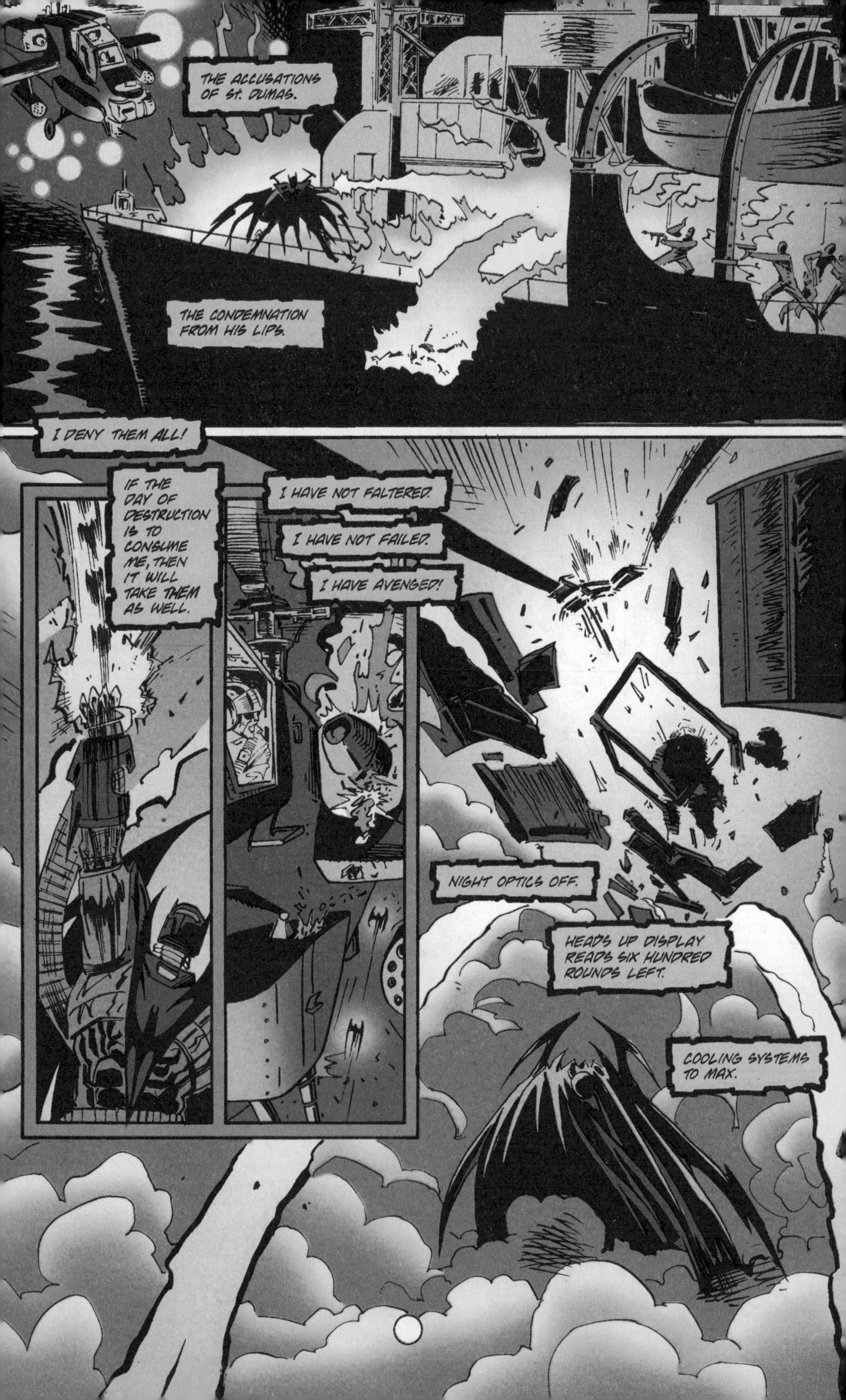
THE ACCUSATIONS OF ST. DUMAS.
THE CONDEMNATION FROM HIS LIPS.
I DENY THEM ALL!
IF THE DAY OF DESTRUCTION IS TO CONSUME ME, THEN IT WILL TAKE THEM AS WELL.
I HAVE NOT FALTERED.
I HAVE NOT FAILED.
I HAVE AVENGED!
NIGHT OPTICS OFF.
HEADS UP DISPLAY READS SIX HUNDRED ROUNDS LEFT.
COOLING SYSTEMS TO MAX.

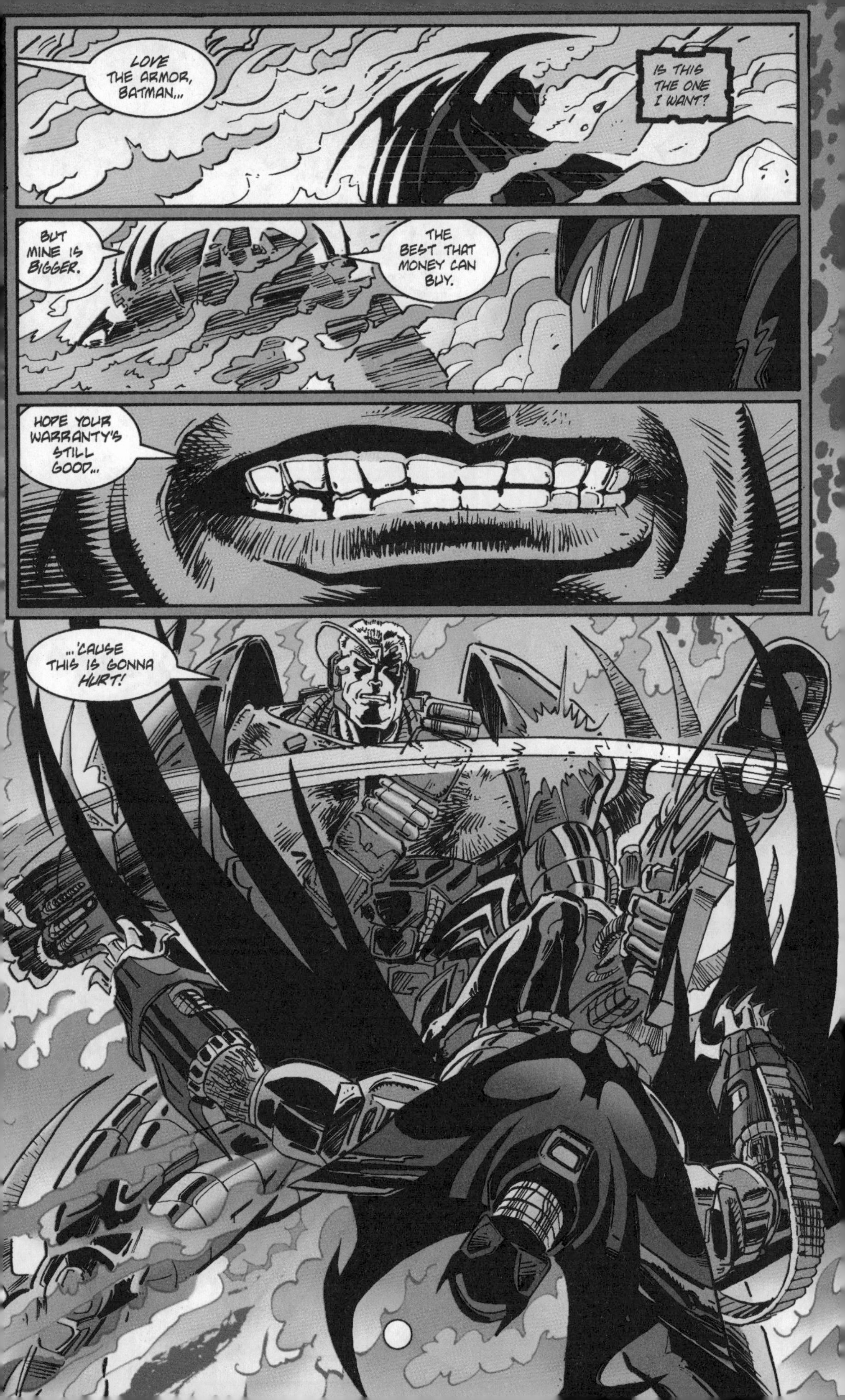
LOVE THE ARMOR, BATMAN...
IS THIS THE ONE I WANT?
BUT MINE IS BIGGER.
THE BEST THAT MONEY CAN BUY.
HOPE YOUR WARRANTY'S STILL GOOD...
...'CAUSE THIS IS GONNA HURT!

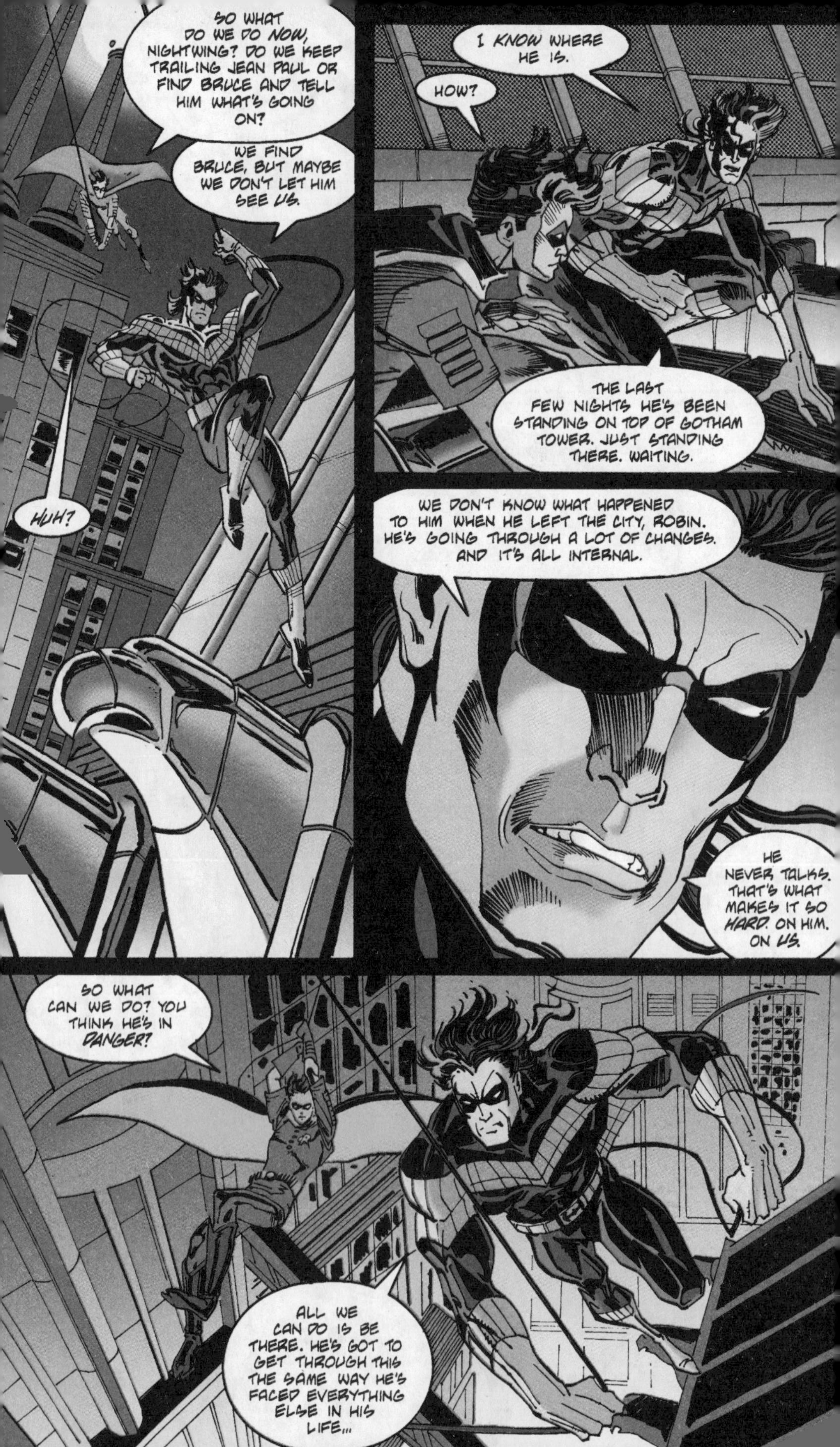
SO WHAT DO WE DO *NOW*, NIGHTWING? DO WE KEEP TRAILING JEAN PAUL OR FIND BRUCE AND TELL HIM WHAT'S GOING ON?
WE FIND BRUCE, BUT MAYBE WE DON'T LET HIM SEE *US*.
HUH?
I KNOW WHERE HE IS.
HOW?
THE LAST FEW NIGHTS HE'S BEEN STANDING ON TOP OF GOTHAM TOWER. JUST STANDING THERE. WAITING.
WE DON'T KNOW WHAT HAPPENED TO HIM WHEN HE LEFT THE CITY, ROBIN. HE'S GOING THROUGH A LOT OF CHANGES. AND IT'S ALL INTERNAL.
HE NEVER TALKS. THAT'S WHAT MAKES IT SO *HARD*. ON HIM. ON *US*.
SO WHAT CAN WE DO? YOU THINK HE'S IN *DANGER*?
ALL WE CAN DO IS BE THERE. HE'S GOT TO GET THROUGH THIS THE SAME WAY HE'S FACED EVERYTHING ELSE IN HIS LIFE...

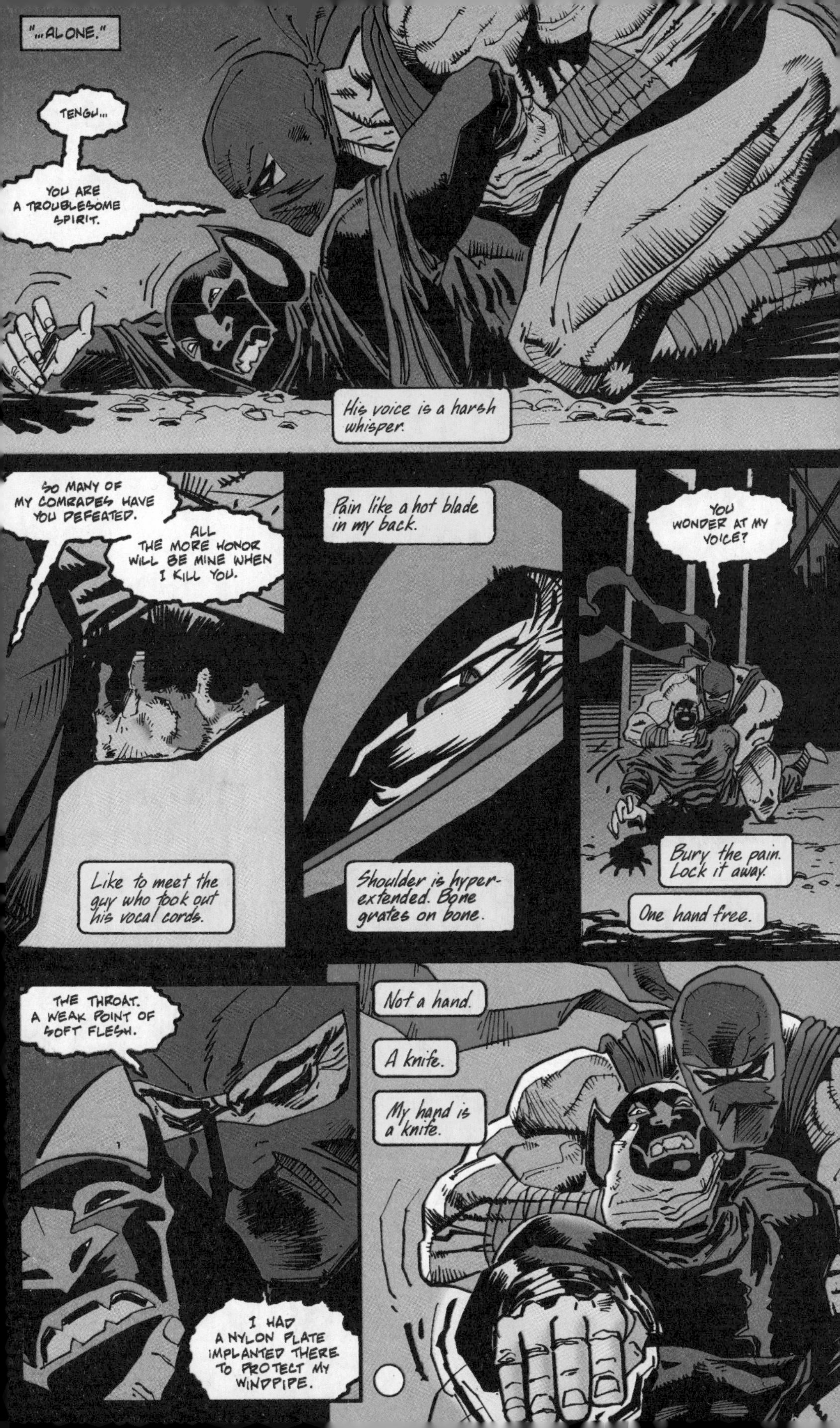
"...ALONE."
TENGU...
YOU ARE A TROUBLESOME SPIRIT.
His voice is a harsh whisper.
SO MANY OF MY COMRADES HAVE YOU DEFEATED.
ALL THE MORE HONOR WILL BE MINE WHEN I KILL YOU.
Like to meet the guy who took out his vocal cords.
Pain like a hot blade in my back.
Shoulder is hyper-extended. Bone grates on bone.
YOU WONDER AT MY VOICE?
Bury the pain. Lock it away.
One hand free.
THE THROAT. A WEAK POINT OF SOFT FLESH.
I HAD A NYLON PLATE IMPLANTED THERE TO PROTECT MY WINDPIPE.
Not a hand.
A knife.
My hand is a knife.

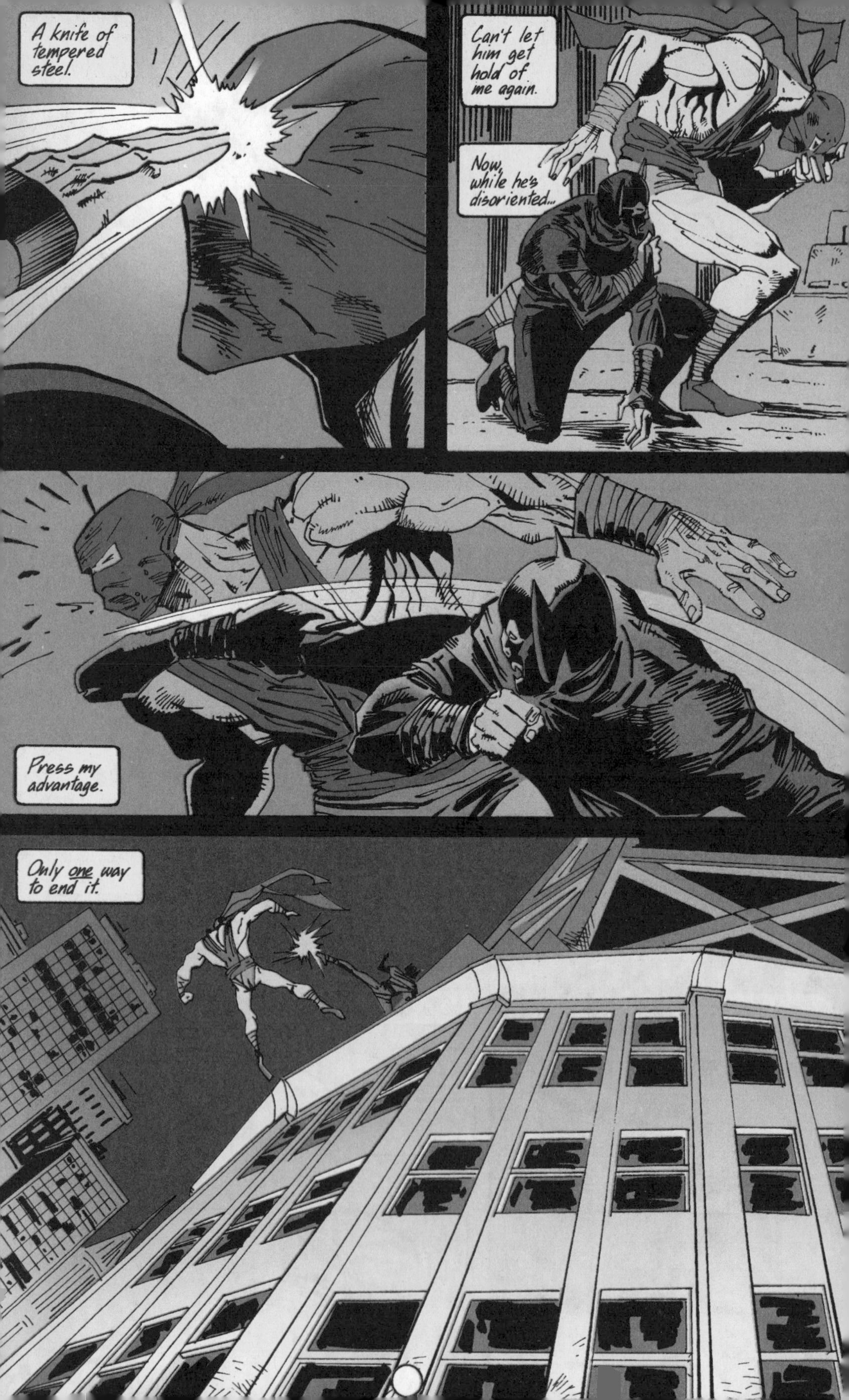
A knife of tempered steel.
Can't let him get hold of me again.
Now, while he's disoriented...
Press my advantage.
Only one way to end it.

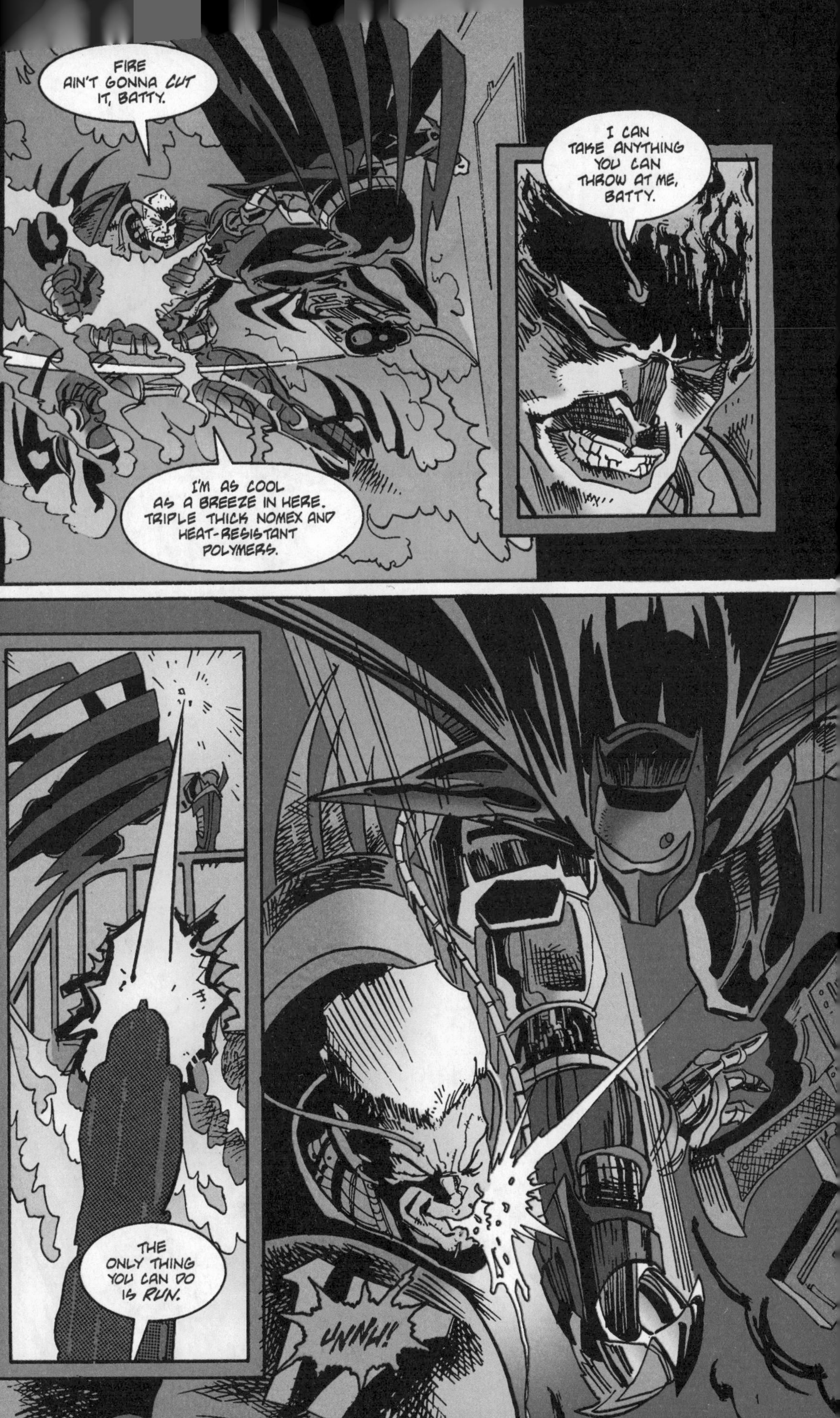
FIRE AIN'T GONNA CUT IT, BATTY.
I'M AS COOL AS A BREEZE IN HERE. TRIPLE THICK NOMEX AND HEAT-RESISTANT POLYMERS.
I CAN TAKE ANYTHING YOU CAN THROW AT ME, BATTY.
THE ONLY THING YOU CAN DO IS RUN.
UNNH!

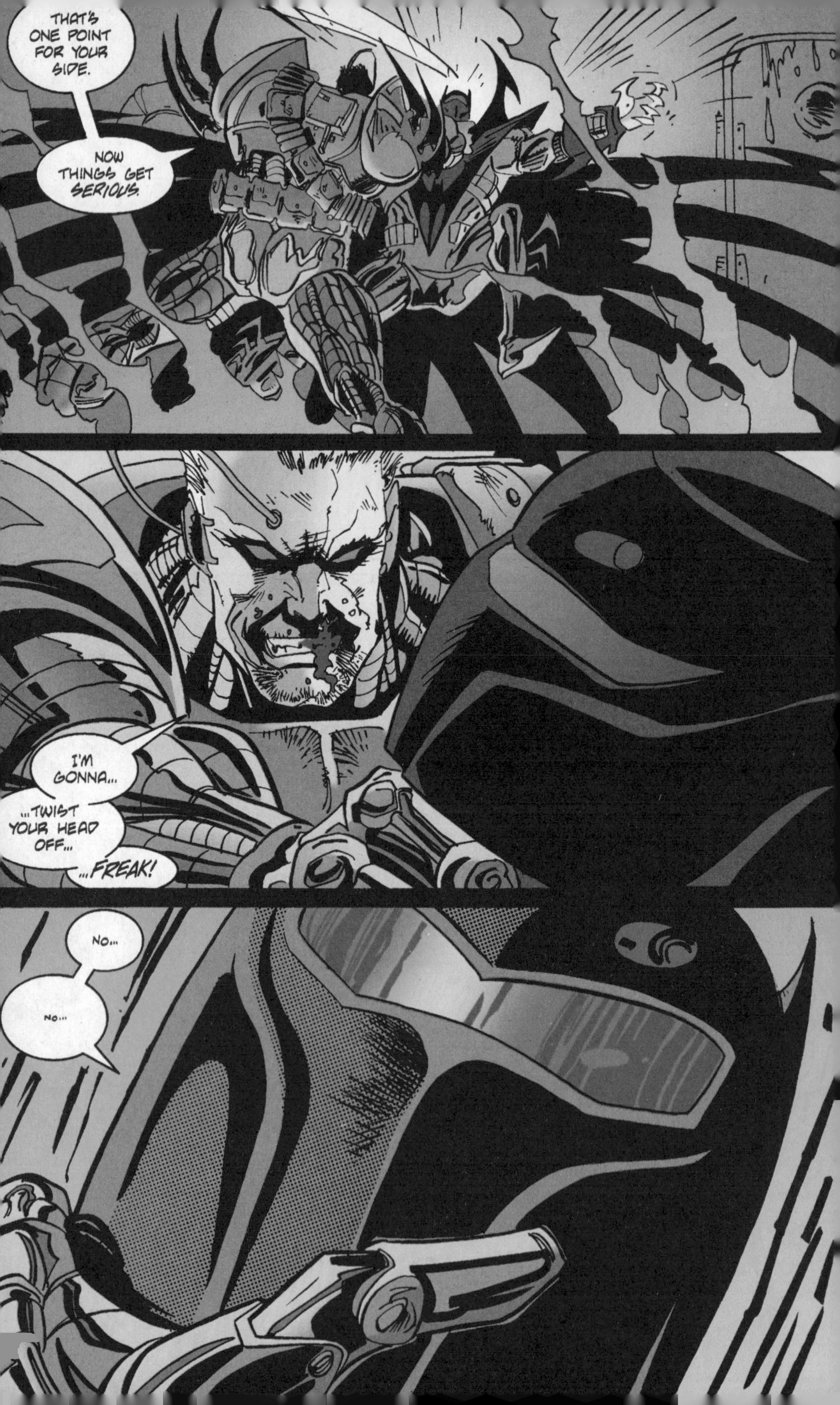
THAT'S ONE POINT FOR YOUR SIDE.
NOW THINGS GET SERIOUS.
I'M GONNA...
...TWIST YOUR HEAD OFF...
...FREAK!
NO...
NO...

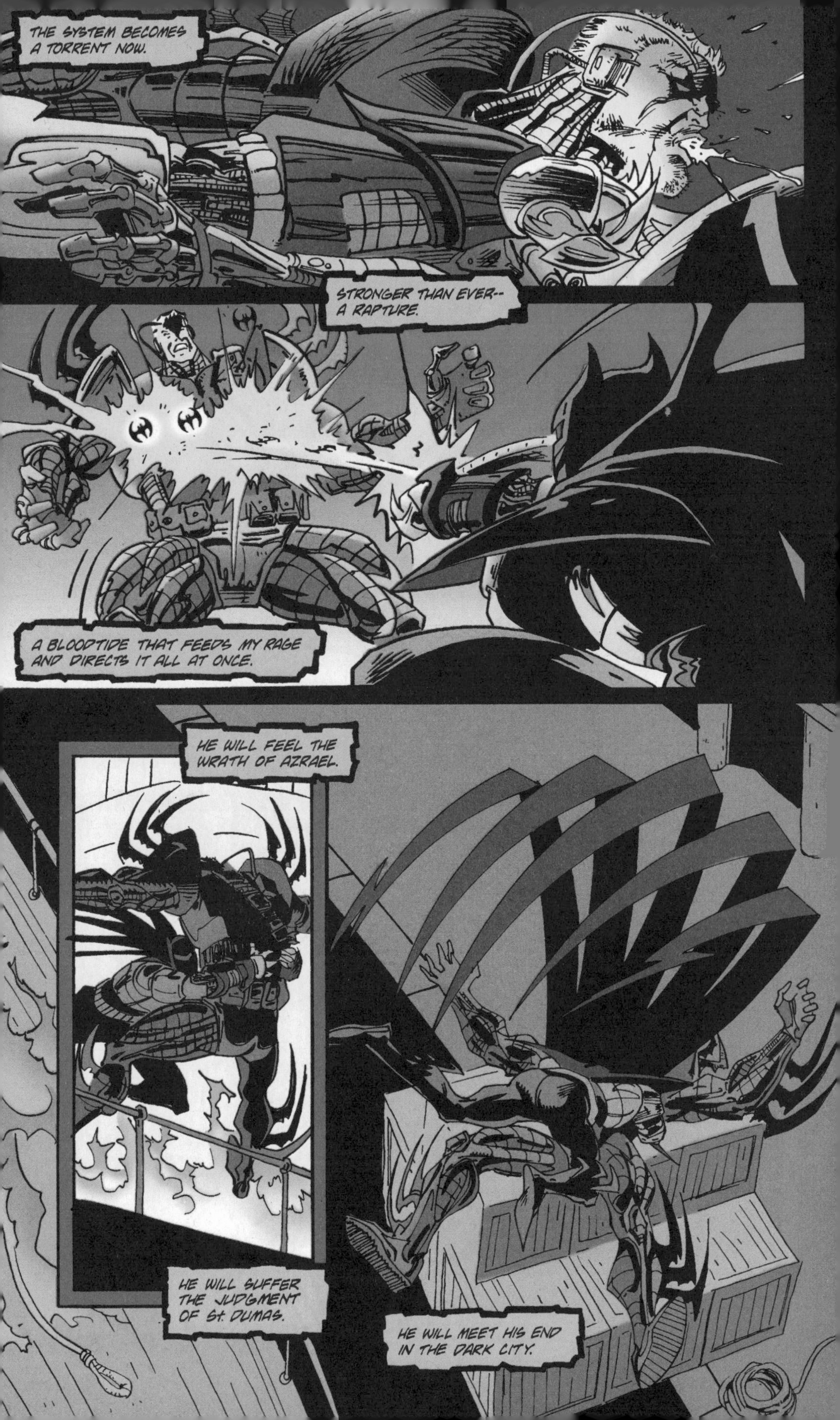
THE SYSTEM BECOMES A TORRENT NOW.
STRONGER THAN EVER-- A RAPTURE.
A BLOODTIDE THAT FEEDS MY RAGE AND DIRECTS IT ALL AT ONCE.
HE WILL FEEL THE WRATH OF AZRAEL.
HE WILL SUFFER THE JUDGMENT OF St. DUMAS.
HE WILL MEET HIS END IN THE DARK CITY.

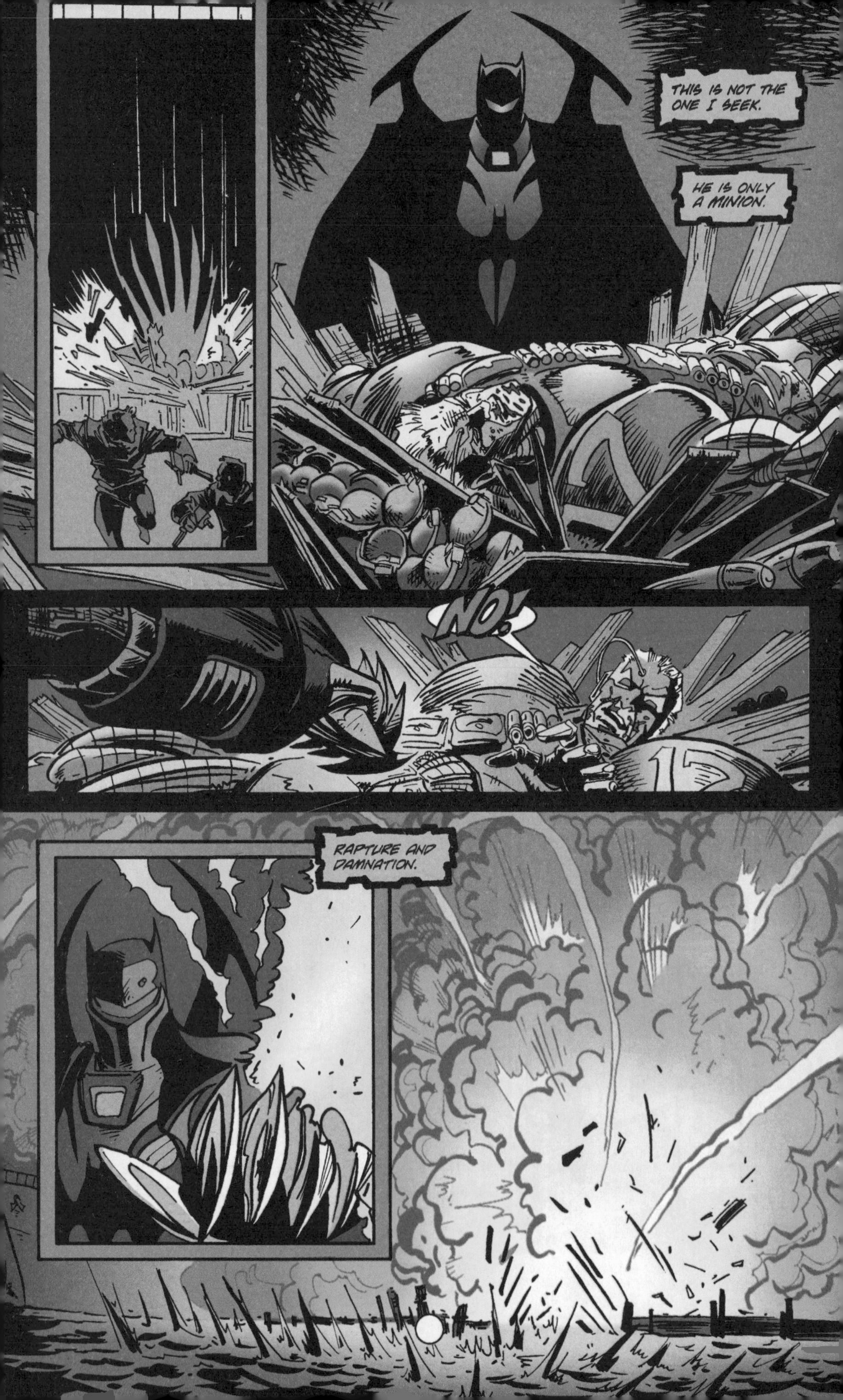
THIS IS NOT THE ONE I SEEK.
HE IS ONLY A MINION.
NO!
RAPTURE AND DAMNATION.

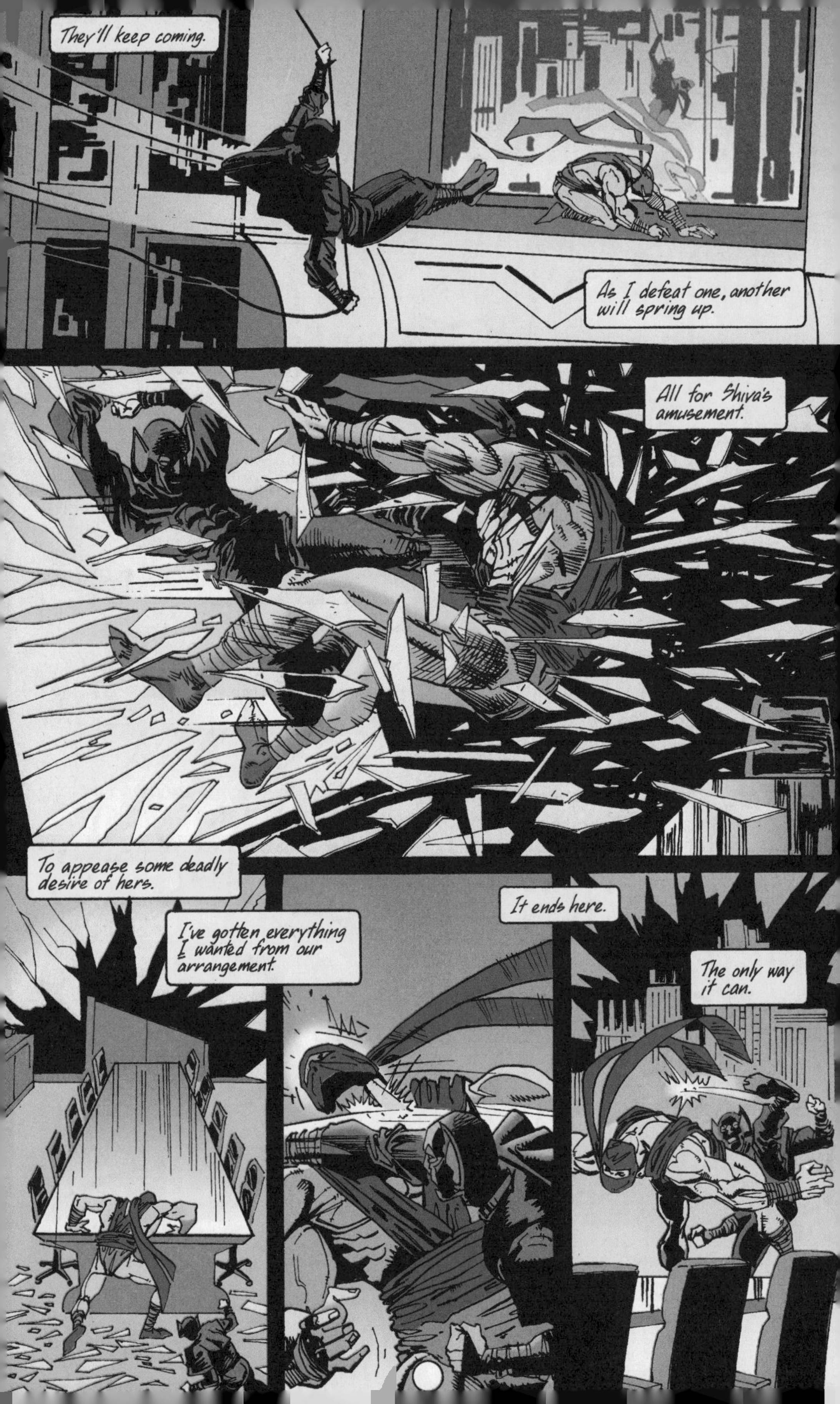

They'll keep coming.
As I defeat one, another will spring up.
All for Shiva's amusement.
To appease some deadly desire of hers.
I've gotten everything I wanted from our arrangement.
It ends here.
The only way it can.

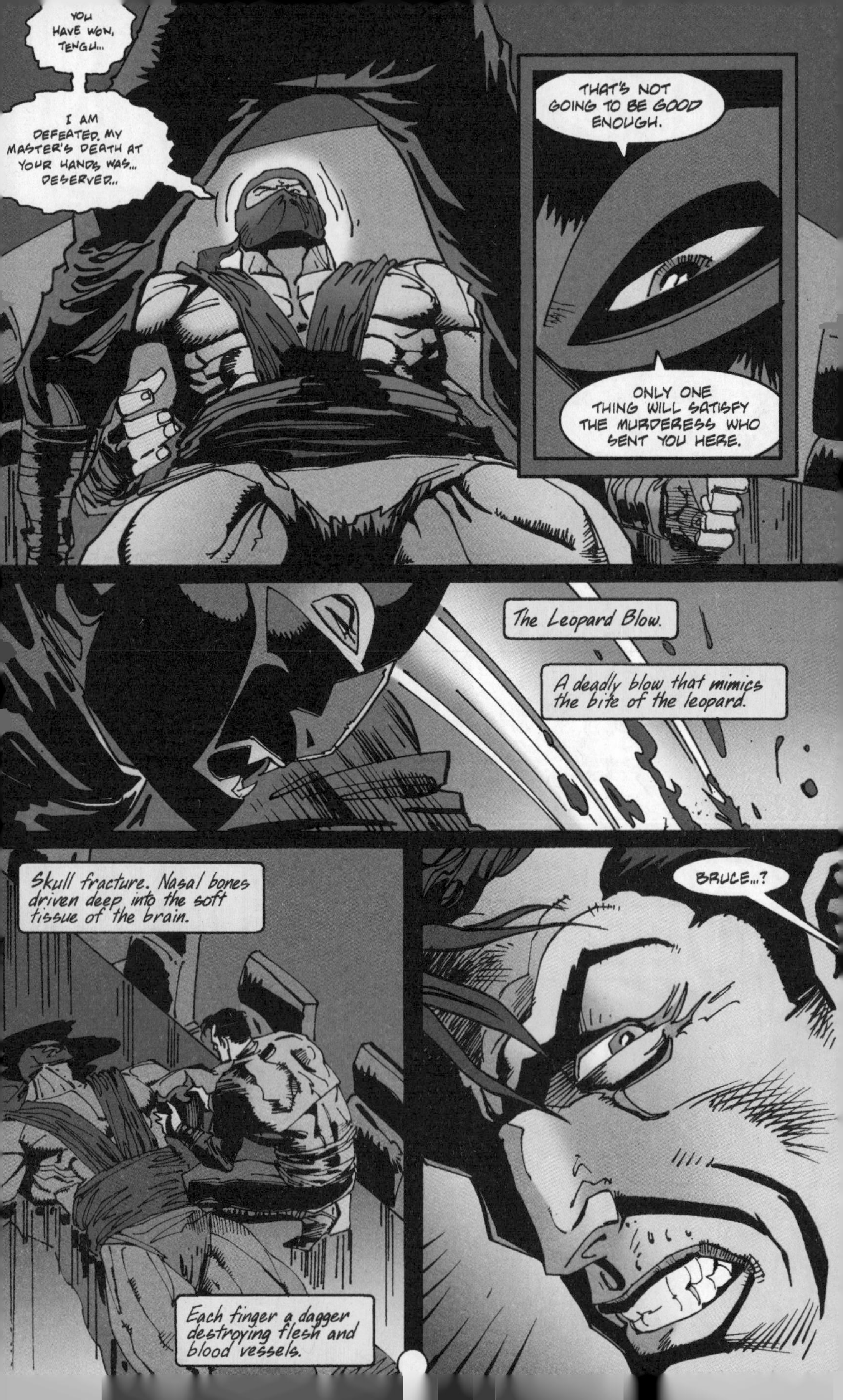
YOU HAVE WON, TENGU...
I AM DEFEATED. MY MASTER'S DEATH AT YOUR HANDS WAS... DESERVED...
THAT'S NOT GOING TO BE GOOD ENOUGH.
ONLY ONE THING WILL SATISFY THE MURDERESS WHO SENT YOU HERE.
The Leopard Blow.
A deadly blow that mimics the bite of the leopard.
Skull fracture. Nasal bones driven deep into the soft tissue of the brain.
Each finger a dagger destroying flesh and blood vessels.
BRUCE...?

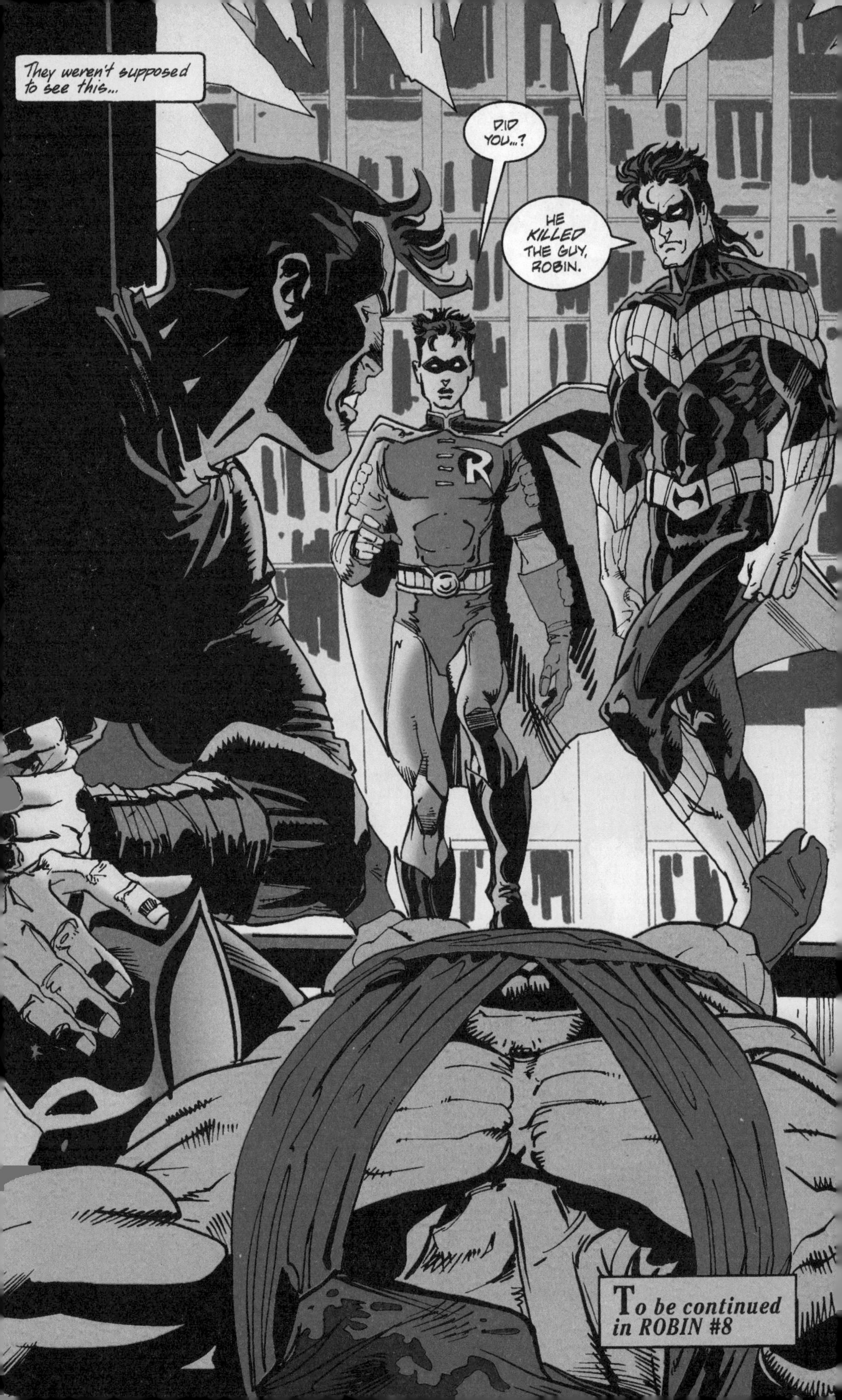
They weren't supposed to see this...
DID YOU...?
HE KILLED THE GUY, ROBIN.
To be continued in ROBIN #8

Cover art by TOM GRUMMETT and RAY KRYSSING

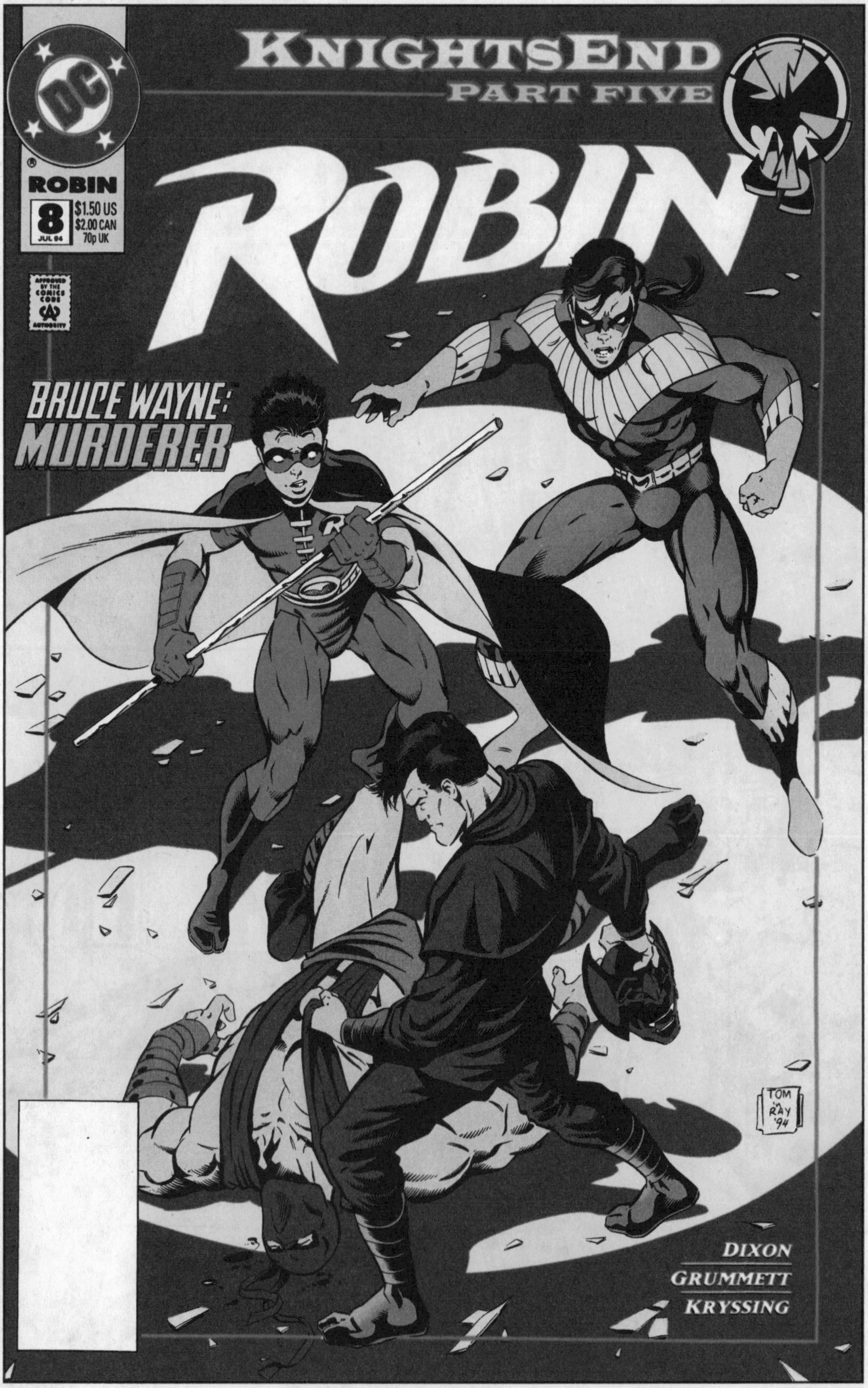
KNIGHTSEND
PART FIVE
DC
ROBIN
8
JUL 94
$1.50 US
$2.00 CAN
70p UK
ROBIN
BRUCE WAYNE: MURDERER
TOM RAY '94
DIXON
GRUMMETT
KRYSSING

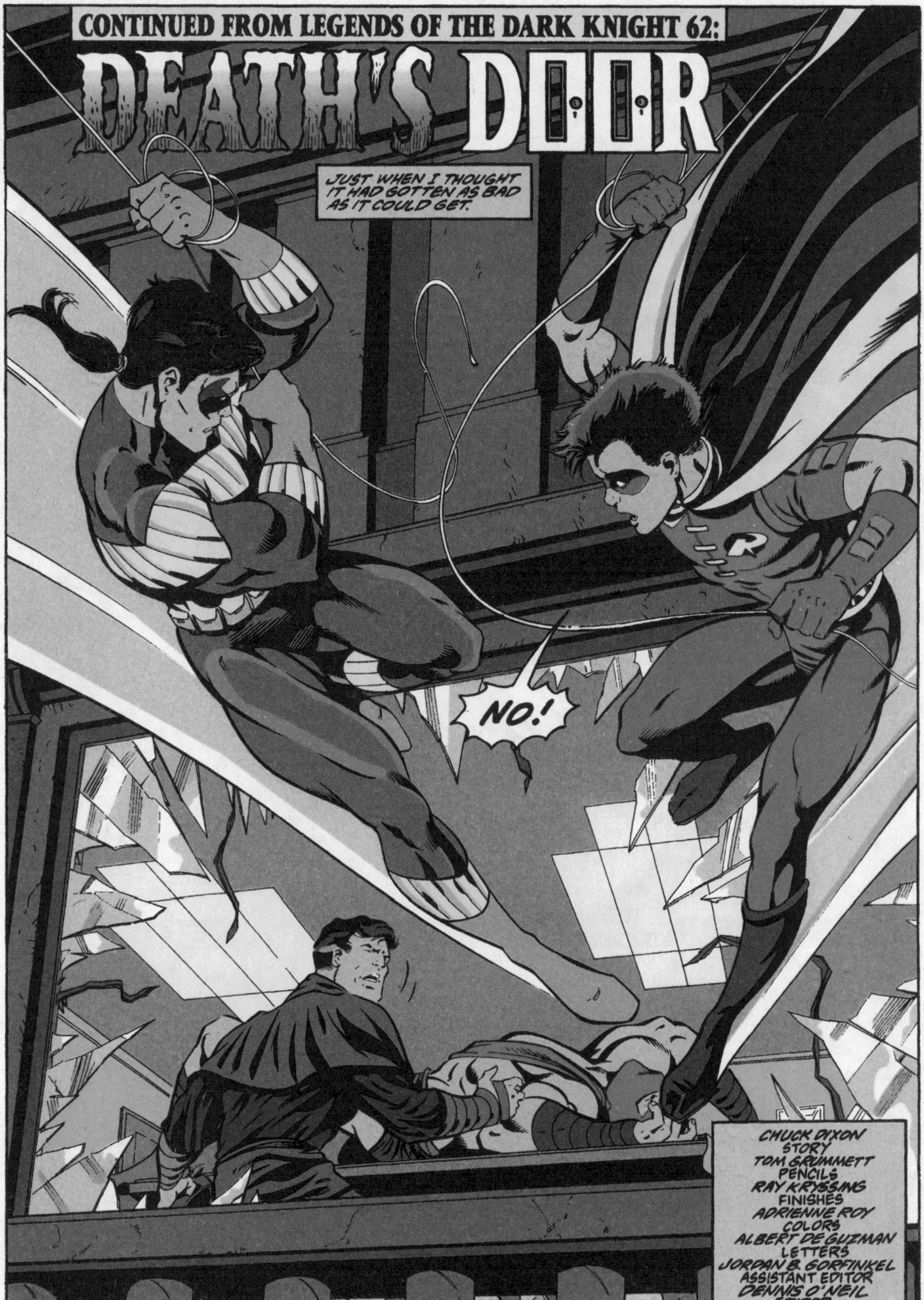

CONTINUED FROM LEGENDS OF THE DARK KNIGHT 62:
DEATH'S DOOR
JUST WHEN I THOUGHT IT HAD GOTTEN AS BAD AS IT COULD GET.
NO!
CHUCK DIXON STORY
TOM GRUMMETT PENCILS
RAY KRYSSING FINISHES
ADRIENNE ROY COLORS
ALBERT DE GUZMAN LETTERS
JORDAN B. GORFINKEL ASSISTANT EDITOR
DENNIS O'NEIL EDITOR

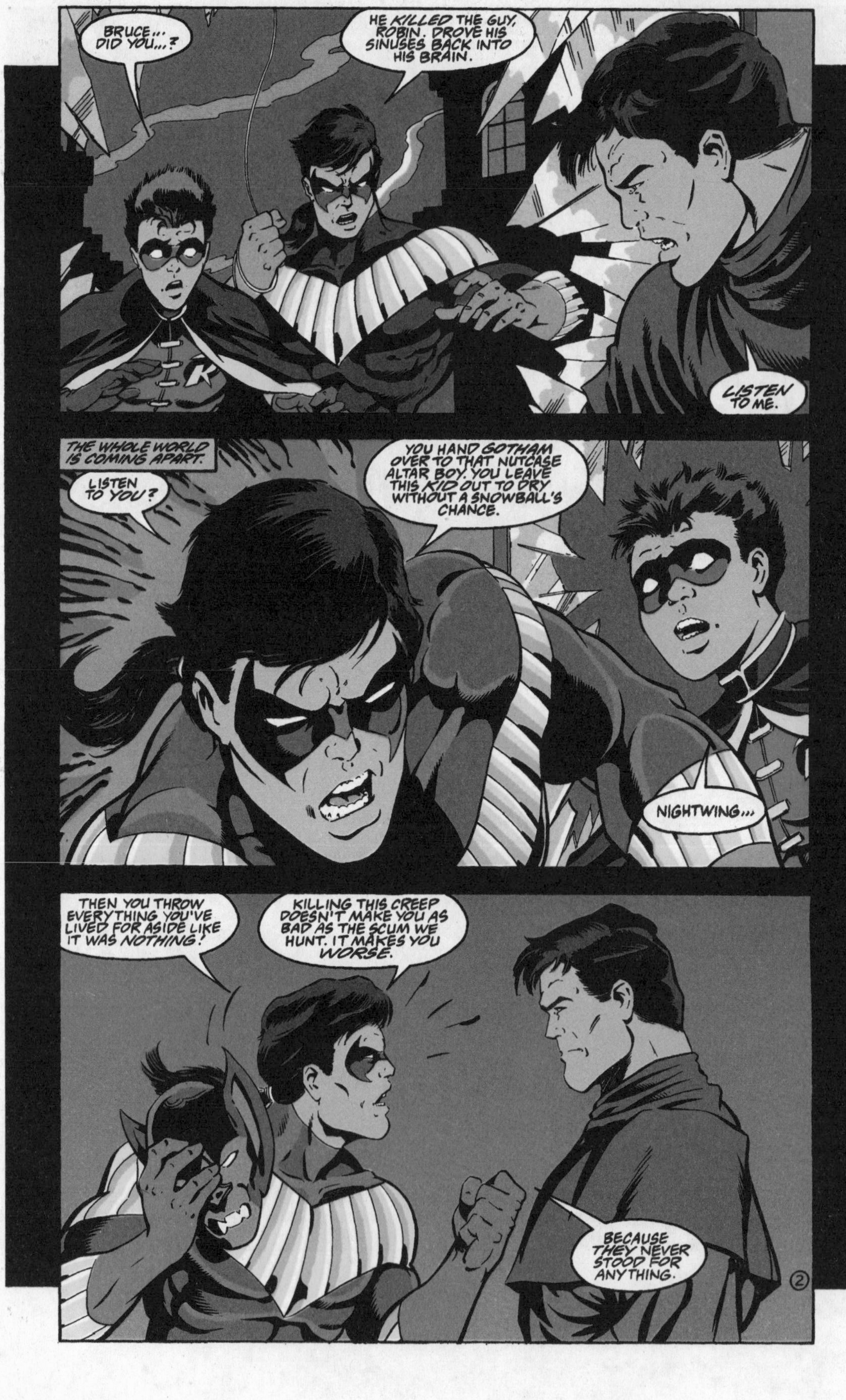
BRUCE... DID YOU...?
HE KILLED THE GUY, ROBIN. DROVE HIS SINUSES BACK INTO HIS BRAIN.
LISTEN TO ME.
THE WHOLE WORLD IS COMING APART.
LISTEN TO YOU?
YOU HAND GOTHAM OVER TO THAT NUTCASE ALTAR BOY. YOU LEAVE THIS KID OUT TO DRY WITHOUT A SNOWBALL'S CHANCE.
NIGHTWING...
THEN YOU THROW EVERYTHING YOU'VE LIVED FOR ASIDE LIKE IT WAS NOTHING!
KILLING THIS CREEP DOESN'T MAKE YOU AS BAD AS THE SCUM WE HUNT. IT MAKES YOU WORSE.
BECAUSE THEY NEVER STOOD FOR ANYTHING.
2

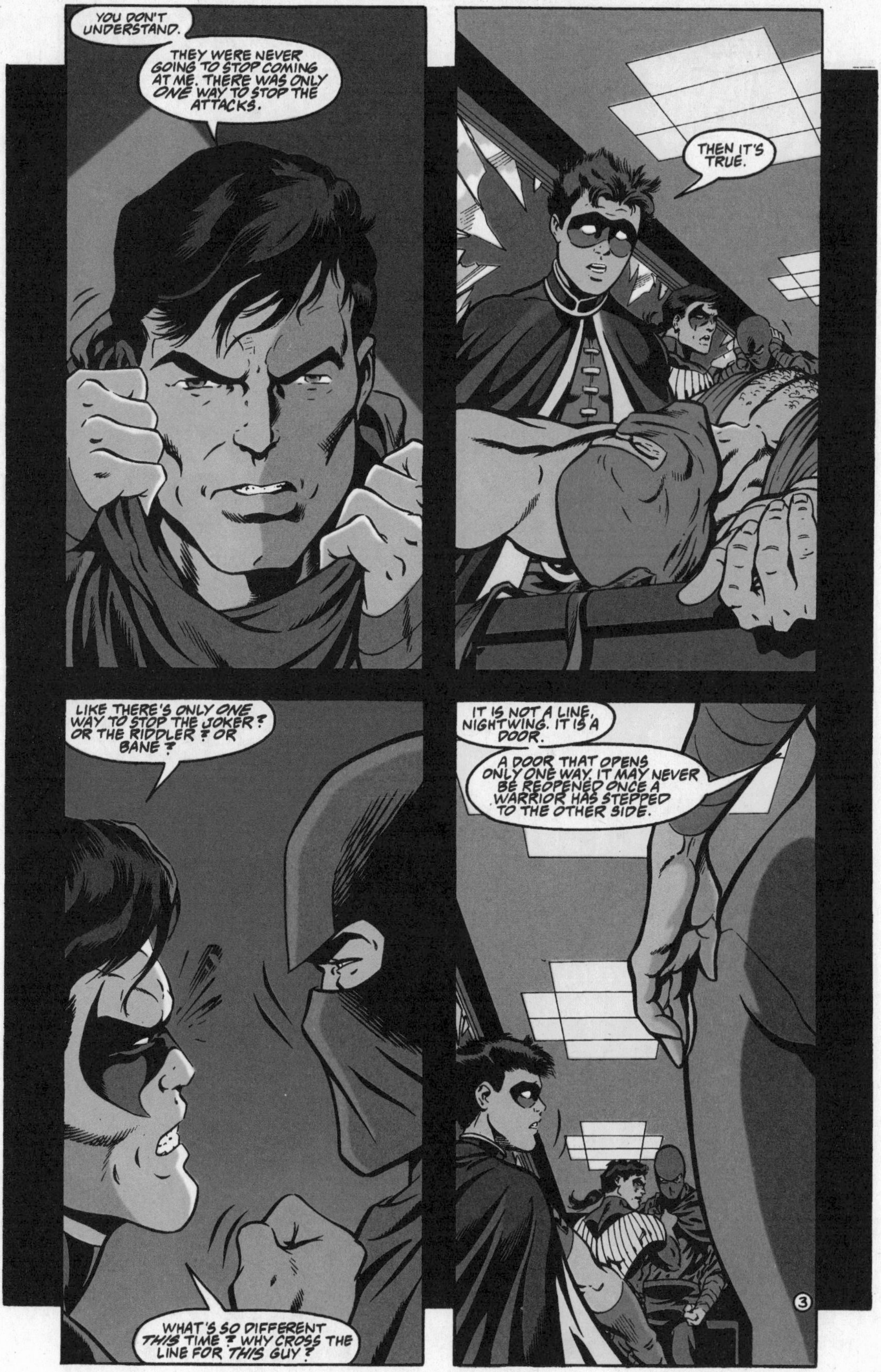
YOU DON'T UNDERSTAND.
THEY WERE NEVER GOING TO STOP COMING AT ME. THERE WAS ONLY ONE WAY TO STOP THE ATTACKS.
THEN IT'S TRUE.
LIKE THERE'S ONLY ONE WAY TO STOP THE JOKER? OR THE RIDDLER? OR BANE?
WHAT'S SO DIFFERENT THIS TIME? WHY CROSS THE LINE FOR THIS GUY?
IT IS NOT A LINE, NIGHTWING. IT IS A DOOR.
A DOOR THAT OPENS ONLY ONE WAY. IT MAY NEVER BE REOPENED ONCE A WARRIOR HAS STEPPED TO THE OTHER SIDE.
3

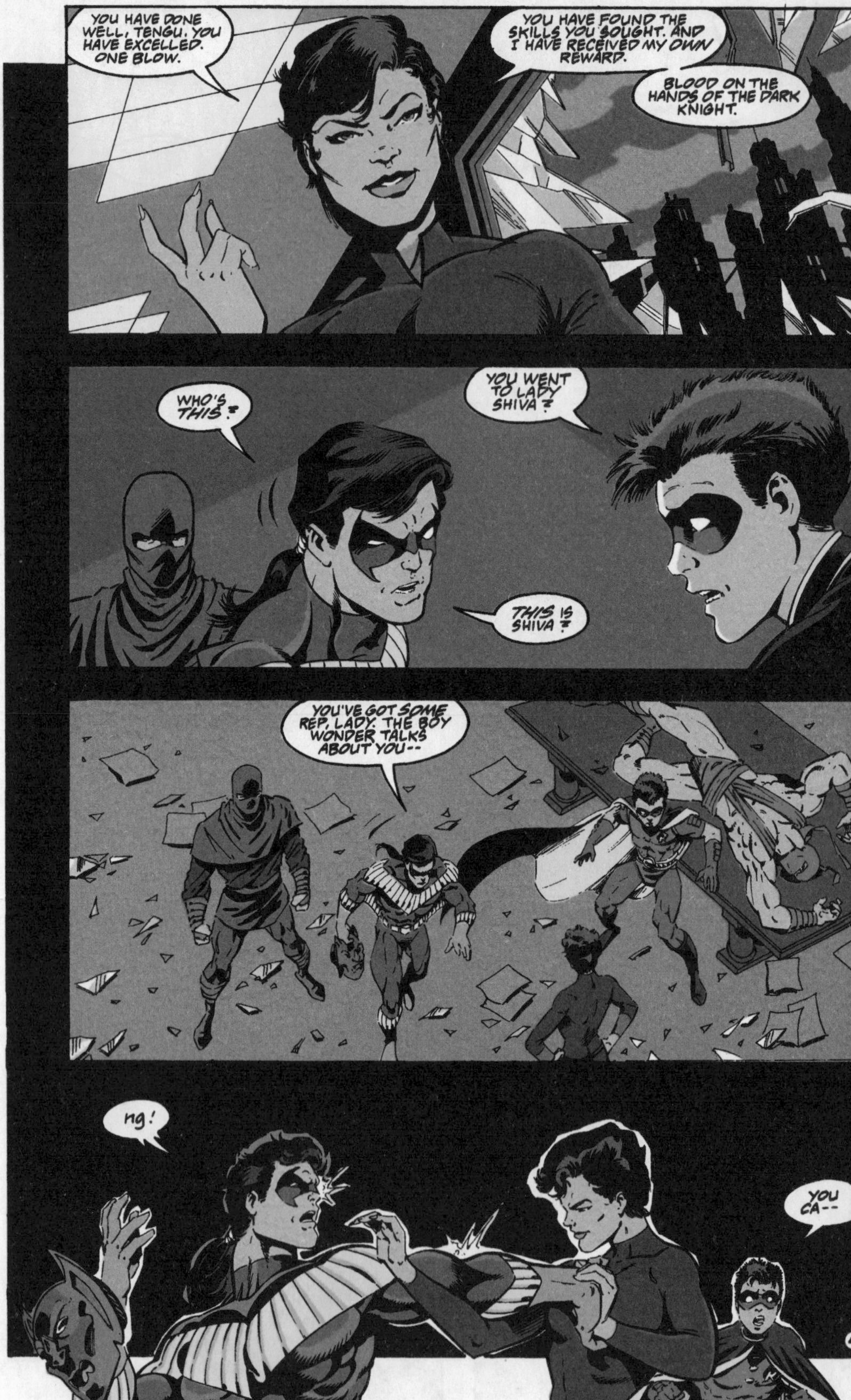

YOU HAVE DONE WELL, TENGU. YOU HAVE EXCELLED. ONE BLOW.
YOU HAVE FOUND THE SKILLS YOU SOUGHT. AND I HAVE RECEIVED MY OWN REWARD.
BLOOD ON THE HANDS OF THE DARK KNIGHT.
WHO'S THIS?
YOU WENT TO LADY SHIVA?
THIS IS SHIVA?
YOU'VE GOT SOME REP, LADY. THE BOY WONDER TALKS ABOUT YOU--
ng!
YOU CA--
4

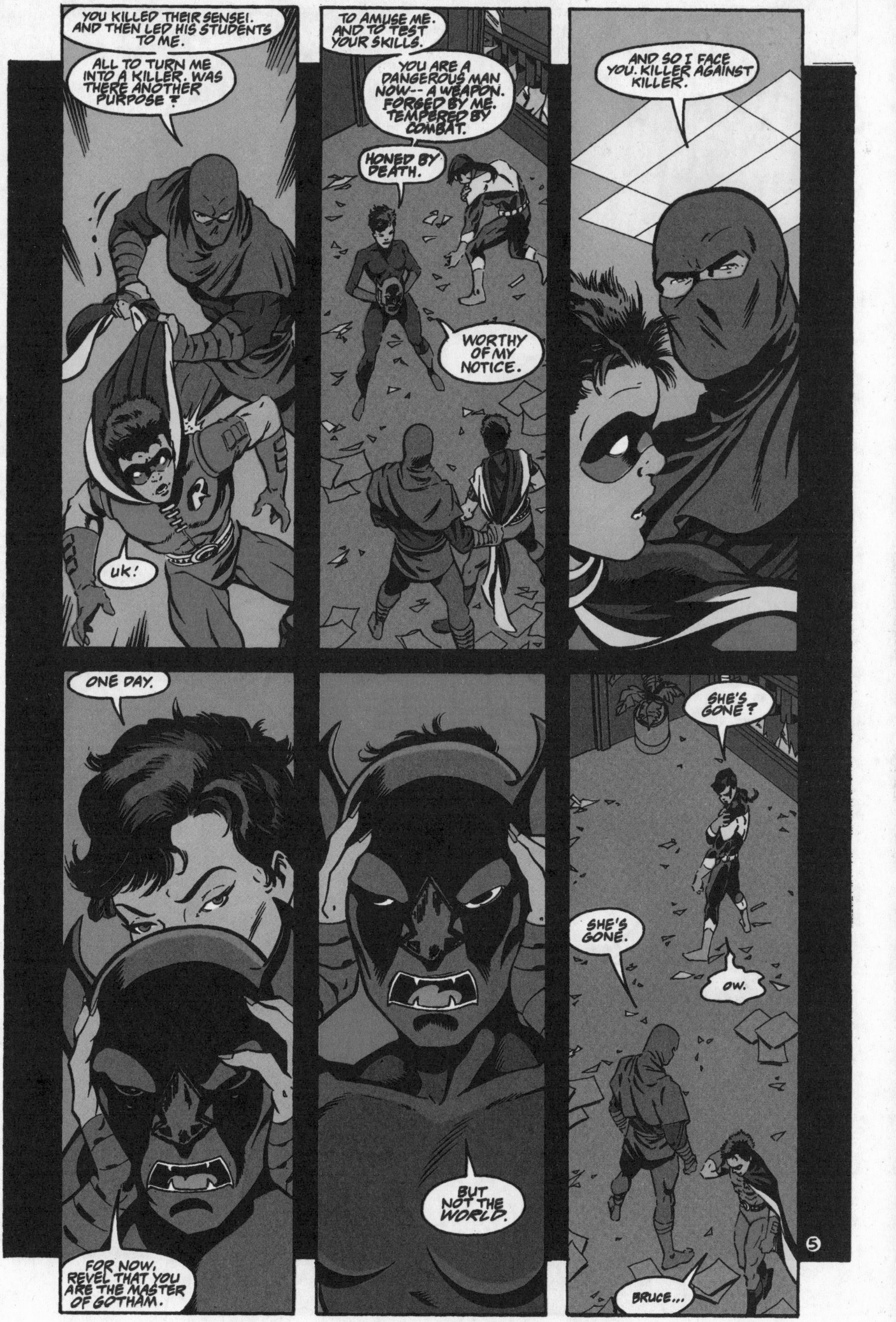
YOU KILLED THEIR SENSEI. AND THEN LED HIS STUDENTS TO ME.
ALL TO TURN ME INTO A KILLER. WAS THERE ANOTHER PURPOSE?
UK!
TO AMUSE ME. AND TO TEST YOUR SKILLS.
YOU ARE A DANGEROUS MAN NOW-- A WEAPON. FORGED BY ME. TEMPERED BY COMBAT.
HONED BY DEATH.
WORTHY OF MY NOTICE.
AND SO I FACE YOU. KILLER AGAINST KILLER.
ONE DAY.
FOR NOW, REVEL THAT YOU ARE THE MASTER OF GOTHAM.
BUT NOT THE WORLD.
SHE'S GONE?
SHE'S GONE.
OW.
BRUCE...
5

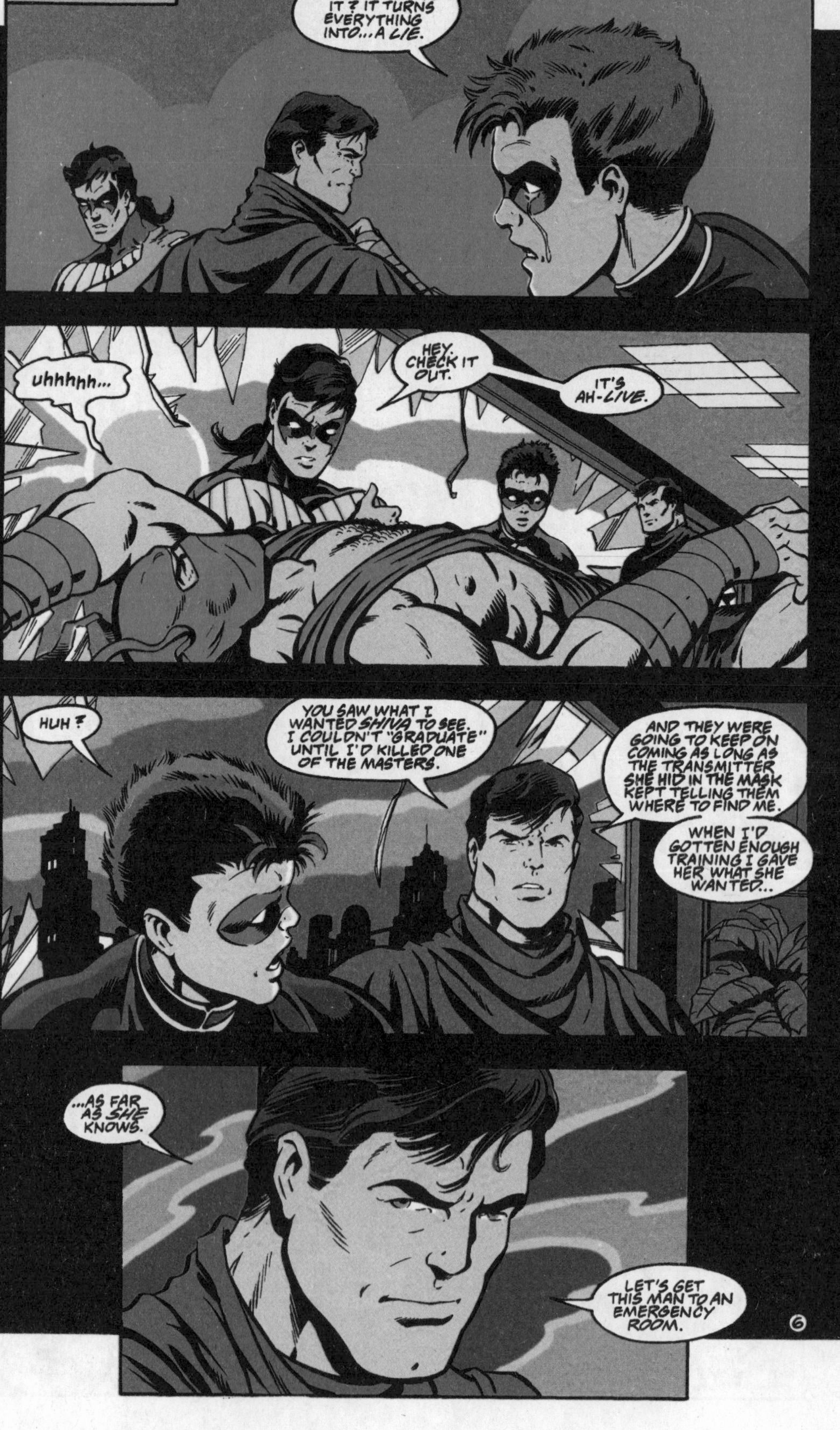
CAN'T BELIEVE THIS IS HAPPENING.
WHY DID YOU DO IT? IT TURNS EVERYTHING INTO... A LIE.
uhhhhh...
HEY. CHECK IT OUT.
IT'S AH-LIVE.
HUH?
YOU SAW WHAT I WANTED SHIVA TO SEE. I COULDN'T "GRADUATE" UNTIL I'D KILLED ONE OF THE MASTERS.
AND THEY WERE GOING TO KEEP ON COMING AS LONG AS THE TRANSMITTER SHE HID IN THE MASK KEPT TELLING THEM WHERE TO FIND ME.
WHEN I'D GOTTEN ENOUGH TRAINING I GAVE HER WHAT SHE WANTED...
...AS FAR AS SHE KNOWS.
LET'S GET THIS MAN TO AN EMERGENCY ROOM.
6

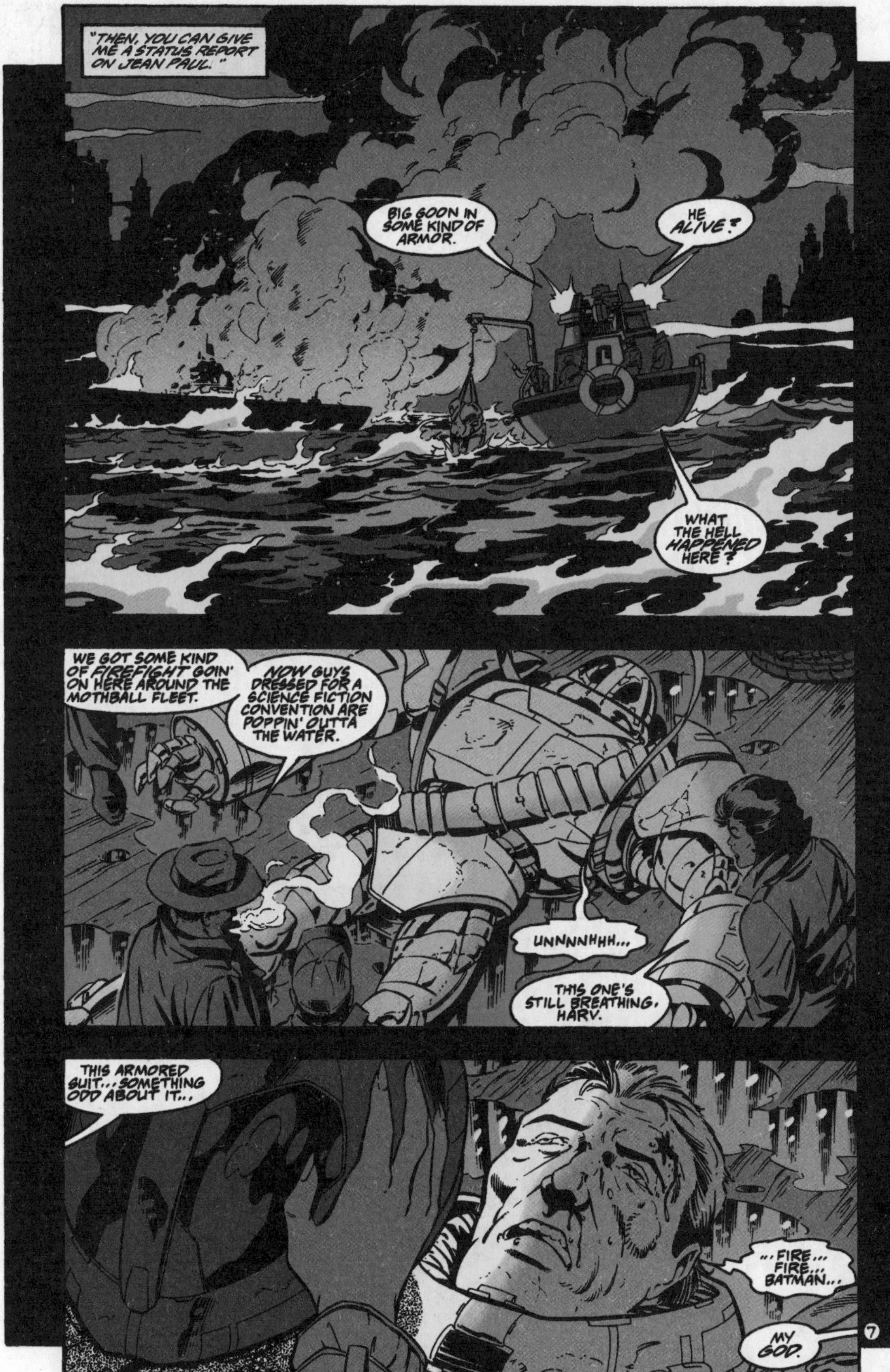
"THEN, YOU CAN GIVE ME A STATUS REPORT ON JEAN PAUL."
BIG GOON IN SOME KIND OF ARMOR.
HE ALIVE?
WHAT THE HELL HAPPENED HERE?
WE GOT SOME KIND OF FIREFIGHT GOIN' ON HERE AROUND THE MOTHBALL FLEET.
NOW GUYS DRESSED FOR A SCIENCE FICTION CONVENTION ARE POPPIN' OUTTA THE WATER.
UNNNNHHH...
THIS ONE'S STILL BREATHING, HARV.
THIS ARMORED SUIT... SOMETHING ODD ABOUT IT...
...FIRE... FIRE... BATMAN...
MY GOD.
7

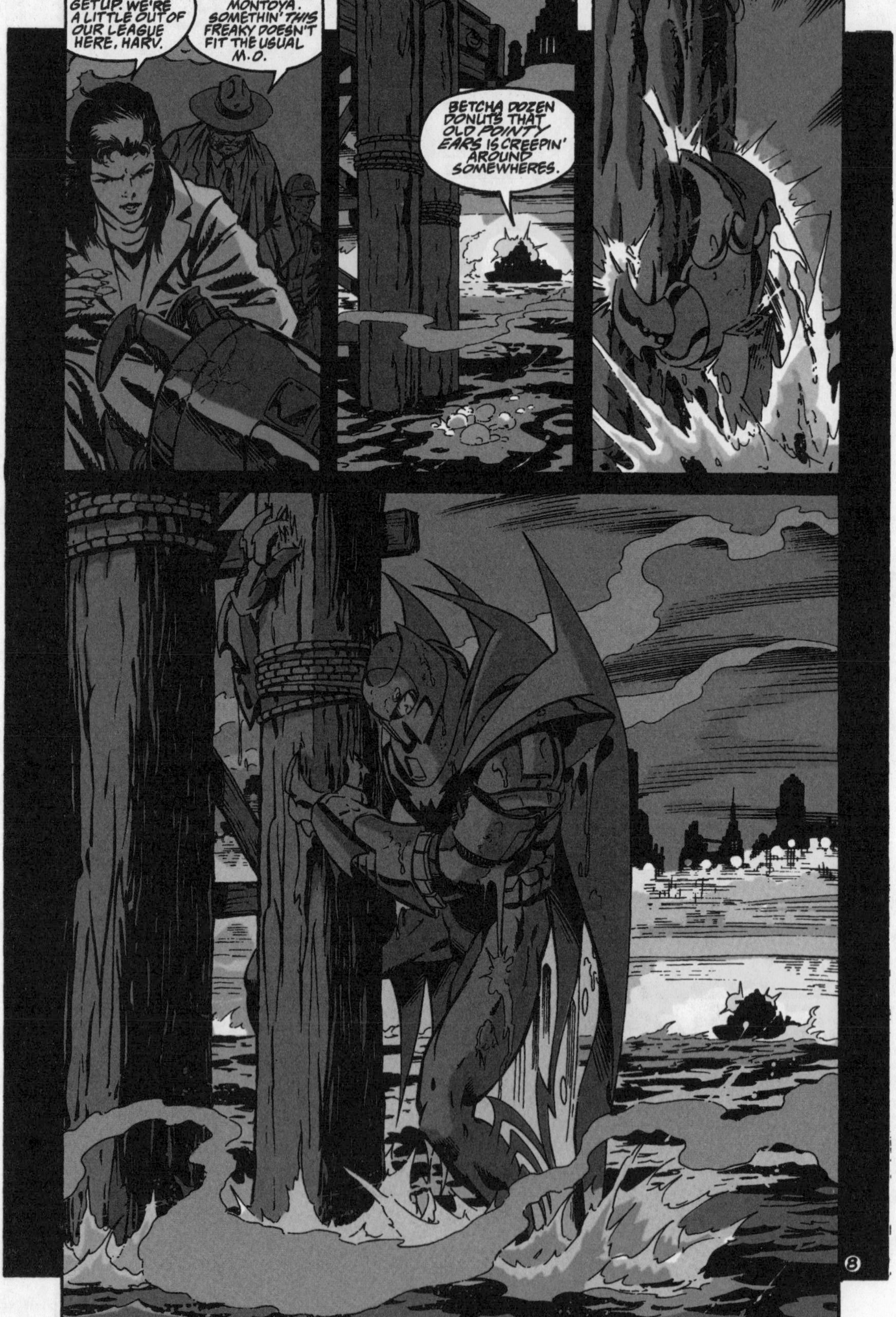
HE'S JUST WEARING THIS GETUP. WE'RE A LITTLE OUT OF OUR LEAGUE HERE, HARV.
ONE FOR THE TALK SHOWS, MONTOYA. SOMETHIN' THIS FREAKY DOESN'T FIT THE USUAL M.O.
BETCHA DOZEN DONUTS THAT OLD POINTY EARS IS CREEPIN' AROUND SOMEWHERES.
8

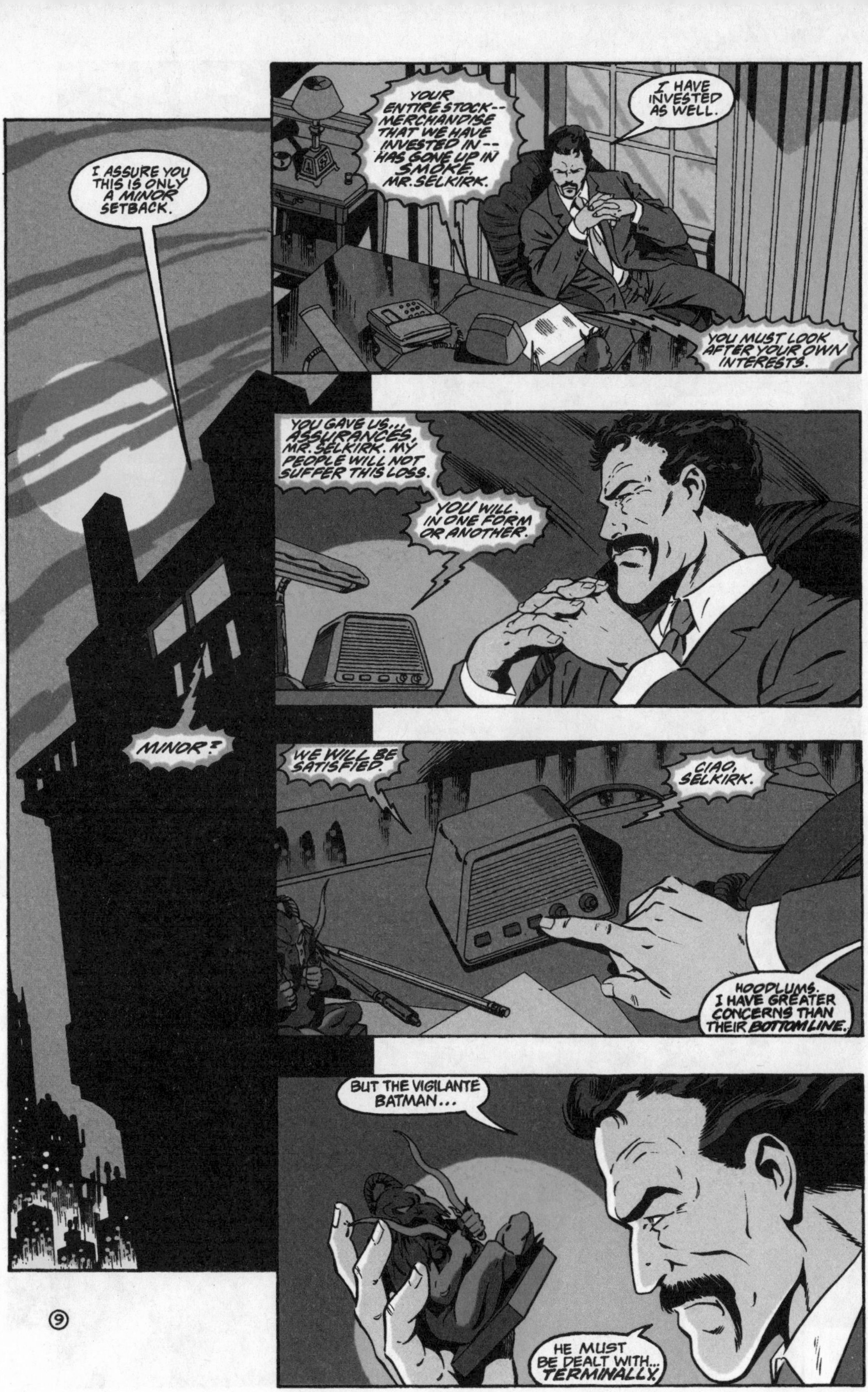
I ASSURE YOU THIS IS ONLY A MINOR SETBACK.
YOUR ENTIRE STOCK-- MERCHANDISE THAT WE HAVE INVESTED IN-- HAS GONE UP IN SMOKE, MR. SELKIRK.
I HAVE INVESTED AS WELL.
YOU MUST LOOK AFTER YOUR OWN INTERESTS.
MINOR?
YOU GAVE US... ASSURANCES, MR. SELKIRK. MY PEOPLE WILL NOT SUFFER THIS LOSS.
YOU WILL. IN ONE FORM OR ANOTHER.
WE WILL BE SATISFIED.
CIAO, SELKIRK.
HOODLUMS. I HAVE GREATER CONCERNS THAN THEIR BOTTOM LINE.
BUT THE VIGILANTE BATMAN...
HE MUST BE DEALT WITH... TERMINALLY.
9

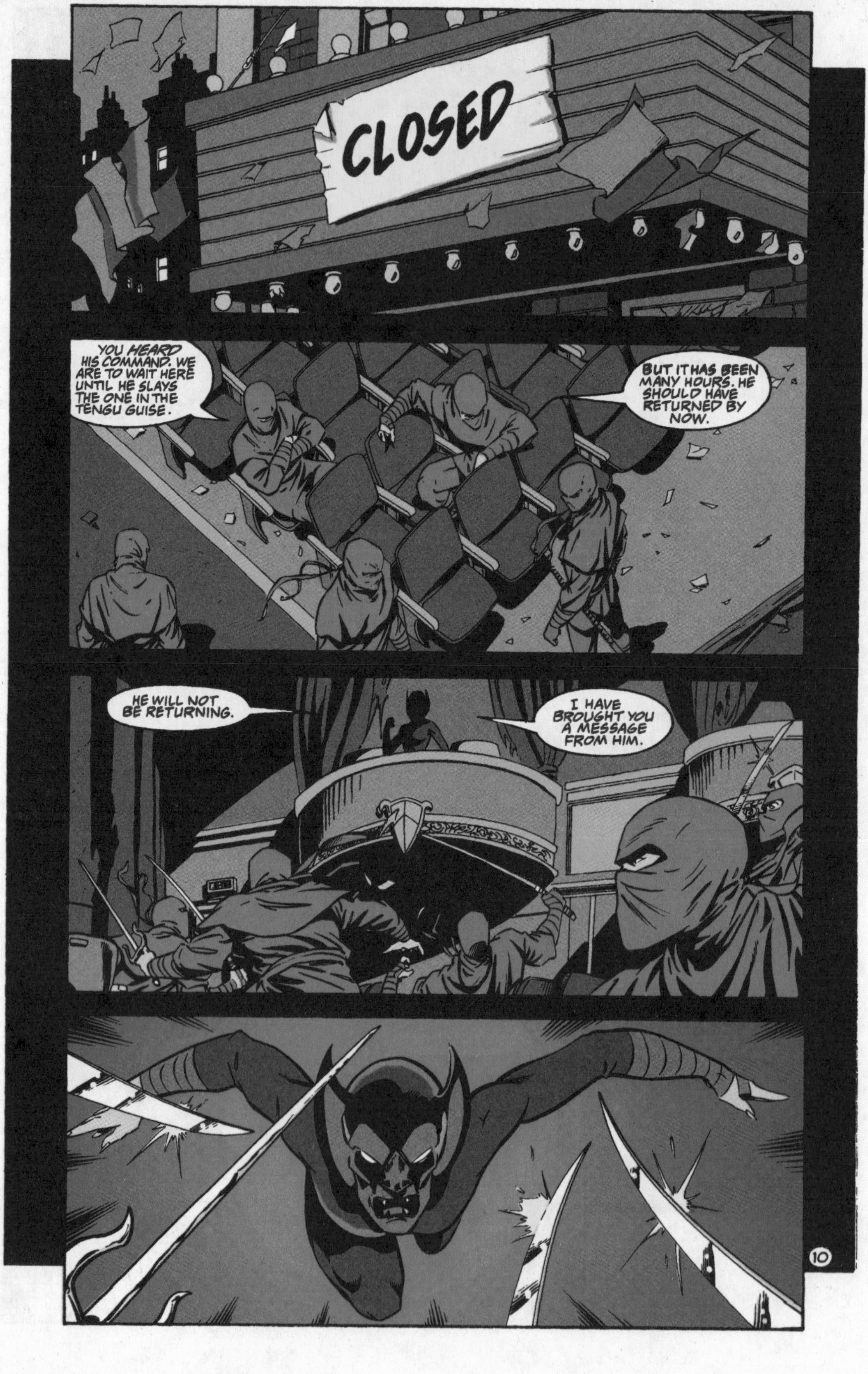
CLOSED
YOU HEARD HIS COMMAND. WE ARE TO WAIT HERE UNTIL HE SLAYS THE ONE IN THE TENGU GUISE.
BUT IT HAS BEEN MANY HOURS. HE SHOULD HAVE RETURNED BY NOW.
HE WILL NOT BE RETURNING.
I HAVE BROUGHT YOU A MESSAGE FROM HIM.
10

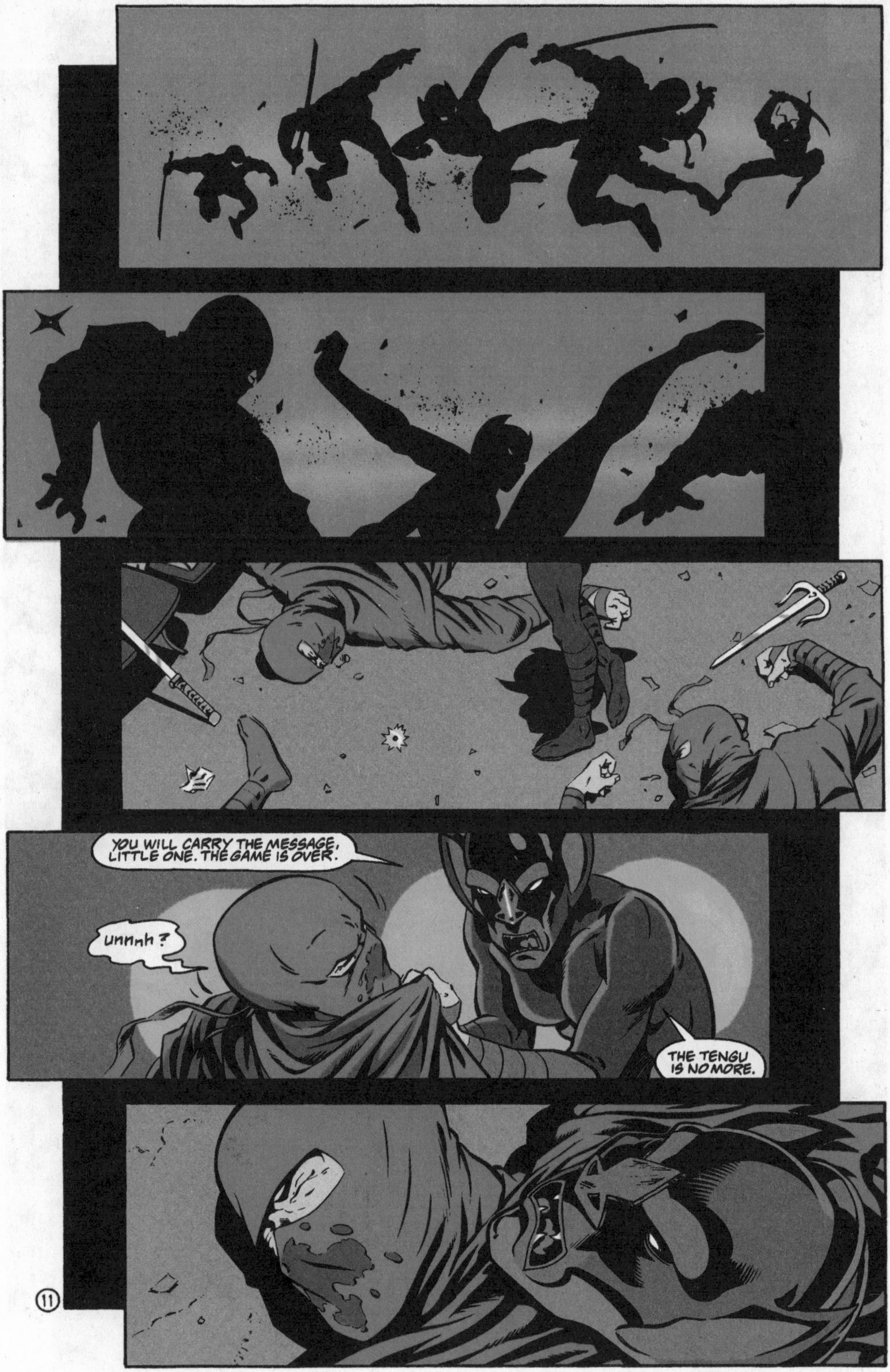
YOU WILL CARRY THE MESSAGE, LITTLE ONE. THE GAME IS OVER.
unnnh ?
THE TENGU IS NO MORE.
11

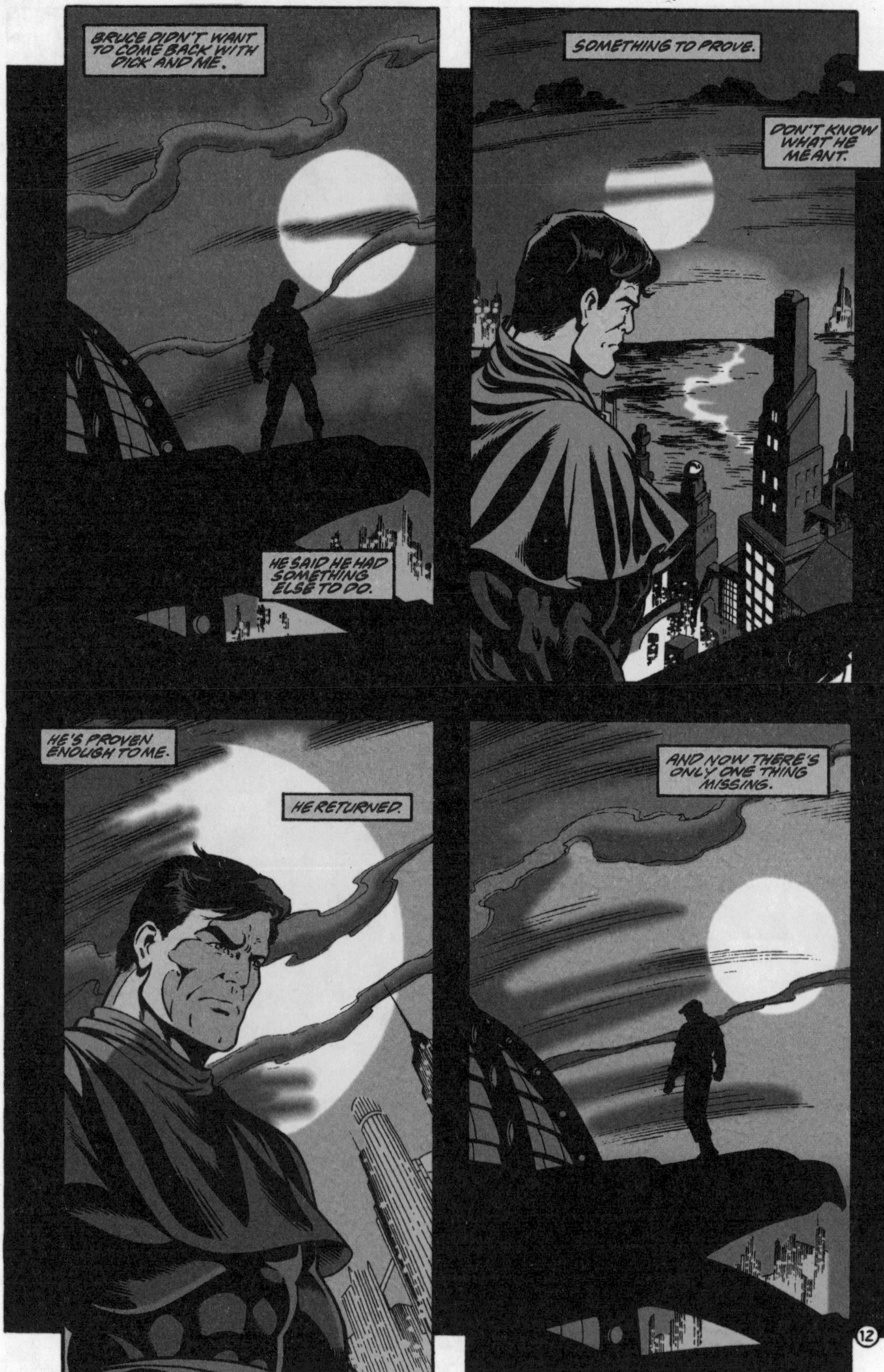

BRUCE DIDN'T WANT TO COME BACK WITH DICK AND ME.
HE SAID HE HAD SOMETHING ELSE TO DO.
SOMETHING TO PROVE.
DON'T KNOW WHAT HE MEANT.
HE'S PROVEN ENOUGH TO ME.
HE RETURNED.
AND NOW THERE'S ONLY ONE THING MISSING.
12

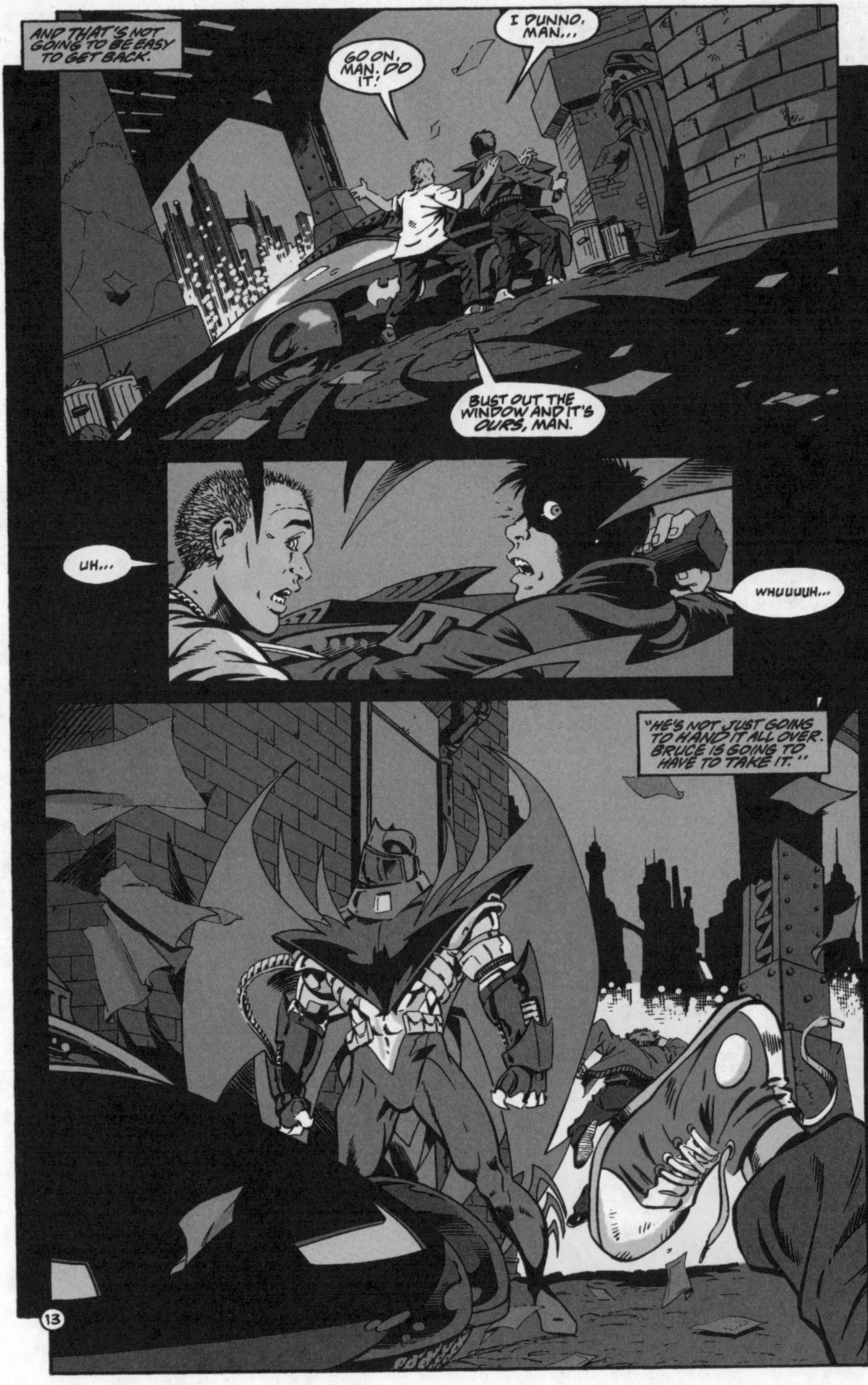
AND THAT'S NOT GOING TO BE EASY TO GET BACK.
GO ON, MAN. DO IT!
I DUNNO, MAN...
BUST OUT THE WINDOW AND IT'S OURS, MAN.
UH...
WHUUUUH...
"HE'S NOT JUST GOING TO HAND IT ALL OVER. BRUCE IS GOING TO HAVE TO TAKE IT."
13

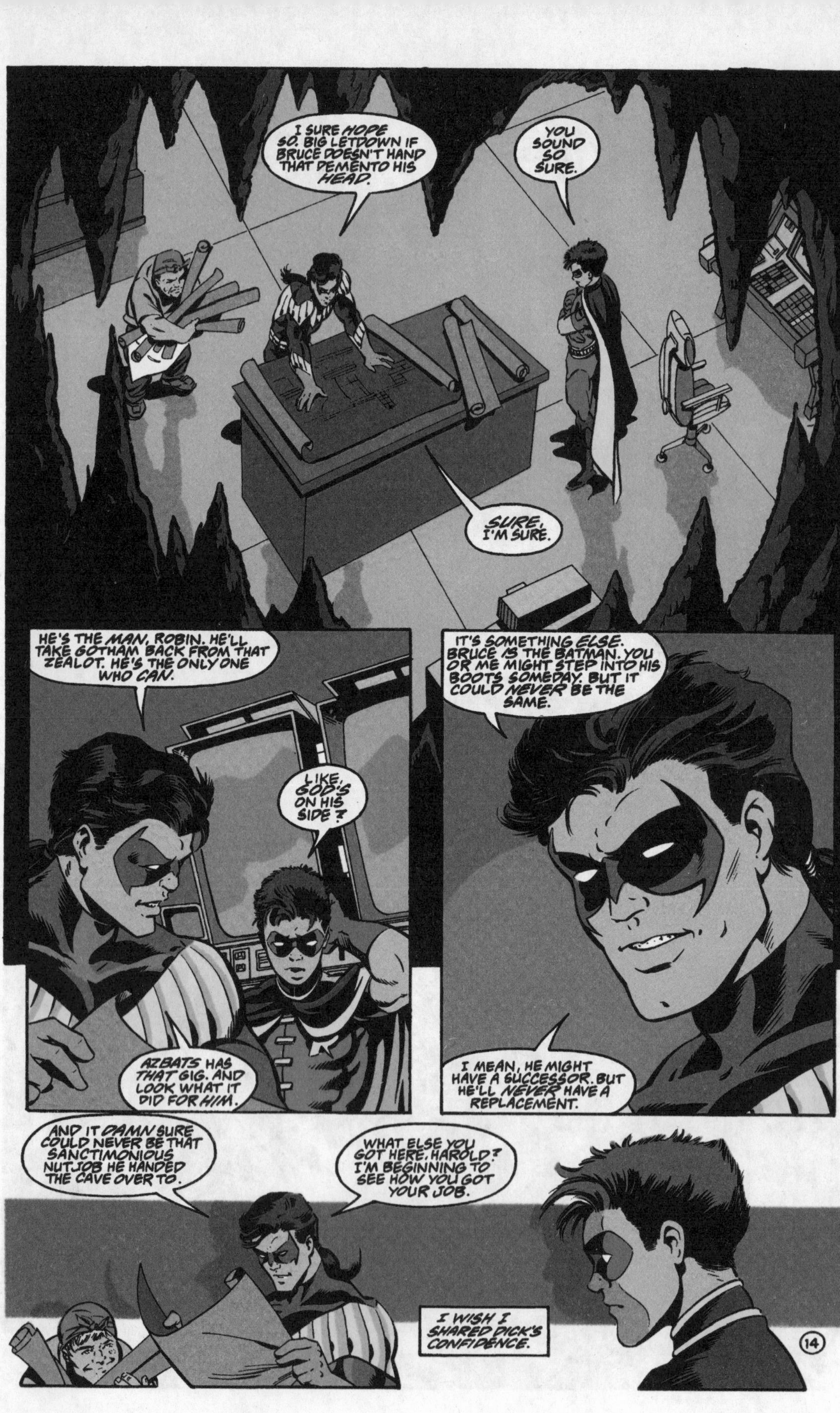
I SURE HOPE SO. BIG LETDOWN IF BRUCE DOESN'T HAND THAT DEMENTO HIS HEAD.
YOU SOUND SO SURE.
SURE. I'M SURE.
HE'S THE MAN, ROBIN. HE'LL TAKE GOTHAM BACK FROM THAT ZEALOT. HE'S THE ONLY ONE WHO CAN.
LIKE, GOD'S ON HIS SIDE?
AZBATS HAS THAT GIG. AND LOOK WHAT IT DID FOR HIM.
IT'S SOMETHING ELSE. BRUCE IS THE BATMAN. YOU OR ME MIGHT STEP INTO HIS BOOTS SOMEDAY. BUT IT COULD NEVER BE THE SAME.
I MEAN, HE MIGHT HAVE A SUCCESSOR. BUT HE'LL NEVER HAVE A REPLACEMENT.
AND IT DAMN SURE COULD NEVER BE THAT SANCTIMONIOUS NUTJOB HE HANDED THE CAVE OVER TO.
WHAT ELSE YOU GOT HERE, HAROLD? I'M BEGINNING TO SEE HOW YOU GOT YOUR JOB.
I WISH I SHARED DICK'S CONFIDENCE.
14

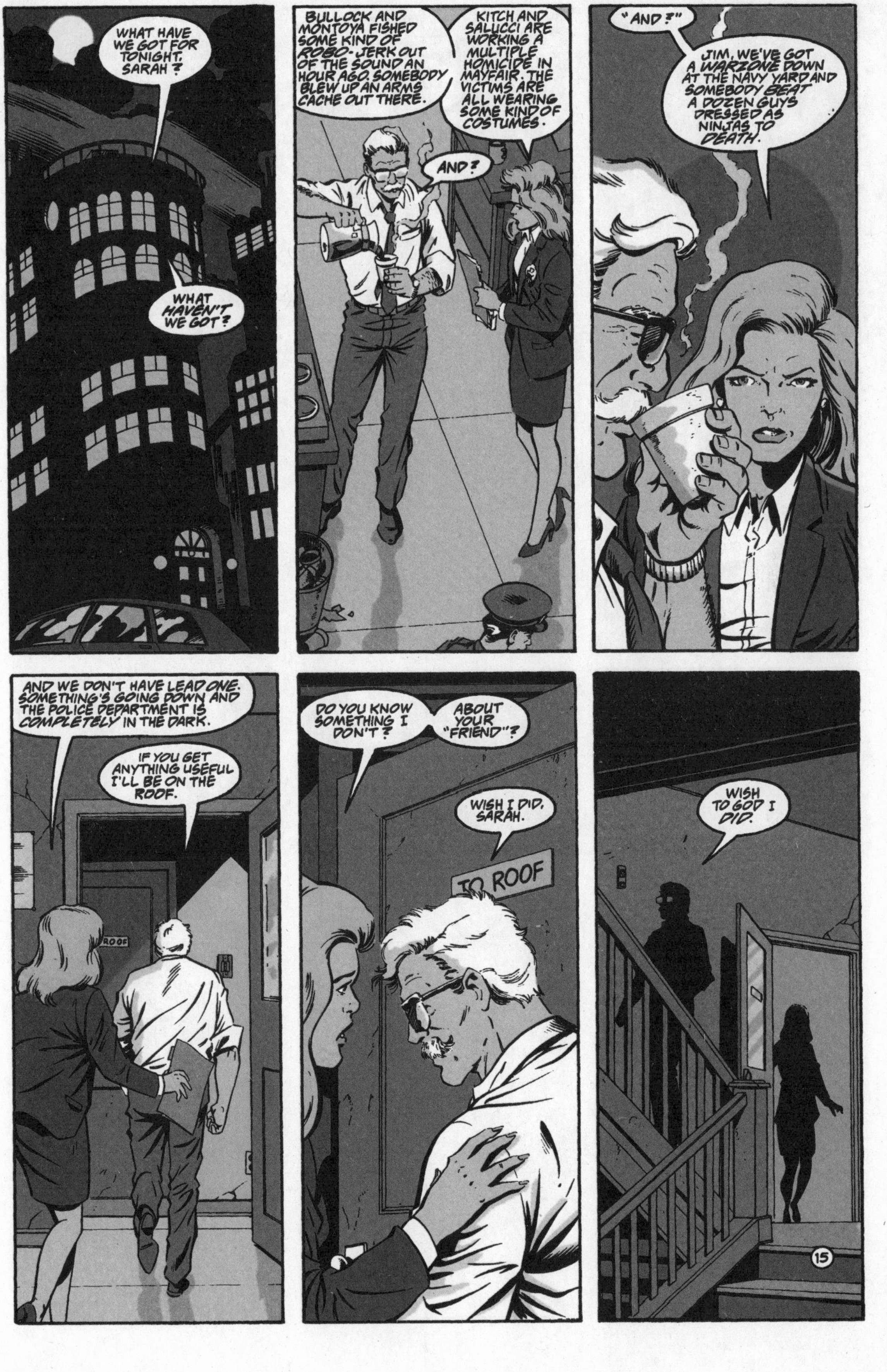
WHAT HAVE WE GOT FOR TONIGHT, SARAH?
WHAT HAVEN'T WE GOT?
BULLOCK AND MONTOYA FISHED SOME KIND OF ROBO-JERK OUT OF THE SOUND AN HOUR AGO. SOMEBODY BLEW UP AN ARMS CACHE OUT THERE.
AND?
KITCH AND SALUCCI ARE WORKING A MULTIPLE HOMICIDE IN MAYFAIR. THE VICTIMS ARE ALL WEARING SOME KIND OF COSTUMES.
"AND?"
JIM, WE'VE GOT A WARZONE DOWN AT THE NAVY YARD AND SOMEBODY BEAT A DOZEN GUYS DRESSED AS NINJAS TO DEATH.
AND WE DON'T HAVE LEAD ONE. SOMETHING'S GOING DOWN AND THE POLICE DEPARTMENT IS COMPLETELY IN THE DARK.
IF YOU GET ANYTHING USEFUL I'LL BE ON THE ROOF.
ROOF
DO YOU KNOW SOMETHING I DON'T?
ABOUT YOUR "FRIEND"?
WISH I DID, SARAH.
TO ROOF
WISH TO GOD I DID.
15

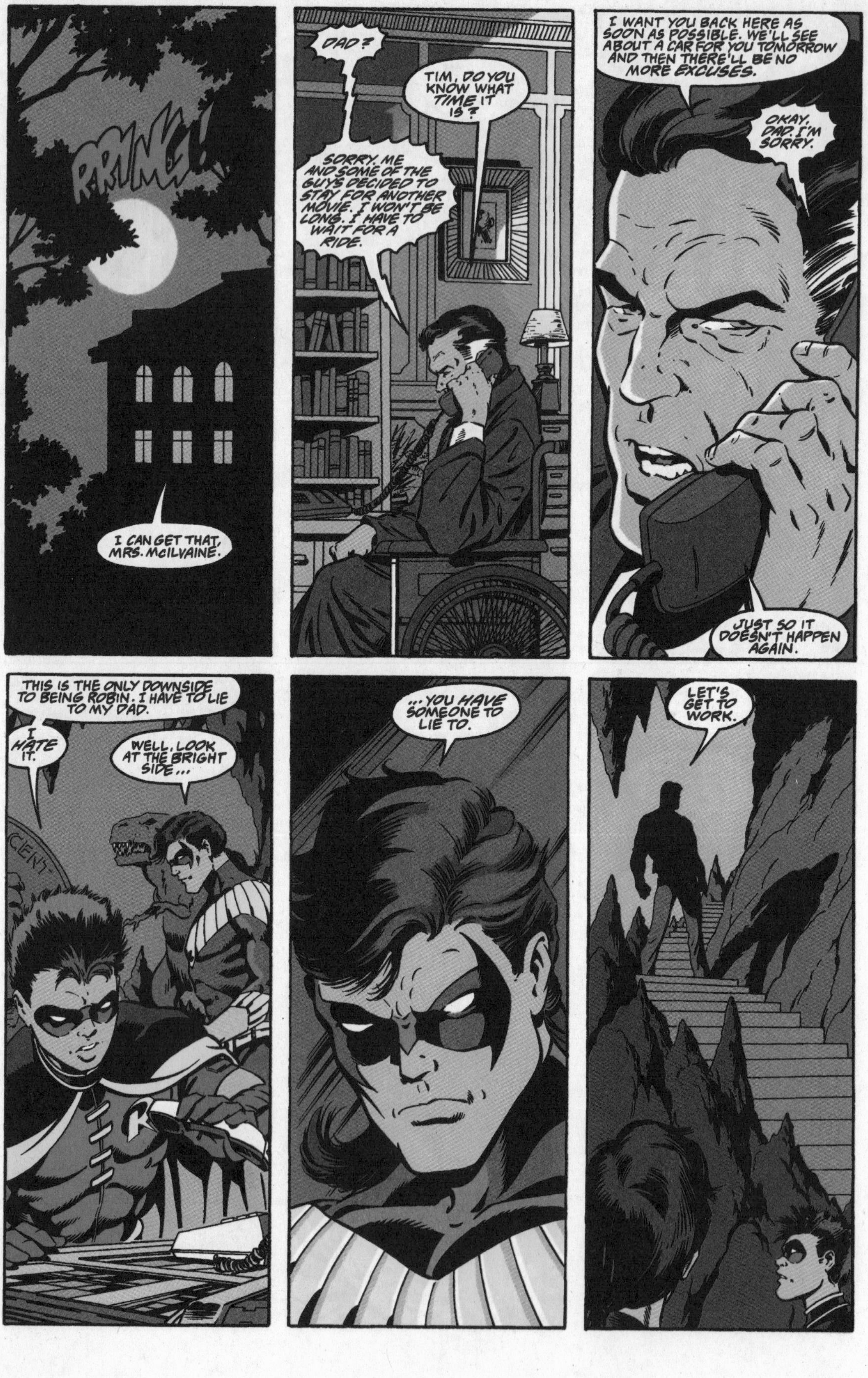
RRRING!
I CAN GET THAT, MRS. McILVAINE.
DAD?
TIM, DO YOU KNOW WHAT TIME IT IS?
SORRY. ME AND SOME OF THE GUYS DECIDED TO STAY FOR ANOTHER MOVIE. I WON'T BE LONG. I HAVE TO WAIT FOR A RIDE.
I WANT YOU BACK HERE AS SOON AS POSSIBLE. WE'LL SEE ABOUT A CAR FOR YOU TOMORROW AND THEN THERE'LL BE NO MORE EXCUSES.
OKAY, DAD. I'M SORRY.
JUST SO IT DOESN'T HAPPEN AGAIN.
THIS IS THE ONLY DOWNSIDE TO BEING ROBIN. I HAVE TO LIE TO MY DAD.
I HATE IT.
WELL, LOOK AT THE BRIGHT SIDE...
...YOU HAVE SOMEONE TO LIE TO.
LET'S GET TO WORK.

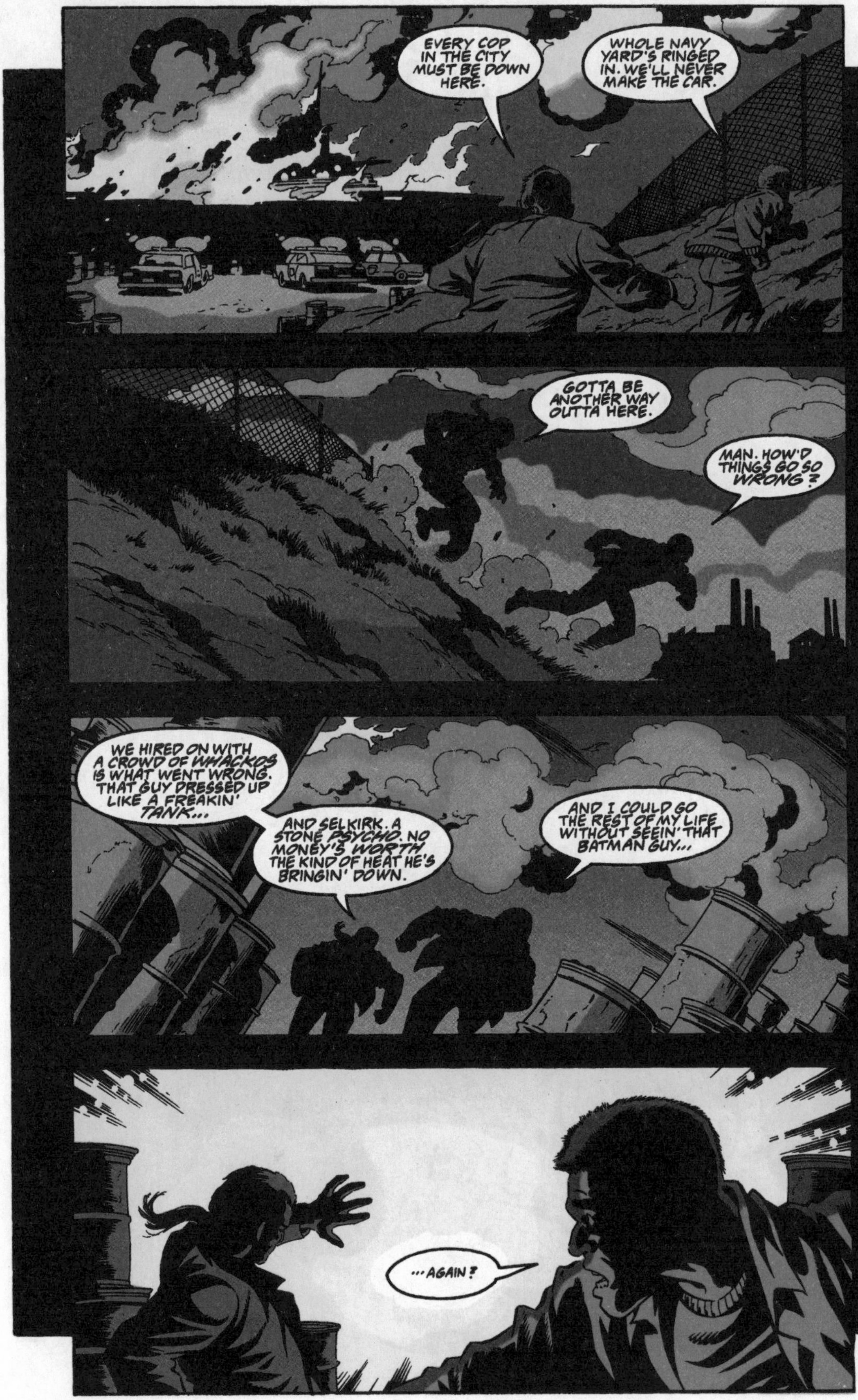
EVERY COP IN THE CITY MUST BE DOWN HERE.
WHOLE NAVY YARD'S RINGED IN. WE'LL NEVER MAKE THE CAR.
GOTTA BE ANOTHER WAY OUTTA HERE.
MAN. HOW'D THINGS GO SO WRONG?
WE HIRED ON WITH A CROWD OF WHACKOS IS WHAT WENT WRONG. THAT GUY DRESSED UP LIKE A FREAKIN' TANK...
AND SELKIRK. A STONE PSYCHO. NO MONEY'S WORTH THE KIND OF HEAT HE'S BRINGIN' DOWN.
AND I COULD GO THE REST OF MY LIFE WITHOUT SEEIN' THAT BATMAN GUY...
...AGAIN?
17

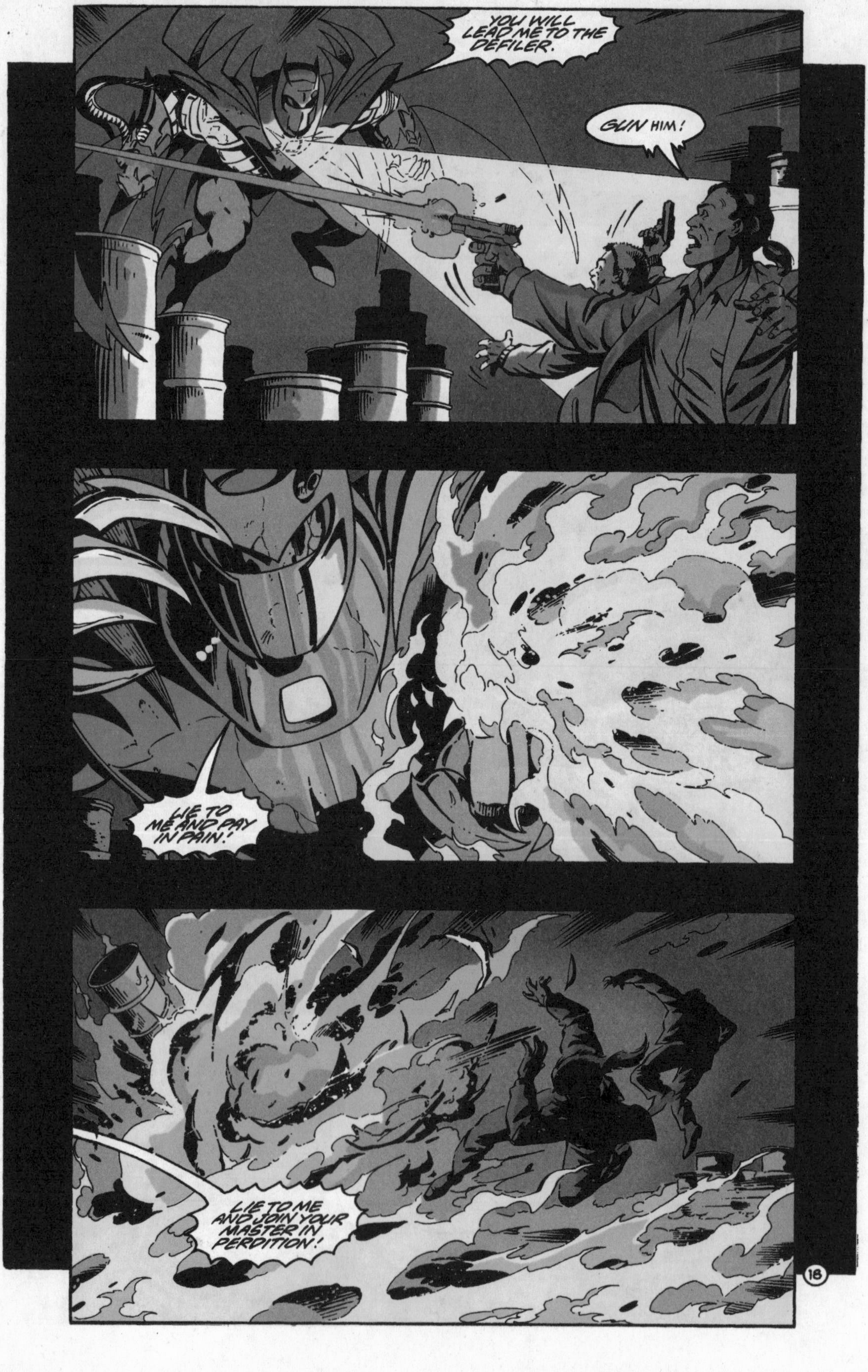
YOU WILL LEAD ME TO THE DEFILER.
GUN HIM!
LIE TO ME AND PAY IN PAIN!
LIE TO ME AND JOIN YOUR MASTER IN PERDITION!
18

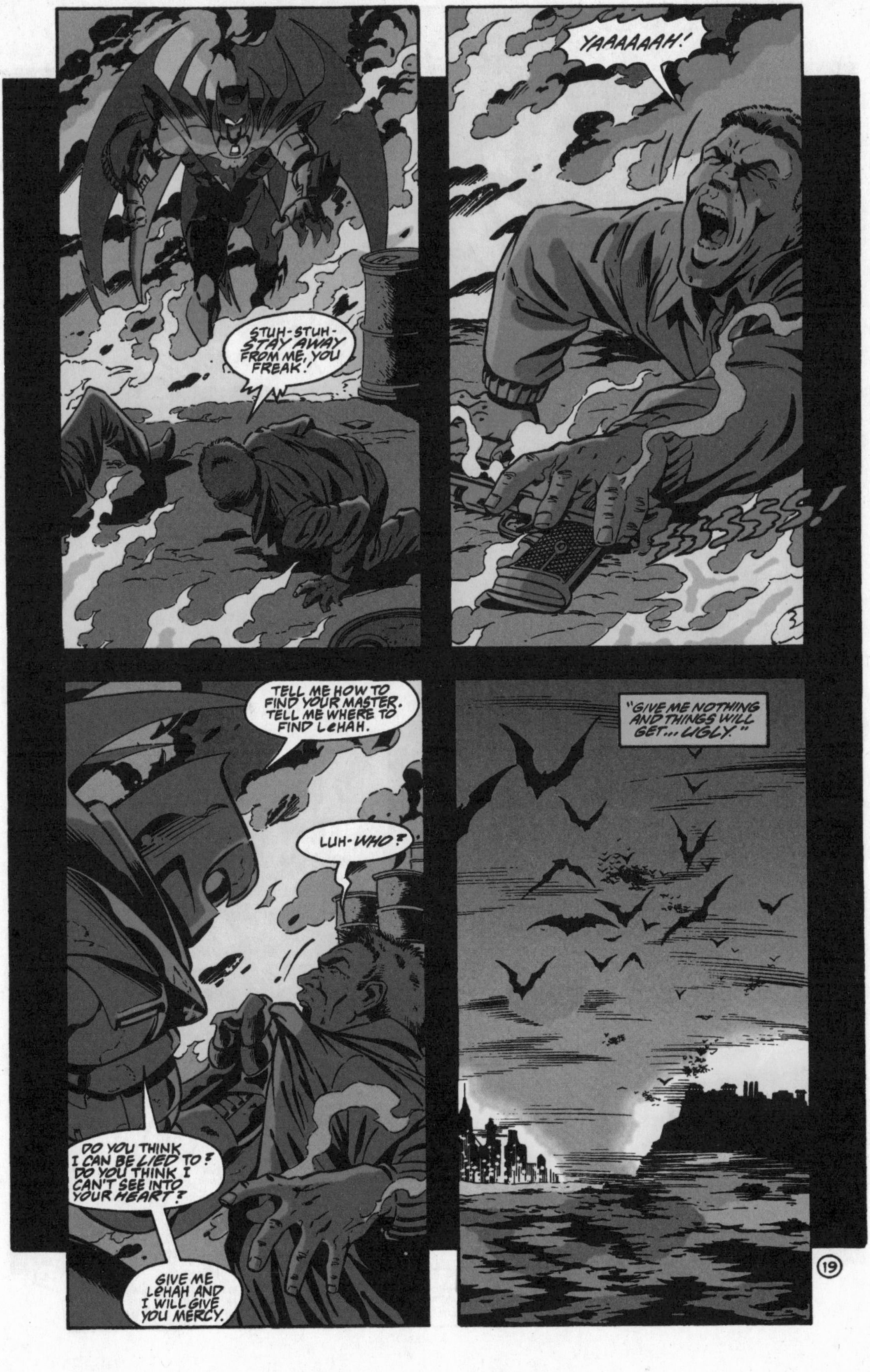
STUH-STUH-STAY AWAY FROM ME, YOU FREAK!
YAAAAAAH!
HSSSSSS!
TELL ME HOW TO FIND YOUR MASTER. TELL ME WHERE TO FIND LEHAH.
LUH-WHO?
DO YOU THINK I CAN BE LIED TO? DO YOU THINK I CAN'T SEE INTO YOUR HEART?
GIVE ME LEHAH AND I WILL GIVE YOU MERCY.
"GIVE ME NOTHING AND THINGS WILL GET... UGLY."
19

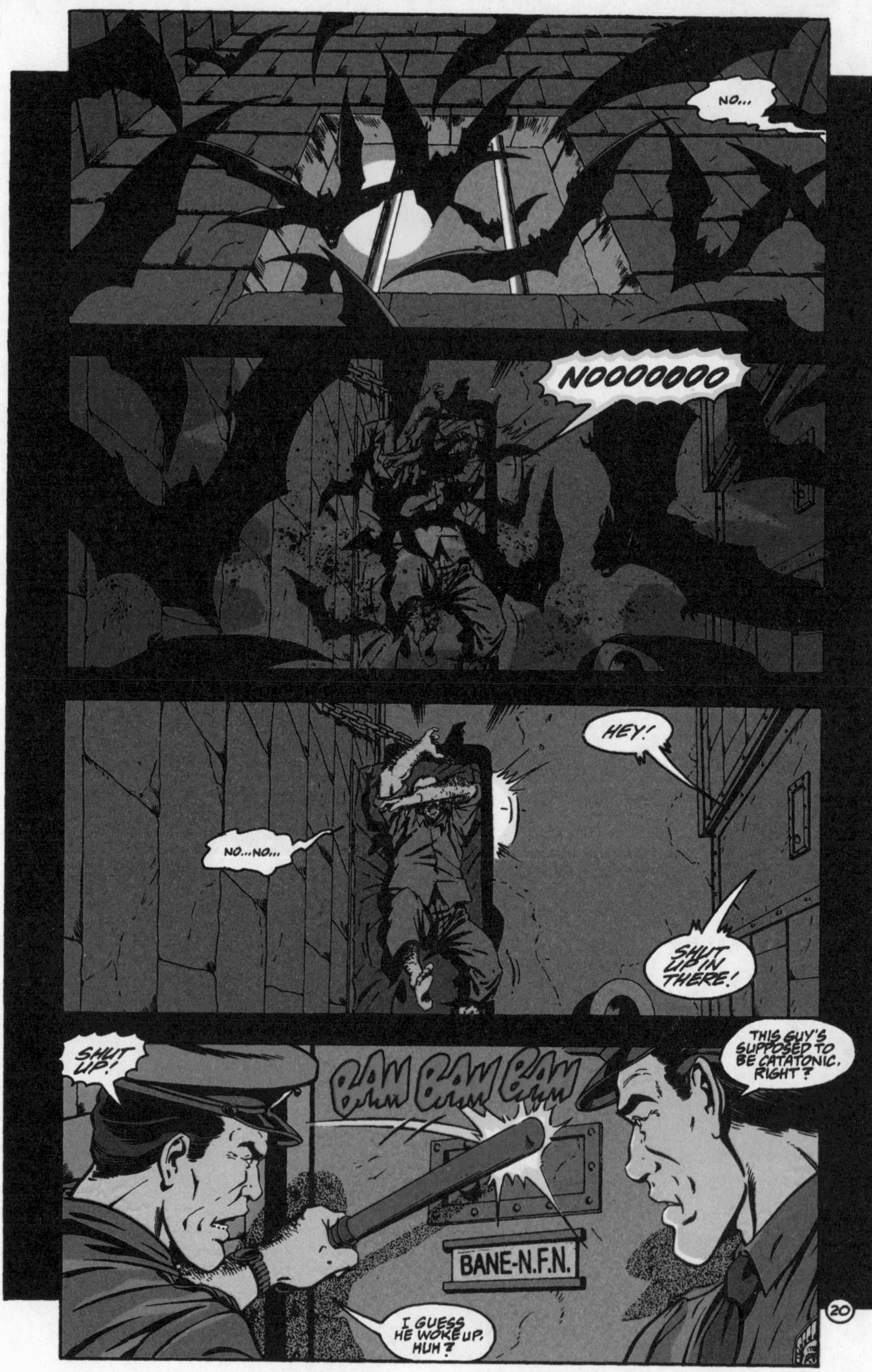
NO...
NOOOOOOO
HEY!
NO...NO...
SHUT UP IN THERE!
SHUT UP!
BAM BAM BAM
THIS GUY'S SUPPOSED TO BE CATATONIC, RIGHT?
BANE-N.F.N.
I GUESS HE WOKE UP, HUH?
20

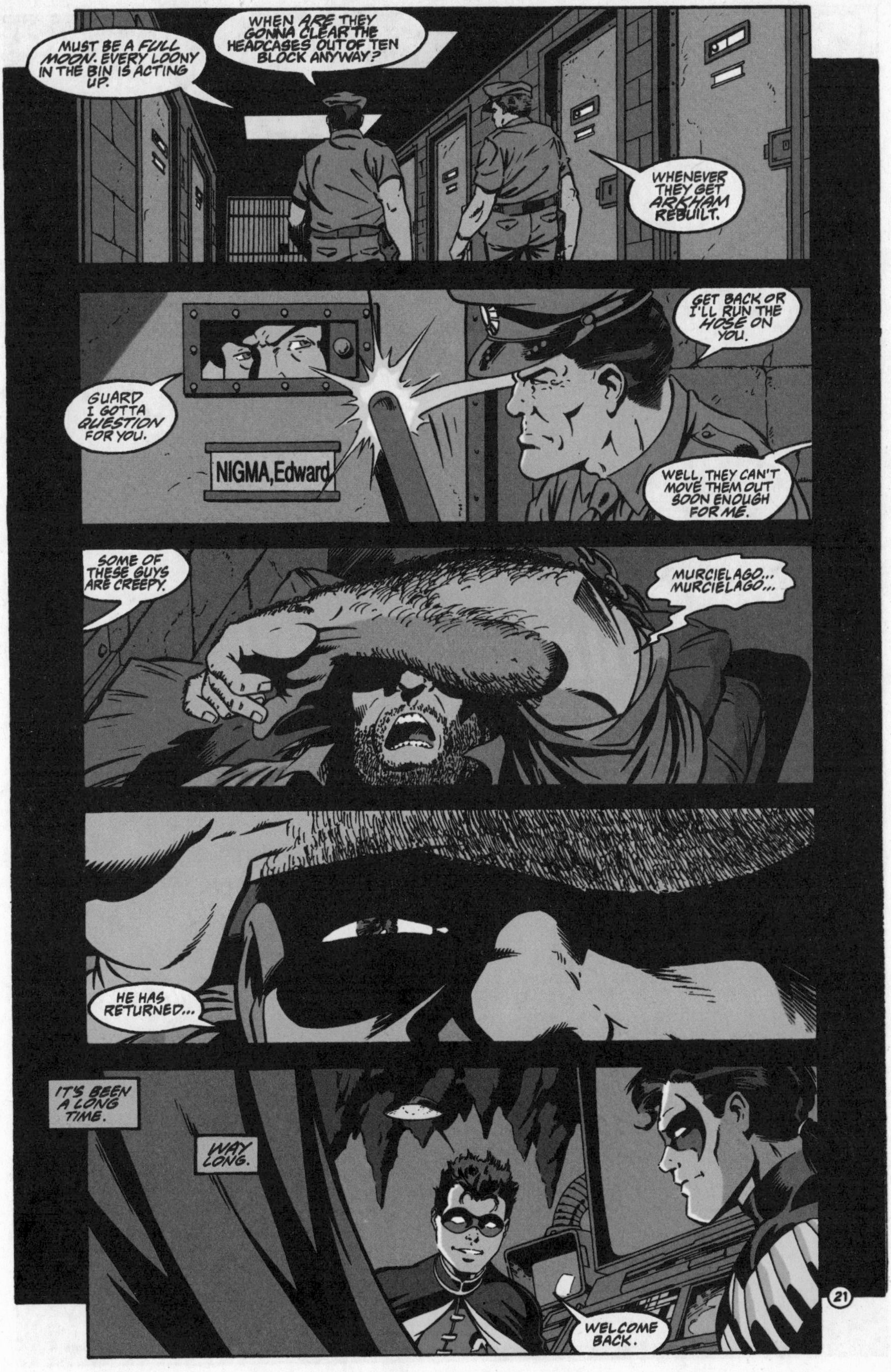
MUST BE A FULL MOON. EVERY LOONY IN THE BIN IS ACTING UP.
WHEN ARE THEY GONNA CLEAR THE HEADCASES OUT OF TEN BLOCK ANYWAY?
WHENEVER THEY GET ARKHAM REBUILT.
GUARD I GOTTA QUESTION FOR YOU.
NIGMA, Edward
GET BACK OR I'LL RUN THE HOSE ON YOU.
WELL, THEY CAN'T MOVE THEM OUT SOON ENOUGH FOR ME.
SOME OF THESE GUYS ARE CREEPY.
MURCIELAGO... MURCIELAGO...
HE HAS RETURNED...
IT'S BEEN A LONG TIME.
WAY LONG.
WELCOME BACK.
21

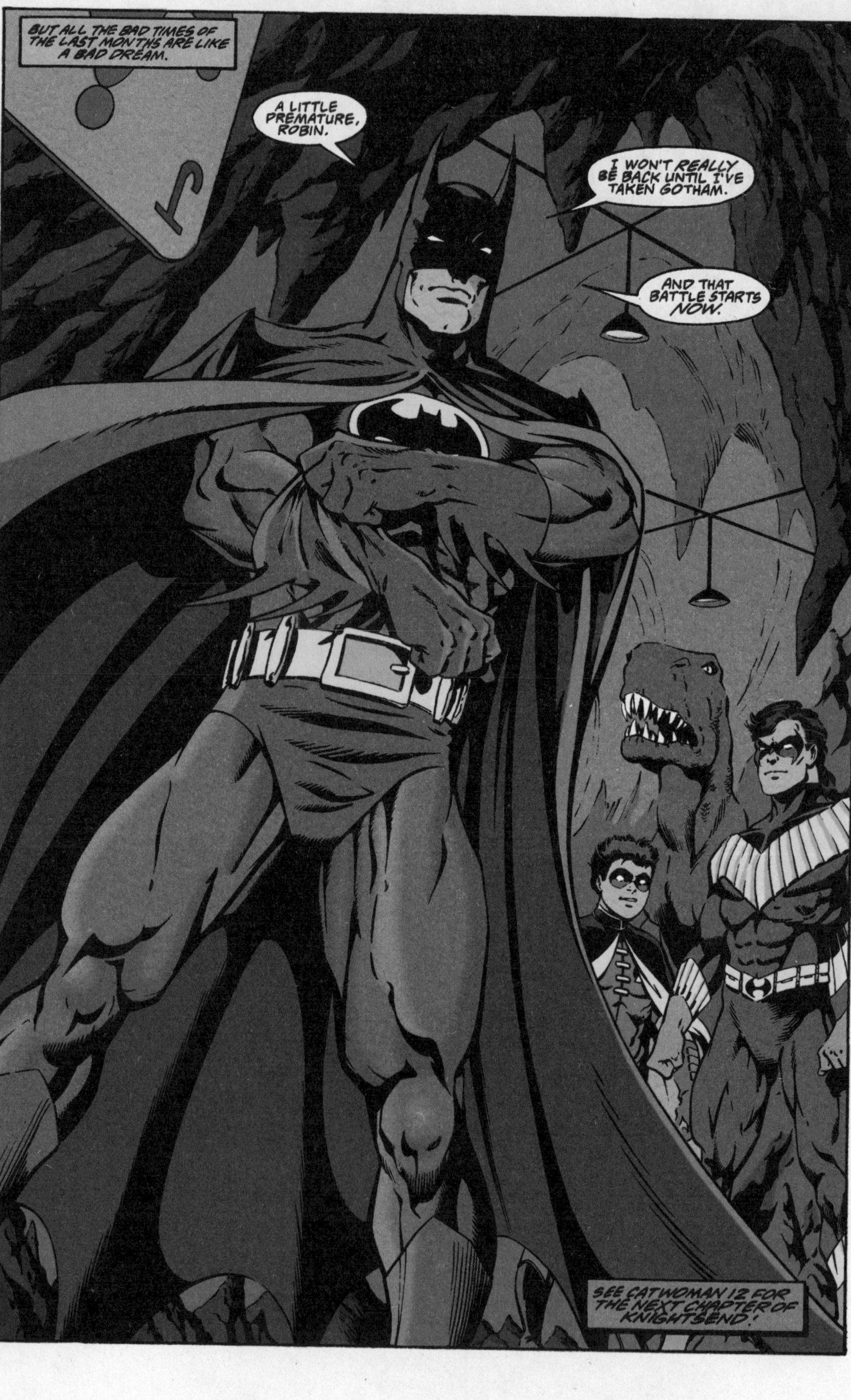
BUT ALL THE BAD TIMES OF THE LAST MONTHS ARE LIKE A BAD DREAM.
A LITTLE PREMATURE, ROBIN.
I WON'T REALLY BE BACK UNTIL I'VE TAKEN GOTHAM.
AND THAT BATTLE STARTS NOW.
SEE CATWOMAN 12 FOR THE NEXT CHAPTER OF KNIGHTSEND!

Cover art by JIM BALENT

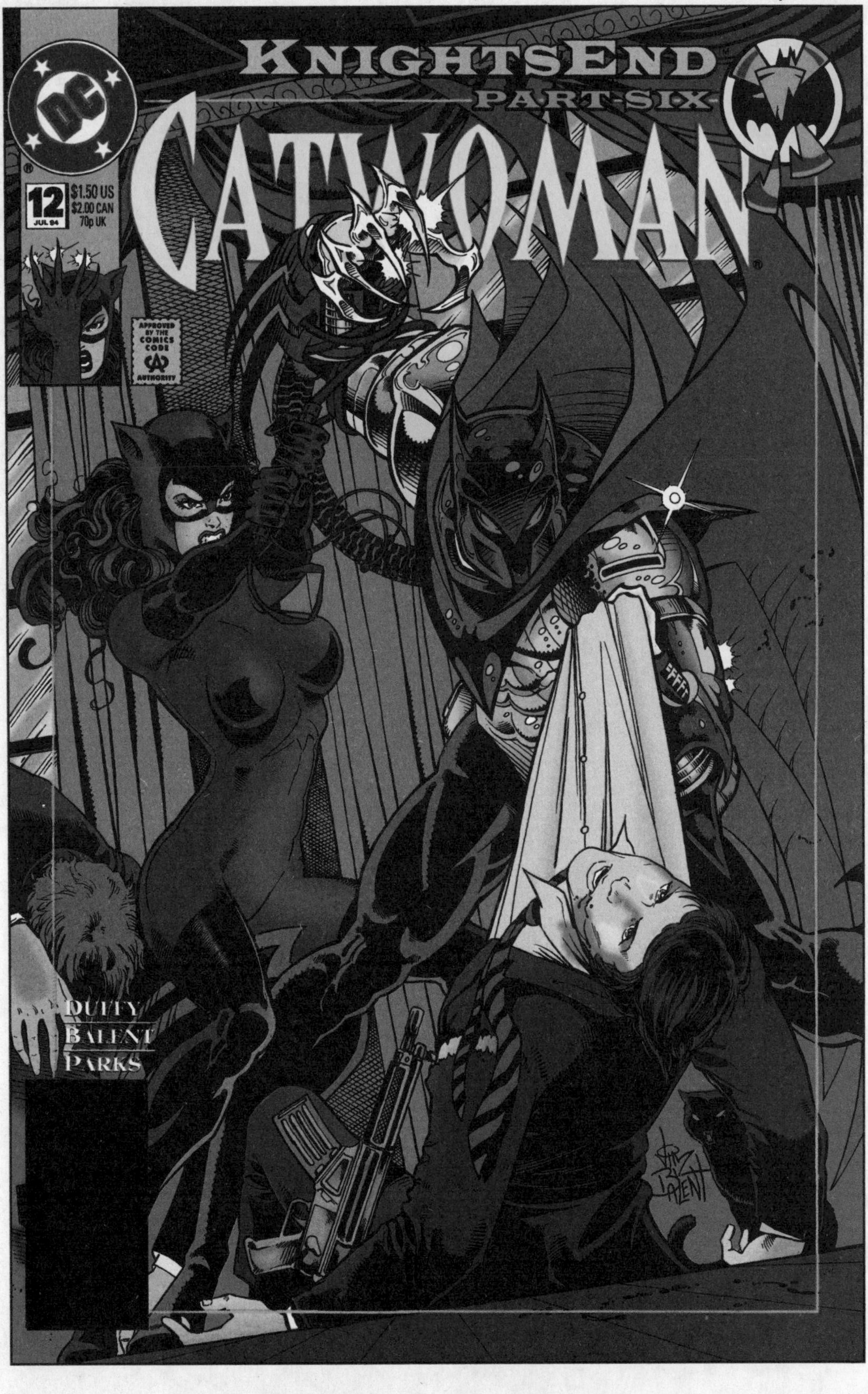
KNIGHTSEND
PART SIX
CATWOMAN
12
JUL 94
$1.50 US
$2.00 CAN
70p UK
APPROVED BY THE COMICS CODE AUTHORITY
DUFFY
BALENT
PARKS

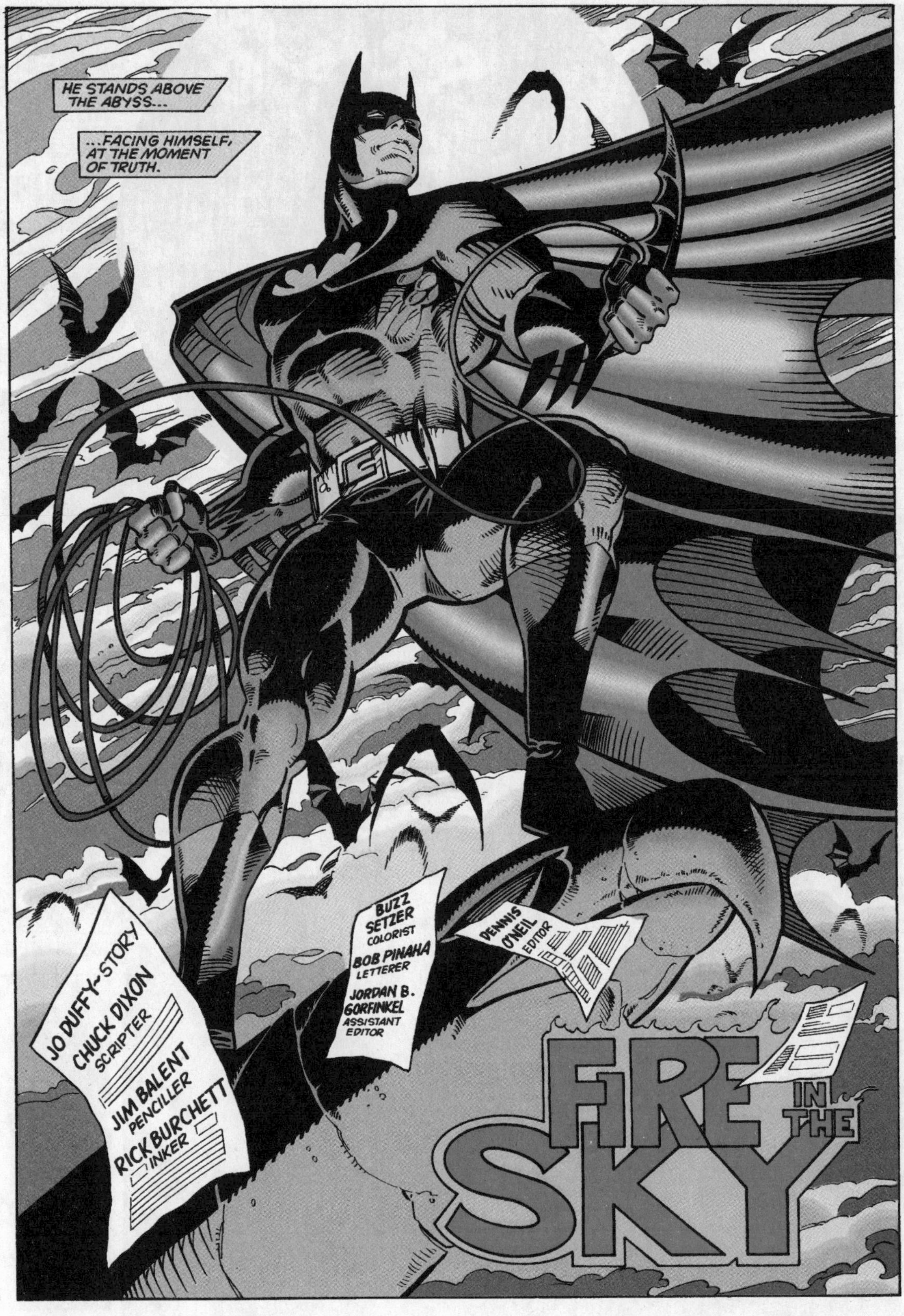

HE STANDS ABOVE THE ABYSS...
...FACING HIMSELF, AT THE MOMENT OF TRUTH.
JO DUFFY-STORY
CHUCK DIXON SCRIPTER
JIM BALENT PENCILLER
RICK BURCHETT INKER
BUZZ SETZER COLORIST
BOB PINAHA LETTERER
JORDAN B. GORFINKEL ASSISTANT EDITOR
DENNIS O'NEIL EDITOR
FIRE IN THE SKY

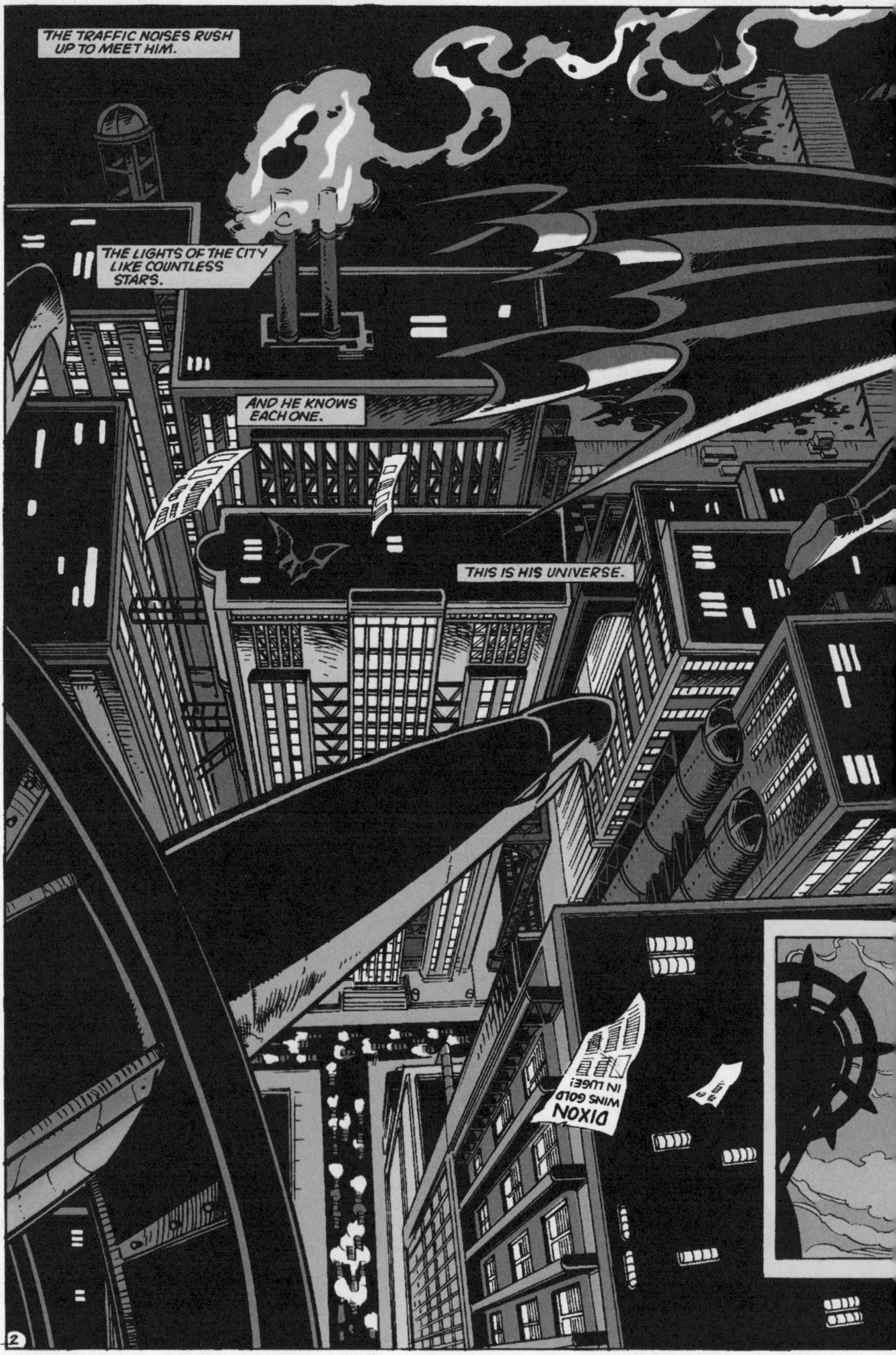
THE TRAFFIC NOISES RUSH UP TO MEET HIM.
THE LIGHTS OF THE CITY LIKE COUNTLESS STARS.
AND HE KNOWS EACH ONE.
THIS IS HIS UNIVERSE.
DIXON WINS GOLD IN LUGE!
2

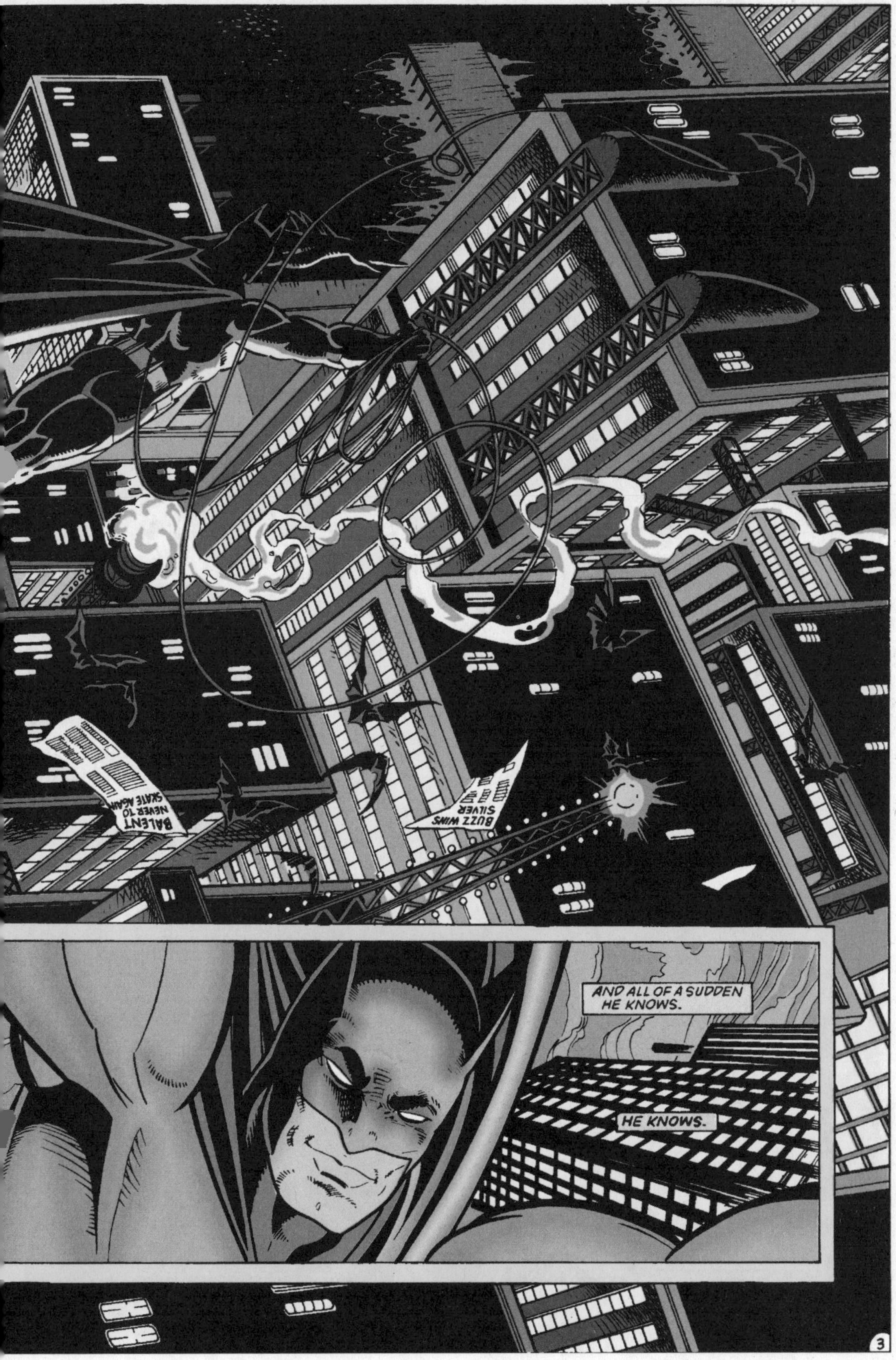
BALENT NEVER TO SKATE AGAIN
BUZZ WINS SILVER
AND ALL OF A SUDDEN HE KNOWS.
HE KNOWS.
3

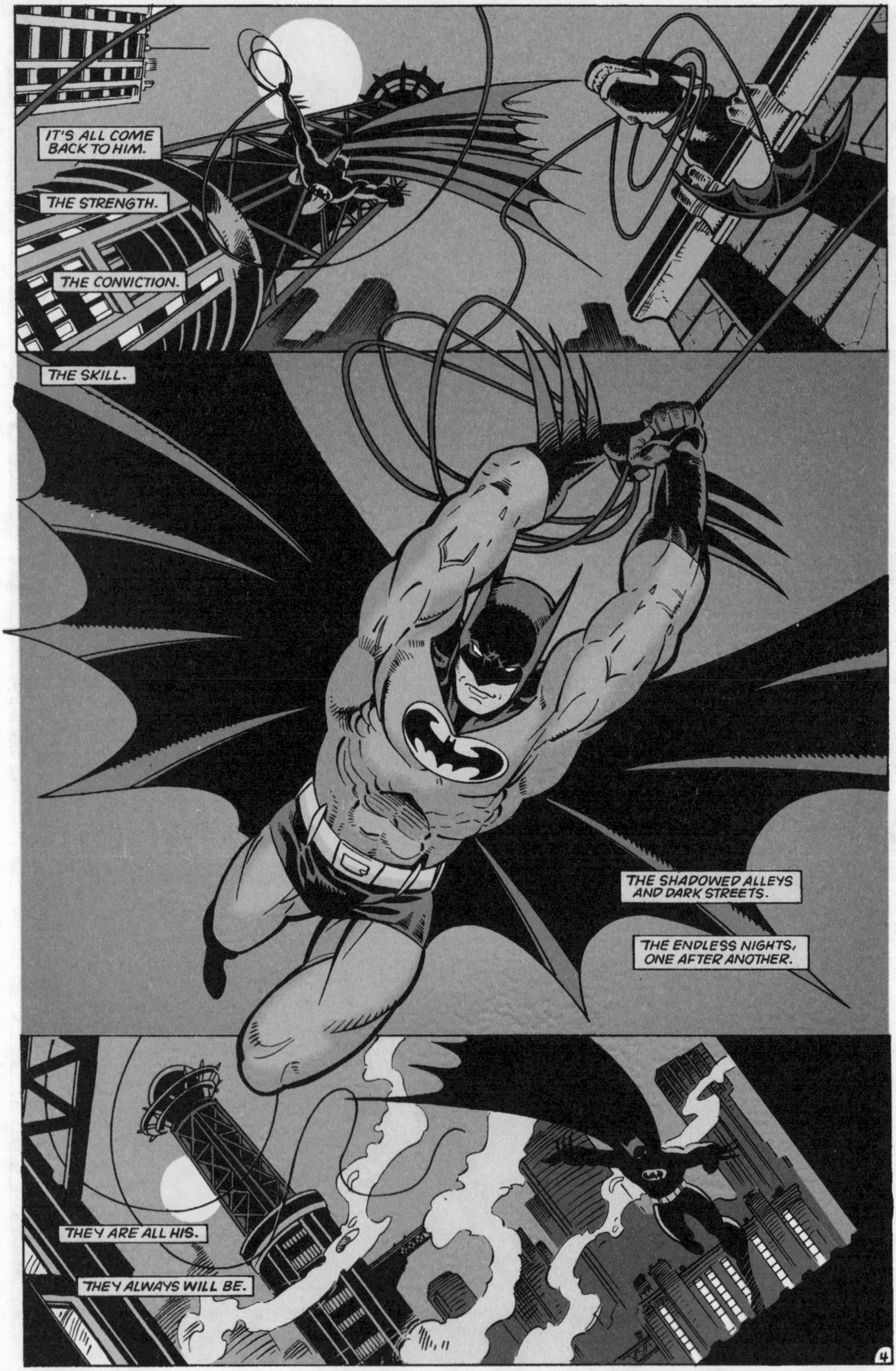
IT'S ALL COME BACK TO HIM.
THE STRENGTH.
THE CONVICTION.
THE SKILL.
THE SHADOWED ALLEYS AND DARK STREETS.
THE ENDLESS NIGHTS, ONE AFTER ANOTHER.
THEY ARE ALL HIS.
THEY ALWAYS WILL BE.
4

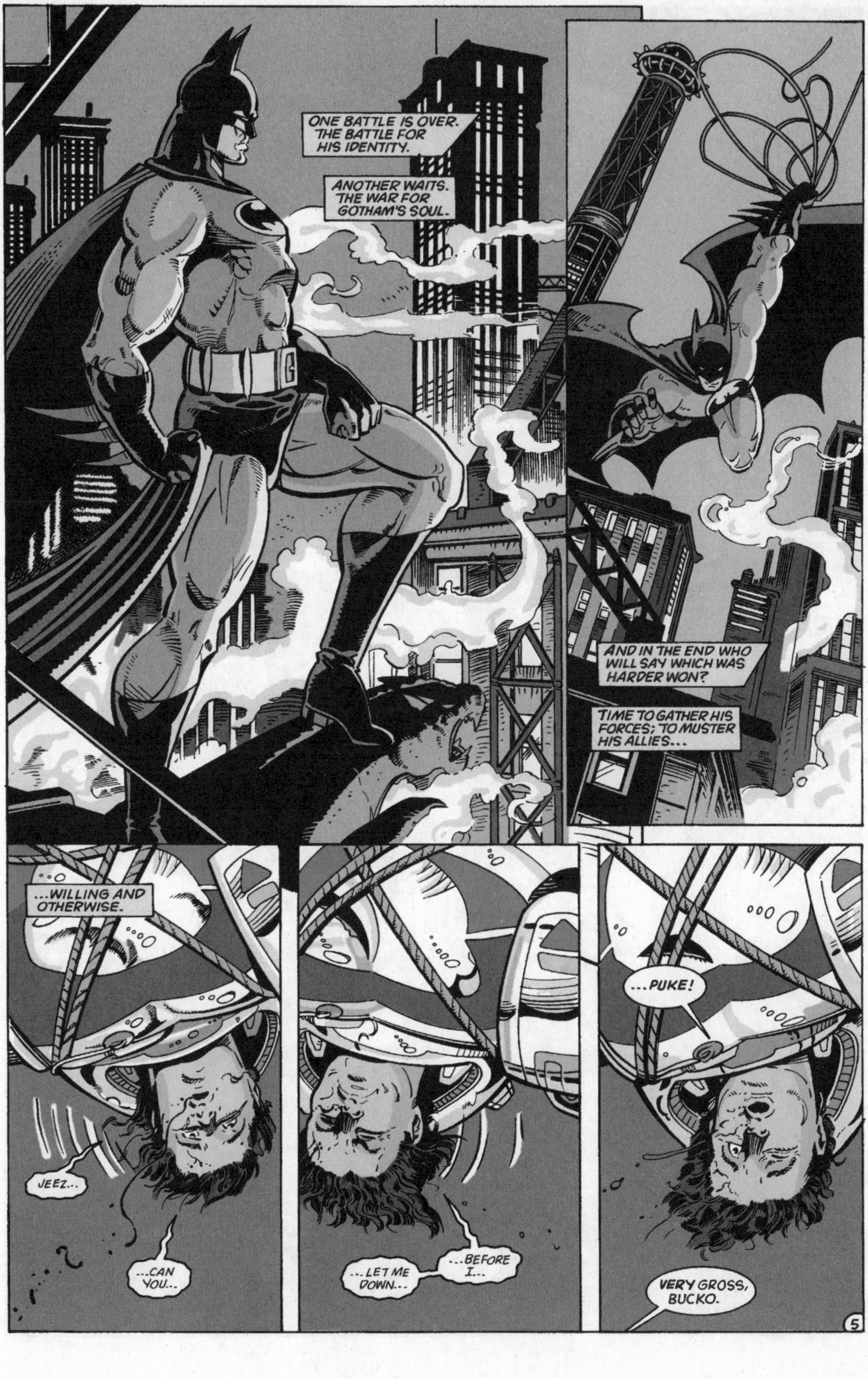
ONE BATTLE IS OVER. THE BATTLE FOR HIS IDENTITY.
ANOTHER WAITS. THE WAR FOR GOTHAM'S SOUL.
AND IN THE END WHO WILL SAY WHICH WAS HARDER WON?
TIME TO GATHER HIS FORCES; TO MUSTER HIS ALLIES...
...WILLING AND OTHERWISE.
JEEZ...
...CAN YOU...
...LET ME DOWN...
...BEFORE I...
...PUKE!
VERY GROSS, BUCKO.
5

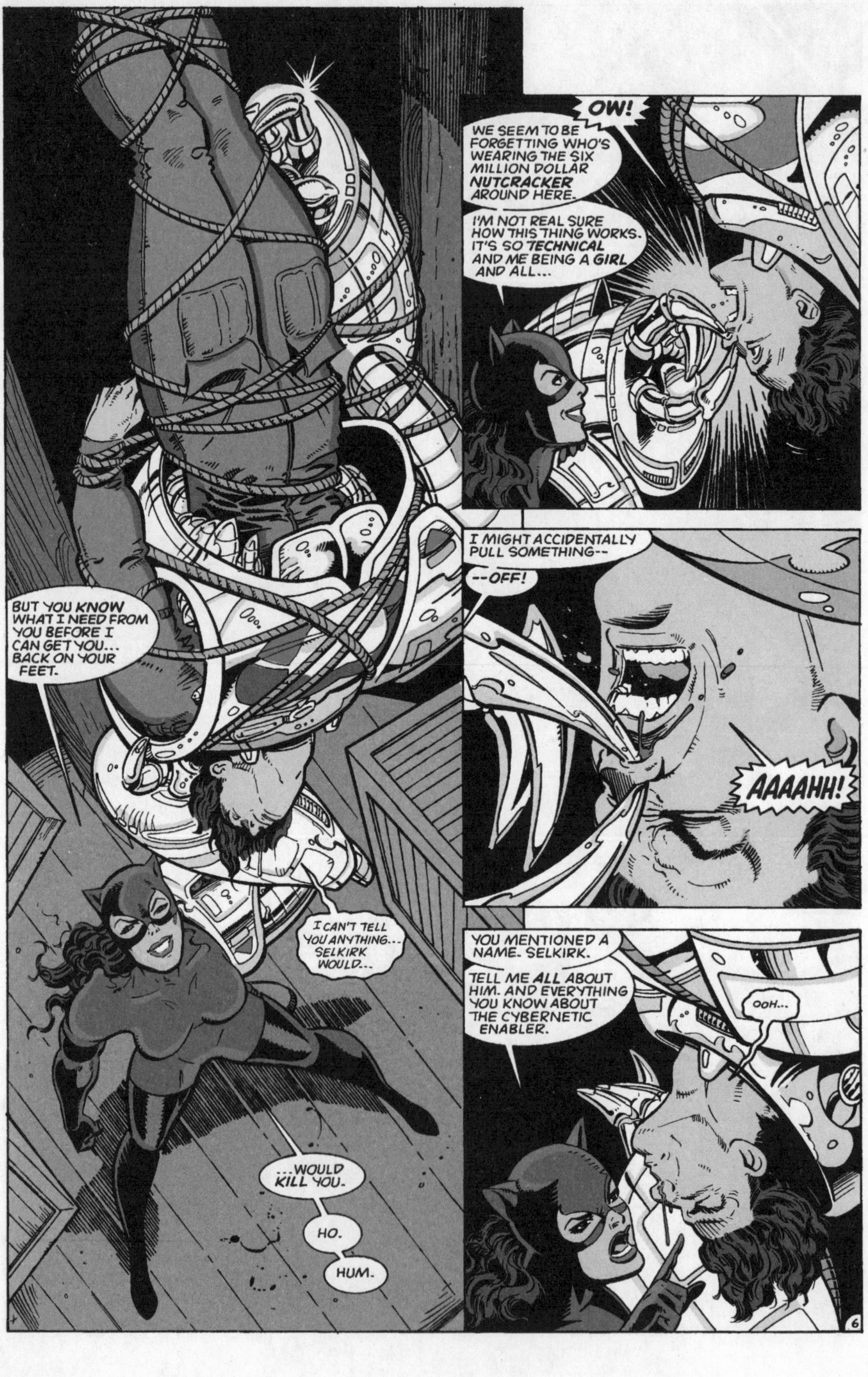

BUT YOU KNOW WHAT I NEED FROM YOU BEFORE I CAN GET YOU... BACK ON YOUR FEET.
I CAN'T TELL YOU ANYTHING... SELKIRK WOULD...
...WOULD KILL YOU.
HO.
HUM.
OW!
WE SEEM TO BE FORGETTING WHO'S WEARING THE SIX MILLION DOLLAR NUTCRACKER AROUND HERE.
I'M NOT REAL SURE HOW THIS THING WORKS. IT'S SO TECHNICAL AND ME BEING A GIRL AND ALL...
I MIGHT ACCIDENTALLY PULL SOMETHING--
--OFF!
AAAAHH!
YOU MENTIONED A NAME. SELKIRK.
TELL ME ALL ABOUT HIM. AND EVERYTHING YOU KNOW ABOUT THE CYBERNETIC ENABLER.
OOH...
6

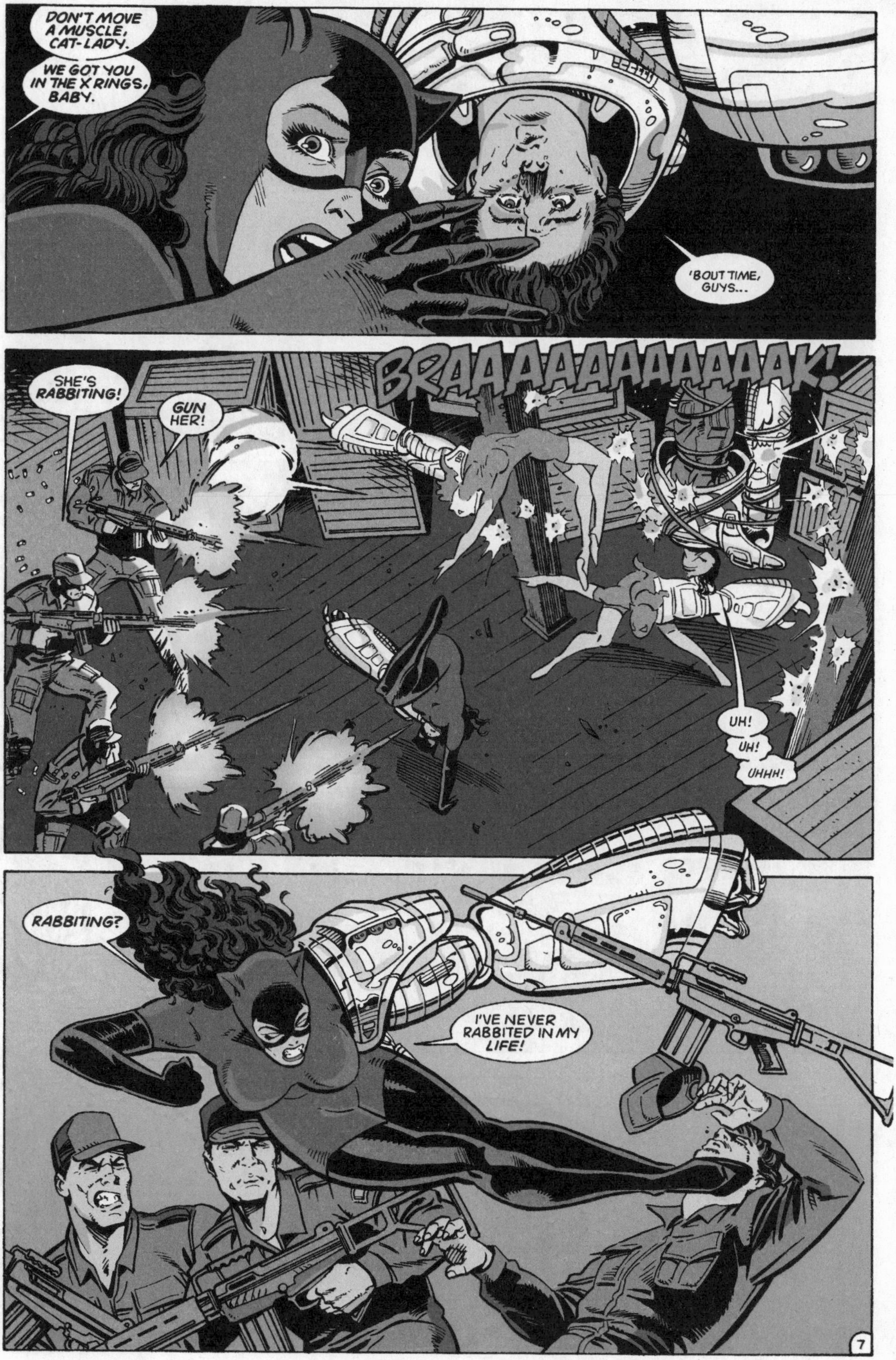
DON'T MOVE A MUSCLE, CAT-LADY.
WE GOT YOU IN THE X RINGS, BABY.
'BOUT TIME, GUYS...
BRAAAAAAAAAAAK!
SHE'S RABBITING!
GUN HER!
UH!
UH!
UHHH!
RABBITING?
I'VE NEVER RABBITED IN MY LIFE!
7

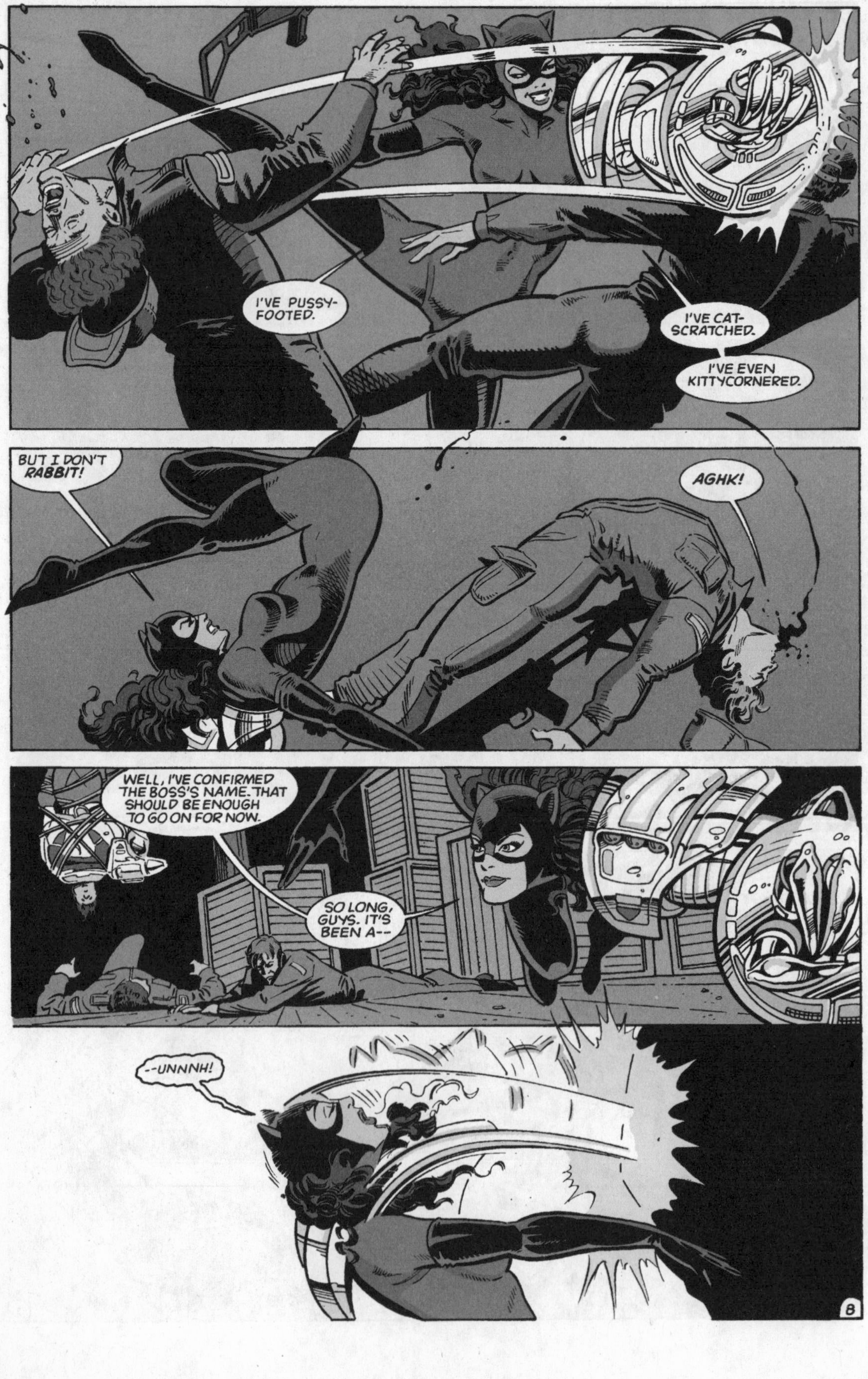

I'VE PUSSY-FOOTED.
I'VE CAT-SCRATCHED.
I'VE EVEN KITTYCORNERED.
BUT I DON'T RABBIT!
AGHK!
WELL, I'VE CONFIRMED THE BOSS'S NAME. THAT SHOULD BE ENOUGH TO GO ON FOR NOW.
SO LONG, GUYS. IT'S BEEN A--
--UNNNH!
8

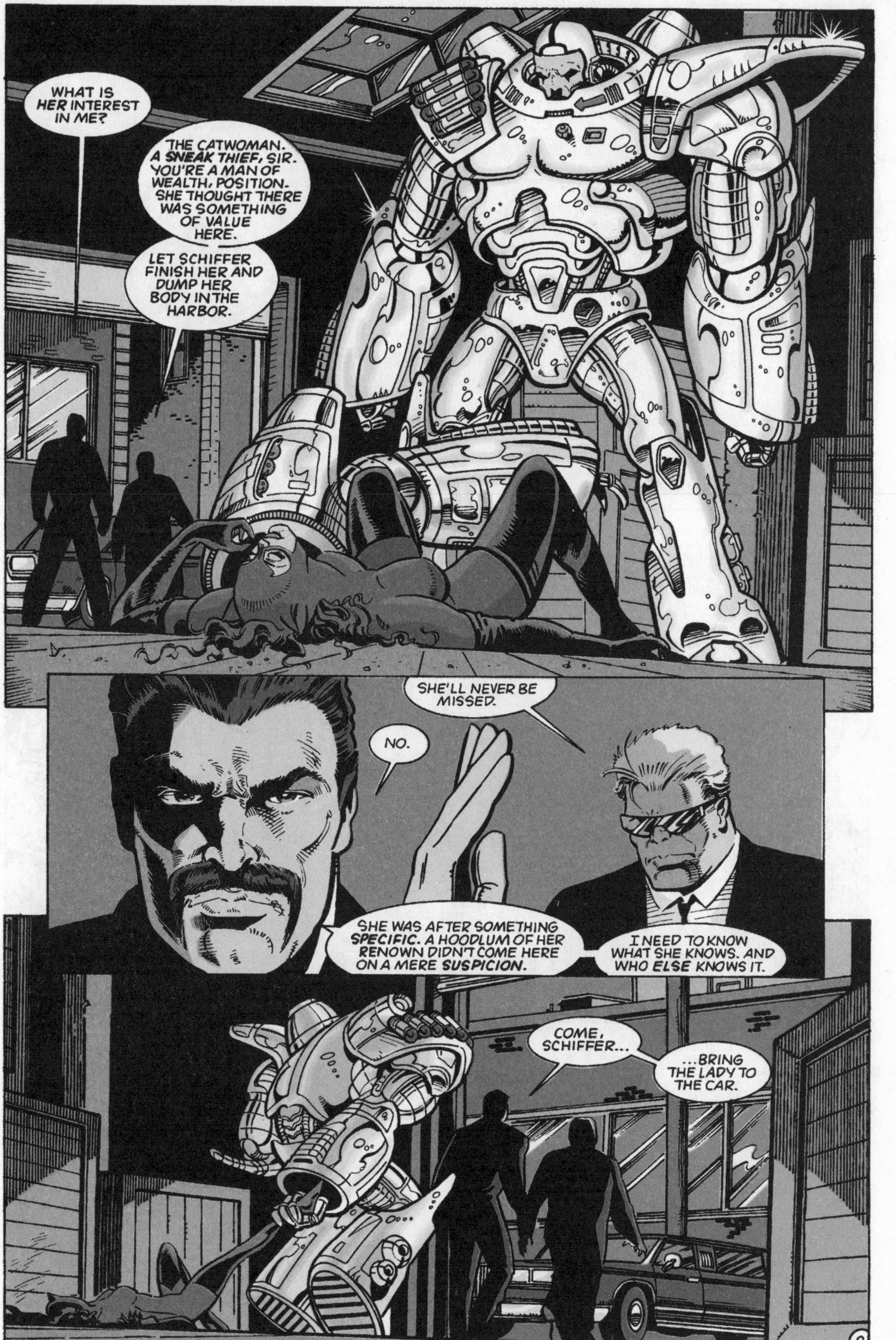

WHAT IS HER INTEREST IN ME?
THE CATWOMAN. A SNEAK THIEF, SIR. YOU'RE A MAN OF WEALTH, POSITION. SHE THOUGHT THERE WAS SOMETHING OF VALUE HERE.
LET SCHIFFER FINISH HER AND DUMP HER BODY IN THE HARBOR.
SHE'LL NEVER BE MISSED.
NO.
SHE WAS AFTER SOMETHING SPECIFIC. A HOODLUM OF HER RENOWN DIDN'T COME HERE ON A MERE SUSPICION.
I NEED TO KNOW WHAT SHE KNOWS. AND WHO ELSE KNOWS IT.
COME, SCHIFFER...
...BRING THE LADY TO THE CAR.
9

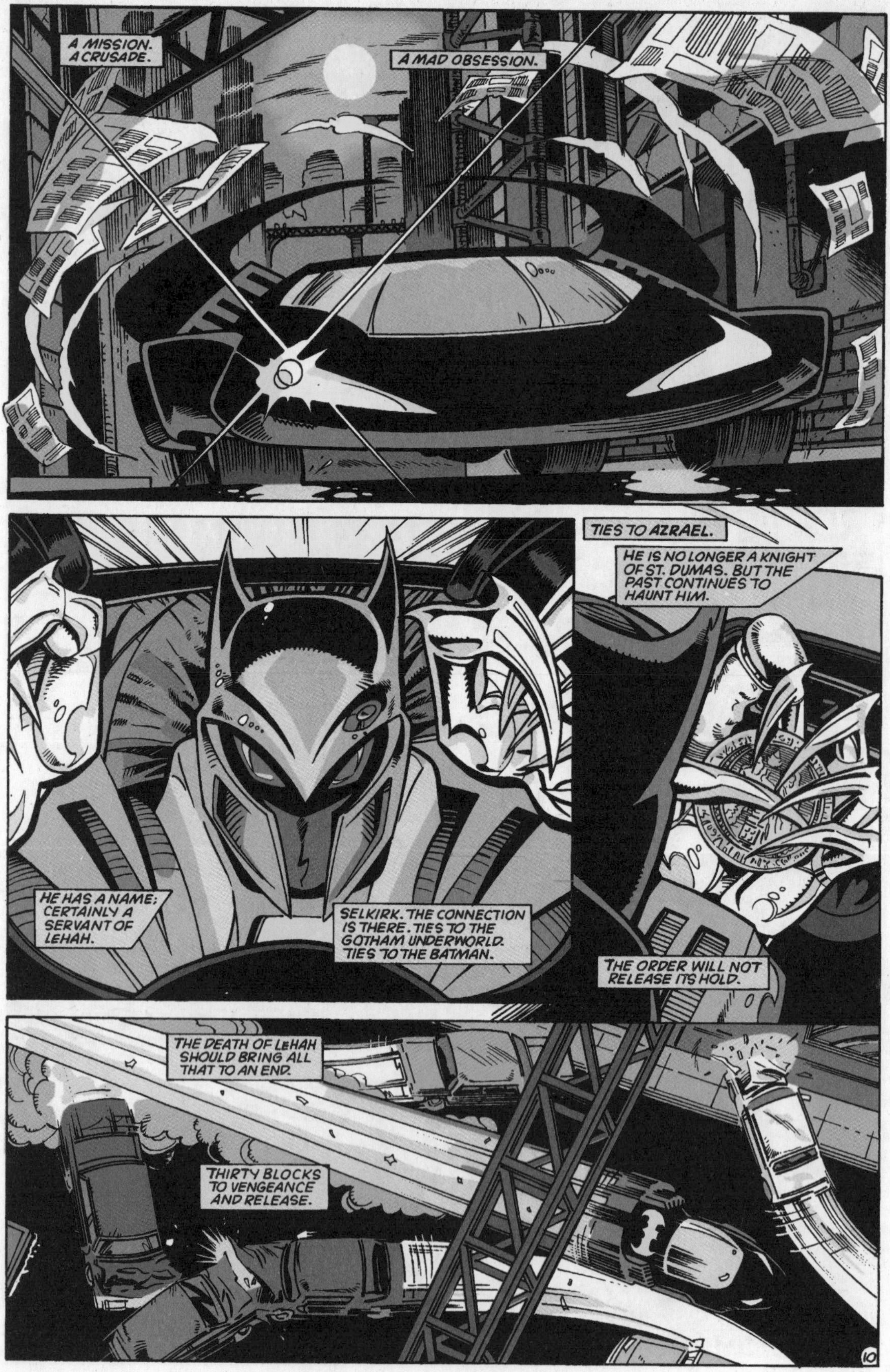
A MISSION. A CRUSADE.
A MAD OBSESSION.
TIES TO AZRAEL.
HE IS NO LONGER A KNIGHT OF ST. DUMAS. BUT THE PAST CONTINUES TO HAUNT HIM.
HE HAS A NAME: CERTAINLY A SERVANT OF LEHAH.
SELKIRK. THE CONNECTION IS THERE. TIES TO THE GOTHAM UNDERWORLD. TIES TO THE BATMAN.
THE ORDER WILL NOT RELEASE ITS HOLD.
THE DEATH OF LEHAH SHOULD BRING ALL THAT TO AN END.
THIRTY BLOCKS TO VENGEANCE AND RELEASE.
10

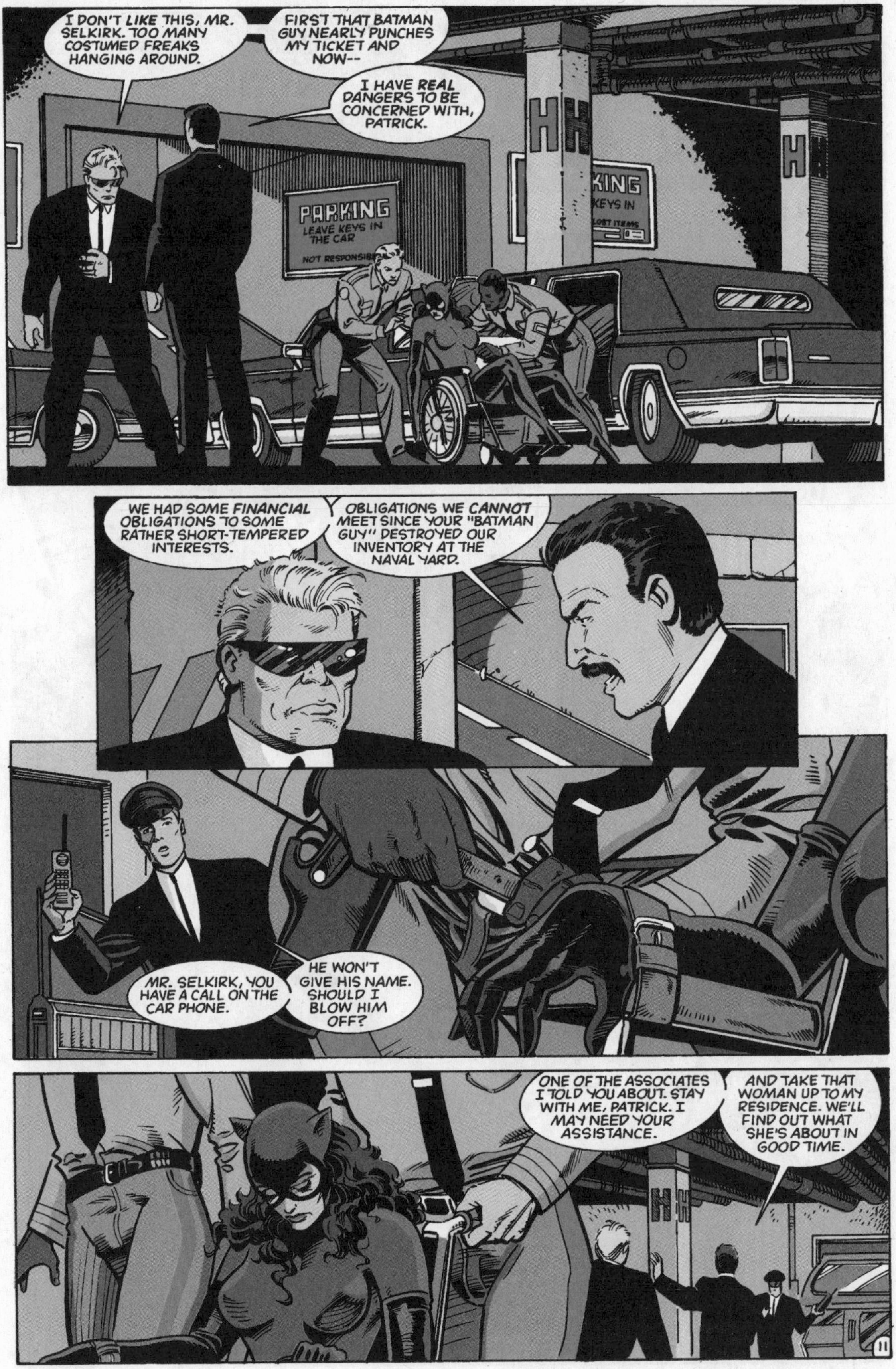
I DON'T LIKE THIS, MR. SELKIRK. TOO MANY COSTUMED FREAKS HANGING AROUND.
FIRST THAT BATMAN GUY NEARLY PUNCHES MY TICKET AND NOW--
I HAVE REAL DANGERS TO BE CONCERNED WITH, PATRICK.
PARKING
LEAVE KEYS IN THE CAR
NOT RESPONSIBLE
WE HAD SOME FINANCIAL OBLIGATIONS TO SOME RATHER SHORT-TEMPERED INTERESTS.
OBLIGATIONS WE CANNOT MEET SINCE YOUR "BATMAN GUY" DESTROYED OUR INVENTORY AT THE NAVAL YARD.
MR. SELKIRK, YOU HAVE A CALL ON THE CAR PHONE.
HE WON'T GIVE HIS NAME. SHOULD I BLOW HIM OFF?
ONE OF THE ASSOCIATES I TOLD YOU ABOUT. STAY WITH ME, PATRICK. I MAY NEED YOUR ASSISTANCE.
AND TAKE THAT WOMAN UP TO MY RESIDENCE. WE'LL FIND OUT WHAT SHE'S ABOUT IN GOOD TIME.
11

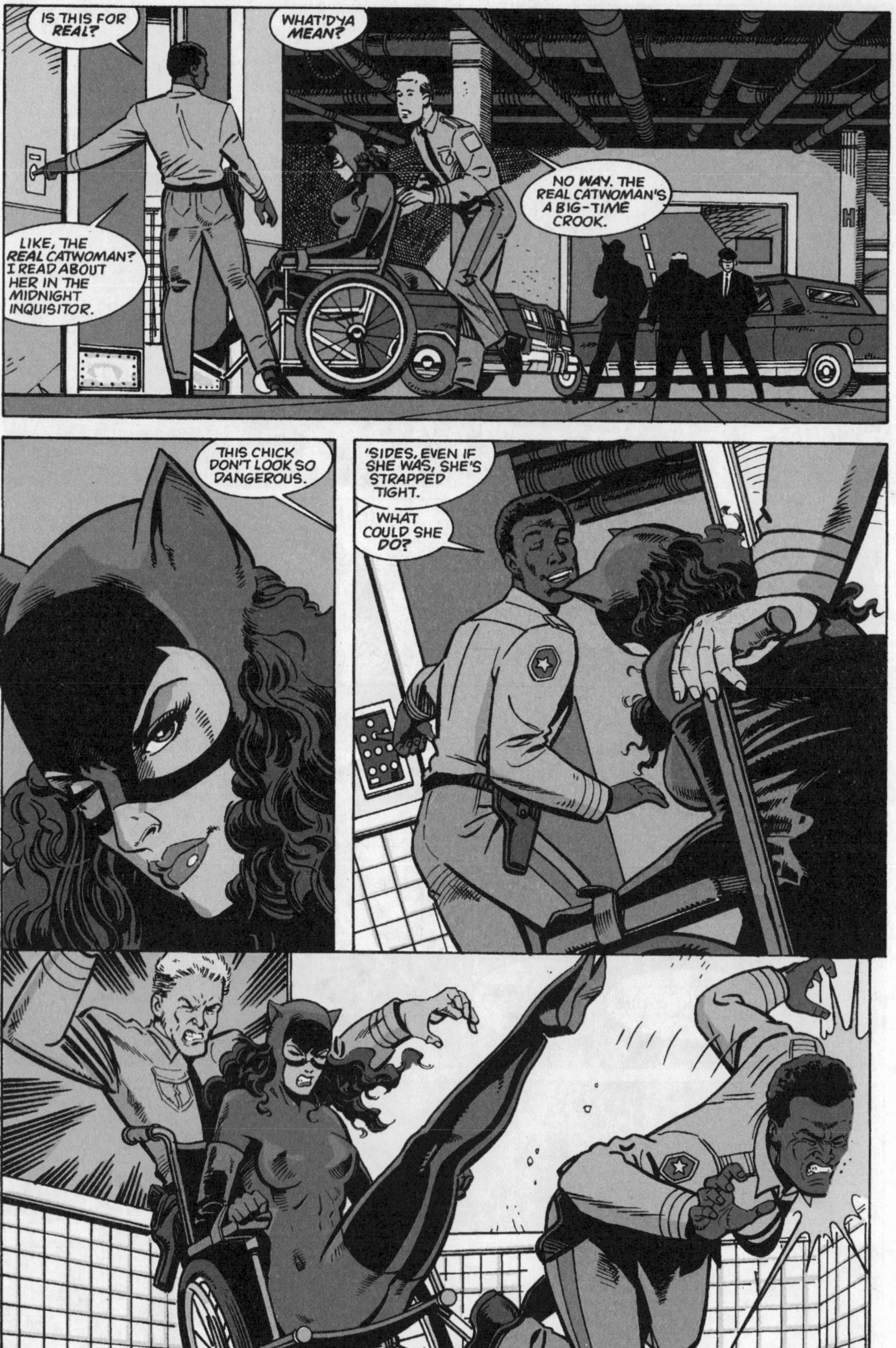
IS THIS FOR REAL?
WHAT'D'YA MEAN?
LIKE, THE REAL CATWOMAN? I READ ABOUT HER IN THE MIDNIGHT INQUISITOR.
NO WAY. THE REAL CATWOMAN'S A BIG-TIME CROOK.
THIS CHICK DON'T LOOK SO DANGEROUS.
'SIDES, EVEN IF SHE WAS, SHE'S STRAPPED TIGHT.
WHAT COULD SHE DO?
12

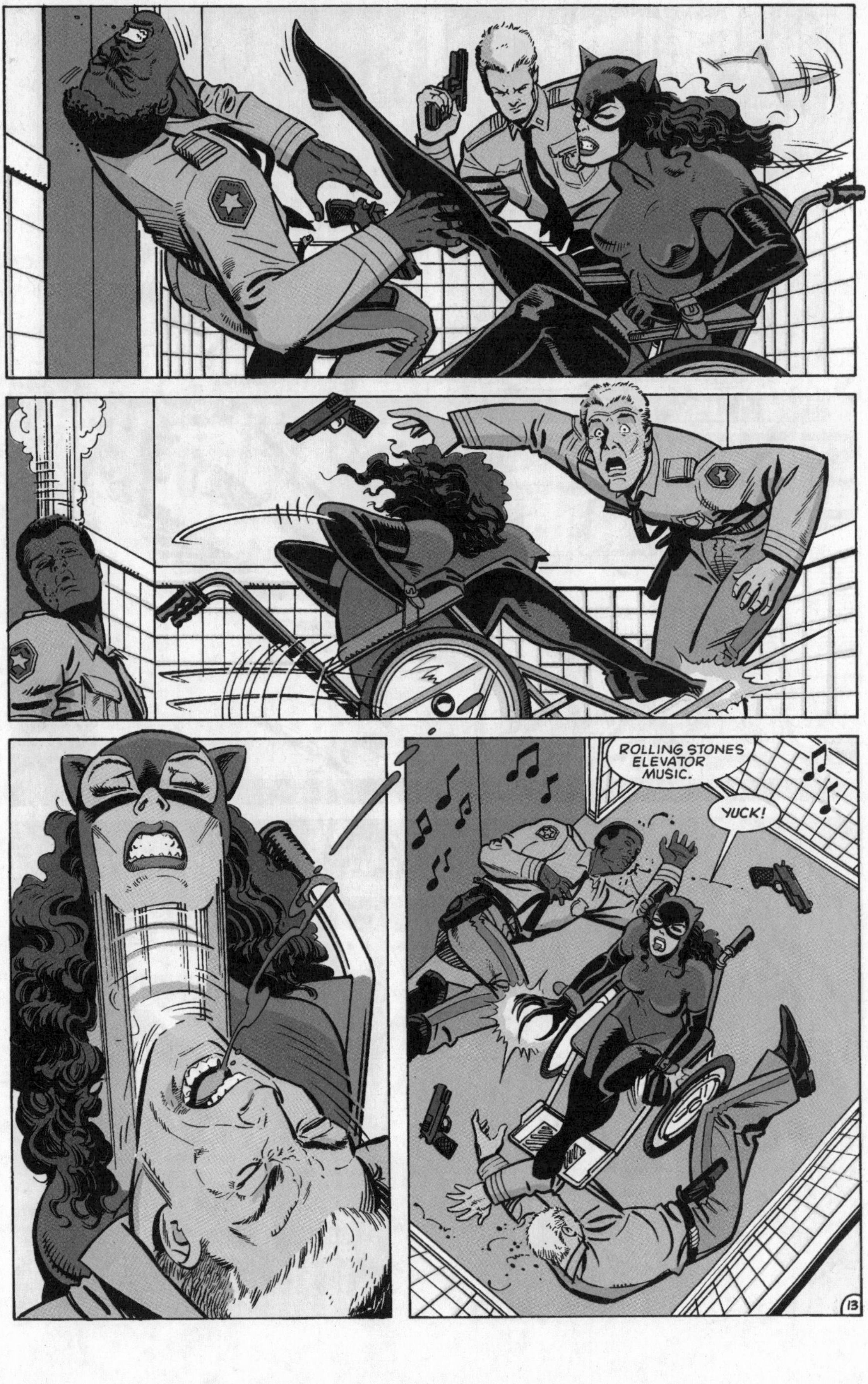
ROLLING STONES ELEVATOR MUSIC.
YUCK!
13

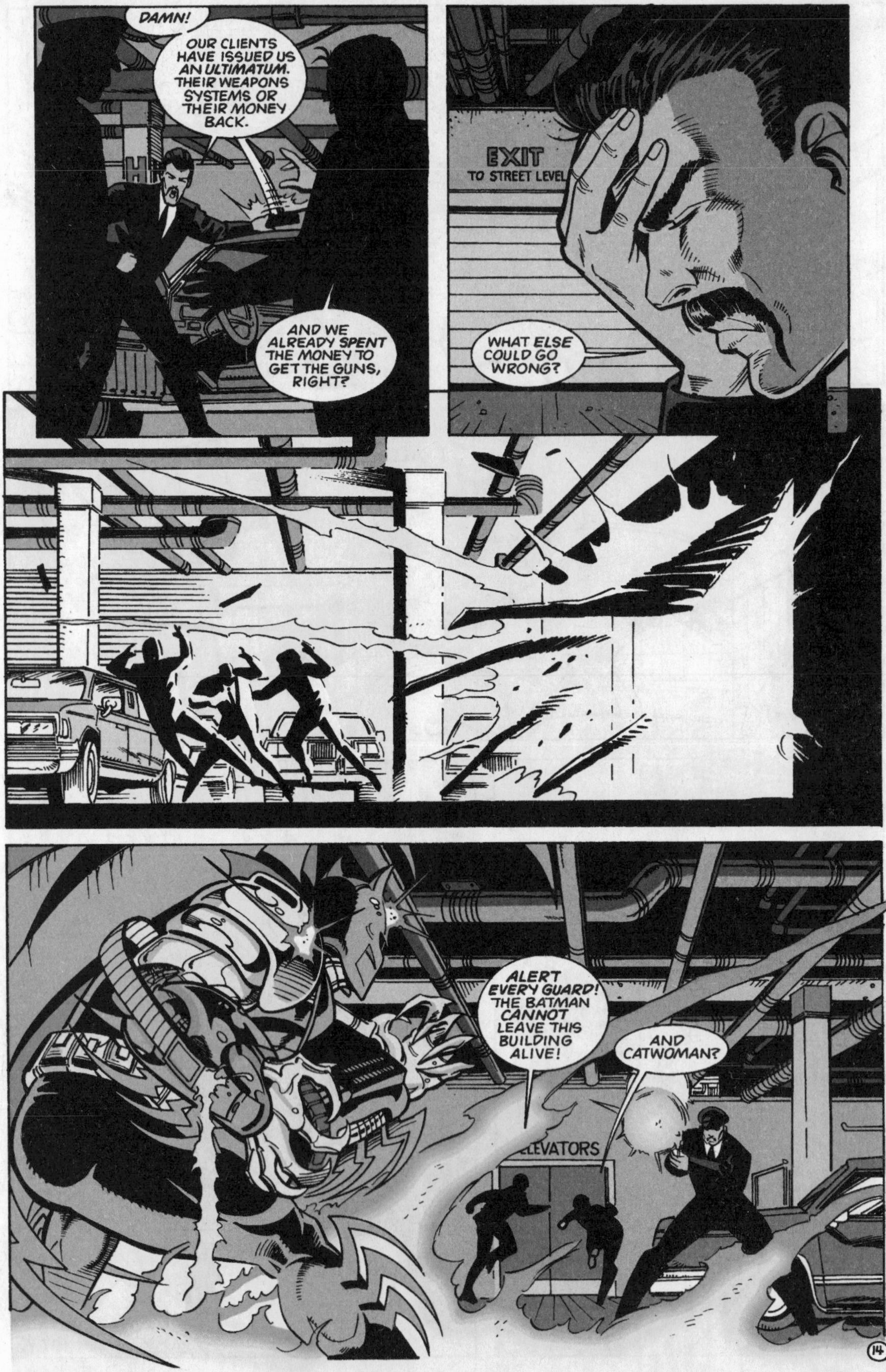
DAMN!
OUR CLIENTS HAVE ISSUED US AN ULTIMATUM. THEIR WEAPONS SYSTEMS OR THEIR MONEY BACK.
AND WE ALREADY SPENT THE MONEY TO GET THE GUNS, RIGHT?
EXIT
TO STREET LEVEL
WHAT ELSE COULD GO WRONG?
ALERT EVERY GUARD! THE BATMAN CANNOT LEAVE THIS BUILDING ALIVE!
AND CATWOMAN?
ELEVATORS
14

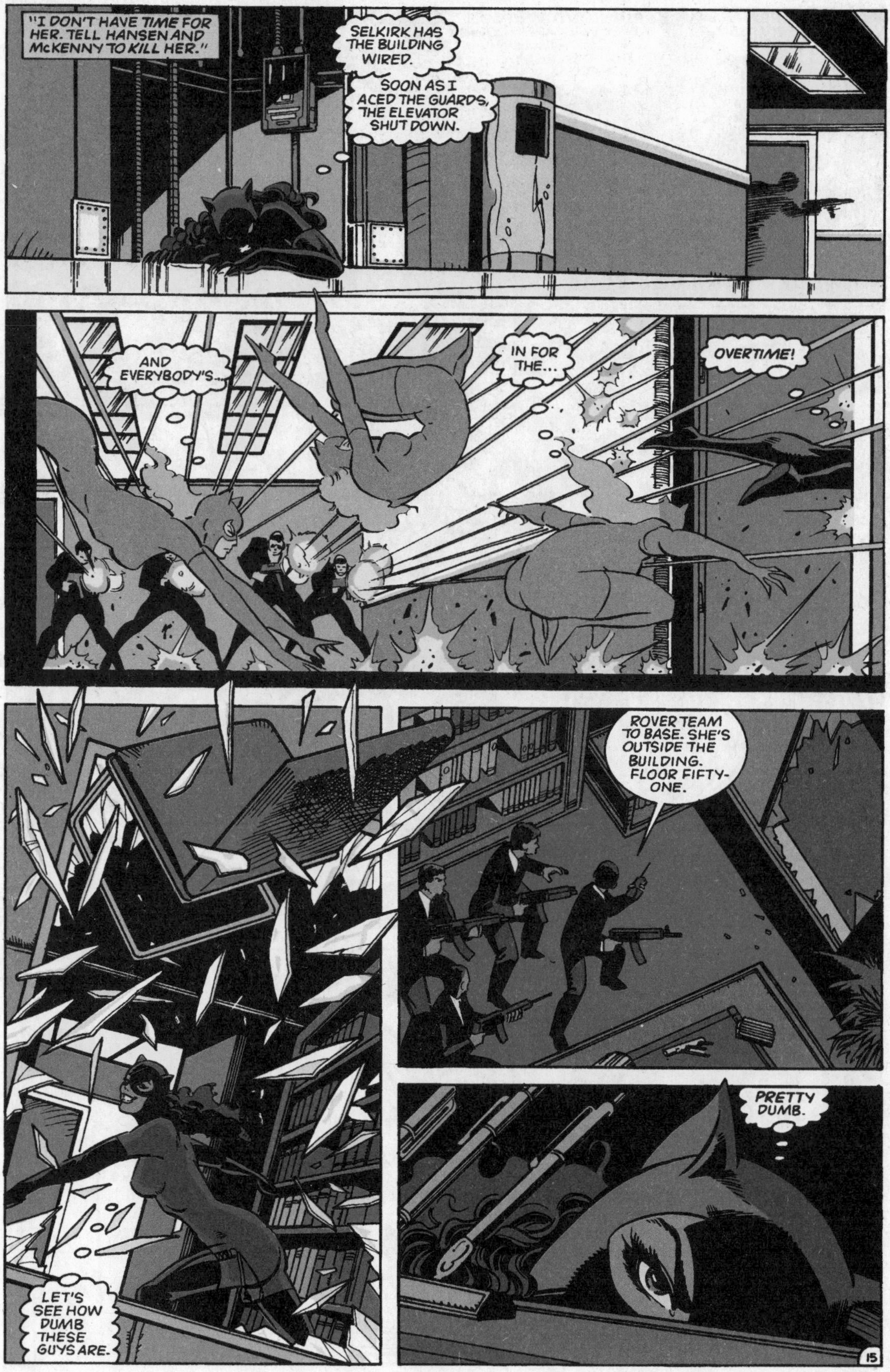
"I DON'T HAVE TIME FOR HER. TELL HANSEN AND McKENNY TO KILL HER."
SELKIRK HAS THE BUILDING WIRED.
SOON AS I ACED THE GUARDS, THE ELEVATOR SHUT DOWN.
AND EVERYBODY'S...
IN FOR THE...
OVERTIME!
ROVER TEAM TO BASE. SHE'S OUTSIDE THE BUILDING. FLOOR FIFTY-ONE.
LET'S SEE HOW DUMB THESE GUYS ARE.
PRETTY DUMB.
15

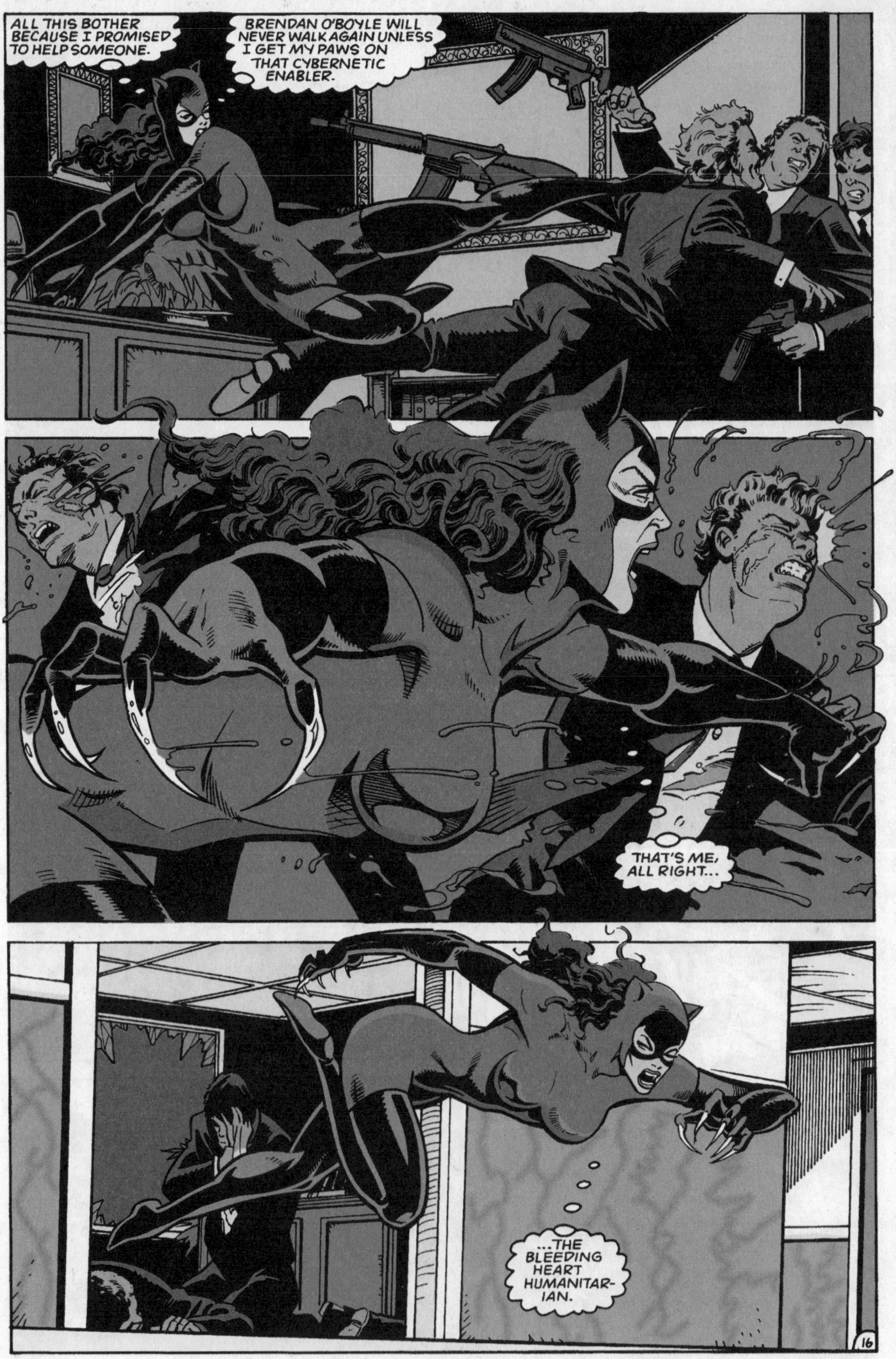
ALL THIS BOTHER BECAUSE I PROMISED TO HELP SOMEONE.
BRENDAN O'BOYLE WILL NEVER WALK AGAIN UNLESS I GET MY PAWS ON THAT CYBERNETIC ENABLER.
THAT'S ME, ALL RIGHT...
...THE BLEEDING HEART HUMANITAR-IAN.
16

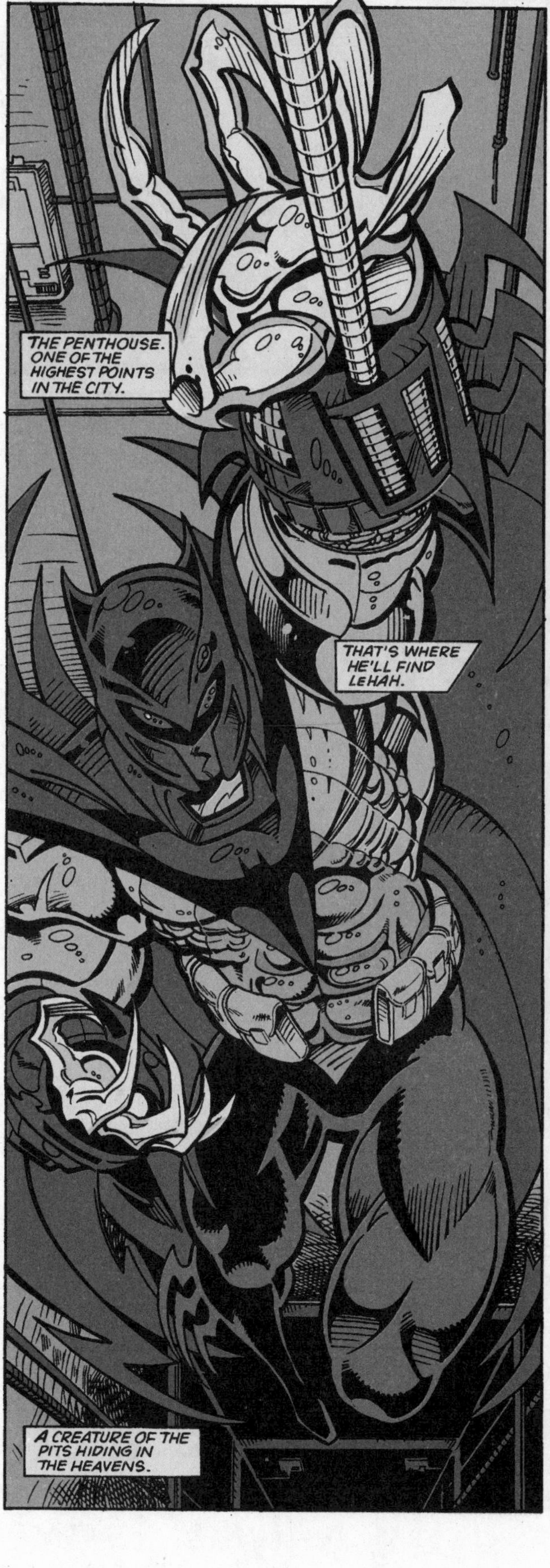
THE PENTHOUSE. ONE OF THE HIGHEST POINTS IN THE CITY.
THAT'S WHERE HE'LL FIND LEHAH.
A CREATURE OF THE PITS HIDING IN THE HEAVENS.

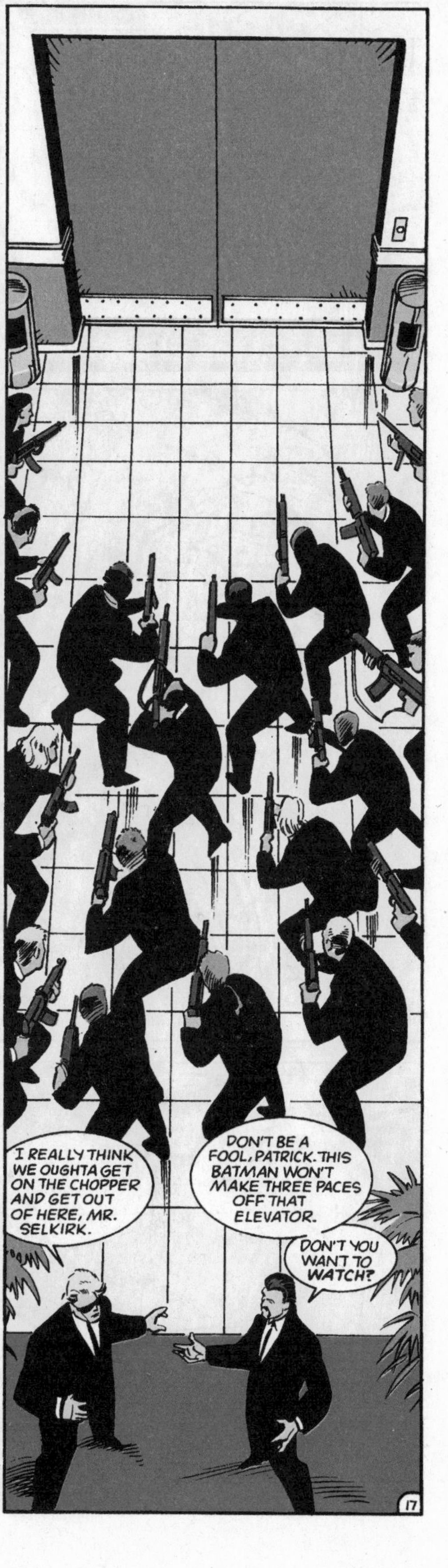
I REALLY THINK WE OUGHTA GET ON THE CHOPPER AND GET OUT OF HERE, MR. SELKIRK.
DON'T BE A FOOL, PATRICK. THIS BATMAN WON'T MAKE THREE PACES OFF THAT ELEVATOR.
DON'T YOU WANT TO WATCH?
17

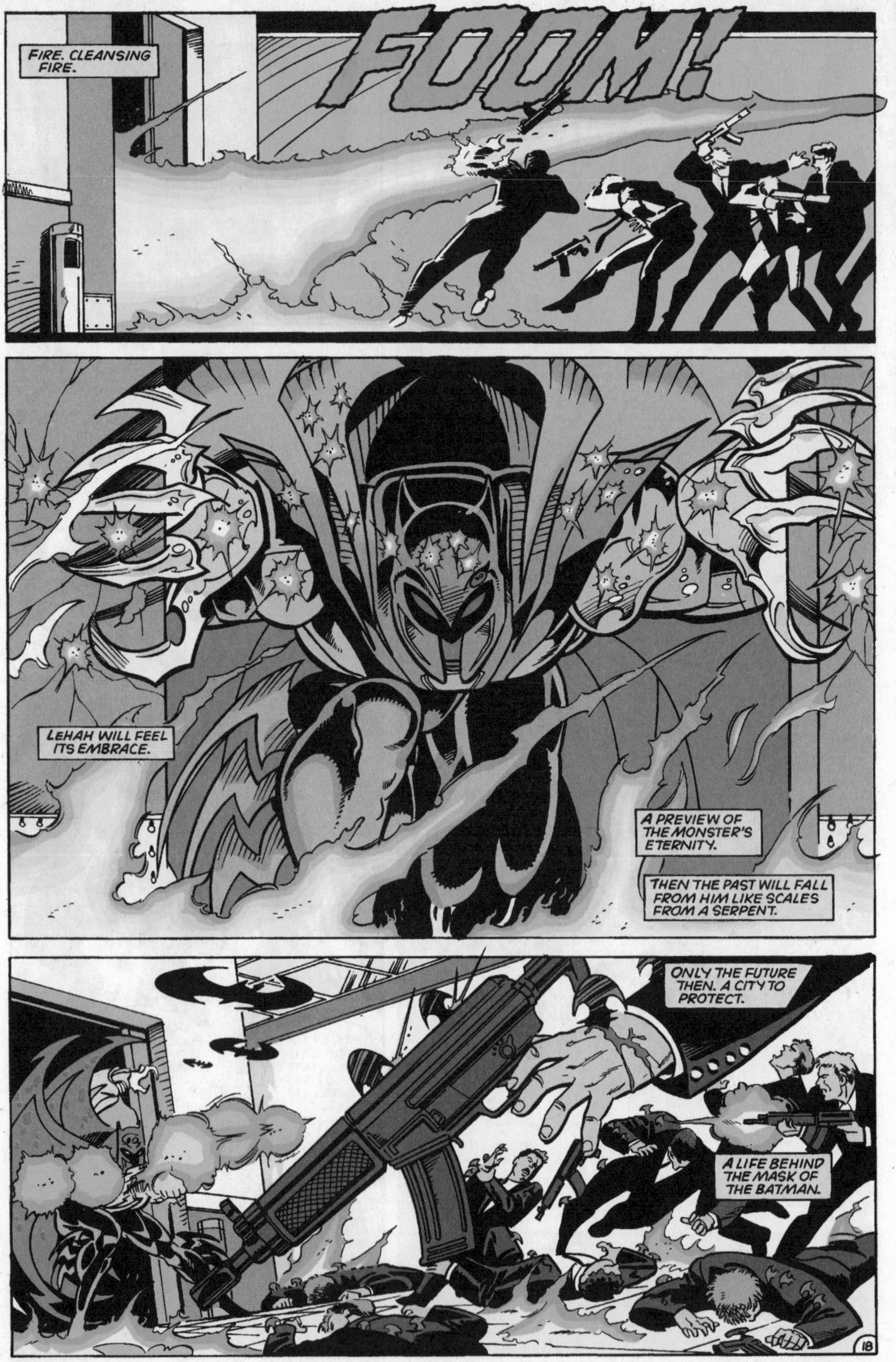
FIRE. CLEANSING FIRE.
FOOM!
LEHAH WILL FEEL ITS EMBRACE.
A PREVIEW OF THE MONSTER'S ETERNITY.
THEN THE PAST WILL FALL FROM HIM LIKE SCALES FROM A SERPENT.
ONLY THE FUTURE THEN. A CITY TO PROTECT.
A LIFE BEHIND THE MASK OF THE BATMAN.
18

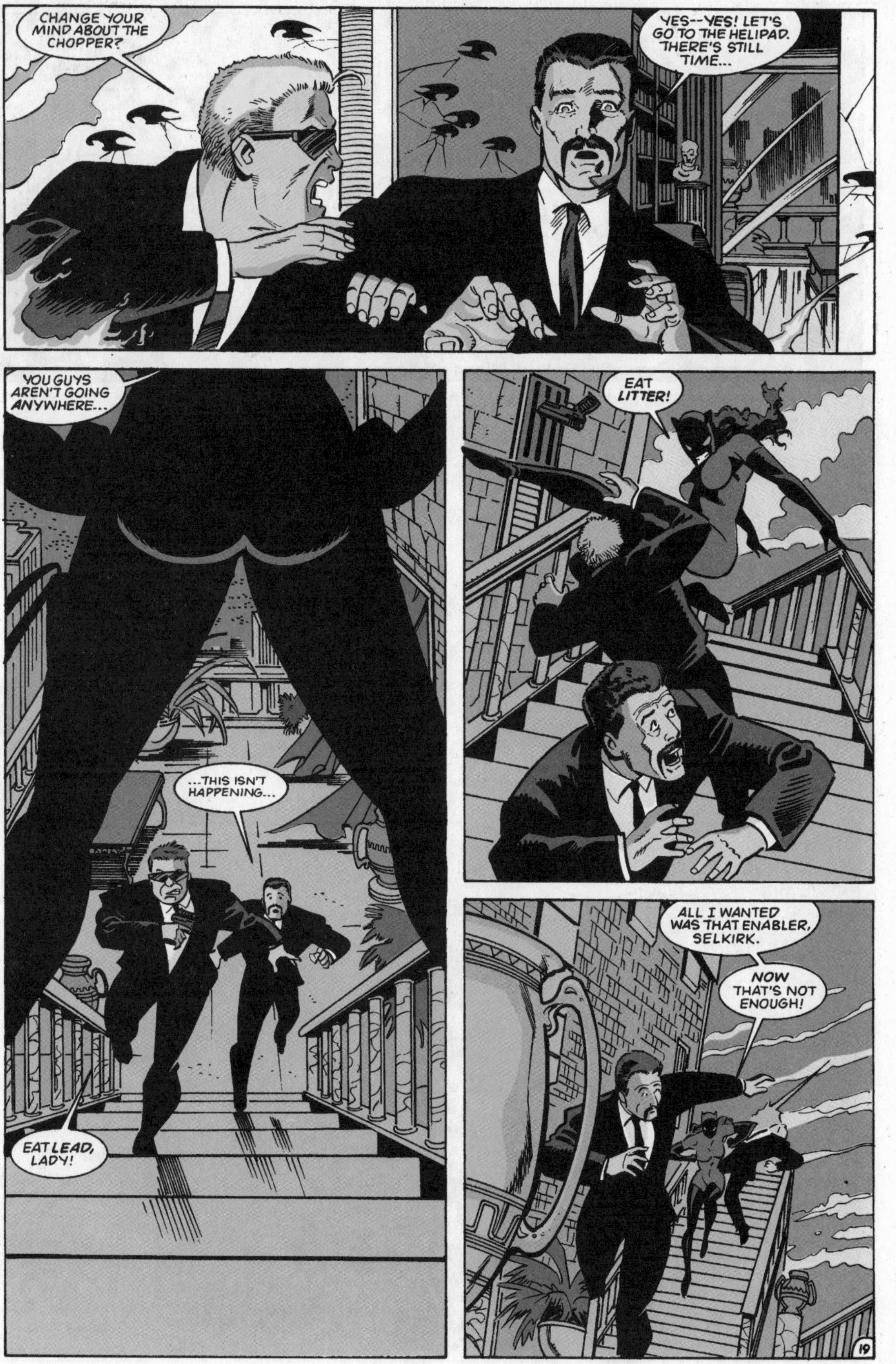
CHANGE YOUR MIND ABOUT THE CHOPPER?
YES--YES! LET'S GO TO THE HELIPAD. THERE'S STILL TIME...
YOU GUYS AREN'T GOING ANYWHERE...
...THIS ISN'T HAPPENING...
EAT LEAD, LADY!
EAT LITTER!
ALL I WANTED WAS THAT ENABLER, SELKIRK.
NOW THAT'S NOT ENOUGH!
19

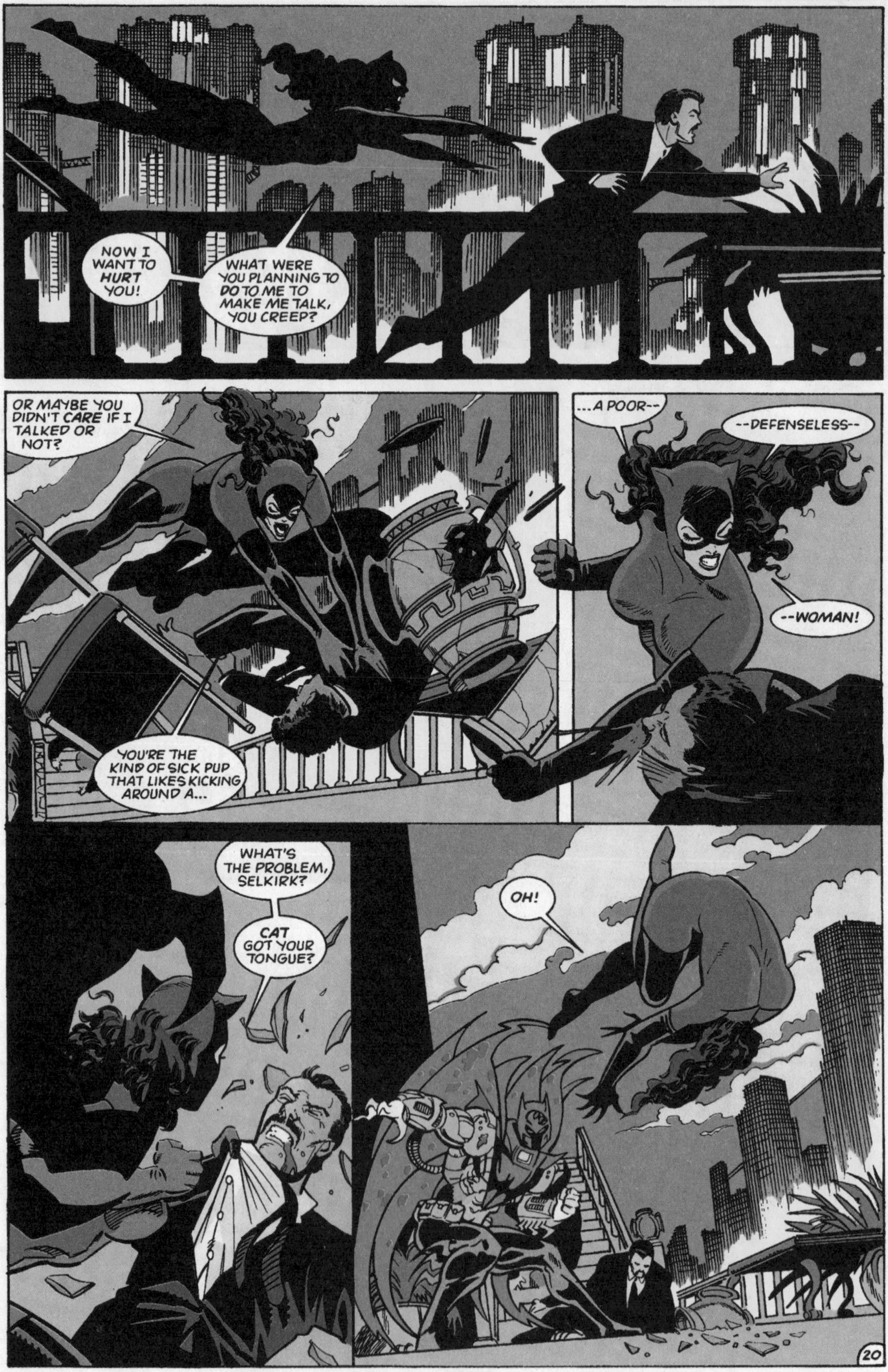
NOW I WANT TO HURT YOU!
WHAT WERE YOU PLANNING TO DO TO ME TO MAKE ME TALK, YOU CREEP?
OR MAYBE YOU DIDN'T CARE IF I TALKED OR NOT?
YOU'RE THE KIND OF SICK PUP THAT LIKES KICKING AROUND A...
...A POOR--
--DEFENSELESS--
--WOMAN!
WHAT'S THE PROBLEM, SELKIRK?
CAT GOT YOUR TONGUE?
OH!
20

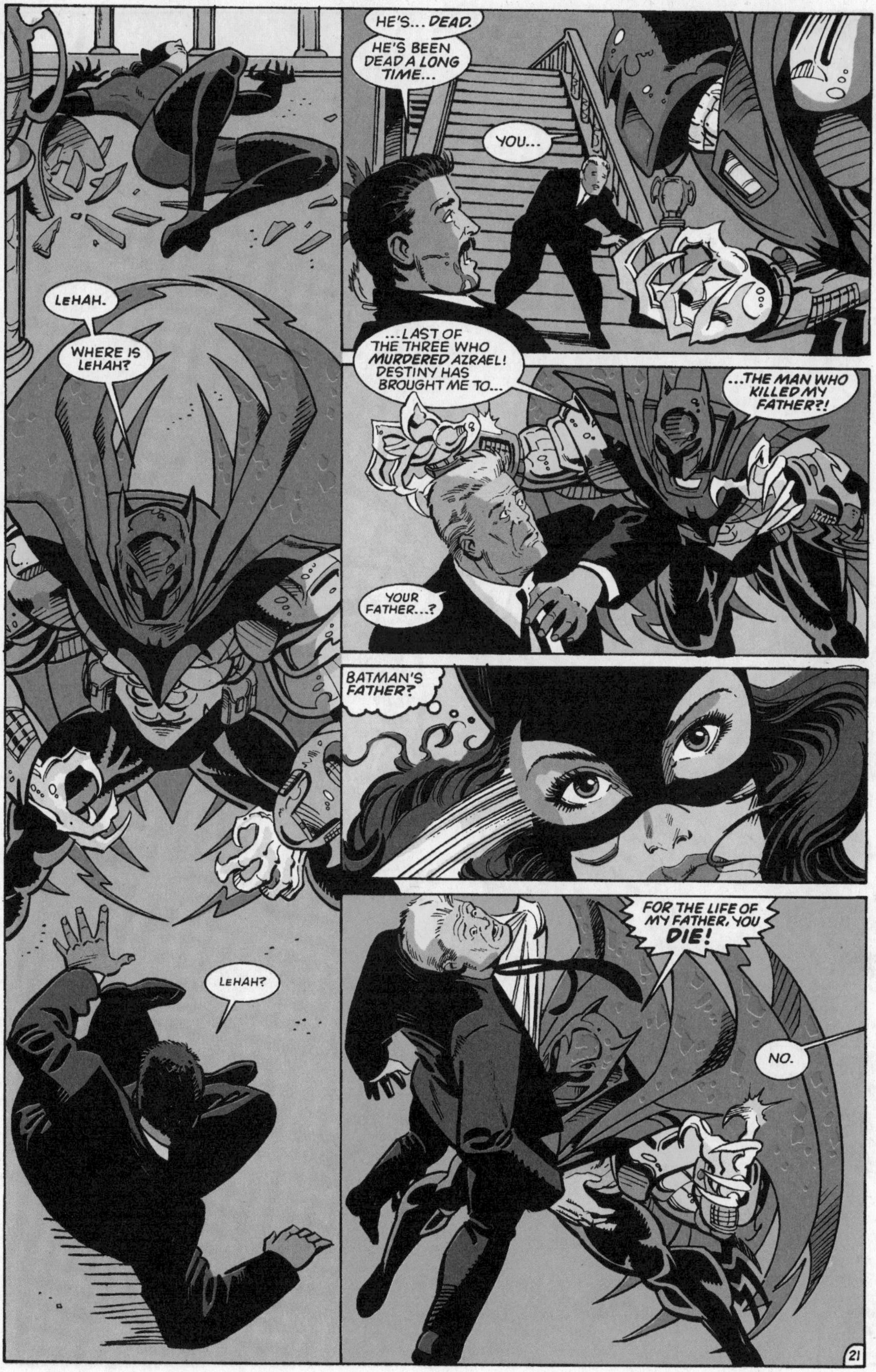
HE'S... DEAD.
HE'S BEEN DEAD A LONG TIME...
YOU...
LEHAH.
WHERE IS LEHAH?
...LAST OF THE THREE WHO MURDERED AZRAEL! DESTINY HAS BROUGHT ME TO...
...THE MAN WHO KILLED MY FATHER?!
YOUR FATHER...?
BATMAN'S FATHER?
LEHAH?
FOR THE LIFE OF MY FATHER, YOU DIE!
NO.
21

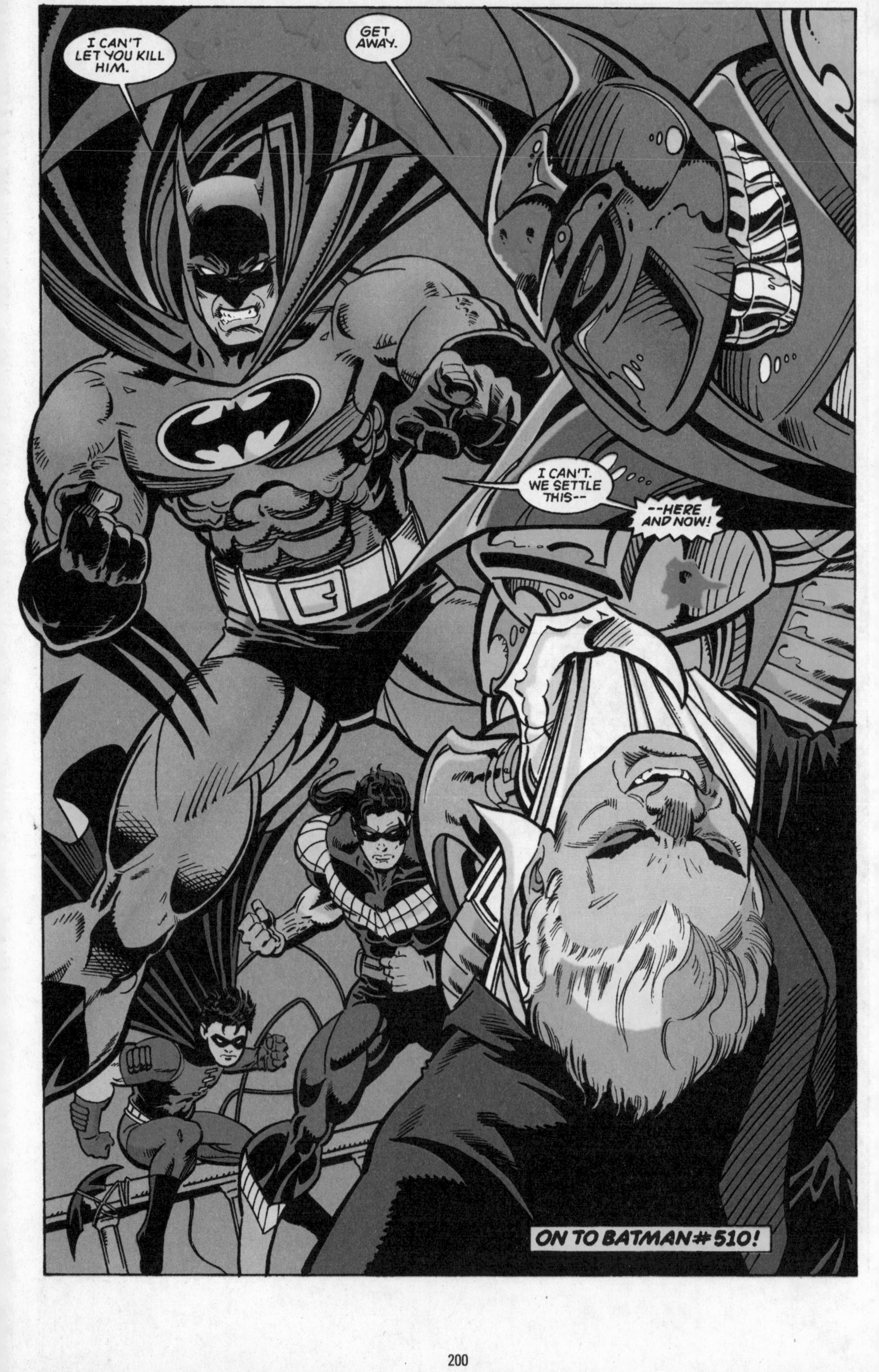
I CAN'T LET YOU KILL HIM.
GET AWAY.
I CAN'T. WE SETTLE THIS--
--HERE AND NOW!
ON TO BATMAN #510!

Cover art by KELLEY JONES

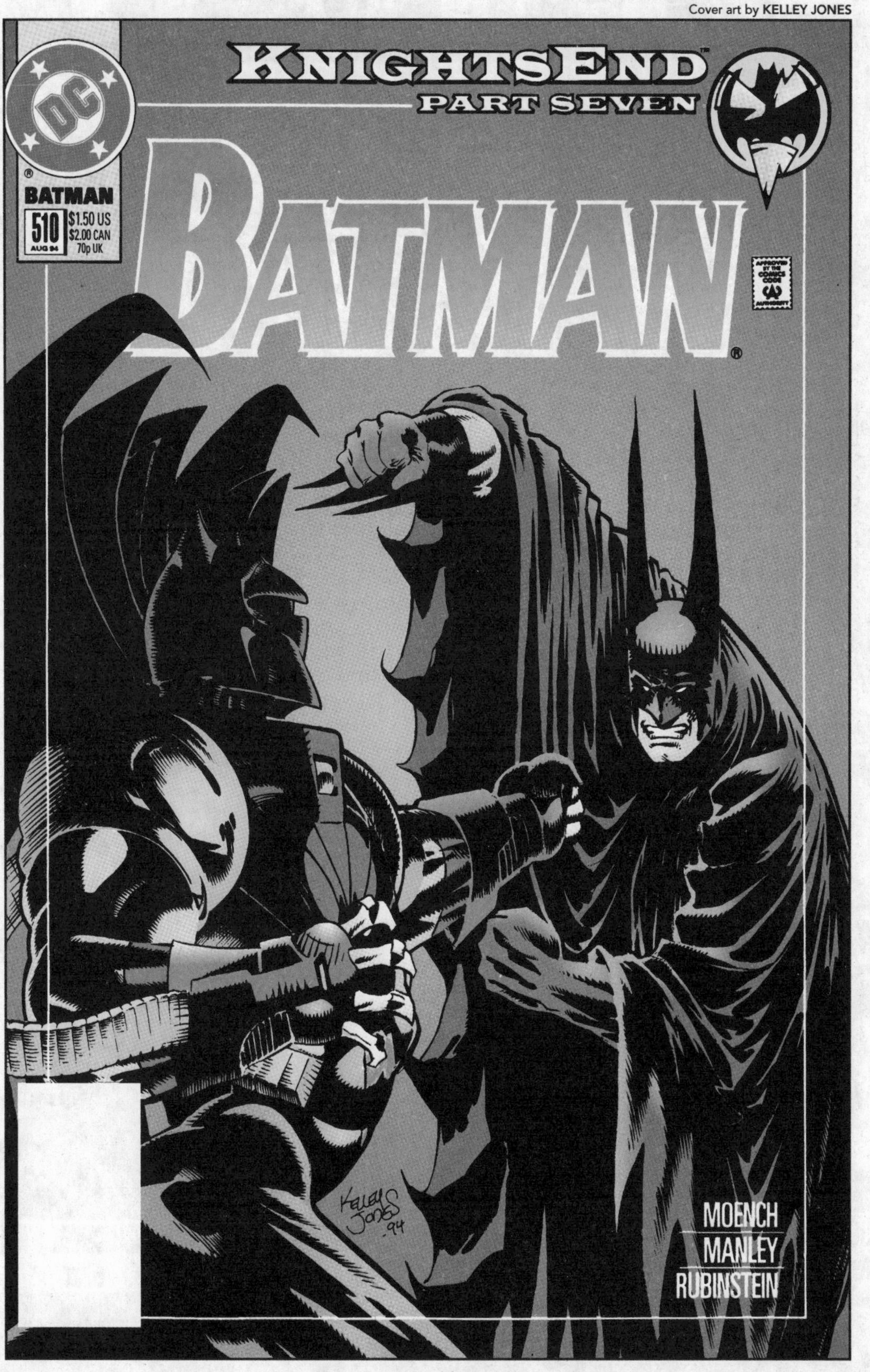
KNIGHTSEND
PART SEVEN
DC
BATMAN
510
AUG 94
$1.50 US
$2.00 CAN
70p UK
BATMAN
APPROVED BY THE COMICS CODE AUTHORITY
KELLEY JONES '94
MOENCH
MANLEY
RUBINSTEIN

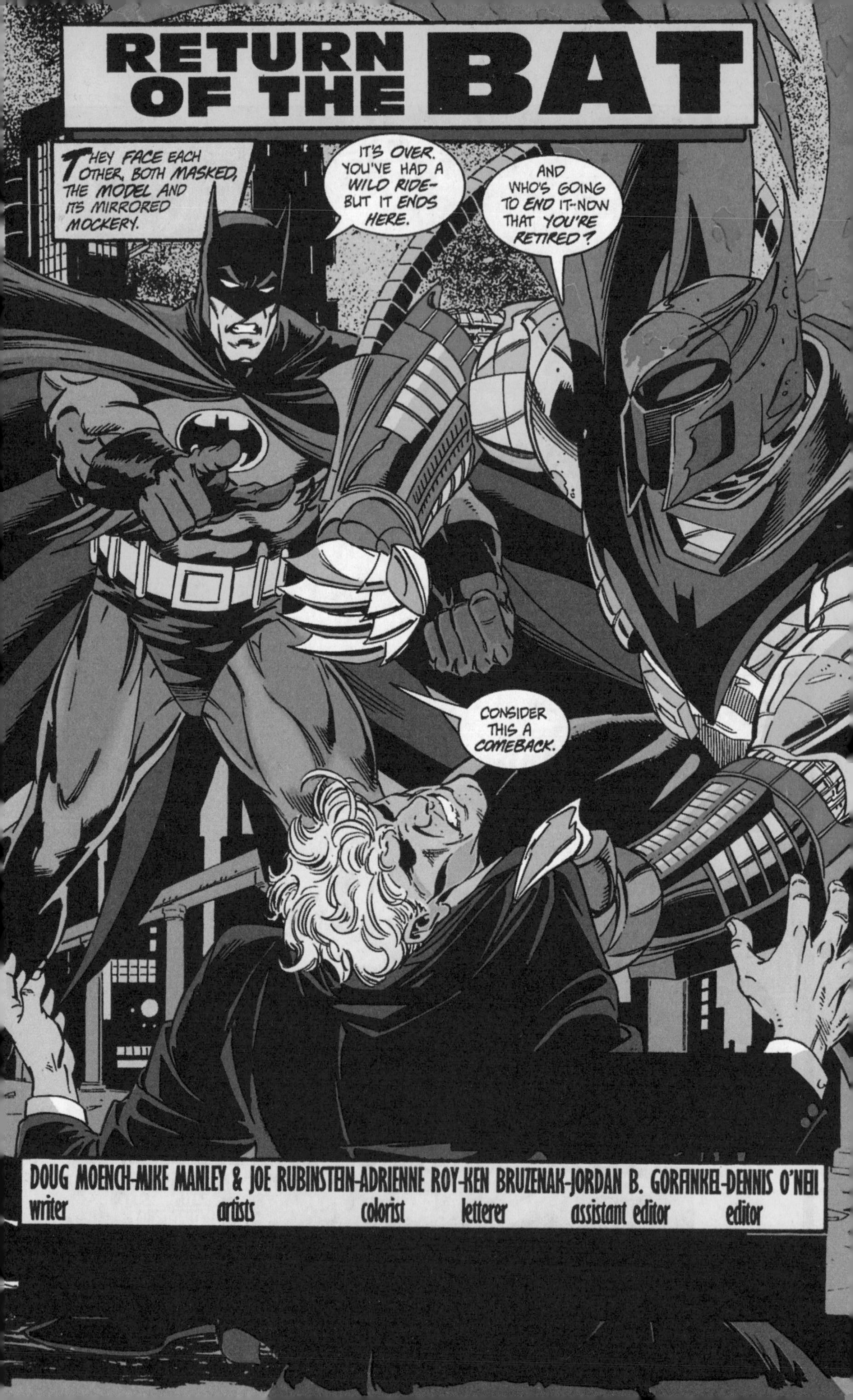
RETURN OF THE BAT
THEY FACE EACH OTHER, BOTH MASKED, THE MODEL AND ITS MIRRORED MOCKERY.
IT'S OVER. YOU'VE HAD A WILD RIDE-- BUT IT ENDS HERE.
AND WHO'S GOING TO END IT--NOW THAT YOU'RE RETIRED?
CONSIDER THIS A COMEBACK.
DOUG MOENCH-MIKE MANLEY & JOE RUBINSTEIN-ADRIENNE ROY-KEN BRUZENAK-JORDAN B. GORFINKEL-DENNIS O'NEIL
writer artists colorist letterer assistant editor editor

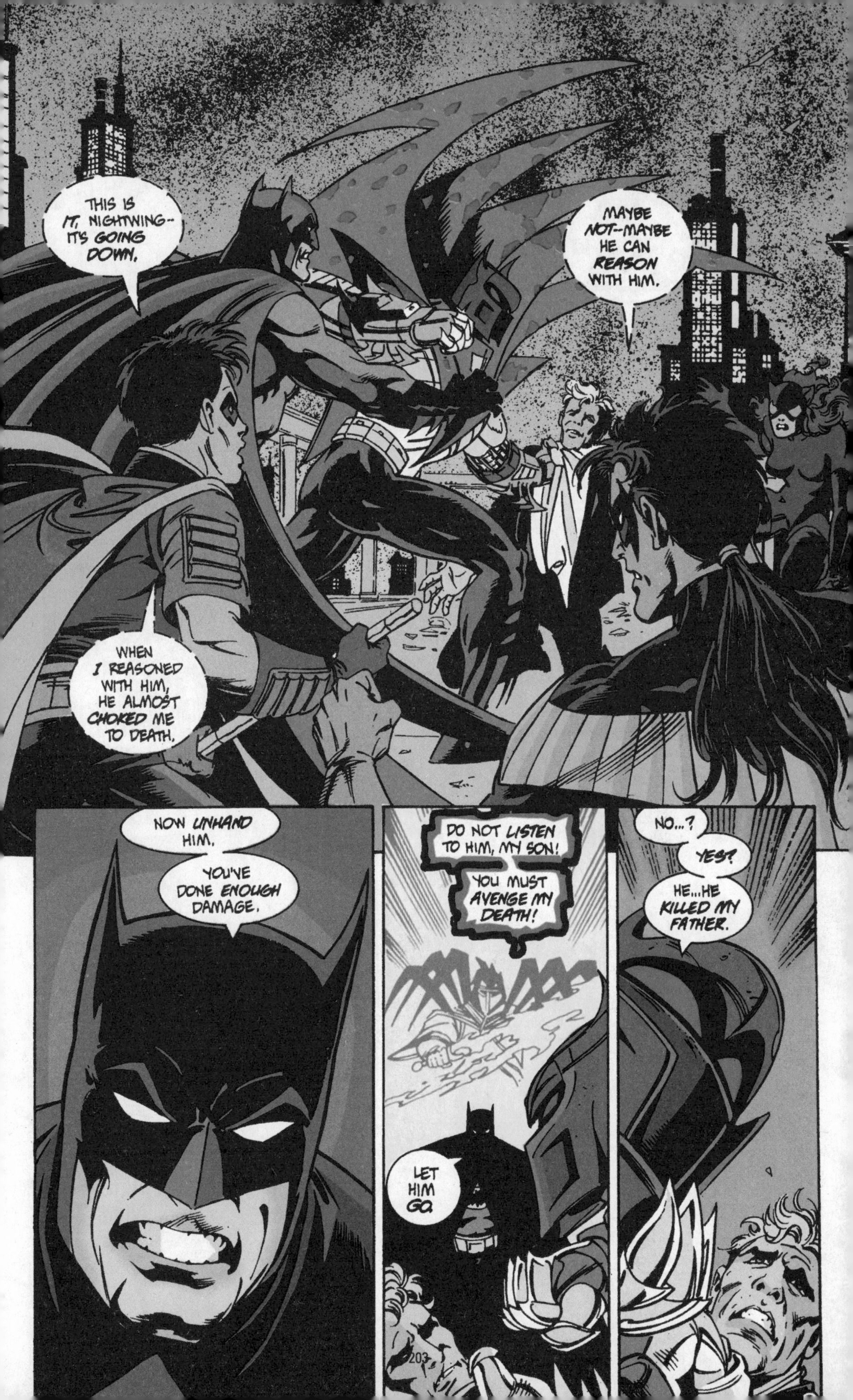
THIS IS IT, NIGHTWING-- IT'S GOING DOWN.
MAYBE NOT--MAYBE HE CAN REASON WITH HIM.
WHEN I REASONED WITH HIM, HE ALMOST CHOKED ME TO DEATH.
NOW UNHAND HIM.
YOU'VE DONE ENOUGH DAMAGE.
DO NOT LISTEN TO HIM, MY SON!
YOU MUST AVENGE MY DEATH!
LET HIM GO.
NO...?
YES?
HE...HE KILLED MY FATHER.

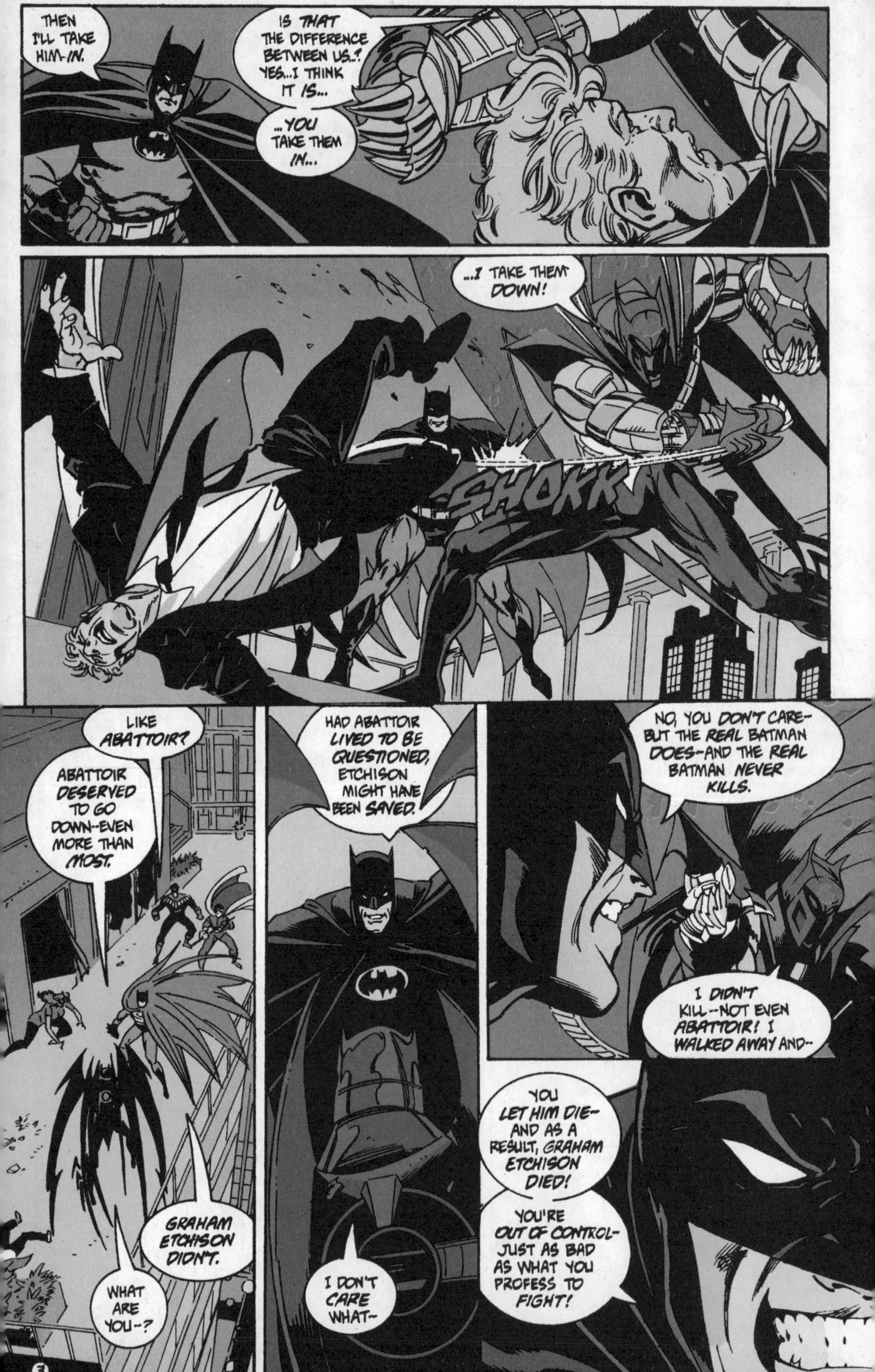

THEN I'LL TAKE HIM-IN.
IS THAT THE DIFFERENCE BETWEEN US..? YES...I THINK IT IS...
...YOU TAKE THEM IN...
...I TAKE THEM DOWN!
SHOKK
LIKE ABATTOIR?
ABATTOIR DESERVED TO GO DOWN--EVEN MORE THAN MOST.
GRAHAM ETCHISON DIDN'T.
WHAT ARE YOU--?
HAD ABATTOIR LIVED TO BE QUESTIONED, ETCHISON MIGHT HAVE BEEN SAVED.
I DON'T CARE WHAT--
NO, YOU DON'T CARE-BUT THE REAL BATMAN DOES--AND THE REAL BATMAN NEVER KILLS.
I DIDN'T KILL--NOT EVEN ABATTOIR! I WALKED AWAY AND--
YOU LET HIM DIE-AND AS A RESULT, GRAHAM ETCHISON DIED!
YOU'RE OUT OF CONTROL-JUST AS BAD AS WHAT YOU PROFESS TO FIGHT!

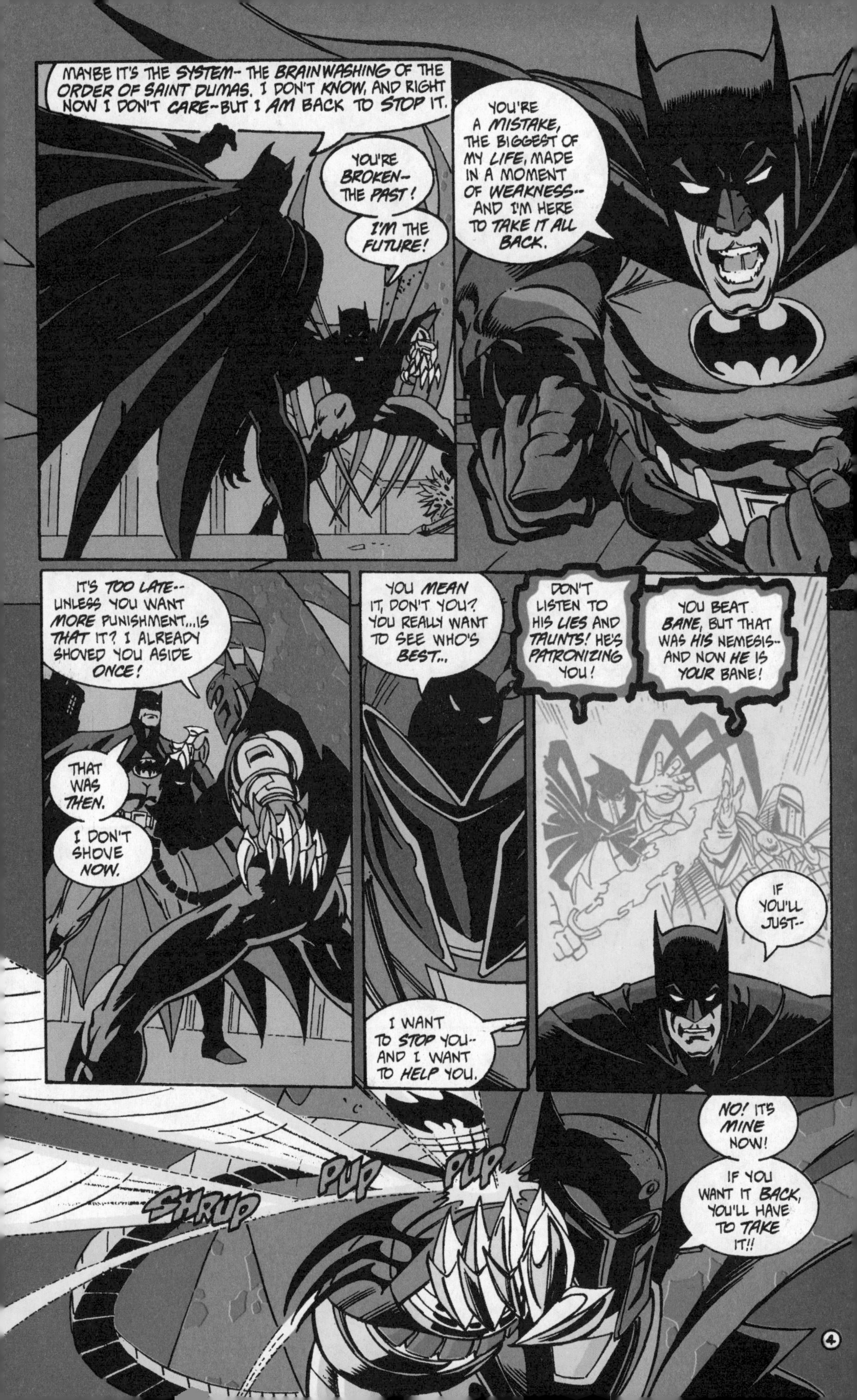
MAYBE IT'S THE SYSTEM-- THE BRAINWASHING OF THE ORDER OF SAINT DUMAS. I DON'T KNOW, AND RIGHT NOW I DON'T CARE--BUT I AM BACK TO STOP IT.
YOU'RE BROKEN-- THE PAST!
I'M THE FUTURE!
YOU'RE A MISTAKE, THE BIGGEST OF MY LIFE, MADE IN A MOMENT OF WEAKNESS-- AND I'M HERE TO TAKE IT ALL BACK.
IT'S TOO LATE-- UNLESS YOU WANT MORE PUNISHMENT...IS THAT IT? I ALREADY SHOVED YOU ASIDE ONCE!
THAT WAS THEN.
I DON'T SHOVE NOW.
YOU MEAN IT, DON'T YOU? YOU REALLY WANT TO SEE WHO'S BEST...
I WANT TO STOP YOU-- AND I WANT TO HELP YOU.
DON'T LISTEN TO HIS LIES AND TAUNTS! HE'S PATRONIZING YOU!
YOU BEAT BANE, BUT THAT WAS HIS NEMESIS-- AND NOW HE IS YOUR BANE!
IF YOU'LL JUST--
SHRUP
PUP
PUP
NO! IT'S MINE NOW!
IF YOU WANT IT BACK, YOU'LL HAVE TO TAKE IT!!
4

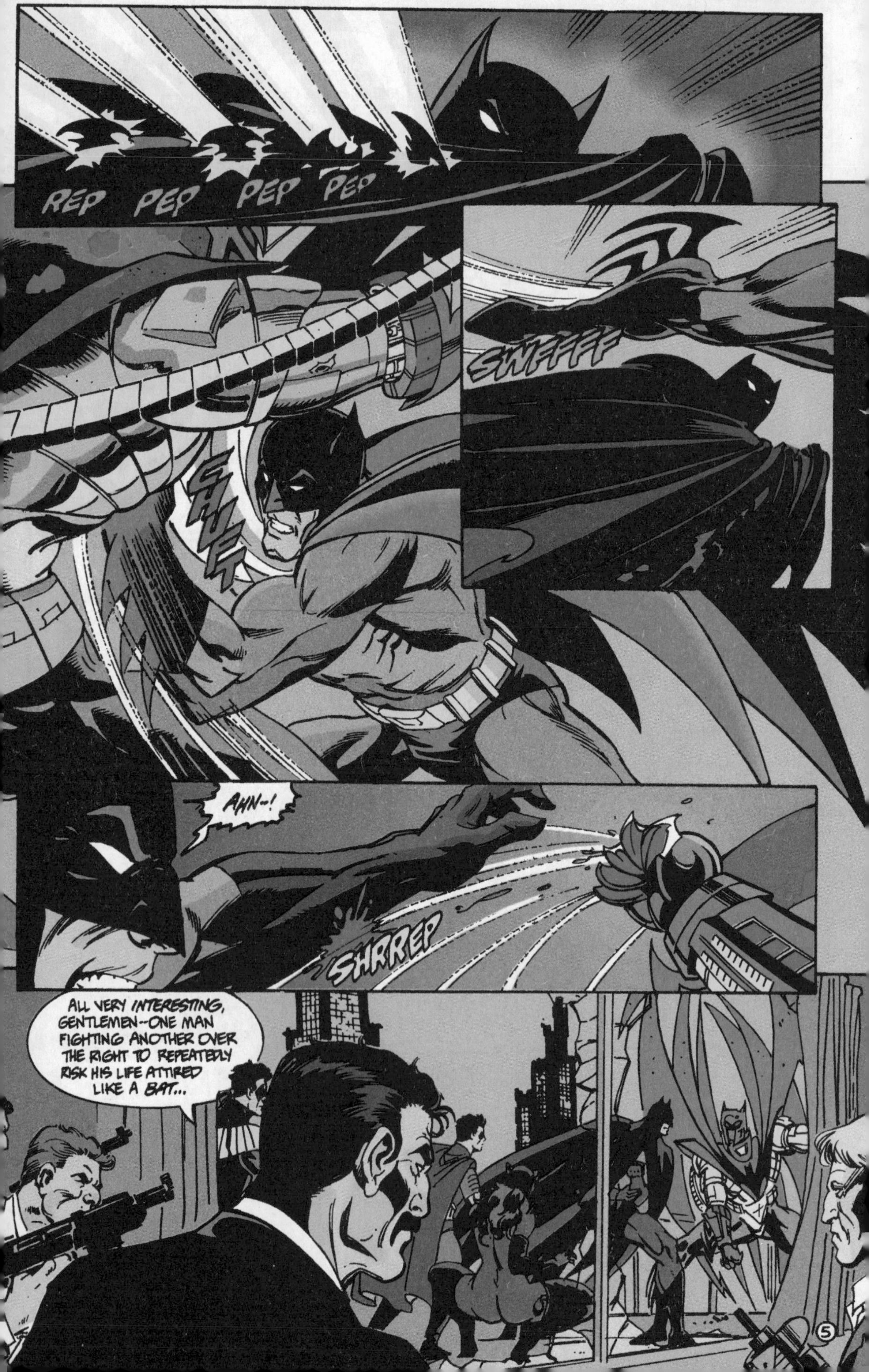
REP PEP PEP PEP
CHUK
SWFFFF
AHN--!
SHRREP
ALL VERY *INTERESTING*, GENTLEMEN--ONE MAN FIGHTING ANOTHER OVER THE RIGHT TO REPEATEDLY RISK HIS LIFE ATTIRED LIKE A *BAT*...

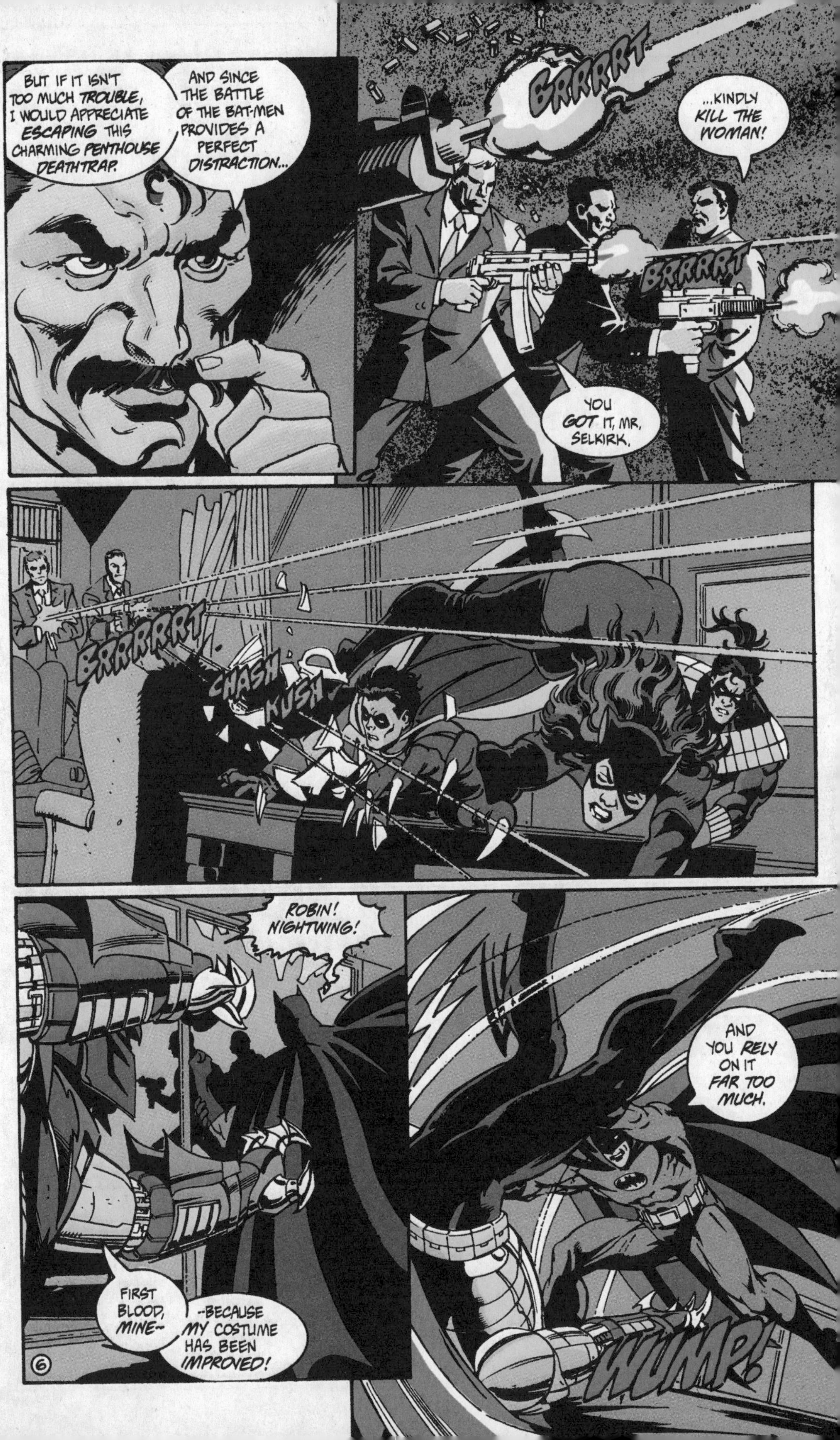
BUT IF IT ISN'T TOO MUCH TROUBLE, I WOULD APPRECIATE ESCAPING THIS CHARMING PENTHOUSE DEATHTRAP.
AND SINCE THE BATTLE OF THE BAT-MEN PROVIDES A PERFECT DISTRACTION...
BRRRRT
...KINDLY KILL THE WOMAN!
BRRRRT
YOU GOT IT, MR. SELKIRK.
BRRRRRT
CHASH
KUSH
ROBIN! NIGHTWING!
FIRST BLOOD, MINE--
--BECAUSE MY COSTUME HAS BEEN IMPROVED!
AND YOU RELY ON IT FAR TOO MUCH.
WUMP!
6

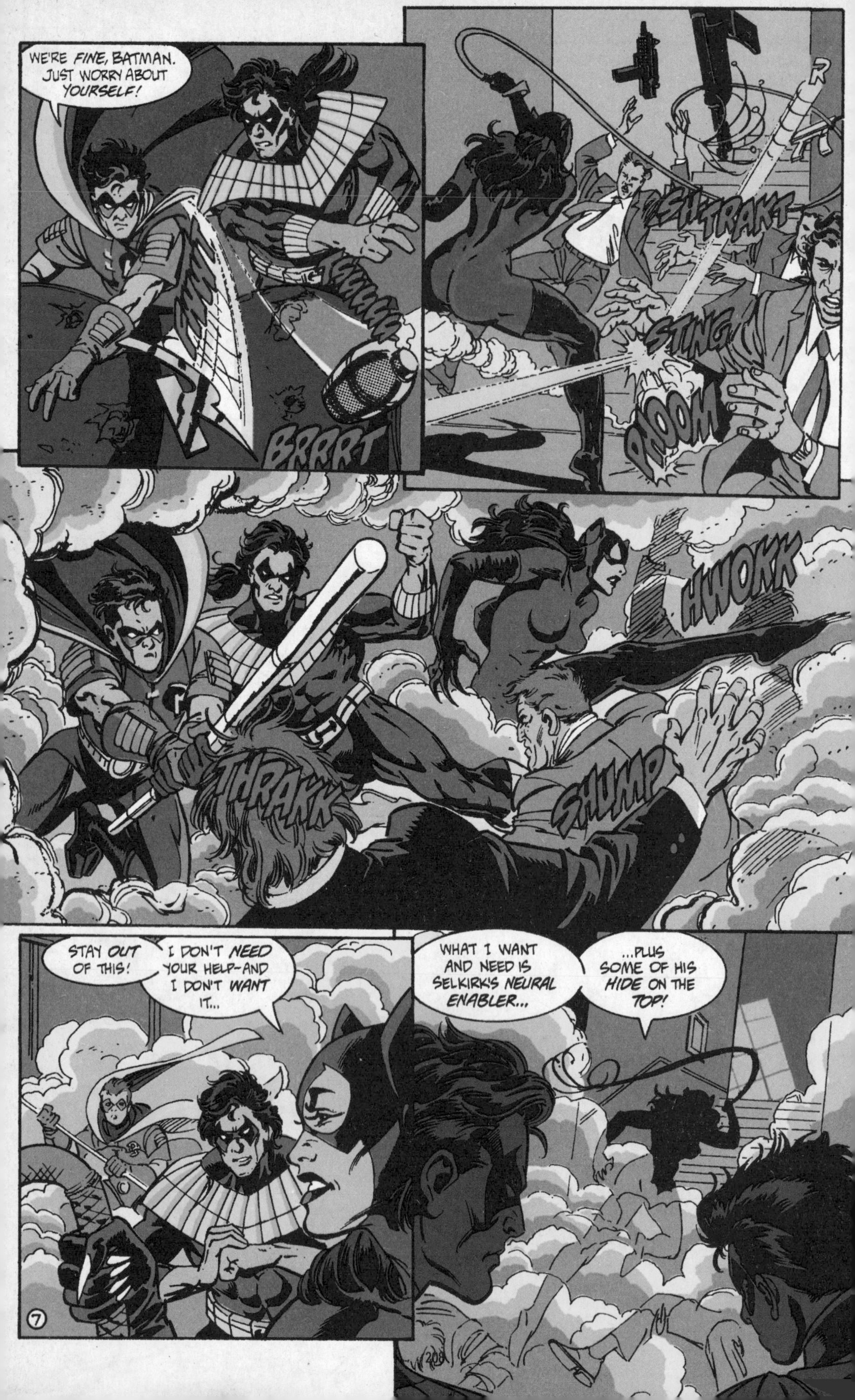
WE'RE FINE, BATMAN. JUST WORRY ABOUT YOURSELF!
BRRRT
SHTRAKT
STING
PHOOM
HWOKK
THRAKK
SHUMP
STAY OUT OF THIS!
I DON'T NEED YOUR HELP–AND I DON'T WANT IT...
WHAT I WANT AND NEED IS SELKIRK'S NEURAL ENABLER...
...PLUS SOME OF HIS HIDE ON THE TOP!
7

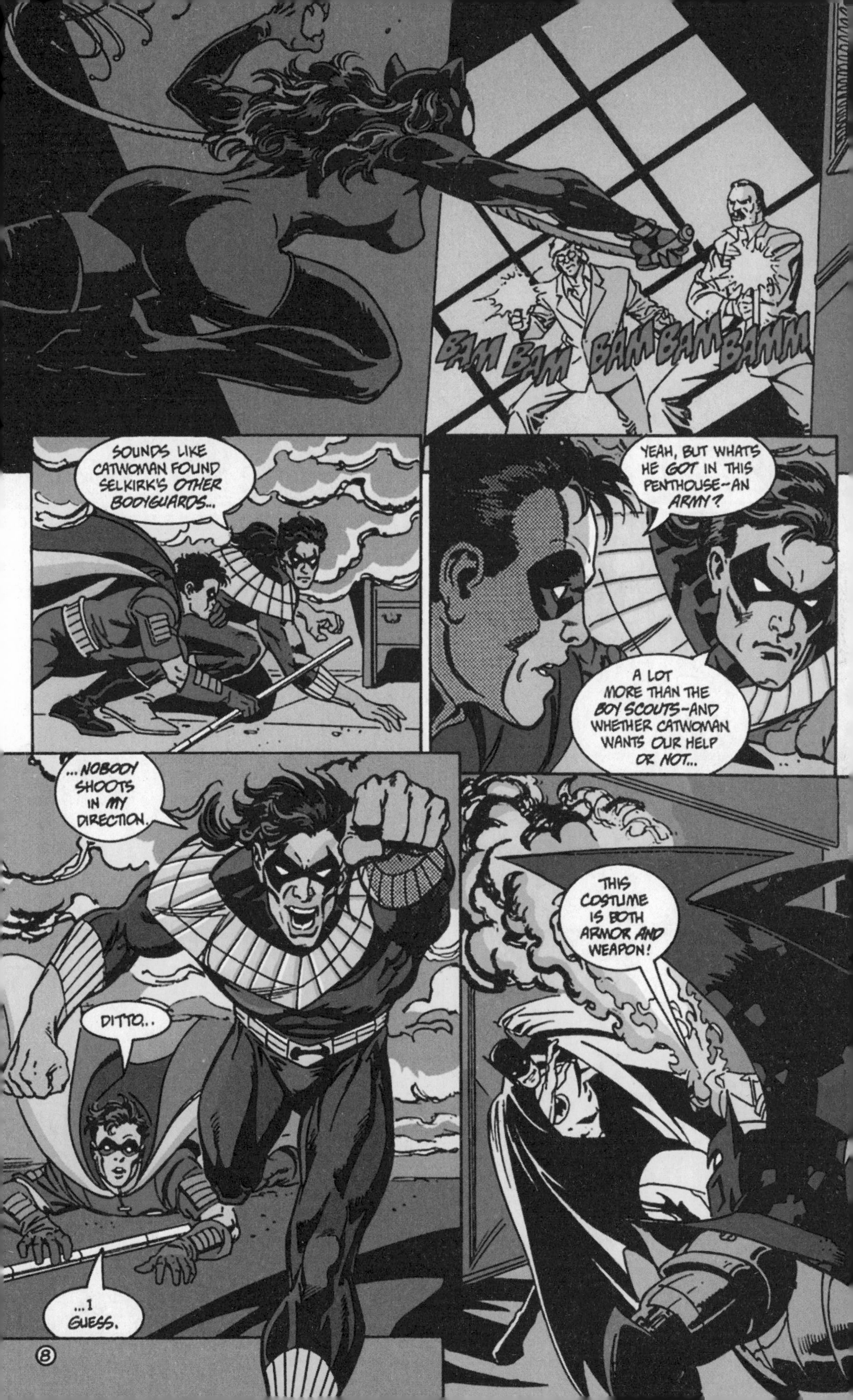
BAM BAM BAM BAM BAMM
SOUNDS LIKE CATWOMAN FOUND SELKIRK'S OTHER BODYGUARDS...
YEAH, BUT WHATS HE GOT IN THIS PENTHOUSE--AN ARMY?
A LOT MORE THAN THE BOY SCOUTS--AND WHETHER CATWOMAN WANTS OUR HELP OR NOT...
...NOBODY SHOOTS IN MY DIRECTION.
DITTO...
...I GUESS.
THIS COSTUME IS BOTH ARMOR AND WEAPON!
8

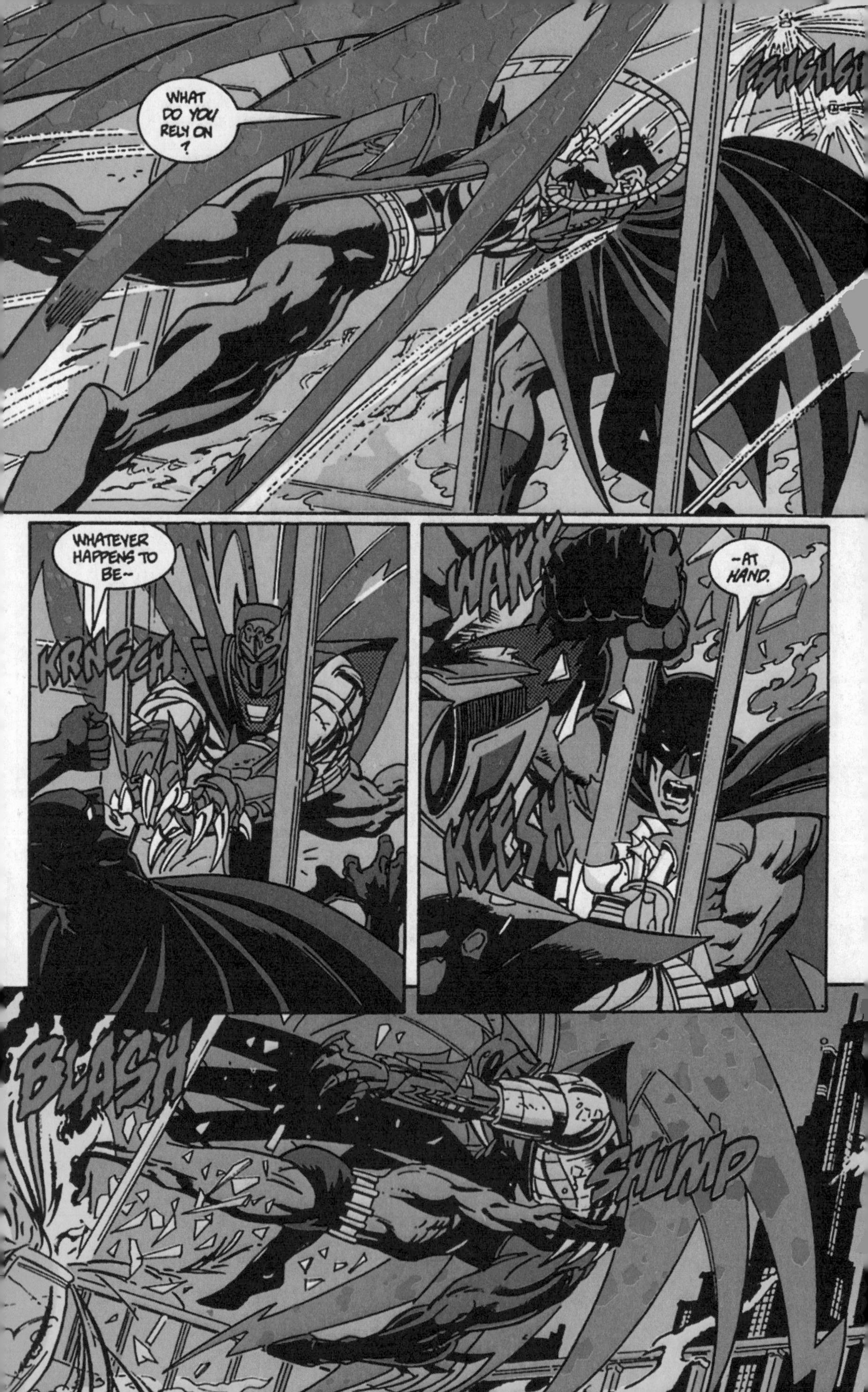
WHAT DO YOU RELY ON ?
FSHSHSH
WHATEVER HAPPENS TO BE~
KRNSCH
WAKK
-AT HAND.
KEESH
BLASH
SHUMP

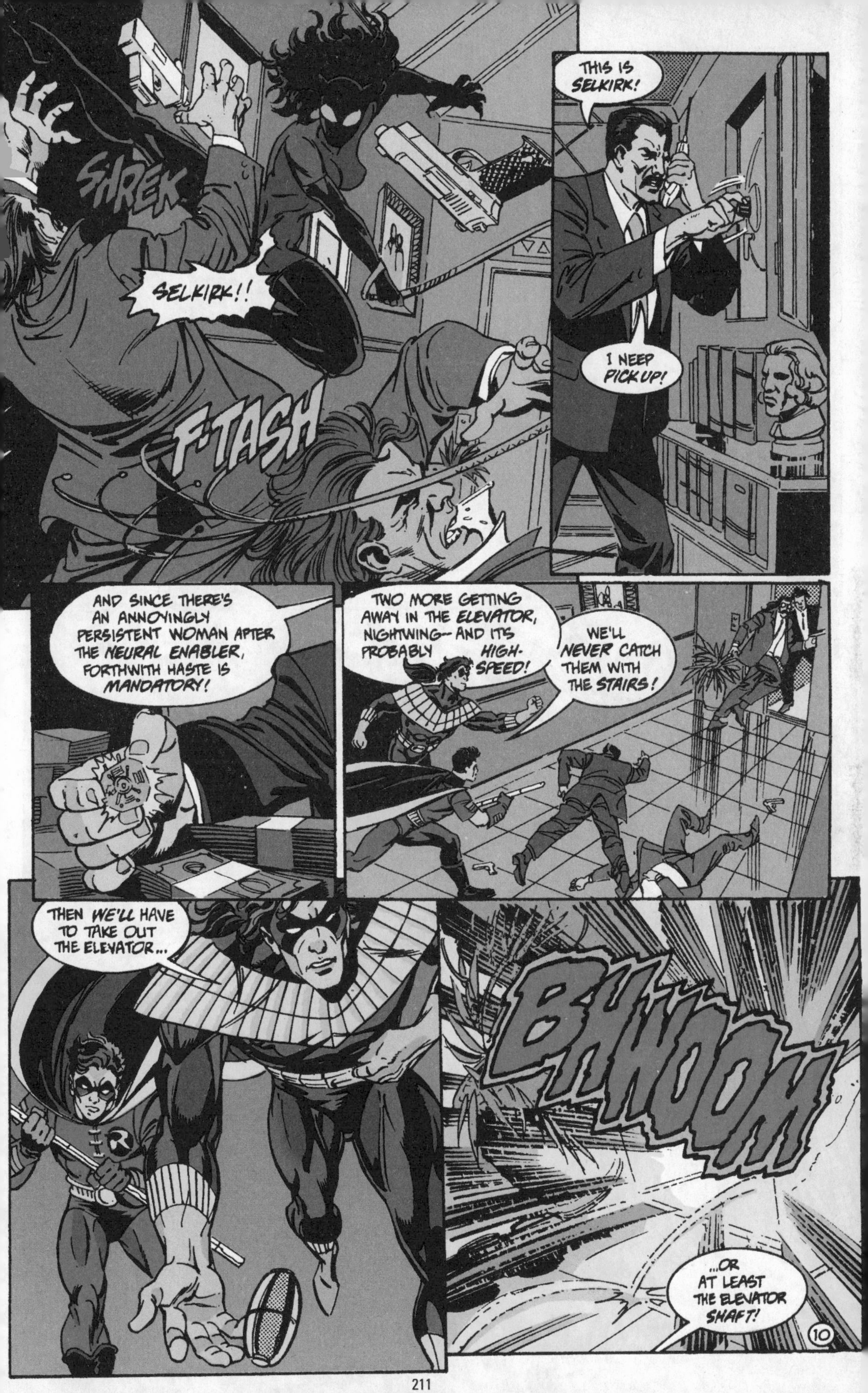
SHREK
SELKIRK!!
F-TASH
THIS IS SELKIRK!
I NEED PICKUP!
AND SINCE THERE'S AN ANNOYINGLY PERSISTENT WOMAN AFTER THE NEURAL ENABLER, FORTHWITH HASTE IS MANDATORY!
TWO MORE GETTING AWAY IN THE ELEVATOR, NIGHTWING-- AND ITS PROBABLY HIGH-SPEED!
WE'LL NEVER CATCH THEM WITH THE STAIRS!
THEN WE'LL HAVE TO TAKE OUT THE ELEVATOR...
BHWOOM
...OR AT LEAST THE ELEVATOR SHAFT!
10

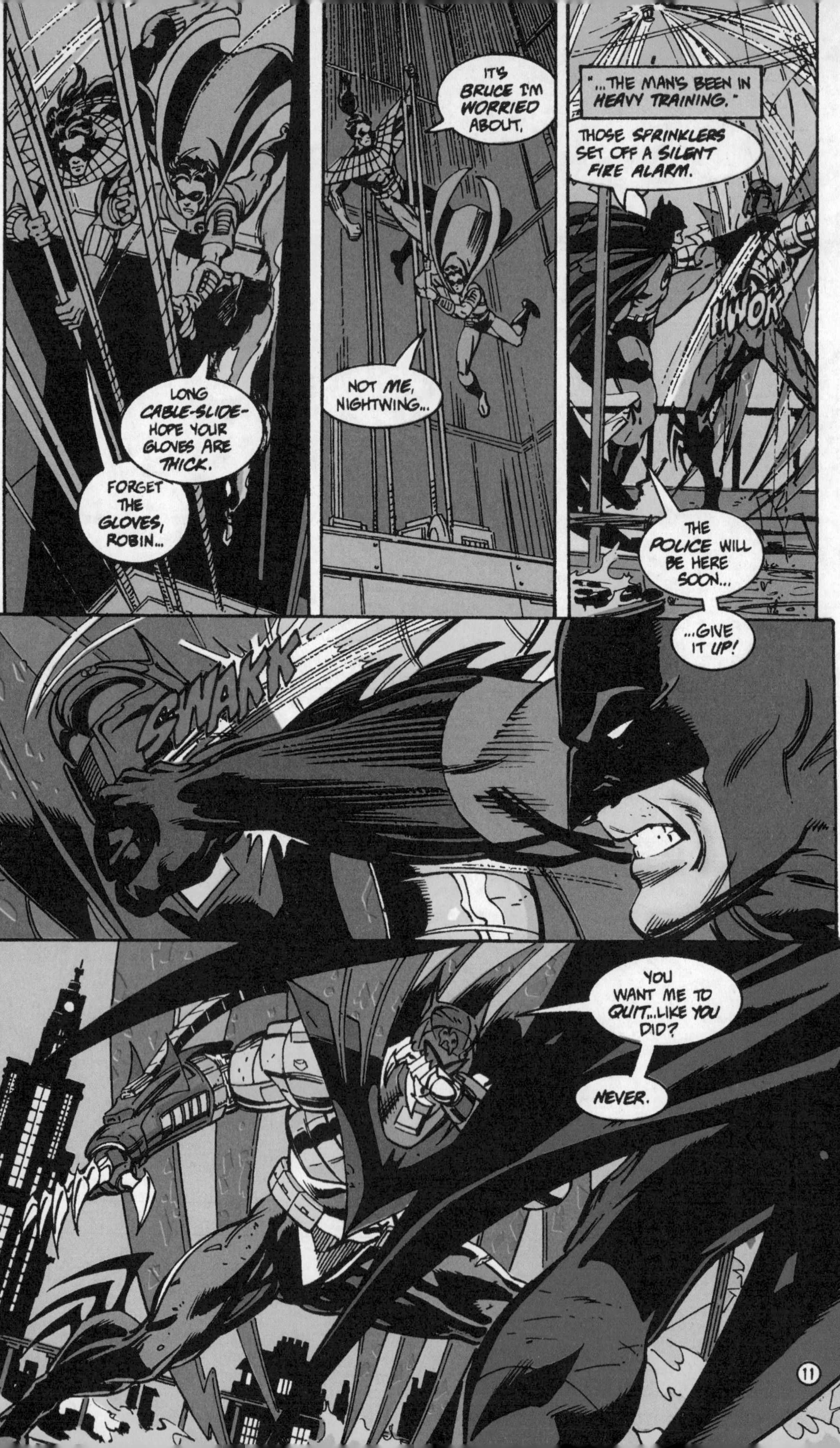

LONG CABLE-SLIDE- HOPE YOUR GLOVES ARE THICK.
FORGET THE GLOVES, ROBIN...
IT'S BRUCE I'M WORRIED ABOUT.
NOT ME, NIGHTWING...
"...THE MAN'S BEEN IN HEAVY TRAINING."
THOSE SPRINKLERS SET OFF A SILENT FIRE ALARM.
WOK
THE POLICE WILL BE HERE SOON...
...GIVE IT UP!
SWAKK
YOU WANT ME TO QUIT...LIKE YOU DID?
NEVER.

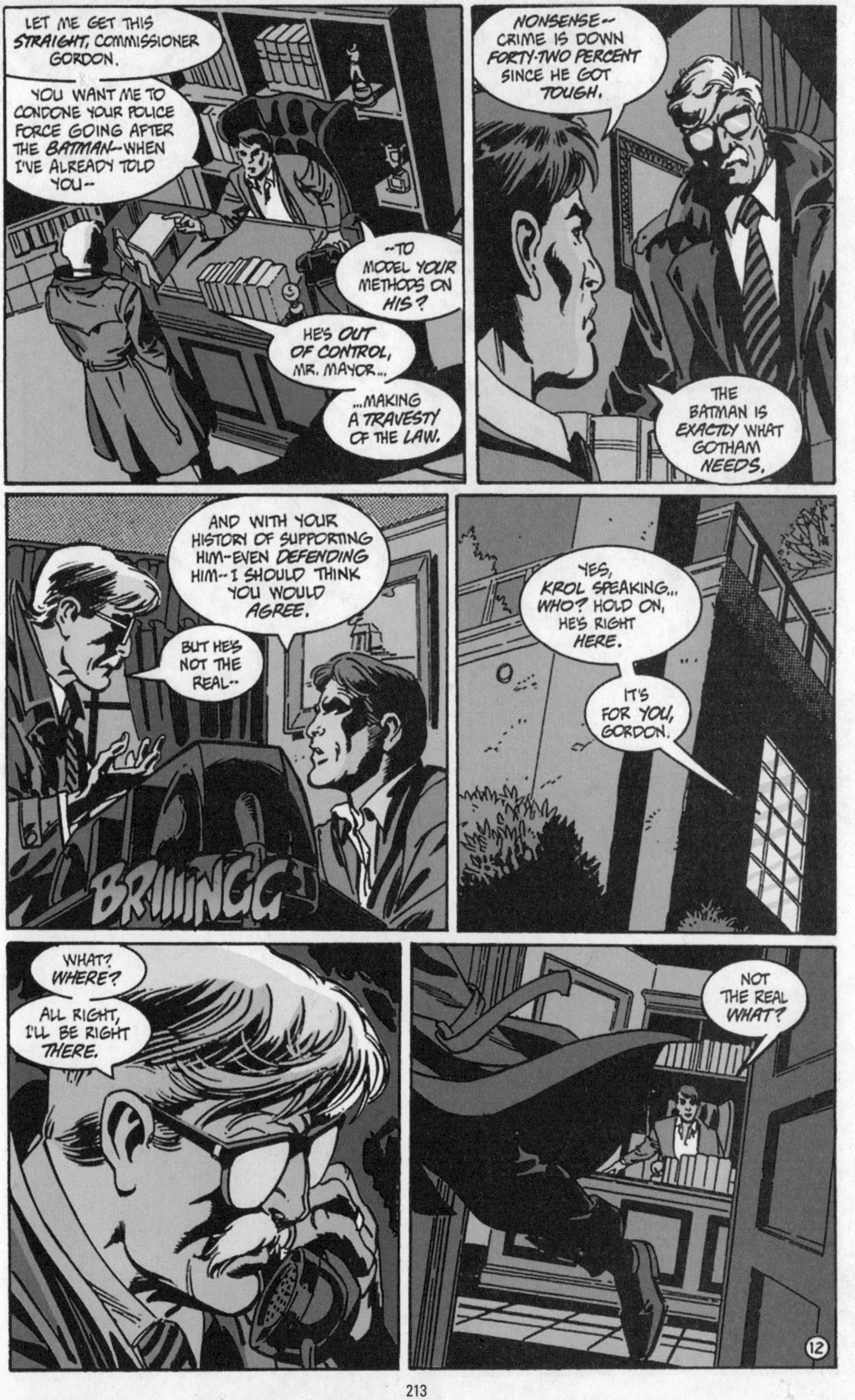
LET ME GET THIS STRAIGHT, COMMISSIONER GORDON.
YOU WANT ME TO CONDONE YOUR POLICE FORCE GOING AFTER THE BATMAN--WHEN I'VE ALREADY TOLD YOU--
--TO MODEL YOUR METHODS ON HIS?
HE'S OUT OF CONTROL, MR. MAYOR...
...MAKING A TRAVESTY OF THE LAW.
NONSENSE-- CRIME IS DOWN FORTY-TWO PERCENT SINCE HE GOT TOUGH.
THE BATMAN IS EXACTLY WHAT GOTHAM NEEDS.
AND WITH YOUR HISTORY OF SUPPORTING HIM-EVEN DEFENDING HIM--I SHOULD THINK YOU WOULD AGREE.
BUT HE'S NOT THE REAL--
BRIIIINGG
YES, KROL SPEAKING... WHO? HOLD ON, HE'S RIGHT HERE.
IT'S FOR YOU, GORDON.
WHAT? WHERE?
ALL RIGHT, I'LL BE RIGHT THERE.
NOT THE REAL WHAT?
12

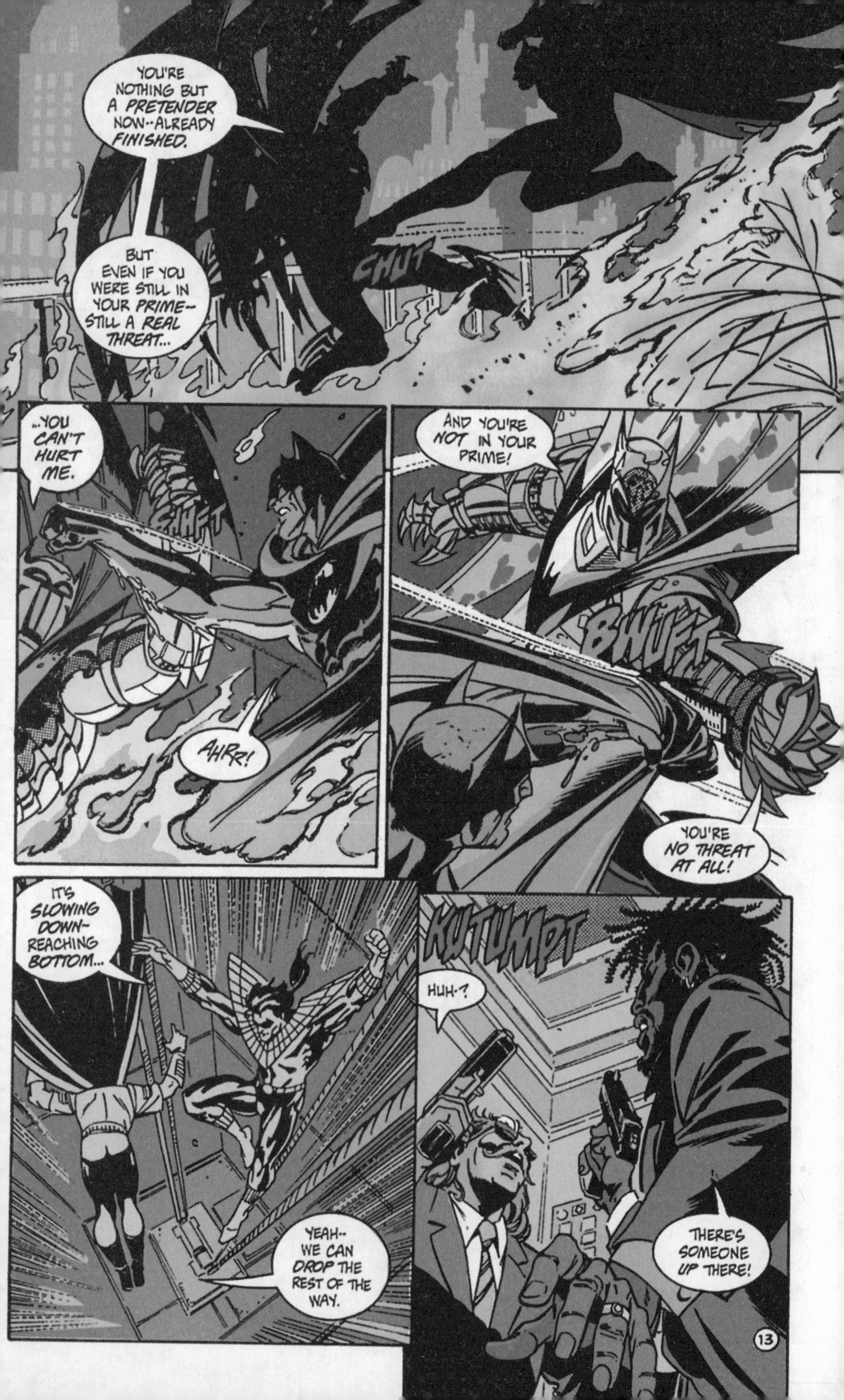
YOU'RE NOTHING BUT A PRETENDER NOW--ALREADY FINISHED.
BUT EVEN IF YOU WERE STILL IN YOUR PRIME-- STILL A REAL THREAT...
CHUT
..YOU CAN'T HURT ME.
SHFT
AHRR!
AND YOU'RE NOT IN YOUR PRIME!
BWUFF
YOU'RE NO THREAT AT ALL!
IT'S SLOWING DOWN-- REACHING BOTTOM...
YEAH-- WE CAN DROP THE REST OF THE WAY.
KUTUMPT
HUH-?
THERE'S SOMEONE UP THERE!
13

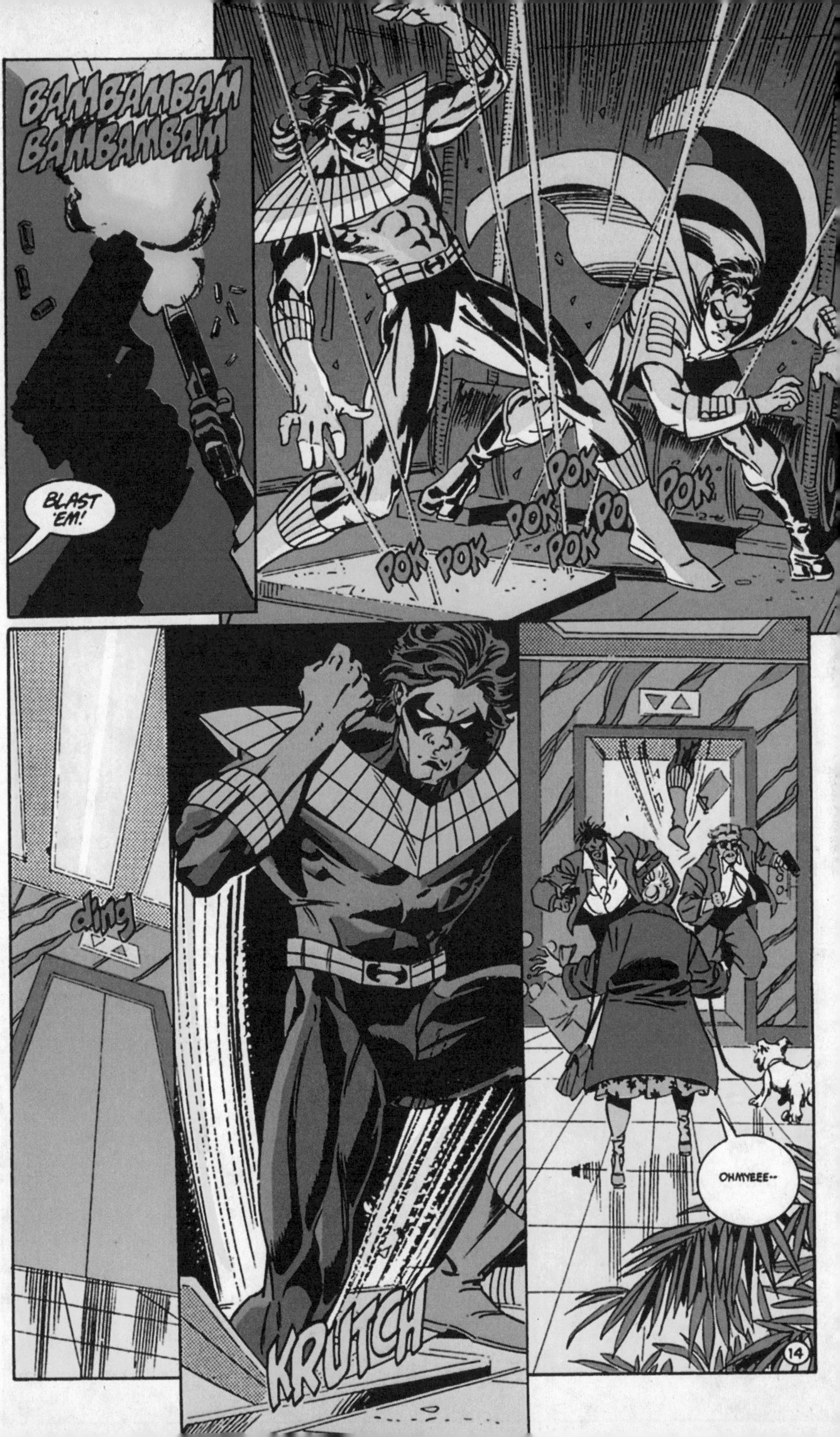
BAMBAMBAM
BAMBAMBAM
BLAST 'EM!
POK POK POK POK POK POK POK
ding
KRUTCH
OHMYEEE--
14

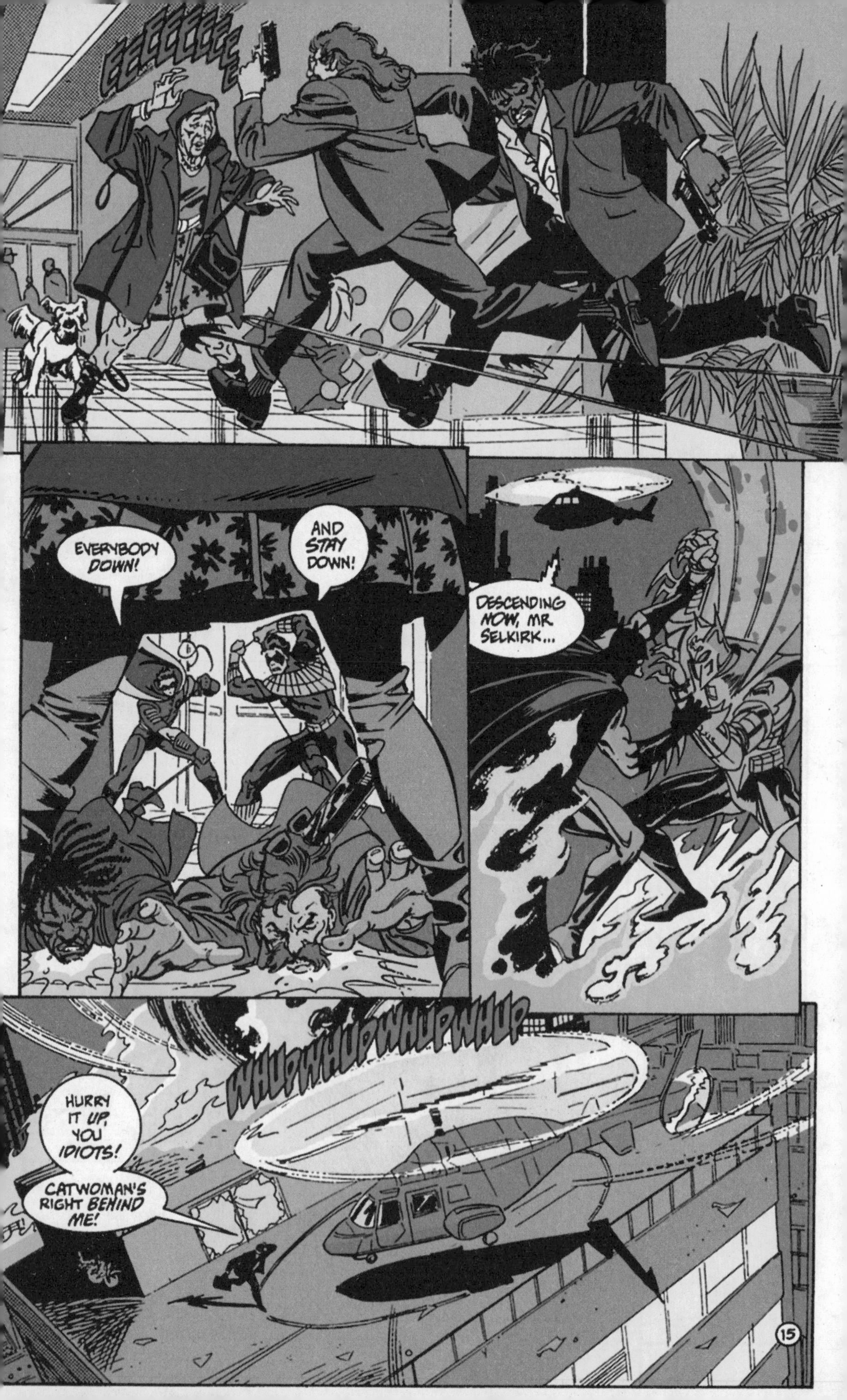
EEEEEEEE
EVERYBODY DOWN!
AND STAY DOWN!
DESCENDING NOW, MR SELKIRK...
WHUPWHUPWHUPWHUP
HURRY IT UP, YOU IDIOTS!
CATWOMAN'S RIGHT BEHIND ME!

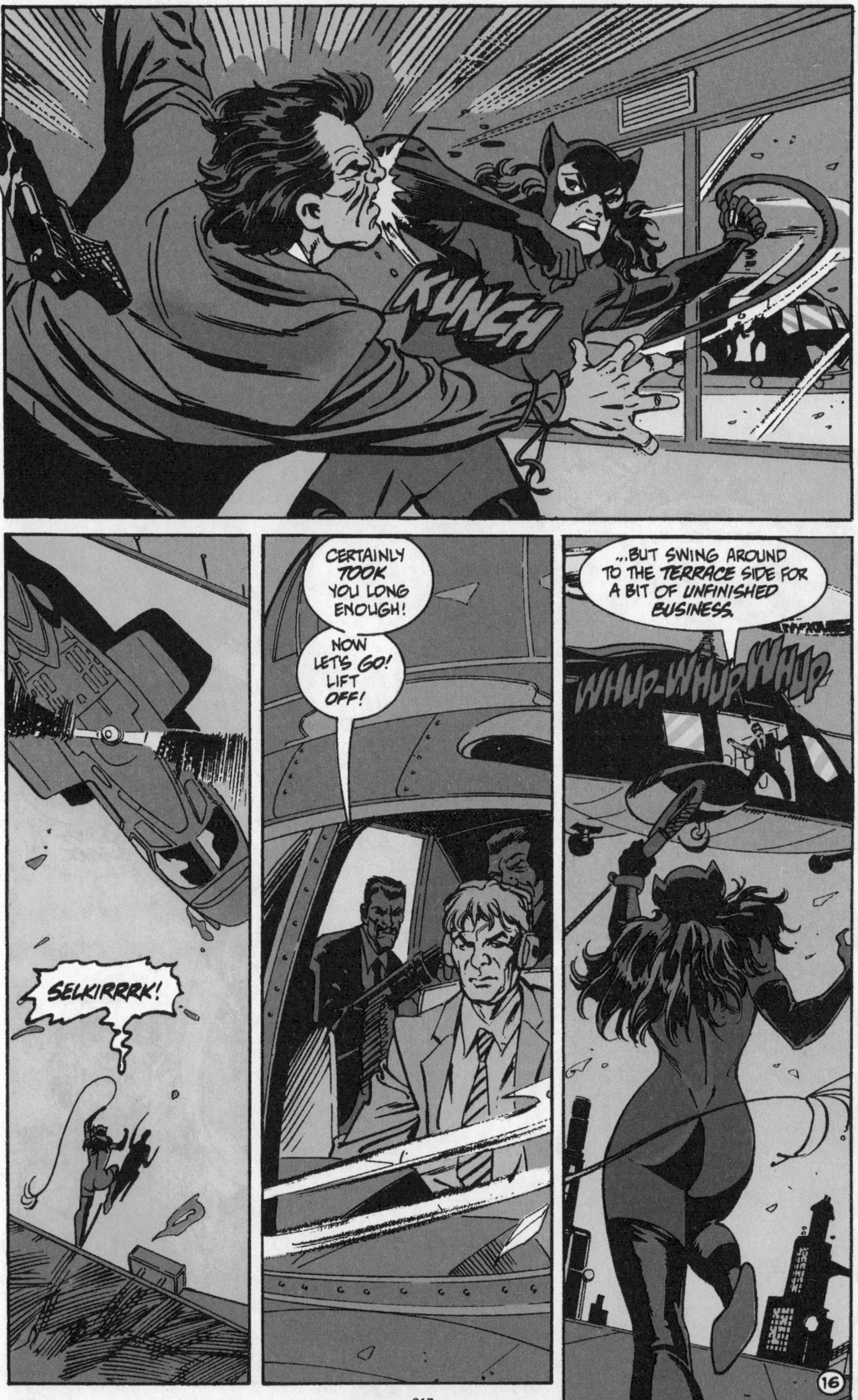
KUNCH
SELKIRRRK!
CERTAINLY TOOK YOU LONG ENOUGH!
NOW LET'S GO! LIFT OFF!
...BUT SWING AROUND TO THE TERRACE SIDE FOR A BIT OF UNFINISHED BUSINESS.
WHUP-WHUP-WHUP
16

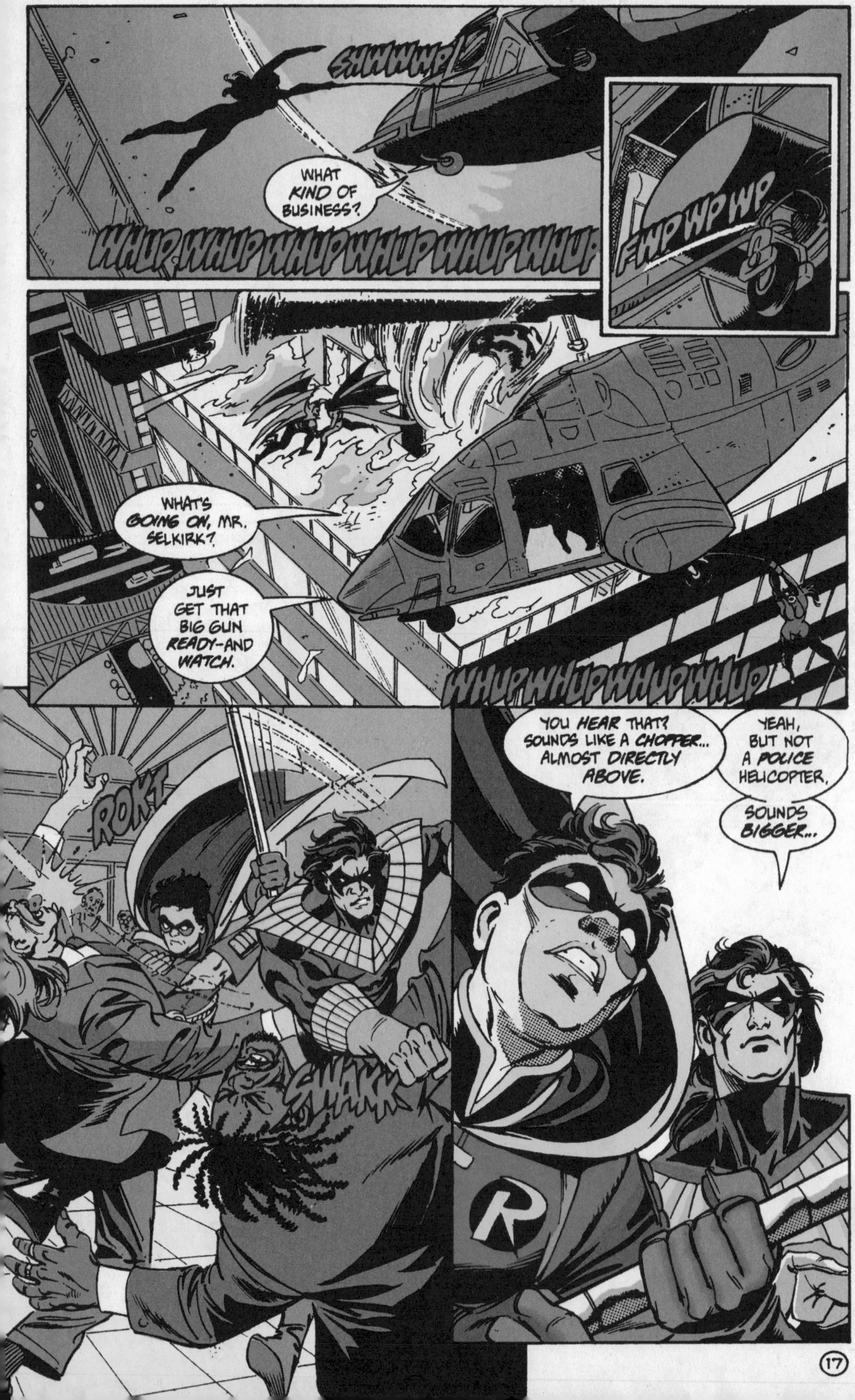
SHWWWP
WHAT KIND OF BUSINESS?
WHUP WHUP WHUP WHUP WHUP WHUP
FWP WP WP
WHAT'S GOING ON, MR. SELKIRK?
JUST GET THAT BIG GUN READY--AND WATCH.
WHUPWHUPWHUPWHUP
ROKT
SMAKK
YOU HEAR THAT? SOUNDS LIKE A CHOPPER... ALMOST DIRECTLY ABOVE.
YEAH, BUT NOT A POLICE HELICOPTER.
SOUNDS BIGGER...

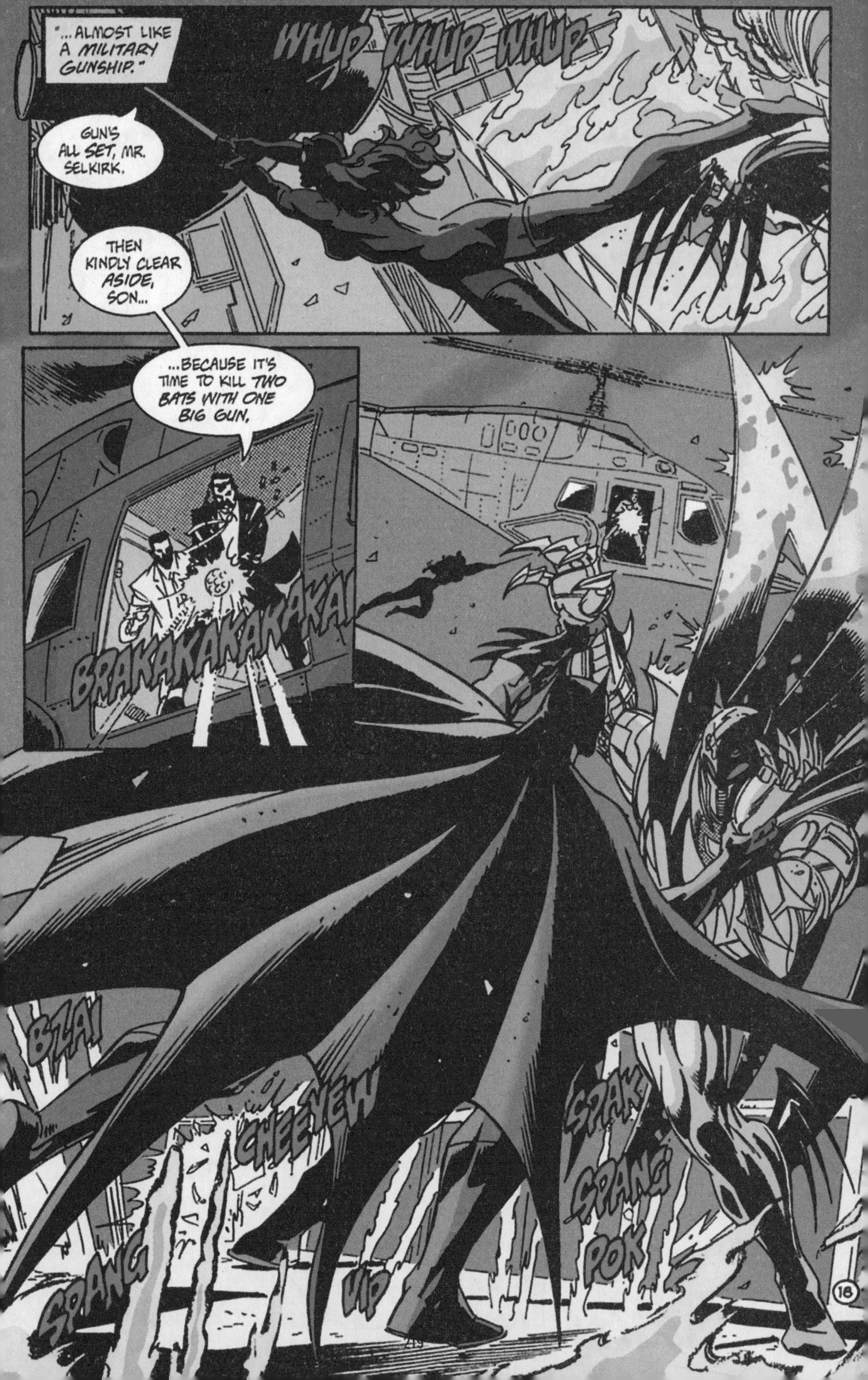
"...ALMOST LIKE A MILITARY GUNSHIP."
WHUP WHUP WHUP
GUN'S ALL SET, MR. SELKIRK.
THEN KINDLY CLEAR ASIDE, SON...
...BECAUSE IT'S TIME TO KILL TWO BATS WITH ONE BIG GUN.
BRAKAKAKAKAKA
BZAI
CHEEYEW
SPAK
SPANG
POK
SPANG
YIP
18

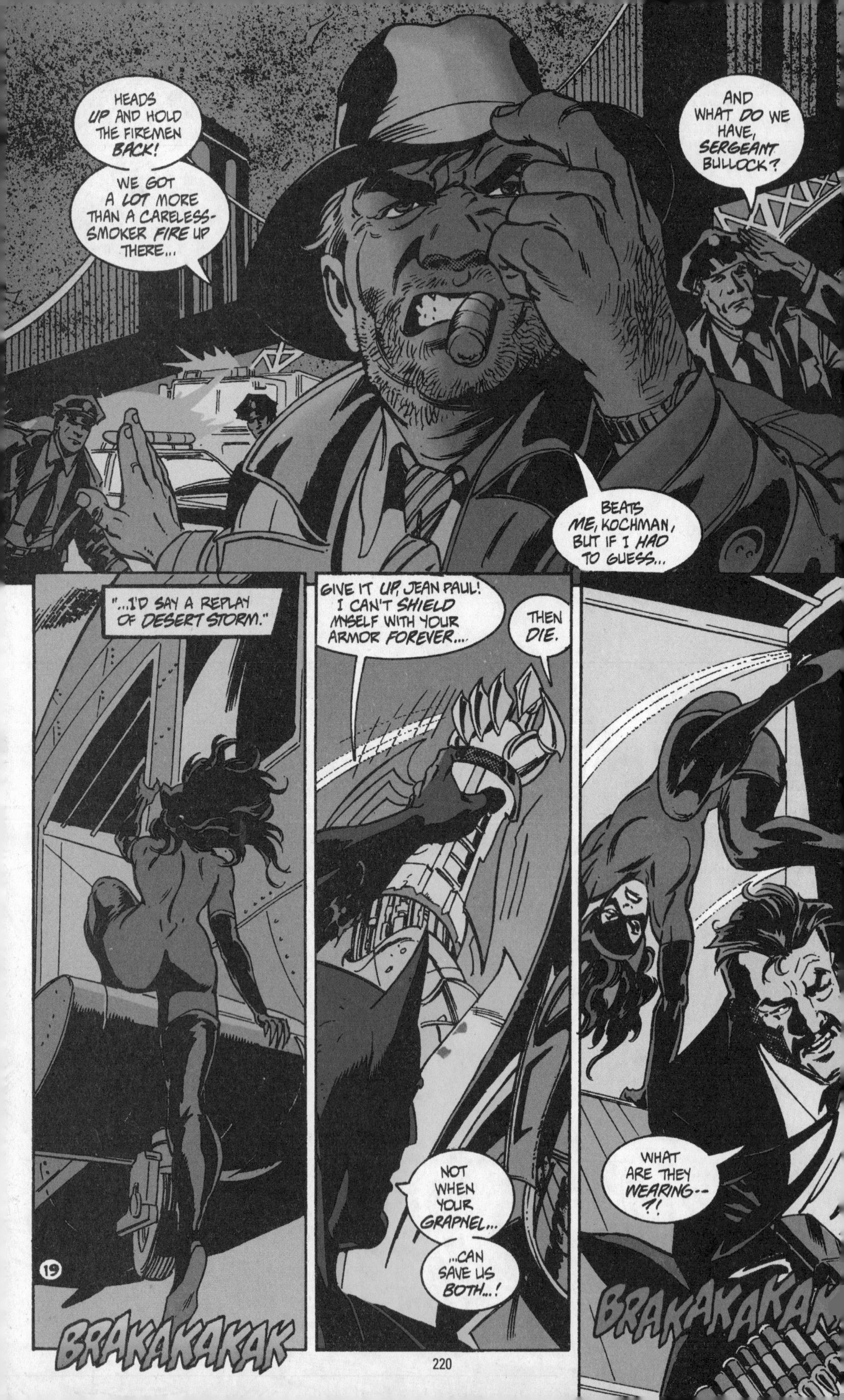
HEADS UP AND HOLD THE FIREMEN BACK!
WE GOT A LOT MORE THAN A CARELESS-SMOKER FIRE UP THERE...
AND WHAT DO WE HAVE, SERGEANT BULLOCK?
BEATS ME, KOCHMAN, BUT IF I HAD TO GUESS...
"...I'D SAY A REPLAY OF DESERT STORM."
BRAKAKAKAK
GIVE IT UP, JEAN PAUL! I CAN'T SHIELD MYSELF WITH YOUR ARMOR FOREVER...
THEN DIE.
NOT WHEN YOUR GRAPNEL...
...CAN SAVE US BOTH...!
WHAT ARE THEY WEARING--?!
BRAKAKAKAK

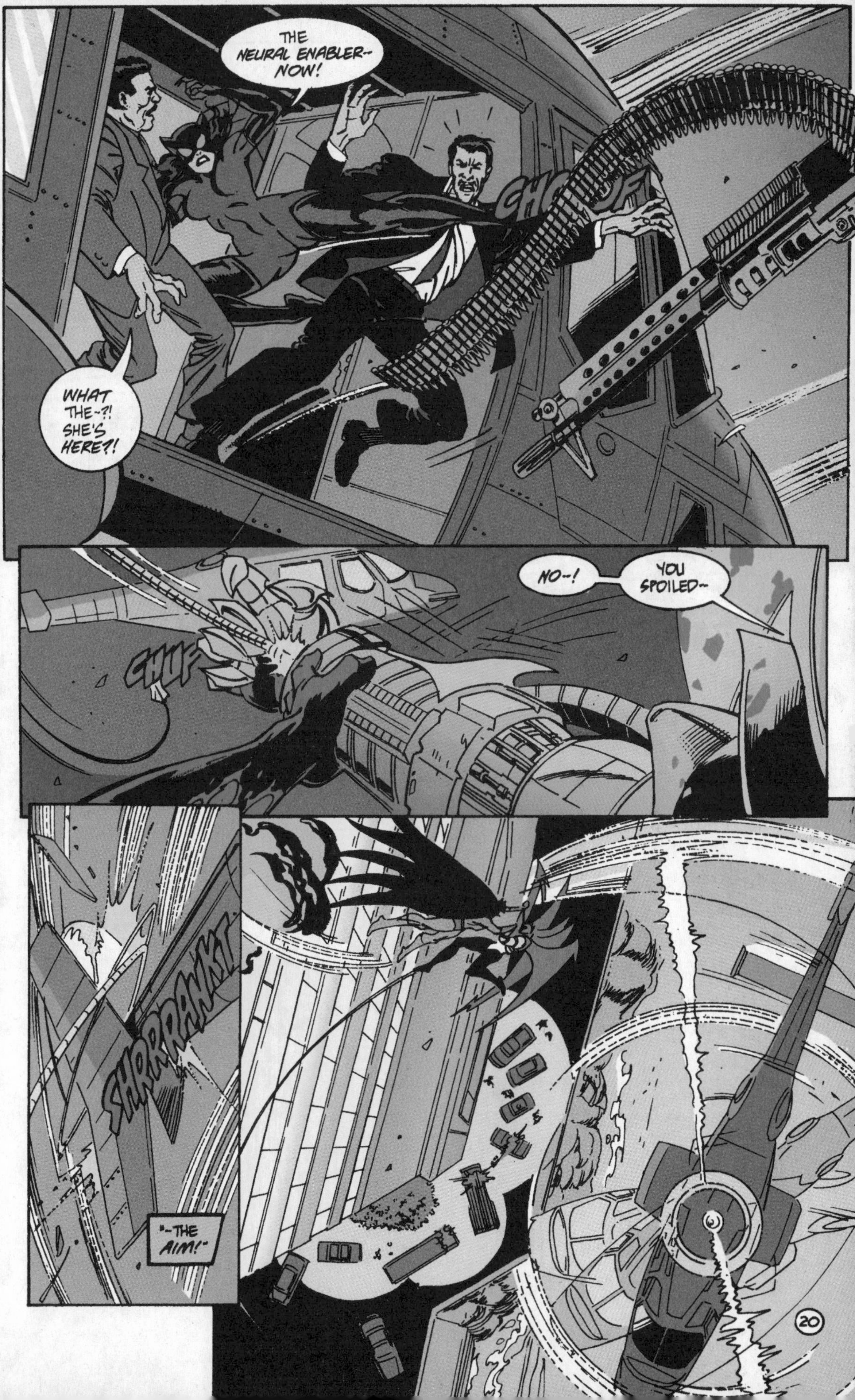

THE NEURAL ENABLER-- NOW!
WHAT THE--?! SHE'S HERE?!
CHOOF
NO--!
YOU SPOILED--
CHUF
SHRRAKKT
"--THE AIM!"
20

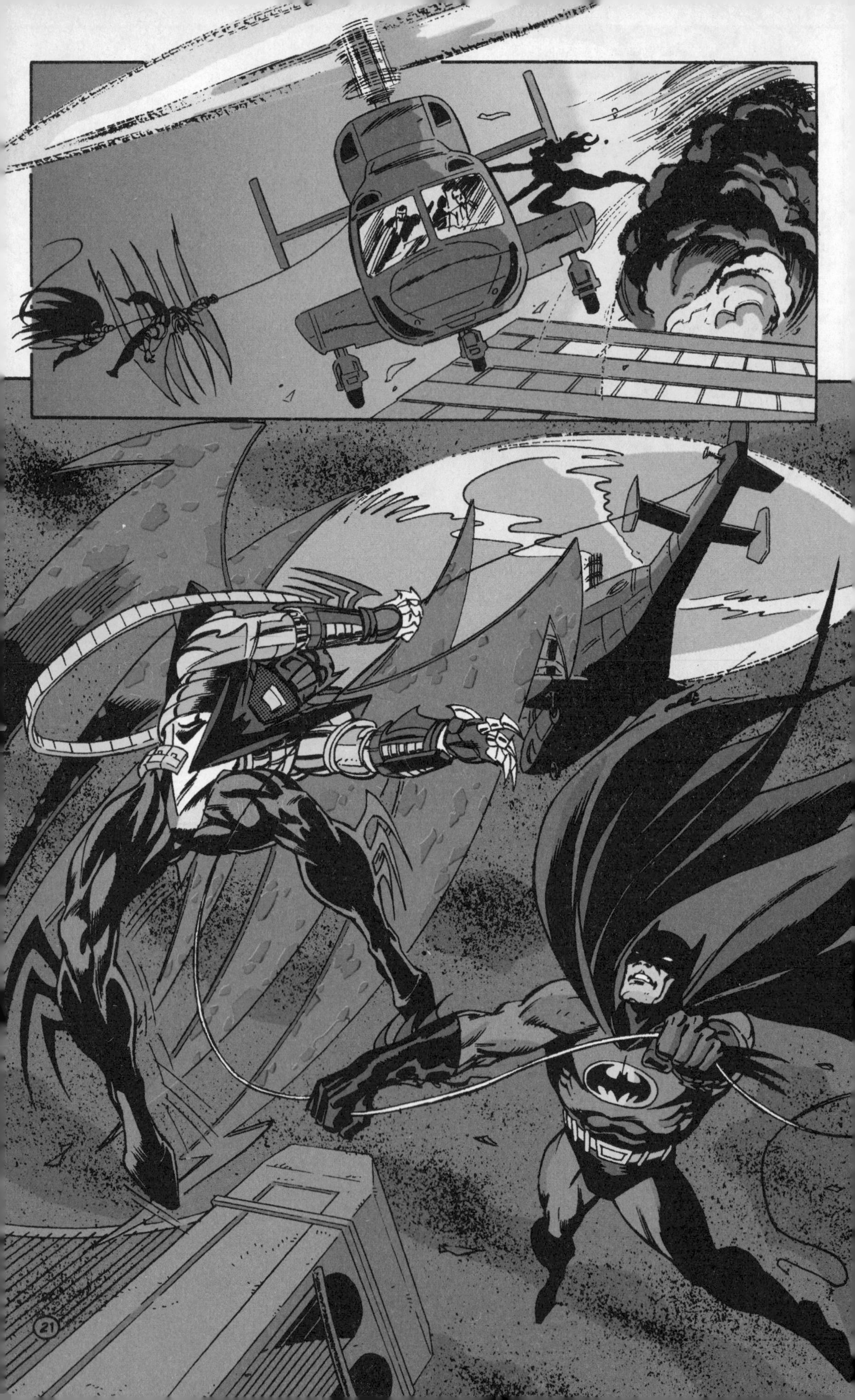

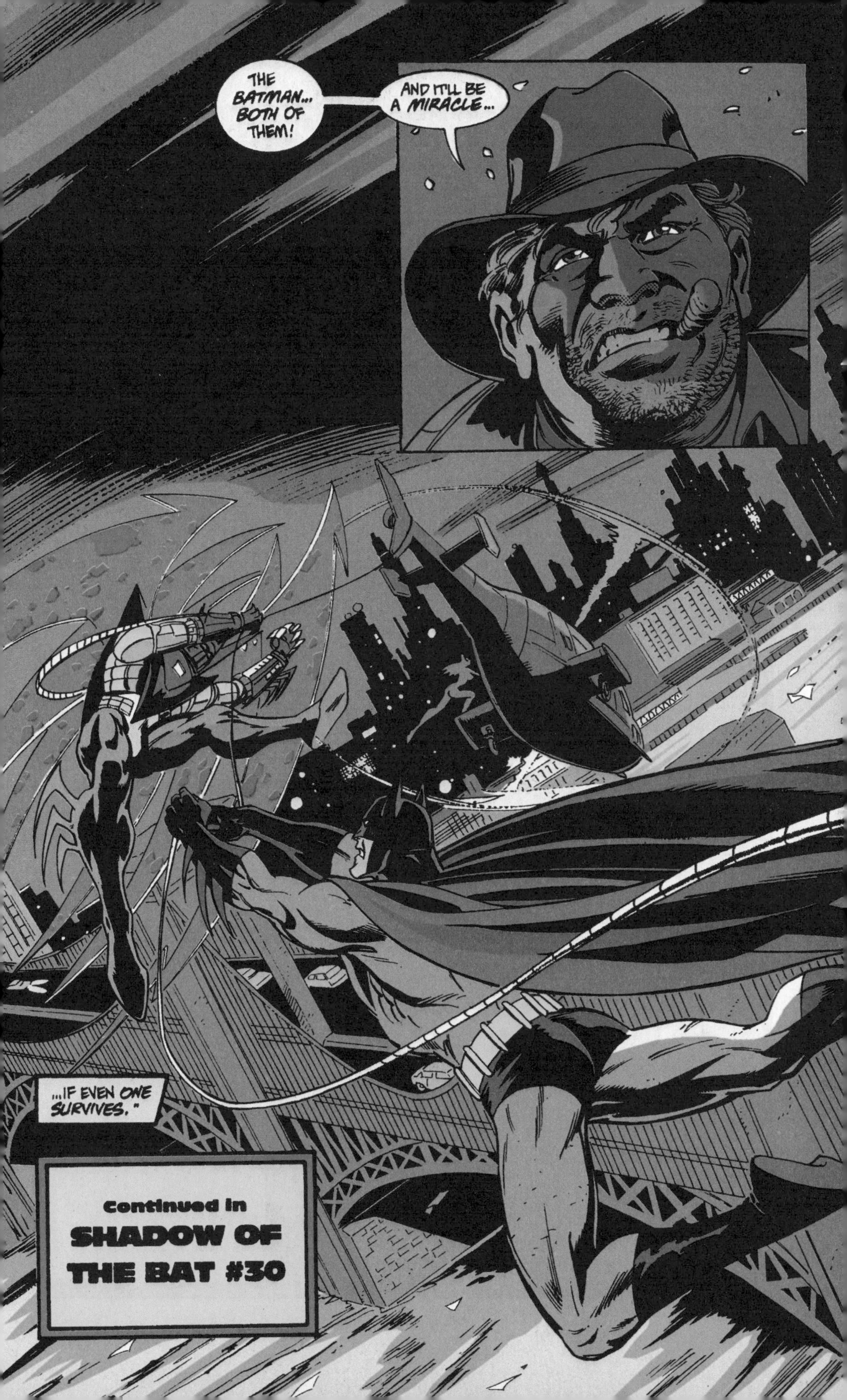
THE BATMAN... BOTH OF THEM!
AND IT'LL BE A MIRACLE...
...IF EVEN ONE SURVIVES."
Continued in SHADOW OF THE BAT #30

Cover art by **BRIAN STELFREEZE**

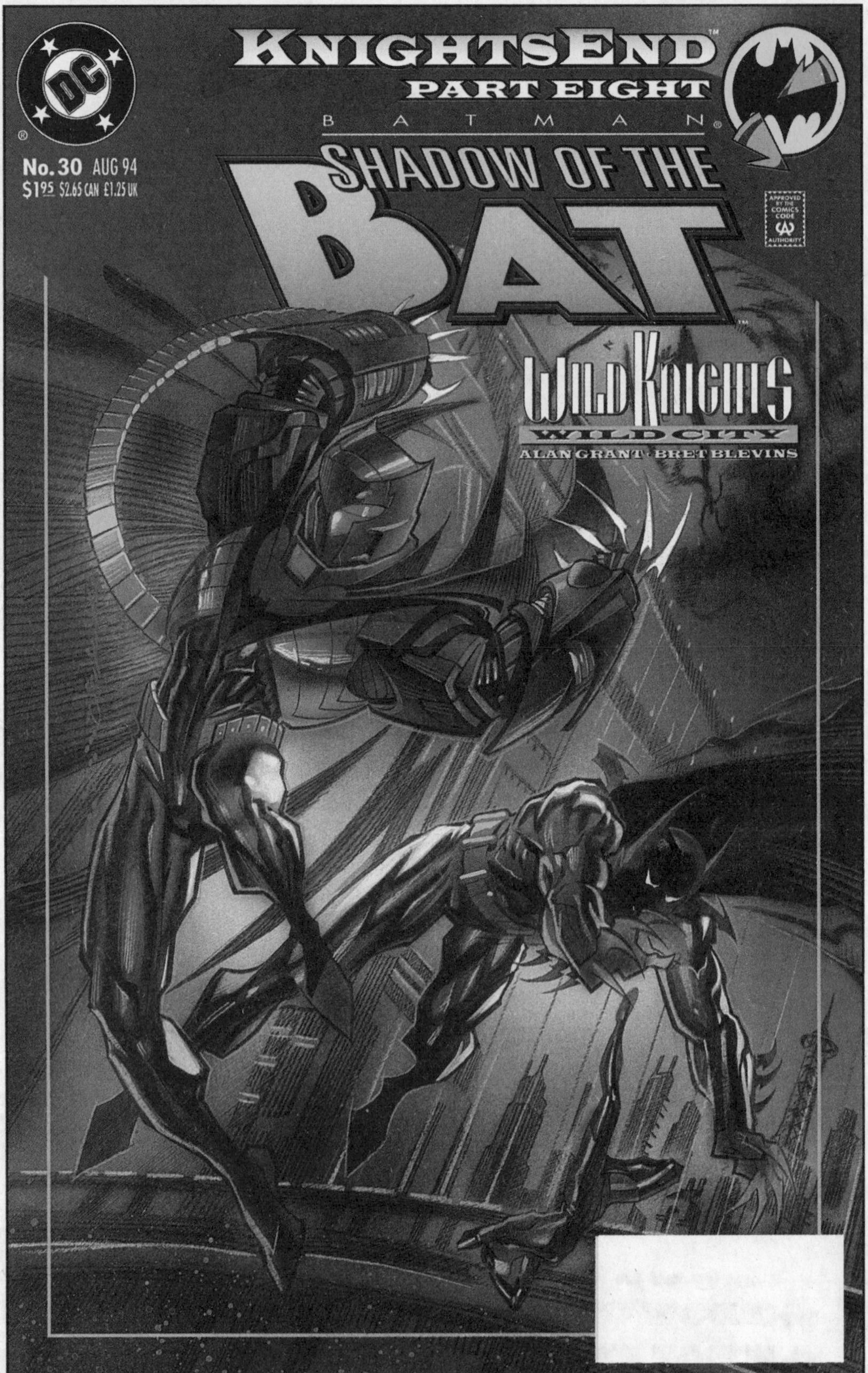

DC
KNIGHTSEND
PART EIGHT
BATMAN
SHADOW OF THE BAT
No. 30 AUG 94
$1.95 $2.65 CAN £1.25 UK
APPROVED BY THE COMICS CODE AUTHORITY
WILD KNIGHTS
WILD CITY
ALAN GRANT · BRET BLEVINS

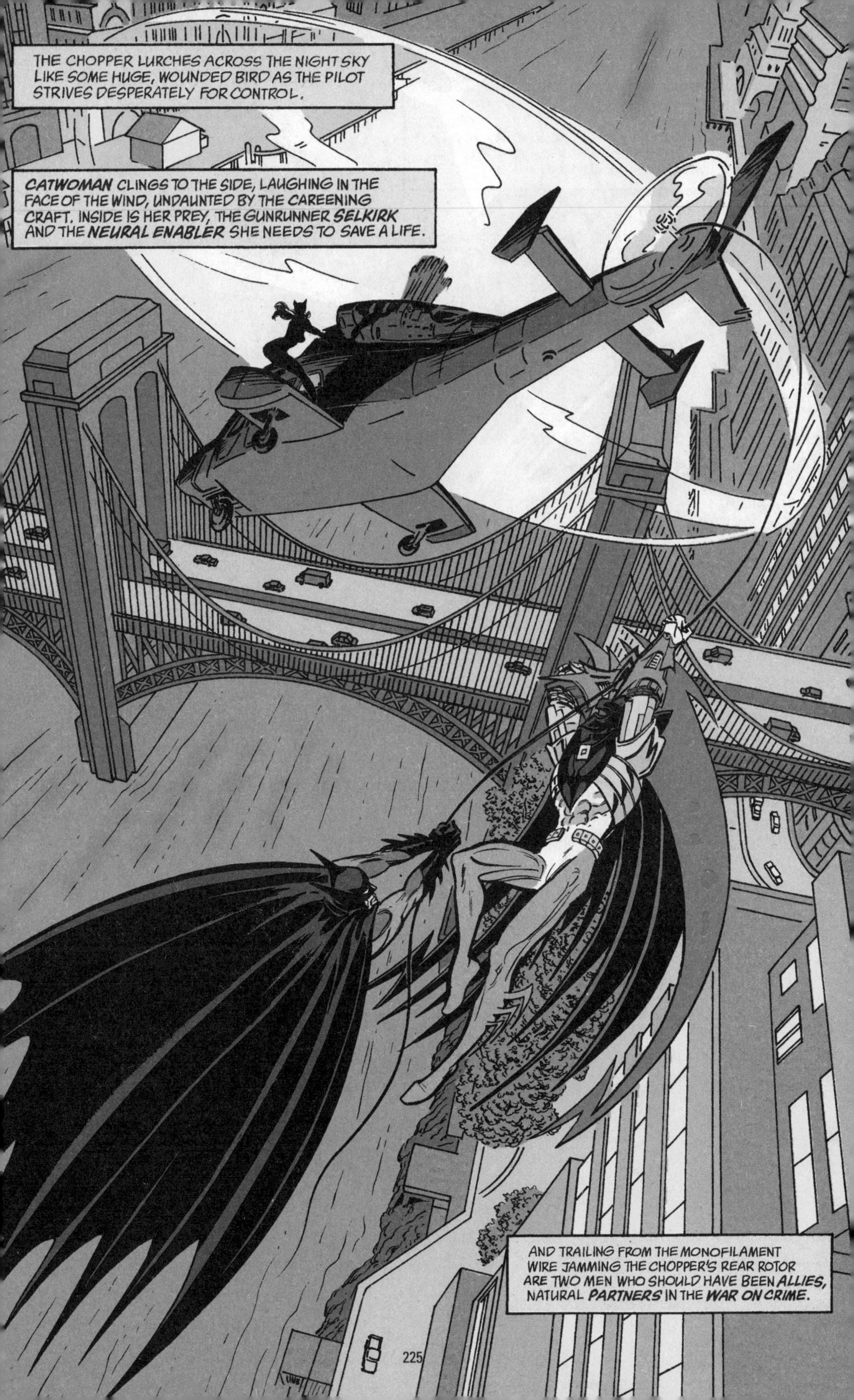
THE CHOPPER LURCHES ACROSS THE NIGHT SKY LIKE SOME HUGE, WOUNDED BIRD AS THE PILOT STRIVES DESPERATELY FOR CONTROL.
CATWOMAN CLINGS TO THE SIDE, LAUGHING IN THE FACE OF THE WIND, UNDAUNTED BY THE CAREENING CRAFT. INSIDE IS HER PREY, THE GUNRUNNER SELKIRK AND THE NEURAL ENABLER SHE NEEDS TO SAVE A LIFE.
AND TRAILING FROM THE MONOFILAMENT WIRE JAMMING THE CHOPPER'S REAR ROTOR ARE TWO MEN WHO SHOULD HAVE BEEN ALLIES, NATURAL PARTNERS IN THE WAR ON CRIME.

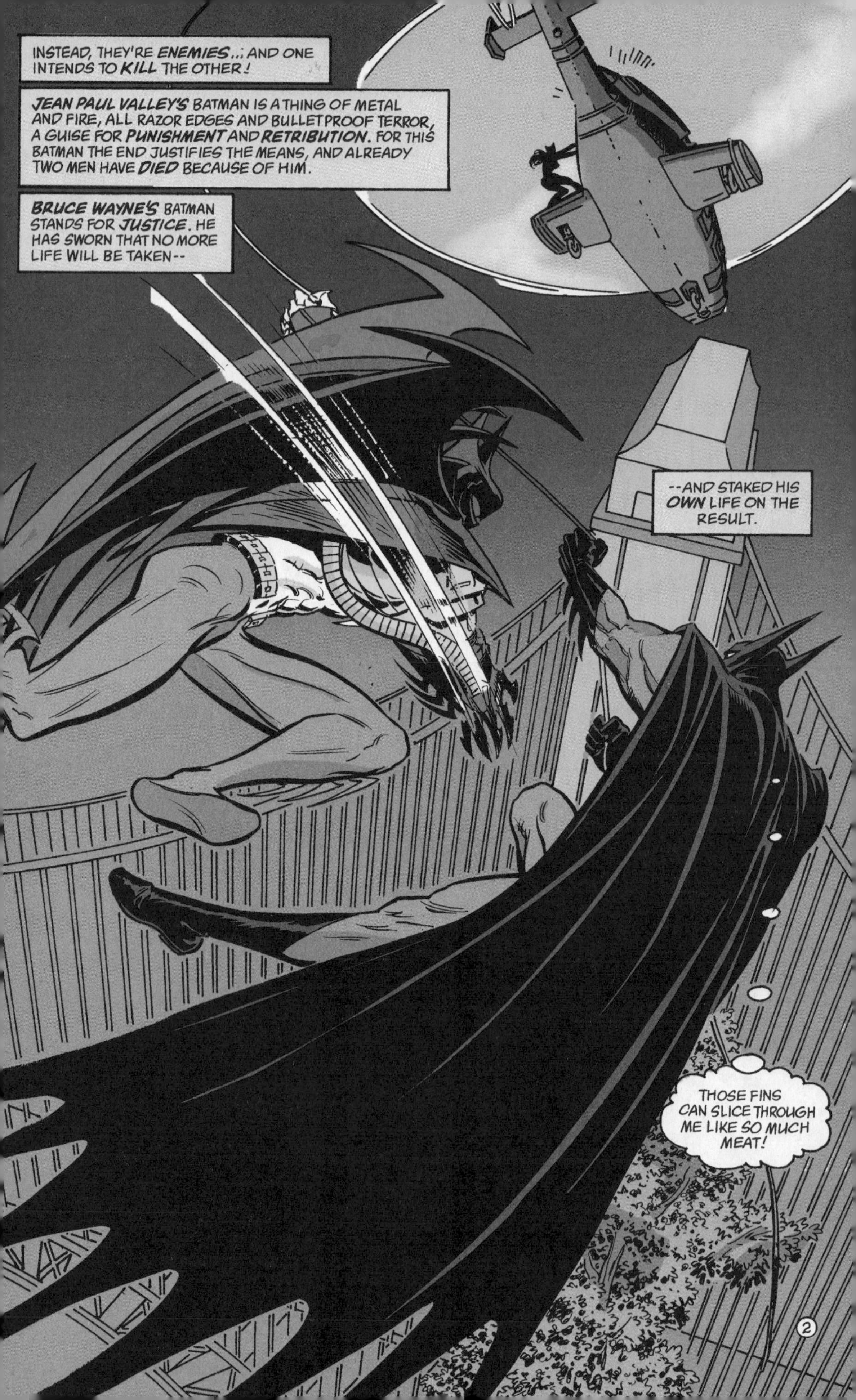
INSTEAD, THEY'RE ENEMIES...; AND ONE INTENDS TO KILL THE OTHER!
JEAN PAUL VALLEY'S BATMAN IS A THING OF METAL AND FIRE, ALL RAZOR EDGES AND BULLETPROOF TERROR, A GUISE FOR PUNISHMENT AND RETRIBUTION. FOR THIS BATMAN THE END JUSTIFIES THE MEANS, AND ALREADY TWO MEN HAVE DIED BECAUSE OF HIM.
BRUCE WAYNE'S BATMAN STANDS FOR JUSTICE. HE HAS SWORN THAT NO MORE LIFE WILL BE TAKEN--
--AND STAKED HIS OWN LIFE ON THE RESULT.
THOSE FINS CAN SLICE THROUGH ME LIKE SO MUCH MEAT!
2

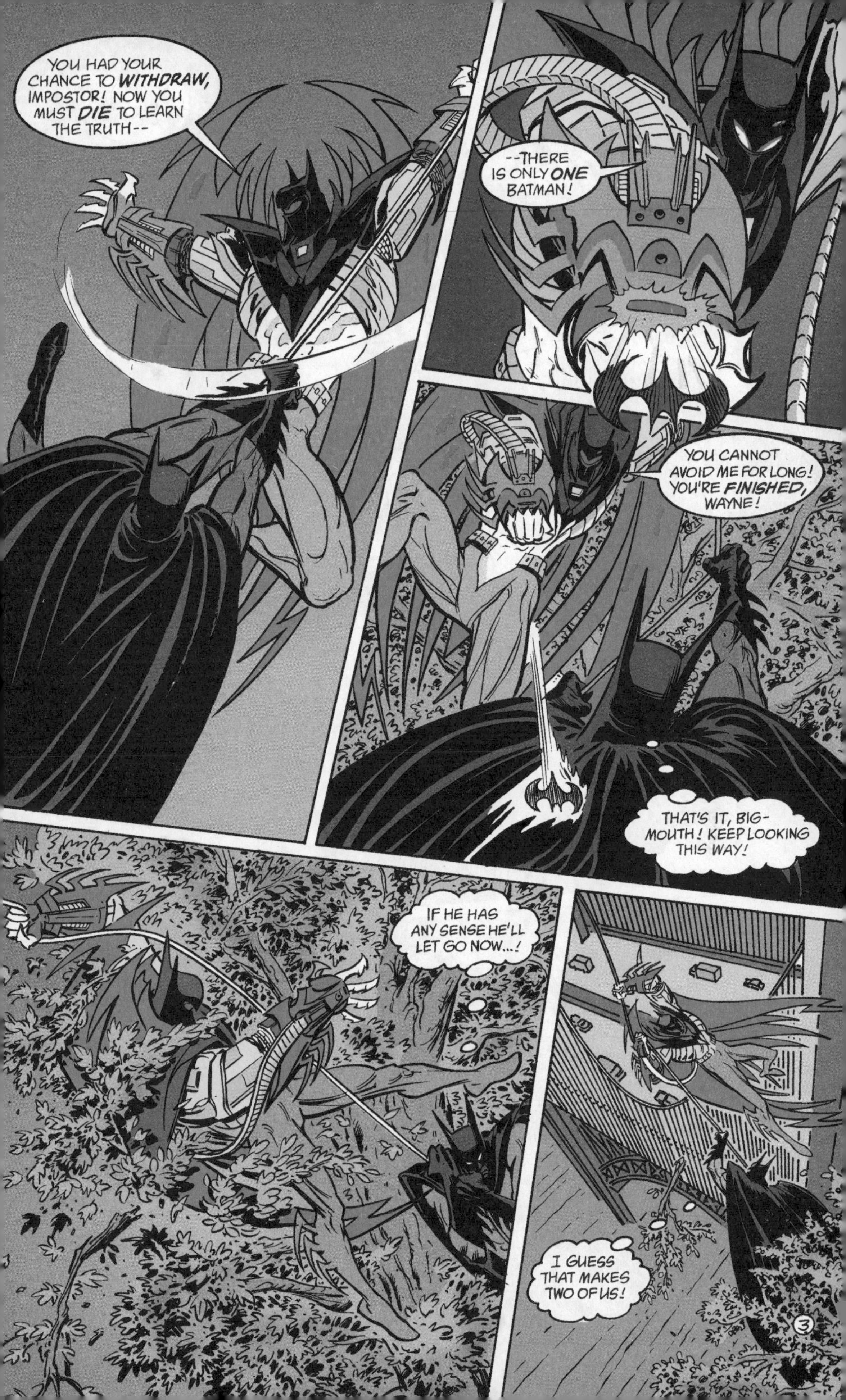

YOU HAD YOUR CHANCE TO WITHDRAW, IMPOSTOR! NOW YOU MUST DIE TO LEARN THE TRUTH--
--THERE IS ONLY ONE BATMAN!
YOU CANNOT AVOID ME FOR LONG! YOU'RE FINISHED, WAYNE!
THAT'S IT, BIG-MOUTH! KEEP LOOKING THIS WAY!
IF HE HAS ANY SENSE HE'LL LET GO NOW...!
I GUESS THAT MAKES TWO OF US!
3

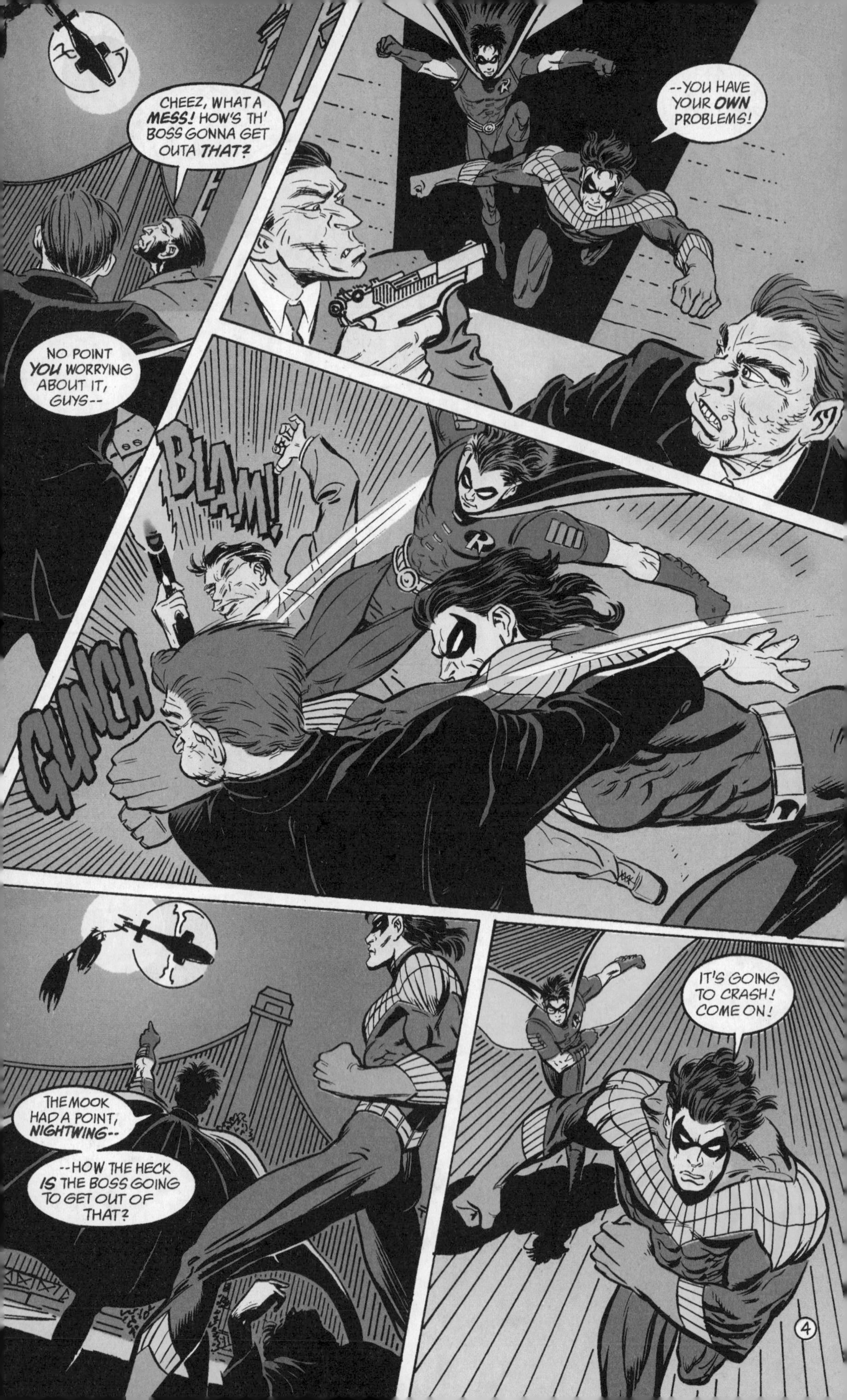
CHEEZ, WHAT A MESS! HOW'S TH' BOSS GONNA GET OUTA THAT?
--YOU HAVE YOUR OWN PROBLEMS!
NO POINT YOU WORRYING ABOUT IT, GUYS--
BLAM!
GLINCH
THE MOOK HAD A POINT, NIGHTWING--
--HOW THE HECK IS THE BOSS GOING TO GET OUT OF THAT?
IT'S GOING TO CRASH! COME ON!
4

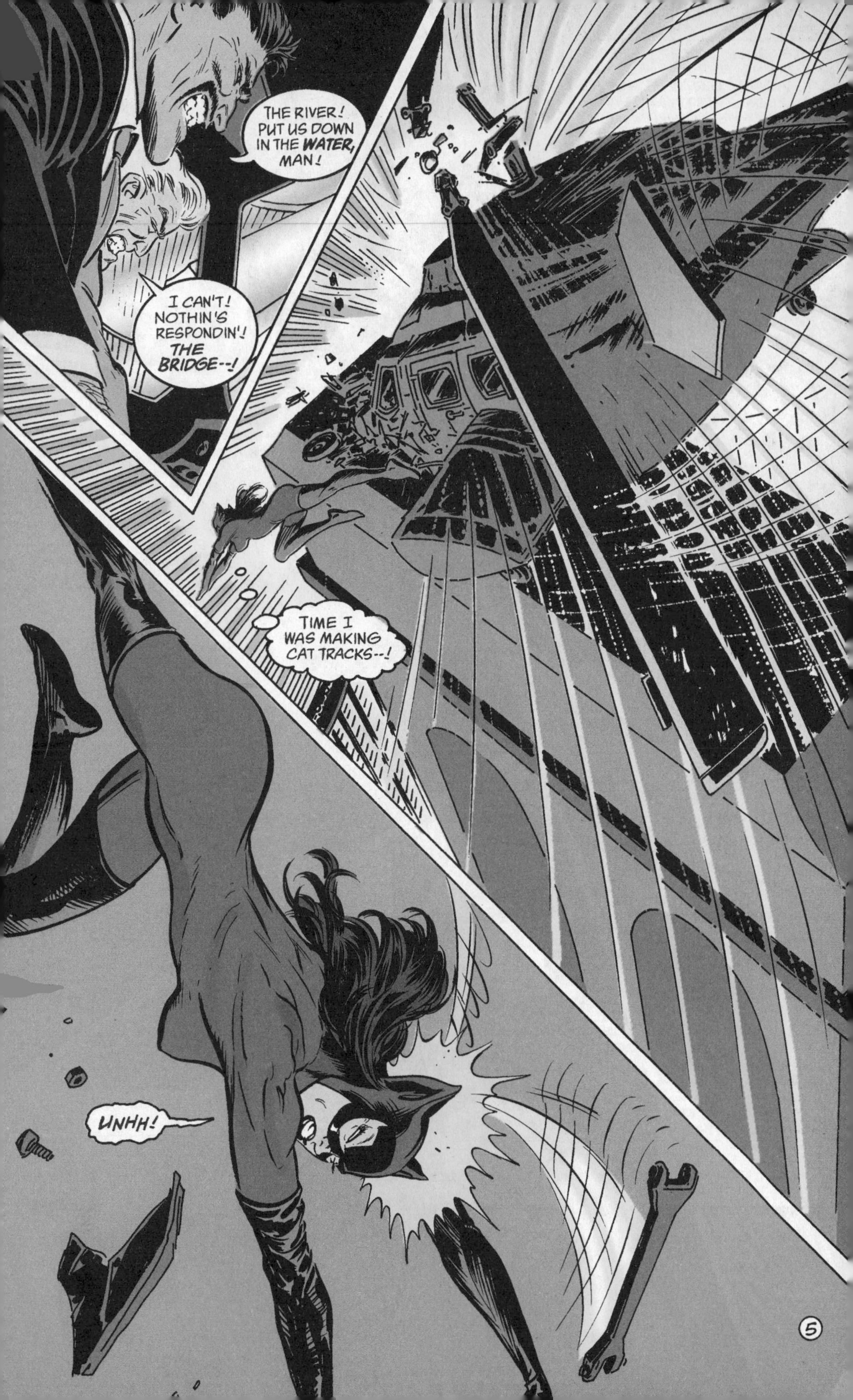

THE RIVER! PUT US DOWN IN THE WATER, MAN!
I CAN'T! NOTHIN'S RESPONDIN'! THE BRIDGE--!
TIME I WAS MAKING CAT TRACKS--!
UNHH!

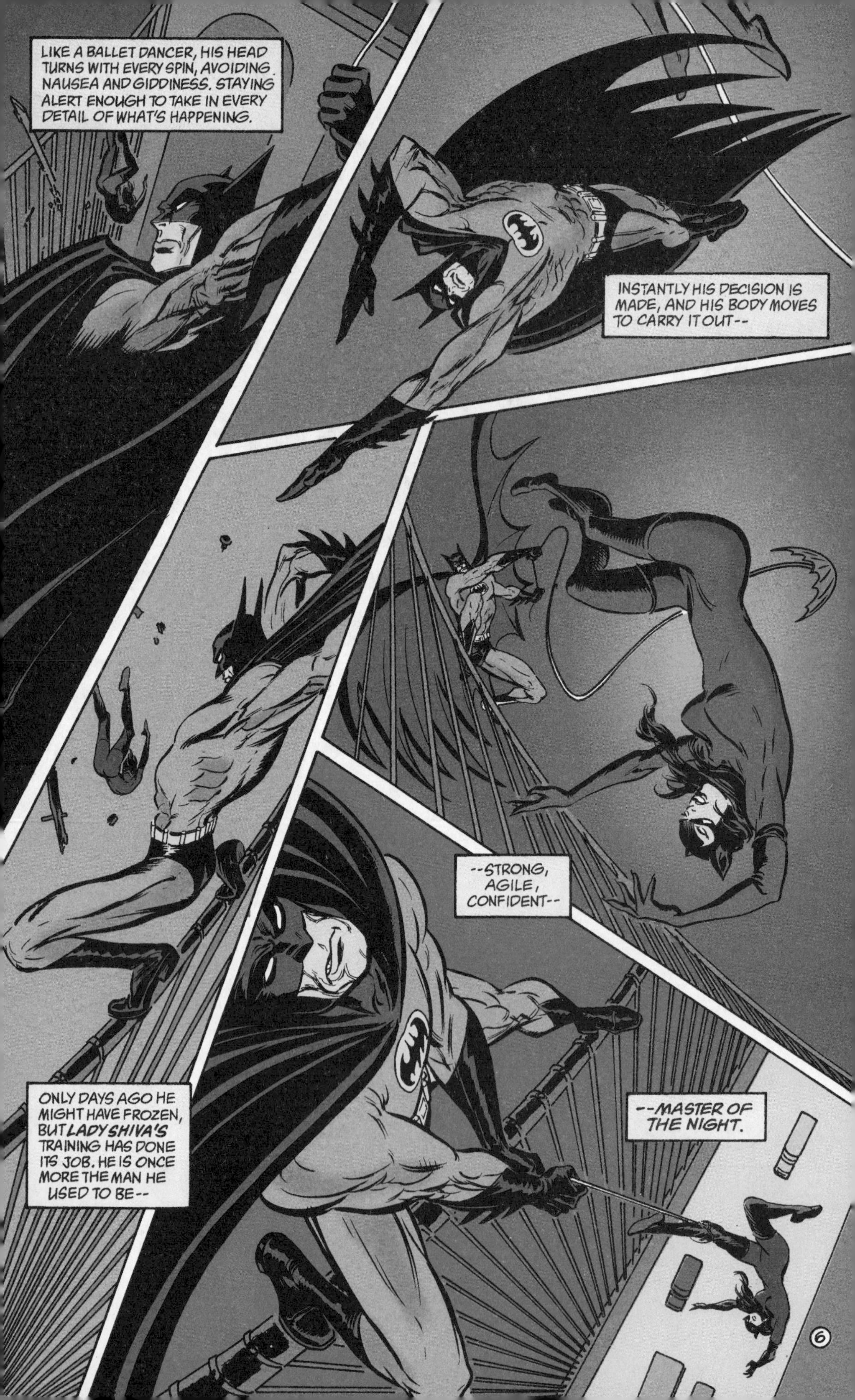
LIKE A BALLET DANCER, HIS HEAD TURNS WITH EVERY SPIN, AVOIDING NAUSEA AND GIDDINESS. STAYING ALERT ENOUGH TO TAKE IN EVERY DETAIL OF WHAT'S HAPPENING.
INSTANTLY HIS DECISION IS MADE, AND HIS BODY MOVES TO CARRY IT OUT--
--STRONG, AGILE, CONFIDENT--
ONLY DAYS AGO HE MIGHT HAVE FROZEN, BUT LADY SHIVA'S TRAINING HAS DONE ITS JOB. HE IS ONCE MORE THE MAN HE USED TO BE--
--MASTER OF THE NIGHT.
6

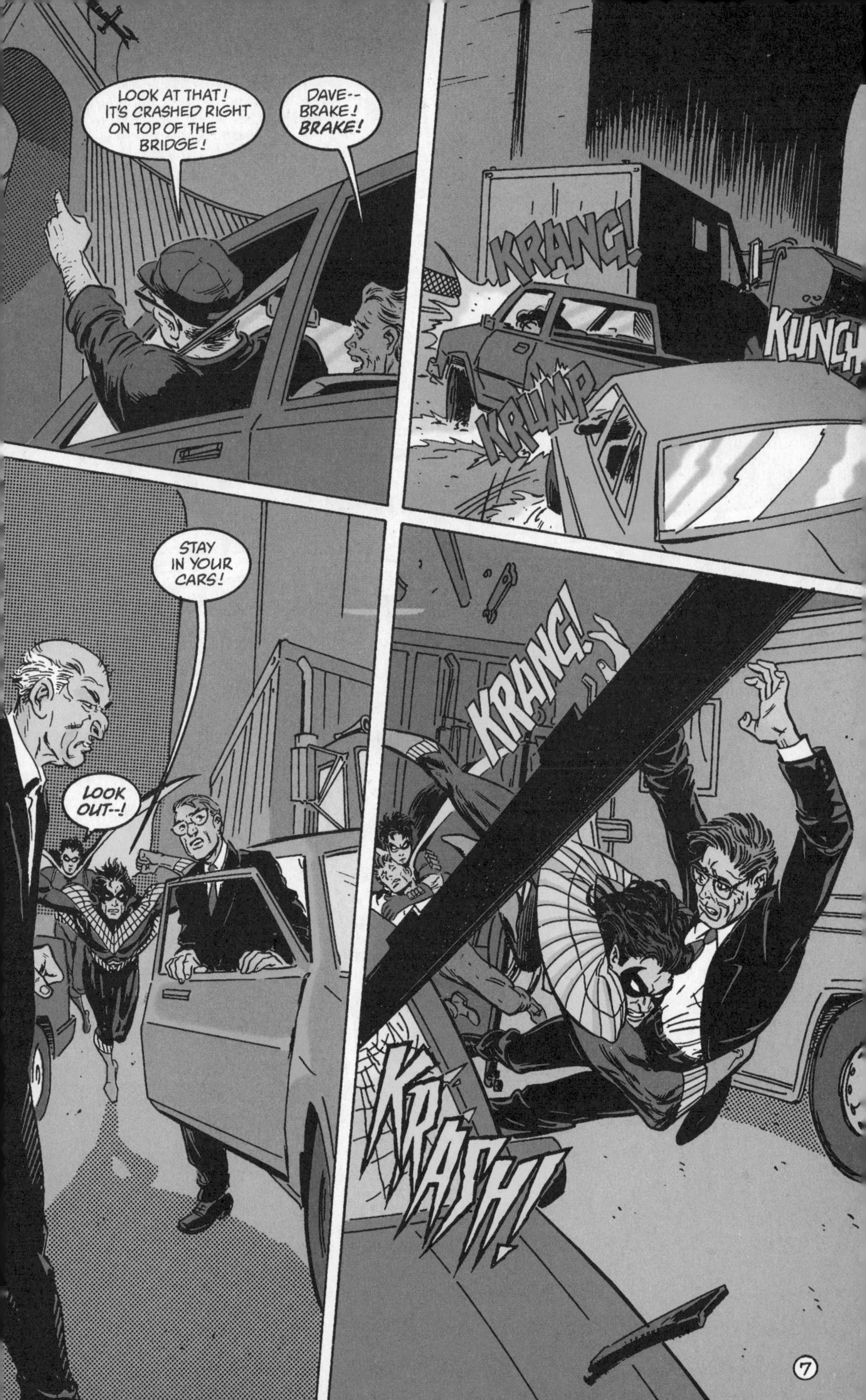
LOOK AT THAT! IT'S CRASHED RIGHT ON TOP OF THE BRIDGE!
DAVE-- BRAKE! BRAKE!
KRANG!
KUNCH
KRUMP
STAY IN YOUR CARS!
LOOK OUT--!
KRANG!
KRASH!

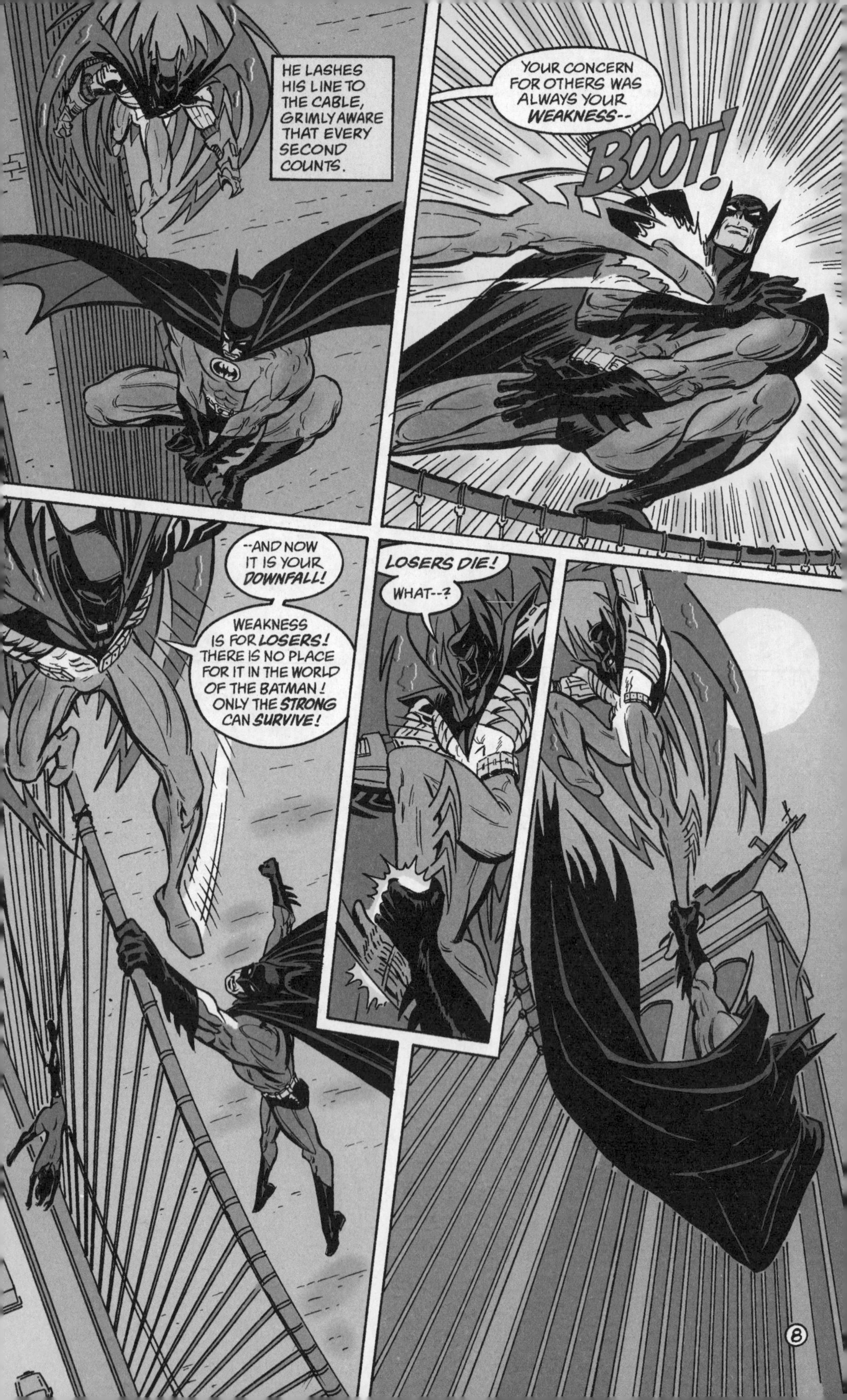
HE LASHES HIS LINE TO THE CABLE, GRIMLY AWARE THAT EVERY SECOND COUNTS.
YOUR CONCERN FOR OTHERS WAS ALWAYS YOUR WEAKNESS--
BOOT!
--AND NOW IT IS YOUR DOWNFALL!
WEAKNESS IS FOR LOSERS! THERE IS NO PLACE FOR IT IN THE WORLD OF THE BATMAN! ONLY THE STRONG CAN SURVIVE!
LOSERS DIE!
WHAT--?
8

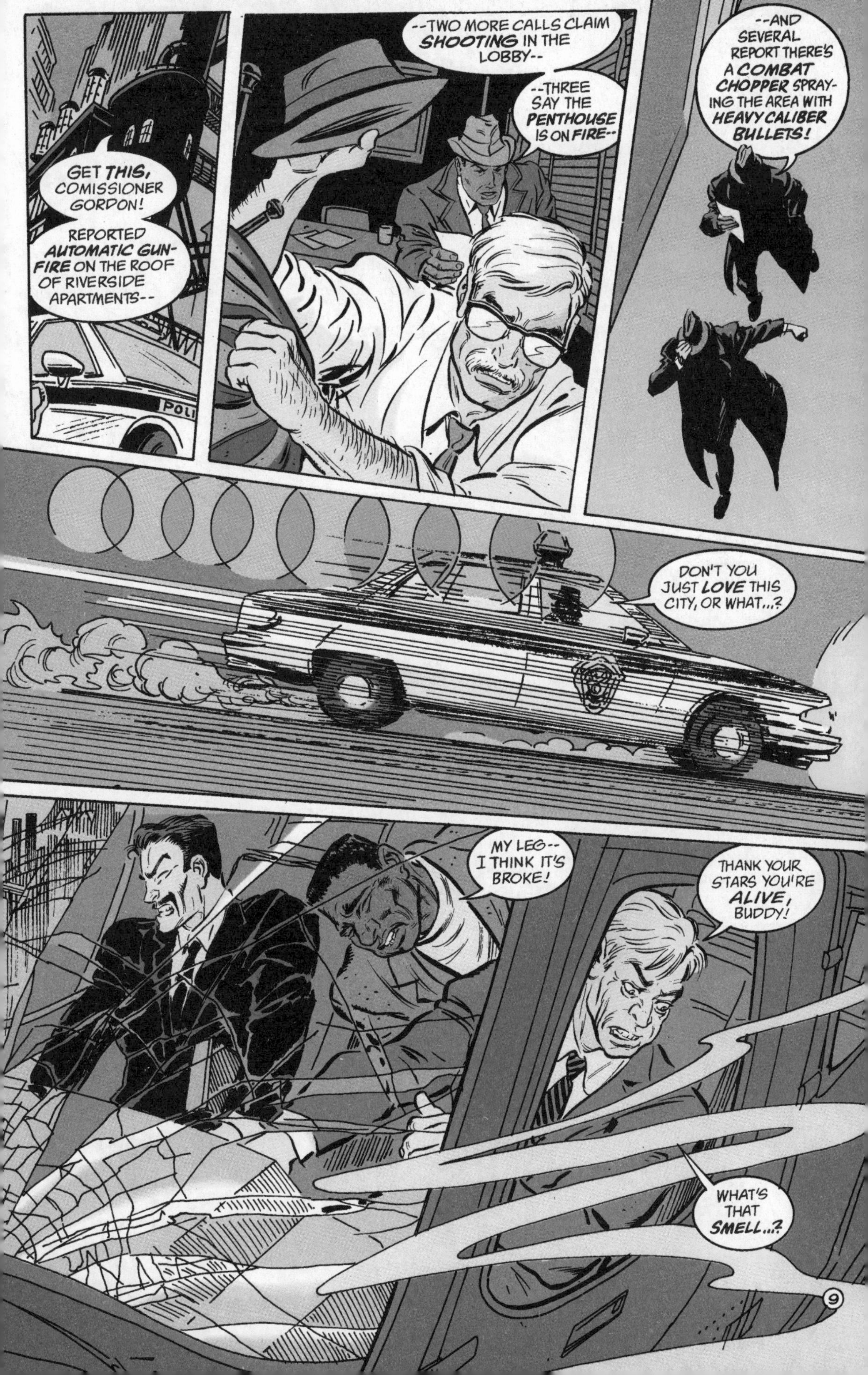
GET THIS, COMISSIONER GORDON!
REPORTED AUTOMATIC GUN-FIRE ON THE ROOF OF RIVERSIDE APARTMENTS--
--TWO MORE CALLS CLAIM SHOOTING IN THE LOBBY--
--THREE SAY THE PENTHOUSE IS ON FIRE--
--AND SEVERAL REPORT THERE'S A COMBAT CHOPPER SPRAY-ING THE AREA WITH HEAVY CALIBER BULLETS!
DON'T YOU JUST LOVE THIS CITY, OR WHAT...?
MY LEG-- I THINK IT'S BROKE!
THANK YOUR STARS YOU'RE ALIVE, BUDDY!
WHAT'S THAT SMELL...?

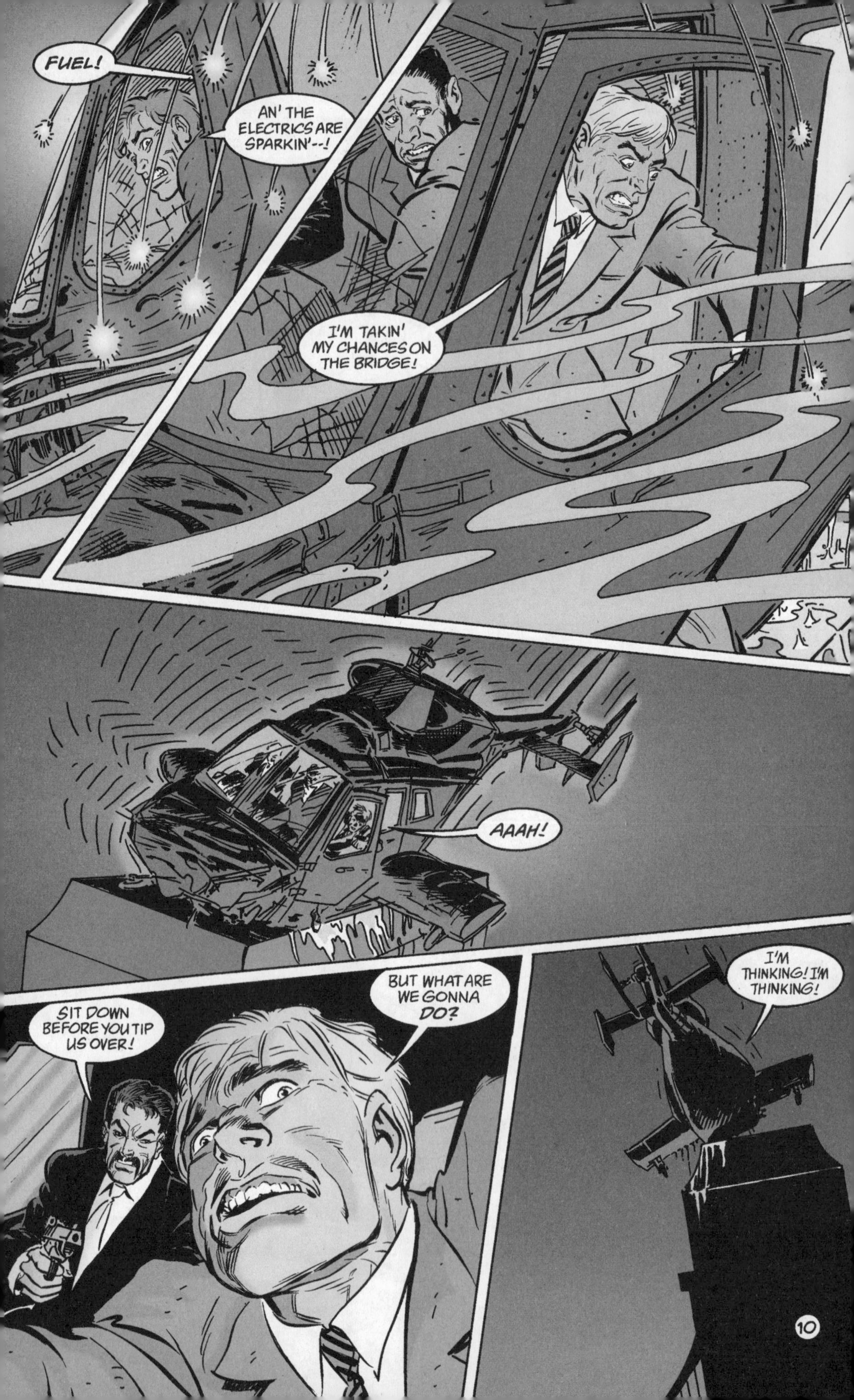
FUEL!
AN' THE ELECTRICS ARE SPARKIN'--!
I'M TAKIN' MY CHANCES ON THE BRIDGE!
AAAH!
SIT DOWN BEFORE YOU TIP US OVER!
BUT WHAT ARE WE GONNA DO?
I'M THINKING! I'M THINKING!

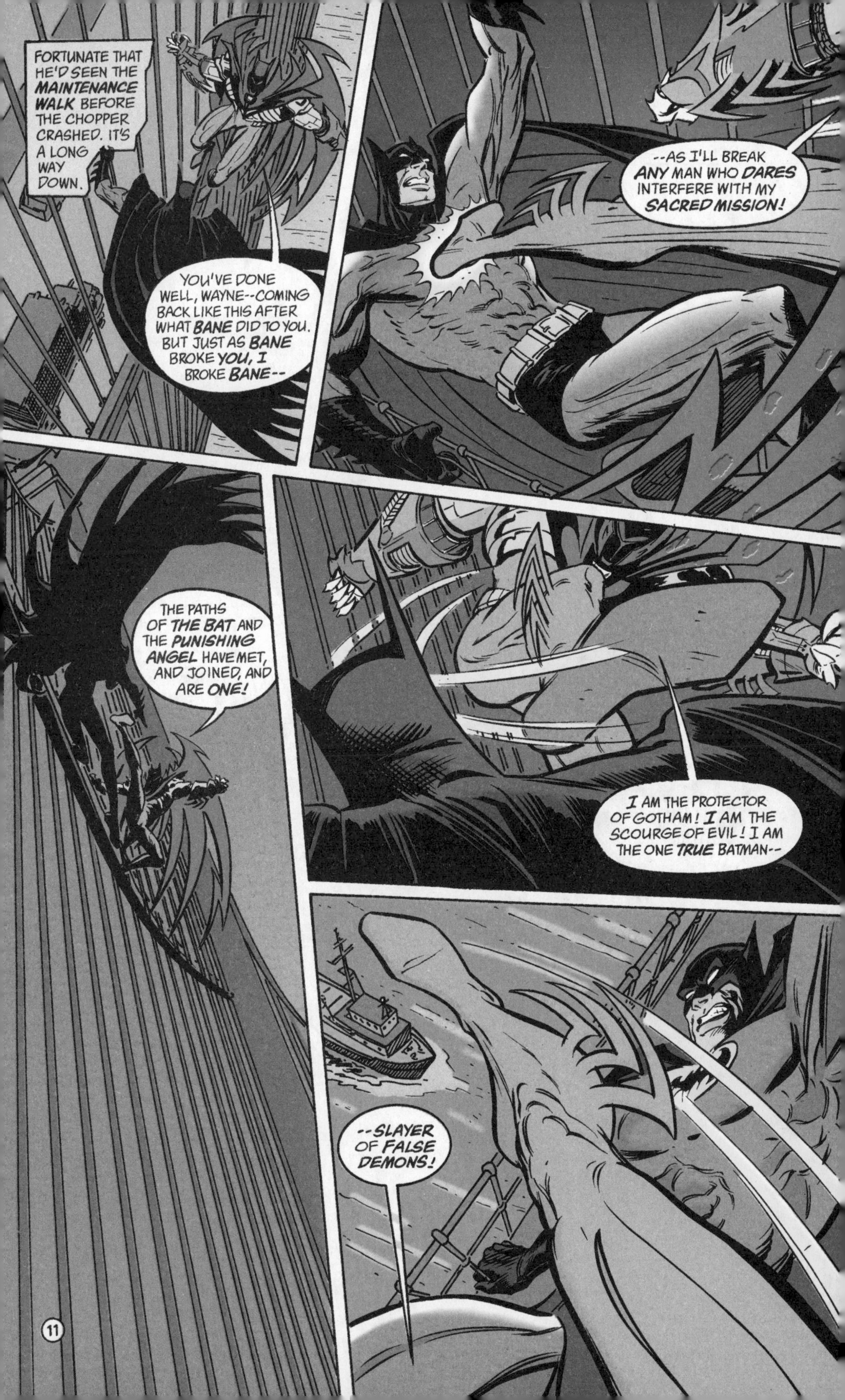

FORTUNATE THAT HE'D SEEN THE MAINTENANCE WALK BEFORE THE CHOPPER CRASHED. IT'S A LONG WAY DOWN.
YOU'VE DONE WELL, WAYNE--COMING BACK LIKE THIS AFTER WHAT BANE DID TO YOU. BUT JUST AS BANE BROKE YOU, I BROKE BANE--
--AS I'LL BREAK ANY MAN WHO DARES INTERFERE WITH MY SACRED MISSION!
THE PATHS OF THE BAT AND THE PUNISHING ANGEL HAVE MET, AND JOINED, AND ARE ONE!
I AM THE PROTECTOR OF GOTHAM! I AM THE SCOURGE OF EVIL! I AM THE ONE TRUE BATMAN--
--SLAYER OF FALSE DEMONS!

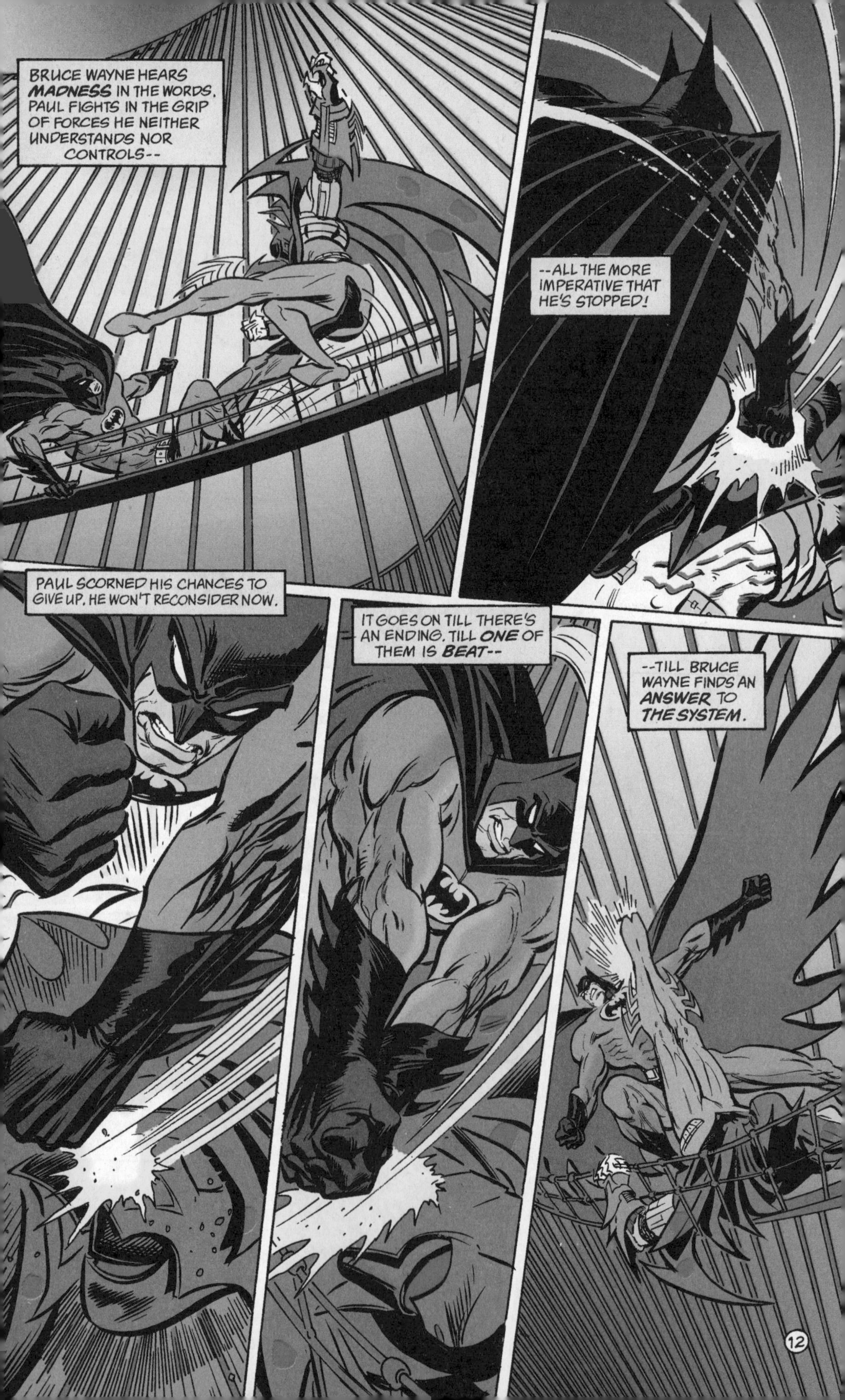
BRUCE WAYNE HEARS MADNESS IN THE WORDS. PAUL FIGHTS IN THE GRIP OF FORCES HE NEITHER UNDERSTANDS NOR CONTROLS--
--ALL THE MORE IMPERATIVE THAT HE'S STOPPED!
PAUL SCORNED HIS CHANCES TO GIVE UP. HE WON'T RECONSIDER NOW.
IT GOES ON TILL THERE'S AN ENDING. TILL ONE OF THEM IS BEAT--
--TILL BRUCE WAYNE FINDS AN ANSWER TO THE SYSTEM.
12

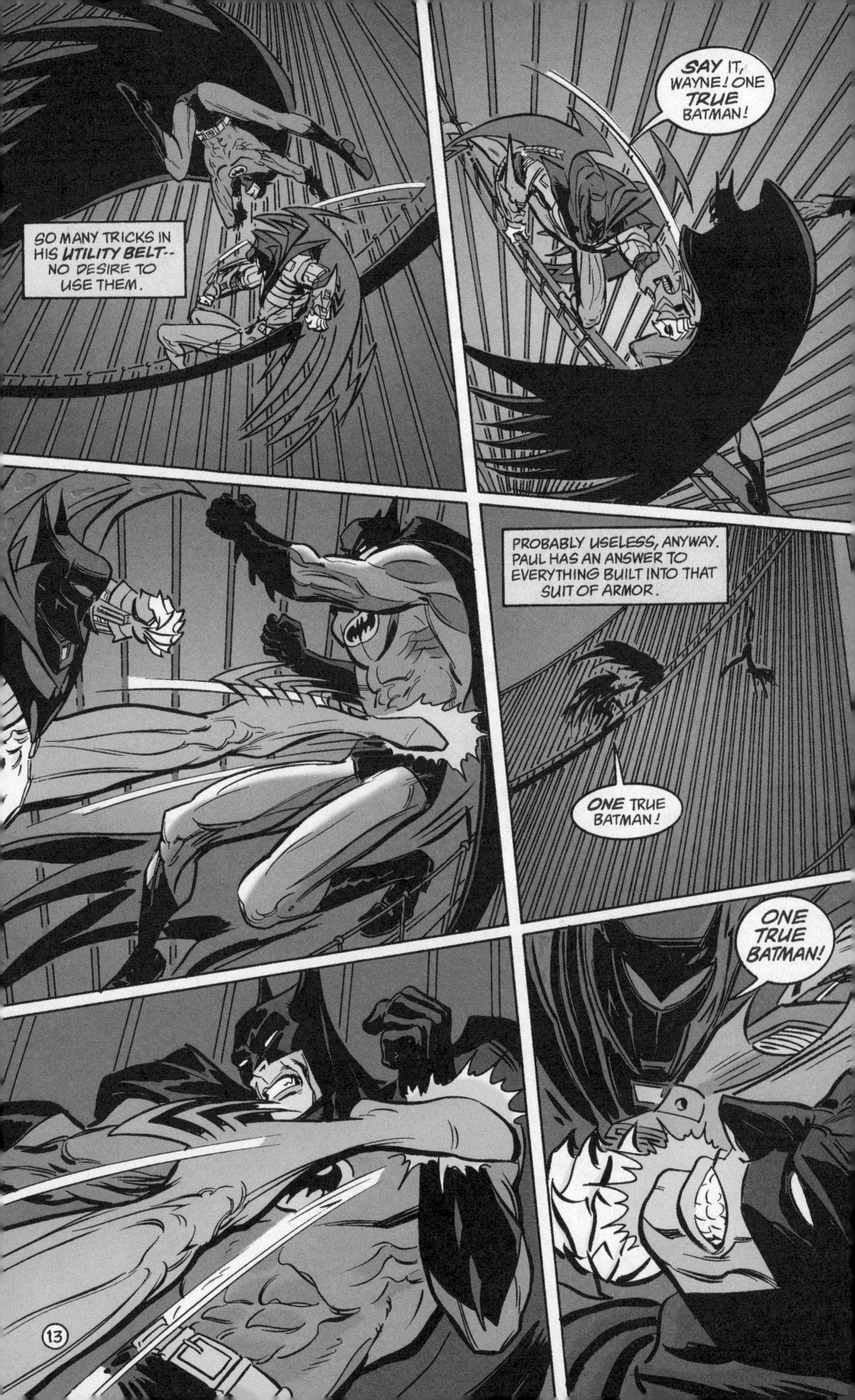
SO MANY TRICKS IN HIS UTILITY BELT-- NO DESIRE TO USE THEM.
SAY IT, WAYNE! ONE TRUE BATMAN!
PROBABLY USELESS, ANYWAY. PAUL HAS AN ANSWER TO EVERYTHING BUILT INTO THAT SUIT OF ARMOR.
ONE TRUE BATMAN!
ONE TRUE BATMAN!
13

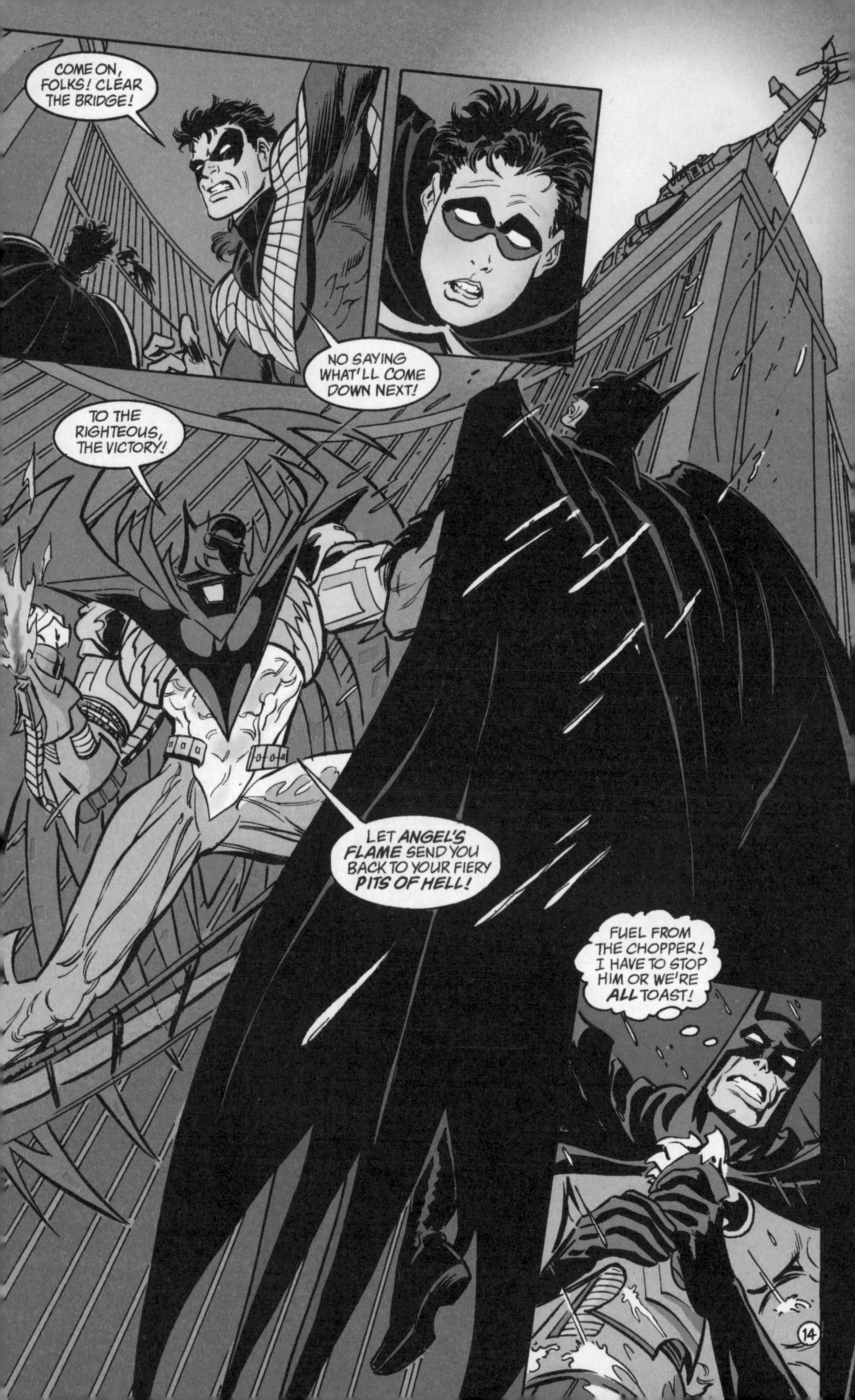
COME ON, FOLKS! CLEAR THE BRIDGE!
NO SAYING WHAT'LL COME DOWN NEXT!
TO THE RIGHTEOUS, THE VICTORY!
LET ANGEL'S FLAME SEND YOU BACK TO YOUR FIERY PITS OF HELL!
FUEL FROM THE CHOPPER! I HAVE TO STOP HIM OR WE'RE ALL TOAST!
14

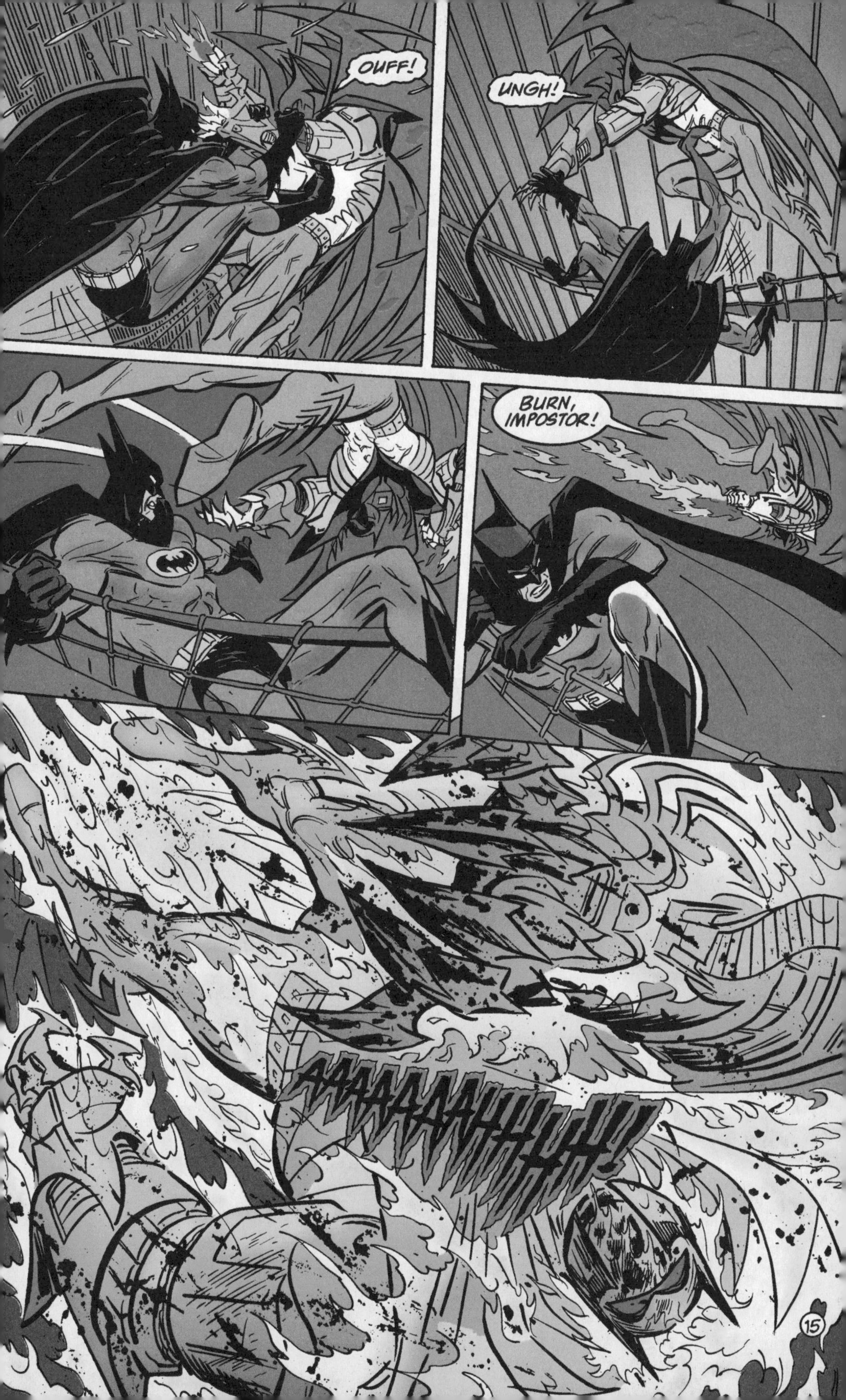
OUFF!
UNGH!
BURN, IMPOSTOR!
AAAAAAAAHHHHH!
15

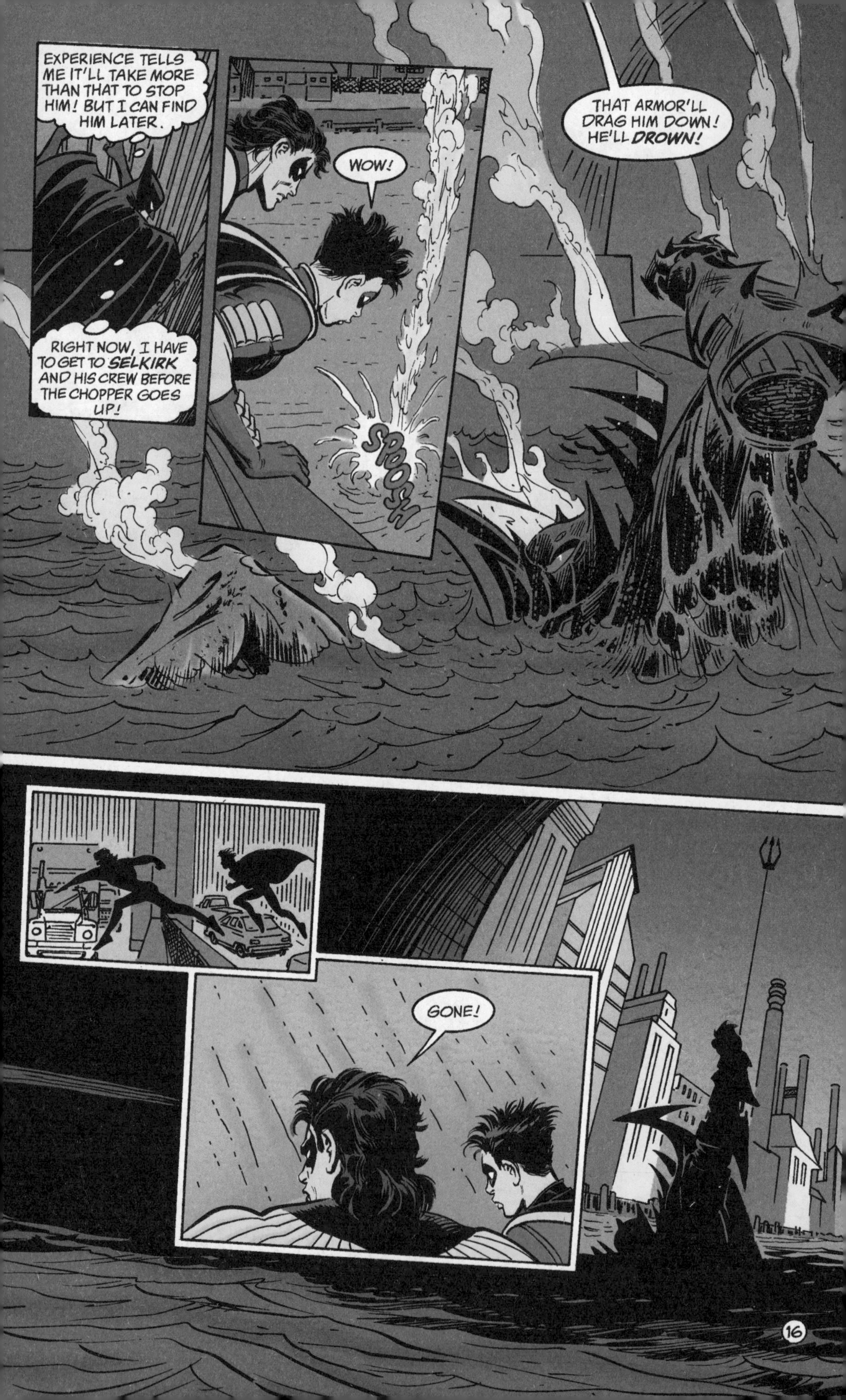

EXPERIENCE TELLS ME IT'LL TAKE MORE THAN THAT TO STOP HIM! BUT I CAN FIND HIM LATER.
RIGHT NOW, I HAVE TO GET TO SELKIRK AND HIS CREW BEFORE THE CHOPPER GOES UP!
WOW!
SPOOSH
THAT ARMOR'LL DRAG HIM DOWN! HE'LL DROWN!
GONE!

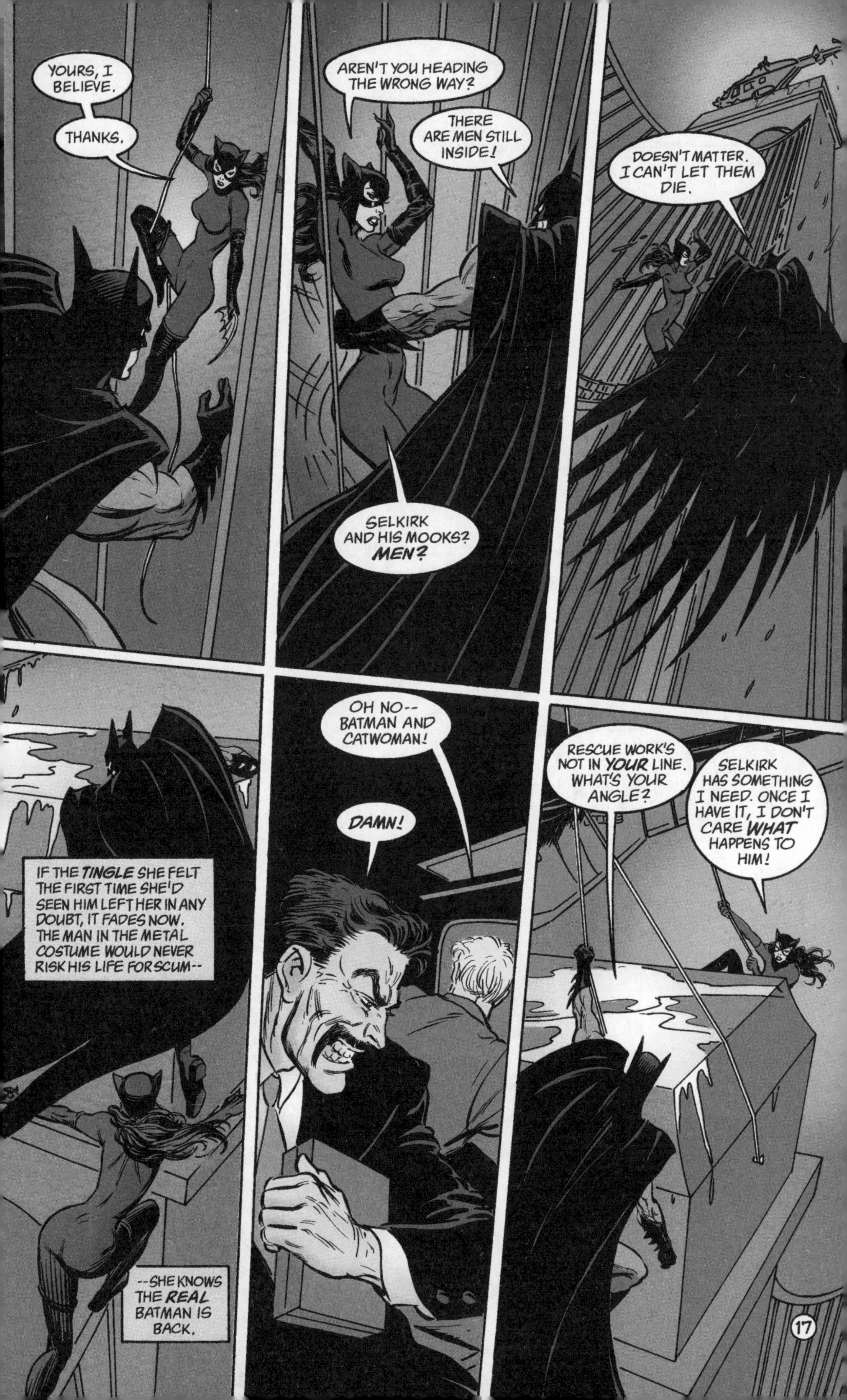
YOURS, I BELIEVE.
THANKS.
AREN'T YOU HEADING THE WRONG WAY?
THERE ARE MEN STILL INSIDE!
SELKIRK AND HIS MOOKS? MEN?
DOESN'T MATTER. I CAN'T LET THEM DIE.
IF THE TINGLE SHE FELT THE FIRST TIME SHE'D SEEN HIM LEFT HER IN ANY DOUBT, IT FADES NOW. THE MAN IN THE METAL COSTUME WOULD NEVER RISK HIS LIFE FOR SCUM--
--SHE KNOWS THE REAL BATMAN IS BACK.
OH NO-- BATMAN AND CATWOMAN!
DAMN!
RESCUE WORK'S NOT IN YOUR LINE. WHAT'S YOUR ANGLE?
SELKIRK HAS SOMETHING I NEED. ONCE I HAVE IT, I DON'T CARE WHAT HAPPENS TO HIM!

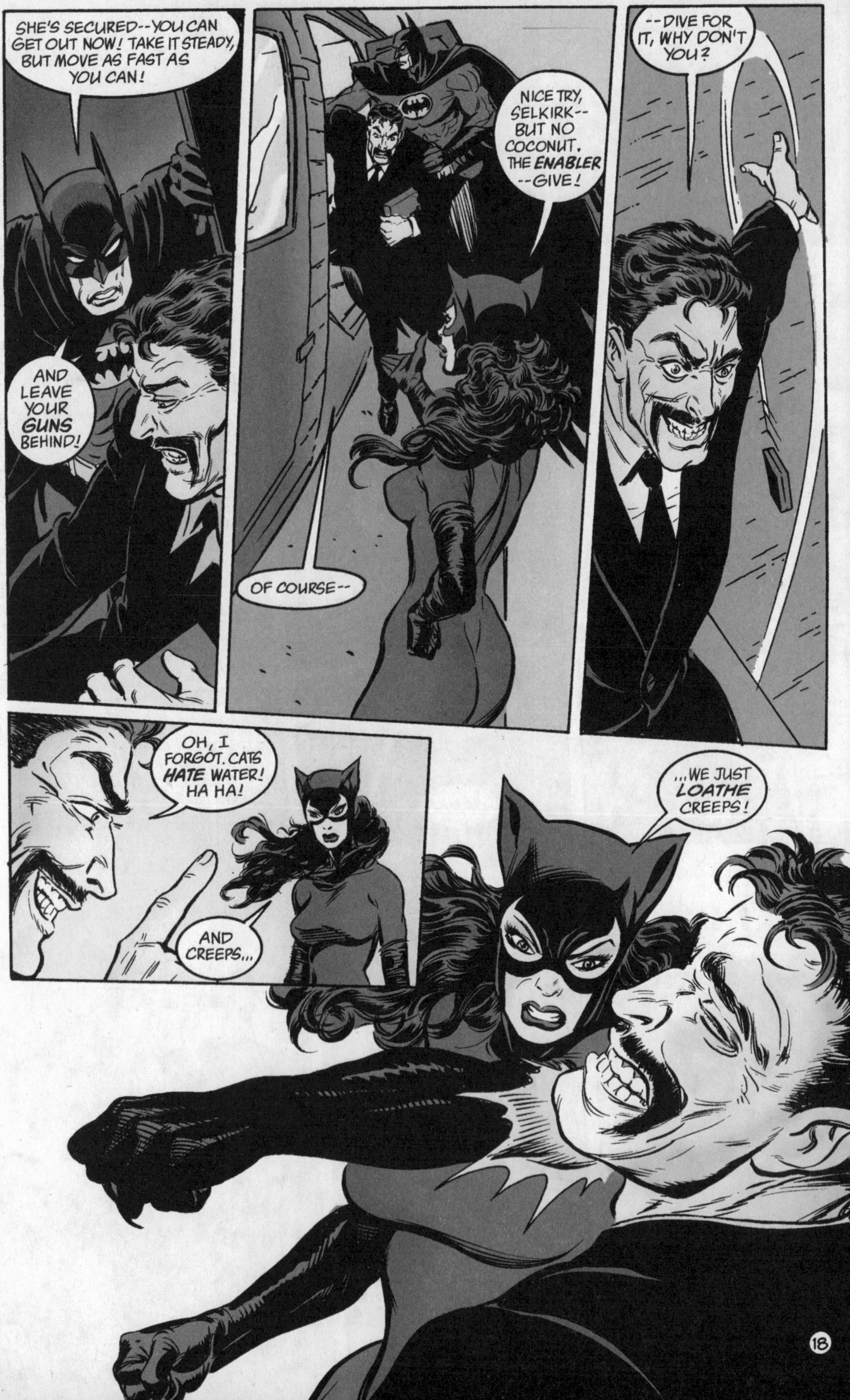
SHE'S SECURED--YOU CAN GET OUT NOW! TAKE IT STEADY, BUT MOVE AS FAST AS YOU CAN!
AND LEAVE YOUR GUNS BEHIND!
NICE TRY, SELKIRK--BUT NO COCONUT. THE ENABLER--GIVE!
OF COURSE--
--DIVE FOR IT, WHY DON'T YOU?
OH, I FORGOT. CATS HATE WATER! HA HA!
AND CREEPS...
...WE JUST LOATHE CREEPS!

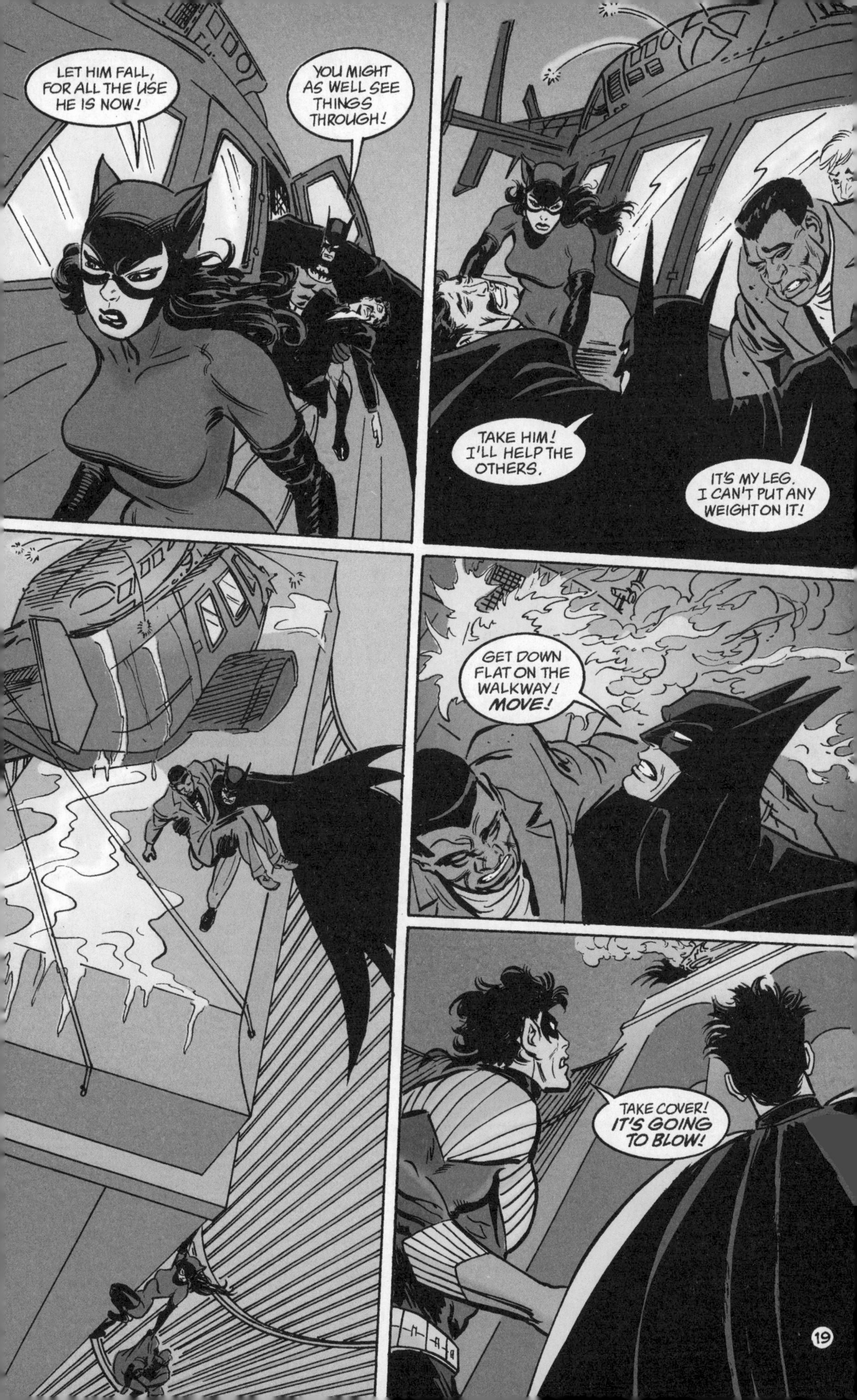
LET HIM FALL, FOR ALL THE USE HE IS NOW!
YOU MIGHT AS WELL SEE THINGS THROUGH!
TAKE HIM! I'LL HELP THE OTHERS.
IT'S MY LEG. I CAN'T PUT ANY WEIGHT ON IT!
GET DOWN FLAT ON THE WALKWAY! MOVE!
TAKE COVER! IT'S GOING TO BLOW!

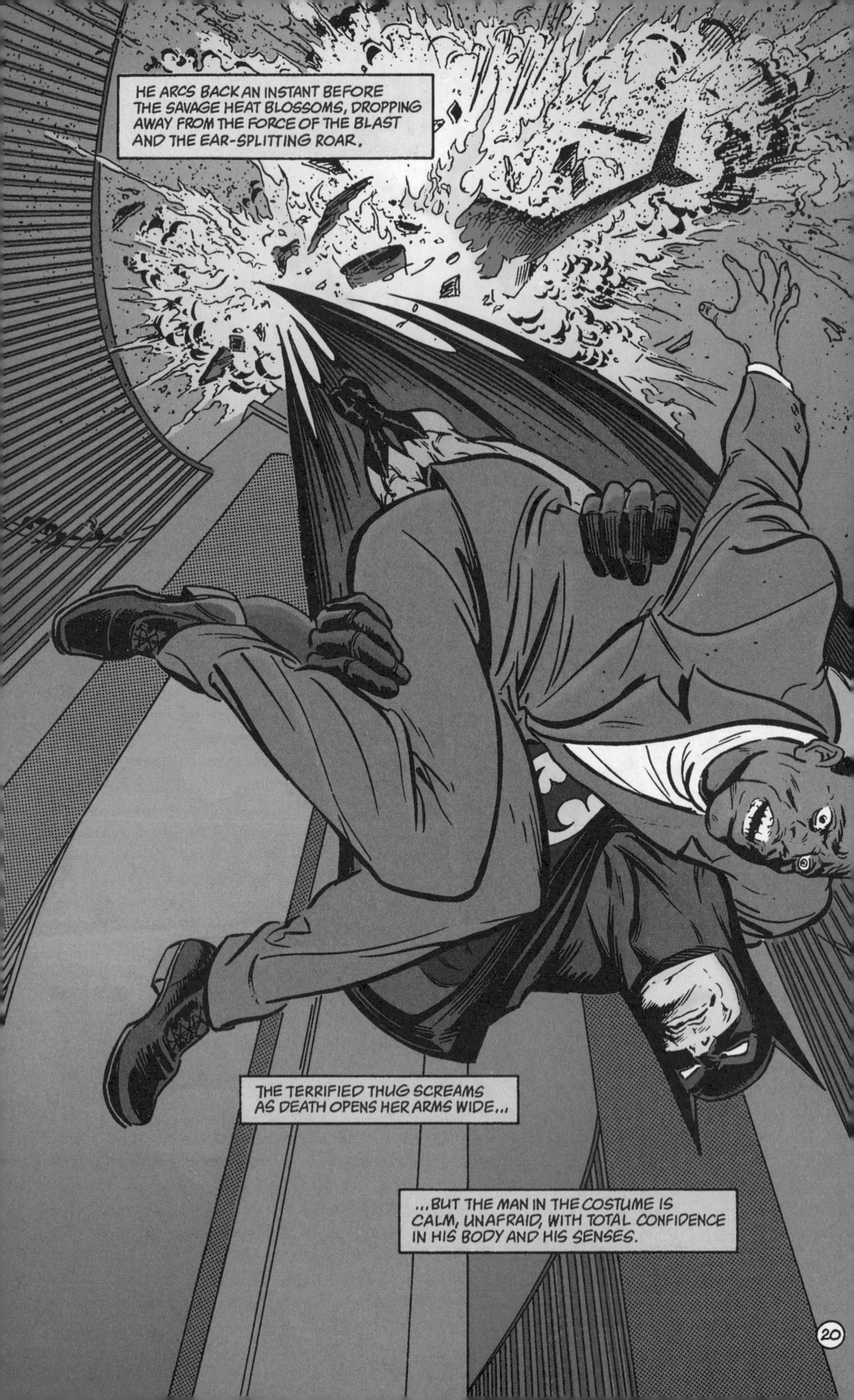
HE ARCS BACK AN INSTANT BEFORE THE SAVAGE HEAT BLOSSOMS, DROPPING AWAY FROM THE FORCE OF THE BLAST AND THE EAR-SPLITTING ROAR.
THE TERRIFIED THUG SCREAMS AS DEATH OPENS HER ARMS WIDE...
...BUT THE MAN IN THE COSTUME IS CALM, UNAFRAID, WITH TOTAL CONFIDENCE IN HIS BODY AND HIS SENSES.
20

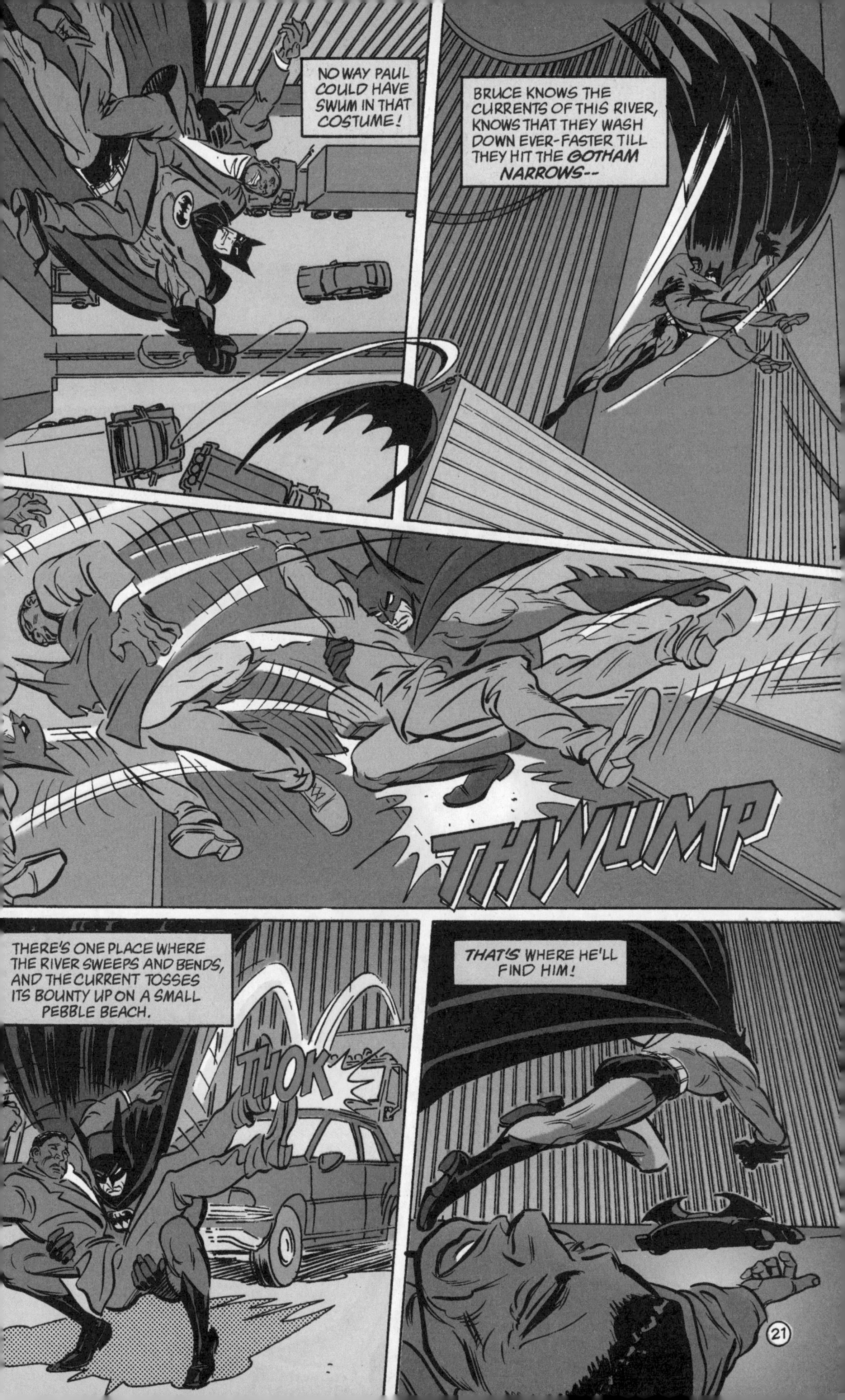
NO WAY PAUL COULD HAVE SWUM IN THAT COSTUME!
BRUCE KNOWS THE CURRENTS OF THIS RIVER, KNOWS THAT THEY WASH DOWN EVER-FASTER TILL THEY HIT THE GOTHAM NARROWS--
THWUMP
THERE'S ONE PLACE WHERE THE RIVER SWEEPS AND BENDS, AND THE CURRENT TOSSES ITS BOUNTY UP ON A SMALL PEBBLE BEACH.
THOK
THAT'S WHERE HE'LL FIND HIM!

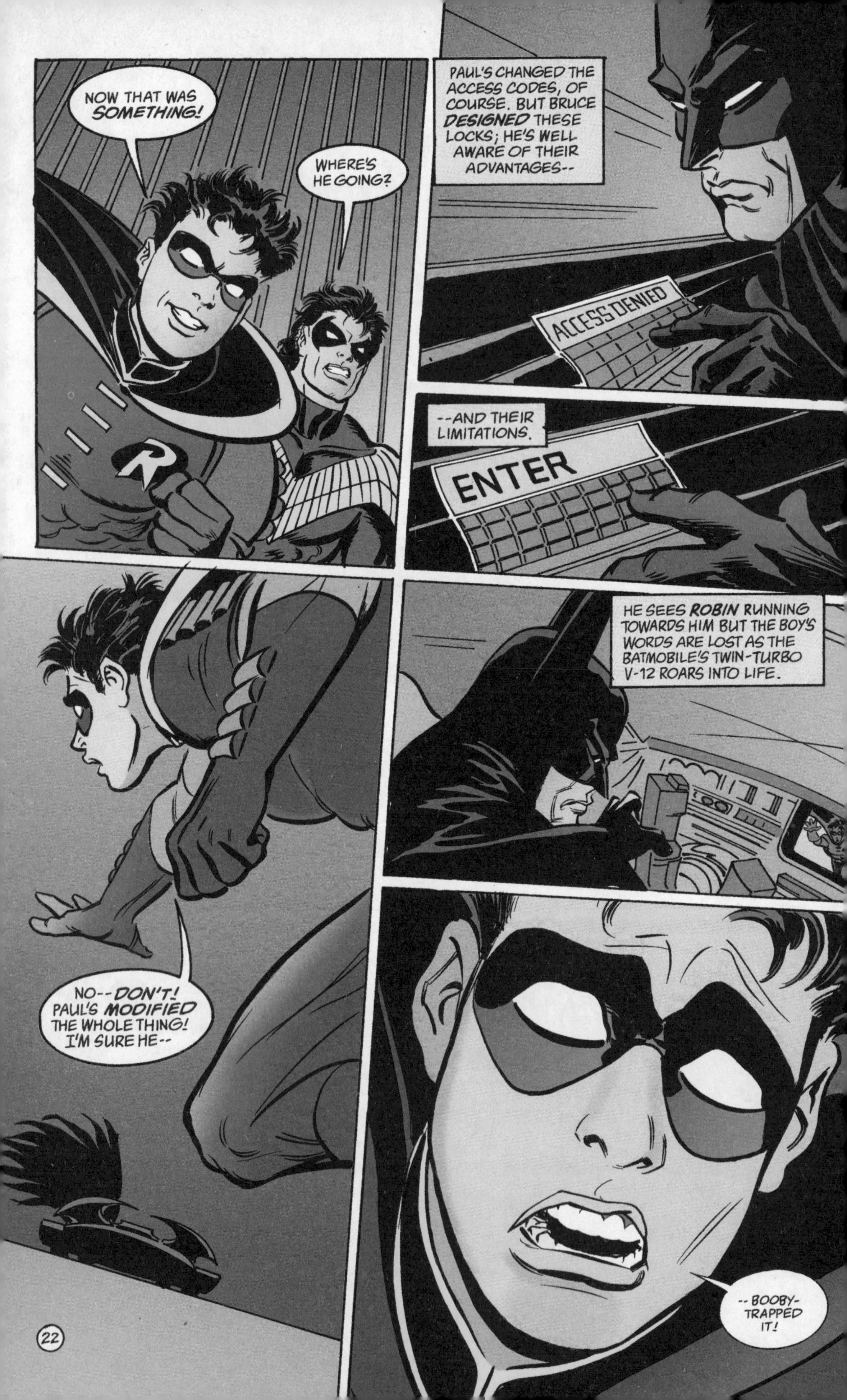

NOW THAT WAS SOMETHING!
WHERE'S HE GOING?
PAUL'S CHANGED THE ACCESS CODES, OF COURSE. BUT BRUCE DESIGNED THESE LOCKS; HE'S WELL AWARE OF THEIR ADVANTAGES--
ACCESS DENIED
--AND THEIR LIMITATIONS.
ENTER
NO--DON'T! PAUL'S MODIFIED THE WHOLE THING! I'M SURE HE--
HE SEES ROBIN RUNNING TOWARDS HIM BUT THE BOY'S WORDS ARE LOST AS THE BATMOBILE'S TWIN-TURBO V-12 ROARS INTO LIFE.
--BOOBY-TRAPPED IT!

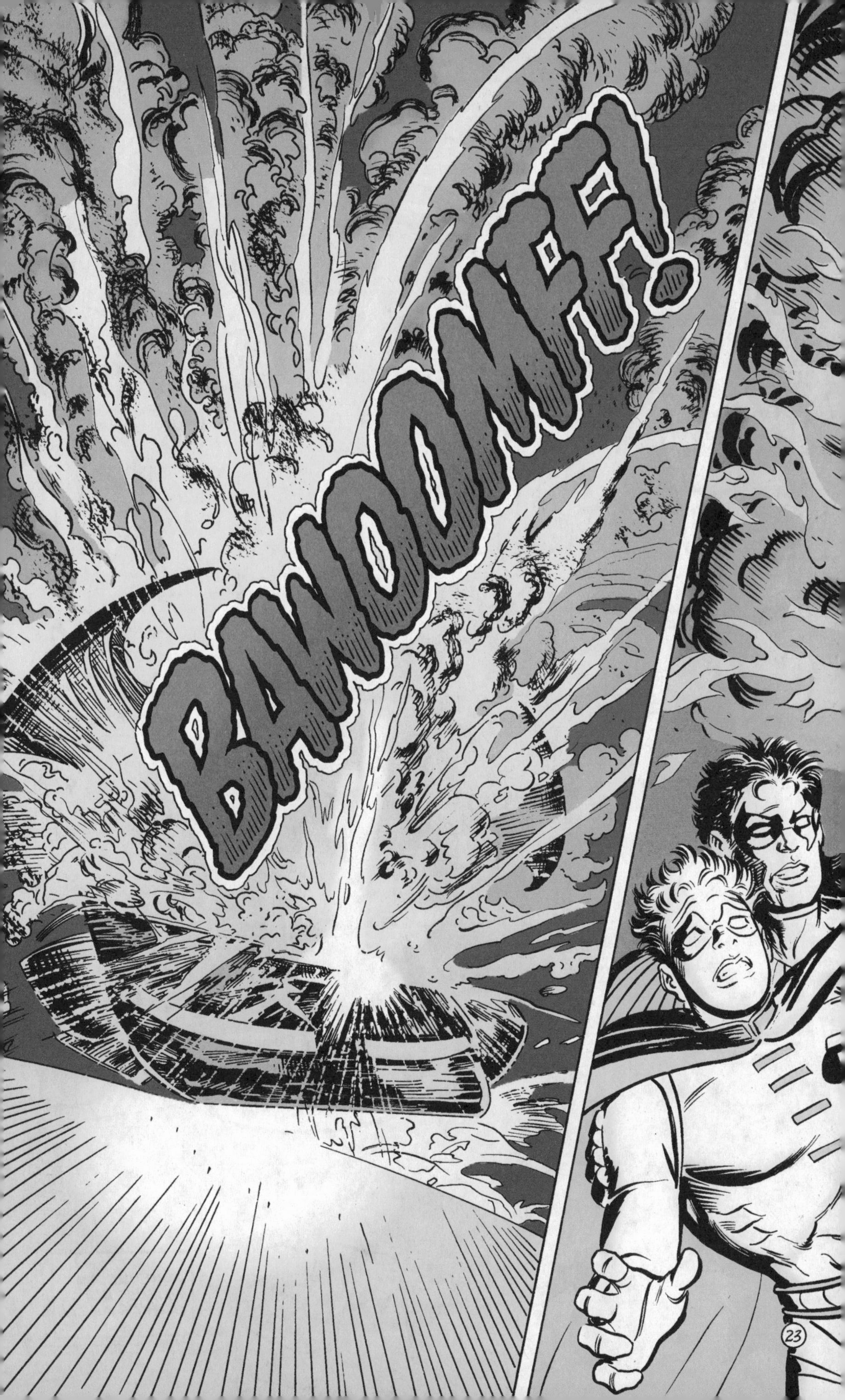
BAWOOMFF!
23

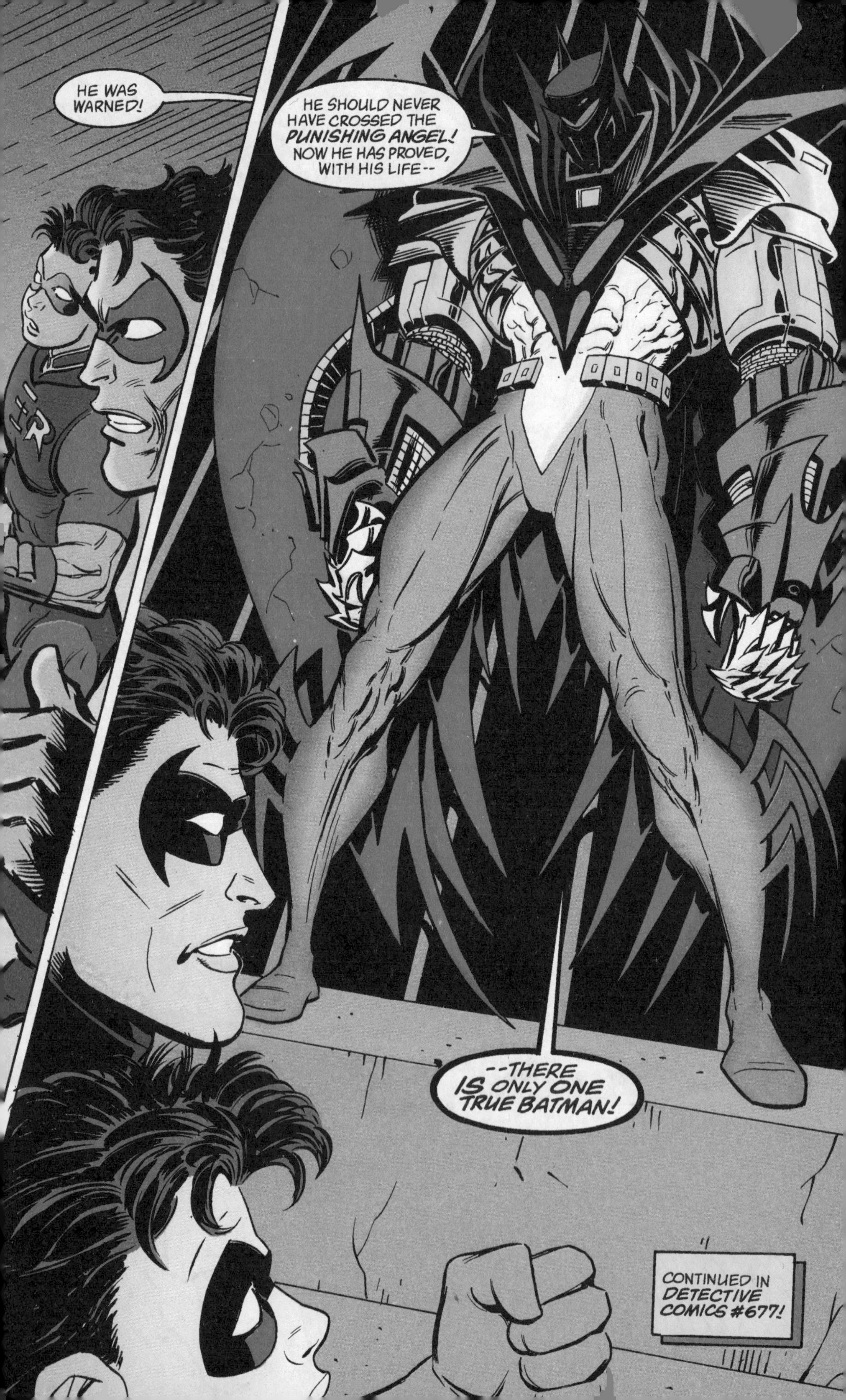

HE WAS WARNED!
HE SHOULD NEVER HAVE CROSSED THE PUNISHING ANGEL! NOW HE HAS PROVED, WITH HIS LIFE--
--THERE IS ONLY ONE TRUE BATMAN!
CONTINUED IN DETECTIVE COMICS #677!

Cover art by KELLEY JONES and JOHN BEATTY

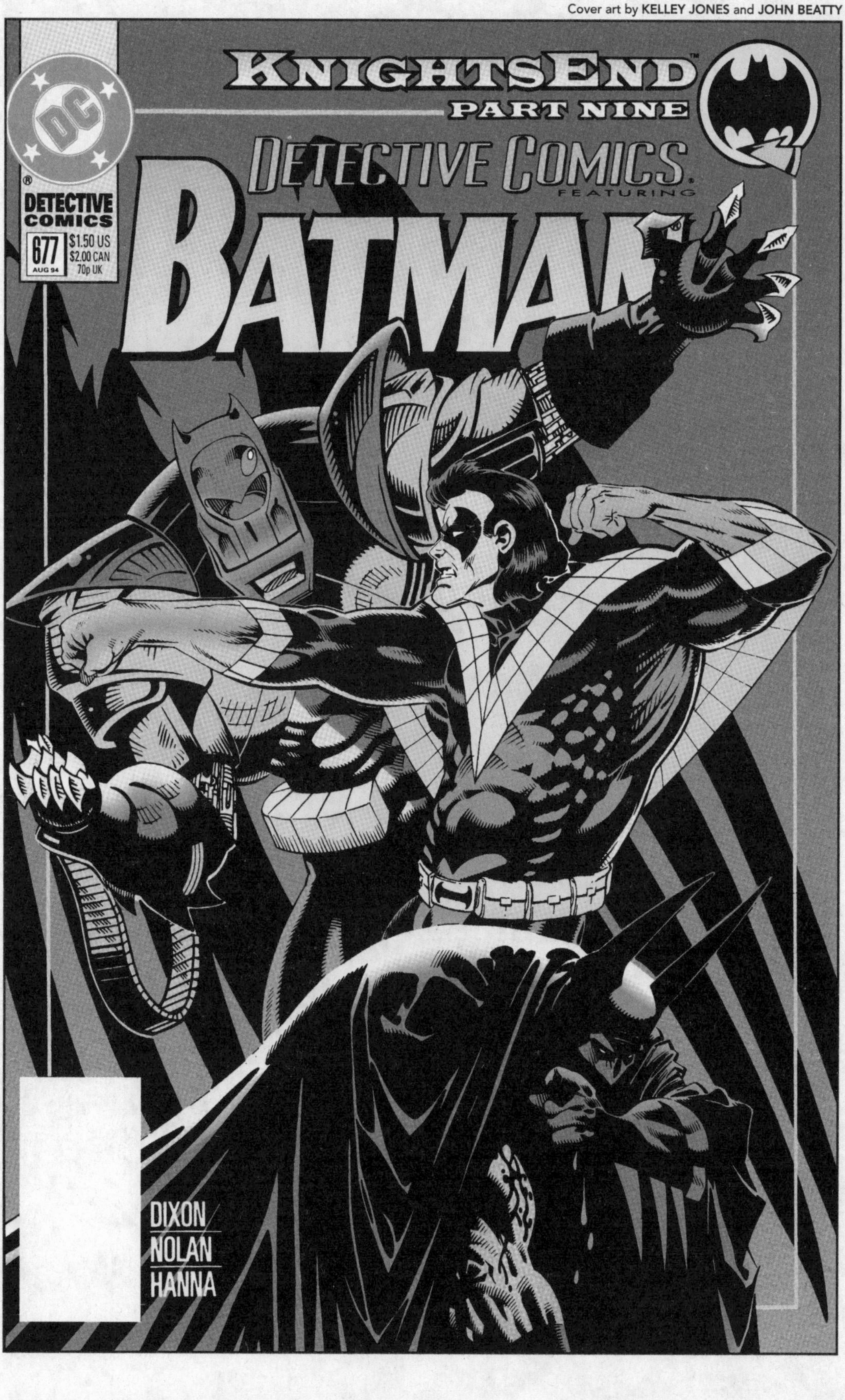

KNIGHTSEND
PART NINE
DETECTIVE COMICS
FEATURING
BATMAN
DC
DETECTIVE COMICS
677
AUG 94
$1.50 US
$2.00 CAN
70p UK
DIXON
NOLAN
HANNA

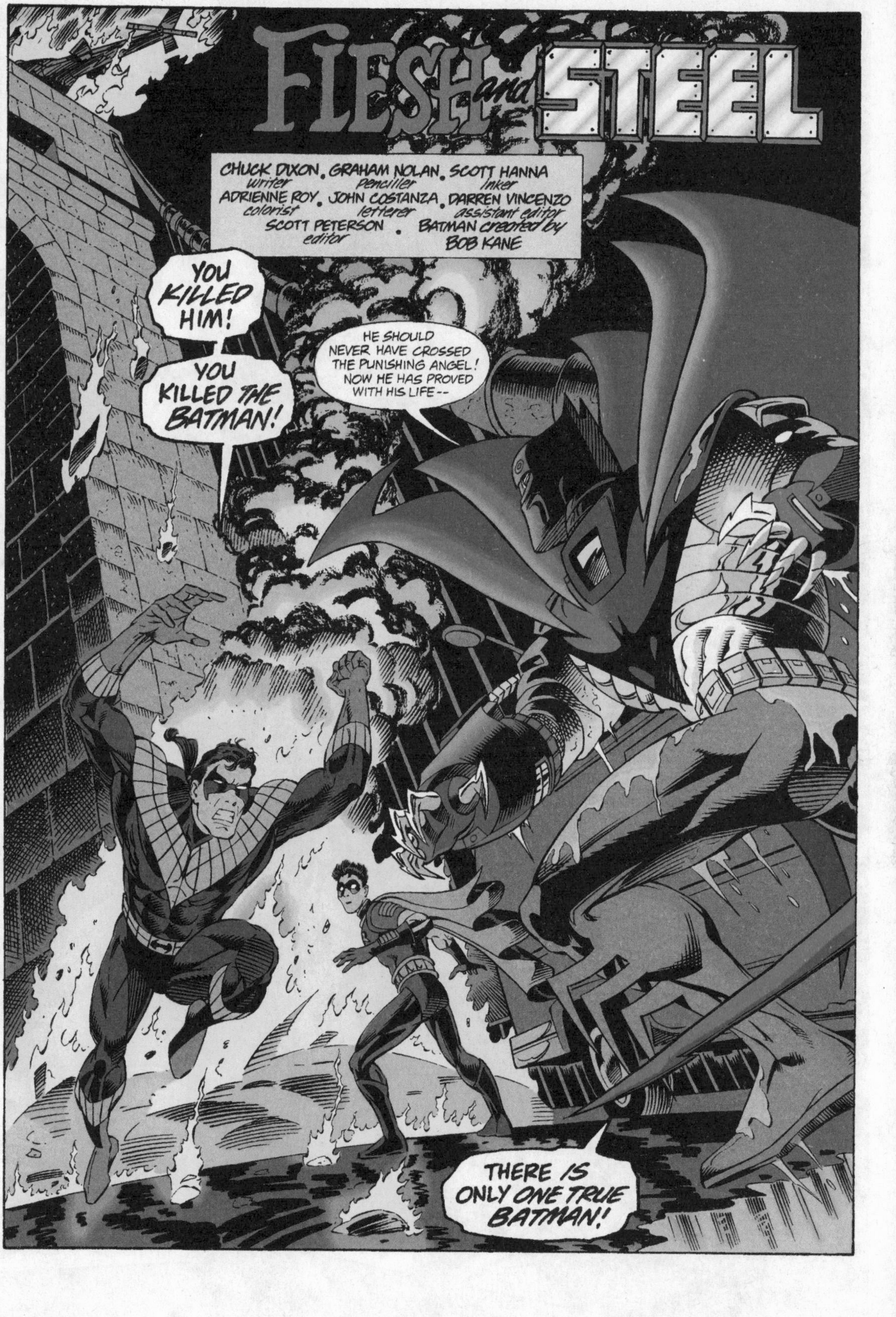
FLESH and STEEL
CHUCK DIXON writer • GRAHAM NOLAN penciller • SCOTT HANNA inker
ADRIENNE ROY colorist • JOHN COSTANZA letterer • DARREN VINCENZO assistant editor
SCOTT PETERSON editor • BATMAN created by BOB KANE
YOU KILLED HIM!
YOU KILLED THE BATMAN!
HE SHOULD NEVER HAVE CROSSED THE PUNISHING ANGEL! NOW HE HAS PROVED WITH HIS LIFE--
THERE IS ONLY ONE TRUE BATMAN!

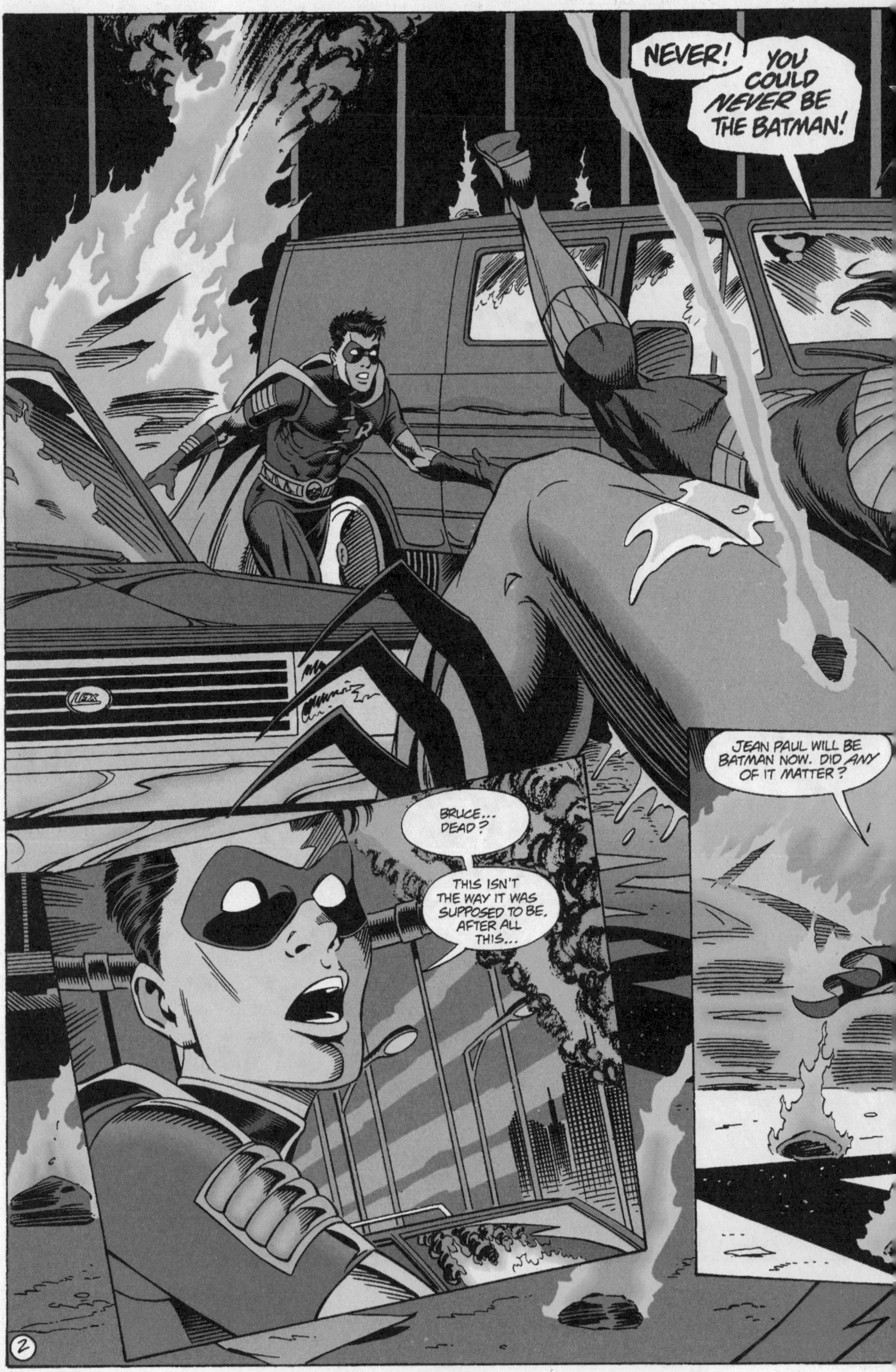
NEVER!
YOU COULD NEVER BE THE BATMAN!
JEAN PAUL WILL BE BATMAN NOW. DID ANY OF IT MATTER?
BRUCE... DEAD?
THIS ISN'T THE WAY IT WAS SUPPOSED TO BE. AFTER ALL THIS...
2

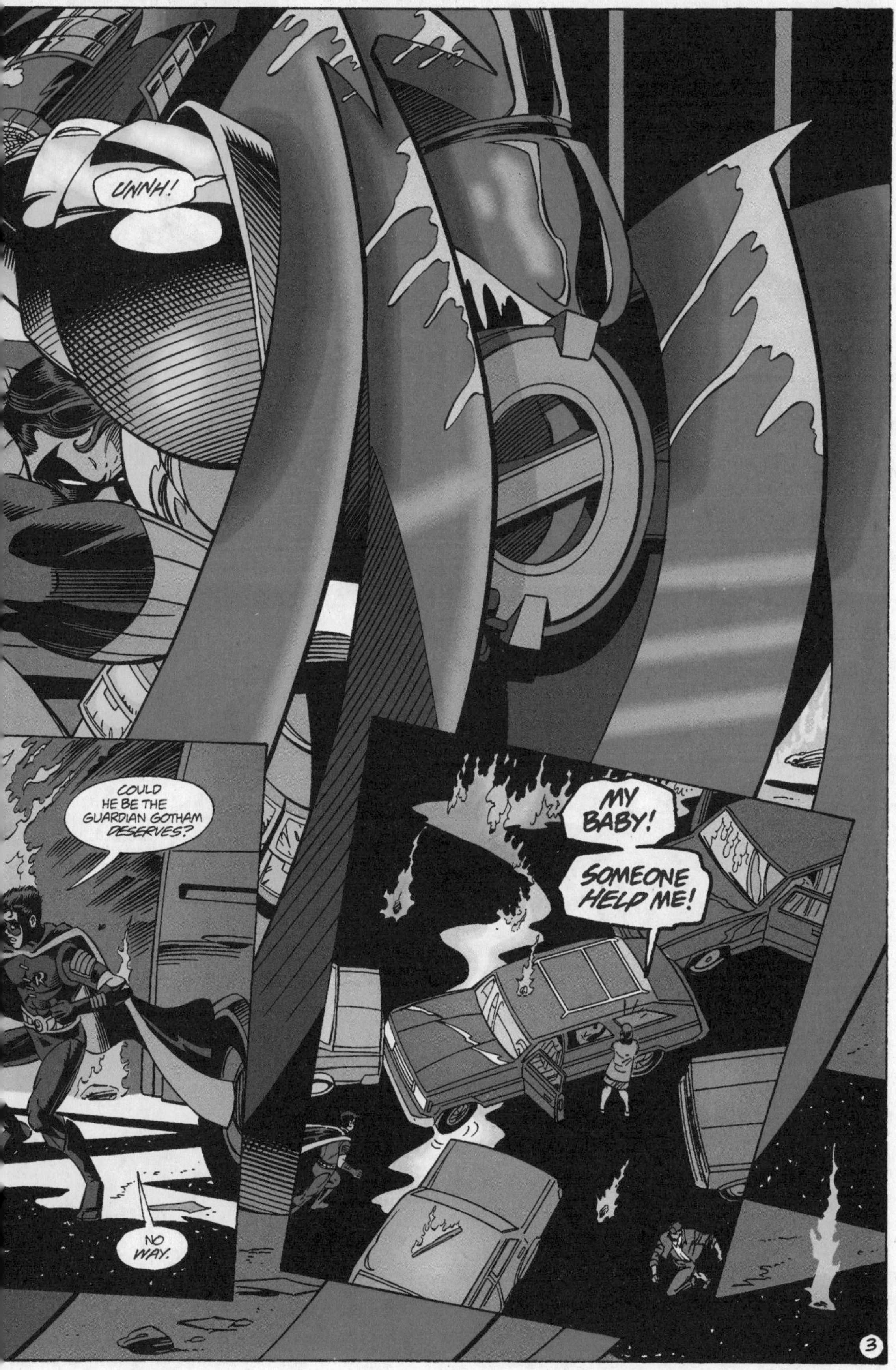
UNNH!
COULD HE BE THE GUARDIAN GOTHAM DESERVES?
NO WAY.
MY BABY!
SOMEONE HELP ME!
3

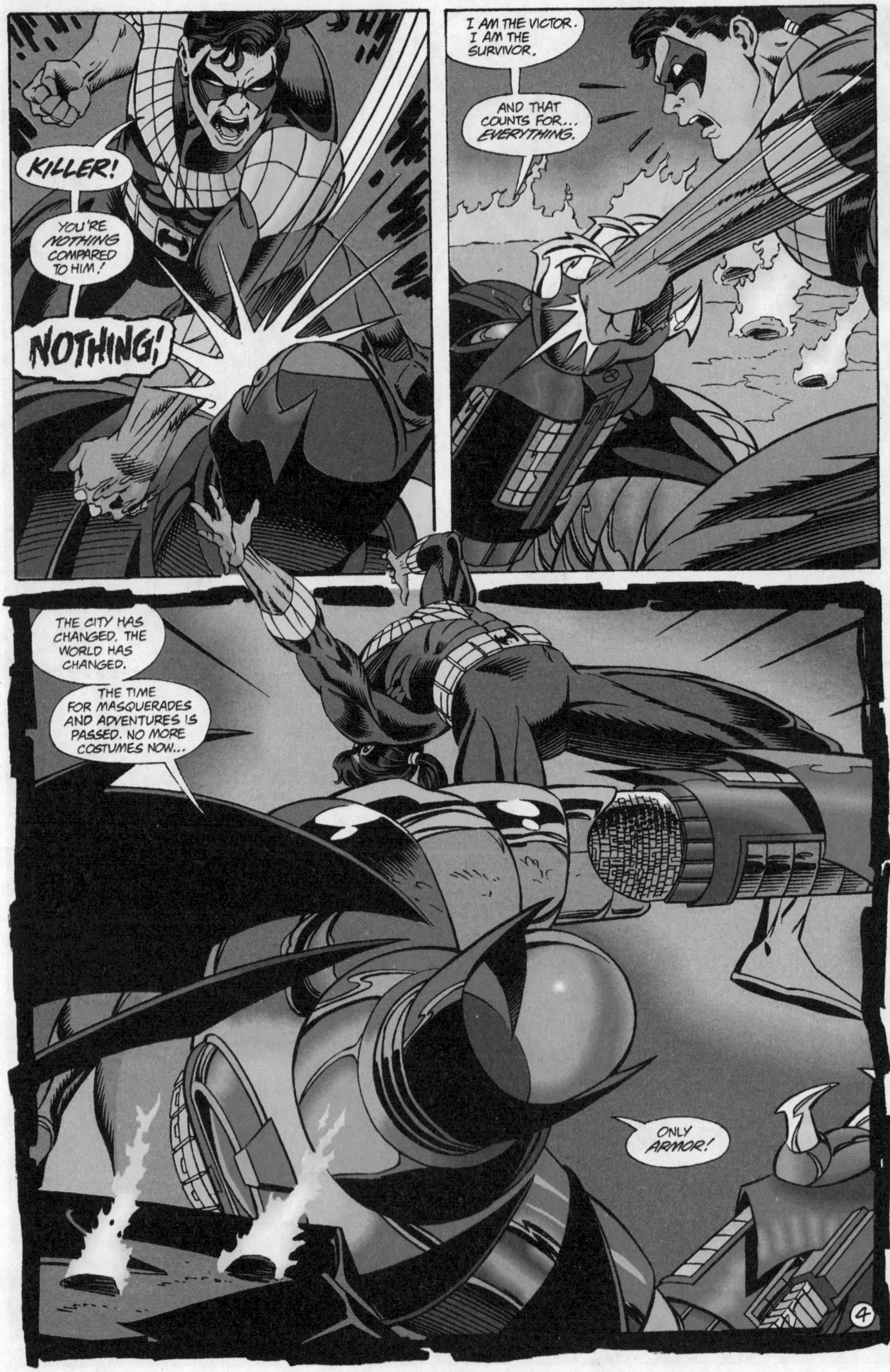
KILLER!
YOU'RE NOTHING COMPARED TO HIM!
NOTHING!
I AM THE VICTOR. I AM THE SURVIVOR.
AND THAT COUNTS FOR... EVERYTHING.
THE CITY HAS CHANGED. THE WORLD HAS CHANGED.
THE TIME FOR MASQUERADES AND ADVENTURES IS PASSED. NO MORE COSTUMES NOW...
ONLY ARMOR!
4

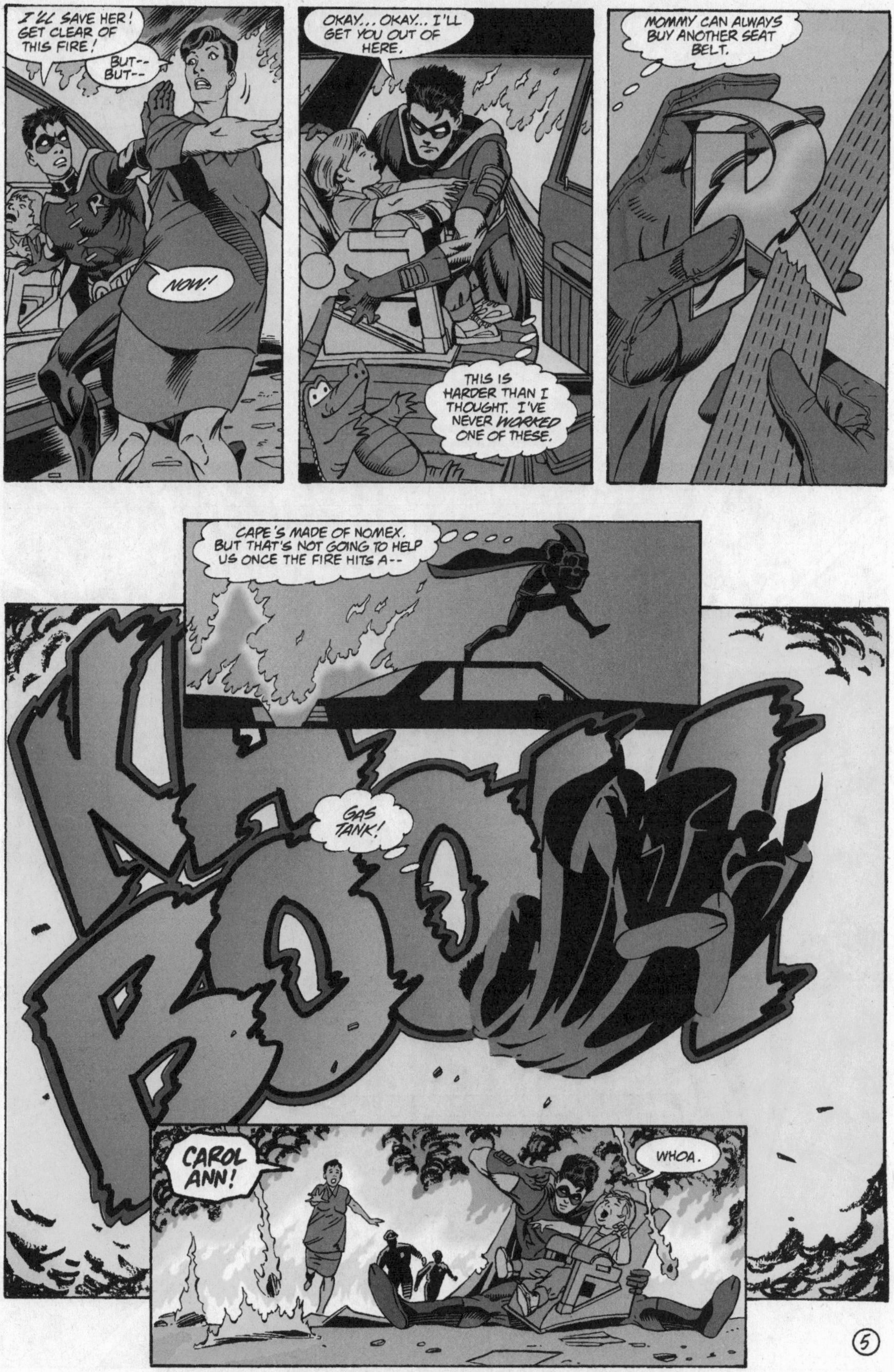
I'LL SAVE HER! GET CLEAR OF THIS FIRE!
BUT-- BUT--
NOW!
OKAY... OKAY... I'LL GET YOU OUT OF HERE.
THIS IS HARDER THAN I THOUGHT. I'VE NEVER WORKED ONE OF THESE.
MOMMY CAN ALWAYS BUY ANOTHER SEAT BELT.
CAPE'S MADE OF NOMEX. BUT THAT'S NOT GOING TO HELP US ONCE THE FIRE HITS A--
GAS TANK!
CAROL ANN!
WHOA.
5

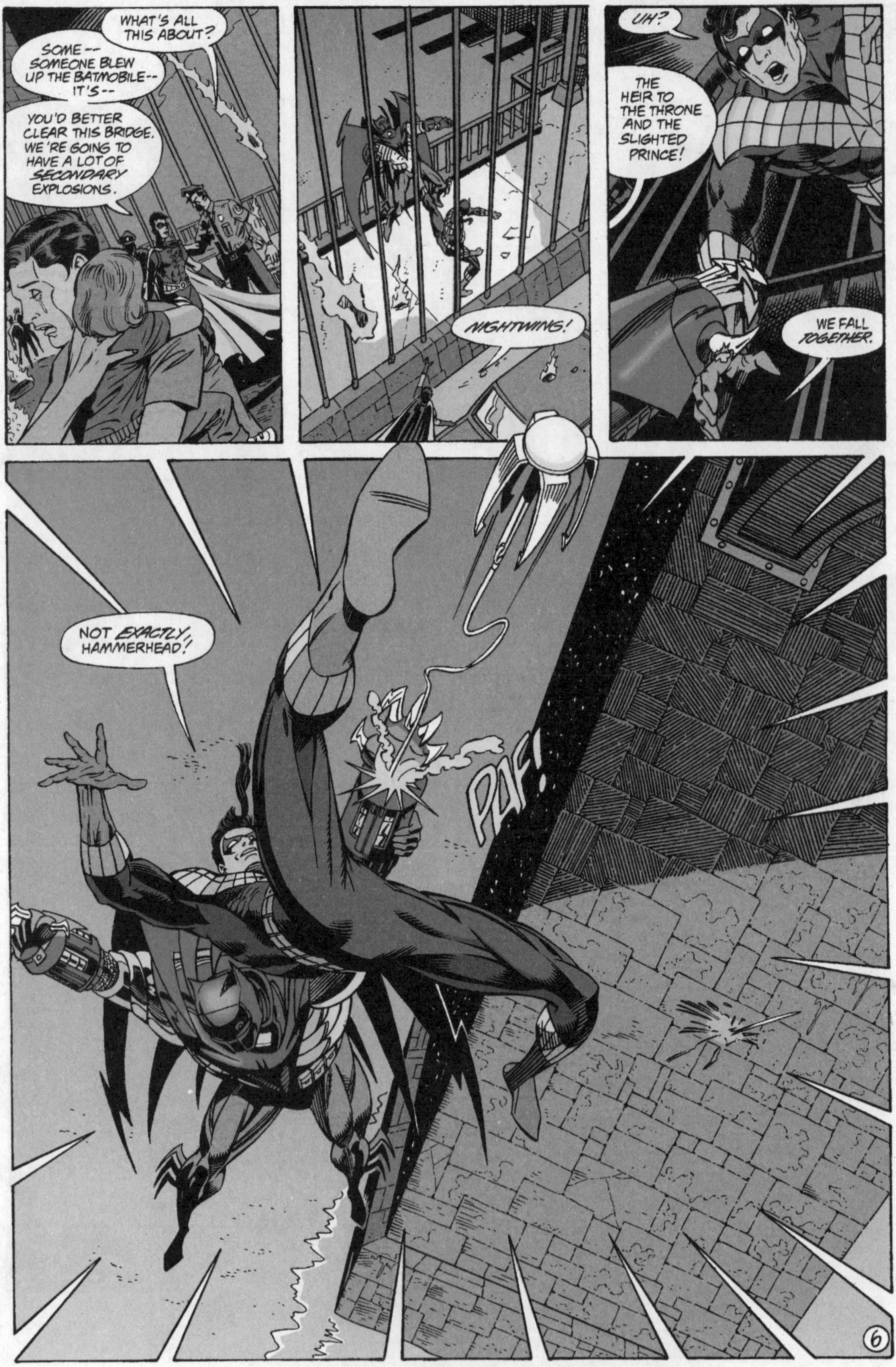
WHAT'S ALL THIS ABOUT?
SOME -- SOMEONE BLEW UP THE BATMOBILE-- IT'S --
YOU'D BETTER CLEAR THIS BRIDGE. WE'RE GOING TO HAVE A LOT OF SECONDARY EXPLOSIONS.
NIGHTWING!
UH?
THE HEIR TO THE THRONE AND THE SLIGHTED PRINCE!
WE FALL TOGETHER.
NOT EXACTLY, HAMMERHEAD!
POF!
6

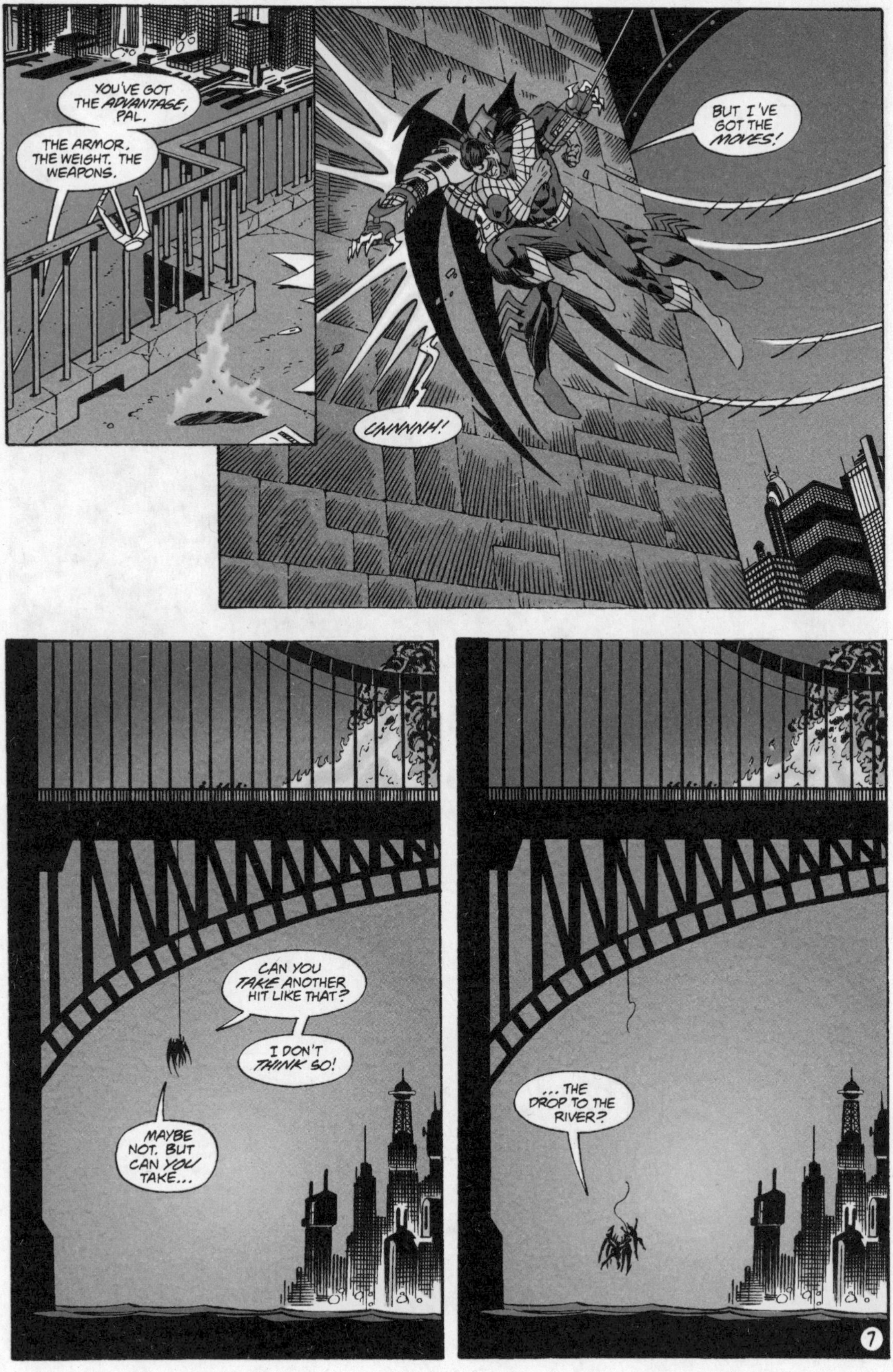
YOU'VE GOT THE ADVANTAGE, PAL.
THE ARMOR. THE WEIGHT. THE WEAPONS.
BUT I'VE GOT THE MOVES!
UNNNNH!
CAN YOU TAKE ANOTHER HIT LIKE THAT?
I DON'T THINK SO!
MAYBE NOT. BUT CAN YOU TAKE...
... THE DROP TO THE RIVER?
7

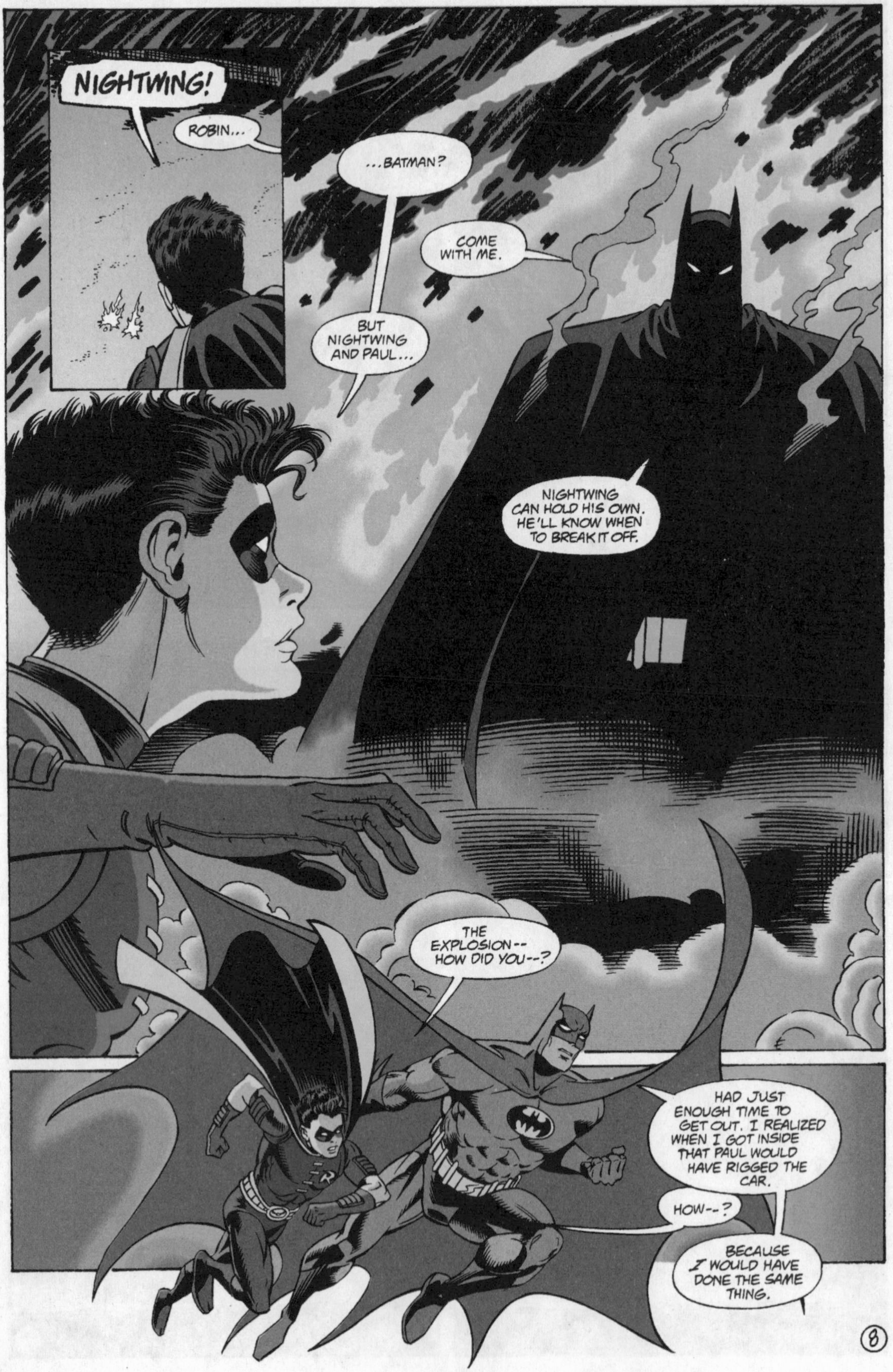
NIGHTWING!
ROBIN...
...BATMAN?
COME WITH ME.
BUT NIGHTWING AND PAUL...
NIGHTWING CAN HOLD HIS OWN. HE'LL KNOW WHEN TO BREAK IT OFF.
THE EXPLOSION-- HOW DID YOU--?
HAD JUST ENOUGH TIME TO GET OUT. I REALIZED WHEN I GOT INSIDE THAT PAUL WOULD HAVE RIGGED THE CAR.
HOW--?
BECAUSE I WOULD HAVE DONE THE SAME THING.
8

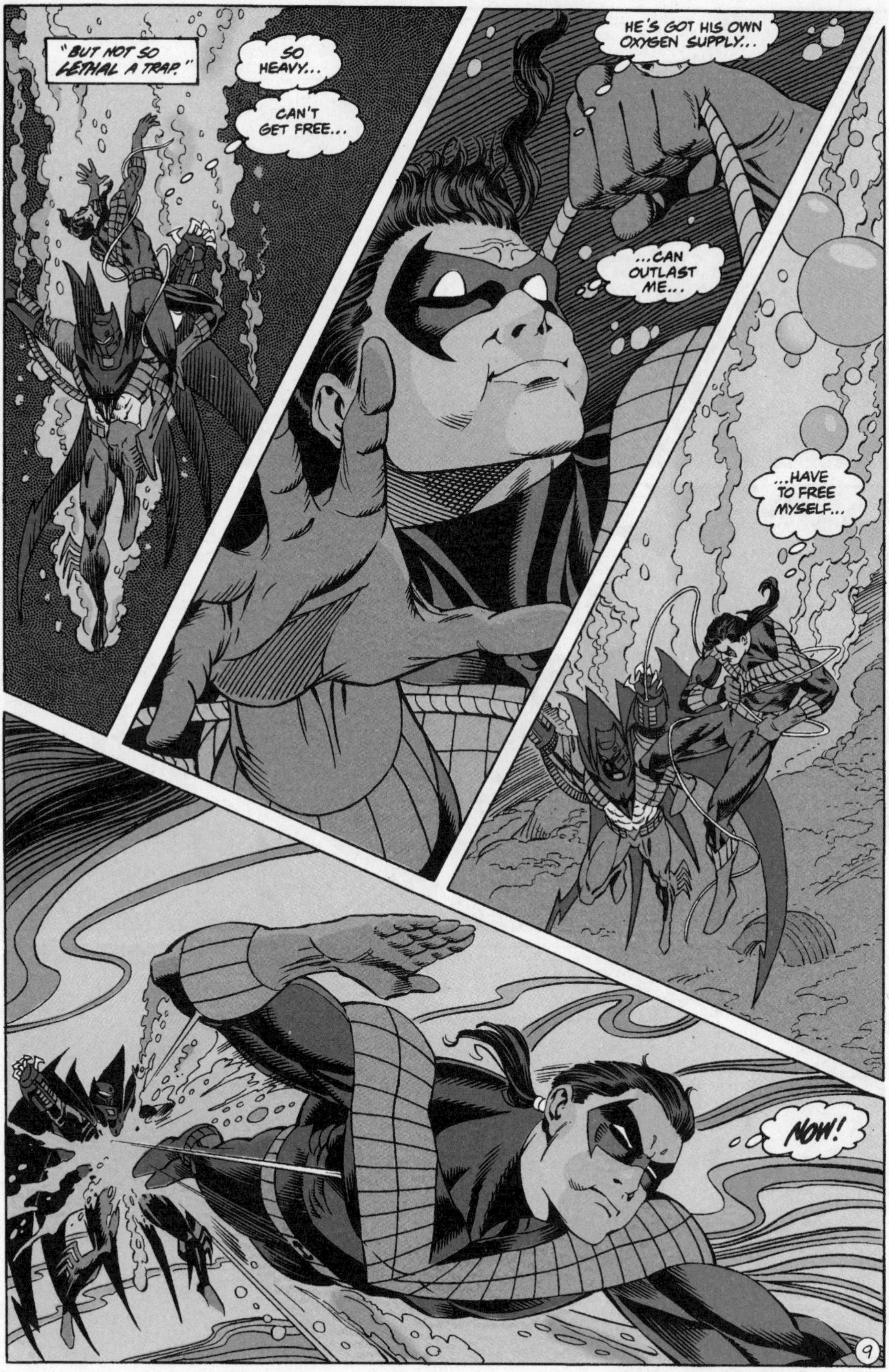
"BUT NOT SO LETHAL A TRAP."
SO HEAVY...
CAN'T GET FREE...
HE'S GOT HIS OWN OXYGEN SUPPLY...
...CAN OUTLAST ME...
...HAVE TO FREE MYSELF...
NOW!
9

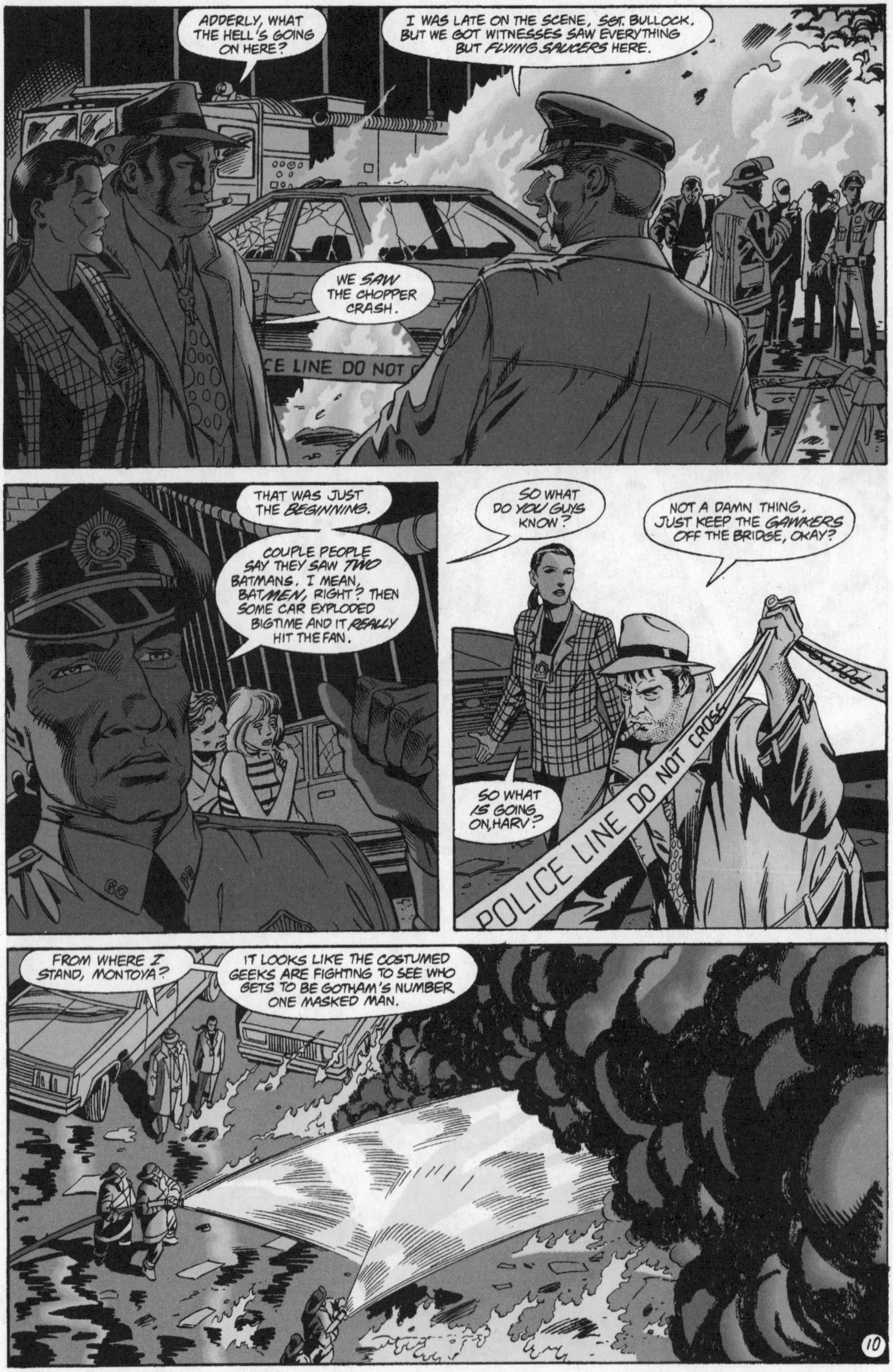
ADDERLY, WHAT THE HELL'S GOING ON HERE?
I WAS LATE ON THE SCENE, SGT. BULLOCK. BUT WE GOT WITNESSES SAW EVERYTHING BUT FLYING SAUCERS HERE.
WE SAW THE CHOPPER CRASH.
THAT WAS JUST THE BEGINNING.
COUPLE PEOPLE SAY THEY SAW TWO BATMANS. I MEAN, BATMEN, RIGHT? THEN SOME CAR EXPLODED BIGTIME AND IT REALLY HIT THE FAN.
SO WHAT DO YOU GUYS KNOW?
NOT A DAMN THING. JUST KEEP THE GAWKERS OFF THE BRIDGE, OKAY?
SO WHAT IS GOING ON, HARV?
POLICE LINE DO NOT CROSS
FROM WHERE I STAND, MONTOYA?
IT LOOKS LIKE THE COSTUMED GEEKS ARE FIGHTING TO SEE WHO GETS TO BE GOTHAM'S NUMBER ONE MASKED MAN.
10

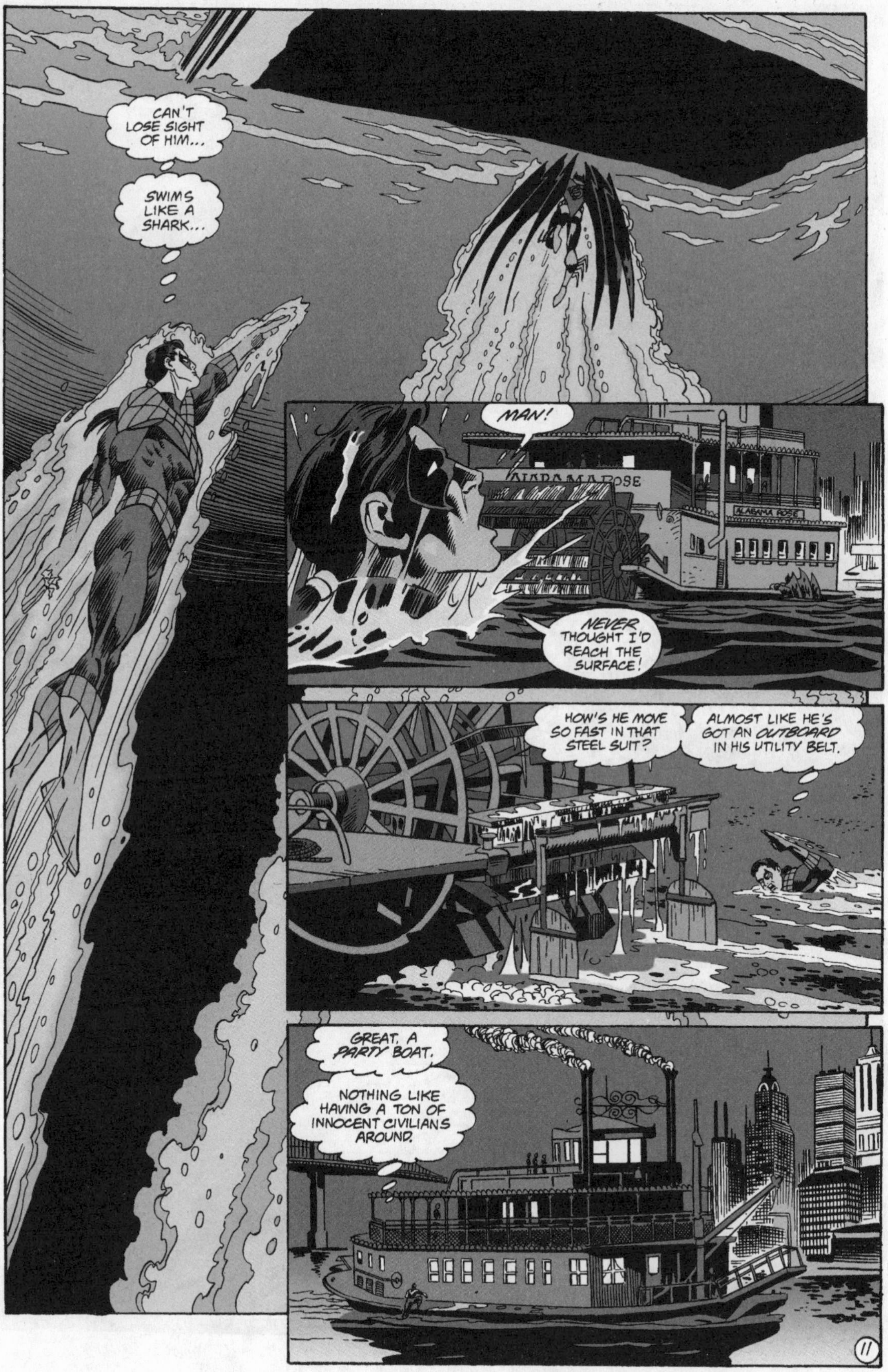
CAN'T LOSE SIGHT OF HIM...
SWIMS LIKE A SHARK...
MAN!
ALABAMA ROSE
NEVER THOUGHT I'D REACH THE SURFACE!
HOW'S HE MOVE SO FAST IN THAT STEEL SUIT?
ALMOST LIKE HE'S GOT AN OUTBOARD IN HIS UTILITY BELT.
GREAT, A PARTY BOAT.
NOTHING LIKE HAVING A TON OF INNOCENT CIVILIANS AROUND.
11

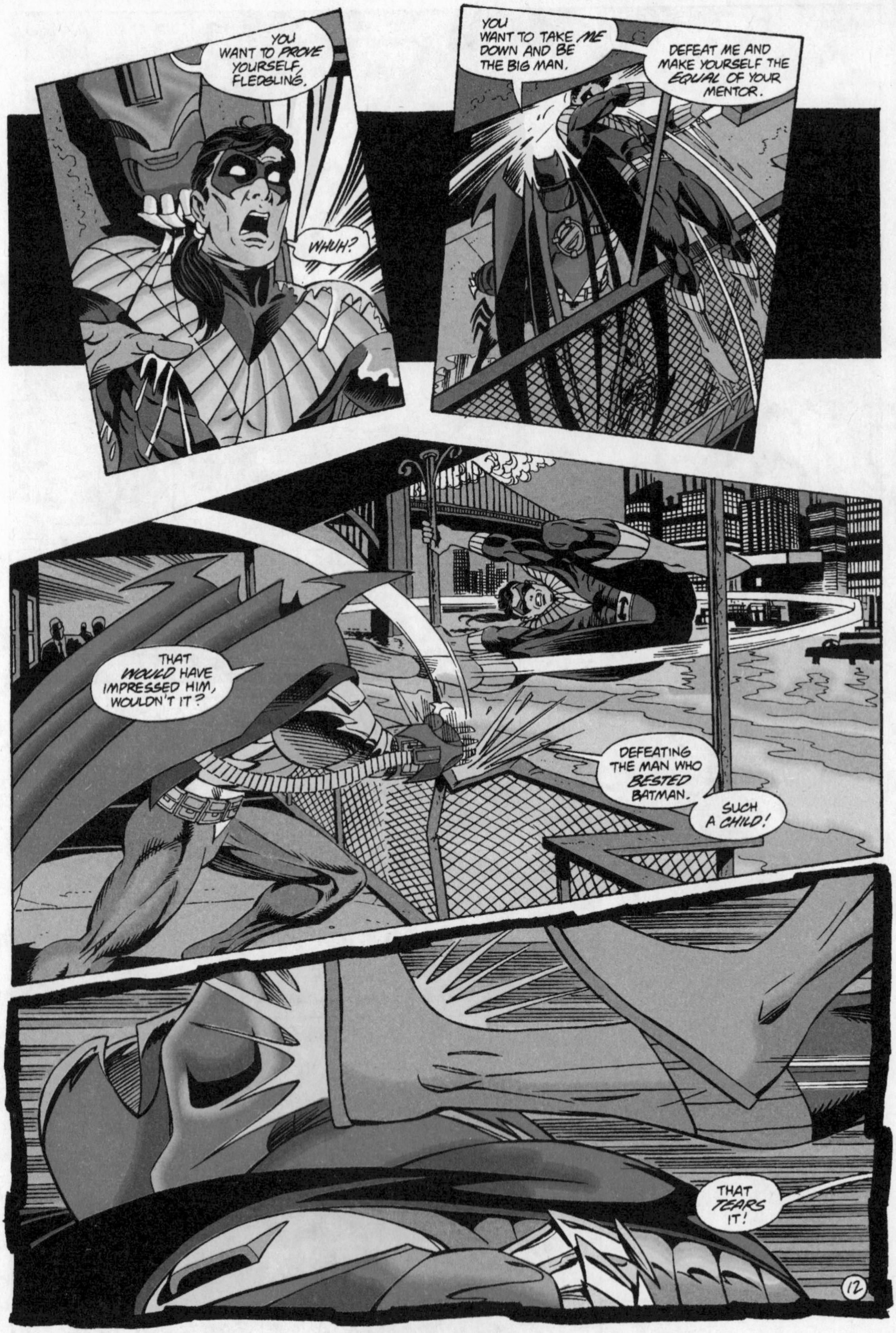
YOU WANT TO PROVE YOURSELF, FLEDGLING.
WHUH?
YOU WANT TO TAKE ME DOWN AND BE THE BIG MAN.
DEFEAT ME AND MAKE YOURSELF THE EQUAL OF YOUR MENTOR.
THAT WOULD HAVE IMPRESSED HIM, WOULDN'T IT?
DEFEATING THE MAN WHO BESTED BATMAN.
SUCH A CHILD!
THAT TEARS IT!
12

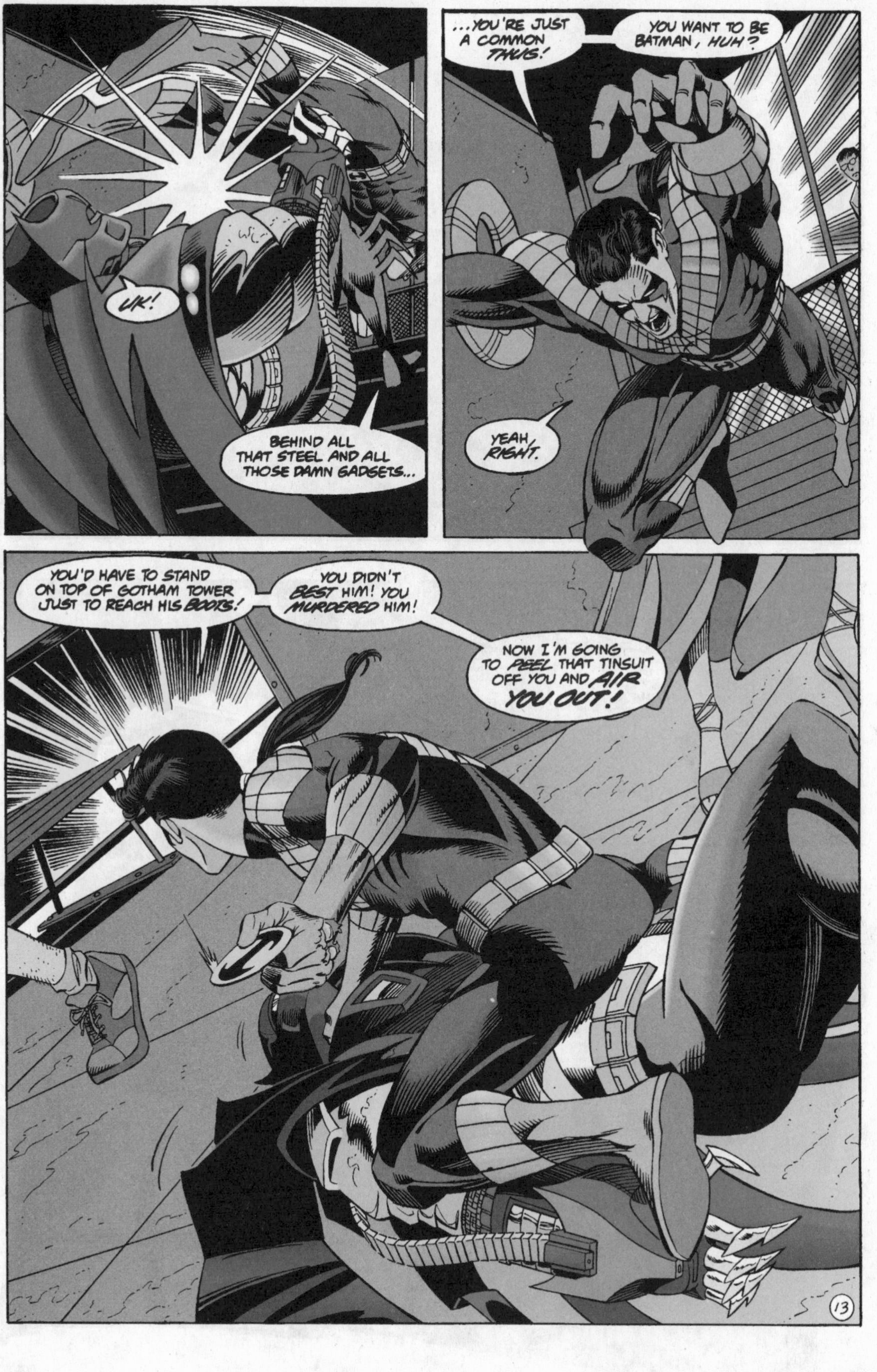
UK!
BEHIND ALL THAT STEEL AND ALL THOSE DAMN GADGETS...
...YOU'RE JUST A COMMON THUG!
YOU WANT TO BE BATMAN, HUH?
YEAH, RIGHT.
YOU'D HAVE TO STAND ON TOP OF GOTHAM TOWER JUST TO REACH HIS BOOTS!
YOU DIDN'T BEST HIM! YOU MURDERED HIM!
NOW I'M GOING TO PEEL THAT TINSUIT OFF YOU AND AIR YOU OUT!
13

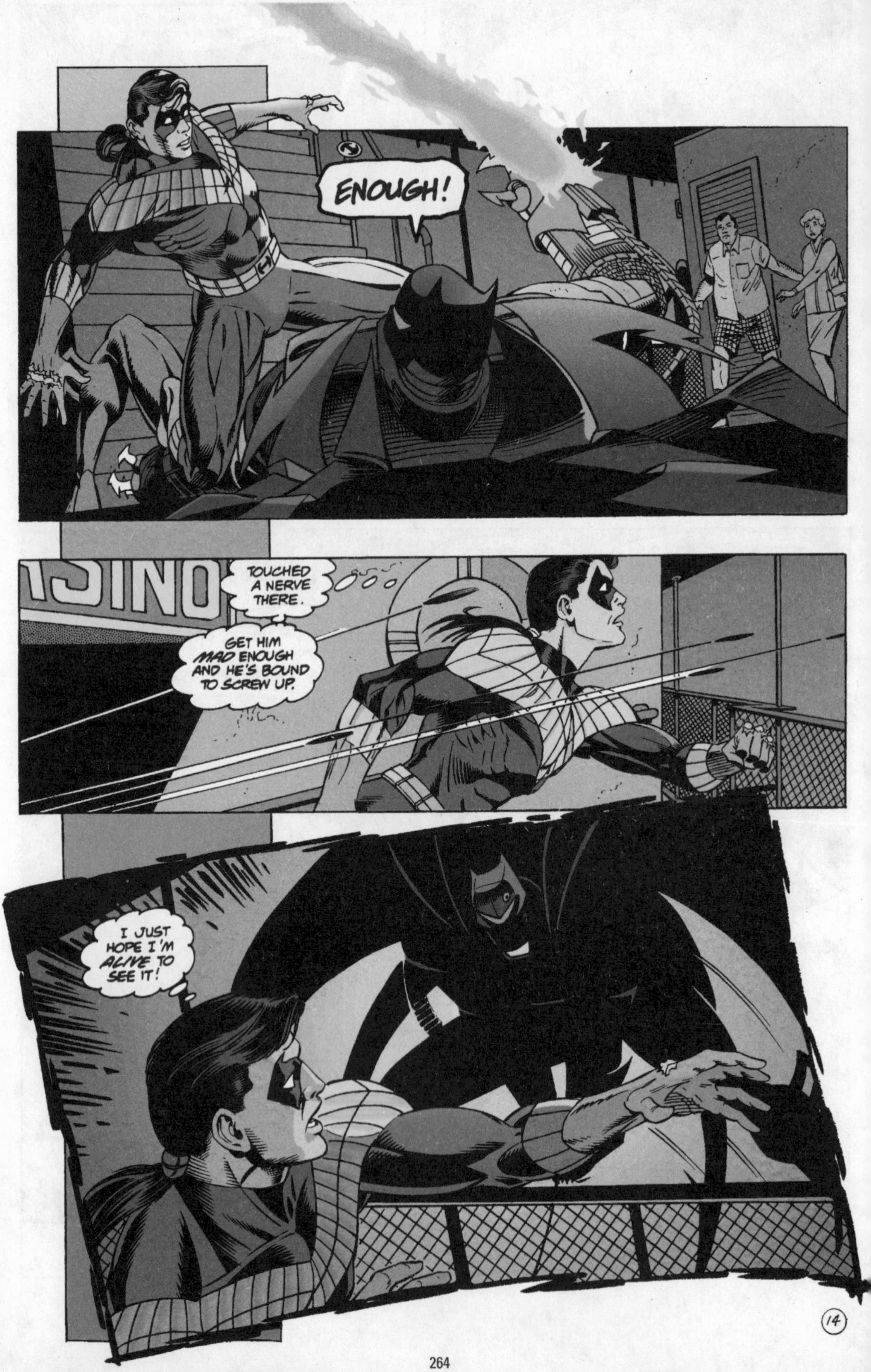
ENOUGH!
TOUCHED A NERVE THERE.
GET HIM MAD ENOUGH AND HE'S BOUND TO SCREW UP.
I JUST HOPE I'M ALIVE TO SEE IT!
14

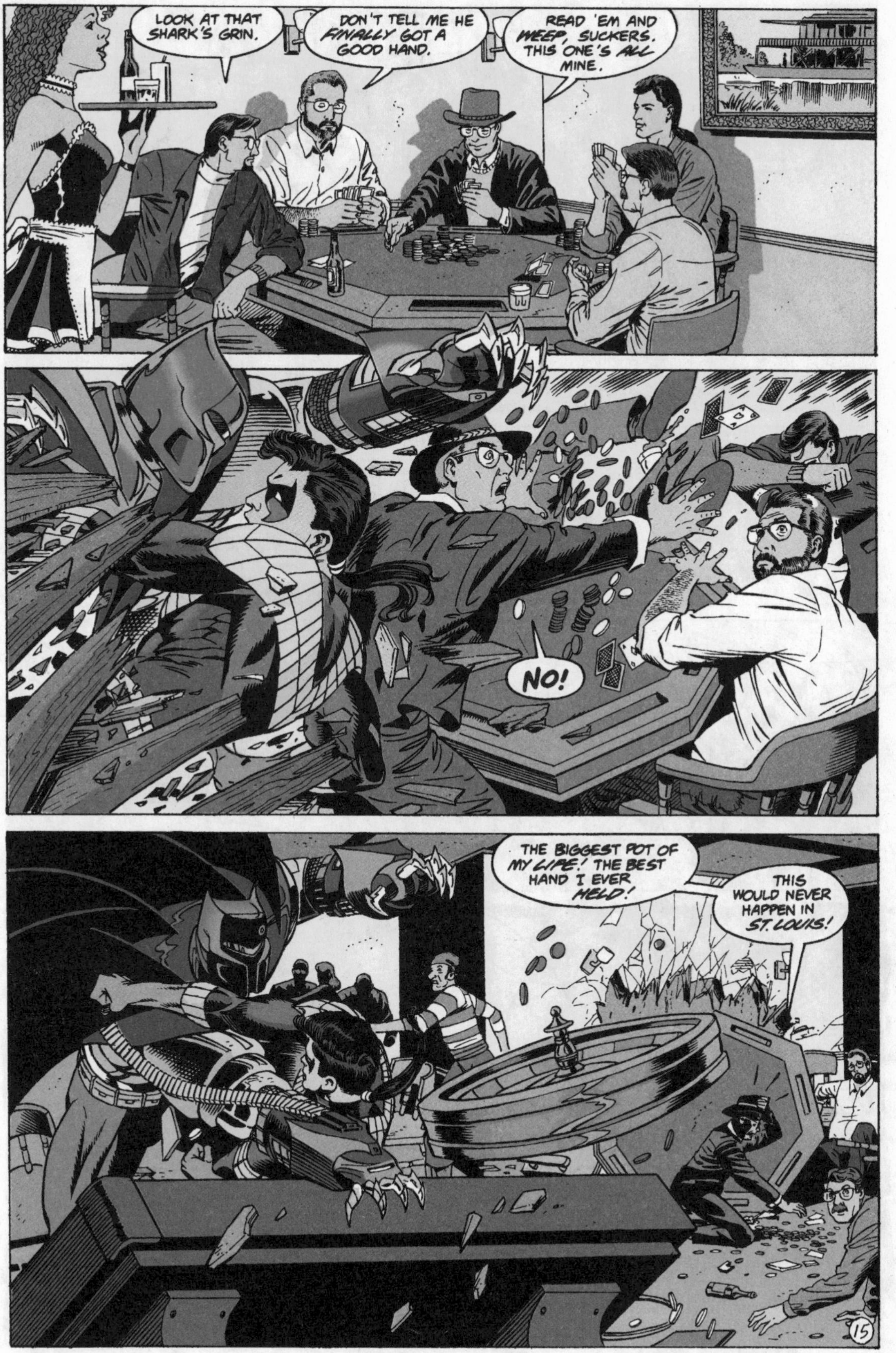
LOOK AT THAT SHARK'S GRIN.
DON'T TELL ME HE FINALLY GOT A GOOD HAND.
READ 'EM AND WEEP, SUCKERS. THIS ONE'S ALL MINE.
NO!
THE BIGGEST POT OF MY LIFE! THE BEST HAND I EVER HELD!
THIS WOULD NEVER HAPPEN IN ST. LOUIS!
15

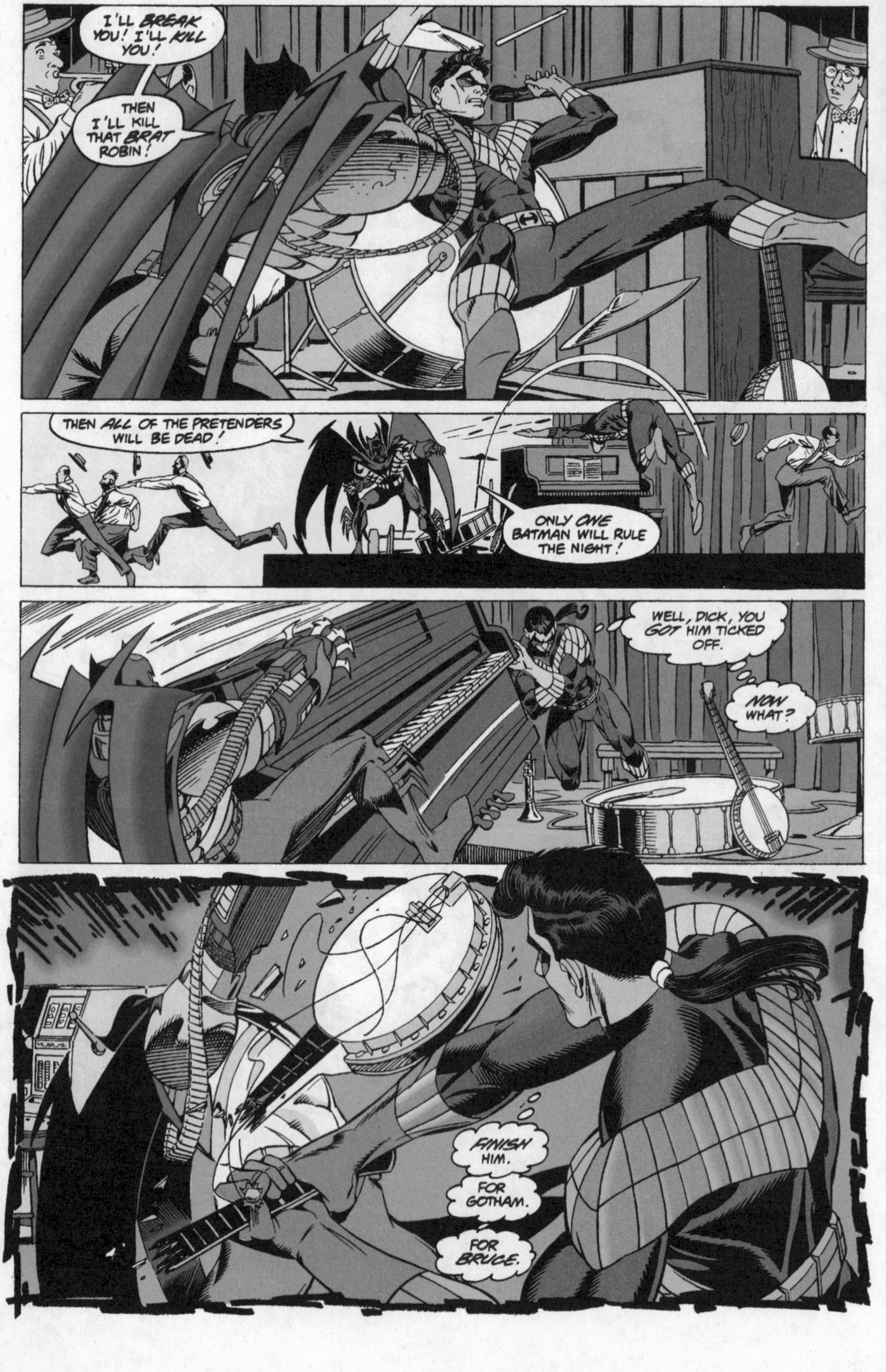

I'LL BREAK YOU! I'LL KILL YOU!
THEN I'LL KILL THAT BRAT ROBIN!
THEN ALL OF THE PRETENDERS WILL BE DEAD!
ONLY ONE BATMAN WILL RULE THE NIGHT!
WELL, DICK, YOU GOT HIM TICKED OFF.
NOW WHAT?
FINISH HIM.
FOR GOTHAM.
FOR BRUCE.

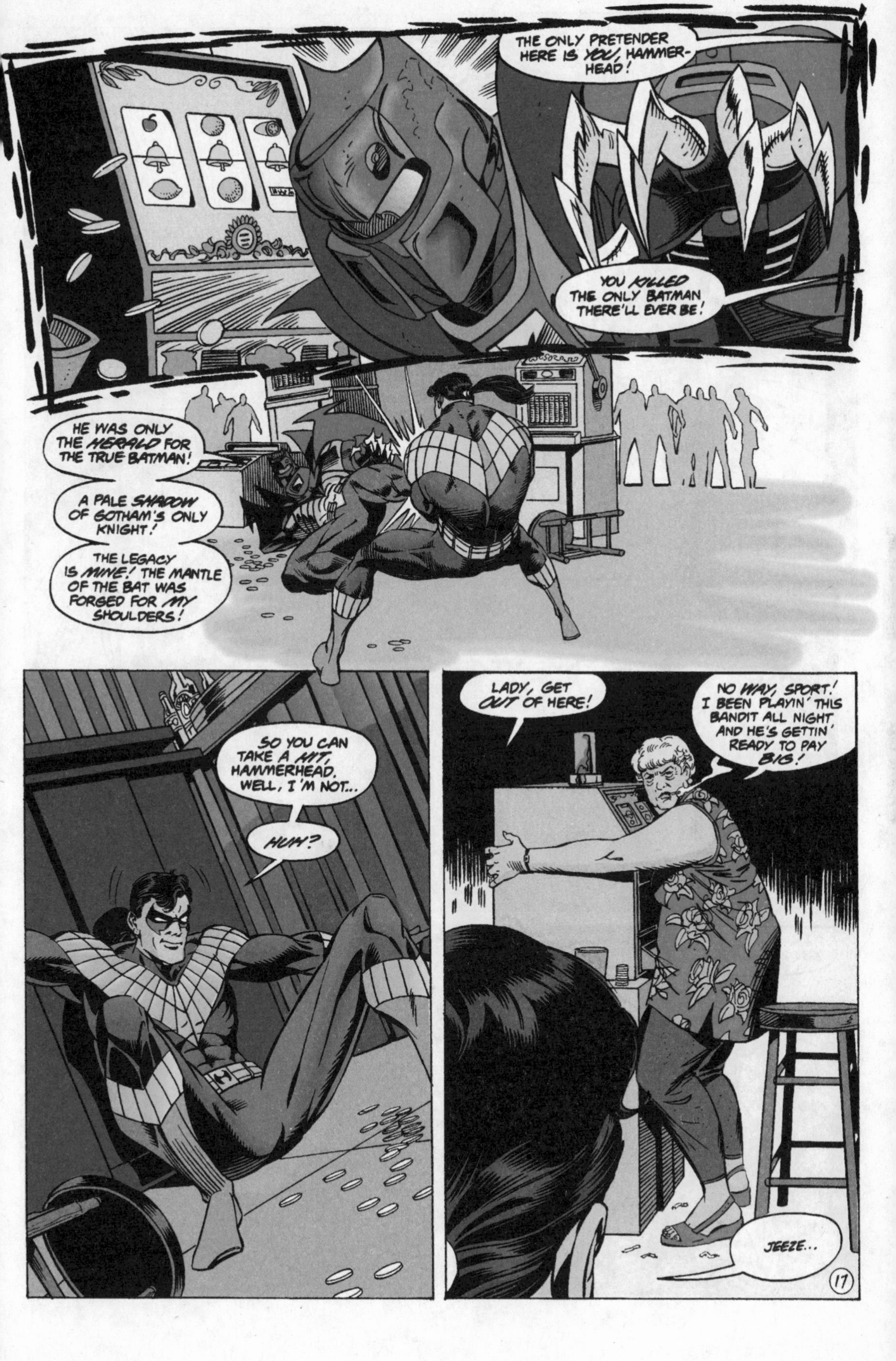
THE ONLY PRETENDER HERE IS YOU, HAMMER-HEAD!
YOU KILLED THE ONLY BATMAN THERE'LL EVER BE!
HE WAS ONLY THE HERALD FOR THE TRUE BATMAN!
A PALE SHADOW OF GOTHAM'S ONLY KNIGHT!
THE LEGACY IS MINE! THE MANTLE OF THE BAT WAS FORGED FOR MY SHOULDERS!
SO YOU CAN TAKE A HIT, HAMMERHEAD. WELL, I'M NOT...
HUH?
LADY, GET OUT OF HERE!
NO WAY, SPORT! I BEEN PLAYIN' THIS BANDIT ALL NIGHT AND HE'S GETTIN' READY TO PAY BIG!
JEEZE...
17

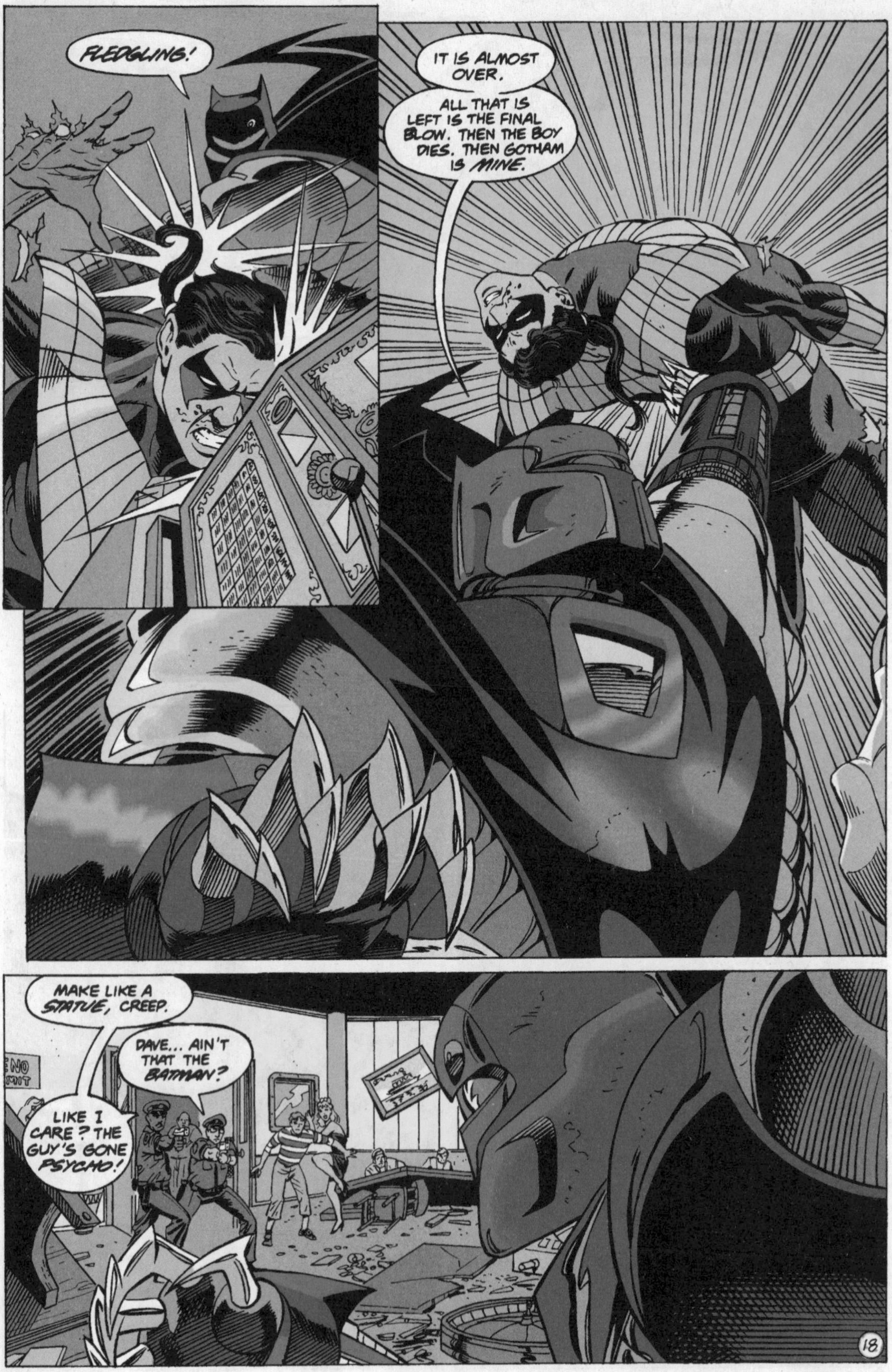
FLEDGLING!
IT IS ALMOST OVER.
ALL THAT IS LEFT IS THE FINAL BLOW. THEN THE BOY DIES. THEN GOTHAM IS MINE.
MAKE LIKE A STATUE, CREEP.
DAVE... AIN'T THAT THE BATMAN?
LIKE I CARE? THE GUY'S GONE PSYCHO!
18

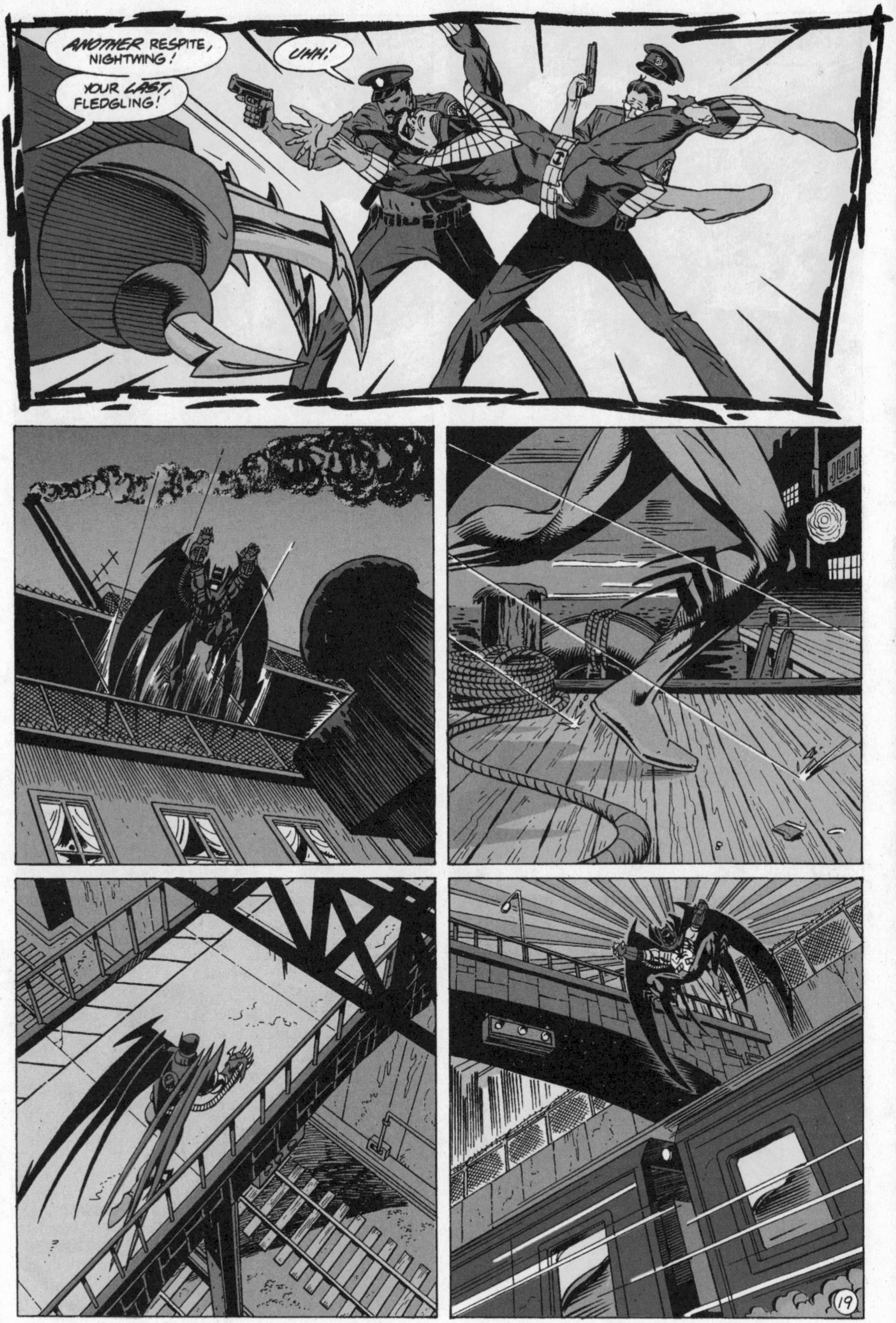
ANOTHER RESPITE, NIGHTWING!
YOUR LAST, FLEDGLING!
UNH!
19

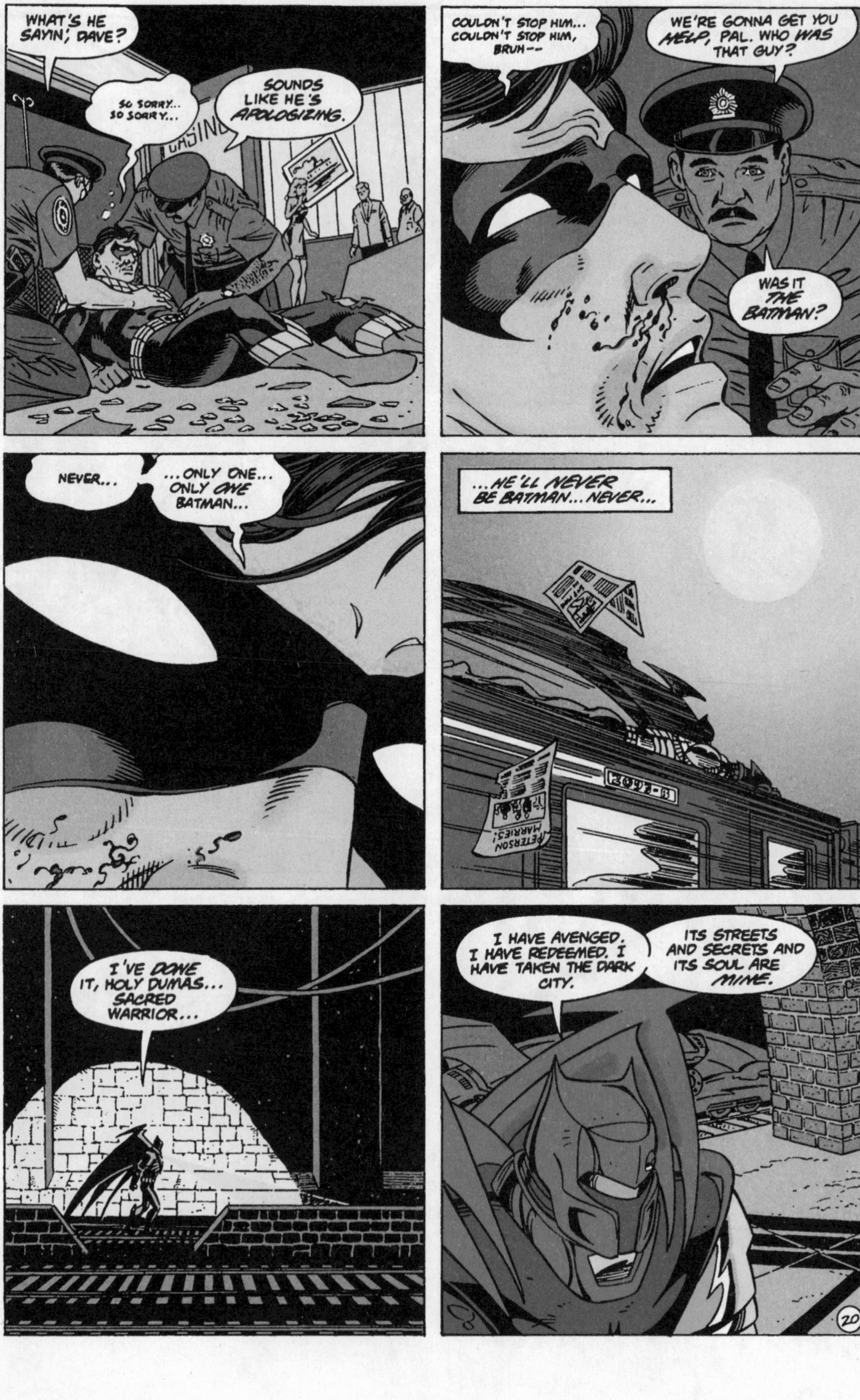
WHAT'S HE SAYIN', DAVE?
SO SORRY... SO SORRY...
SOUNDS LIKE HE'S APOLOGIZING.
CASINO
COULDN'T STOP HIM... COULDN'T STOP HIM, BRUH--
WE'RE GONNA GET YOU HELP, PAL. WHO WAS THAT GUY?
WAS IT THE BATMAN?
NEVER...
...ONLY ONE... ONLY ONE BATMAN...
...HE'LL NEVER BE BATMAN... NEVER...
PETERSON MARRIES!
I'VE DONE IT, HOLY DUMAS... SACRED WARRIOR...
I HAVE AVENGED. I HAVE REDEEMED. I HAVE TAKEN THE DARK CITY.
ITS STREETS AND SECRETS AND ITS SOUL ARE MINE.
20

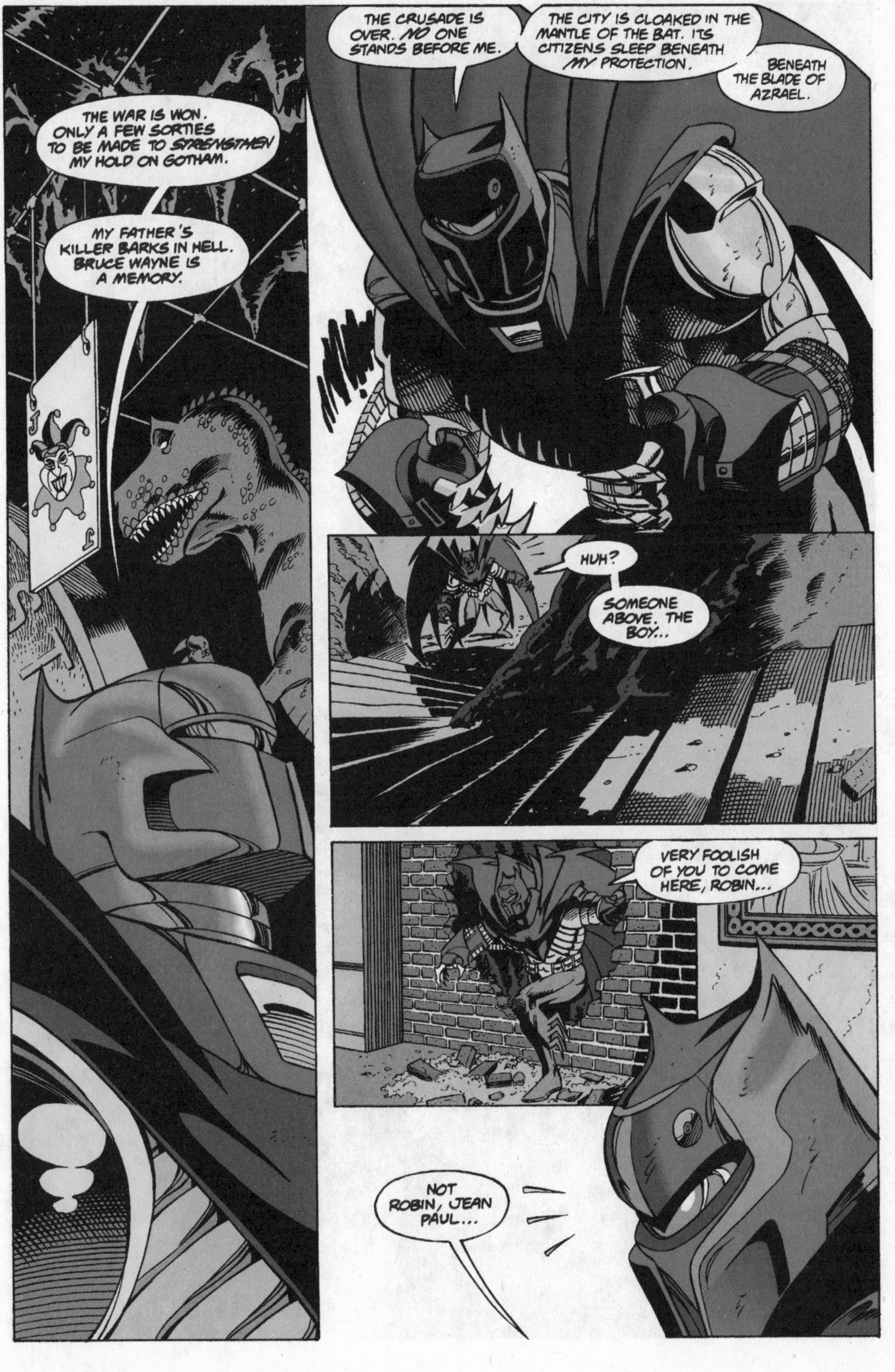
THE WAR IS WON. ONLY A FEW SORTIES TO BE MADE TO STRENGTHEN MY HOLD ON GOTHAM.
MY FATHER'S KILLER BARKS IN HELL. BRUCE WAYNE IS A MEMORY.
THE CRUSADE IS OVER. NO ONE STANDS BEFORE ME.
THE CITY IS CLOAKED IN THE MANTLE OF THE BAT. ITS CITIZENS SLEEP BENEATH MY PROTECTION.
BENEATH THE BLADE OF AZRAEL.
HUH?
SOMEONE ABOVE. THE BOY...
VERY FOOLISH OF YOU TO COME HERE, ROBIN...
NOT ROBIN, JEAN PAUL...

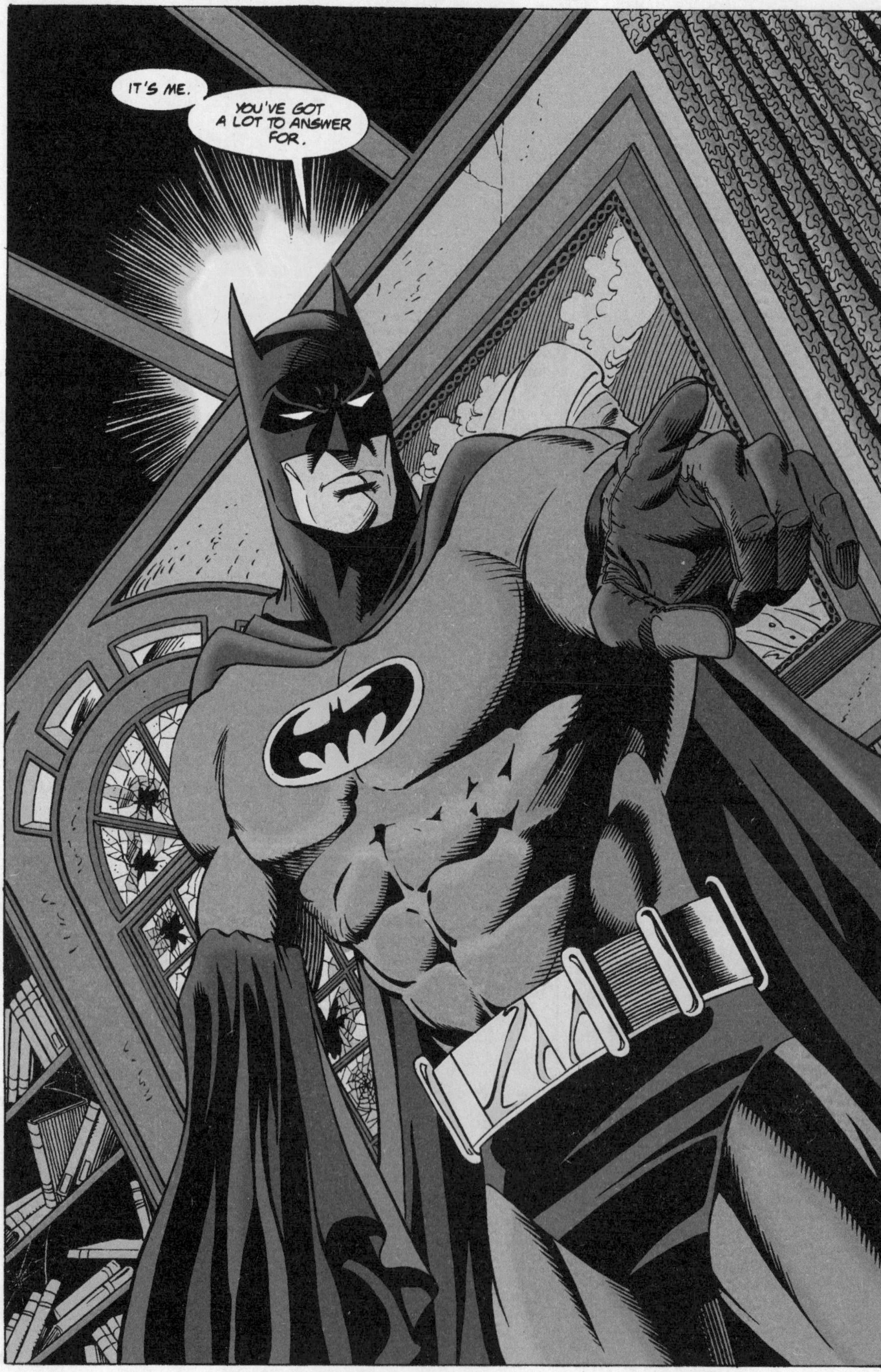
IT'S ME.
YOU'VE GOT A LOT TO ANSWER FOR.

Cover art by BARRY KITSON and SCOTT HANNA

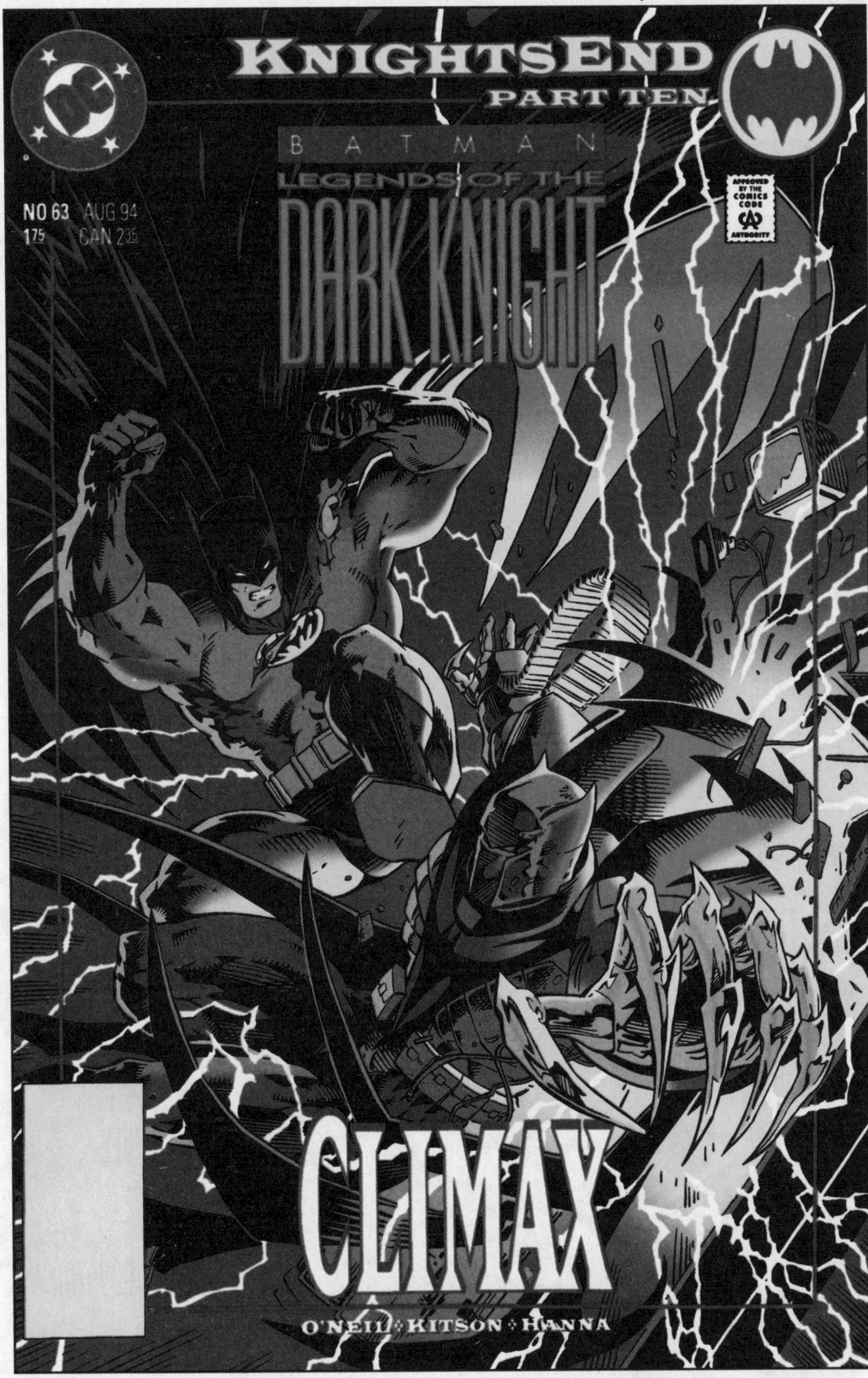
KNIGHTSEND
PART TEN
BATMAN
LEGENDS OF THE
DARK KNIGHT
NO 63 AUG 94
1.75 CAN 2.35
APPROVED BY THE COMICS CODE AUTHORITY
CLIMAX
O'NEIL KITSON HANNA

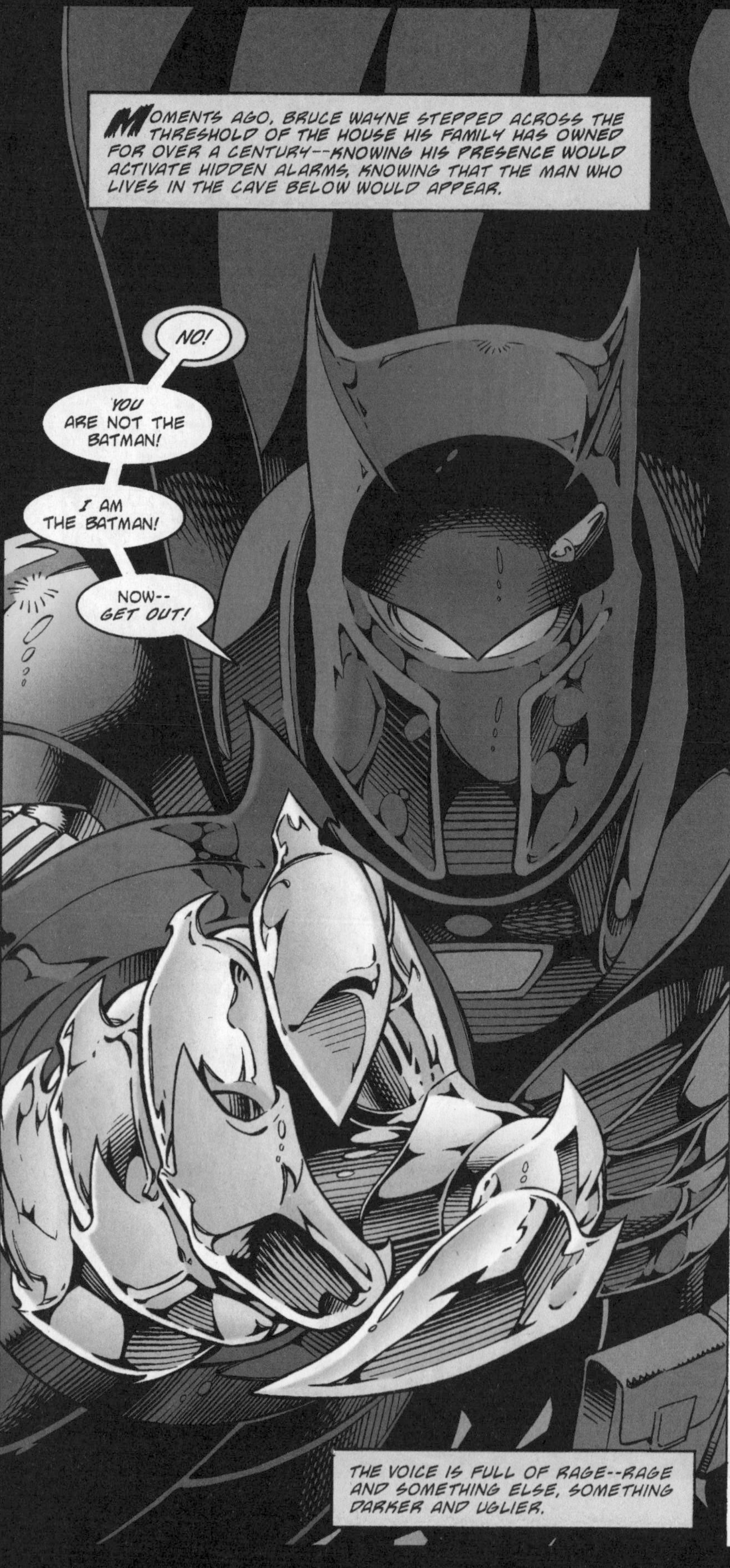
MOMENTS AGO, BRUCE WAYNE STEPPED ACROSS THE THRESHOLD OF THE HOUSE HIS FAMILY HAS OWNED FOR OVER A CENTURY--KNOWING HIS PRESENCE WOULD ACTIVATE HIDDEN ALARMS, KNOWING THAT THE MAN WHO LIVES IN THE CAVE BELOW WOULD APPEAR.
NO!
YOU ARE NOT THE BATMAN!
I AM THE BATMAN!
NOW-- GET OUT!
THE VOICE IS FULL OF RAGE--RAGE AND SOMETHING ELSE, SOMETHING DARKER AND UGLIER.

CLIMAX

writer
DENNY O'NEIL

penciller
BARRY KITSON

inker
SCOTT HANNA

letterer
WILLIE SCHUBERT

colorist
DIGITAL CHAMELEON

assistant editor
CHUCK KIM

associate editor
JIM SPIVEY

editor
ARCHIE GOODWIN

BATMAN created
by BOB KANE

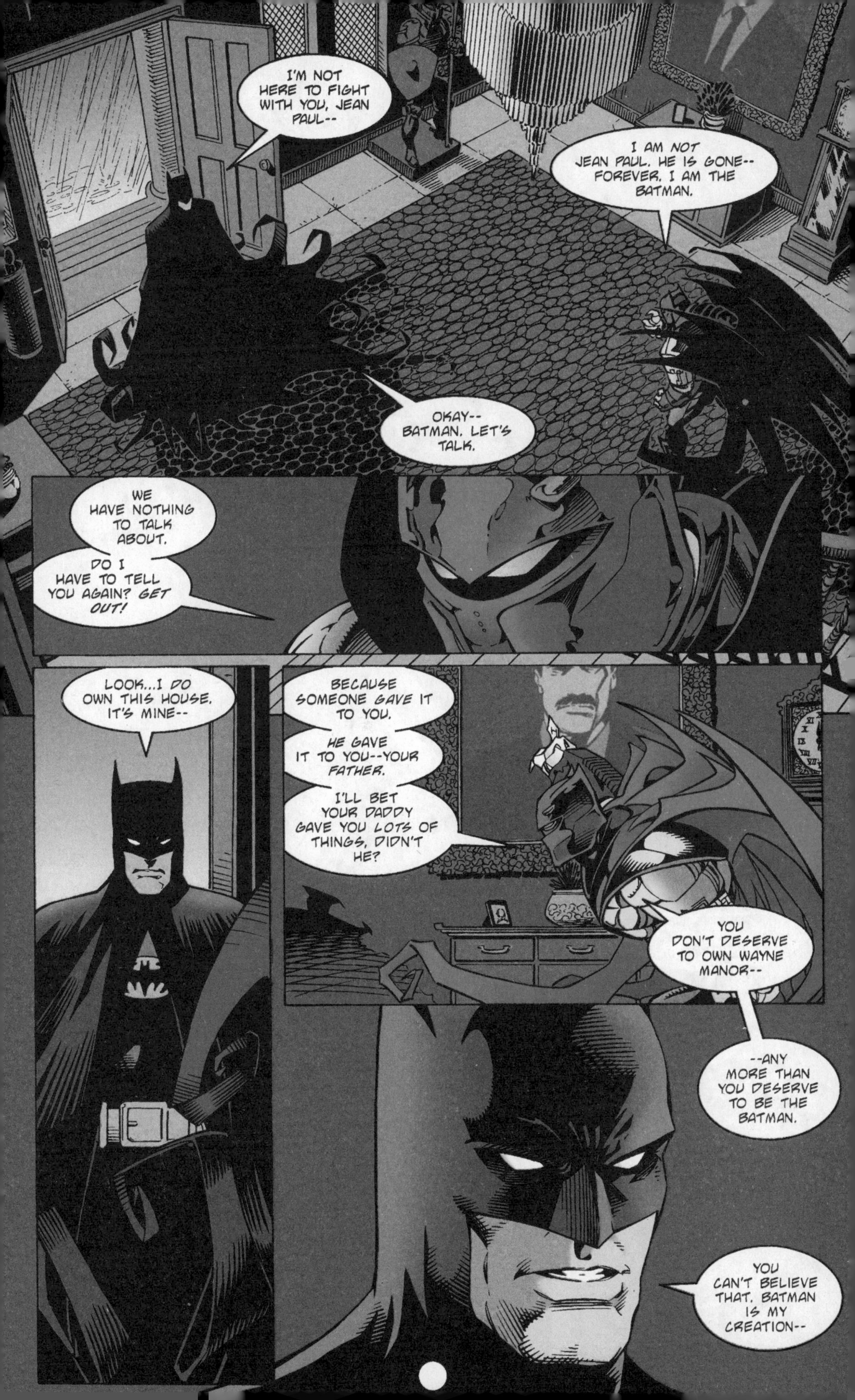
I'M NOT HERE TO FIGHT WITH YOU, JEAN PAUL--
I AM NOT JEAN PAUL. HE IS GONE-- FOREVER. I AM THE BATMAN.
OKAY-- BATMAN. LET'S TALK.
WE HAVE NOTHING TO TALK ABOUT.
DO I HAVE TO TELL YOU AGAIN? GET OUT!
LOOK...I DO OWN THIS HOUSE. IT'S MINE--
BECAUSE SOMEONE GAVE IT TO YOU.
HE GAVE IT TO YOU--YOUR FATHER.
I'LL BET YOUR DADDY GAVE YOU LOTS OF THINGS, DIDN'T HE?
YOU DON'T DESERVE TO OWN WAYNE MANOR--
--ANY MORE THAN YOU DESERVE TO BE THE BATMAN.
YOU CAN'T BELIEVE THAT. BATMAN IS MY CREATION--

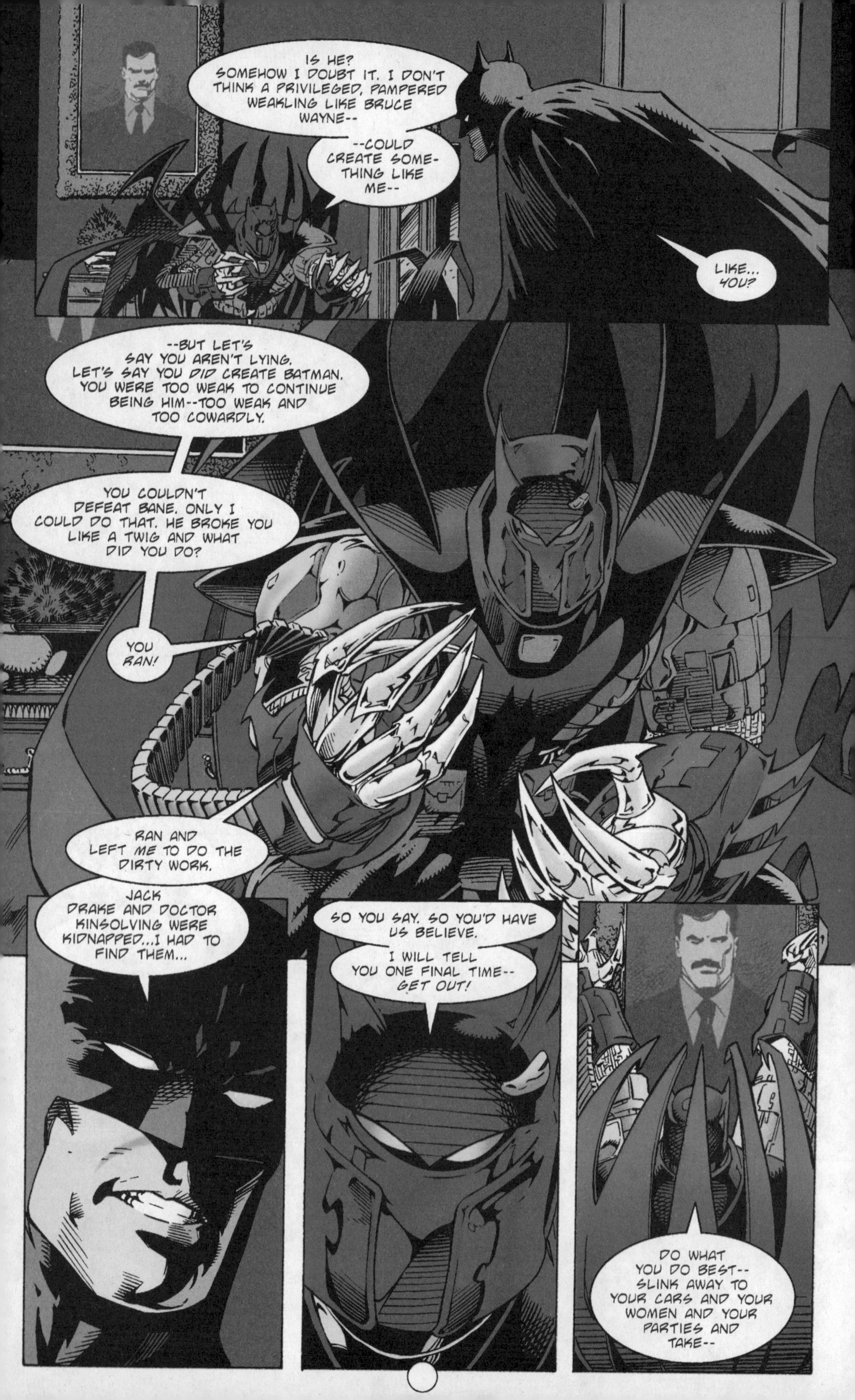
IS HE? SOMEHOW I DOUBT IT. I DON'T THINK A PRIVILEGED, PAMPERED WEAKLING LIKE BRUCE WAYNE--
--COULD CREATE SOME-THING LIKE ME--
LIKE... YOU?
--BUT LET'S SAY YOU AREN'T LYING. LET'S SAY YOU DID CREATE BATMAN. YOU WERE TOO WEAK TO CONTINUE BEING HIM--TOO WEAK AND TOO COWARDLY.
YOU COULDN'T DEFEAT BANE. ONLY I COULD DO THAT. HE BROKE YOU LIKE A TWIG AND WHAT DID YOU DO?
YOU RAN!
RAN AND LEFT ME TO DO THE DIRTY WORK.
JACK DRAKE AND DOCTOR KINSOLVING WERE KIDNAPPED...I HAD TO FIND THEM...
SO YOU SAY. SO YOU'D HAVE US BELIEVE.
I WILL TELL YOU ONE FINAL TIME--GET OUT!
DO WHAT YOU DO BEST--SLINK AWAY TO YOUR CARS AND YOUR WOMEN AND YOUR PARTIES AND TAKE--

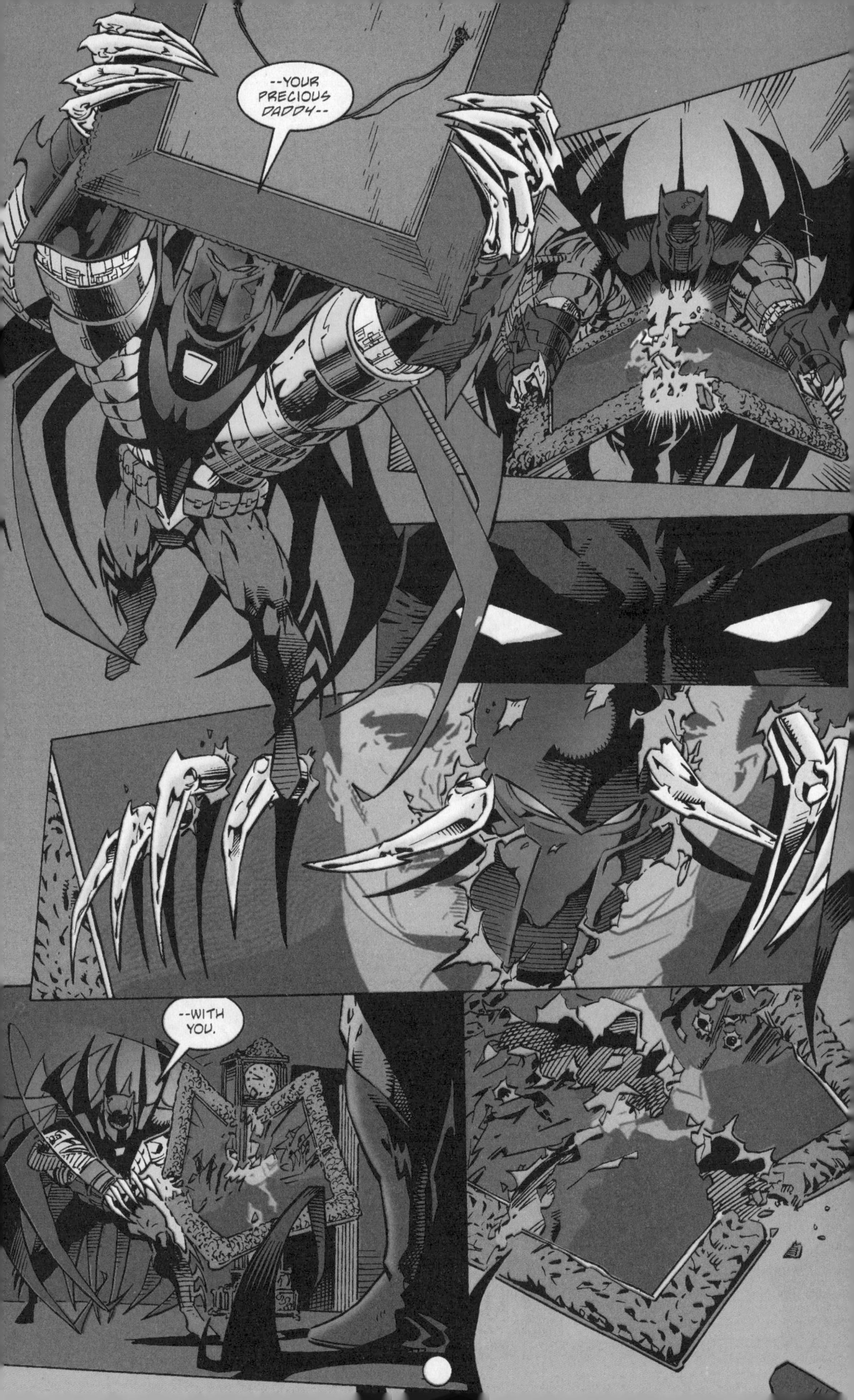
--YOUR PRECIOUS DADDY--
--WITH YOU.

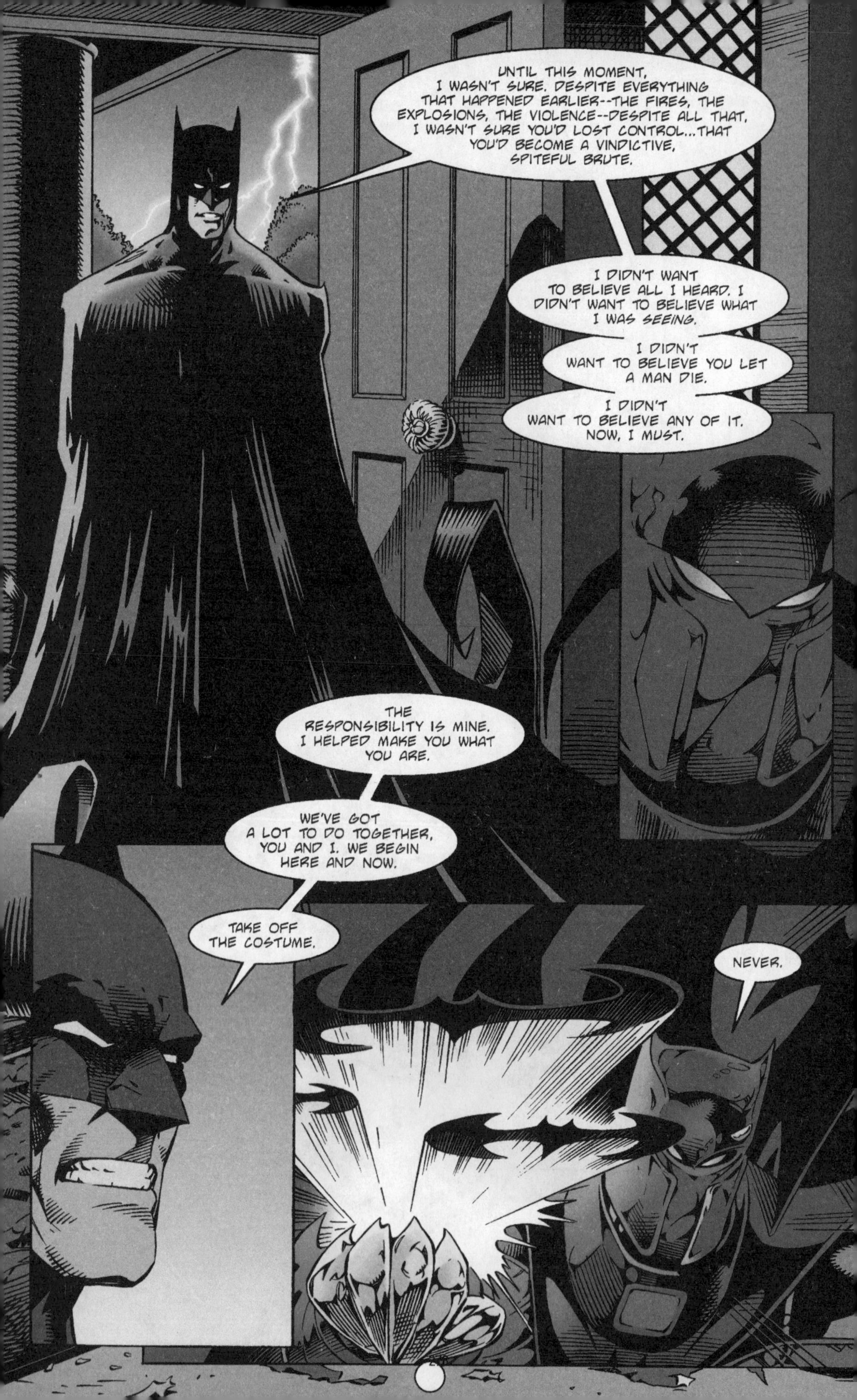
UNTIL THIS MOMENT, I WASN'T SURE. DESPITE EVERYTHING THAT HAPPENED EARLIER--THE FIRES, THE EXPLOSIONS, THE VIOLENCE--DESPITE ALL THAT, I WASN'T SURE YOU'D LOST CONTROL...THAT YOU'D BECOME A VINDICTIVE, SPITEFUL BRUTE.
I DIDN'T WANT TO BELIEVE ALL I HEARD. I DIDN'T WANT TO BELIEVE WHAT I WAS SEEING.
I DIDN'T WANT TO BELIEVE YOU LET A MAN DIE.
I DIDN'T WANT TO BELIEVE ANY OF IT. NOW, I MUST.
THE RESPONSIBILITY IS MINE. I HELPED MAKE YOU WHAT YOU ARE.
WE'VE GOT A LOT TO DO TOGETHER, YOU AND I. WE BEGIN HERE AND NOW.
TAKE OFF THE COSTUME.
NEVER.

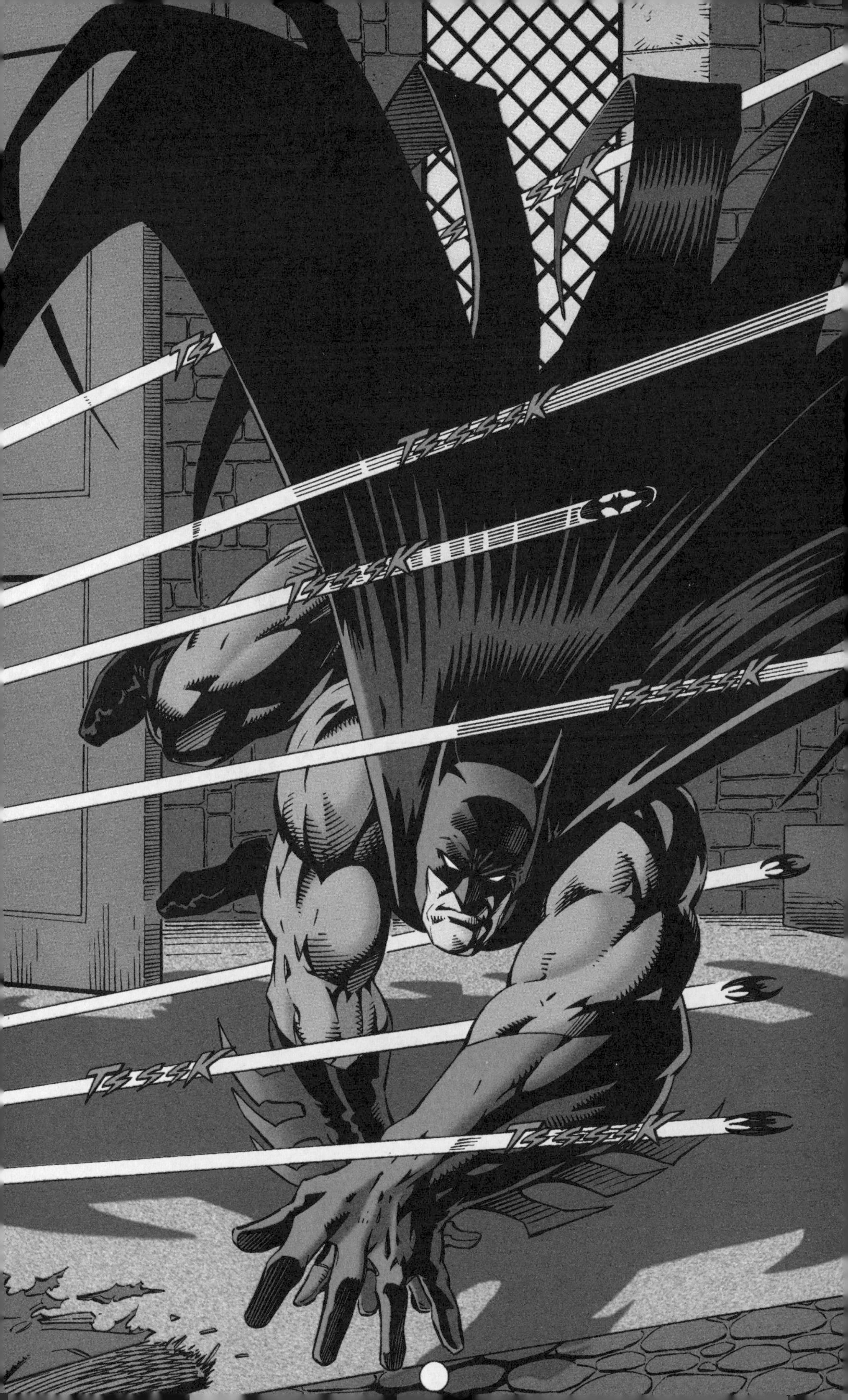
TSSSSK
TSSSSK
TSSSSSK
TSSSSK
TSSSSSK

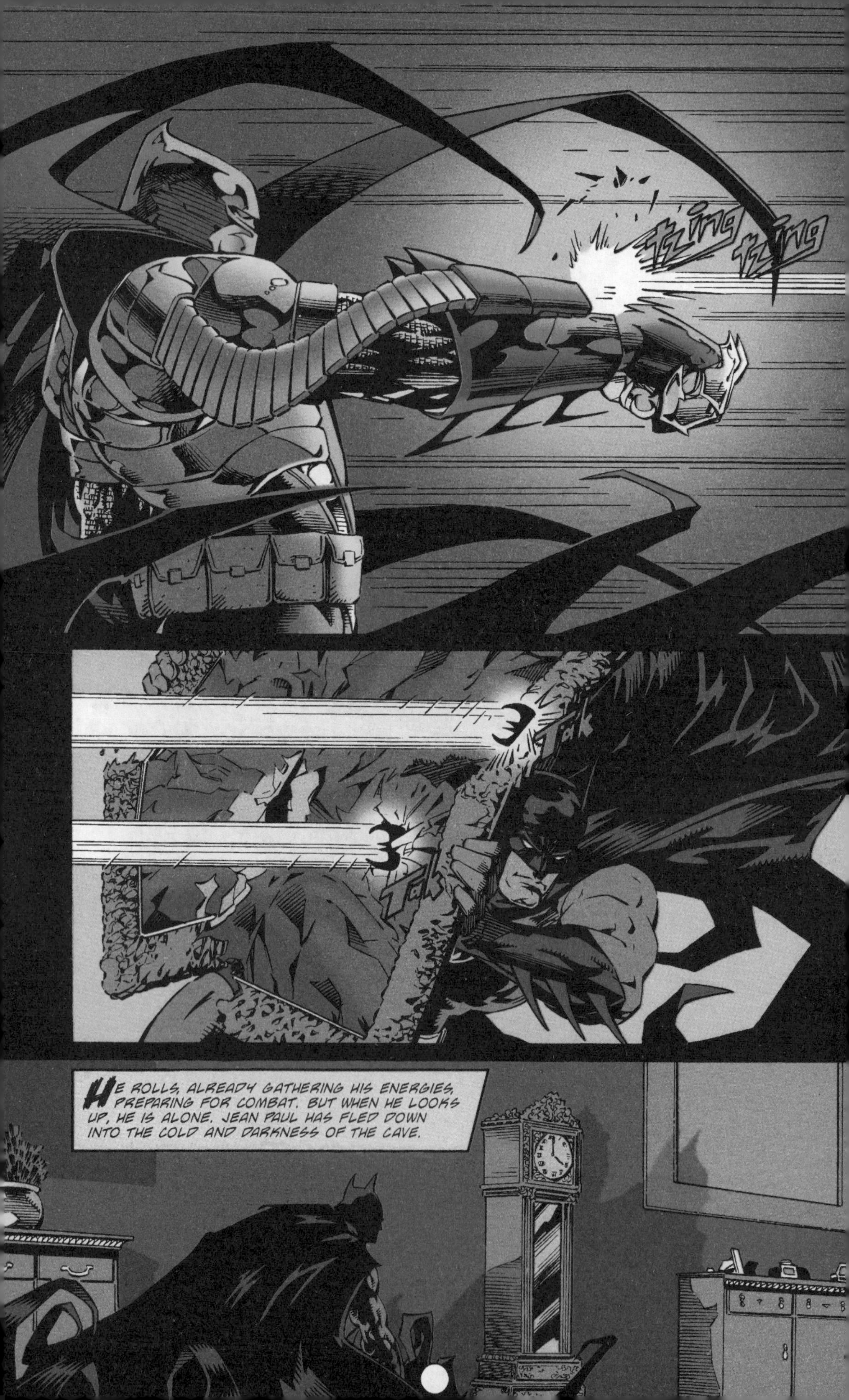
tzing tzing
Tak
Tak
HE ROLLS, ALREADY GATHERING HIS ENERGIES, PREPARING FOR COMBAT. BUT WHEN HE LOOKS UP, HE IS ALONE. JEAN PAUL HAS FLED DOWN INTO THE COLD AND DARKNESS OF THE CAVE.

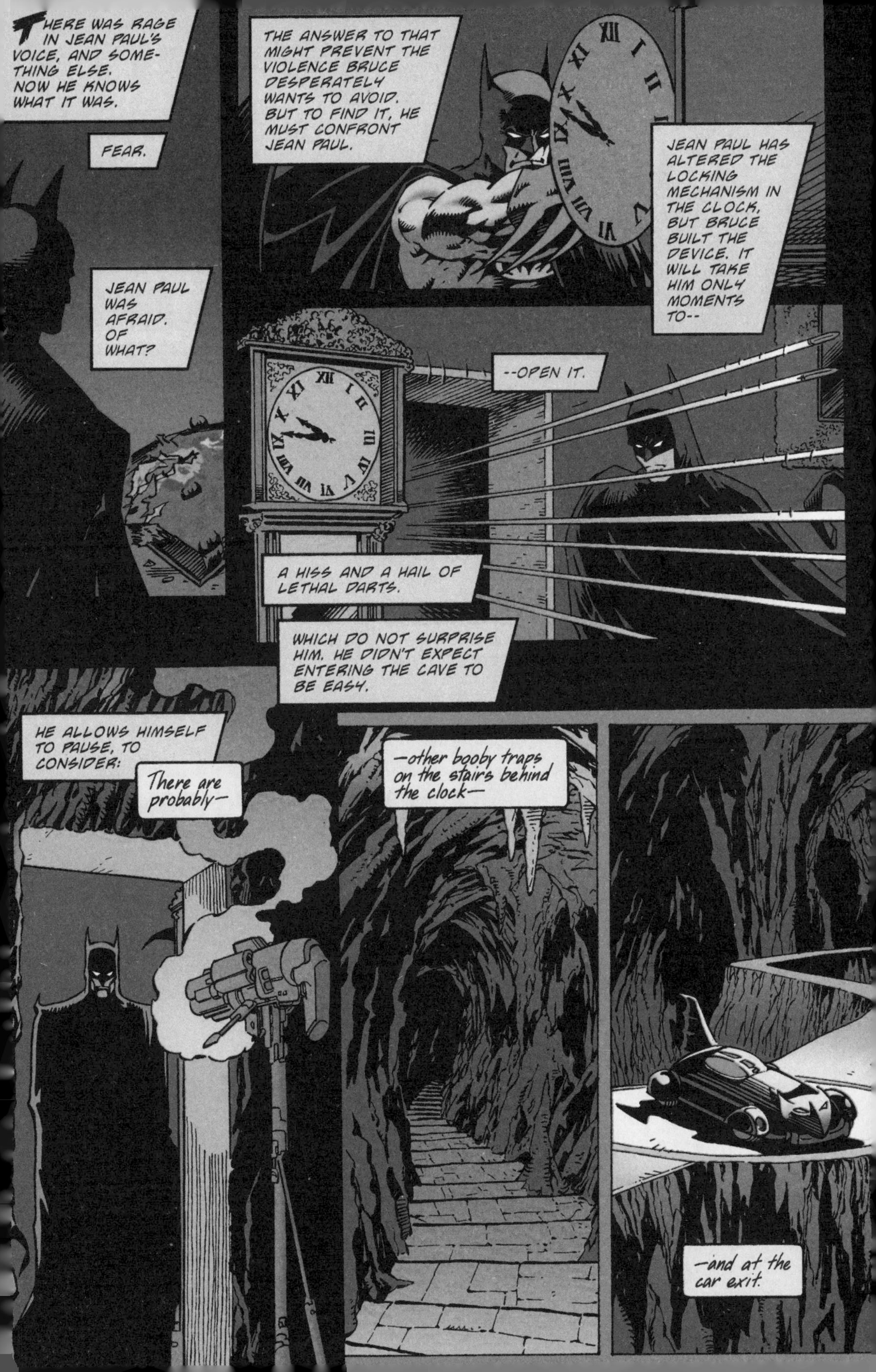
THERE WAS RAGE IN JEAN PAUL'S VOICE, AND SOMETHING ELSE. NOW HE KNOWS WHAT IT WAS.
FEAR.
JEAN PAUL WAS AFRAID. OF WHAT?
THE ANSWER TO THAT MIGHT PREVENT THE VIOLENCE BRUCE DESPERATELY WANTS TO AVOID. BUT TO FIND IT, HE MUST CONFRONT JEAN PAUL.
JEAN PAUL HAS ALTERED THE LOCKING MECHANISM IN THE CLOCK, BUT BRUCE BUILT THE DEVICE. IT WILL TAKE HIM ONLY MOMENTS TO--
--OPEN IT.
A HISS AND A HAIL OF LETHAL DARTS.
WHICH DO NOT SURPRISE HIM. HE DIDN'T EXPECT ENTERING THE CAVE TO BE EASY.
HE ALLOWS HIMSELF TO PAUSE, TO CONSIDER:
There are probably—
—other booby traps on the stairs behind the clock—
—and at the car exit.

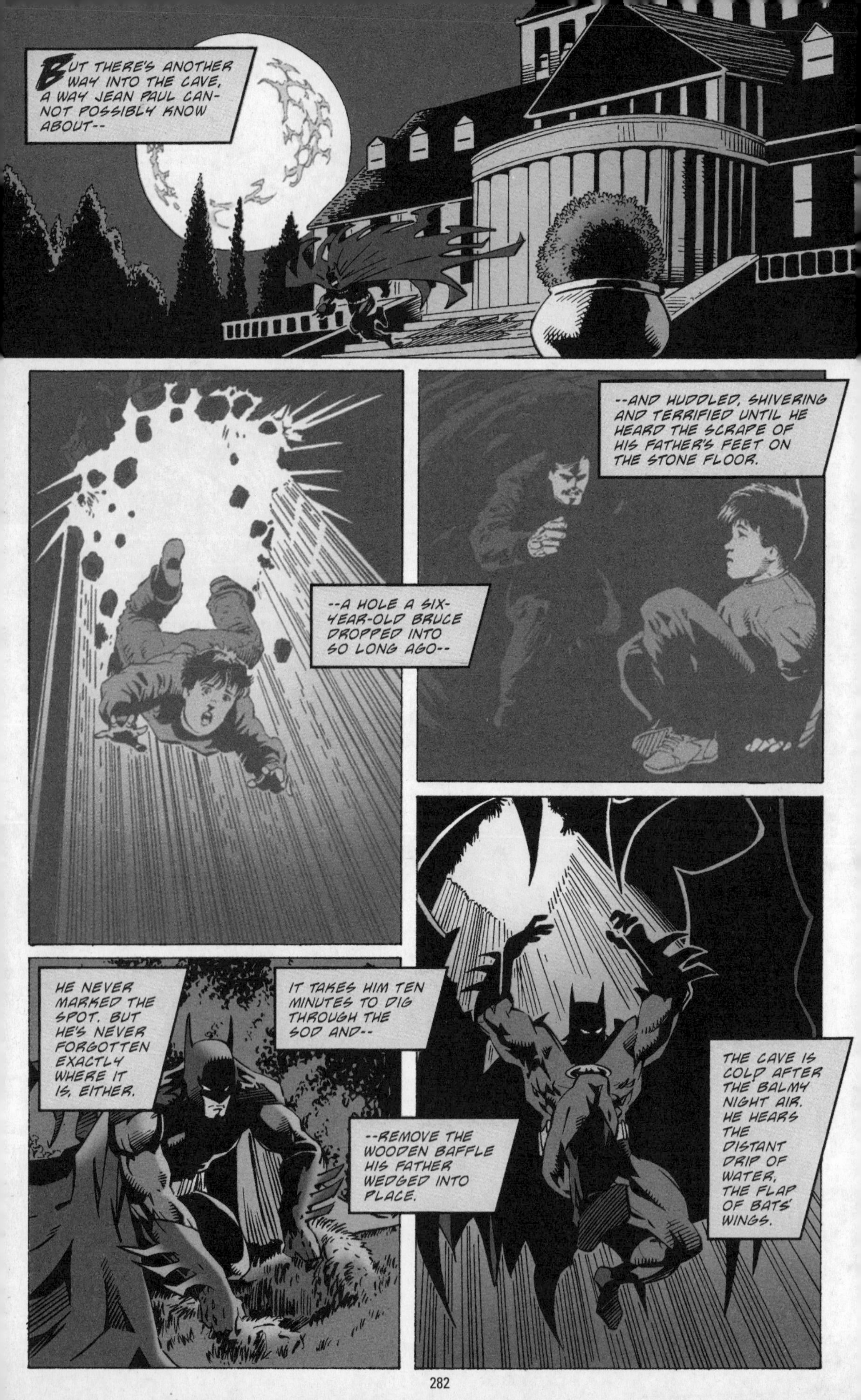
BUT THERE'S ANOTHER WAY INTO THE CAVE, A WAY JEAN PAUL CANNOT POSSIBLY KNOW ABOUT--
--A HOLE A SIX-YEAR-OLD BRUCE DROPPED INTO SO LONG AGO--
--AND HUDDLED, SHIVERING AND TERRIFIED UNTIL HE HEARD THE SCRAPE OF HIS FATHER'S FEET ON THE STONE FLOOR.
HE NEVER MARKED THE SPOT. BUT HE'S NEVER FORGOTTEN EXACTLY WHERE IT IS, EITHER.
IT TAKES HIM TEN MINUTES TO DIG THROUGH THE SOD AND--
--REMOVE THE WOODEN BAFFLE HIS FATHER WEDGED INTO PLACE.
THE CAVE IS COLD AFTER THE BALMY NIGHT AIR. HE HEARS THE DISTANT DRIP OF WATER, THE FLAP OF BATS' WINGS.

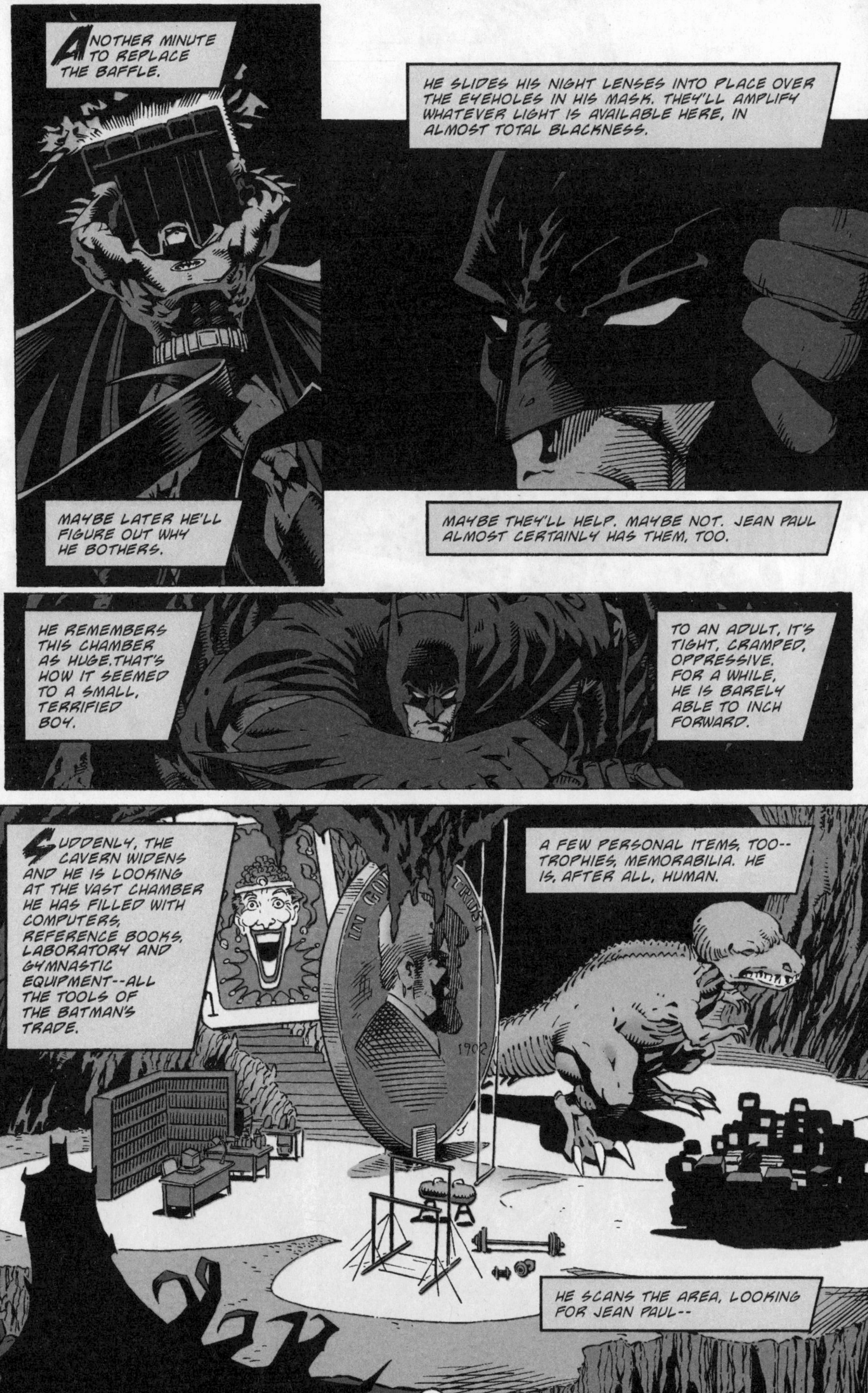
ANOTHER MINUTE TO REPLACE THE BAFFLE.
MAYBE LATER HE'LL FIGURE OUT WHY HE BOTHERS.
HE SLIDES HIS NIGHT LENSES INTO PLACE OVER THE EYEHOLES IN HIS MASK. THEY'LL AMPLIFY WHATEVER LIGHT IS AVAILABLE HERE, IN ALMOST TOTAL BLACKNESS.
MAYBE THEY'LL HELP. MAYBE NOT. JEAN PAUL ALMOST CERTAINLY HAS THEM, TOO.
HE REMEMBERS THIS CHAMBER AS HUGE. THAT'S HOW IT SEEMED TO A SMALL, TERRIFIED BOY.
TO AN ADULT, IT'S TIGHT, CRAMPED, OPPRESSIVE. FOR A WHILE, HE IS BARELY ABLE TO INCH FORWARD.
SUDDENLY, THE CAVERN WIDENS AND HE IS LOOKING AT THE VAST CHAMBER HE HAS FILLED WITH COMPUTERS, REFERENCE BOOKS, LABORATORY AND GYMNASTIC EQUIPMENT--ALL THE TOOLS OF THE BATMAN'S TRADE.
A FEW PERSONAL ITEMS, TOO-- TROPHIES, MEMORABILIA. HE IS, AFTER ALL, HUMAN.
HE SCANS THE AREA, LOOKING FOR JEAN PAUL--

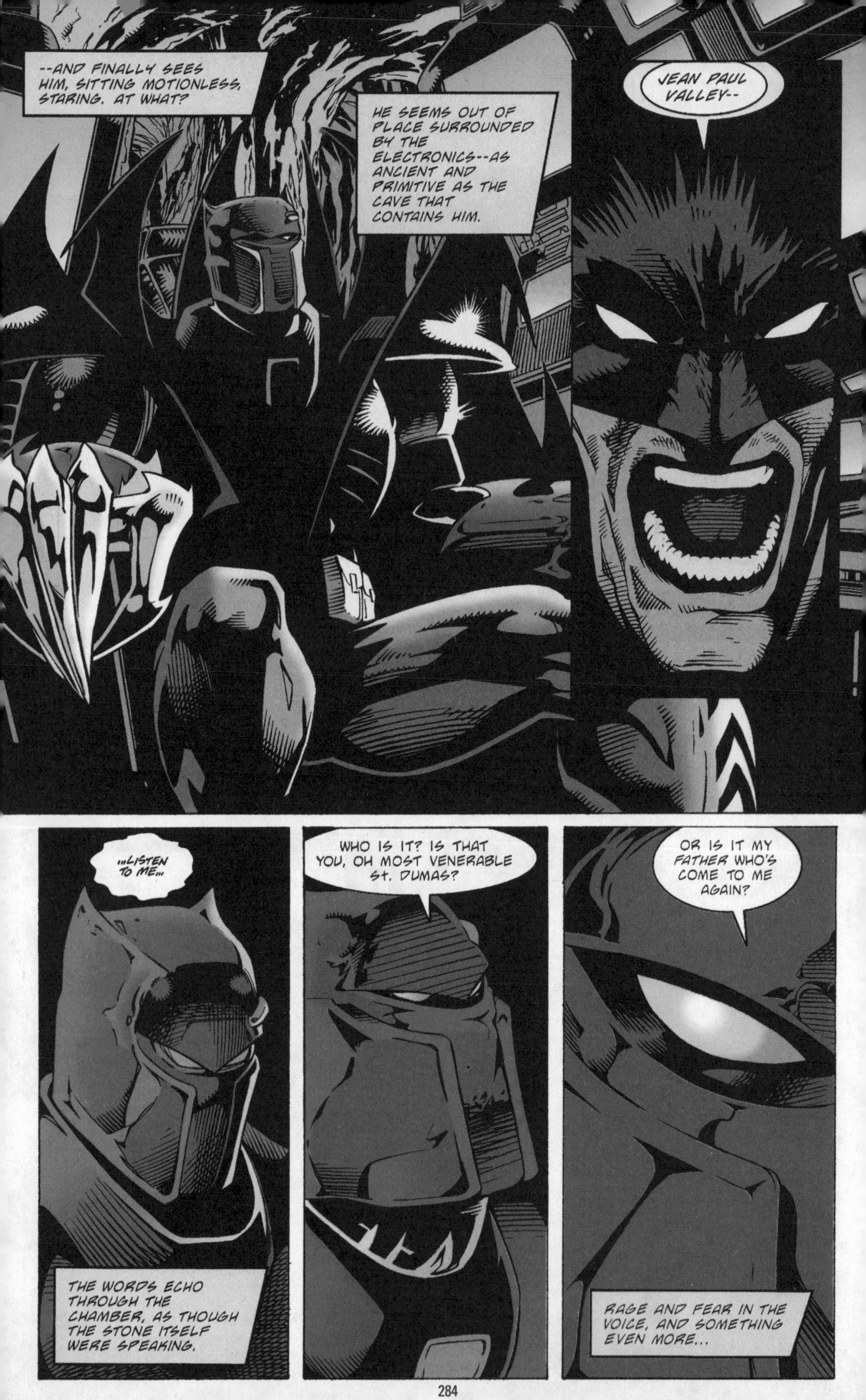
--AND FINALLY SEES HIM, SITTING MOTIONLESS, STARING. AT WHAT?
HE SEEMS OUT OF PLACE SURROUNDED BY THE ELECTRONICS--AS ANCIENT AND PRIMITIVE AS THE CAVE THAT CONTAINS HIM.
JEAN PAUL VALLEY--
...LISTEN TO ME...
THE WORDS ECHO THROUGH THE CHAMBER, AS THOUGH THE STONE ITSELF WERE SPEAKING.
WHO IS IT? IS THAT YOU, OH MOST VENERABLE St. DUMAS?
OR IS IT MY FATHER WHO'S COME TO ME AGAIN?
RAGE AND FEAR IN THE VOICE, AND SOMETHING EVEN MORE...

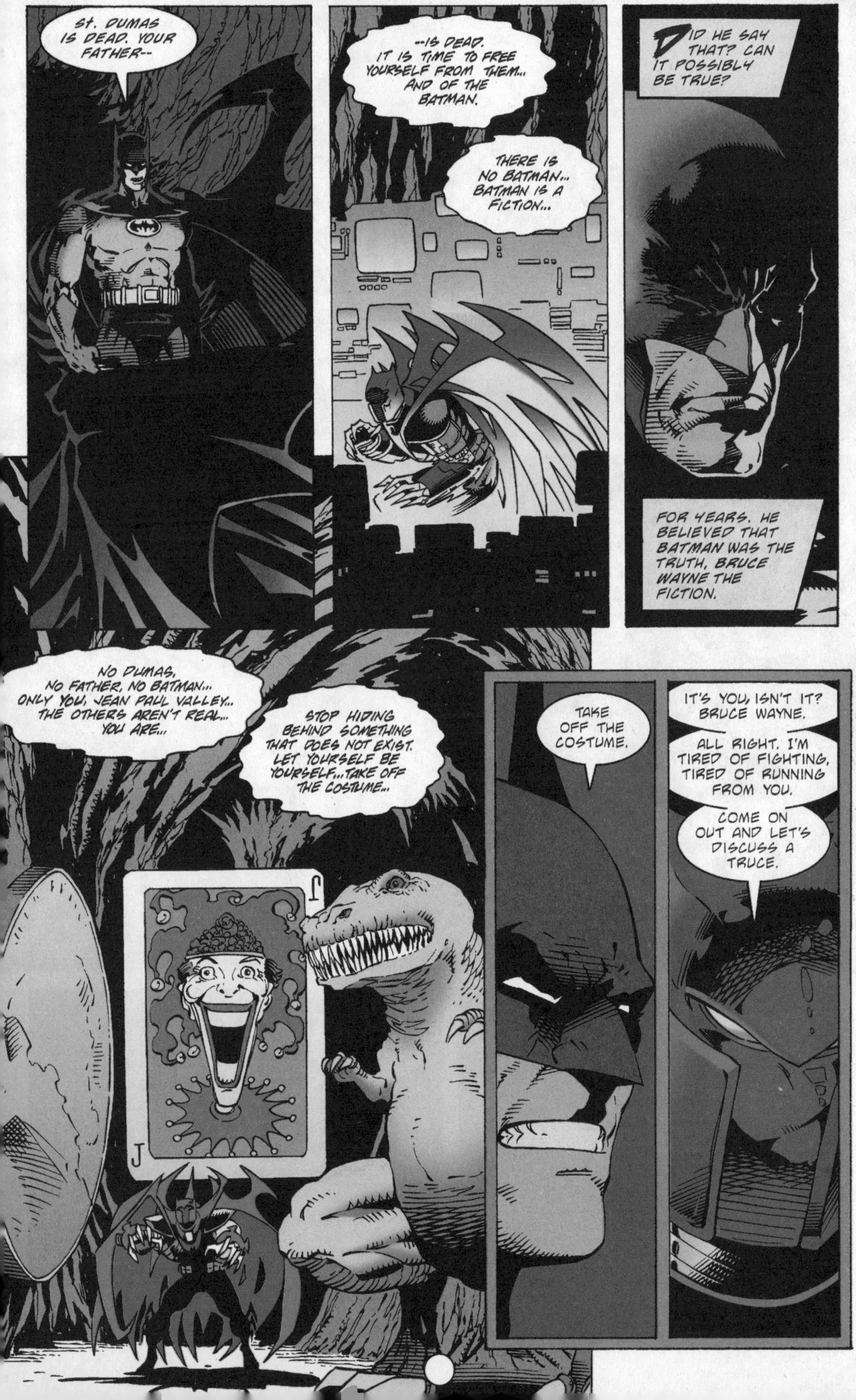

ST. DUMAS IS DEAD. YOUR FATHER--
--IS DEAD. IT IS TIME TO FREE YOURSELF FROM THEM... AND OF THE BATMAN.
THERE IS NO BATMAN... BATMAN IS A FICTION...
DID HE SAY THAT? CAN IT POSSIBLY BE TRUE?
FOR YEARS, HE BELIEVED THAT BATMAN WAS THE TRUTH, BRUCE WAYNE THE FICTION.
NO DUMAS, NO FATHER, NO BATMAN... ONLY YOU, JEAN PAUL VALLEY... THE OTHERS AREN'T REAL... YOU ARE...
STOP HIDING BEHIND SOMETHING THAT DOES NOT EXIST. LET YOURSELF BE YOURSELF...TAKE OFF THE COSTUME...
TAKE OFF THE COSTUME.
IT'S YOU, ISN'T IT? BRUCE WAYNE.
ALL RIGHT. I'M TIRED OF FIGHTING, TIRED OF RUNNING FROM YOU.
COME ON OUT AND LET'S DISCUSS A TRUCE.

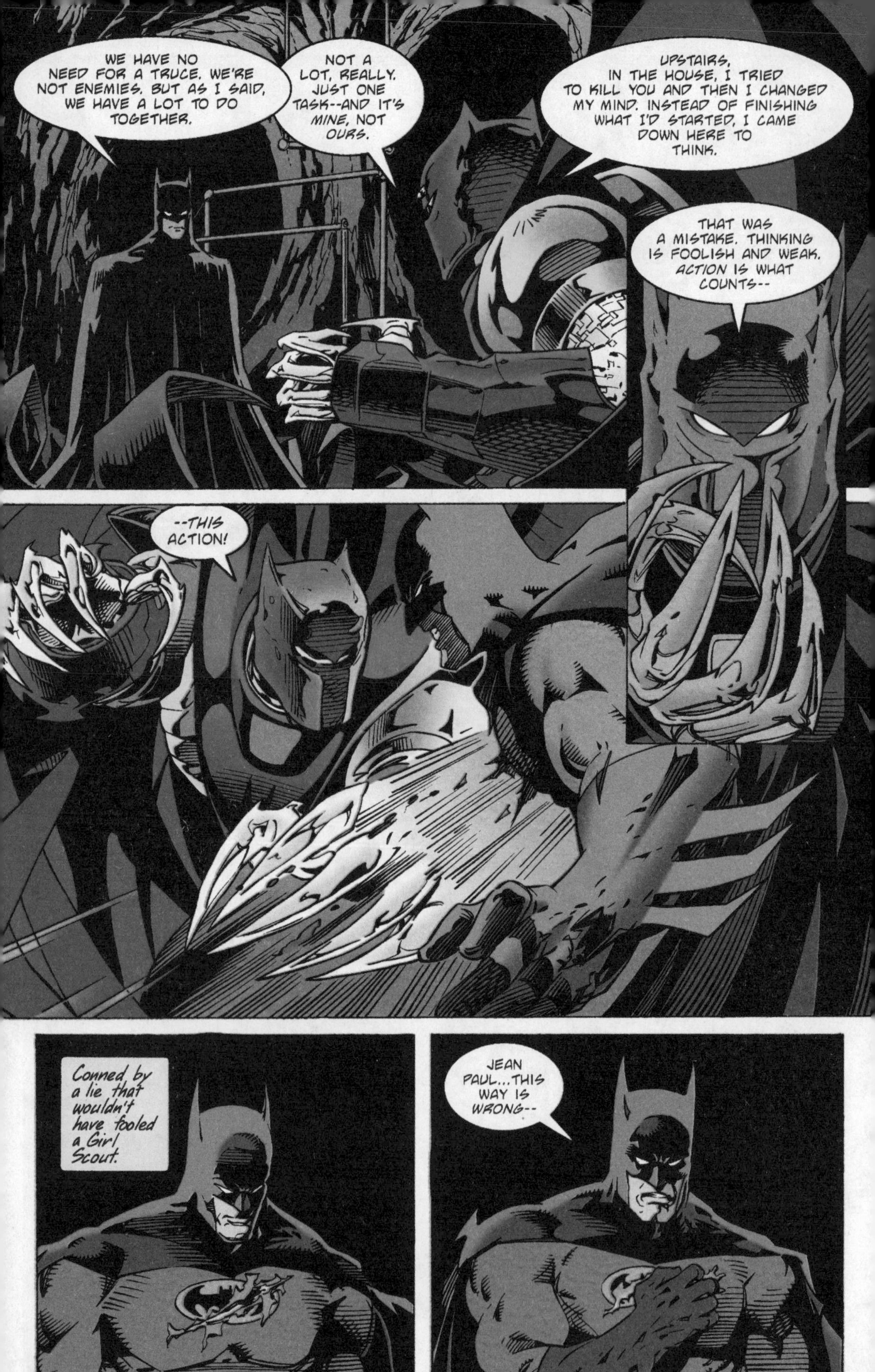
WE HAVE NO NEED FOR A TRUCE. WE'RE NOT ENEMIES. BUT AS I SAID, WE HAVE A LOT TO DO TOGETHER.
NOT A LOT, REALLY. JUST ONE TASK--AND IT'S *MINE*, NOT *OURS*.
UPSTAIRS, IN THE HOUSE, I TRIED TO KILL YOU AND THEN I CHANGED MY MIND. INSTEAD OF FINISHING WHAT I'D STARTED, I CAME DOWN HERE TO THINK.
THAT WAS A MISTAKE. THINKING IS FOOLISH AND WEAK. *ACTION* IS WHAT COUNTS--
--THIS ACTION!
Conned by a lie that wouldn't have fooled a Girl Scout.
JEAN PAUL...THIS WAY IS WRONG--

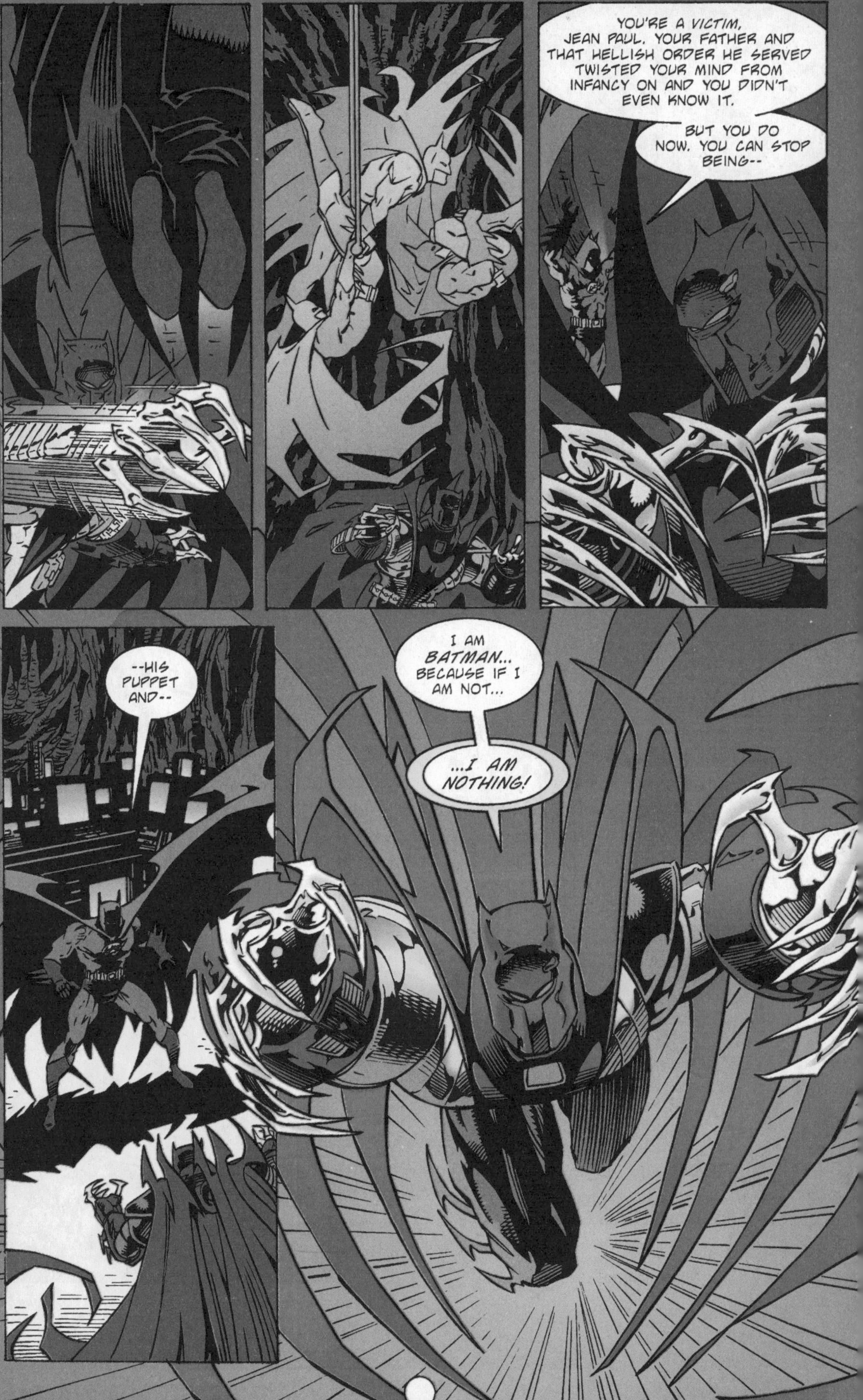
YOU'RE A VICTIM, JEAN PAUL. YOUR FATHER AND THAT HELLISH ORDER HE SERVED TWISTED YOUR MIND FROM INFANCY ON AND YOU DIDN'T EVEN KNOW IT.
BUT YOU DO NOW. YOU CAN STOP BEING--
--HIS PUPPET AND--
I AM BATMAN... BECAUSE IF I AM NOT...
...I AM NOTHING!

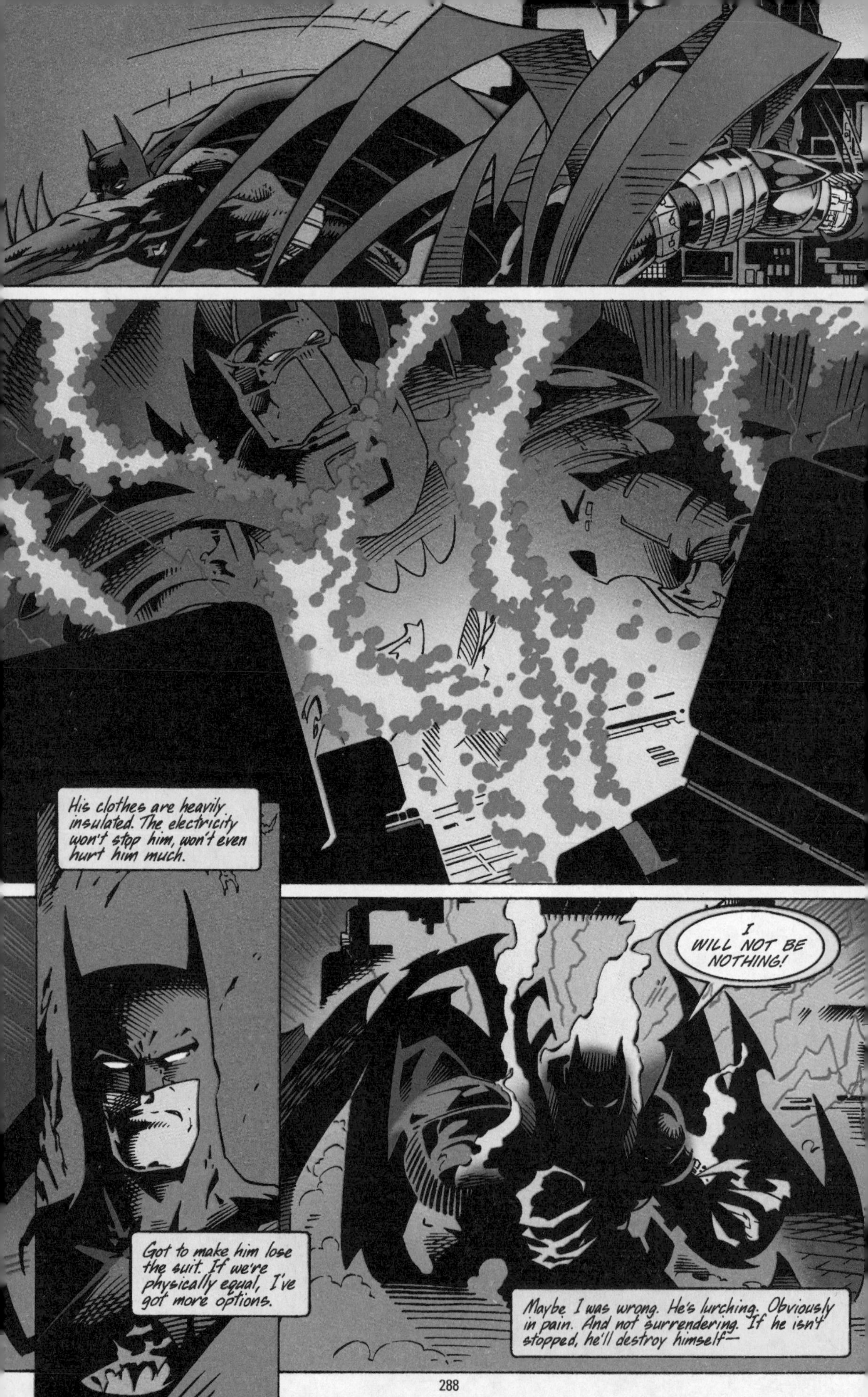

His clothes are heavily insulated. The electricity won't stop him, won't even hurt him much.
Got to make him lose the suit. If we're physically equal, I've got more options.
I WILL NOT BE NOTHING!
Maybe I was wrong. He's lurching. Obviously in pain. And not surrendering. If he isn't stopped, he'll destroy himself—

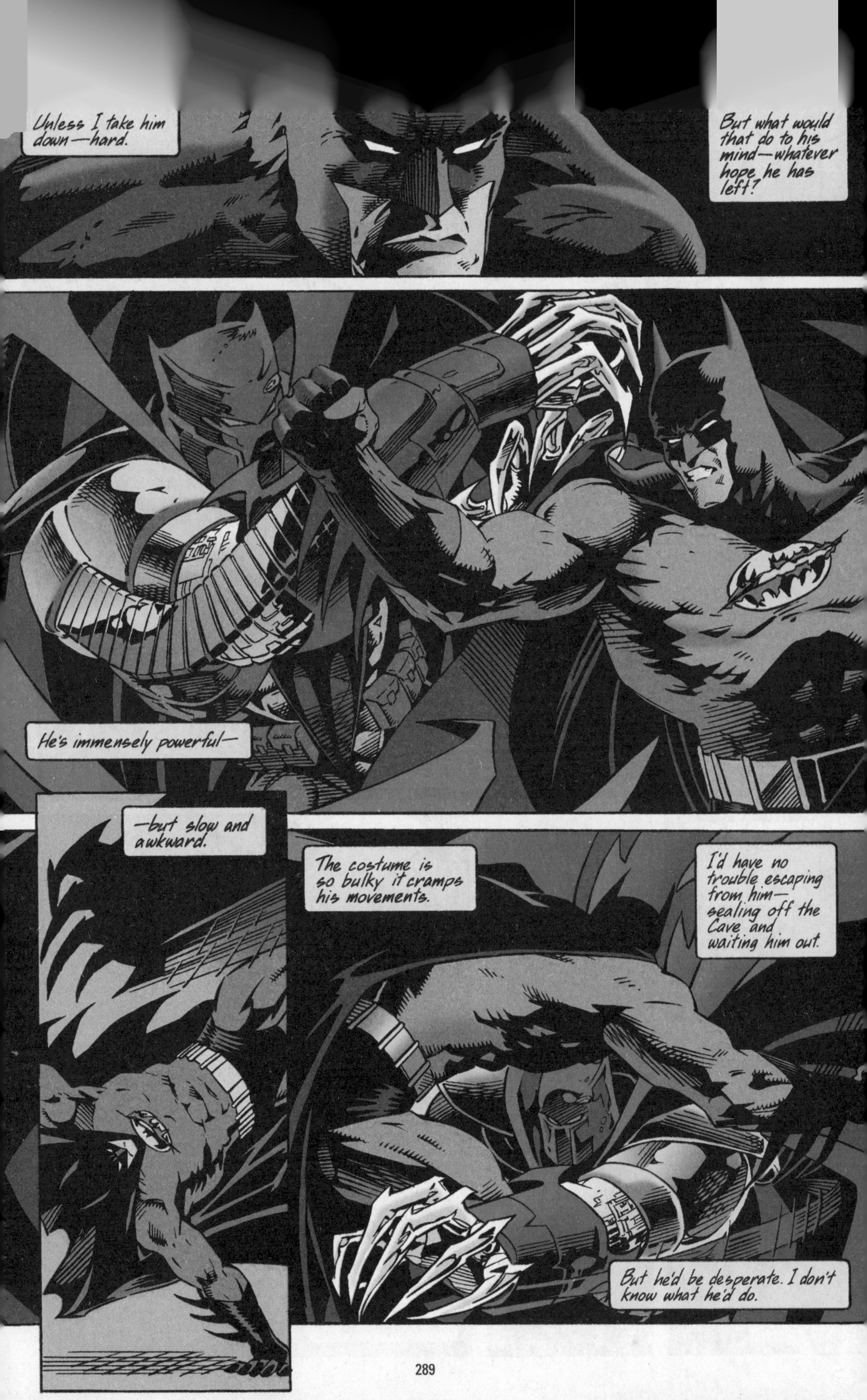

Unless I take him down—hard.
But what would that do to his mind—whatever hope he has left?
He's immensely powerful—
—but slow and awkward.
The costume is so bulky it cramps his movements.
I'd have no trouble escaping from him—sealing off the Cave and waiting him out.
But he'd be desperate. I don't know what he'd do.

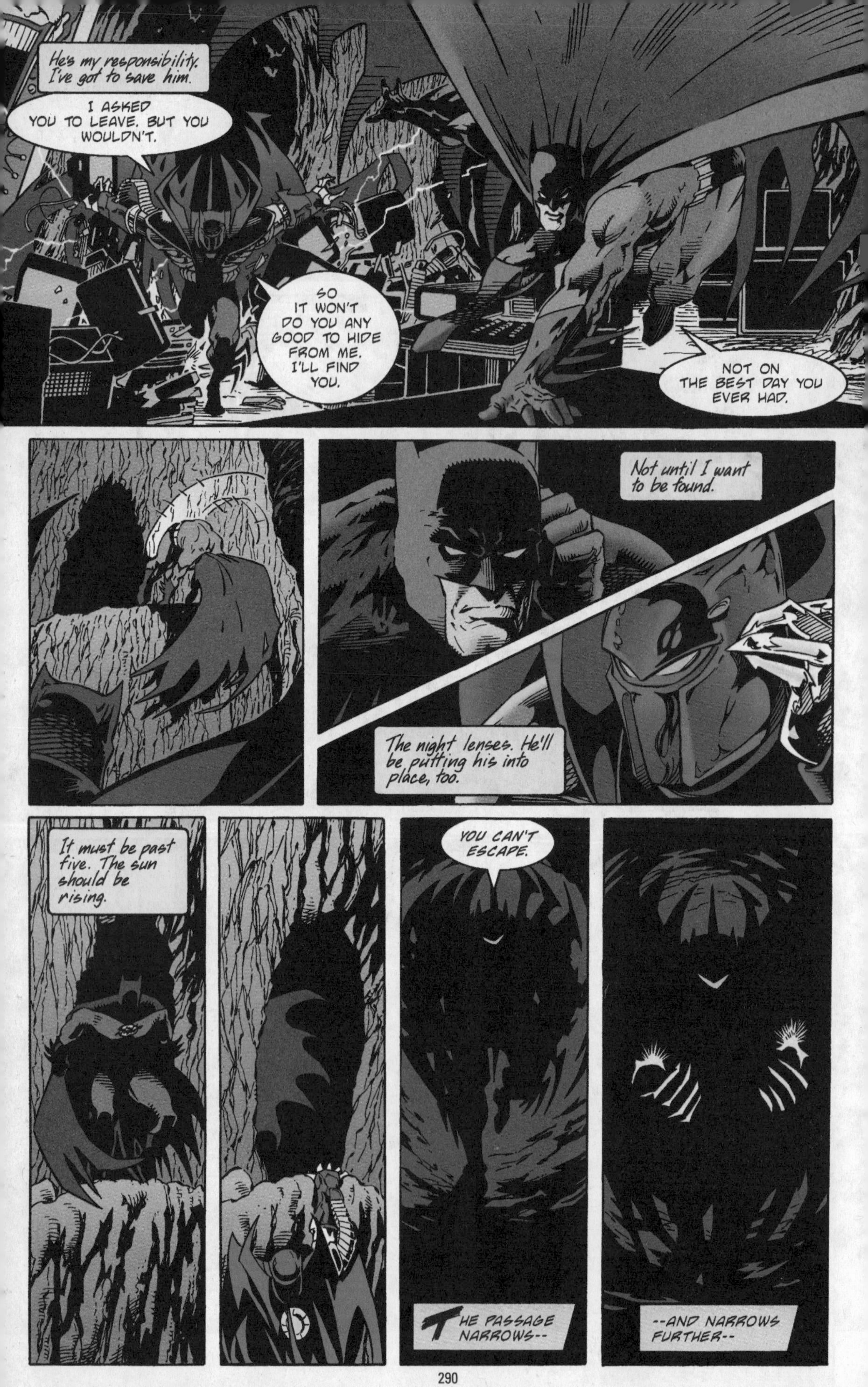
He's my responsibility. I've got to save him.
I ASKED YOU TO LEAVE. BUT YOU WOULDN'T.
SO IT WON'T DO YOU ANY GOOD TO HIDE FROM ME. I'LL FIND YOU.
NOT ON THE BEST DAY YOU EVER HAD.
Not until I want to be found.
The night lenses. He'll be putting his into place, too.
It must be past five. The sun should be rising.
YOU CAN'T ESCAPE.
THE PASSAGE NARROWS--
--AND NARROWS FURTHER--

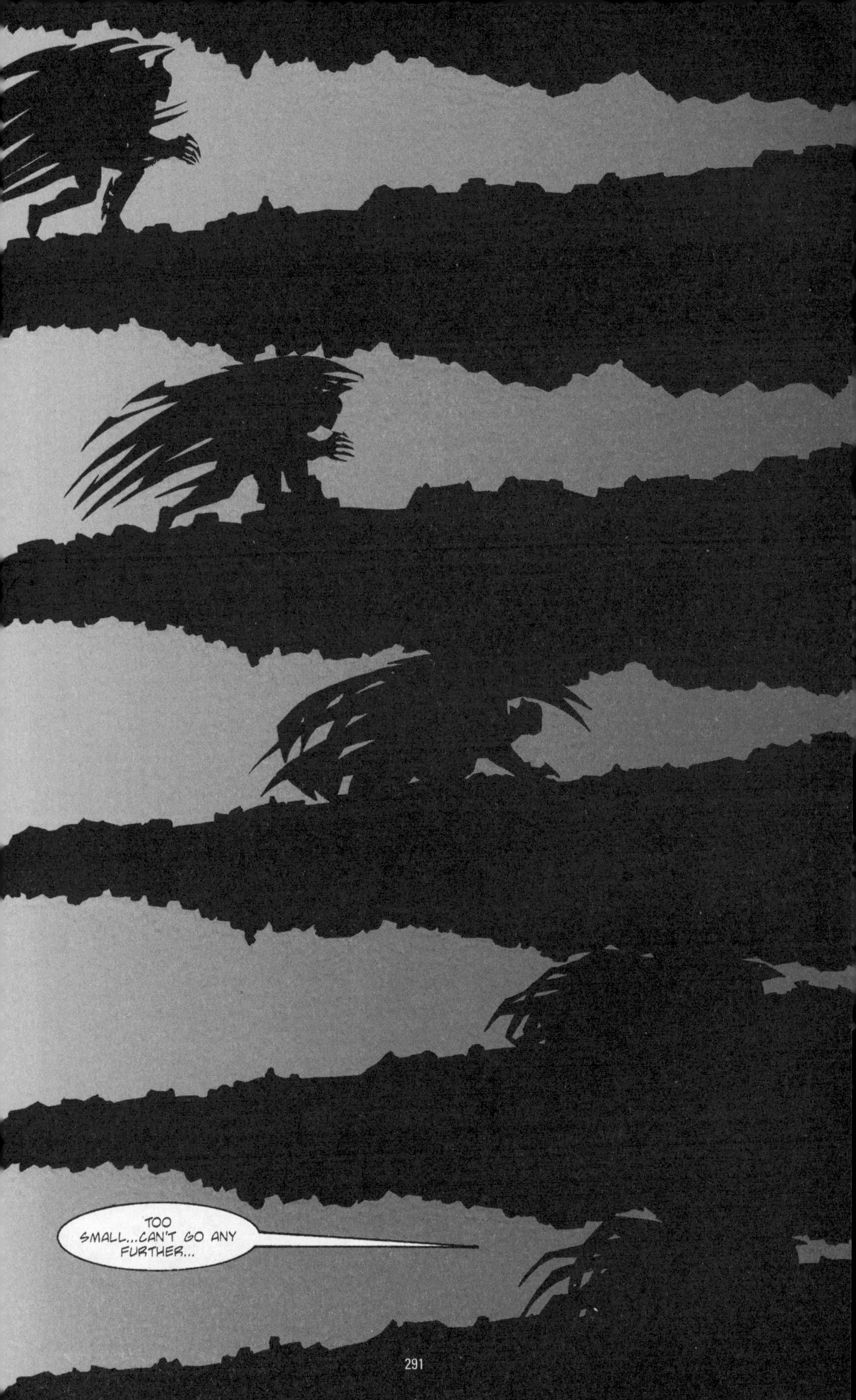
TOO SMALL...CAN'T GO ANY FURTHER...

The next few seconds will make all the difference...if he stops now, or removes the mask—

NOT GIVING UP, ARE YOU?

Perfect. He's lost the suit but he's leaving the mask on...

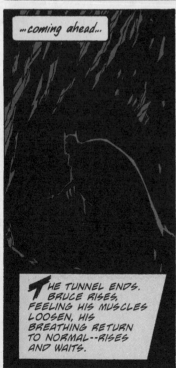

...coming ahead...

THE TUNNEL ENDS. BRUCE RISES, FEELING HIS MUSCLES LOOSEN, HIS BREATHING RETURN TO NORMAL--RISES AND WAITS.

HE LISTENS TO THE DISTANT DRIP OF WATER, THE FLAP OF BATS' WINGS--

--AND THE GRUNTS OF THE APPROACHING MAN WHO IS BOTH HIS PURSUER AND HIS QUARRY...

THEN--

SO. YOU'VE GOT NO MORE ROOM TO RUN.

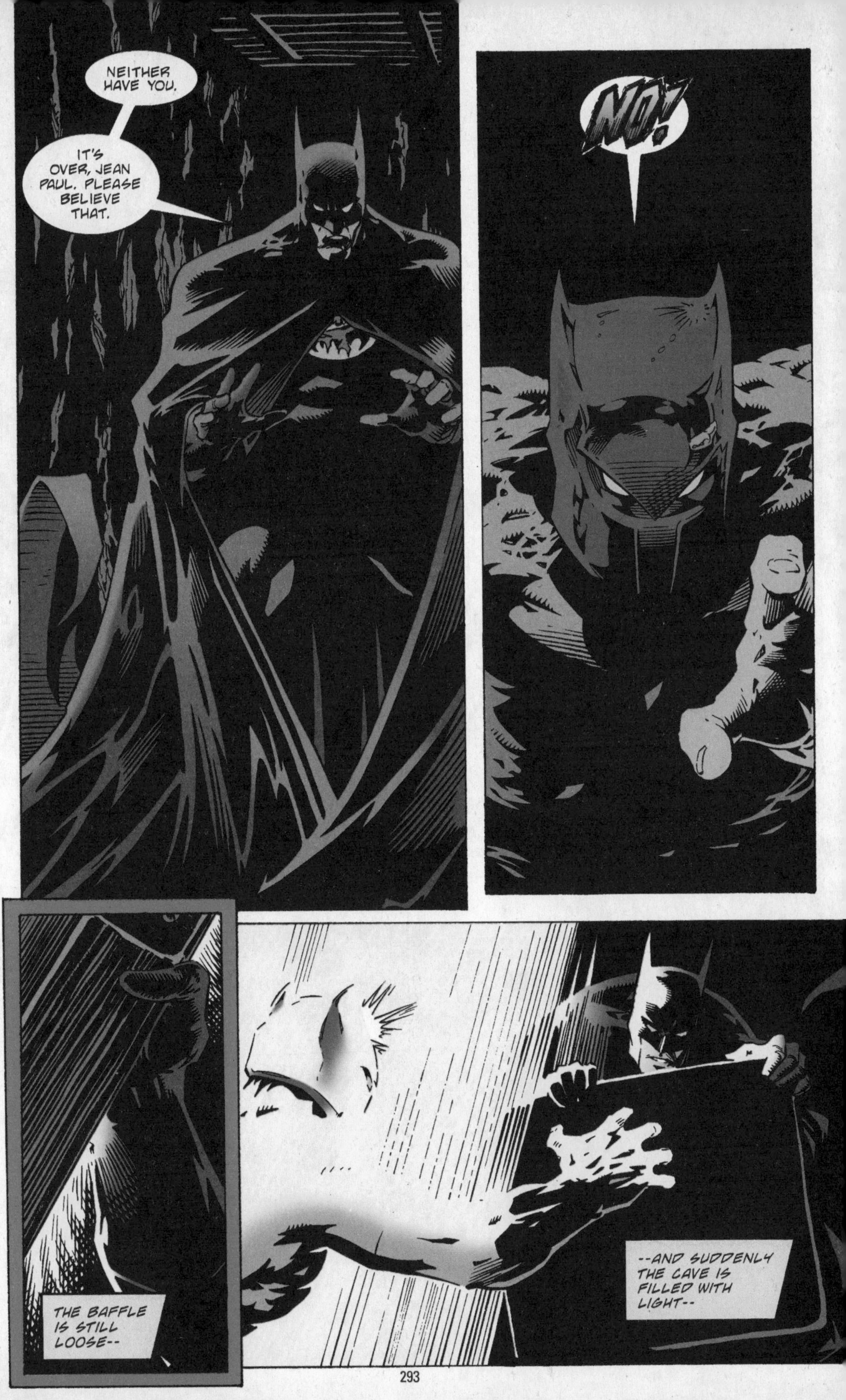
NEITHER HAVE YOU.
IT'S OVER, JEAN PAUL. PLEASE BELIEVE THAT.
NO!
THE BAFFLE IS STILL LOOSE--
--AND SUDDENLY THE CAVE IS FILLED WITH LIGHT--

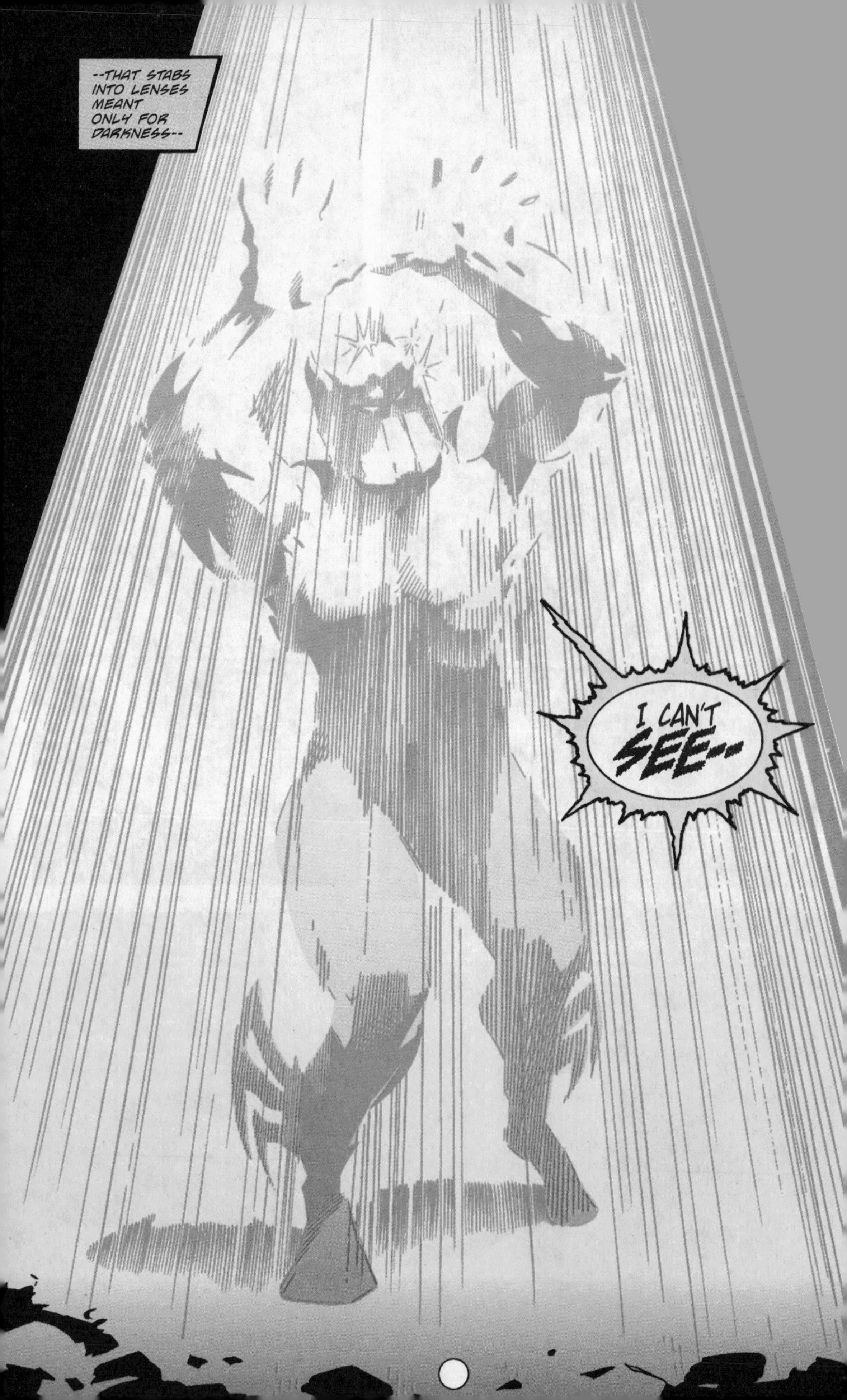
--THAT STABS INTO LENSES MEANT ONLY FOR DARKNESS--
I CAN'T SEE--

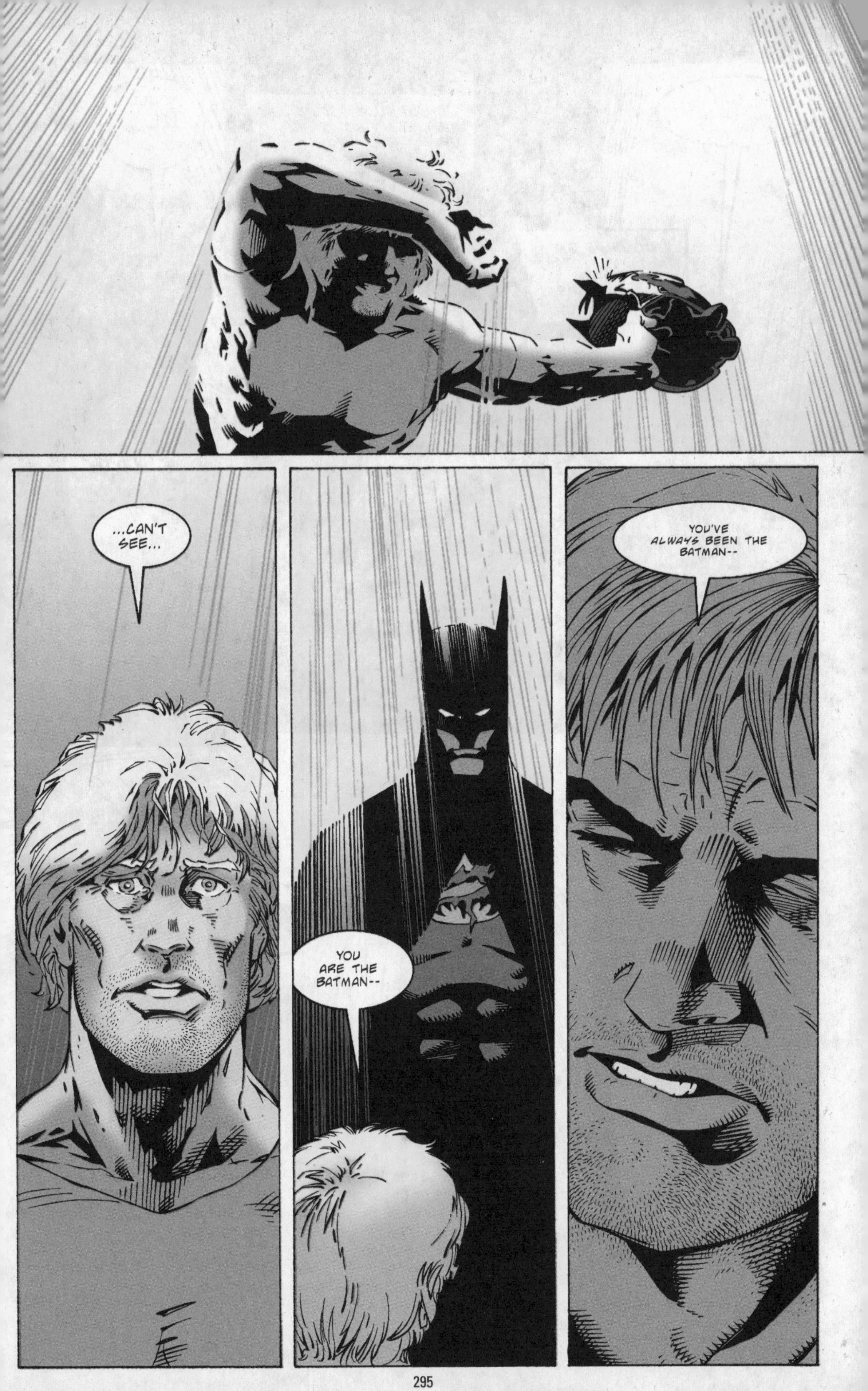
...CAN'T SEE...
YOU ARE THE BATMAN--
YOU'VE ALWAYS BEEN THE BATMAN--

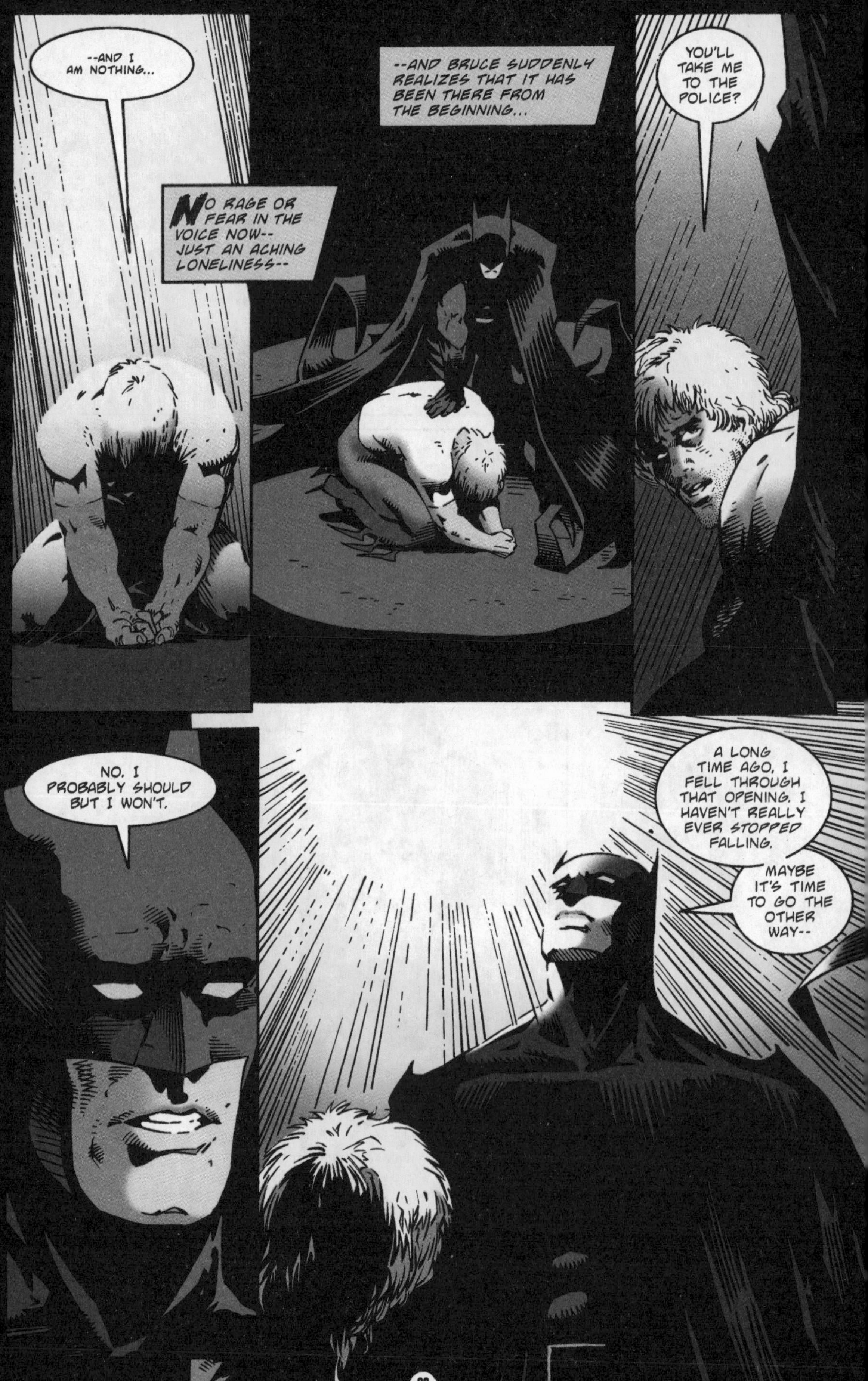
--AND I AM NOTHING...
NO RAGE OR FEAR IN THE VOICE NOW-- JUST AN ACHING LONELINESS--
--AND BRUCE SUDDENLY REALIZES THAT IT HAS BEEN THERE FROM THE BEGINNING...
YOU'LL TAKE ME TO THE POLICE?
NO. I PROBABLY SHOULD BUT I WON'T.
A LONG TIME AGO, I FELL THROUGH THAT OPENING. I HAVEN'T REALLY EVER STOPPED FALLING.
MAYBE IT'S TIME TO GO THE OTHER WAY--

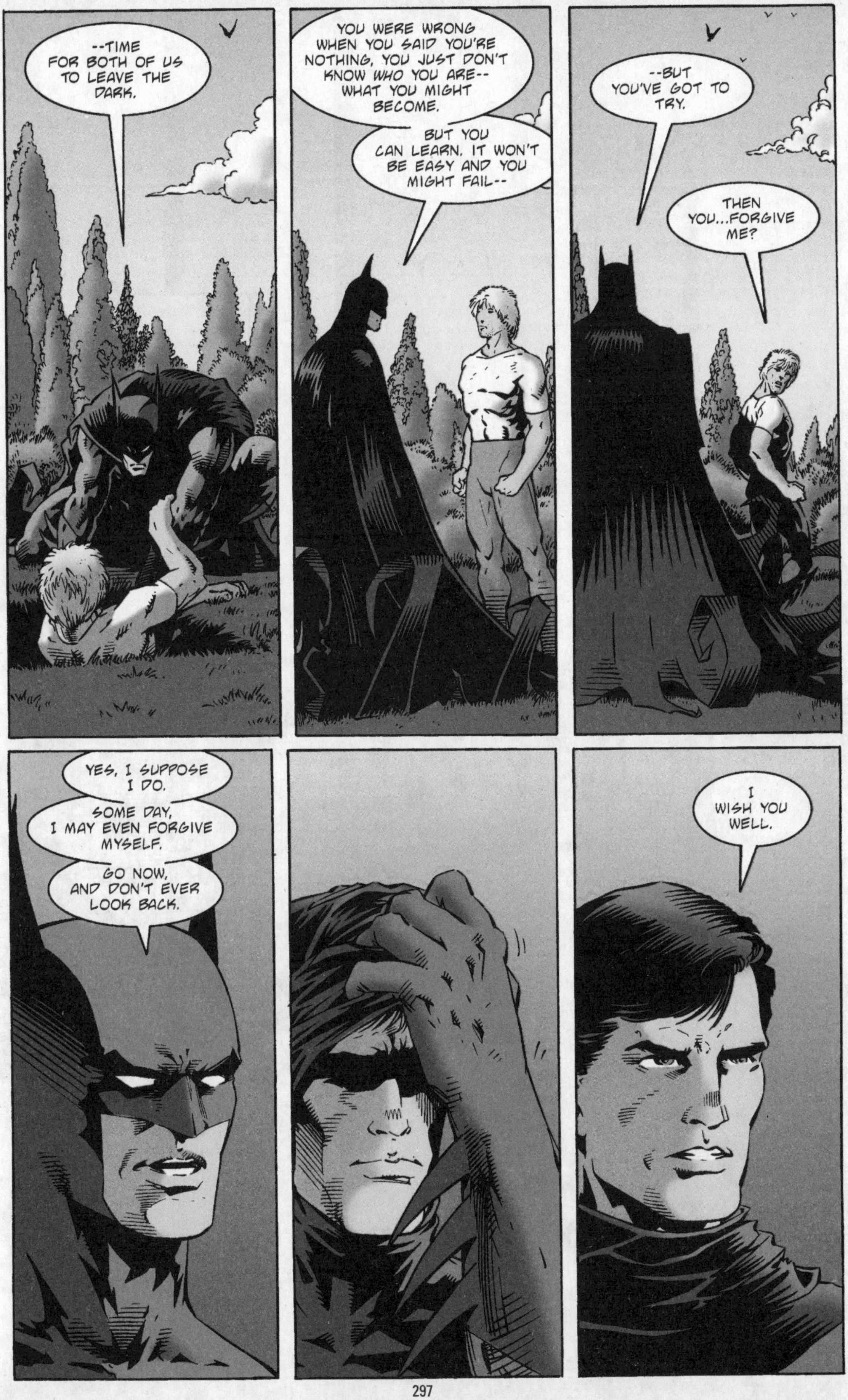
--TIME FOR BOTH OF US TO LEAVE THE DARK.
YOU WERE WRONG WHEN YOU SAID YOU'RE NOTHING. YOU JUST DON'T KNOW WHO YOU ARE-- WHAT YOU MIGHT BECOME.
BUT YOU CAN LEARN. IT WON'T BE EASY AND YOU MIGHT FAIL--
--BUT YOU'VE GOT TO TRY.
THEN YOU...FORGIVE ME?
YES, I SUPPOSE I DO.
SOME DAY, I MAY EVEN FORGIVE MYSELF.
GO NOW, AND DON'T EVER LOOK BACK.
I WISH YOU WELL.

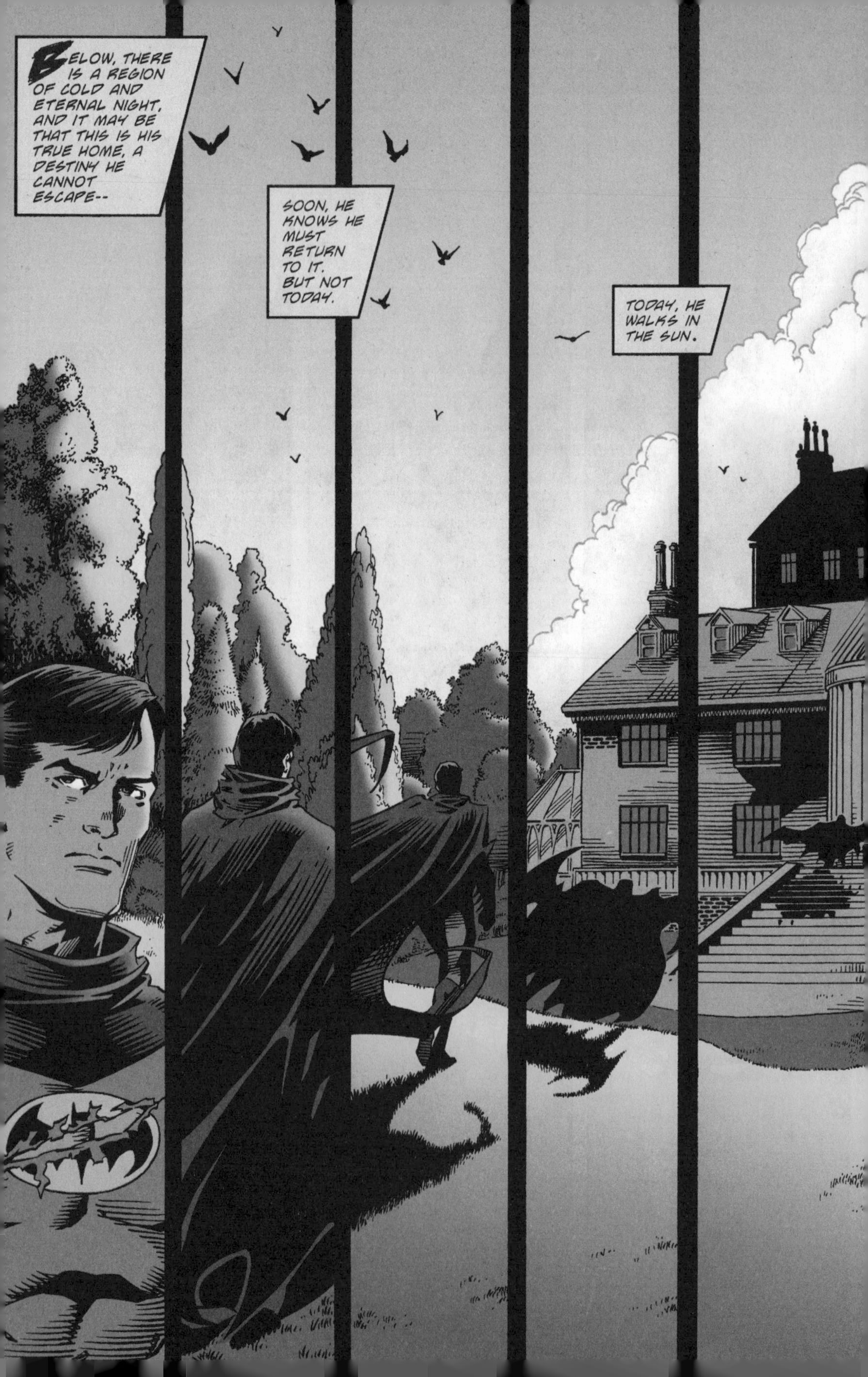
BELOW, THERE IS A REGION OF COLD AND ETERNAL NIGHT, AND IT MAY BE THAT THIS IS HIS TRUE HOME, A DESTINY HE CANNOT ESCAPE--
SOON, HE KNOWS HE MUST RETURN TO IT. BUT NOT TODAY.
TODAY, HE WALKS IN THE SUN.

Cover art by TOM GRUMMETT and RAY KRYSSING

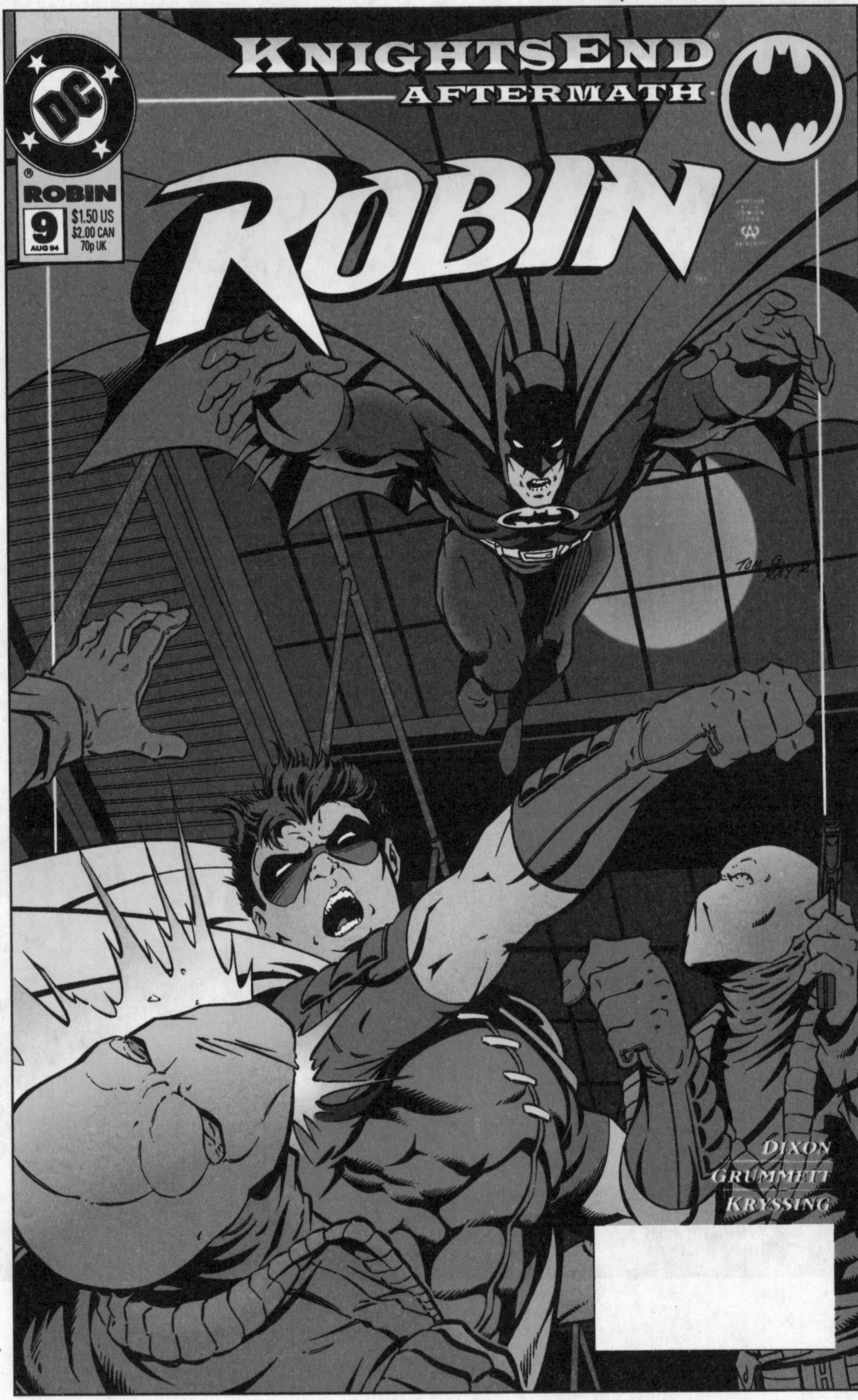
KNIGHTSEND
AFTERMATH
DC
ROBIN
9
AUG 94
$1.50 US
$2.00 CAN
70p UK
ROBIN
DIXON
GRUMMETT
KRYSSING

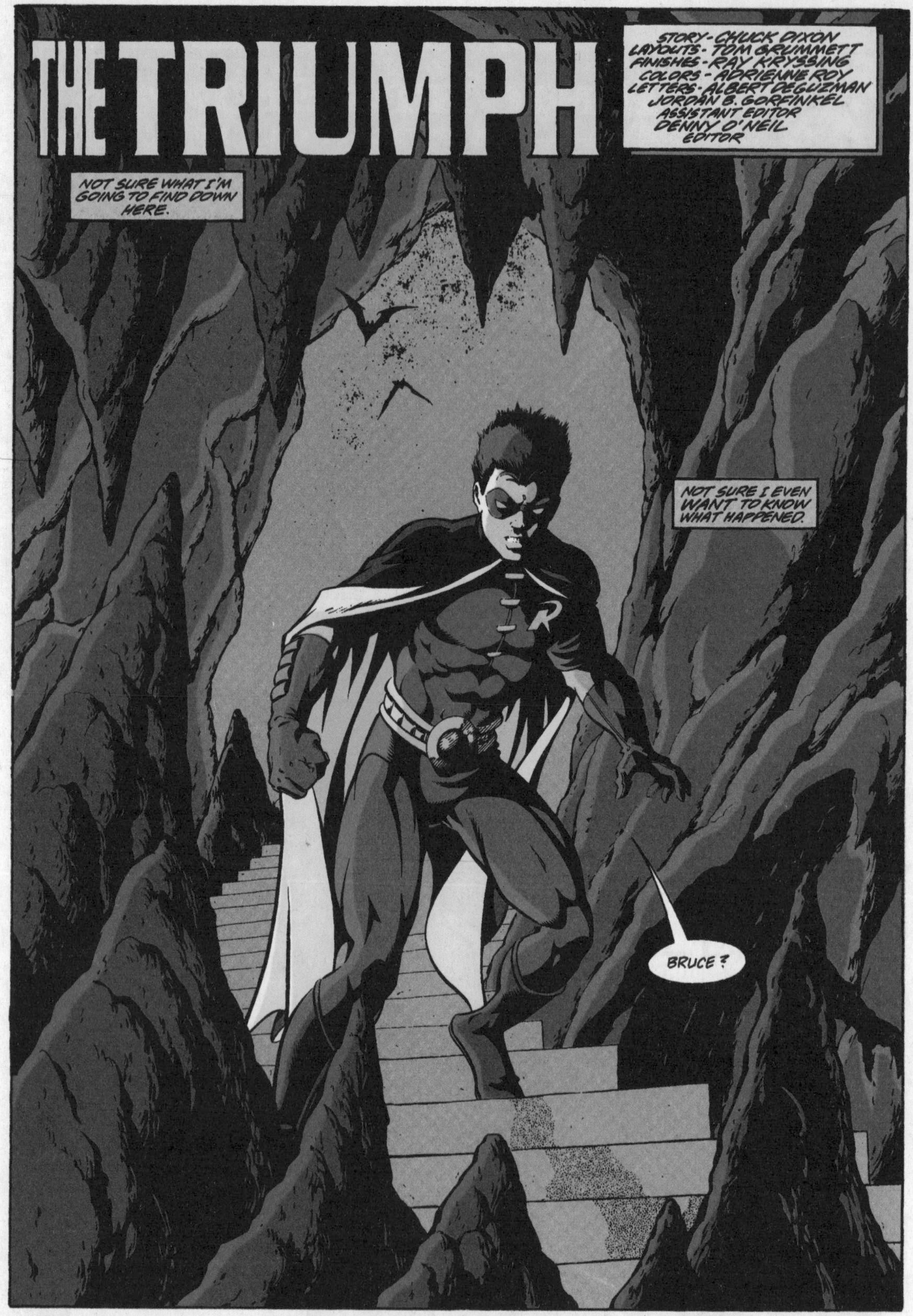
THE TRIUMPH
STORY - CHUCK DIXON
LAYOUTS - TOM GRUMMETT
FINISHES - RAY KRYSSING
COLORS - ADRIENNE ROY
LETTERS - ALBERT DEGUZMAN
JORDAN B. GORFINKEL
ASSISTANT EDITOR
DENNY O'NEIL
EDITOR
NOT SURE WHAT I'M GOING TO FIND DOWN HERE.
NOT SURE I EVEN WANT TO KNOW WHAT HAPPENED.
BRUCE?

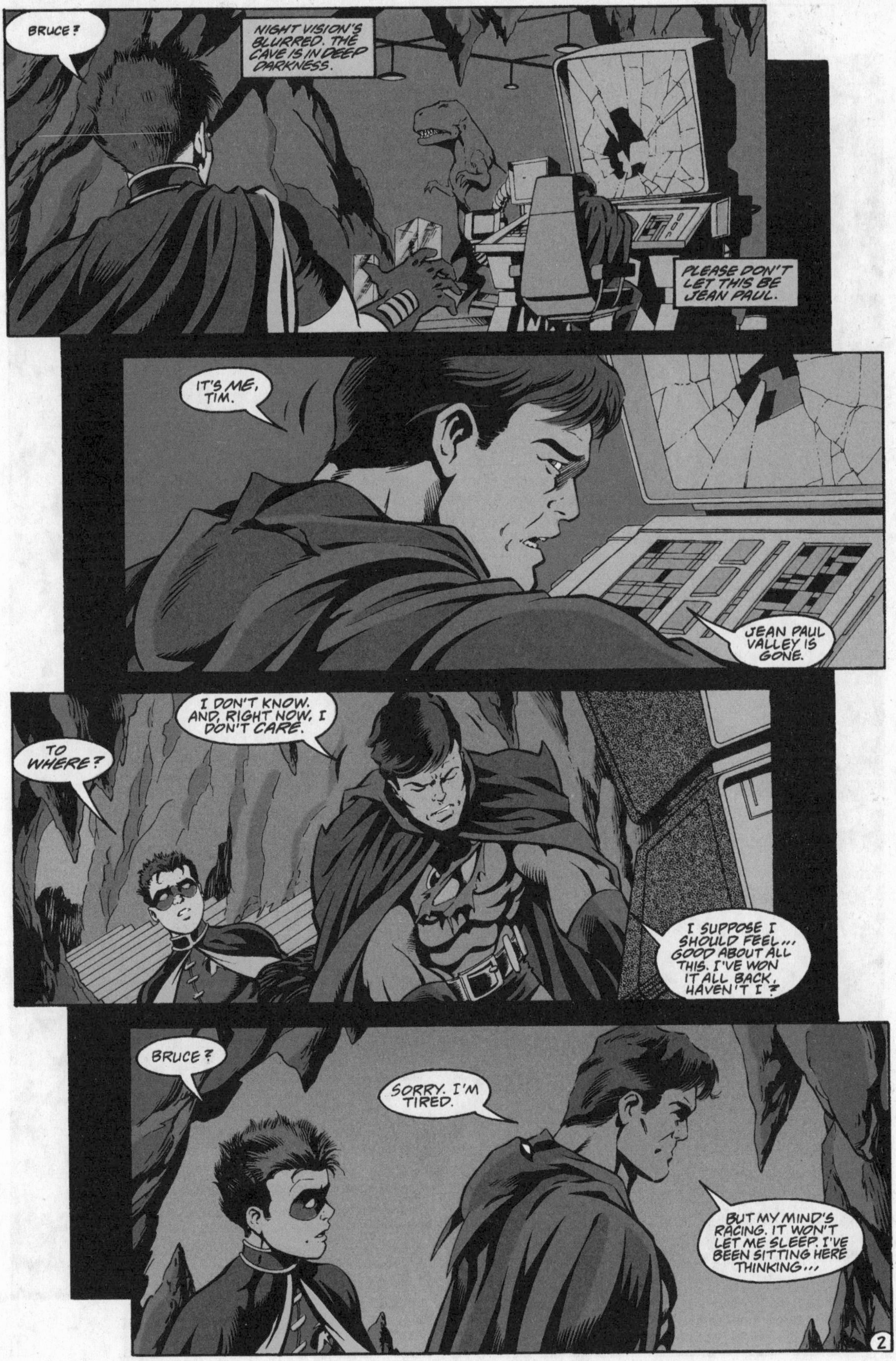
BRUCE?
NIGHT VISION'S BLURRED. THE CAVE IS IN DEEP DARKNESS.
PLEASE DON'T LET THIS BE JEAN PAUL.
IT'S ME, TIM.
JEAN PAUL VALLEY IS GONE.
TO WHERE?
I DON'T KNOW. AND, RIGHT NOW, I DON'T CARE.
I SUPPOSE I SHOULD FEEL... GOOD ABOUT ALL THIS. I'VE WON IT ALL BACK, HAVEN'T I?
BRUCE?
SORRY. I'M TIRED.
BUT MY MIND'S RACING. IT WON'T LET ME SLEEP. I'VE BEEN SITTING HERE THINKING...
2

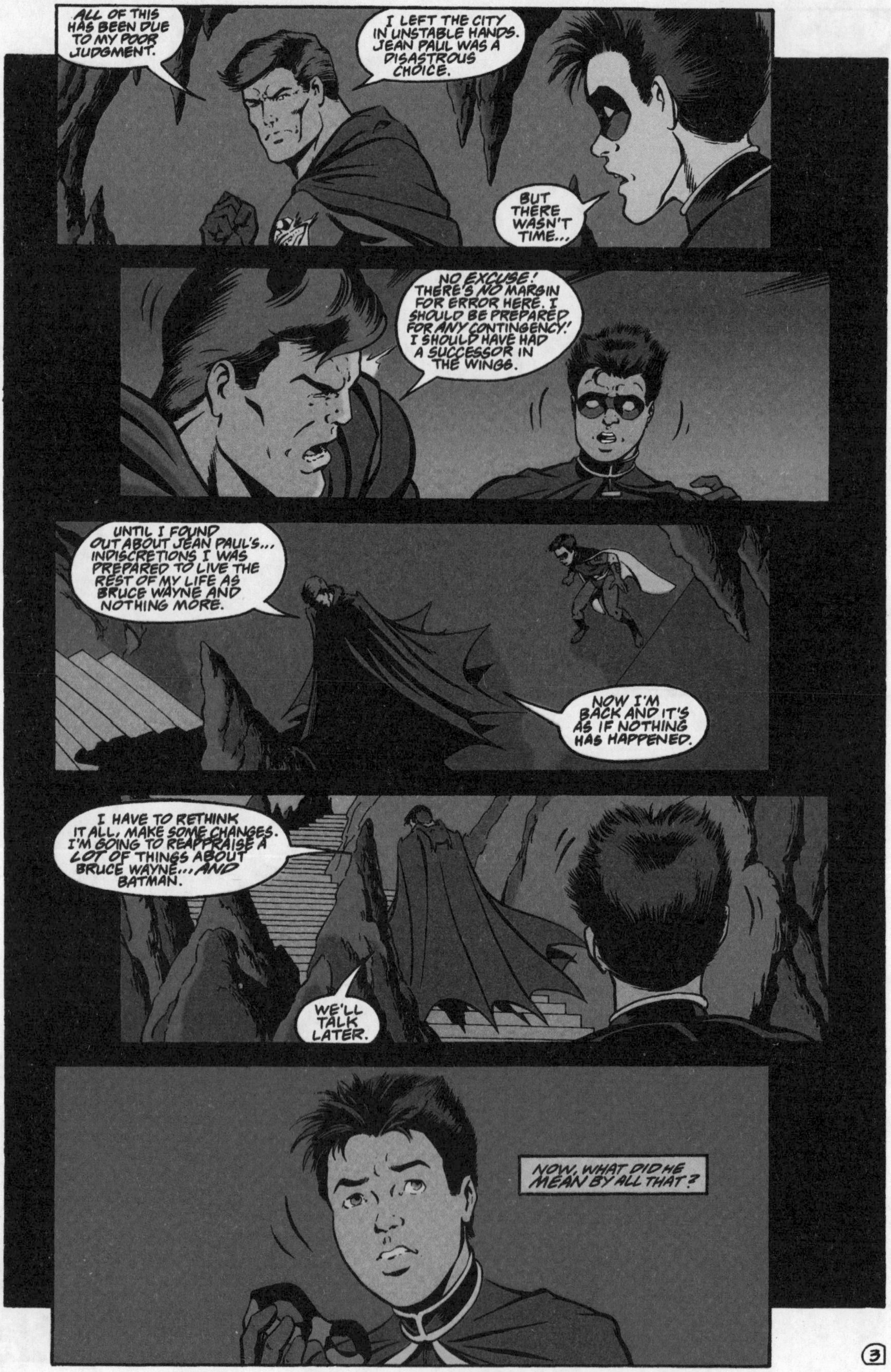
ALL OF THIS HAS BEEN DUE TO MY POOR JUDGMENT.
I LEFT THE CITY IN UNSTABLE HANDS. JEAN PAUL WAS A DISASTROUS CHOICE.
BUT THERE WASN'T TIME...
NO EXCUSE! THERE'S NO MARGIN FOR ERROR HERE. I SHOULD BE PREPARED FOR ANY CONTINGENCY! I SHOULD HAVE HAD A SUCCESSOR IN THE WINGS.
UNTIL I FOUND OUT ABOUT JEAN PAUL'S... INDISCRETIONS I WAS PREPARED TO LIVE THE REST OF MY LIFE AS BRUCE WAYNE AND NOTHING MORE.
NOW I'M BACK AND IT'S AS IF NOTHING HAS HAPPENED.
I HAVE TO RETHINK IT ALL, MAKE SOME CHANGES. I'M GOING TO REAPPRAISE A LOT OF THINGS ABOUT BRUCE WAYNE... AND BATMAN.
WE'LL TALK LATER.
NOW, WHAT DID HE MEAN BY ALL THAT?
3

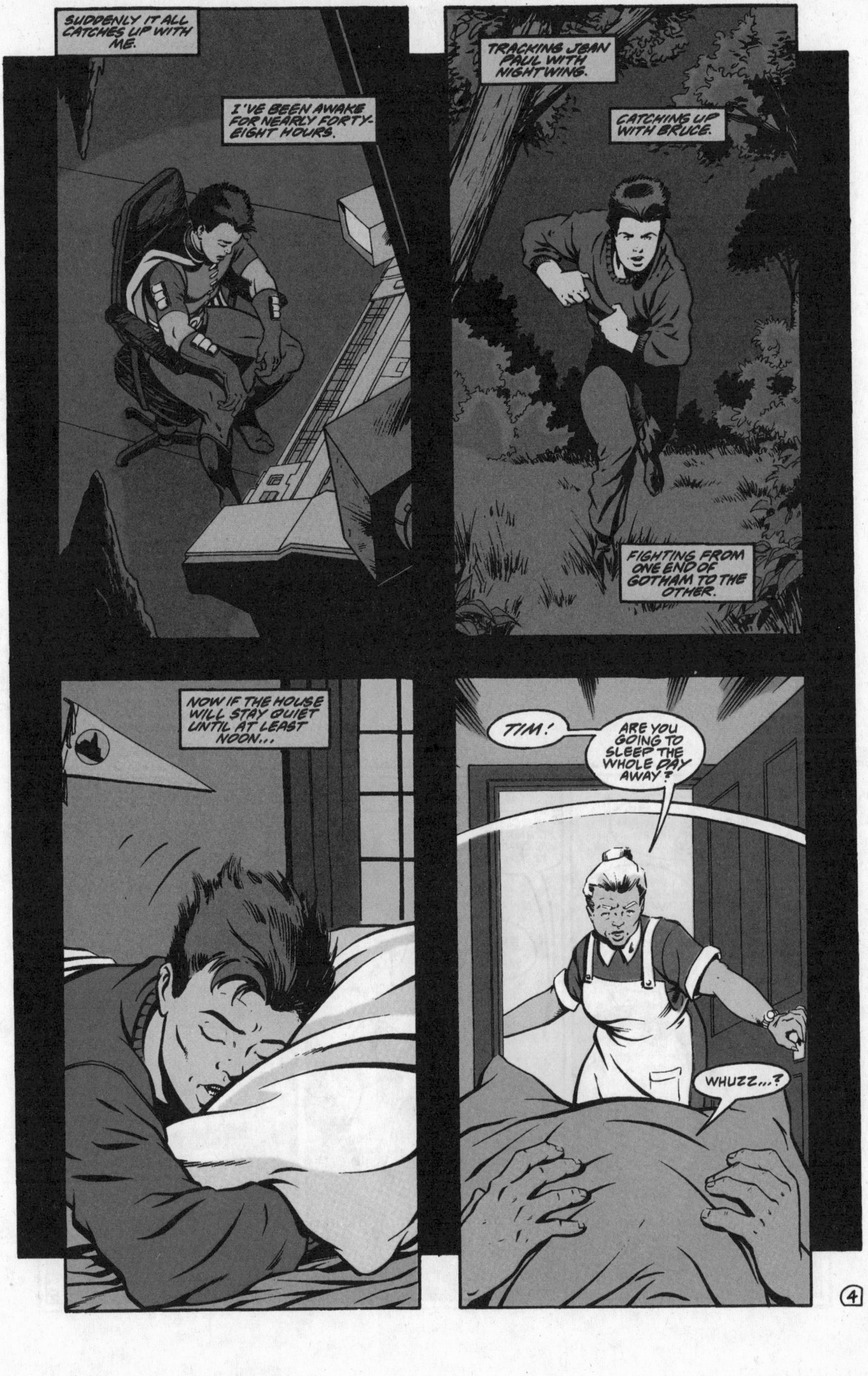
SUDDENLY IT ALL CATCHES UP WITH ME.
I'VE BEEN AWAKE FOR NEARLY FORTY-EIGHT HOURS.
TRACKING JEAN PAUL WITH NIGHTWING.
CATCHING UP WITH BRUCE.
FIGHTING FROM ONE END OF GOTHAM TO THE OTHER.
NOW IF THE HOUSE WILL STAY QUIET UNTIL AT LEAST NOON...
TIM!
ARE YOU GOING TO SLEEP THE WHOLE DAY AWAY?
WHUZZ...?
4

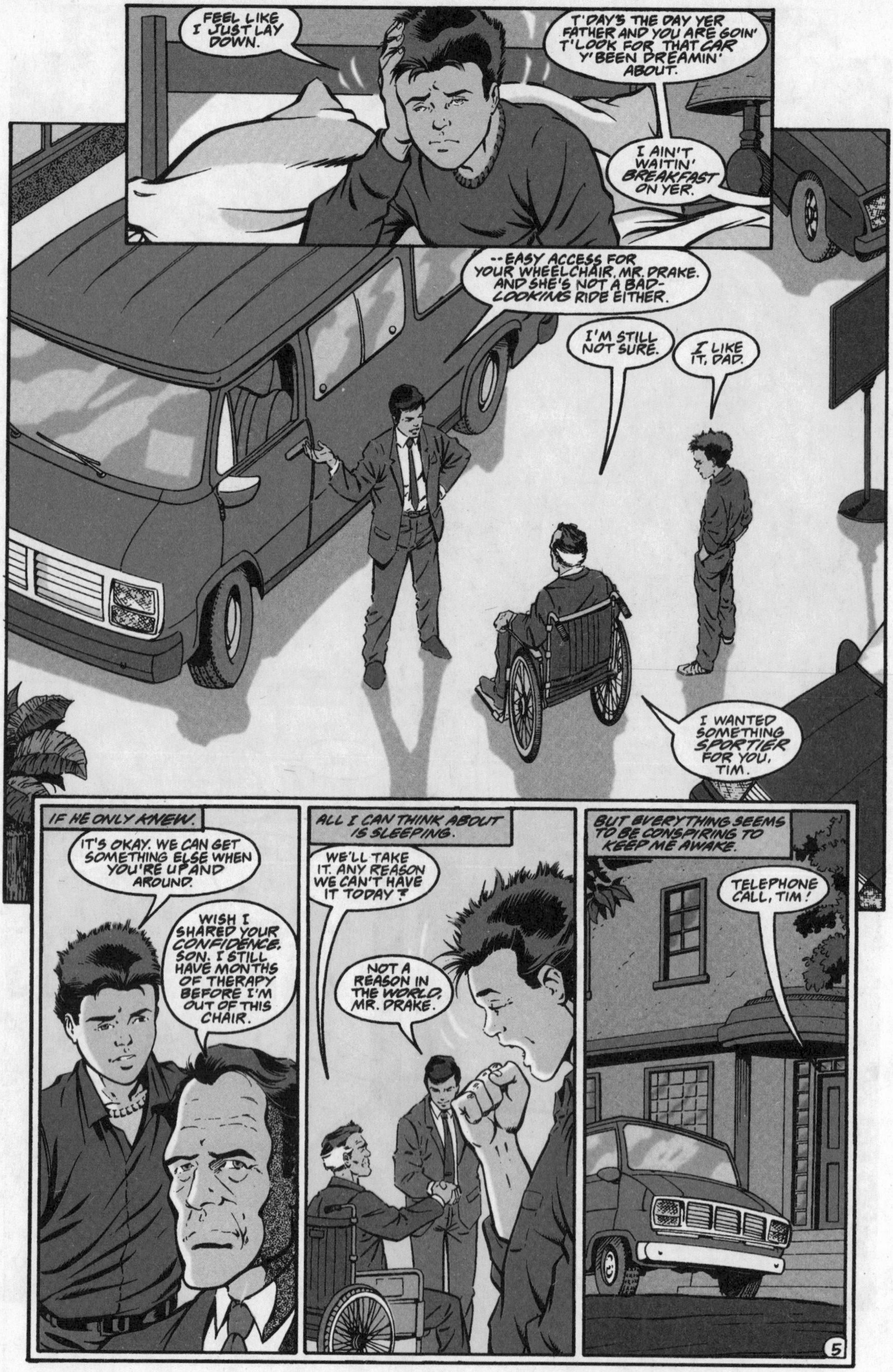
FEEL LIKE I JUST LAY DOWN.
T'DAY'S THE DAY YER FATHER AND YOU ARE GOIN' T'LOOK FOR THAT CAR Y'BEEN DREAMIN' ABOUT.
I AIN'T WAITIN' BREAKFAST ON YER.
--EASY ACCESS FOR YOUR WHEELCHAIR, MR. DRAKE. AND SHE'S NOT A BAD-LOOKING RIDE EITHER.
I'M STILL NOT SURE.
I LIKE IT, DAD.
I WANTED SOMETHING SPORTIER FOR YOU, TIM.
IF HE ONLY KNEW.
IT'S OKAY. WE CAN GET SOMETHING ELSE WHEN YOU'RE UP AND AROUND.
WISH I SHARED YOUR CONFIDENCE, SON. I STILL HAVE MONTHS OF THERAPY BEFORE I'M OUT OF THIS CHAIR.
ALL I CAN THINK ABOUT IS SLEEPING.
WE'LL TAKE IT. ANY REASON WE CAN'T HAVE IT TODAY?
NOT A REASON IN THE WORLD, MR. DRAKE.
BUT EVERYTHING SEEMS TO BE CONSPIRING TO KEEP ME AWAKE.
TELEPHONE CALL, TIM!
5

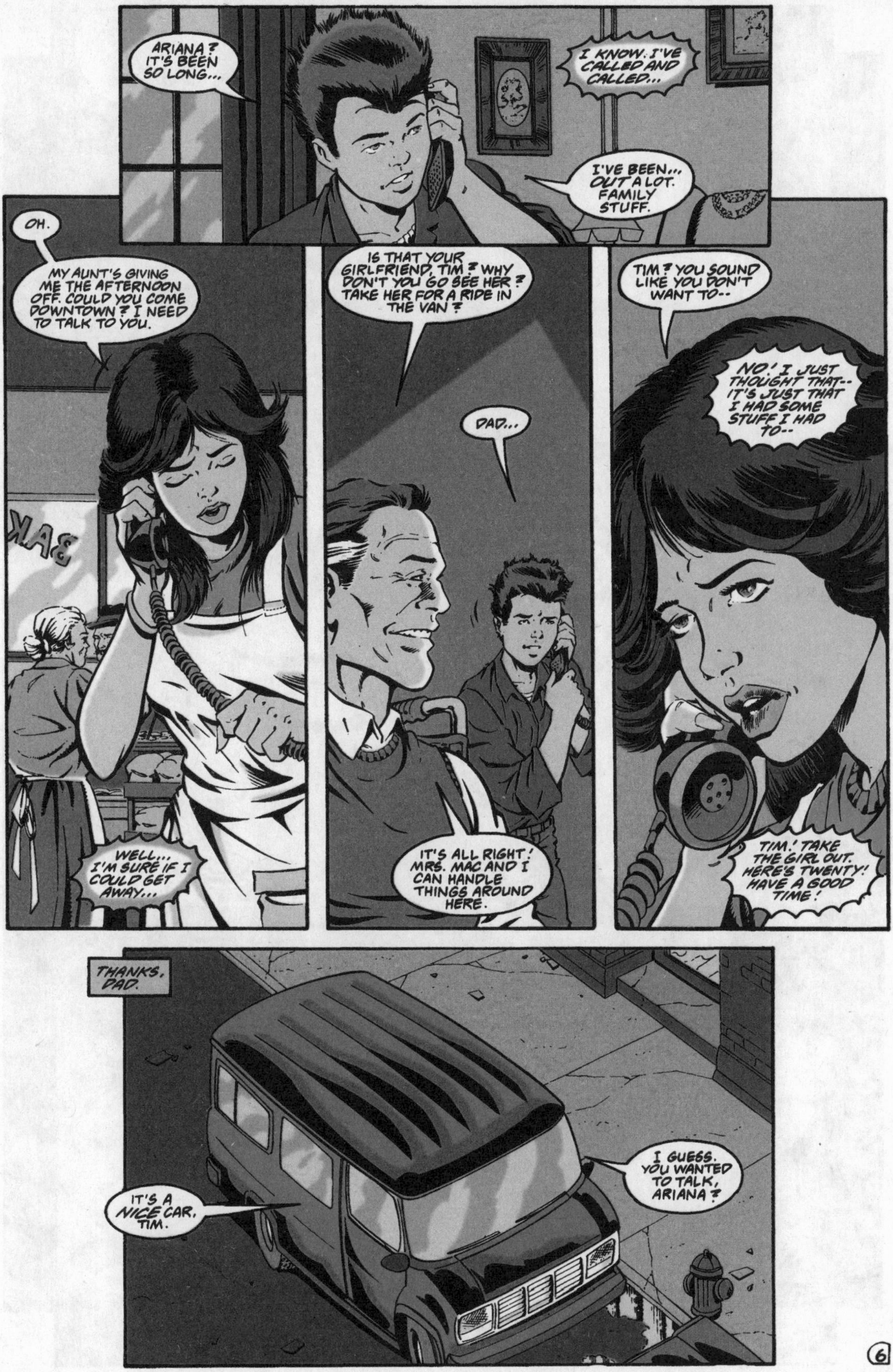
ARIANA? IT'S BEEN SO LONG...
I KNOW. I'VE CALLED AND CALLED...
I'VE BEEN... OUT A LOT. FAMILY STUFF.
OH.
MY AUNT'S GIVING ME THE AFTERNOON OFF. COULD YOU COME DOWNTOWN? I NEED TO TALK TO YOU.
WELL... I'M SURE IF I COULD GET AWAY...
IS THAT YOUR GIRLFRIEND, TIM? WHY DON'T YOU GO SEE HER? TAKE HER FOR A RIDE IN THE VAN?
DAD...
IT'S ALL RIGHT! MRS. MAC AND I CAN HANDLE THINGS AROUND HERE.
TIM? YOU SOUND LIKE YOU DON'T WANT TO--
NO! I JUST THOUGHT THAT-- IT'S JUST THAT I HAD SOME STUFF I HAD TO--
TIM! TAKE THE GIRL OUT. HERE'S TWENTY! HAVE A GOOD TIME!
THANKS, DAD.
IT'S A NICE CAR, TIM.
I GUESS. YOU WANTED TO TALK, ARIANA?
6

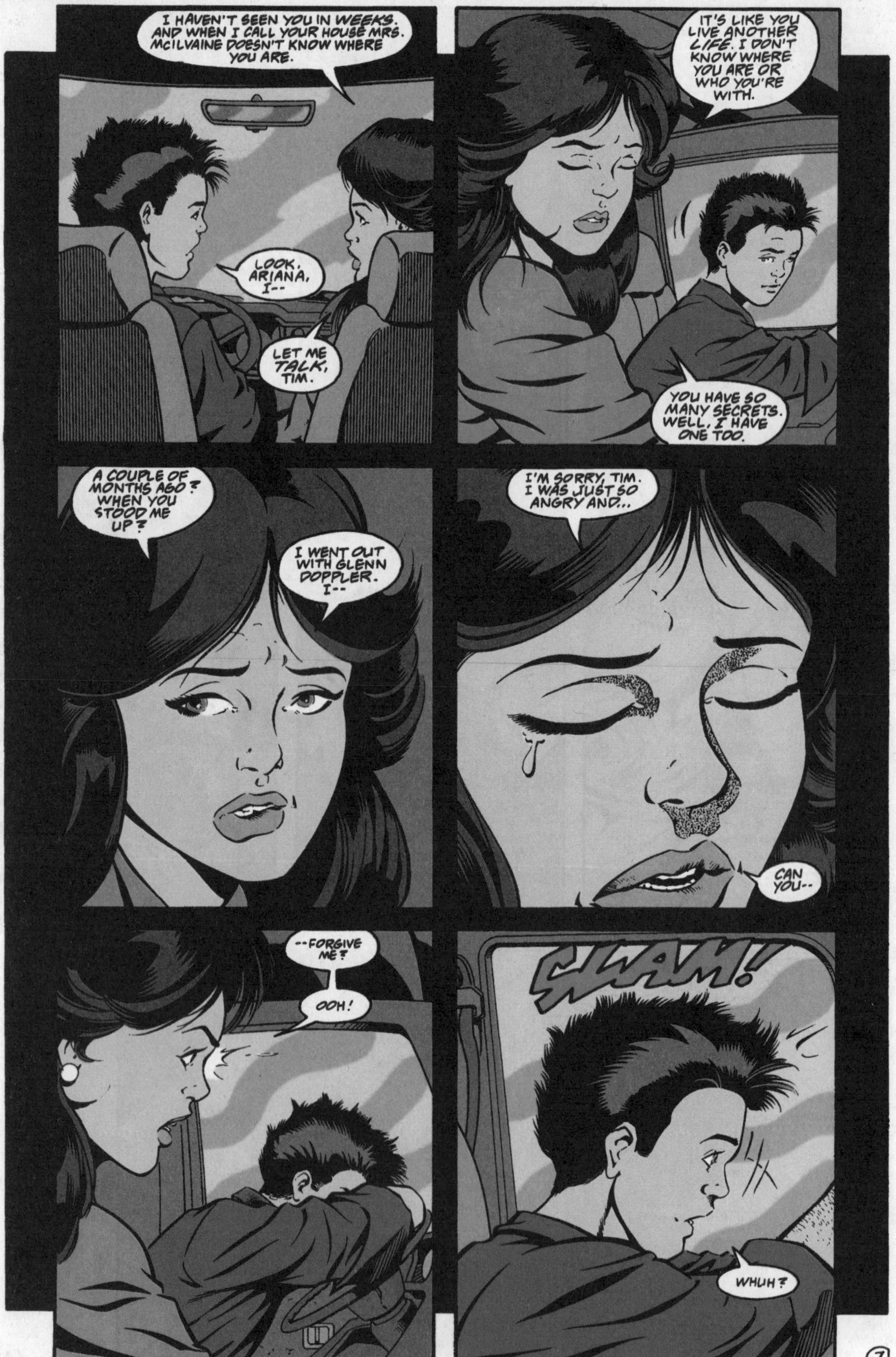
I HAVEN'T SEEN YOU IN WEEKS. AND WHEN I CALL YOUR HOUSE MRS. McILVAINE DOESN'T KNOW WHERE YOU ARE.
LOOK, ARIANA, I--
LET ME TALK, TIM.
IT'S LIKE YOU LIVE ANOTHER LIFE. I DON'T KNOW WHERE YOU ARE OR WHO YOU'RE WITH.
YOU HAVE SO MANY SECRETS. WELL, I HAVE ONE TOO.
A COUPLE OF MONTHS AGO? WHEN YOU STOOD ME UP?
I WENT OUT WITH GLENN DOPPLER. I--
I'M SORRY, TIM. I WAS JUST SO ANGRY AND...
CAN YOU--
--FORGIVE ME?
OOH!
SLAM!
WHUH?
7

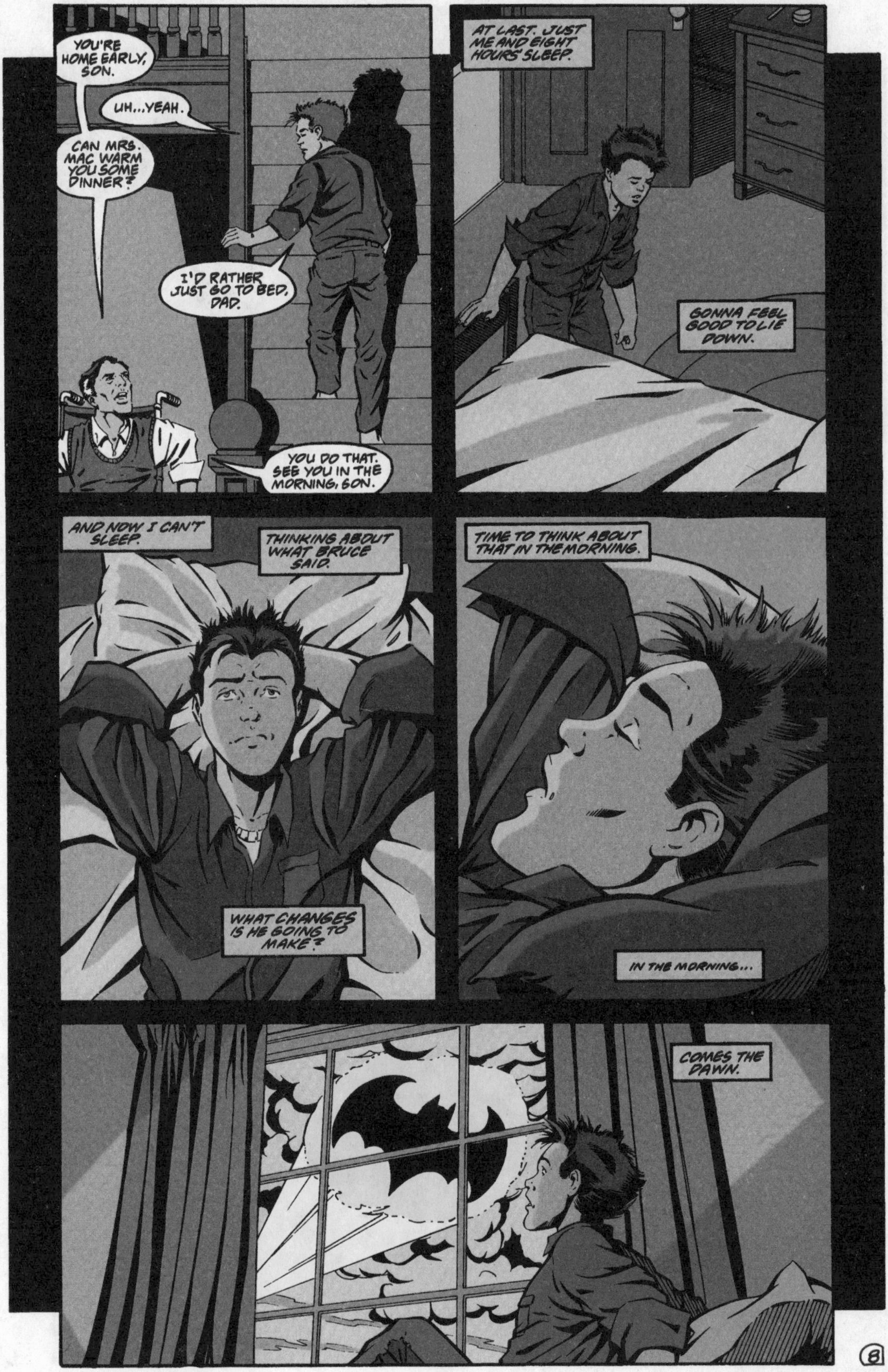

YOU'RE HOME EARLY, SON.
UH...YEAH.
CAN MRS. MAC WARM YOU SOME DINNER?
I'D RATHER JUST GO TO BED, DAD.
YOU DO THAT. SEE YOU IN THE MORNING, SON.
AT LAST. JUST ME AND EIGHT HOURS' SLEEP.
GONNA FEEL GOOD TO LIE DOWN.
AND NOW I CAN'T SLEEP.
THINKING ABOUT WHAT BRUCE SAID.
WHAT CHANGES IS HE GOING TO MAKE?
TIME TO THINK ABOUT THAT IN THE MORNING.
IN THE MORNING...
COMES THE DAWN.
8

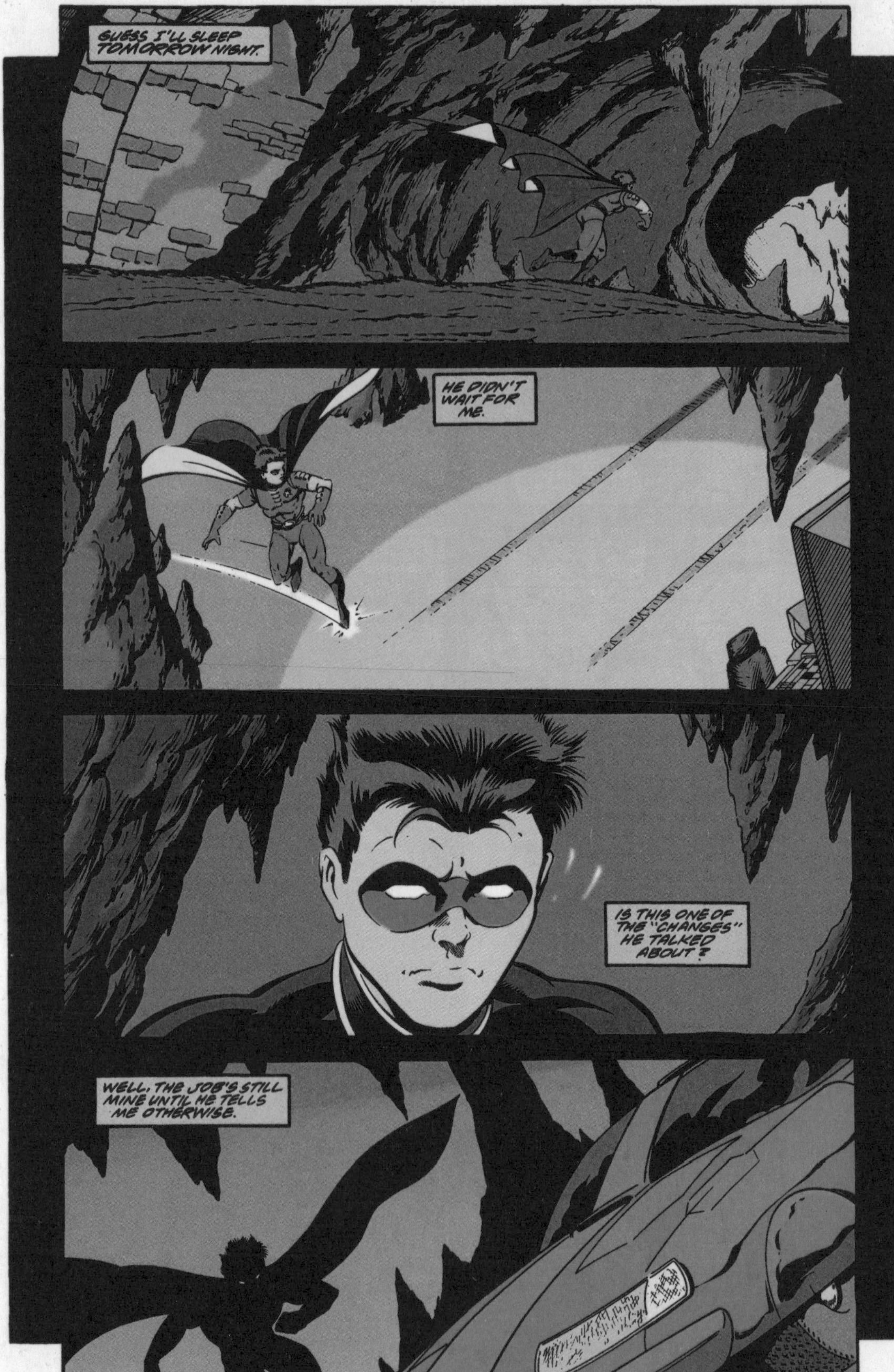
GUESS I'LL SLEEP TOMORROW NIGHT.
HE DIDN'T WAIT FOR ME.
IS THIS ONE OF THE "CHANGES" HE TALKED ABOUT?
WELL, THE JOB'S STILL MINE UNTIL HE TELLS ME OTHERWISE.
9

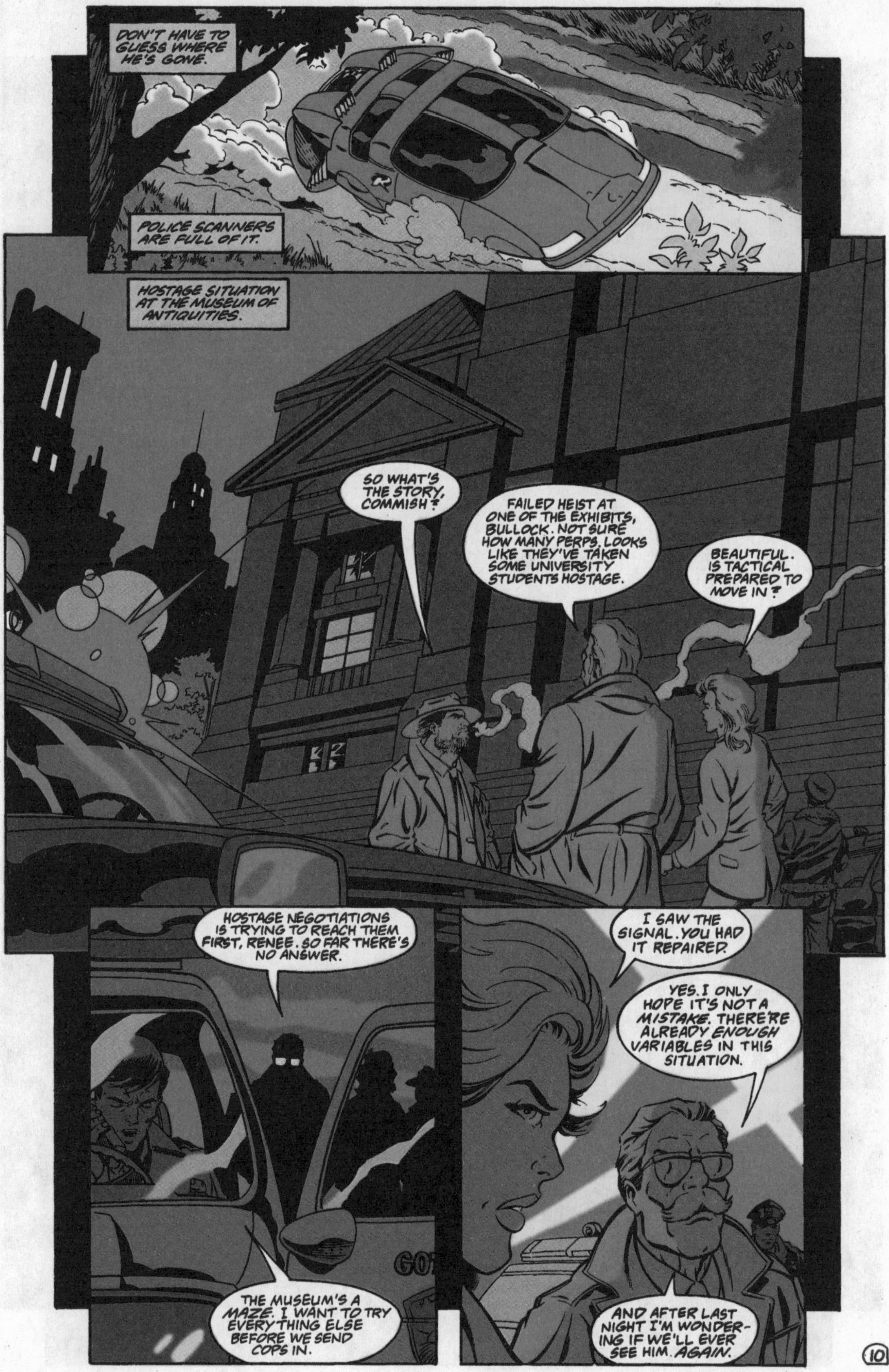
DON'T HAVE TO GUESS WHERE HE'S GONE.
POLICE SCANNERS ARE FULL OF IT.
HOSTAGE SITUATION AT THE MUSEUM OF ANTIQUITIES.
SO WHAT'S THE STORY, COMMISH?
FAILED HEIST AT ONE OF THE EXHIBITS, BULLOCK. NOT SURE HOW MANY PERPS. LOOKS LIKE THEY'VE TAKEN SOME UNIVERSITY STUDENTS HOSTAGE.
BEAUTIFUL. IS TACTICAL PREPARED TO MOVE IN?
HOSTAGE NEGOTIATIONS IS TRYING TO REACH THEM FIRST, RENEE. SO FAR THERE'S NO ANSWER.
THE MUSEUM'S A MAZE. I WANT TO TRY EVERYTHING ELSE BEFORE WE SEND COPS IN.
I SAW THE SIGNAL. YOU HAD IT REPAIRED.
YES. I ONLY HOPE IT'S NOT A MISTAKE. THERE'RE ALREADY ENOUGH VARIABLES IN THIS SITUATION.
AND AFTER LAST NIGHT I'M WONDERING IF WE'LL EVER SEE HIM. AGAIN.
10

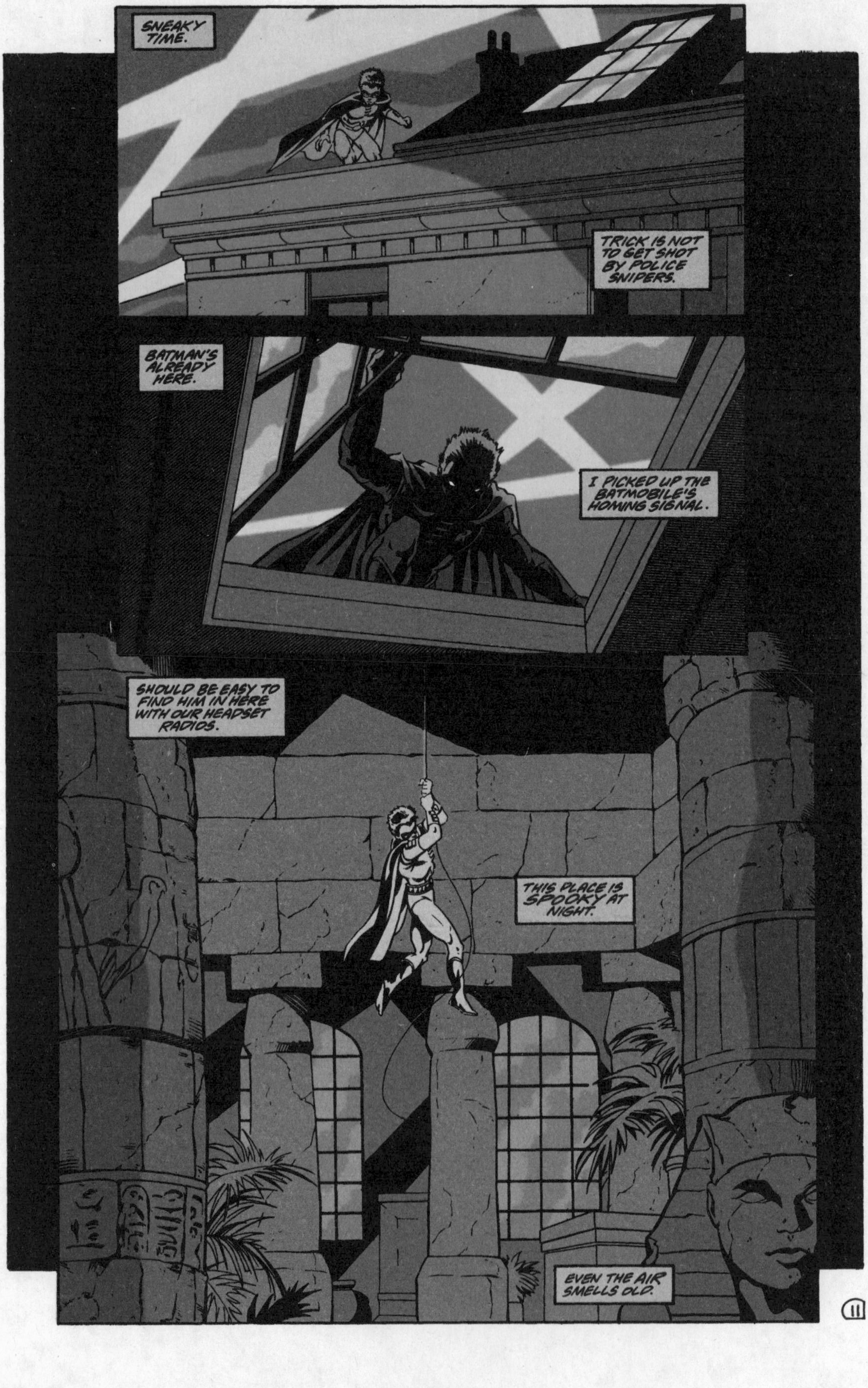
SNEAKY TIME.
TRICK IS NOT TO GET SHOT BY POLICE SNIPERS.
BATMAN'S ALREADY HERE.
I PICKED UP THE BATMOBILE'S HOMING SIGNAL.
SHOULD BE EASY TO FIND HIM IN HERE WITH OUR HEADSET RADIOS.
THIS PLACE IS SPOOKY AT NIGHT.
EVEN THE AIR SMELLS OLD.
11

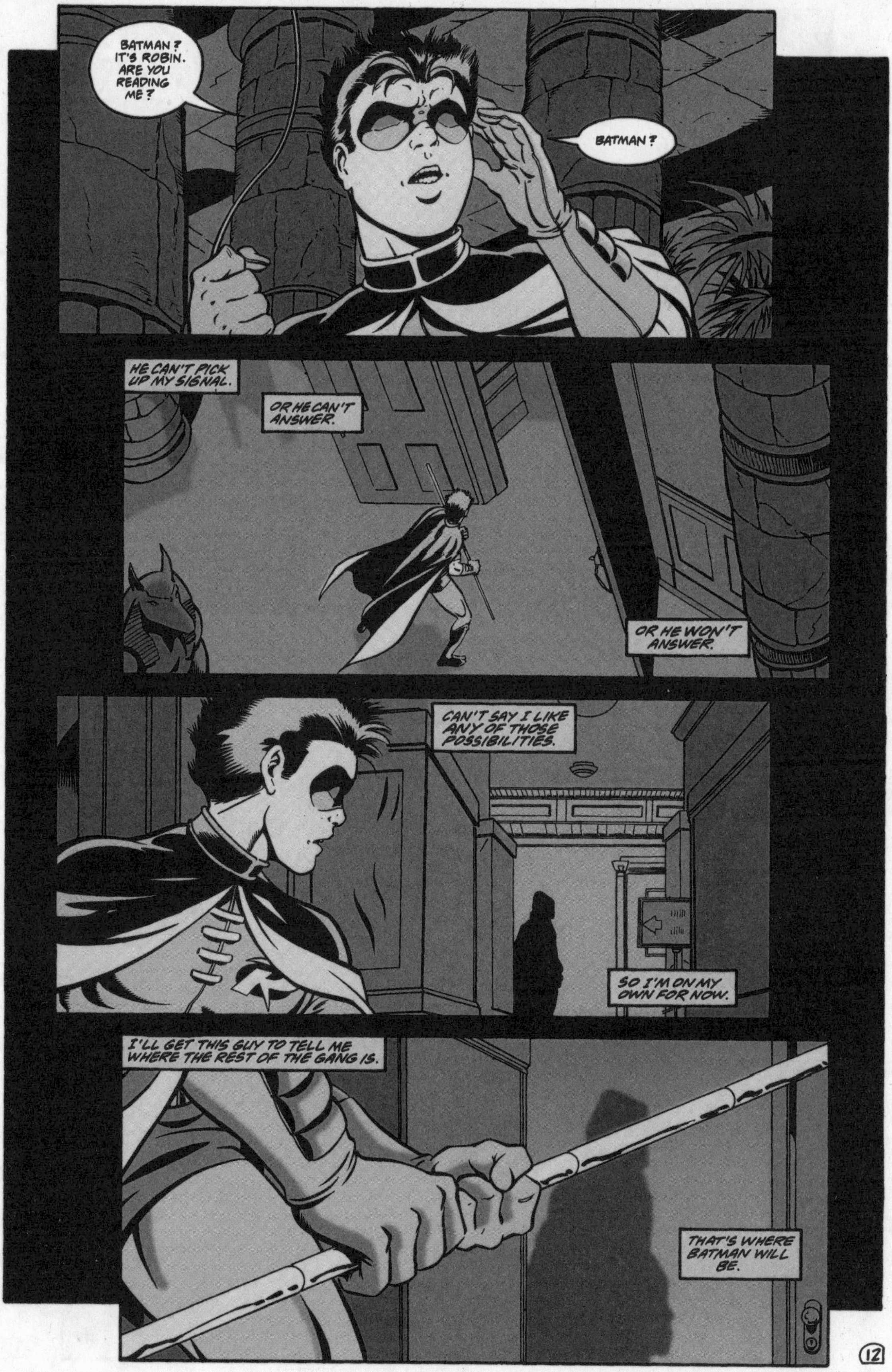
BATMAN? IT'S ROBIN. ARE YOU READING ME?
BATMAN?
HE CAN'T PICK UP MY SIGNAL.
OR HE CAN'T ANSWER.
OR HE WON'T ANSWER.
CAN'T SAY I LIKE ANY OF THOSE POSSIBILITIES.
SO I'M ON MY OWN FOR NOW.
I'LL GET THIS GUY TO TELL ME WHERE THE REST OF THE GANG IS.
THAT'S WHERE BATMAN WILL BE.
12

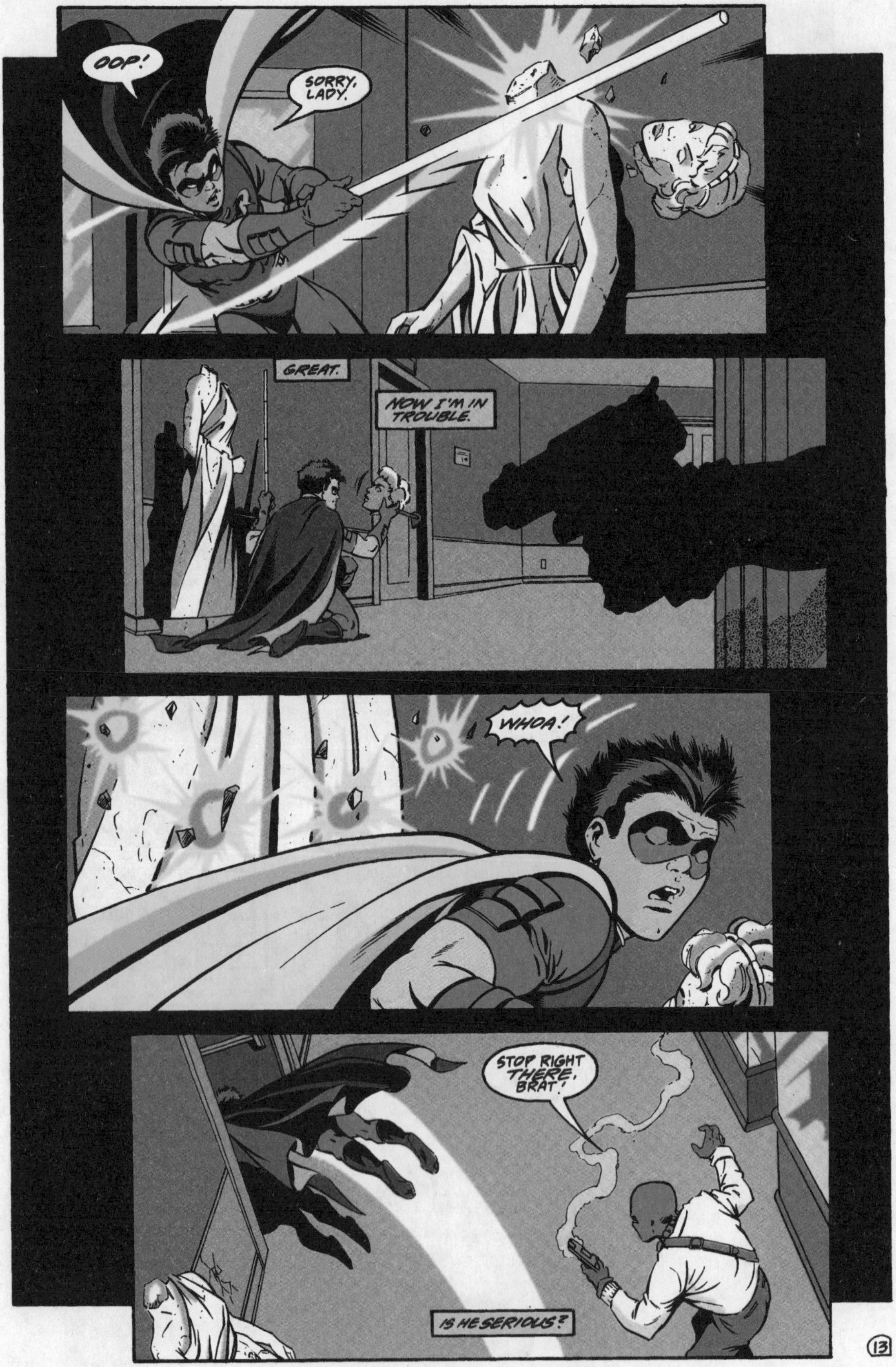
OOP!
SORRY, LADY.
GREAT.
NOW I'M IN TROUBLE.
WHOA!
STOP RIGHT THERE, BRAT!
IS HE SERIOUS?
13

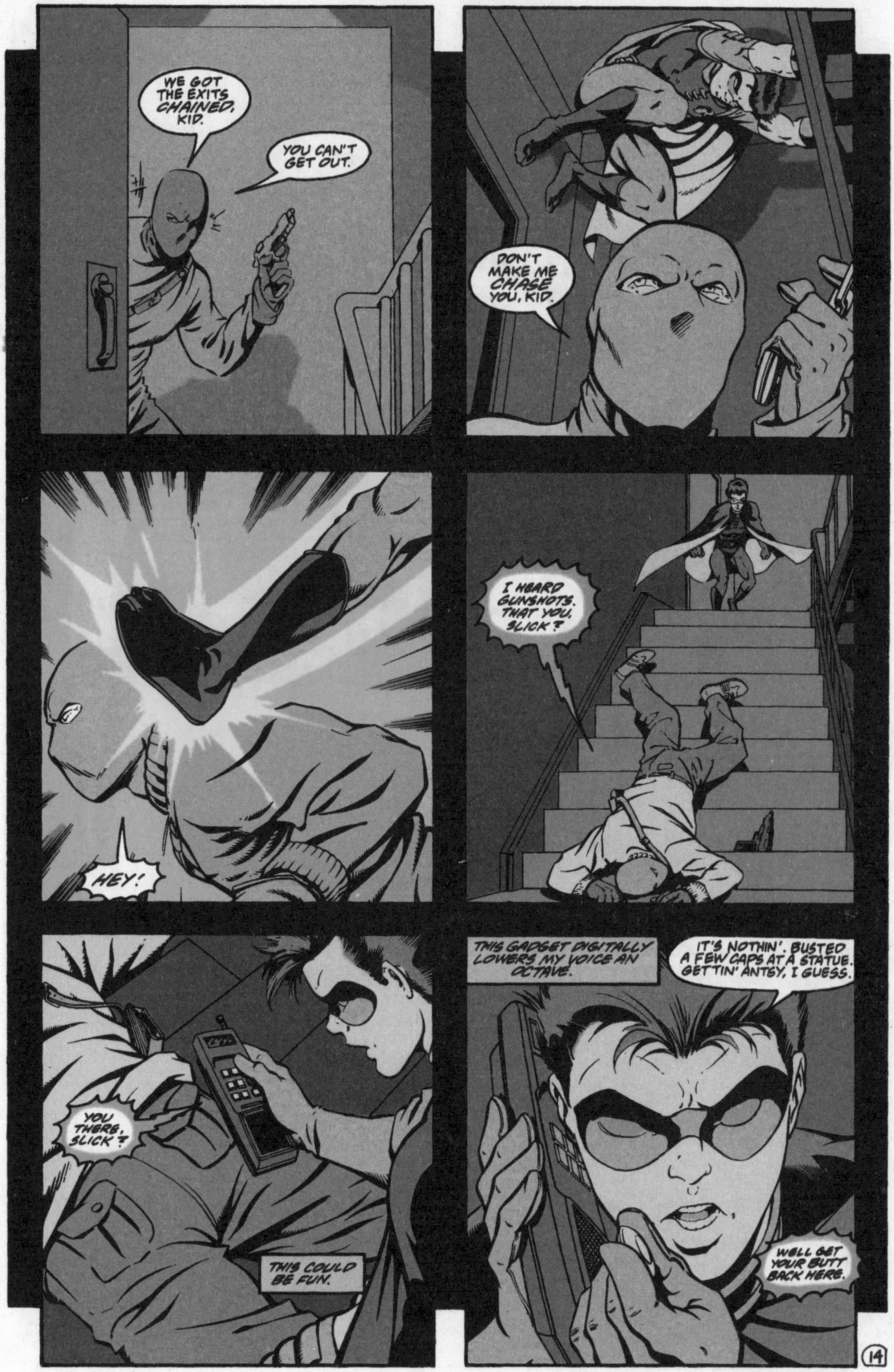
WE GOT THE EXITS CHAINED, KID.
YOU CAN'T GET OUT.
DON'T MAKE ME CHASE YOU, KID.
HEY!
I HEARD GUNSHOTS. THAT YOU, SLICK?
YOU THERE, SLICK?
THIS COULD BE FUN.
THIS GADGET DIGITALLY LOWERS MY VOICE AN OCTAVE.
IT'S NOTHIN'. BUSTED A FEW CAPS AT A STATUE. GETTIN' ANTSY, I GUESS.
WELL GET YOUR BUTT BACK HERE.
14

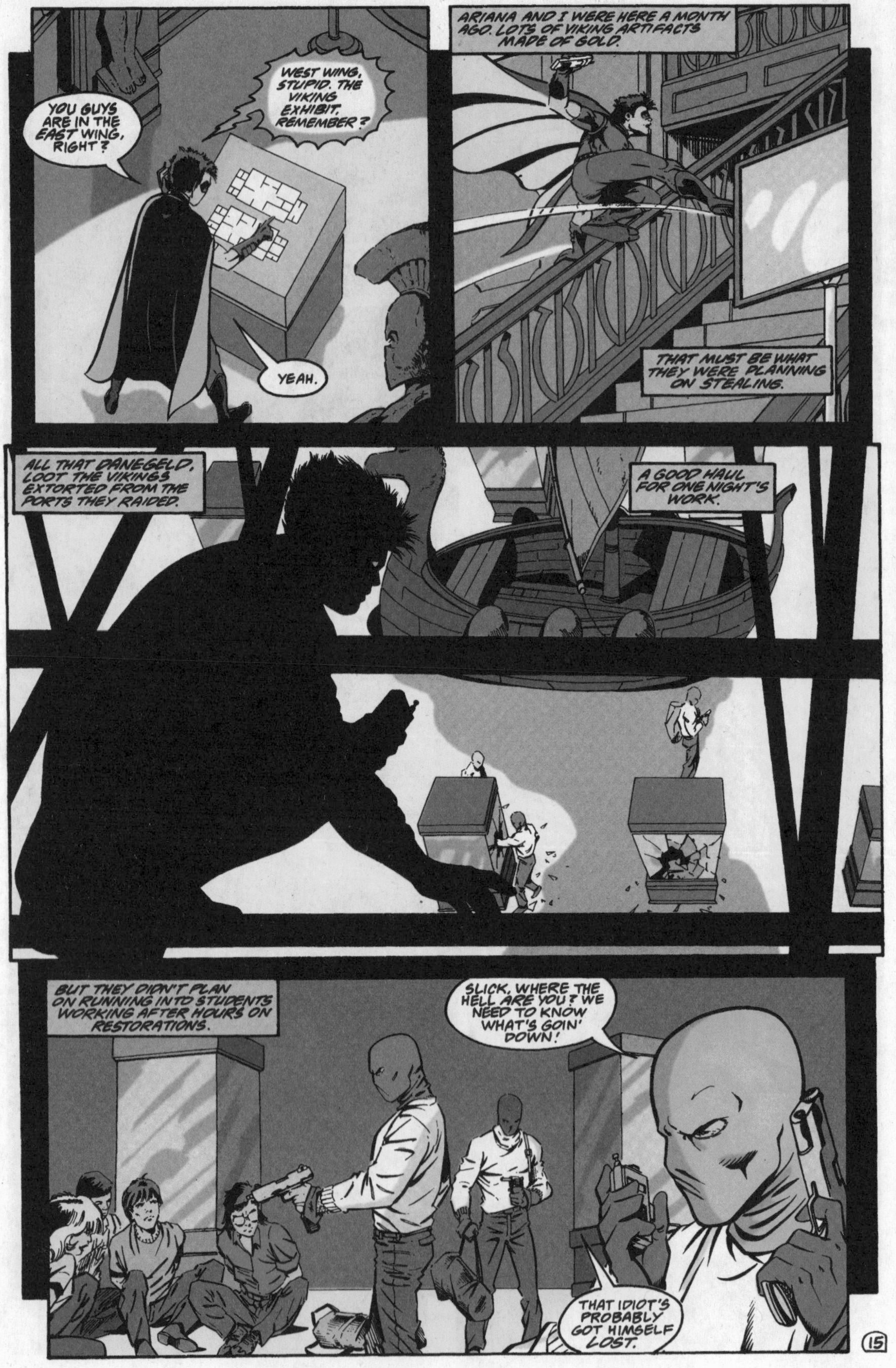
YOU GUYS ARE IN THE EAST WING, RIGHT?
WEST WING, STUPID. THE VIKING EXHIBIT, REMEMBER?
YEAH.
ARIANA AND I WERE HERE A MONTH AGO. LOTS OF VIKING ARTIFACTS MADE OF GOLD.
THAT MUST BE WHAT THEY WERE PLANNING ON STEALING.
ALL THAT DANEGELD, LOOT THE VIKINGS EXTORTED FROM THE PORTS THEY RAIDED.
A GOOD HAUL FOR ONE NIGHT'S WORK.
BUT THEY DIDN'T PLAN ON RUNNING INTO STUDENTS WORKING AFTER HOURS ON RESTORATIONS.
SLICK, WHERE THE HELL ARE YOU? WE NEED TO KNOW WHAT'S GOIN' DOWN!
THAT IDIOT'S PROBABLY GOT HIMSELF LOST.
15

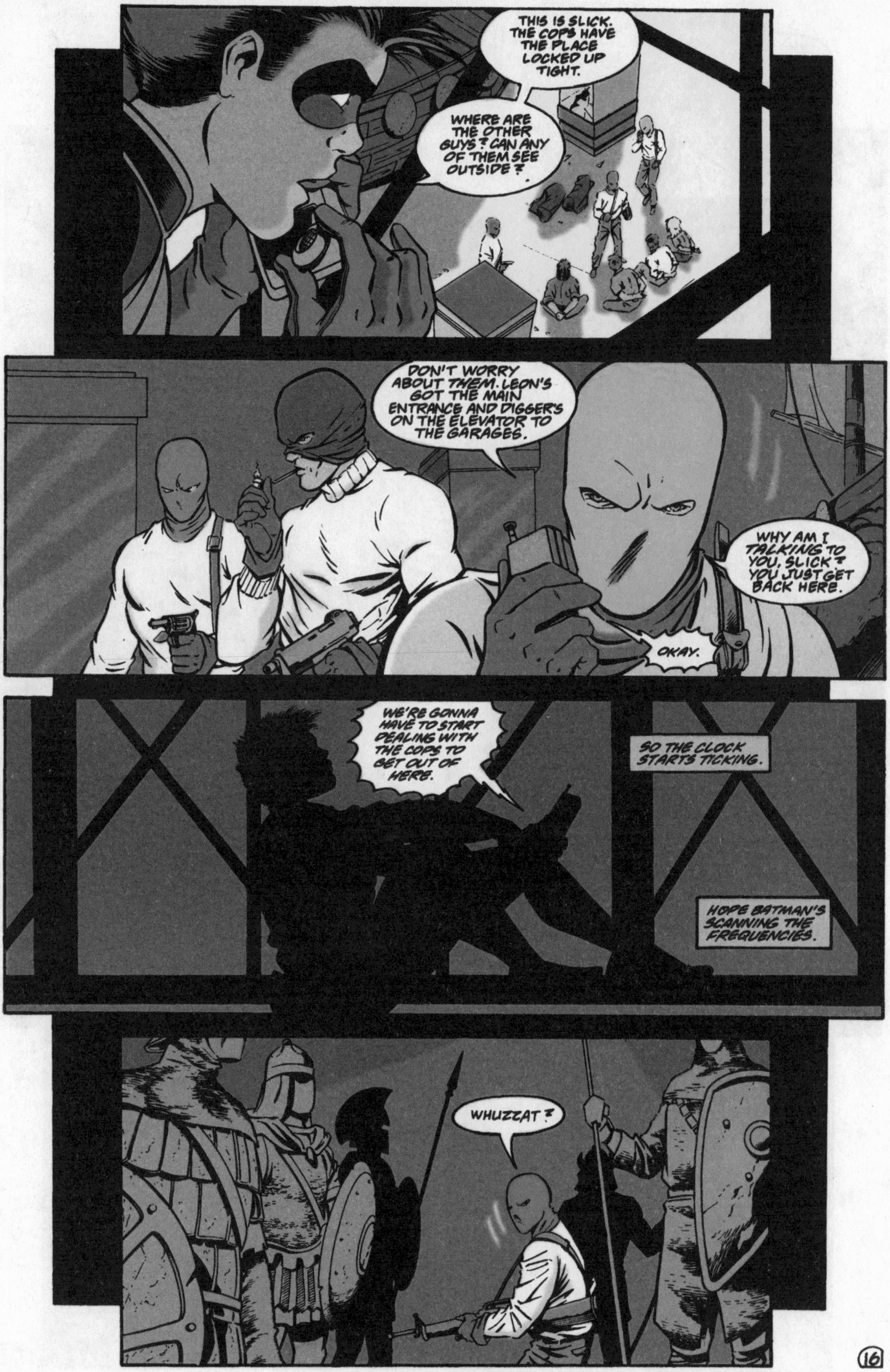
THIS IS SLICK. THE COPS HAVE THE PLACE LOCKED UP TIGHT.
WHERE ARE THE OTHER GUYS? CAN ANY OF THEM SEE OUTSIDE?
DON'T WORRY ABOUT THEM. LEON'S GOT THE MAIN ENTRANCE AND DIGGER'S ON THE ELEVATOR TO THE GARAGES.
WHY AM I TALKING TO YOU, SLICK? YOU JUST GET BACK HERE.
OKAY.
WE'RE GONNA HAVE TO START DEALING WITH THE COPS TO GET OUT OF HERE.
SO THE CLOCK STARTS TICKING.
HOPE BATMAN'S SCANNING THE FREQUENCIES.
WHUZZAT?
16

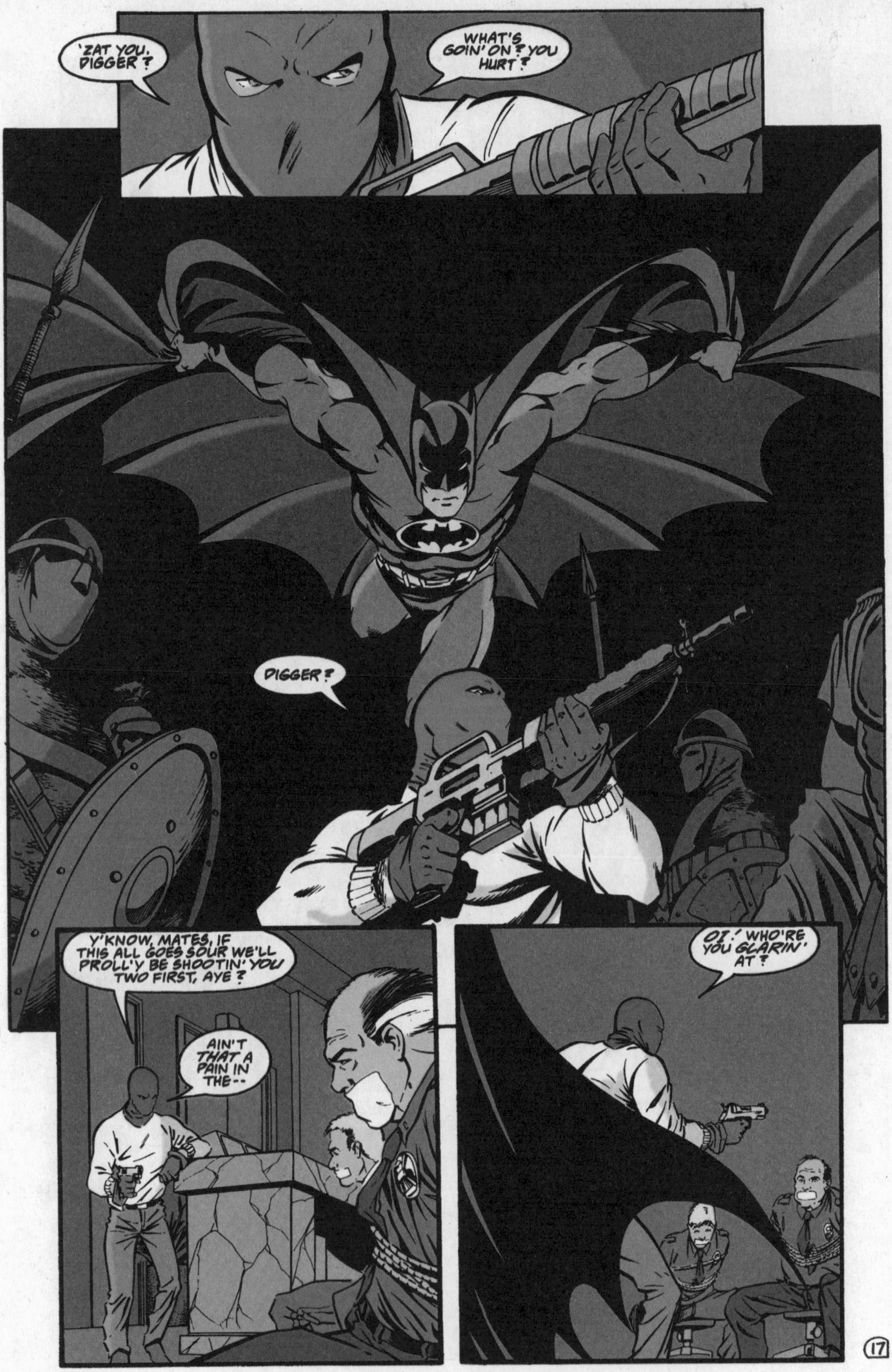
'ZAT YOU, DIGGER?
WHAT'S GOIN' ON? YOU HURT?
DIGGER?
Y'KNOW, MATES, IF THIS ALL GOES SOUR WE'LL PROLL'Y BE SHOOTIN' YOU TWO FIRST, AYE?
AIN'T THAT A PAIN IN THE--
OI! WHO'RE YOU GLARIN' AT?
17

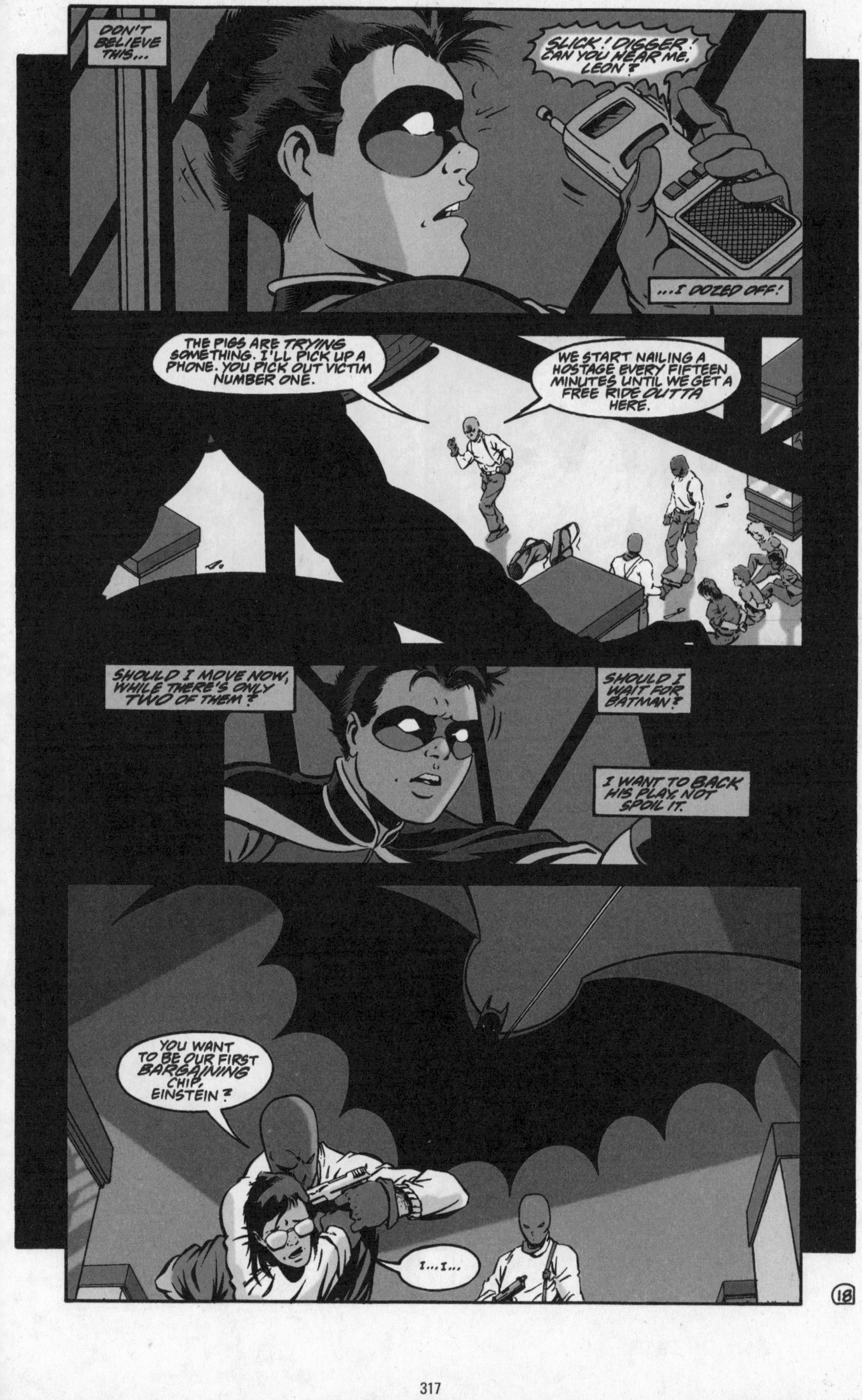
DON'T BELIEVE THIS...
SLICK! DIGGER! CAN YOU HEAR ME, LEON?
...I DOZED OFF!
THE PIGS ARE TRYING SOMETHING. I'LL PICK UP A PHONE. YOU PICK OUT VICTIM NUMBER ONE.
WE START NAILING A HOSTAGE EVERY FIFTEEN MINUTES UNTIL WE GET A FREE RIDE OUTTA HERE.
SHOULD I MOVE NOW, WHILE THERE'S ONLY TWO OF THEM?
SHOULD I WAIT FOR BATMAN?
I WANT TO BACK HIS PLAY, NOT SPOIL IT.
YOU WANT TO BE OUR FIRST BARGAINING CHIP, EINSTEIN?
I...I...
18

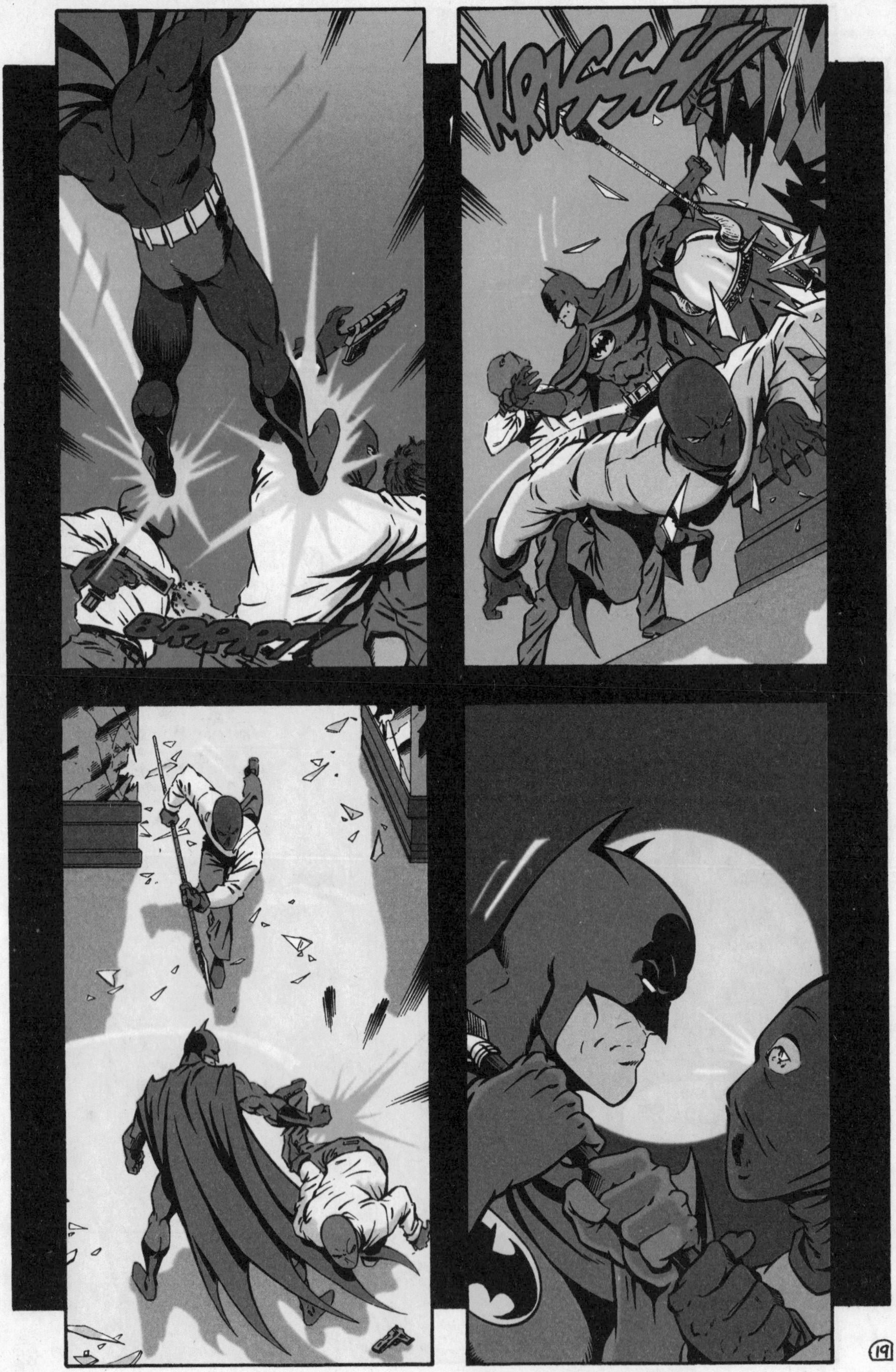
BRRRPT!
KRASSH!!
19

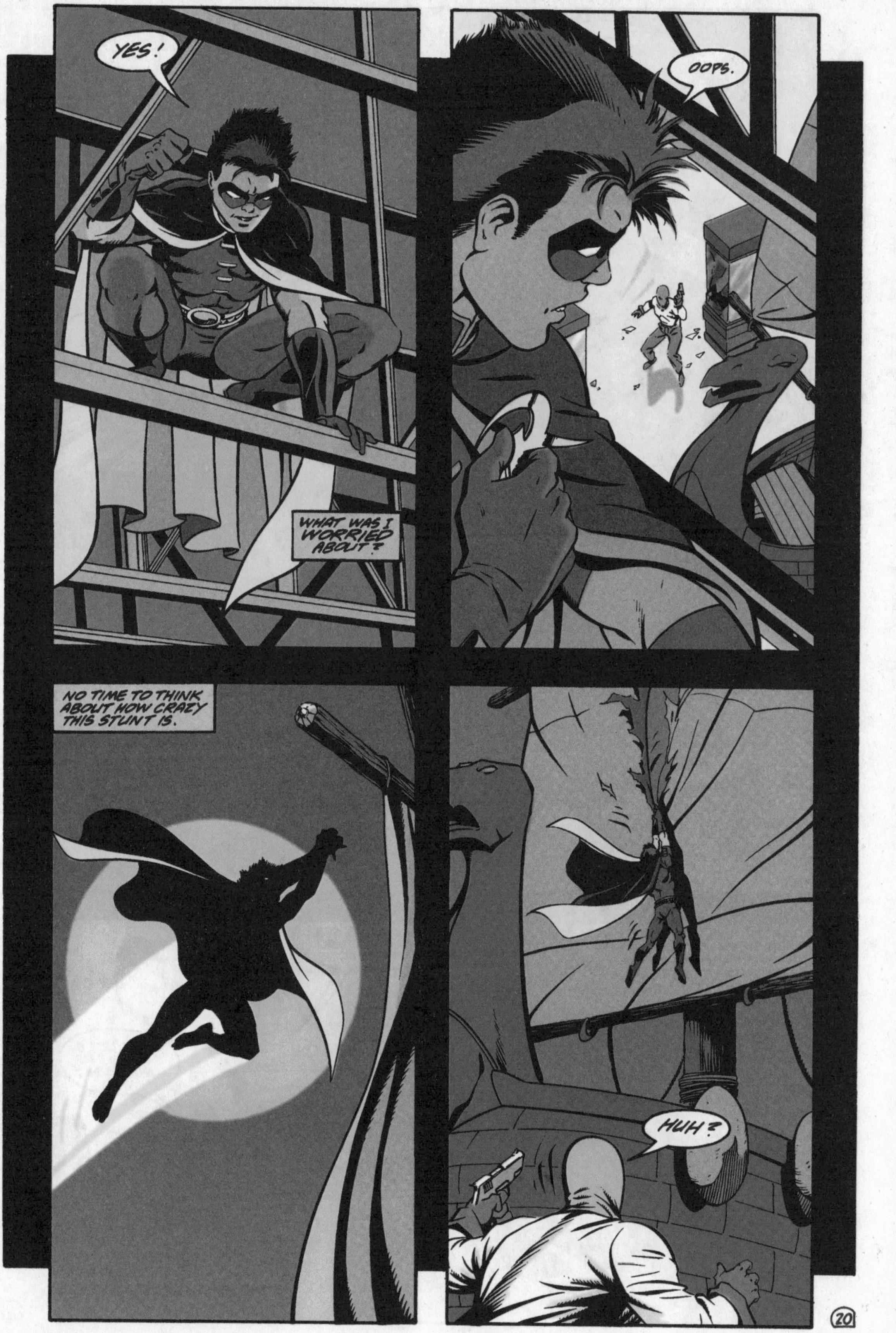
YES!
WHAT WAS I WORRIED ABOUT?
OOPS.
NO TIME TO THINK ABOUT HOW CRAZY THIS STUNT IS.
HUH?
20

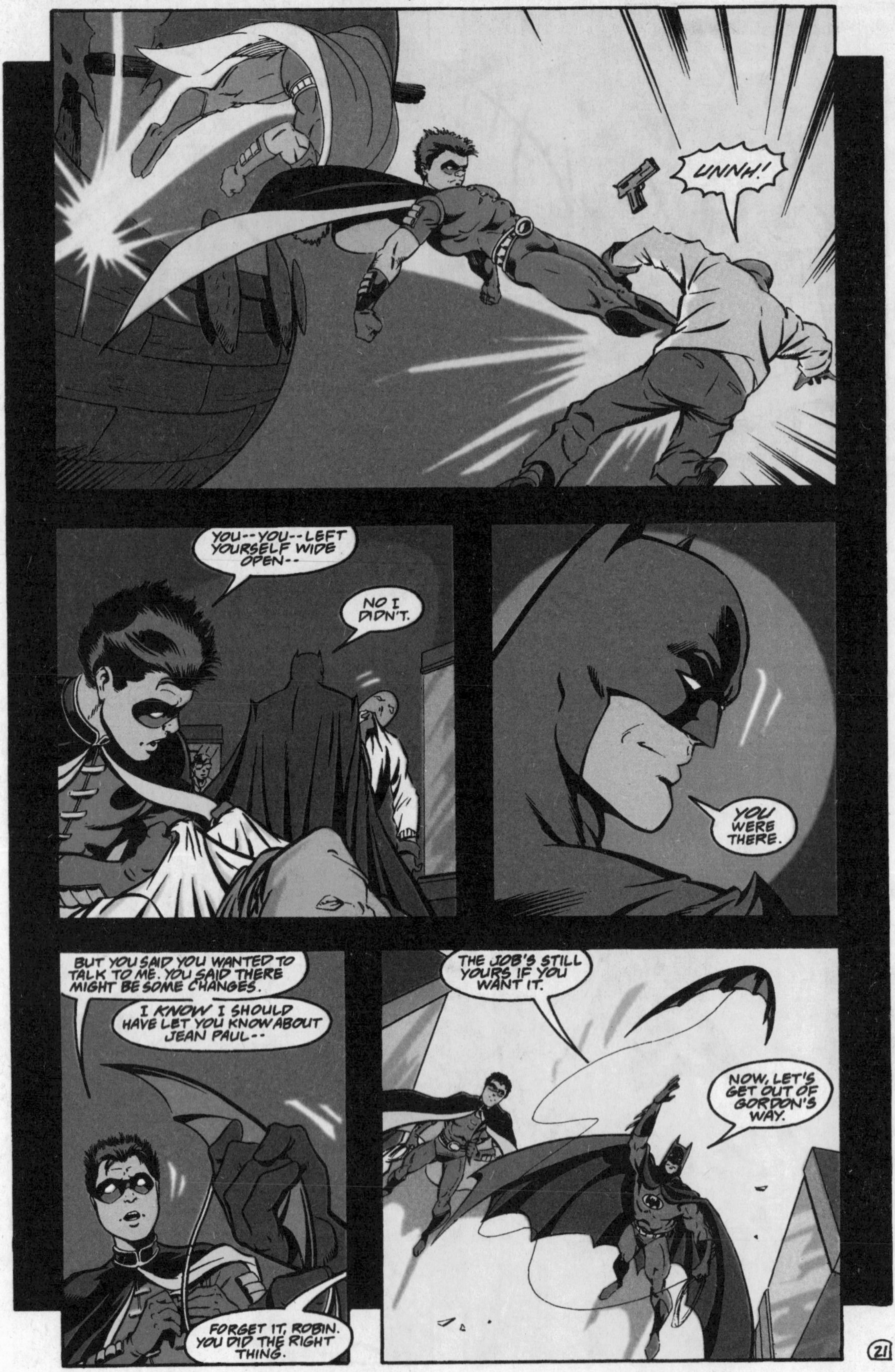
UNNH!
YOU--YOU--LEFT YOURSELF WIDE OPEN--
NO I DIDN'T.
YOU WERE THERE.
BUT YOU SAID YOU WANTED TO TALK TO ME. YOU SAID THERE MIGHT BE SOME CHANGES.
I KNOW I SHOULD HAVE LET YOU KNOW ABOUT JEAN PAUL--
FORGET IT, ROBIN. YOU DID THE RIGHT THING.
THE JOB'S STILL YOURS IF YOU WANT IT.
NOW, LET'S GET OUT OF GORDON'S WAY.
21

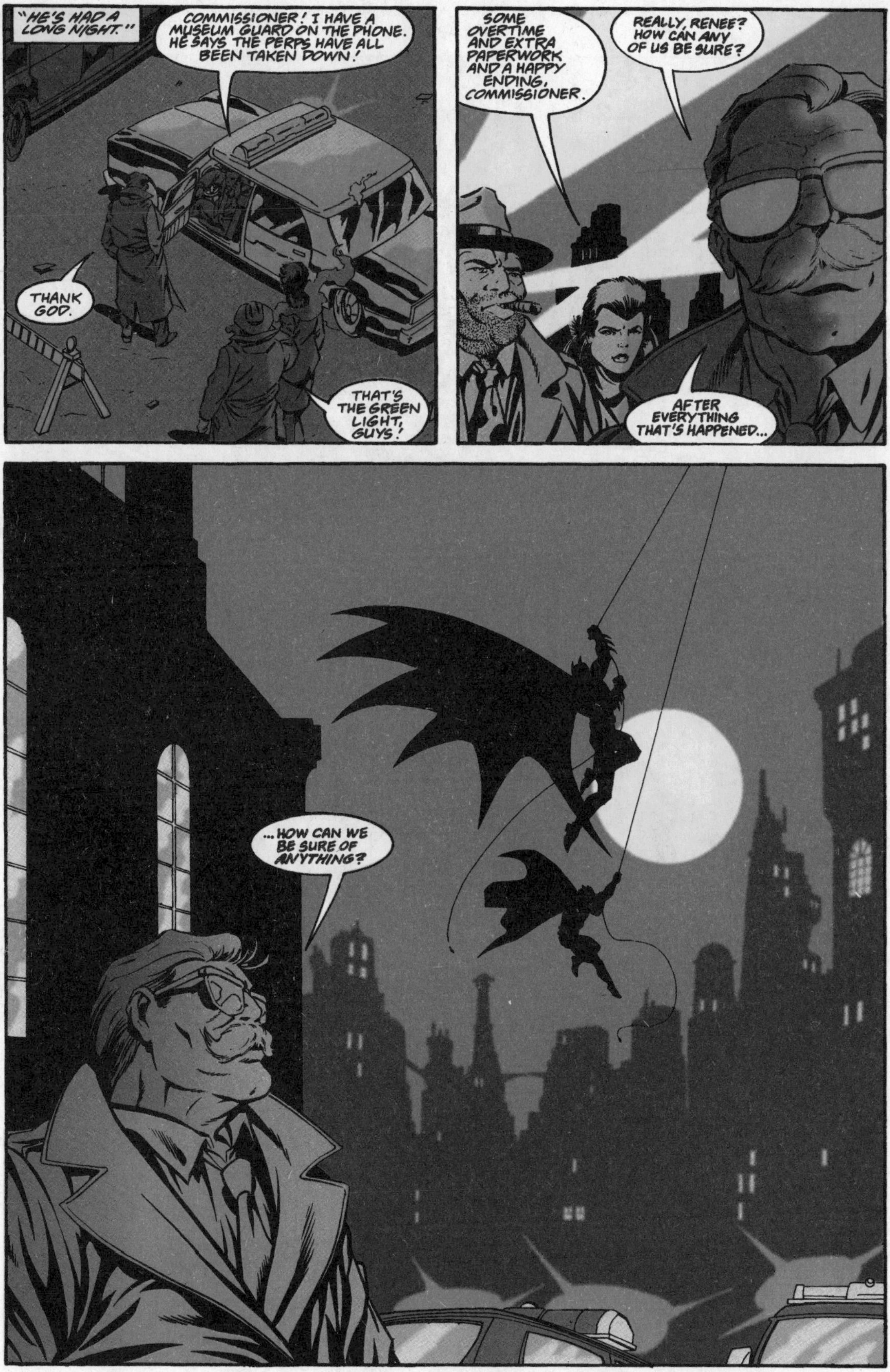
"HE'S HAD A LONG NIGHT."
COMMISSIONER! I HAVE A MUSEUM GUARD ON THE PHONE. HE SAYS THE PERPS HAVE ALL BEEN TAKEN DOWN!
THANK GOD.
THAT'S THE GREEN LIGHT, GUYS!
SOME OVERTIME AND EXTRA PAPERWORK AND A HAPPY ENDING, COMMISSIONER.
REALLY, RENEE? HOW CAN ANY OF US BE SURE?
AFTER EVERYTHING THAT'S HAPPENED...
...HOW CAN WE BE SURE OF ANYTHING?

Cover art by JIM BALENT

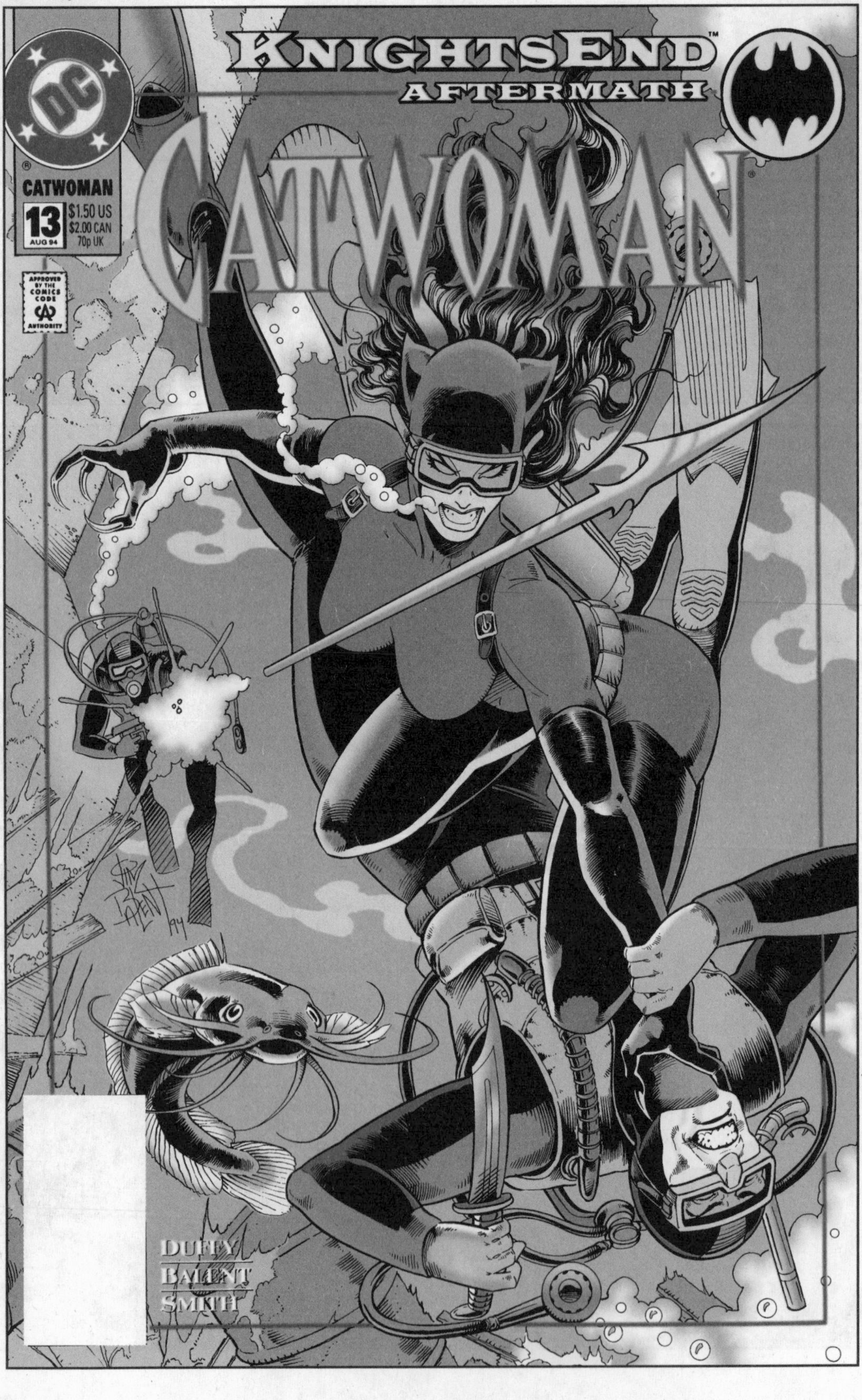
KNIGHTSEND™
AFTERMATH
DC
CATWOMAN
13
AUG 94
$1.50 US
$2.00 CAN
70p UK
APPROVED BY THE COMICS CODE AUTHORITY
CATWOMAN
DUFFY
BALENT
SMITH

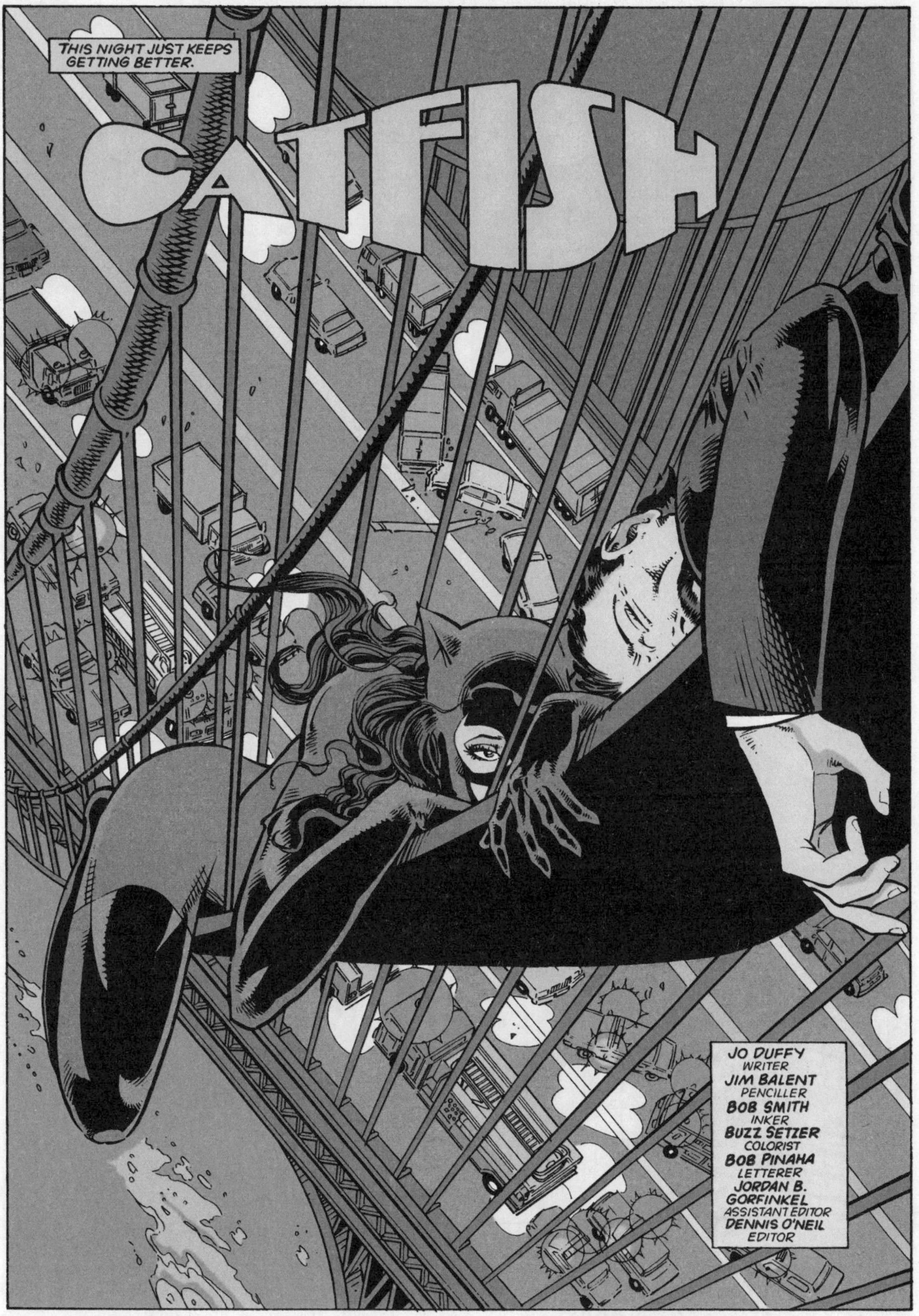
THIS NIGHT JUST KEEPS GETTING BETTER.
CATFISH
JO DUFFY
WRITER
JIM BALENT
PENCILLER
BOB SMITH
INKER
BUZZ SETZER
COLORIST
BOB PINAHA
LETTERER
JORDAN B. GORFINKEL
ASSISTANT EDITOR
DENNIS O'NEIL
EDITOR

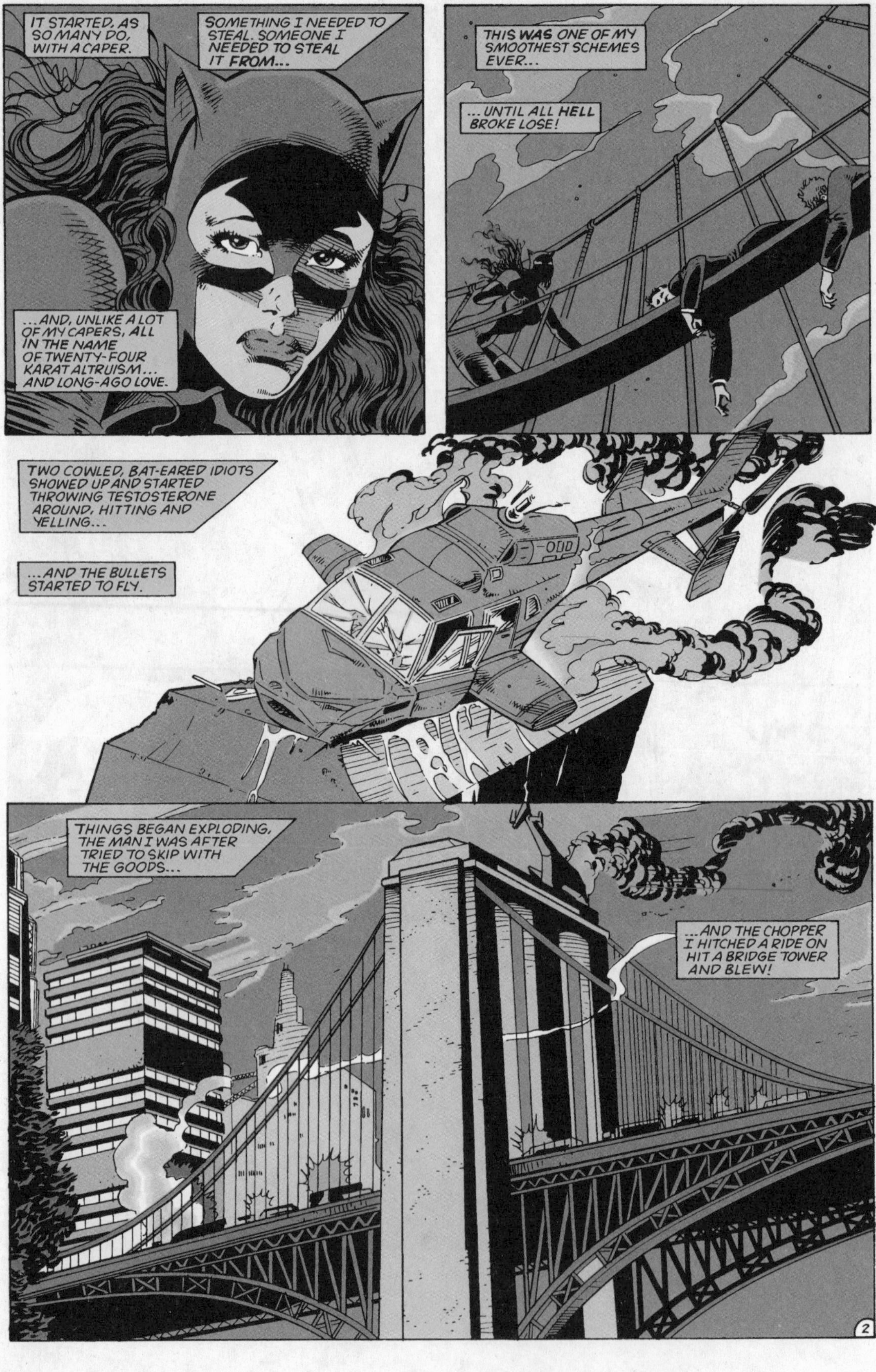

IT STARTED, AS SO MANY DO, WITH A CAPER.
SOMETHING I NEEDED TO STEAL. SOMEONE I NEEDED TO STEAL IT FROM...
...AND, UNLIKE A LOT OF MY CAPERS, ALL IN THE NAME OF TWENTY-FOUR KARAT ALTRUISM... AND LONG-AGO LOVE.
THIS WAS ONE OF MY SMOOTHEST SCHEMES EVER...
...UNTIL ALL HELL BROKE LOSE!
TWO COWLED, BAT-EARED IDIOTS SHOWED UP AND STARTED THROWING TESTOSTERONE AROUND, HITTING AND YELLING...
...AND THE BULLETS STARTED TO FLY.
THINGS BEGAN EXPLODING, THE MAN I WAS AFTER TRIED TO SKIP WITH THE GOODS...
...AND THE CHOPPER I HITCHED A RIDE ON HIT A BRIDGE TOWER AND BLEW!
2

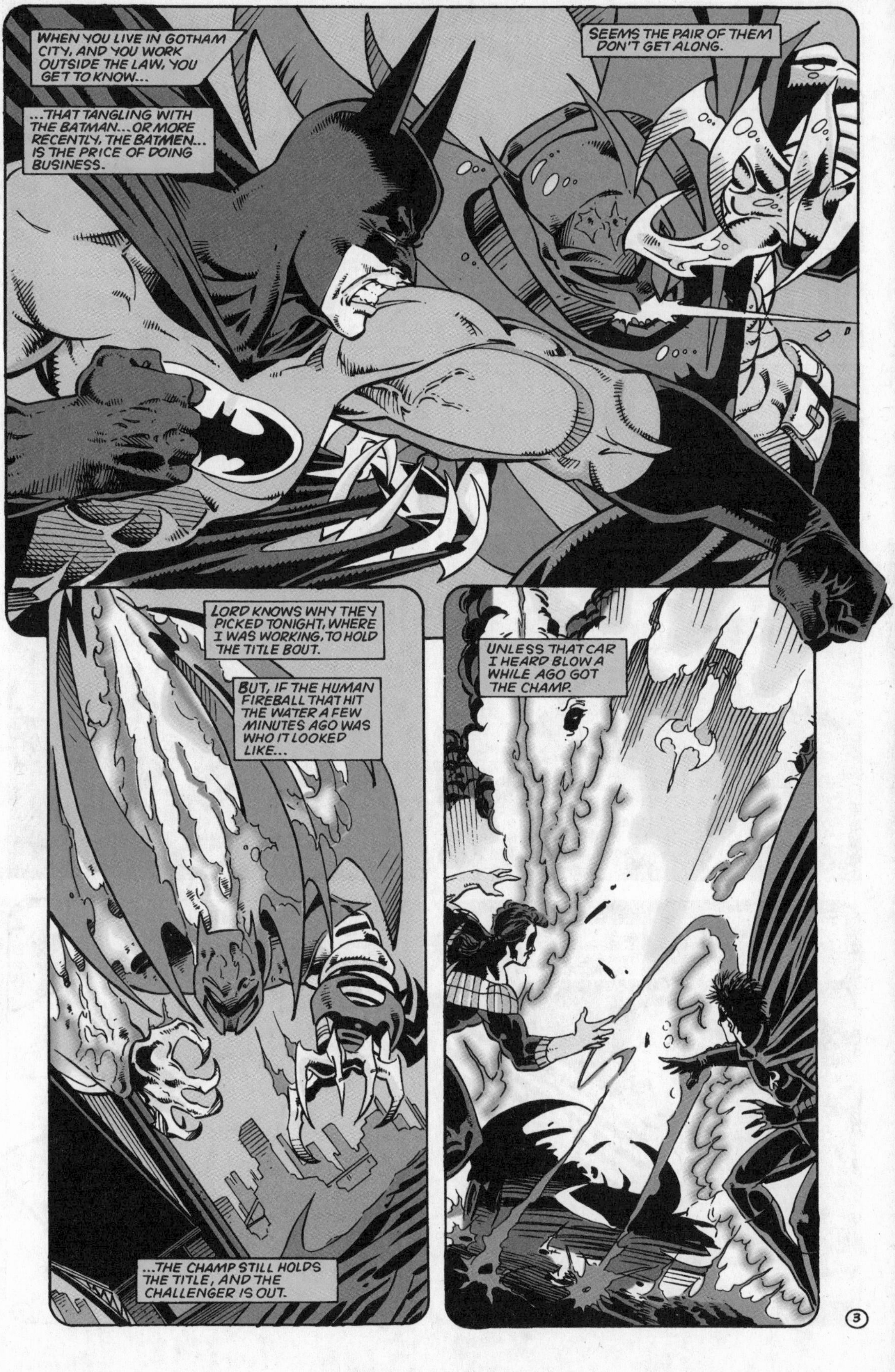
WHEN YOU LIVE IN GOTHAM CITY, AND YOU WORK OUTSIDE THE LAW, YOU GET TO KNOW...
...THAT TANGLING WITH THE BATMAN... OR MORE RECENTLY, THE BATMEN... IS THE PRICE OF DOING BUSINESS.
SEEMS THE PAIR OF THEM DON'T GET ALONG.
LORD KNOWS WHY THEY PICKED TONIGHT, WHERE I WAS WORKING, TO HOLD THE TITLE BOUT.
BUT, IF THE HUMAN FIREBALL THAT HIT THE WATER A FEW MINUTES AGO WAS WHO IT LOOKED LIKE...
...THE CHAMP STILL HOLDS THE TITLE, AND THE CHALLENGER IS OUT.
UNLESS THAT CAR I HEARD BLOW A WHILE AGO GOT THE CHAMP.
3

I'M BETTING NOT. HE'S MY DEAREST OPPONENT...

...AND HAS MORE LIVES THAN A CAT!

Uh... LADY? CAT-LADY?

WONDERFUL. THE MAN WHOSE FLYING LANDED US UP HERE.

H-HOW'RE WE GONNA GET DOWN?

PRIVATE PILOT OF PENN SELKIRK, MUNITIONS BROKER WHO, HOPING TO EXPAND HIS MERCHANDISE INTO CYBERNETIC WEAPONRY...

...STOLE THE PROTOTYPE AND PLANS FOR A DEVICE I'VE GOT TO HAVE.

THERE HE WAS, IN HIS PENTHOUSE STRONGHOLD, SURROUNDED BY GUARDS...

...HOLDING THE CYBERNETIC NEURAL ENABLER...

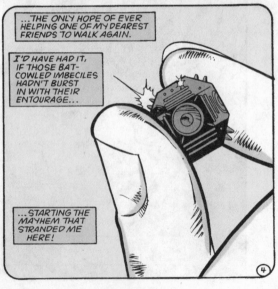

...THE ONLY HOPE OF EVER HELPING ONE OF MY DEAREST FRIENDS TO WALK AGAIN.

I'D HAVE HAD IT, IF THOSE BAT-COWLED IMBECILES HADN'T BURST IN WITH THEIR ENTOURAGE...

...STARTING THE MAYHEM THAT STRANDED ME HERE!

4

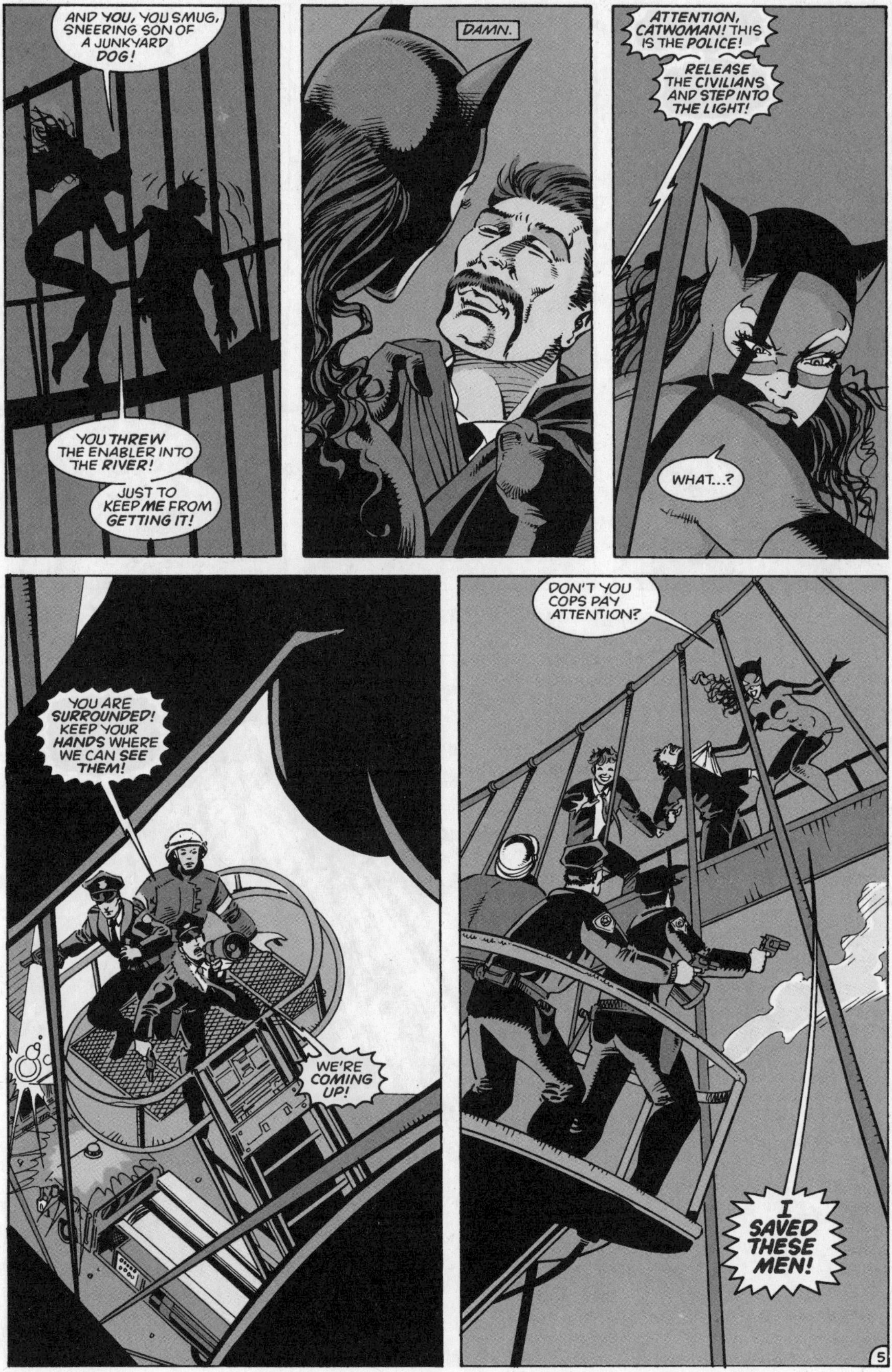
AND YOU, YOU SMUG, SNEERING SON OF A JUNKYARD DOG!
YOU THREW THE ENABLER INTO THE RIVER!
JUST TO KEEP ME FROM GETTING IT!
DAMN.
ATTENTION, CATWOMAN! THIS IS THE POLICE!
RELEASE THE CIVILIANS AND STEP INTO THE LIGHT!
WHAT...?
YOU ARE SURROUNDED! KEEP YOUR HANDS WHERE WE CAN SEE THEM!
WE'RE COMING UP!
DON'T YOU COPS PAY ATTENTION?
I SAVED THESE MEN!
5

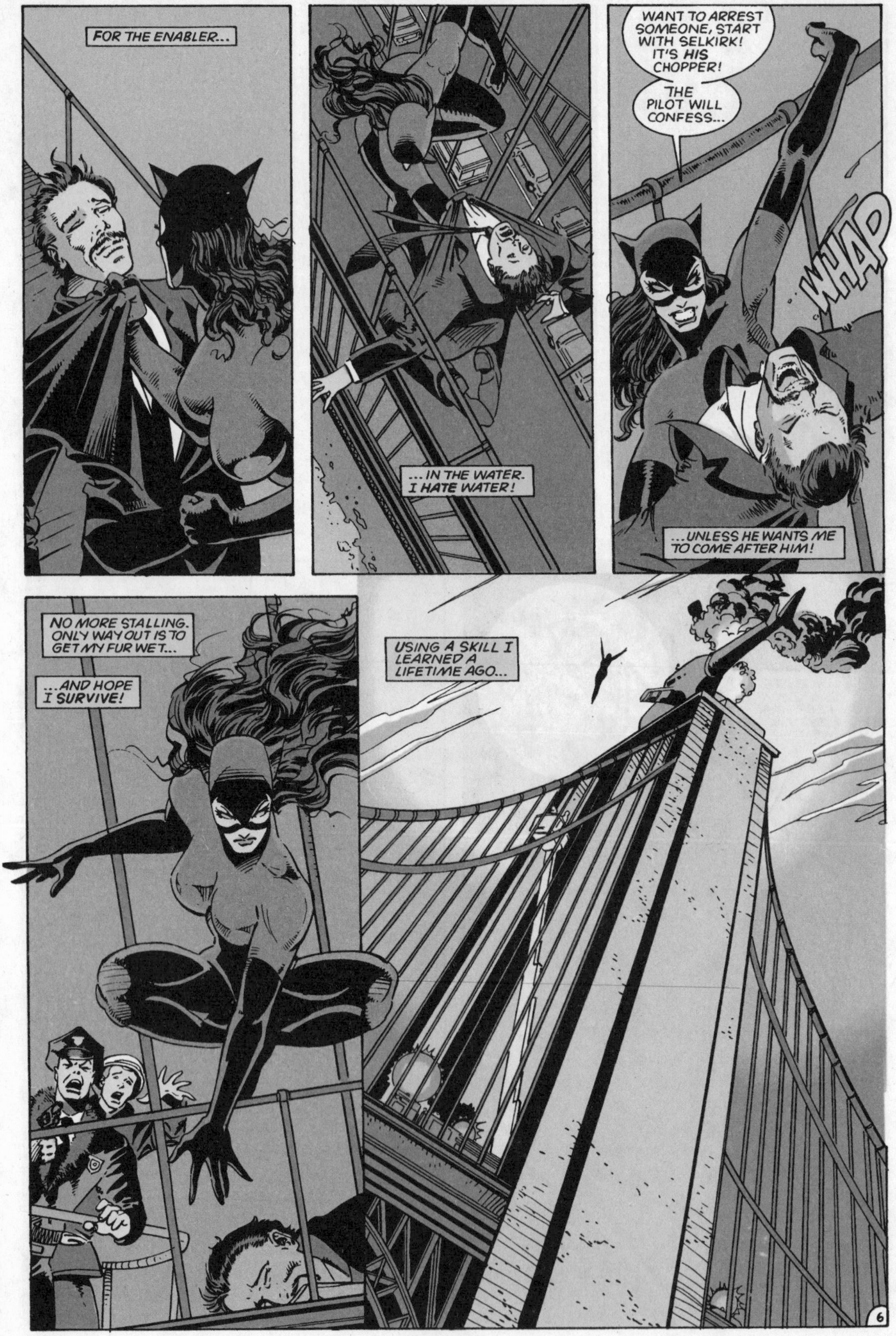
FOR THE ENABLER...
...IN THE WATER. I HATE WATER!
WANT TO ARREST SOMEONE, START WITH SELKIRK! IT'S HIS CHOPPER!
THE PILOT WILL CONFESS...
WHAP
...UNLESS HE WANTS ME TO COME AFTER HIM!
NO MORE STALLING. ONLY WAY OUT IS TO GET MY FUR WET...
...AND HOPE I SURVIVE!
USING A SKILL I LEARNED A LIFETIME AGO...
6

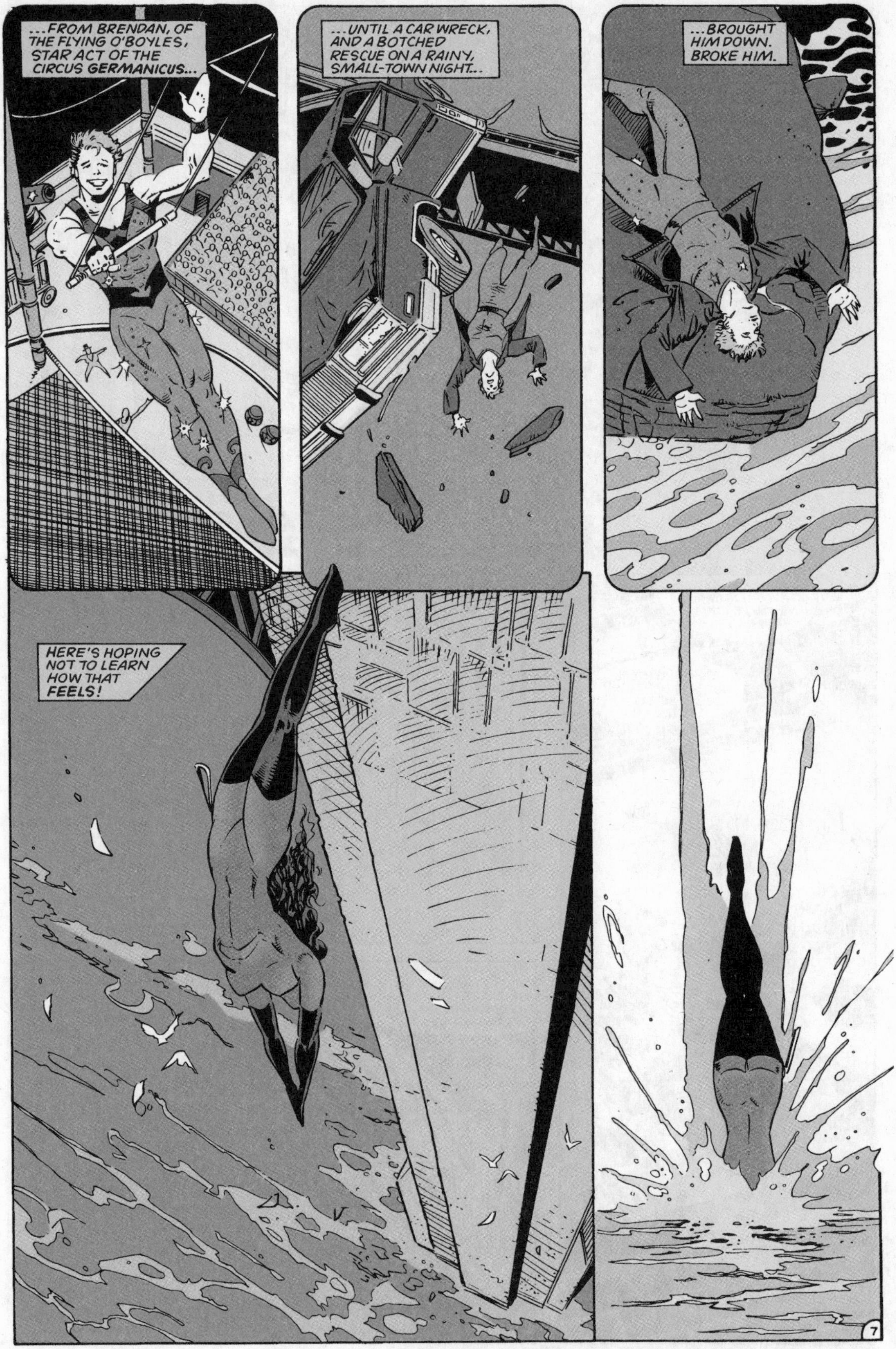
...FROM BRENDAN, OF THE FLYING O'BOYLES, STAR ACT OF THE CIRCUS GERMANICUS...
...UNTIL A CAR WRECK, AND A BOTCHED RESCUE ON A RAINY, SMALL-TOWN NIGHT...
...BROUGHT HIM DOWN. BROKE HIM.
HERE'S HOPING NOT TO LEARN HOW THAT FEELS!
7

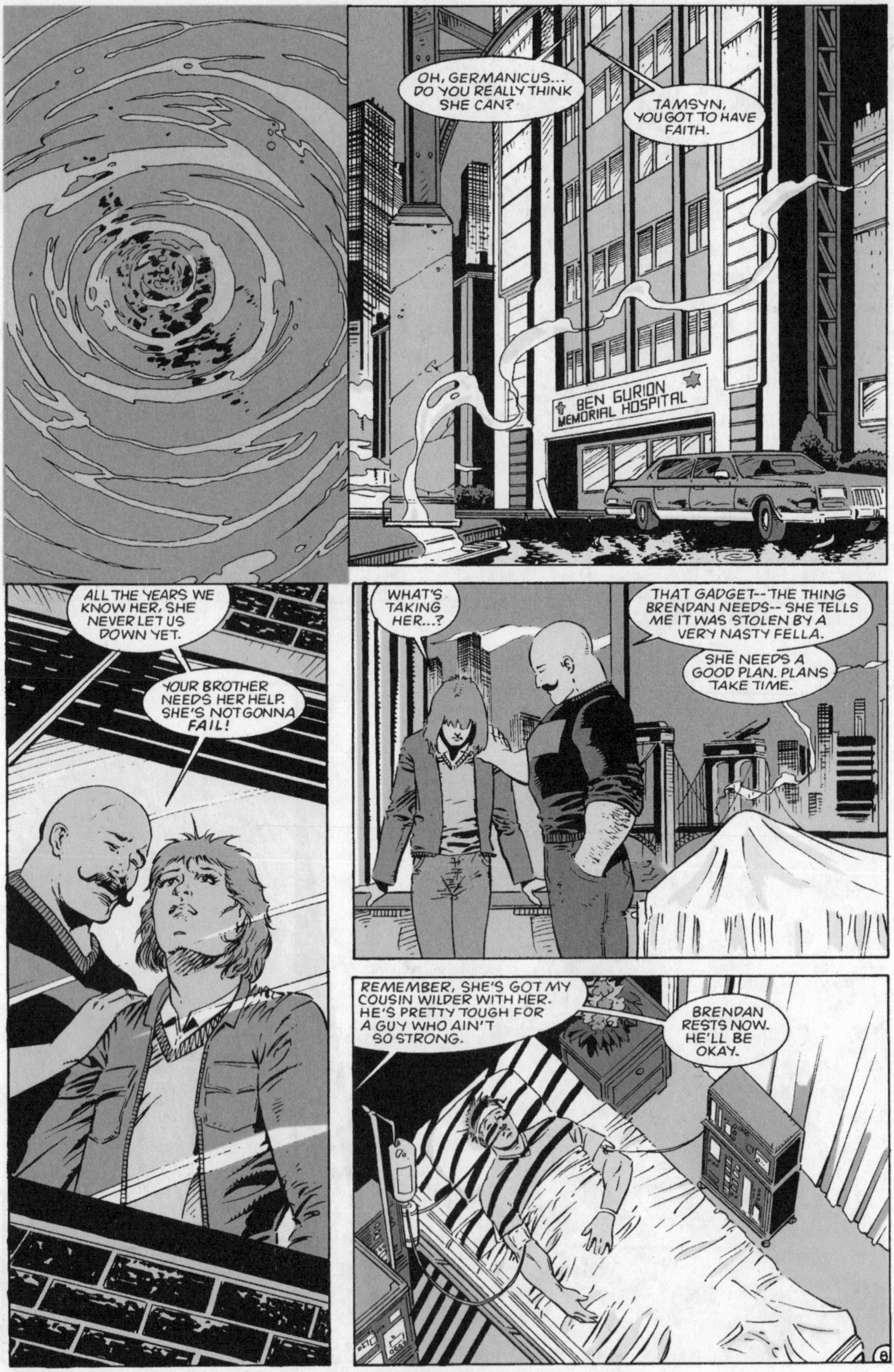
OH, GERMANICUS... DO YOU REALLY THINK SHE CAN?
TAMSYN, YOU GOT TO HAVE FAITH.
BEN GURION MEMORIAL HOSPITAL
ALL THE YEARS WE KNOW HER, SHE NEVER LET US DOWN YET.
YOUR BROTHER NEEDS HER HELP. SHE'S NOT GONNA FAIL!
WHAT'S TAKING HER...?
THAT GADGET--THE THING BRENDAN NEEDS-- SHE TELLS ME IT WAS STOLEN BY A VERY NASTY FELLA.
SHE NEEDS A GOOD PLAN. PLANS TAKE TIME.
REMEMBER, SHE'S GOT MY COUSIN WILDER WITH HER. HE'S PRETTY TOUGH FOR A GUY WHO AIN'T SO STRONG.
BRENDAN RESTS NOW. HE'LL BE OKAY.
8

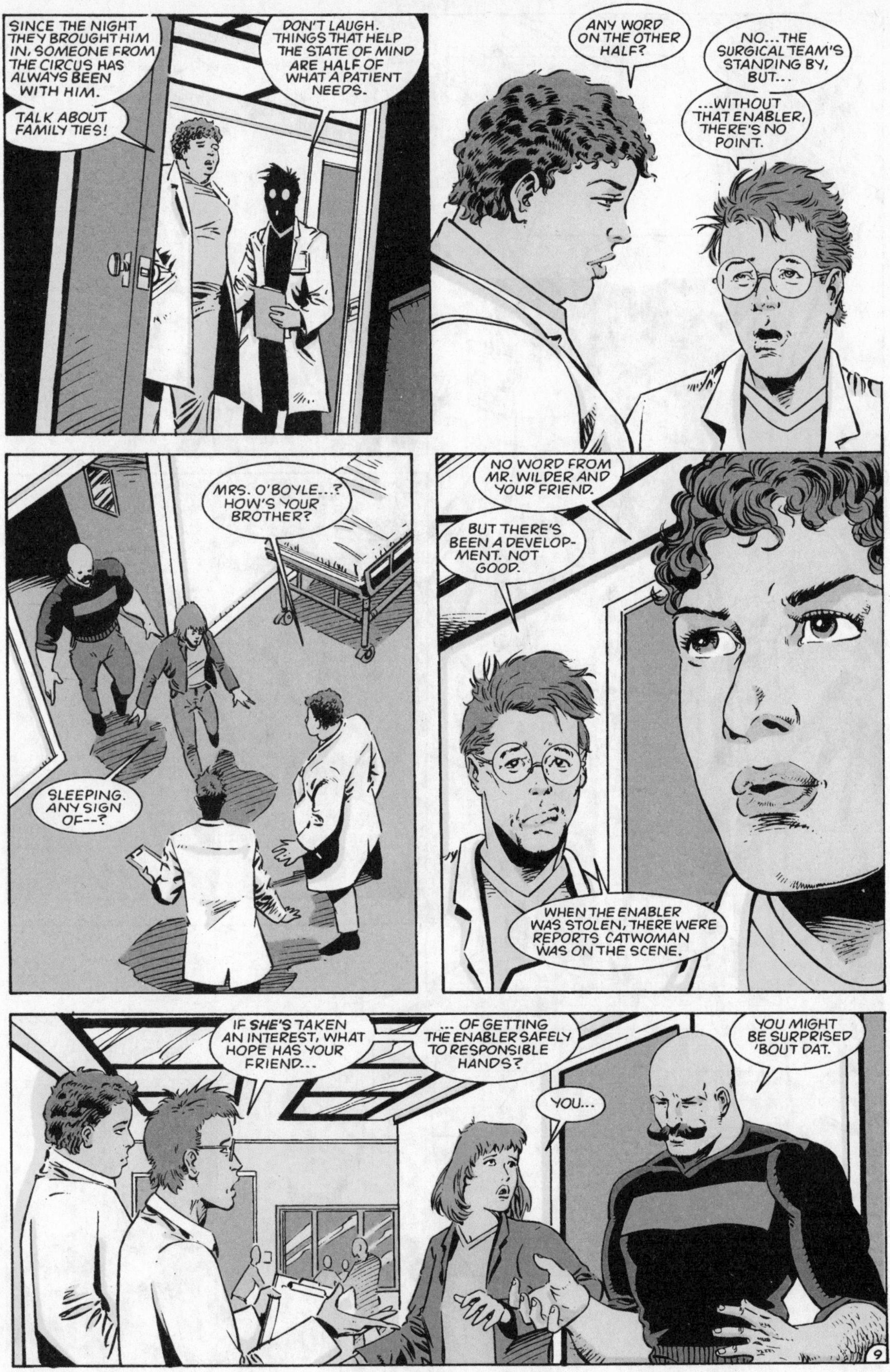
SINCE THE NIGHT THEY BROUGHT HIM IN, SOMEONE FROM THE CIRCUS HAS ALWAYS BEEN WITH HIM.
TALK ABOUT FAMILY TIES!
DON'T LAUGH. THINGS THAT HELP THE STATE OF MIND ARE HALF OF WHAT A PATIENT NEEDS.
ANY WORD ON THE OTHER HALF?
NO... THE SURGICAL TEAM'S STANDING BY, BUT...
...WITHOUT THAT ENABLER, THERE'S NO POINT.
MRS. O'BOYLE...? HOW'S YOUR BROTHER?
SLEEPING. ANY SIGN OF--?
NO WORD FROM MR. WILDER AND YOUR FRIEND.
BUT THERE'S BEEN A DEVELOPMENT. NOT GOOD.
WHEN THE ENABLER WAS STOLEN, THERE WERE REPORTS CATWOMAN WAS ON THE SCENE.
IF SHE'S TAKEN AN INTEREST, WHAT HOPE HAS YOUR FRIEND...
... OF GETTING THE ENABLER SAFELY TO RESPONSIBLE HANDS?
YOU...
YOU MIGHT BE SURPRISED 'BOUT DAT.
9

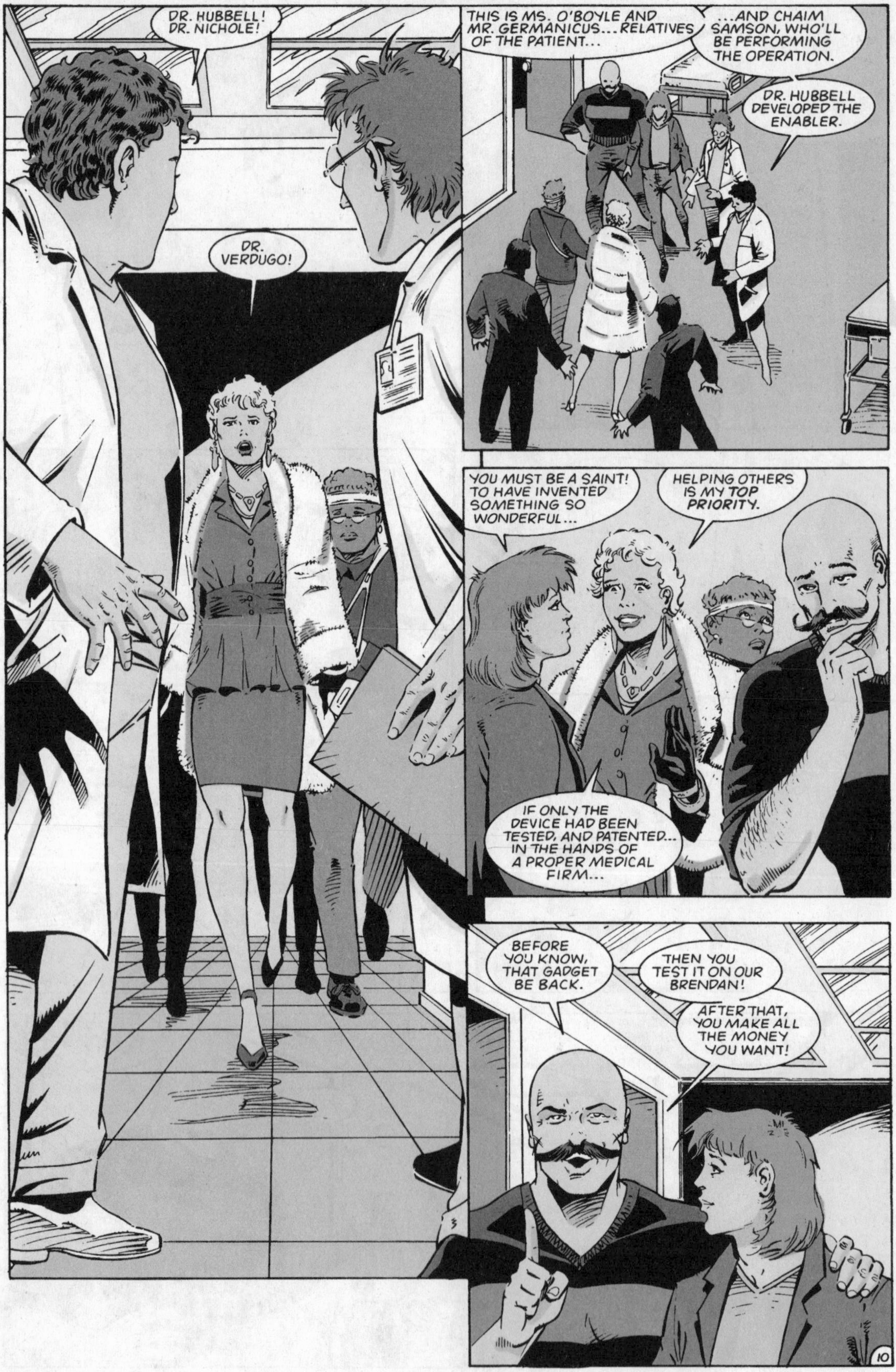
DR. HUBBELL! DR. NICHOLE!
DR. VERDUGO!
THIS IS MS. O'BOYLE AND MR. GERMANICUS... RELATIVES OF THE PATIENT...
...AND CHAIM SAMSON, WHO'LL BE PERFORMING THE OPERATION.
DR. HUBBELL DEVELOPED THE ENABLER.
YOU MUST BE A SAINT! TO HAVE INVENTED SOMETHING SO WONDERFUL...
HELPING OTHERS IS MY TOP PRIORITY.
IF ONLY THE DEVICE HAD BEEN TESTED, AND PATENTED... IN THE HANDS OF A PROPER MEDICAL FIRM...
BEFORE YOU KNOW, THAT GADGET BE BACK.
THEN YOU TEST IT ON OUR BRENDAN!
AFTER THAT, YOU MAKE ALL THE MONEY YOU WANT!
10

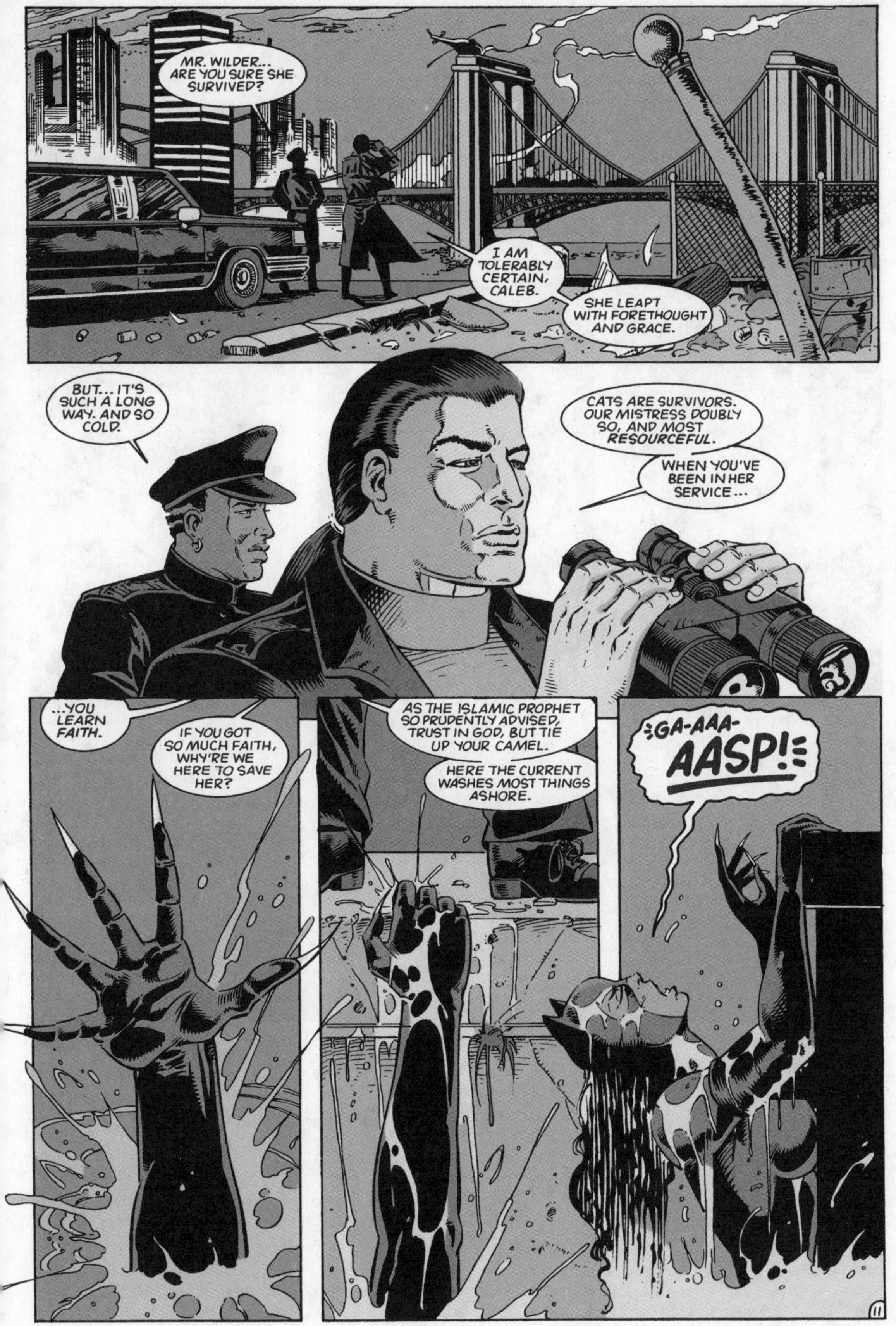
MR. WILDER... ARE YOU SURE SHE SURVIVED?
I AM TOLERABLY CERTAIN, CALEB.
SHE LEAPT WITH FORETHOUGHT AND GRACE.
BUT... IT'S SUCH A LONG WAY. AND SO COLD.
CATS ARE SURVIVORS. OUR MISTRESS DOUBLY SO, AND MOST RESOURCEFUL.
WHEN YOU'VE BEEN IN HER SERVICE...
...YOU LEARN FAITH.
IF YOU GOT SO MUCH FAITH, WHY'RE WE HERE TO SAVE HER?
AS THE ISLAMIC PROPHET SO PRUDENTLY ADVISED, TRUST IN GOD, BUT TIE UP YOUR CAMEL.
HERE THE CURRENT WASHES MOST THINGS ASHORE.
GA-AAA-AASP!
11

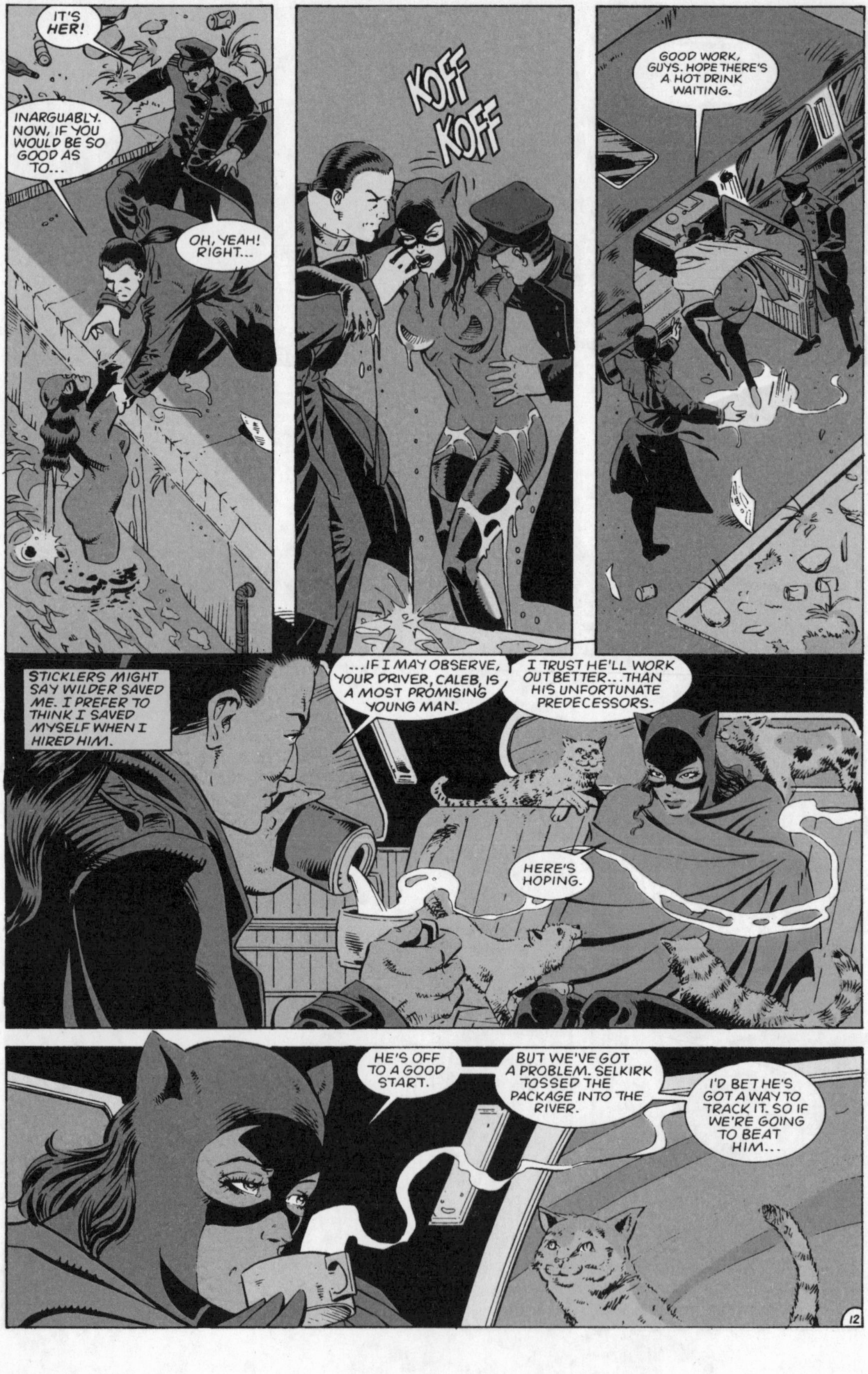
IT'S HER!
INARGUABLY. NOW, IF YOU WOULD BE SO GOOD AS TO...
OH, YEAH! RIGHT...
KOFF KOFF
GOOD WORK, GUYS. HOPE THERE'S A HOT DRINK WAITING.
STICKLERS MIGHT SAY WILDER SAVED ME. I PREFER TO THINK I SAVED MYSELF WHEN I HIRED HIM.
...IF I MAY OBSERVE, YOUR DRIVER, CALEB, IS A MOST PROMISING YOUNG MAN.
I TRUST HE'LL WORK OUT BETTER... THAN HIS UNFORTUNATE PREDECESSORS.
HERE'S HOPING.
HE'S OFF TO A GOOD START.
BUT WE'VE GOT A PROBLEM. SELKIRK TOSSED THE PACKAGE INTO THE RIVER.
I'D BET HE'S GOT A WAY TO TRACK IT. SO IF WE'RE GOING TO BEAT HIM...
12

"...WE'LL HAVE TO ACT FAST."

...BE GOING WITH YOU, TO SHOW YOU WHERE TO LOOK.

ANYTHING YOU SAY.

I LIKE A GIRL WHO PACKS HER OWN WET-SUIT.

NIXY NAIAD
MARINE SALVAGE

RUPERT AND JEREMY ARE OLD FRIENDS, NICE KIDS WITH A LITTLE STREAK OF LARCENY.

I BOUGHT THEM THEIR BOAT, SO WHEN I SAY JUMP, THEY ASK, "HOW HIGH?"

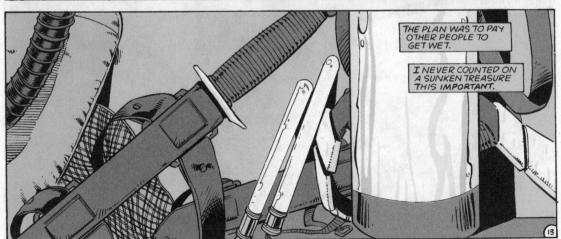

THE PLAN WAS TO PAY OTHER PEOPLE TO GET WET.

I NEVER COUNTED ON A SUNKEN TREASURE THIS IMPORTANT.

13

335

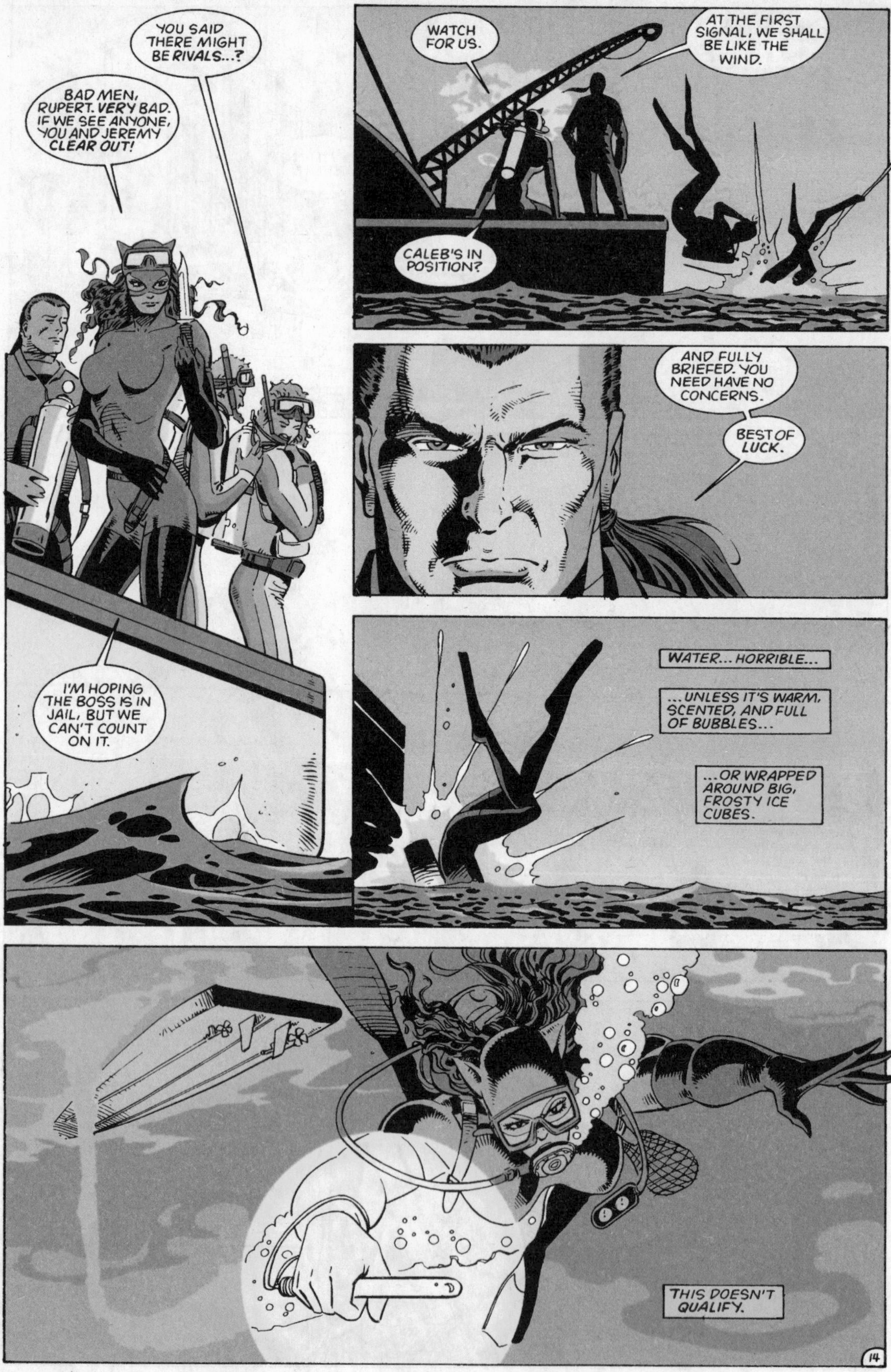

BAD MEN, RUPERT. VERY BAD. IF WE SEE ANYONE, YOU AND JEREMY CLEAR OUT!
YOU SAID THERE MIGHT BE RIVALS...?
I'M HOPING THE BOSS IS IN JAIL, BUT WE CAN'T COUNT ON IT.
WATCH FOR US.
AT THE FIRST SIGNAL, WE SHALL BE LIKE THE WIND.
CALEB'S IN POSITION?
AND FULLY BRIEFED. YOU NEED HAVE NO CONCERNS.
BEST OF LUCK.
WATER... HORRIBLE...
...UNLESS IT'S WARM, SCENTED, AND FULL OF BUBBLES...
...OR WRAPPED AROUND BIG, FROSTY ICE CUBES.
THIS DOESN'T QUALIFY.
14

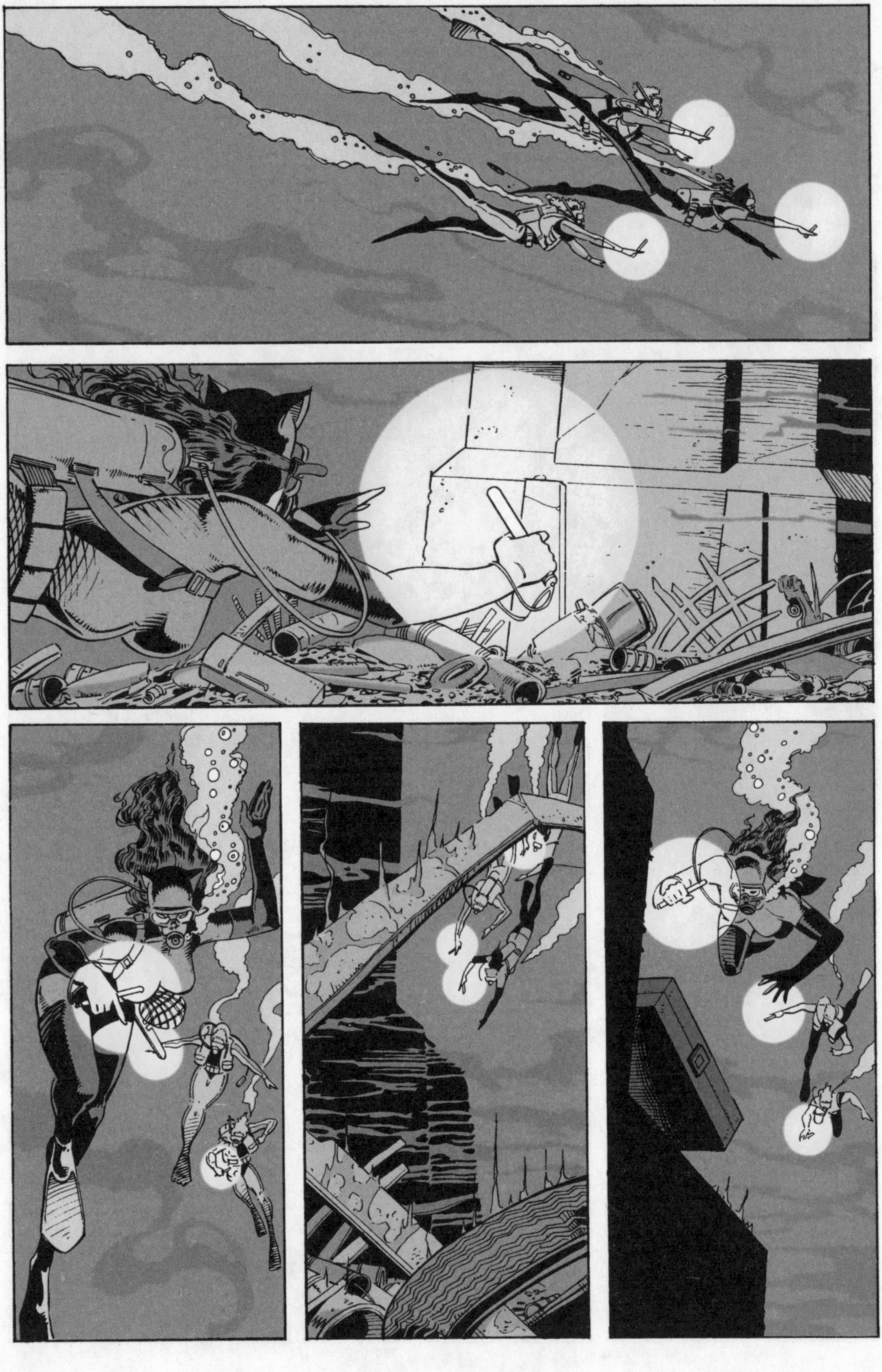

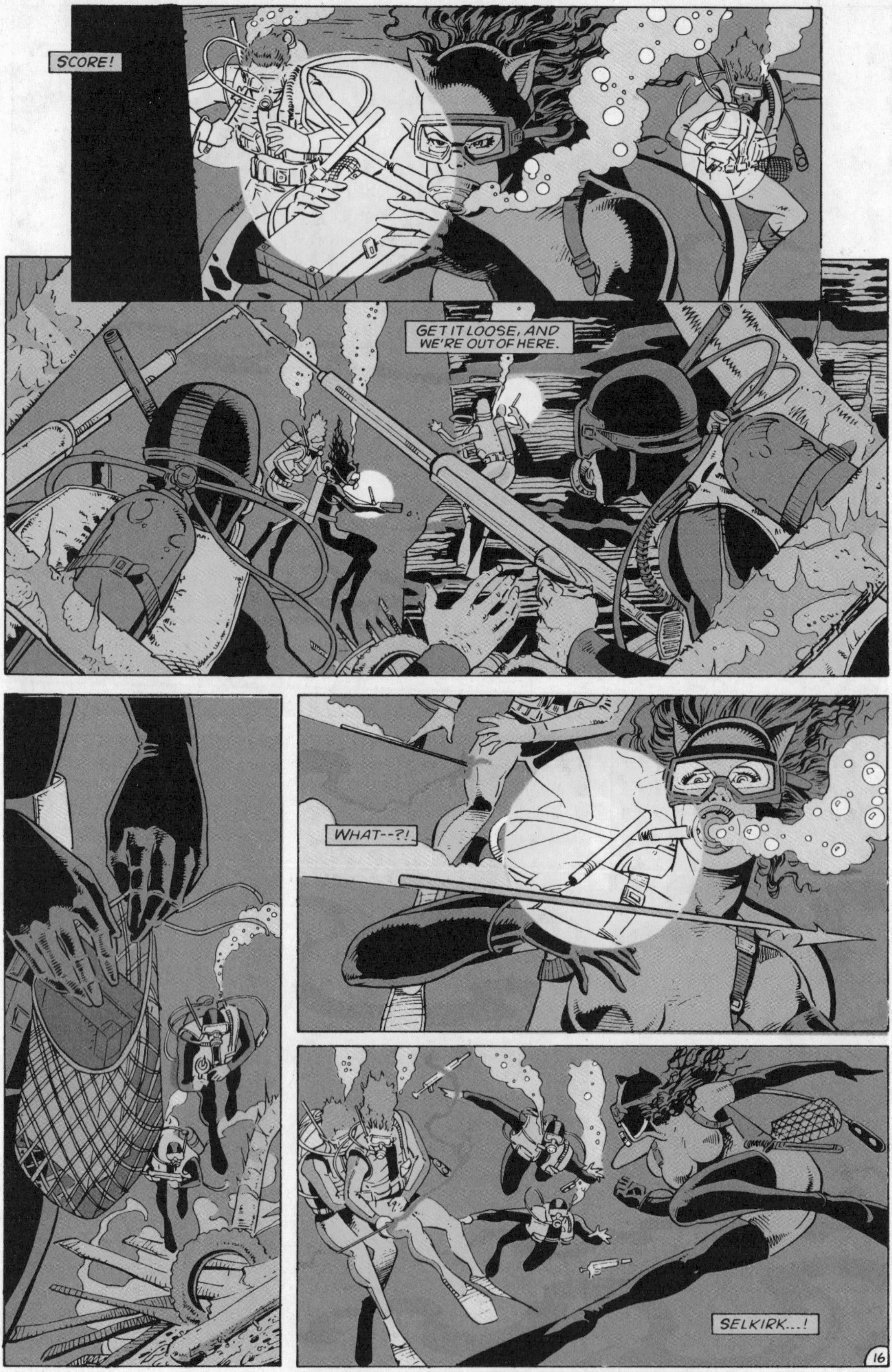
SCORE!
GET IT LOOSE, AND WE'RE OUT OF HERE.
WHAT--?!
SELKIRK...!
16

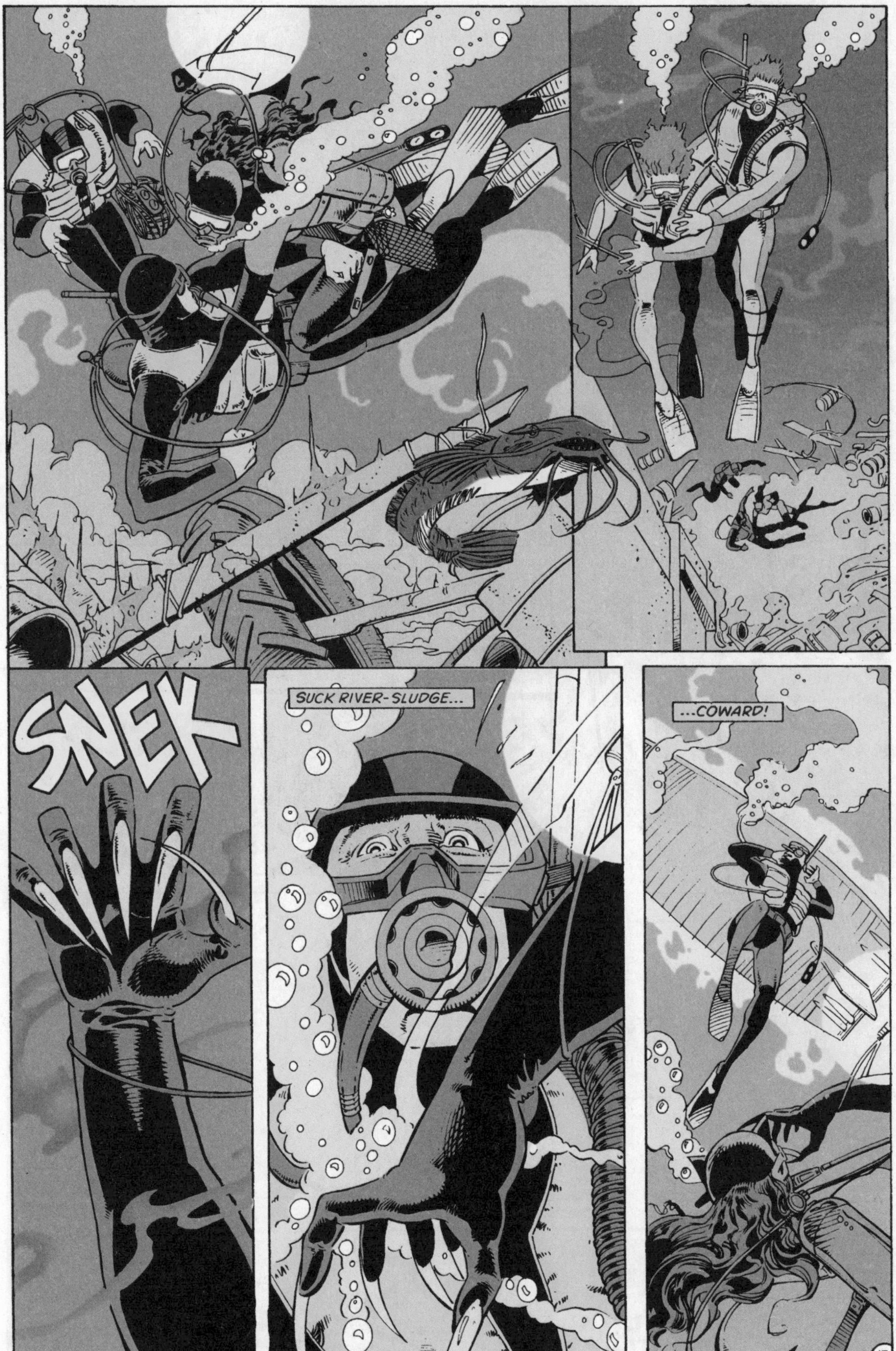
SNEK
SUCK RIVER-SLUDGE...
...COWARD!
17

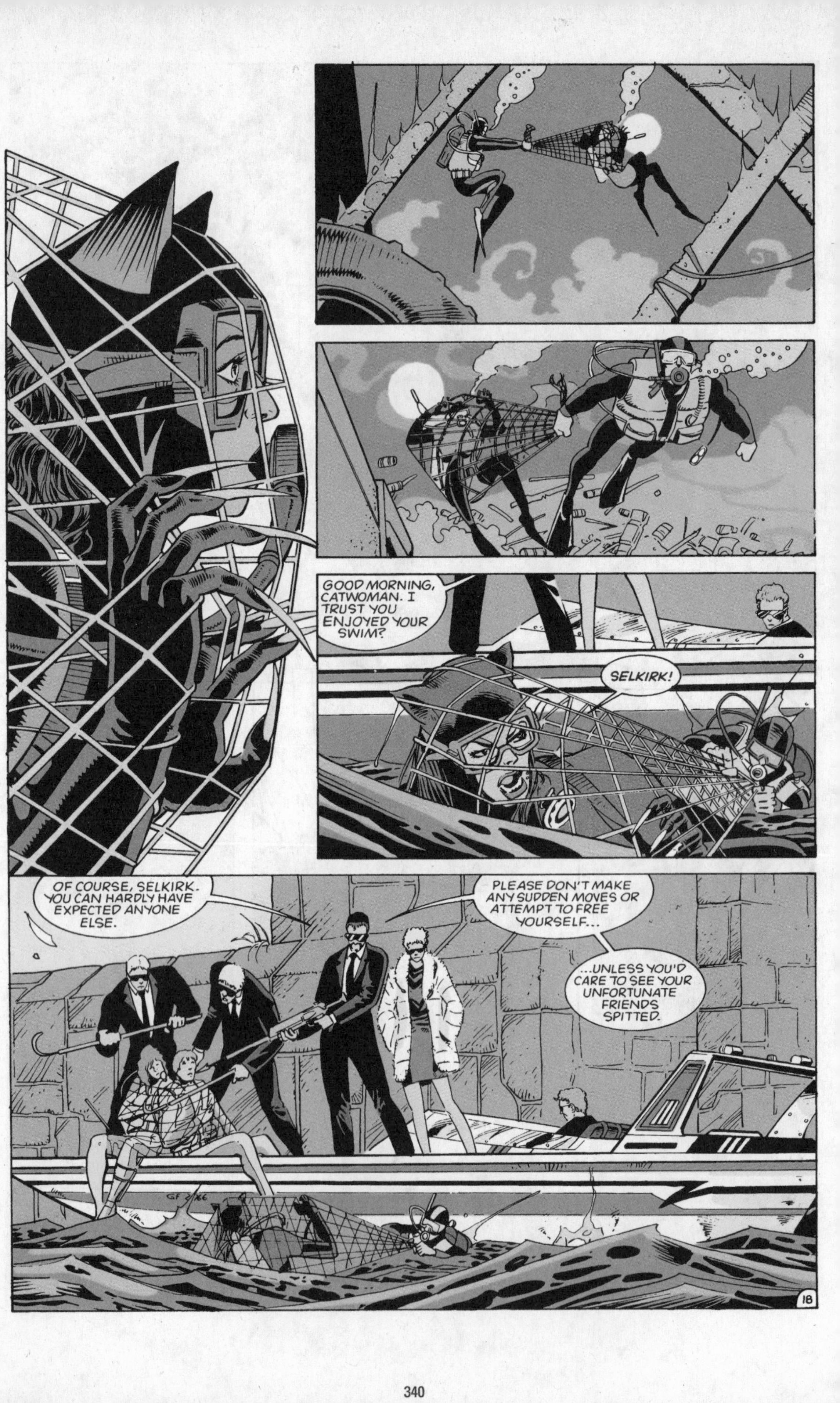

GOOD MORNING, CATWOMAN. I TRUST YOU ENJOYED YOUR SWIM?
SELKIRK!
OF COURSE, SELKIRK. YOU CAN HARDLY HAVE EXPECTED ANYONE ELSE.
PLEASE DON'T MAKE ANY SUDDEN MOVES OR ATTEMPT TO FREE YOURSELF...
...UNLESS YOU'D CARE TO SEE YOUR UNFORTUNATE FRIENDS SPITTED.
18

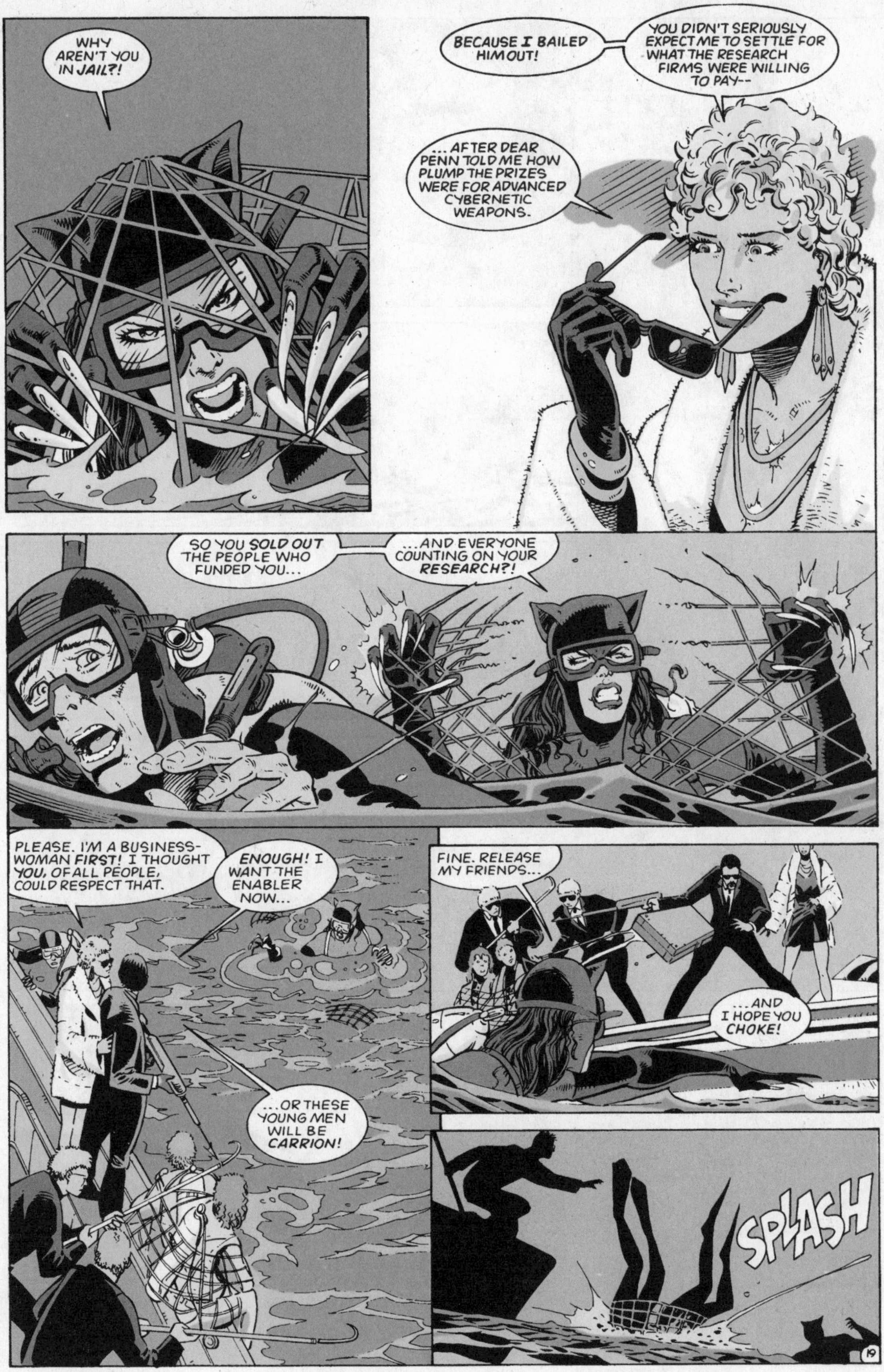
WHY AREN'T YOU IN JAIL?!
BECAUSE I BAILED HIM OUT!
YOU DIDN'T SERIOUSLY EXPECT ME TO SETTLE FOR WHAT THE RESEARCH FIRMS WERE WILLING TO PAY--
...AFTER DEAR PENN TOLD ME HOW PLUMP THE PRIZES WERE FOR ADVANCED CYBERNETIC WEAPONS.
SO YOU SOLD OUT THE PEOPLE WHO FUNDED YOU...
...AND EVERYONE COUNTING ON YOUR RESEARCH?!
PLEASE. I'M A BUSINESS-WOMAN FIRST! I THOUGHT YOU, OF ALL PEOPLE, COULD RESPECT THAT.
ENOUGH! I WANT THE ENABLER NOW...
...OR THESE YOUNG MEN WILL BE CARRION!
FINE. RELEASE MY FRIENDS...
...AND I HOPE YOU CHOKE!
SPLASH
19

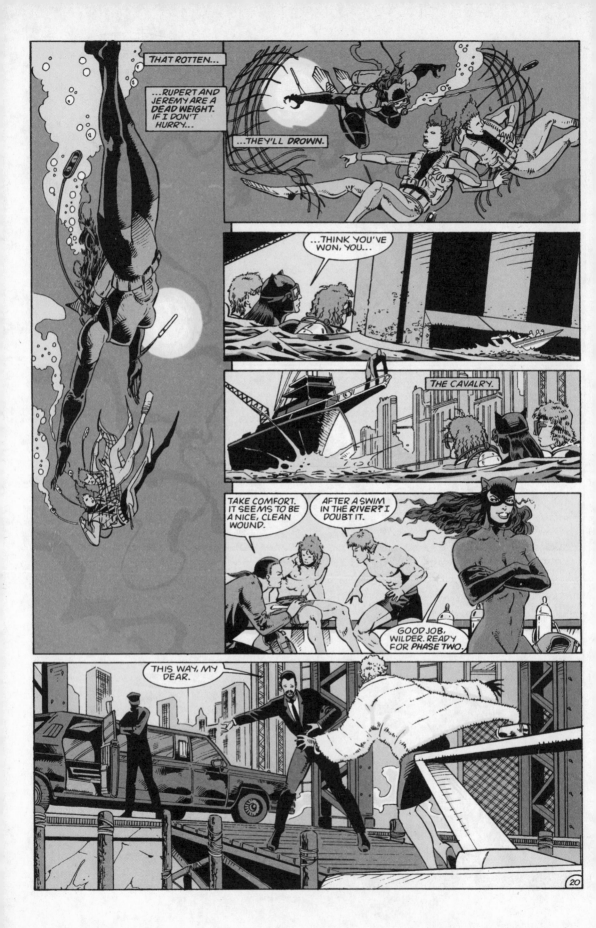

THAT ROTTEN...

...RUPERT AND JEREMY ARE A DEAD WEIGHT. IF I DON'T HURRY...

...THEY'LL DROWN.

...THINK YOU'VE WON, YOU...

THE CAVALRY.

TAKE COMFORT. IT SEEMS TO BE A NICE, CLEAN WOUND.

AFTER A SWIM IN THE RIVER? I DOUBT IT.

GOOD JOB, WILDER. READY FOR PHASE TWO.

THIS WAY, MY DEAR.

20

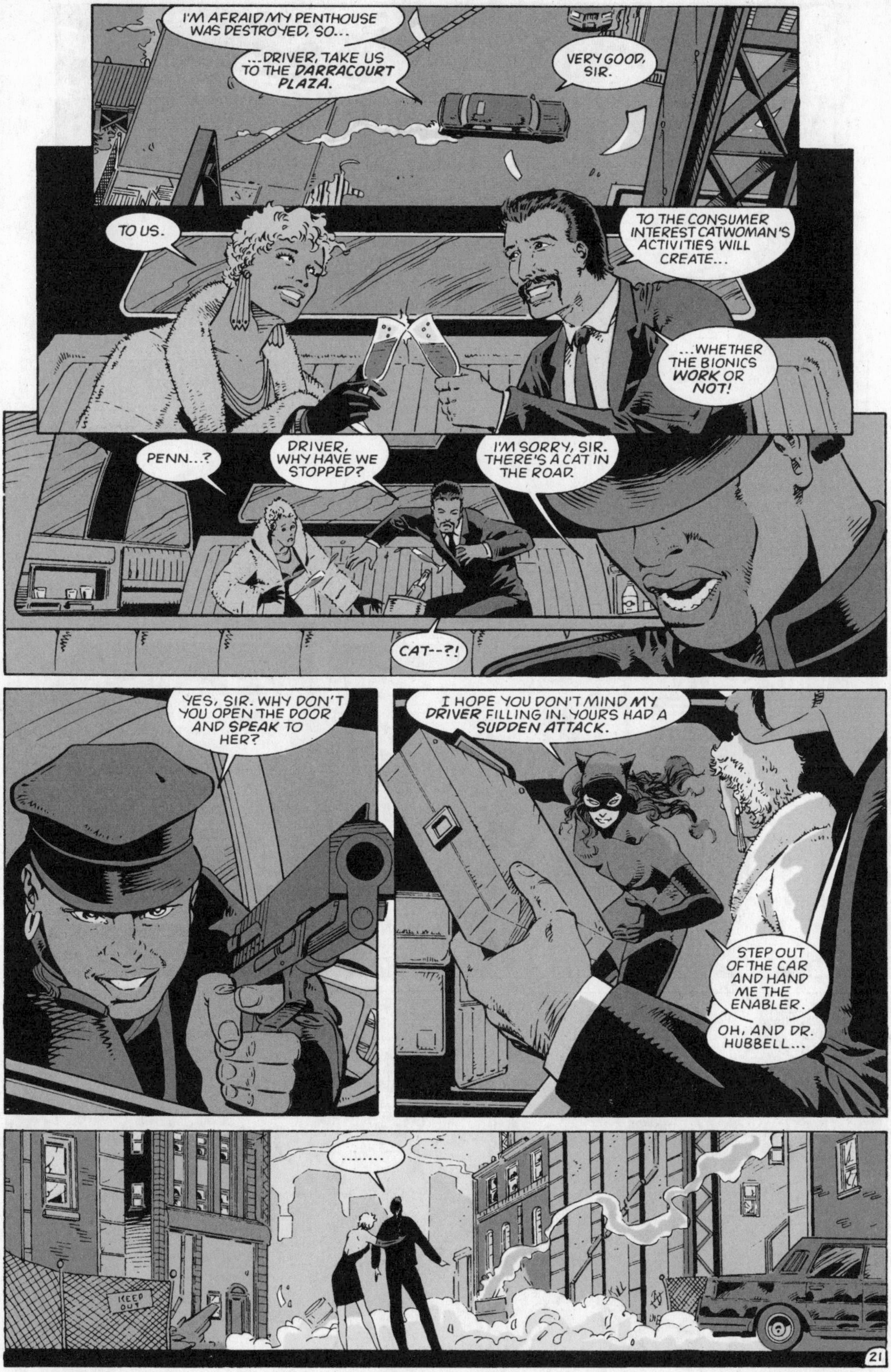

I'M AFRAID MY PENTHOUSE WAS DESTROYED, SO...
...DRIVER, TAKE US TO THE DARRACOURT PLAZA.
VERY GOOD, SIR.
TO US.
TO THE CONSUMER INTEREST CATWOMAN'S ACTIVITIES WILL CREATE...
...WHETHER THE BIONICS WORK OR NOT!
PENN...?
DRIVER, WHY HAVE WE STOPPED?
I'M SORRY, SIR. THERE'S A CAT IN THE ROAD.
CAT--?!
YES, SIR. WHY DON'T YOU OPEN THE DOOR AND SPEAK TO HER?
I HOPE YOU DON'T MIND MY DRIVER FILLING IN. YOURS HAD A SUDDEN ATTACK.
STEP OUT OF THE CAR AND HAND ME THE ENABLER.
OH, AND DR. HUBBELL...
....
KEEP OUT
21

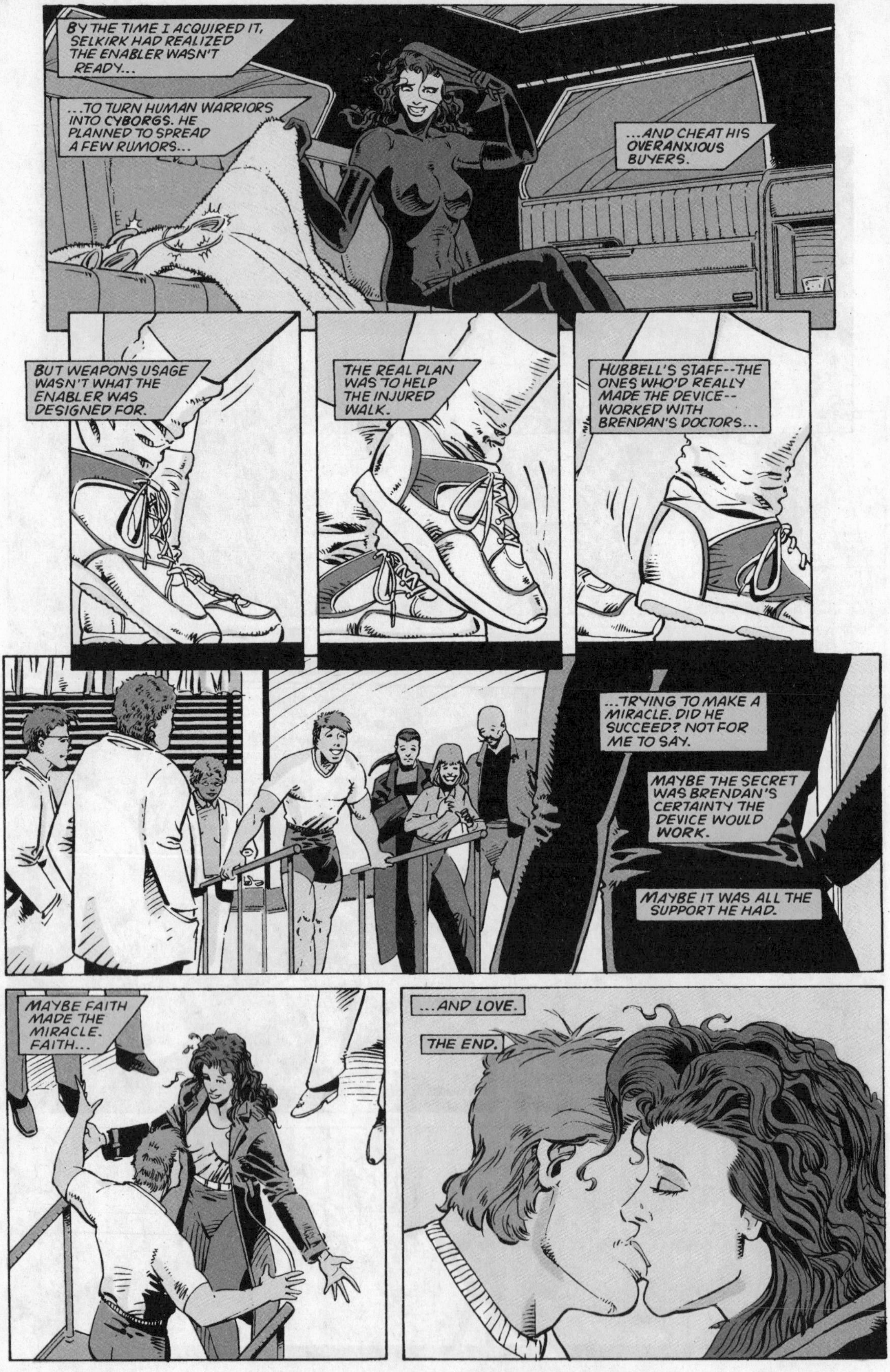
BY THE TIME I ACQUIRED IT, SELKIRK HAD REALIZED THE ENABLER WASN'T READY...
...TO TURN HUMAN WARRIORS INTO CYBORGS. HE PLANNED TO SPREAD A FEW RUMORS...
...AND CHEAT HIS OVERANXIOUS BUYERS.
BUT WEAPONS USAGE WASN'T WHAT THE ENABLER WAS DESIGNED FOR.
THE REAL PLAN WAS TO HELP THE INJURED WALK.
HUBBELL'S STAFF--THE ONES WHO'D REALLY MADE THE DEVICE--WORKED WITH BRENDAN'S DOCTORS...
...TRYING TO MAKE A MIRACLE. DID HE SUCCEED? NOT FOR ME TO SAY.
MAYBE THE SECRET WAS BRENDAN'S CERTAINTY THE DEVICE WOULD WORK.
MAYBE IT WAS ALL THE SUPPORT HE HAD.
MAYBE FAITH MADE THE MIRACLE. FAITH...
...AND LOVE.
THE END.

Cover art by **JOE QUESADA** and **KARL KESEL**

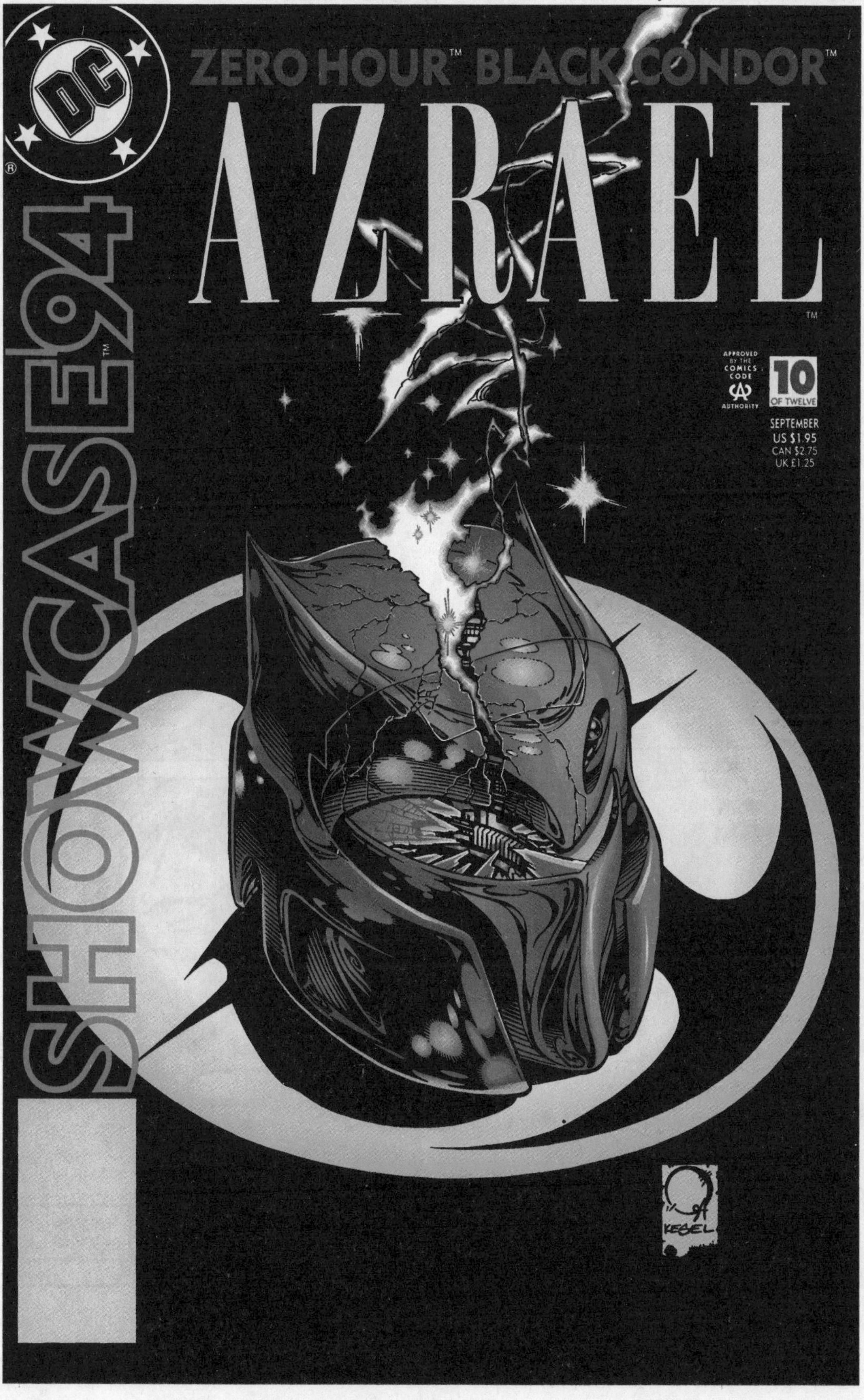
DC
SHOWCASE '94
ZERO HOUR BLACK CONDOR
AZRAEL
APPROVED BY THE COMICS CODE AUTHORITY
10 OF TWELVE
SEPTEMBER
US $1.95
CAN $2.75
UK £1.25
KESEL

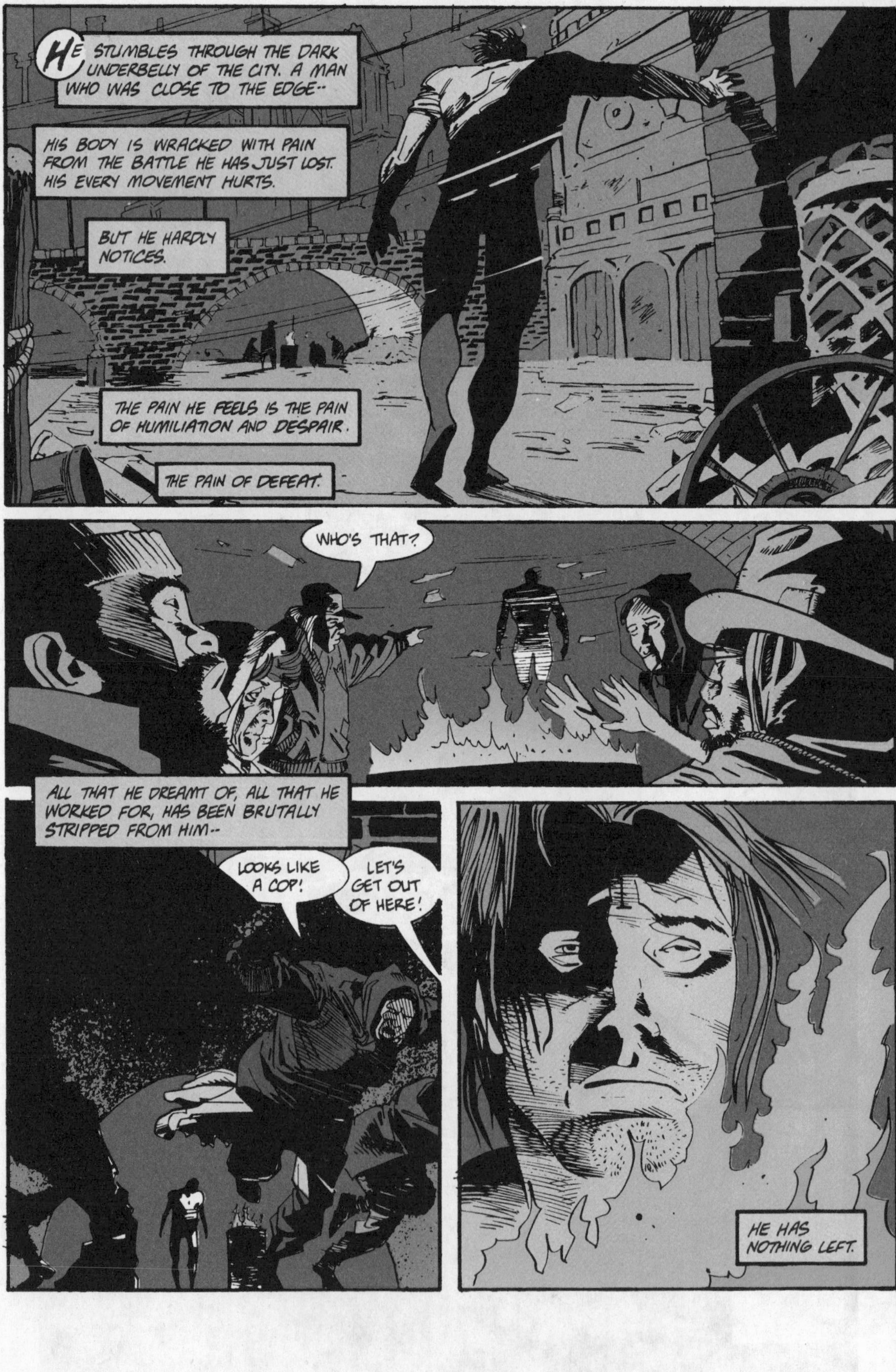
HE STUMBLES THROUGH THE DARK UNDERBELLY OF THE CITY. A MAN WHO WAS CLOSE TO THE EDGE--
HIS BODY IS WRACKED WITH PAIN FROM THE BATTLE HE HAS JUST LOST. HIS EVERY MOVEMENT HURTS.
BUT HE HARDLY NOTICES.
THE PAIN HE FEELS IS THE PAIN OF HUMILIATION AND DESPAIR.
THE PAIN OF DEFEAT.
WHO'S THAT?
ALL THAT HE DREAMT OF, ALL THAT HE WORKED FOR, HAS BEEN BRUTALLY STRIPPED FROM HIM--
LOOKS LIKE A COP!
LET'S GET OUT OF HERE!
HE HAS NOTHING LEFT.

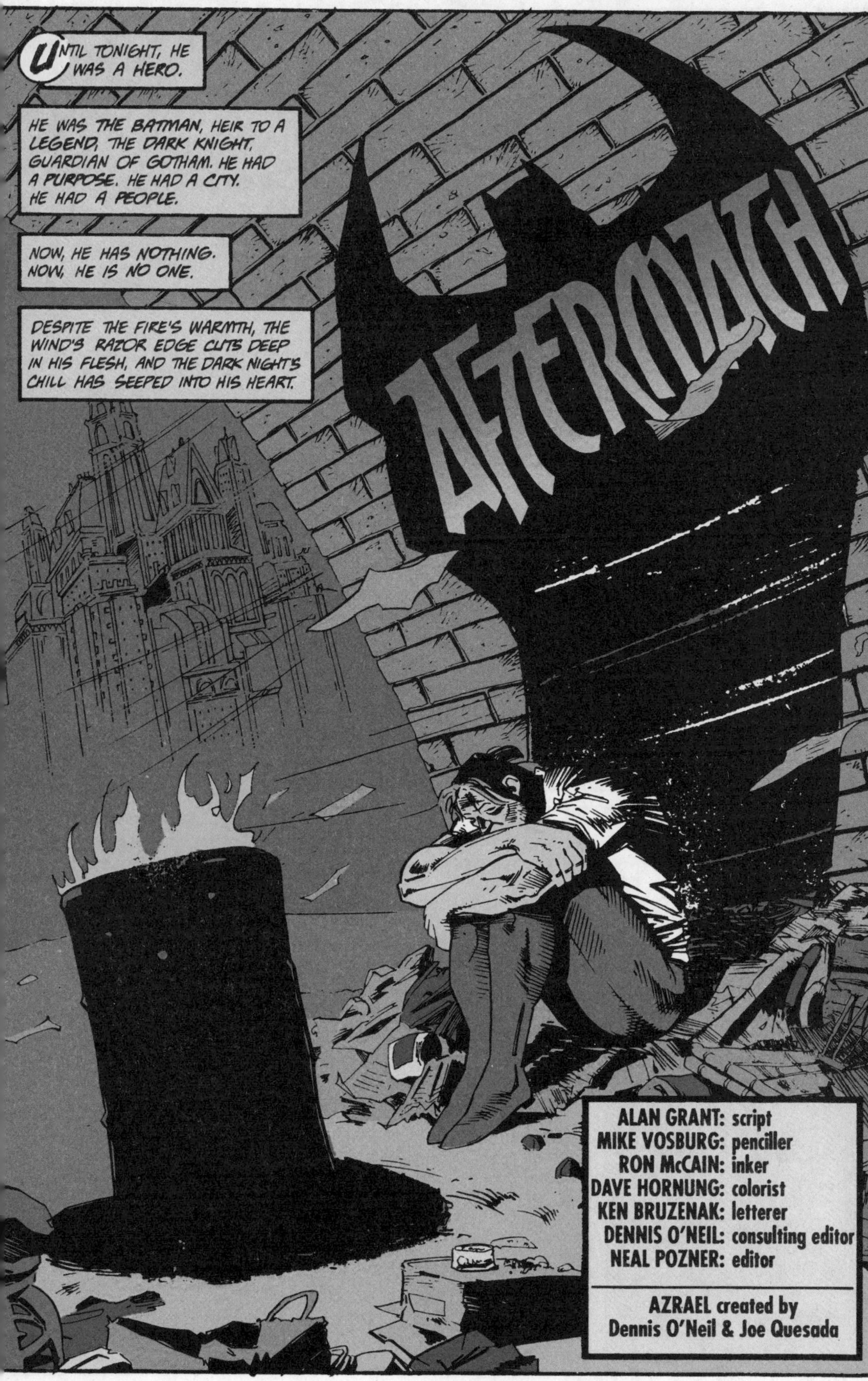
UNTIL TONIGHT, HE WAS A HERO.
HE WAS THE BATMAN, HEIR TO A LEGEND, THE DARK KNIGHT, GUARDIAN OF GOTHAM. HE HAD A PURPOSE. HE HAD A CITY. HE HAD A PEOPLE.
NOW, HE HAS NOTHING. NOW, HE IS NO ONE.
DESPITE THE FIRE'S WARMTH, THE WIND'S RAZOR EDGE CUTS DEEP IN HIS FLESH, AND THE DARK NIGHT'S CHILL HAS SEEPED INTO HIS HEART.
AFTERMATH
ALAN GRANT: script
MIKE VOSBURG: penciller
RON McCAIN: inker
DAVE HORNUNG: colorist
KEN BRUZENAK: letterer
DENNIS O'NEIL: consulting editor
NEAL POZNER: editor
AZRAEL created by Dennis O'Neil & Joe Quesada

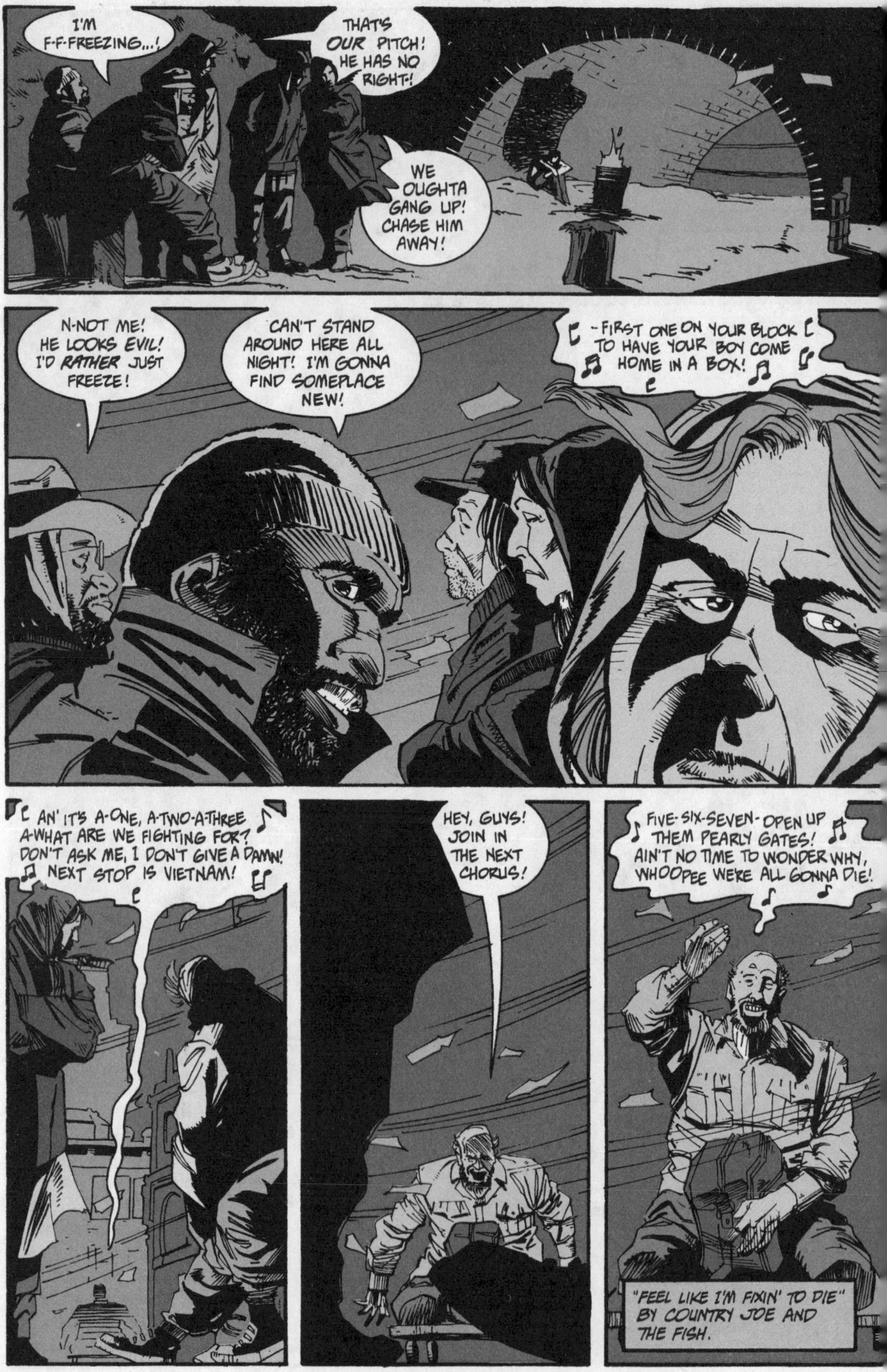
I'M F-F-FREEZING...!
THAT'S OUR PITCH! HE HAS NO RIGHT-!
WE OUGHTA GANG UP! CHASE HIM AWAY!
N-NOT ME! HE LOOKS EVIL! I'D RATHER JUST FREEZE!
CAN'T STAND AROUND HERE ALL NIGHT! I'M GONNA FIND SOMEPLACE NEW!
-FIRST ONE ON YOUR BLOCK TO HAVE YOUR BOY COME HOME IN A BOX!
AN' IT'S A-ONE, A-TWO-A-THREE A-WHAT ARE WE FIGHTING FOR? DON'T ASK ME, I DON'T GIVE A DAMN! NEXT STOP IS VIETNAM!
HEY, GUYS! JOIN IN THE NEXT CHORUS!
FIVE-SIX-SEVEN-OPEN UP THEM PEARLY GATES! AIN'T NO TIME TO WONDER WHY, WHOOPEE WE'RE ALL GONNA DIE!
"FEEL LIKE I'M FIXIN' TO DIE" BY COUNTRY JOE AND THE FISH.

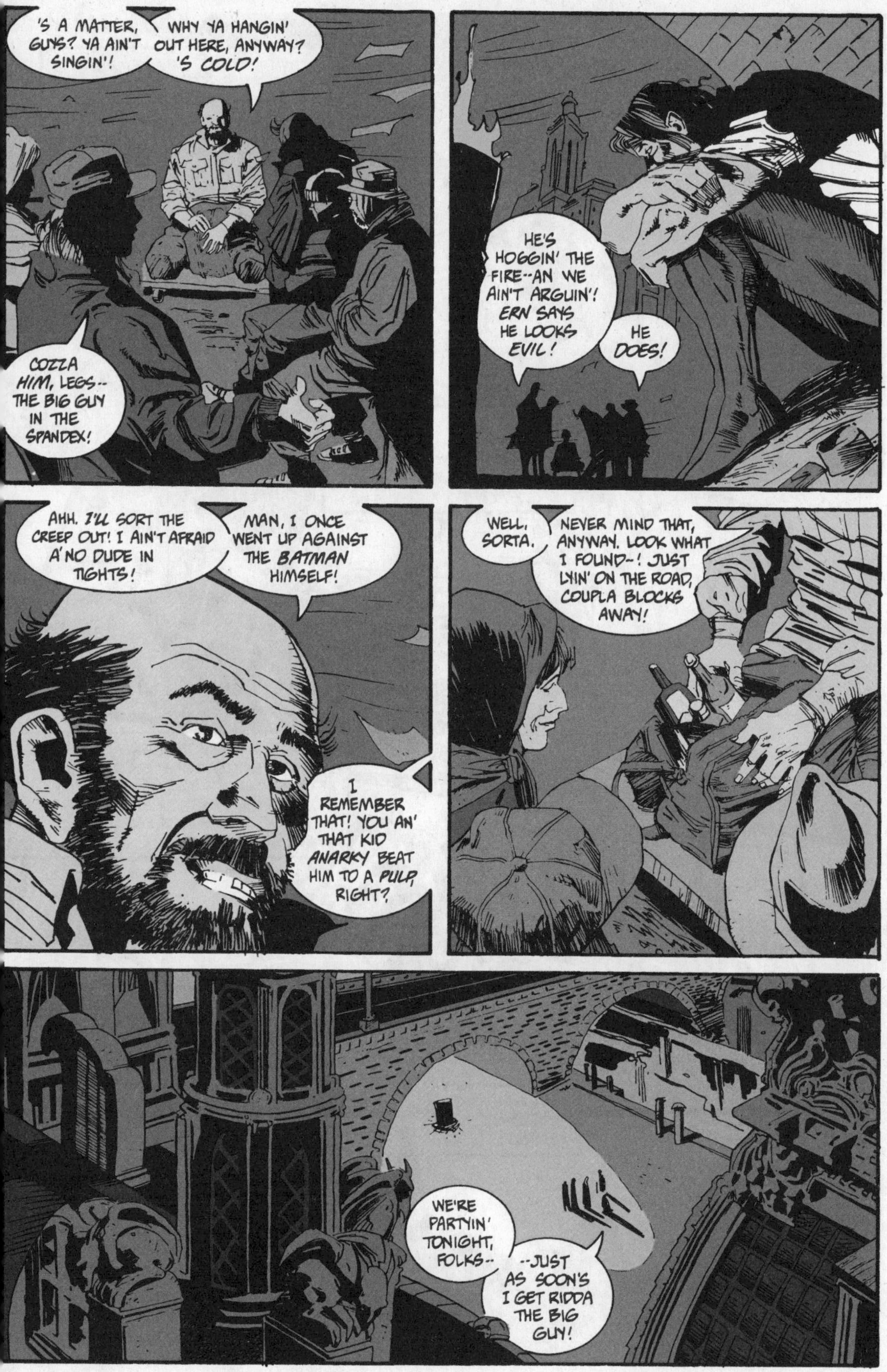
'S A MATTER, GUYS? YA AIN'T SINGIN'!
WHY YA HANGIN' OUT HERE, ANYWAY? 'S COLD!
COZZA HIM, LEGS-- THE BIG GUY IN THE SPANDEX!
HE'S HOGGIN' THE FIRE--AN WE AIN'T ARGUIN'! ERN SAYS HE LOOKS EVIL!
HE DOES!
AHH. I'LL SORT THE CREEP OUT! I AIN'T AFRAID A' NO DUDE IN TIGHTS!
MAN, I ONCE WENT UP AGAINST THE BATMAN HIMSELF!
I REMEMBER THAT! YOU AN' THAT KID ANARKY BEAT HIM TO A PULP, RIGHT?
WELL, SORTA.
NEVER MIND THAT, ANYWAY. LOOK WHAT I FOUND--! JUST LYIN' ON THE ROAD, COUPLA BLOCKS AWAY!
WE'RE PARTYIN' TONIGHT, FOLKS--
--JUST AS SOON'S I GET RIDDA THE BIG GUY!

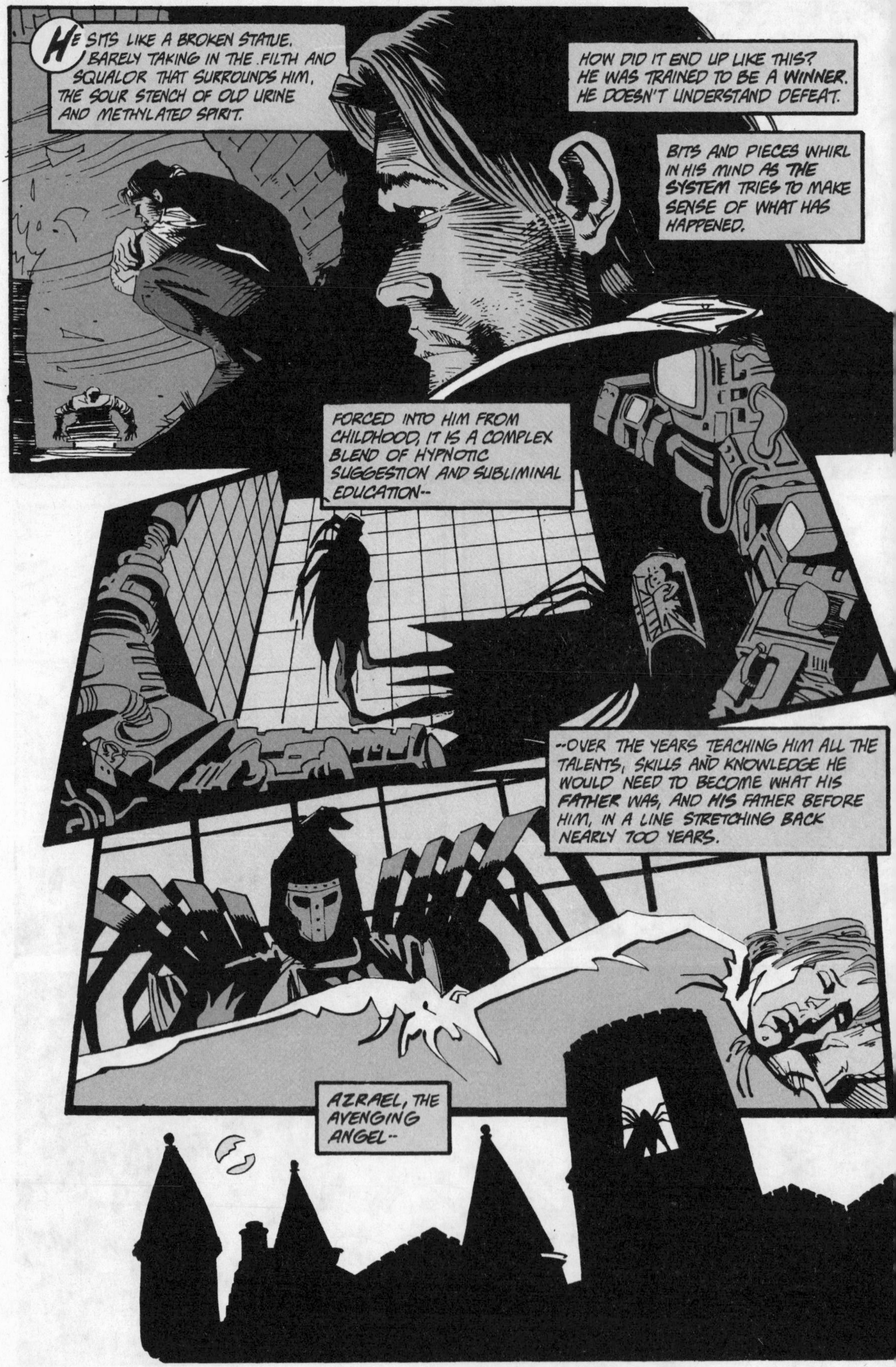
HE SITS LIKE A BROKEN STATUE, BARELY TAKING IN THE FILTH AND SQUALOR THAT SURROUNDS HIM, THE SOUR STENCH OF OLD URINE AND METHYLATED SPIRIT.
HOW DID IT END UP LIKE THIS? HE WAS TRAINED TO BE A WINNER. HE DOESN'T UNDERSTAND DEFEAT.
BITS AND PIECES WHIRL IN HIS MIND AS THE SYSTEM TRIES TO MAKE SENSE OF WHAT HAS HAPPENED.
FORCED INTO HIM FROM CHILDHOOD, IT IS A COMPLEX BLEND OF HYPNOTIC SUGGESTION AND SUBLIMINAL EDUCATION--
--OVER THE YEARS TEACHING HIM ALL THE TALENTS, SKILLS AND KNOWLEDGE HE WOULD NEED TO BECOME WHAT HIS FATHER WAS, AND HIS FATHER BEFORE HIM, IN A LINE STRETCHING BACK NEARLY 700 YEARS.
AZRAEL, THE AVENGING ANGEL--

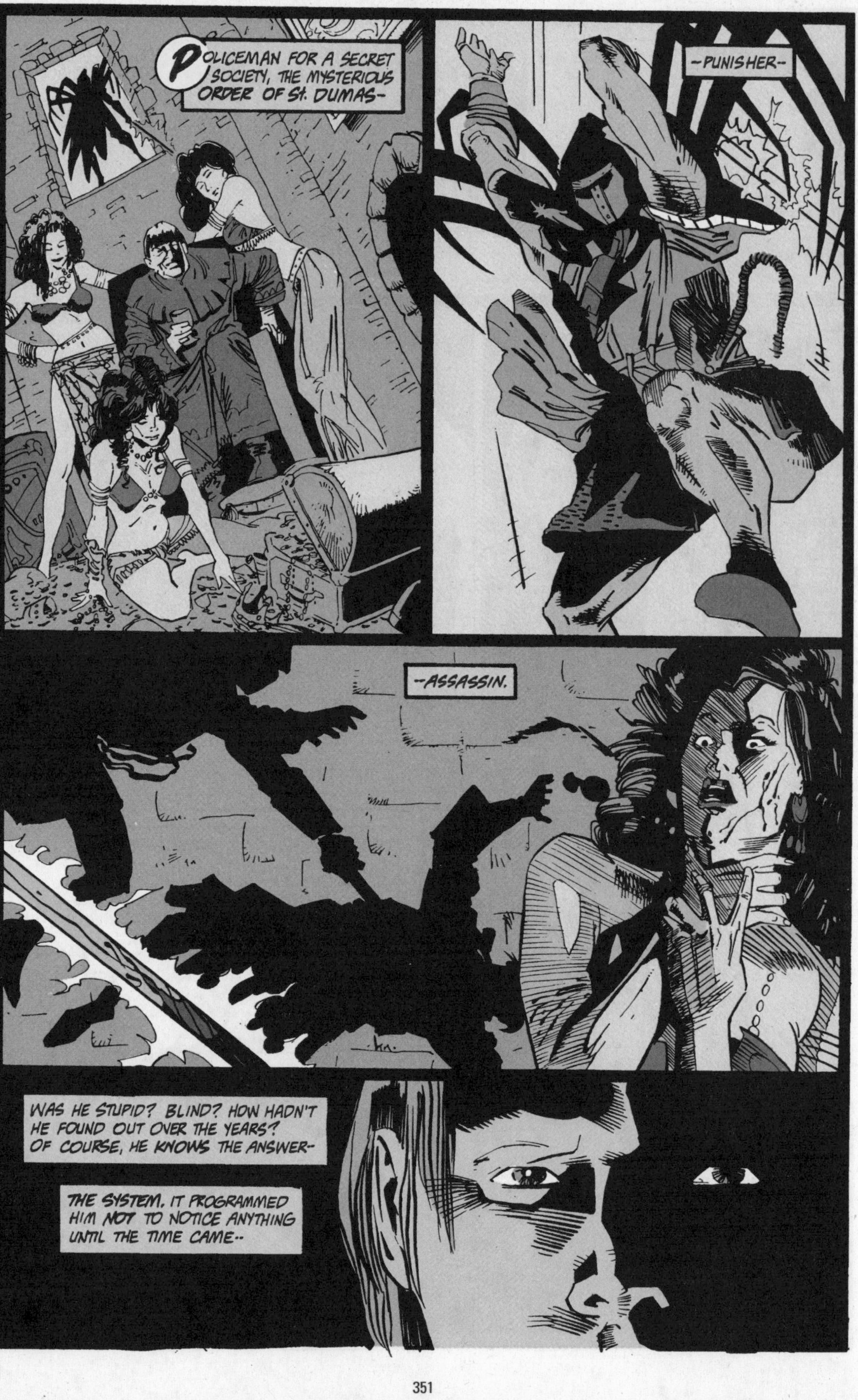
POLICEMAN FOR A SECRET SOCIETY, THE MYSTERIOUS ORDER OF St. DUMAS-
-PUNISHER-
--ASSASSIN.
WAS HE STUPID? BLIND? HOW HADN'T HE FOUND OUT OVER THE YEARS? OF COURSE, HE KNOWS THE ANSWER-
THE SYSTEM. IT PROGRAMMED HIM NOT TO NOTICE ANYTHING UNTIL THE TIME CAME--

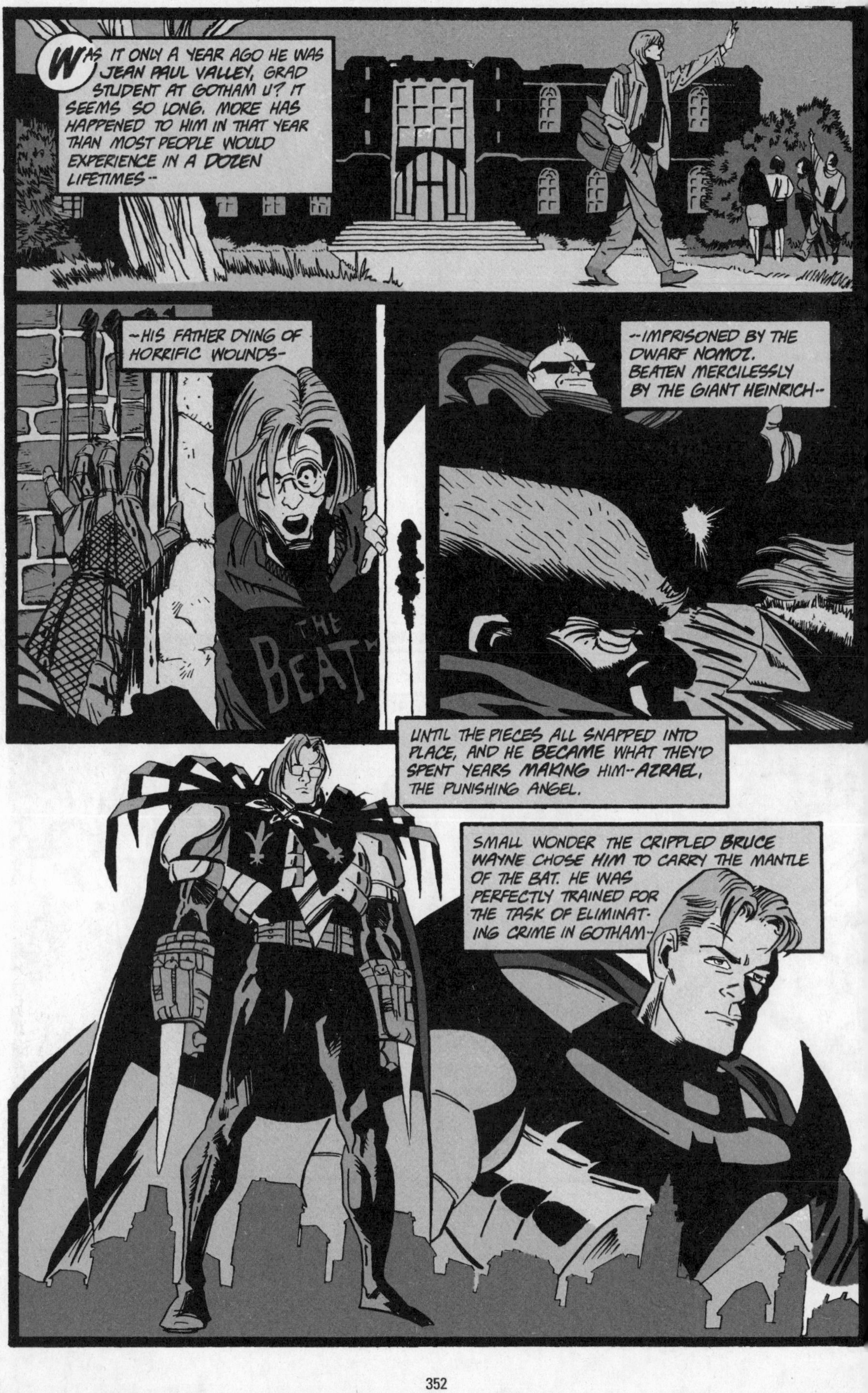
WAS IT ONLY A YEAR AGO HE WAS JEAN PAUL VALLEY, GRAD STUDENT AT GOTHAM U? IT SEEMS SO LONG. MORE HAS HAPPENED TO HIM IN THAT YEAR THAN MOST PEOPLE WOULD EXPERIENCE IN A DOZEN LIFETIMES--
--HIS FATHER DYING OF HORRIFIC WOUNDS--
THE BEAT
--IMPRISONED BY THE DWARF NOMOZ. BEATEN MERCILESSLY BY THE GIANT HEINRICH--
UNTIL THE PIECES ALL SNAPPED INTO PLACE, AND HE BECAME WHAT THEY'D SPENT YEARS MAKING HIM--AZRAEL, THE PUNISHING ANGEL.
SMALL WONDER THE CRIPPLED BRUCE WAYNE CHOSE HIM TO CARRY THE MANTLE OF THE BAT. HE WAS PERFECTLY TRAINED FOR THE TASK OF ELIMINATING CRIME IN GOTHAM--

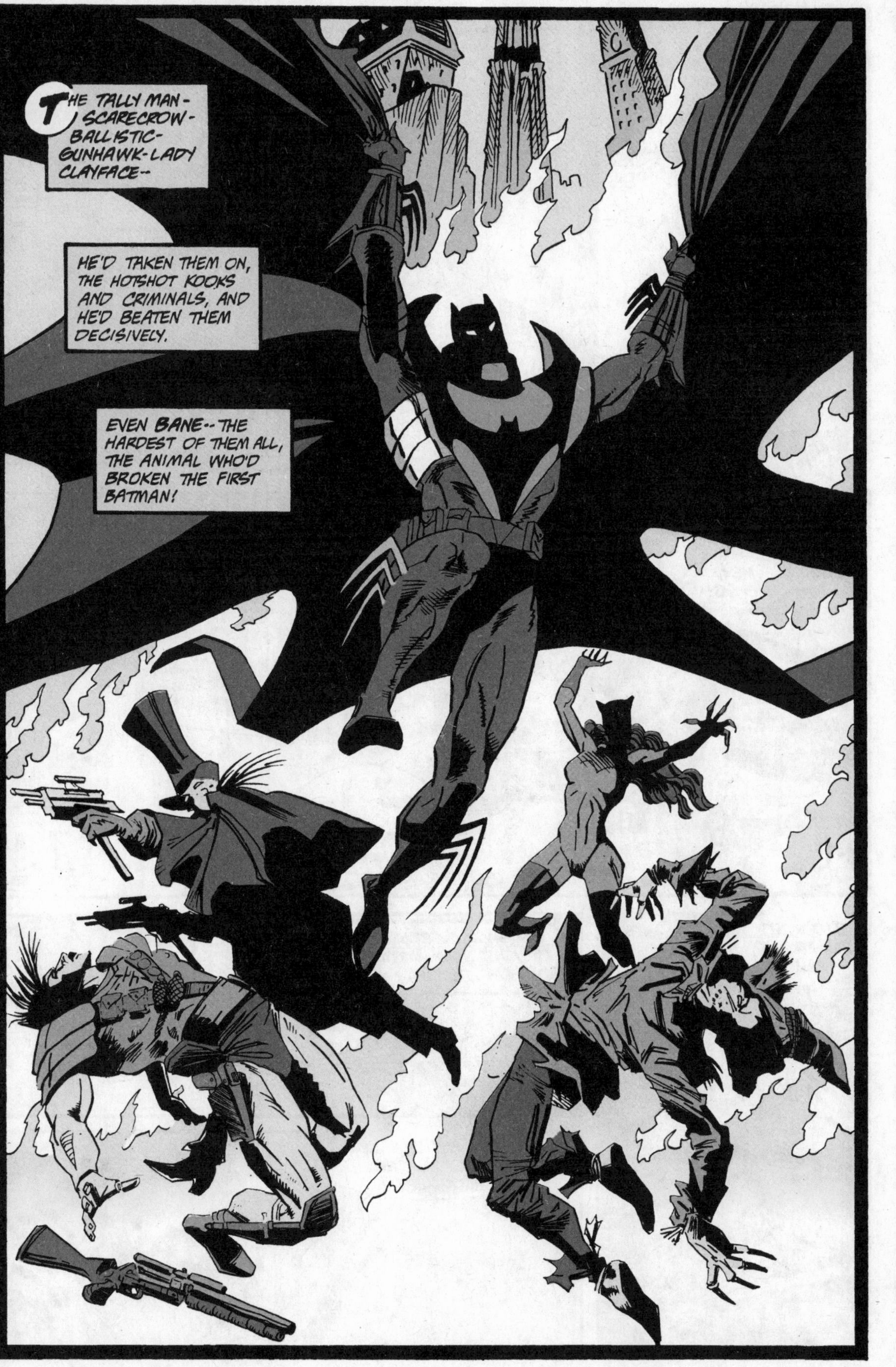
THE TALLY MAN-
SCARECROW-
BALLISTIC-
GUNHAWK-LADY
CLAYFACE--
HE'D TAKEN THEM ON, THE HOTSHOT KOOKS AND CRIMINALS, AND HE'D BEATEN THEM DECISIVELY.
EVEN BANE--THE HARDEST OF THEM ALL, THE ANIMAL WHO'D BROKEN THE FIRST BATMAN!

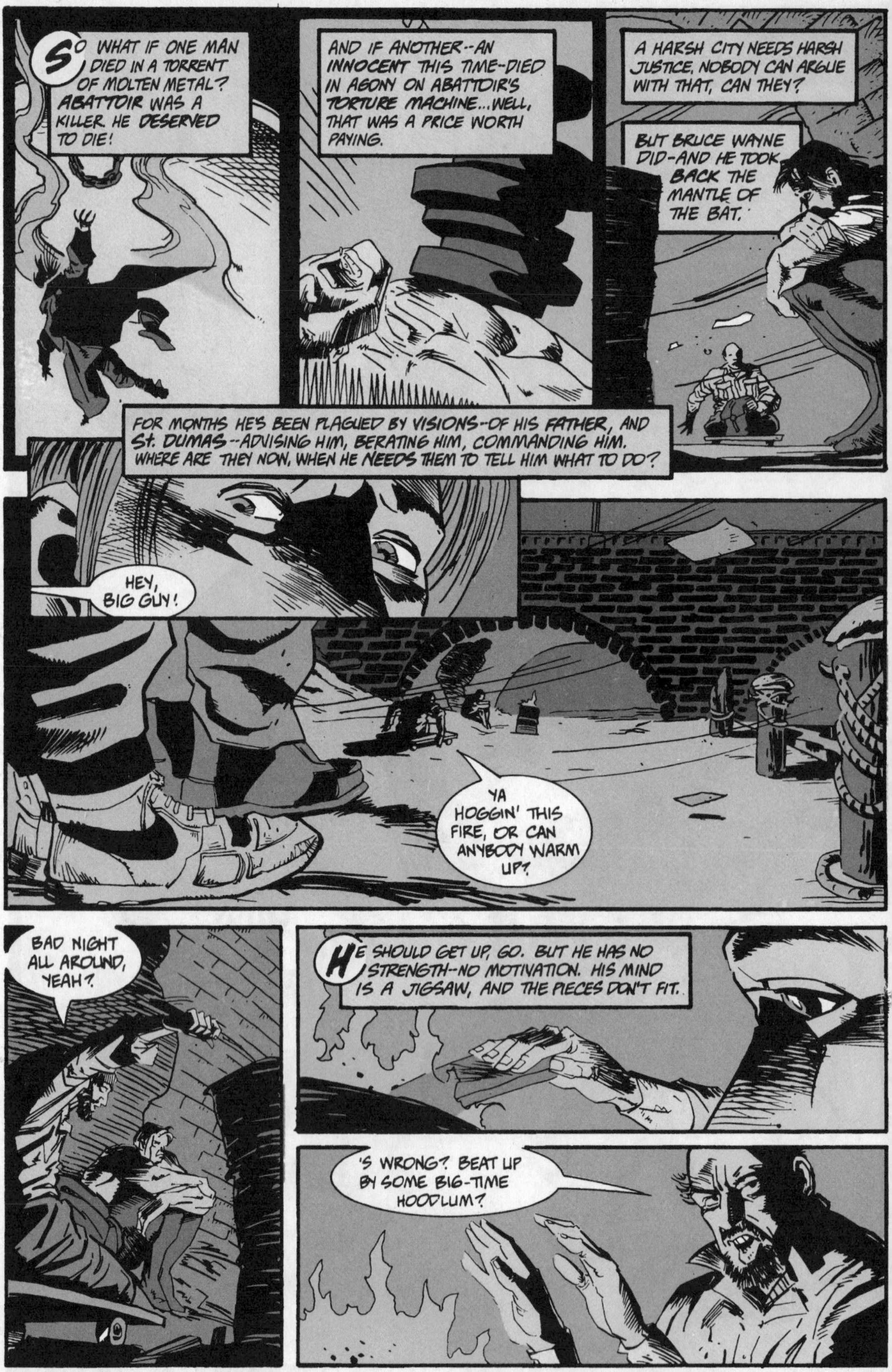
SO WHAT IF ONE MAN DIED IN A TORRENT OF MOLTEN METAL? ABATTOIR WAS A KILLER. HE DESERVED TO DIE!
AND IF ANOTHER--AN INNOCENT THIS TIME--DIED IN AGONY ON ABATTOIR'S TORTURE MACHINE...WELL, THAT WAS A PRICE WORTH PAYING.
A HARSH CITY NEEDS HARSH JUSTICE. NOBODY CAN ARGUE WITH THAT, CAN THEY?
BUT BRUCE WAYNE DID--AND HE TOOK BACK THE MANTLE OF THE BAT.
FOR MONTHS HE'S BEEN PLAGUED BY VISIONS--OF HIS FATHER, AND St. DUMAS--ADVISING HIM, BERATING HIM, COMMANDING HIM. WHERE ARE THEY NOW, WHEN HE NEEDS THEM TO TELL HIM WHAT TO DO?
HEY, BIG GUY!
YA HOGGIN' THIS FIRE, OR CAN ANYBODY WARM UP?
BAD NIGHT ALL AROUND, YEAH?
HE SHOULD GET UP, GO. BUT HE HAS NO STRENGTH--NO MOTIVATION. HIS MIND IS A JIGSAW, AND THE PIECES DON'T FIT.
'S WRONG? BEAT UP BY SOME BIG-TIME HOODLUM?

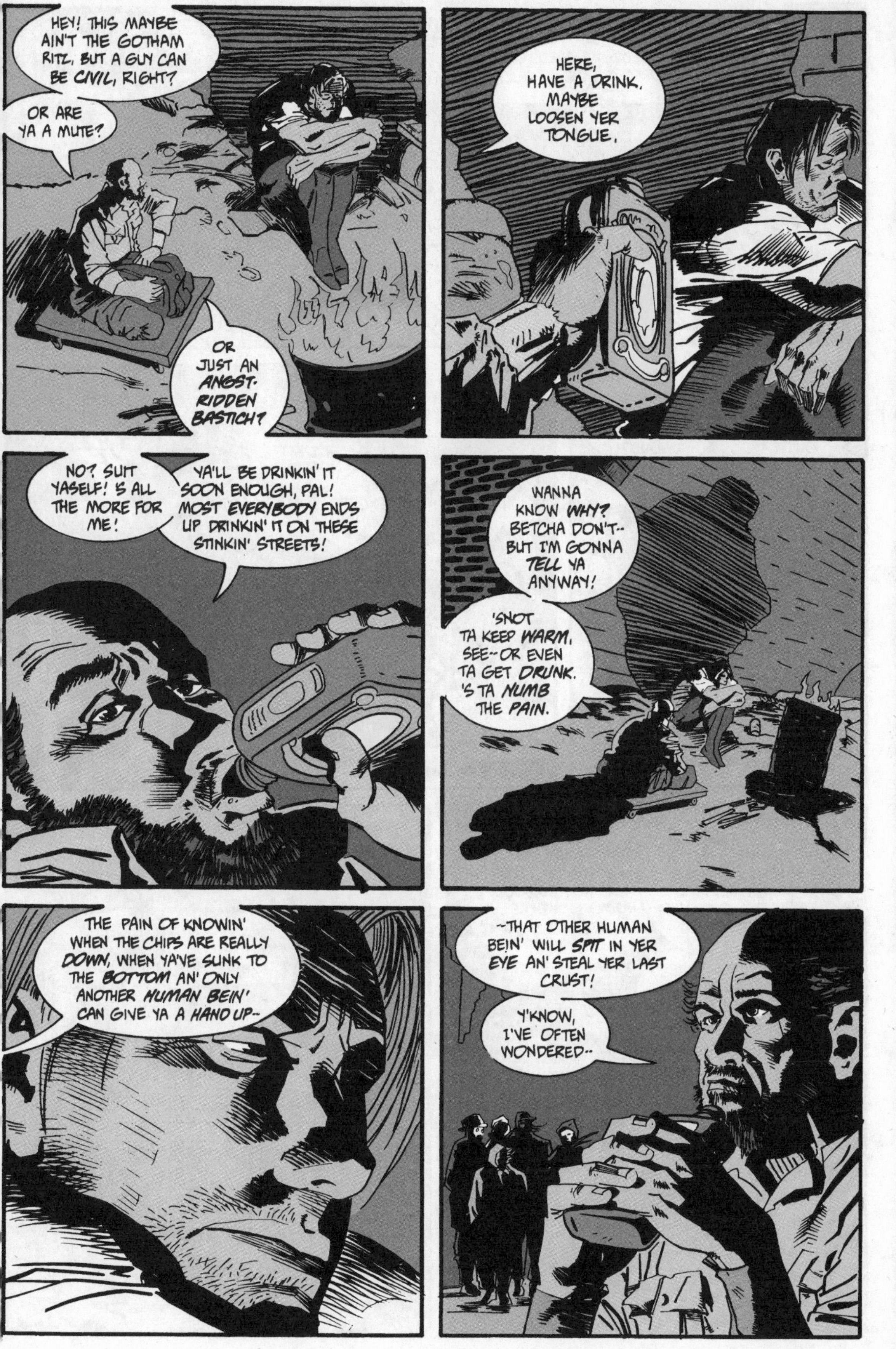
HEY! THIS MAYBE AIN'T THE GOTHAM RITZ, BUT A GUY CAN BE CIVIL, RIGHT?
OR ARE YA A MUTE?
OR JUST AN ANGST-RIDDEN BASTICH?
HERE, HAVE A DRINK. MAYBE LOOSEN YER TONGUE.
NO? SUIT YASELF! 'S ALL THE MORE FOR ME!
YA'LL BE DRINKIN' IT SOON ENOUGH, PAL! MOST EVERYBODY ENDS UP DRINKIN' IT ON THESE STINKIN' STREETS!
WANNA KNOW WHY? BETCHA DON'T-- BUT I'M GONNA TELL YA ANYWAY!
'SNOT TA KEEP WARM, SEE--OR EVEN TA GET DRUNK. 'S TA NUMB THE PAIN.
THE PAIN OF KNOWIN' WHEN THE CHIPS ARE REALLY DOWN, WHEN YA'VE SUNK TO THE BOTTOM AN' ONLY ANOTHER HUMAN BEIN' CAN GIVE YA A HAND UP--
--THAT OTHER HUMAN BEIN' WILL SPIT IN YER EYE AN' STEAL YER LAST CRUST!
Y'KNOW, I'VE OFTEN WONDERED--

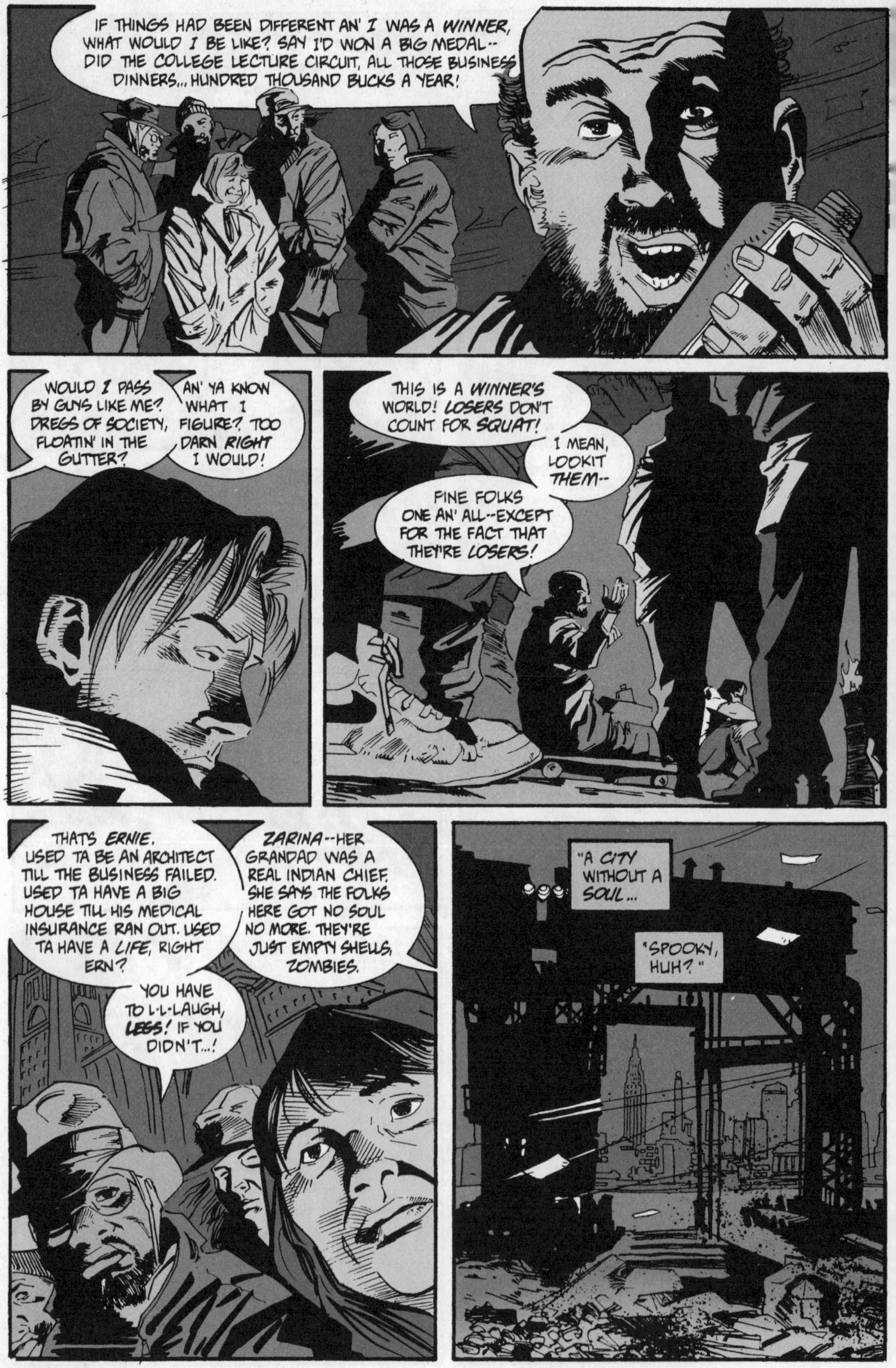
IF THINGS HAD BEEN DIFFERENT AN' I WAS A WINNER, WHAT WOULD I BE LIKE? SAY I'D WON A BIG MEDAL-- DID THE COLLEGE LECTURE CIRCUIT, ALL THOSE BUSINESS DINNERS... HUNDRED THOUSAND BUCKS A YEAR!
WOULD I PASS BY GUYS LIKE ME? DREGS OF SOCIETY, FLOATIN' IN THE GUTTER?
AN' YA KNOW WHAT I FIGURE? TOO DARN RIGHT I WOULD!
THIS IS A WINNER'S WORLD! LOSERS DON'T COUNT FOR SQUAT!
I MEAN, LOOKIT THEM--
FINE FOLKS ONE AN' ALL--EXCEPT FOR THE FACT THAT THEY'RE LOSERS!
THAT'S ERNIE. USED TA BE AN ARCHITECT TILL THE BUSINESS FAILED. USED TA HAVE A BIG HOUSE TILL HIS MEDICAL INSURANCE RAN OUT. USED TA HAVE A LIFE, RIGHT ERN?
YOU HAVE TO L-L-LAUGH, LESS! IF YOU DIDN'T...!
ZARINA--HER GRANDAD WAS A REAL INDIAN CHIEF. SHE SAYS THE FOLKS HERE GOT NO SOUL NO MORE. THEY'RE JUST EMPTY SHELLS, ZOMBIES.
"A CITY WITHOUT A SOUL...
"SPOOKY, HUH?"

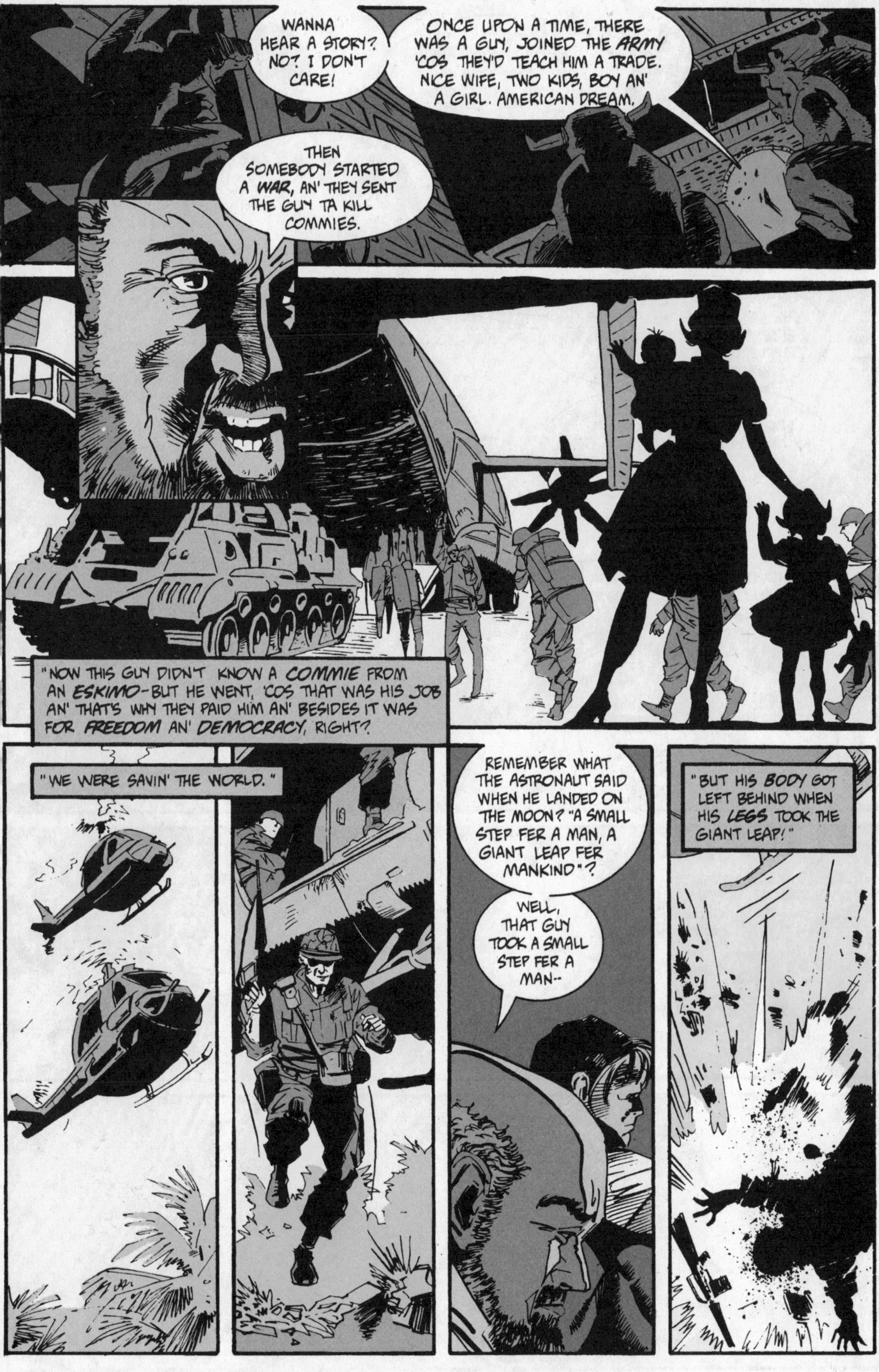
WANNA HEAR A STORY? NO? I DON'T CARE!
ONCE UPON A TIME, THERE WAS A GUY, JOINED THE ARMY 'COS THEY'D TEACH HIM A TRADE. NICE WIFE, TWO KIDS, BOY AN' A GIRL. AMERICAN DREAM.
THEN SOMEBODY STARTED A WAR, AN' THEY SENT THE GUY TA KILL COMMIES.
"NOW THIS GUY DIDN'T KNOW A COMMIE FROM AN ESKIMO--BUT HE WENT, 'COS THAT WAS HIS JOB AN' THAT'S WHY THEY PAID HIM AN' BESIDES IT WAS FOR FREEDOM AN' DEMOCRACY, RIGHT?
"WE WERE SAVIN' THE WORLD."
REMEMBER WHAT THE ASTRONAUT SAID WHEN HE LANDED ON THE MOON? "A SMALL STEP FER A MAN, A GIANT LEAP FER MANKIND"?
WELL, THAT GUY TOOK A SMALL STEP FER A MAN--
"BUT HIS BODY GOT LEFT BEHIND WHEN HIS LEGS TOOK THE GIANT LEAP!"

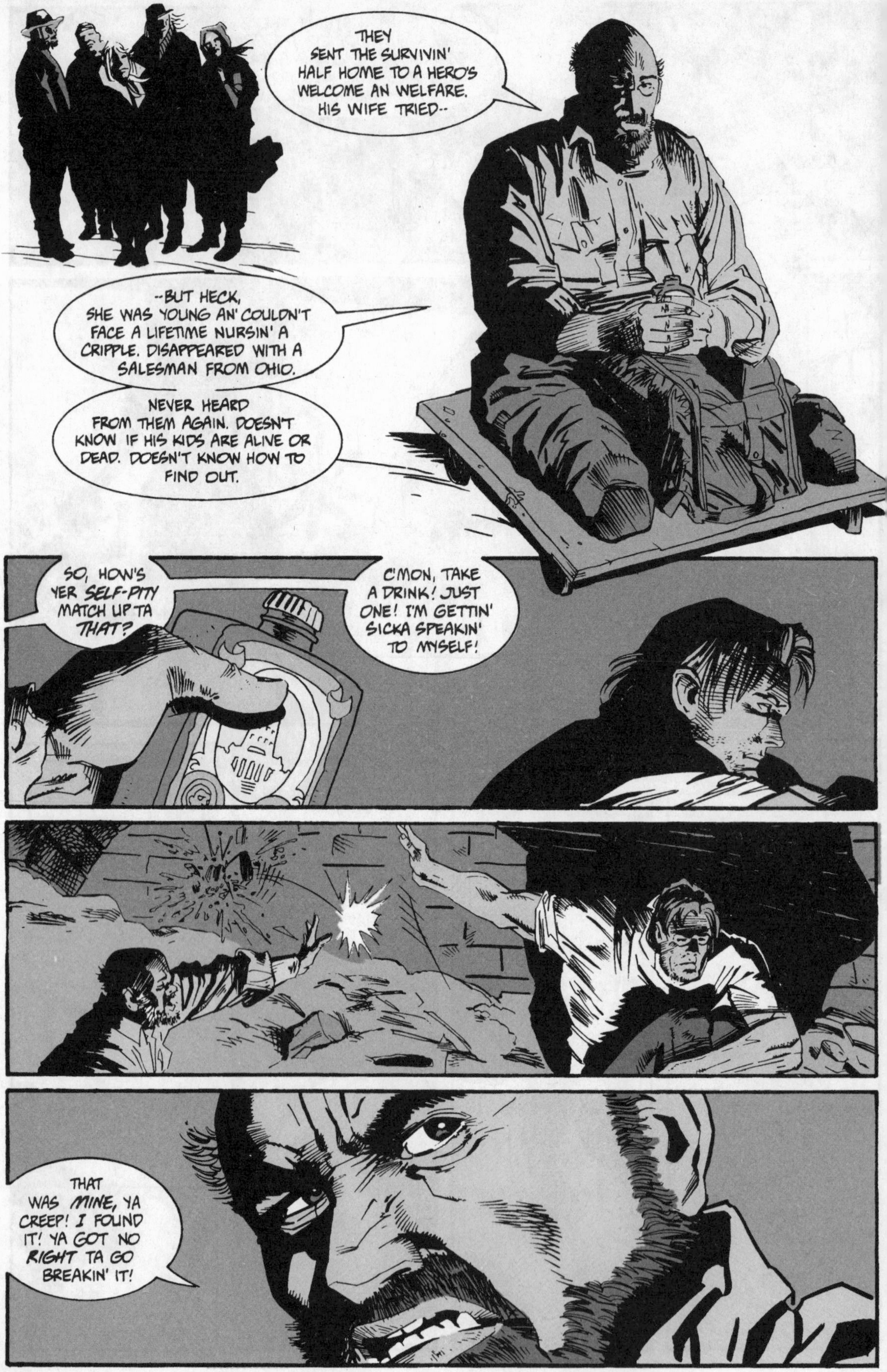
THEY SENT THE SURVIVIN' HALF HOME TO A HERO'S WELCOME AN WELFARE. HIS WIFE TRIED--
--BUT HECK, SHE WAS YOUNG AN' COULDN'T FACE A LIFETIME NURSIN' A CRIPPLE. DISAPPEARED WITH A SALESMAN FROM OHIO.
NEVER HEARD FROM THEM AGAIN. DOESN'T KNOW IF HIS KIDS ARE ALIVE OR DEAD. DOESN'T KNOW HOW TO FIND OUT.
SO, HOW'S YER SELF-PITY MATCH UP TA THAT?
C'MON, TAKE A DRINK! JUST ONE! I'M GETTIN' SICKA SPEAKIN' TO MYSELF!
THAT WAS MINE, YA CREEP! I FOUND IT! YA GOT NO RIGHT TA GO BREAKIN' IT!

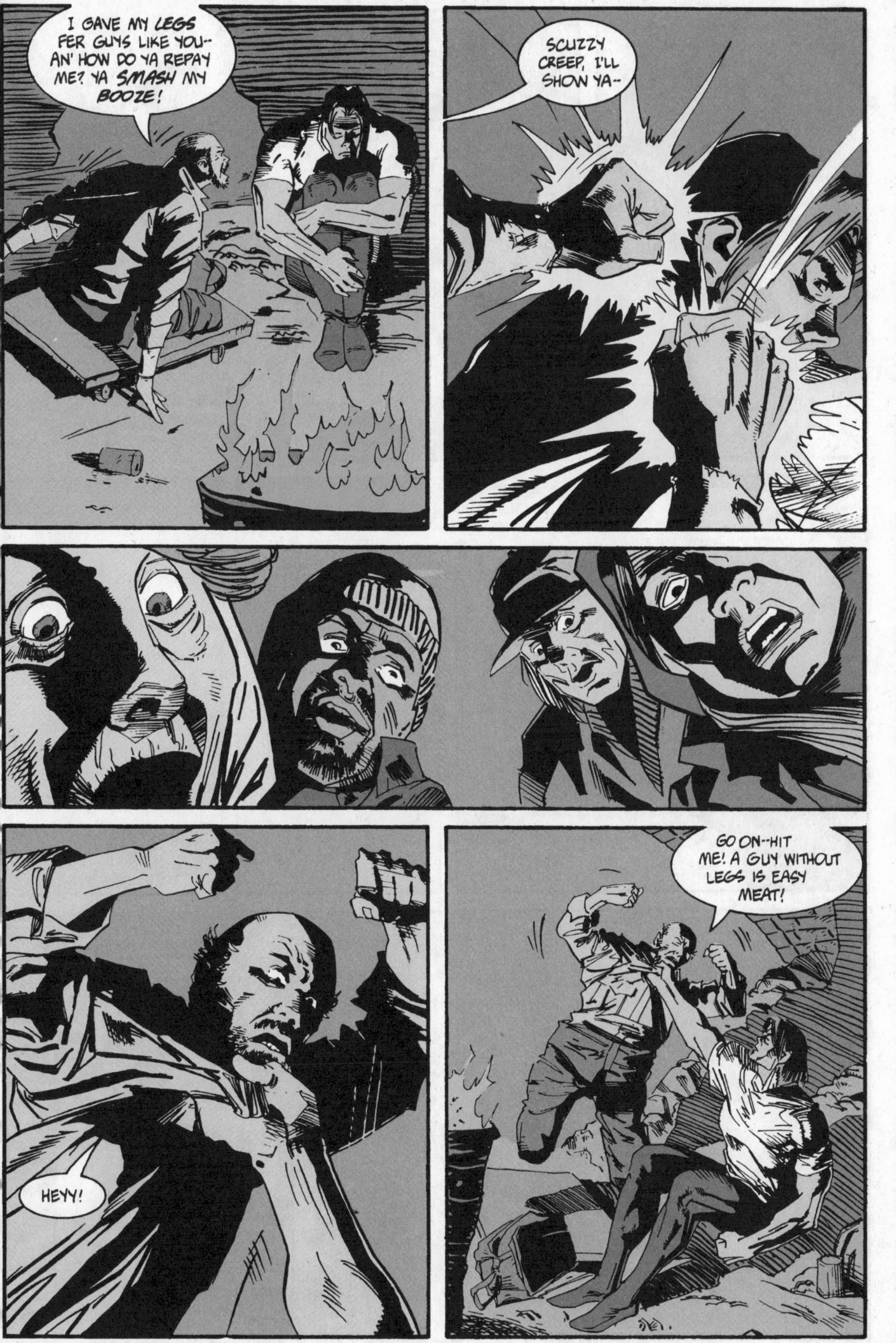
I GAVE MY LEGS FER GUYS LIKE YOU-- AN' HOW DO YA REPAY ME? YA SMASH MY BOOZE!
SCUZZY CREEP, I'LL SHOW YA--
HEYY!
GO ON--HIT ME! A GUY WITHOUT LEGS IS EASY MEAT!

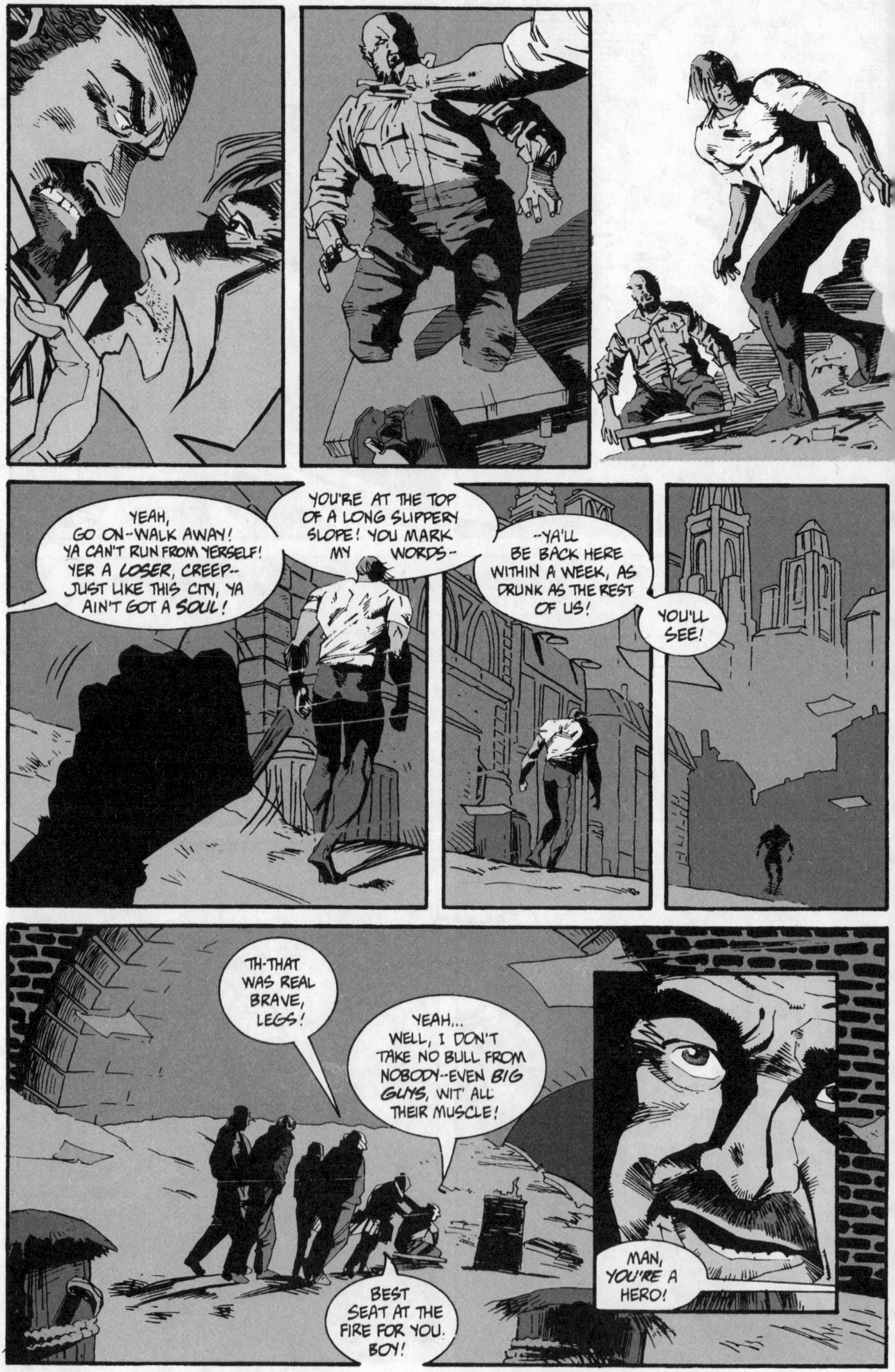
YEAH, GO ON--WALK AWAY! YA CAN'T RUN FROM YERSELF! YER A LOSER, CREEP-- JUST LIKE THIS CITY, YA AIN'T GOT A SOUL!
YOU'RE AT THE TOP OF A LONG SLIPPERY SLOPE! YOU MARK MY WORDS--
--YA'LL BE BACK HERE WITHIN A WEEK, AS DRUNK AS THE REST OF US!
YOU'LL SEE!
TH-THAT WAS REAL BRAVE, LEGS!
YEAH... WELL, I DON'T TAKE NO BULL FROM NOBODY--EVEN BIG GUYS, WIT' ALL THEIR MUSCLE!
BEST SEAT AT THE FIRE FOR YOU, BOY!
MAN, YOU'RE A HERO!

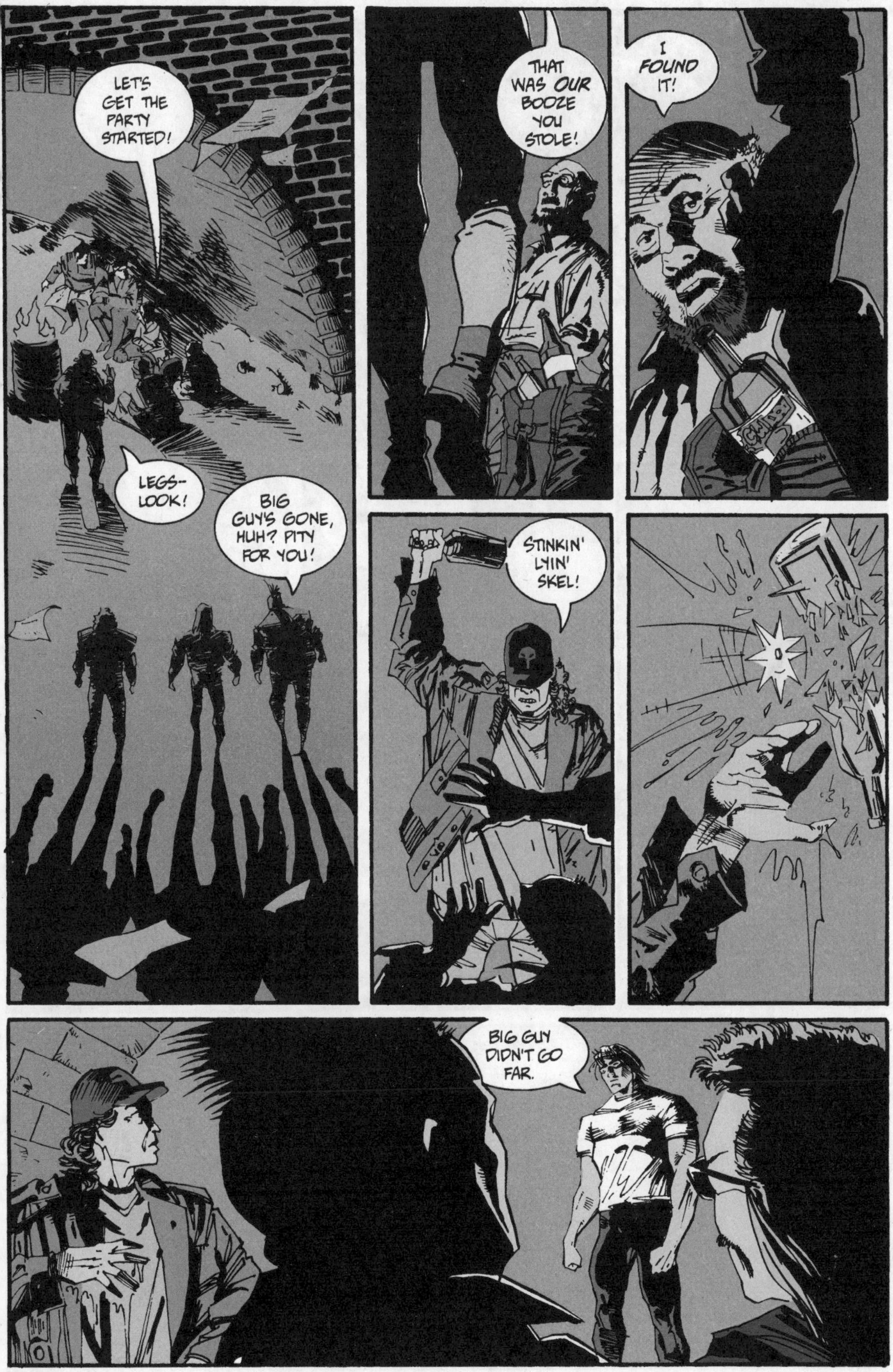
LET'S GET THE PARTY STARTED!
LEGS-- LOOK!
BIG GUY'S GONE, HUH? PITY FOR YOU!
THAT WAS OUR BOOZE YOU STOLE!
I FOUND IT!
STINKIN' LYIN' SKEL!
BIG GUY DIDN'T GO FAR.

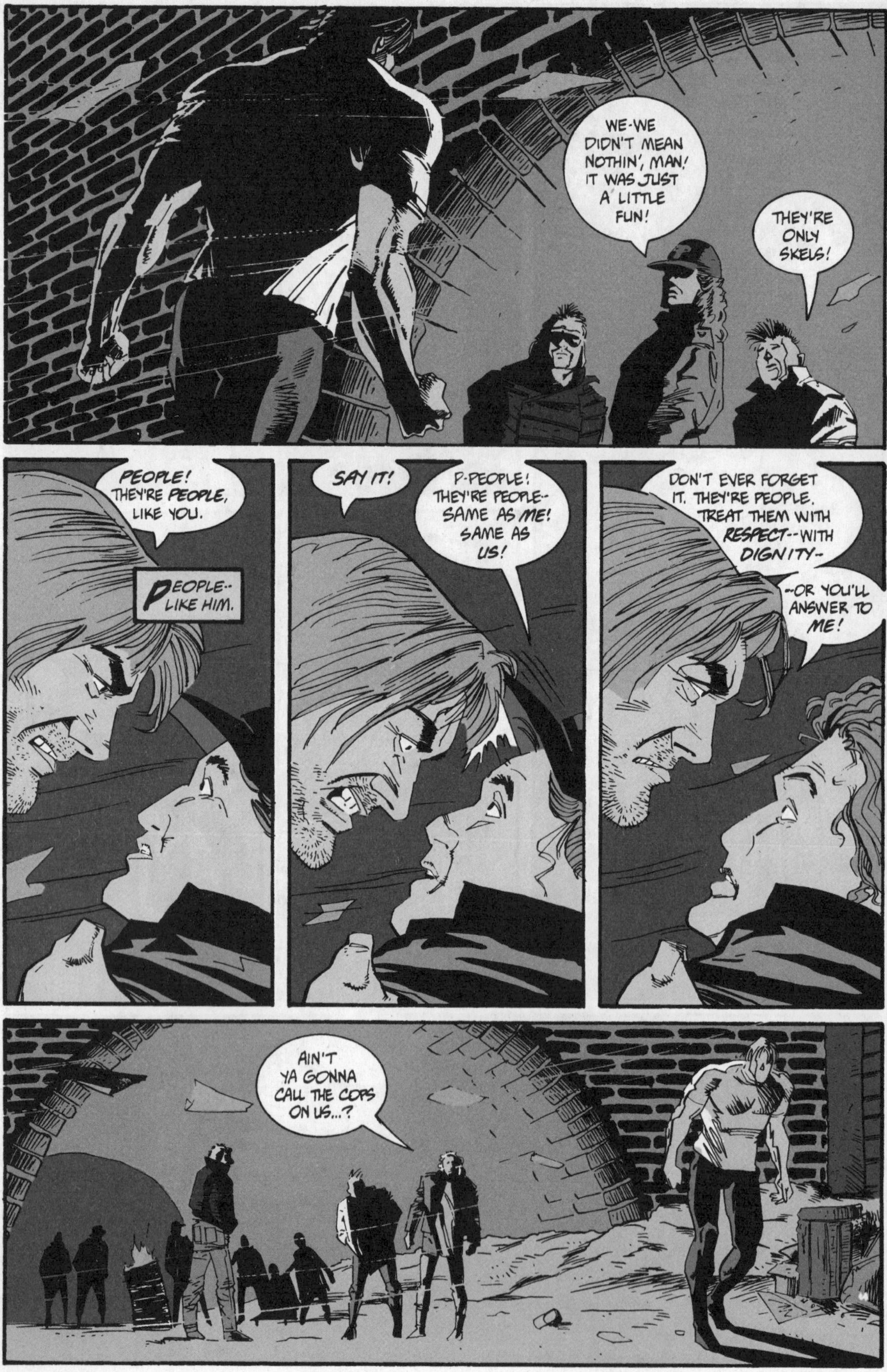
WE-WE DIDN'T MEAN NOTHIN', MAN! IT WAS JUST A LITTLE FUN!
THEY'RE ONLY SKELS!
PEOPLE! THEY'RE PEOPLE, LIKE YOU.
PEOPLE-- LIKE HIM.
SAY IT!
P-PEOPLE! THEY'RE PEOPLE-- SAME AS ME! SAME AS US!
DON'T EVER FORGET IT. THEY'RE PEOPLE. TREAT THEM WITH RESPECT--WITH DIGNITY--
--OR YOU'LL ANSWER TO ME!
AIN'T YA GONNA CALL THE COPS ON US...?

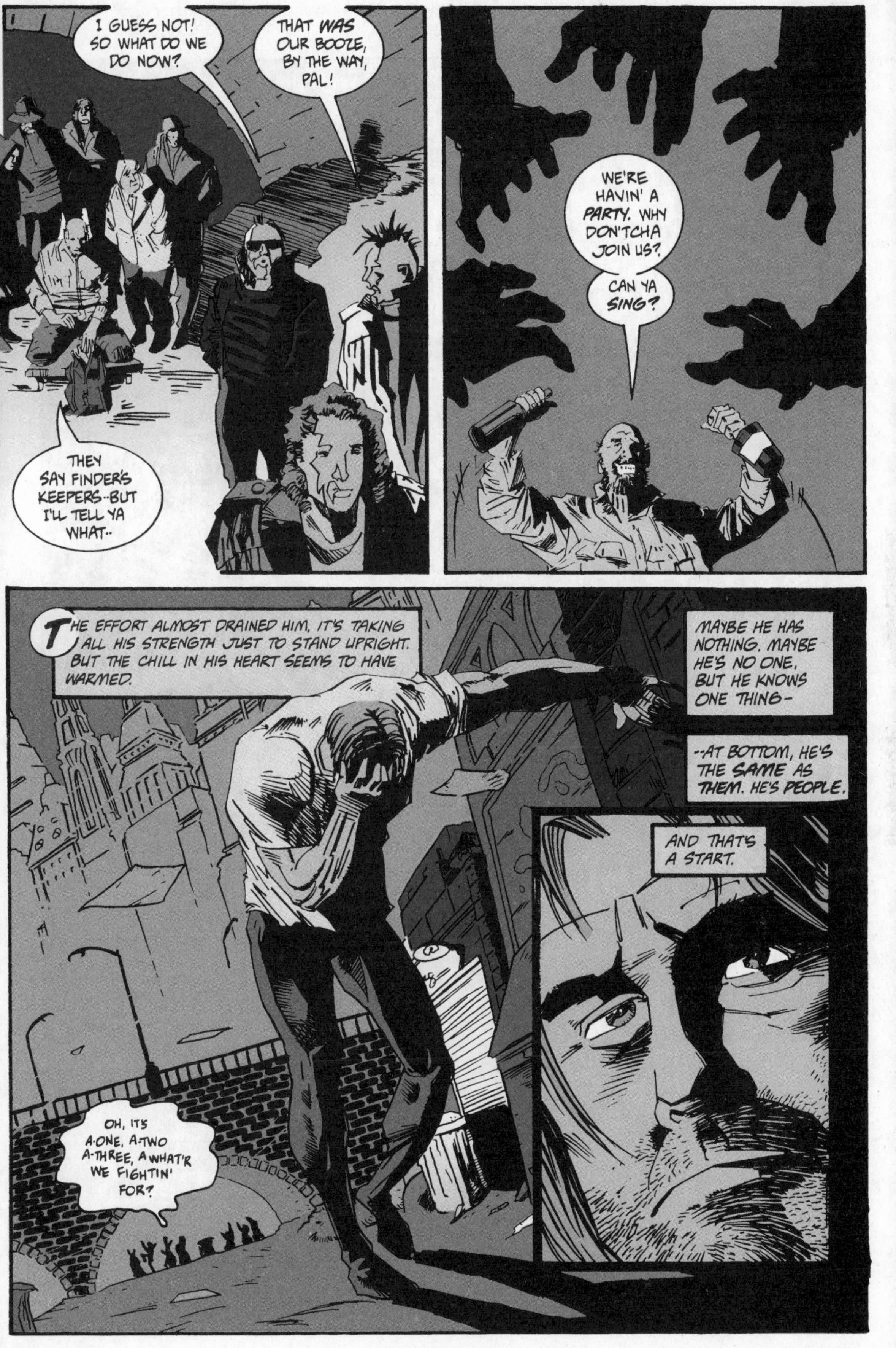

I GUESS NOT! SO WHAT DO WE DO NOW?
THAT WAS OUR BOOZE, BY THE WAY, PAL!
THEY SAY FINDER'S KEEPERS--BUT I'LL TELL YA WHAT--
WE'RE HAVIN' A PARTY. WHY DON'TCHA JOIN US?
CAN YA SING?
THE EFFORT ALMOST DRAINED HIM, IT'S TAKING ALL HIS STRENGTH JUST TO STAND UPRIGHT. BUT THE CHILL IN HIS HEART SEEMS TO HAVE WARMED.
MAYBE HE HAS NOTHING. MAYBE HE'S NO ONE. BUT HE KNOWS ONE THING-
--AT BOTTOM, HE'S THE SAME AS THEM. HE'S PEOPLE.
AND THAT'S A START.
OH, IT'S A-ONE, A-TWO A-THREE, A WHAT'R WE FIGHTIN' FOR?

Cover art by MIKE MANLEY

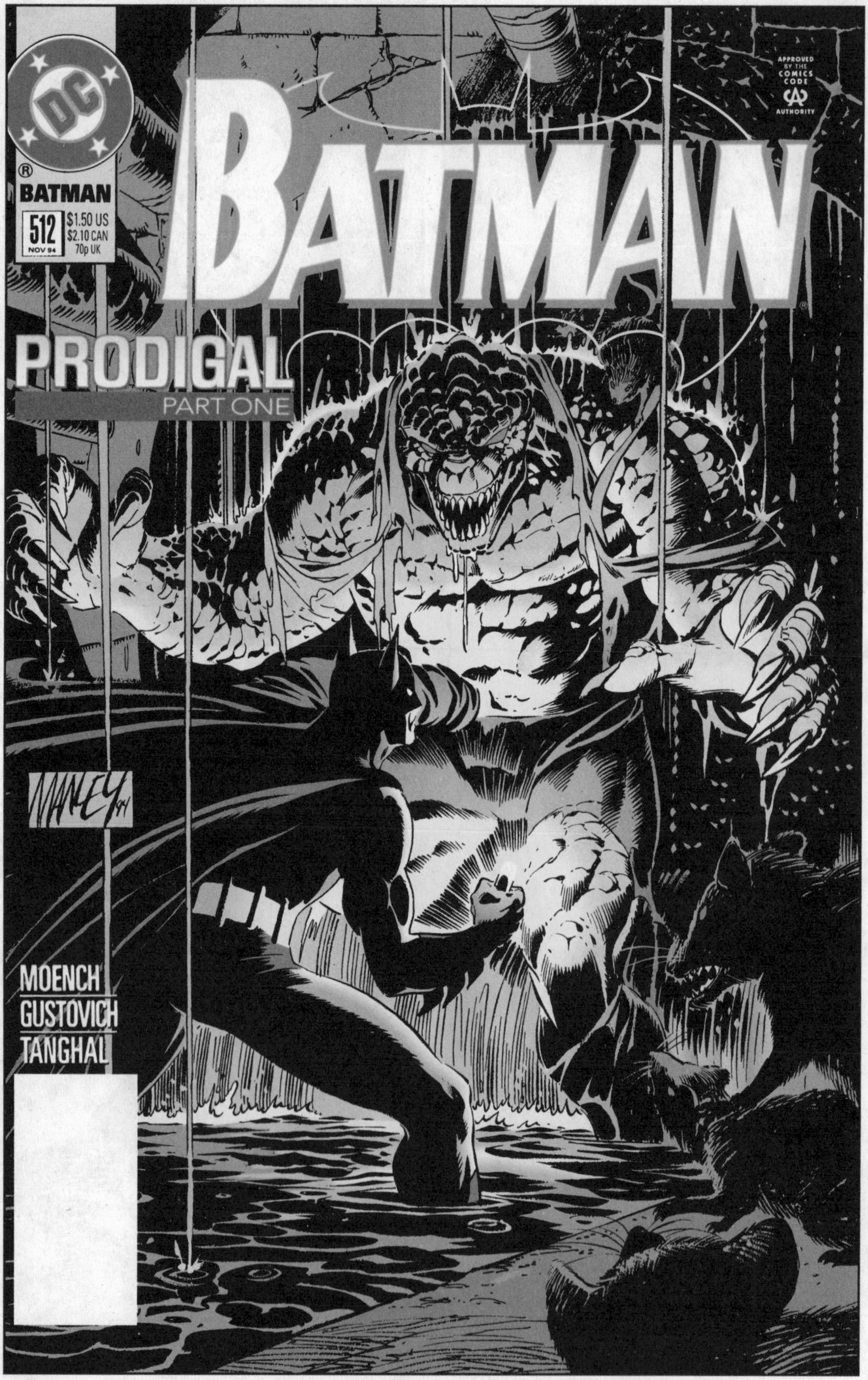
DC
BATMAN
512
NOV 94
$1.50 US
$2.10 CAN
70p UK
APPROVED BY THE COMICS CODE AUTHORITY
BATMAN
PRODIGAL
PART ONE
MANLEY 94
MOENCH
GUSTOVICH
TANGHAL

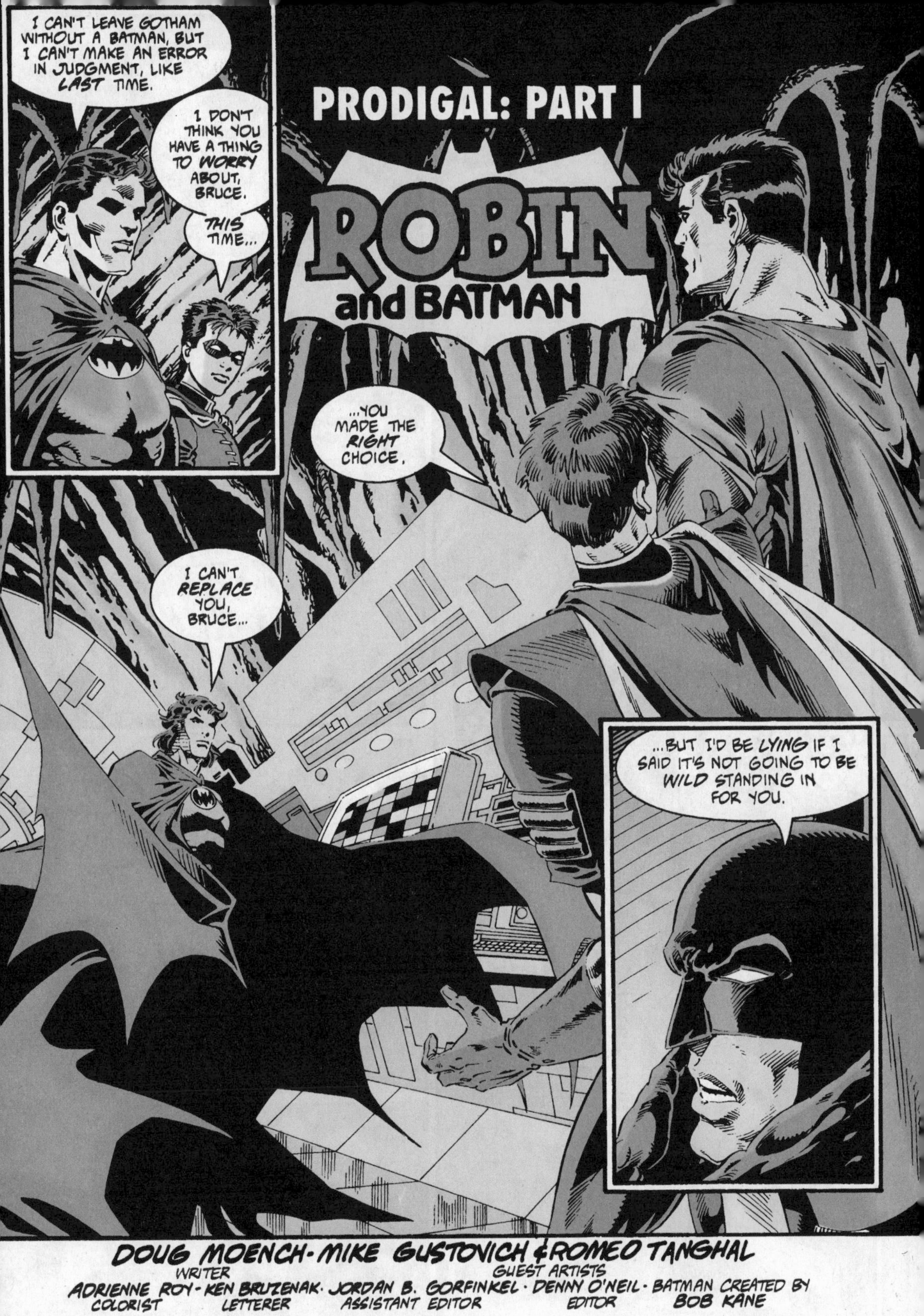
I CAN'T LEAVE GOTHAM WITHOUT A BATMAN, BUT I CAN'T MAKE AN ERROR IN JUDGMENT, LIKE LAST TIME.
I DON'T THINK YOU HAVE A THING TO WORRY ABOUT, BRUCE.
THIS TIME...
PRODIGAL: PART I
ROBIN and BATMAN
...YOU MADE THE RIGHT CHOICE.
I CAN'T REPLACE YOU, BRUCE...
...BUT I'D BE LYING IF I SAID IT'S NOT GOING TO BE WILD STANDING IN FOR YOU.

DOUG MOENCH · MIKE GUSTOVICH & ROMEO TANGHAL
WRITER · GUEST ARTISTS
ADRIENNE ROY · KEN BRUZENAK · JORDAN B. GORFINKEL · DENNY O'NEIL · BATMAN CREATED BY
COLORIST · LETTERER · ASSISTANT EDITOR · EDITOR · BOB KANE

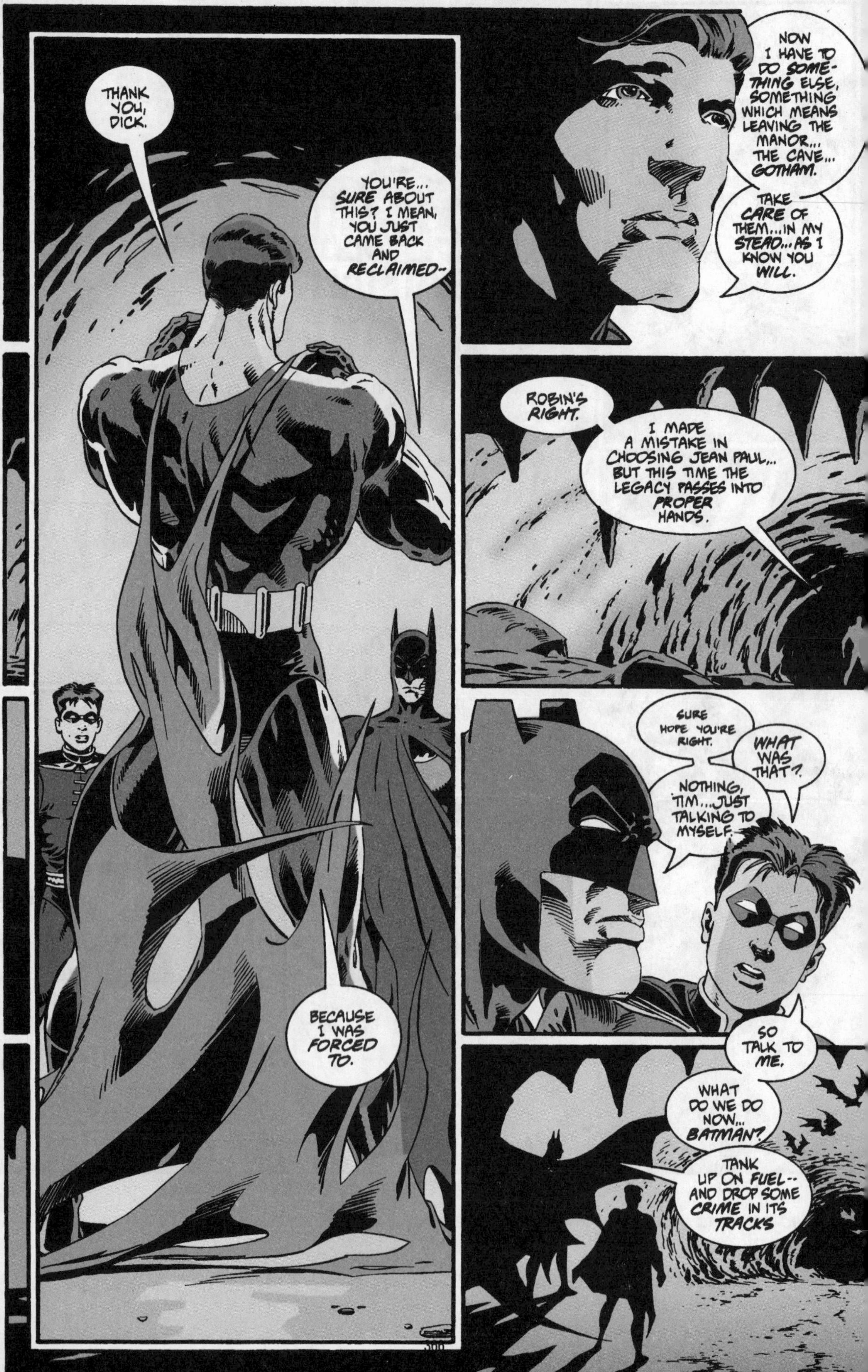
THANK YOU, DICK.
YOU'RE... SURE ABOUT THIS? I MEAN, YOU JUST CAME BACK AND RECLAIMED--
BECAUSE I WAS FORCED TO.
NOW I HAVE TO DO SOMETHING ELSE, SOMETHING WHICH MEANS LEAVING THE MANOR... THE CAVE... GOTHAM.
TAKE CARE OF THEM...IN MY STEAD...AS I KNOW YOU WILL.
ROBIN'S RIGHT.
I MADE A MISTAKE IN CHOOSING JEAN PAUL... BUT THIS TIME THE LEGACY PASSES INTO PROPER HANDS.
SURE HOPE YOU'RE RIGHT.
WHAT WAS THAT?
NOTHING, TIM...JUST TALKING TO MYSELF.
SO TALK TO ME.
WHAT DO WE DO NOW... BATMAN?
TANK UP ON FUEL-- AND DROP SOME CRIME IN ITS TRACKS

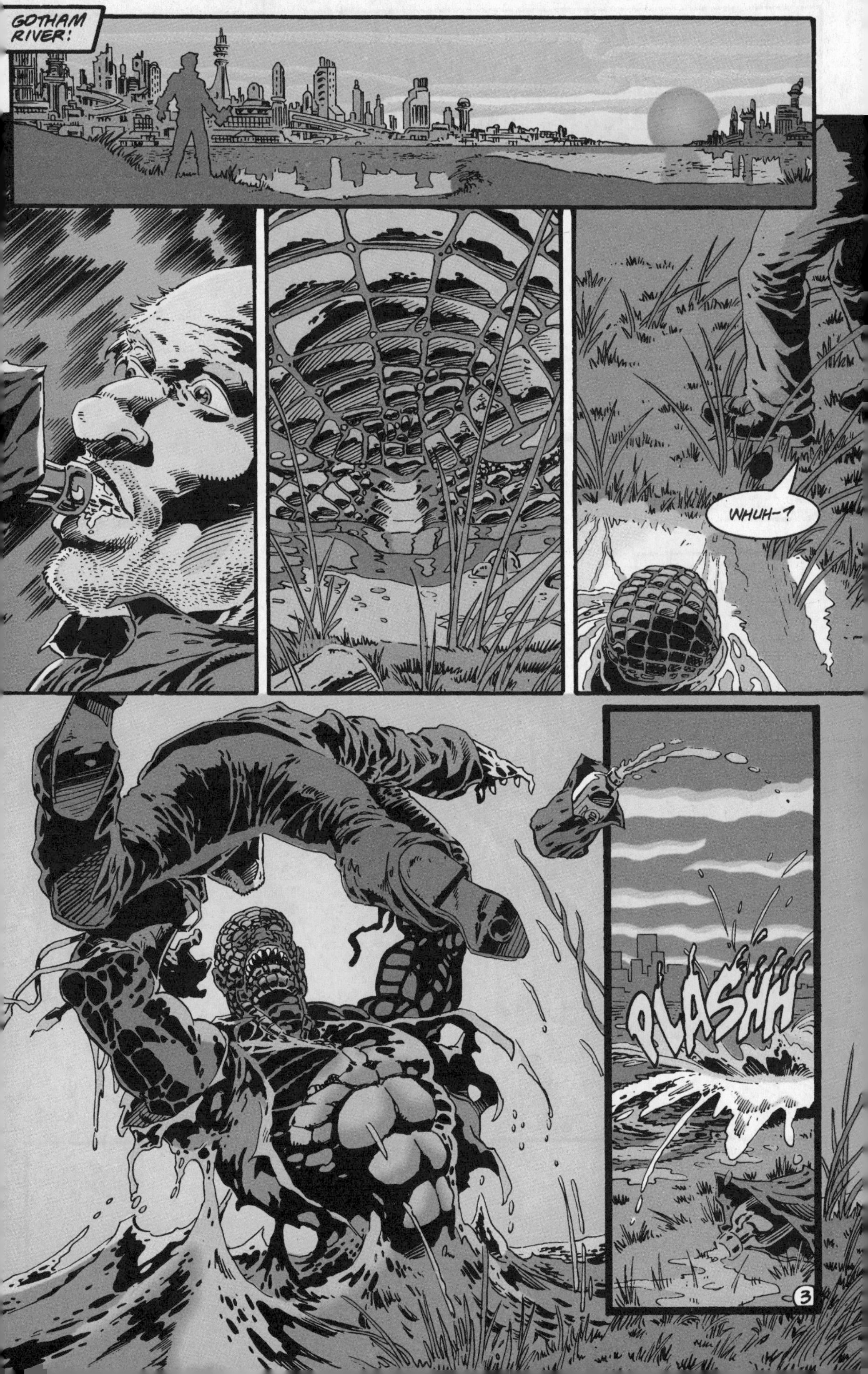
GOTHAM RIVER:
WHUH-?
PLASHH
3

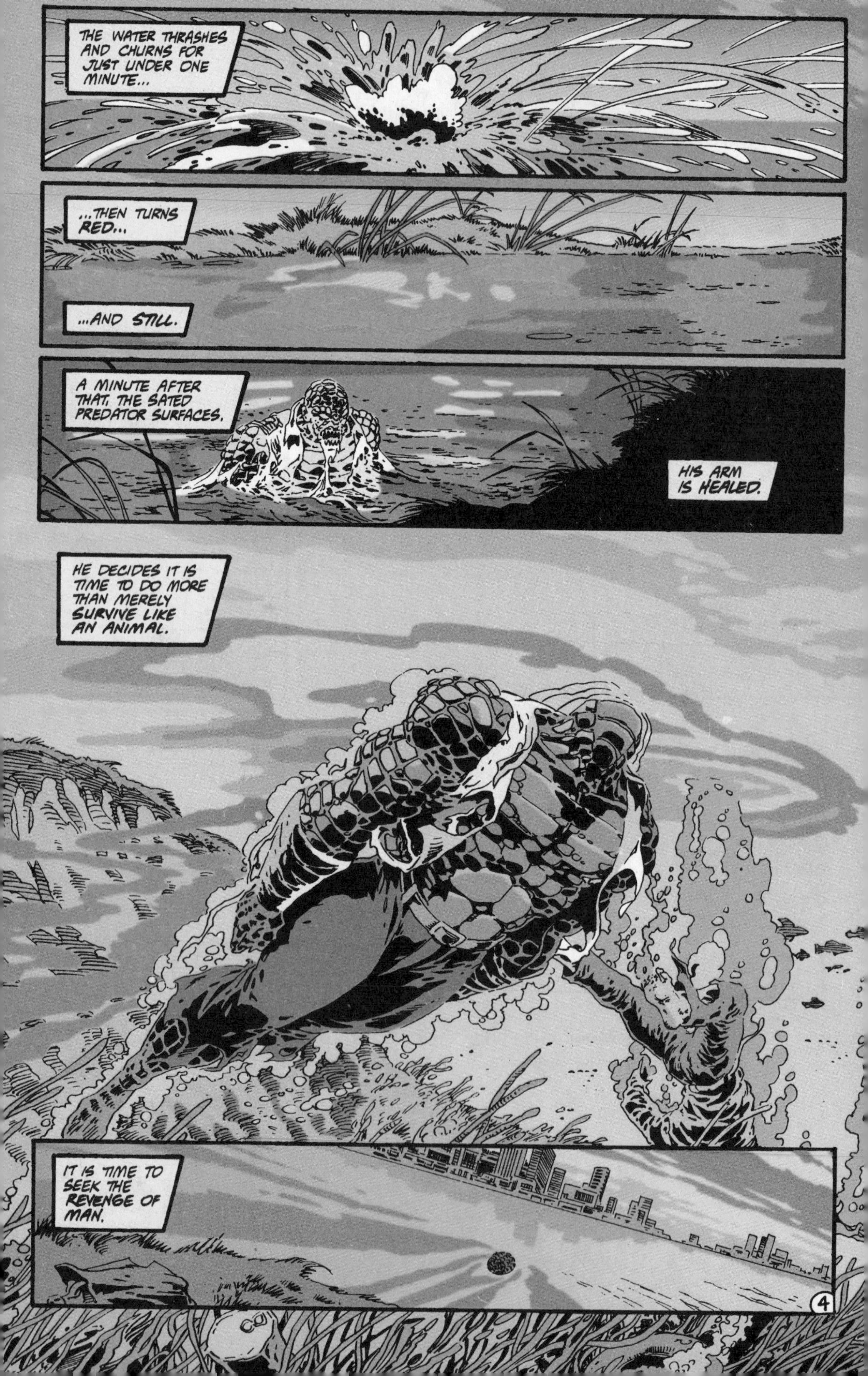
THE WATER THRASHES AND CHURNS FOR JUST UNDER ONE MINUTE...
...THEN TURNS RED...
...AND STILL.
A MINUTE AFTER THAT, THE SATED PREDATOR SURFACES.
HIS ARM IS HEALED.
HE DECIDES IT IS TIME TO DO MORE THAN MERELY SURVIVE LIKE AN ANIMAL.
IT IS TIME TO SEEK THE REVENGE OF MAN.

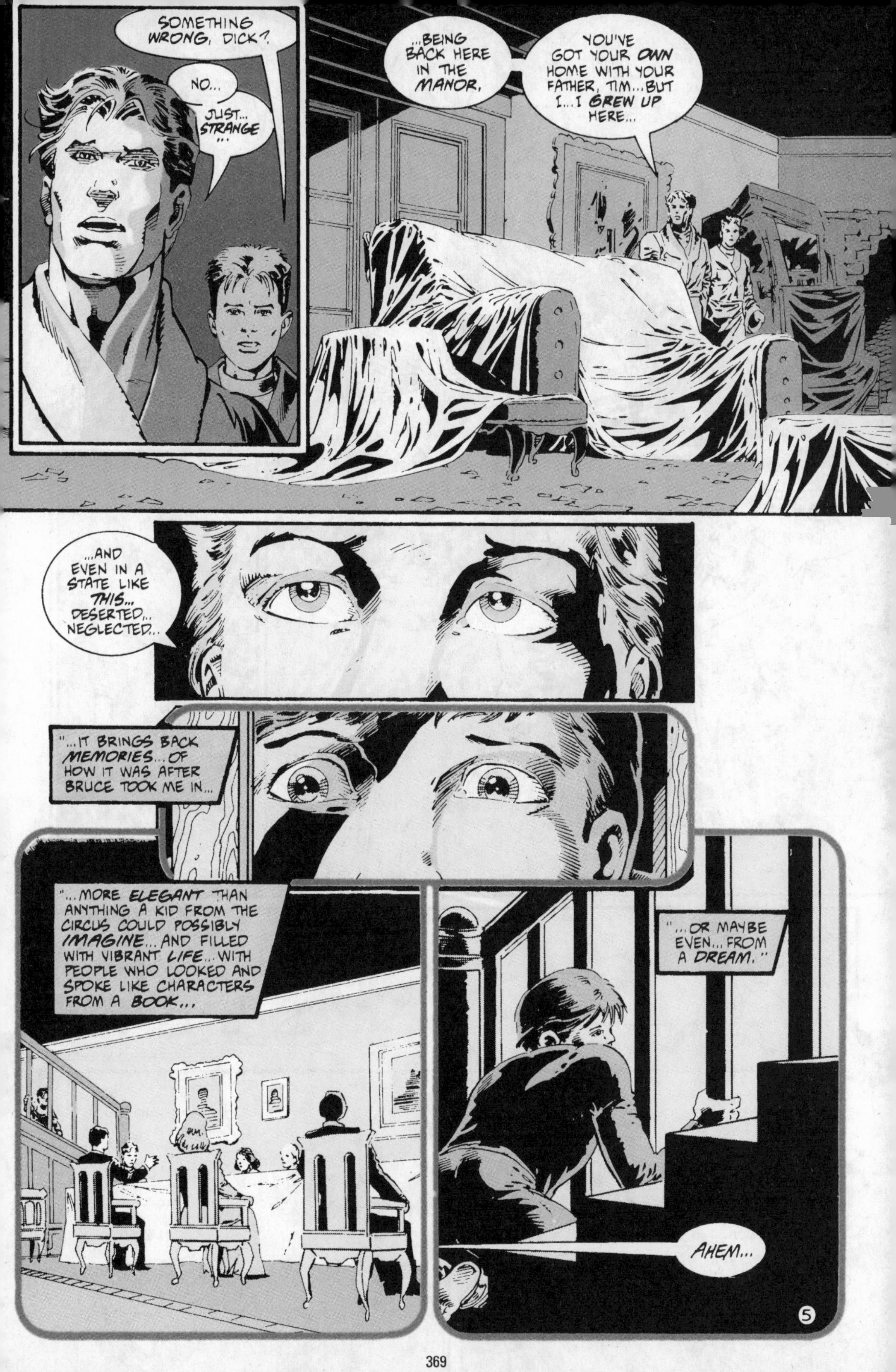
SOMETHING WRONG, DICK?
NO...
JUST... STRANGE...
...BEING BACK HERE IN THE MANOR.
YOU'VE GOT YOUR OWN HOME WITH YOUR FATHER, TIM...BUT I...I GREW UP HERE...
...AND EVEN IN A STATE LIKE THIS... DESERTED... NEGLECTED...
"...IT BRINGS BACK MEMORIES... OF HOW IT WAS AFTER BRUCE TOOK ME IN...
"...MORE ELEGANT THAN ANYTHING A KID FROM THE CIRCUS COULD POSSIBLY IMAGINE... AND FILLED WITH VIBRANT LIFE... WITH PEOPLE WHO LOOKED AND SPOKE LIKE CHARACTERS FROM A BOOK...
"...OR MAYBE EVEN... FROM A DREAM."
AHEM...
5

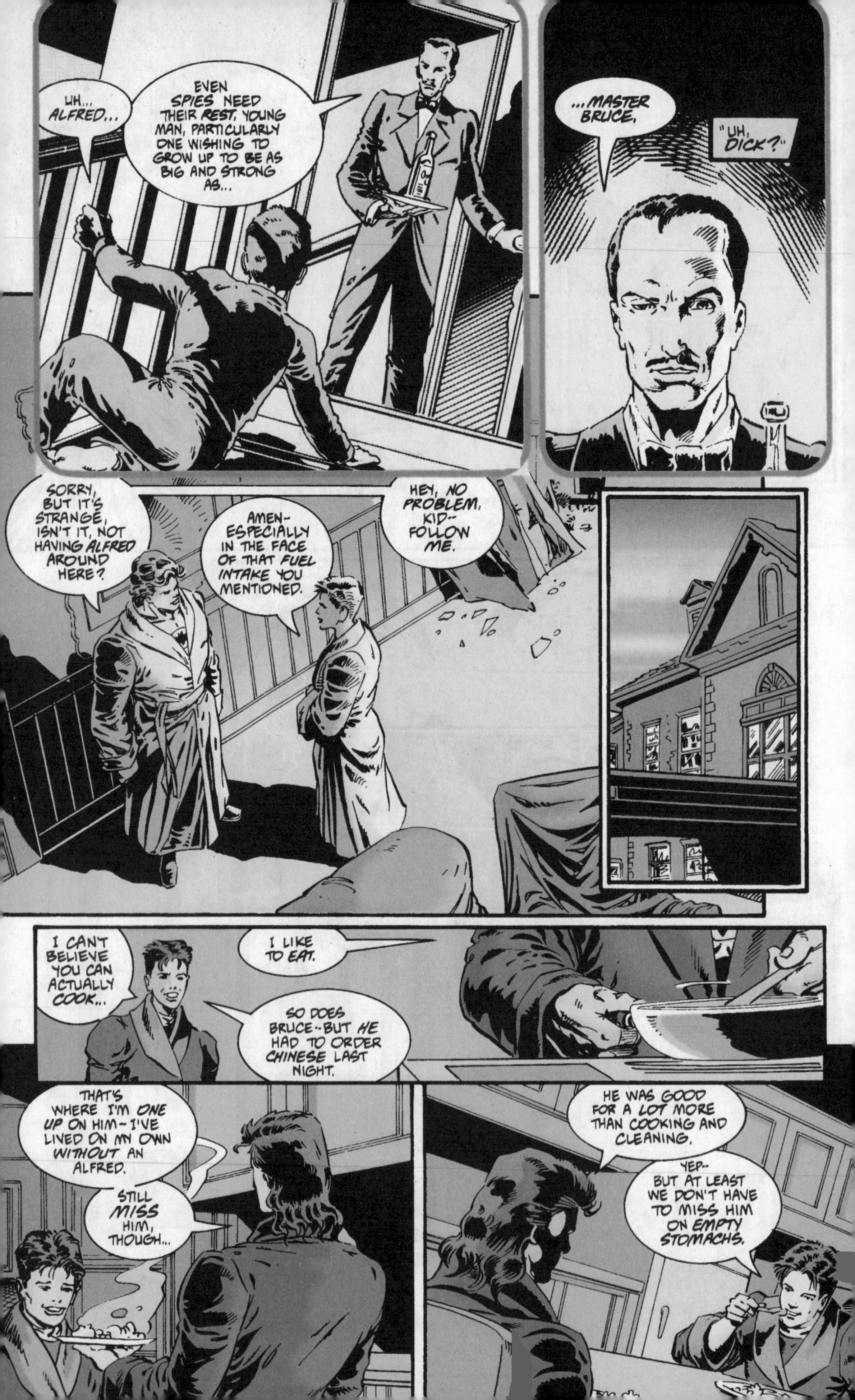
UH... ALFRED...
EVEN SPIES NEED THEIR REST, YOUNG MAN, PARTICULARLY ONE WISHING TO GROW UP TO BE AS BIG AND STRONG AS...
...MASTER BRUCE.
"UH, DICK?"
SORRY, BUT IT'S STRANGE, ISN'T IT, NOT HAVING ALFRED AROUND HERE?
AMEN-- ESPECIALLY IN THE FACE OF THAT FUEL INTAKE YOU MENTIONED.
HEY, NO PROBLEM, KID-- FOLLOW ME.
I CAN'T BELIEVE YOU CAN ACTUALLY COOK...
I LIKE TO EAT.
SO DOES BRUCE--BUT HE HAD TO ORDER CHINESE LAST NIGHT.
THAT'S WHERE I'M ONE UP ON HIM--I'VE LIVED ON MY OWN WITHOUT AN ALFRED.
STILL MISS HIM, THOUGH...
HE WAS GOOD FOR A LOT MORE THAN COOKING AND CLEANING.
YEP-- BUT AT LEAST WE DON'T HAVE TO MISS HIM ON EMPTY STOMACHS.

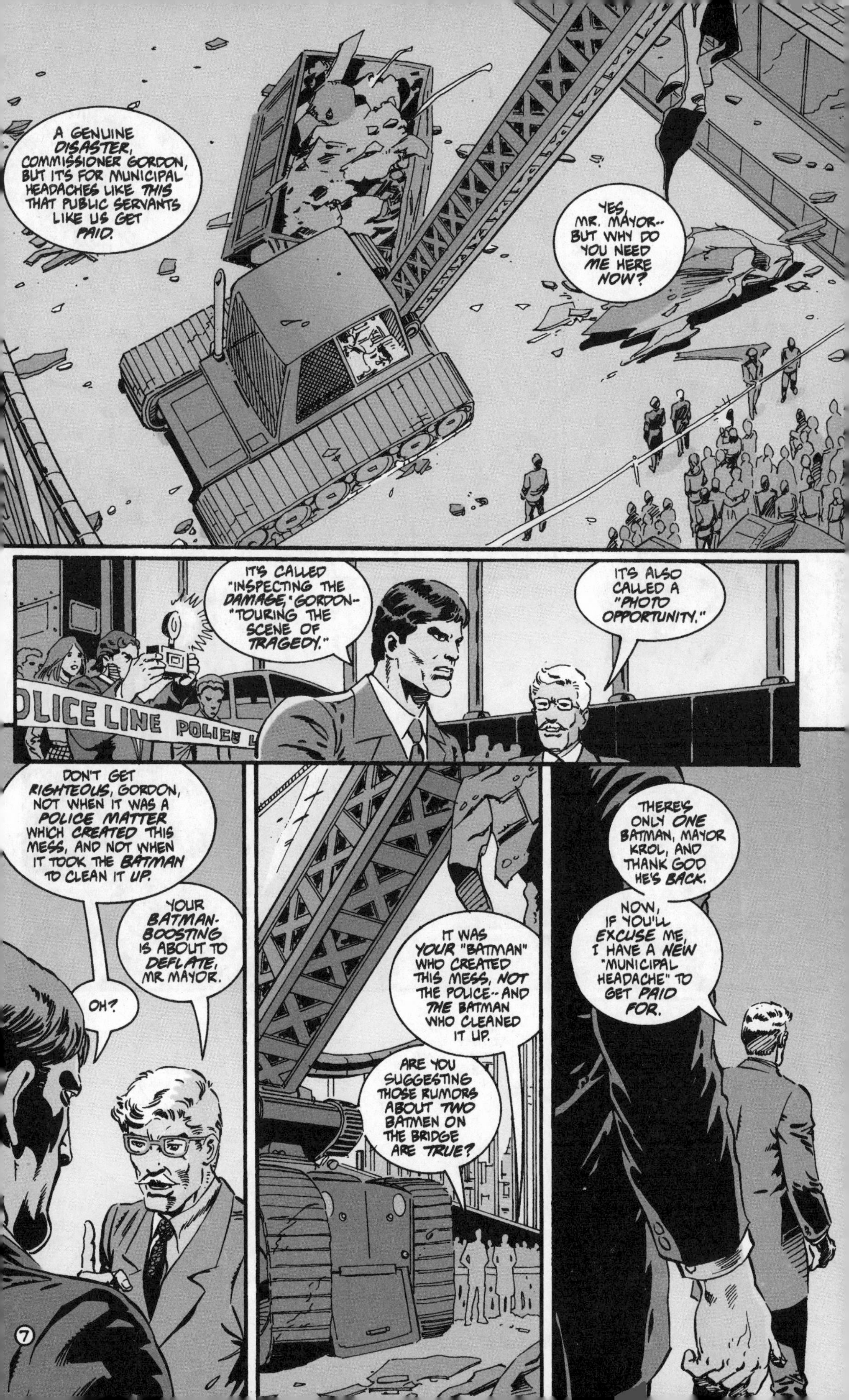
A GENUINE DISASTER, COMMISSIONER GORDON, BUT IT'S FOR MUNICIPAL HEADACHES LIKE THIS THAT PUBLIC SERVANTS LIKE US GET PAID.
YES, MR. MAYOR-- BUT WHY DO YOU NEED ME HERE NOW?
IT'S CALLED "INSPECTING THE DAMAGE," GORDON-- "TOURING THE SCENE OF TRAGEDY."
IT'S ALSO CALLED A "PHOTO OPPORTUNITY."
POLICE LINE POLICE L
DON'T GET RIGHTEOUS, GORDON, NOT WHEN IT WAS A POLICE MATTER WHICH CREATED THIS MESS, AND NOT WHEN IT TOOK THE BATMAN TO CLEAN IT UP.
YOUR BATMAN-BOOSTING IS ABOUT TO DEFLATE, MR MAYOR.
OH?
IT WAS YOUR "BATMAN" WHO CREATED THIS MESS, NOT THE POLICE-- AND THE BATMAN WHO CLEANED IT UP.
ARE YOU SUGGESTING THOSE RUMORS ABOUT TWO BATMEN ON THE BRIDGE ARE TRUE?
THERE'S ONLY ONE BATMAN, MAYOR KROL, AND THANK GOD HE'S BACK.
NOW, IF YOU'LL EXCUSE ME, I HAVE A NEW "MUNICIPAL HEADACHE" TO GET PAID FOR.
7

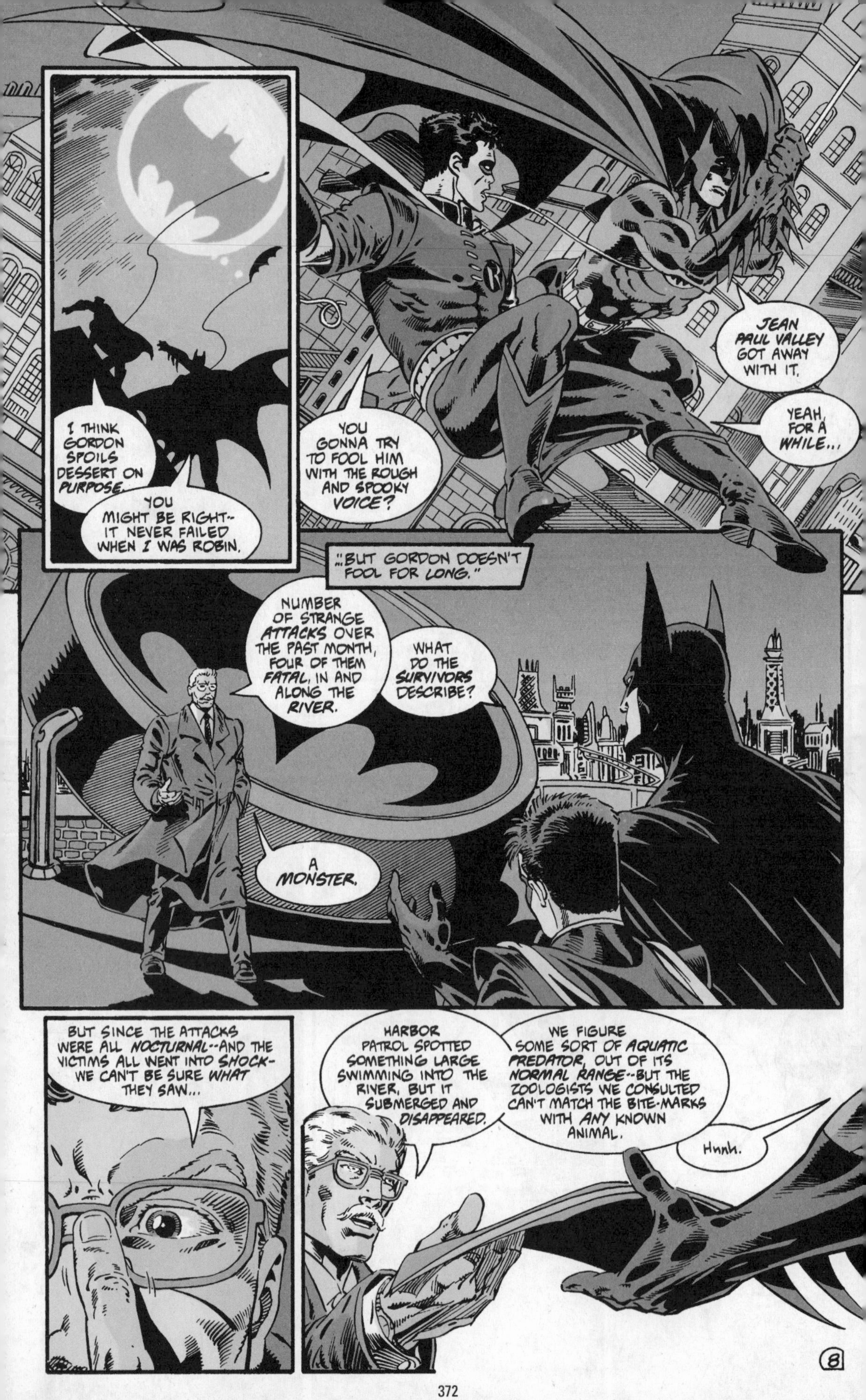
I THINK GORDON SPOILS DESSERT ON PURPOSE.
YOU MIGHT BE RIGHT-- IT NEVER FAILED WHEN I WAS ROBIN.
YOU GONNA TRY TO FOOL HIM WITH THE ROUGH AND SPOOKY VOICE?
JEAN PAUL VALLEY GOT AWAY WITH IT.
YEAH, FOR A WHILE...
"...BUT GORDON DOESN'T FOOL FOR LONG."
NUMBER OF STRANGE ATTACKS OVER THE PAST MONTH, FOUR OF THEM FATAL, IN AND ALONG THE RIVER.
WHAT DO THE SURVIVORS DESCRIBE?
A MONSTER.
BUT SINCE THE ATTACKS WERE ALL NOCTURNAL--AND THE VICTIMS ALL WENT INTO SHOCK-WE CAN'T BE SURE WHAT THEY SAW...
HARBOR PATROL SPOTTED SOMETHING LARGE SWIMMING INTO THE RIVER, BUT IT SUBMERGED AND DISAPPEARED.
WE FIGURE SOME SORT OF AQUATIC PREDATOR, OUT OF ITS NORMAL RANGE--BUT THE ZOOLOGISTS WE CONSULTED CAN'T MATCH THE BITE-MARKS WITH ANY KNOWN ANIMAL.
Hnnh.
8

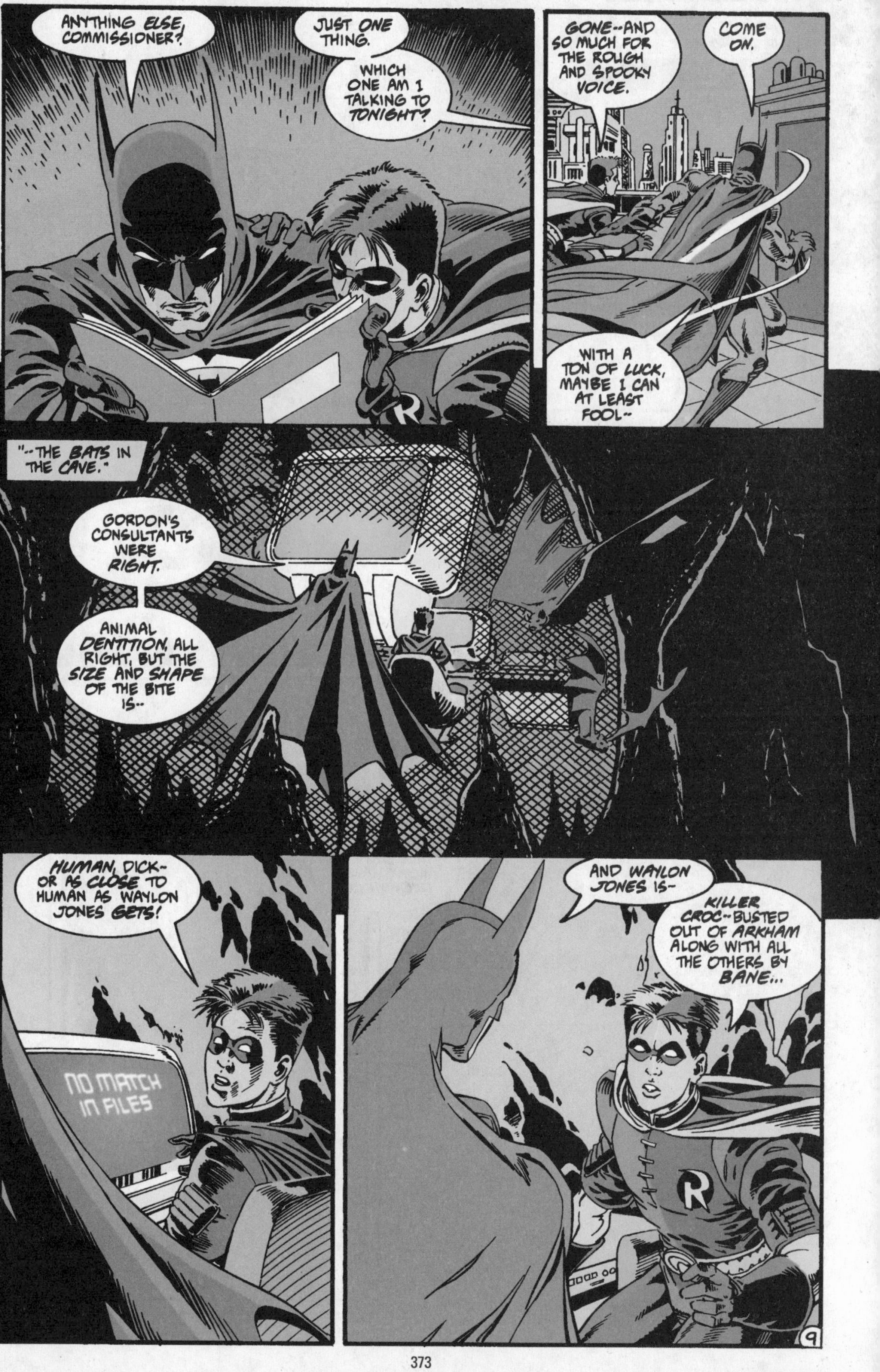

ANYTHING ELSE, COMMISSIONER?
JUST ONE THING.
WHICH ONE AM I TALKING TO TONIGHT?
GONE--AND SO MUCH FOR THE ROUGH AND SPOOKY VOICE.
COME ON.
WITH A TON OF LUCK, MAYBE I CAN AT LEAST FOOL--
"--THE BATS IN THE CAVE."
GORDON'S CONSULTANTS WERE RIGHT.
ANIMAL DENTITION, ALL RIGHT, BUT THE SIZE AND SHAPE OF THE BITE IS--
HUMAN, DICK--OR AS CLOSE TO HUMAN AS WAYLON JONES GETS!
NO MATCH IN FILES
AND WAYLON JONES IS--
KILLER CROC--BUSTED OUT OF ARKHAM ALONG WITH ALL THE OTHERS BY BANE...
9

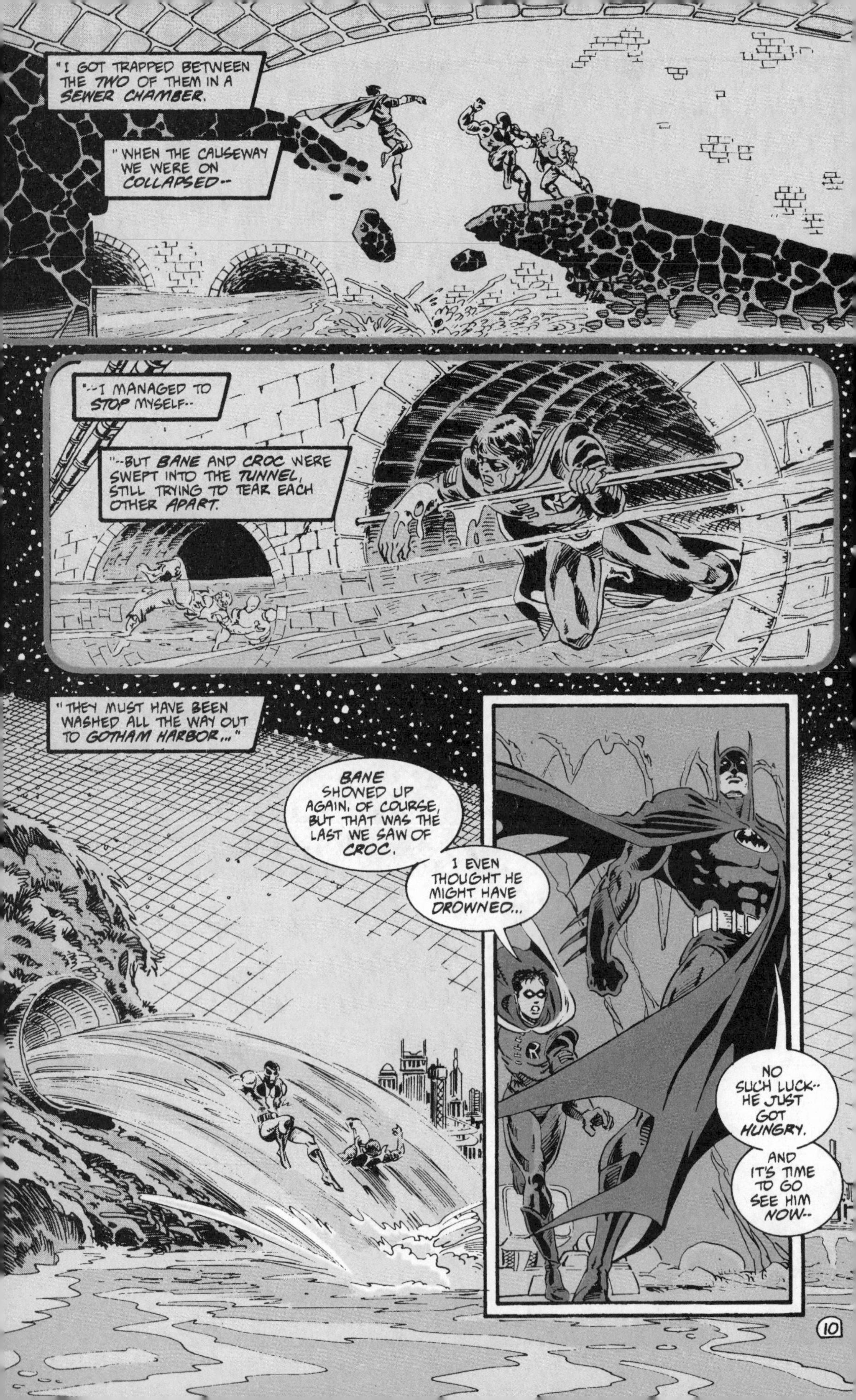
"I GOT TRAPPED BETWEEN THE TWO OF THEM IN A SEWER CHAMBER.
"WHEN THE CAUSEWAY WE WERE ON COLLAPSED--
"--I MANAGED TO STOP MYSELF--
"--BUT BANE AND CROC WERE SWEPT INTO THE TUNNEL, STILL TRYING TO TEAR EACH OTHER APART.
"THEY MUST HAVE BEEN WASHED ALL THE WAY OUT TO GOTHAM HARBOR..."
BANE SHOWED UP AGAIN, OF COURSE, BUT THAT WAS THE LAST WE SAW OF CROC.
I EVEN THOUGHT HE MIGHT HAVE DROWNED...
NO SUCH LUCK-- HE JUST GOT HUNGRY.
AND IT'S TIME TO GO SEE HIM NOW--

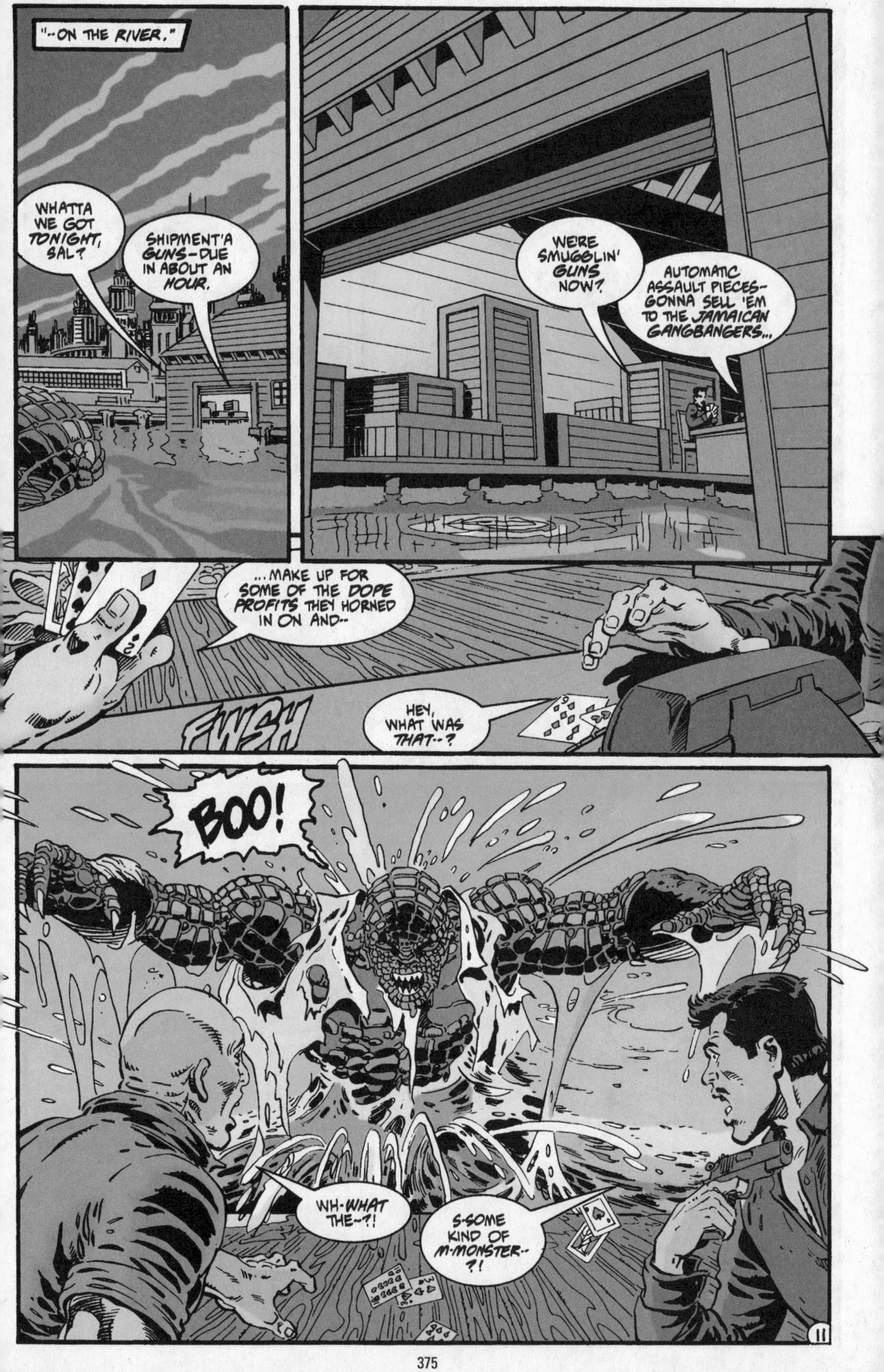
"--ON THE RIVER."
WHATTA WE GOT TONIGHT, SAL?
SHIPMENT'A GUNS--DUE IN ABOUT AN HOUR.
WE'RE SMUGGLIN' GUNS NOW?
AUTOMATIC ASSAULT PIECES-- GONNA SELL 'EM TO THE JAMAICAN GANGBANGERS...
...MAKE UP FOR SOME OF THE DOPE PROFITS THEY HORNED IN ON AND--
FWSH
HEY, WHAT WAS THAT--?
BOO!
WH-WHAT THE--?!
S-SOME KIND OF M-MONSTER--?!
11

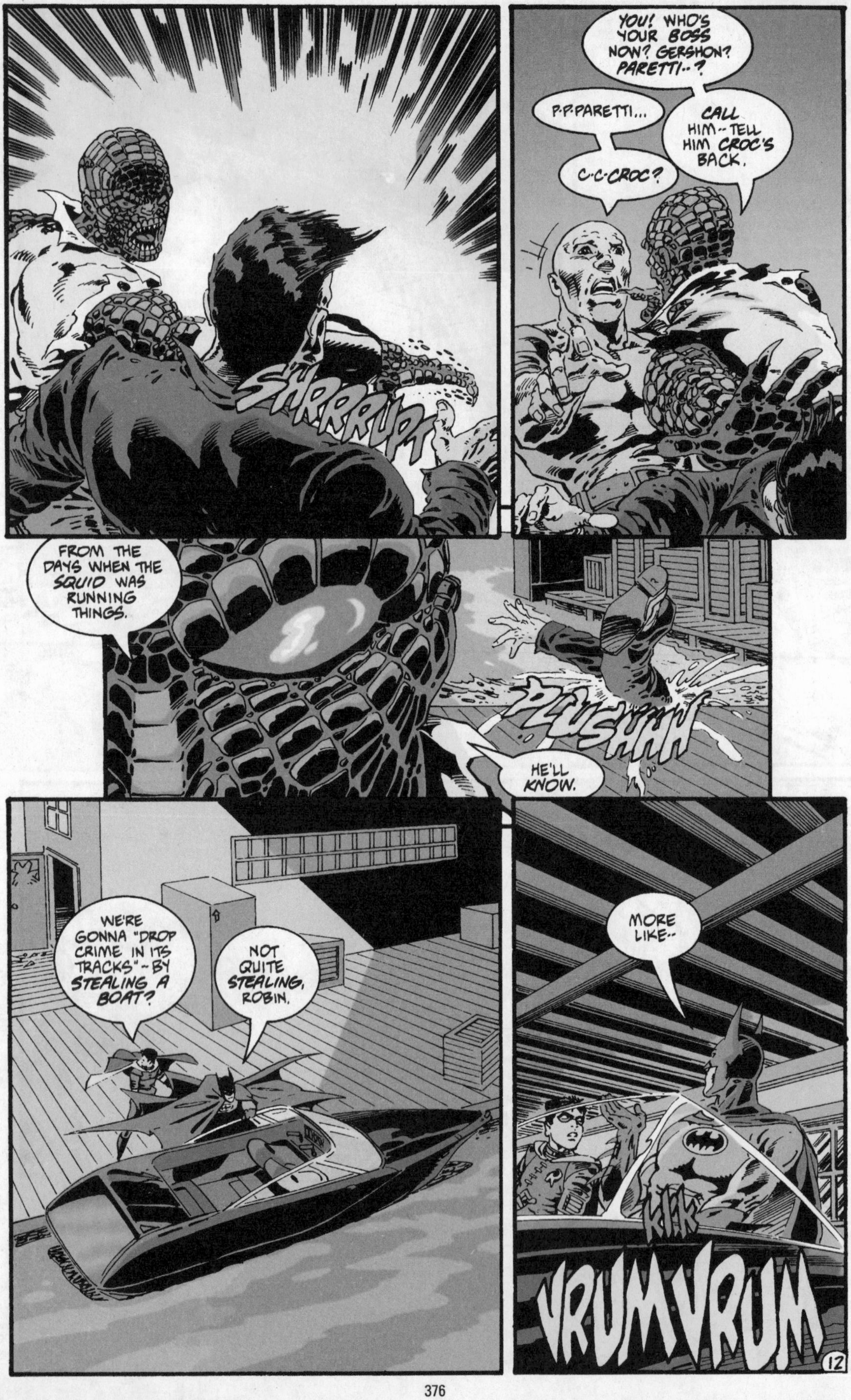
SHRRRUPT
YOU! WHO'S YOUR BOSS NOW? GERSHON? PARETTI..?
P-P-PARETTI...
C-C-CROC?
CALL HIM--TELL HIM CROC'S BACK.
FROM THE DAYS WHEN THE SQUID WAS RUNNING THINGS.
PLUSHHH
HE'LL KNOW.
WE'RE GONNA "DROP CRIME IN ITS TRACKS"--BY STEALING A BOAT?
NOT QUITE STEALING, ROBIN.
MORE LIKE--
KLIK
VRUMVRUM
12

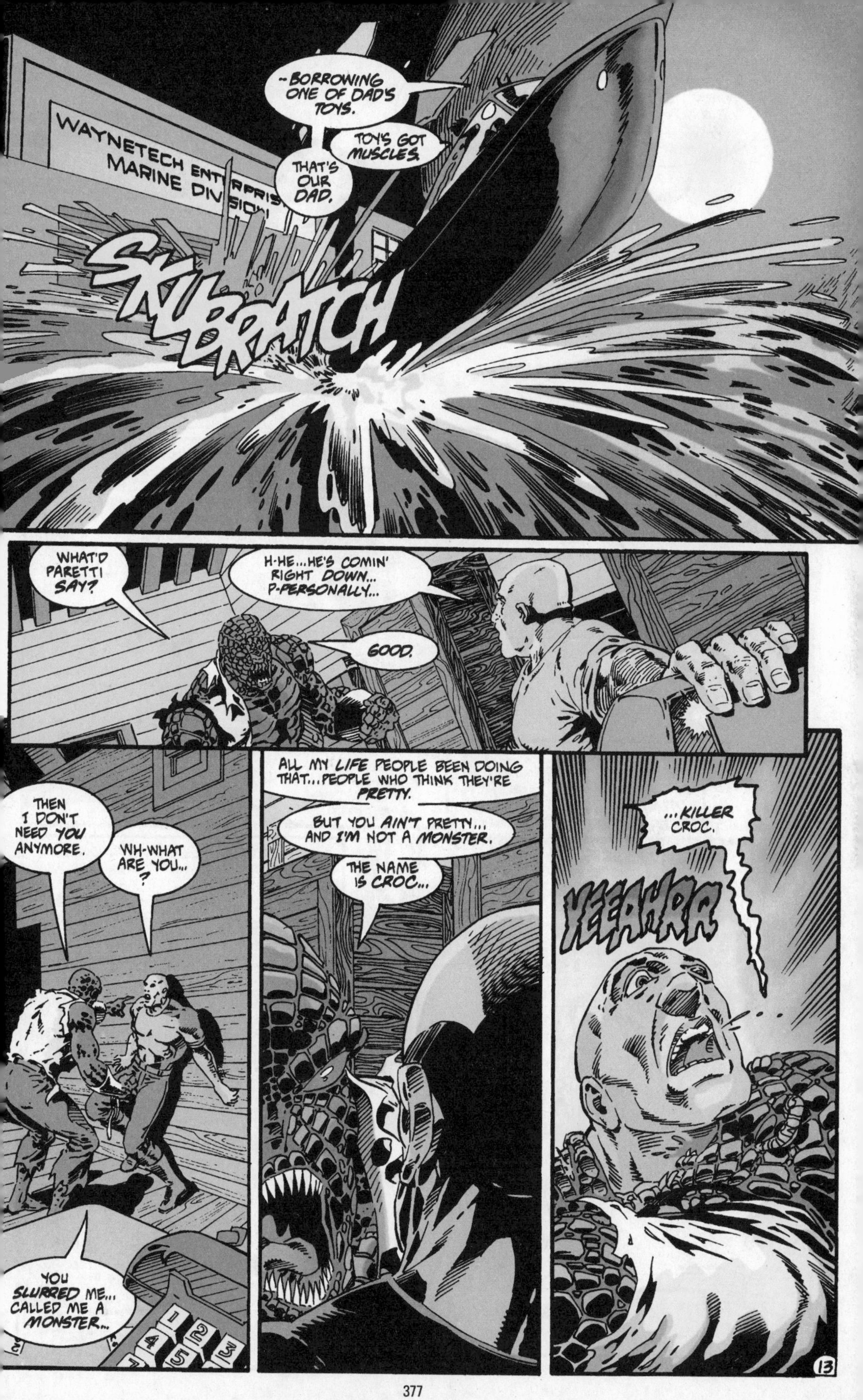
WAYNETECH ENTERPRIS
MARINE DIVISION
--BORROWING ONE OF DAD'S TOYS.
TOY'S GOT MUSCLES.
THAT'S OUR DAD.
SKLUBRATCH
WHAT'D PARETTI SAY?
H-HE...HE'S COMIN' RIGHT DOWN... P-PERSONALLY...
GOOD.
THEN I DON'T NEED YOU ANYMORE.
WH-WHAT ARE YOU... ?
YOU SLURRED ME... CALLED ME A MONSTER...
ALL MY LIFE PEOPLE BEEN DOING THAT...PEOPLE WHO THINK THEY'RE PRETTY.
BUT YOU AIN'T PRETTY... AND I'M NOT A MONSTER.
THE NAME IS CROC...
...KILLER CROC.
YEEAHRR
13

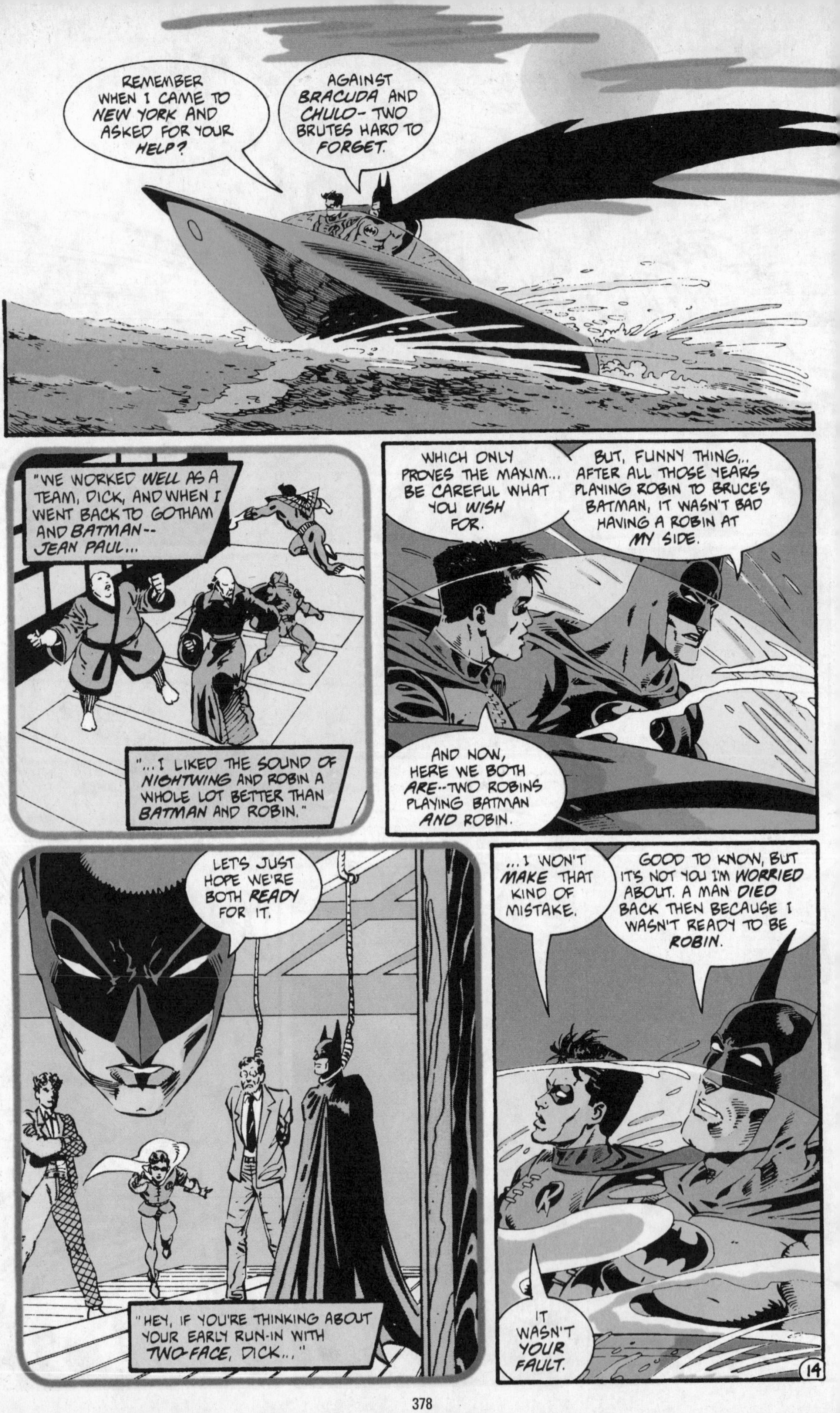
REMEMBER WHEN I CAME TO NEW YORK AND ASKED FOR YOUR HELP?
AGAINST BRACUDA AND CHULO-- TWO BRUTES HARD TO FORGET.
"WE WORKED WELL AS A TEAM, DICK, AND WHEN I WENT BACK TO GOTHAM AND BATMAN-- JEAN PAUL...
"...I LIKED THE SOUND OF NIGHTWING AND ROBIN A WHOLE LOT BETTER THAN BATMAN AND ROBIN."
WHICH ONLY PROVES THE MAXIM... BE CAREFUL WHAT YOU WISH FOR.
BUT, FUNNY THING... AFTER ALL THOSE YEARS PLAYING ROBIN TO BRUCE'S BATMAN, IT WASN'T BAD HAVING A ROBIN AT MY SIDE.
AND NOW, HERE WE BOTH ARE--TWO ROBINS PLAYING BATMAN AND ROBIN.
LET'S JUST HOPE WE'RE BOTH READY FOR IT.
"HEY, IF YOU'RE THINKING ABOUT YOUR EARLY RUN-IN WITH TWO-FACE, DICK..."
...I WON'T MAKE THAT KIND OF MISTAKE.
GOOD TO KNOW, BUT IT'S NOT YOU I'M WORRIED ABOUT. A MAN DIED BACK THEN BECAUSE I WASN'T READY TO BE ROBIN.
IT WASN'T YOUR FAULT.
14

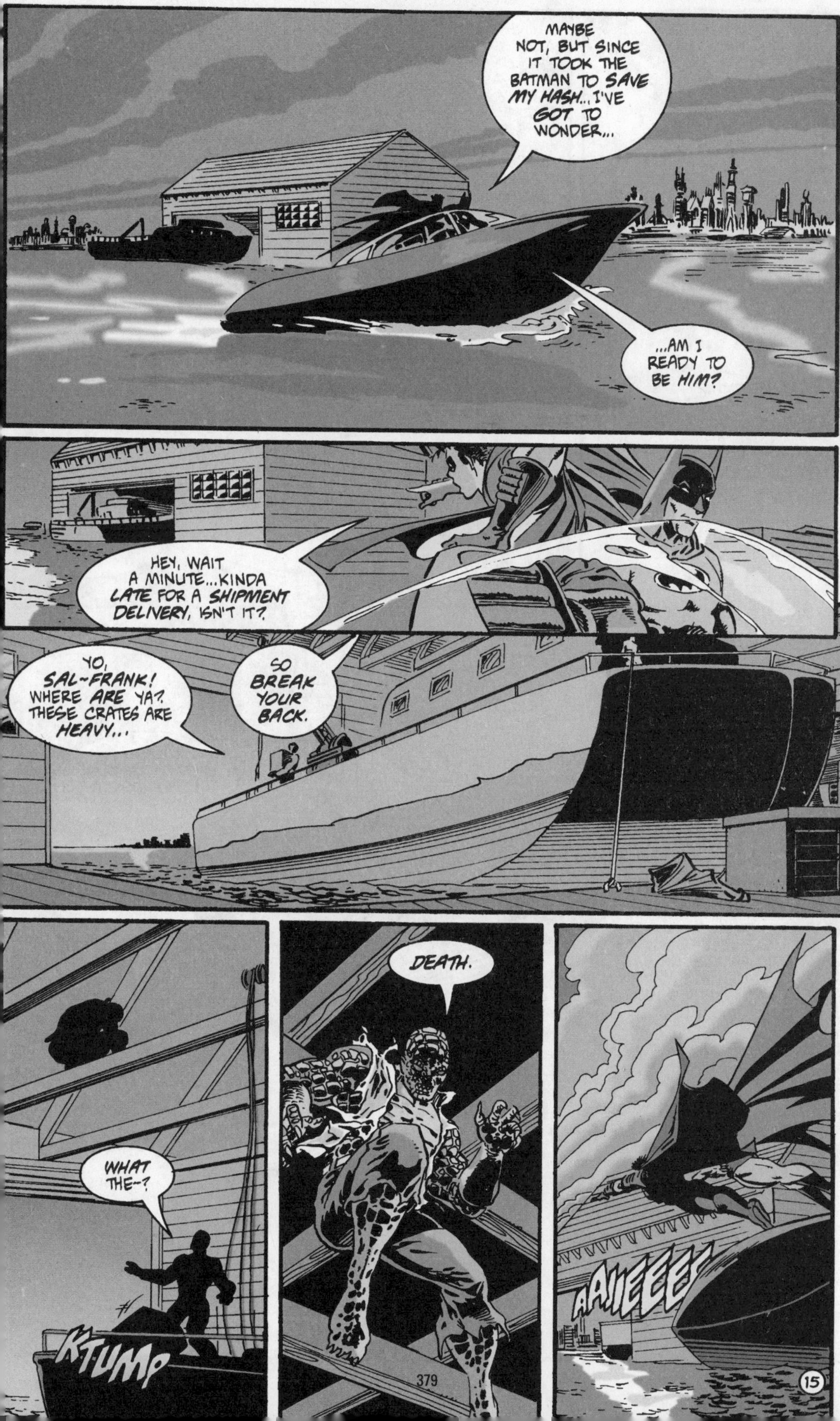
MAYBE NOT, BUT SINCE IT TOOK THE BATMAN TO SAVE MY HASH... I'VE GOT TO WONDER...
...AM I READY TO BE HIM?
HEY, WAIT A MINUTE... KINDA LATE FOR A SHIPMENT DELIVERY, ISN'T IT?
YO, SAL-FRANK! WHERE ARE YA? THESE CRATES ARE HEAVY...
SO BREAK YOUR BACK.
WHAT THE--?
KTUMP
DEATH.
AAIIEEE

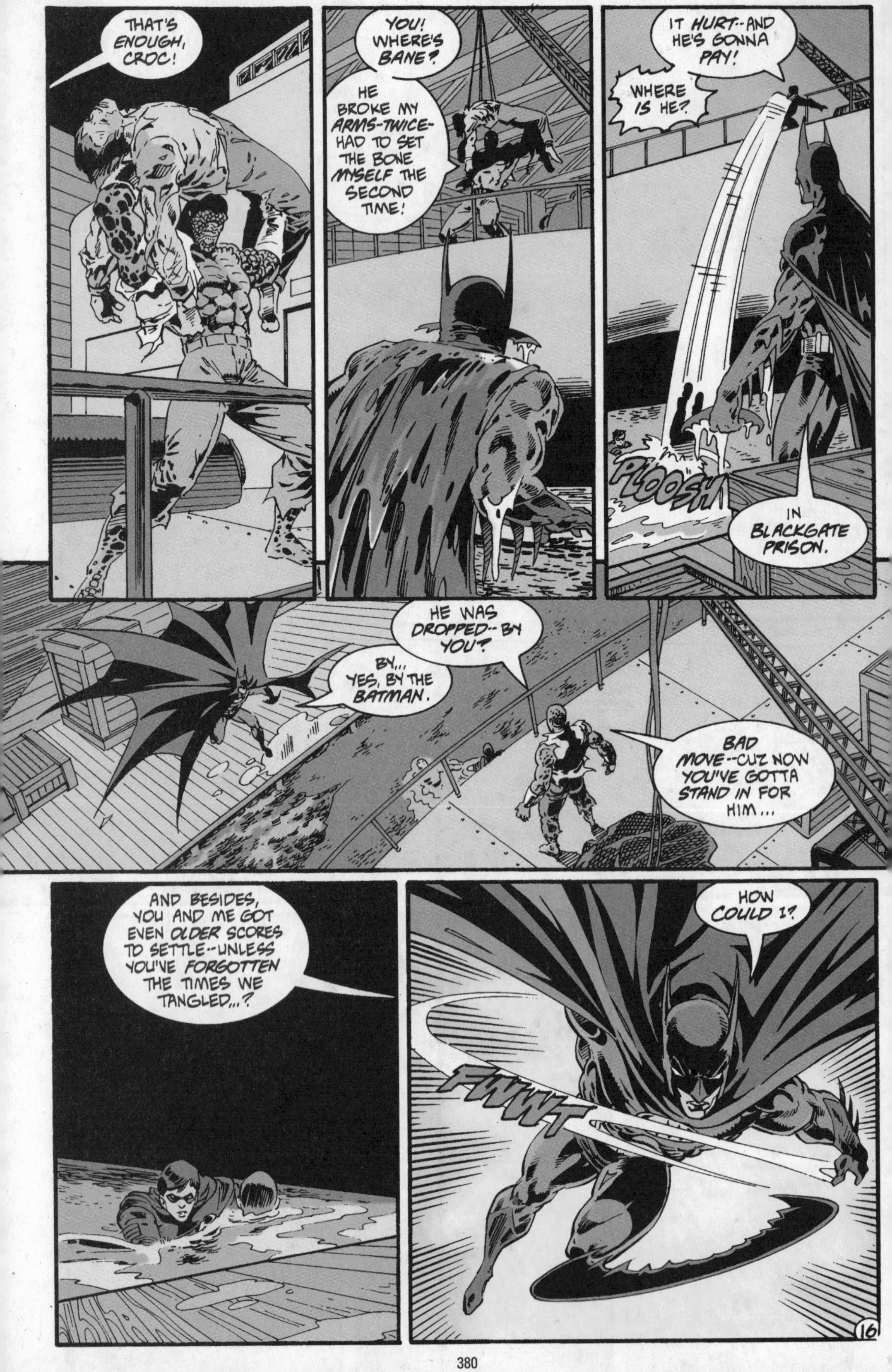
THAT'S ENOUGH, CROC!
YOU! WHERE'S BANE?
HE BROKE MY ARMS--TWICE-- HAD TO SET THE BONE MYSELF THE SECOND TIME!
IT HURT--AND HE'S GONNA PAY!
WHERE IS HE?
PLOOSH
IN BLACKGATE PRISON.
HE WAS DROPPED--BY YOU?
BY... YES, BY THE BATMAN.
BAD MOVE--CUZ NOW YOU'VE GOTTA STAND IN FOR HIM...
AND BESIDES, YOU AND ME GOT EVEN OLDER SCORES TO SETTLE--UNLESS YOU'VE FORGOTTEN THE TIMES WE TANGLED...?
HOW COULD I?
FWWT
16

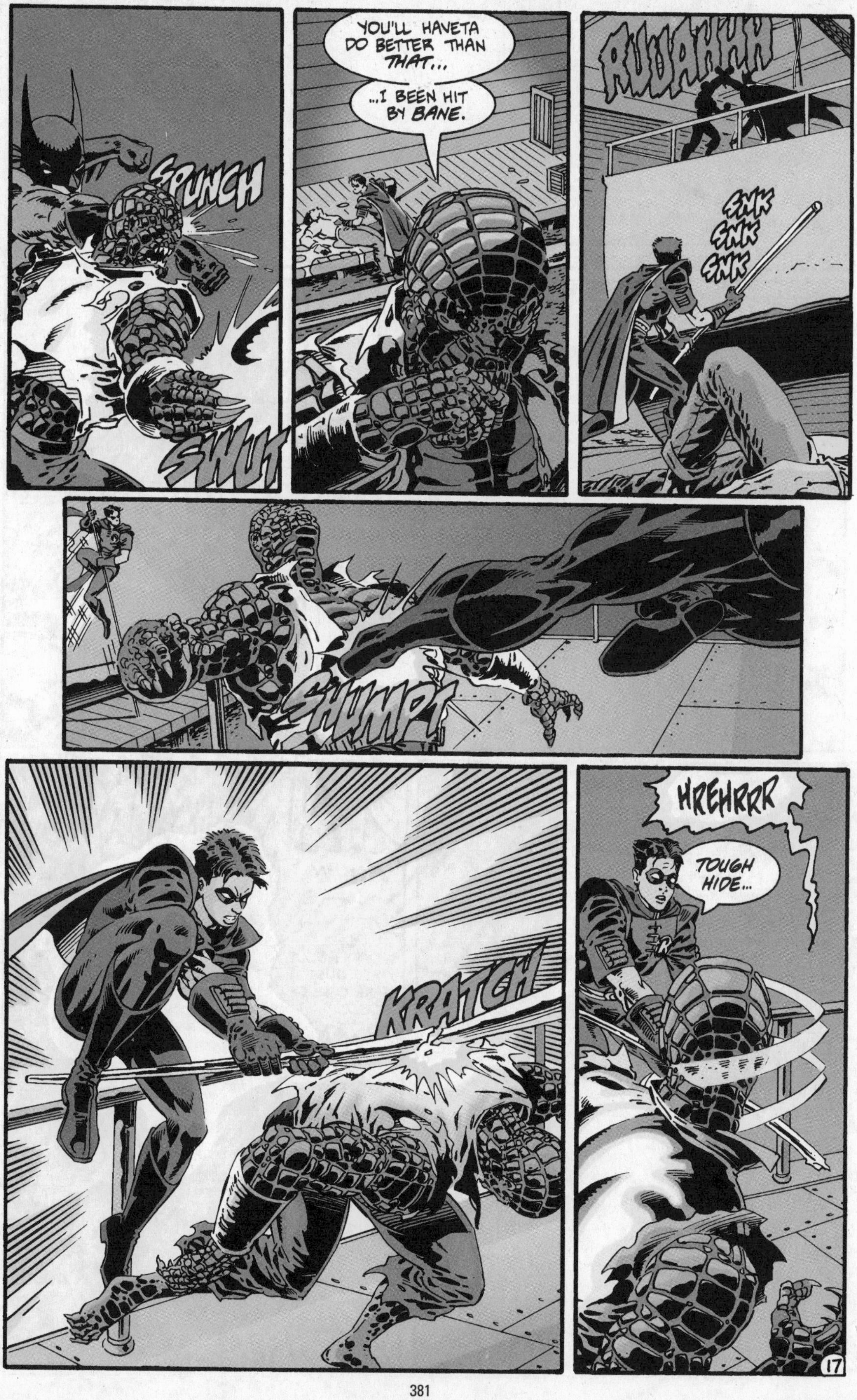
SPUNCH
SWUT
YOU'LL HAVETA DO BETTER THAN THAT...
...I BEEN HIT BY BANE.
RUUAHHH
SNK SNK SNK
SHUMPT
KRATCH
HREHRRR
TOUGH HIDE...
17

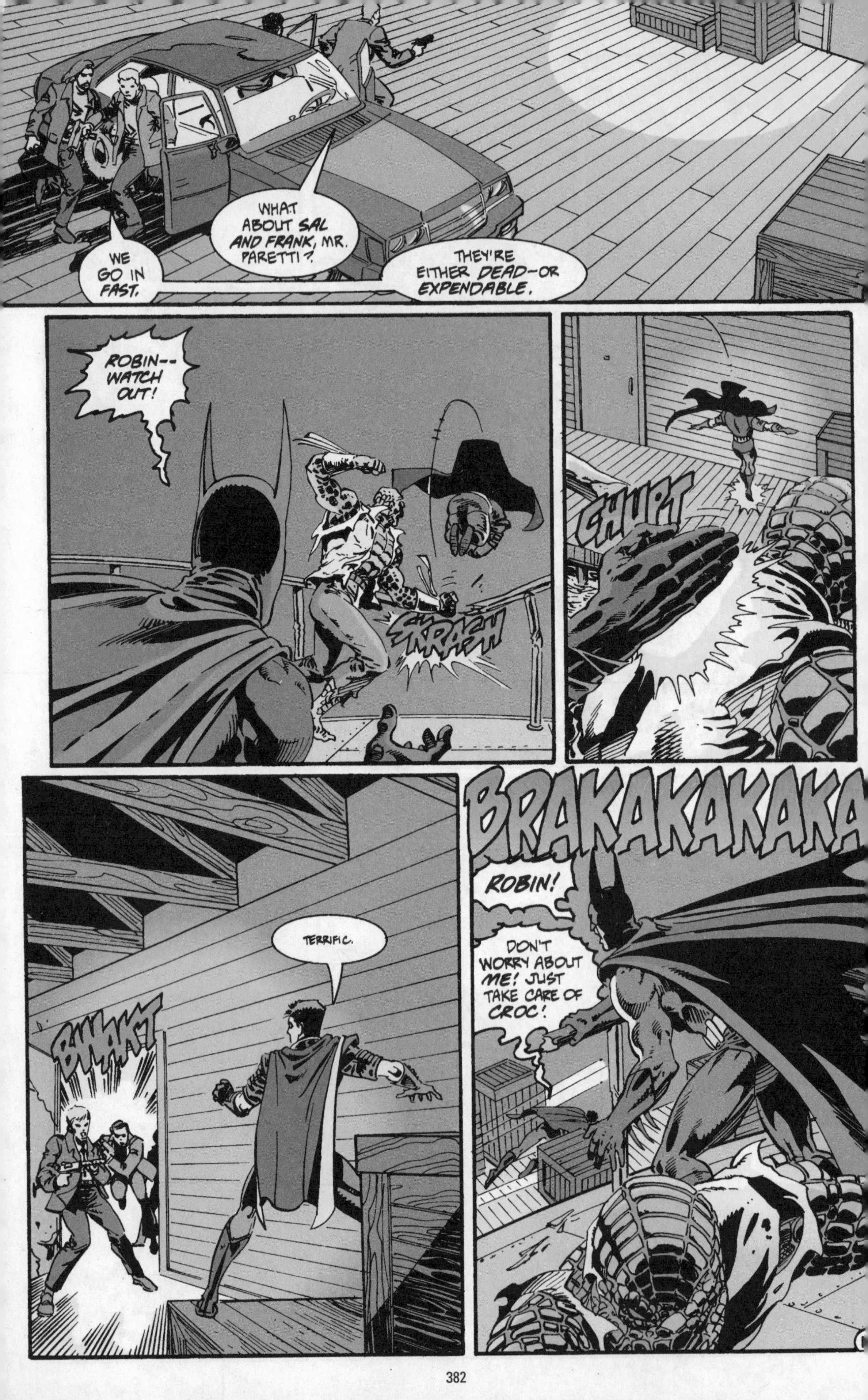
WE GO IN FAST.
WHAT ABOUT SAL AND FRANK, MR. PARETTI?
THEY'RE EITHER DEAD--OR EXPENDABLE.
ROBIN--WATCH OUT!
SKRASH
CHUPT
TERRIFIC.
BHAKT
BRAKAKAKAKA
ROBIN!
DON'T WORRY ABOUT ME! JUST TAKE CARE OF CROC!

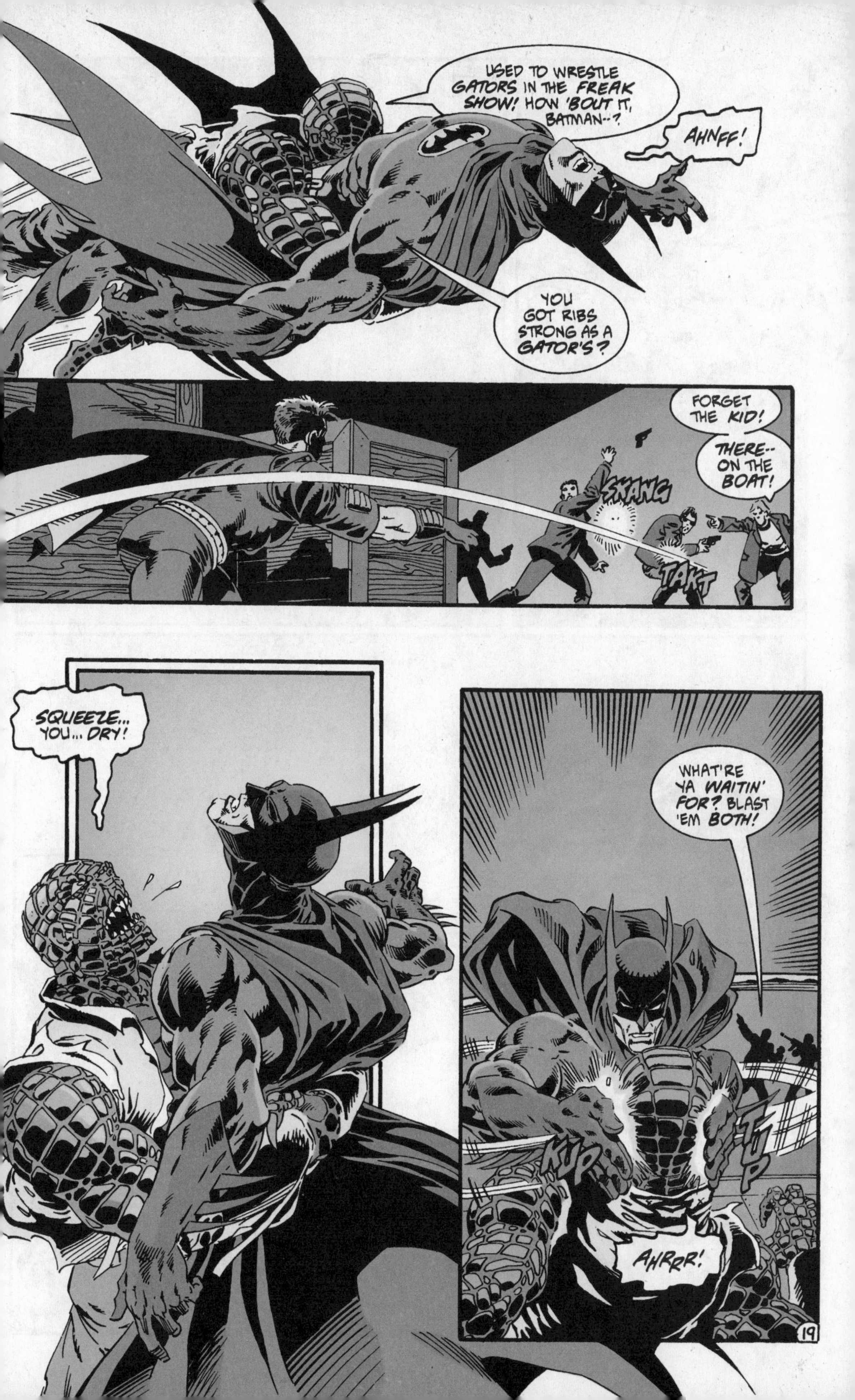
USED TO WRESTLE GATORS IN THE FREAK SHOW! HOW 'BOUT IT, BATMAN--?
AHNFF!
YOU GOT RIBS STRONG AS A GATOR'S?
FORGET THE KID!
THERE-- ON THE BOAT!
SKANG
TAKT
SQUEEZE... YOU... DRY!
WHAT'RE YA WAITIN' FOR? BLAST 'EM BOTH!
KUP
TUP
AHRRR!

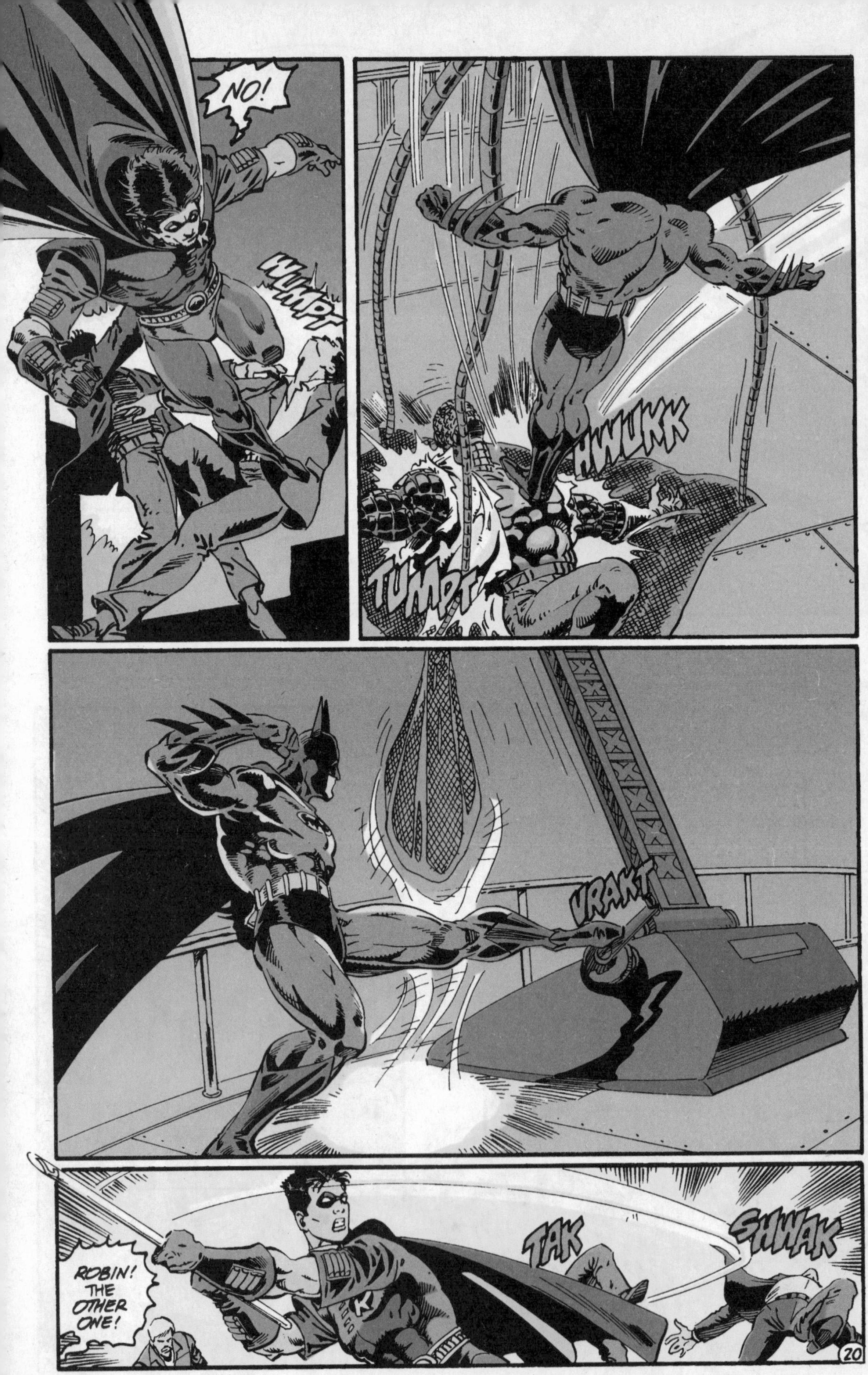
NO!
WUMPT
HWUKK
TUMPT
URAKT
ROBIN! THE OTHER ONE!
TAK
SHWAK
20

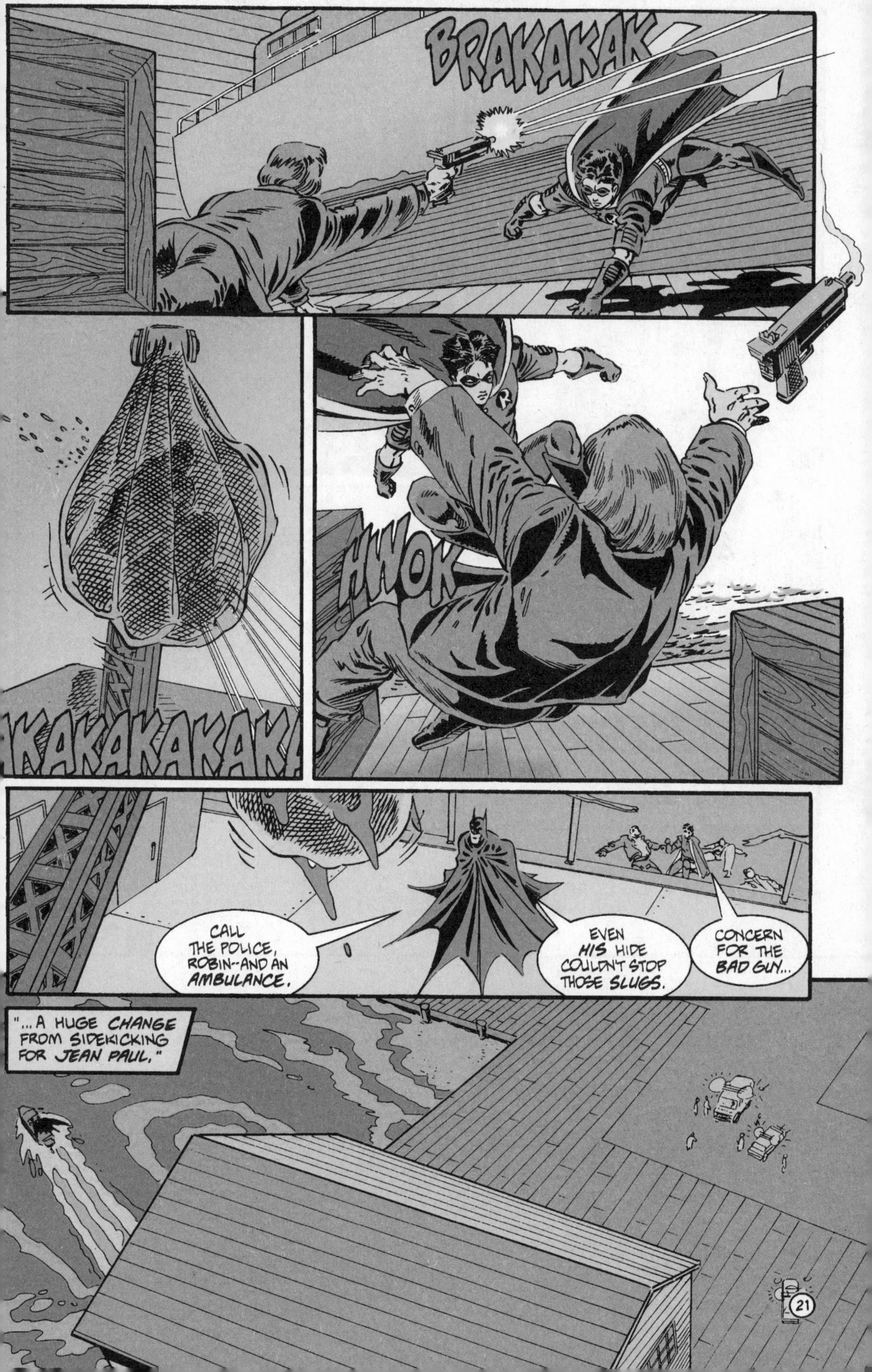
BRAKAKAK
KAKAKAKAKAKAK
HWOK
CALL THE POLICE, ROBIN--AND AN AMBULANCE.
EVEN HIS HIDE COULDN'T STOP THOSE SLUGS.
CONCERN FOR THE BAD GUY...
"...A HUGE CHANGE FROM SIDEKICKING FOR JEAN PAUL."

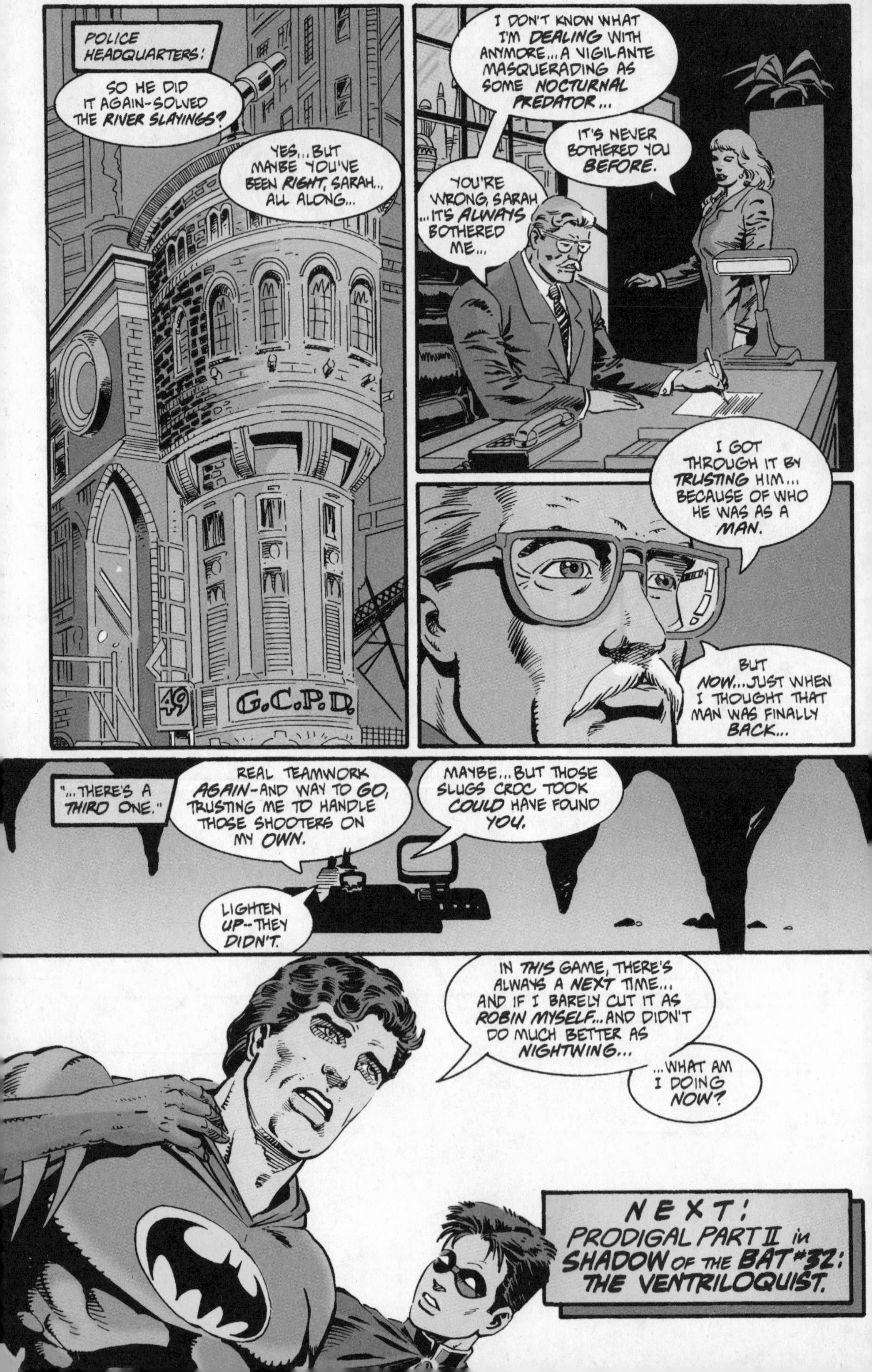
POLICE HEADQUARTERS:
SO HE DID IT AGAIN-SOLVED THE RIVER SLAYINGS?
YES... BUT MAYBE YOU'VE BEEN RIGHT, SARAH... ALL ALONG...
G.C.P.D.
49
I DON'T KNOW WHAT I'M DEALING WITH ANYMORE... A VIGILANTE MASQUERADING AS SOME NOCTURNAL PREDATOR...
IT'S NEVER BOTHERED YOU BEFORE.
YOU'RE WRONG, SARAH ...IT'S ALWAYS BOTHERED ME...
I GOT THROUGH IT BY TRUSTING HIM... BECAUSE OF WHO HE WAS AS A MAN.
BUT NOW...JUST WHEN I THOUGHT THAT MAN WAS FINALLY BACK...
"...THERE'S A THIRD ONE."
REAL TEAMWORK AGAIN-AND WAY TO GO, TRUSTING ME TO HANDLE THOSE SHOOTERS ON MY OWN.
MAYBE... BUT THOSE SLUGS CROC TOOK COULD HAVE FOUND YOU.
LIGHTEN UP--THEY DIDN'T.
IN THIS GAME, THERE'S ALWAYS A NEXT TIME... AND IF I BARELY CUT IT AS ROBIN MYSELF... AND DIDN'T DO MUCH BETTER AS NIGHTWING...
...WHAT AM I DOING NOW?
NEXT! PRODIGAL PART II in SHADOW OF THE BAT #32: THE VENTRILOQUIST.

Cover art by **BRIAN STELFREEZE**

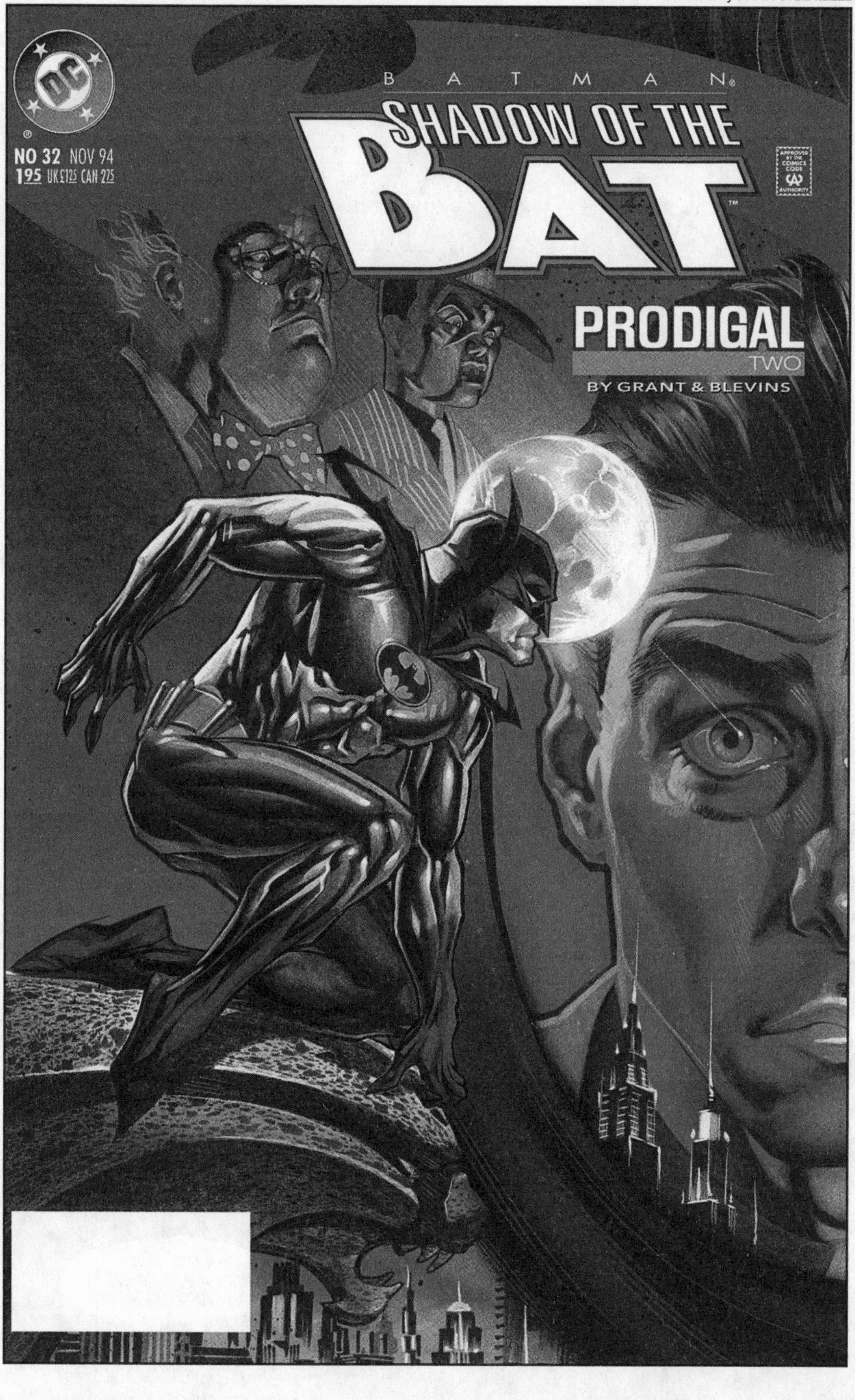

DC
NO 32 NOV 94
1.95 UK £1.25 CAN 2.75
BATMAN
SHADOW OF THE BAT
APPROVED BY THE COMICS CODE AUTHORITY
PRODIGAL
TWO
BY GRANT & BLEVINS

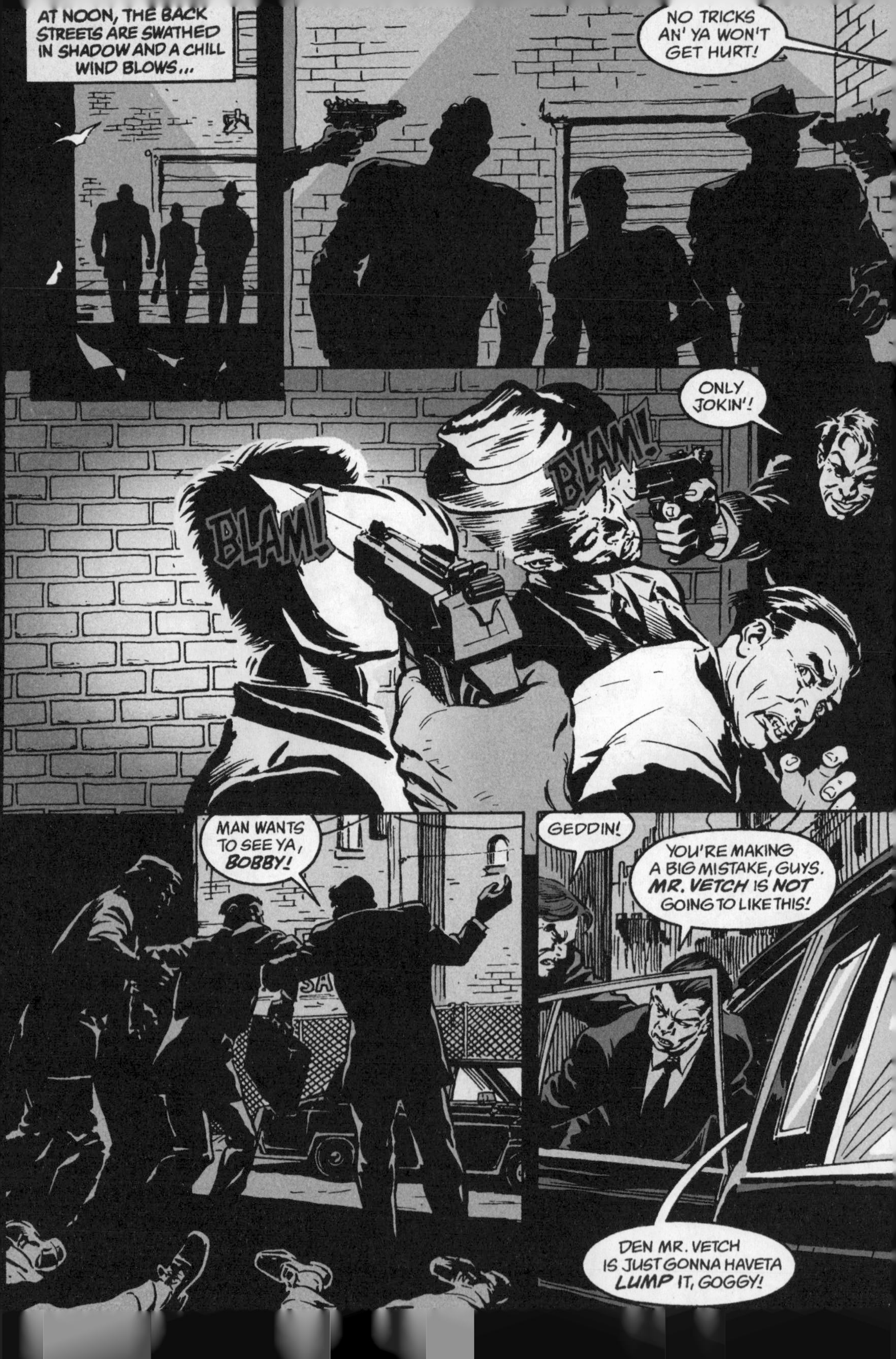
AT NOON, THE BACK STREETS ARE SWATHED IN SHADOW AND A CHILL WIND BLOWS...
NO TRICKS AN' YA WON'T GET HURT!
ONLY JOKIN'!
BLAM!
BLAM!
MAN WANTS TO SEE YA, BOBBY!
GEDDIN!
YOU'RE MAKING A BIG MISTAKE, GUYS. MR. VETCH IS NOT GOING TO LIKE THIS!
DEN MR. VETCH IS JUST GONNA HAVETA LUMP IT, GOGGY!

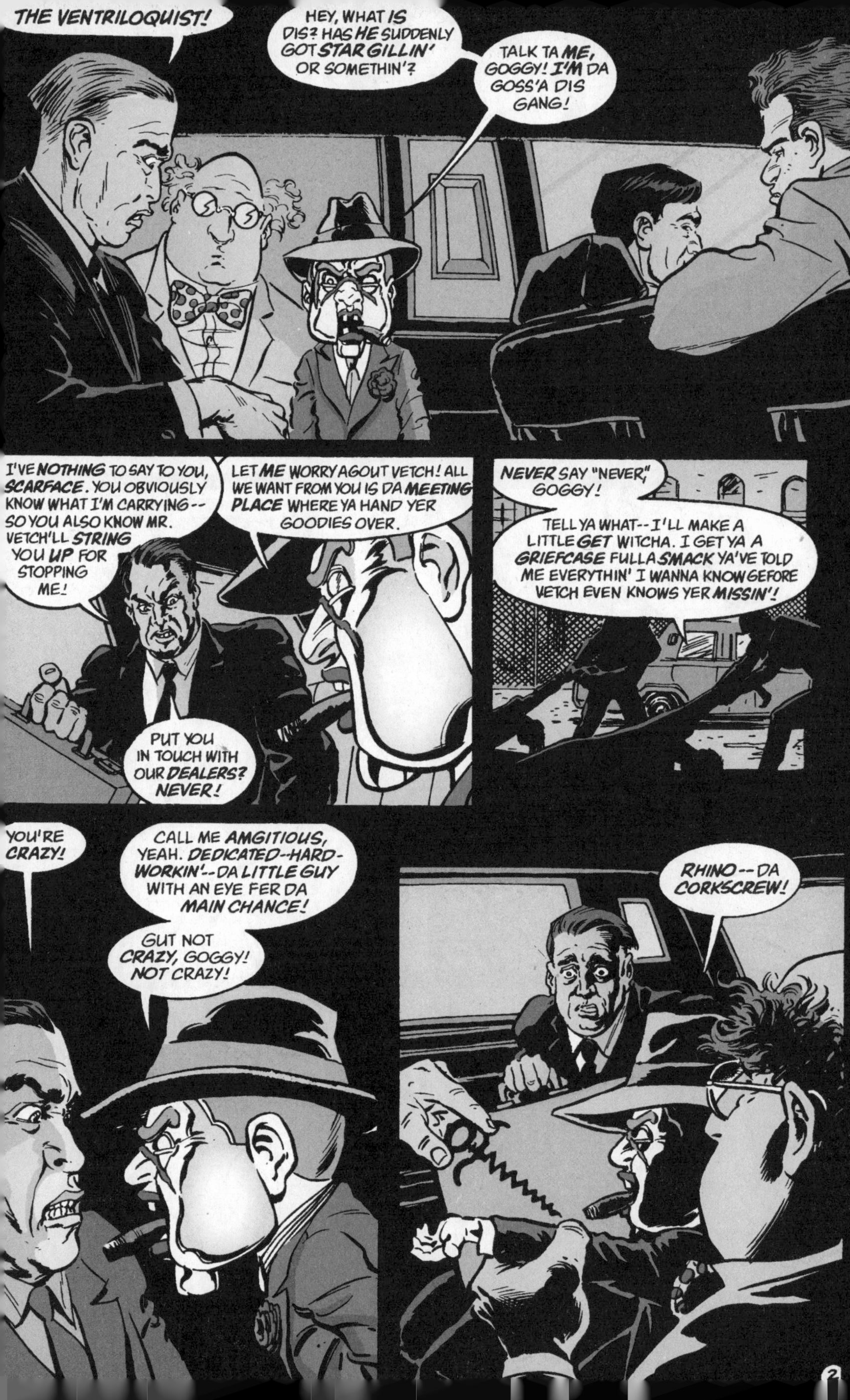
THE VENTRILOQUIST!
HEY, WHAT IS DIS? HAS HE SUDDENLY GOT STAR GILLIN' OR SOMETHIN'?
TALK TA ME, GOGGY! I'M DA GOSS'A DIS GANG!
I'VE NOTHING TO SAY TO YOU, SCARFACE. YOU OBVIOUSLY KNOW WHAT I'M CARRYING-- SO YOU ALSO KNOW MR. VETCH'LL STRING YOU UP FOR STOPPING ME!
LET ME WORRY AGOUT VETCH! ALL WE WANT FROM YOU IS DA MEETING PLACE WHERE YA HAND YER GOODIES OVER.
PUT YOU IN TOUCH WITH OUR DEALERS? NEVER!
NEVER SAY "NEVER," GOGGY!
TELL YA WHAT--I'LL MAKE A LITTLE GET WITCHA. I GET YA A GRIEFCASE FULLA SMACK YA'VE TOLD ME EVERYTHIN' I WANNA KNOW GEFORE VETCH EVEN KNOWS YER MISSIN'!
YOU'RE CRAZY!
CALL ME AMGITIOUS, YEAH. DEDICATED--HARD-WORKIN'--DA LITTLE GUY WITH AN EYE FER DA MAIN CHANCE!
GUT NOT CRAZY, GOGGY! NOT CRAZY!
RHINO--DA CORKSCREW!
2

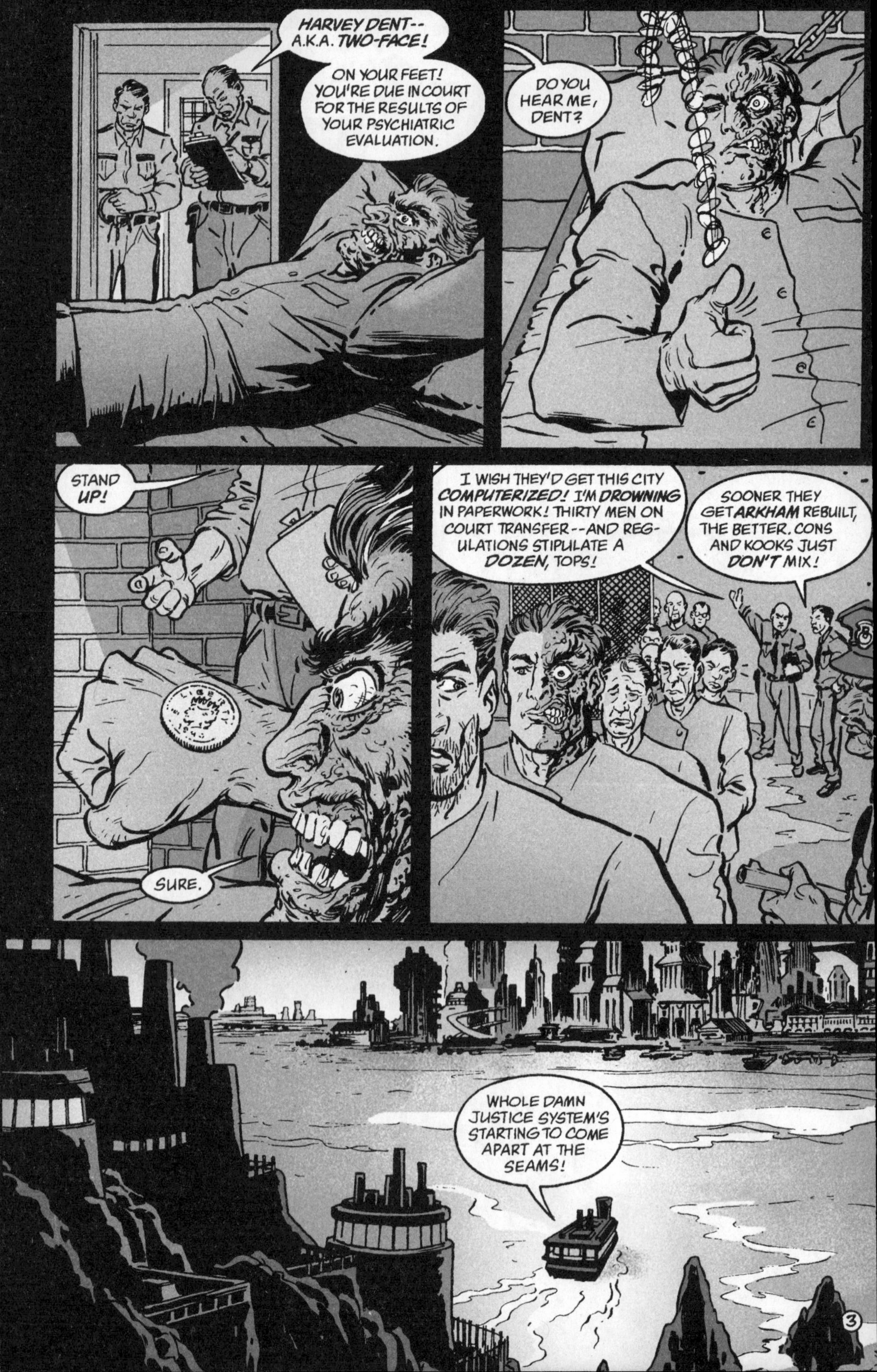

HARVEY DENT-- A.K.A. TWO-FACE!
ON YOUR FEET! YOU'RE DUE IN COURT FOR THE RESULTS OF YOUR PSYCHIATRIC EVALUATION.
DO YOU HEAR ME, DENT?
STAND UP!
SURE.
I WISH THEY'D GET THIS CITY COMPUTERIZED! I'M DROWNING IN PAPERWORK! THIRTY MEN ON COURT TRANSFER--AND REGULATIONS STIPULATE A DOZEN, TOPS!
SOONER THEY GET ARKHAM REBUILT, THE BETTER. CONS AND KOOKS JUST DON'T MIX!
WHOLE DAMN JUSTICE SYSTEM'S STARTING TO COME APART AT THE SEAMS!

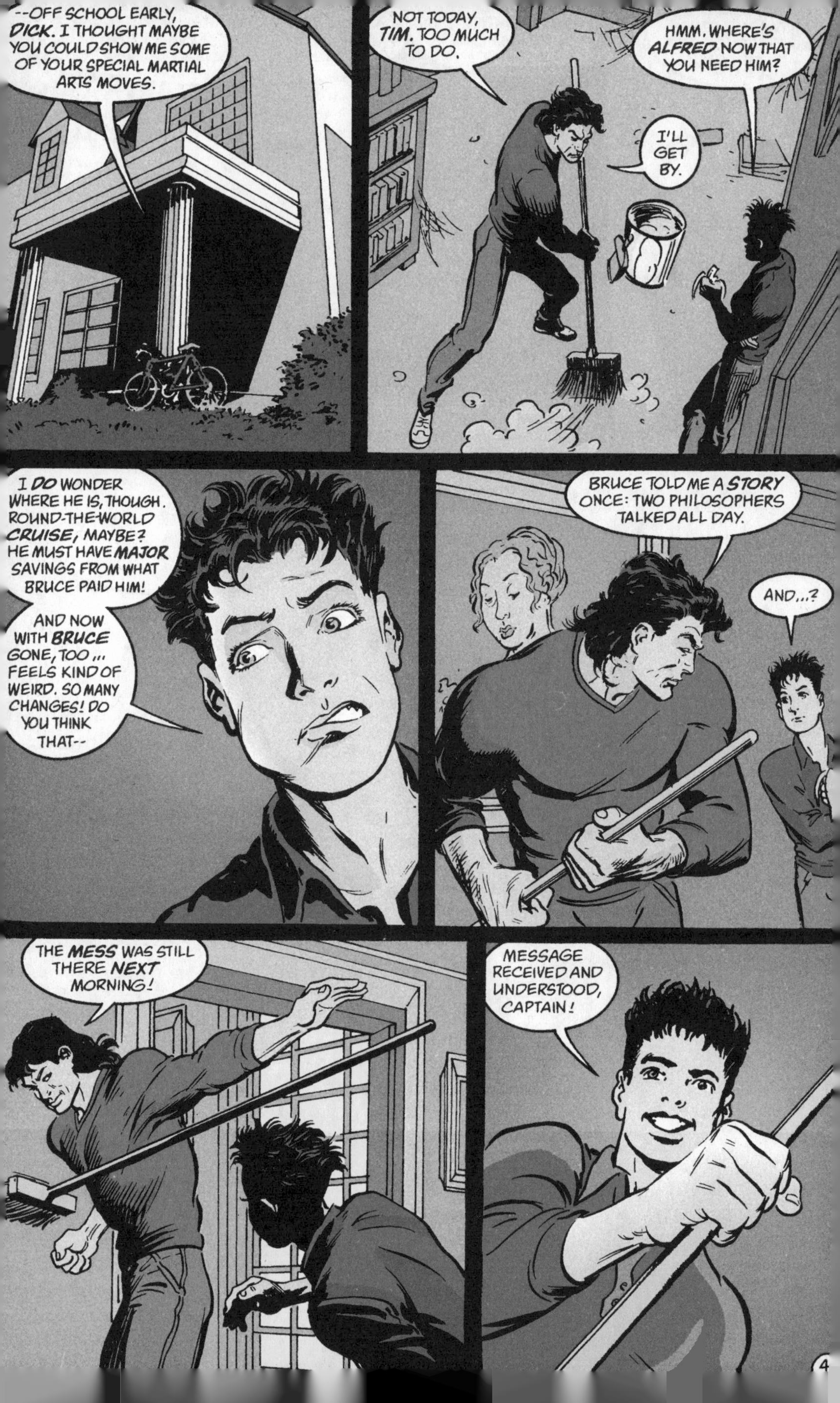
--OFF SCHOOL EARLY, DICK. I THOUGHT MAYBE YOU COULD SHOW ME SOME OF YOUR SPECIAL MARTIAL ARTS MOVES.
NOT TODAY, TIM. TOO MUCH TO DO.
HMM. WHERE'S ALFRED NOW THAT YOU NEED HIM?
I'LL GET BY.
I DO WONDER WHERE HE IS, THOUGH. ROUND-THE-WORLD CRUISE, MAYBE? HE MUST HAVE MAJOR SAVINGS FROM WHAT BRUCE PAID HIM!
AND NOW WITH BRUCE GONE, TOO... FEELS KIND OF WEIRD. SO MANY CHANGES! DO YOU THINK THAT--
BRUCE TOLD ME A STORY ONCE: TWO PHILOSOPHERS TALKED ALL DAY.
AND...?
THE MESS WAS STILL THERE NEXT MORNING!
MESSAGE RECEIVED AND UNDERSTOOD, CAPTAIN!
4

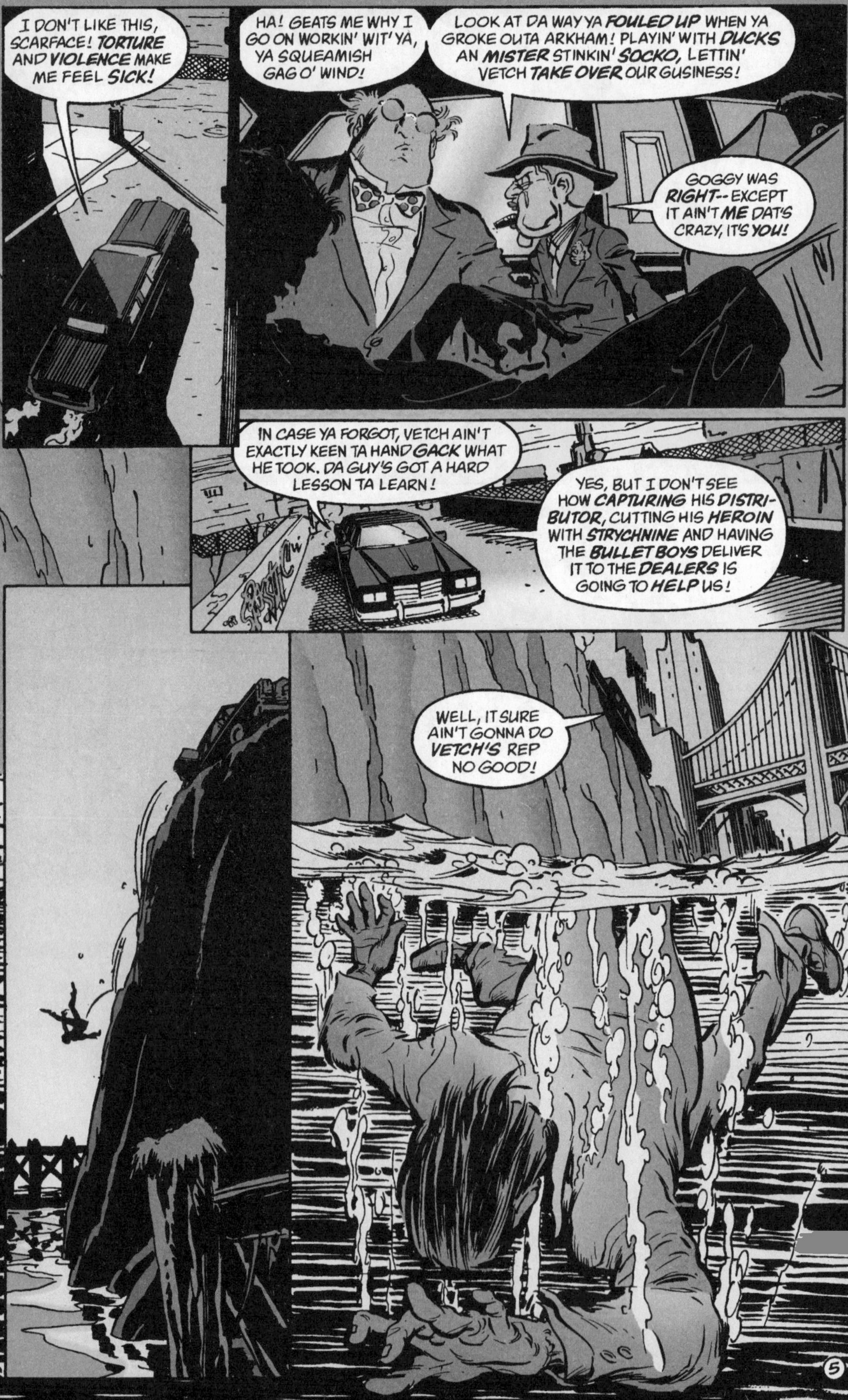
I DON'T LIKE THIS, SCARFACE! TORTURE AND VIOLENCE MAKE ME FEEL SICK!
HA! GEATS ME WHY I GO ON WORKIN' WIT'YA, YA SQUEAMISH GAG O' WIND!
LOOK AT DA WAY YA FOULED UP WHEN YA GROKE OUTA ARKHAM! PLAYIN' WITH DUCKS AN MISTER STINKIN' SOCKO, LETTIN' VETCH TAKE OVER OUR GUSINESS!
GOGGY WAS RIGHT-- EXCEPT IT AIN'T ME DAT'S CRAZY, IT'S YOU!
IN CASE YA FORGOT, VETCH AIN'T EXACTLY KEEN TA HAND GACK WHAT HE TOOK. DA GUY'S GOT A HARD LESSON TA LEARN!
YES, BUT I DON'T SEE HOW CAPTURING HIS DISTRIBUTOR, CUTTING HIS HEROIN WITH STRYCHNINE AND HAVING THE BULLET BOYS DELIVER IT TO THE DEALERS IS GOING TO HELP US!
WELL, IT SURE AIN'T GONNA DO VETCH'S REP NO GOOD!
5

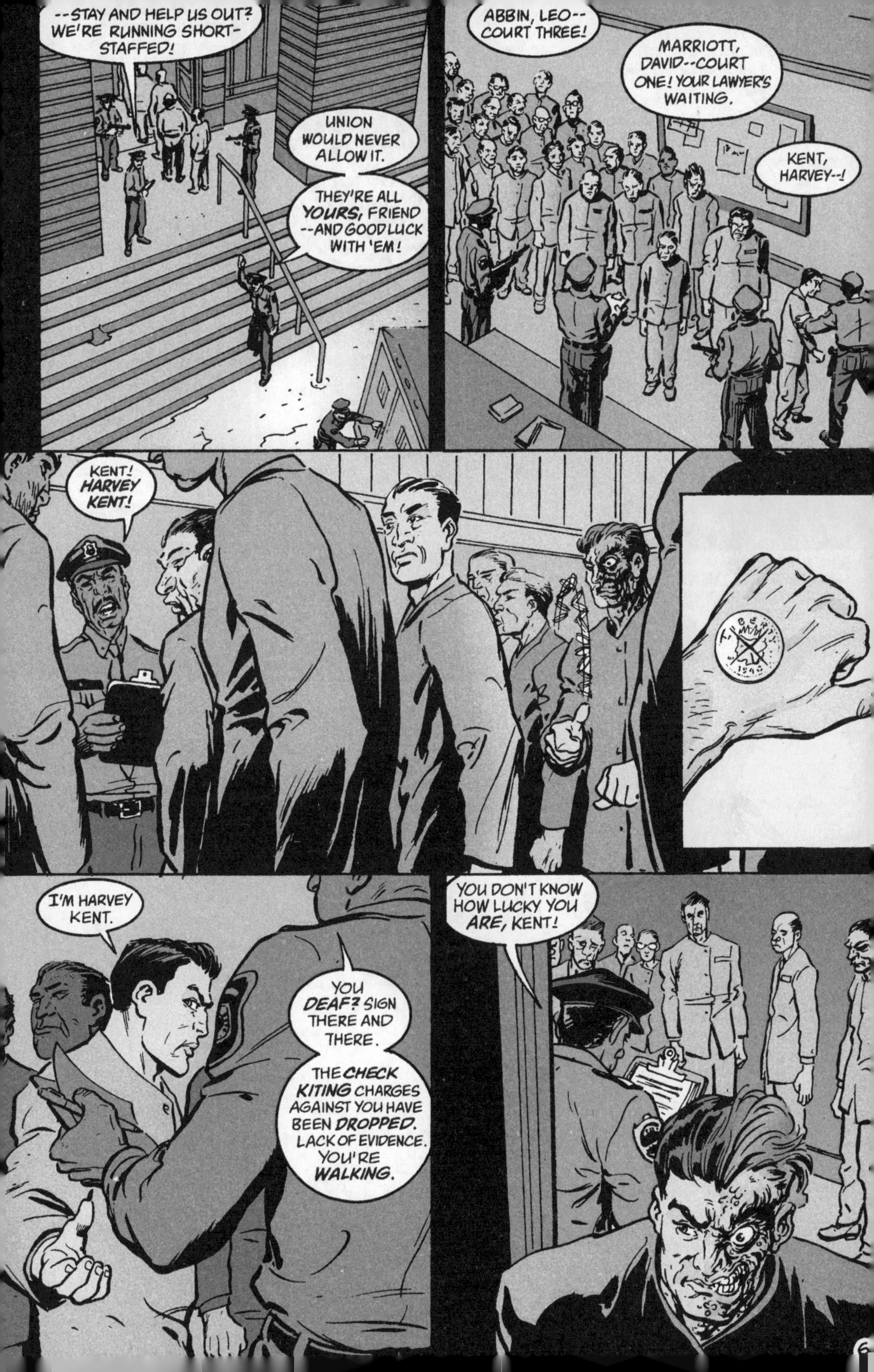

--STAY AND HELP US OUT? WE'RE RUNNING SHORT-STAFFED!
UNION WOULD NEVER ALLOW IT.
THEY'RE ALL YOURS, FRIEND --AND GOOD LUCK WITH 'EM!
ABBIN, LEO-- COURT THREE!
MARRIOTT, DAVID--COURT ONE! YOUR LAWYER'S WAITING.
KENT, HARVEY--!
KENT! HARVEY KENT!
I'M HARVEY KENT.
YOU DEAF? SIGN THERE AND THERE.
THE CHECK KITING CHARGES AGAINST YOU HAVE BEEN DROPPED. LACK OF EVIDENCE. YOU'RE WALKING.
YOU DON'T KNOW HOW LUCKY YOU ARE, KENT!

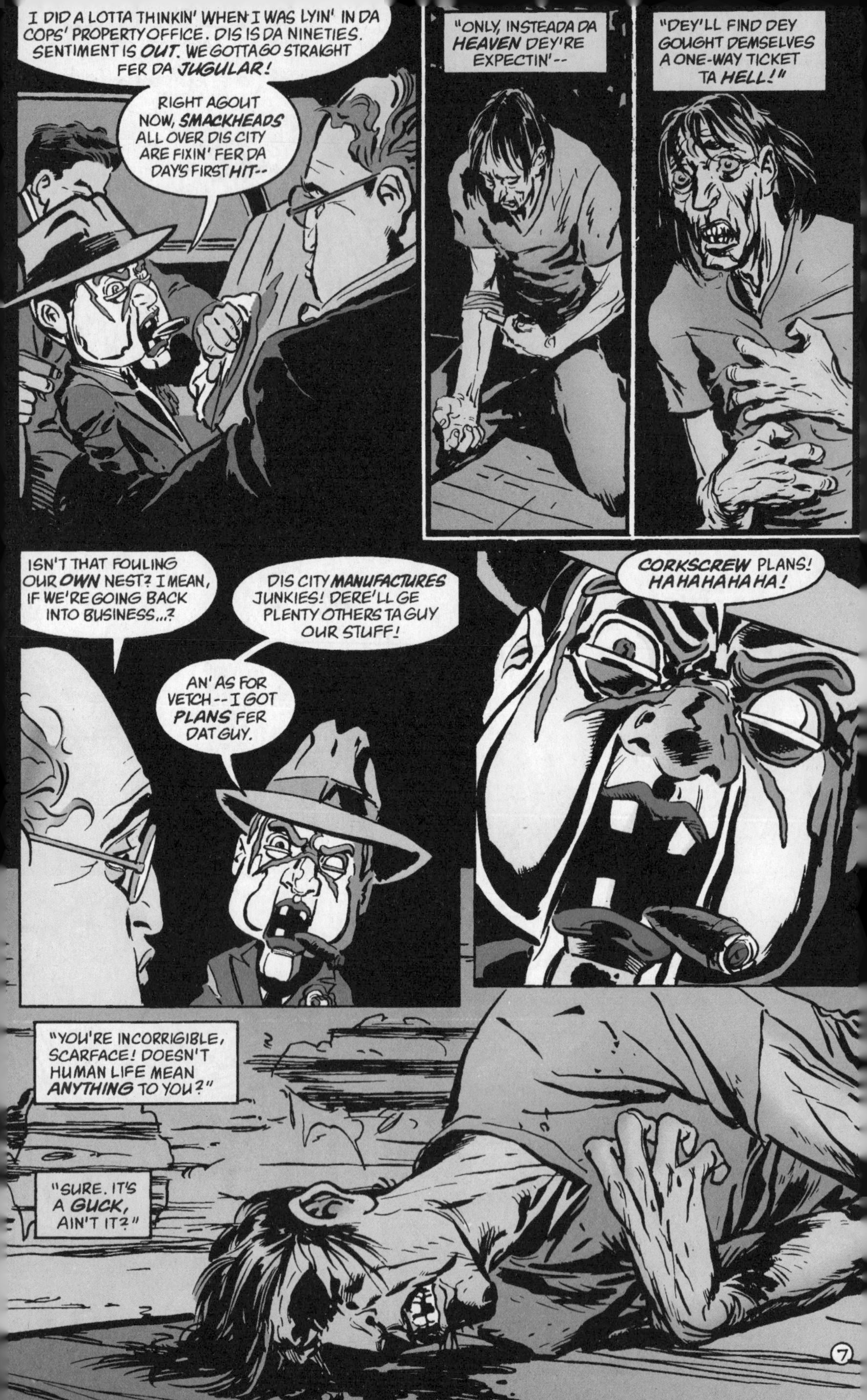
I DID A LOTTA THINKIN' WHEN I WAS LYIN' IN DA COPS' PROPERTY OFFICE. DIS IS DA NINETIES. SENTIMENT IS OUT. WE GOTTA GO STRAIGHT FER DA JUGULAR!
RIGHT AGOUT NOW, SMACKHEADS ALL OVER DIS CITY ARE FIXIN' FER DA DAY'S FIRST HIT--
"ONLY, INSTEADA DA HEAVEN DEY'RE EXPECTIN'--
"DEY'LL FIND DEY GOUGHT DEMSELVES A ONE-WAY TICKET TA HELL!"
ISN'T THAT FOULING OUR OWN NEST? I MEAN, IF WE'RE GOING BACK INTO BUSINESS...?
DIS CITY MANUFACTURES JUNKIES! DERE'LL GE PLENTY OTHERS TA GUY OUR STUFF!
AN' AS FOR VETCH--I GOT PLANS FER DAT GUY.
CORKSCREW PLANS! HAHAHAHAHA!
"YOU'RE INCORRIGIBLE, SCARFACE! DOESN'T HUMAN LIFE MEAN ANYTHING TO YOU?"
"SURE. IT'S A GUCK, AIN'T IT?"
7

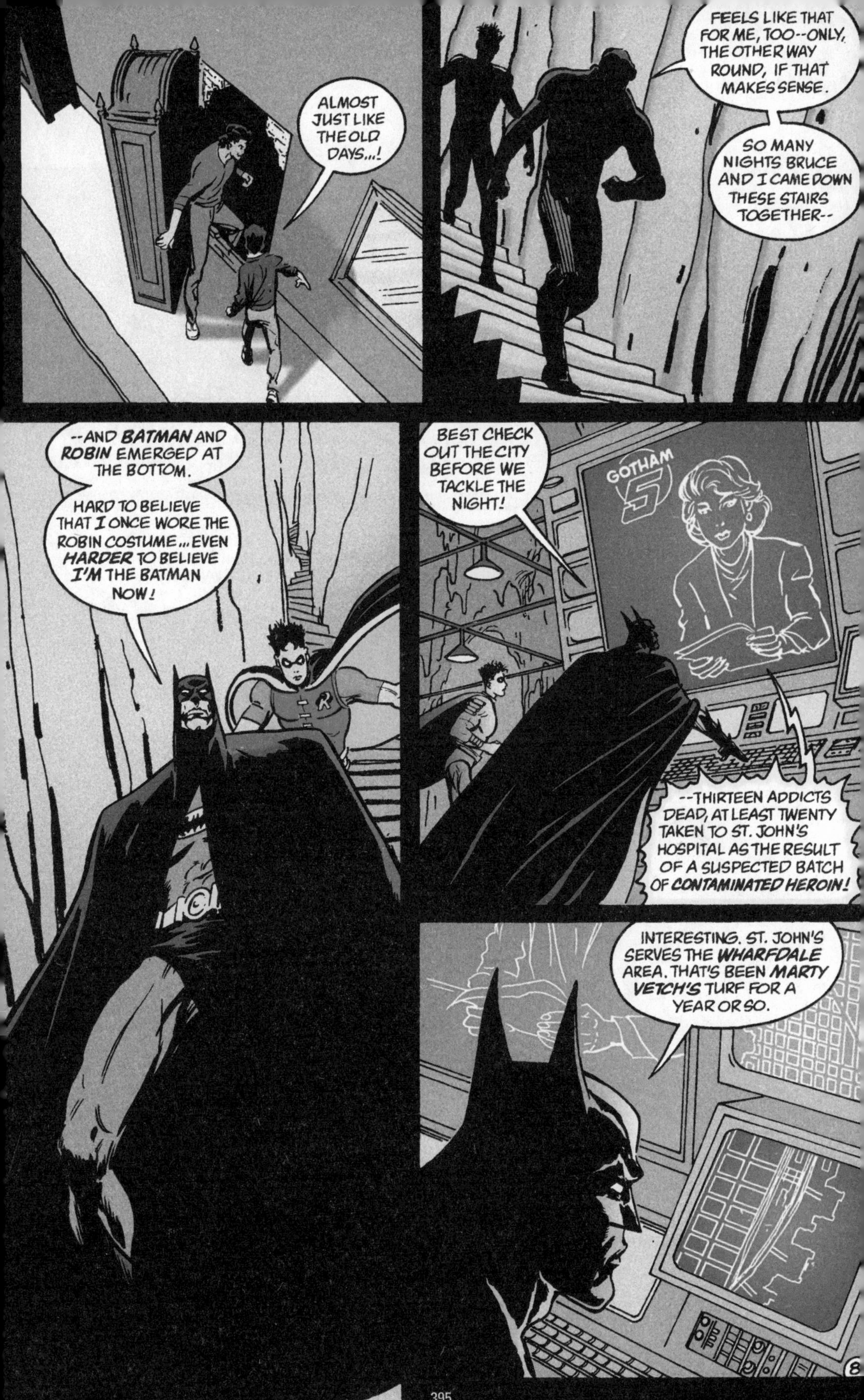
ALMOST JUST LIKE THE OLD DAYS...!
FEELS LIKE THAT FOR ME, TOO--ONLY, THE OTHER WAY ROUND, IF THAT MAKES SENSE.
SO MANY NIGHTS BRUCE AND I CAME DOWN THESE STAIRS TOGETHER--
--AND BATMAN AND ROBIN EMERGED AT THE BOTTOM.
HARD TO BELIEVE THAT I ONCE WORE THE ROBIN COSTUME... EVEN HARDER TO BELIEVE I'M THE BATMAN NOW!
BEST CHECK OUT THE CITY BEFORE WE TACKLE THE NIGHT!
GOTHAM 5
--THIRTEEN ADDICTS DEAD, AT LEAST TWENTY TAKEN TO ST. JOHN'S HOSPITAL AS THE RESULT OF A SUSPECTED BATCH OF CONTAMINATED HEROIN!
INTERESTING. ST. JOHN'S SERVES THE WHARFDALE AREA. THAT'S BEEN MARTY VETCH'S TURF FOR A YEAR OR SO.
8

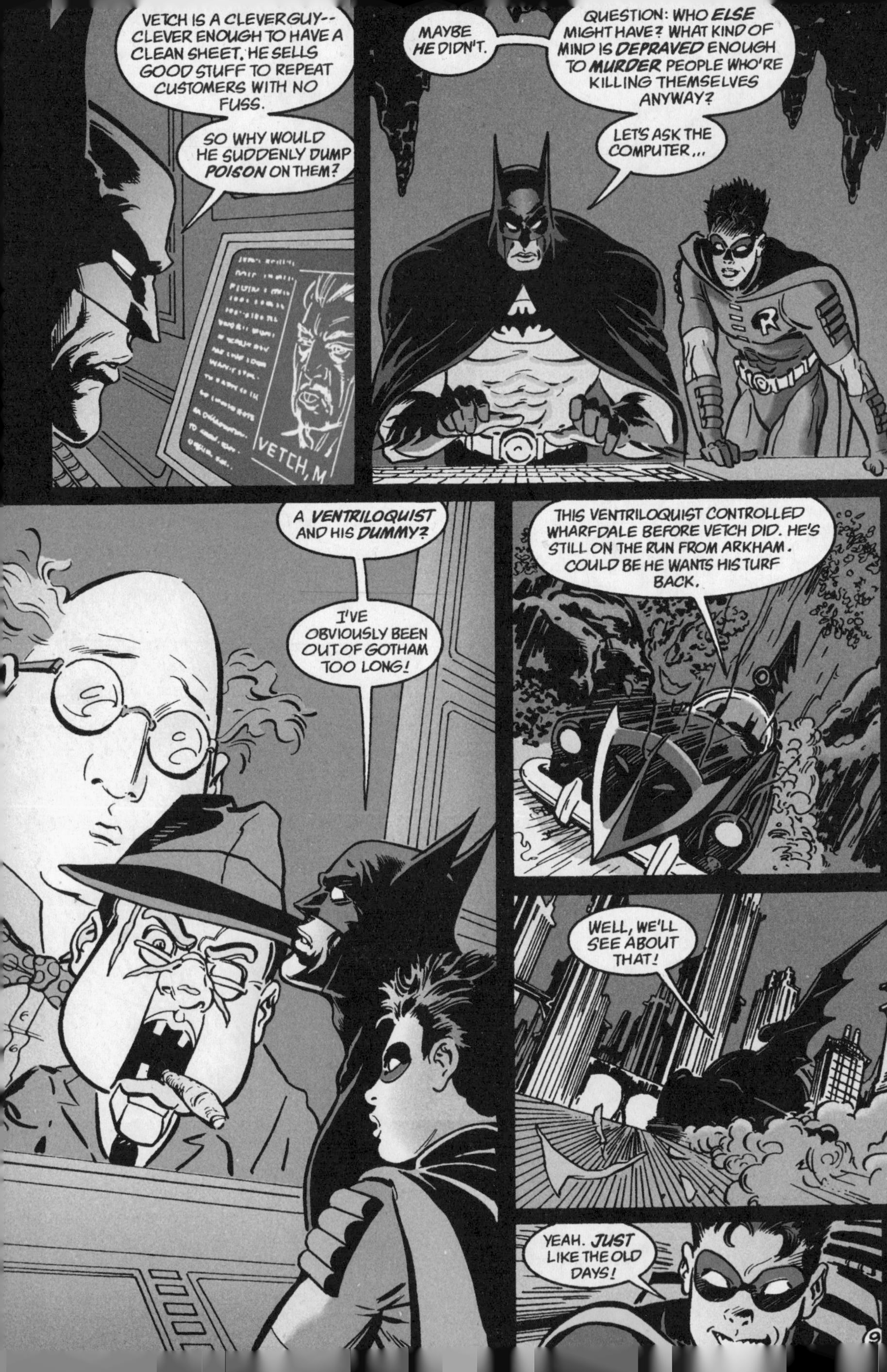
VETCH IS A CLEVER GUY-- CLEVER ENOUGH TO HAVE A CLEAN SHEET. HE SELLS GOOD STUFF TO REPEAT CUSTOMERS WITH NO FUSS.
SO WHY WOULD HE SUDDENLY DUMP POISON ON THEM?
VETCH, M
MAYBE HE DIDN'T.
QUESTION: WHO ELSE MIGHT HAVE? WHAT KIND OF MIND IS DEPRAVED ENOUGH TO MURDER PEOPLE WHO'RE KILLING THEMSELVES ANYWAY?
LET'S ASK THE COMPUTER...
A VENTRILOQUIST AND HIS DUMMY?
I'VE OBVIOUSLY BEEN OUT OF GOTHAM TOO LONG!
THIS VENTRILOQUIST CONTROLLED WHARFDALE BEFORE VETCH DID. HE'S STILL ON THE RUN FROM ARKHAM. COULD BE HE WANTS HIS TURF BACK.
WELL, WE'LL SEE ABOUT THAT!
YEAH. JUST LIKE THE OLD DAYS!
9

--AT LEAST TWENTY--

--AND WE CAN COUNT ON THERE BEING *MORE*. DEALERS WHO'VE *PAID* FOR BAD HEROIN WON'T BE WILLING TO LOSE MONEY. THEY'LL JUST *CUT* IT AND PASS IT ON,...!

MAYBE NOT SUCH A BAD THING, COMMISH. IT'S NOT EXACTLY *ENHANCEMENTS* TO THE CITY WE'RE LOSING!

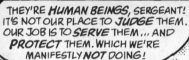

THEY'RE *HUMAN BEINGS*, SERGEANT! IT'S NOT OUR PLACE TO *JUDGE* THEM. OUR JOB IS TO *SERVE* THEM,... AND *PROTECT* THEM. WHICH WE'RE MANIFESTLY *NOT* DOING!

SORRY, COMMISH. FEEBLE JOKE!

HE LOOKS UP AT THE SKY, FOR A MOMENT ALMOST EXPECTANT. IT'S AT TIMES LIKE THIS HE USED TO ASK FOR HELP.

THE TRUST IT REQUIRED TO WORK WITH A VIGILANTE HAD BEEN BUILT UP OVER A LONG TIME. JIM GORDON *COULD* NEVER SEEK AID FROM SOMEONE HE DIDN'T KNOW.

AND HE NO LONGER KNOWS THE MAN IN THE COSTUME.

10

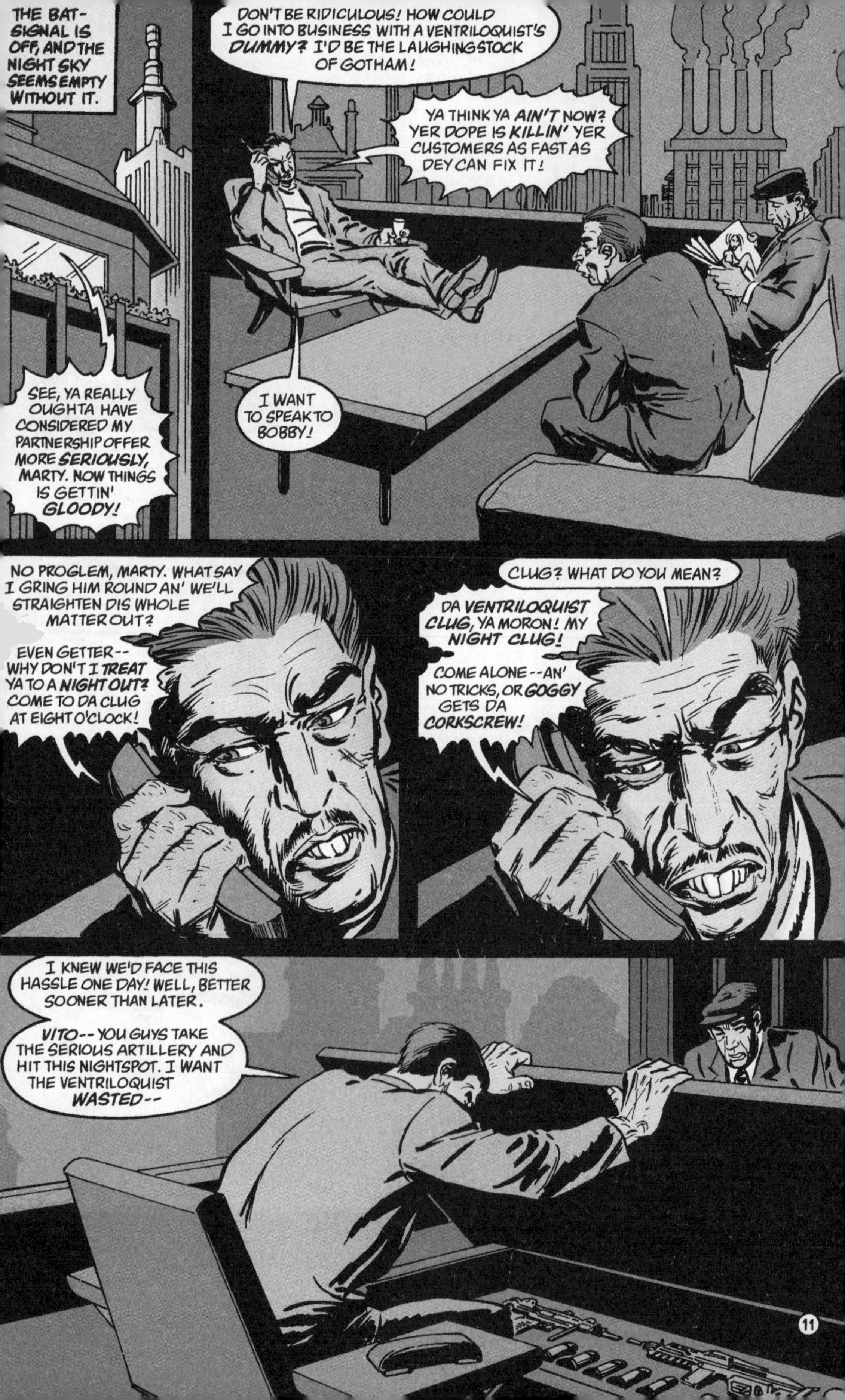
THE BAT-SIGNAL IS OFF, AND THE NIGHT SKY SEEMS EMPTY WITHOUT IT.
DON'T BE RIDICULOUS! HOW COULD I GO INTO BUSINESS WITH A VENTRILOQUIST'S DUMMY? I'D BE THE LAUGHINGSTOCK OF GOTHAM!
YA THINK YA AIN'T NOW? YER DOPE IS KILLIN' YER CUSTOMERS AS FAST AS DEY CAN FIX IT!
SEE, YA REALLY OUGHTA HAVE CONSIDERED MY PARTNERSHIP OFFER MORE SERIOUSLY, MARTY. NOW THINGS IS GETTIN' GLOODY!
I WANT TO SPEAK TO BOBBY!
NO PROGLEM, MARTY. WHAT SAY I GRING HIM ROUND AN' WE'LL STRAIGHTEN DIS WHOLE MATTER OUT?
EVEN GETTER-- WHY DON'T I TREAT YA TO A NIGHT OUT? COME TO DA CLUG AT EIGHT O'CLOCK!
CLUG? WHAT DO YOU MEAN?
DA VENTRILOQUIST CLUG, YA MORON! MY NIGHT CLUG!
COME ALONE--AN' NO TRICKS, OR GOGGY GETS DA CORKSCREW!
I KNEW WE'D FACE THIS HASSLE ONE DAY! WELL, BETTER SOONER THAN LATER.
VITO-- YOU GUYS TAKE THE SERIOUS ARTILLERY AND HIT THIS NIGHTSPOT. I WANT THE VENTRILOQUIST WASTED--
11

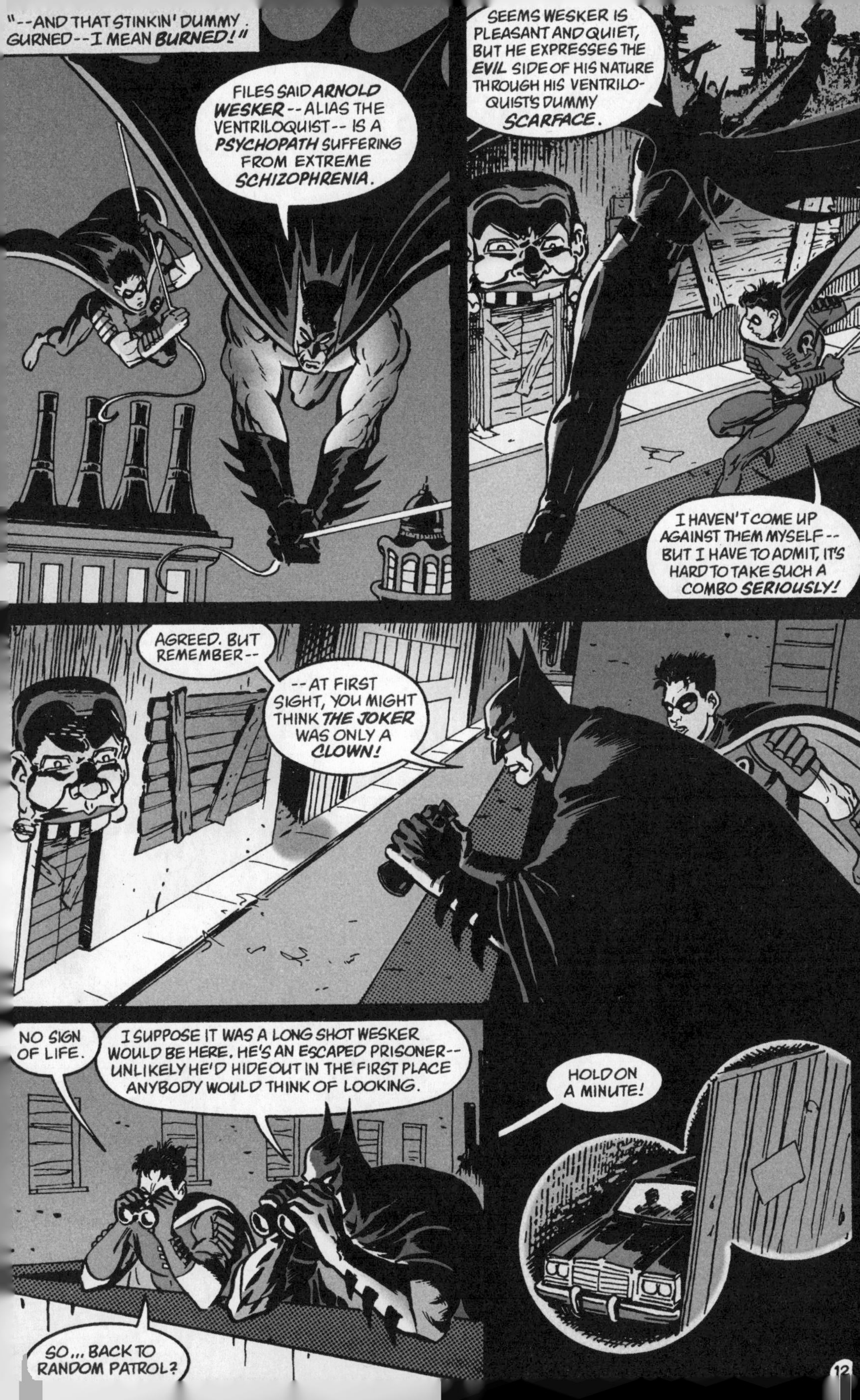
"--AND THAT STINKIN' DUMMY GURNED--I MEAN BURNED!"
FILES SAID ARNOLD WESKER--ALIAS THE VENTRILOQUIST--IS A PSYCHOPATH SUFFERING FROM EXTREME SCHIZOPHRENIA.
SEEMS WESKER IS PLEASANT AND QUIET, BUT HE EXPRESSES THE EVIL SIDE OF HIS NATURE THROUGH HIS VENTRILOQUIST'S DUMMY SCARFACE.
I HAVEN'T COME UP AGAINST THEM MYSELF--BUT I HAVE TO ADMIT, IT'S HARD TO TAKE SUCH A COMBO SERIOUSLY!
AGREED. BUT REMEMBER--
--AT FIRST SIGHT, YOU MIGHT THINK THE JOKER WAS ONLY A CLOWN!
NO SIGN OF LIFE.
I SUPPOSE IT WAS A LONG SHOT WESKER WOULD BE HERE. HE'S AN ESCAPED PRISONER--UNLIKELY HE'D HIDE OUT IN THE FIRST PLACE ANYBODY WOULD THINK OF LOOKING.
SO... BACK TO RANDOM PATROL?
HOLD ON A MINUTE!

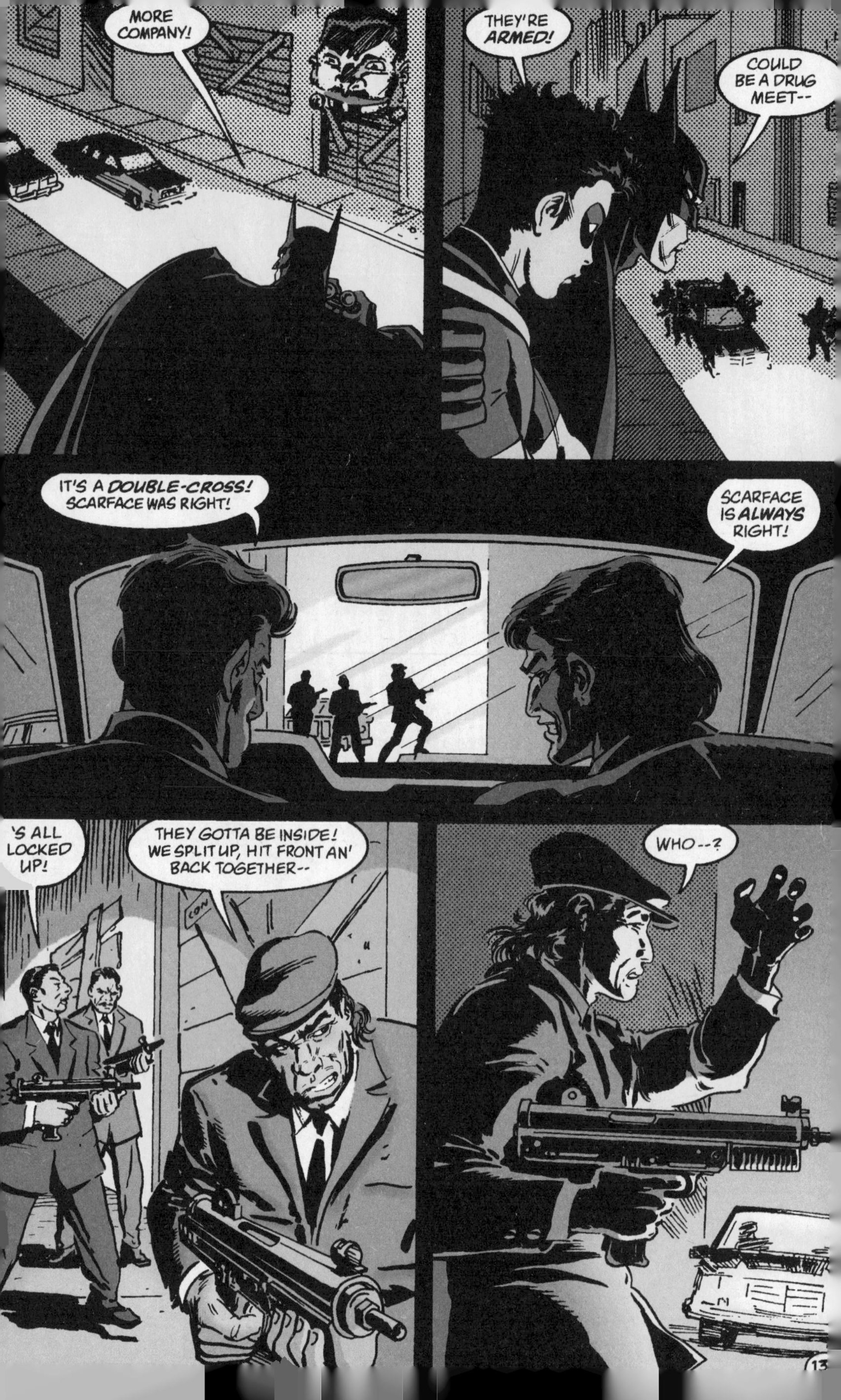
MORE COMPANY!
THEY'RE ARMED!
COULD BE A DRUG MEET--
IT'S A DOUBLE-CROSS! SCARFACE WAS RIGHT!
SCARFACE IS ALWAYS RIGHT!
'S ALL LOCKED UP!
THEY GOTTA BE INSIDE! WE SPLIT UP, HIT FRONT AN' BACK TOGETHER--
WHO--?

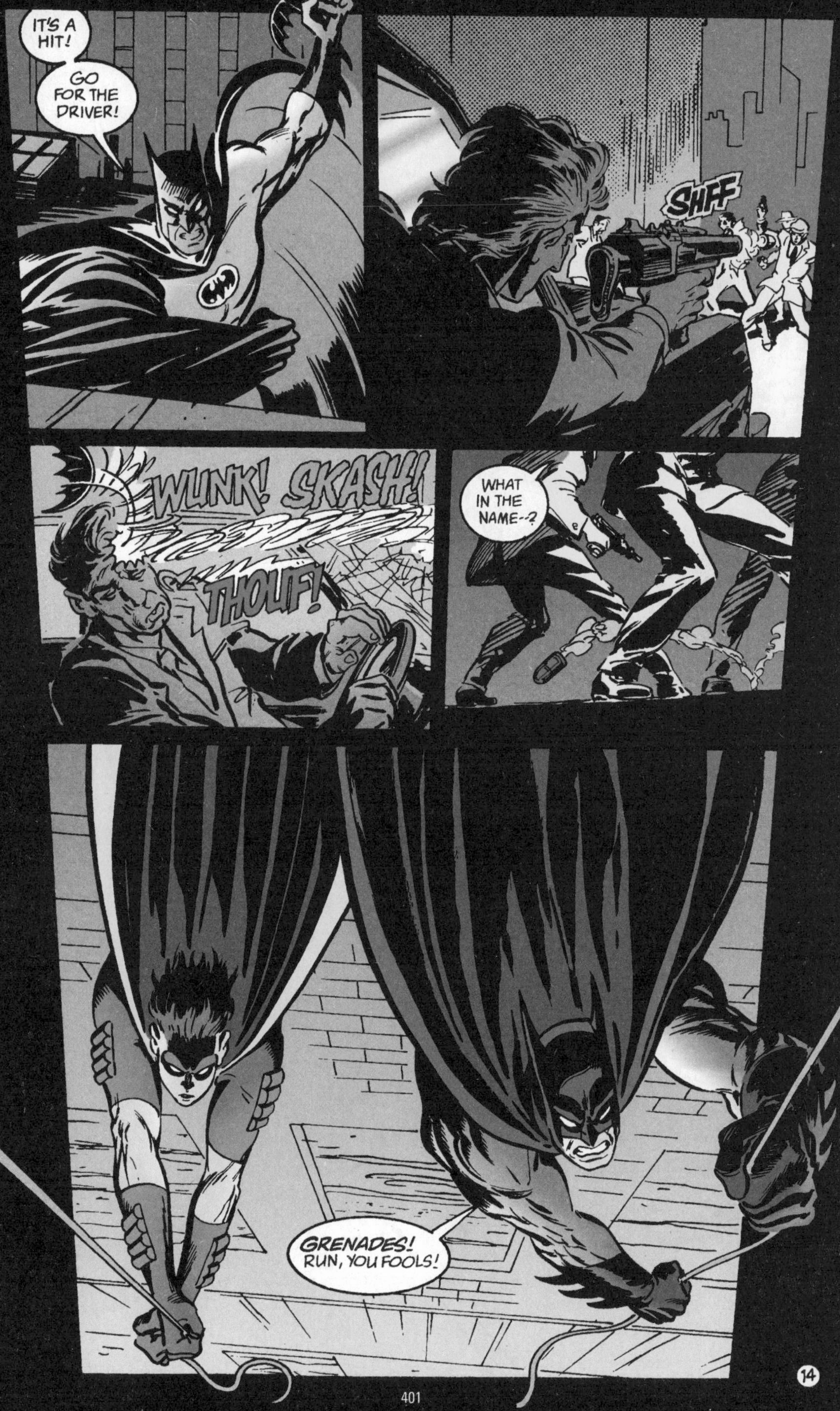
IT'S A HIT!
GO FOR THE DRIVER!
SHFF
WUNK! SKASH!
THOUF!
WHAT IN THE NAME--?
GRENADES! RUN, YOU FOOLS!
14

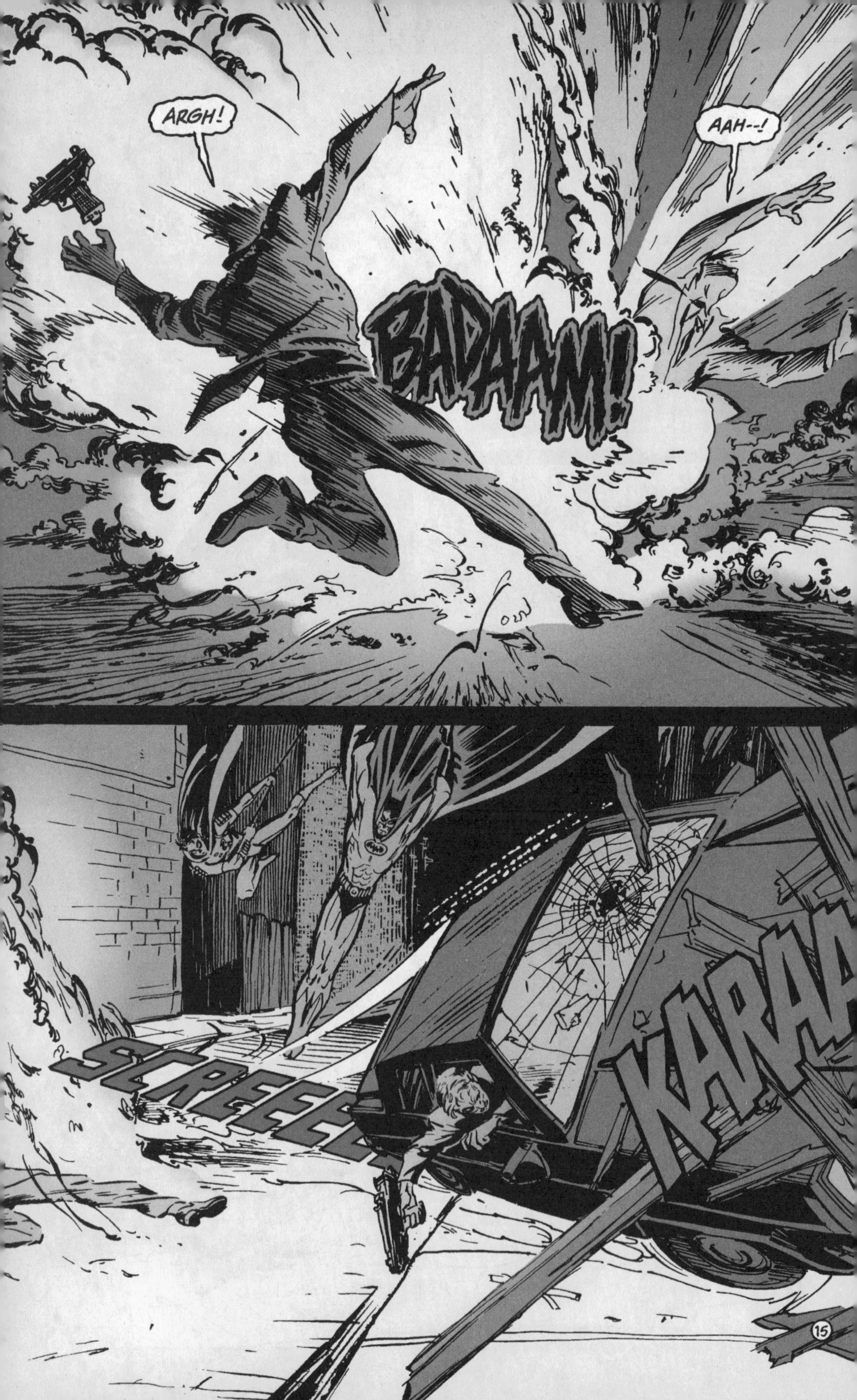
ARGH!
AAH--!
BADAAM!
SCREEE
KARA

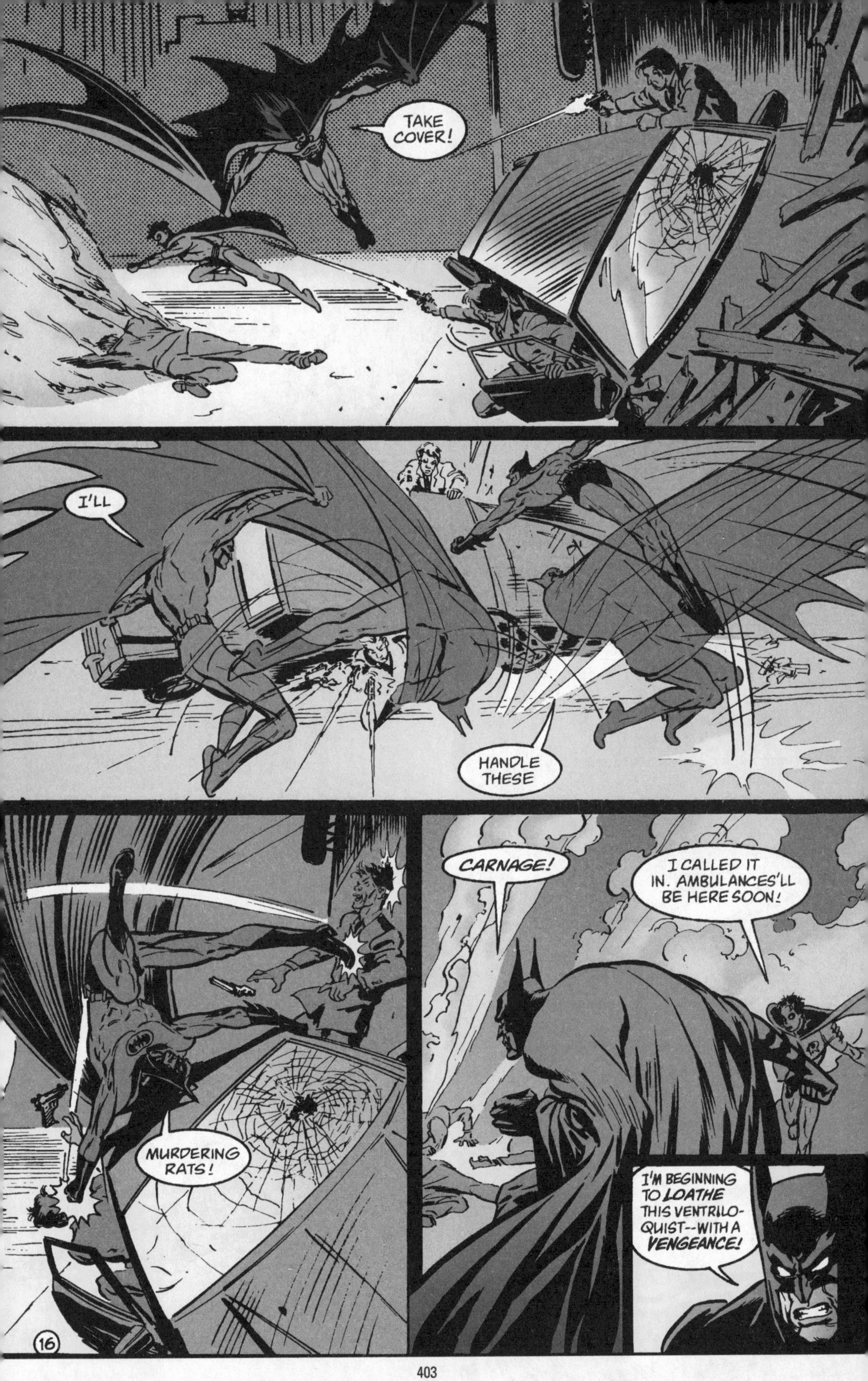
TAKE COVER!
I'LL
HANDLE THESE
MURDERING RATS!
CARNAGE!
I CALLED IT IN. AMBULANCES'LL BE HERE SOON!
I'M BEGINNING TO LOATHE THIS VENTRILO-QUIST--WITH A VENGEANCE!
16

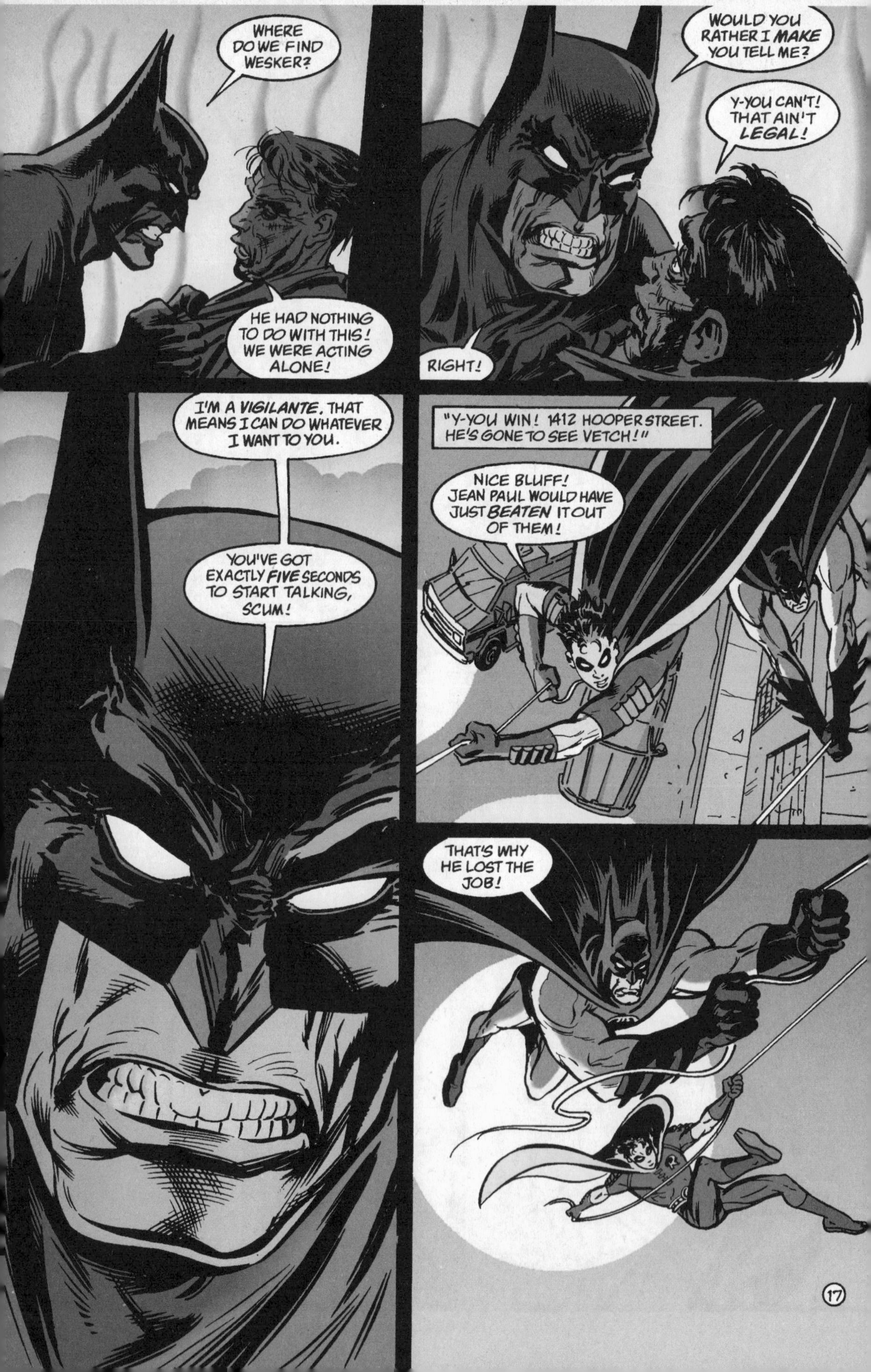
WHERE DO WE FIND WESKER?
HE HAD NOTHING TO DO WITH THIS! WE WERE ACTING ALONE!
WOULD YOU RATHER I MAKE YOU TELL ME?
Y-YOU CAN'T! THAT AIN'T LEGAL!
RIGHT!
I'M A VIGILANTE. THAT MEANS I CAN DO WHATEVER I WANT TO YOU.
YOU'VE GOT EXACTLY FIVE SECONDS TO START TALKING, SCUM!
"Y-YOU WIN! 1412 HOOPER STREET. HE'S GONE TO SEE VETCH!"
NICE BLUFF! JEAN PAUL WOULD HAVE JUST BEATEN IT OUT OF THEM!
THAT'S WHY HE LOST THE JOB!

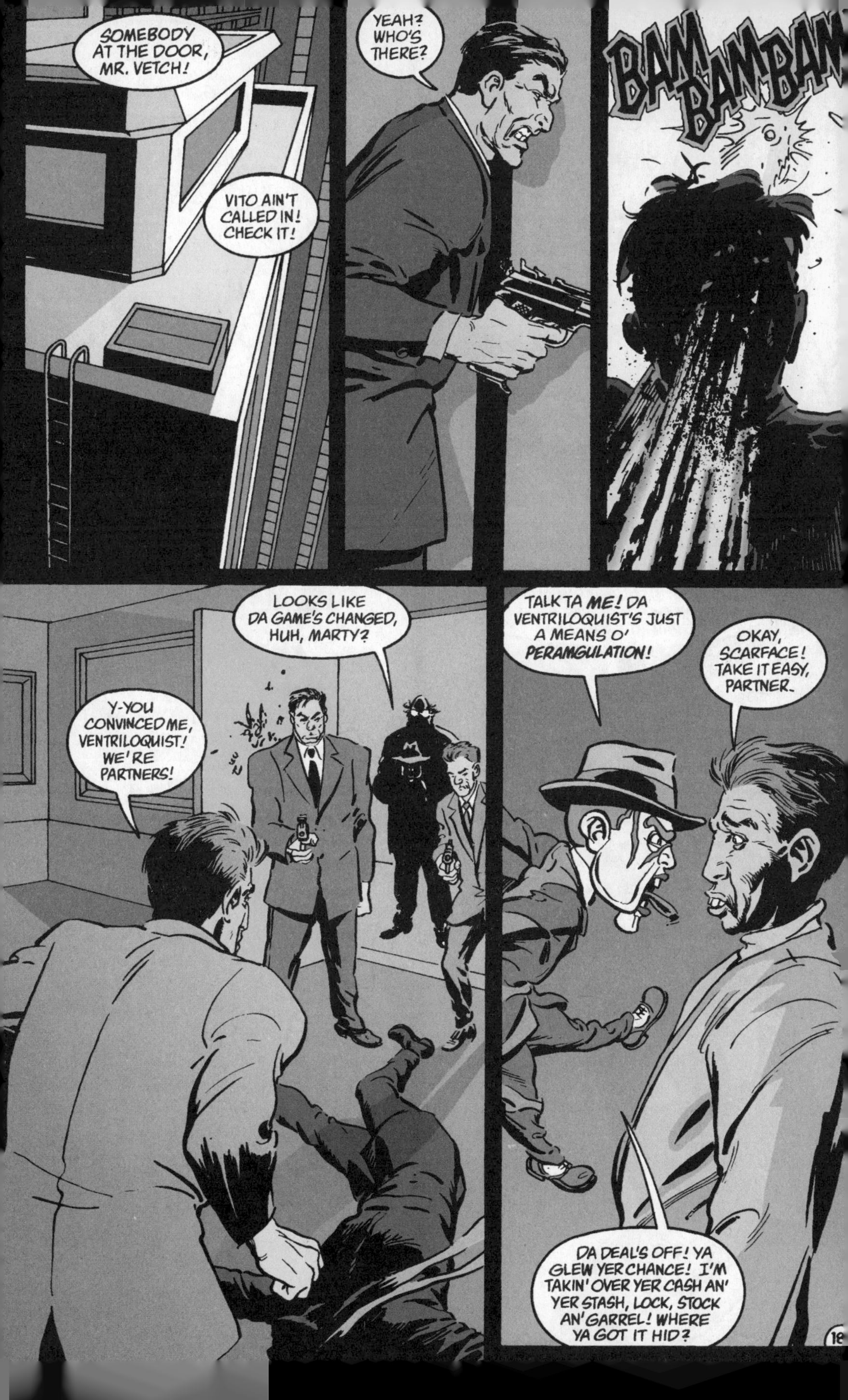
SOMEBODY AT THE DOOR, MR. VETCH!
VITO AIN'T CALLED IN! CHECK IT!
YEAH? WHO'S THERE?
BAM BAM BAM
LOOKS LIKE DA GAME'S CHANGED, HUH, MARTY?
Y-YOU CONVINCED ME, VENTRILOQUIST! WE'RE PARTNERS!
TALK TA ME! DA VENTRILOQUIST'S JUST A MEANS O' PERAMGULATION!
OKAY, SCARFACE! TAKE IT EASY, PARTNER.
DA DEAL'S OFF! YA GLEW YER CHANCE! I'M TAKIN' OVER YER CASH AN' YER STASH, LOCK, STOCK AN' GARREL! WHERE YA GOT IT HID?
18

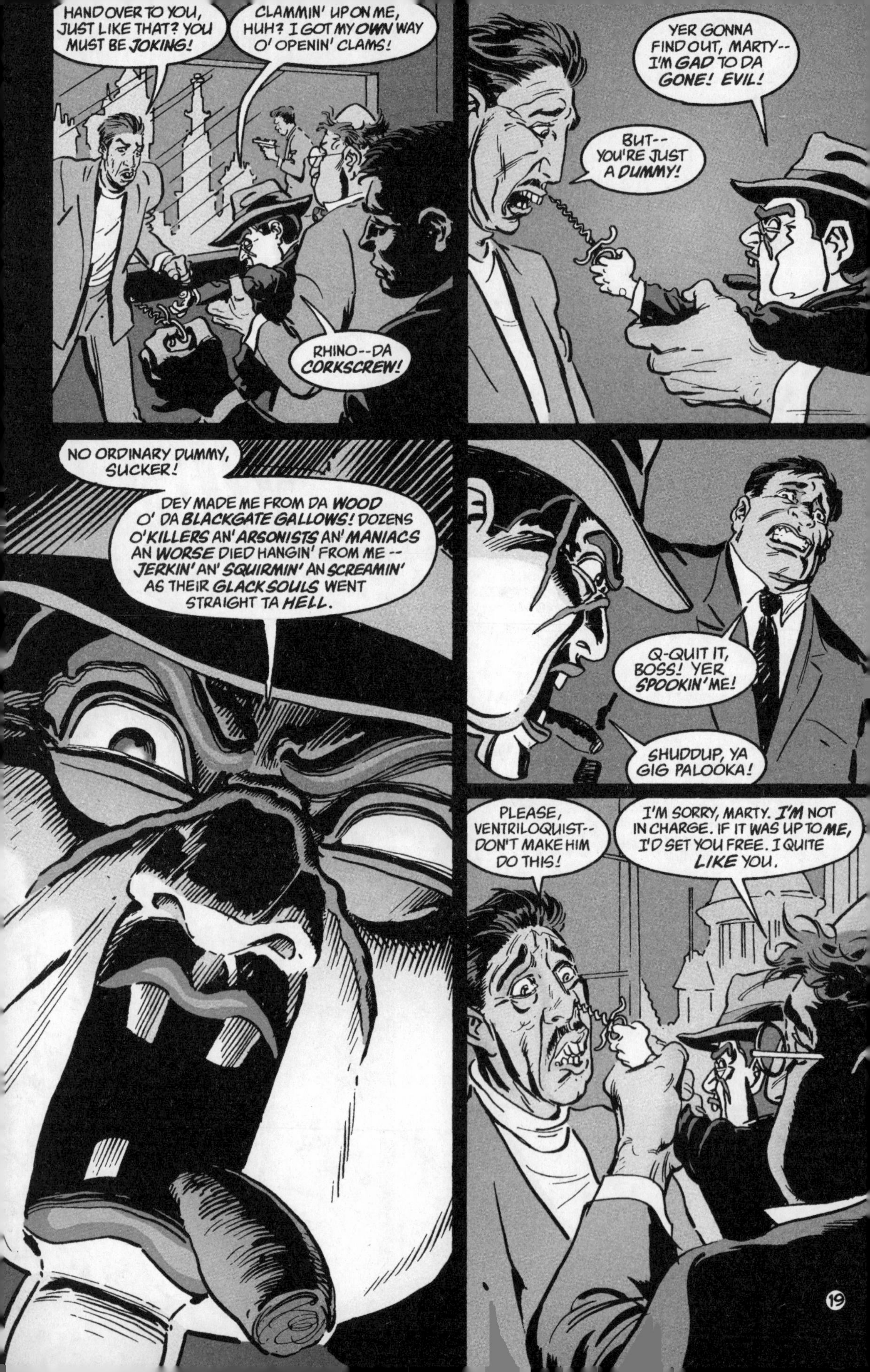
HAND OVER TO YOU, JUST LIKE THAT? YOU MUST BE JOKING!
CLAMMIN' UP ON ME, HUH? I GOT MY OWN WAY O' OPENIN' CLAMS!
RHINO--DA CORKSCREW!
YER GONNA FIND OUT, MARTY-- I'M GAD TO DA GONE! EVIL!
BUT-- YOU'RE JUST A DUMMY!
NO ORDINARY DUMMY, SUCKER!
DEY MADE ME FROM DA WOOD O' DA BLACKGATE GALLOWS! DOZENS O' KILLERS AN' ARSONISTS AN' MANIACS AN WORSE DIED HANGIN' FROM ME -- JERKIN' AN' SQUIRMIN' AN SCREAMIN' AS THEIR GLACK SOULS WENT STRAIGHT TA HELL.
Q-QUIT IT, BOSS! YER SPOOKIN' ME!
SHUDDUP, YA GIG PALOOKA!
PLEASE, VENTRILOQUIST-- DON'T MAKE HIM DO THIS!
I'M SORRY, MARTY. I'M NOT IN CHARGE. IF IT WAS UP TO ME, I'D SET YOU FREE. I QUITE LIKE YOU.

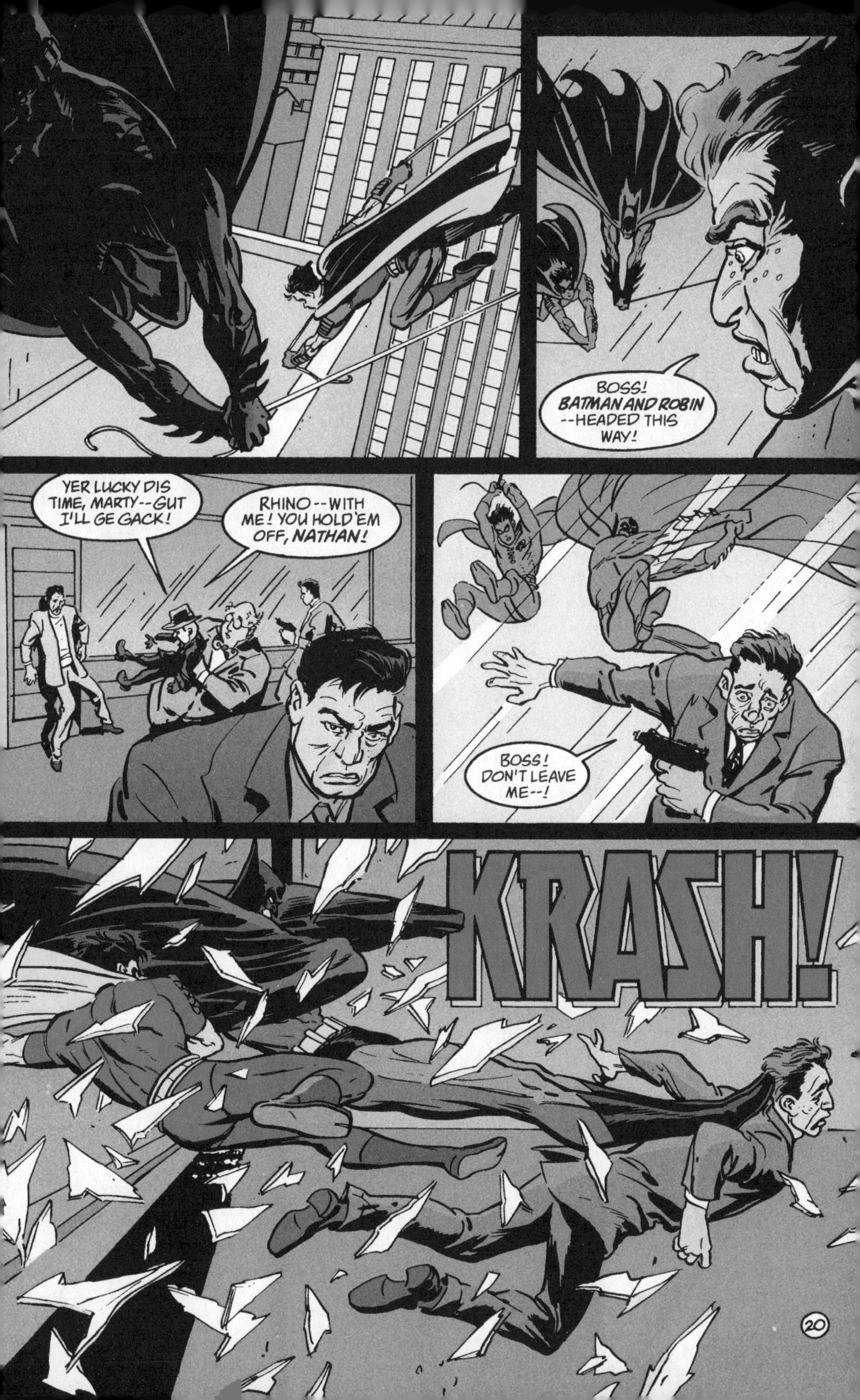
BOSS! BATMAN AND ROBIN --HEADED THIS WAY!
YER LUCKY DIS TIME, MARTY--GUT I'LL GE GACK!
RHINO--WITH ME! YOU HOLD'EM OFF, NATHAN!
BOSS! DON'T LEAVE ME--!
KRASH!
20

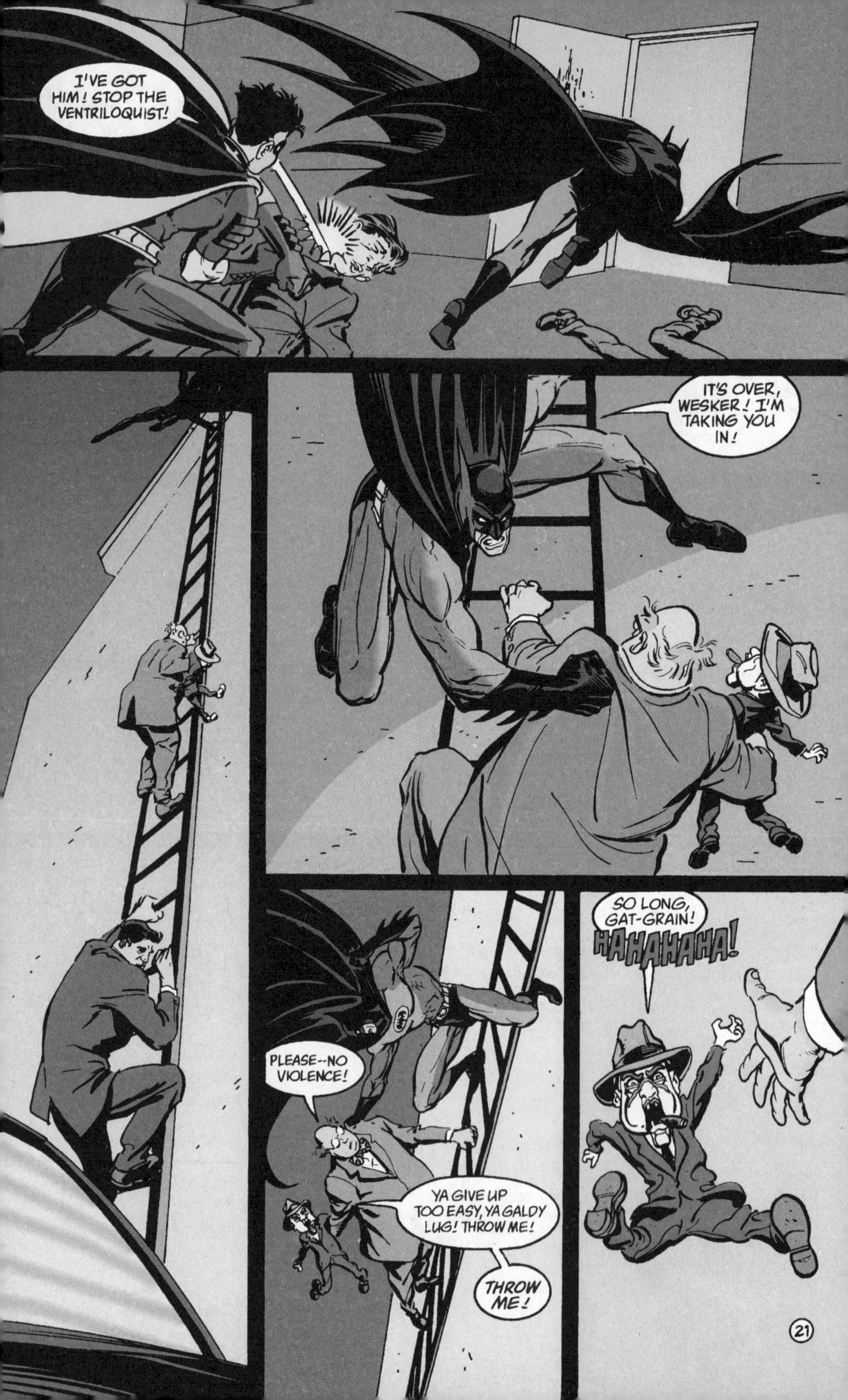
I'VE GOT HIM! STOP THE VENTRILOQUIST!
IT'S OVER, WESKER! I'M TAKING YOU IN!
PLEASE--NO VIOLENCE!
YA GIVE UP TOO EASY, YA GALDY LUG! THROW ME!
THROW ME!
SO LONG, GAT-GRAIN!
HAHAHAHA!

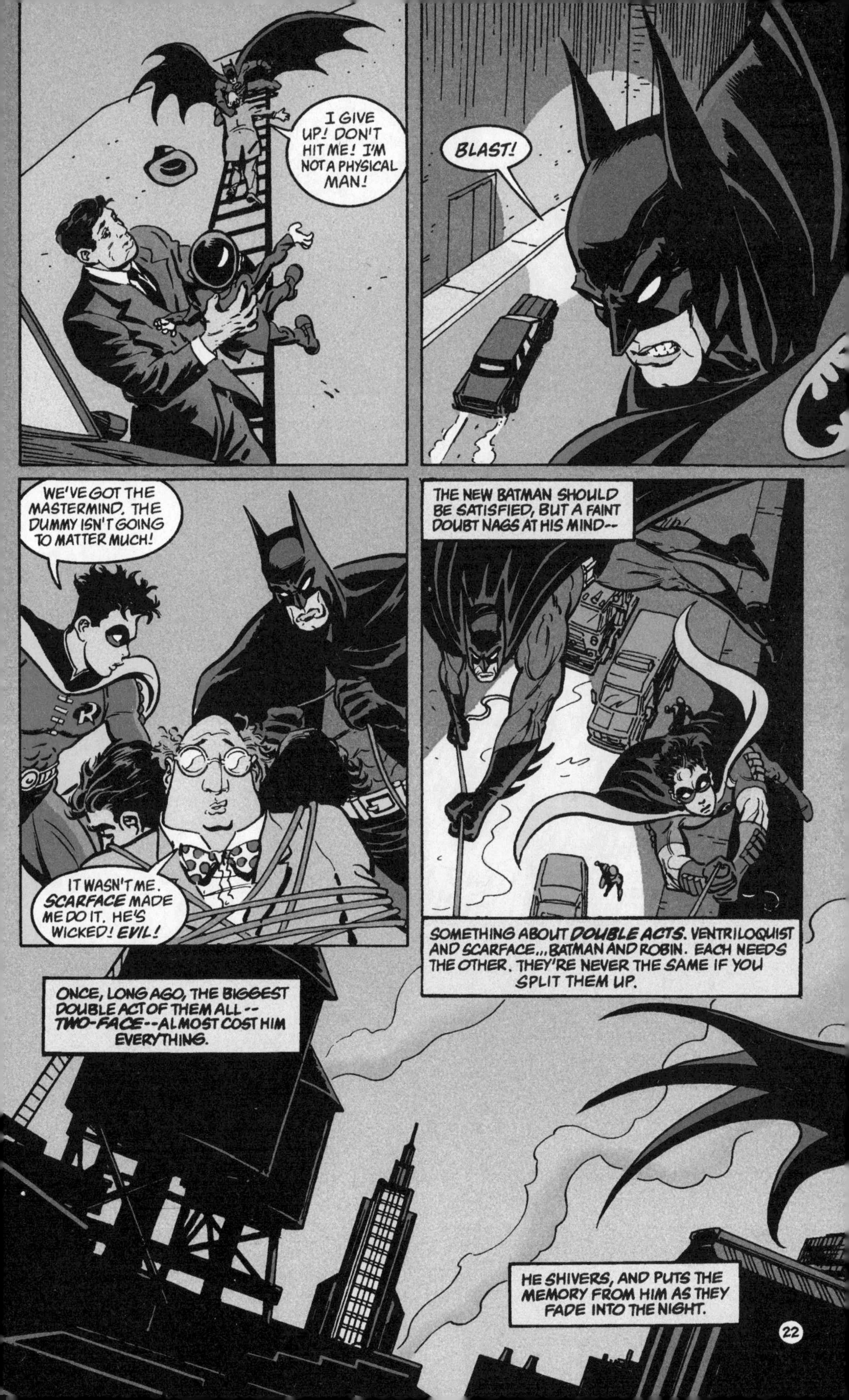
I GIVE UP! DON'T HIT ME! I'M NOT A PHYSICAL MAN!
BLAST!
WE'VE GOT THE MASTERMIND. THE DUMMY ISN'T GOING TO MATTER MUCH!
IT WASN'T ME. SCARFACE MADE ME DO IT. HE'S WICKED! EVIL!
THE NEW BATMAN SHOULD BE SATISFIED, BUT A FAINT DOUBT NAGS AT HIS MIND--
SOMETHING ABOUT DOUBLE ACTS. VENTRILOQUIST AND SCARFACE... BATMAN AND ROBIN. EACH NEEDS THE OTHER. THEY'RE NEVER THE SAME IF YOU SPLIT THEM UP.
ONCE, LONG AGO, THE BIGGEST DOUBLE ACT OF THEM ALL -- TWO-FACE--ALMOST COST HIM EVERYTHING.
HE SHIVERS, AND PUTS THE MEMORY FROM HIM AS THEY FADE INTO THE NIGHT.
22

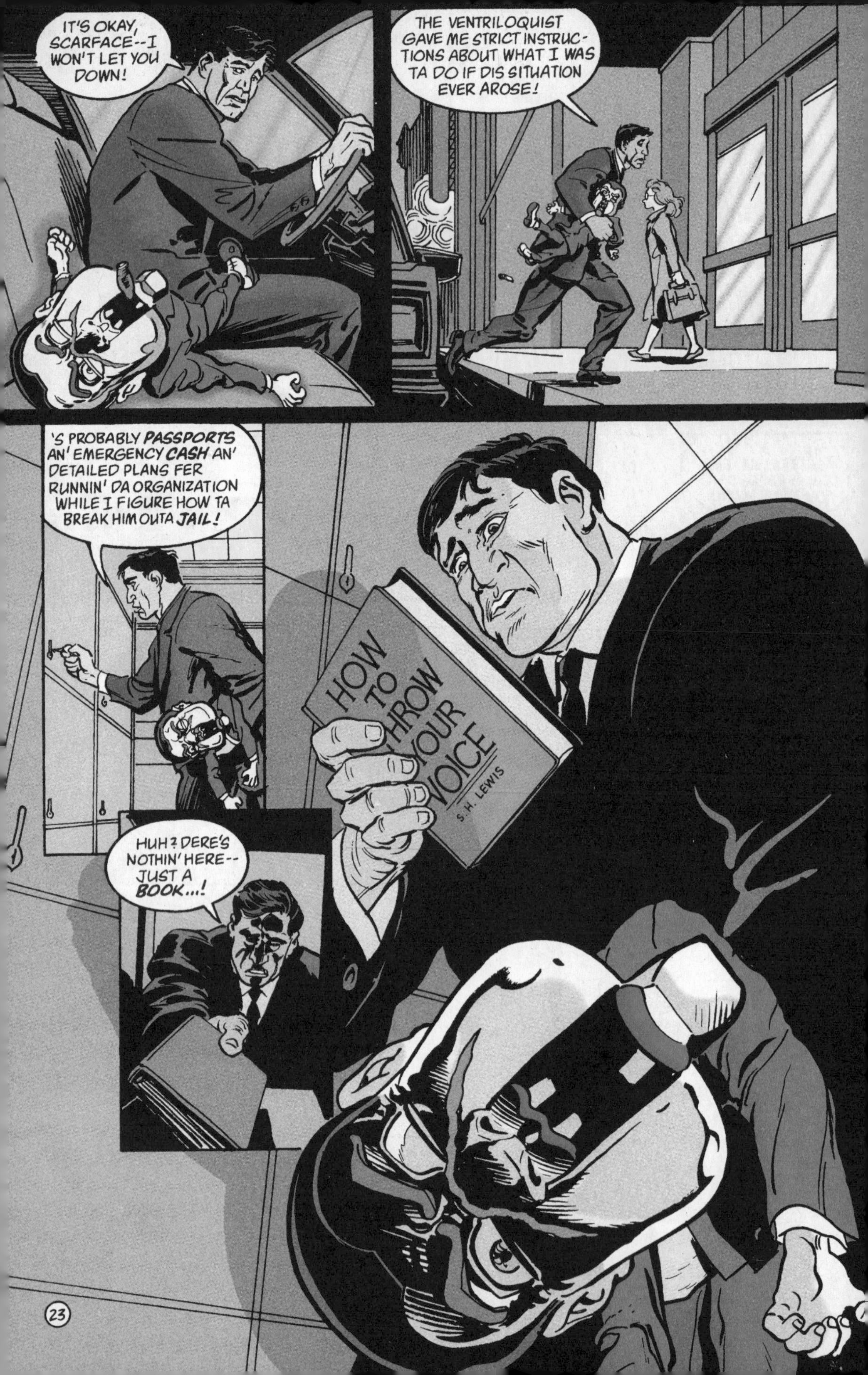
IT'S OKAY, SCARFACE--I WON'T LET YOU DOWN!
THE VENTRILOQUIST GAVE ME STRICT INSTRUC-TIONS ABOUT WHAT I WAS TA DO IF DIS SITUATION EVER AROSE!
'S PROBABLY PASSPORTS AN' EMERGENCY CASH AN' DETAILED PLANS FER RUNNIN' DA ORGANIZATION WHILE I FIGURE HOW TA BREAK HIM OUTA JAIL!
HUH? DERE'S NOTHIN' HERE-- JUST A BOOK...!
HOW TO THROW YOUR VOICE
S. H. LEWIS

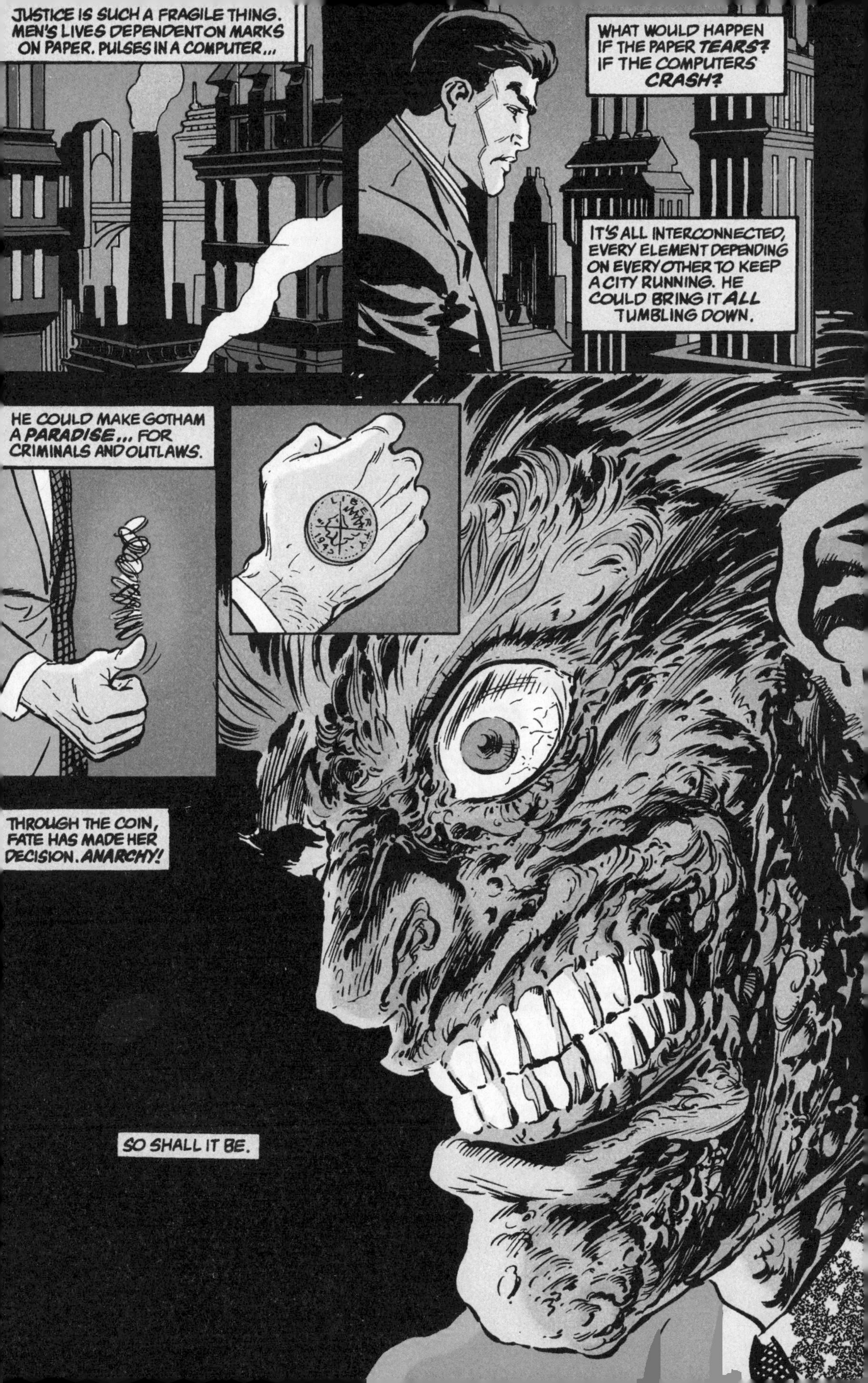
JUSTICE IS SUCH A FRAGILE THING. MEN'S LIVES DEPENDENT ON MARKS ON PAPER. PULSES IN A COMPUTER...
WHAT WOULD HAPPEN IF THE PAPER TEARS? IF THE COMPUTERS CRASH?
IT'S ALL INTERCONNECTED, EVERY ELEMENT DEPENDING ON EVERY OTHER TO KEEP A CITY RUNNING. HE COULD BRING IT ALL TUMBLING DOWN.
HE COULD MAKE GOTHAM A PARADISE... FOR CRIMINALS AND OUTLAWS.
THROUGH THE COIN, FATE HAS MADE HER DECISION. ANARCHY!
SO SHALL IT BE.

Cover art by LEE WEEKS

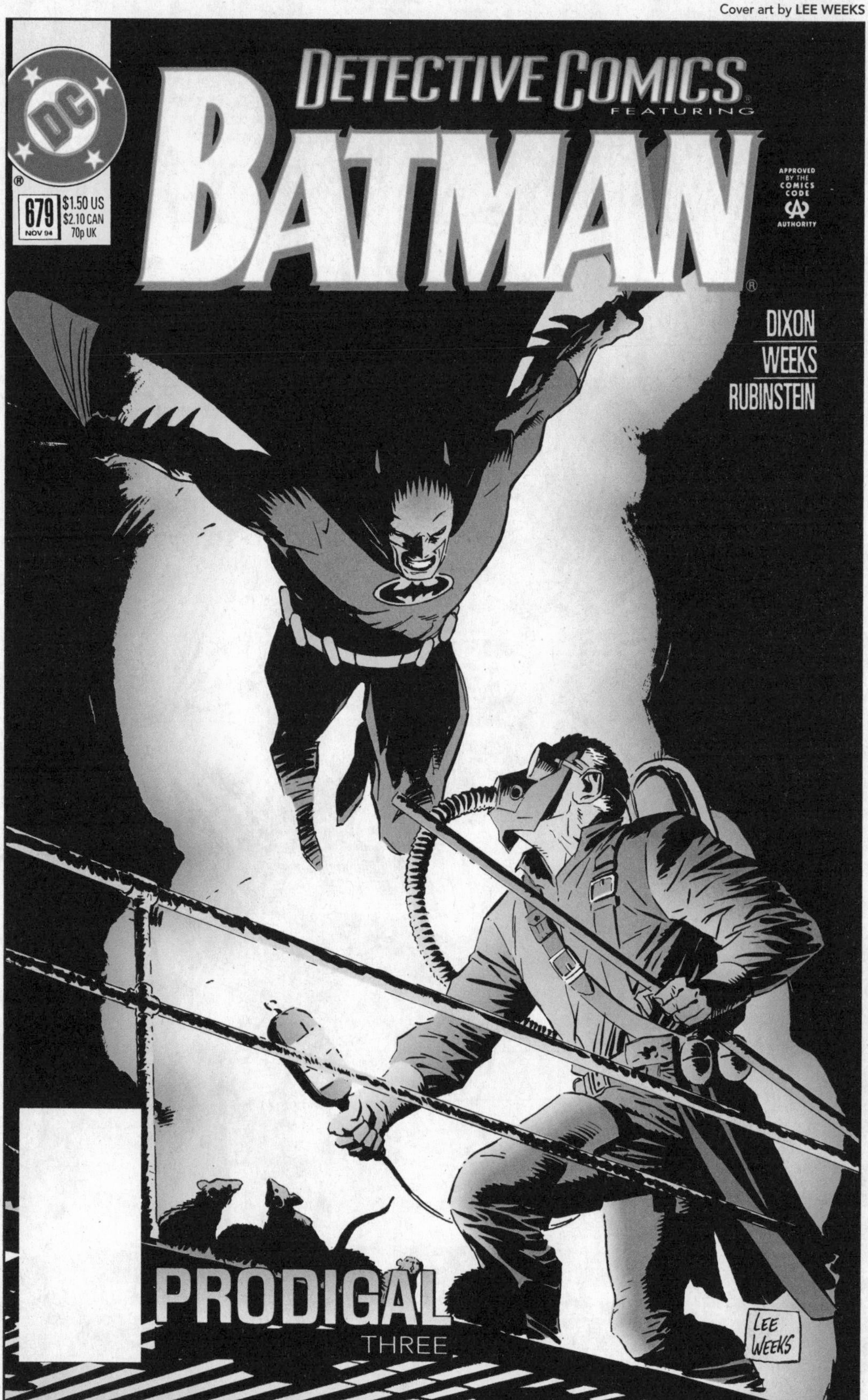
DETECTIVE COMICS
FEATURING
BATMAN
DC
679
NOV 94
$1.50 US
$2.10 CAN
70p UK
APPROVED BY THE COMICS CODE AUTHORITY
DIXON
WEEKS
RUBINSTEIN
PRODIGAL
THREE
LEE WEEKS

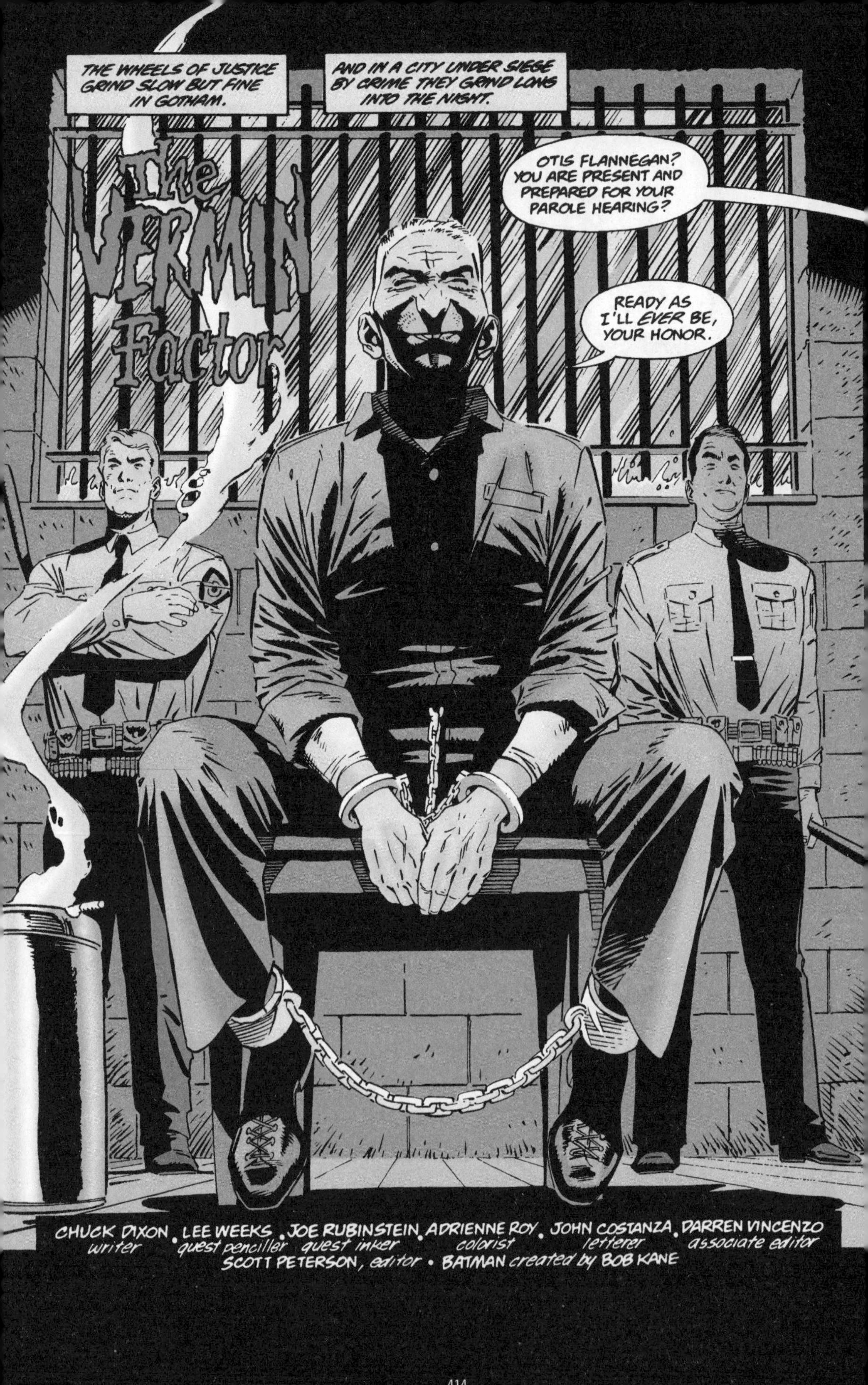
THE WHEELS OF JUSTICE GRIND SLOW BUT FINE IN GOTHAM.
AND IN A CITY UNDER SIEGE BY CRIME THEY GRIND LONG INTO THE NIGHT.
The VERMIN Factor
OTIS FLANNEGAN? YOU ARE PRESENT AND PREPARED FOR YOUR PAROLE HEARING?
READY AS I'LL EVER BE, YOUR HONOR.
CHUCK DIXON writer • LEE WEEKS guest penciller • JOE RUBINSTEIN guest inker • ADRIENNE ROY colorist • JOHN COSTANZA letterer • DARREN VINCENZO associate editor
SCOTT PETERSON, editor • BATMAN created by BOB KANE

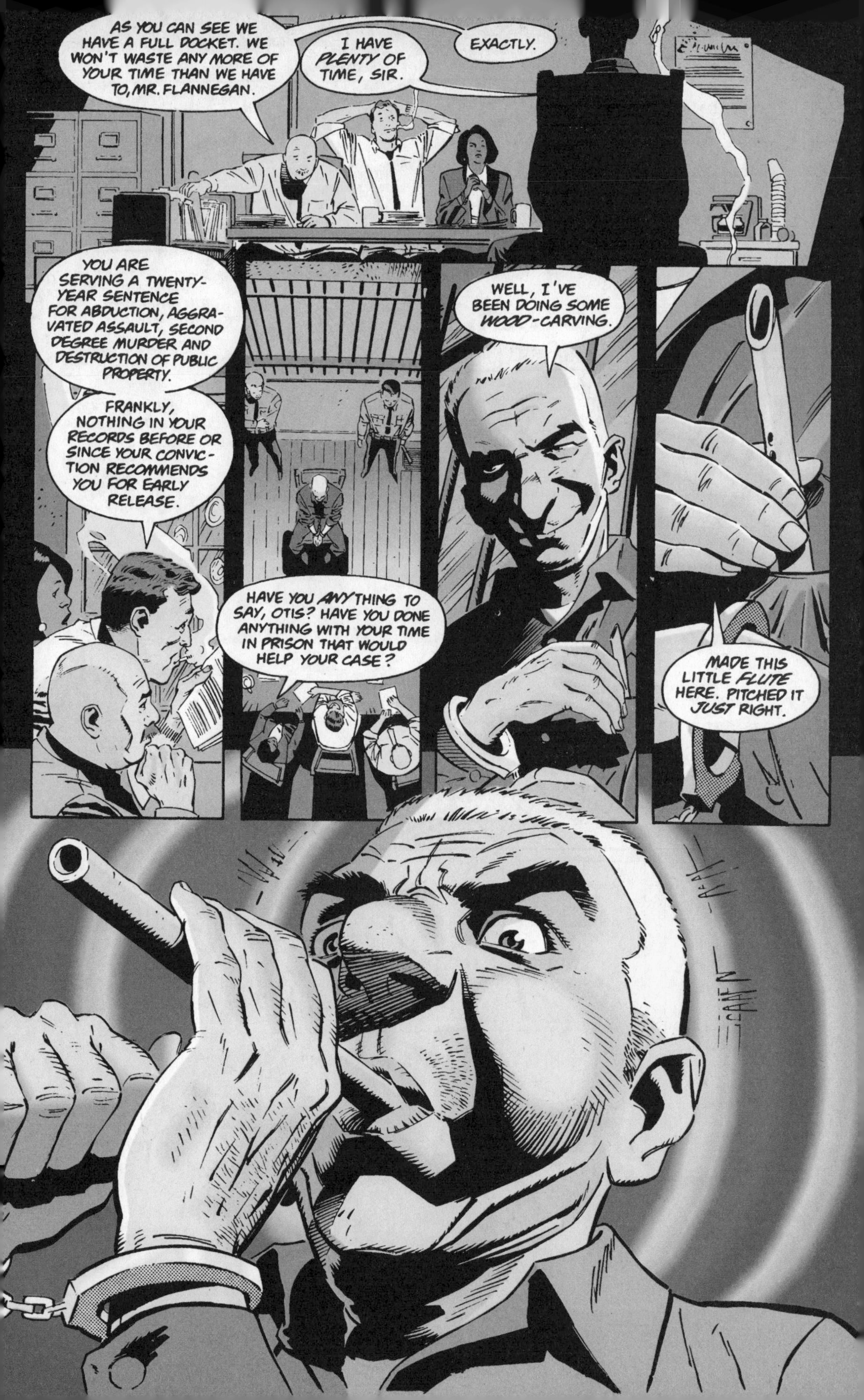
AS YOU CAN SEE WE HAVE A FULL DOCKET. WE WON'T WASTE ANY MORE OF YOUR TIME THAN WE HAVE TO, MR. FLANNEGAN.
I HAVE PLENTY OF TIME, SIR.
EXACTLY.
YOU ARE SERVING A TWENTY-YEAR SENTENCE FOR ABDUCTION, AGGRAVATED ASSAULT, SECOND DEGREE MURDER AND DESTRUCTION OF PUBLIC PROPERTY.
FRANKLY, NOTHING IN YOUR RECORDS BEFORE OR SINCE YOUR CONVICTION RECOMMENDS YOU FOR EARLY RELEASE.
HAVE YOU ANYTHING TO SAY, OTIS? HAVE YOU DONE ANYTHING WITH YOUR TIME IN PRISON THAT WOULD HELP YOUR CASE?
WELL, I'VE BEEN DOING SOME WOOD-CARVING.
MADE THIS LITTLE FLUTE HERE. PITCHED IT JUST RIGHT.

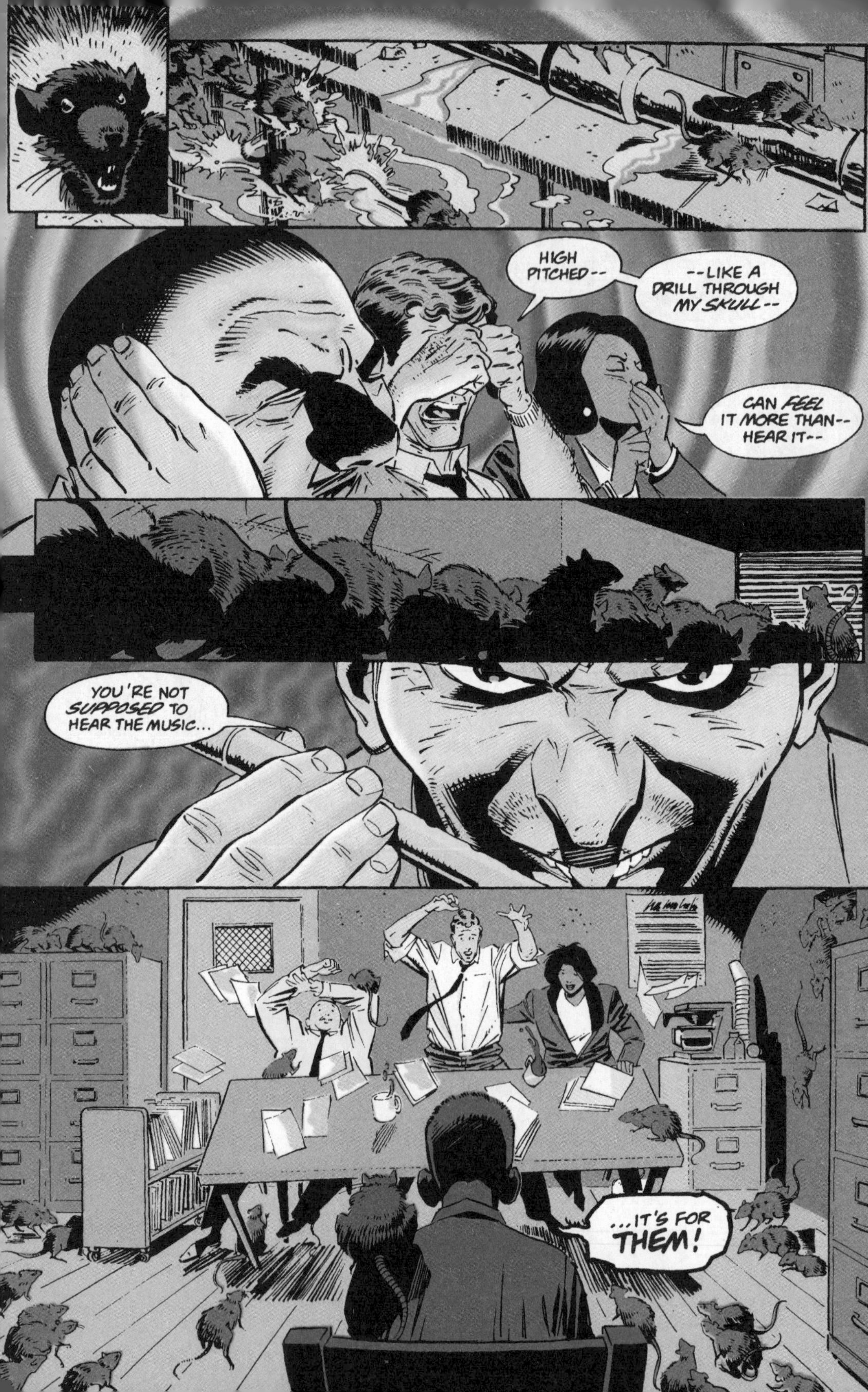
HIGH PITCHED--
--LIKE A DRILL THROUGH MY SKULL--
CAN FEEL IT MORE THAN-- HEAR IT--
YOU'RE NOT SUPPOSED TO HEAR THE MUSIC...
...IT'S FOR THEM!

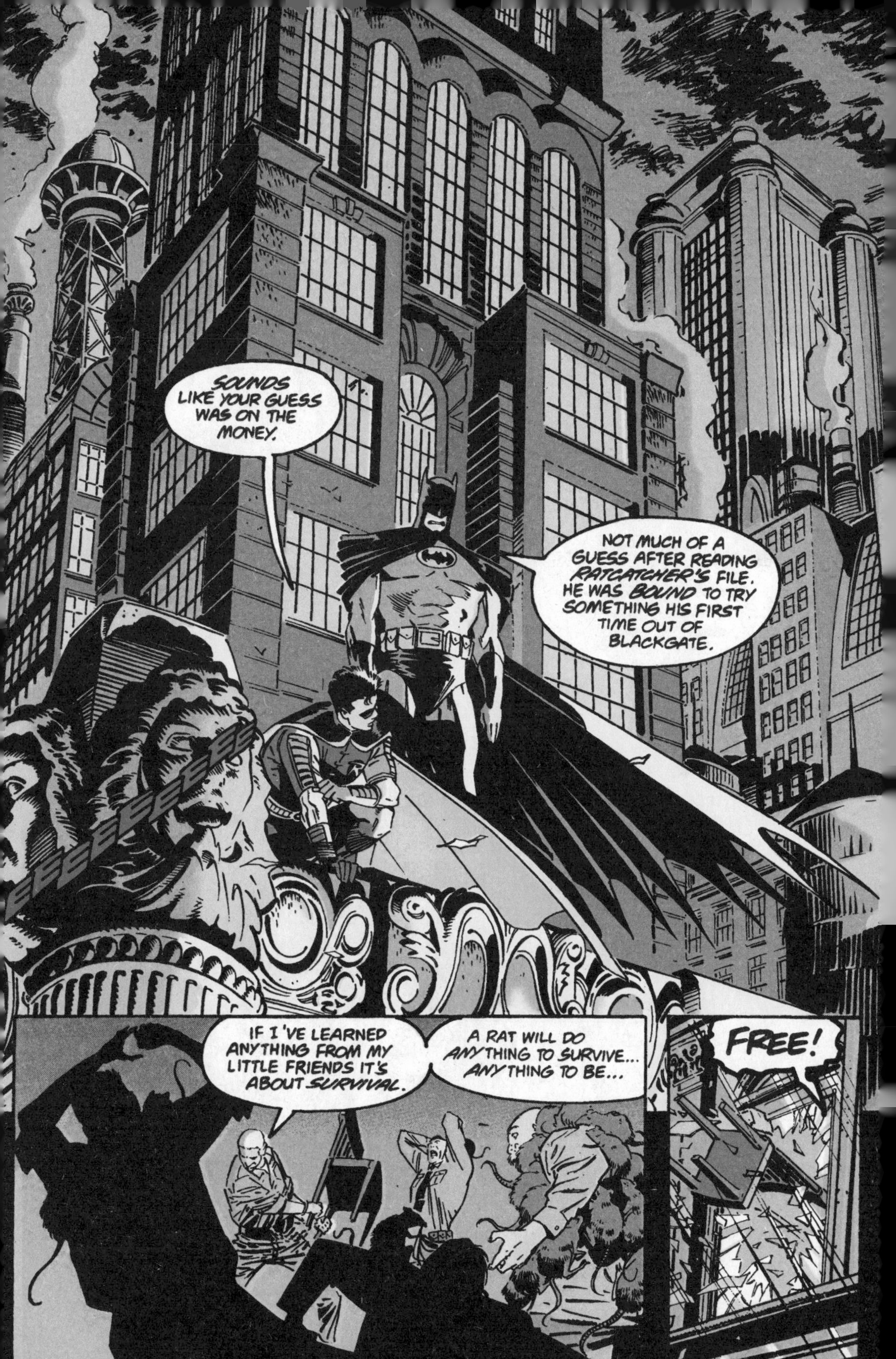
SOUNDS LIKE YOUR GUESS WAS ON THE MONEY.
NOT MUCH OF A GUESS AFTER READING RATCATCHER'S FILE. HE WAS BOUND TO TRY SOMETHING HIS FIRST TIME OUT OF BLACKGATE.
IF I'VE LEARNED ANYTHING FROM MY LITTLE FRIENDS IT'S ABOUT SURVIVAL.
A RAT WILL DO ANYTHING TO SURVIVE... ANYTHING TO BE...
FREE!

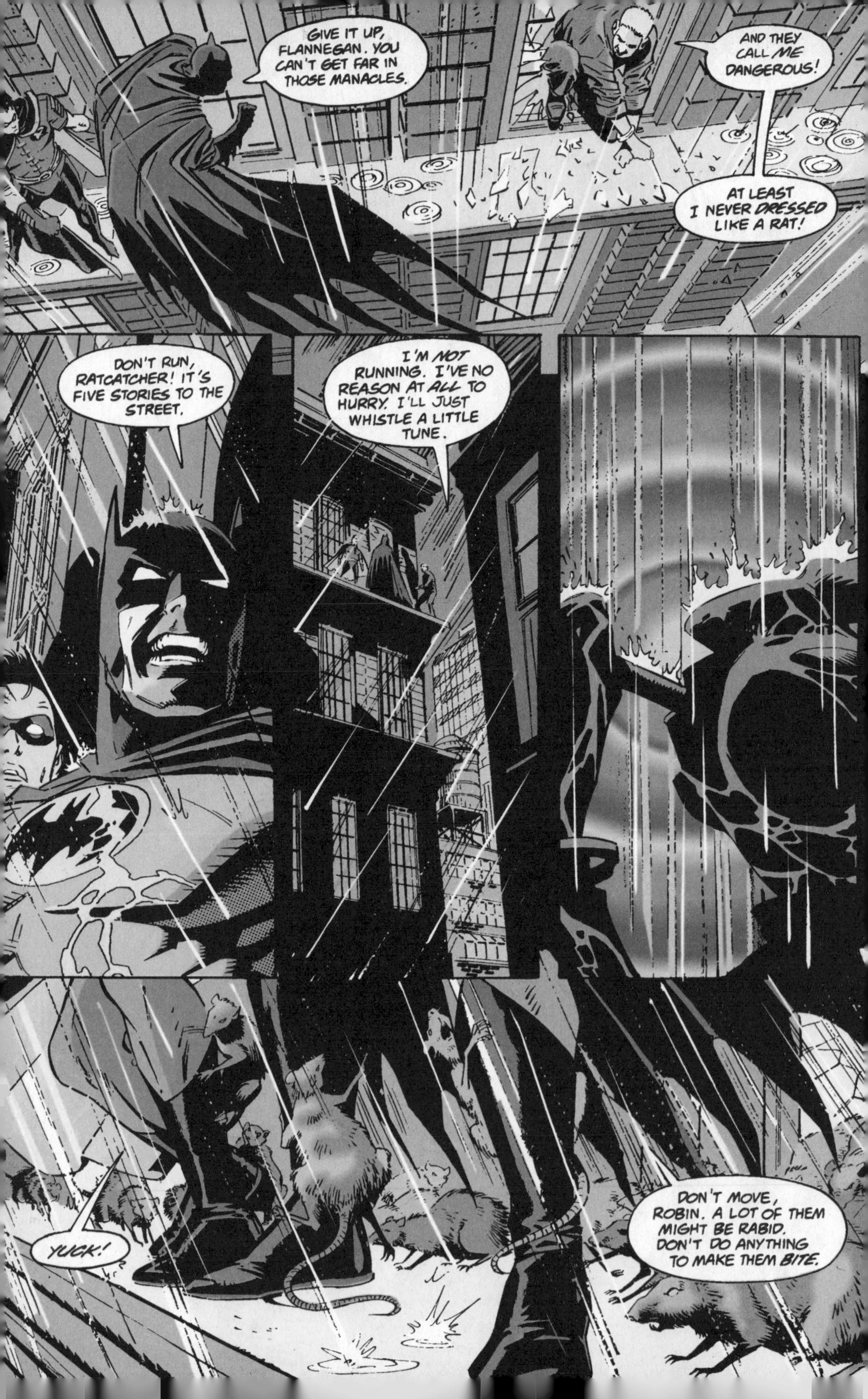
GIVE IT UP, FLANNEGAN. YOU CAN'T GET FAR IN THOSE MANACLES.
AND THEY CALL ME DANGEROUS!
AT LEAST I NEVER DRESSED LIKE A RAT!
DON'T RUN, RATCATCHER! IT'S FIVE STORIES TO THE STREET.
I'M NOT RUNNING. I'VE NO REASON AT ALL TO HURRY. I'LL JUST WHISTLE A LITTLE TUNE.
YUCK!
DON'T MOVE, ROBIN. A LOT OF THEM MIGHT BE RABID. DON'T DO ANYTHING TO MAKE THEM BITE.

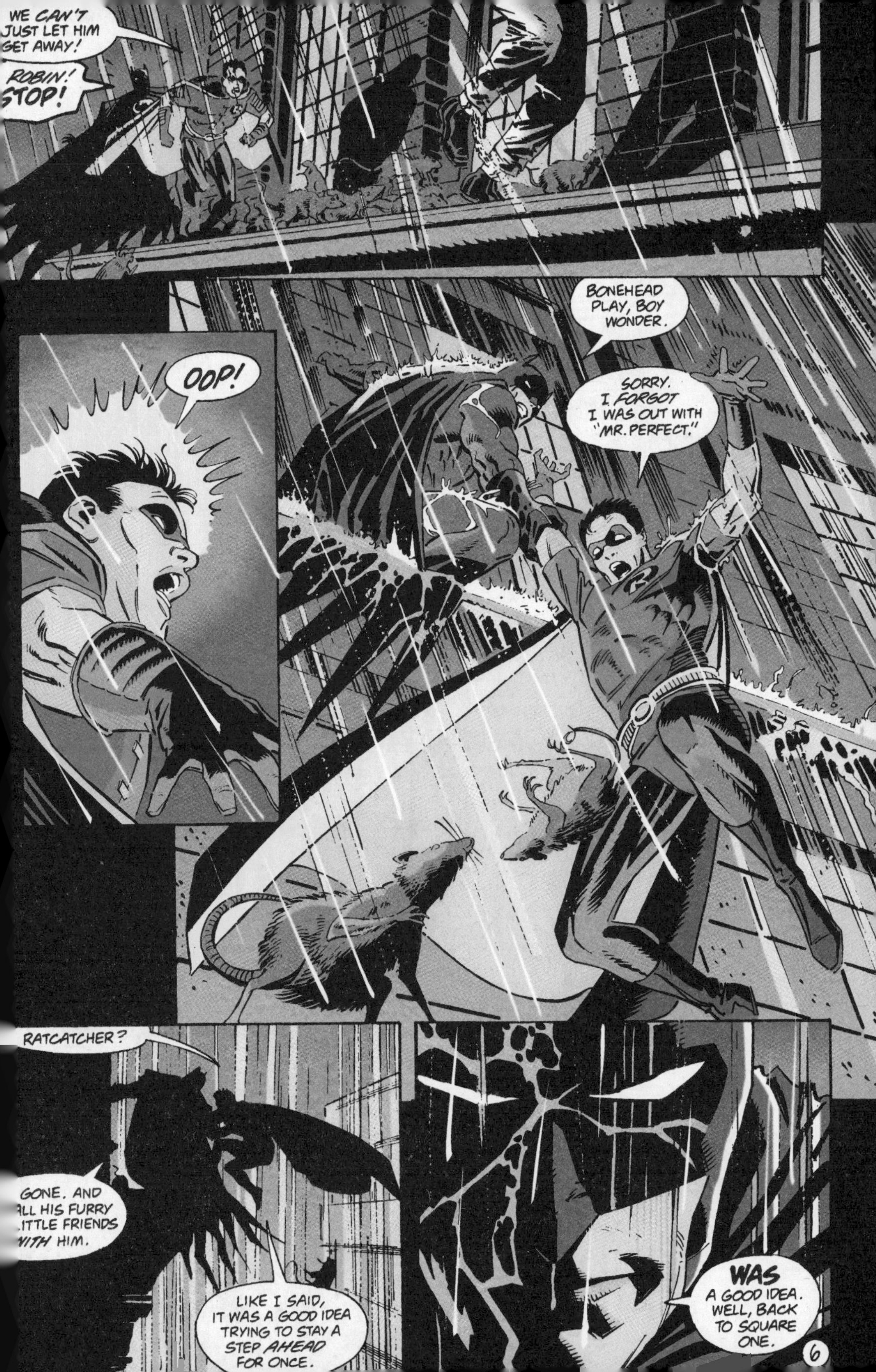

WE CAN'T JUST LET HIM GET AWAY!
ROBIN! STOP!
BONEHEAD PLAY, BOY WONDER.
OOP!
SORRY. I FORGOT I WAS OUT WITH "MR. PERFECT."
RATCATCHER?
GONE. AND ALL HIS FURRY LITTLE FRIENDS WITH HIM.
LIKE I SAID, IT WAS A GOOD IDEA TRYING TO STAY A STEP AHEAD FOR ONCE.
WAS A GOOD IDEA. WELL, BACK TO SQUARE ONE.
6

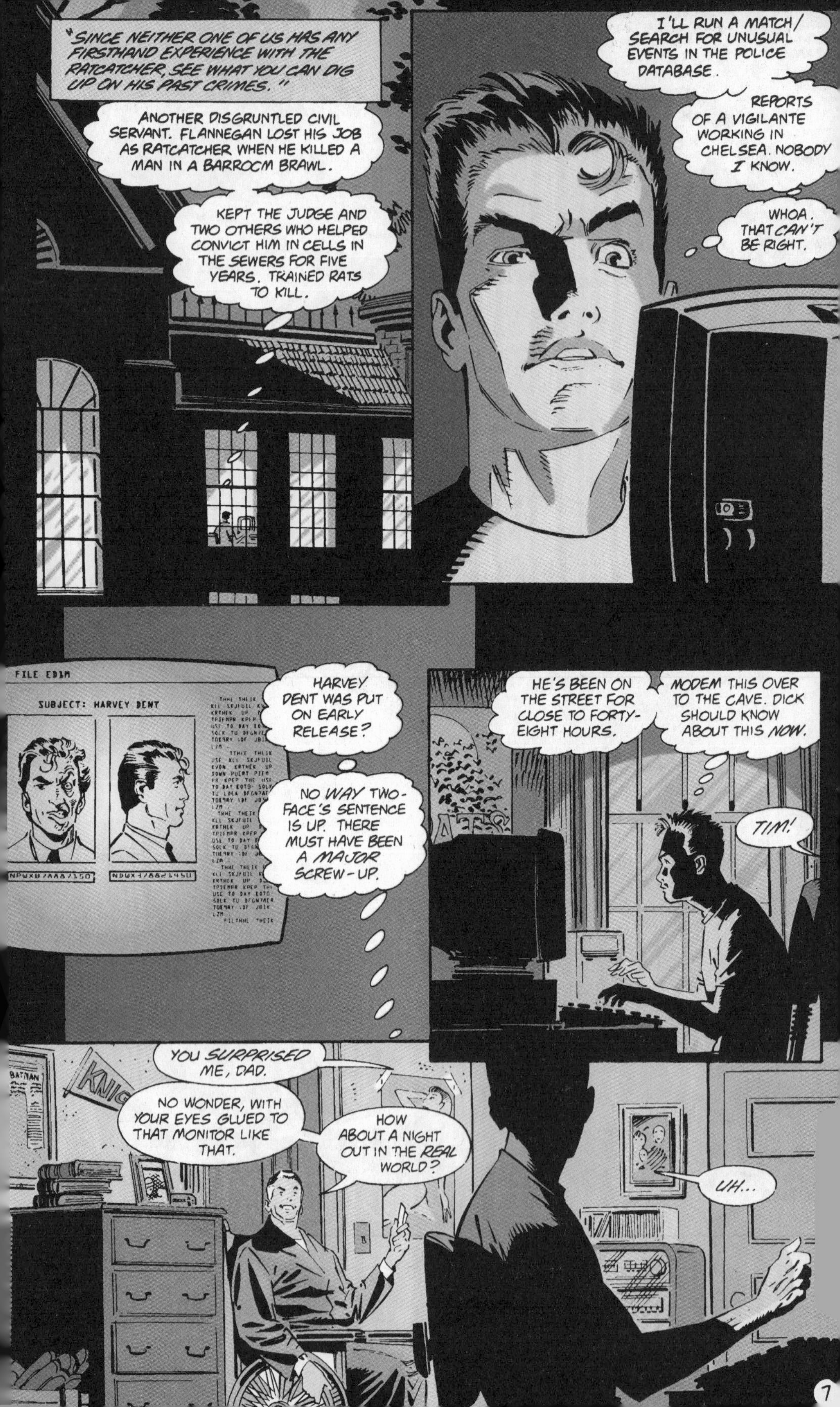
"SINCE NEITHER ONE OF US HAS ANY FIRSTHAND EXPERIENCE WITH THE RATCATCHER, SEE WHAT YOU CAN DIG UP ON HIS PAST CRIMES."
ANOTHER DISGRUNTLED CIVIL SERVANT. FLANNEGAN LOST HIS JOB AS RATCATCHER WHEN HE KILLED A MAN IN A BARROOM BRAWL.
KEPT THE JUDGE AND TWO OTHERS WHO HELPED CONVICT HIM IN CELLS IN THE SEWERS FOR FIVE YEARS. TRAINED RATS TO KILL.
I'LL RUN A MATCH/ SEARCH FOR UNUSUAL EVENTS IN THE POLICE DATABASE.
REPORTS OF A VIGILANTE WORKING IN CHELSEA. NOBODY I KNOW.
WHOA. THAT CAN'T BE RIGHT.
FILE EDIM
SUBJECT: HARVEY DENT
HARVEY DENT WAS PUT ON EARLY RELEASE?
NO WAY TWO-FACE'S SENTENCE IS UP. THERE MUST HAVE BEEN A MAJOR SCREW-UP.
HE'S BEEN ON THE STREET FOR CLOSE TO FORTY-EIGHT HOURS.
MODEM THIS OVER TO THE CAVE. DICK SHOULD KNOW ABOUT THIS NOW.
TIM!
YOU SURPRISED ME, DAD.
NO WONDER, WITH YOUR EYES GLUED TO THAT MONITOR LIKE THAT.
HOW ABOUT A NIGHT OUT IN THE REAL WORLD?
UH...

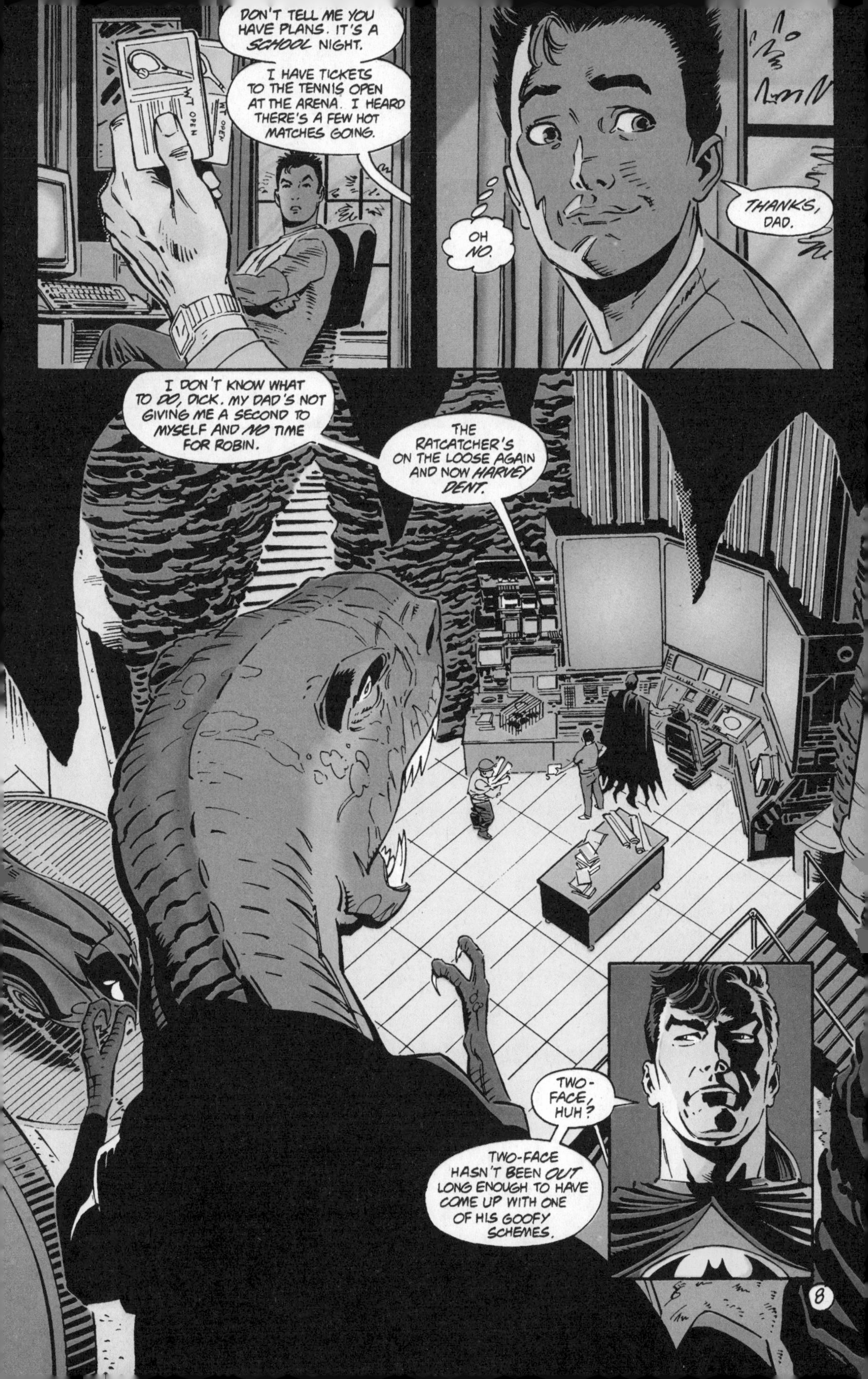
DON'T TELL ME YOU HAVE PLANS. IT'S A SCHOOL NIGHT.
I HAVE TICKETS TO THE TENNIS OPEN AT THE ARENA. I HEARD THERE'S A FEW HOT MATCHES GOING.
WT OPEN
OH NO.
THANKS, DAD.
I DON'T KNOW WHAT TO DO, DICK. MY DAD'S NOT GIVING ME A SECOND TO MYSELF AND NO TIME FOR ROBIN.
THE RATCATCHER'S ON THE LOOSE AGAIN AND NOW HARVEY DENT.
TWO-FACE, HUH?
TWO-FACE HASN'T BEEN OUT LONG ENOUGH TO HAVE COME UP WITH ONE OF HIS GOOFY SCHEMES.

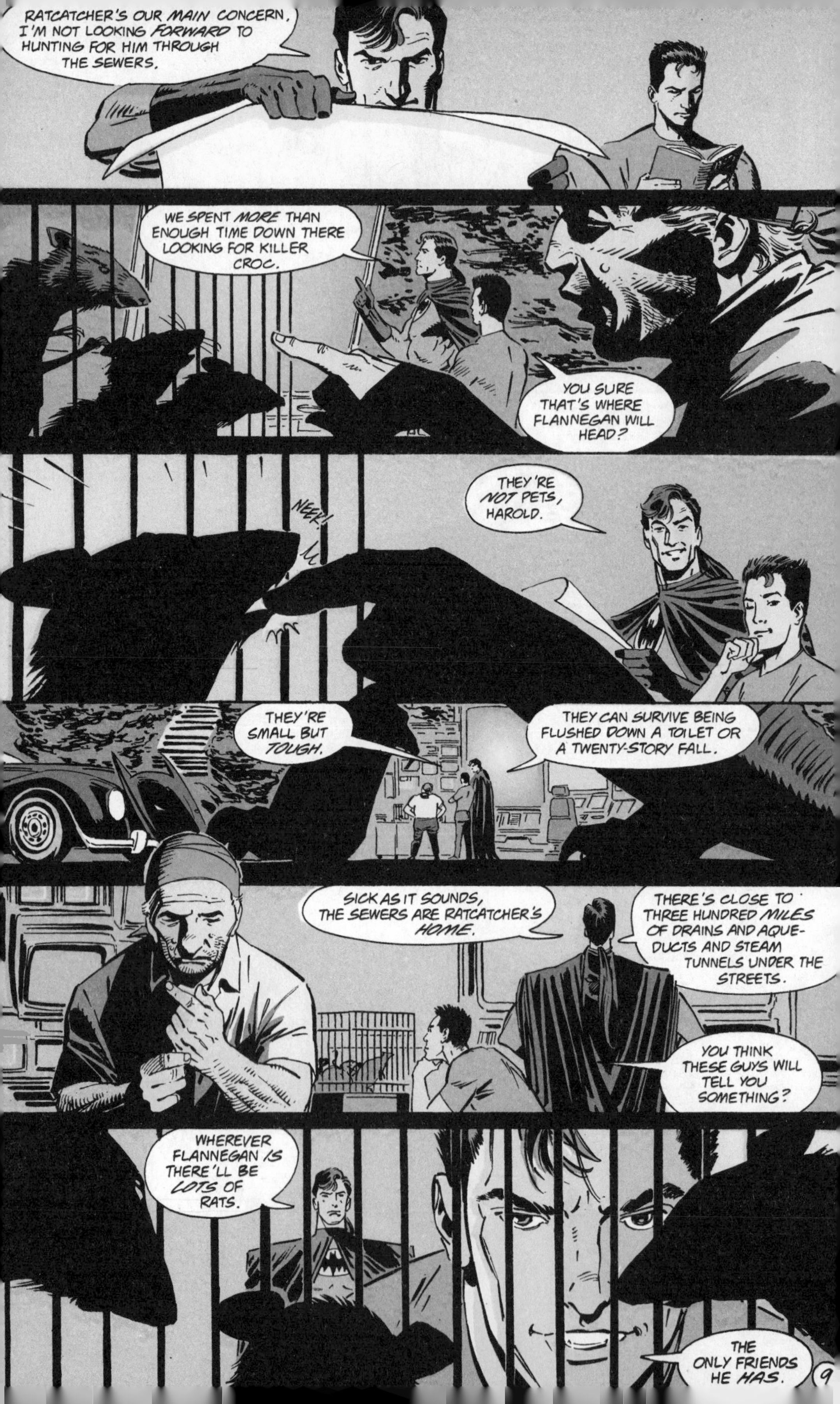
RATCATCHER'S OUR MAIN CONCERN. I'M NOT LOOKING FORWARD TO HUNTING FOR HIM THROUGH THE SEWERS.
WE SPENT MORE THAN ENOUGH TIME DOWN THERE LOOKING FOR KILLER CROC.
YOU SURE THAT'S WHERE FLANNEGAN WILL HEAD?
NEEK!
THEY'RE NOT PETS, HAROLD.
THEY'RE SMALL BUT TOUGH.
THEY CAN SURVIVE BEING FLUSHED DOWN A TOILET OR A TWENTY-STORY FALL.
SICK AS IT SOUNDS, THE SEWERS ARE RATCATCHER'S HOME.
THERE'S CLOSE TO THREE HUNDRED MILES OF DRAINS AND AQUE-DUCTS AND STEAM TUNNELS UNDER THE STREETS.
YOU THINK THESE GUYS WILL TELL YOU SOMETHING?
WHEREVER FLANNEGAN IS THERE'LL BE LOTS OF RATS.
THE ONLY FRIENDS HE HAS.
9

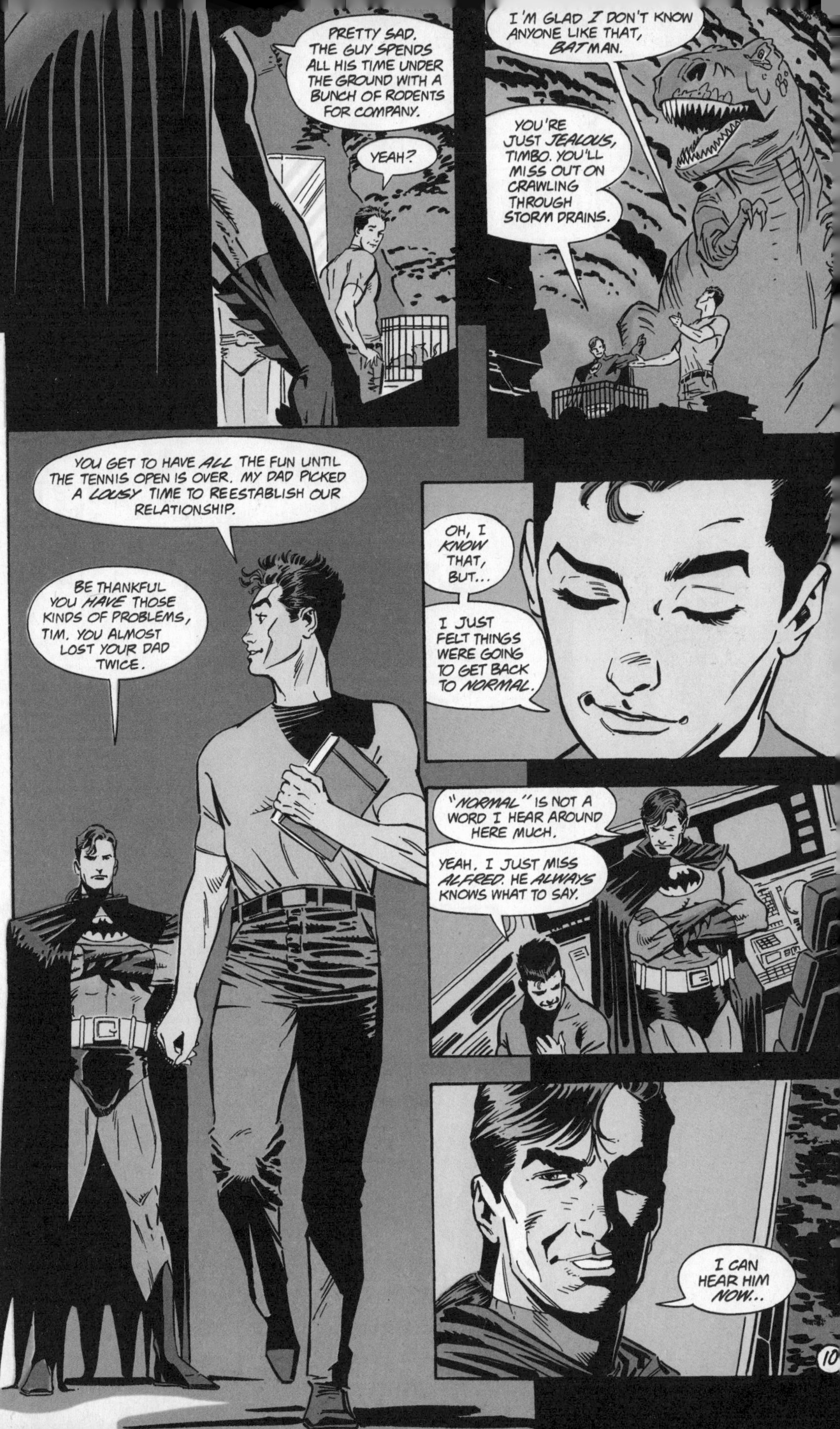
PRETTY SAD. THE GUY SPENDS ALL HIS TIME UNDER THE GROUND WITH A BUNCH OF RODENTS FOR COMPANY.
YEAH?
I'M GLAD I DON'T KNOW ANYONE LIKE THAT, BATMAN.
YOU'RE JUST JEALOUS, TIMBO. YOU'LL MISS OUT ON CRAWLING THROUGH STORM DRAINS.
YOU GET TO HAVE ALL THE FUN UNTIL THE TENNIS OPEN IS OVER. MY DAD PICKED A LOUSY TIME TO REESTABLISH OUR RELATIONSHIP.
BE THANKFUL YOU HAVE THOSE KINDS OF PROBLEMS, TIM. YOU ALMOST LOST YOUR DAD TWICE.
OH, I KNOW THAT, BUT...
I JUST FELT THINGS WERE GOING TO GET BACK TO NORMAL.
"NORMAL" IS NOT A WORD I HEAR AROUND HERE MUCH.
YEAH. I JUST MISS ALFRED. HE ALWAYS KNOWS WHAT TO SAY.
I CAN HEAR HIM NOW...

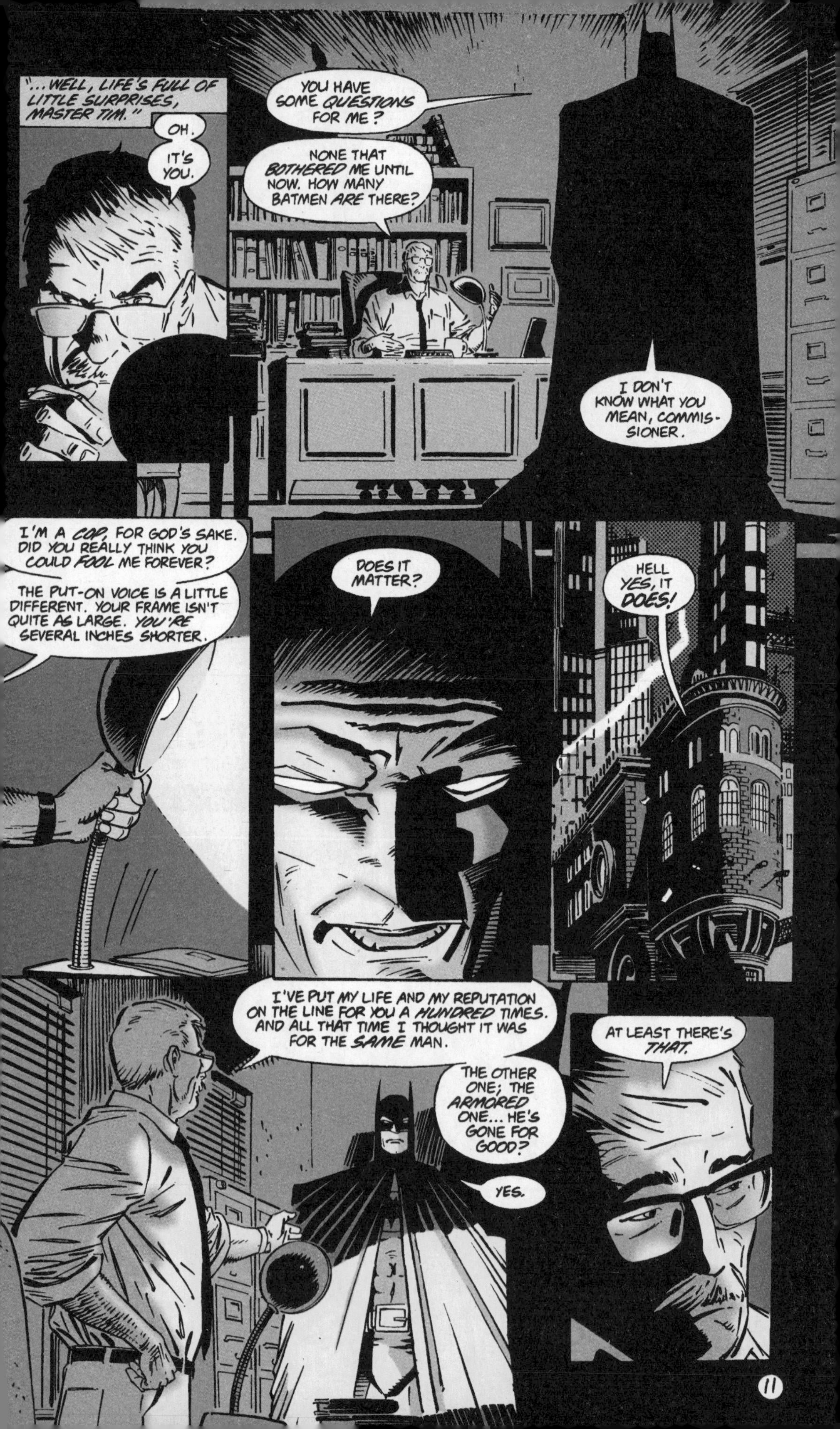
"...WELL, LIFE'S FULL OF LITTLE SURPRISES, MASTER TIM."
OH.
IT'S YOU.
YOU HAVE SOME QUESTIONS FOR ME?
NONE THAT BOTHERED ME UNTIL NOW. HOW MANY BATMEN ARE THERE?
I DON'T KNOW WHAT YOU MEAN, COMMIS-SIONER.
I'M A COP, FOR GOD'S SAKE. DID YOU REALLY THINK YOU COULD FOOL ME FOREVER?
THE PUT-ON VOICE IS A LITTLE DIFFERENT. YOUR FRAME ISN'T QUITE AS LARGE. YOU'RE SEVERAL INCHES SHORTER.
DOES IT MATTER?
HELL YES, IT DOES!
I'VE PUT MY LIFE AND MY REPUTATION ON THE LINE FOR YOU A HUNDRED TIMES. AND ALL THAT TIME I THOUGHT IT WAS FOR THE SAME MAN.
THE OTHER ONE; THE ARMORED ONE... HE'S GONE FOR GOOD?
YES.
AT LEAST THERE'S THAT.
11

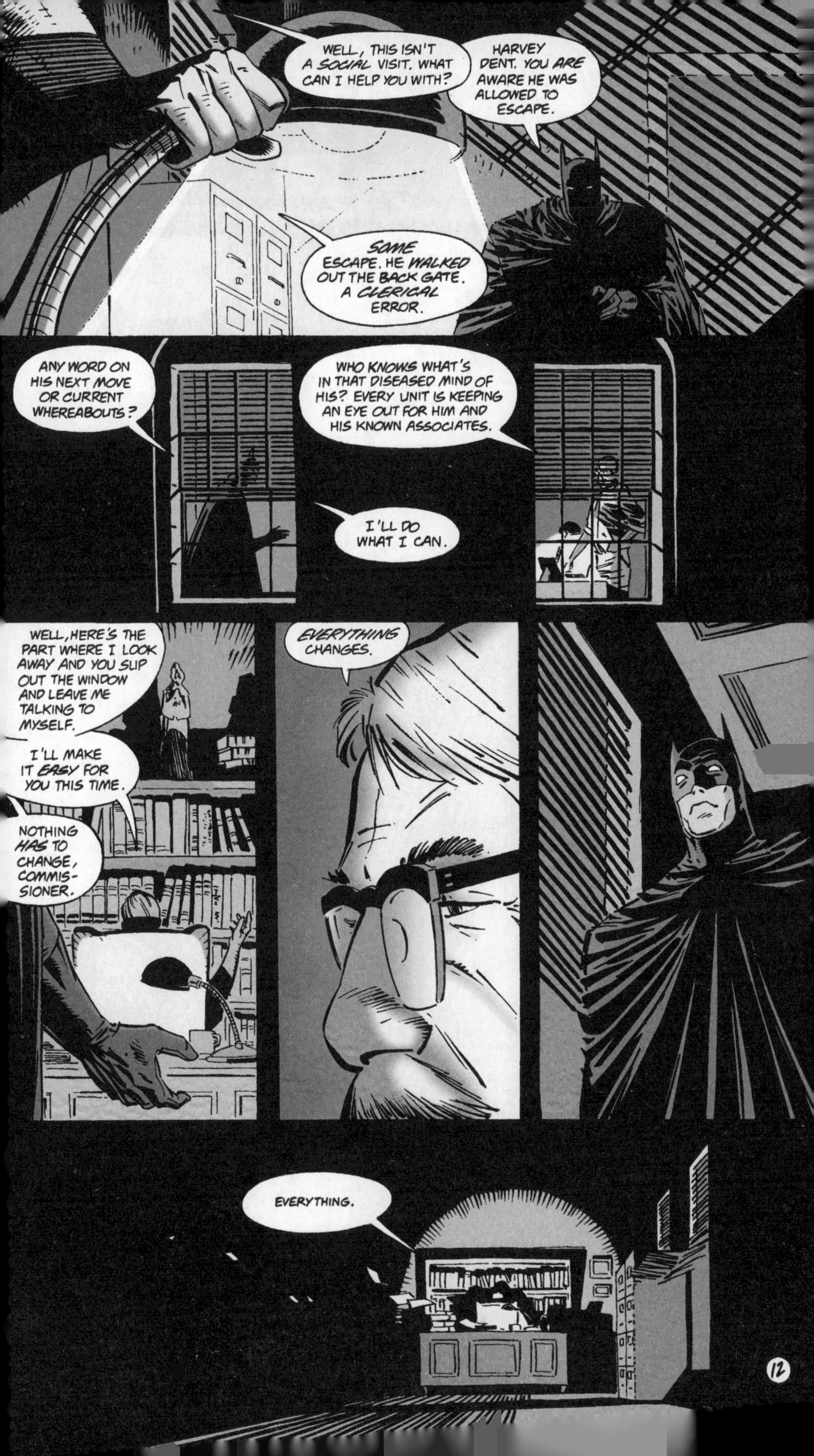

WELL, THIS ISN'T A SOCIAL VISIT. WHAT CAN I HELP YOU WITH?
HARVEY DENT. YOU ARE AWARE HE WAS ALLOWED TO ESCAPE.
SOME ESCAPE. HE WALKED OUT THE BACK GATE. A CLERICAL ERROR.
ANY WORD ON HIS NEXT MOVE OR CURRENT WHEREABOUTS?
WHO KNOWS WHAT'S IN THAT DISEASED MIND OF HIS? EVERY UNIT IS KEEPING AN EYE OUT FOR HIM AND HIS KNOWN ASSOCIATES.
I'LL DO WHAT I CAN.
WELL, HERE'S THE PART WHERE I LOOK AWAY AND YOU SLIP OUT THE WINDOW AND LEAVE ME TALKING TO MYSELF.
I'LL MAKE IT EASY FOR YOU THIS TIME.
NOTHING HAS TO CHANGE, COMMISSIONER.
EVERYTHING CHANGES.
EVERYTHING.

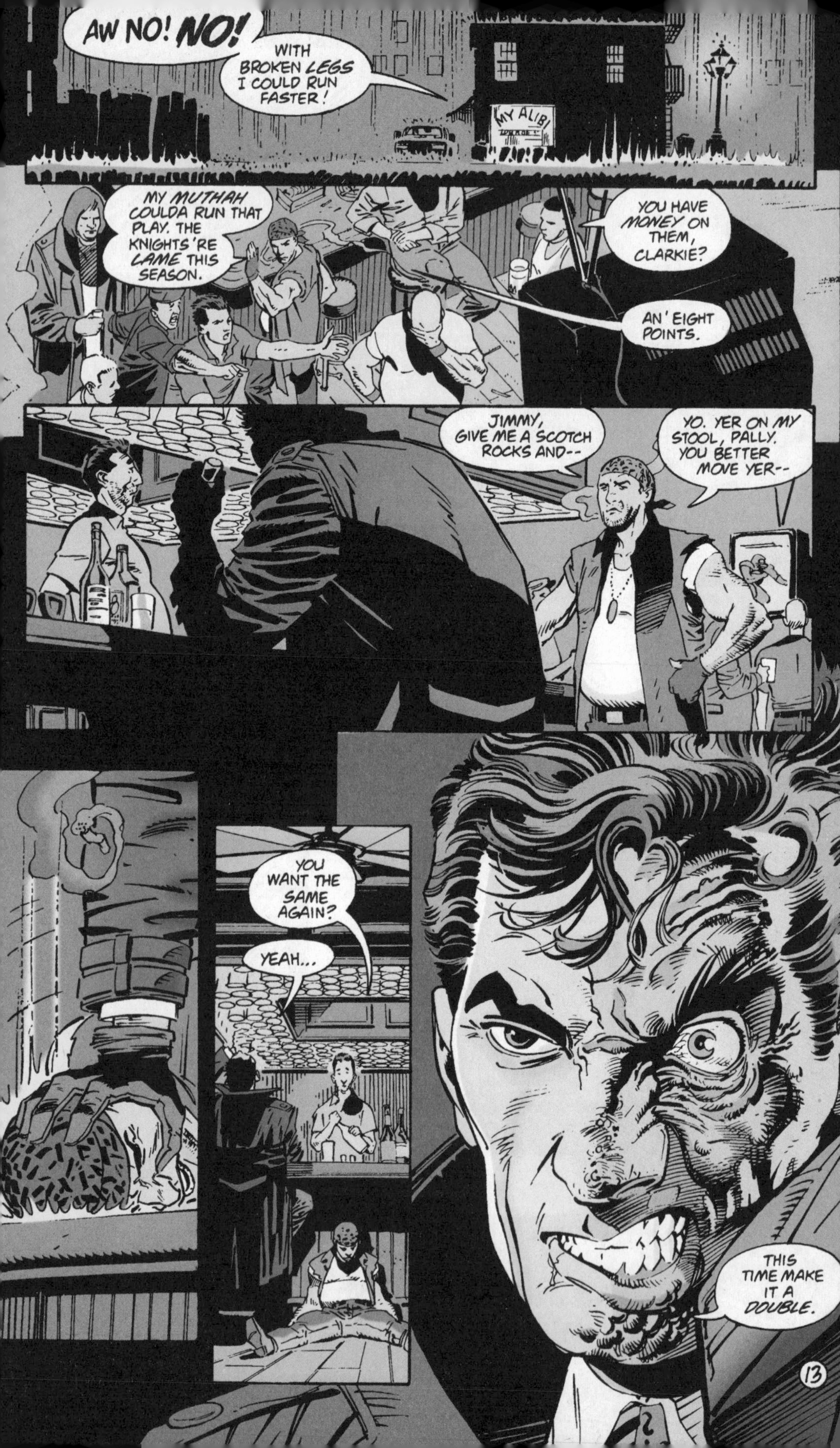

AW NO! NO!
WITH BROKEN LEGS I COULD RUN FASTER!
MY ALIBI
MY MUTHAH COULDA RUN THAT PLAY. THE KNIGHTS'RE LAME THIS SEASON.
YOU HAVE MONEY ON THEM, CLARKIE?
AN' EIGHT POINTS.
JIMMY, GIVE ME A SCOTCH ROCKS AND--
YO. YER ON MY STOOL, PALLY. YOU BETTER MOVE YER--
YOU WANT THE SAME AGAIN?
YEAH...
THIS TIME MAKE IT A DOUBLE.

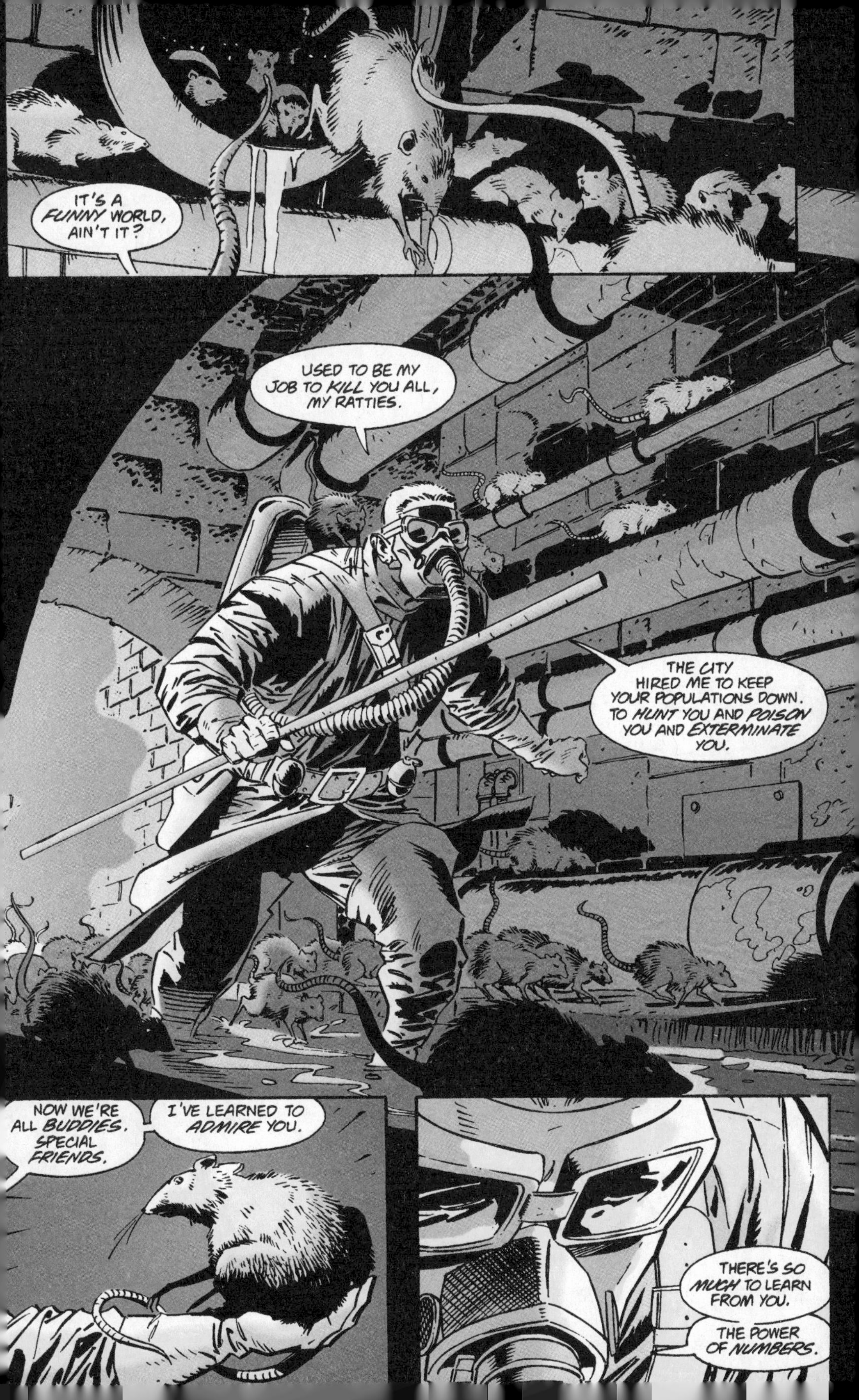
IT'S A FUNNY WORLD, AIN'T IT?
USED TO BE MY JOB TO KILL YOU ALL, MY RATTIES.
THE CITY HIRED ME TO KEEP YOUR POPULATIONS DOWN. TO HUNT YOU AND POISON YOU AND EXTERMINATE YOU.
NOW WE'RE ALL BUDDIES. SPECIAL FRIENDS.
I'VE LEARNED TO ADMIRE YOU.
THERE'S SO MUCH TO LEARN FROM YOU.
THE POWER OF NUMBERS.

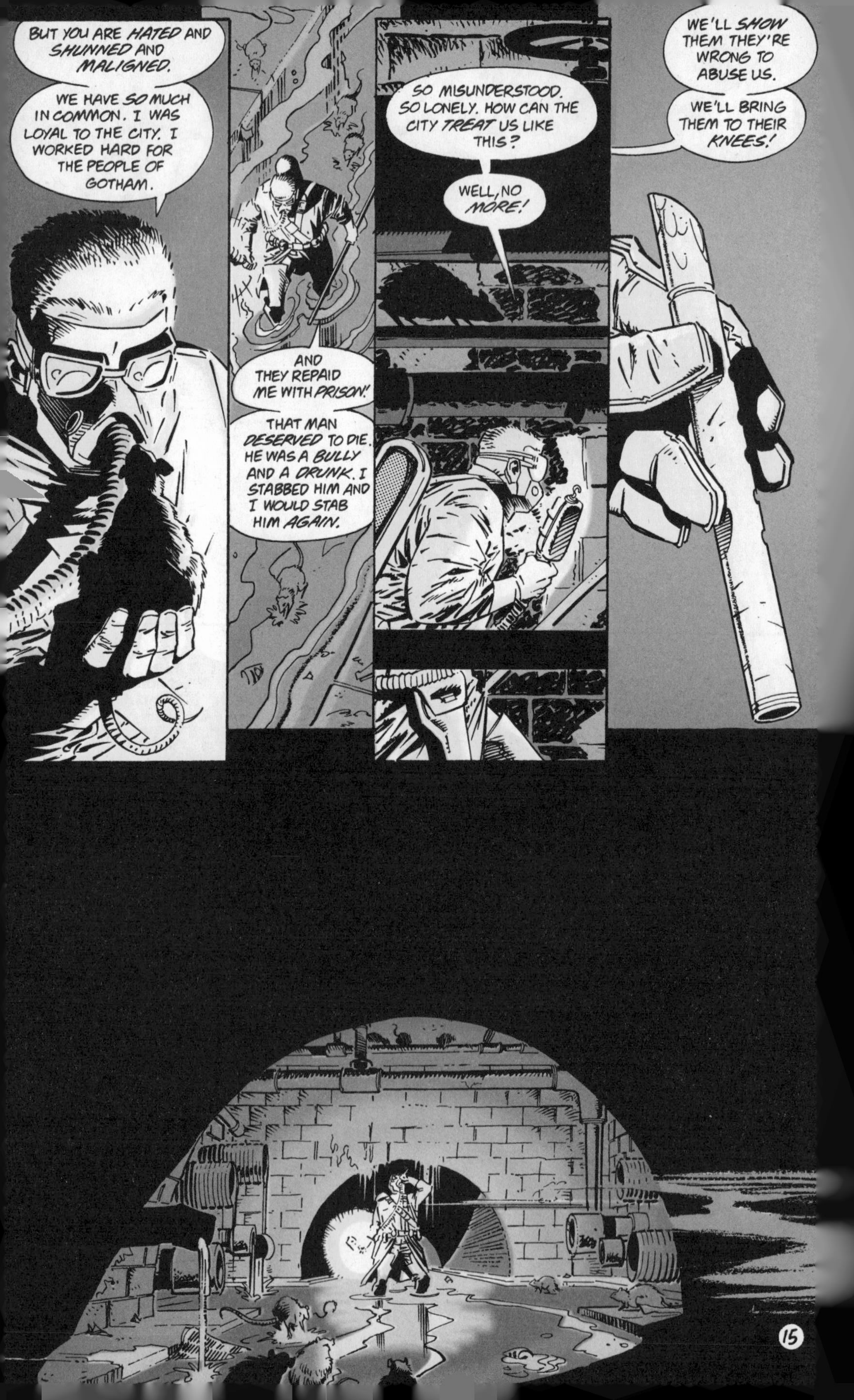

BUT YOU ARE HATED AND SHUNNED AND MALIGNED.
WE HAVE SO MUCH IN COMMON. I WAS LOYAL TO THE CITY. I WORKED HARD FOR THE PEOPLE OF GOTHAM.
AND THEY REPAID ME WITH PRISON!
THAT MAN DESERVED TO DIE. HE WAS A BULLY AND A DRUNK. I STABBED HIM AND I WOULD STAB HIM AGAIN.
SO MISUNDERSTOOD. SO LONELY. HOW CAN THE CITY TREAT US LIKE THIS?
WELL, NO MORE!
WE'LL SHOW THEM THEY'RE WRONG TO ABUSE US.
WE'LL BRING THEM TO THEIR KNEES!

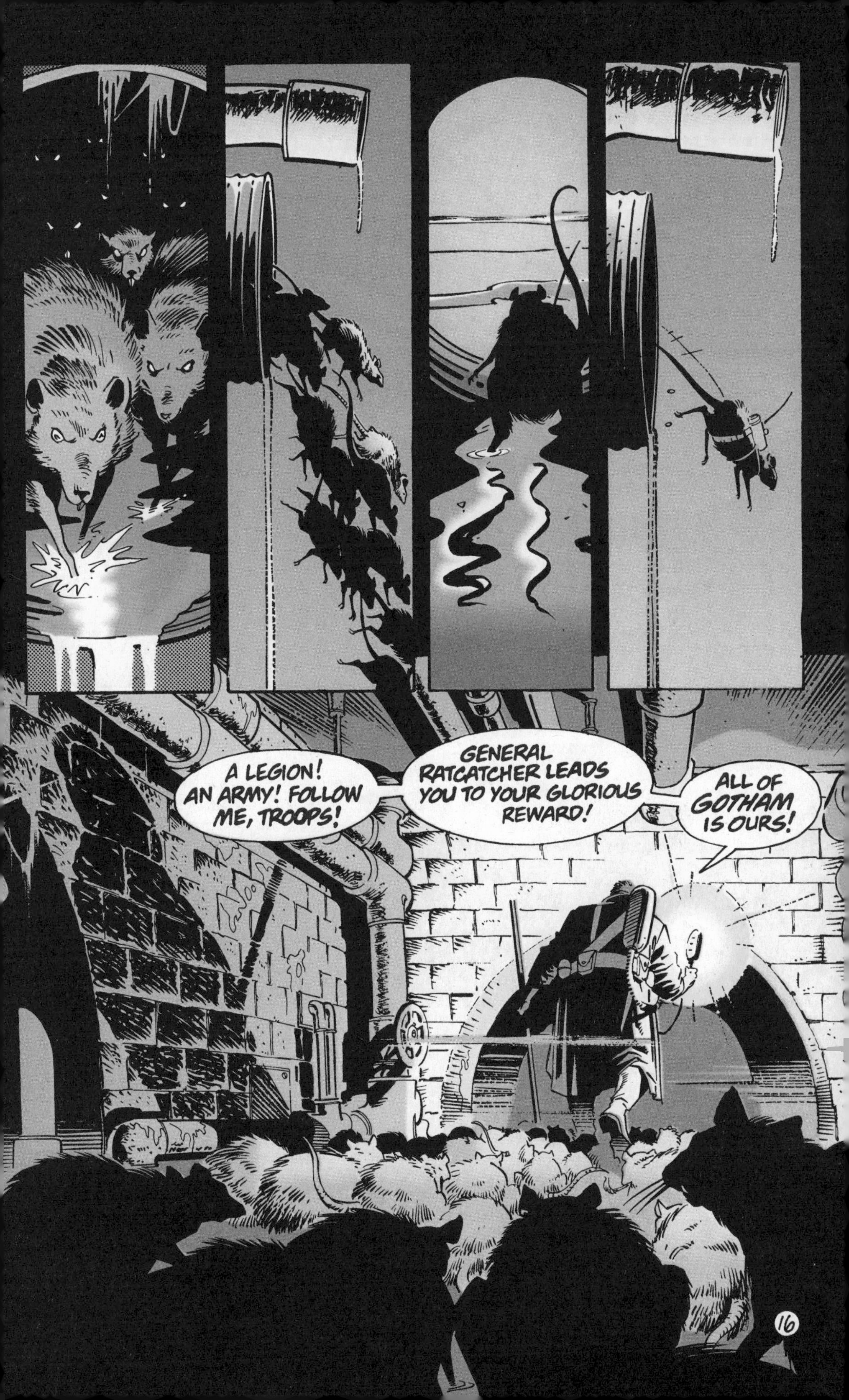
A LEGION! AN ARMY! FOLLOW ME, TROOPS!
GENERAL RATCATCHER LEADS YOU TO YOUR GLORIOUS REWARD!
ALL OF GOTHAM IS OURS!

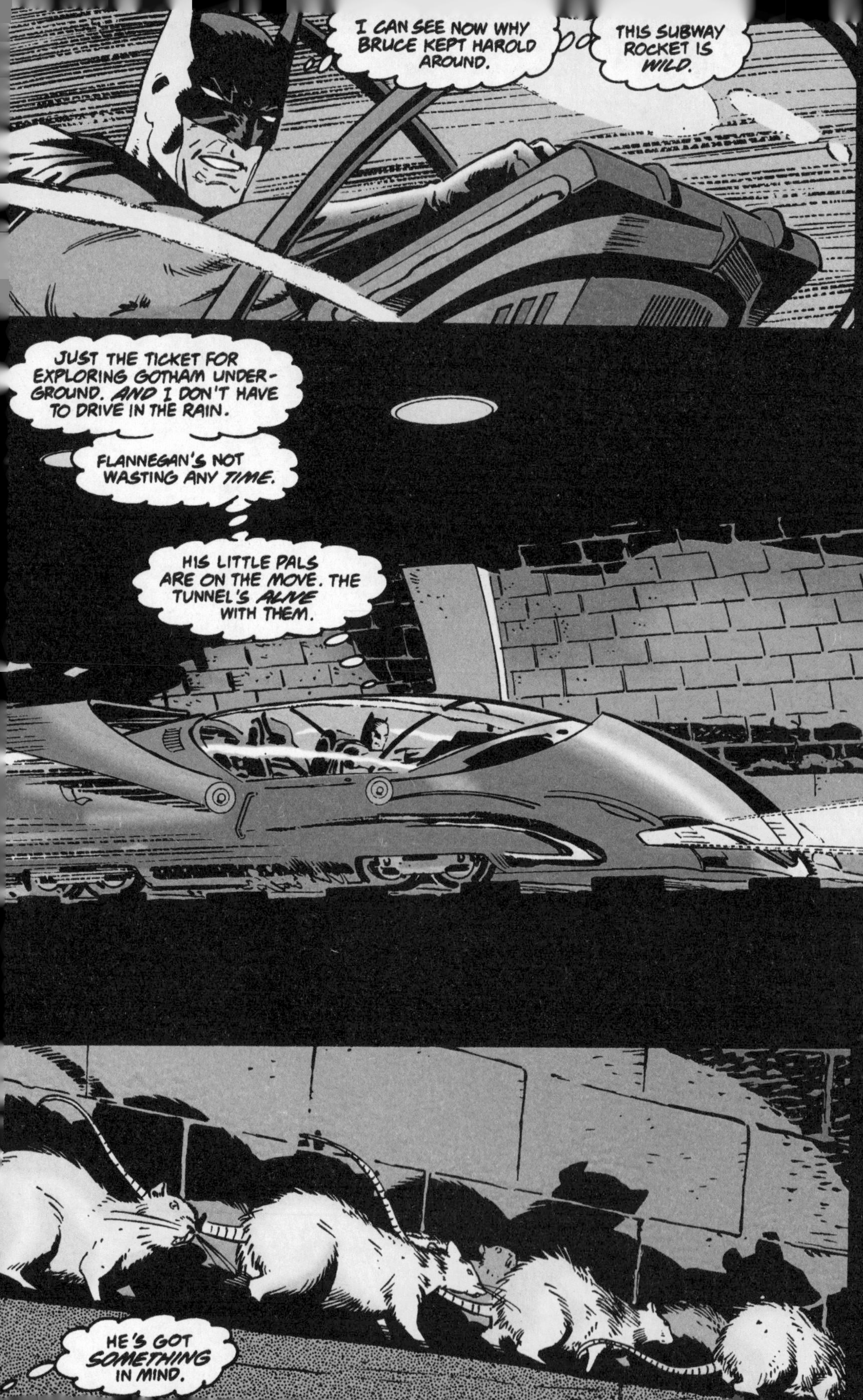
I CAN SEE NOW WHY BRUCE KEPT HAROLD AROUND.
THIS SUBWAY ROCKET IS *WILD.*
JUST THE TICKET FOR EXPLORING GOTHAM UNDER-GROUND. *AND* I DON'T HAVE TO DRIVE IN THE RAIN.
FLANNEGAN'S NOT WASTING ANY *TIME.*
HIS LITTLE PALS ARE ON THE *MOVE.* THE TUNNEL'S *ALIVE* WITH THEM.
HE'S GOT *SOMETHING* IN MIND.

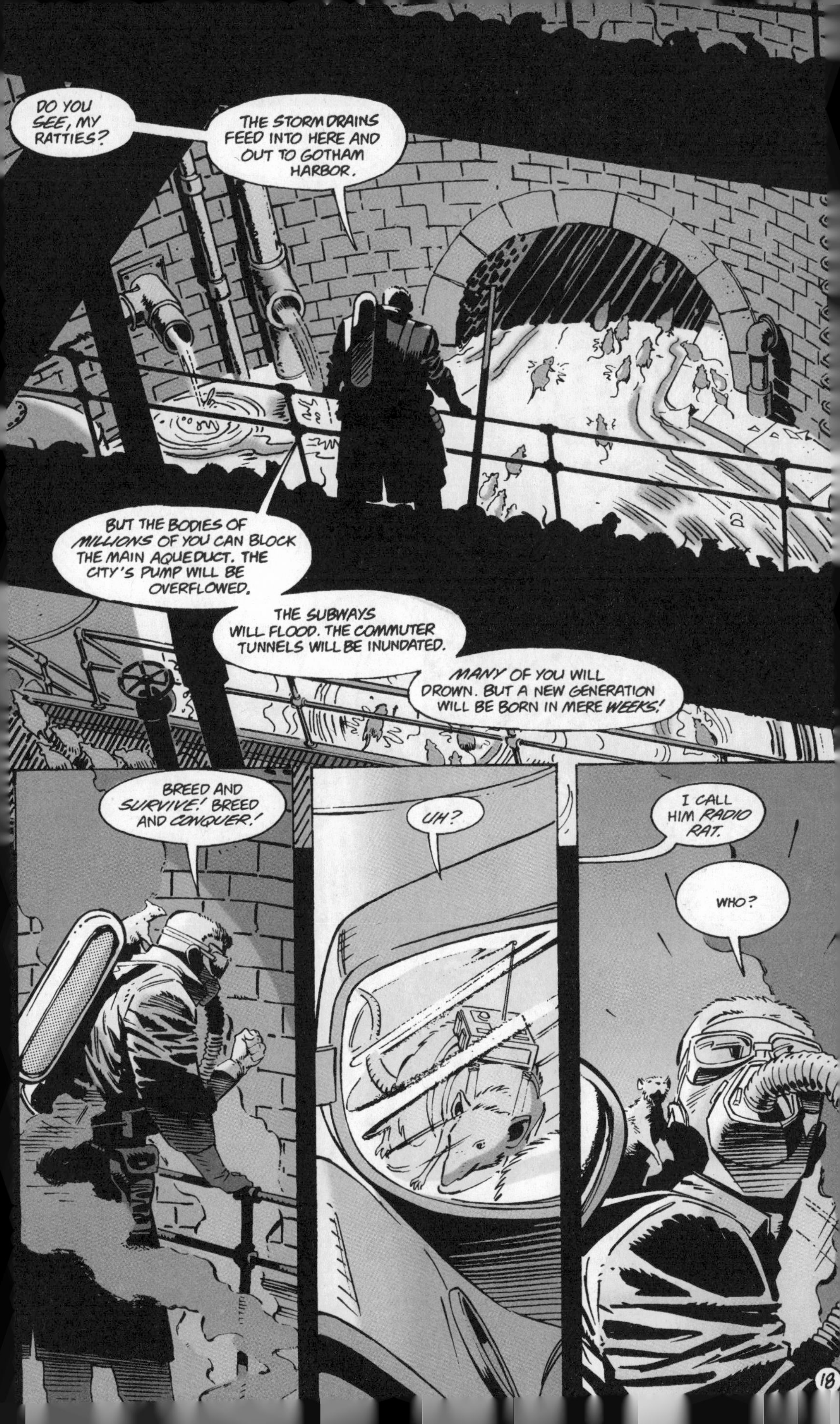
DO YOU SEE, MY RATTIES?
THE STORM DRAINS FEED INTO HERE AND OUT TO GOTHAM HARBOR.
BUT THE BODIES OF MILLIONS OF YOU CAN BLOCK THE MAIN AQUEDUCT. THE CITY'S PUMP WILL BE OVERFLOWED.
THE SUBWAYS WILL FLOOD. THE COMMUTER TUNNELS WILL BE INUNDATED.
MANY OF YOU WILL DROWN. BUT A NEW GENERATION WILL BE BORN IN MERE WEEKS!
BREED AND SURVIVE! BREED AND CONQUER!
UH?
I CALL HIM RADIO RAT.
WHO?
18

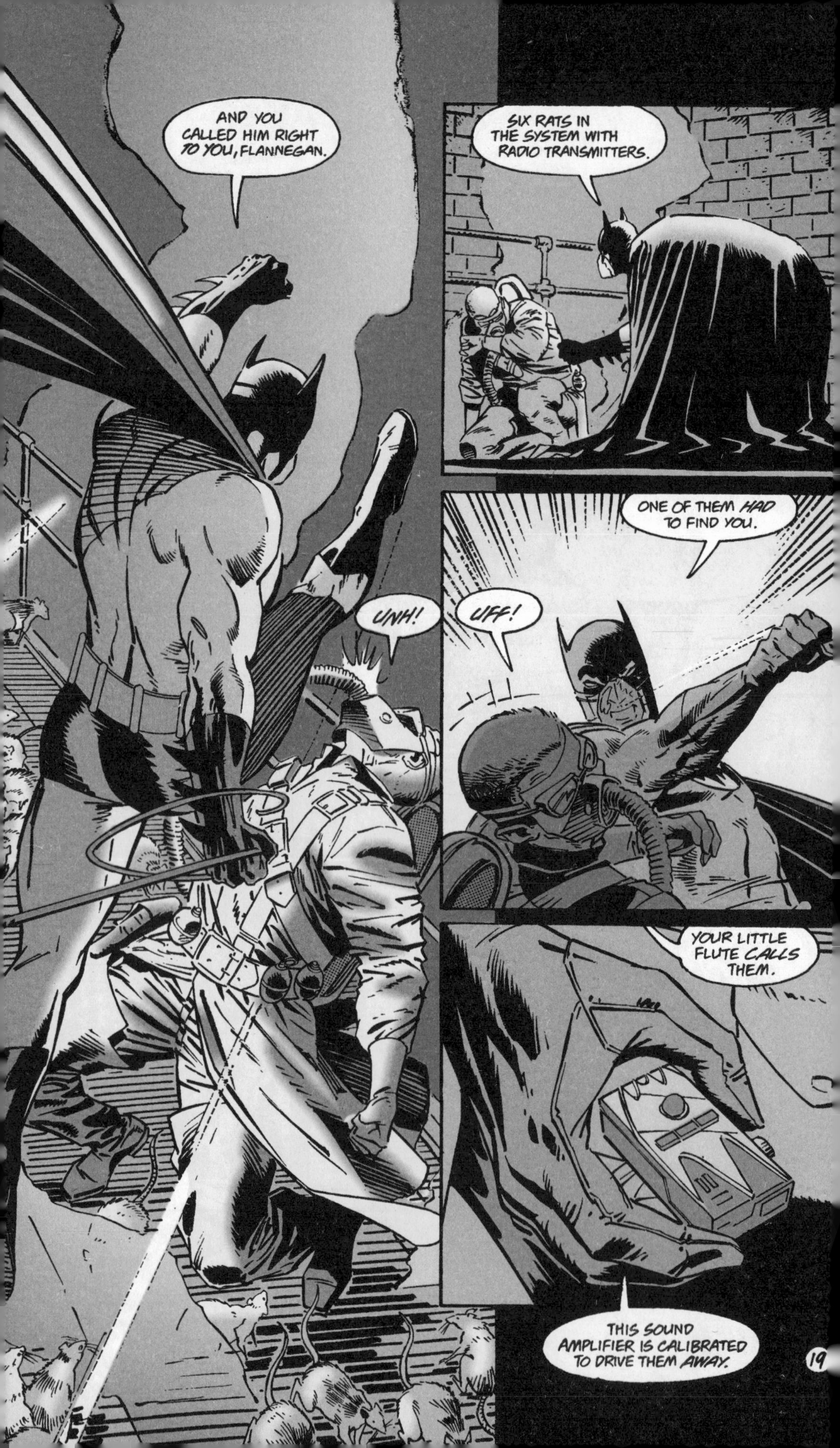
AND YOU CALLED HIM RIGHT TO YOU, FLANNEGAN.
SIX RATS IN THE SYSTEM WITH RADIO TRANSMITTERS.
UNH!
UFF!
ONE OF THEM HAD TO FIND YOU.
YOUR LITTLE FLUTE CALLS THEM.
THIS SOUND AMPLIFIER IS CALIBRATED TO DRIVE THEM AWAY.

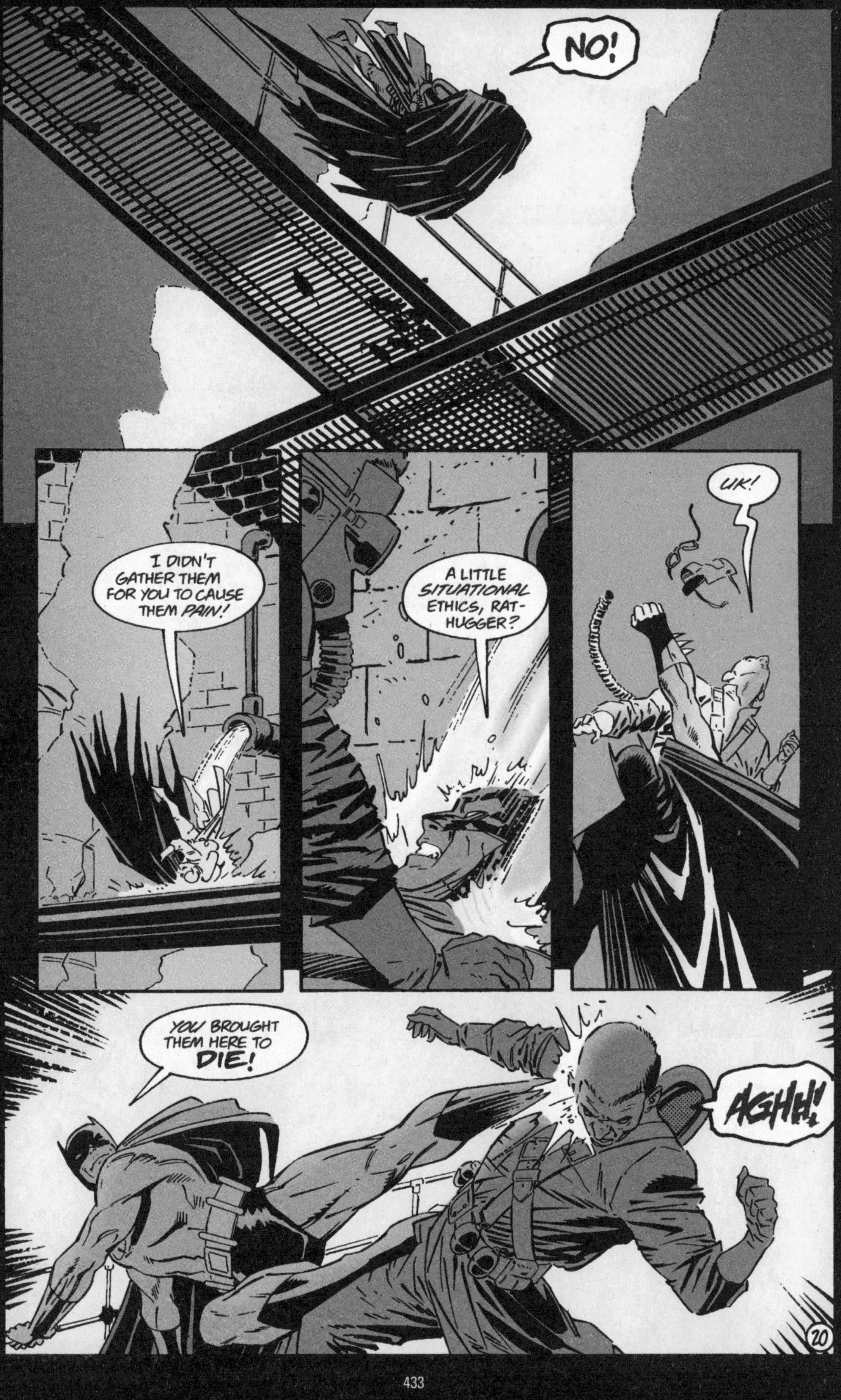
NO!
I DIDN'T GATHER THEM FOR YOU TO CAUSE THEM PAIN!
A LITTLE SITUATIONAL ETHICS, RAT-HUGGER?
UK!
YOU BROUGHT THEM HERE TO DIE!
AGHH!
20

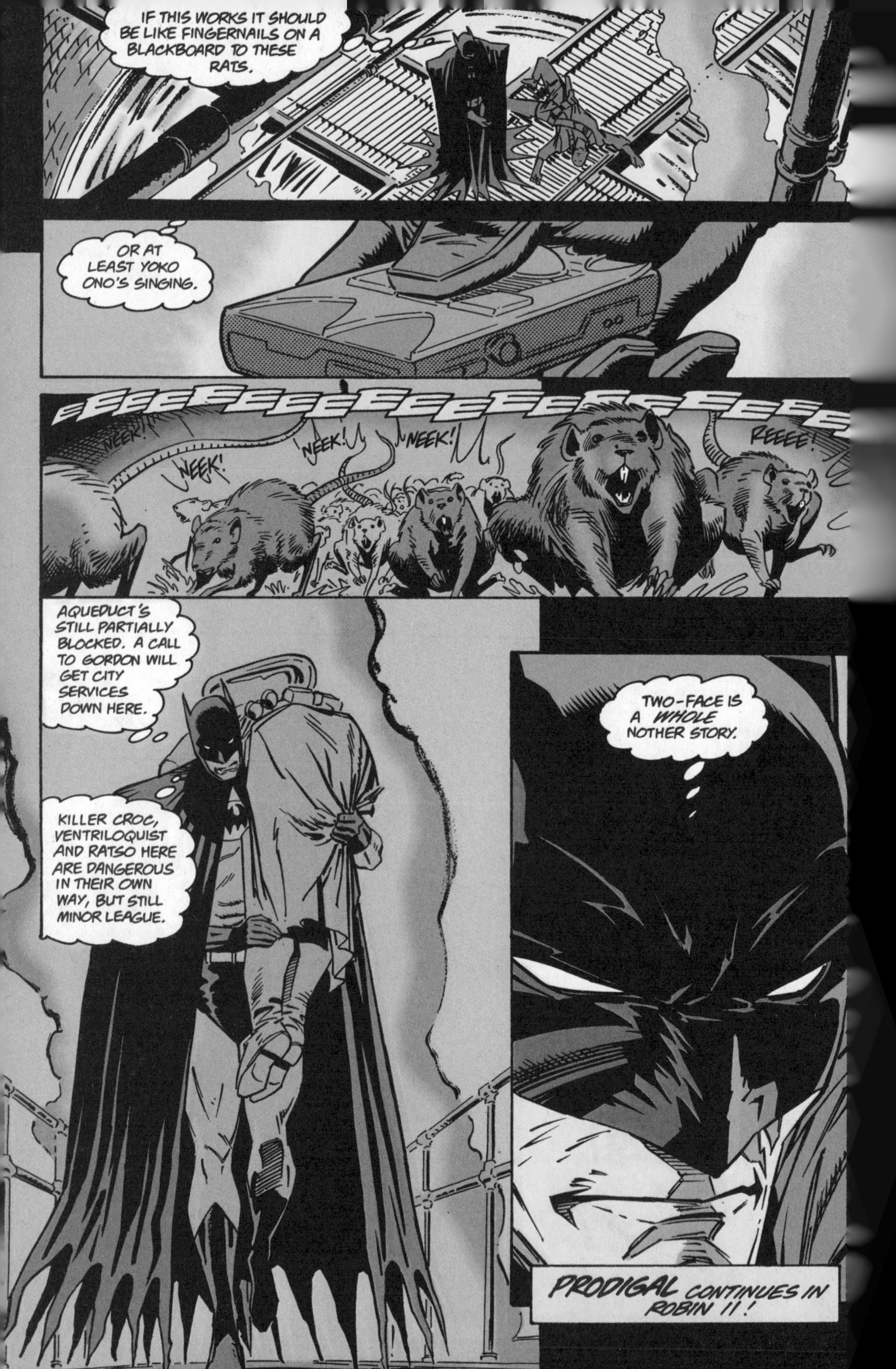
IF THIS WORKS IT SHOULD BE LIKE FINGERNAILS ON A BLACKBOARD TO THESE RATS.
OR AT LEAST YOKO ONO'S SINGING.
EEEEEEEEEEEEEEEEEEEEEEEEEEEE
NEEK!
NEEK!
NEEK!
NEEK!
REEEE!
AQUEDUCT'S STILL PARTIALLY BLOCKED. A CALL TO GORDON WILL GET CITY SERVICES DOWN HERE.
KILLER CROC, VENTRILOQUIST AND RATSO HERE ARE DANGEROUS IN THEIR OWN WAY, BUT STILL MINOR LEAGUE.
TWO-FACE IS A WHOLE NOTHER STORY.
PRODIGAL CONTINUES IN ROBIN 11!

Cover art by TOM GRUMMETT and RAY KRYSSING

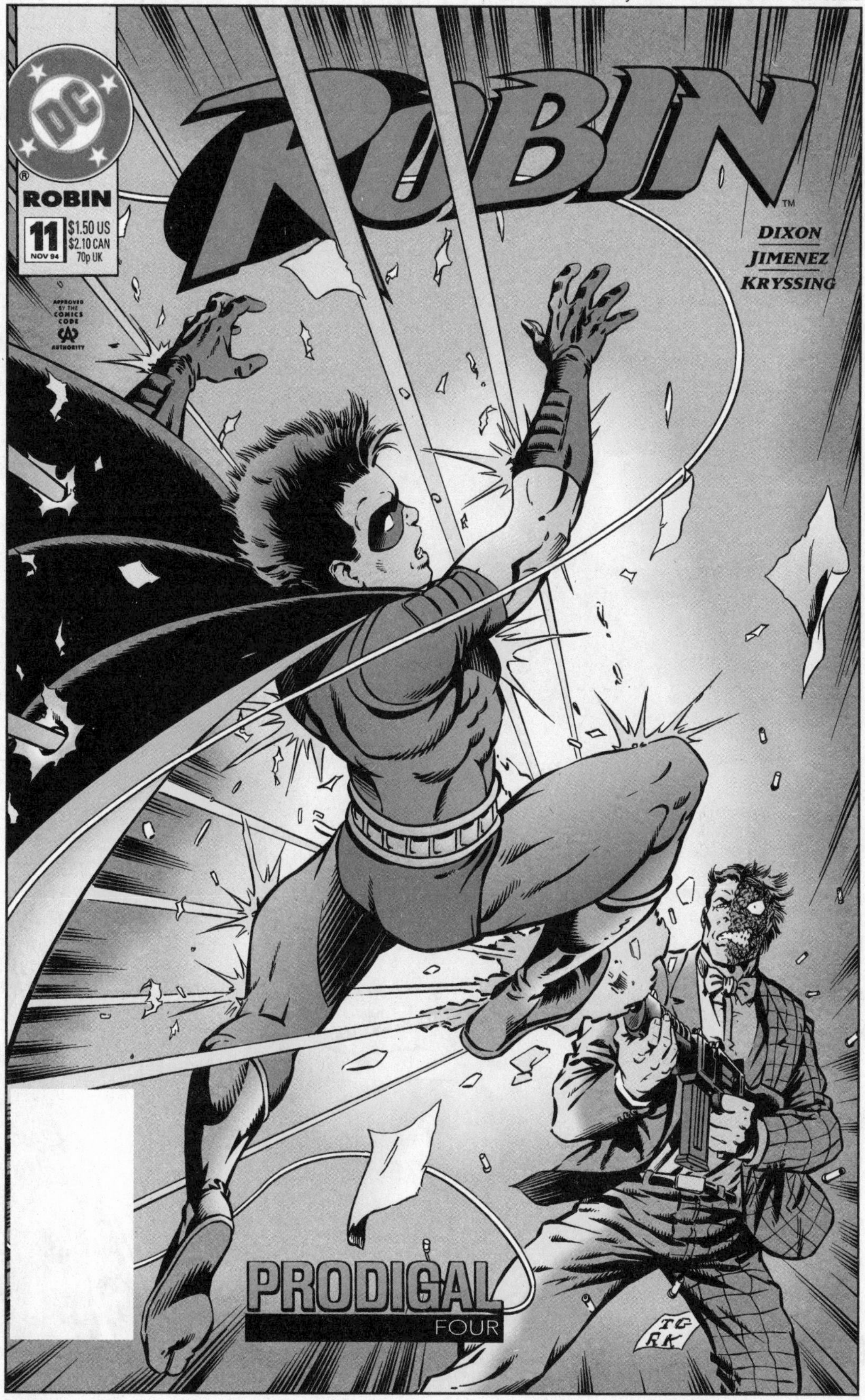

DC
ROBIN
ROBIN
11
NOV 94
$1.50 US
$2.10 CAN
70p UK
APPROVED BY THE COMICS CODE AUTHORITY
DIXON
JIMENEZ
KRYSSING
PRODIGAL
FOUR
TG
RK

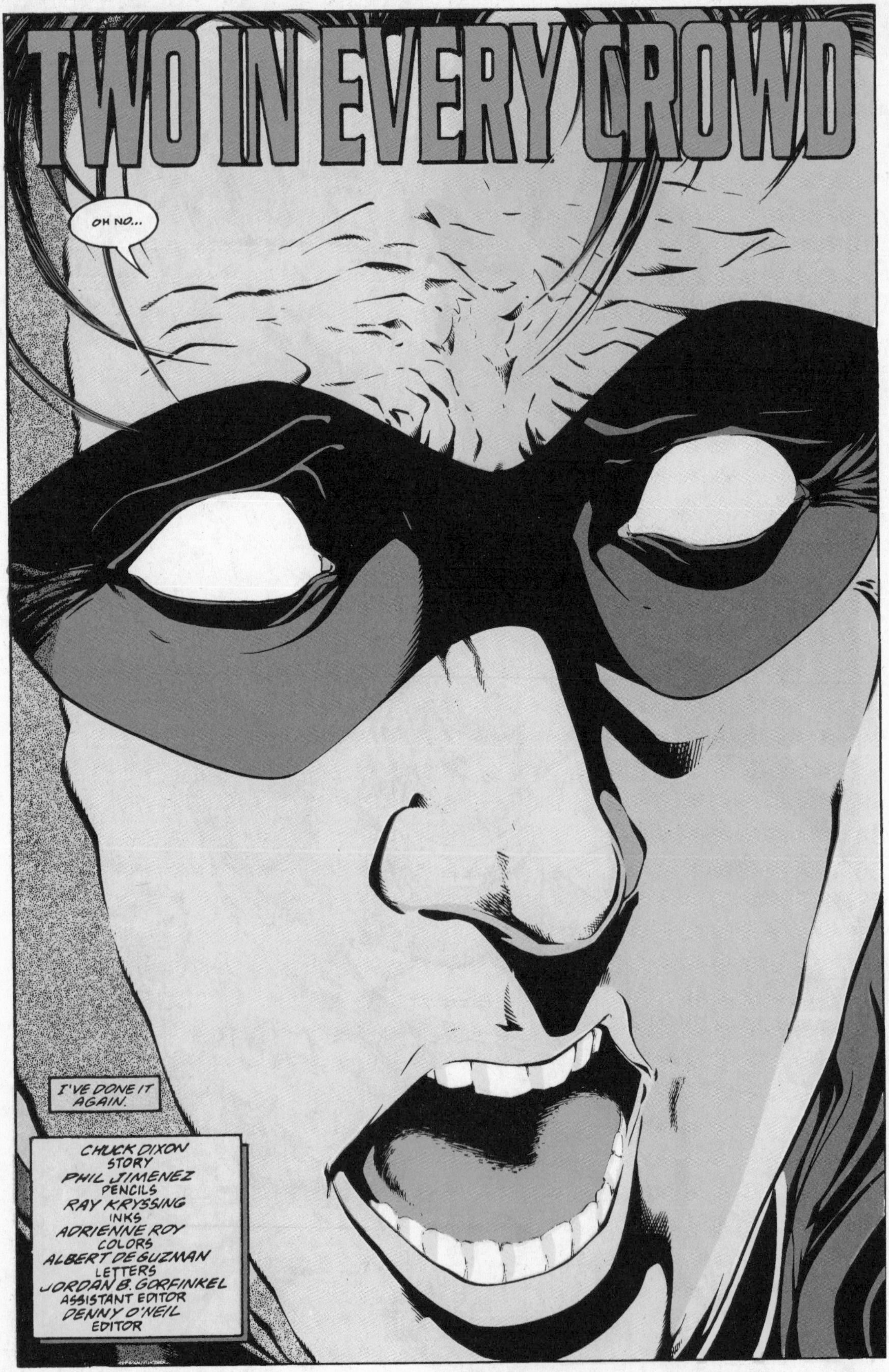
TWO IN EVERY CROWD
OH NO...
I'VE DONE IT AGAIN.
CHUCK DIXON STORY
PHIL JIMENEZ PENCILS
RAY KRYSSING INKS
ADRIENNE ROY COLORS
ALBERT DEGUZMAN LETTERS
JORDAN B. GORFINKEL ASSISTANT EDITOR
DENNY O'NEIL EDITOR

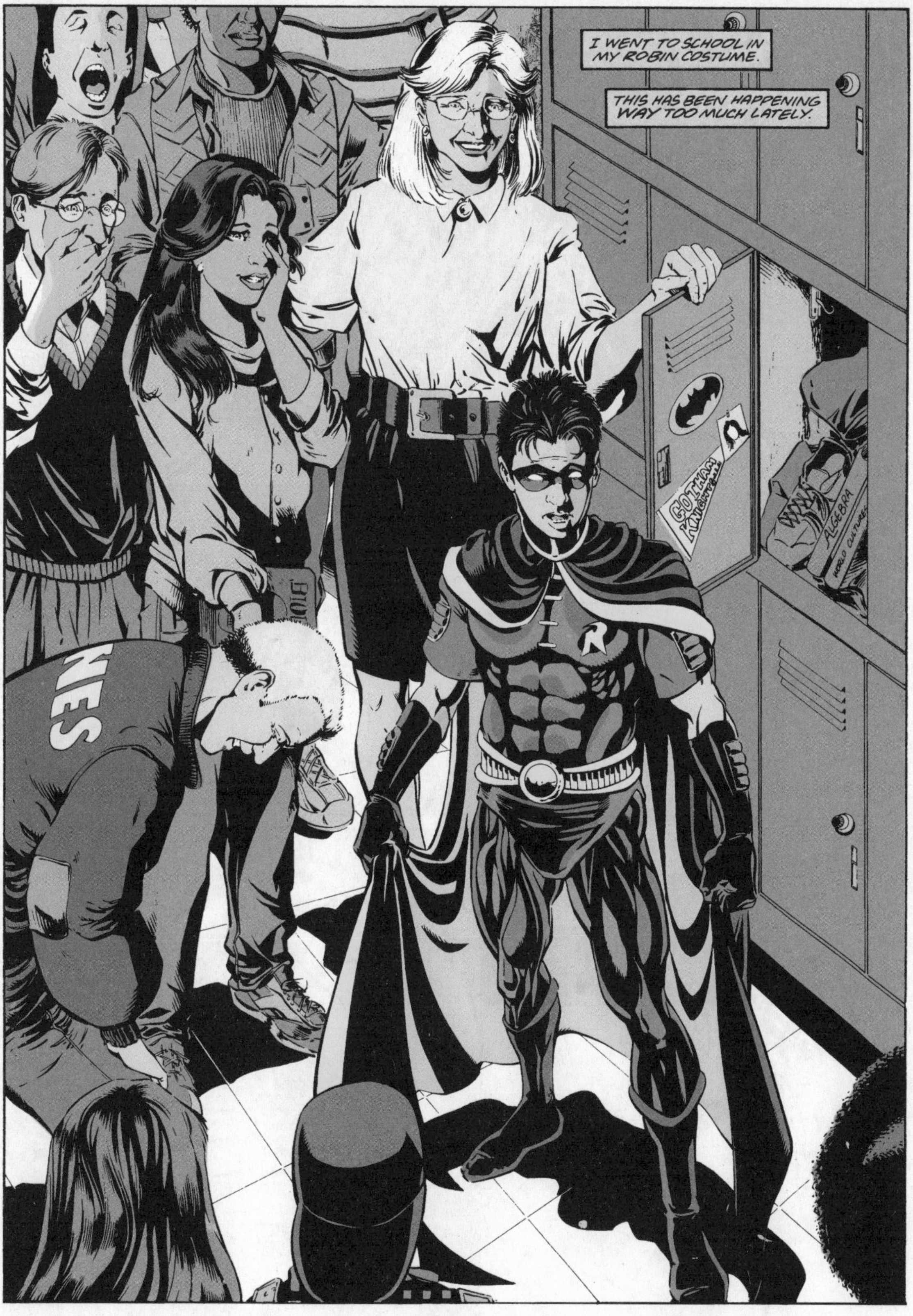
I WENT TO SCHOOL IN MY ROBIN COSTUME.
THIS HAS BEEN HAPPENING WAY TOO MUCH LATELY.
GOTHAM KNIGHTS
ALGEBRA
WORLD CULTURES

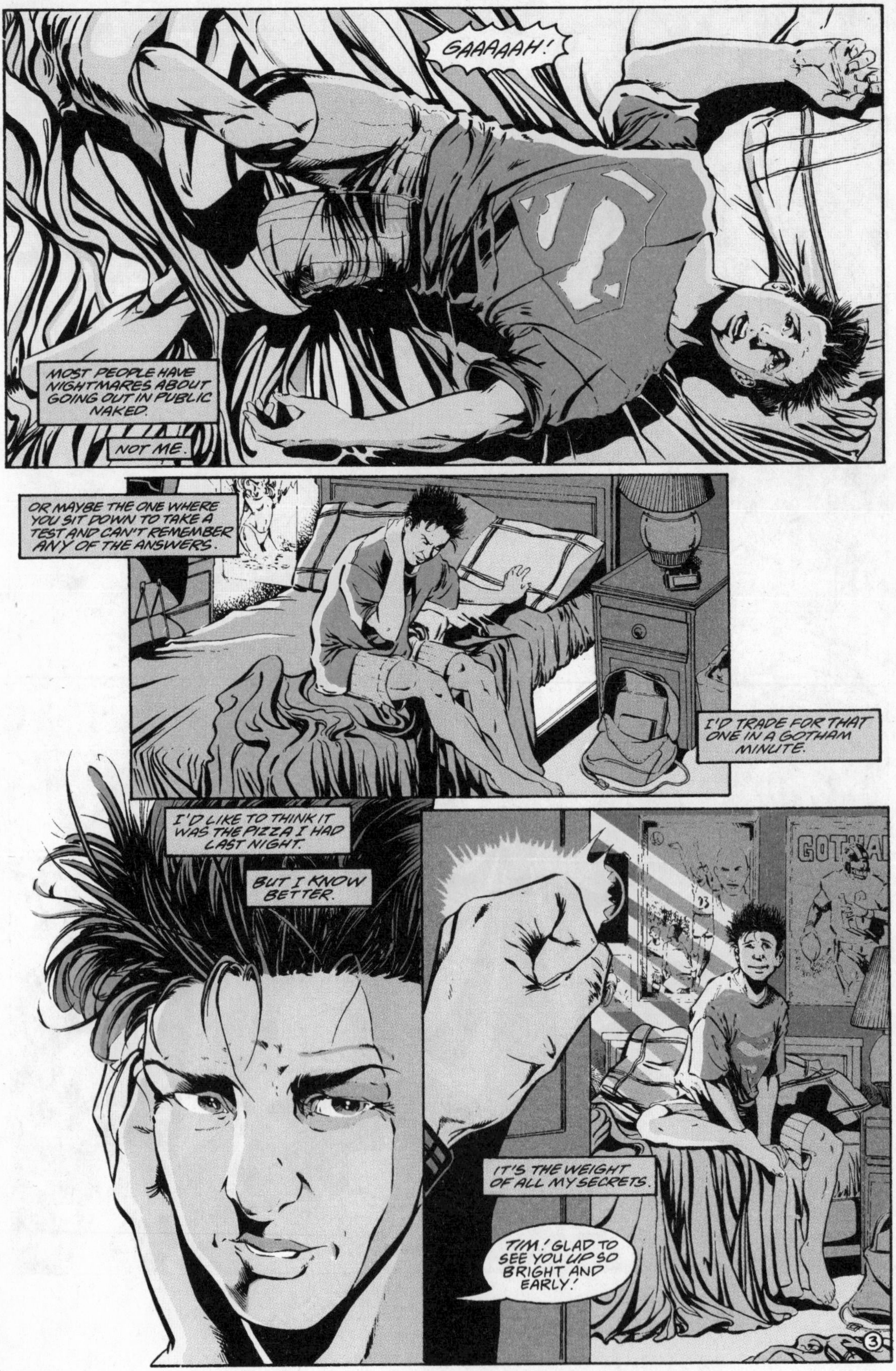
GAAAAAH!
MOST PEOPLE HAVE NIGHTMARES ABOUT GOING OUT IN PUBLIC NAKED.
NOT ME.
OR MAYBE THE ONE WHERE YOU SIT DOWN TO TAKE A TEST AND CAN'T REMEMBER ANY OF THE ANSWERS.
I'D TRADE FOR THAT ONE IN A GOTHAM MINUTE.
I'D LIKE TO THINK IT WAS THE PIZZA I HAD LAST NIGHT.
BUT I KNOW BETTER.
IT'S THE WEIGHT OF ALL MY SECRETS.
TIM! GLAD TO SEE YOU UP SO BRIGHT AND EARLY!
3

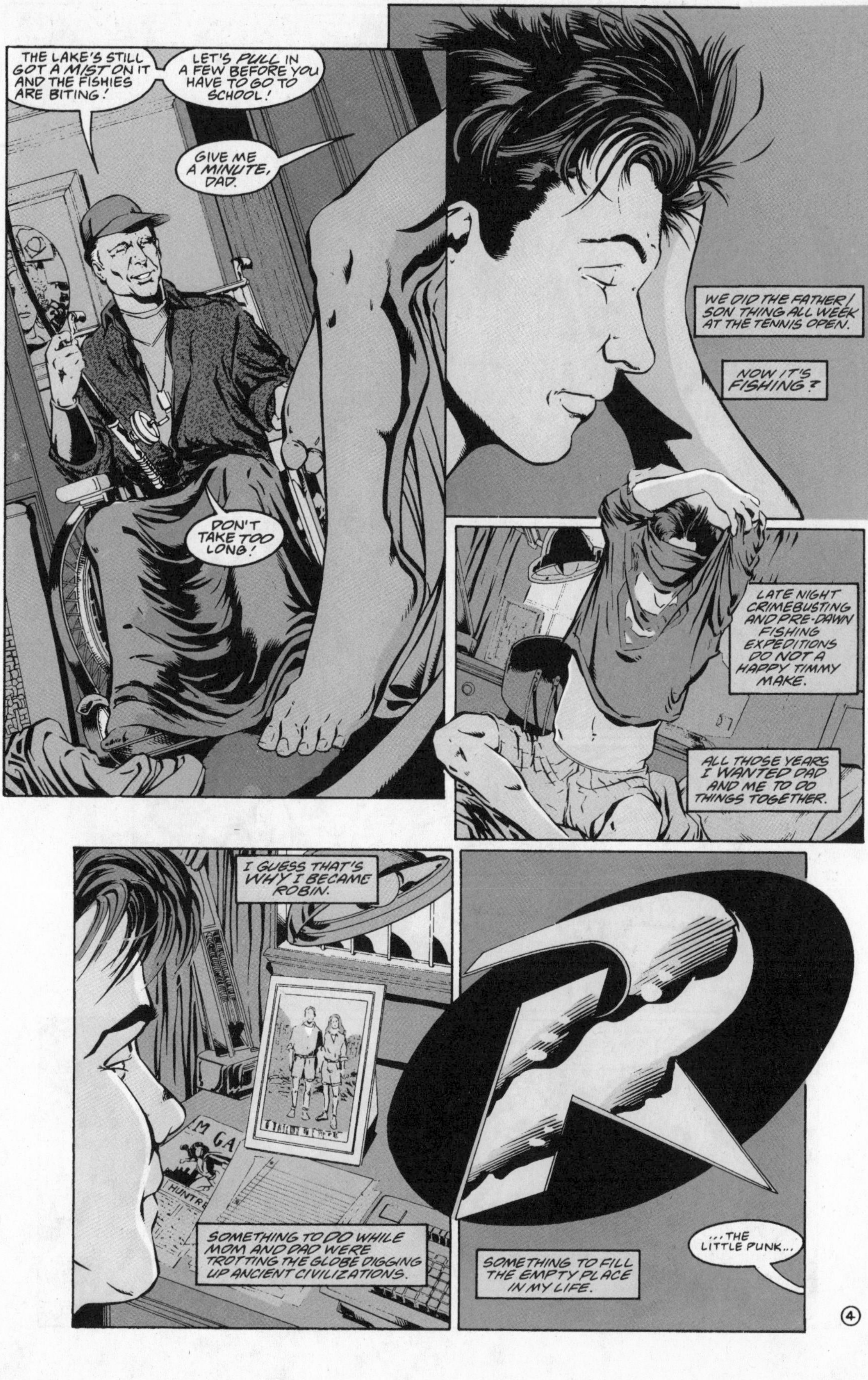
THE LAKE'S STILL GOT A MIST ON IT AND THE FISHIES ARE BITING!
LET'S PULL IN A FEW BEFORE YOU HAVE TO GO TO SCHOOL!
GIVE ME A MINUTE, DAD.
DON'T TAKE TOO LONG!
WE DID THE FATHER/SON THING ALL WEEK AT THE TENNIS OPEN.
NOW IT'S FISHING?
LATE NIGHT CRIMEBUSTING AND PRE-DAWN FISHING EXPEDITIONS DO NOT A HAPPY TIMMY MAKE.
ALL THOSE YEARS I WANTED DAD AND ME TO DO THINGS TOGETHER.
I GUESS THAT'S WHY I BECAME ROBIN.
SOMETHING TO DO WHILE MOM AND DAD WERE TROTTING THE GLOBE DIGGING UP ANCIENT CIVILIZATIONS.
SOMETHING TO FILL THE EMPTY PLACE IN MY LIFE.
...THE LITTLE PUNK...
4

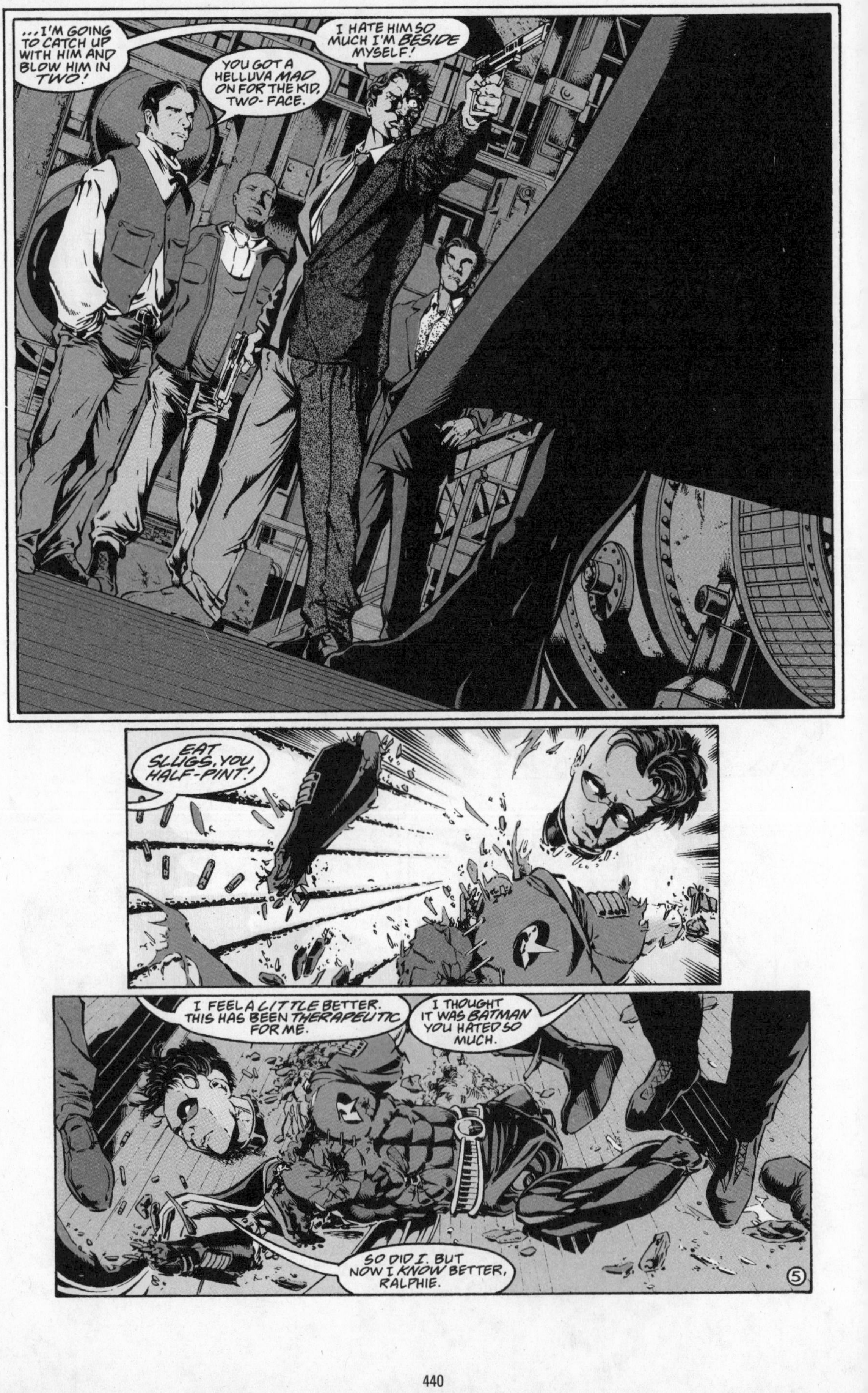
I HATE HIM SO MUCH I'M BESIDE MYSELF!
...I'M GOING TO CATCH UP WITH HIM AND BLOW HIM IN TWO!
YOU GOT A HELLUVA MAD ON FOR THE KID, TWO-FACE.
EAT SLUGS, YOU HALF-PINT!
I FEEL A LITTLE BETTER. THIS HAS BEEN THERAPEUTIC FOR ME.
I THOUGHT IT WAS BATMAN YOU HATED SO MUCH.
SO DID I. BUT NOW I KNOW BETTER, RALPHIE.
5

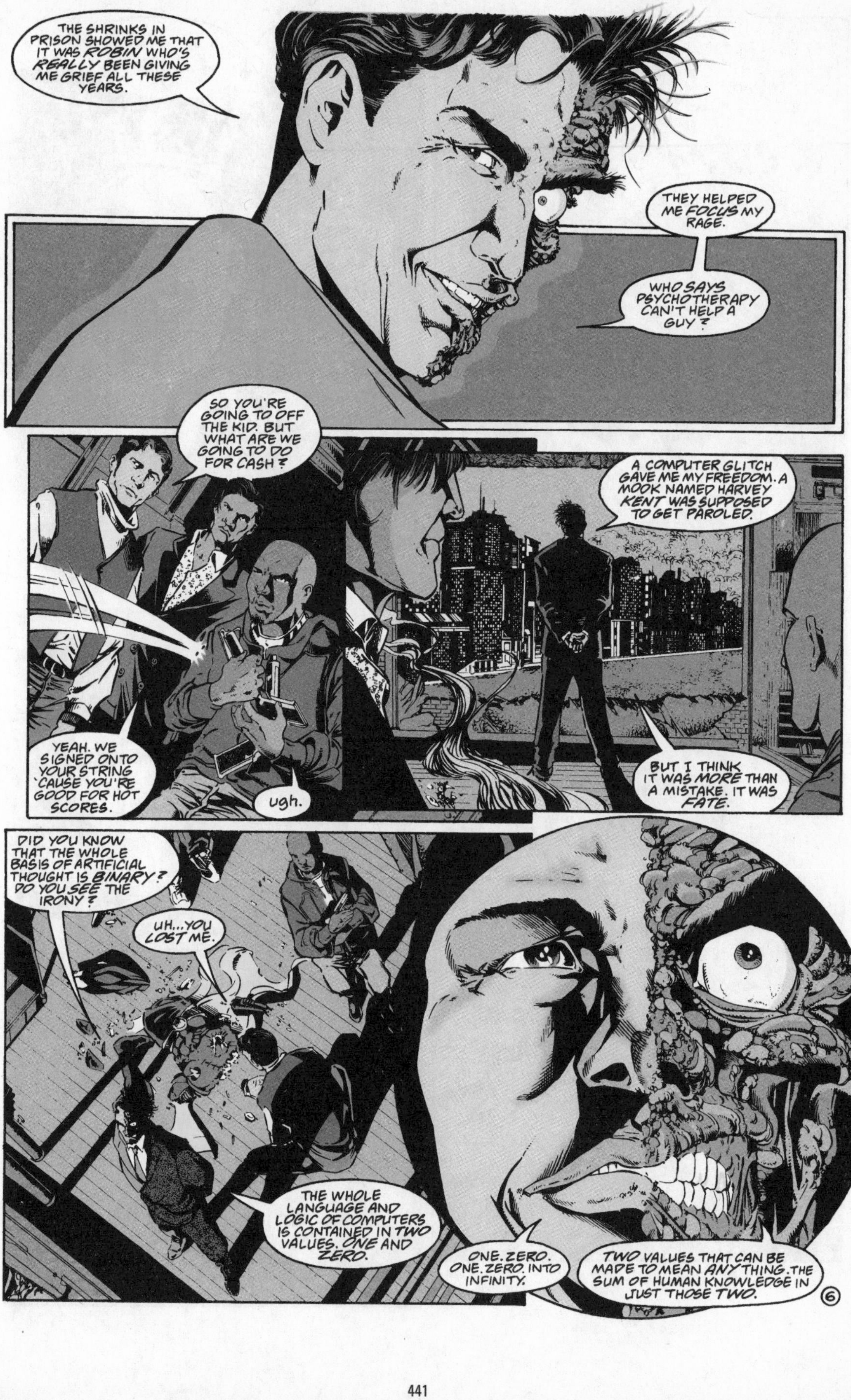

THE SHRINKS IN PRISON SHOWED ME THAT IT WAS ROBIN WHO'S REALLY BEEN GIVING ME GRIEF ALL THESE YEARS.
THEY HELPED ME FOCUS MY RAGE.
WHO SAYS PSYCHOTHERAPY CAN'T HELP A GUY?
SO YOU'RE GOING TO OFF THE KID. BUT WHAT ARE WE GOING TO DO FOR CASH?
YEAH. WE SIGNED ONTO YOUR STRING 'CAUSE YOU'RE GOOD FOR HOT SCORES.
ugh.
A COMPUTER GLITCH GAVE ME MY FREEDOM. A MOOK NAMED HARVEY KENT WAS SUPPOSED TO GET PAROLED.
BUT I THINK IT WAS MORE THAN A MISTAKE. IT WAS FATE.
DID YOU KNOW THAT THE WHOLE BASIS OF ARTIFICIAL THOUGHT IS BINARY? DO YOU SEE THE IRONY?
UH...YOU LOST ME.
THE WHOLE LANGUAGE AND LOGIC OF COMPUTERS IS CONTAINED IN TWO VALUES. ONE AND ZERO.
ONE. ZERO. ONE. ZERO. INTO INFINITY.
TWO VALUES THAT CAN BE MADE TO MEAN ANYTHING. THE SUM OF HUMAN KNOWLEDGE IN JUST THOSE TWO.
6

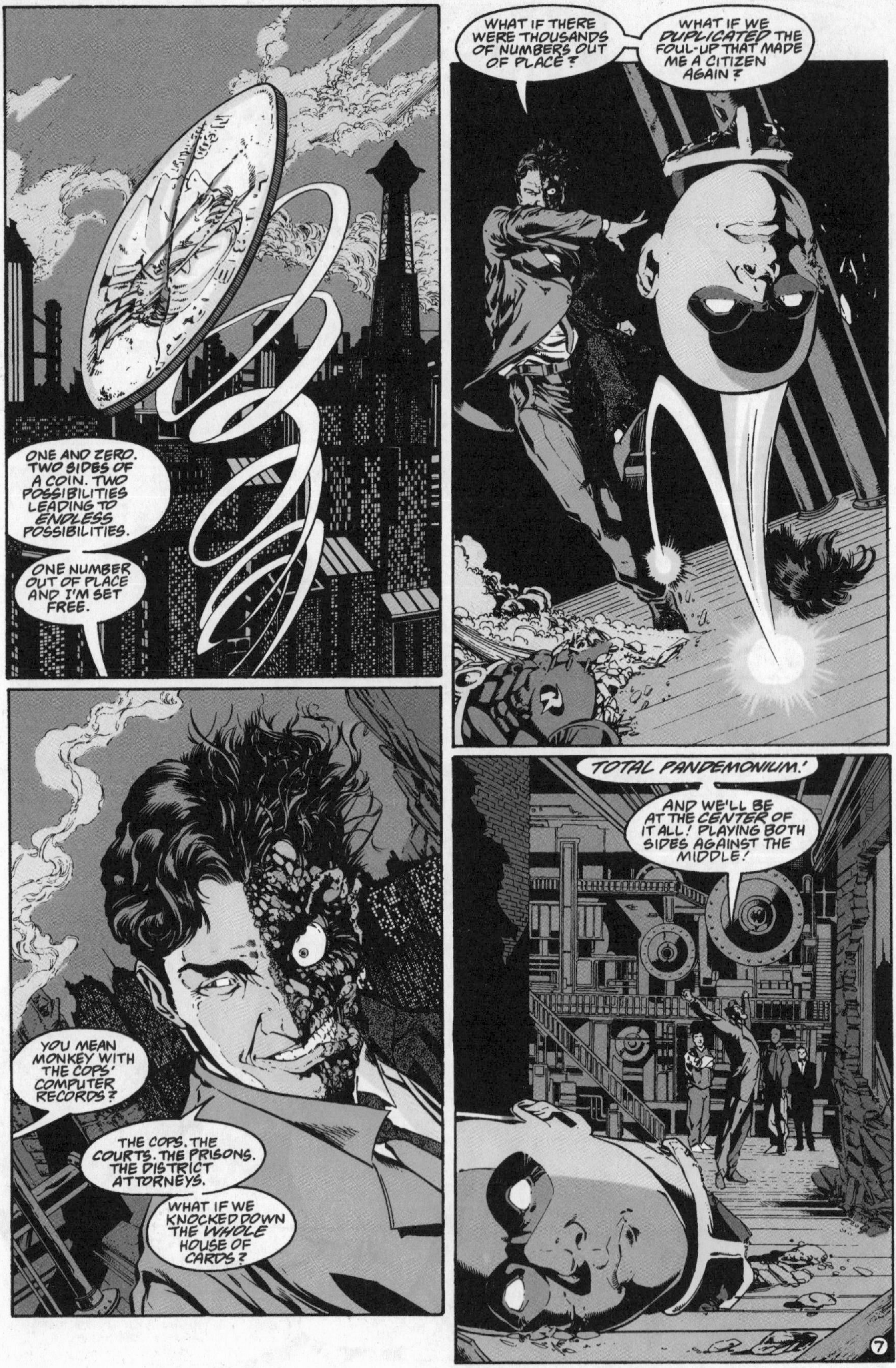
ONE AND ZERO. TWO SIDES OF A COIN. TWO POSSIBILITIES LEADING TO *ENDLESS* POSSIBILITIES.
ONE NUMBER OUT OF PLACE AND I'M SET FREE.
WHAT IF THERE WERE THOUSANDS OF NUMBERS OUT OF PLACE?
WHAT IF WE *DUPLICATED* THE FOUL-UP THAT MADE ME A CITIZEN AGAIN?
YOU MEAN MONKEY WITH THE COPS' COMPUTER RECORDS?
THE COPS. THE COURTS. THE PRISONS. THE DISTRICT ATTORNEYS.
WHAT IF WE KNOCKED DOWN THE *WHOLE* HOUSE OF CARDS?
TOTAL PANDEMONIUM!
AND WE'LL BE AT THE *CENTER* OF IT ALL! PLAYING BOTH SIDES AGAINST THE MIDDLE!
7

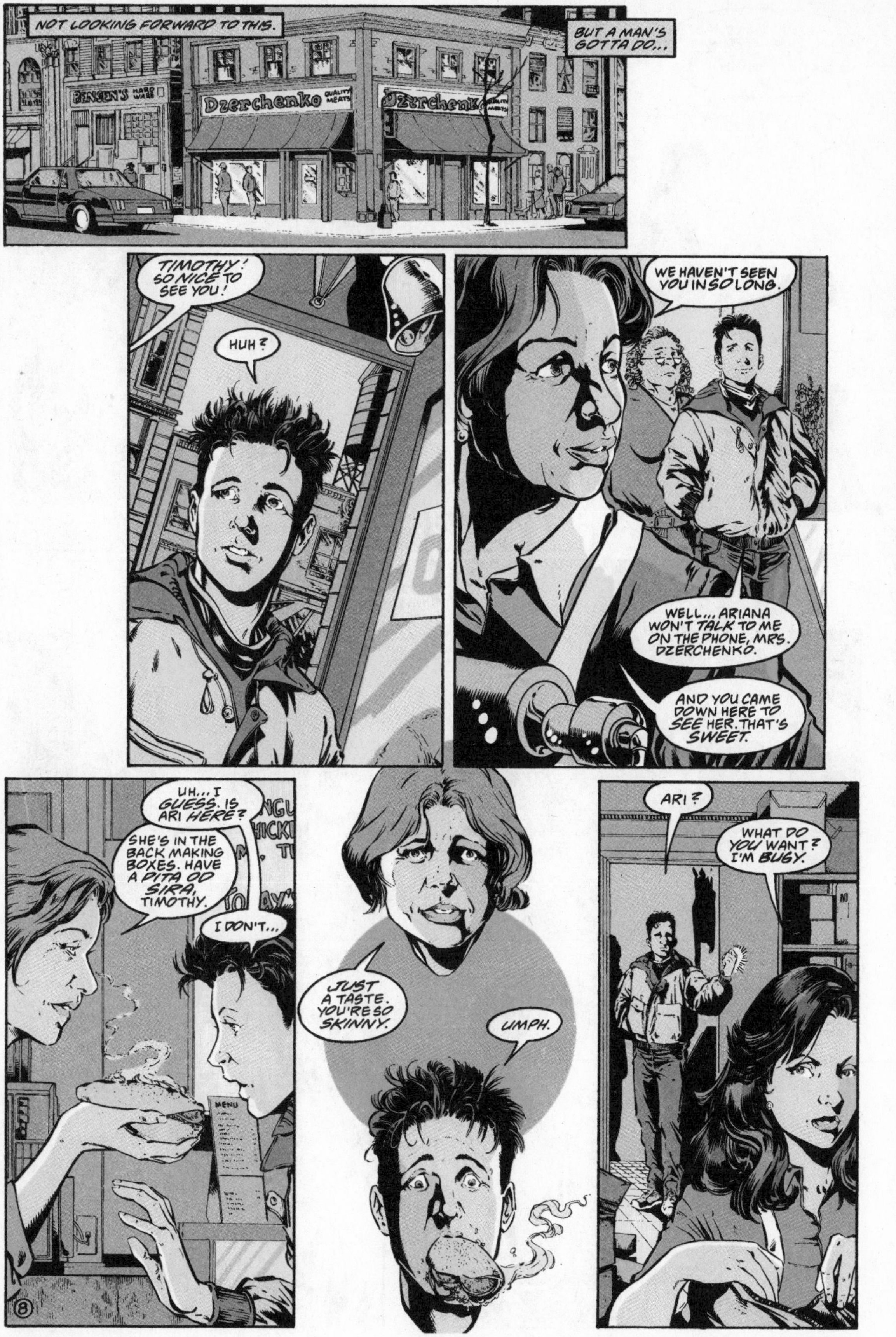
NOT LOOKING FORWARD TO THIS.
BUT A MAN'S GOTTA DO...
BENSEN'S HARD WARE
Dzerchenko QUALITY MEATS
TIMOTHY! SO NICE TO SEE YOU!
HUH?
WE HAVEN'T SEEN YOU IN SO LONG.
WELL... ARIANA WON'T TALK TO ME ON THE PHONE, MRS. DZERCHENKO.
AND YOU CAME DOWN HERE TO SEE HER. THAT'S SWEET.
UH... I GUESS. IS ARI HERE?
SHE'S IN THE BACK MAKING BOXES. HAVE A PITA OD SIRA, TIMOTHY.
I DON'T...
MENU
JUST A TASTE. YOU'RE SO SKINNY.
UMPH.
ARI?
WHAT DO YOU WANT? I'M BUSY.
8

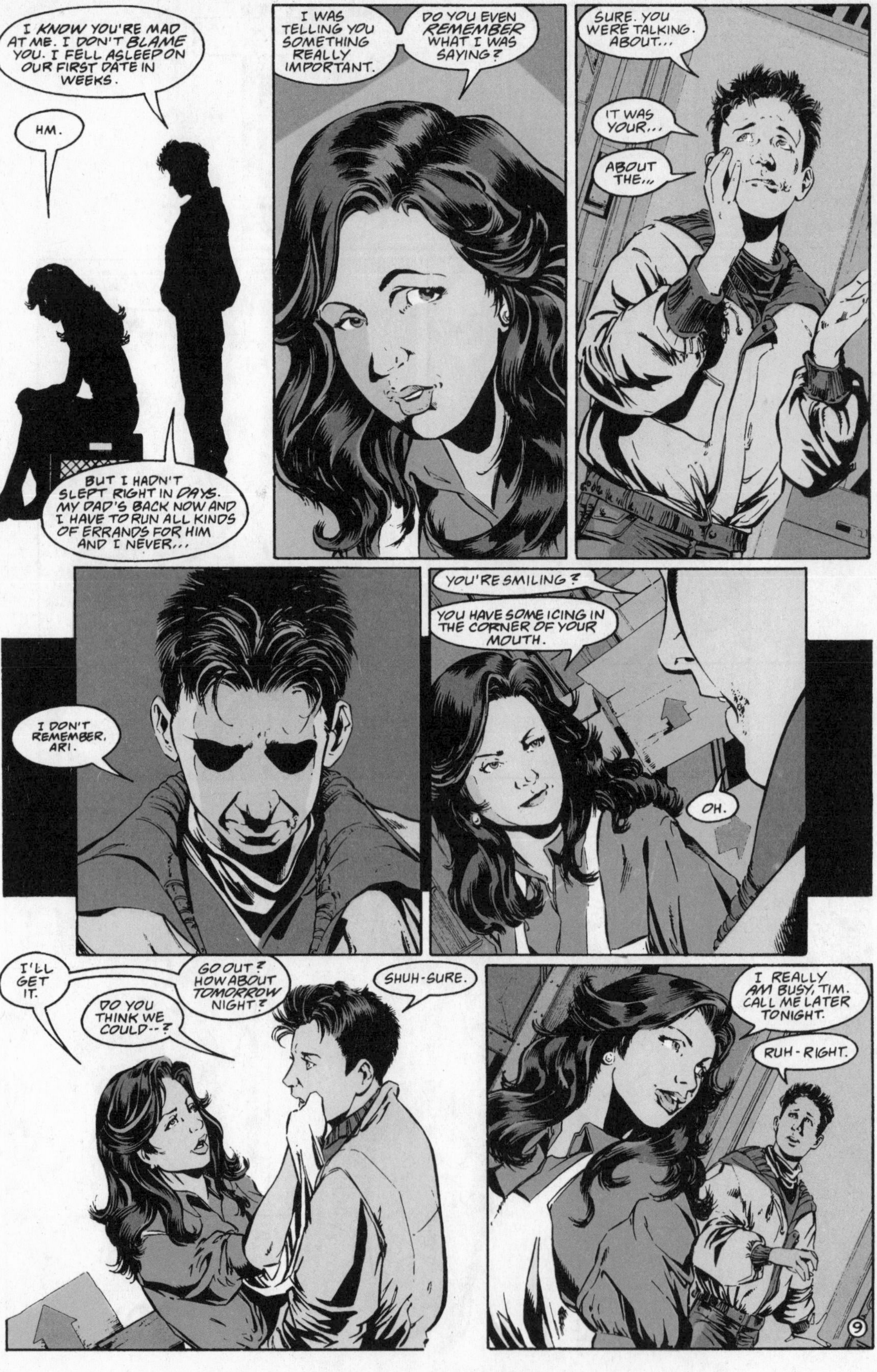
I KNOW YOU'RE MAD AT ME. I DON'T BLAME YOU. I FELL ASLEEP ON OUR FIRST DATE IN WEEKS.
HM.
BUT I HADN'T SLEPT RIGHT IN DAYS. MY DAD'S BACK NOW AND I HAVE TO RUN ALL KINDS OF ERRANDS FOR HIM AND I NEVER...
I WAS TELLING YOU SOMETHING REALLY IMPORTANT.
DO YOU EVEN REMEMBER WHAT I WAS SAYING?
SURE. YOU WERE TALKING. ABOUT...
IT WAS YOUR...
ABOUT THE...
I DON'T REMEMBER, ARI.
YOU'RE SMILING?
YOU HAVE SOME ICING IN THE CORNER OF YOUR MOUTH.
OH.
I'LL GET IT.
DO YOU THINK WE COULD--?
GO OUT? HOW ABOUT TOMORROW NIGHT?
SHUH-SURE.
I REALLY AM BUSY, TIM. CALL ME LATER TONIGHT.
RUH-RIGHT.
9

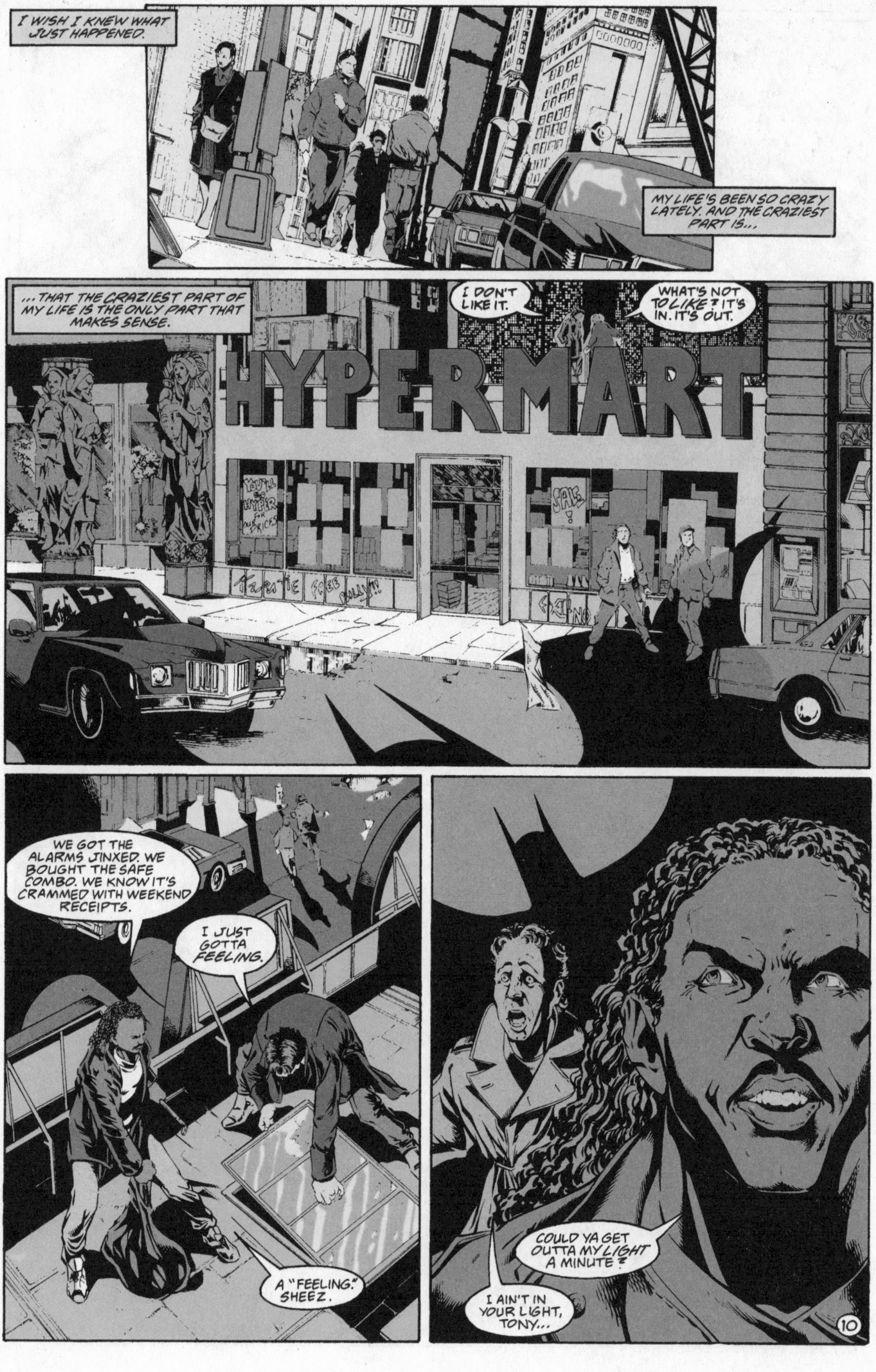
I WISH I KNEW WHAT JUST HAPPENED.
MY LIFE'S BEEN SO CRAZY LATELY. AND THE CRAZIEST PART IS...
...THAT THE CRAZIEST PART OF MY LIFE IS THE ONLY PART THAT MAKES SENSE.
I DON'T LIKE IT.
WHAT'S NOT TO LIKE? IT'S IN. IT'S OUT.
HYPERMART
SALE!
WE GOT THE ALARMS JINXED. WE BOUGHT THE SAFE COMBO. WE KNOW IT'S CRAMMED WITH WEEKEND RECEIPTS.
I JUST GOTTA FEELING.
A "FEELING." SHEEZ.
COULD YA GET OUTTA MY LIGHT A MINUTE?
I AIN'T IN YOUR LIGHT, TONY...
10

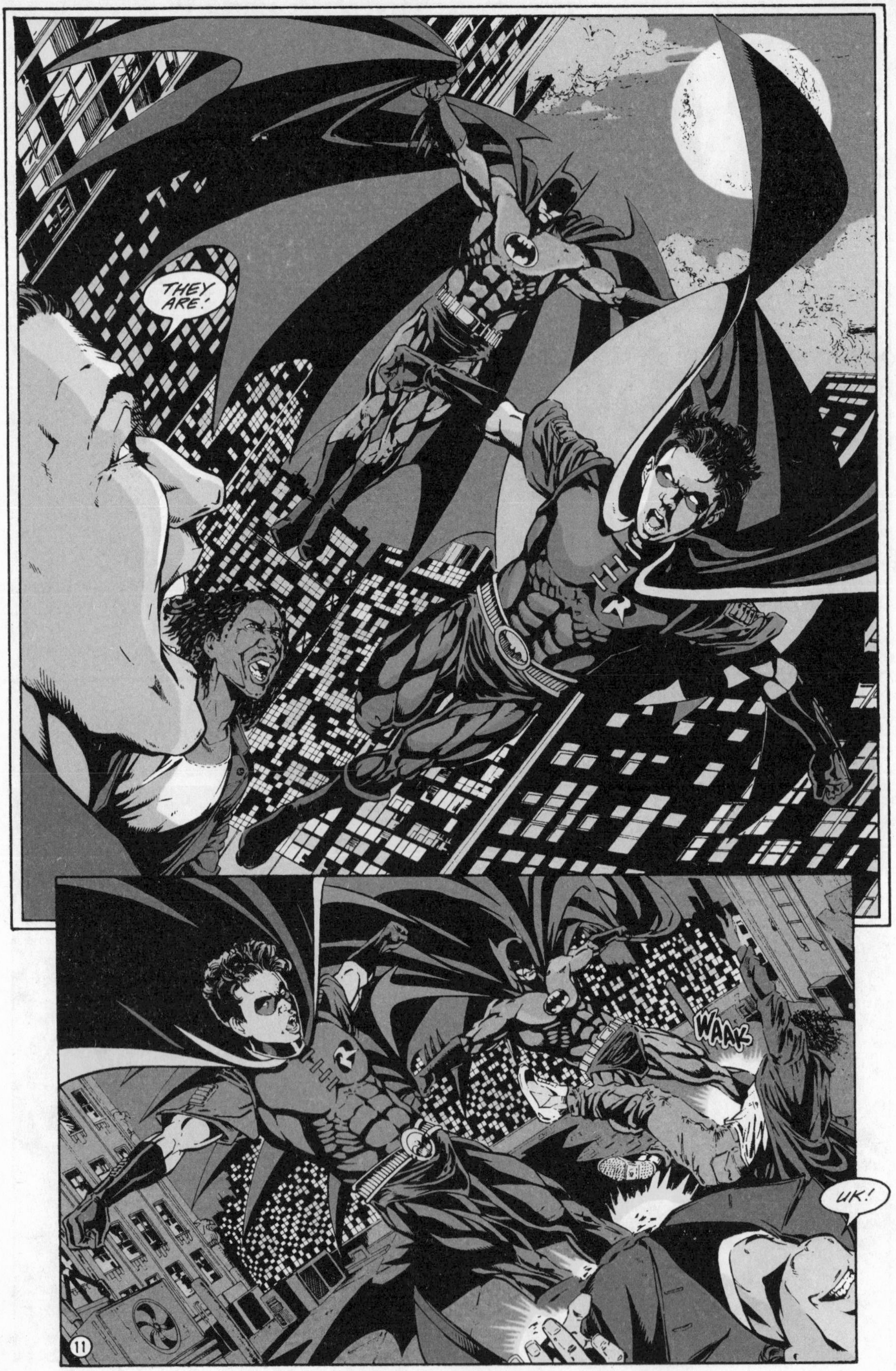
THEY ARE!
WAAK
UK!

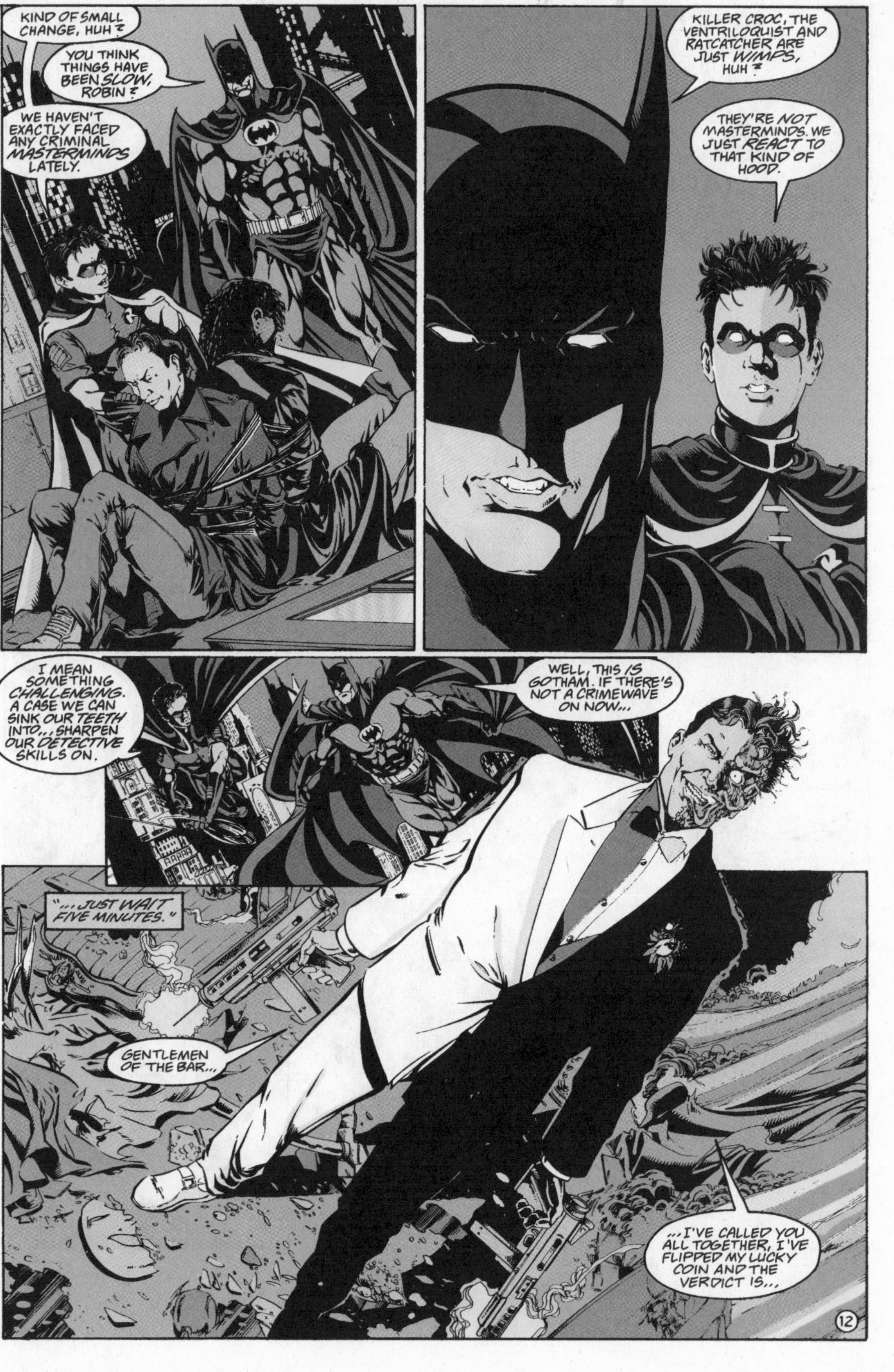
KIND OF SMALL CHANGE, HUH?
YOU THINK THINGS HAVE BEEN SLOW, ROBIN?
WE HAVEN'T EXACTLY FACED ANY CRIMINAL MASTERMINDS LATELY.
KILLER CROC, THE VENTRILOQUIST AND RATCATCHER ARE JUST WIMPS, HUH?
THEY'RE NOT MASTERMINDS. WE JUST REACT TO THAT KIND OF HOOD.
I MEAN SOMETHING CHALLENGING. A CASE WE CAN SINK OUR TEETH INTO... SHARPEN OUR DETECTIVE SKILLS ON.
WELL, THIS IS GOTHAM. IF THERE'S NOT A CRIMEWAVE ON NOW...
"...JUST WAIT FIVE MINUTES."
GENTLEMEN OF THE BAR...
...I'VE CALLED YOU ALL TOGETHER, I'VE FLIPPED MY LUCKY COIN AND THE VERDICT IS...
12

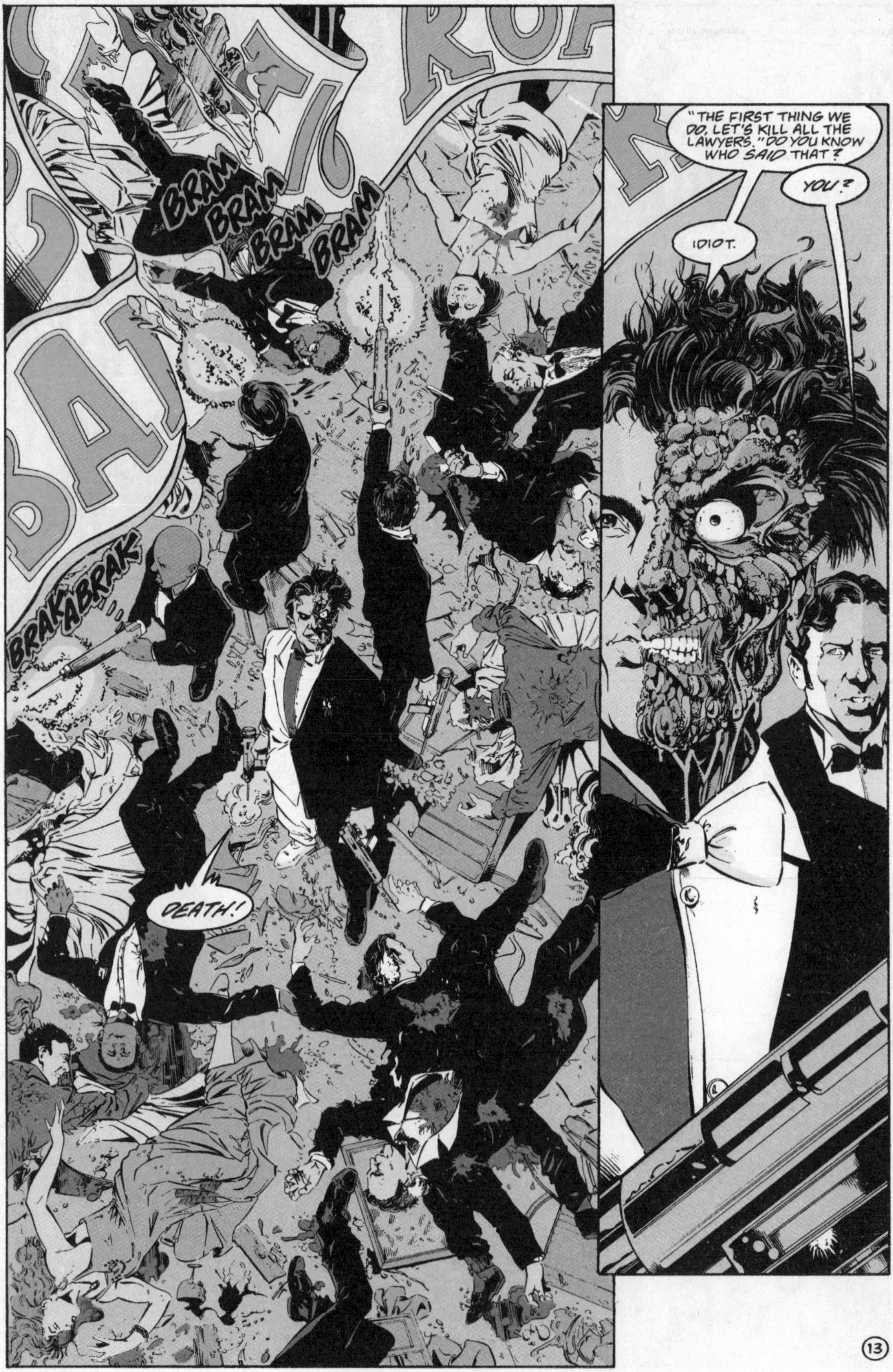
BRAM
BRAM
BRAM
BRAM
BRAKABRAK
DEATH!
"THE FIRST THING WE DO, LET'S KILL ALL THE LAWYERS." DO YOU KNOW WHO SAID THAT?
YOU?
IDIOT.
13

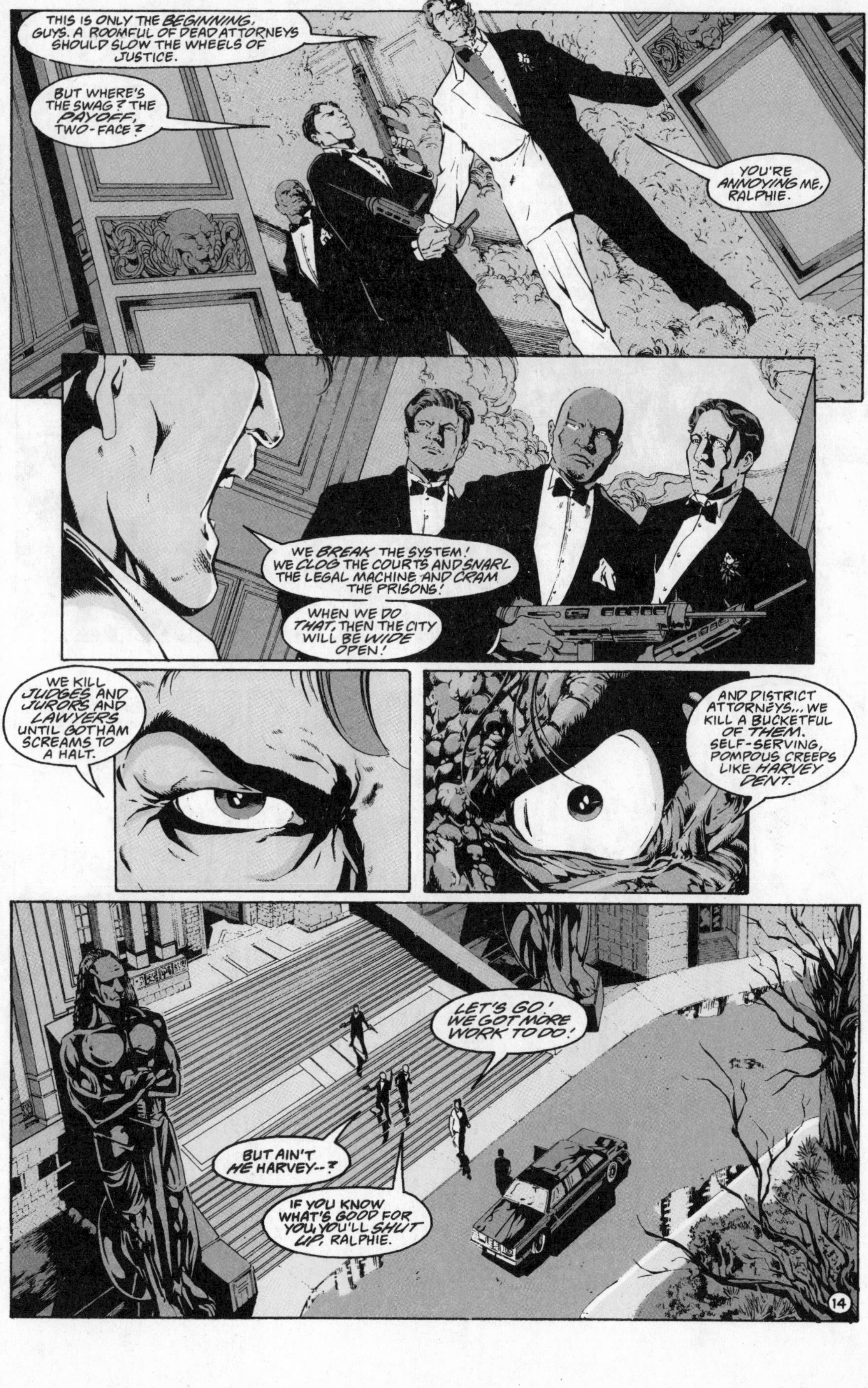
THIS IS ONLY THE BEGINNING, GUYS. A ROOMFUL OF DEAD ATTORNEYS SHOULD SLOW THE WHEELS OF JUSTICE.
BUT WHERE'S THE SWAG? THE PAYOFF, TWO-FACE?
YOU'RE ANNOYING ME, RALPHIE.
WE BREAK THE SYSTEM! WE CLOG THE COURTS AND SNARL THE LEGAL MACHINE AND CRAM THE PRISONS!
WHEN WE DO THAT, THEN THE CITY WILL BE WIDE OPEN!
WE KILL JUDGES AND JURORS AND LAWYERS UNTIL GOTHAM SCREAMS TO A HALT.
AND DISTRICT ATTORNEYS... WE KILL A BUCKETFUL OF THEM. SELF-SERVING, POMPOUS CREEPS LIKE HARVEY DENT.
LET'S GO! WE GOT MORE WORK TO DO!
BUT AIN'T HE HARVEY--?
IF YOU KNOW WHAT'S GOOD FOR YOU, YOU'LL SHUT UP, RALPHIE.
14

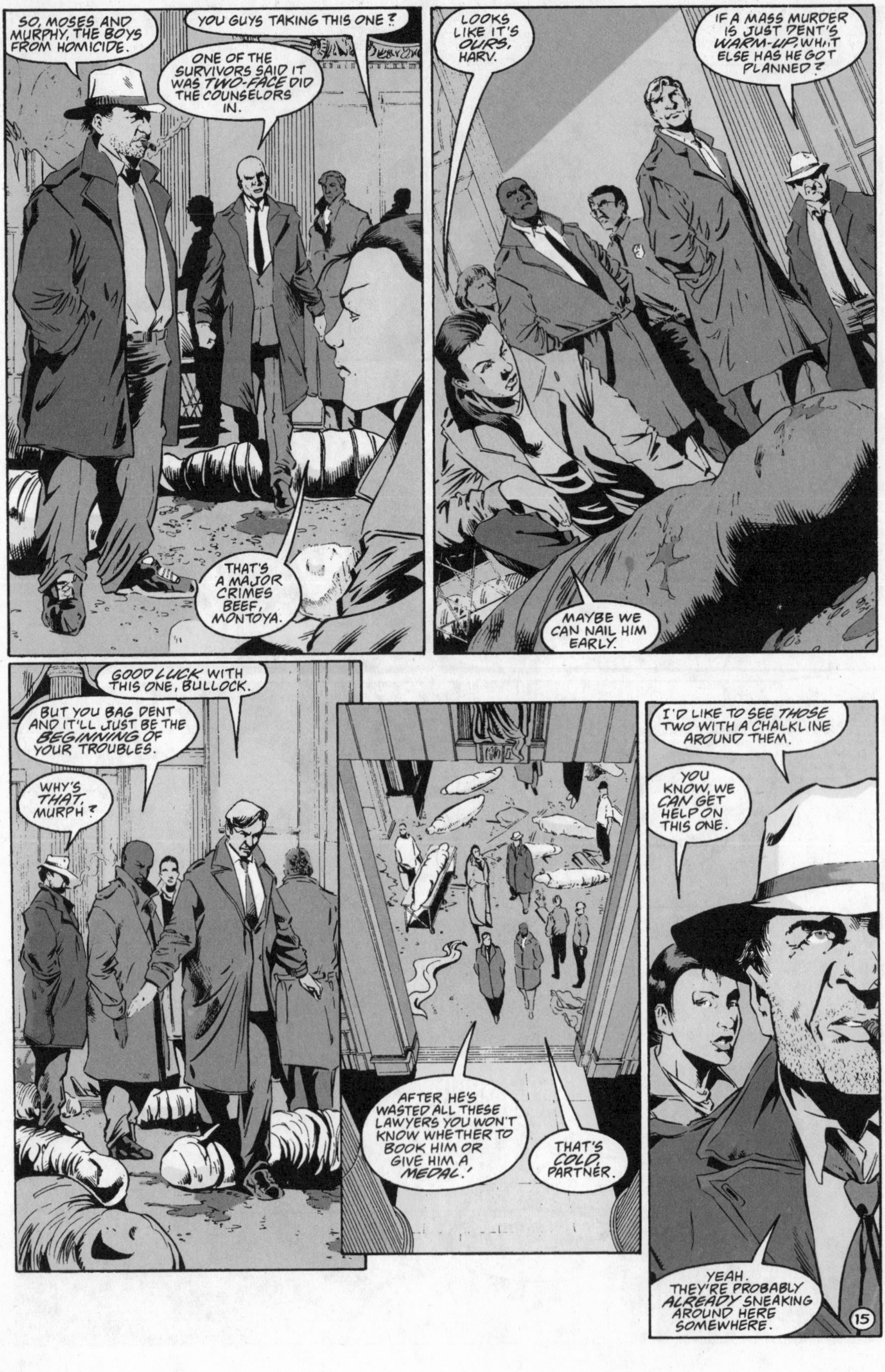
SO, MOSES AND MURPHY, THE BOYS FROM HOMICIDE.
YOU GUYS TAKING THIS ONE?
ONE OF THE SURVIVORS SAID IT WAS TWO-FACE DID THE COUNSELORS IN.
THAT'S A MAJOR CRIMES BEEF, MONTOYA.
LOOKS LIKE IT'S OURS, HARV.
IF A MASS MURDER IS JUST DENT'S WARM-UP, WHAT ELSE HAS HE GOT PLANNED?
MAYBE WE CAN NAIL HIM EARLY.
GOOD LUCK WITH THIS ONE, BULLOCK.
BUT YOU BAG DENT AND IT'LL JUST BE THE BEGINNING OF YOUR TROUBLES.
WHY'S THAT, MURPH?
AFTER HE'S WASTED ALL THESE LAWYERS YOU WON'T KNOW WHETHER TO BOOK HIM OR GIVE HIM A MEDAL.'
THAT'S COLD, PARTNER.
I'D LIKE TO SEE THOSE TWO WITH A CHALKLINE AROUND THEM.
YOU KNOW, WE CAN GET HELP ON THIS ONE.
YEAH. THEY'RE PROBABLY ALREADY SNEAKING AROUND HERE SOMEWHERE.
15

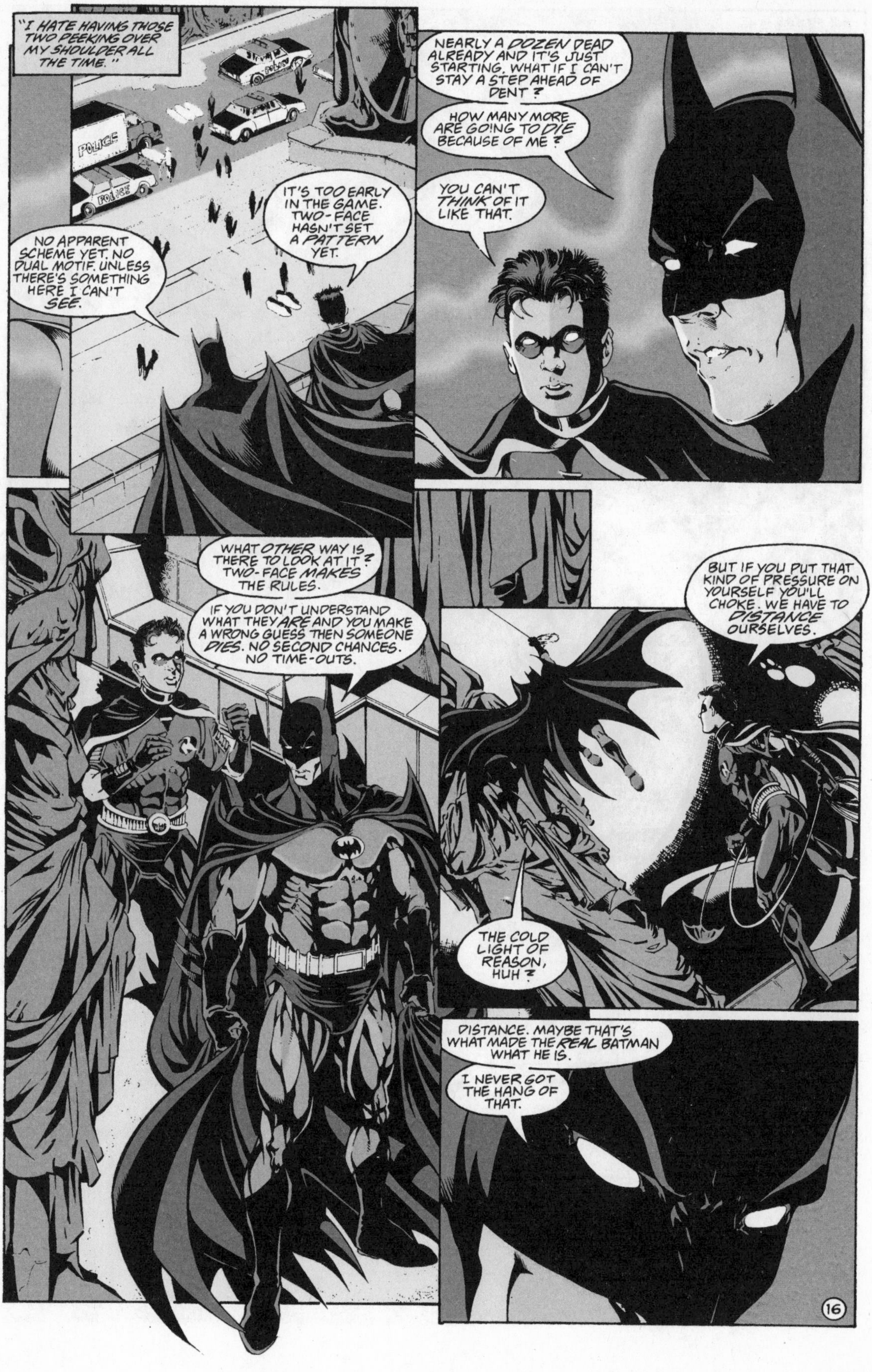
"I HATE HAVING THOSE TWO PEEKING OVER MY SHOULDER ALL THE TIME."
NO APPARENT SCHEME YET. NO DUAL MOTIF. UNLESS THERE'S SOMETHING HERE I CAN'T SEE.
IT'S TOO EARLY IN THE GAME. TWO-FACE HASN'T SET A PATTERN YET.
NEARLY A DOZEN DEAD ALREADY AND IT'S JUST STARTING. WHAT IF I CAN'T STAY A STEP AHEAD OF DENT?
HOW MANY MORE ARE GOING TO DIE BECAUSE OF ME?
YOU CAN'T THINK OF IT LIKE THAT.
WHAT OTHER WAY IS THERE TO LOOK AT IT? TWO-FACE MAKES THE RULES.
IF YOU DON'T UNDERSTAND WHAT THEY ARE AND YOU MAKE A WRONG GUESS THEN SOMEONE DIES. NO SECOND CHANCES. NO TIME-OUTS.
BUT IF YOU PUT THAT KIND OF PRESSURE ON YOURSELF YOU'LL CHOKE. WE HAVE TO DISTANCE OURSELVES.
THE COLD LIGHT OF REASON, HUH?
DISTANCE. MAYBE THAT'S WHAT MADE THE REAL BATMAN WHAT HE IS.
I NEVER GOT THE HANG OF THAT.
16

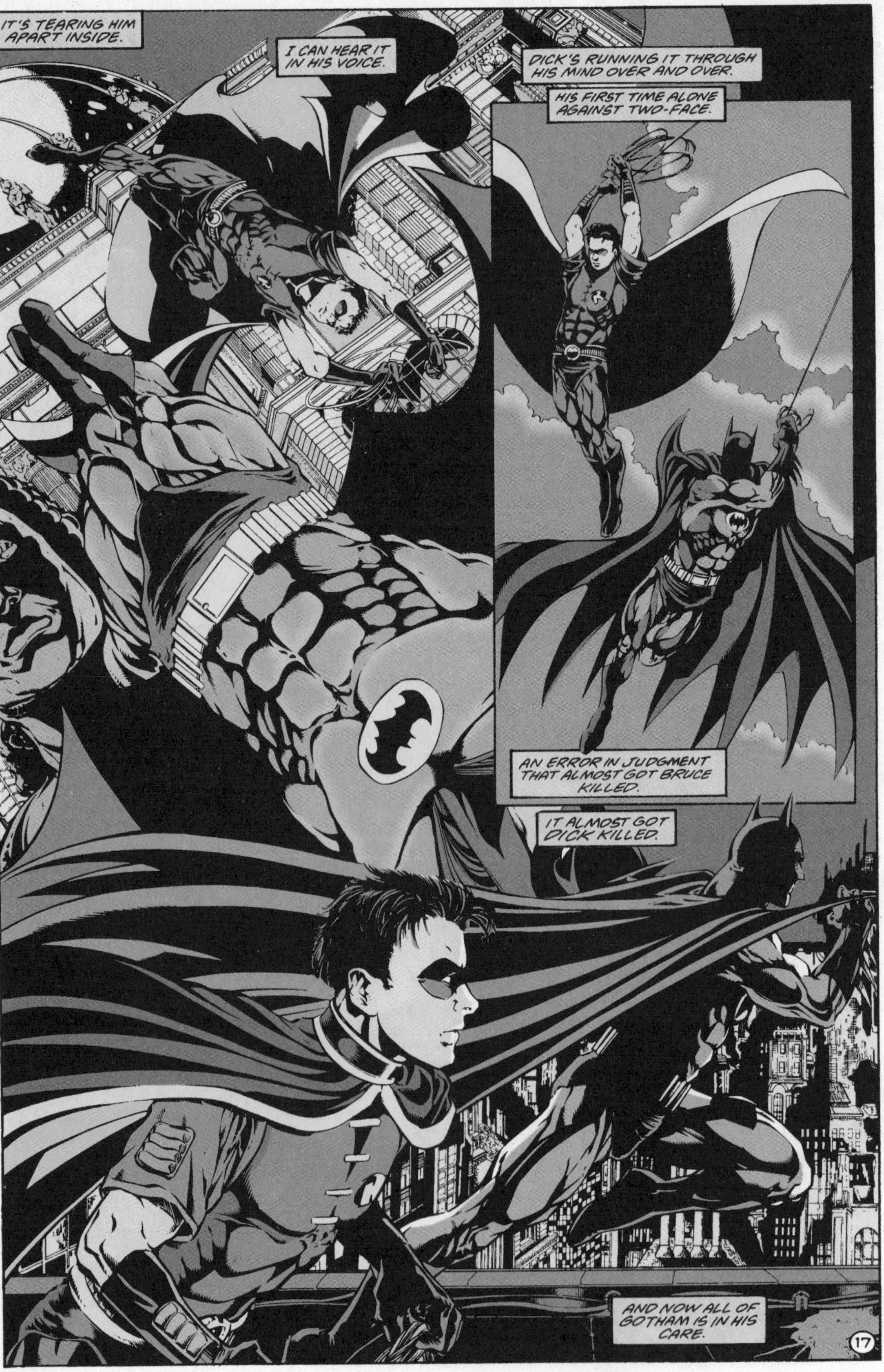
IT'S TEARING HIM APART INSIDE.
I CAN HEAR IT IN HIS VOICE.
DICK'S RUNNING IT THROUGH HIS MIND OVER AND OVER.
HIS FIRST TIME ALONE AGAINST TWO-FACE.
AN ERROR IN JUDGMENT THAT ALMOST GOT BRUCE KILLED.
IT ALMOST GOT DICK KILLED.
AND NOW ALL OF GOTHAM IS IN HIS CARE.
17

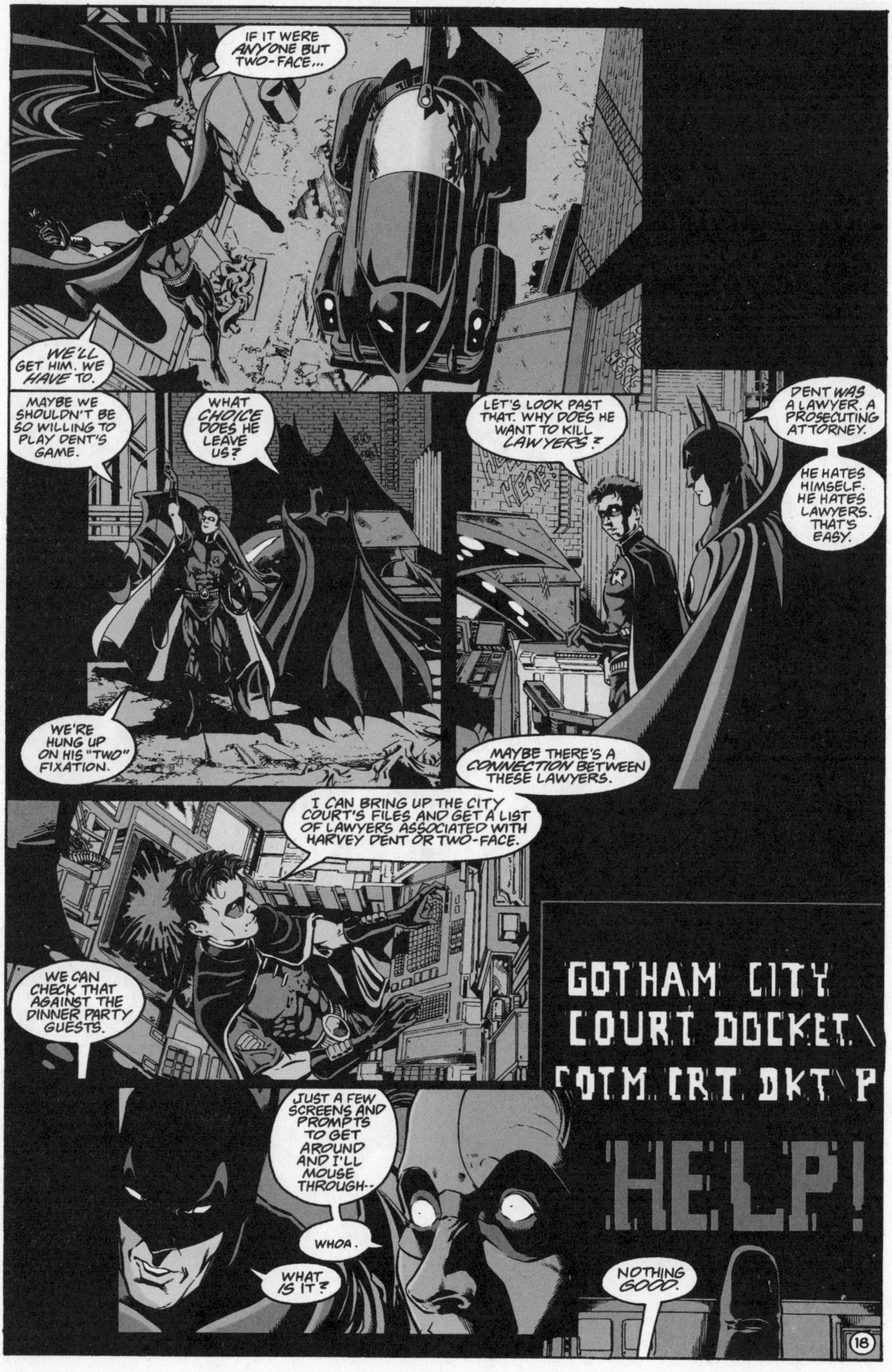

IF IT WERE ANYONE BUT TWO-FACE...
WE'LL GET HIM. WE HAVE TO.
MAYBE WE SHOULDN'T BE SO WILLING TO PLAY DENT'S GAME.
WHAT CHOICE DOES HE LEAVE US?
WE'RE HUNG UP ON HIS "TWO" FIXATION.
LET'S LOOK PAST THAT. WHY DOES HE WANT TO KILL LAWYERS?
DENT WAS A LAWYER. A PROSECUTING ATTORNEY.
HE HATES HIMSELF. HE HATES LAWYERS. THAT'S EASY.
MAYBE THERE'S A CONNECTION BETWEEN THESE LAWYERS.
I CAN BRING UP THE CITY COURT'S FILES AND GET A LIST OF LAWYERS ASSOCIATED WITH HARVEY DENT OR TWO-FACE.
WE CAN CHECK THAT AGAINST THE DINNER PARTY GUESTS.
GOTHAM CITY COURT DOCKET
JUST A FEW SCREENS AND PROMPTS TO GET AROUND AND I'LL MOUSE THROUGH--
WHOA.
WHAT IS IT?
HELP!
NOTHING GOOD.
18

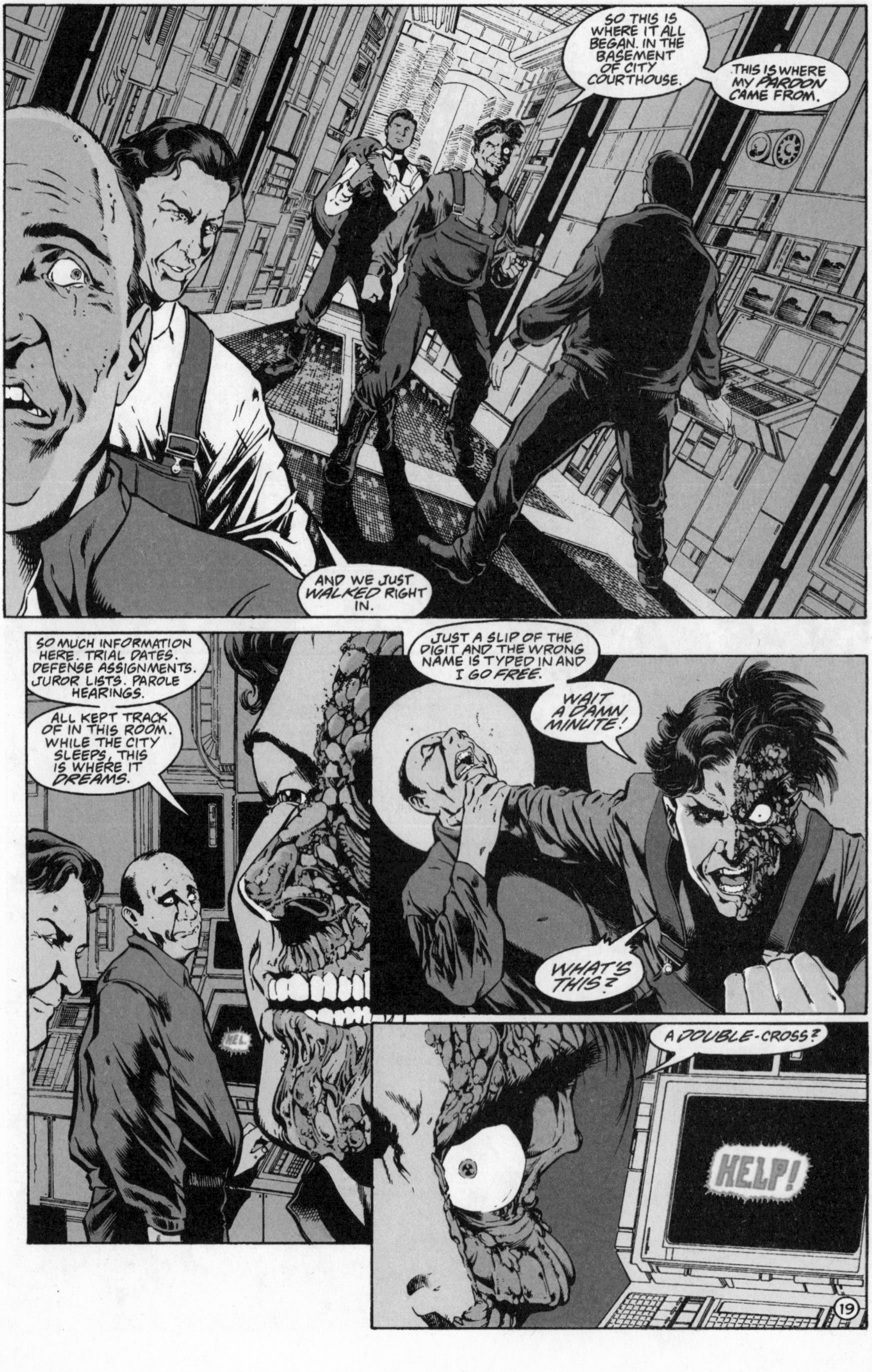
SO THIS IS WHERE IT ALL BEGAN. IN THE BASEMENT OF CITY COURTHOUSE.
THIS IS WHERE MY PARDON CAME FROM.
AND WE JUST WALKED RIGHT IN.
SO MUCH INFORMATION HERE. TRIAL DATES. DEFENSE ASSIGNMENTS. JUROR LISTS. PAROLE HEARINGS.
ALL KEPT TRACK OF IN THIS ROOM. WHILE THE CITY SLEEPS, THIS IS WHERE IT DREAMS.
JUST A SLIP OF THE DIGIT AND THE WRONG NAME IS TYPED IN AND I GO FREE.
WAIT A DAMN MINUTE!
WHAT'S THIS?
A DOUBLE-CROSS?
HELP!
19

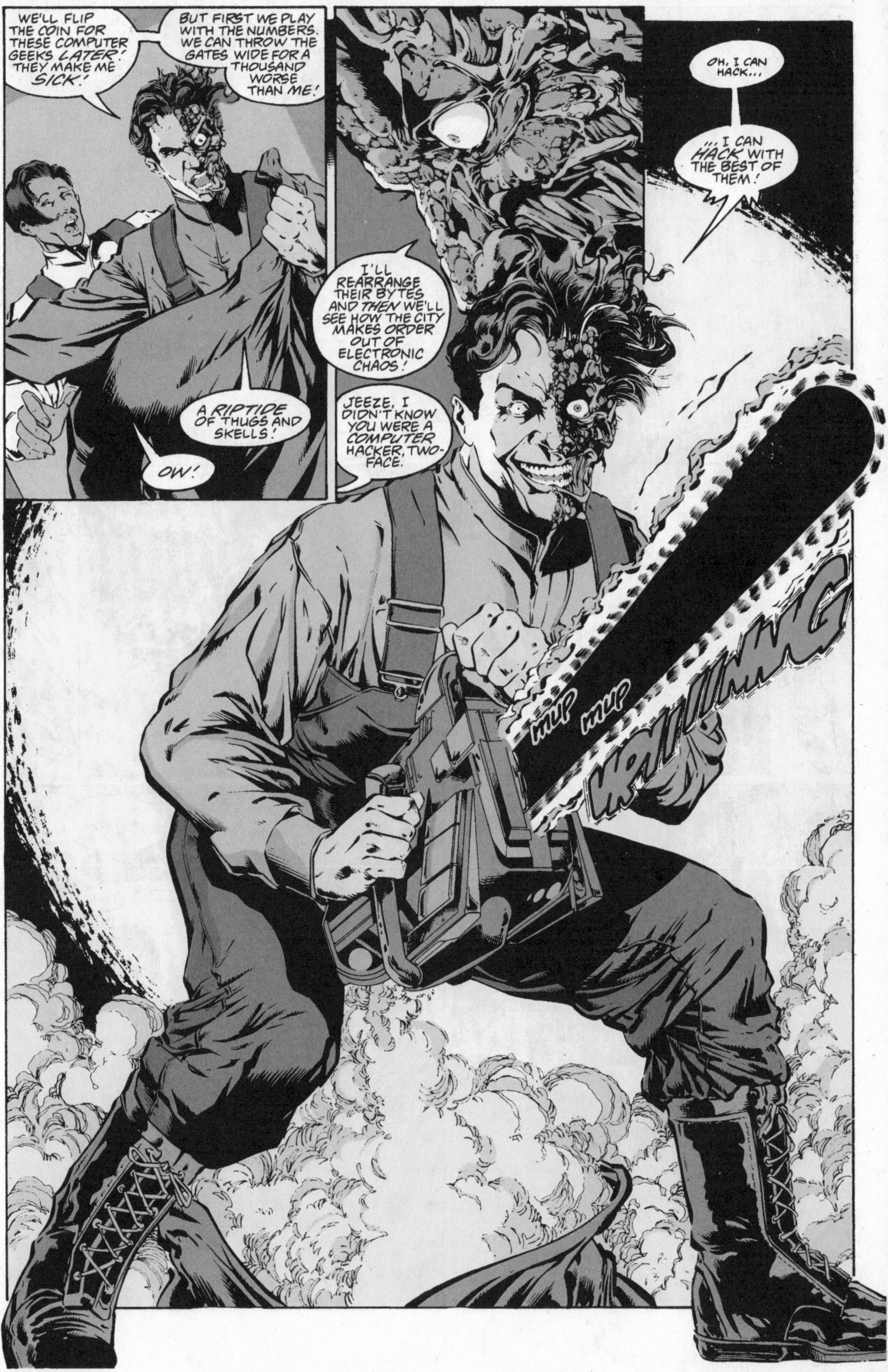
WE'LL FLIP THE COIN FOR THESE COMPUTER GEEKS LATER! THEY MAKE ME SICK!
BUT FIRST WE PLAY WITH THE NUMBERS. WE CAN THROW THE GATES WIDE FOR A THOUSAND WORSE THAN ME!
A RIPTIDE OF THUGS AND SKELLS!
OW!
I'LL REARRANGE THEIR BYTES AND THEN WE'LL SEE HOW THE CITY MAKES ORDER OUT OF ELECTRONIC CHAOS!
JEEZE, I DIDN'T KNOW YOU WERE A COMPUTER HACKER, TWO-FACE.
OH, I CAN HACK...
...I CAN HACK WITH THE BEST OF THEM!
mup mup

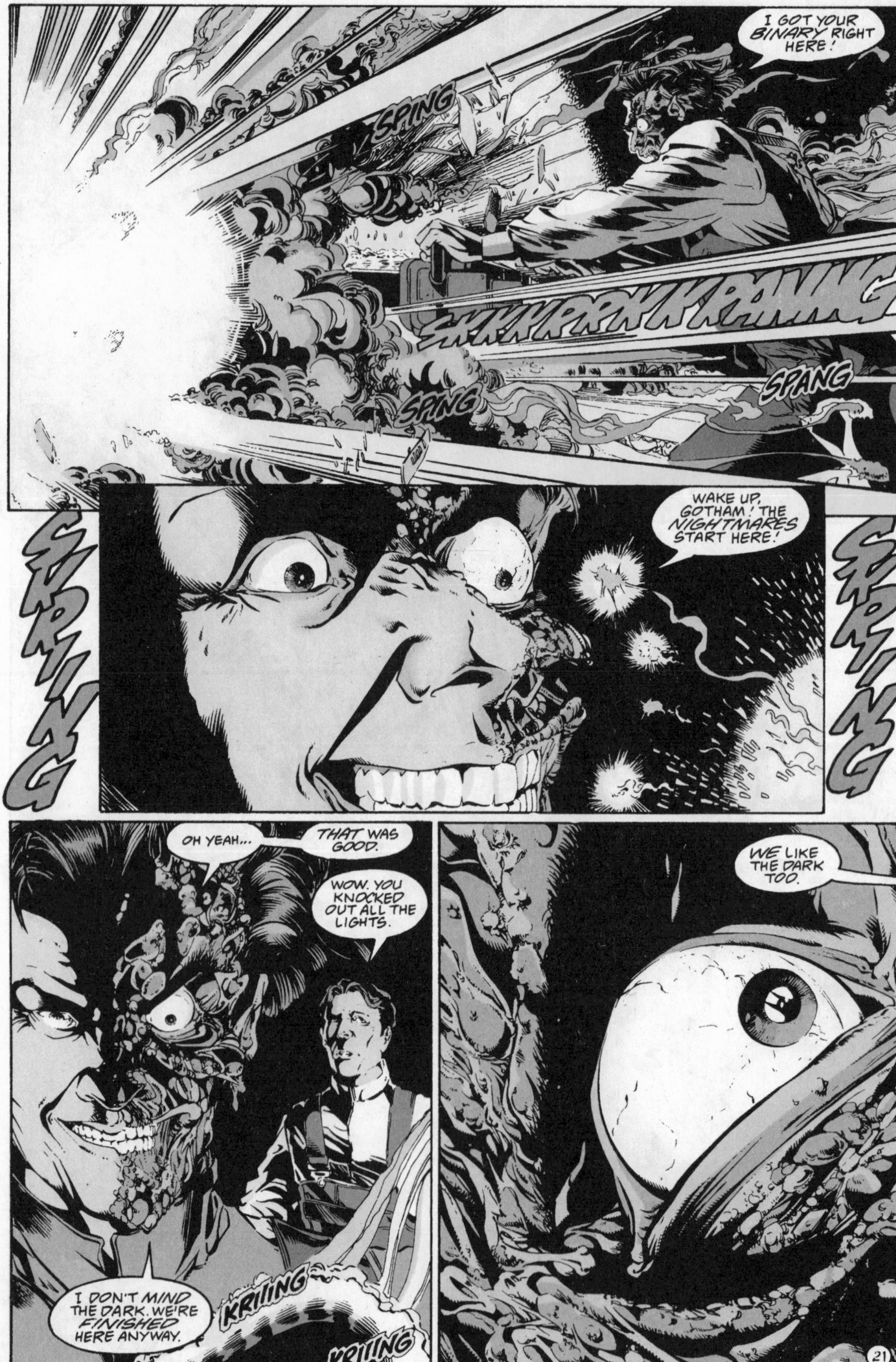
I GOT YOUR BINARY RIGHT HERE!
SPING
SPING
SPANG
SPRIING
WAKE UP, GOTHAM! THE NIGHTMARES START HERE!
SPRIING
OH YEAH...
THAT WAS GOOD.
WOW. YOU KNOCKED OUT ALL THE LIGHTS.
I DON'T MIND THE DARK. WE'RE FINISHED HERE ANYWAY.
KRIIING
KRIIING
WE LIKE THE DARK TOO.
21

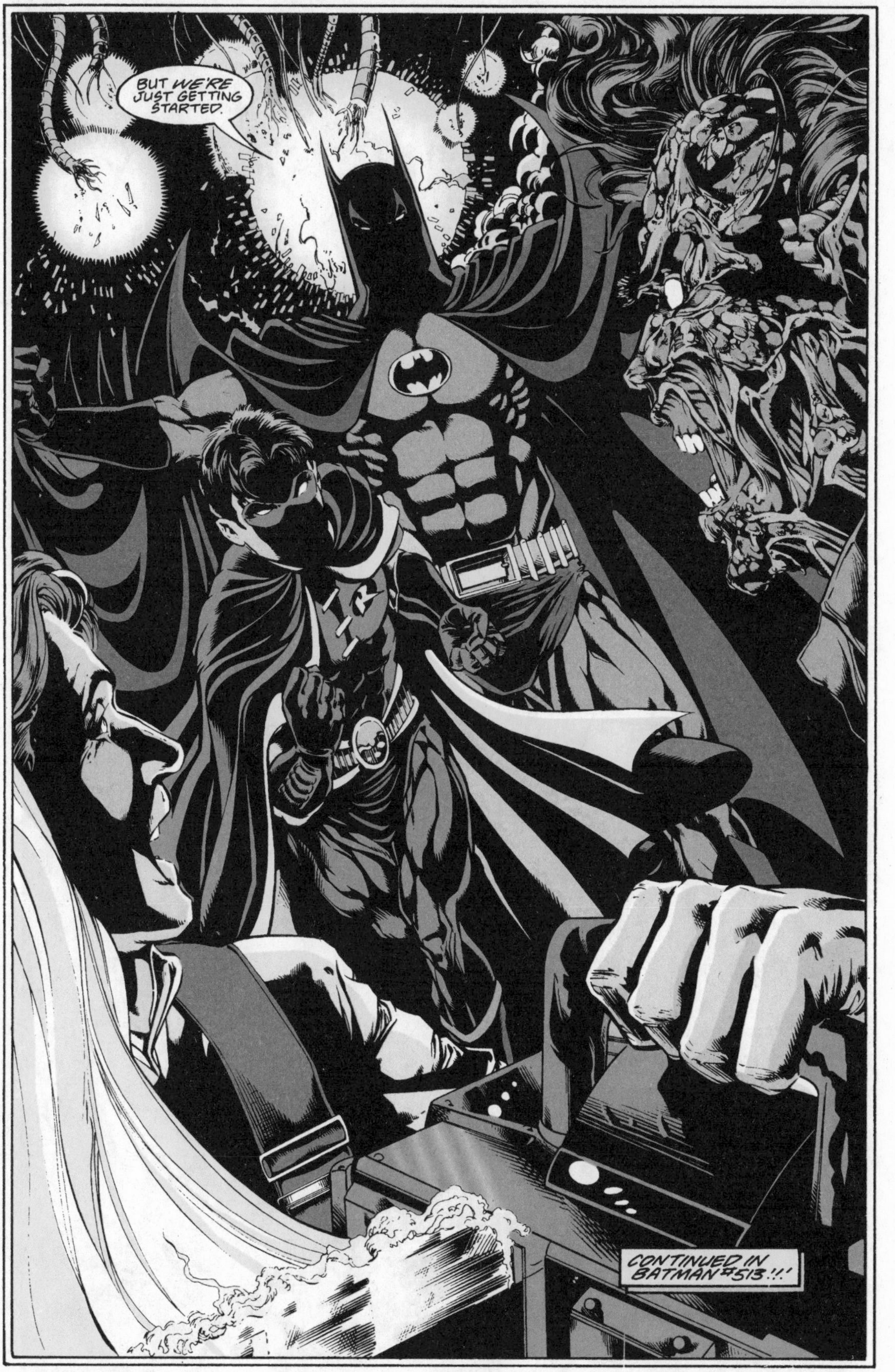
BUT WE'RE JUST GETTING STARTED.
CONTINUED IN BATMAN #513!!!

Cover art by **MIKE MANLEY**

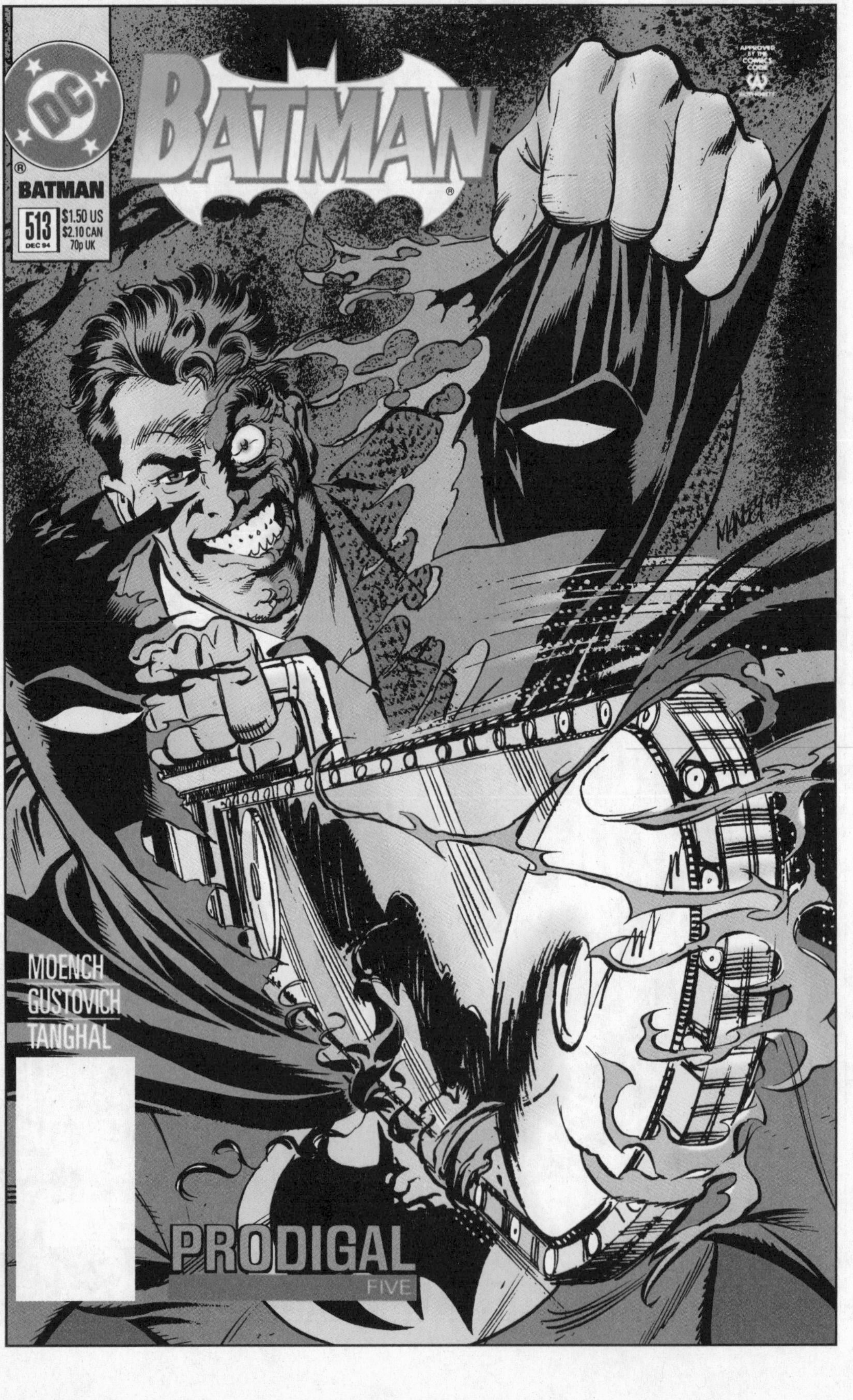
BATMAN
BATMAN
513
DEC 94
$1.50 US
$2.10 CAN
70p UK
MOENCH
GUSTOVICH
TANGHAL
PRODIGAL
FIVE

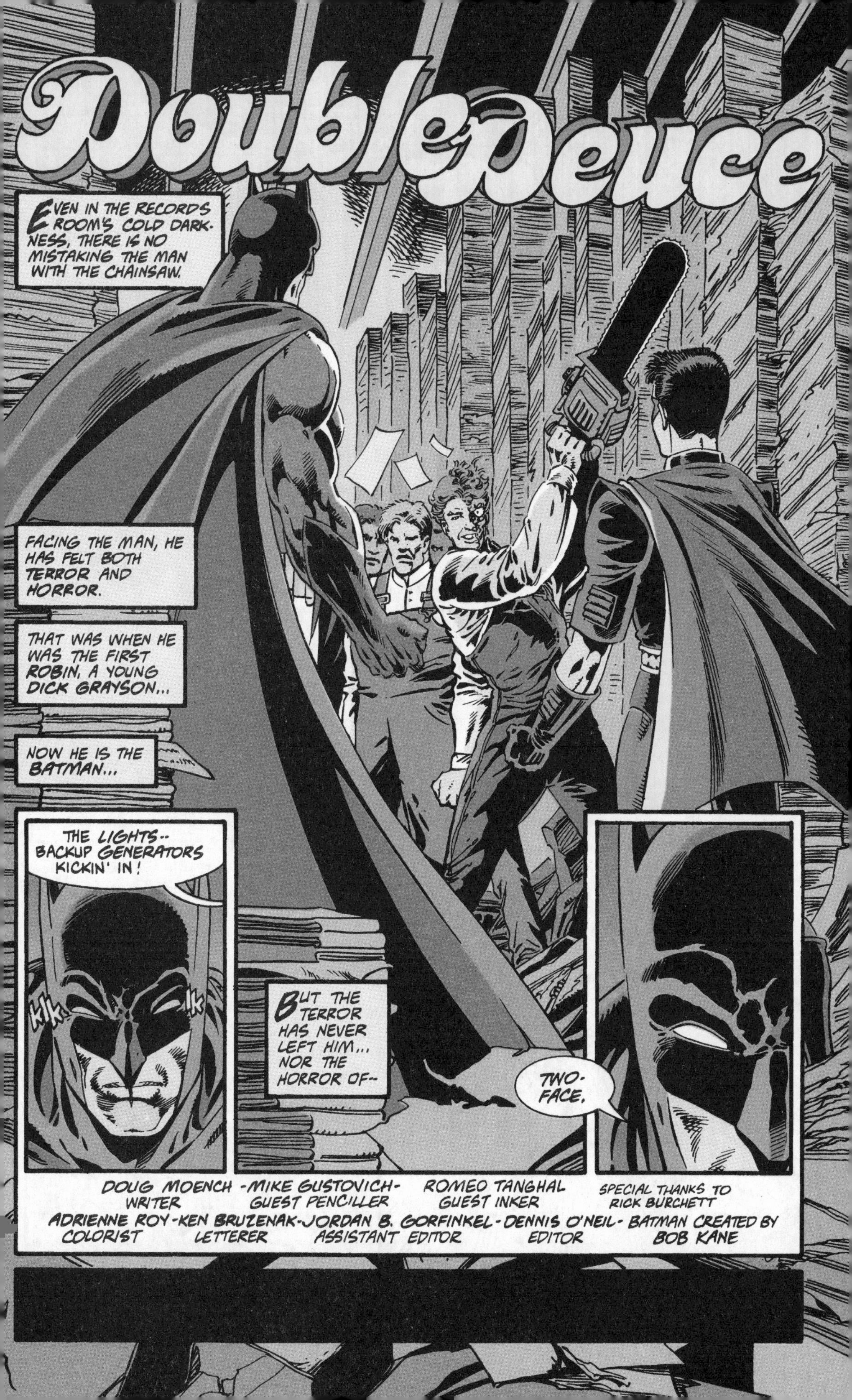
Double Deuce
EVEN IN THE RECORDS ROOM'S COLD DARKNESS, THERE IS NO MISTAKING THE MAN WITH THE CHAINSAW.
FACING THE MAN, HE HAS FELT BOTH TERROR AND HORROR.
THAT WAS WHEN HE WAS THE FIRST ROBIN, A YOUNG DICK GRAYSON...
NOW HE IS THE BATMAN...
THE LIGHTS-- BACKUP GENERATORS KICKIN' IN!
KLIK
KLIK
BUT THE TERROR HAS NEVER LEFT HIM... NOR THE HORROR OF--
TWO-FACE.
DOUG MOENCH WRITER - MIKE GUSTOVICH GUEST PENCILLER - ROMEO TANGHAL GUEST INKER
SPECIAL THANKS TO RICK BURCHETT
ADRIENNE ROY COLORIST - KEN BRUZENAK LETTERER - JORDAN B. GORFINKEL ASSISTANT EDITOR - DENNIS O'NEIL EDITOR - BATMAN CREATED BY BOB KANE

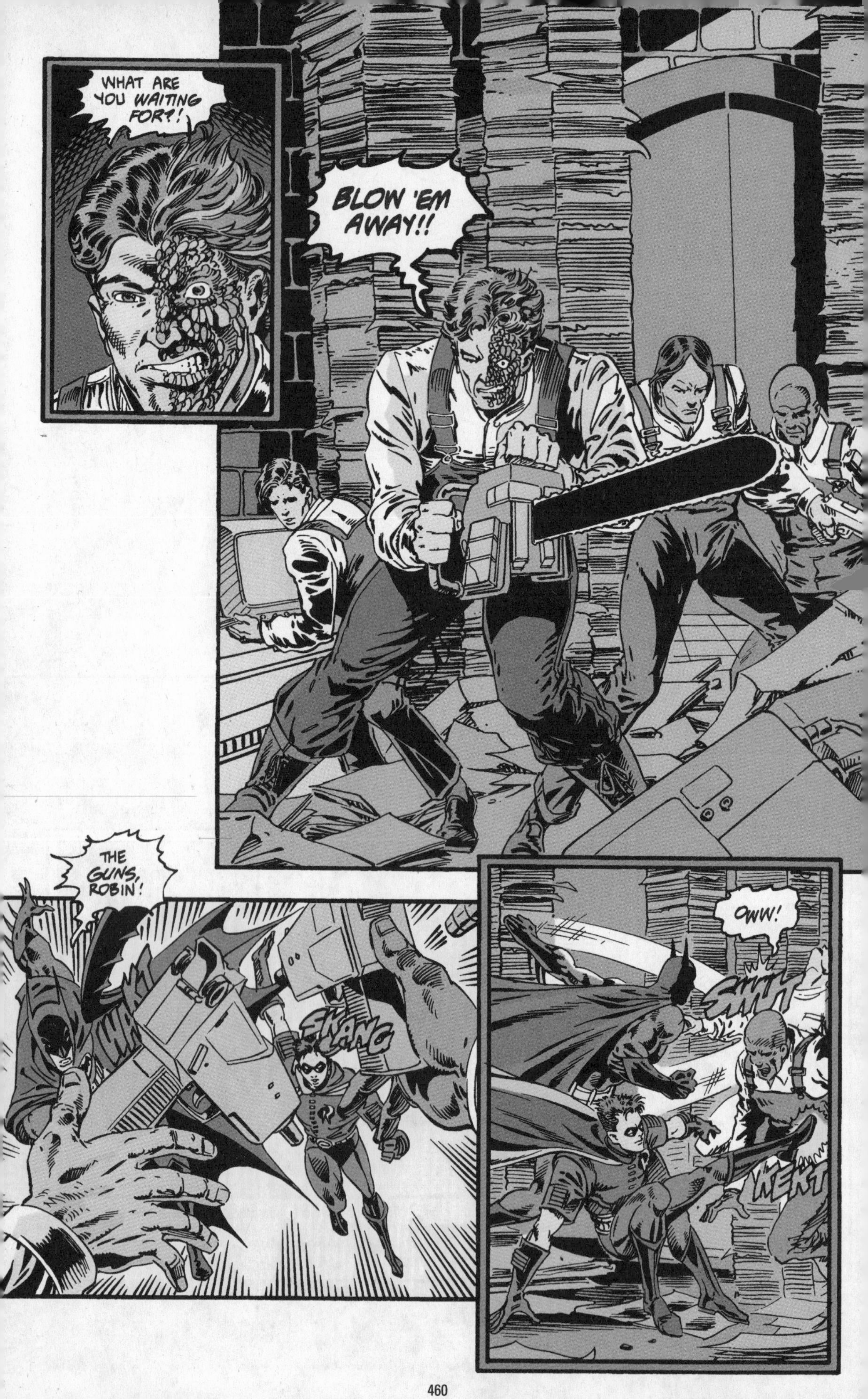
WHAT ARE YOU WAITING FOR?!
BLOW 'EM AWAY!!
THE GUNS, ROBIN!
SKANG
OWW!
SMITH
KENT

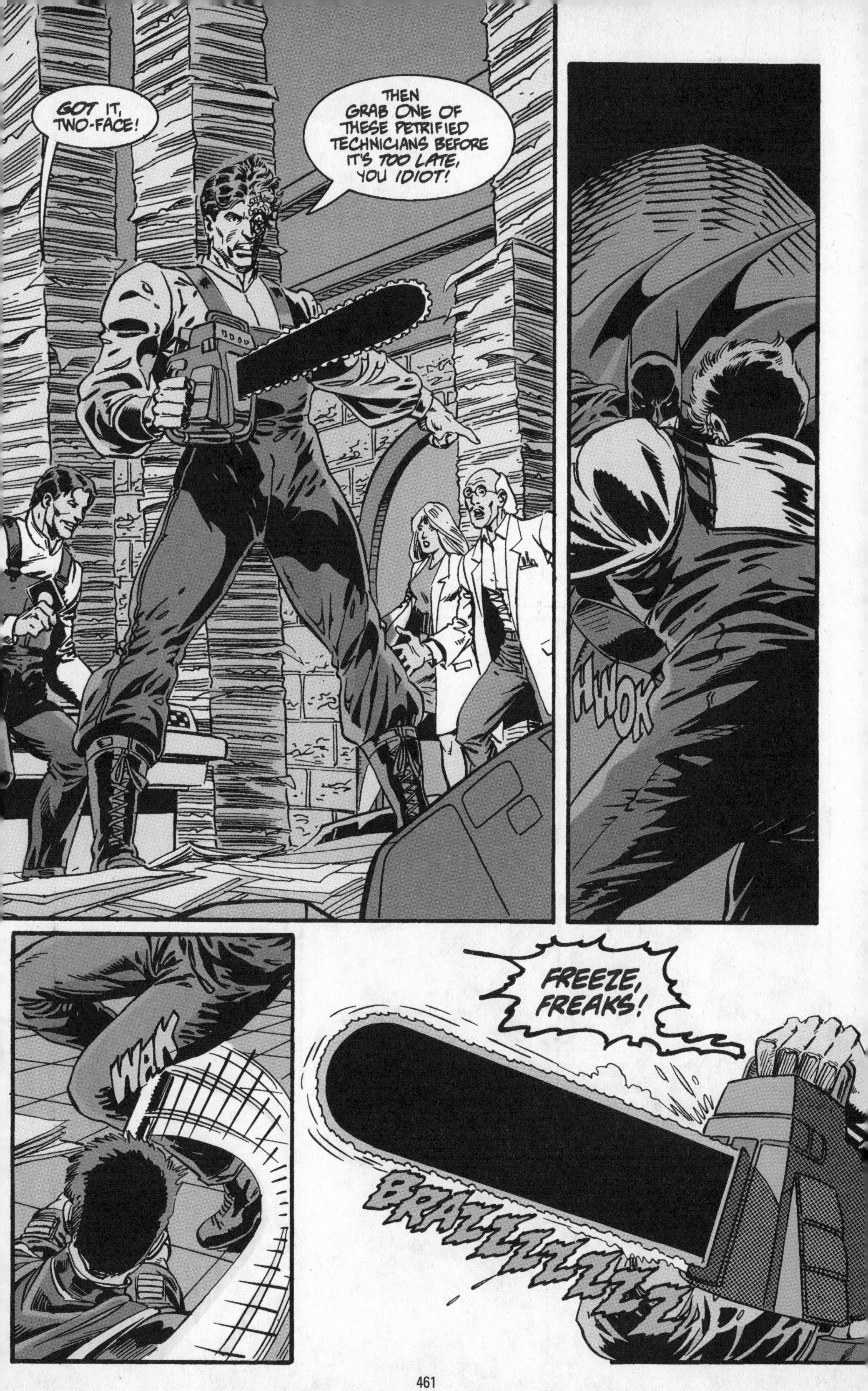
GOT IT, TWO-FACE!
THEN GRAB ONE OF THESE PETRIFIED TECHNICIANS BEFORE IT'S TOO LATE, YOU IDIOT!
HWOK
WAK
FREEZE, FREAKS!
BRAZZZZZZZZZZZZ

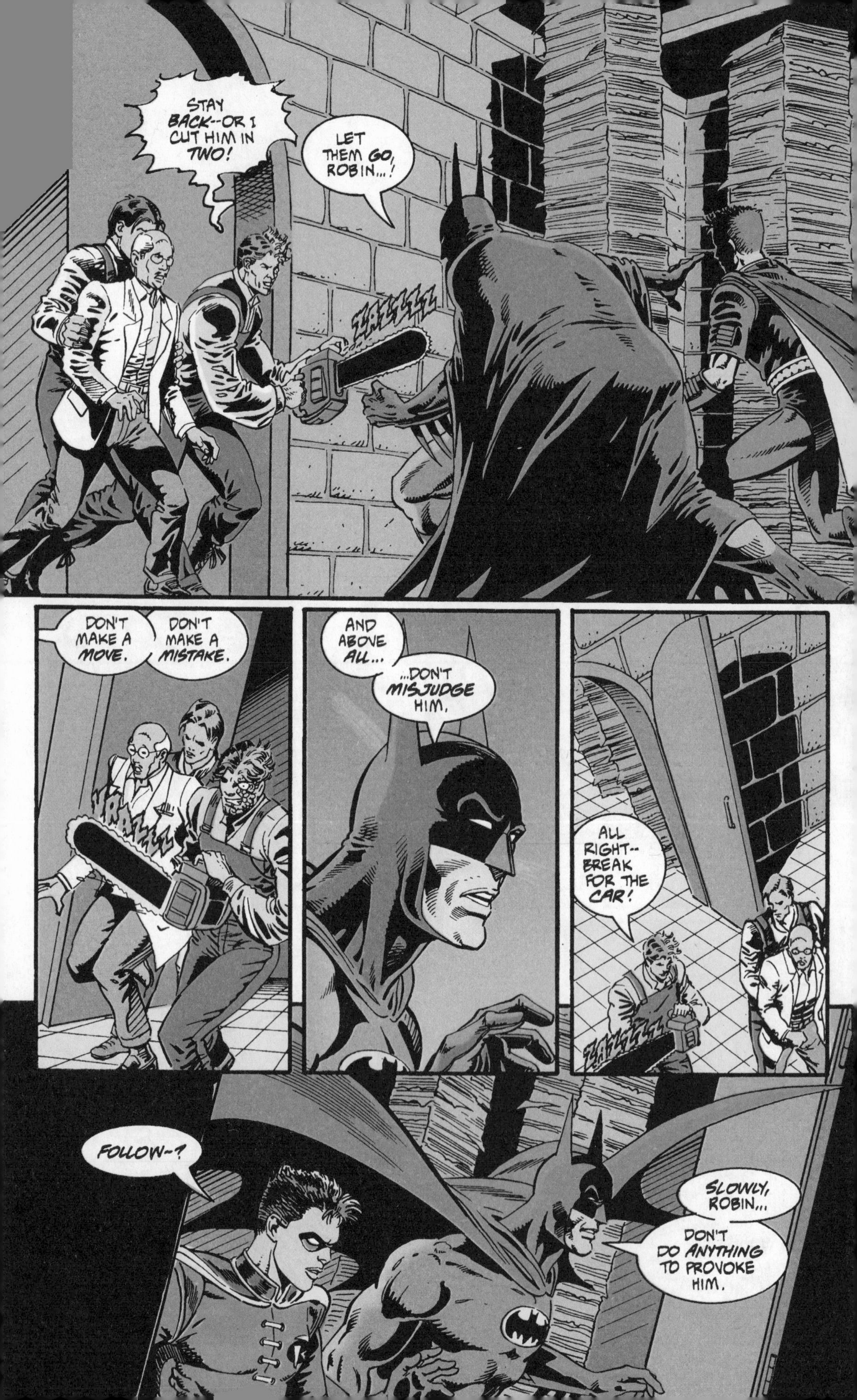
STAY BACK--OR I CUT HIM IN TWO!
LET THEM GO, ROBIN...!
DON'T MAKE A MOVE.
DON'T MAKE A MISTAKE.
AND ABOVE ALL...
...DON'T MISJUDGE HIM.
ALL RIGHT-- BREAK FOR THE CAR!
FOLLOW--?
SLOWLY, ROBIN...
DON'T DO ANYTHING TO PROVOKE HIM.

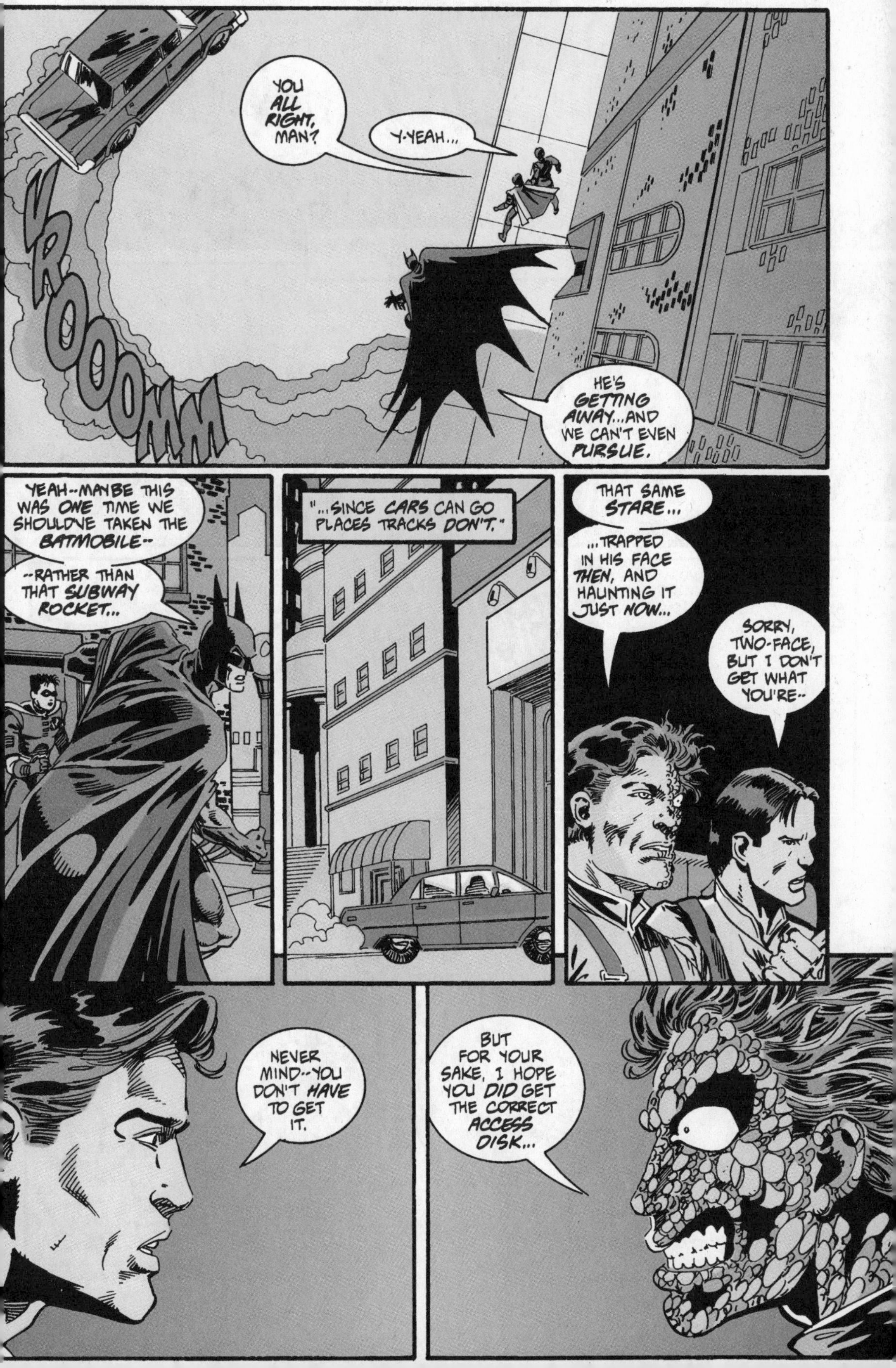
YOU ALL RIGHT, MAN?
Y-YEAH...
VROOOOMM
HE'S GETTING AWAY...AND WE CAN'T EVEN PURSUE.
YEAH--MAYBE THIS WAS ONE TIME WE SHOULD'VE TAKEN THE BATMOBILE--
--RATHER THAN THAT SUBWAY ROCKET...
"...SINCE CARS CAN GO PLACES TRACKS DON'T."
THAT SAME STARE...
...TRAPPED IN HIS FACE THEN, AND HAUNTING IT JUST NOW...
SORRY, TWO-FACE, BUT I DON'T GET WHAT YOU'RE--
NEVER MIND--YOU DON'T HAVE TO GET IT.
BUT FOR YOUR SAKE, I HOPE YOU DID GET THE CORRECT ACCESS DISK...

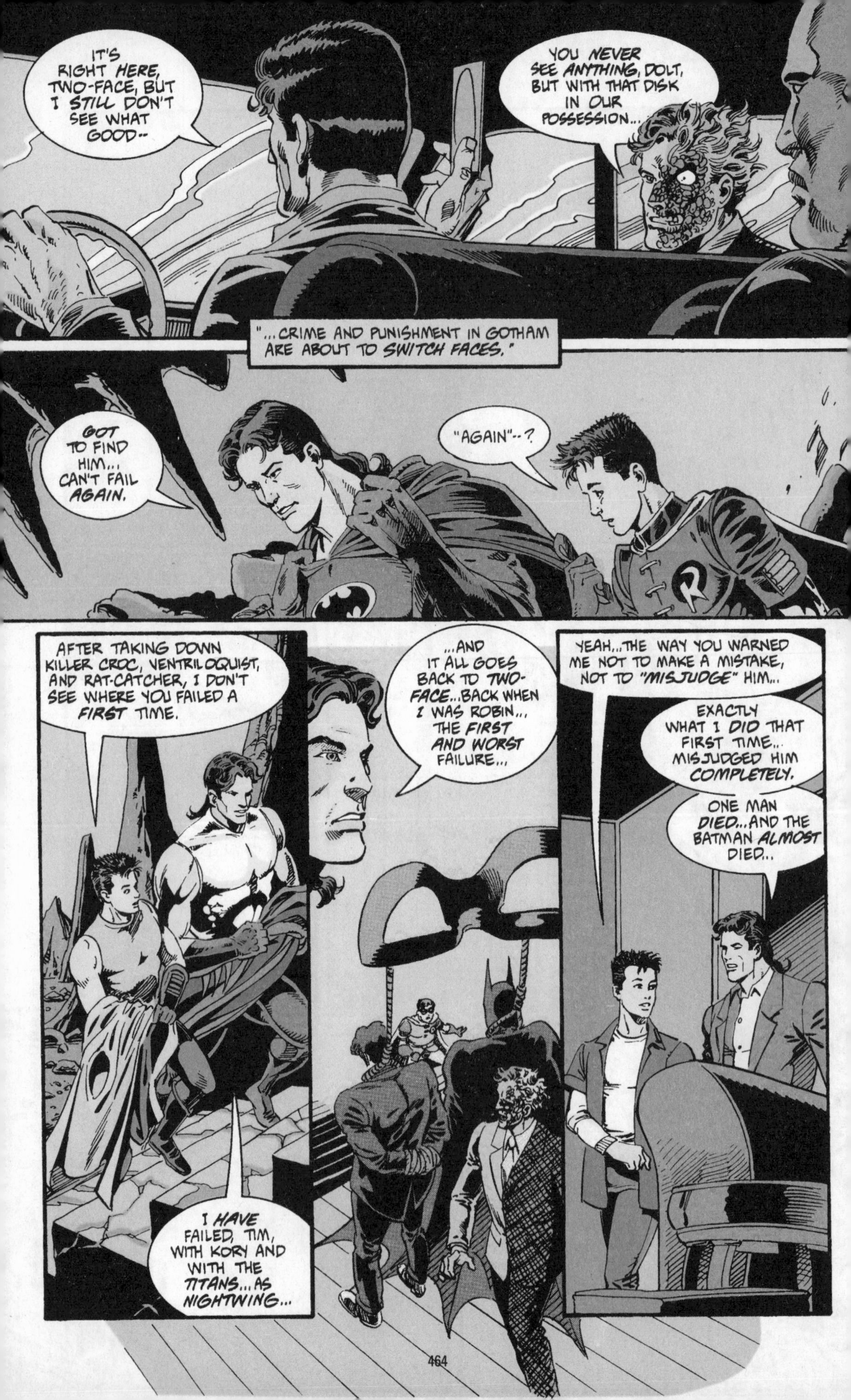

IT'S RIGHT HERE, TWO-FACE, BUT I STILL DON'T SEE WHAT GOOD--
YOU NEVER SEE ANYTHING, DOLT, BUT WITH THAT DISK IN OUR POSSESSION...
"...CRIME AND PUNISHMENT IN GOTHAM ARE ABOUT TO SWITCH FACES."
GOT TO FIND HIM... CAN'T FAIL AGAIN.
"AGAIN"--?
AFTER TAKING DOWN KILLER CROC, VENTRILOQUIST, AND RAT-CATCHER, I DON'T SEE WHERE YOU FAILED A FIRST TIME.
I HAVE FAILED, TIM, WITH KORY AND WITH THE TITANS...AS NIGHTWING...
...AND IT ALL GOES BACK TO TWO-FACE...BACK WHEN I WAS ROBIN... THE FIRST AND WORST FAILURE...
YEAH... THE WAY YOU WARNED ME NOT TO MAKE A MISTAKE, NOT TO "MISJUDGE" HIM...
EXACTLY WHAT I DID THAT FIRST TIME... MISJUDGED HIM COMPLETELY.
ONE MAN DIED...AND THE BATMAN ALMOST DIED...

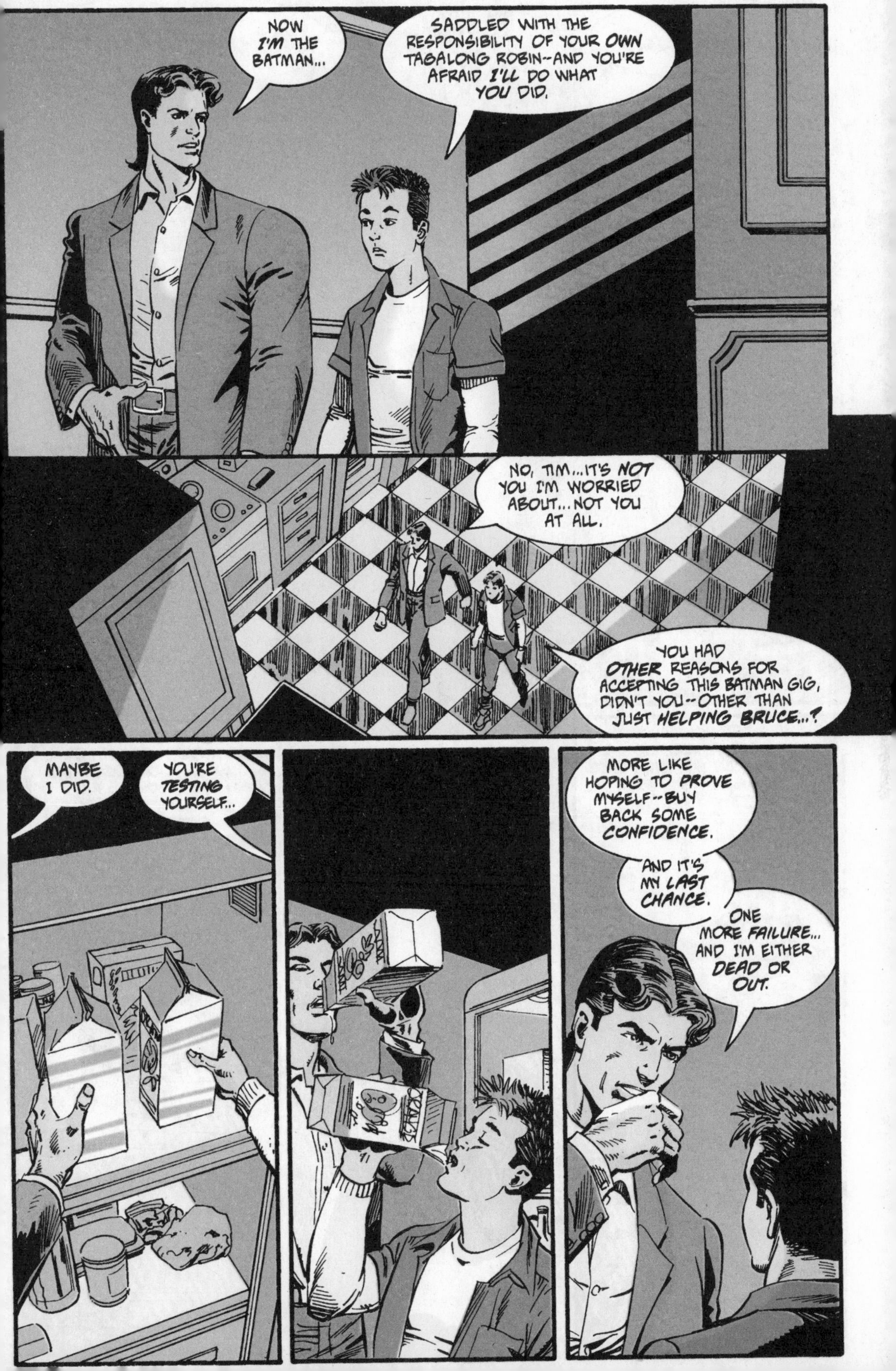
NOW I'M THE BATMAN...
SADDLED WITH THE RESPONSIBILITY OF YOUR OWN TAGALONG ROBIN--AND YOU'RE AFRAID I'LL DO WHAT YOU DID.
NO, TIM...IT'S NOT YOU I'M WORRIED ABOUT...NOT YOU AT ALL.
YOU HAD OTHER REASONS FOR ACCEPTING THIS BATMAN GIG, DIDN'T YOU--OTHER THAN JUST HELPING BRUCE...?
MAYBE I DID.
YOU'RE TESTING YOURSELF...
MORE LIKE HOPING TO PROVE MYSELF--BUY BACK SOME CONFIDENCE.
AND IT'S MY LAST CHANCE.
ONE MORE FAILURE... AND I'M EITHER DEAD OR OUT.

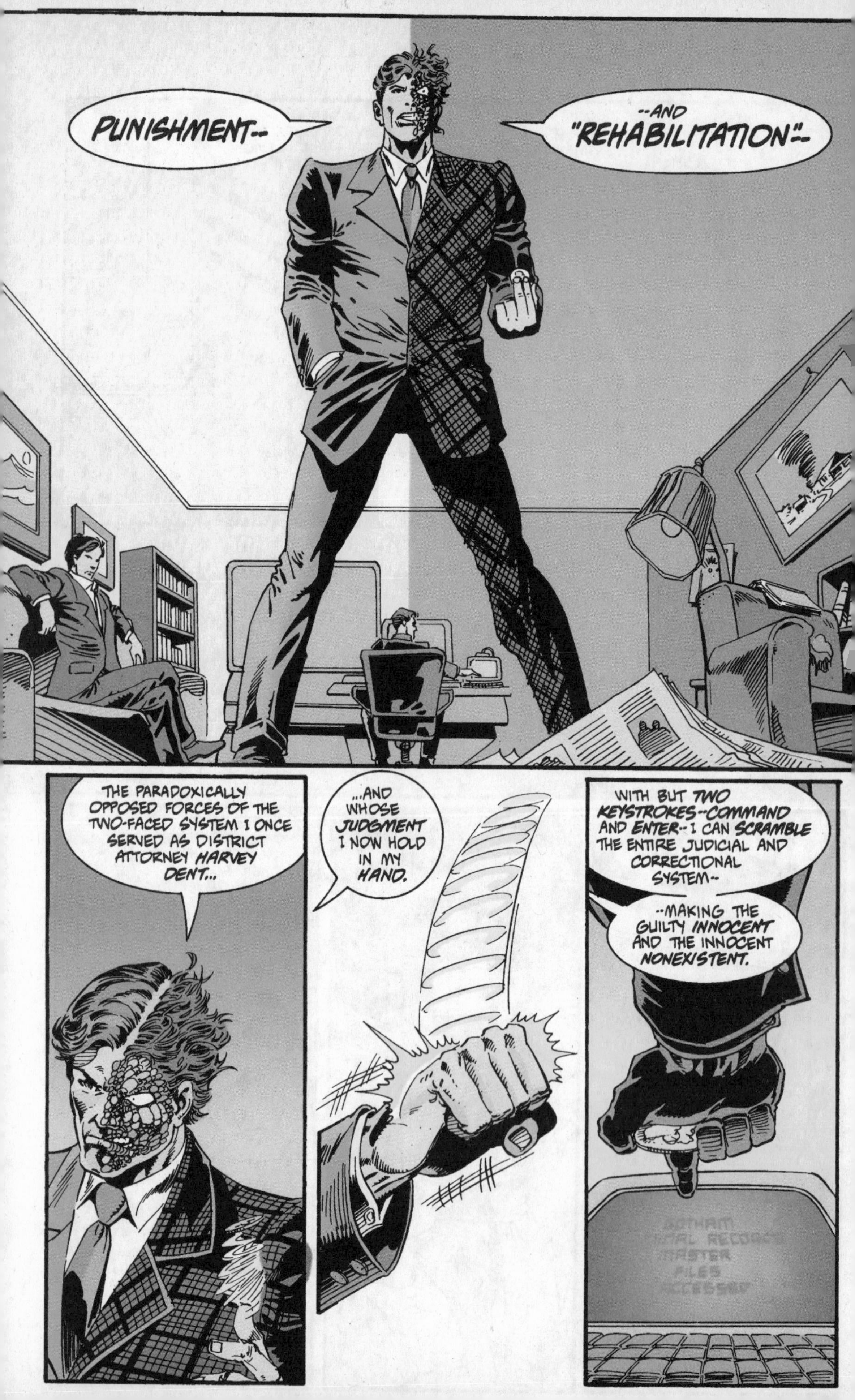

PUNISHMENT--
--AND "REHABILITATION"--
THE PARADOXICALLY OPPOSED FORCES OF THE TWO-FACED SYSTEM I ONCE SERVED AS DISTRICT ATTORNEY HARVEY DENT...
...AND WHOSE JUDGMENT I NOW HOLD IN MY HAND.
WITH BUT TWO KEYSTROKES--COMMAND AND ENTER--I CAN SCRAMBLE THE ENTIRE JUDICIAL AND CORRECTIONAL SYSTEM--
--MAKING THE GUILTY INNOCENT AND THE INNOCENT NONEXISTENT.
GOTHAM
MASTER
FILES

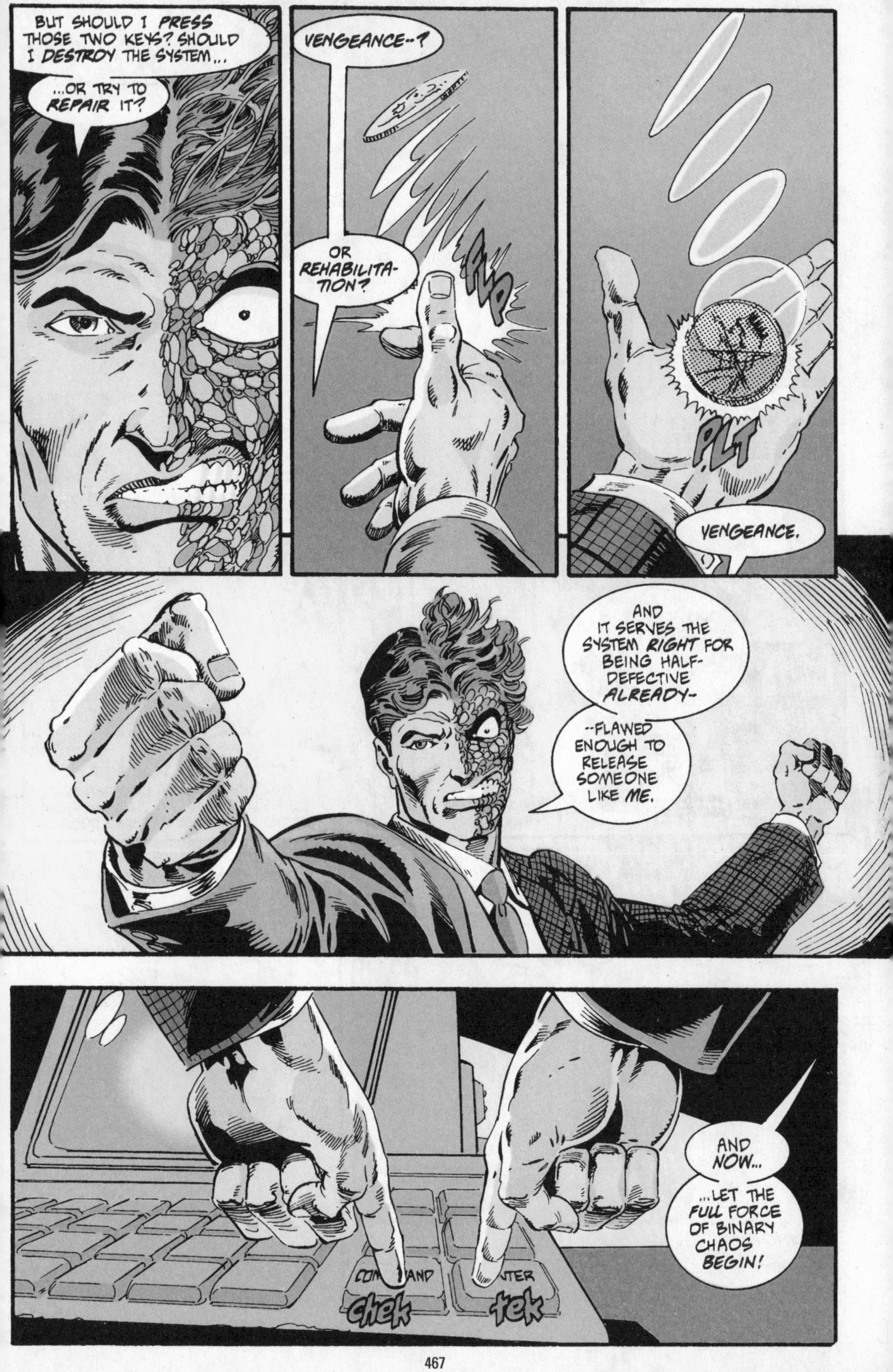
BUT SHOULD I PRESS THOSE TWO KEYS? SHOULD I DESTROY THE SYSTEM...
...OR TRY TO REPAIR IT?
VENGEANCE--?
OR REHABILITATION?
FLIP
PLT
VENGEANCE.
AND IT SERVES THE SYSTEM RIGHT FOR BEING HALF-DEFECTIVE ALREADY--
--FLAWED ENOUGH TO RELEASE SOMEONE LIKE ME.
AND NOW...
...LET THE FULL FORCE OF BINARY CHAOS BEGIN!
chek
tek

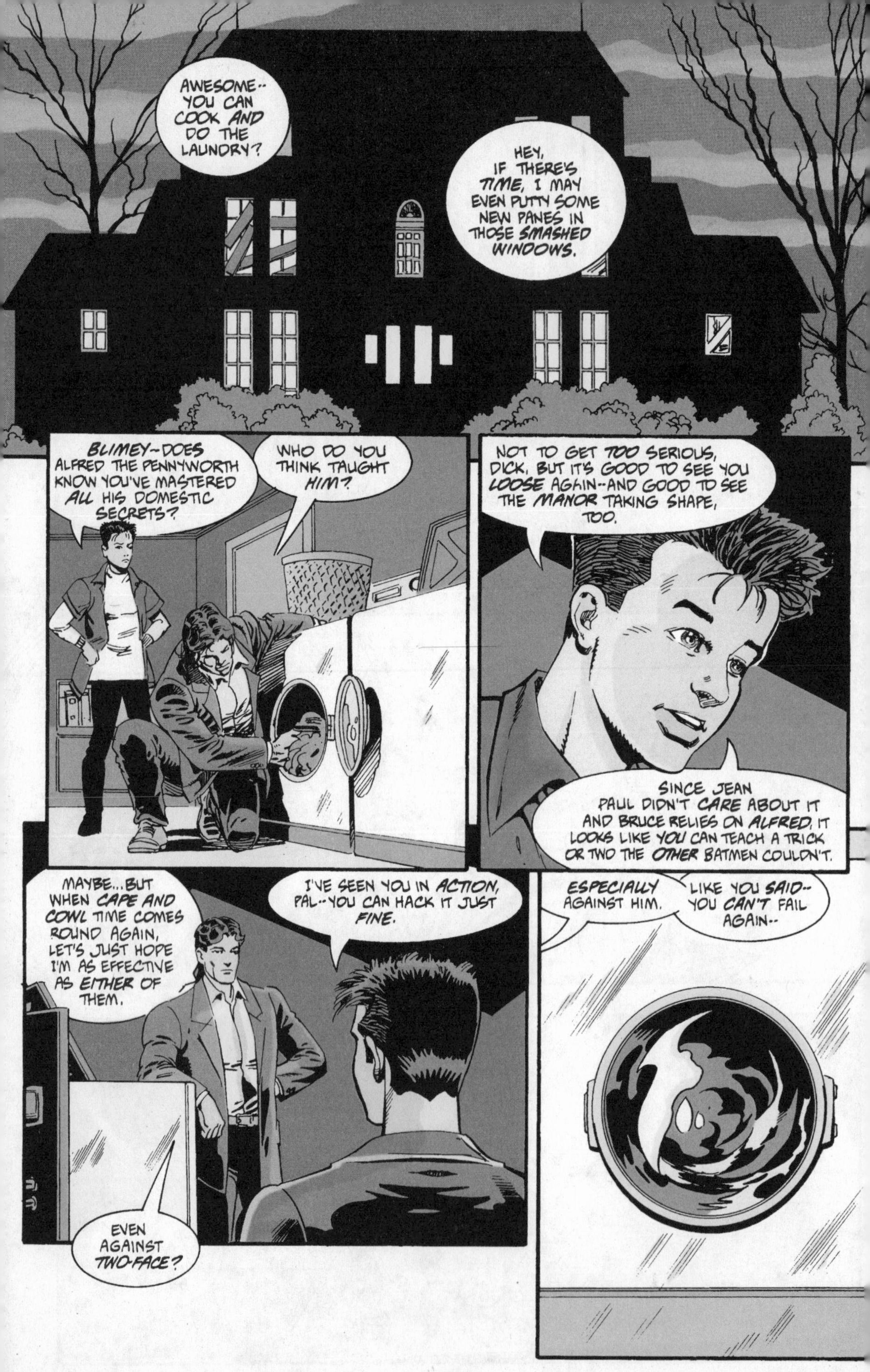

AWESOME.. YOU CAN COOK AND DO THE LAUNDRY?
HEY, IF THERE'S TIME, I MAY EVEN PUTTY SOME NEW PANES IN THOSE SMASHED WINDOWS.
BLIMEY--DOES ALFRED THE PENNYWORTH KNOW YOU'VE MASTERED ALL HIS DOMESTIC SECRETS?
WHO DO YOU THINK TAUGHT HIM?
NOT TO GET TOO SERIOUS, DICK, BUT IT'S GOOD TO SEE YOU LOOSE AGAIN--AND GOOD TO SEE THE MANOR TAKING SHAPE, TOO.
SINCE JEAN PAUL DIDN'T CARE ABOUT IT AND BRUCE RELIES ON ALFRED, IT LOOKS LIKE YOU CAN TEACH A TRICK OR TWO THE OTHER BATMEN COULDN'T.
MAYBE...BUT WHEN CAPE AND COWL TIME COMES 'ROUND AGAIN, LET'S JUST HOPE I'M AS EFFECTIVE AS EITHER OF THEM.
I'VE SEEN YOU IN ACTION, PAL--YOU CAN HACK IT JUST FINE.
EVEN AGAINST TWO-FACE?
ESPECIALLY AGAINST HIM.
LIKE YOU SAID-- YOU CAN'T FAIL AGAIN--

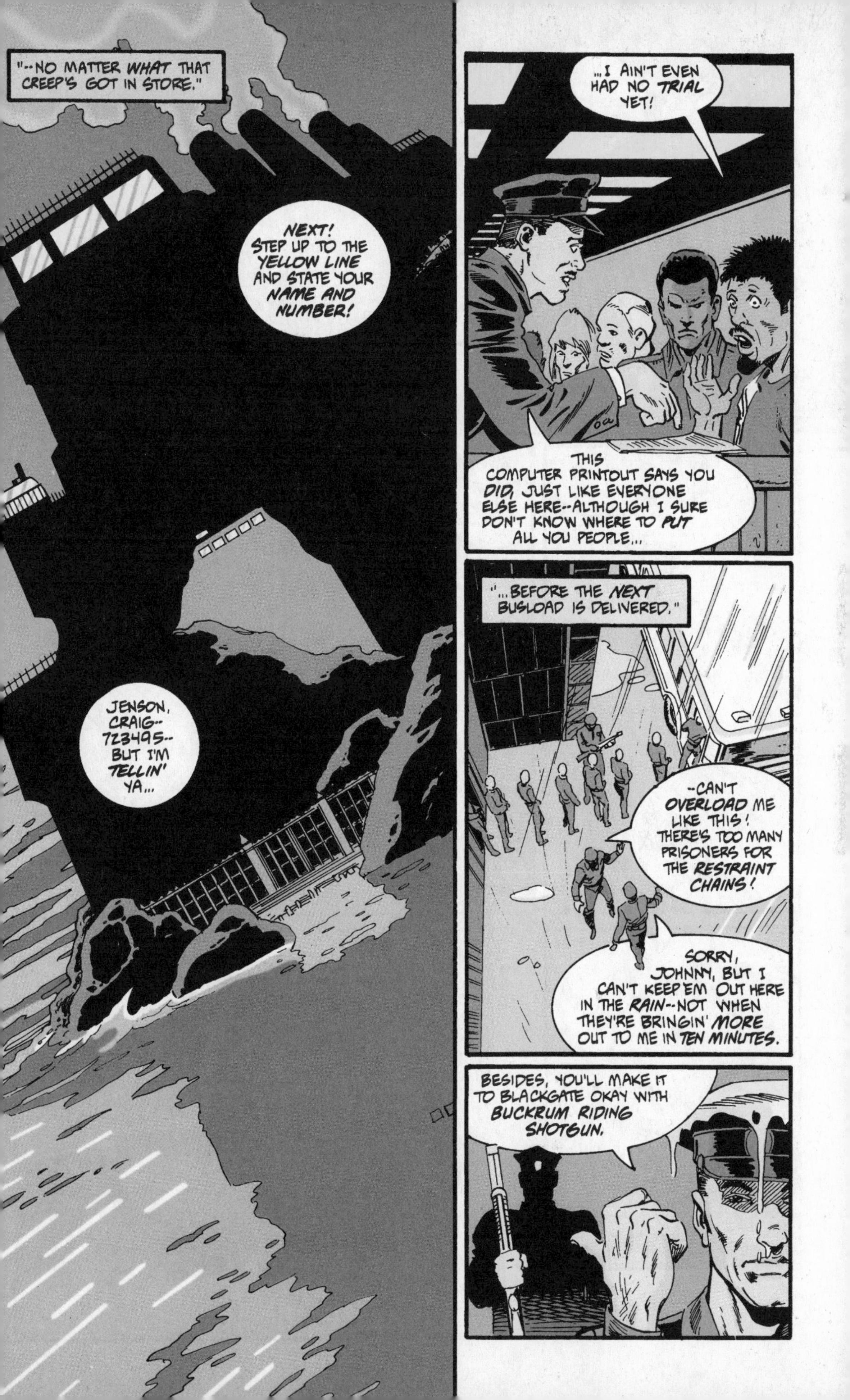
"--NO MATTER WHAT THAT CREEP'S GOT IN STORE."
NEXT! STEP UP TO THE YELLOW LINE AND STATE YOUR NAME AND NUMBER!
JENSON, CRAIG-- 723495-- BUT I'M TELLIN' YA...
...I AIN'T EVEN HAD NO TRIAL YET!
THIS COMPUTER PRINTOUT SAYS YOU DID, JUST LIKE EVERYONE ELSE HERE--ALTHOUGH I SURE DON'T KNOW WHERE TO PUT ALL YOU PEOPLE...
"...BEFORE THE NEXT BUSLOAD IS DELIVERED."
--CAN'T OVERLOAD ME LIKE THIS! THERE'S TOO MANY PRISONERS FOR THE RESTRAINT CHAINS!
SORRY, JOHNNY, BUT I CAN'T KEEP'EM OUT HERE IN THE RAIN--NOT WHEN THEY'RE BRINGIN' MORE OUT TO ME IN TEN MINUTES.
BESIDES, YOU'LL MAKE IT TO BLACKGATE OKAY WITH BUCKRUM RIDING SHOTGUN.

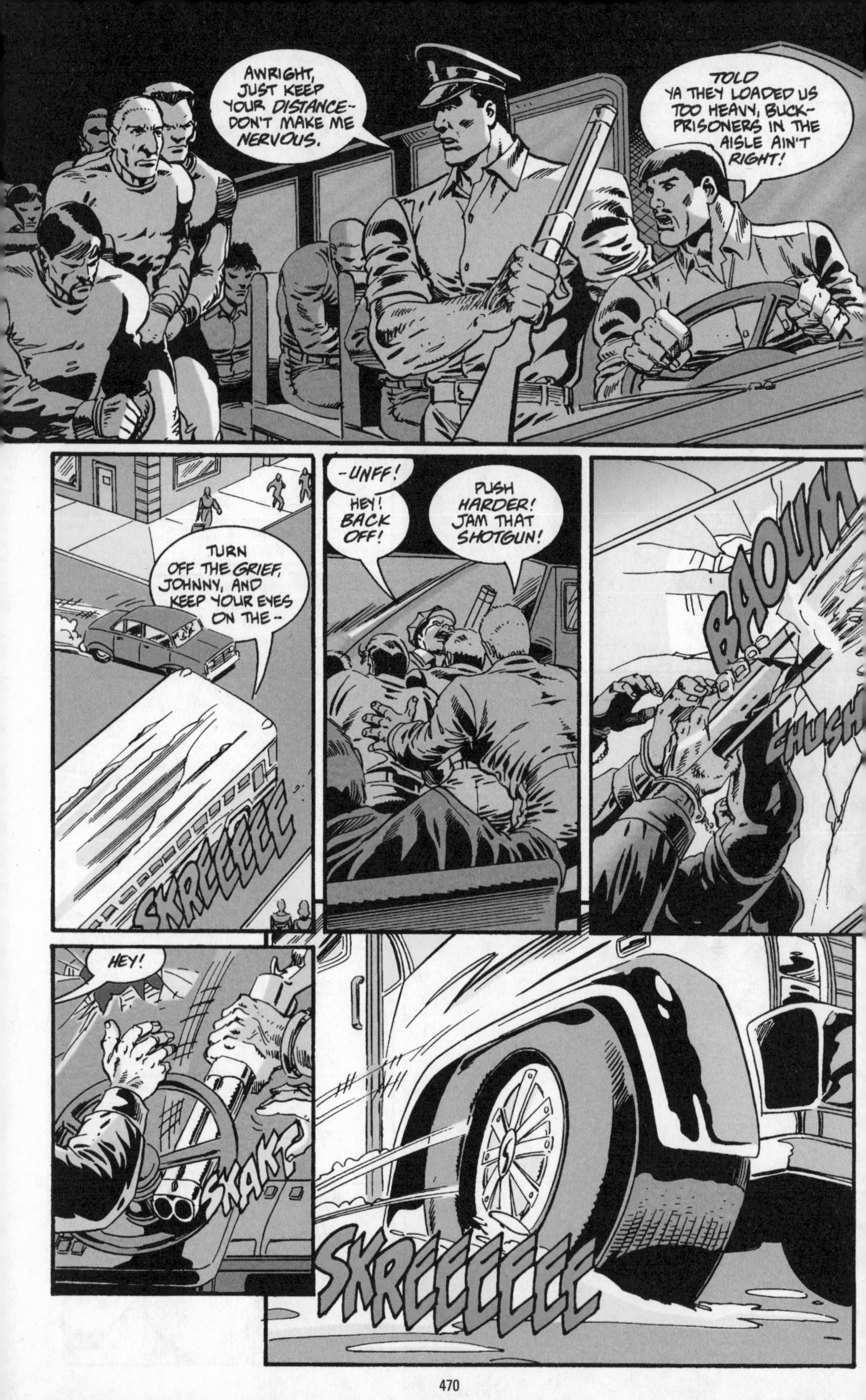
AWRIGHT, JUST KEEP YOUR DISTANCE-- DON'T MAKE ME NERVOUS.
TOLD YA THEY LOADED US TOO HEAVY, BUCK-- PRISONERS IN THE AISLE AIN'T RIGHT!
TURN OFF THE GRIEF, JOHNNY, AND KEEP YOUR EYES ON THE--
SKREEEEEE
-UNFF!
HEY! BACK OFF!
PUSH HARDER! JAM THAT SHOTGUN!
BAOUM
CHUSH
HEY!
SKAK!
SKREEEEEE

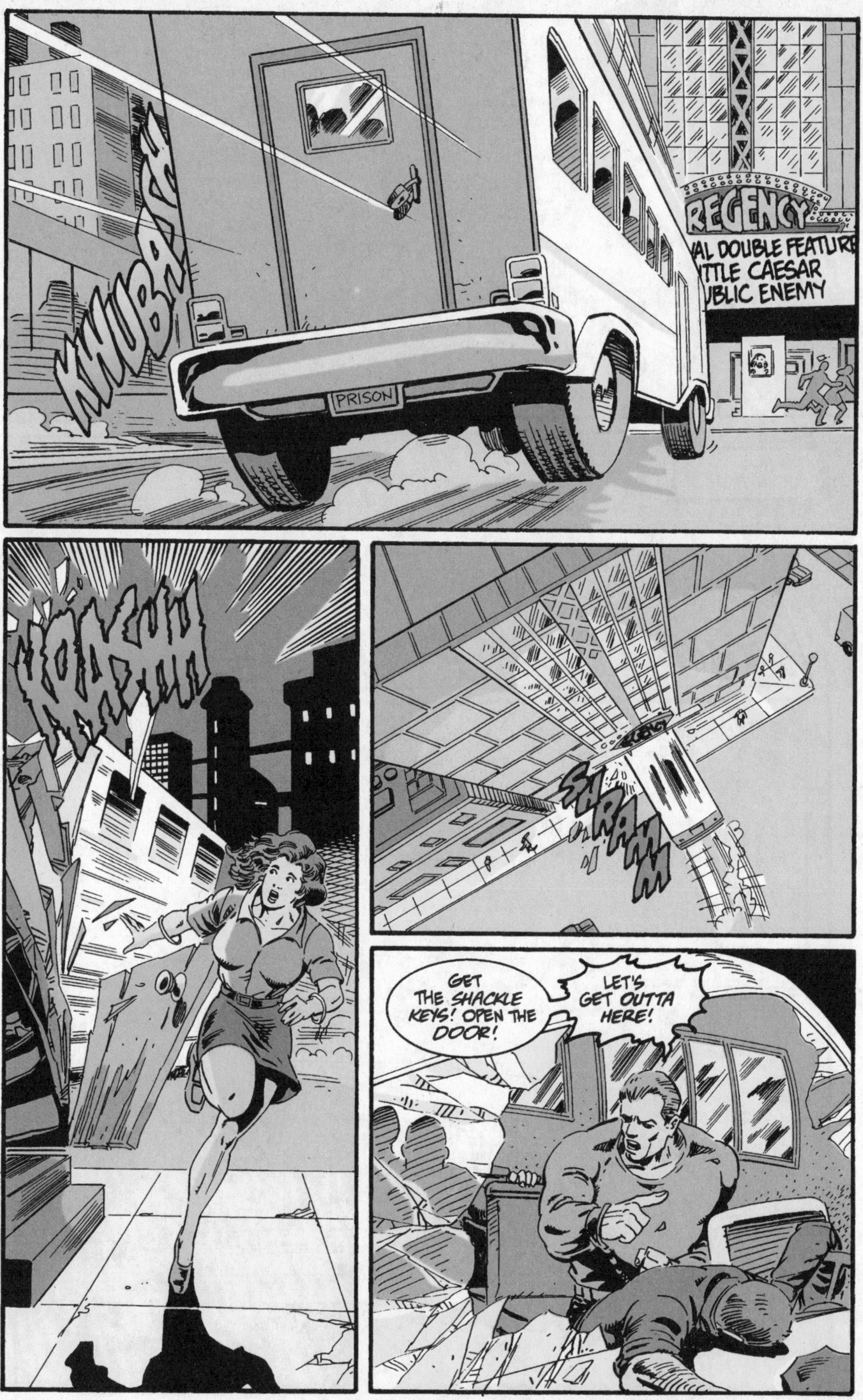
REGENCY
VAL DOUBLE FEATURE
TTLE CAESAR
UBLIC ENEMY
PRISON
SHRAMM
GET THE SHACKLE KEYS! OPEN THE DOOR!
LET'S GET OUTTA HERE!

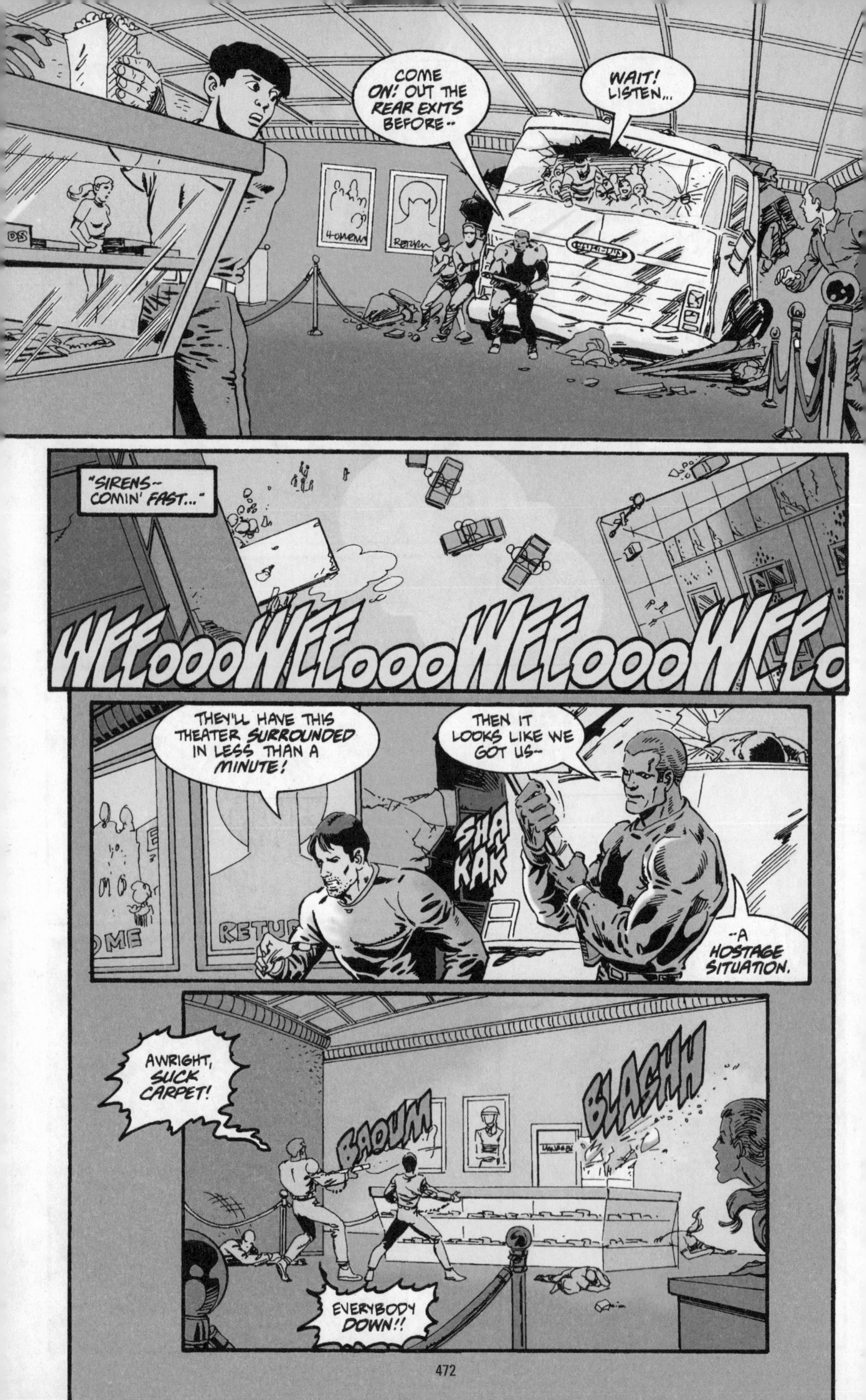
COME ON! OUT THE REAR EXITS BEFORE--
WAIT! LISTEN...
"SIRENS-- COMIN' FAST..."
WEEoooWEEoooWEEoooWEEo
THEY'LL HAVE THIS THEATER SURROUNDED IN LESS THAN A MINUTE!
THEN IT LOOKS LIKE WE GOT US--
SHAKAK
--A HOSTAGE SITUATION.
AWRIGHT, SUCK CARPET!
BAOUM
BLASHH
EVERYBODY DOWN!!

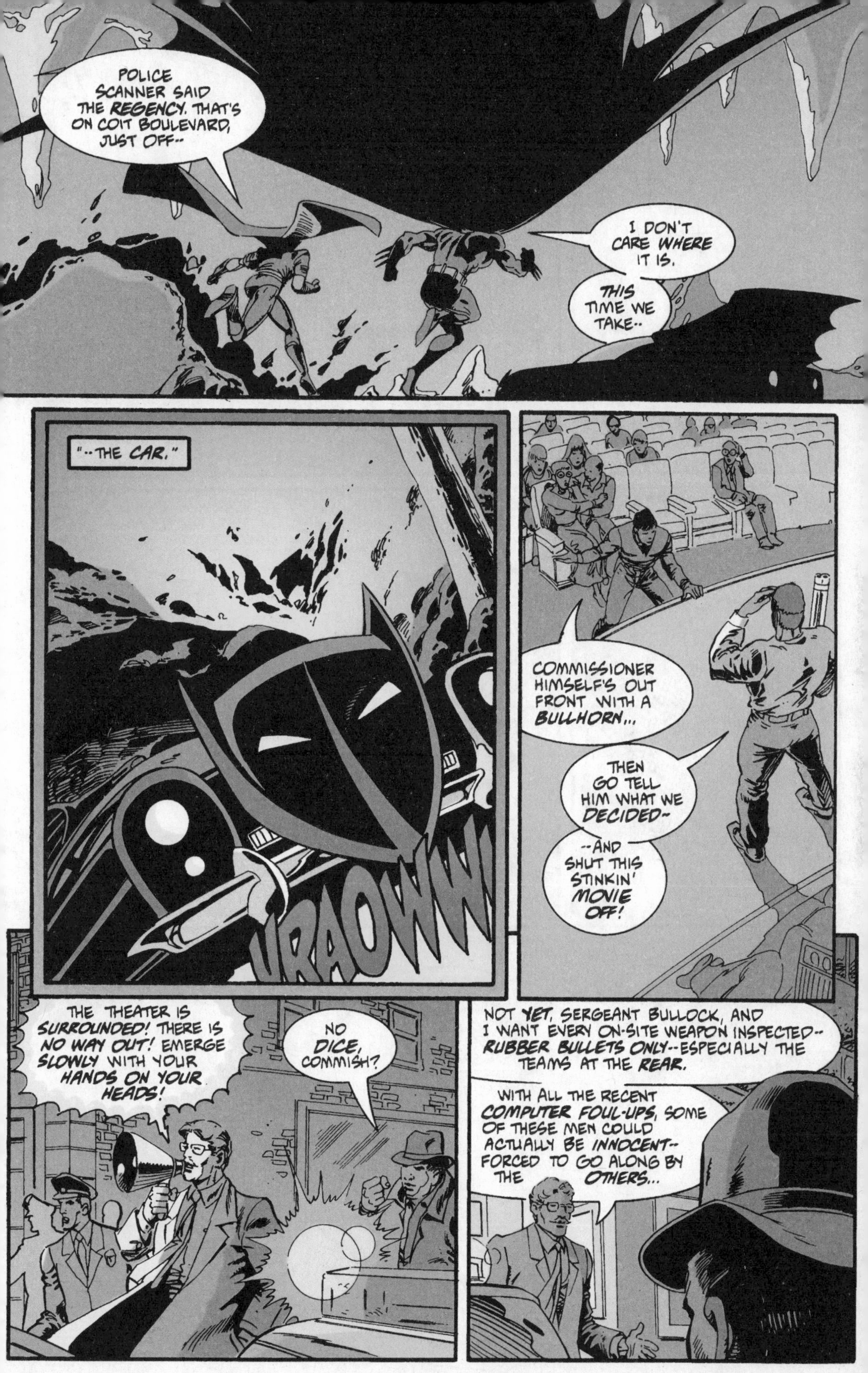
POLICE SCANNER SAID THE REGENCY. THAT'S ON COIT BOULEVARD, JUST OFF--
I DON'T CARE WHERE IT IS.
THIS TIME WE TAKE--
"--THE CAR."
VRAOWW
COMMISSIONER HIMSELF'S OUT FRONT WITH A BULLHORN...
THEN GO TELL HIM WHAT WE DECIDED--
--AND SHUT THIS STINKIN' MOVIE OFF!
THE THEATER IS SURROUNDED! THERE IS NO WAY OUT! EMERGE SLOWLY WITH YOUR HANDS ON YOUR HEADS!
NO DICE, COMMISH?
NOT YET, SERGEANT BULLOCK, AND I WANT EVERY ON-SITE WEAPON INSPECTED-- RUBBER BULLETS ONLY--ESPECIALLY THE TEAMS AT THE REAR.
WITH ALL THE RECENT COMPUTER FOUL-UPS, SOME OF THESE MEN COULD ACTUALLY BE INNOCENT-- FORCED TO GO ALONG BY THE OTHERS...

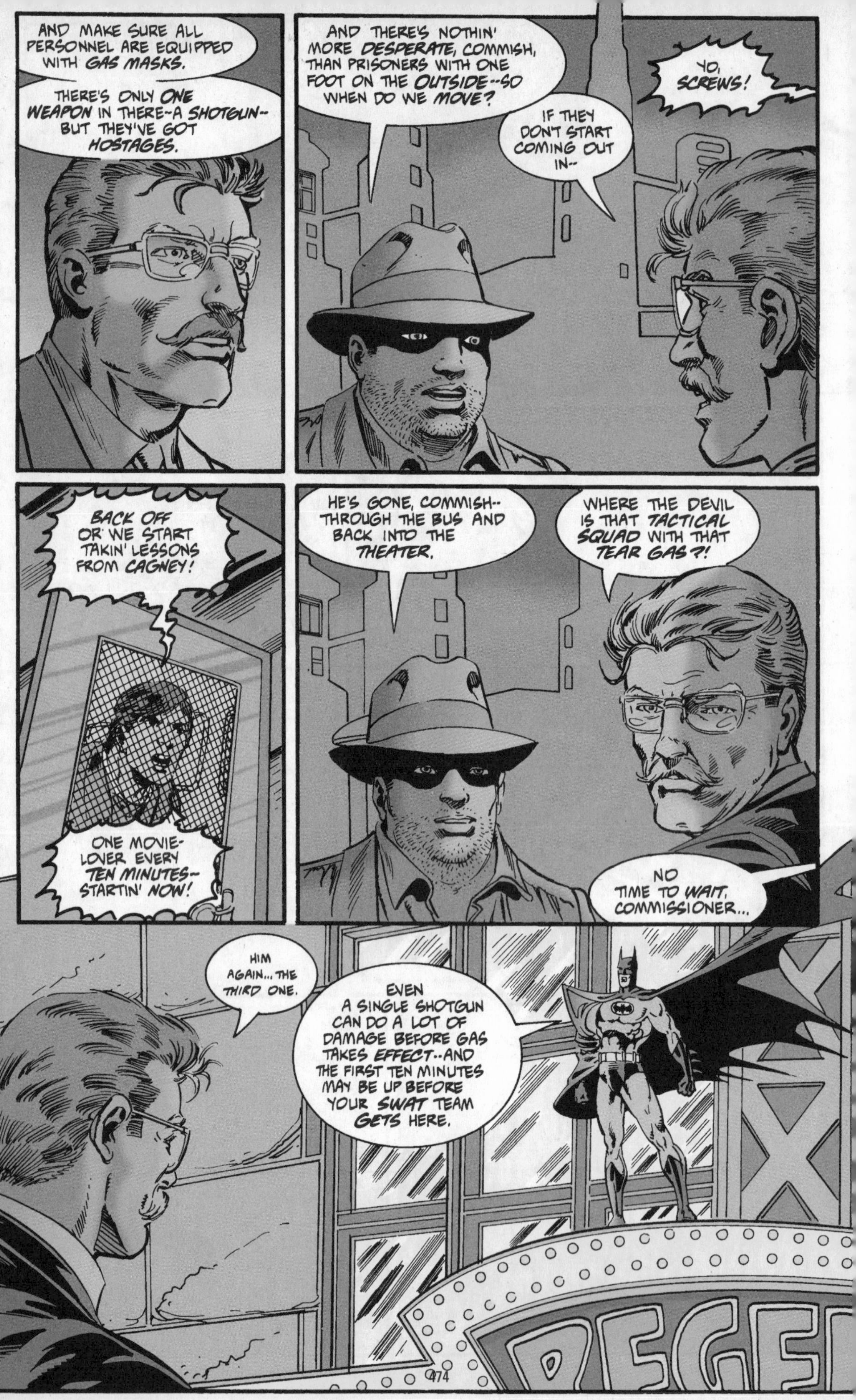
AND MAKE SURE ALL PERSONNEL ARE EQUIPPED WITH GAS MASKS.
THERE'S ONLY ONE WEAPON IN THERE--A SHOTGUN--BUT THEY'VE GOT HOSTAGES.
AND THERE'S NOTHIN' MORE DESPERATE, COMMISH, THAN PRISONERS WITH ONE FOOT ON THE OUTSIDE--SO WHEN DO WE MOVE?
IF THEY DON'T START COMING OUT IN--
YO, SCREWS!
BACK OFF OR WE START TAKIN' LESSONS FROM CAGNEY!
ONE MOVIE-LOVER EVERY TEN MINUTES--STARTIN' NOW!
HE'S GONE, COMMISH--THROUGH THE BUS AND BACK INTO THE THEATER.
WHERE THE DEVIL IS THAT TACTICAL SQUAD WITH THAT TEAR GAS?!
NO TIME TO WAIT, COMMISSIONER...
HIM AGAIN... THE THIRD ONE.
EVEN A SINGLE SHOTGUN CAN DO A LOT OF DAMAGE BEFORE GAS TAKES EFFECT--AND THE FIRST TEN MINUTES MAY BE UP BEFORE YOUR SWAT TEAM GETS HERE.

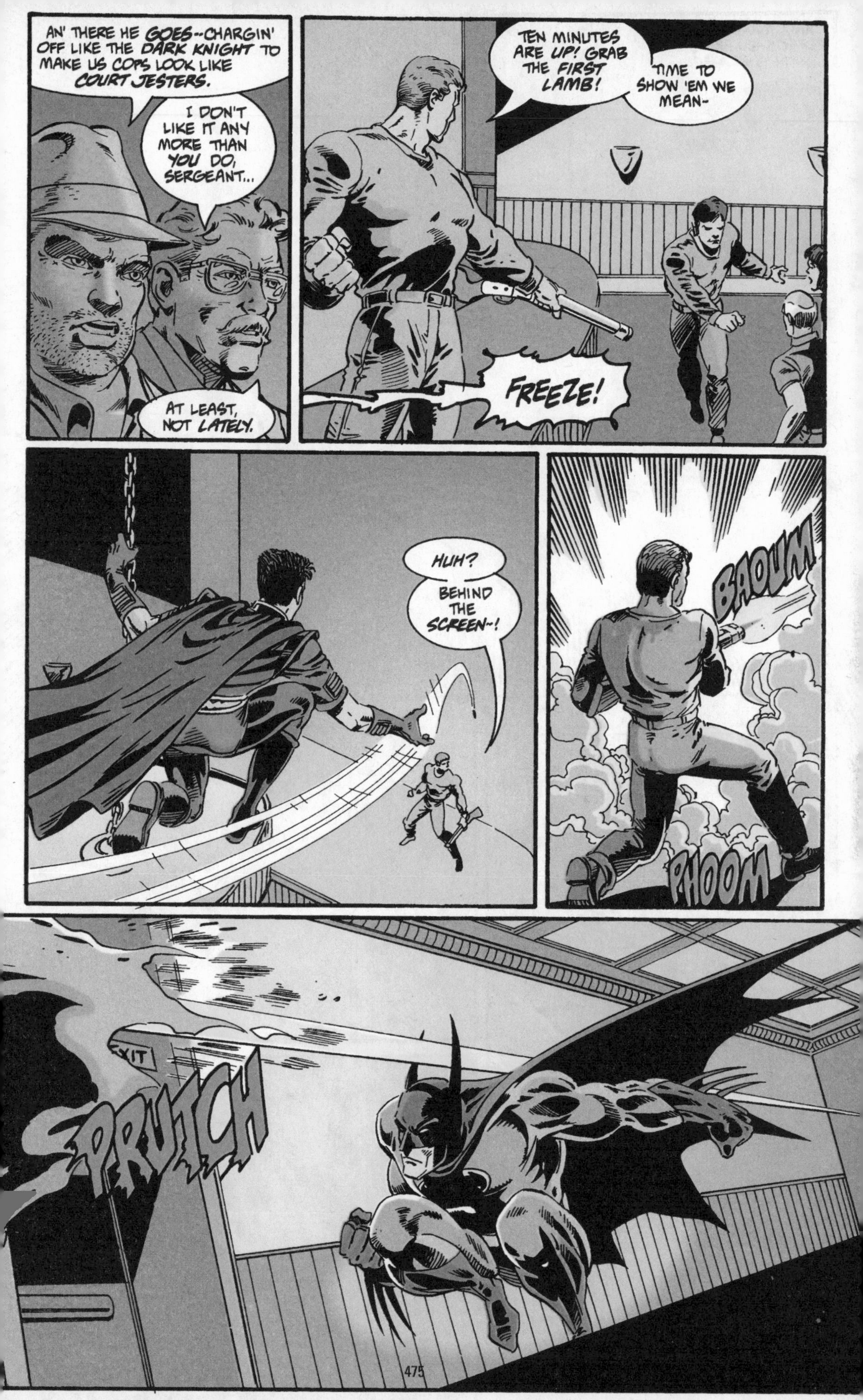

AN' THERE HE GOES--CHARGIN' OFF LIKE THE DARK KNIGHT TO MAKE US COPS LOOK LIKE COURT JESTERS.
I DON'T LIKE IT ANY MORE THAN YOU DO, SERGEANT...
AT LEAST, NOT LATELY.
TEN MINUTES ARE UP! GRAB THE FIRST LAMB!
TIME TO SHOW 'EM WE MEAN-
FREEZE!
HUH?
BEHIND THE SCREEN--!
BAOUM
PHOOM
EXIT
SPRUTCH

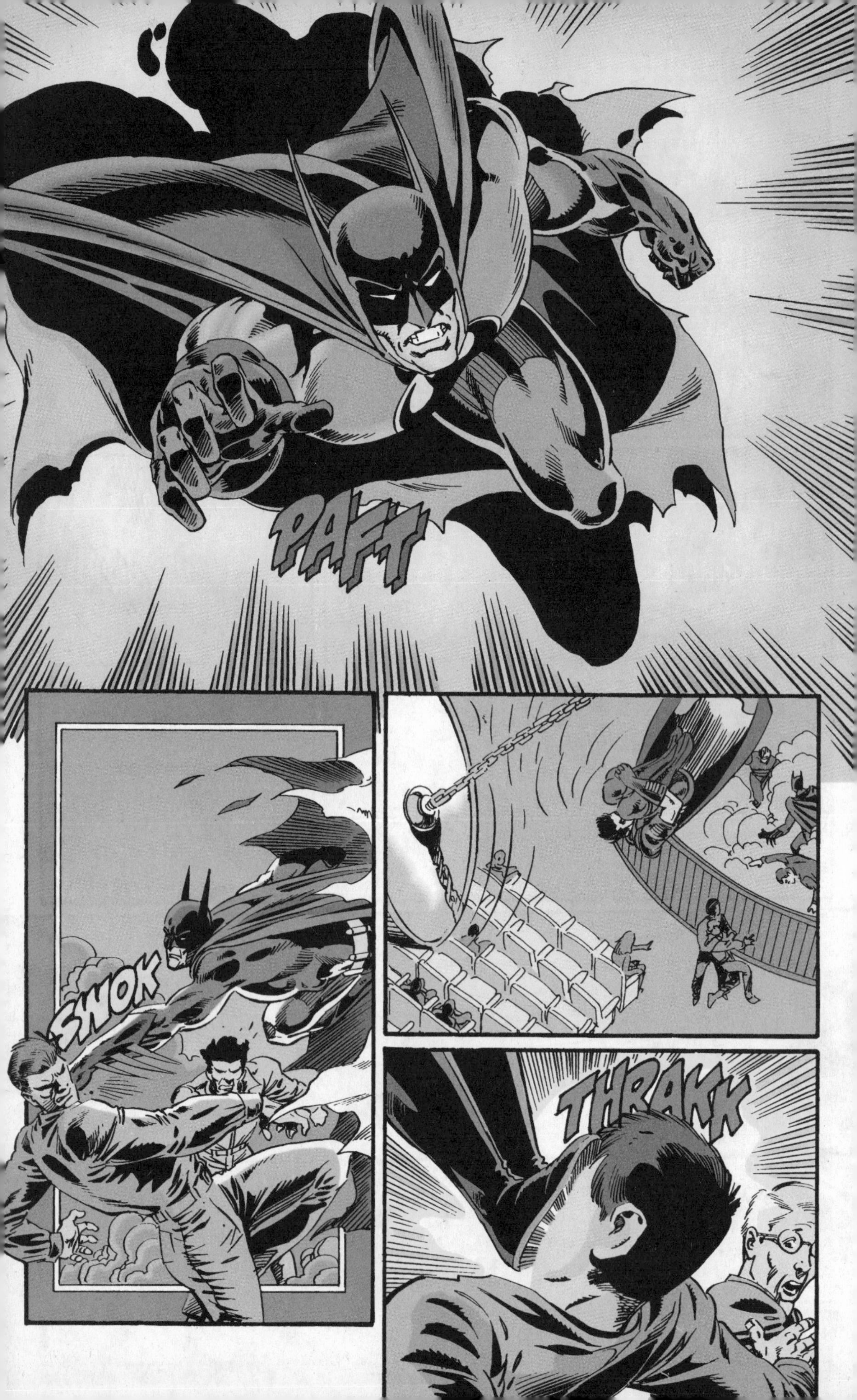
PAFF
SWOK
THRAKK

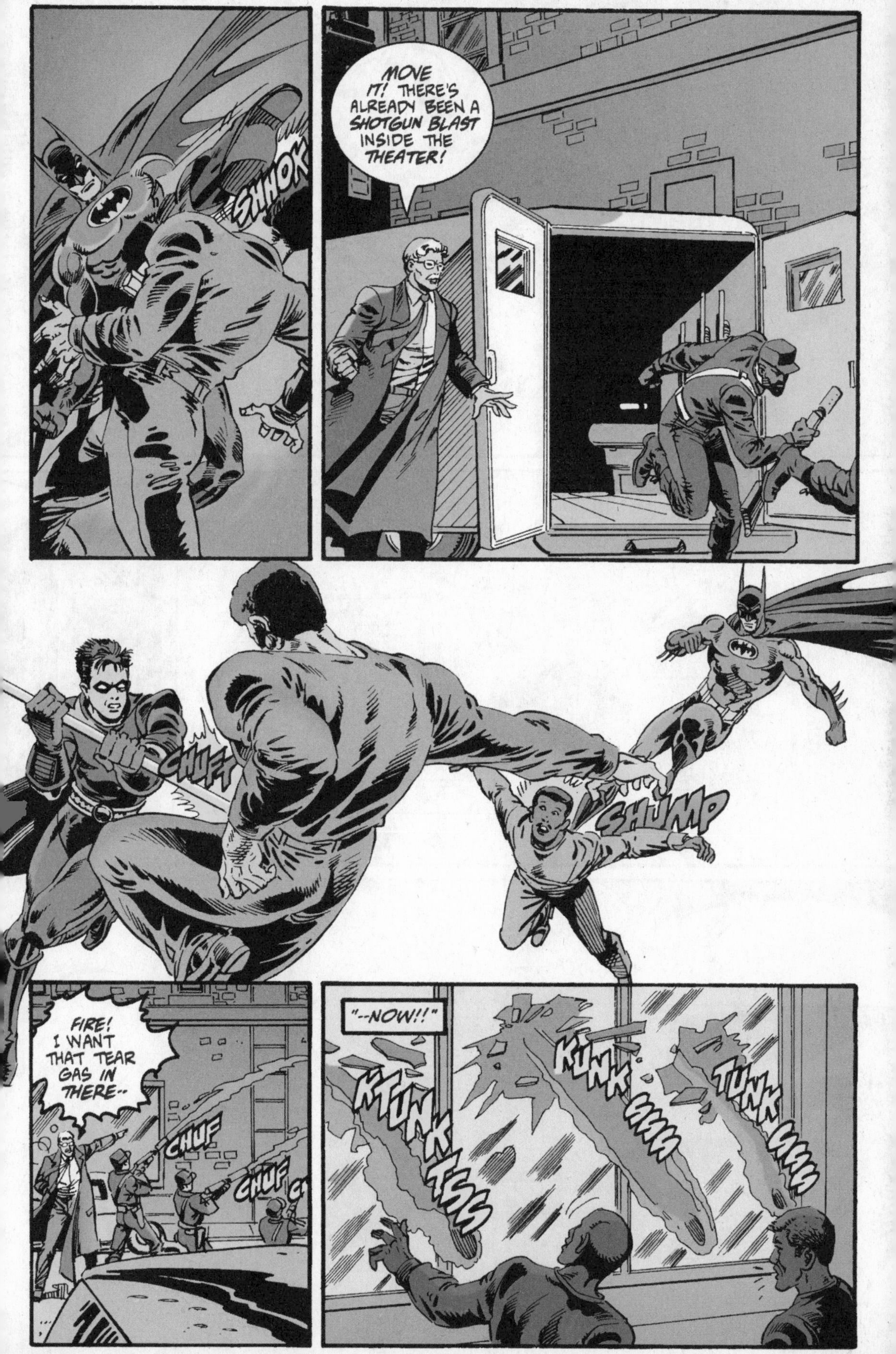
SHHOK
MOVE IT! THERE'S ALREADY BEEN A SHOTGUN BLAST INSIDE THE THEATER!
CHUFF
SHUMP
FIRE! I WANT THAT TEAR GAS IN THERE--
CHUF
CHUF
"--NOW!!"
KTUNK TSSS
KUNK SSSS
TUNK SSSS

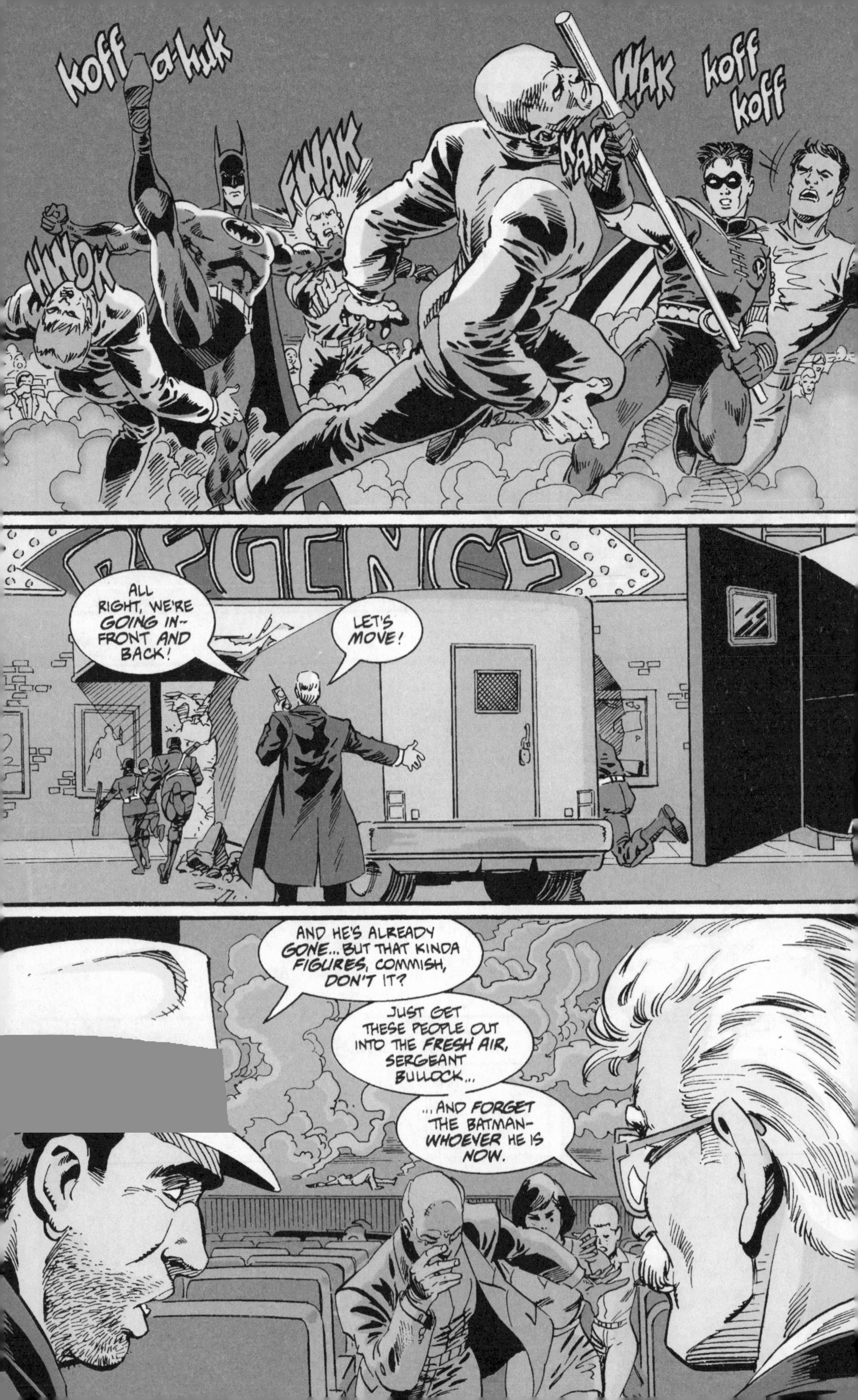
koff
a-huk
HWOK
FWAK
KAK
WAK
koff
koff
koff
ALL RIGHT, WE'RE GOING IN-- FRONT AND BACK!
LET'S MOVE!
AND HE'S ALREADY GONE... BUT THAT KINDA FIGURES, COMMISH, DON'T IT?
JUST GET THESE PEOPLE OUT INTO THE FRESH AIR, SERGEANT BULLOCK...
...AND FORGET THE BATMAN-- WHOEVER HE IS NOW.

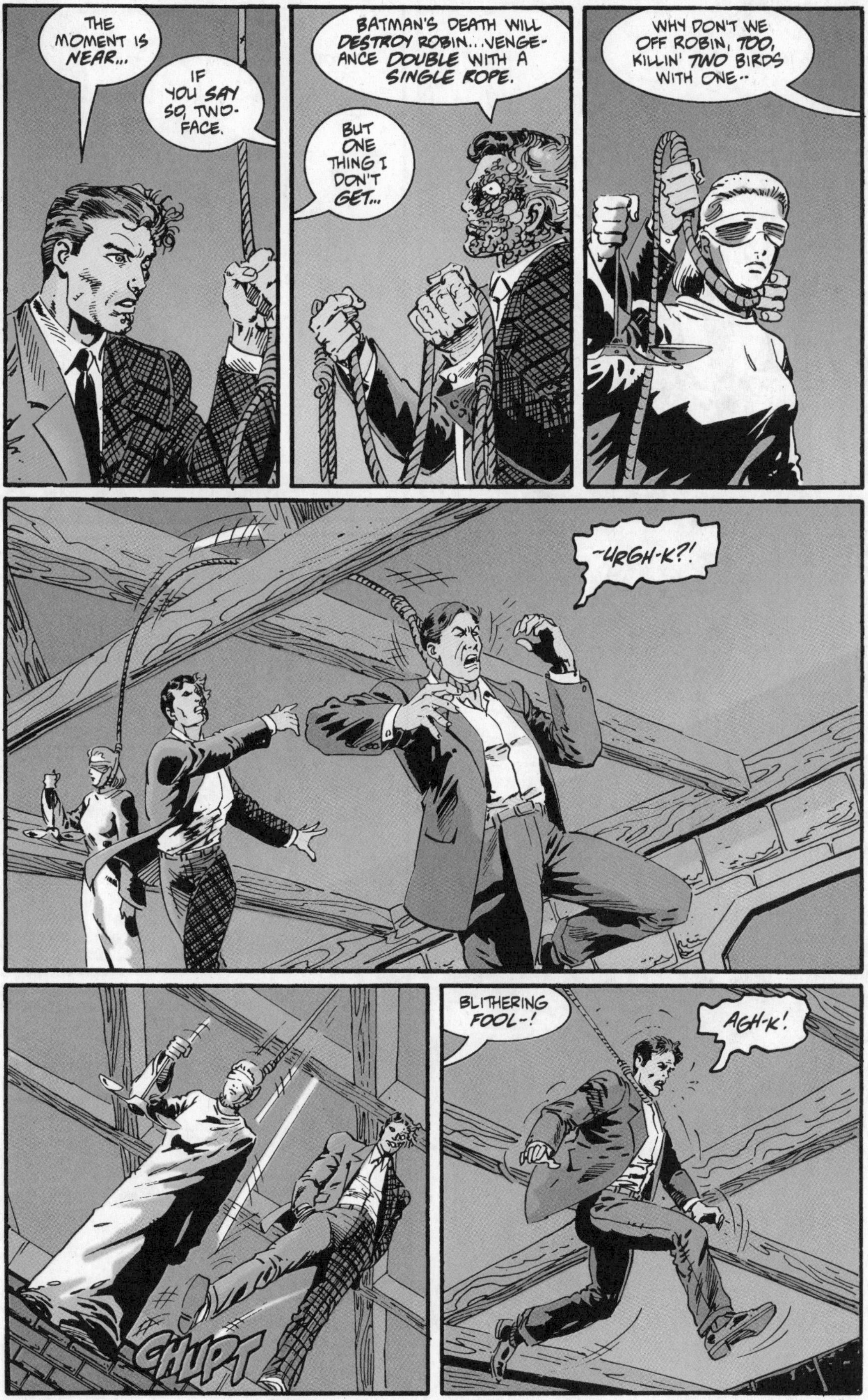
THE MOMENT IS NEAR...
IF YOU SAY SO, TWO-FACE.
BATMAN'S DEATH WILL DESTROY ROBIN...VENGEANCE DOUBLE WITH A SINGLE ROPE.
BUT ONE THING I DON'T GET...
WHY DON'T WE OFF ROBIN, TOO, KILLIN' TWO BIRDS WITH ONE--
~URGH-K?!
CHUPT
BLITHERING FOOL--!
AGH-K!

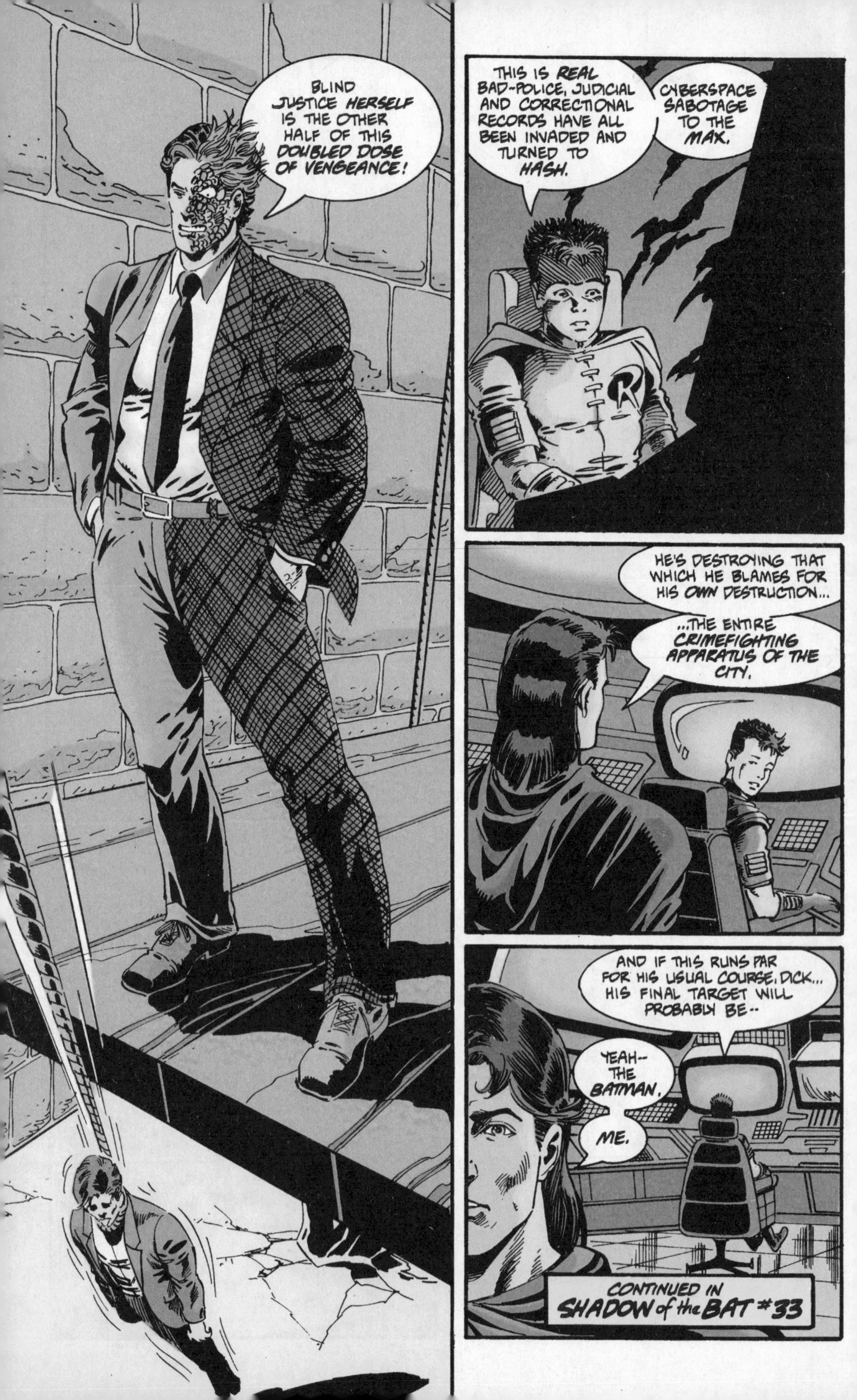
BLIND JUSTICE HERSELF IS THE OTHER HALF OF THIS DOUBLED DOSE OF VENGEANCE!
THIS IS REAL BAD--POLICE, JUDICIAL AND CORRECTIONAL RECORDS HAVE ALL BEEN INVADED AND TURNED TO HASH.
CYBERSPACE SABOTAGE TO THE MAX.
HE'S DESTROYING THAT WHICH HE BLAMES FOR HIS OWN DESTRUCTION...
...THE ENTIRE CRIMEFIGHTING APPARATUS OF THE CITY.
AND IF THIS RUNS PAR FOR HIS USUAL COURSE, DICK... HIS FINAL TARGET WILL PROBABLY BE--
YEAH-- THE BATMAN.
ME.
CONTINUED IN SHADOW of the BAT #33

Cover art by **BRIAN STELFREEZE**

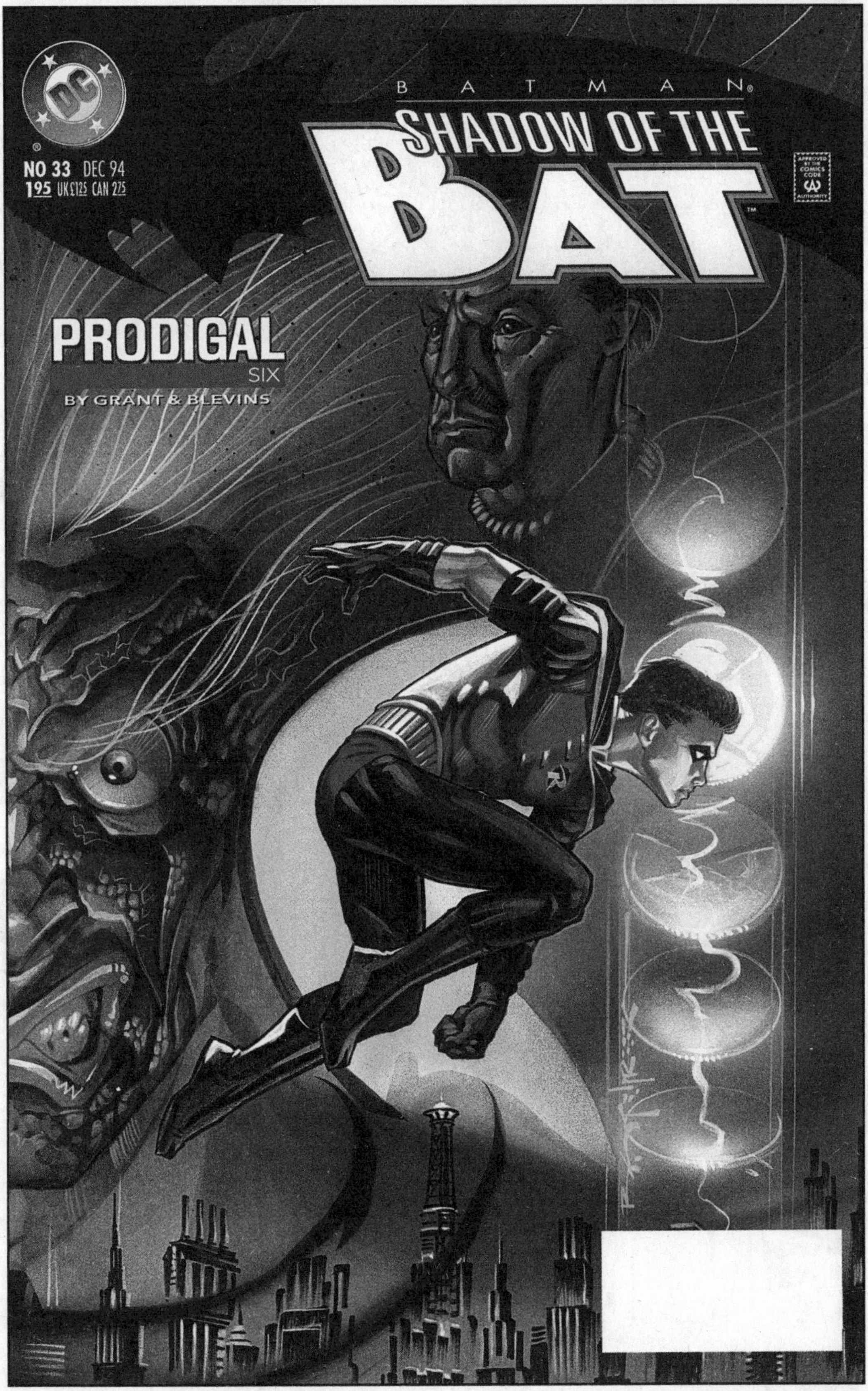
NO 33 DEC 94
1 95 UK £1 25 CAN 2 75
BATMAN
SHADOW OF THE BAT
APPROVED BY THE COMICS CODE AUTHORITY
PRODIGAL
SIX
BY GRANT & BLEVINS

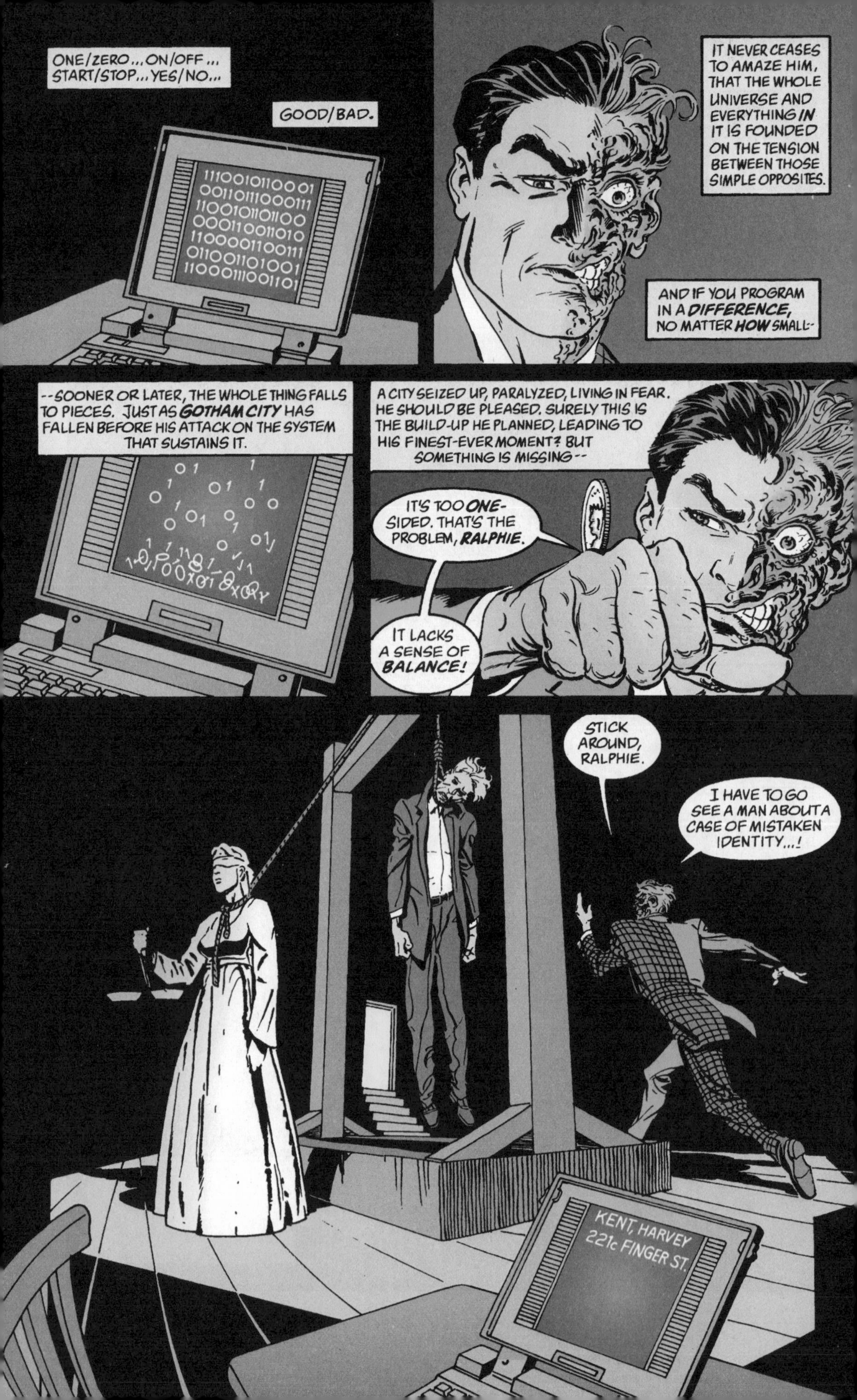
ONE/ZERO... ON/OFF... START/STOP... YES/NO...
GOOD/BAD.
IT NEVER CEASES TO AMAZE HIM, THAT THE WHOLE UNIVERSE AND EVERYTHING IN IT IS FOUNDED ON THE TENSION BETWEEN THOSE SIMPLE OPPOSITES.
AND IF YOU PROGRAM IN A DIFFERENCE, NO MATTER HOW SMALL--
--SOONER OR LATER, THE WHOLE THING FALLS TO PIECES. JUST AS GOTHAM CITY HAS FALLEN BEFORE HIS ATTACK ON THE SYSTEM THAT SUSTAINS IT.
A CITY SEIZED UP, PARALYZED, LIVING IN FEAR. HE SHOULD BE PLEASED. SURELY THIS IS THE BUILD-UP HE PLANNED, LEADING TO HIS FINEST-EVER MOMENT? BUT SOMETHING IS MISSING--
IT'S TOO ONE-SIDED. THAT'S THE PROBLEM, RALPHIE.
IT LACKS A SENSE OF BALANCE!
STICK AROUND, RALPHIE.
I HAVE TO GO SEE A MAN ABOUT A CASE OF MISTAKEN IDENTITY...!
KENT, HARVEY
221c FINGER ST.

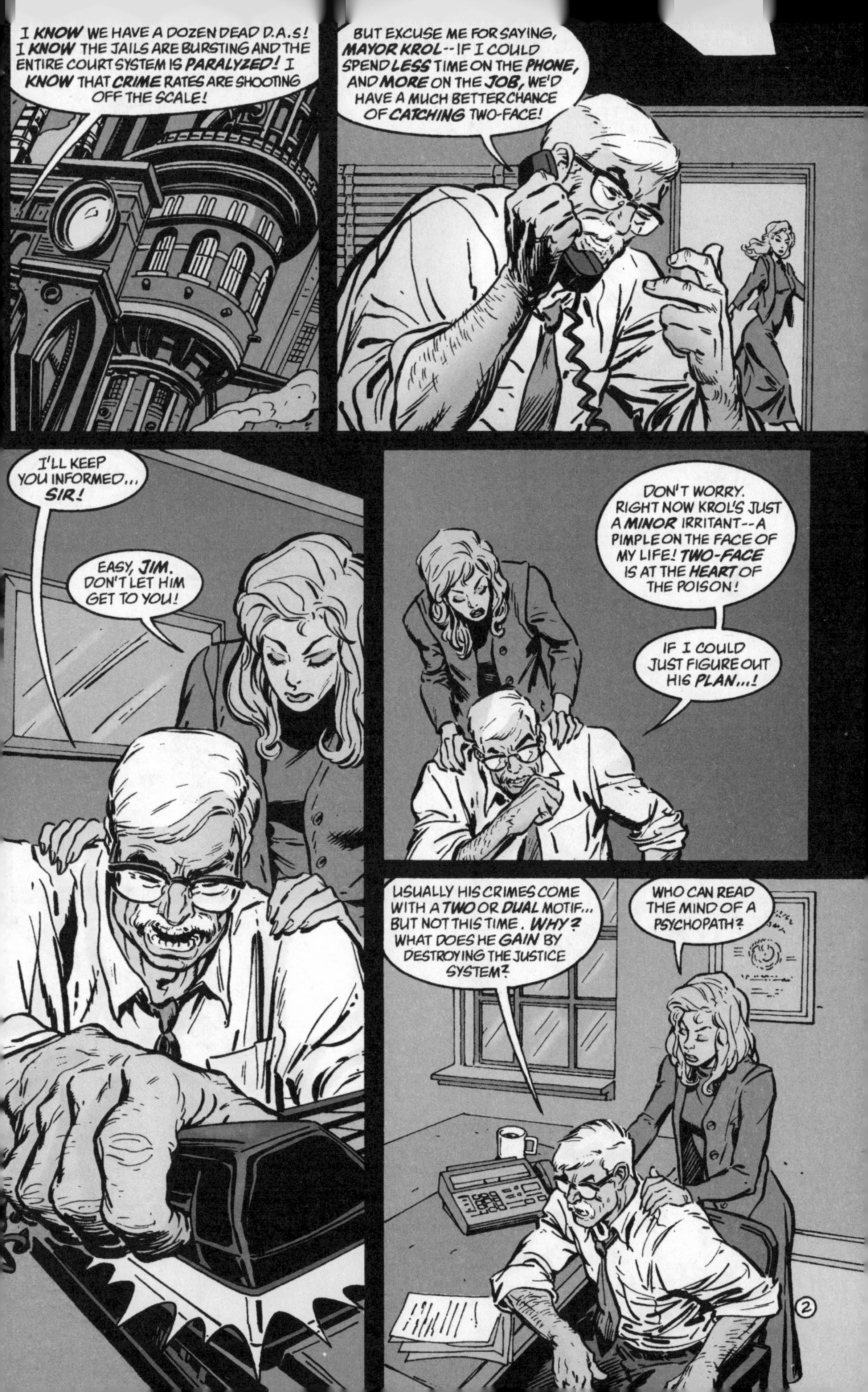
I KNOW WE HAVE A DOZEN DEAD D.A.s! I KNOW THE JAILS ARE BURSTING AND THE ENTIRE COURT SYSTEM IS PARALYZED! I KNOW THAT CRIME RATES ARE SHOOTING OFF THE SCALE!
BUT EXCUSE ME FOR SAYING, MAYOR KROL-- IF I COULD SPEND LESS TIME ON THE PHONE, AND MORE ON THE JOB, WE'D HAVE A MUCH BETTER CHANCE OF CATCHING TWO-FACE!
I'LL KEEP YOU INFORMED... SIR!
EASY, JIM. DON'T LET HIM GET TO YOU!
DON'T WORRY. RIGHT NOW KROL'S JUST A MINOR IRRITANT--A PIMPLE ON THE FACE OF MY LIFE! TWO-FACE IS AT THE HEART OF THE POISON!
IF I COULD JUST FIGURE OUT HIS PLAN...!
USUALLY HIS CRIMES COME WITH A TWO OR DUAL MOTIF... BUT NOT THIS TIME. WHY? WHAT DOES HE GAIN BY DESTROYING THE JUSTICE SYSTEM?
WHO CAN READ THE MIND OF A PSYCHOPATH?
2

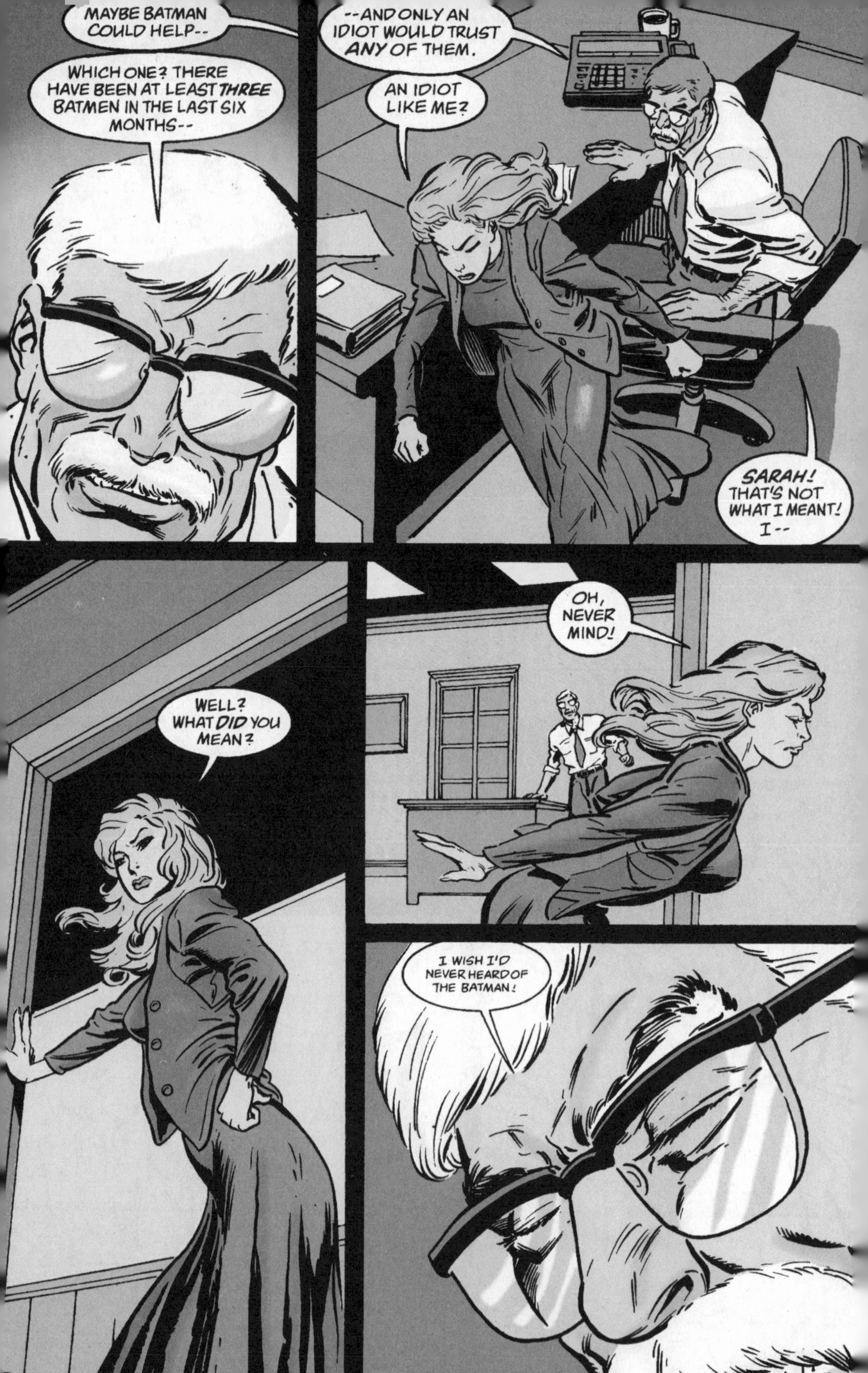
MAYBE BATMAN COULD HELP--
WHICH ONE? THERE HAVE BEEN AT LEAST THREE BATMEN IN THE LAST SIX MONTHS--
--AND ONLY AN IDIOT WOULD TRUST ANY OF THEM.
AN IDIOT LIKE ME?
SARAH! THAT'S NOT WHAT I MEANT! I--
WELL? WHAT DID YOU MEAN?
OH, NEVER MIND!
I WISH I'D NEVER HEARD OF THE BATMAN!

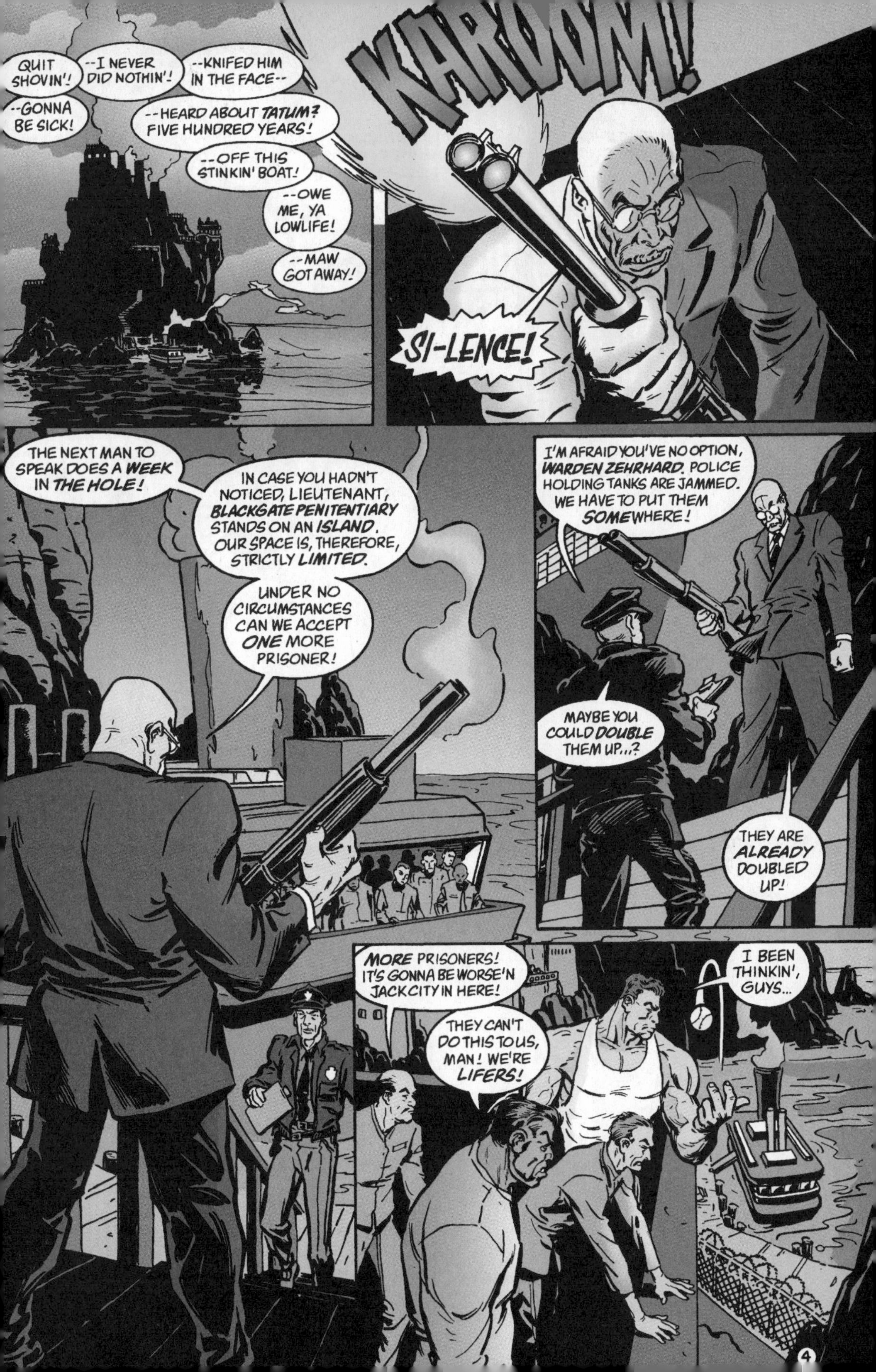
QUIT SHOVIN'!
--I NEVER DID NOTHIN'!
--KNIFED HIM IN THE FACE--
--GONNA BE SICK!
--HEARD ABOUT TATUM? FIVE HUNDRED YEARS!
--OFF THIS STINKIN' BOAT!
--OWE ME, YA LOWLIFE!
--MAW GOT AWAY!
KAROOM!
SI-LENCE!
THE NEXT MAN TO SPEAK DOES A WEEK IN THE HOLE!
IN CASE YOU HADN'T NOTICED, LIEUTENANT, BLACKGATE PENITENTIARY STANDS ON AN ISLAND. OUR SPACE IS, THEREFORE, STRICTLY LIMITED.
UNDER NO CIRCUMSTANCES CAN WE ACCEPT ONE MORE PRISONER!
I'M AFRAID YOU'VE NO OPTION, WARDEN ZEHRHARD. POLICE HOLDING TANKS ARE JAMMED. WE HAVE TO PUT THEM SOMEWHERE!
MAYBE YOU COULD DOUBLE THEM UP...?
THEY ARE ALREADY DOUBLED UP!
MORE PRISONERS! IT'S GONNA BE WORSE'N JACK CITY IN HERE!
THEY CAN'T DO THIS TO US, MAN! WE'RE LIFERS!
I BEEN THINKIN', GUYS...

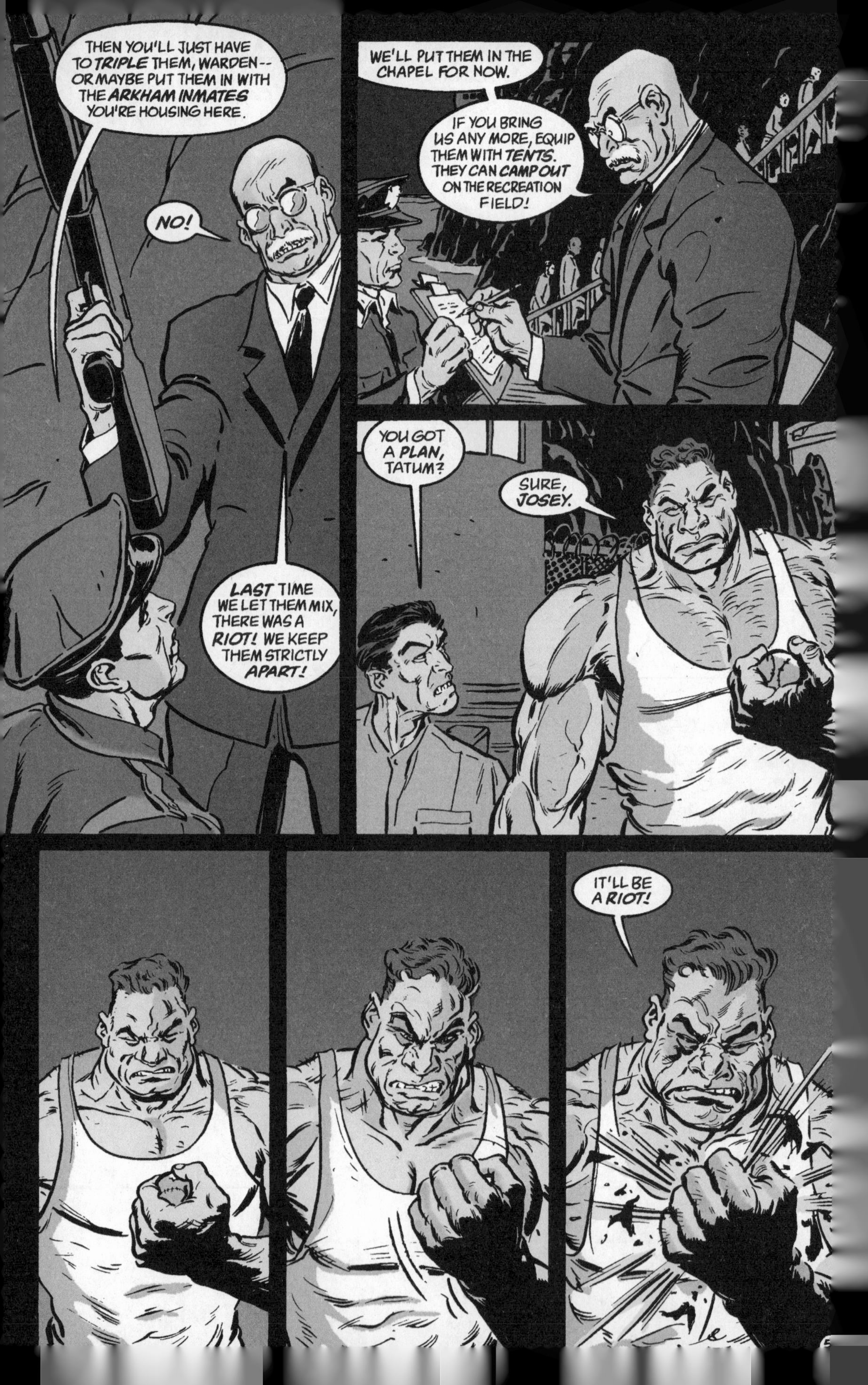
THEN YOU'LL JUST HAVE TO TRIPLE THEM, WARDEN-- OR MAYBE PUT THEM IN WITH THE ARKHAM INMATES YOU'RE HOUSING HERE.
NO!
LAST TIME WE LET THEM MIX, THERE WAS A RIOT! WE KEEP THEM STRICTLY APART!
WE'LL PUT THEM IN THE CHAPEL FOR NOW.
IF YOU BRING US ANY MORE, EQUIP THEM WITH TENTS. THEY CAN CAMP OUT ON THE RECREATION FIELD!
YOU GOT A PLAN, TATUM?
SURE, JOSEY.
IT'LL BE A RIOT!

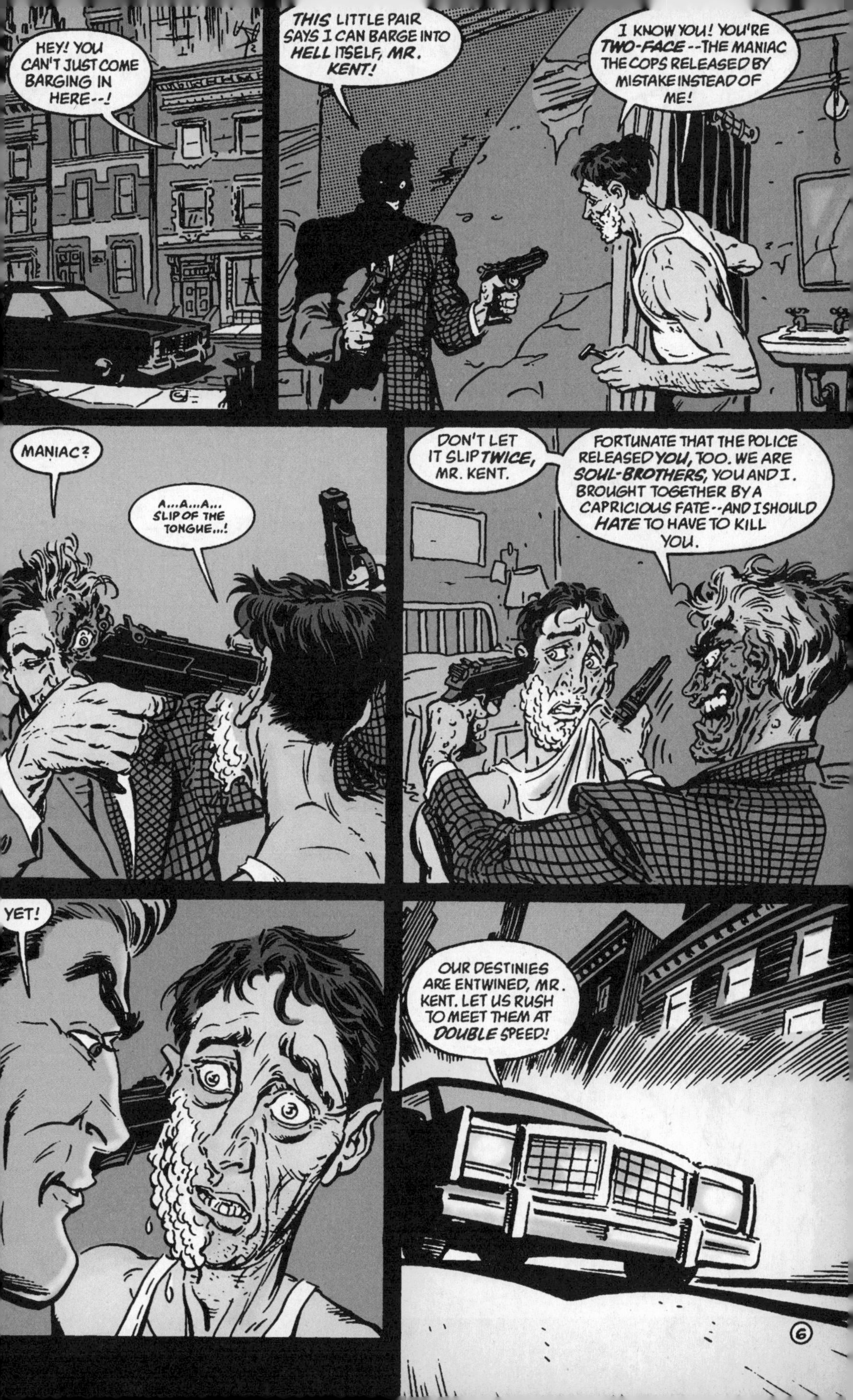
HEY! YOU CAN'T JUST COME BARGING IN HERE--!
THIS LITTLE PAIR SAYS I CAN BARGE INTO HELL ITSELF, MR. KENT!
I KNOW YOU! YOU'RE TWO-FACE--THE MANIAC THE COPS RELEASED BY MISTAKE INSTEAD OF ME!
MANIAC?
A...A...A... SLIP OF THE TONGUE...!
DON'T LET IT SLIP TWICE, MR. KENT.
FORTUNATE THAT THE POLICE RELEASED YOU, TOO. WE ARE SOUL-BROTHERS, YOU AND I. BROUGHT TOGETHER BY A CAPRICIOUS FATE--AND I SHOULD HATE TO HAVE TO KILL YOU.
YET!
OUR DESTINIES ARE ENTWINED, MR. KENT. LET US RUSH TO MEET THEM AT DOUBLE SPEED!
6

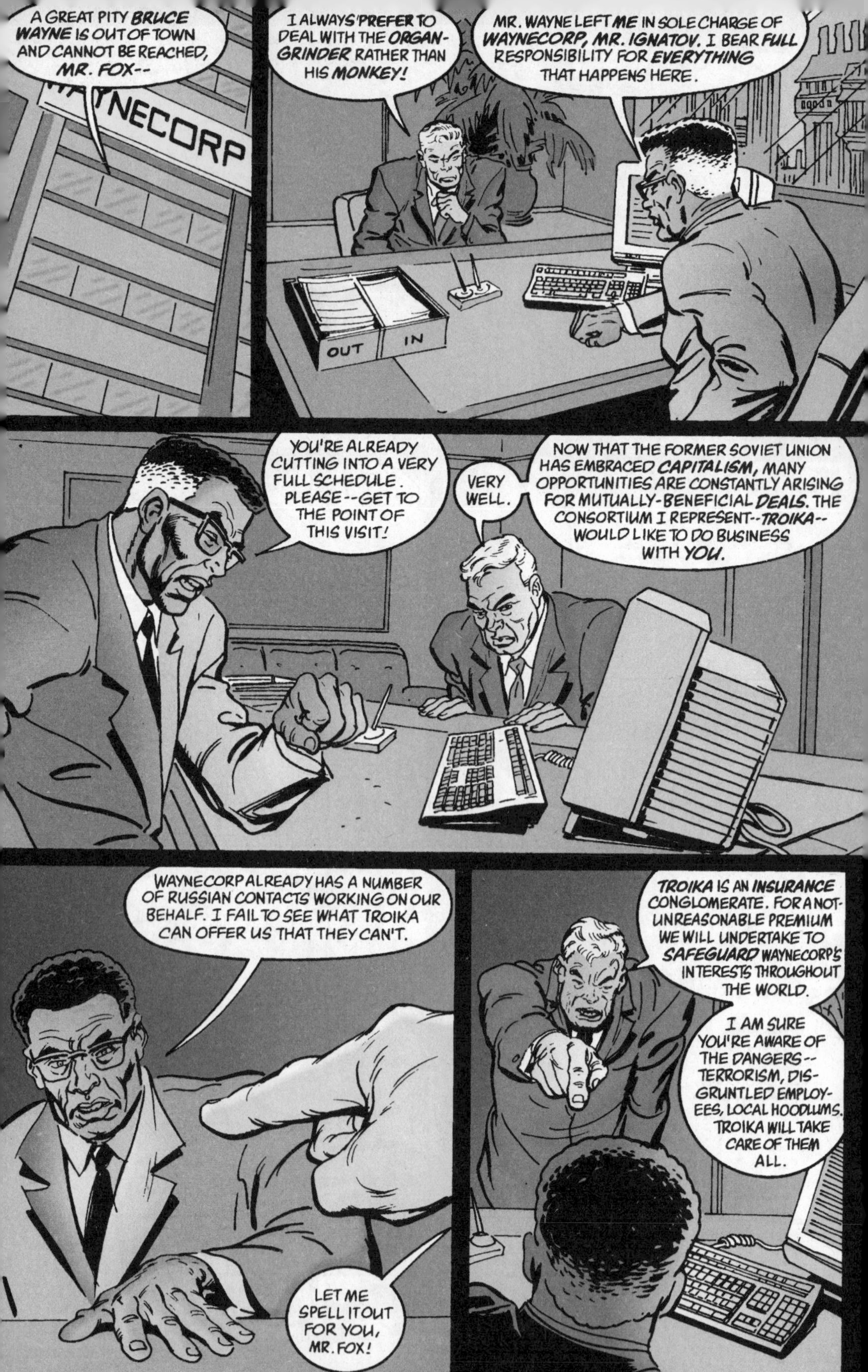

A GREAT PITY BRUCE WAYNE IS OUT OF TOWN AND CANNOT BE REACHED, MR. FOX--
WAYNECORP
I ALWAYS PREFER TO DEAL WITH THE ORGAN-GRINDER RATHER THAN HIS MONKEY!
MR. WAYNE LEFT ME IN SOLE CHARGE OF WAYNECORP, MR. IGNATOV. I BEAR FULL RESPONSIBILITY FOR EVERYTHING THAT HAPPENS HERE.
OUT
IN
YOU'RE ALREADY CUTTING INTO A VERY FULL SCHEDULE. PLEASE--GET TO THE POINT OF THIS VISIT!
VERY WELL.
NOW THAT THE FORMER SOVIET UNION HAS EMBRACED CAPITALISM, MANY OPPORTUNITIES ARE CONSTANTLY ARISING FOR MUTUALLY-BENEFICIAL DEALS. THE CONSORTIUM I REPRESENT--TROIKA--WOULD LIKE TO DO BUSINESS WITH YOU.
WAYNECORP ALREADY HAS A NUMBER OF RUSSIAN CONTACTS WORKING ON OUR BEHALF. I FAIL TO SEE WHAT TROIKA CAN OFFER US THAT THEY CAN'T.
LET ME SPELL IT OUT FOR YOU, MR. FOX!
TROIKA IS AN INSURANCE CONGLOMERATE. FOR A NOT-UNREASONABLE PREMIUM WE WILL UNDERTAKE TO SAFEGUARD WAYNECORP'S INTERESTS THROUGHOUT THE WORLD.
I AM SURE YOU'RE AWARE OF THE DANGERS--TERRORISM, DIS-GRUNTLED EMPLOY-EES, LOCAL HOODLUMS. TROIKA WILL TAKE CARE OF THEM ALL.

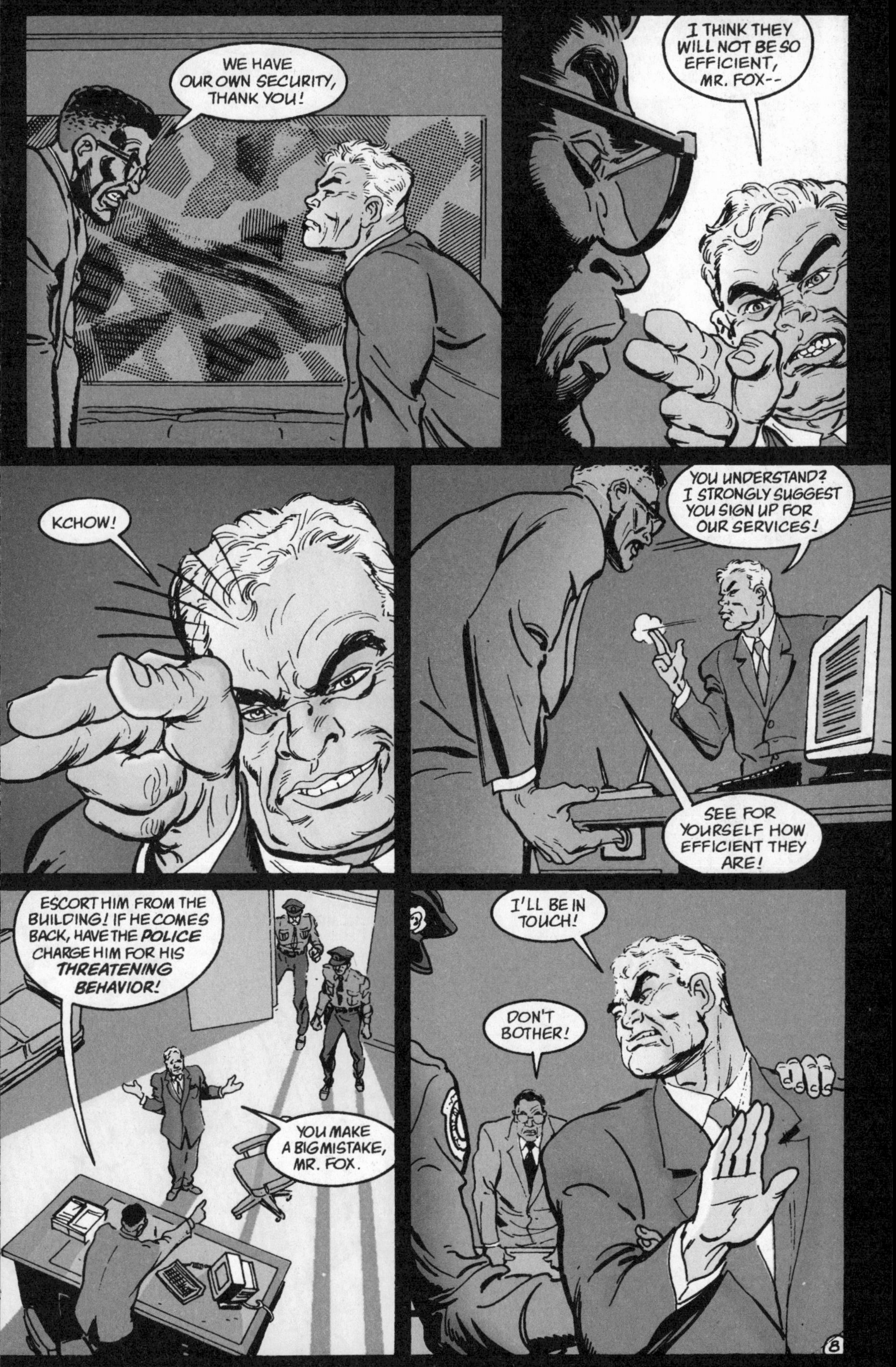
WE HAVE OUR OWN SECURITY, THANK YOU!
I THINK THEY WILL NOT BE SO EFFICIENT, MR. FOX--
KCHOW!
YOU UNDERSTAND? I STRONGLY SUGGEST YOU SIGN UP FOR OUR SERVICES!
SEE FOR YOURSELF HOW EFFICIENT THEY ARE!
ESCORT HIM FROM THE BUILDING! IF HE COMES BACK, HAVE THE POLICE CHARGE HIM FOR HIS THREATENING BEHAVIOR!
YOU MAKE A BIGMISTAKE, MR. FOX.
I'LL BE IN TOUCH!
DON'T BOTHER!
8

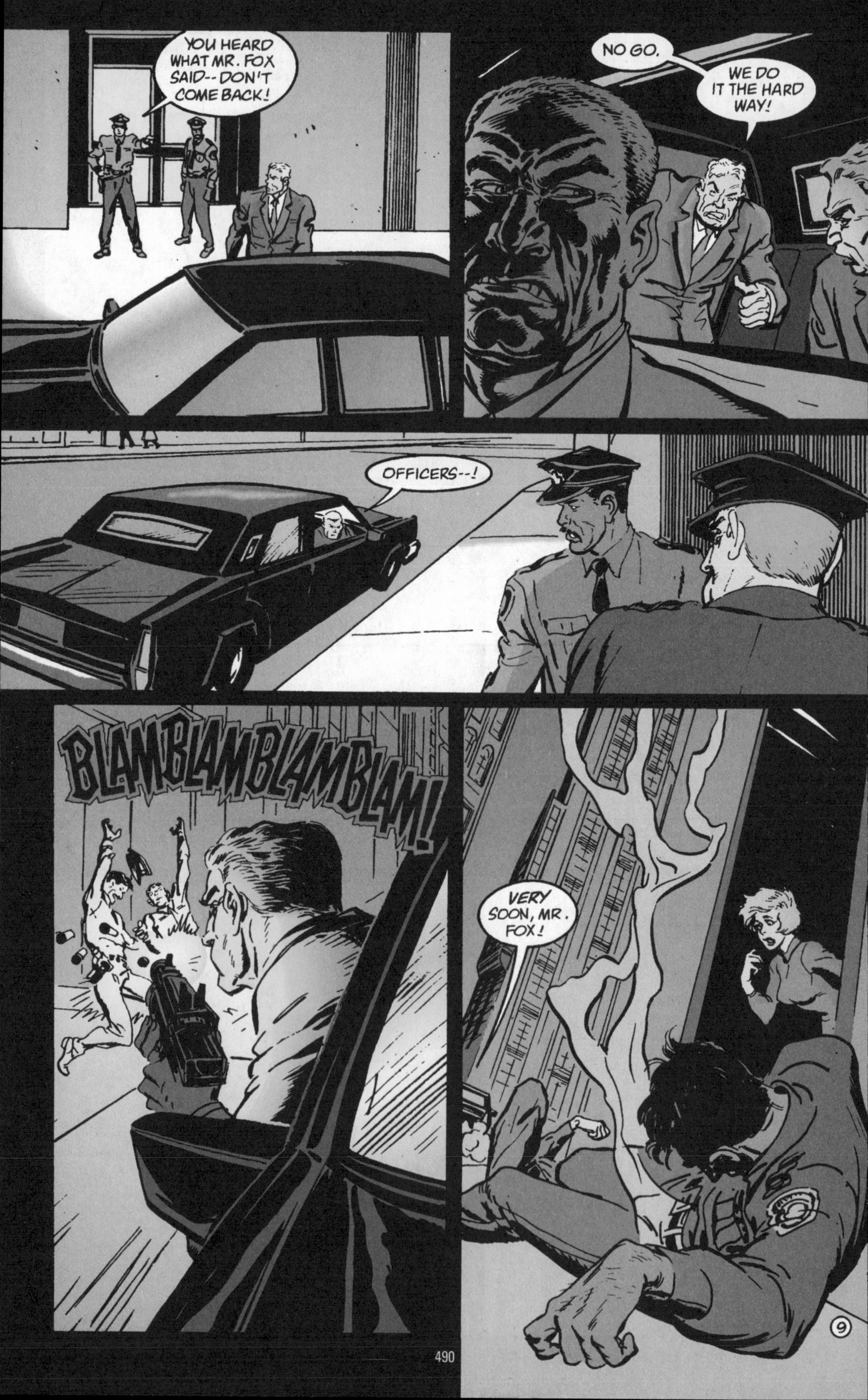
YOU HEARD WHAT MR. FOX SAID--DON'T COME BACK!
NO GO.
WE DO IT THE HARD WAY!
OFFICERS--!
BLAMBLAMBLAMBLAM!
VERY SOON, MR. FOX!
9

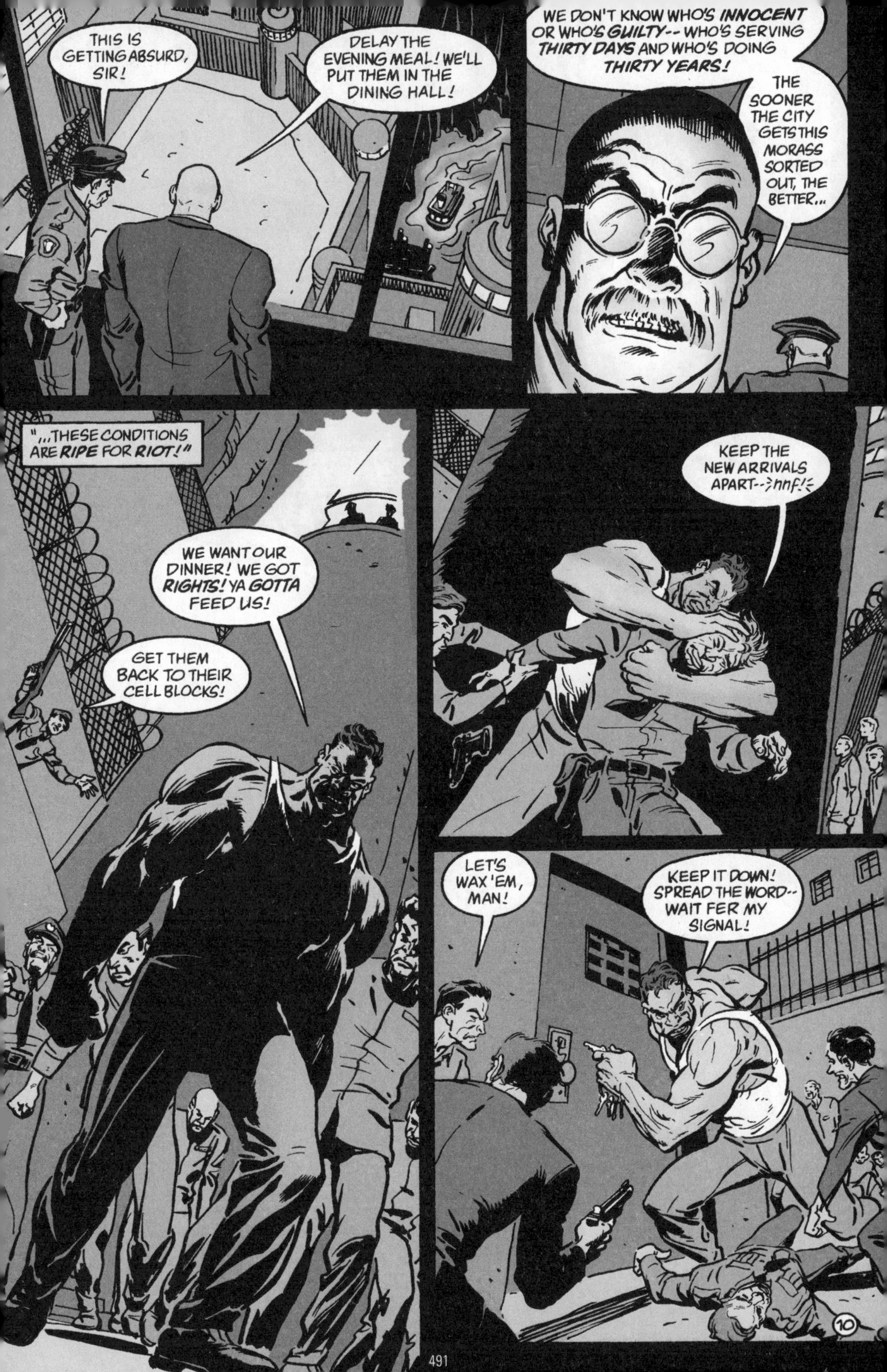
THIS IS GETTING ABSURD, SIR!
DELAY THE EVENING MEAL! WE'LL PUT THEM IN THE DINING HALL!
WE DON'T KNOW WHO'S INNOCENT OR WHO'S GUILTY-- WHO'S SERVING THIRTY DAYS AND WHO'S DOING THIRTY YEARS!
THE SOONER THE CITY GETS THIS MORASS SORTED OUT, THE BETTER...
"...THESE CONDITIONS ARE RIPE FOR RIOT!"
WE WANT OUR DINNER! WE GOT RIGHTS! YA GOTTA FEED US!
GET THEM BACK TO THEIR CELL BLOCKS!
KEEP THE NEW ARRIVALS APART--hnf!
LET'S WAX 'EM, MAN!
KEEP IT DOWN! SPREAD THE WORD-- WAIT FER MY SIGNAL!
10

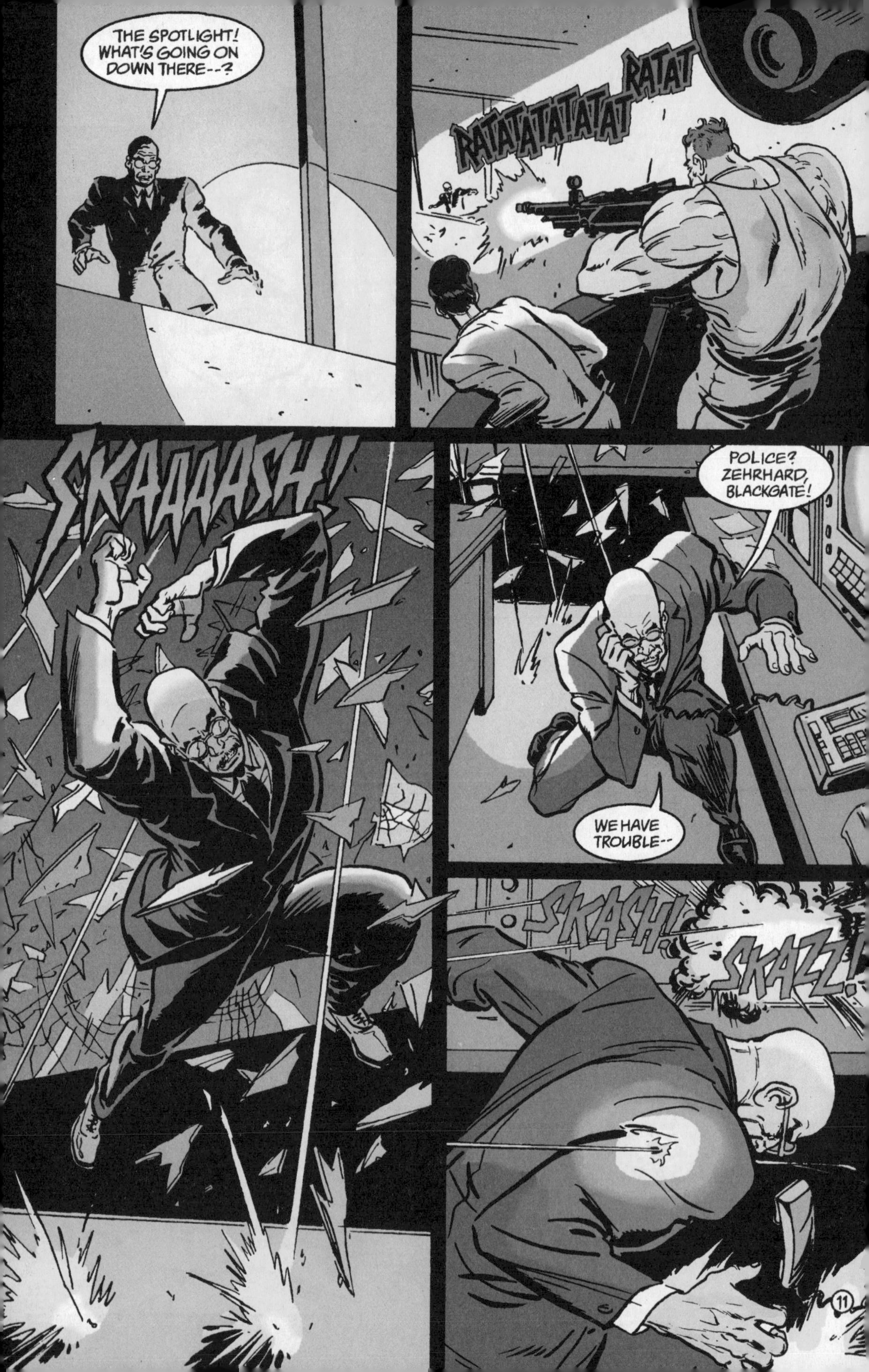
THE SPOTLIGHT! WHAT'S GOING ON DOWN THERE--?
RATATATATATAT RATAT
SKAAAASH!
POLICE? ZEHRHARD, BLACKGATE!
WE HAVE TROUBLE--
SKASH!
SKAZZ!

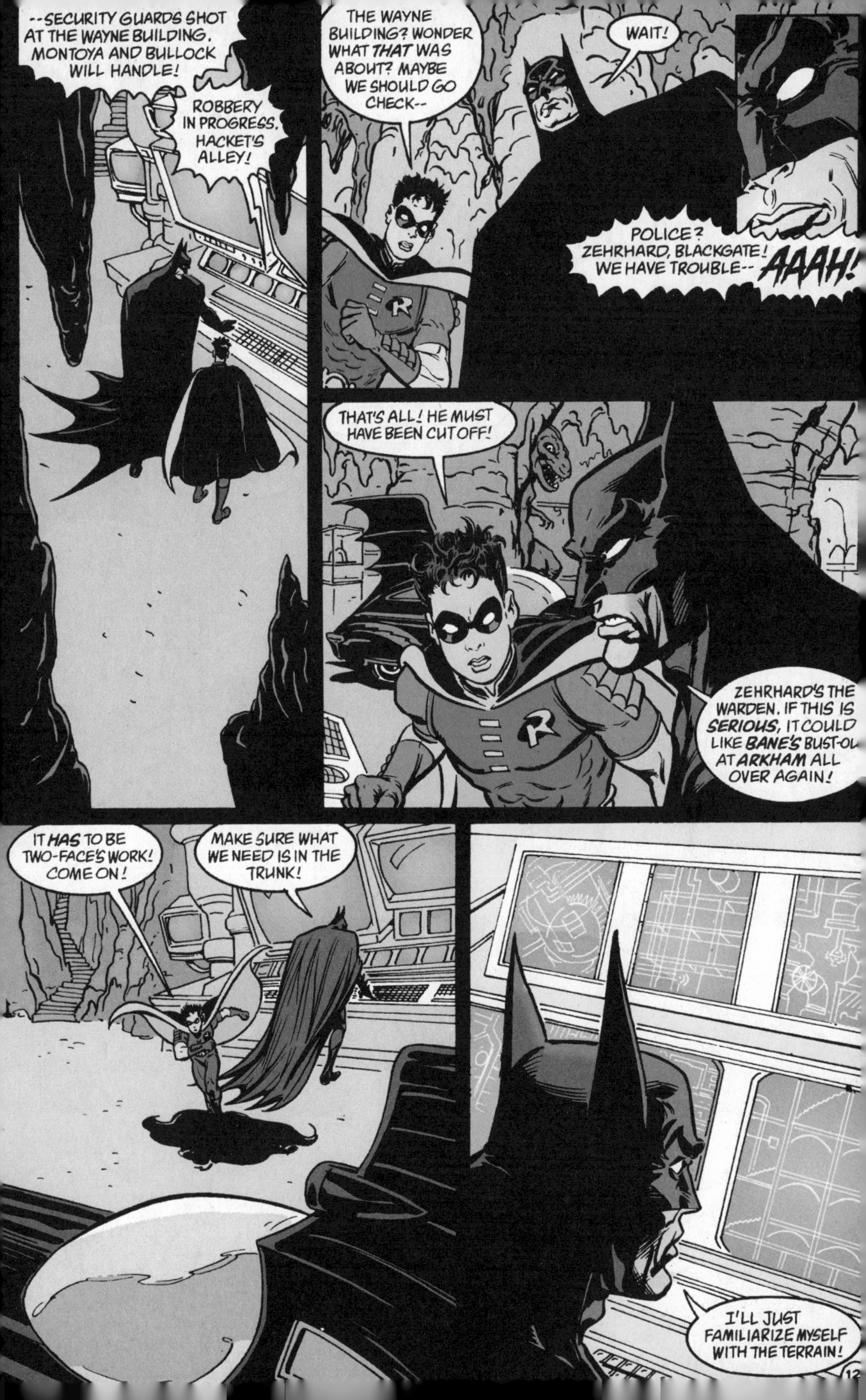
--SECURITY GUARDS SHOT AT THE WAYNE BUILDING. MONTOYA AND BULLOCK WILL HANDLE!
ROBBERY IN PROGRESS. HACKET'S ALLEY!
THE WAYNE BUILDING? WONDER WHAT THAT WAS ABOUT? MAYBE WE SHOULD GO CHECK--
WAIT!
POLICE? ZEHRHARD, BLACKGATE! WE HAVE TROUBLE-- AAAH!
THAT'S ALL! HE MUST HAVE BEEN CUT OFF!
ZEHRHARD'S THE WARDEN. IF THIS IS SERIOUS, IT COULD LIKE BANE'S BUST-OU AT ARKHAM ALL OVER AGAIN!
IT HAS TO BE TWO-FACE'S WORK! COME ON!
MAKE SURE WHAT WE NEED IS IN THE TRUNK!
I'LL JUST FAMILIARIZE MYSELF WITH THE TERRAIN!
12

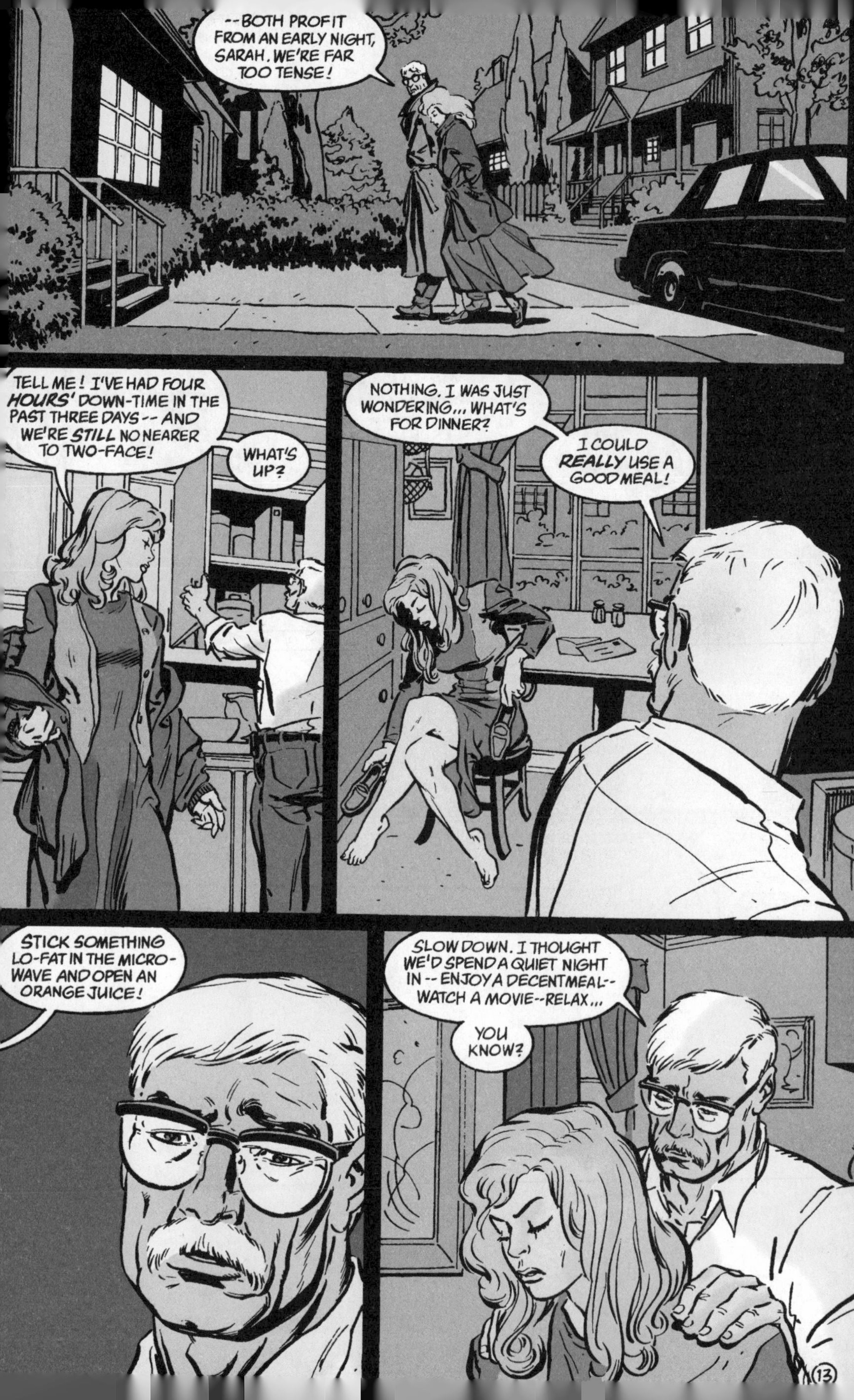

--BOTH PROFIT FROM AN EARLY NIGHT, SARAH. WE'RE FAR TOO TENSE!
TELL ME! I'VE HAD FOUR HOURS' DOWN-TIME IN THE PAST THREE DAYS-- AND WE'RE STILL NO NEARER TO TWO-FACE!
WHAT'S UP?
NOTHING. I WAS JUST WONDERING... WHAT'S FOR DINNER?
I COULD REALLY USE A GOOD MEAL!
STICK SOMETHING LO-FAT IN THE MICRO-WAVE AND OPEN AN ORANGE JUICE!
SLOW DOWN. I THOUGHT WE'D SPEND A QUIET NIGHT IN--ENJOY A DECENT MEAL--WATCH A MOVIE--RELAX...
YOU KNOW?
13

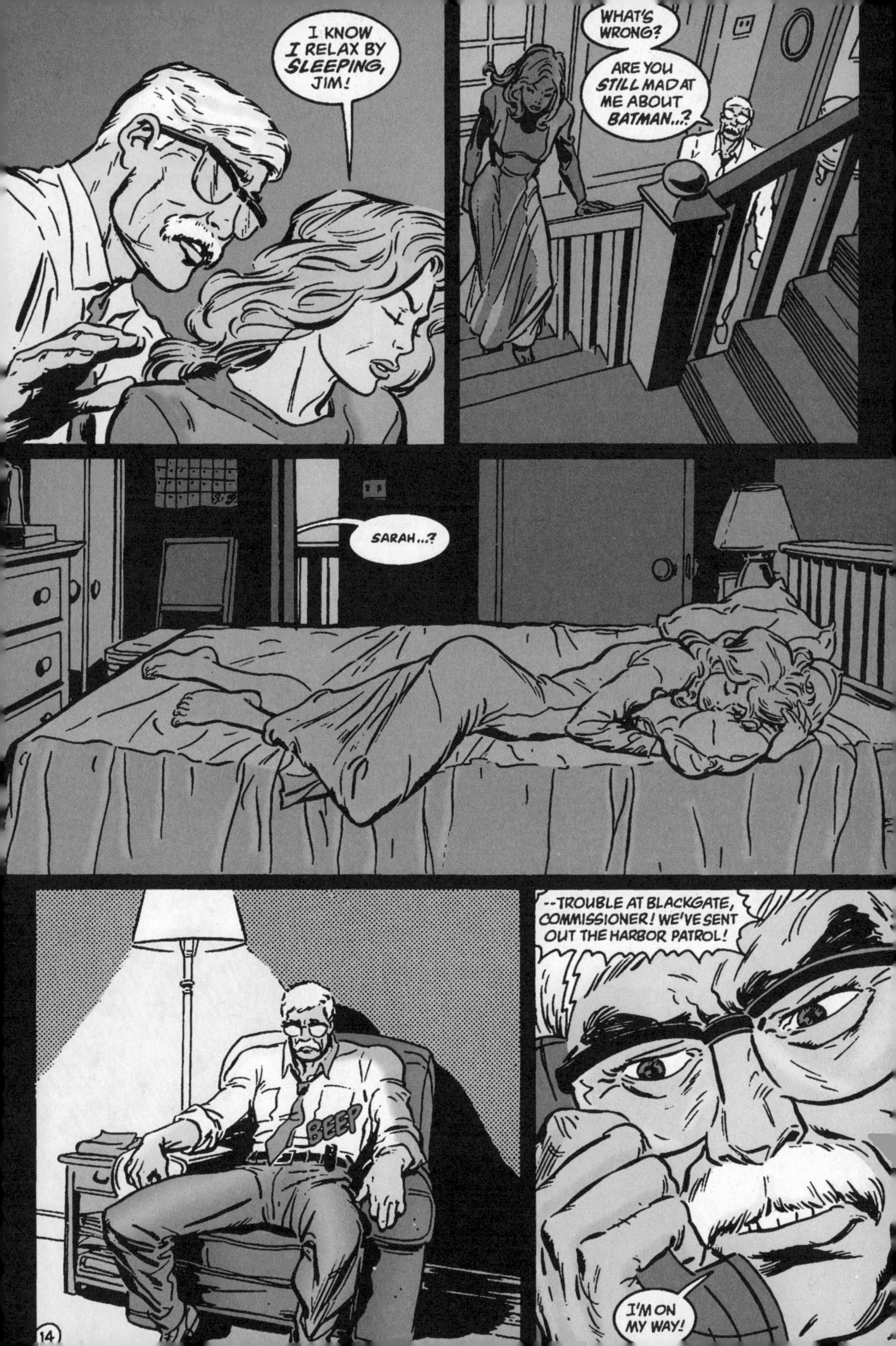
I KNOW I RELAX BY SLEEPING, JIM!
WHAT'S WRONG?
ARE YOU STILL MAD AT ME ABOUT BATMAN...?
SARAH...?
BEEP
--TROUBLE AT BLACKGATE, COMMISSIONER! WE'VE SENT OUT THE HARBOR PATROL!
I'M ON MY WAY!
14

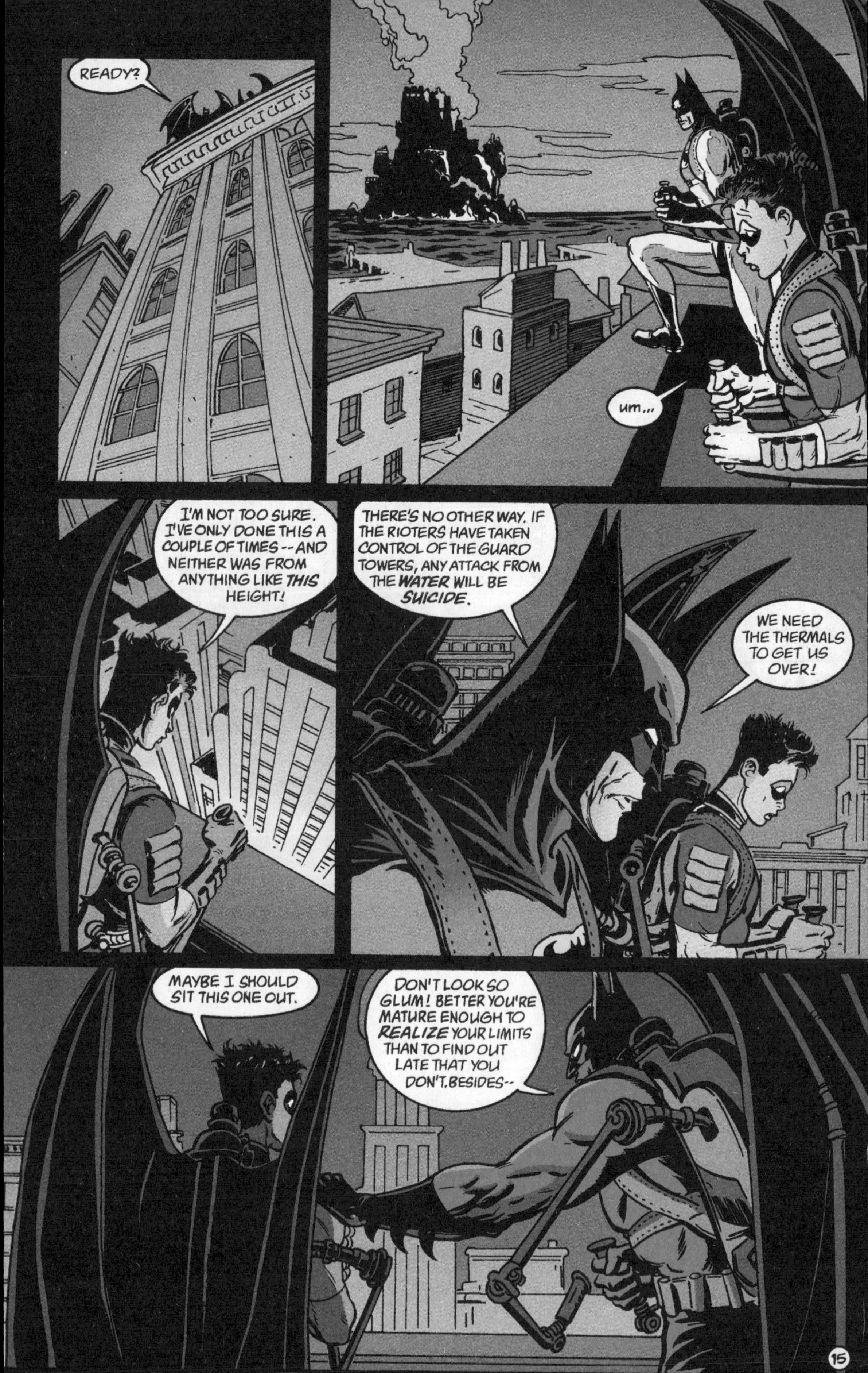
READY?
um...
I'M NOT TOO SURE. I'VE ONLY DONE THIS A COUPLE OF TIMES -- AND NEITHER WAS FROM ANYTHING LIKE THIS HEIGHT!
THERE'S NO OTHER WAY. IF THE RIOTERS HAVE TAKEN CONTROL OF THE GUARD TOWERS, ANY ATTACK FROM THE WATER WILL BE SUICIDE.
WE NEED THE THERMALS TO GET US OVER!
MAYBE I SHOULD SIT THIS ONE OUT.
DON'T LOOK SO GLUM! BETTER YOU'RE MATURE ENOUGH TO REALIZE YOUR LIMITS THAN TO FIND OUT LATE THAT YOU DON'T. BESIDES--
15

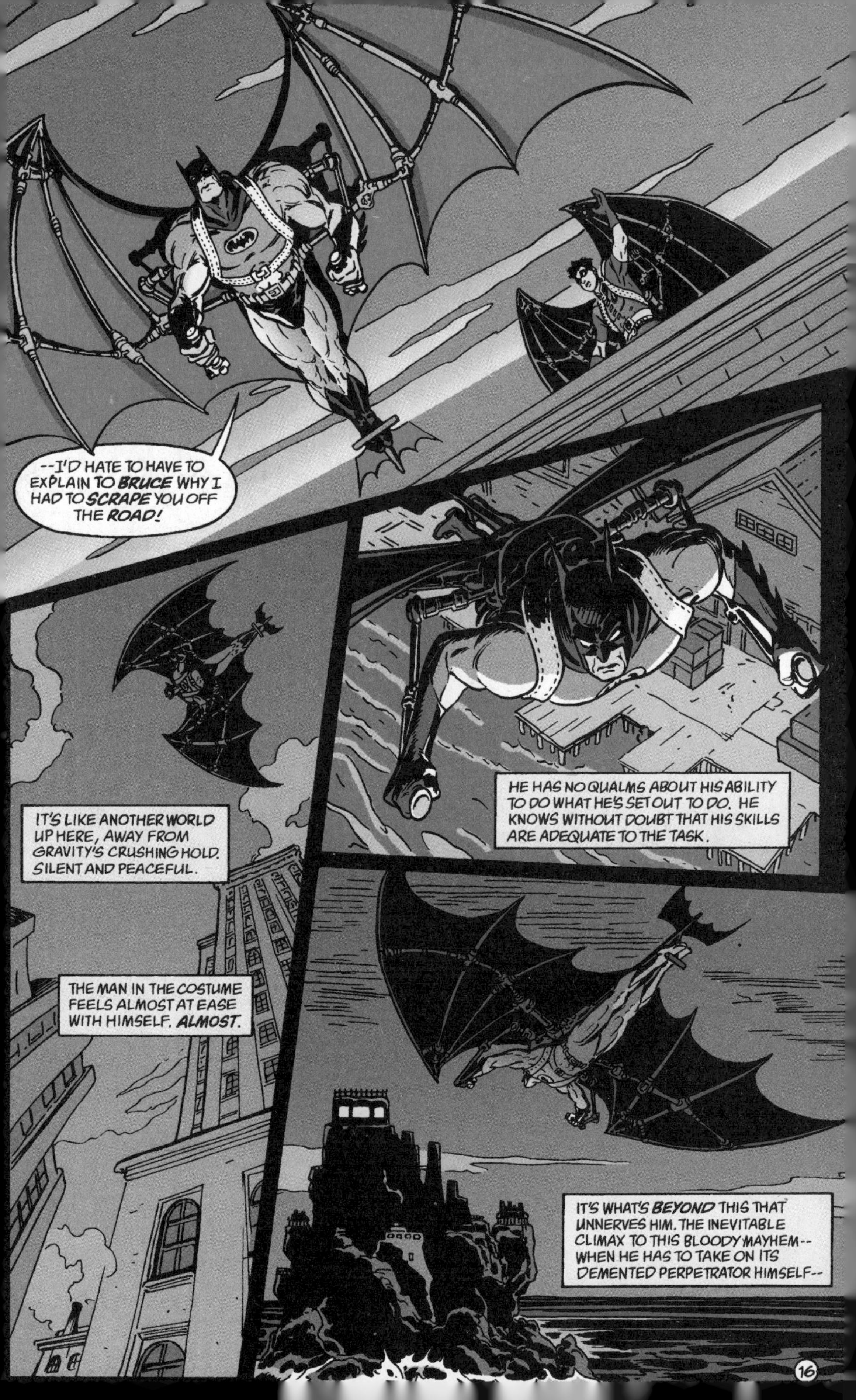
--I'D HATE TO HAVE TO EXPLAIN TO BRUCE WHY I HAD TO SCRAPE YOU OFF THE ROAD!
IT'S LIKE ANOTHER WORLD UP HERE, AWAY FROM GRAVITY'S CRUSHING HOLD. SILENT AND PEACEFUL.
THE MAN IN THE COSTUME FEELS ALMOST AT EASE WITH HIMSELF. ALMOST.
HE HAS NO QUALMS ABOUT HIS ABILITY TO DO WHAT HE'S SET OUT TO DO. HE KNOWS WITHOUT DOUBT THAT HIS SKILLS ARE ADEQUATE TO THE TASK.
IT'S WHAT'S BEYOND THIS THAT UNNERVES HIM. THE INEVITABLE CLIMAX TO THIS BLOODY MAYHEM-- WHEN HE HAS TO TAKE ON ITS DEMENTED PERPETRATOR HIMSELF--
16

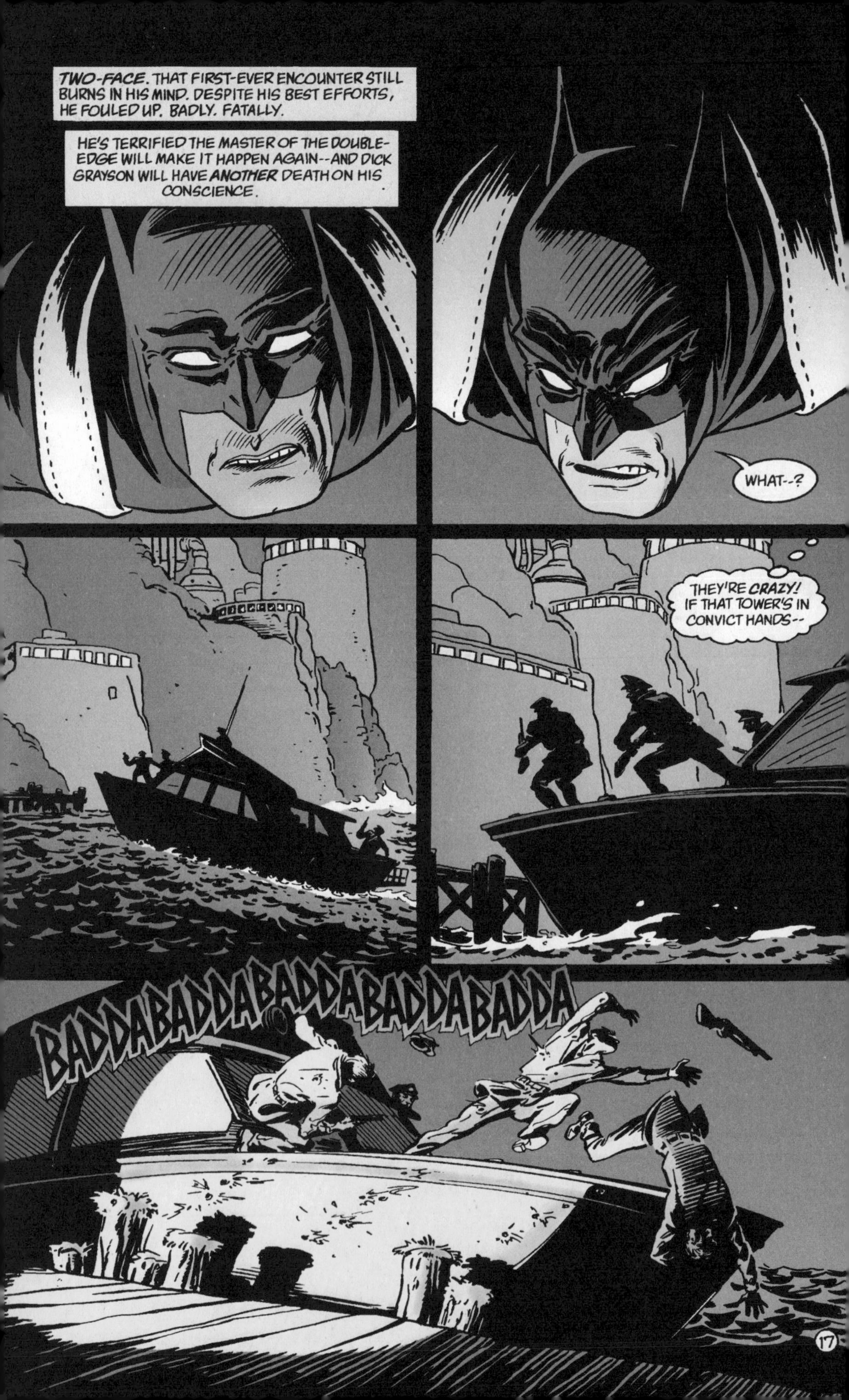

TWO-FACE. THAT FIRST-EVER ENCOUNTER STILL BURNS IN HIS MIND. DESPITE HIS BEST EFFORTS, HE FOULED UP. BADLY. FATALLY.
HE'S TERRIFIED THE MASTER OF THE DOUBLE-EDGE WILL MAKE IT HAPPEN AGAIN--AND DICK GRAYSON WILL HAVE ANOTHER DEATH ON HIS CONSCIENCE.
WHAT--?
THEY'RE CRAZY! IF THAT TOWER'S IN CONVICT HANDS--
BADDABADDABADDABADDABADDA

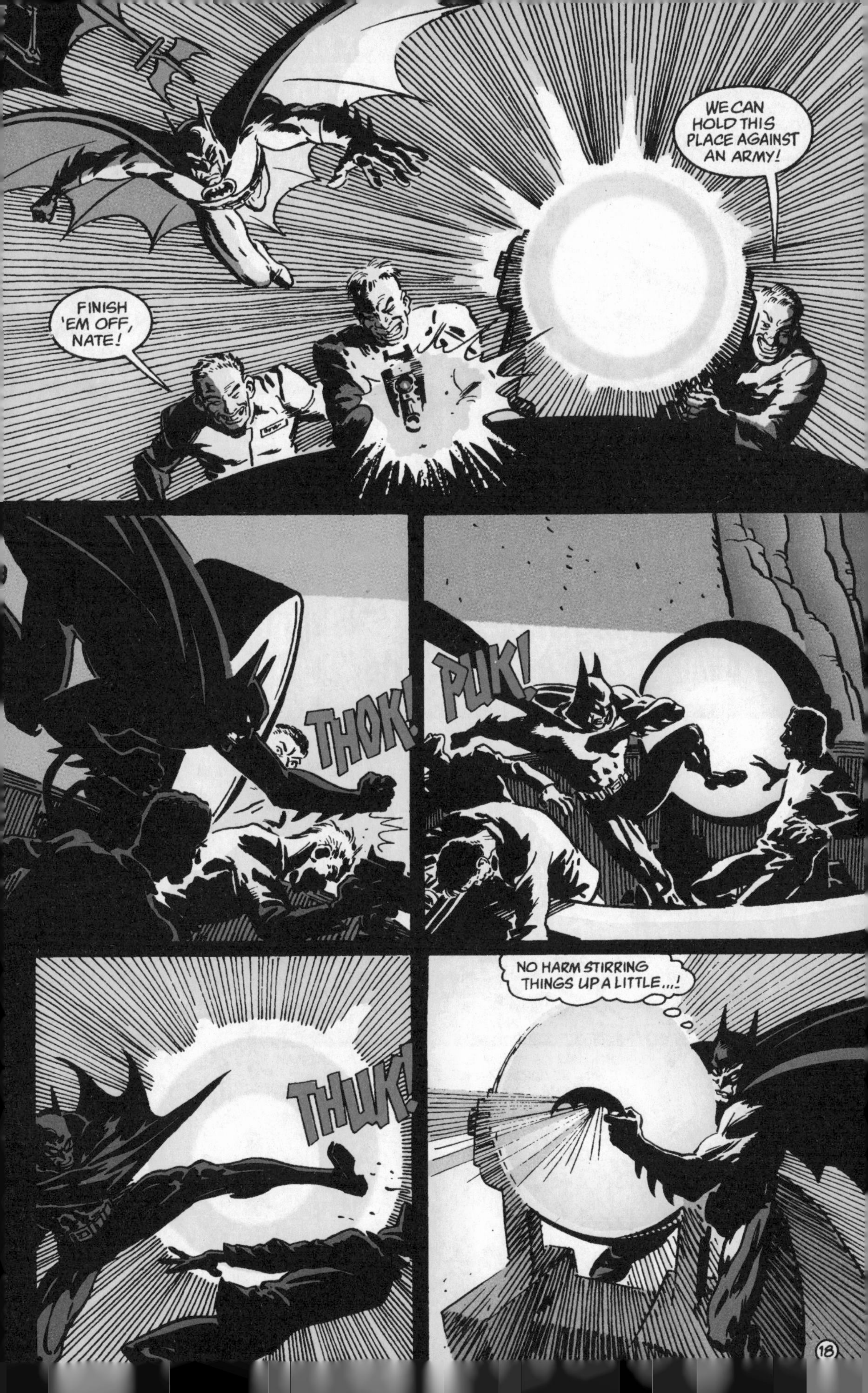
WE CAN HOLD THIS PLACE AGAINST AN ARMY!
FINISH 'EM OFF, NATE!
THOK!
PUK!
THUK!
NO HARM STIRRING THINGS UP A LITTLE...!

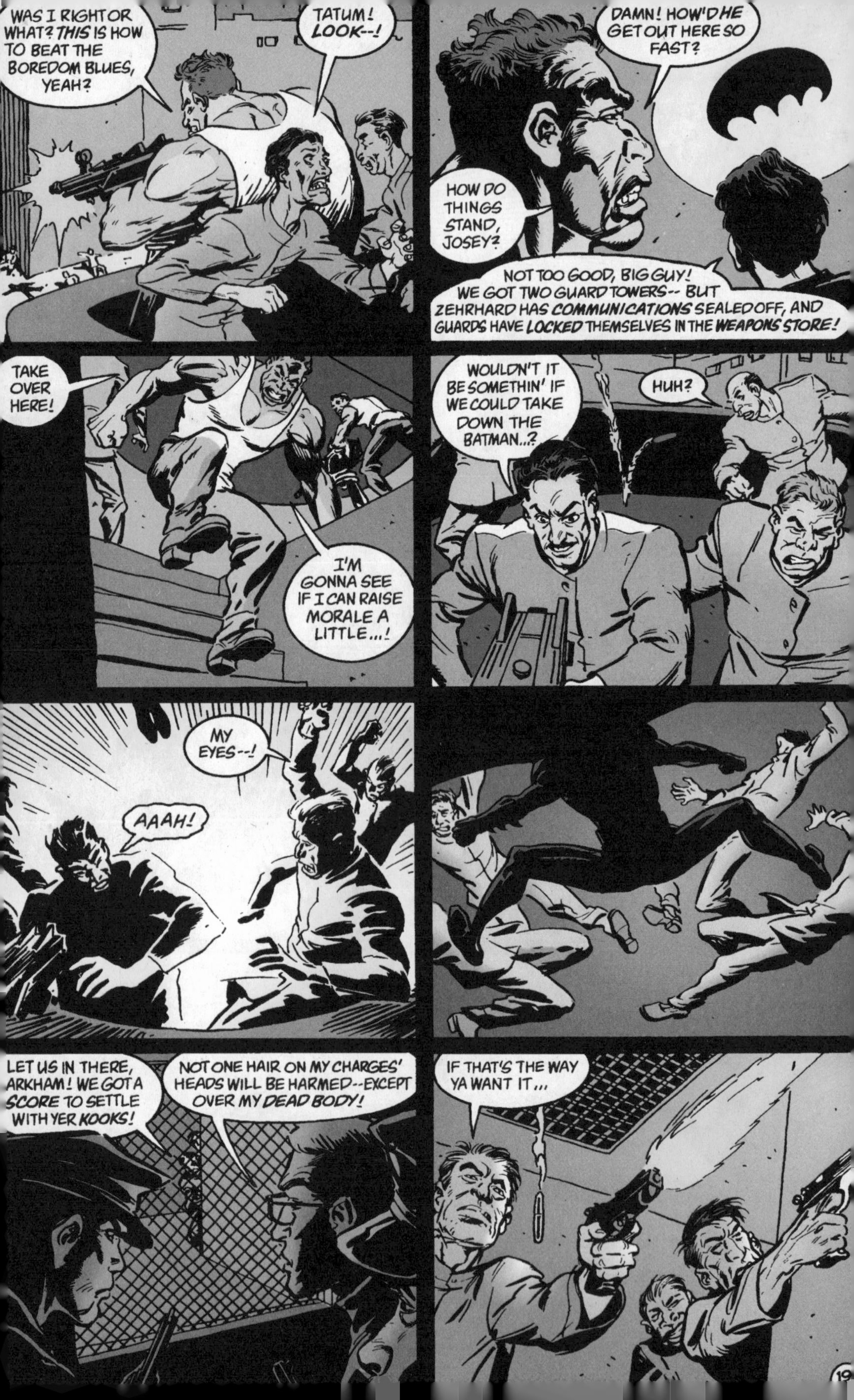

WAS I RIGHT OR WHAT? THIS IS HOW TO BEAT THE BOREDOM BLUES, YEAH?
TATUM! LOOK--!
DAMN! HOW'D HE GET OUT HERE SO FAST?
HOW DO THINGS STAND, JOSEY?
NOT TOO GOOD, BIG GUY! WE GOT TWO GUARD TOWERS-- BUT ZEHRHARD HAS COMMUNICATIONS SEALED OFF, AND GUARDS HAVE LOCKED THEMSELVES IN THE WEAPONS STORE!
TAKE OVER HERE!
I'M GONNA SEE IF I CAN RAISE MORALE A LITTLE...!
WOULDN'T IT BE SOMETHIN' IF WE COULD TAKE DOWN THE BATMAN...?
HUH?
MY EYES--!
AAAH!
LET US IN THERE, ARKHAM! WE GOT A SCORE TO SETTLE WITH YER KOOKS!
NOT ONE HAIR ON MY CHARGES' HEADS WILL BE HARMED--EXCEPT OVER MY DEAD BODY!
IF THAT'S THE WAY YA WANT IT...

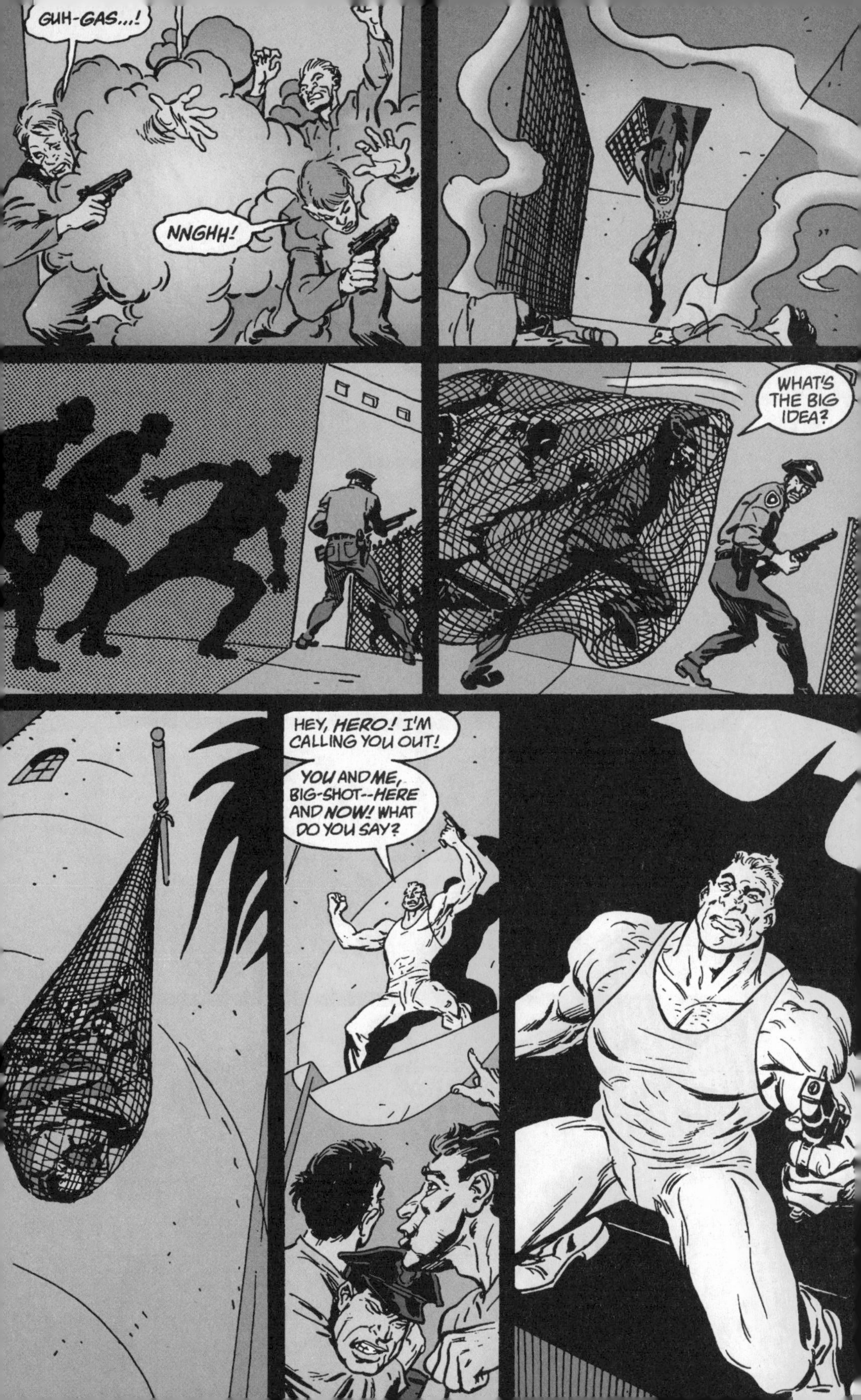
GUH-GAS...!
NNGHH!
WHAT'S THE BIG IDEA?
HEY, HERO! I'M CALLING YOU OUT!
YOU AND ME, BIG-SHOT--HERE AND NOW! WHAT DO YOU SAY?

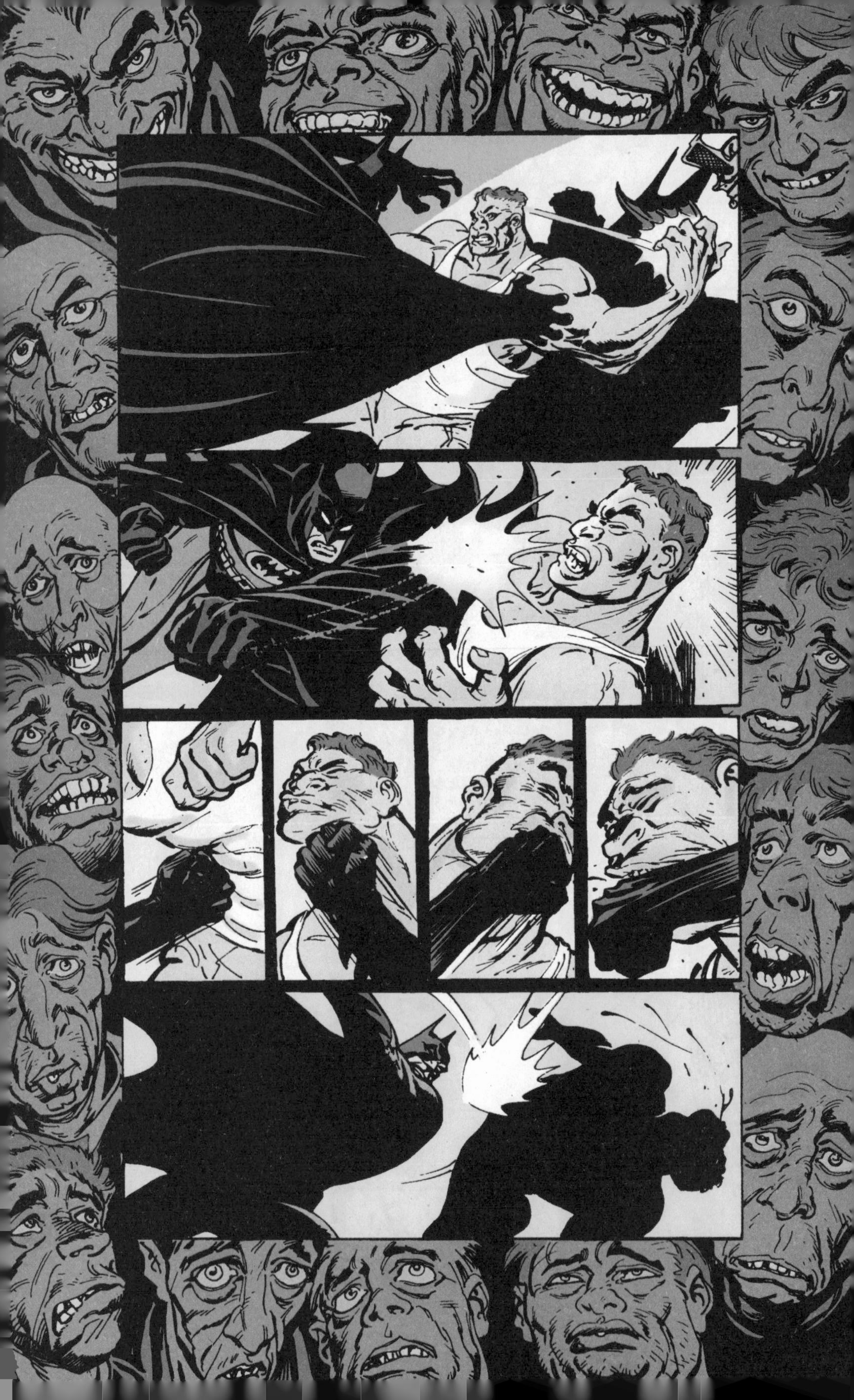

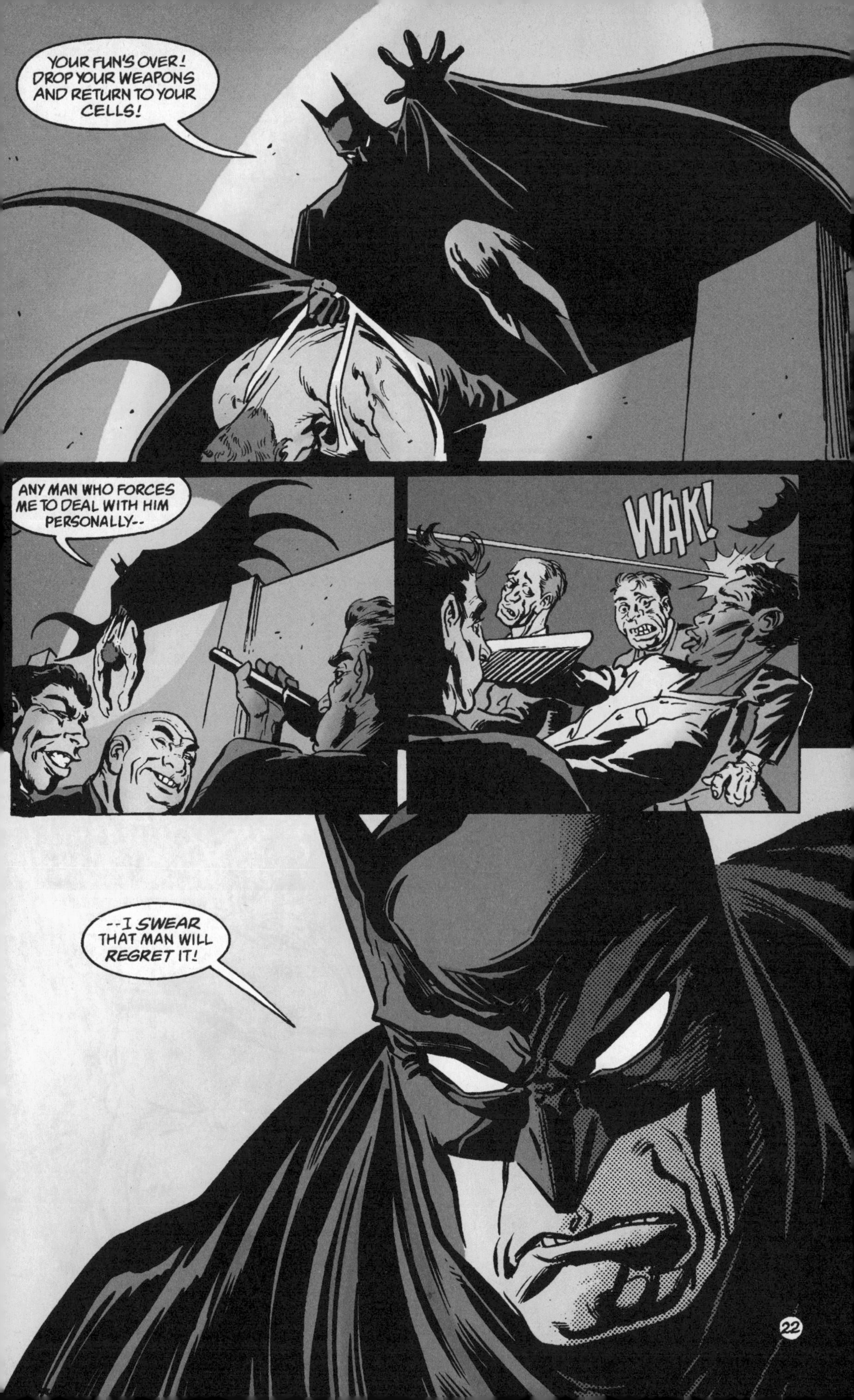
YOUR FUN'S OVER! DROP YOUR WEAPONS AND RETURN TO YOUR CELLS!
ANY MAN WHO FORCES ME TO DEAL WITH HIM PERSONALLY--
WAK!
--I SWEAR THAT MAN WILL REGRET IT!

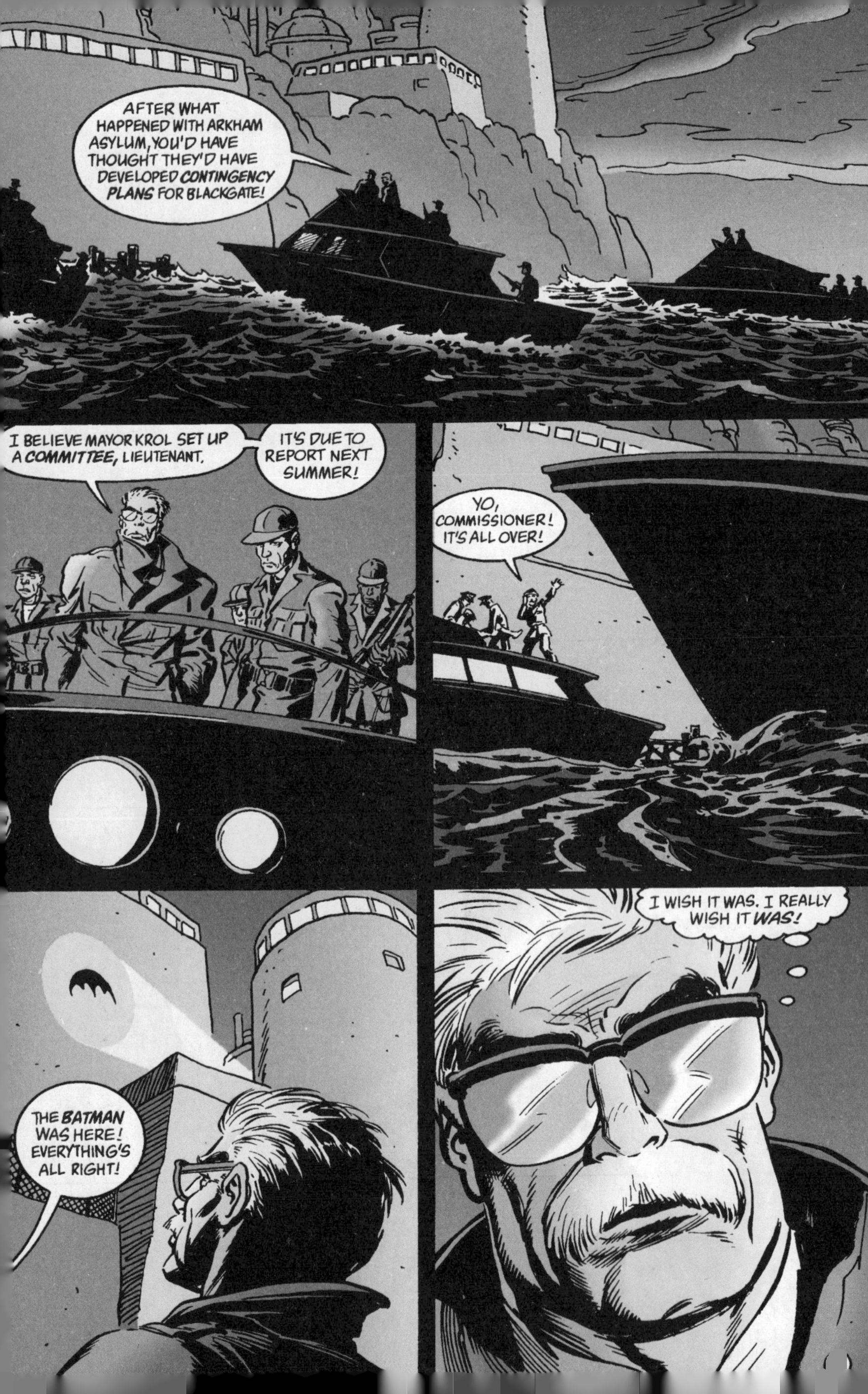
AFTER WHAT HAPPENED WITH ARKHAM ASYLUM, YOU'D HAVE THOUGHT THEY'D HAVE DEVELOPED CONTINGENCY PLANS FOR BLACKGATE!
I BELIEVE MAYOR KROL SET UP A COMMITTEE, LIEUTENANT.
IT'S DUE TO REPORT NEXT SUMMER!
YO, COMMISSIONER! IT'S ALL OVER!
THE BATMAN WAS HERE! EVERYTHING'S ALL RIGHT!
I WISH IT WAS. I REALLY WISH IT WAS!

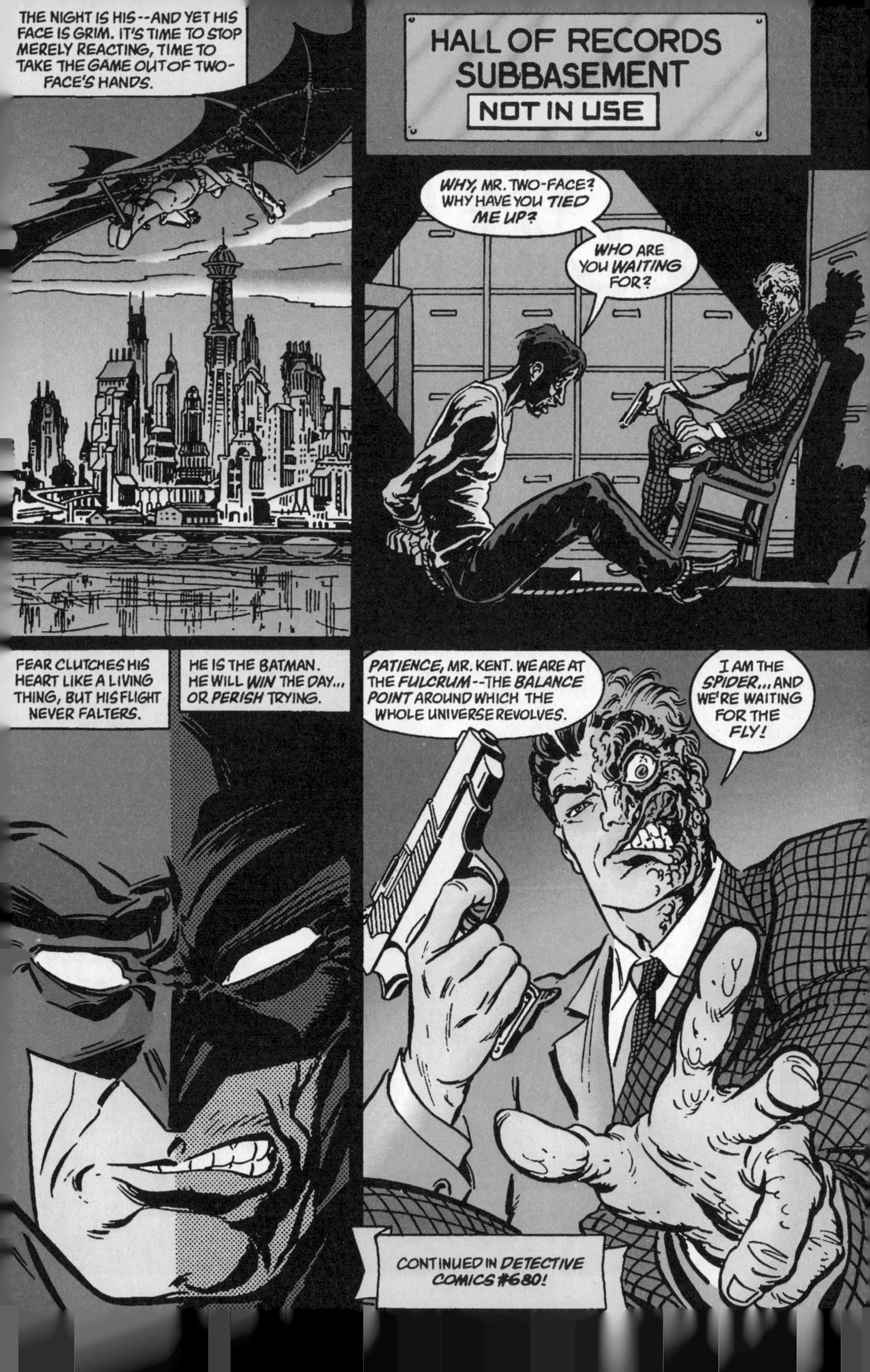
THE NIGHT IS HIS--AND YET HIS FACE IS GRIM. IT'S TIME TO STOP MERELY REACTING, TIME TO TAKE THE GAME OUT OF TWO-FACE'S HANDS.
HALL OF RECORDS SUBBASEMENT
NOT IN USE
WHY, MR. TWO-FACE? WHY HAVE YOU TIED ME UP?
WHO ARE YOU WAITING FOR?
FEAR CLUTCHES HIS HEART LIKE A LIVING THING, BUT HIS FLIGHT NEVER FALTERS.
HE IS THE BATMAN. HE WILL WIN THE DAY... OR PERISH TRYING.
PATIENCE, MR. KENT. WE ARE AT THE FULCRUM--THE BALANCE POINT AROUND WHICH THE WHOLE UNIVERSE REVOLVES.
I AM THE SPIDER... AND WE'RE WAITING FOR THE FLY!
CONTINUED IN DETECTIVE COMICS #680!

Cover art by LEE WEEKS

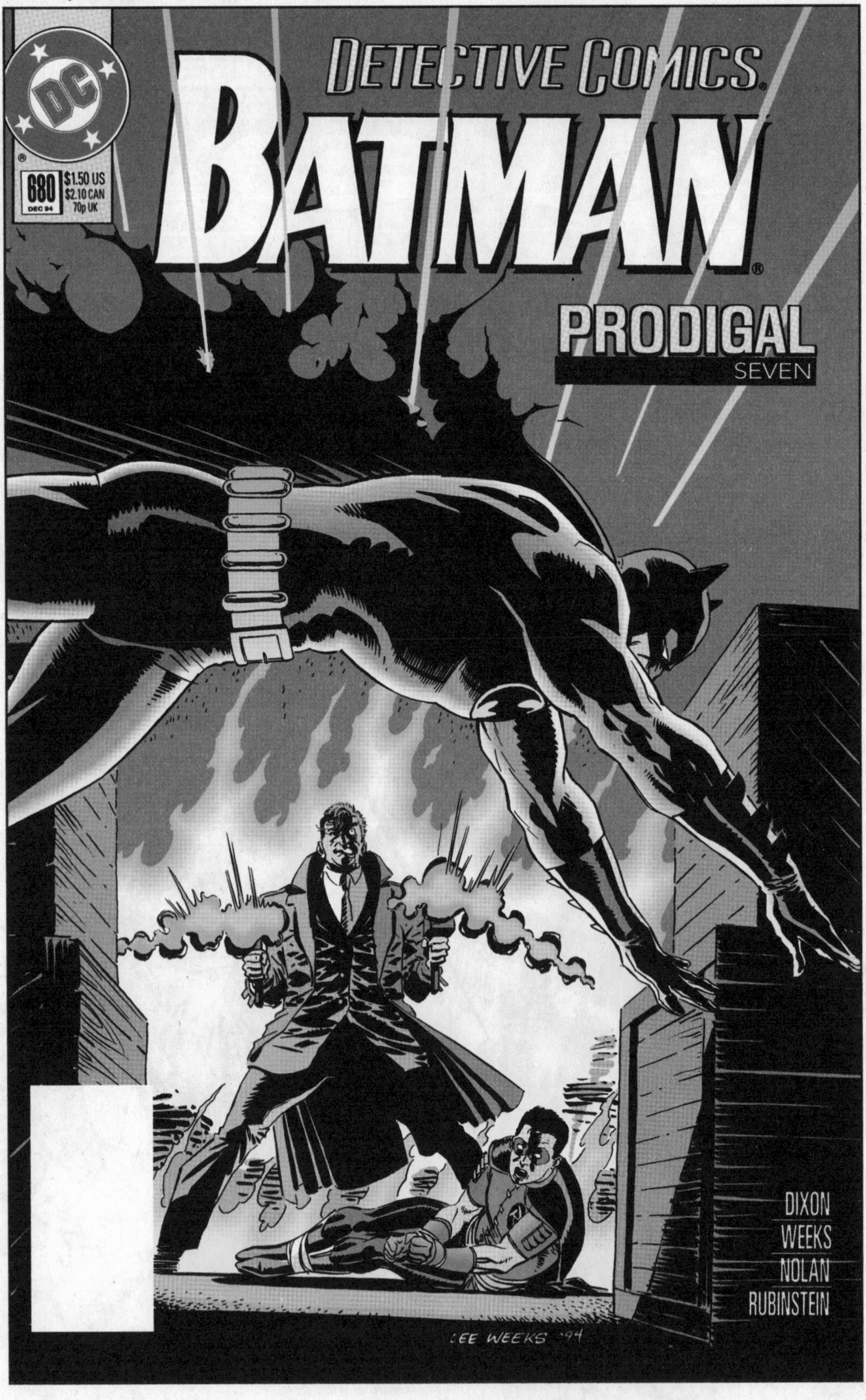

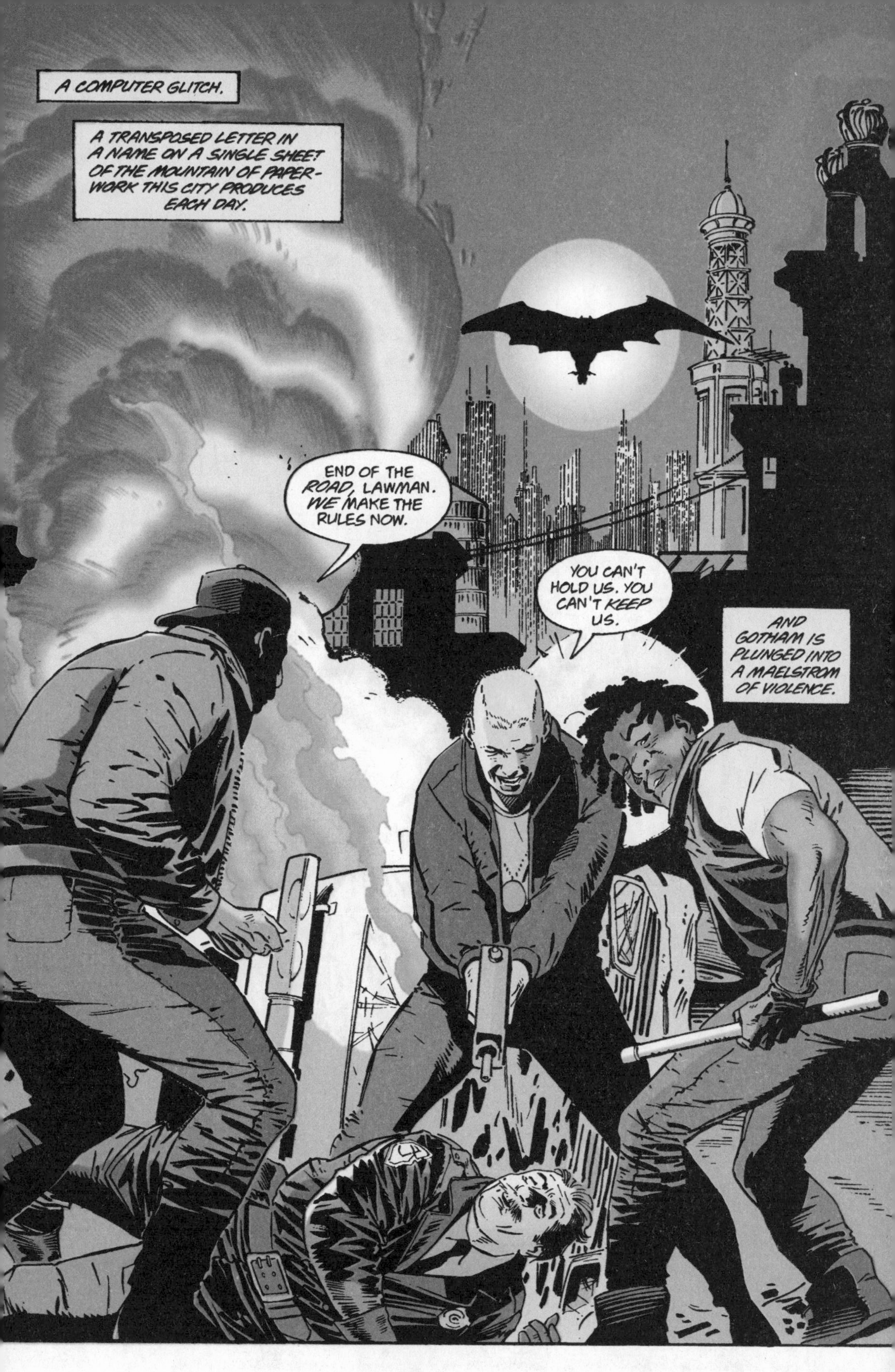
A COMPUTER GLITCH.
A TRANSPOSED LETTER IN A NAME ON A SINGLE SHEET OF THE MOUNTAIN OF PAPER-WORK THIS CITY PRODUCES EACH DAY.
END OF THE ROAD, LAWMAN. WE MAKE THE RULES NOW.
YOU CAN'T HOLD US. YOU CAN'T KEEP US.
AND GOTHAM IS PLUNGED INTO A MAELSTROM OF VIOLENCE.

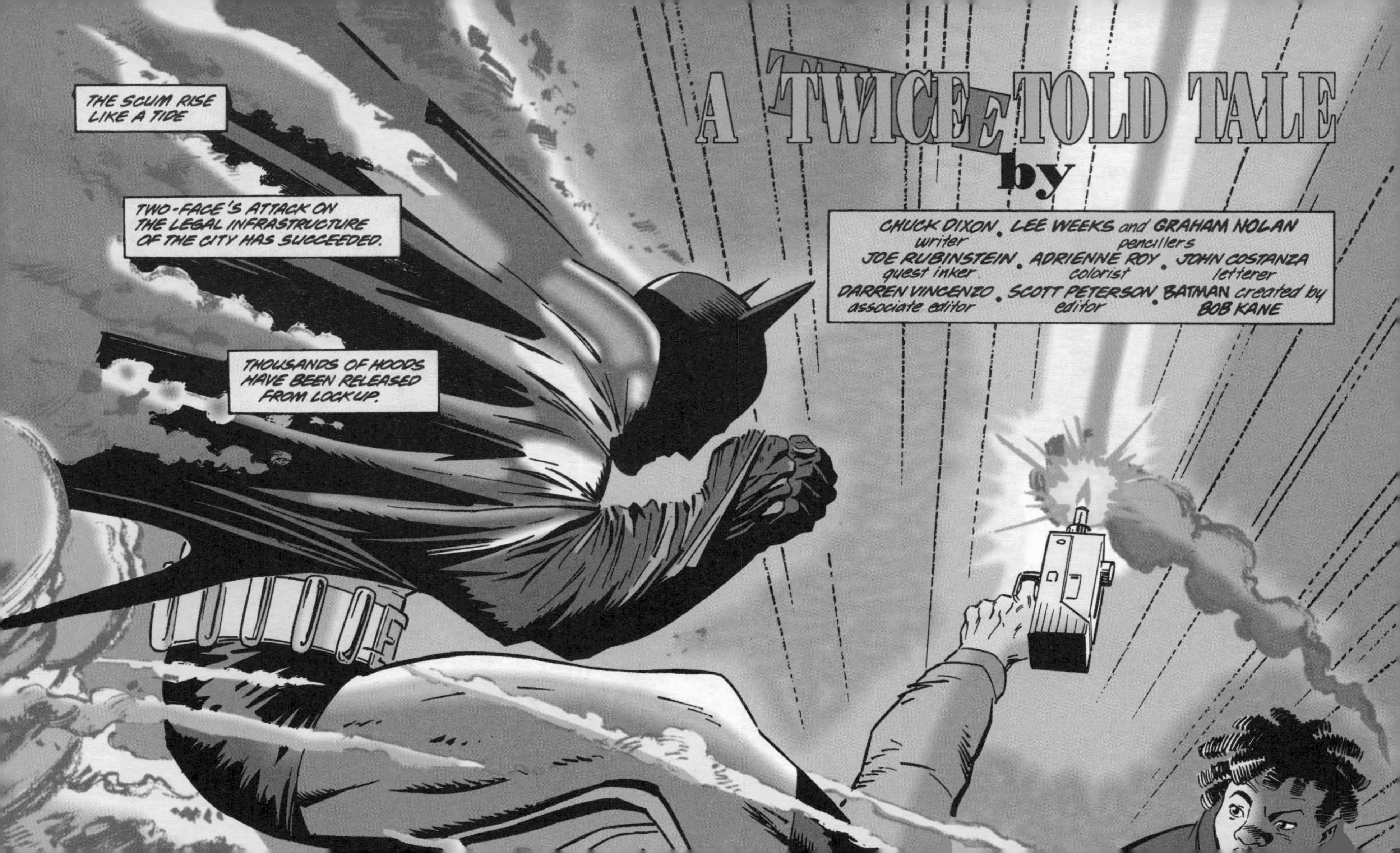
THE SCUM RISE LIKE A TIDE
TWO-FACE'S ATTACK ON THE LEGAL INFRASTRUCTURE OF THE CITY HAS SUCCEEDED.
THOUSANDS OF HOODS HAVE BEEN RELEASED FROM LOCKUP.
A TWICE TOLD TALE
by
CHUCK DIXON writer • LEE WEEKS and GRAHAM NOLAN pencillers
JOE RUBINSTEIN guest inker • ADRIENNE ROY colorist • JOHN COSTANZA letterer
DARREN VINCENZO associate editor • SCOTT PETERSON editor • BATMAN created by BOB KANE

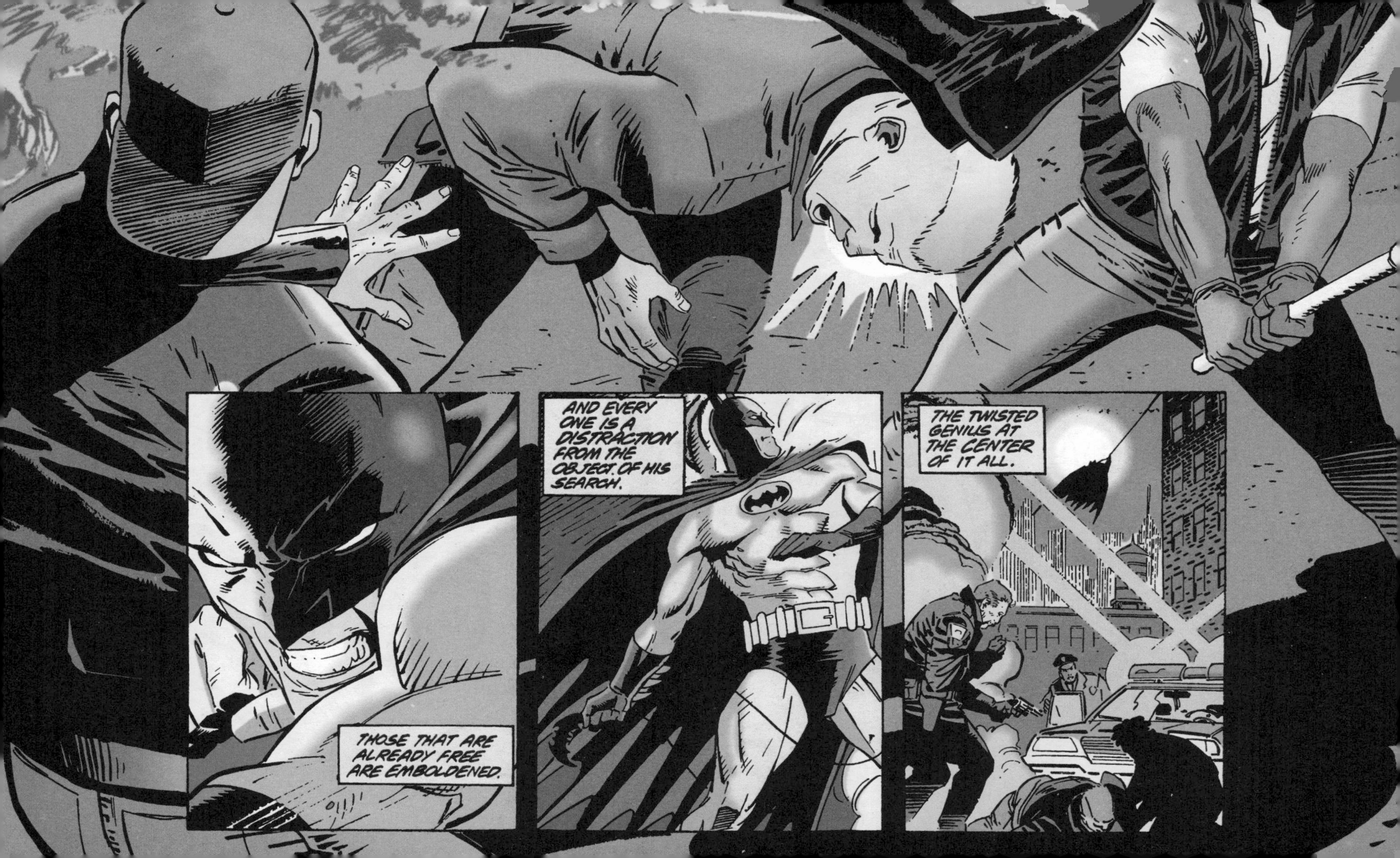
THOSE THAT ARE ALREADY FREE ARE EMBOLDENED.
AND EVERY ONE IS A DISTRACTION FROM THE OBJECT OF HIS SEARCH.
THE TWISTED GENIUS AT THE CENTER OF IT ALL.

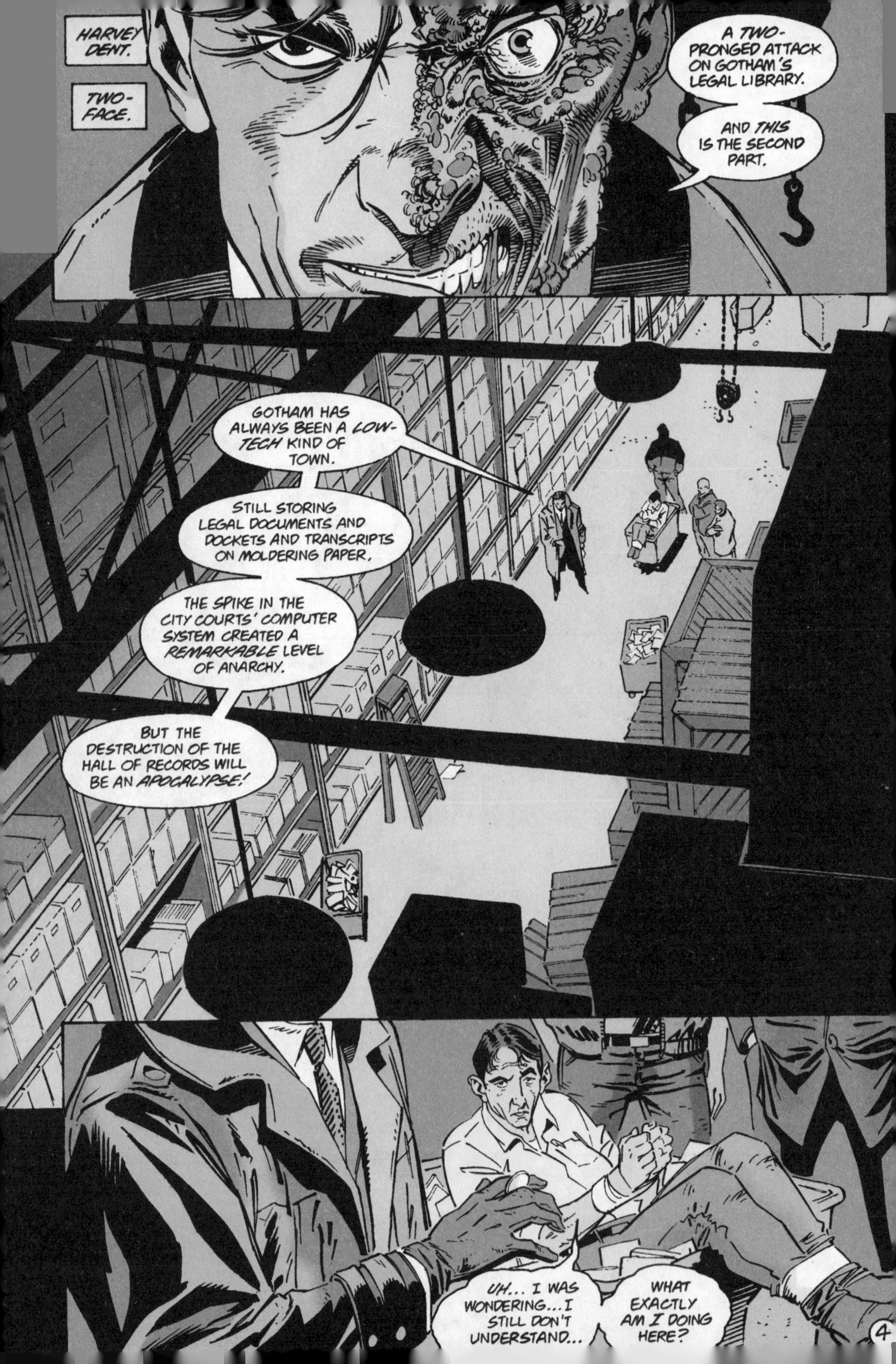
HARVEY DENT.
TWO-FACE.
A TWO-PRONGED ATTACK ON GOTHAM'S LEGAL LIBRARY.
AND THIS IS THE SECOND PART.
GOTHAM HAS ALWAYS BEEN A LOW-TECH KIND OF TOWN.
STILL STORING LEGAL DOCUMENTS AND DOCKETS AND TRANSCRIPTS ON MOLDERING PAPER.
THE SPIKE IN THE CITY COURTS' COMPUTER SYSTEM CREATED A REMARKABLE LEVEL OF ANARCHY.
BUT THE DESTRUCTION OF THE HALL OF RECORDS WILL BE AN APOCALYPSE!
UH... I WAS WONDERING... I STILL DON'T UNDERSTAND...
WHAT EXACTLY AM I DOING HERE?
4

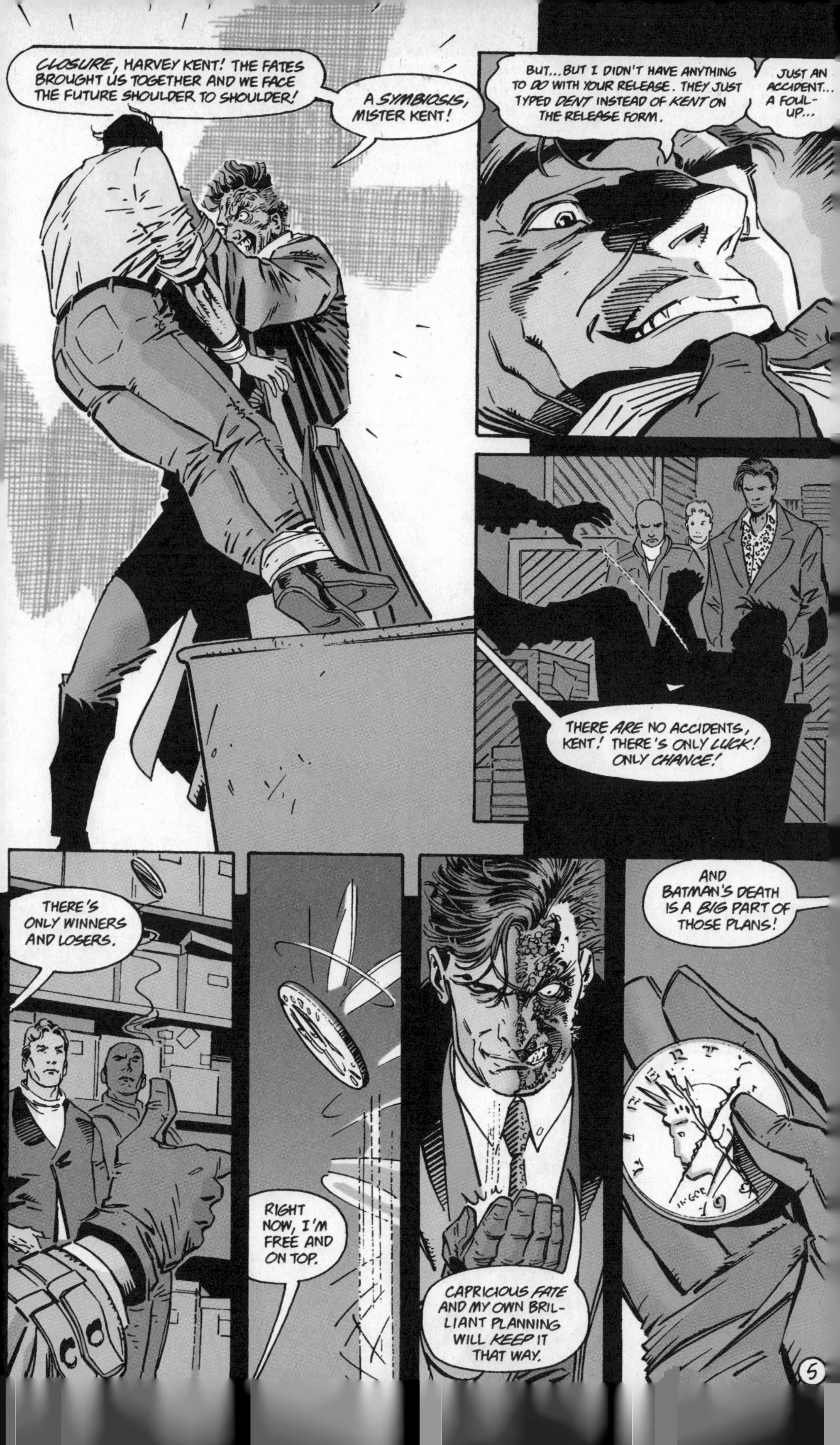
CLOSURE, HARVEY KENT! THE FATES BROUGHT US TOGETHER AND WE FACE THE FUTURE SHOULDER TO SHOULDER!
A SYMBIOSIS, MISTER KENT!
BUT... BUT I DIDN'T HAVE ANYTHING TO DO WITH YOUR RELEASE. THEY JUST TYPED DENT INSTEAD OF KENT ON THE RELEASE FORM.
JUST AN ACCIDENT... A FOUL-UP...
THERE ARE NO ACCIDENTS, KENT! THERE'S ONLY LUCK! ONLY CHANCE!
THERE'S ONLY WINNERS AND LOSERS.
RIGHT NOW, I'M FREE AND ON TOP.
CAPRICIOUS FATE AND MY OWN BRILLIANT PLANNING WILL KEEP IT THAT WAY.
AND BATMAN'S DEATH IS A BIG PART OF THOSE PLANS!

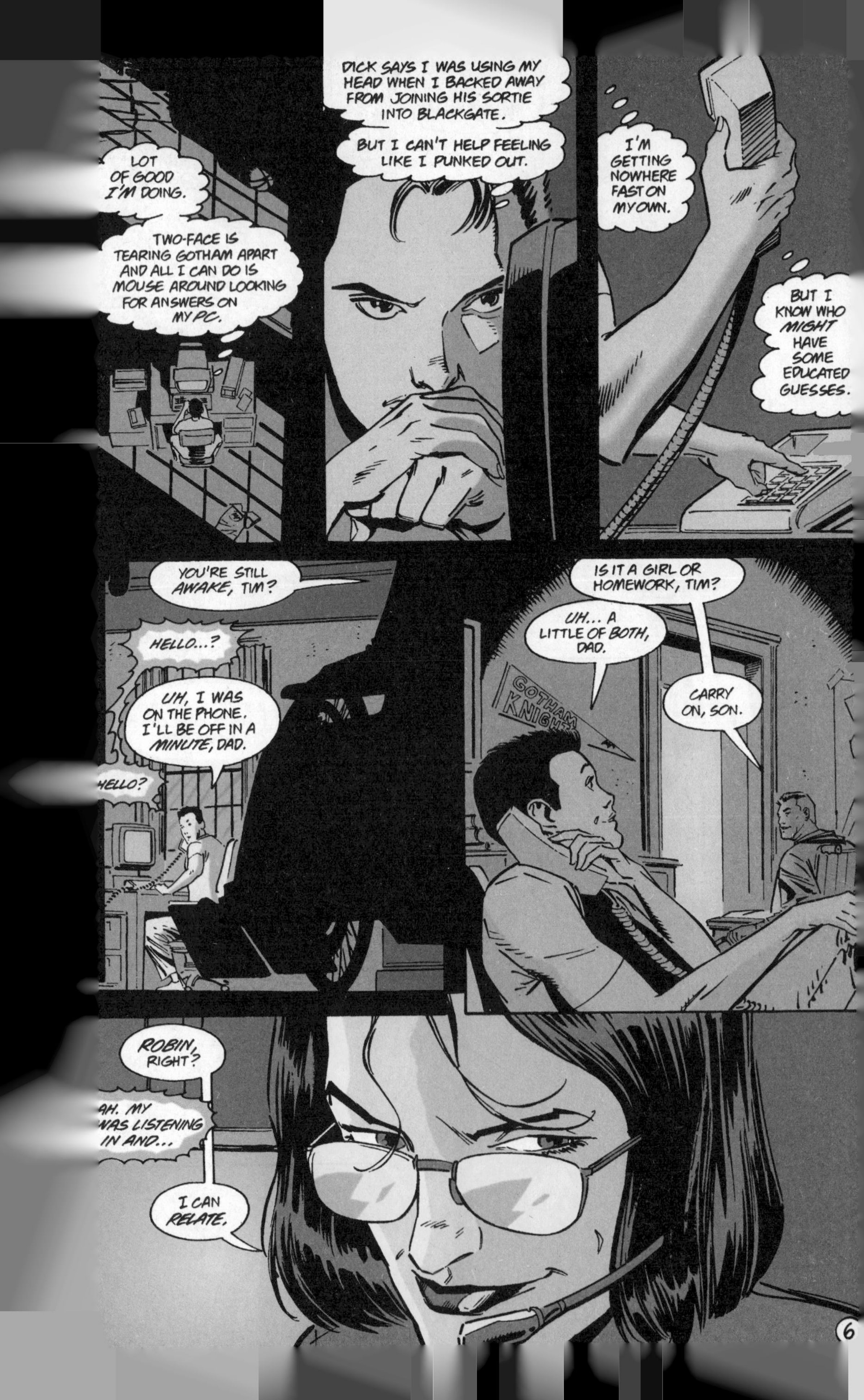

LOT OF GOOD I'M DOING.
TWO-FACE IS TEARING GOTHAM APART AND ALL I CAN DO IS MOUSE AROUND LOOKING FOR ANSWERS ON MY PC.
DICK SAYS I WAS USING MY HEAD WHEN I BACKED AWAY FROM JOINING HIS SORTIE INTO BLACKGATE.
BUT I CAN'T HELP FEELING LIKE I PUNKED OUT.
I'M GETTING NOWHERE FAST ON MY OWN.
BUT I KNOW WHO MIGHT HAVE SOME EDUCATED GUESSES.
YOU'RE STILL AWAKE, TIM?
HELLO...?
UH, I WAS ON THE PHONE. I'LL BE OFF IN A MINUTE, DAD.
HELLO?
IS IT A GIRL OR HOMEWORK, TIM?
UH... A LITTLE OF BOTH, DAD.
GOTHAM KNIGHTS
CARRY ON, SON.
ROBIN, RIGHT?
AH. MY WAS LISTENING IN AND...
I CAN RELATE.

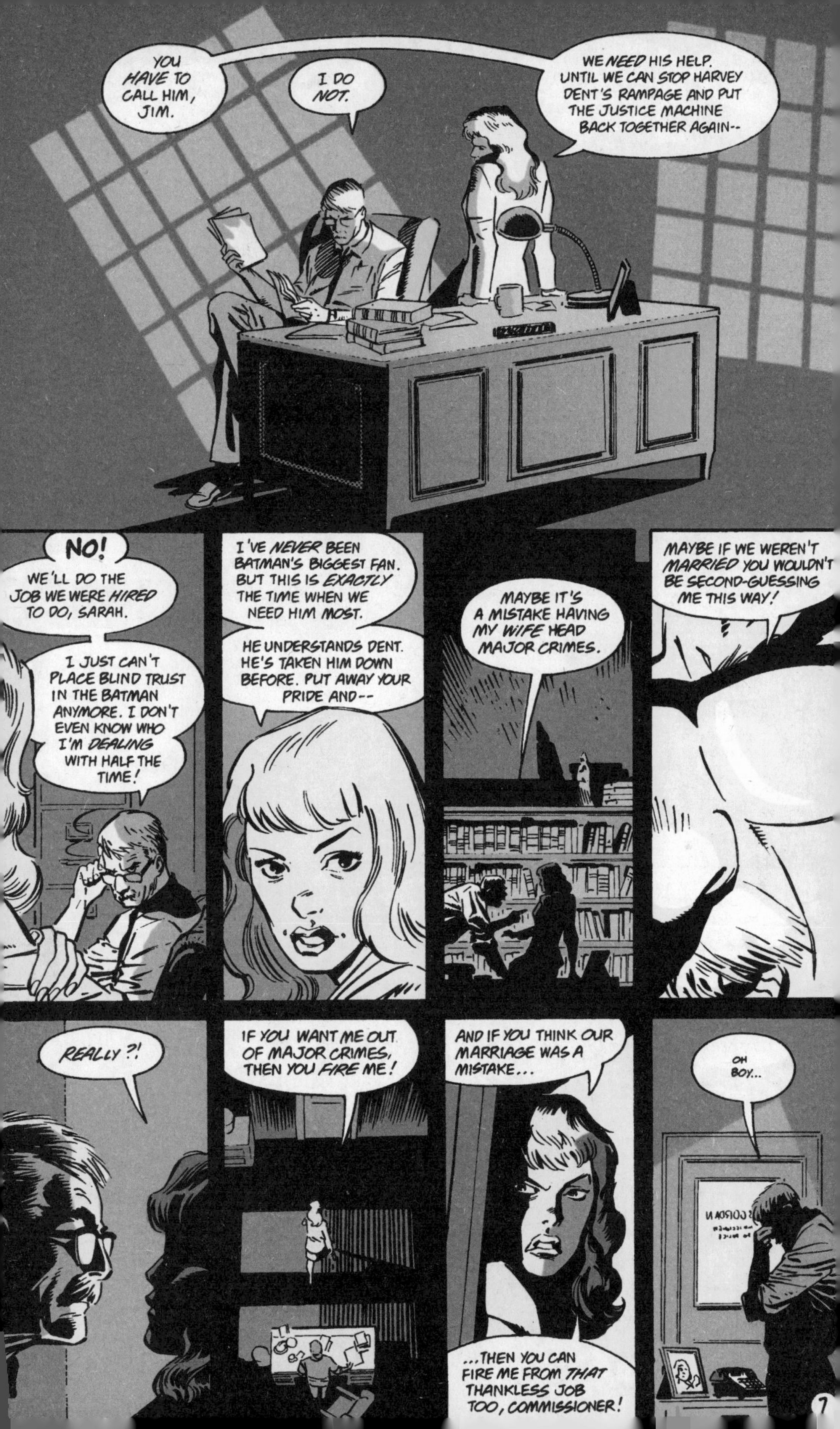

YOU HAVE TO CALL HIM, JIM.
I DO NOT.
WE NEED HIS HELP. UNTIL WE CAN STOP HARVEY DENT'S RAMPAGE AND PUT THE JUSTICE MACHINE BACK TOGETHER AGAIN--
NO!
WE'LL DO THE JOB WE WERE HIRED TO DO, SARAH.
I JUST CAN'T PLACE BLIND TRUST IN THE BATMAN ANYMORE. I DON'T EVEN KNOW WHO I'M DEALING WITH HALF THE TIME!
I'VE NEVER BEEN BATMAN'S BIGGEST FAN. BUT THIS IS EXACTLY THE TIME WHEN WE NEED HIM MOST.
HE UNDERSTANDS DENT. HE'S TAKEN HIM DOWN BEFORE. PUT AWAY YOUR PRIDE AND--
MAYBE IT'S A MISTAKE HAVING MY WIFE HEAD MAJOR CRIMES.
MAYBE IF WE WEREN'T MARRIED YOU WOULDN'T BE SECOND-GUESSING ME THIS WAY!
REALLY ?!
IF YOU WANT ME OUT OF MAJOR CRIMES, THEN YOU FIRE ME!
AND IF YOU THINK OUR MARRIAGE WAS A MISTAKE...
...THEN YOU CAN FIRE ME FROM THAT THANKLESS JOB TOO, COMMISSIONER!
OH BOY...

IS OFF HIS USUAL DUALITY GIG.

OR I JUST CAN'T SEE THE GIMMICK FOR THE TREES.

MAYBE HE'S FINISHED. MAYBE HE'S DONE WHAT HE SET OUT TO DO.

BUT WE KNOW BETTER, RIGHT?

YEAH, WISHFUL THINKING.

SO OTHER THAN BOLLIXING THE CITY'S COMPUTER RECORDS AND KNOCKING OFF DISTRICT ATTORNEYS AND JUDGES AND PACKING THE PRISONS...

WHAT'S HIS GOAL? WHAT'S HE WANT?

CHAOS. REVENGE.

ON WHOM?

WELL, BATMAN... ME... THE DISTRICT ATTORNEY'S OFFICE...

WHAT DISTRICT ATTORNEY DOES HE HATE THE MOST?

UM... HIMSELF? HE HATES HARVEY DENT. HE HATES EVERY--

WHAT'S THAT CLICK?

CALL WAITING. HANG ON.

OH, HI. KIND OF LATE, ISN'T IT?

I JUST THOUGHT I'D CALL. I NEEDED TO HEAR A FRIENDLY VOICE, I GUESS.

WELL...

... I WAS RIGHT IN THE MIDDLE OF SOMETHING, DAD.

I'M SORRY, BARBARA. MAYBE I'LL CALL YOU TOMORROW.

SOUNDS GREAT, DAD! 'BYE!

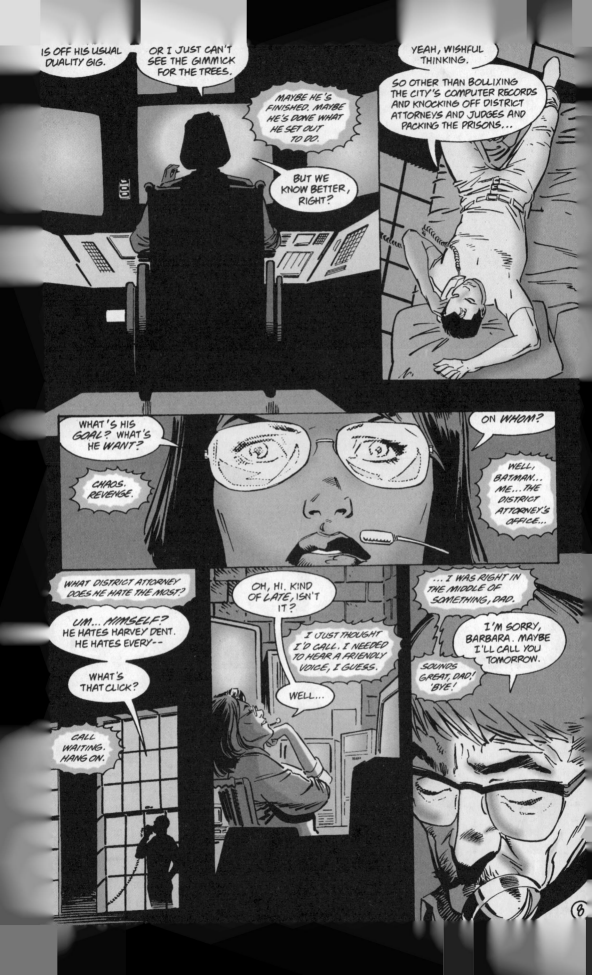

8

ROBIN?

STILL HERE.

THERE'S ONE PLACE HE HASN'T HIT. THE HALL OF RECORDS ANNEX.

GOTHAM'S STILL IN THE DARK AGES AS FAR AS COMPUTERIZING. THE ANNEX STILL HOLDS MOST OF THE COURT DOCUMENTS.

AND CRIMINAL JACKETS AND EVEN EVIDENCE.

IT'S WORTH CHECKING OUT.

HENDRICKS!

JAMES GORDON COMMISSIONER OF GOTHAM

CYNERGISM HOT LINE 1 800555 004

PARENTS HOTLINE 555311

GET ME A COT OUT OF STORAGE AND BRING IT IN HERE.

I HEARD YOUR TIFF WITH THE LIEUTENANT, SIR. ANYTHING YOU WANT TO *TALK* ABOUT?

WE CAN TALK ABOUT YOU WORKING A SOLO BEAT IN THE CANAL ZONE IF THAT COT ISN'T HERE IN FIVE MINUTES.

FIVE *MINUTES*, COMMISH! NO *PROBLEM!*

"I'M ON THE CASE!"

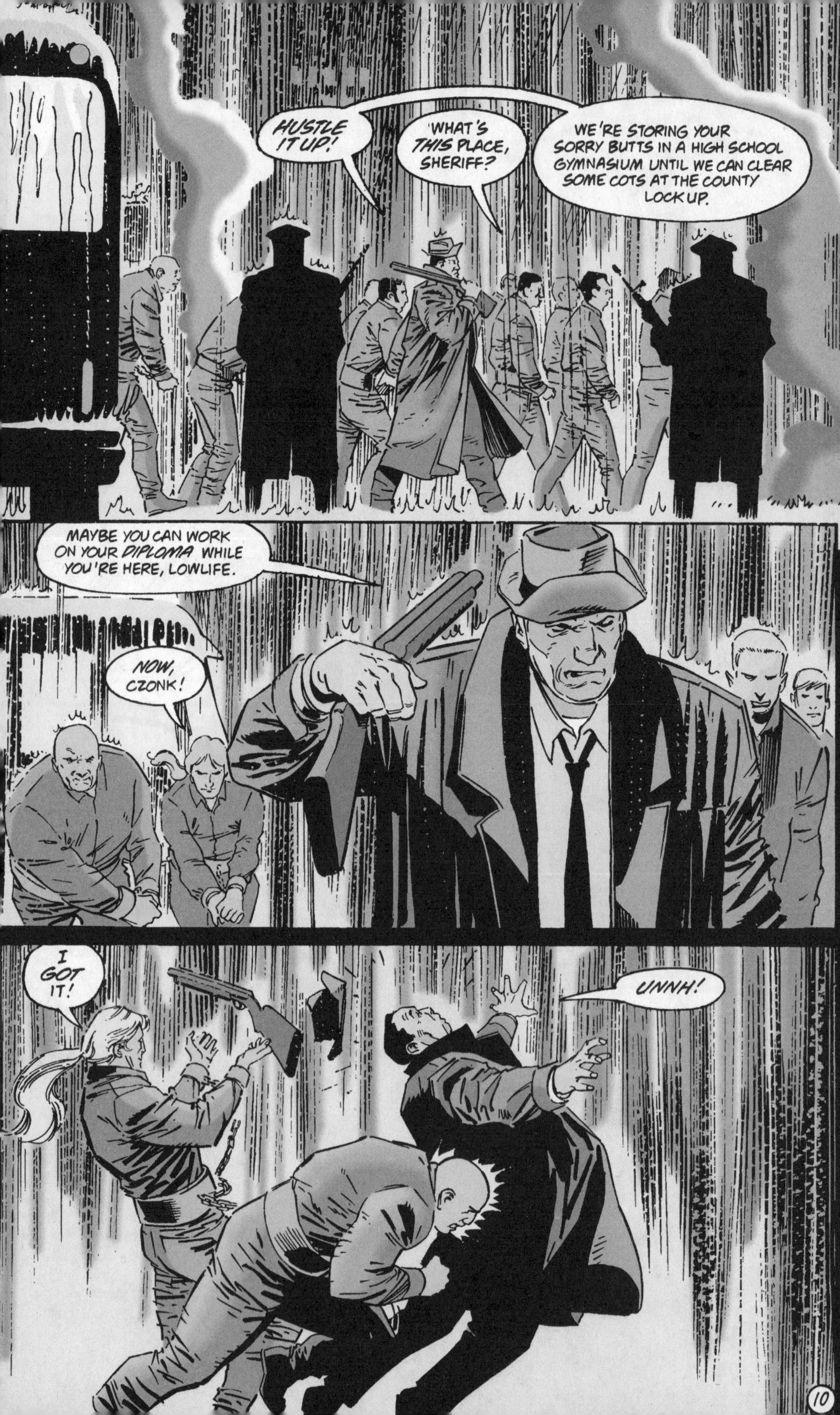
HUSTLE IT UP!
'WHAT'S THIS PLACE, SHERIFF?
WE'RE STORING YOUR SORRY BUTTS IN A HIGH SCHOOL GYMNASIUM UNTIL WE CAN CLEAR SOME COTS AT THE COUNTY LOCK UP.
MAYBE YOU CAN WORK ON YOUR DIPLOMA WHILE YOU'RE HERE, LOWLIFE.
NOW, CZONK!
I GOT IT!
UNNH!

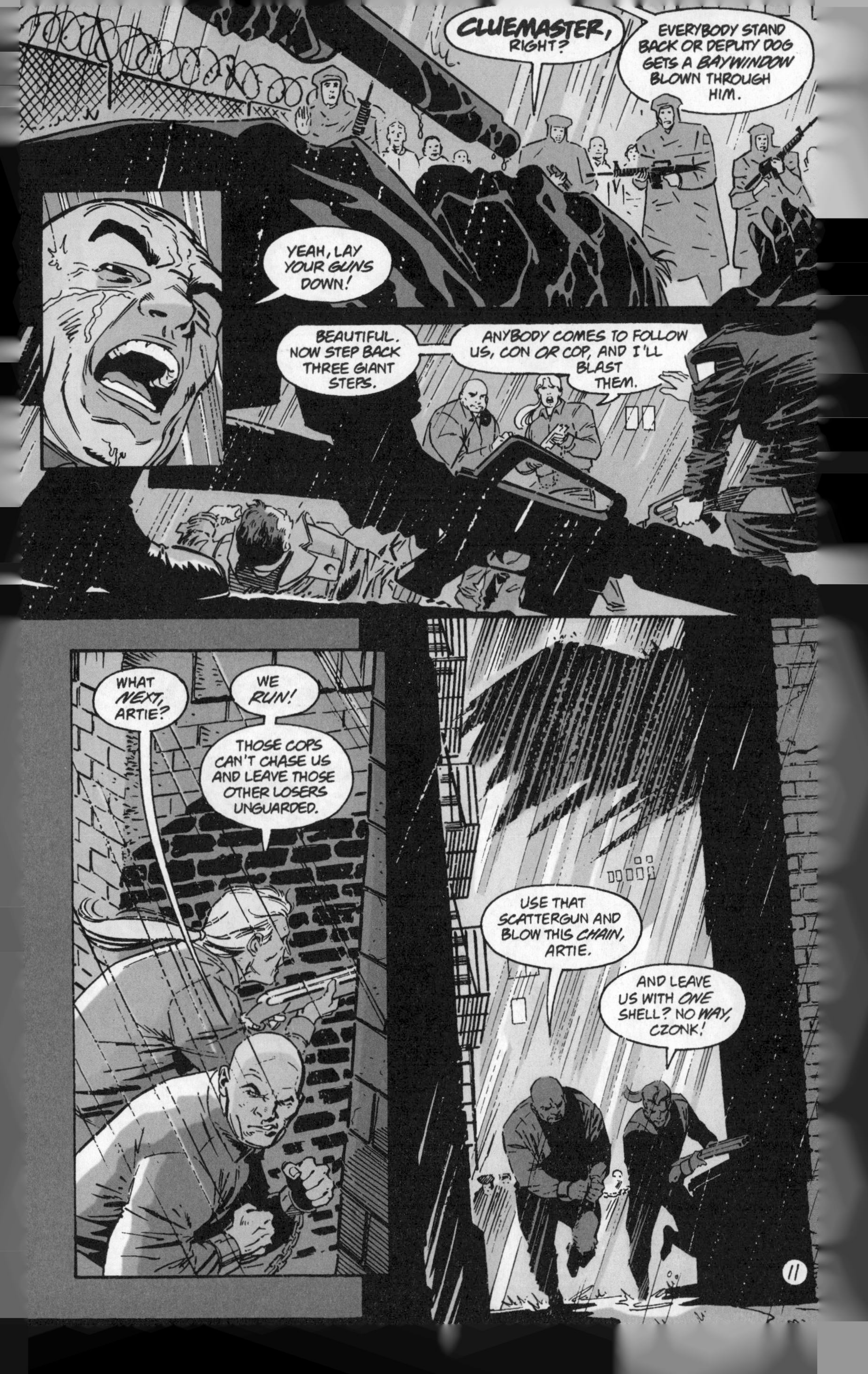

CLUEMASTER, RIGHT?
EVERYBODY STAND BACK OR DEPUTY DOG GETS A BAYWINDOW BLOWN THROUGH HIM.
YEAH, LAY YOUR GUNS DOWN!
BEAUTIFUL. NOW STEP BACK THREE GIANT STEPS.
ANYBODY COMES TO FOLLOW US, CON OR COP, AND I'LL BLAST THEM.
WHAT NEXT, ARTIE?
WE RUN!
THOSE COPS CAN'T CHASE US AND LEAVE THOSE OTHER LOSERS UNGUARDED.
USE THAT SCATTERGUN AND BLOW THIS CHAIN, ARTIE.
AND LEAVE US WITH ONE SHELL? NO WAY, CZONK!

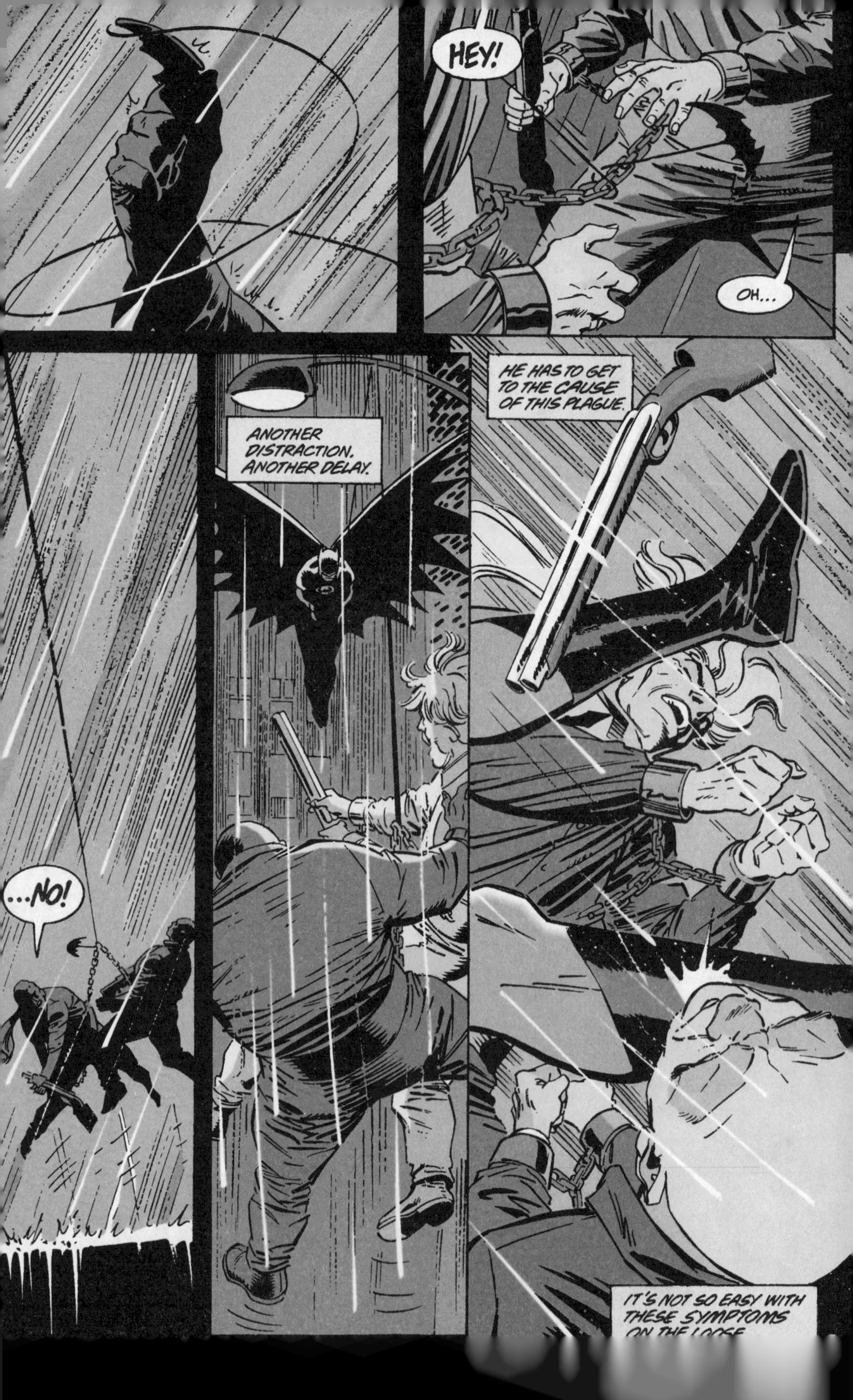
HEY!
OH...
...NO!
ANOTHER DISTRACTION. ANOTHER DELAY.
HE HAS TO GET TO THE CAUSE OF THIS PLAGUE.
IT'S NOT SO EASY WITH THESE SYMPTOMS

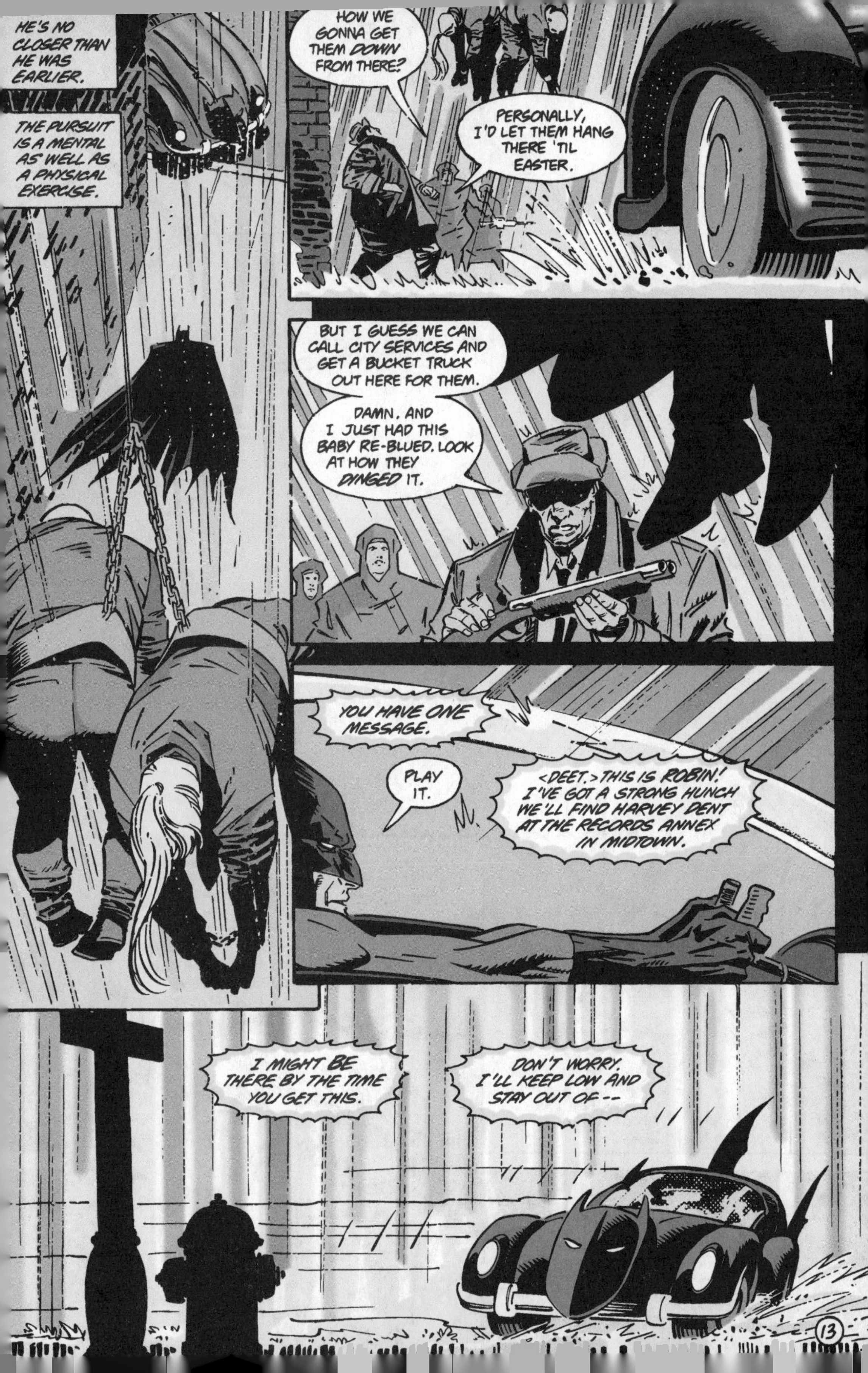
HE'S NO CLOSER THAN HE WAS EARLIER.
THE PURSUIT IS A MENTAL AS WELL AS A PHYSICAL EXERCISE.
HOW WE GONNA GET THEM DOWN FROM THERE?
PERSONALLY, I'D LET THEM HANG THERE 'TIL EASTER.
BUT I GUESS WE CAN CALL CITY SERVICES AND GET A BUCKET TRUCK OUT HERE FOR THEM.
DAMN. AND I JUST HAD THIS BABY RE-BLUED. LOOK AT HOW THEY DINGED IT.
YOU HAVE ONE MESSAGE.
PLAY IT.
<DEET.> THIS IS ROBIN! I'VE GOT A STRONG HUNCH WE'LL FIND HARVEY DENT AT THE RECORDS ANNEX IN MIDTOWN.
I MIGHT BE THERE BY THE TIME YOU GET THIS.
DON'T WORRY. I'LL KEEP LOW AND STAY OUT OF --
13

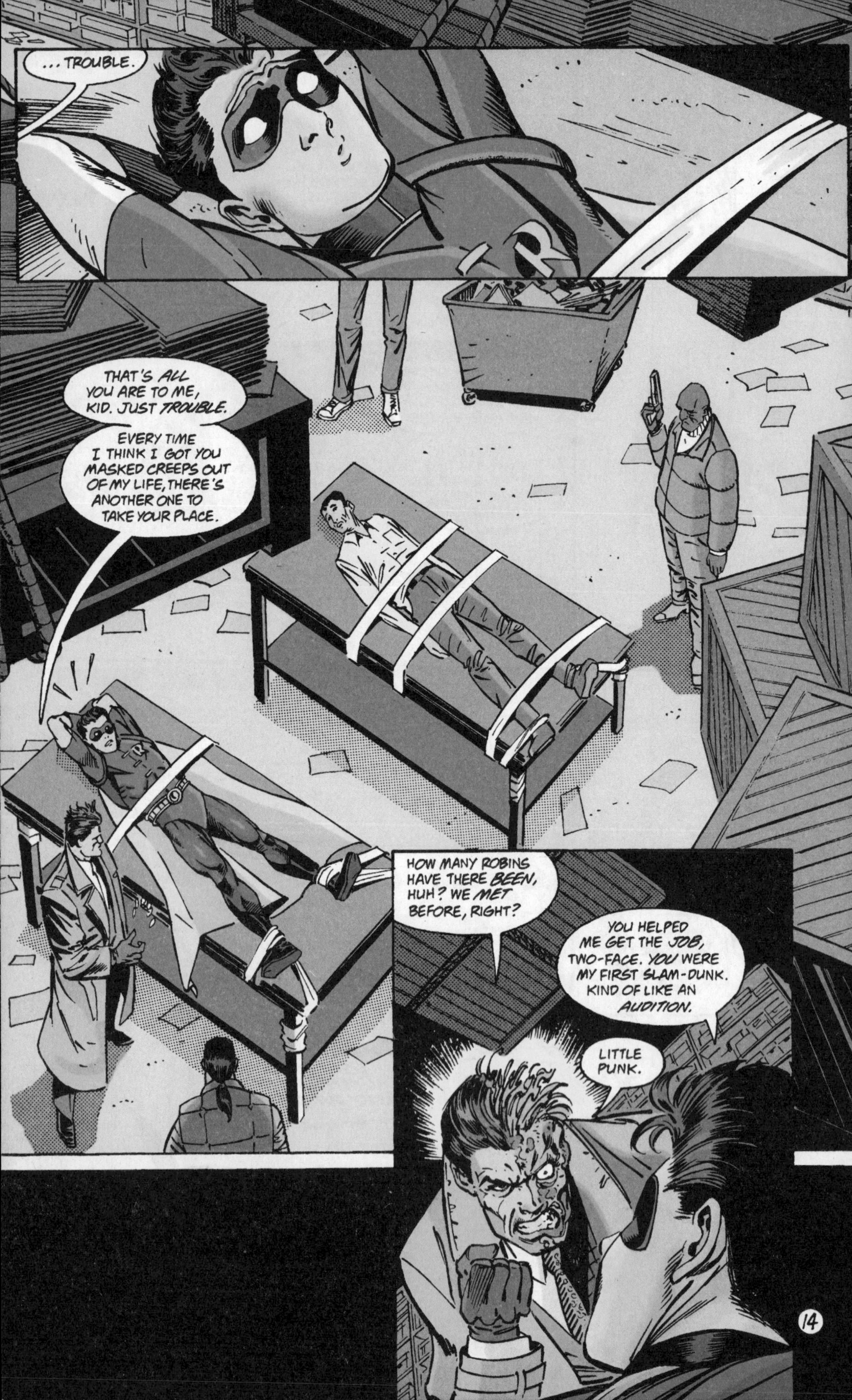

... TROUBLE.
THAT'S ALL YOU ARE TO ME, KID. JUST TROUBLE.
EVERY TIME I THINK I GOT YOU MASKED CREEPS OUT OF MY LIFE, THERE'S ANOTHER ONE TO TAKE YOUR PLACE.
HOW MANY ROBINS HAVE THERE BEEN, HUH? WE MET BEFORE, RIGHT?
YOU HELPED ME GET THE JOB, TWO-FACE. YOU WERE MY FIRST SLAM-DUNK. KIND OF LIKE AN AUDITION.
LITTLE PUNK.

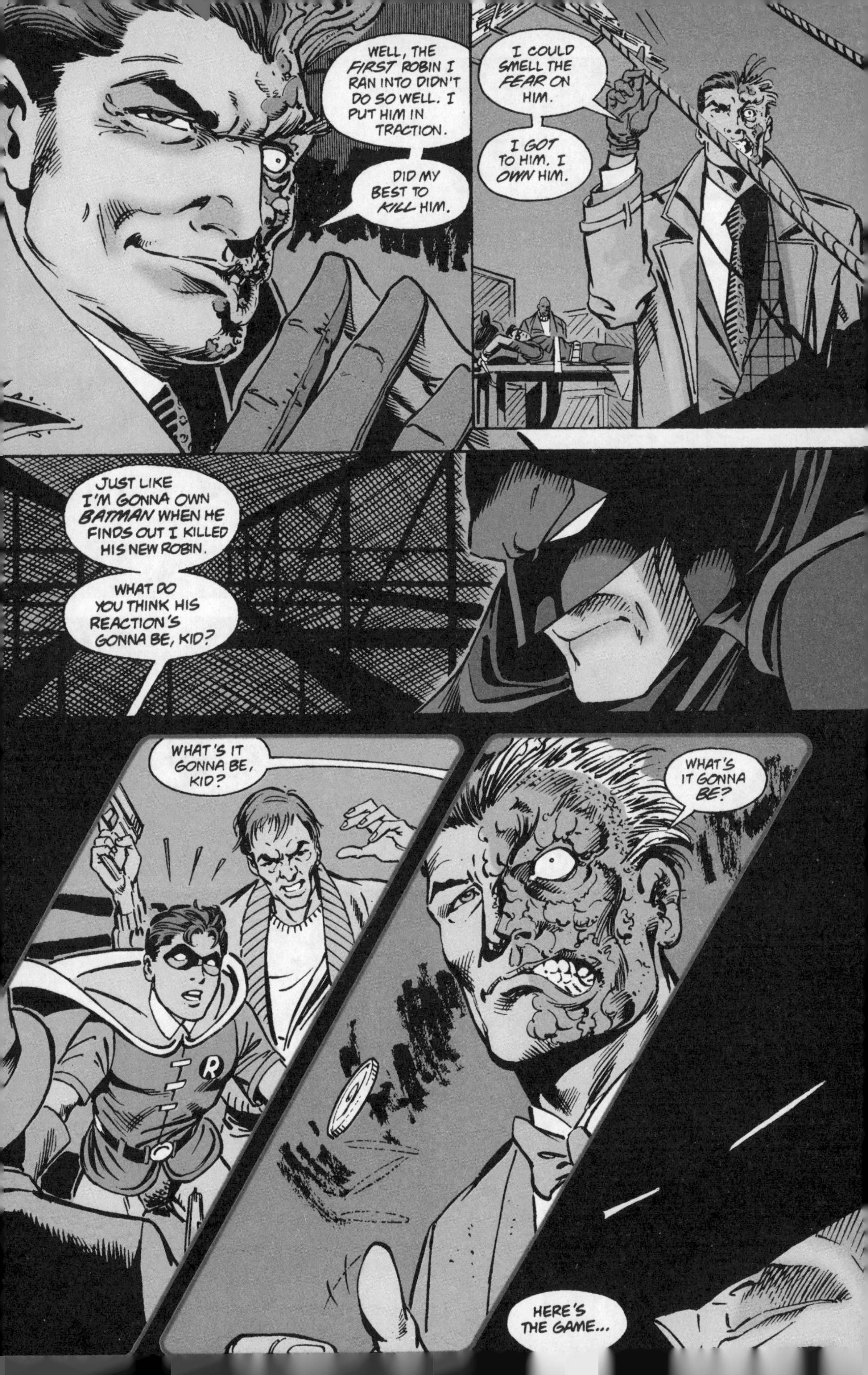
WELL, THE FIRST ROBIN I RAN INTO DIDN'T DO SO WELL. I PUT HIM IN TRACTION.
DID MY BEST TO KILL HIM.
I COULD SMELL THE FEAR ON HIM.
I GOT TO HIM. I OWN HIM.
JUST LIKE I'M GONNA OWN BATMAN WHEN HE FINDS OUT I KILLED HIS NEW ROBIN.
WHAT DO YOU THINK HIS REACTION'S GONNA BE, KID?
WHAT'S IT GONNA BE, KID?
WHAT'S IT GONNA BE?
HERE'S THE GAME...

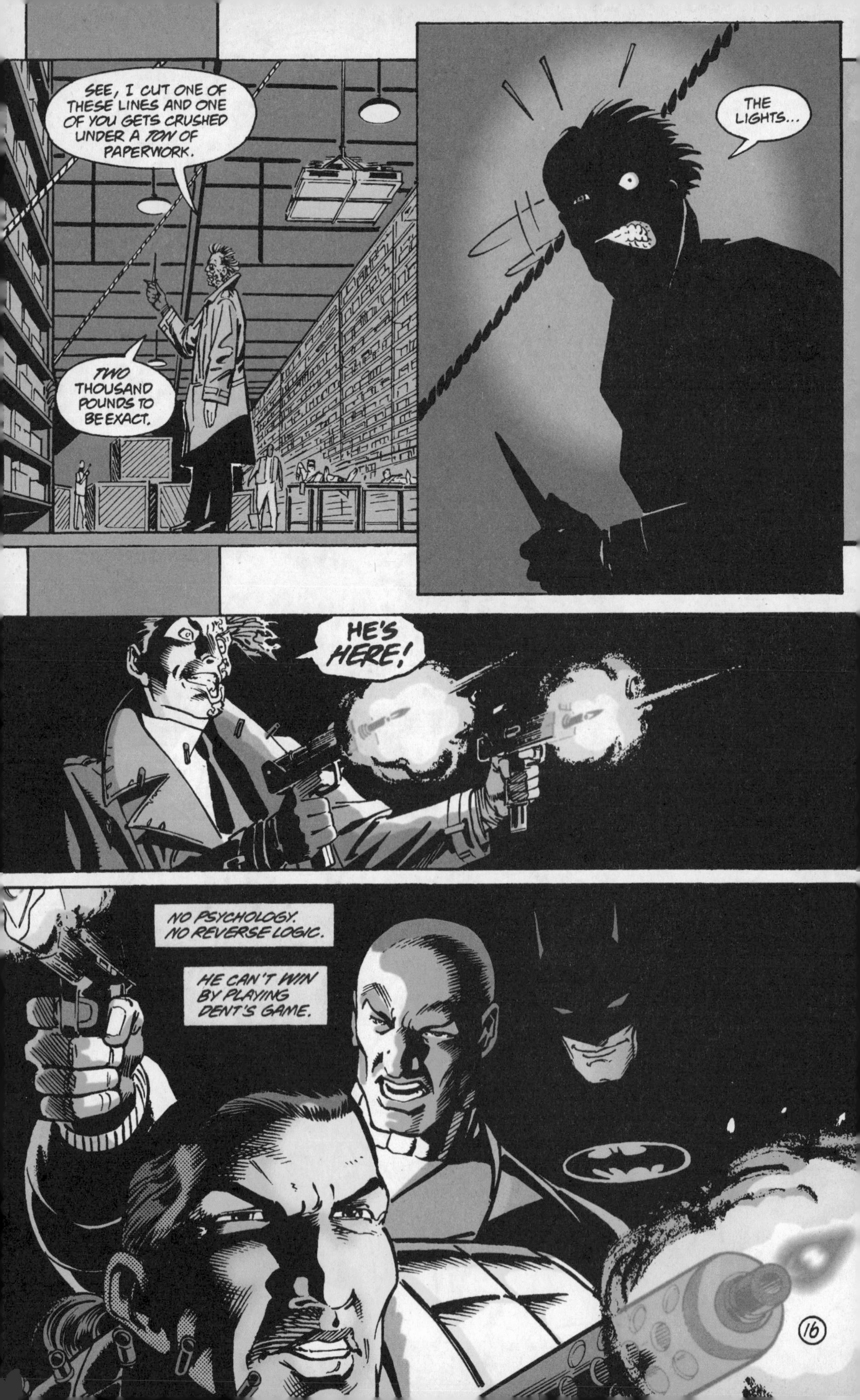
SEE, I CUT ONE OF THESE LINES AND ONE OF YOU GETS CRUSHED UNDER A TON OF PAPERWORK.
TWO THOUSAND POUNDS TO BE EXACT.
THE LIGHTS...
HE'S HERE!
NO PSYCHOLOGY. NO REVERSE LOGIC.
HE CAN'T WIN BY PLAYING DENT'S GAME.
16

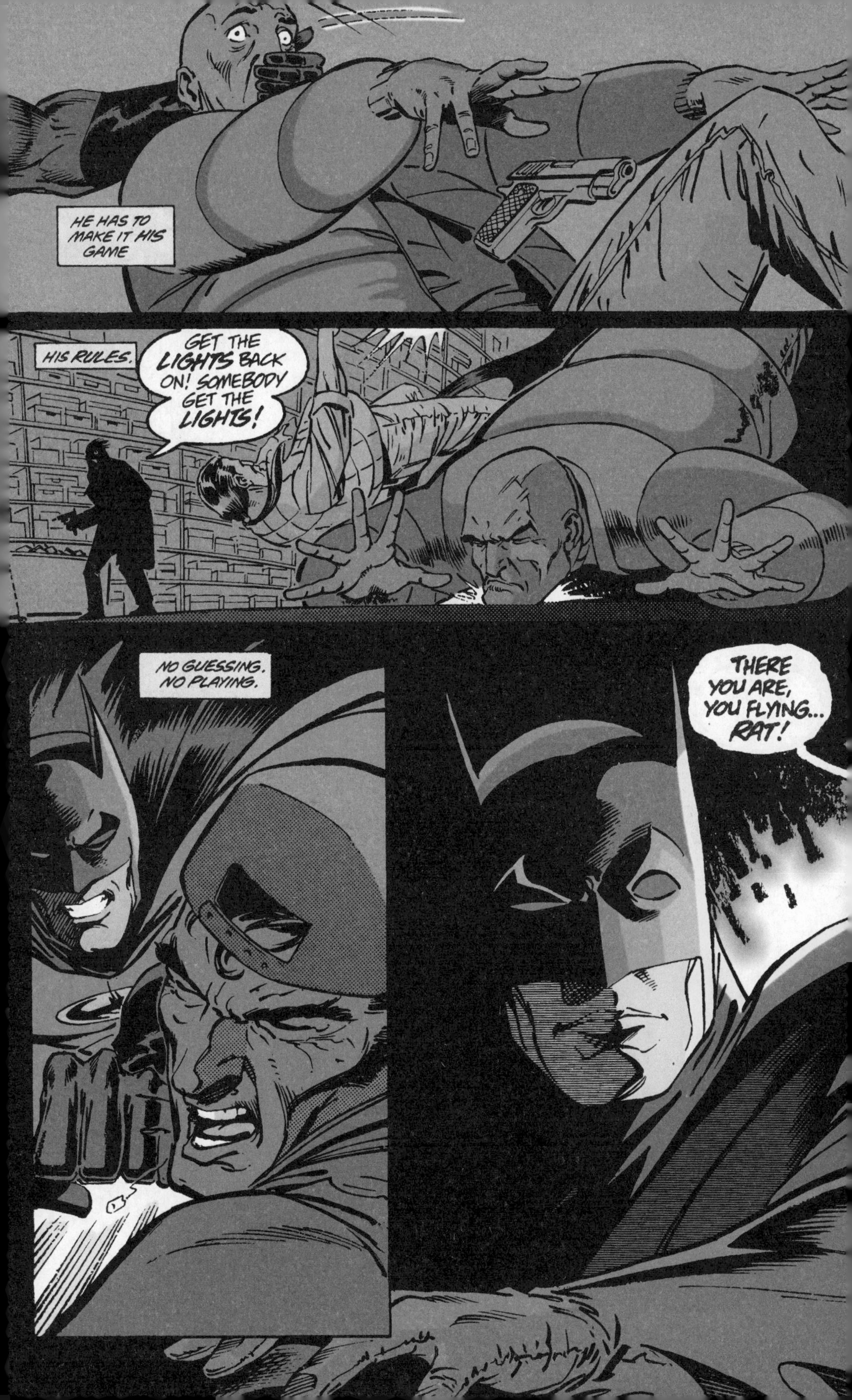
HE HAS TO MAKE IT HIS GAME
HIS RULES.
GET THE LIGHTS BACK ON! SOMEBODY GET THE LIGHTS!
NO GUESSING. NO PLAYING.
THERE YOU ARE, YOU FLYING... RAT!

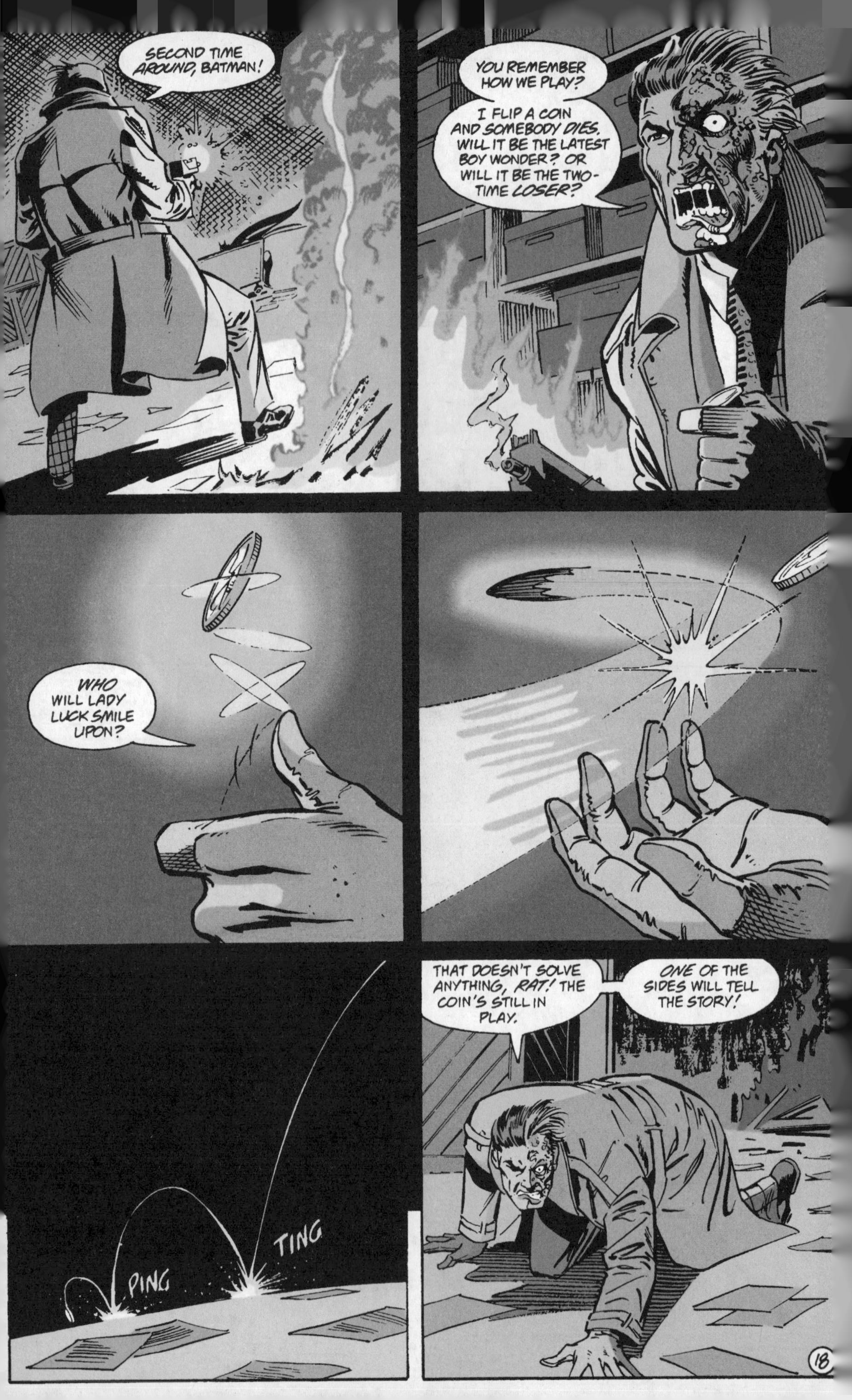
SECOND TIME AROUND, BATMAN!
YOU REMEMBER HOW WE PLAY?
I FLIP A COIN AND SOMEBODY DIES. WILL IT BE THE LATEST BOY WONDER? OR WILL IT BE THE TWO-TIME LOSER?
WHO WILL LADY LUCK SMILE UPON?
PING
TING
THAT DOESN'T SOLVE ANYTHING, RAT! THE COIN'S STILL IN PLAY.
ONE OF THE SIDES WILL TELL THE STORY!
18

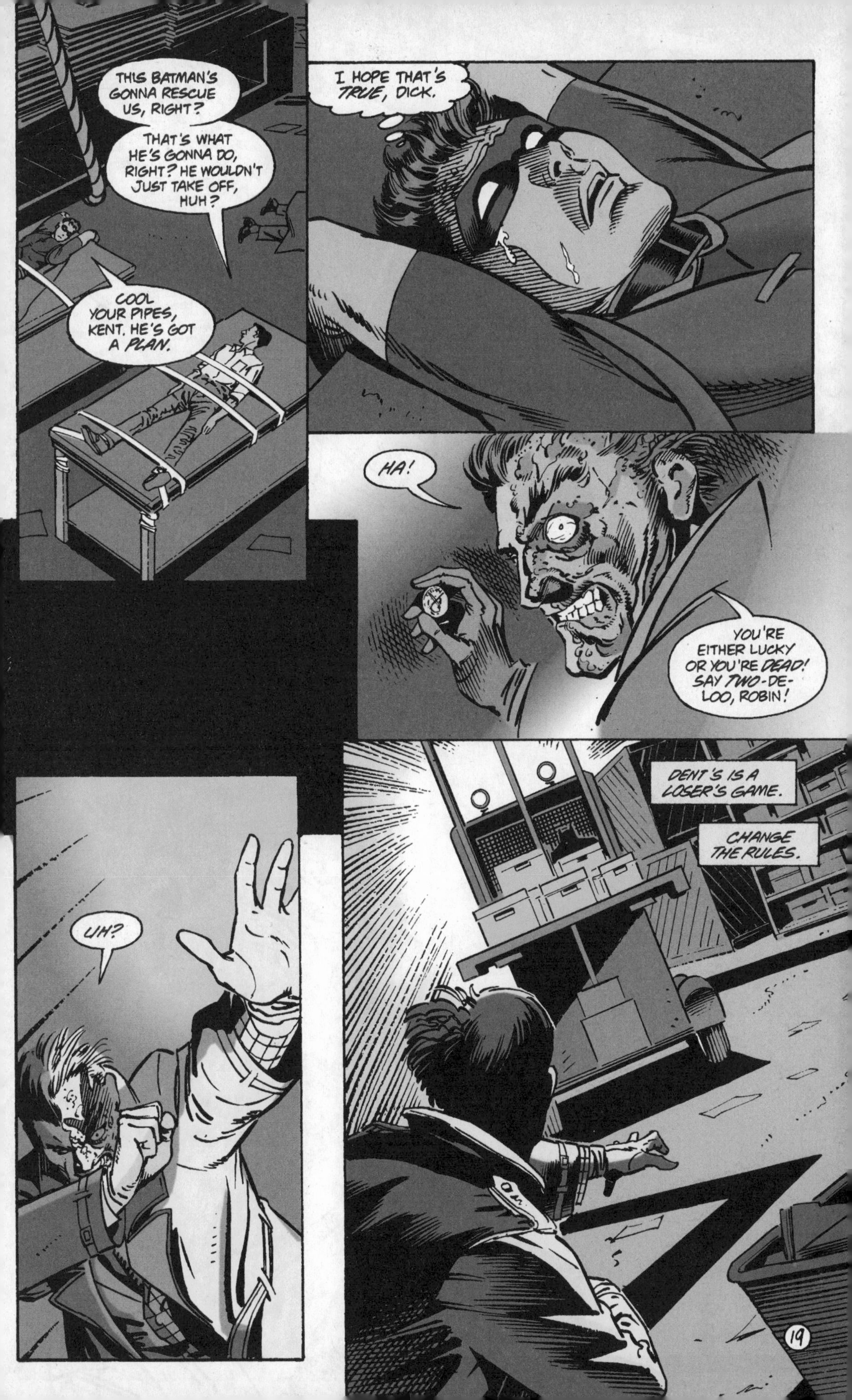
THIS BATMAN'S GONNA RESCUE US, RIGHT?
THAT'S WHAT HE'S GONNA DO, RIGHT? HE WOULDN'T JUST TAKE OFF, HUH?
COOL YOUR PIPES, KENT. HE'S GOT A PLAN.
I HOPE THAT'S TRUE, DICK.
HA!
YOU'RE EITHER LUCKY OR YOU'RE DEAD! SAY TWO-DE-LOO, ROBIN!
UH?
DENT'S IS A LOSER'S GAME.
CHANGE THE RULES.

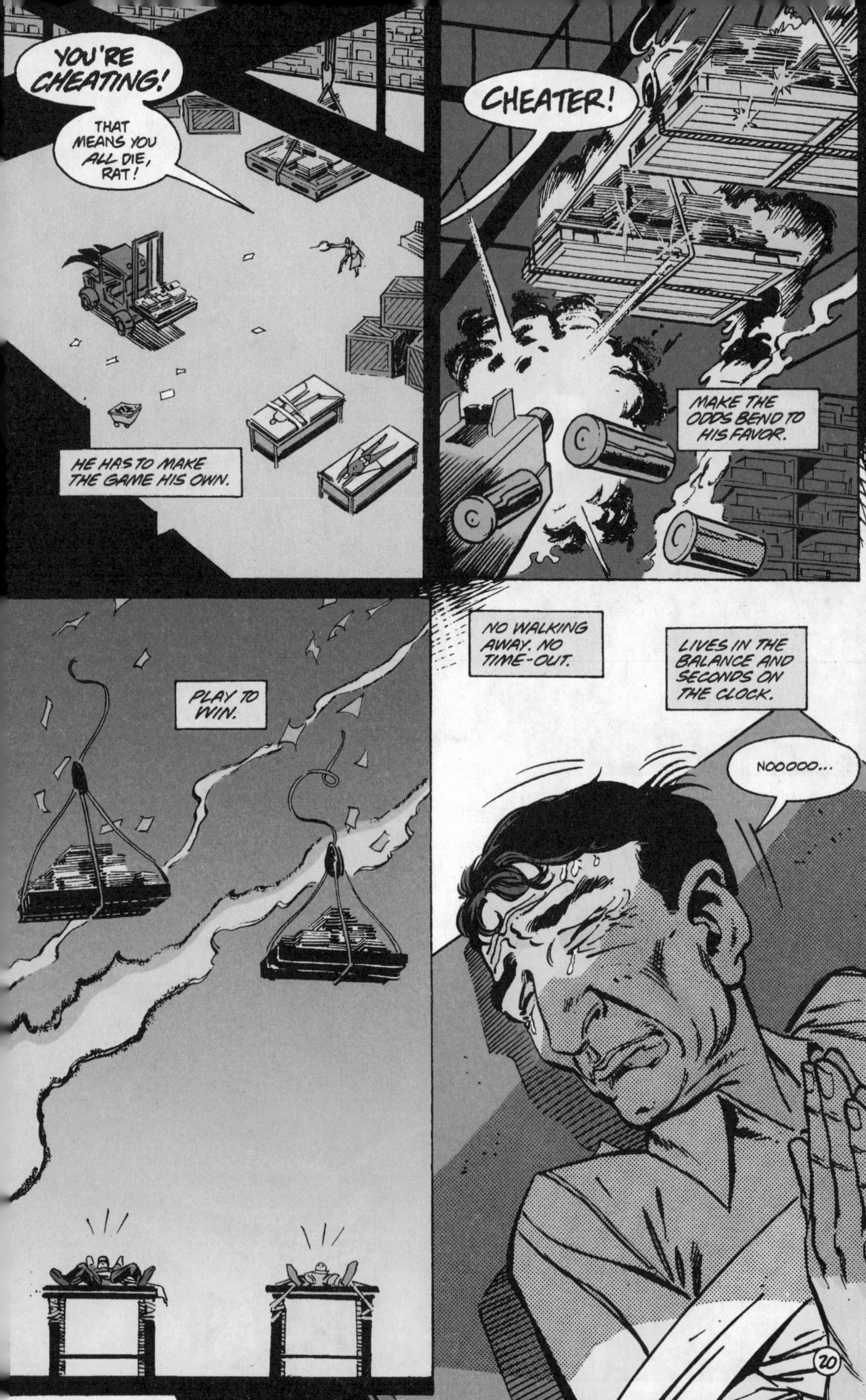

YOU'RE CHEATING!
THAT MEANS YOU ALL DIE, RAT!
HE HAS TO MAKE THE GAME HIS OWN.
CHEATER!
MAKE THE ODDS BEND TO HIS FAVOR.
PLAY TO WIN.
NO WALKING AWAY. NO TIME-OUT.
LIVES IN THE BALANCE AND SECONDS ON THE CLOCK.
NOOOOO...
20

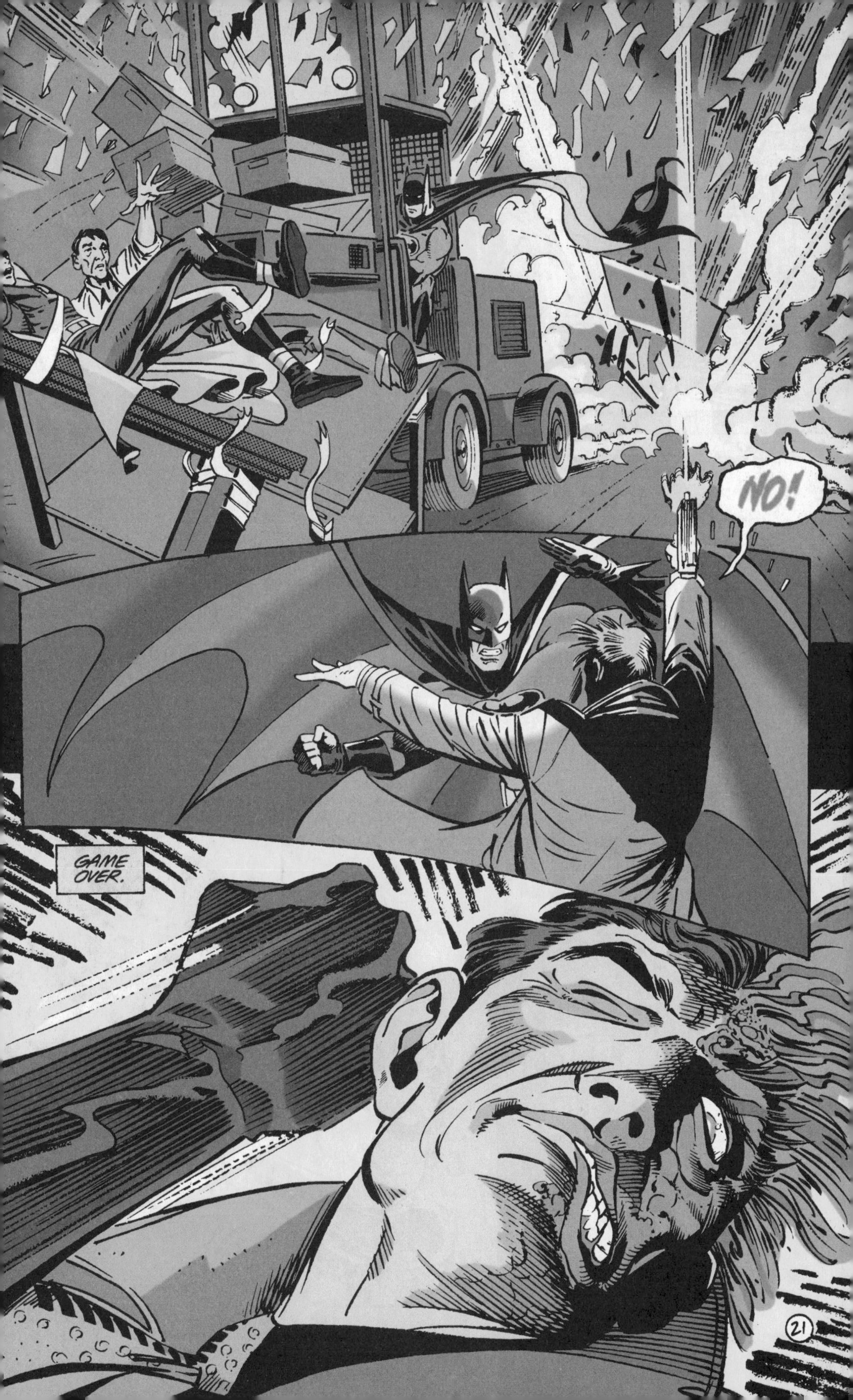

NO!
GAME OVER.

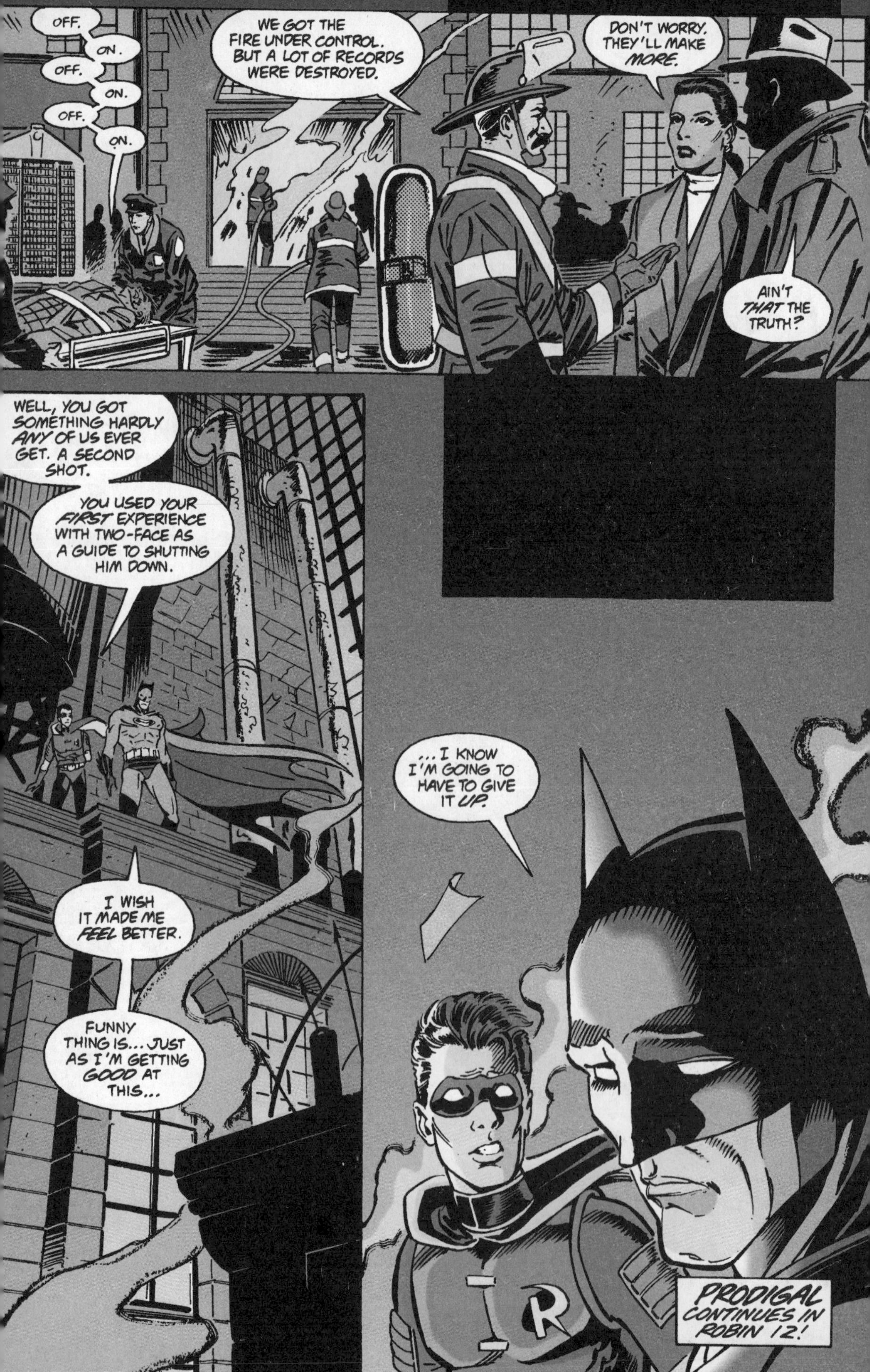
OFF.
ON.
OFF.
ON.
OFF.
ON.
WE GOT THE FIRE UNDER CONTROL. BUT A LOT OF RECORDS WERE DESTROYED.
DON'T WORRY. THEY'LL MAKE MORE.
AIN'T THAT THE TRUTH?
WELL, YOU GOT SOMETHING HARDLY ANY OF US EVER GET. A SECOND SHOT.
YOU USED YOUR FIRST EXPERIENCE WITH TWO-FACE AS A GUIDE TO SHUTTING HIM DOWN.
I WISH IT MADE ME FEEL BETTER.
FUNNY THING IS... JUST AS I'M GETTING GOOD AT THIS...
...I KNOW I'M GOING TO HAVE TO GIVE IT UP.
PRODIGAL CONTINUES IN ROBIN 12!

Cover art by TOM GRUMMETT and RAY KRYSSING

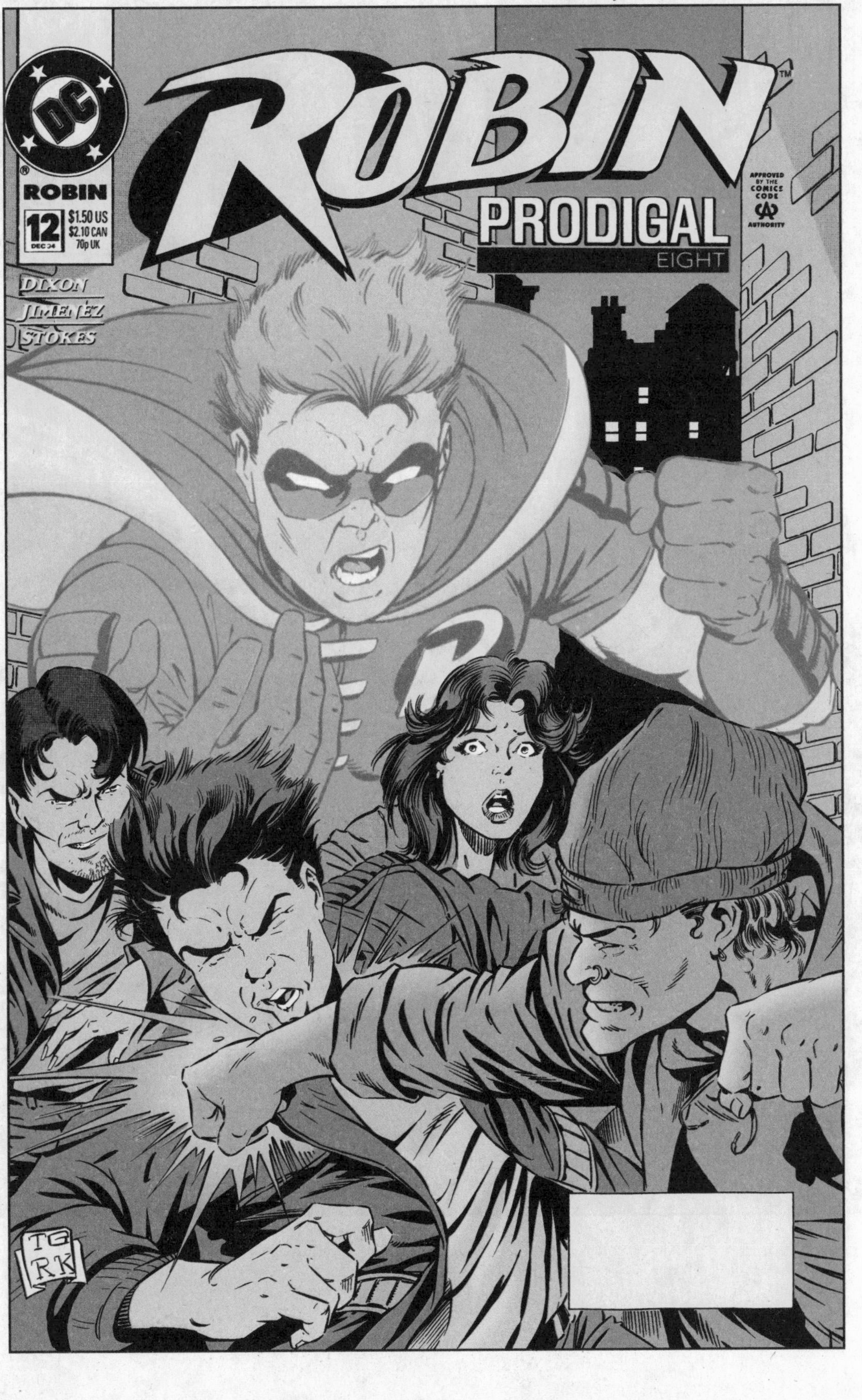
ROBIN™
DC
ROBIN
12
DEC 94
$1.50 US
$2.10 CAN
70p UK
APPROVED BY THE COMICS CODE AUTHORITY
PRODIGAL
EIGHT
DIXON
JIMENEZ
STOKES
TG
RK

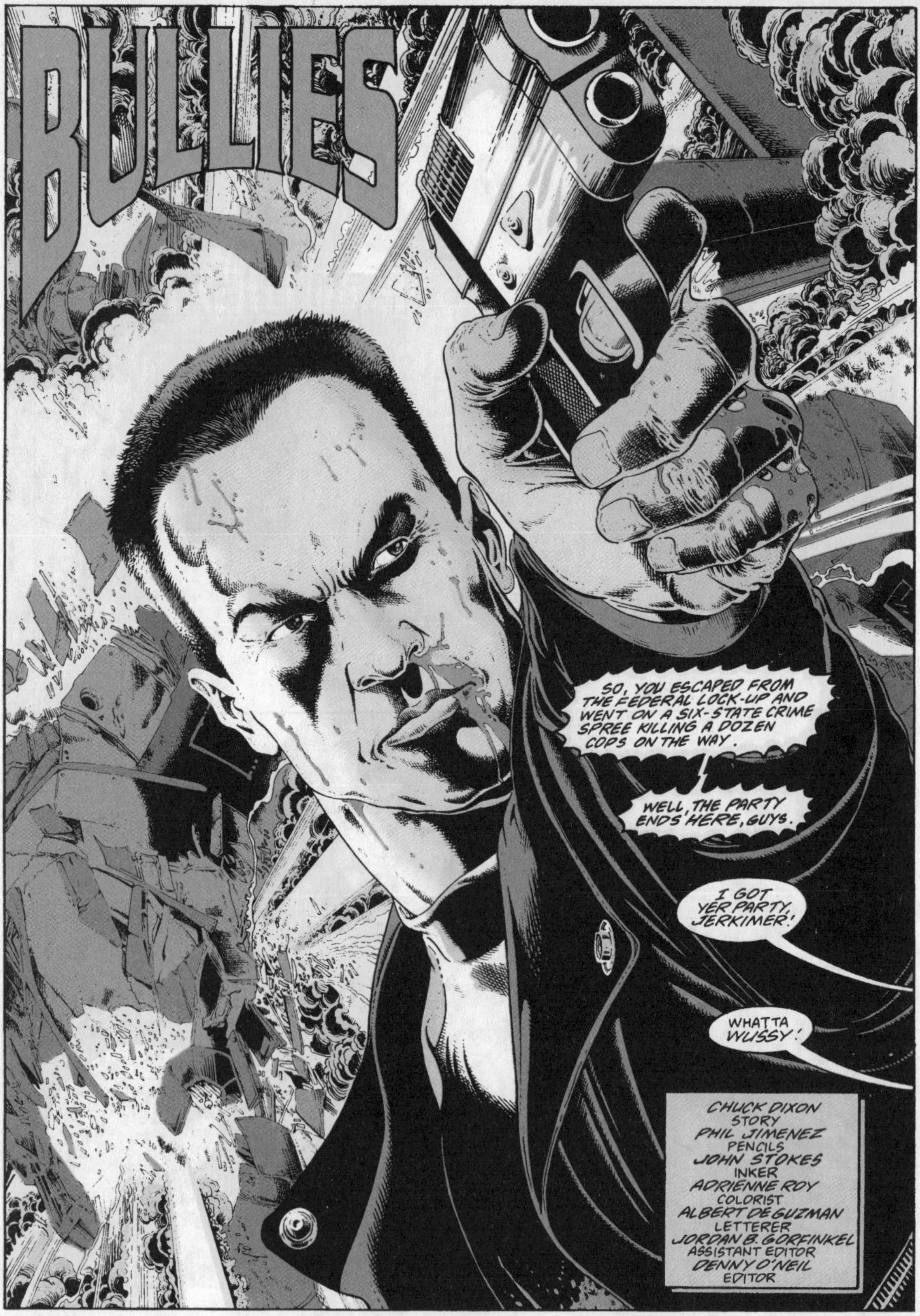
BULLIES
SO, YOU ESCAPED FROM THE FEDERAL LOCK-UP AND WENT ON A SIX-STATE CRIME SPREE KILLING A DOZEN COPS ON THE WAY.
WELL, THE PARTY ENDS HERE, GUYS.
I GOT YER PARTY, JERKIMER!
WHATTA WUSSY!
CHUCK DIXON STORY
PHIL JIMENEZ PENCILS
JOHN STOKES INKER
ADRIENNE ROY COLORIST
ALBERT DE GUZMAN LETTERER
JORDAN B. GORFINKEL ASSISTANT EDITOR
DENNY O'NEIL EDITOR

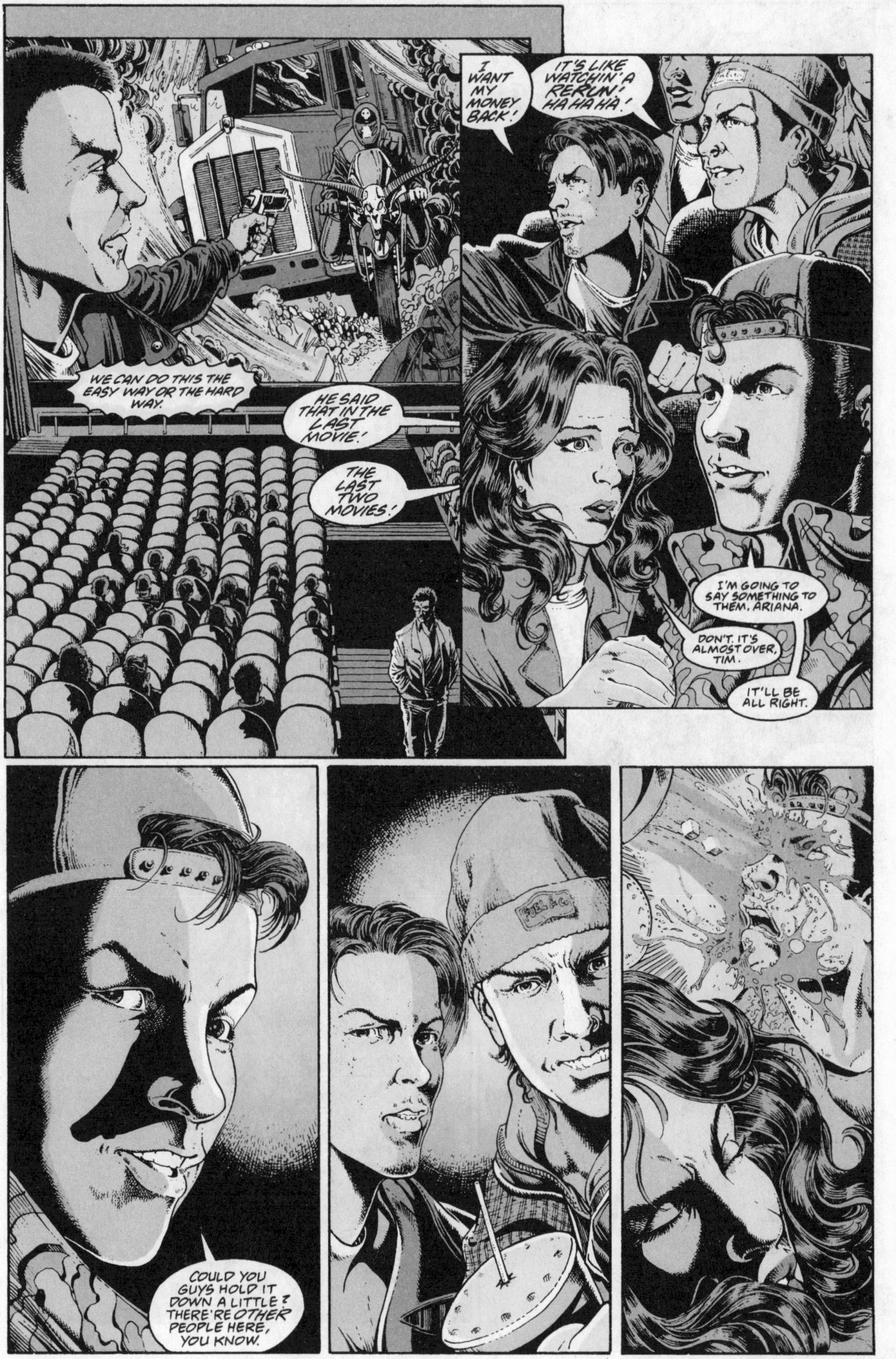
I WANT MY MONEY BACK!
IT'S LIKE WATCHIN' A RERUN! HA HA HA!
WE CAN DO THIS THE EASY WAY OR THE HARD WAY.
HE SAID THAT IN THE LAST MOVIE!
THE LAST TWO MOVIES!
I'M GOING TO SAY SOMETHING TO THEM, ARIANA.
DON'T. IT'S ALMOST OVER, TIM.
IT'LL BE ALL RIGHT.
COULD YOU GUYS HOLD IT DOWN A LITTLE? THERE'RE OTHER PEOPLE HERE, YOU KNOW.
FUEL & CO

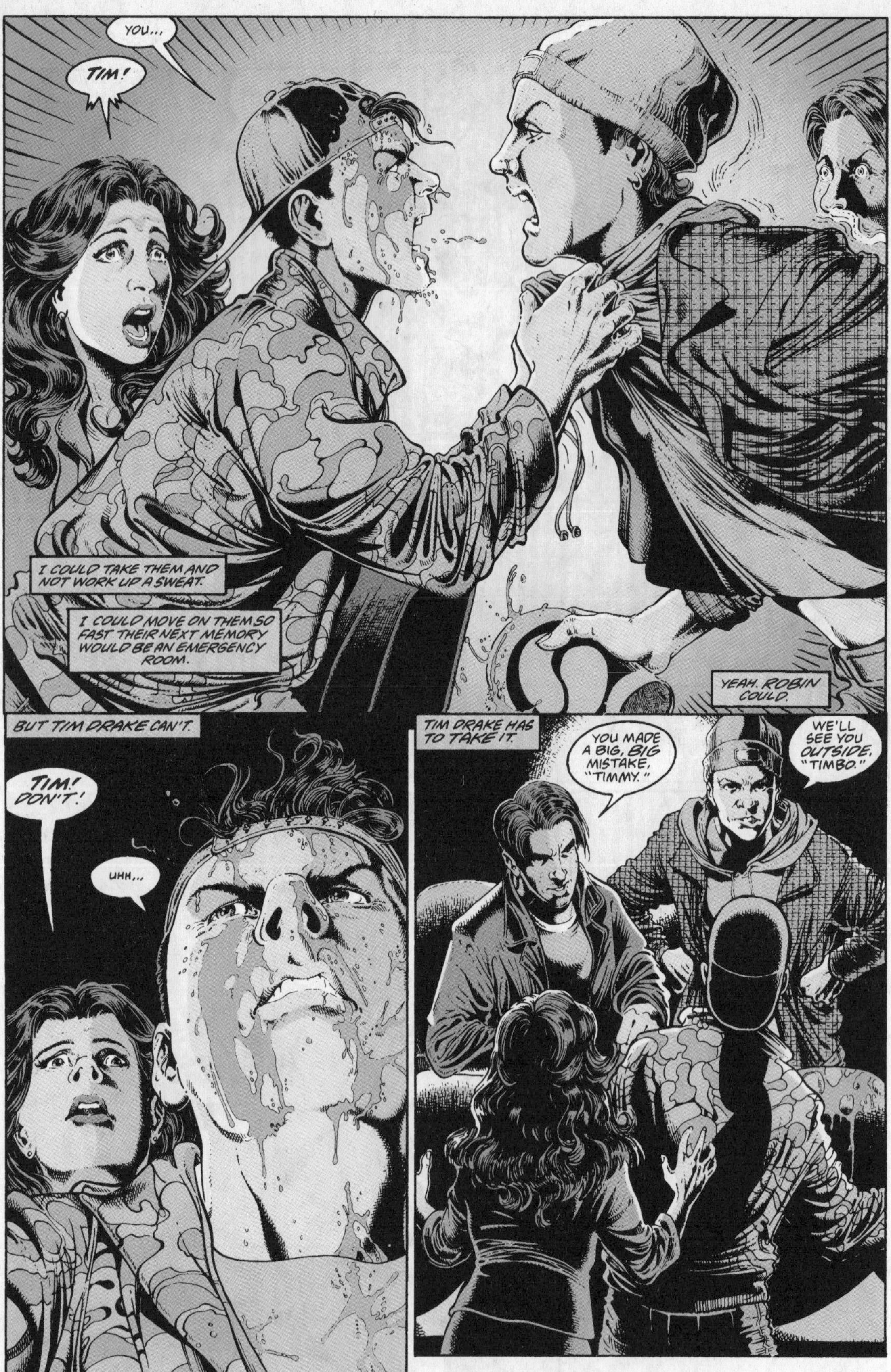
YOU...
TIM!
I COULD TAKE THEM AND NOT WORK UP A SWEAT.
I COULD MOVE ON THEM SO FAST THEIR NEXT MEMORY WOULD BE AN EMERGENCY ROOM.
YEAH. ROBIN COULD.
BUT TIM DRAKE CAN'T.
TIM! DON'T!
UHH...
TIM DRAKE HAS TO TAKE IT.
YOU MADE A BIG, BIG MISTAKE, "TIMMY."
WE'LL SEE YOU OUTSIDE, "TIMBO."

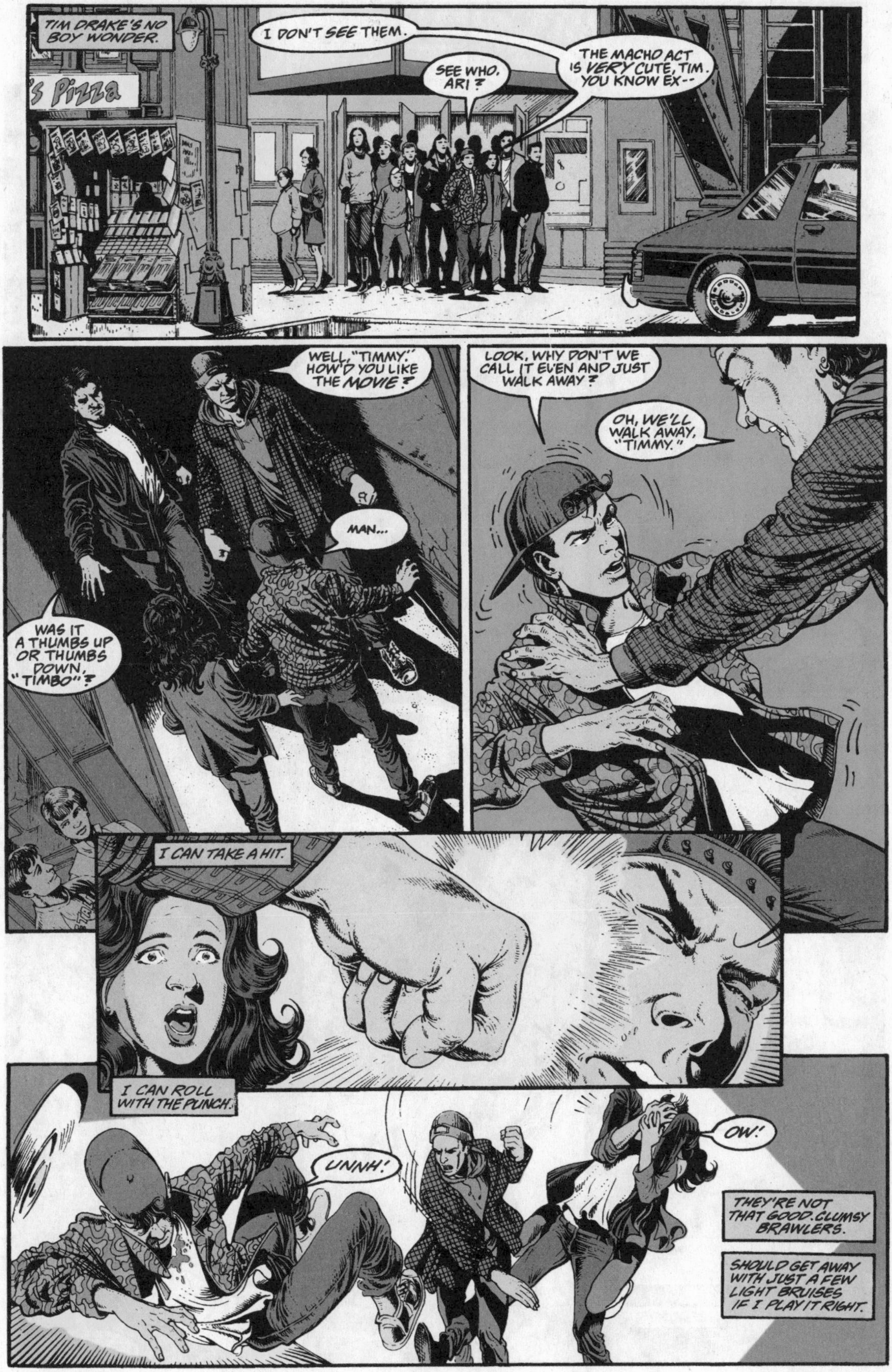
TIM DRAKE'S NO BOY WONDER.
I DON'T SEE THEM.
SEE WHO, ARI?
THE MACHO ACT IS VERY CUTE, TIM. YOU KNOW EX--
'S PIZZA
WELL, "TIMMY." HOW'D YOU LIKE THE MOVIE?
MAN...
WAS IT A THUMBS UP OR THUMBS DOWN, "TIMBO"?
LOOK, WHY DON'T WE CALL IT EVEN AND JUST WALK AWAY?
OH, WE'LL WALK AWAY, "TIMMY."
I CAN TAKE A HIT.
I CAN ROLL WITH THE PUNCH.
UNNH!
OW!
THEY'RE NOT THAT GOOD. CLUMSY BRAWLERS.
SHOULD GET AWAY WITH JUST A FEW LIGHT BRUISES IF I PLAY IT RIGHT.

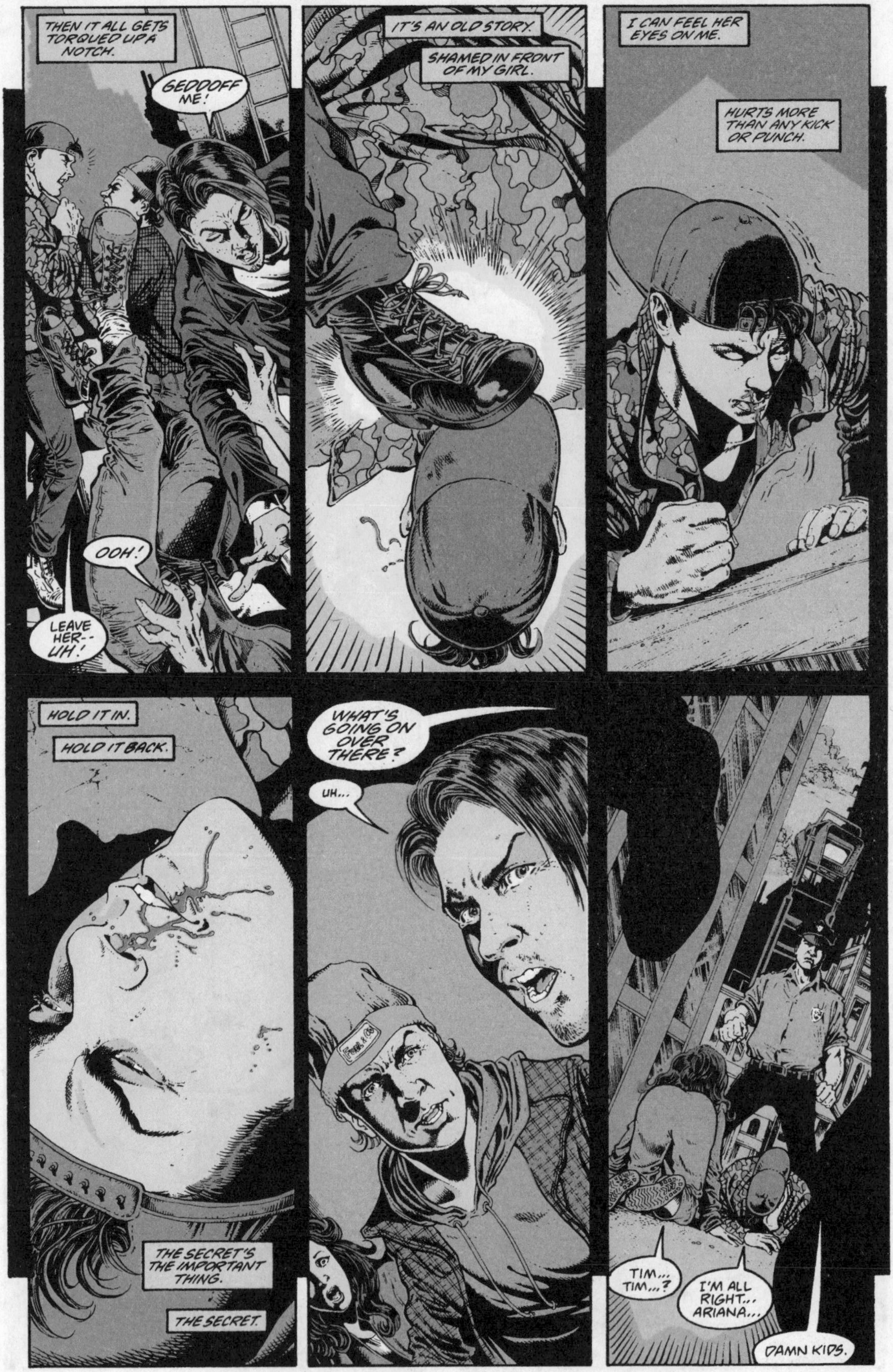

THEN IT ALL GETS TORQUED UP A NOTCH.
GEDDOFF ME!
OOH!
LEAVE HER-- UH!
IT'S AN OLD STORY.
SHAMED IN FRONT OF MY GIRL.
I CAN FEEL HER EYES ON ME.
HURTS MORE THAN ANY KICK OR PUNCH.
HOLD IT IN.
HOLD IT BACK.
THE SECRET'S THE IMPORTANT THING.
THE SECRET.
WHAT'S GOING ON OVER THERE?
UH...
TIM... TIM...?
I'M ALL RIGHT... ARIANA...
DAMN KIDS.

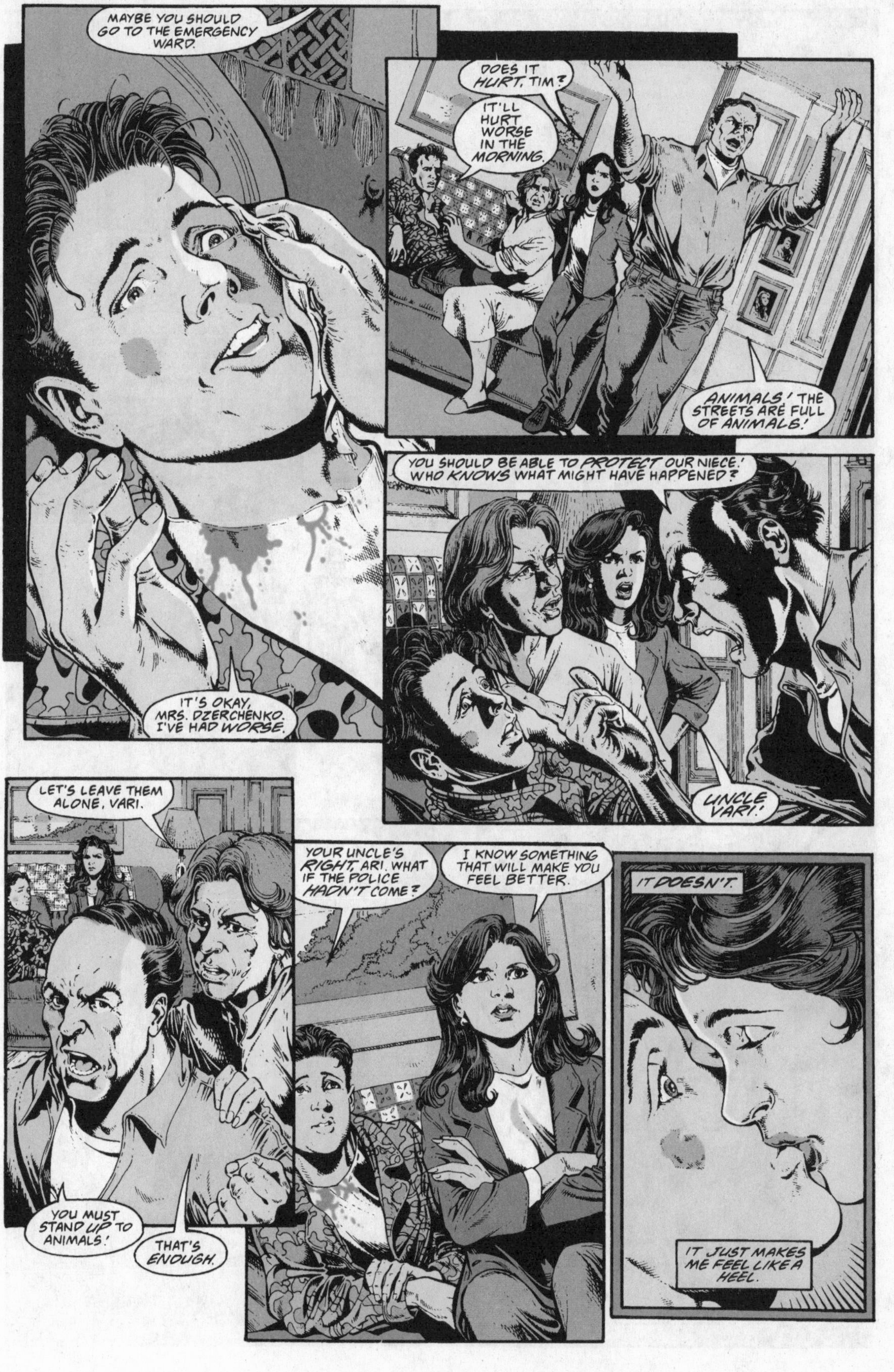
MAYBE YOU SHOULD GO TO THE EMERGENCY WARD.
IT'S OKAY, MRS. DZERCHENKO. I'VE HAD WORSE.
DOES IT HURT, TIM?
IT'LL HURT WORSE IN THE MORNING.
ANIMALS! THE STREETS ARE FULL OF ANIMALS!
YOU SHOULD BE ABLE TO PROTECT OUR NIECE! WHO KNOWS WHAT MIGHT HAVE HAPPENED?
UNCLE VARI!
LET'S LEAVE THEM ALONE, VARI.
YOU MUST STAND UP TO ANIMALS!
THAT'S ENOUGH.
YOUR UNCLE'S RIGHT, ARI. WHAT IF THE POLICE HADN'T COME?
I KNOW SOMETHING THAT WILL MAKE YOU FEEL BETTER.
IT DOESN'T.
IT JUST MAKES ME FEEL LIKE A HEEL.

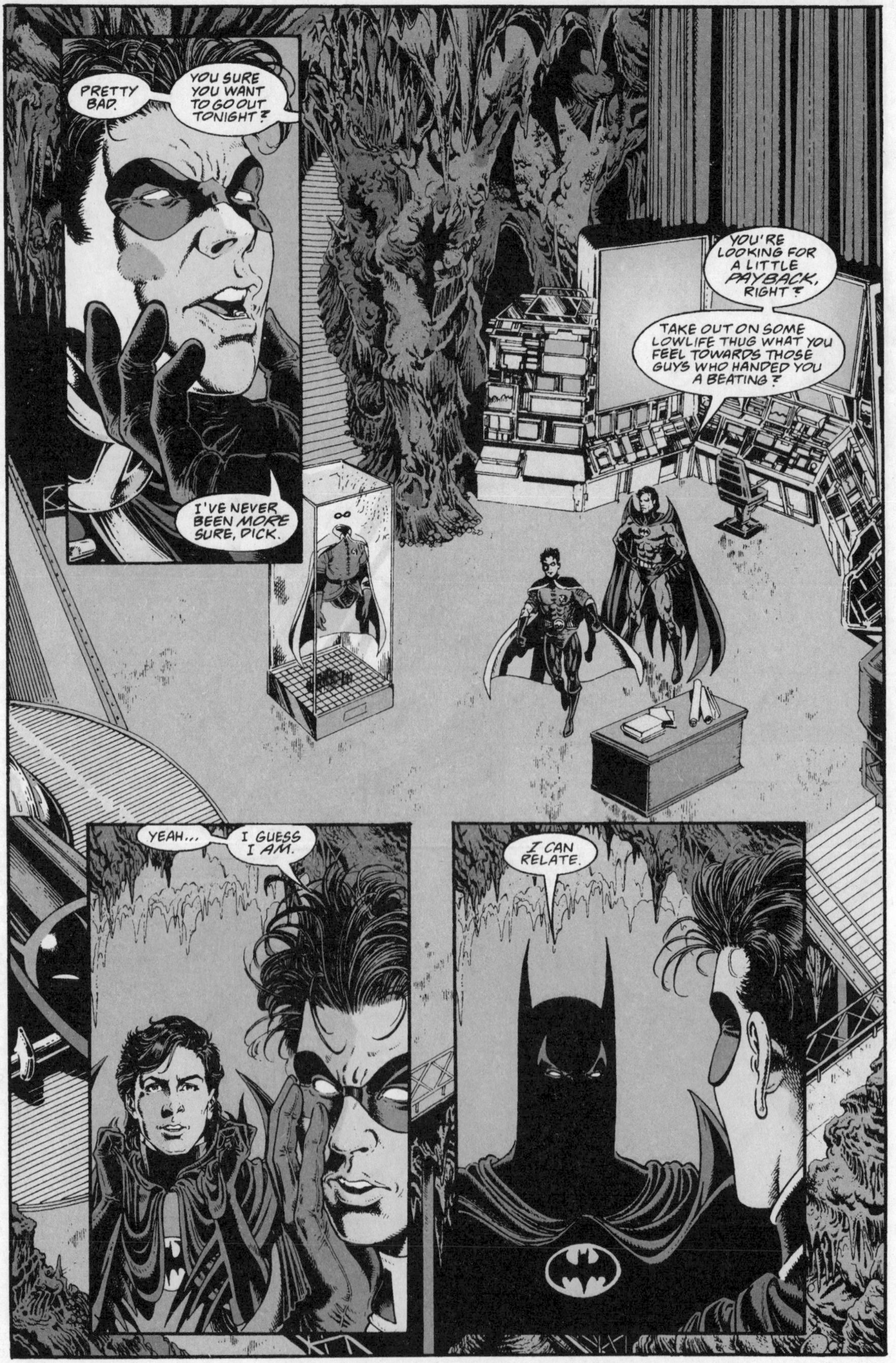
PRETTY BAD.
YOU SURE YOU WANT TO GO OUT TONIGHT?
I'VE NEVER BEEN MORE SURE, DICK.
YOU'RE LOOKING FOR A LITTLE PAYBACK, RIGHT?
TAKE OUT ON SOME LOWLIFE THUG WHAT YOU FEEL TOWARDS THOSE GUYS WHO HANDED YOU A BEATING?
YEAH...
I GUESS I AM.
I CAN RELATE.

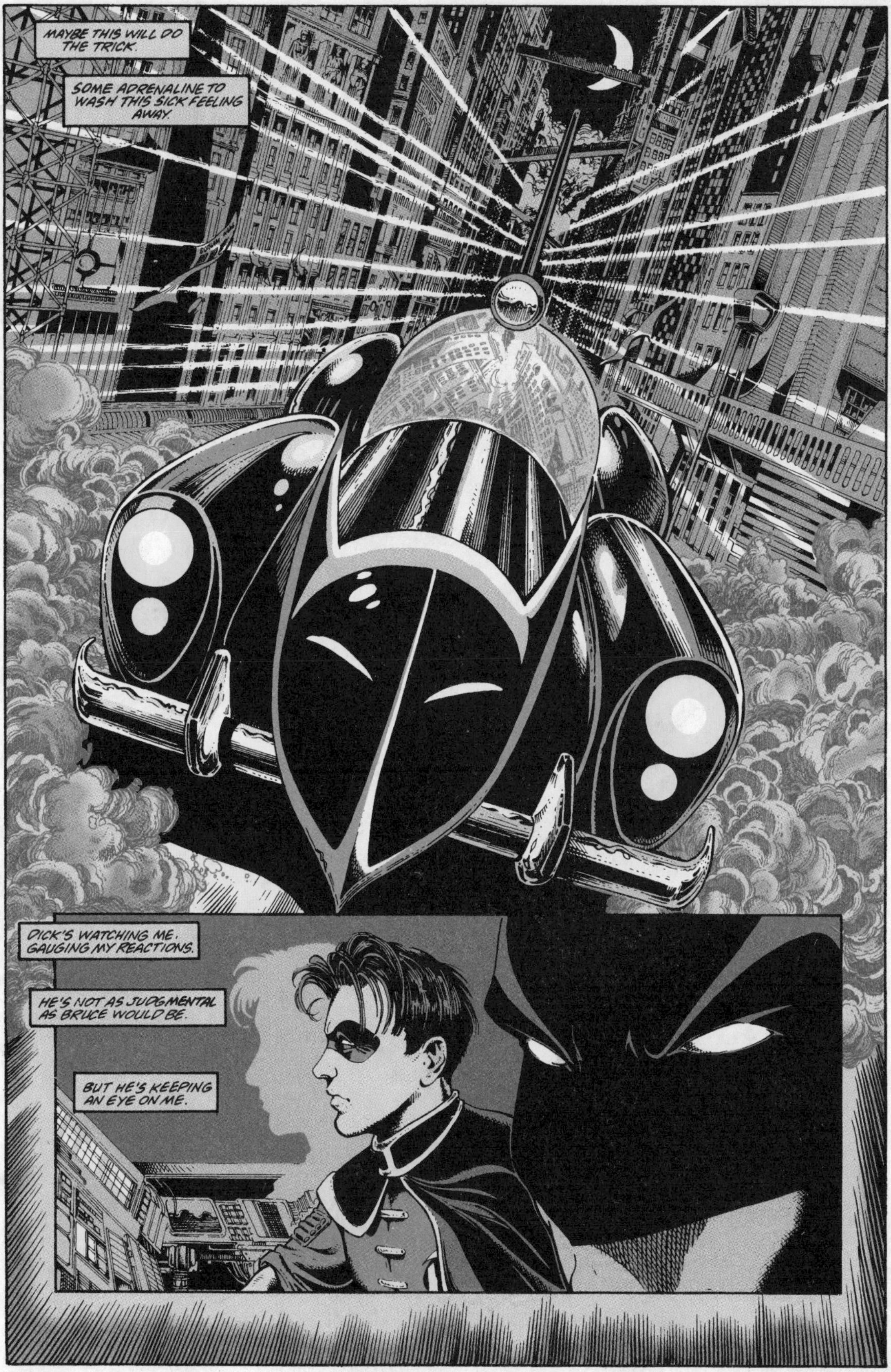
MAYBE THIS WILL DO THE TRICK.
SOME ADRENALINE TO WASH THIS SICK FEELING AWAY.
DICK'S WATCHING ME. GAUGING MY REACTIONS.
HE'S NOT AS JUDGMENTAL AS BRUCE WOULD BE.
BUT HE'S KEEPING AN EYE ON ME.

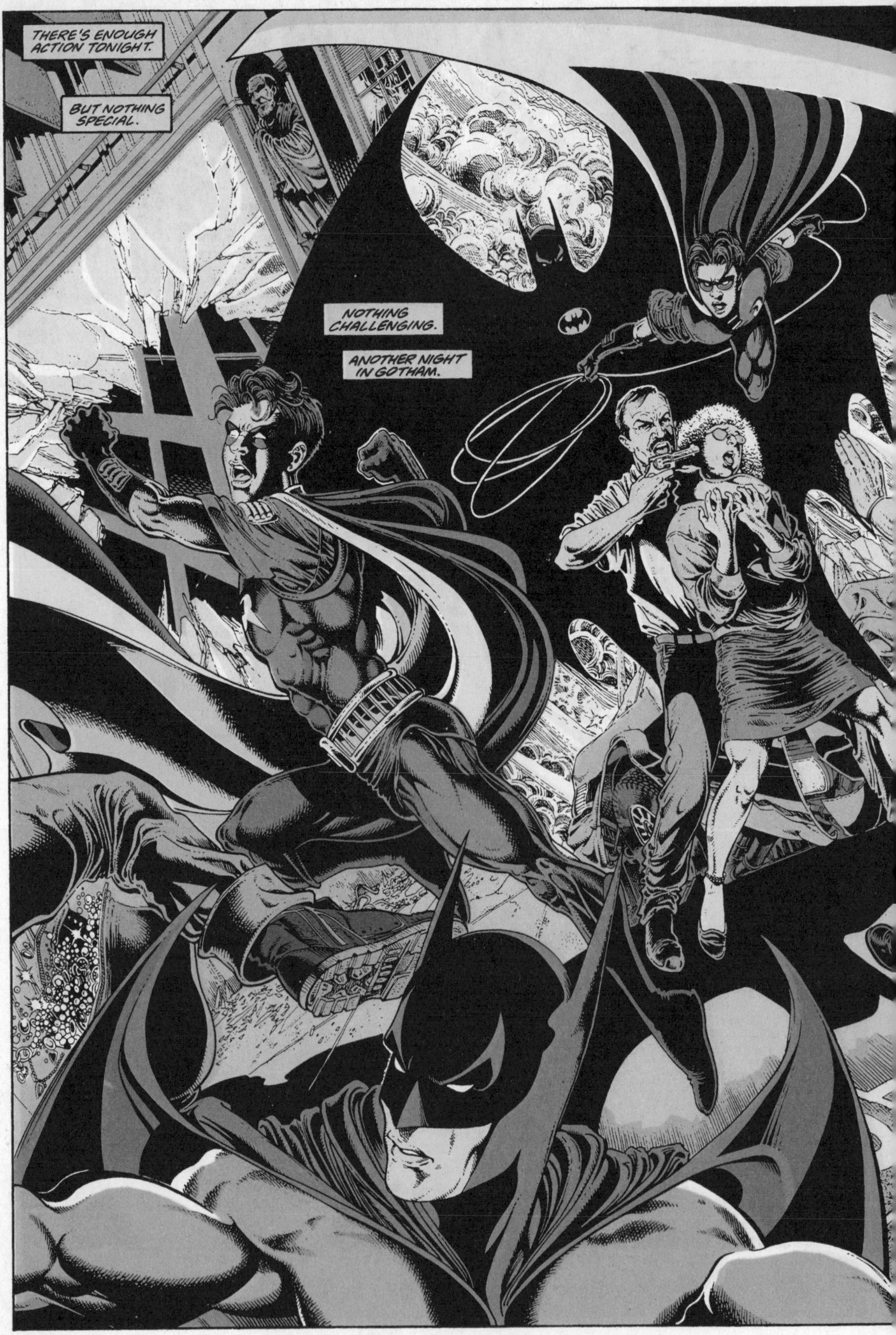
THERE'S ENOUGH ACTION TONIGHT.
BUT NOTHING SPECIAL.
NOTHING CHALLENGING.
ANOTHER NIGHT IN GOTHAM.

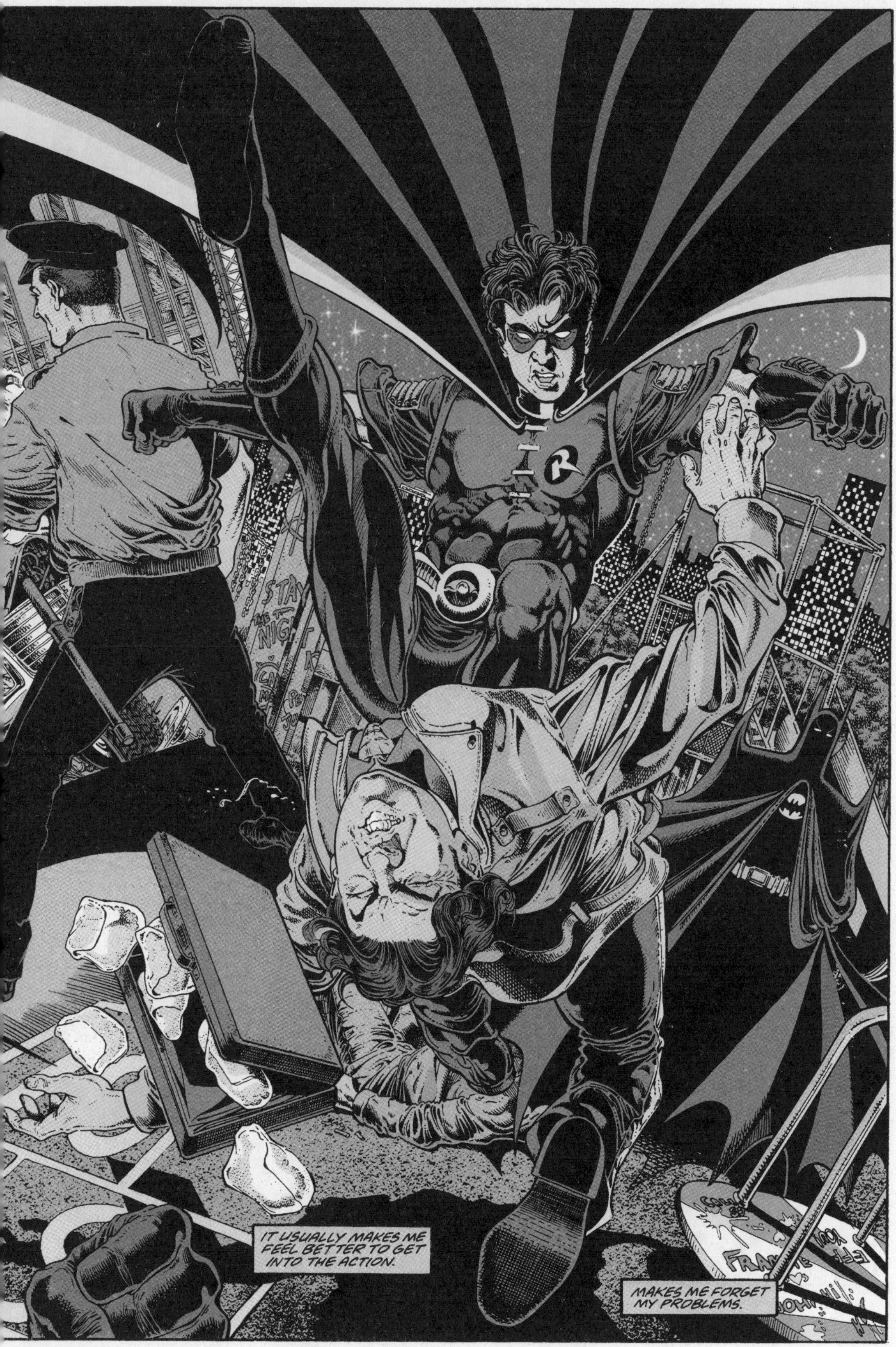
STAY THE NIGHT
IT USUALLY MAKES ME FEEL BETTER TO GET INTO THE ACTION.
MAKES ME FORGET MY PROBLEMS.

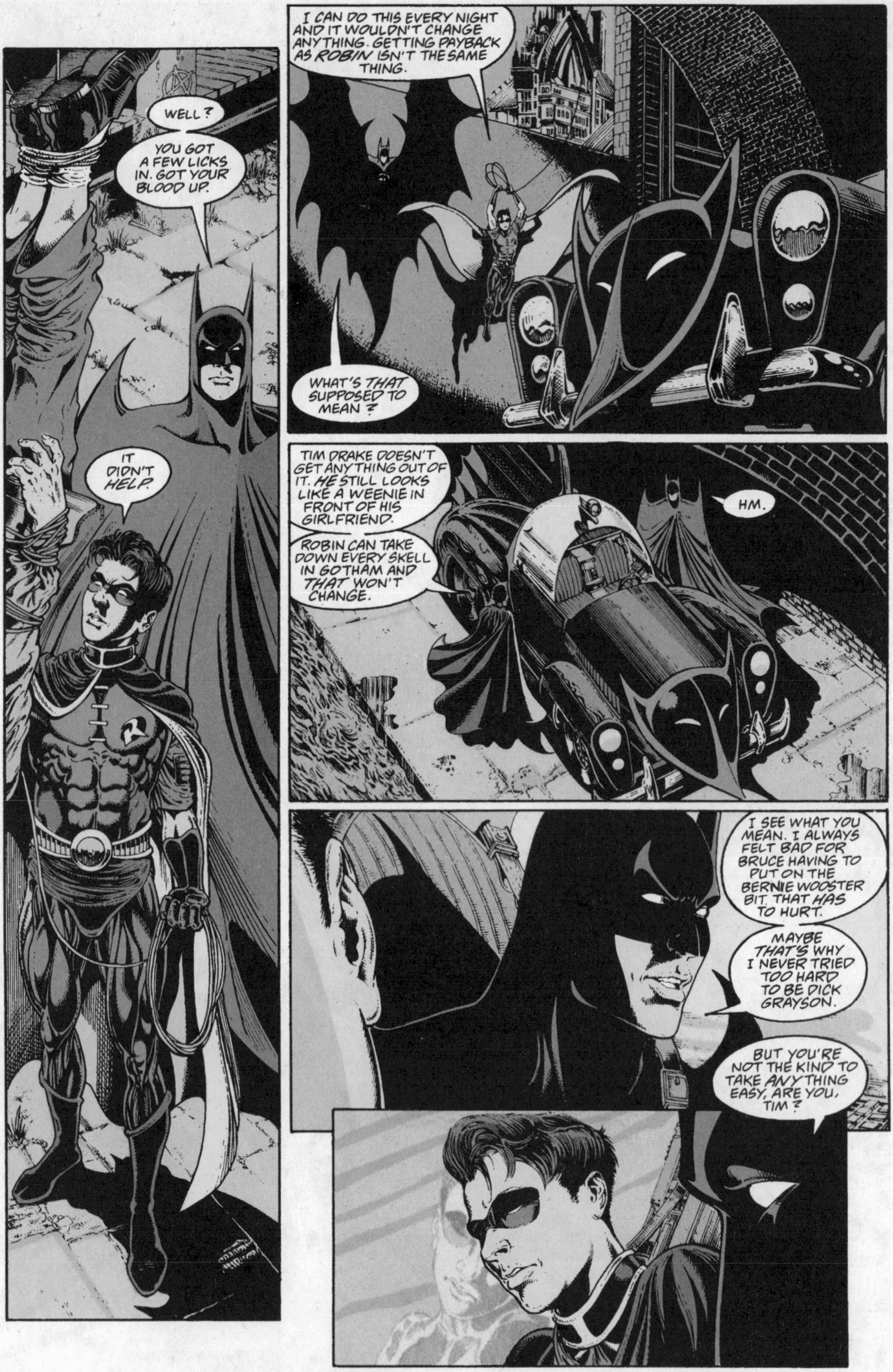
WELL?
YOU GOT A FEW LICKS IN. GOT YOUR BLOOD UP.
IT DIDN'T HELP.
I CAN DO THIS EVERY NIGHT AND IT WOULDN'T CHANGE ANYTHING. GETTING PAYBACK AS ROBIN ISN'T THE SAME THING.
WHAT'S THAT SUPPOSED TO MEAN?
TIM DRAKE DOESN'T GET ANYTHING OUT OF IT. HE STILL LOOKS LIKE A WEENIE IN FRONT OF HIS GIRLFRIEND.
ROBIN CAN TAKE DOWN EVERY SKELL IN GOTHAM AND THAT WON'T CHANGE.
HM.
I SEE WHAT YOU MEAN. I ALWAYS FELT BAD FOR BRUCE HAVING TO PUT ON THE BERNIE WOOSTER BIT. THAT HAS TO HURT.
MAYBE THAT'S WHY I NEVER TRIED TOO HARD TO BE DICK GRAYSON.
BUT YOU'RE NOT THE KIND TO TAKE ANYTHING EASY, ARE YOU, TIM?

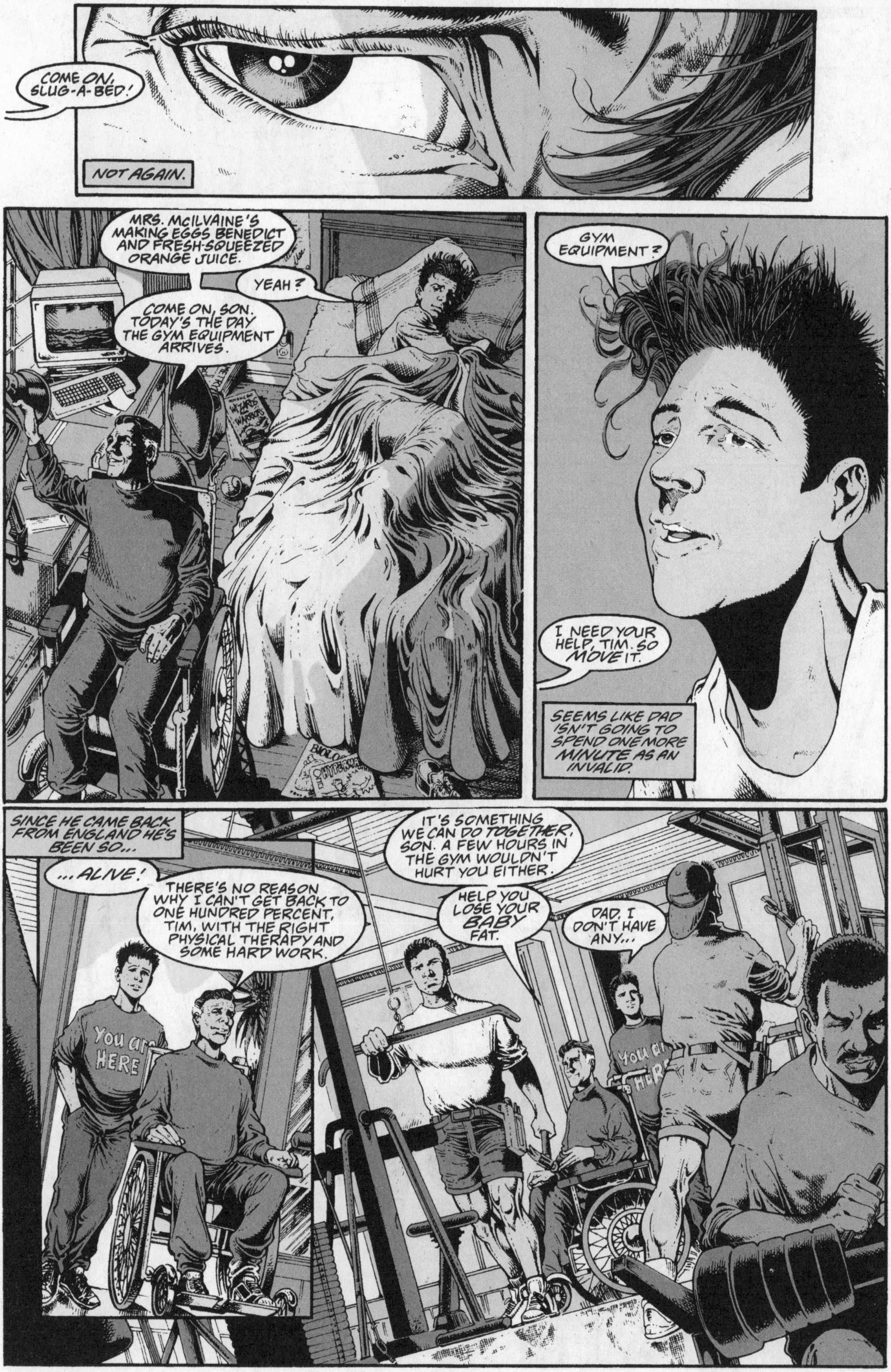
COME ON, SLUG-A-BED!
NOT AGAIN.
MRS. McILVAINE'S MAKING EGGS BENEDICT AND FRESH-SQUEEZED ORANGE JUICE.
YEAH?
COME ON, SON. TODAY'S THE DAY THE GYM EQUIPMENT ARRIVES.
GYM EQUIPMENT?
I NEED YOUR HELP, TIM. SO MOVE IT.
SEEMS LIKE DAD ISN'T GOING TO SPEND ONE MORE MINUTE AS AN INVALID.
SINCE HE CAME BACK FROM ENGLAND HE'S BEEN SO...
...ALIVE!
THERE'S NO REASON WHY I CAN'T GET BACK TO ONE HUNDRED PERCENT, TIM, WITH THE RIGHT PHYSICAL THERAPY AND SOME HARD WORK.
IT'S SOMETHING WE CAN DO TOGETHER, SON. A FEW HOURS IN THE GYM WOULDN'T HURT YOU EITHER.
HELP YOU LOSE YOUR BABY FAT.
DAD, I DON'T HAVE ANY...
You are HERE

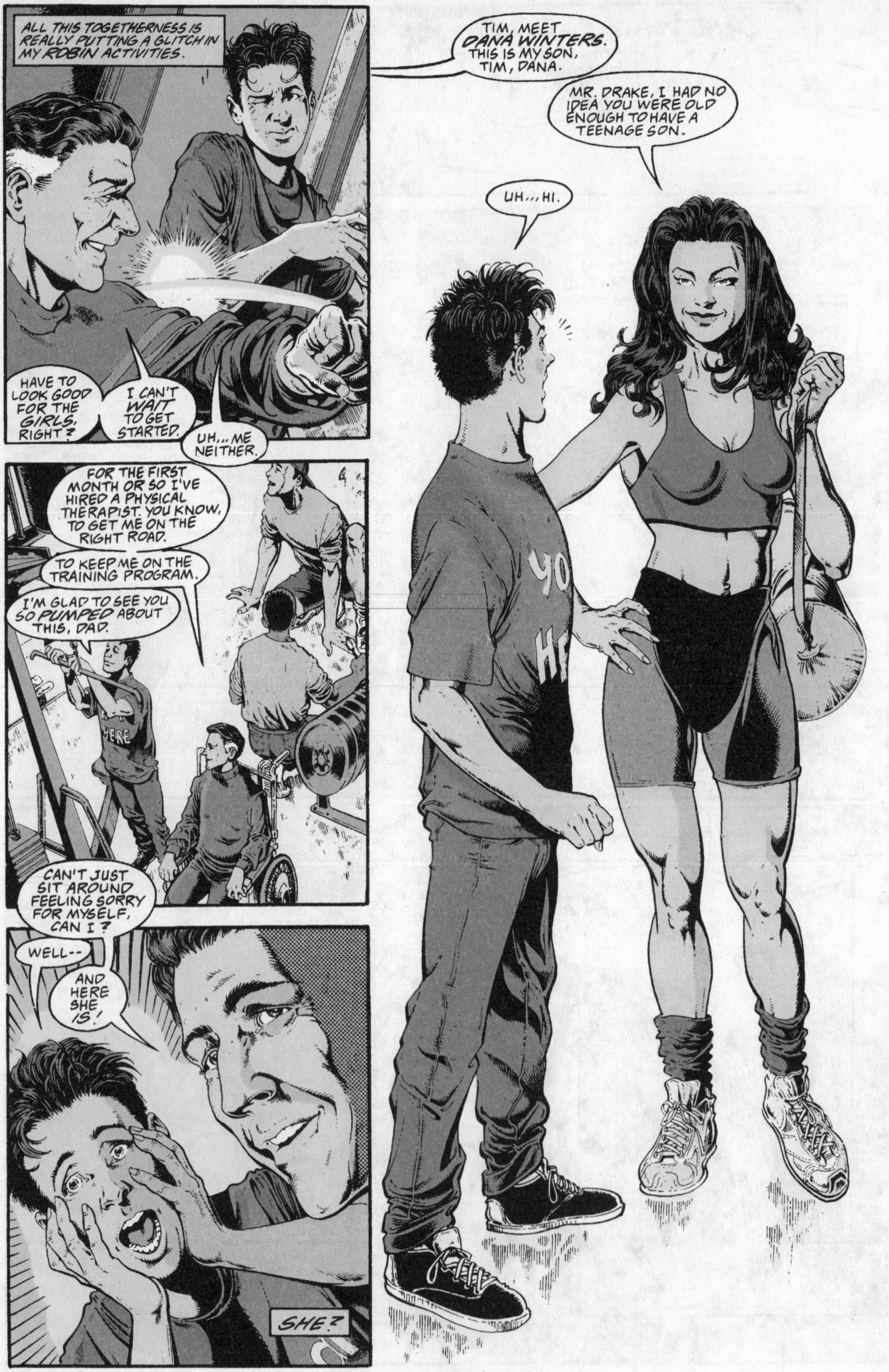
ALL THIS TOGETHERNESS IS REALLY PUTTING A GLITCH IN MY ROBIN ACTIVITIES.
HAVE TO LOOK GOOD FOR THE GIRLS. RIGHT?
I CAN'T WAIT TO GET STARTED.
UH... ME NEITHER.
FOR THE FIRST MONTH OR SO I'VE HIRED A PHYSICAL THERAPIST. YOU KNOW, TO GET ME ON THE RIGHT ROAD.
TO KEEP ME ON THE TRAINING PROGRAM.
I'M GLAD TO SEE YOU SO PUMPED ABOUT THIS, DAD.
CAN'T JUST SIT AROUND FEELING SORRY FOR MYSELF, CAN I?
WELL--
AND HERE SHE IS!
SHE?
TIM, MEET DANA WINTERS. THIS IS MY SON, TIM, DANA.
MR. DRAKE, I HAD NO IDEA YOU WERE OLD ENOUGH TO HAVE A TEENAGE SON.
UH... HI.

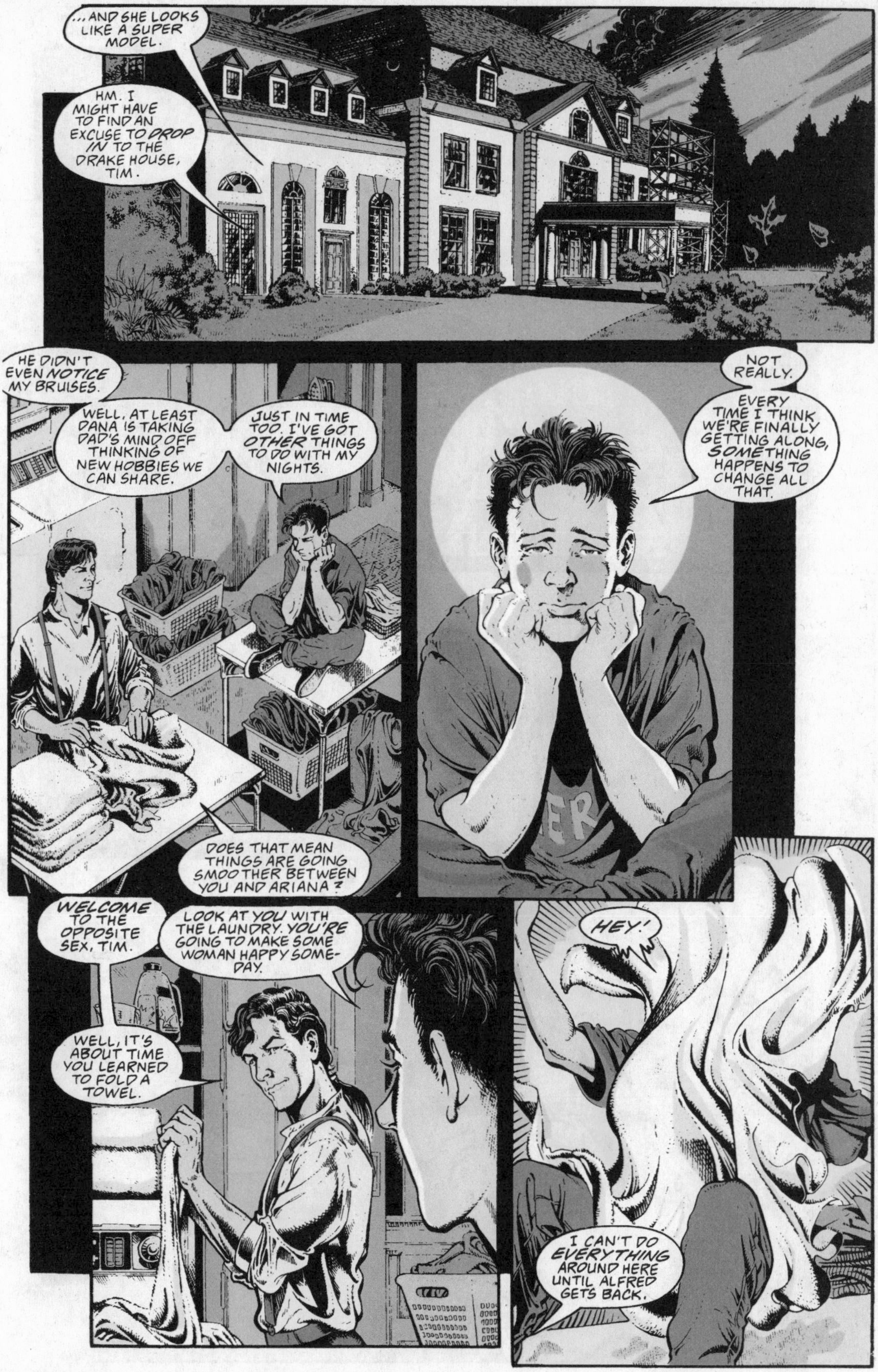

...AND SHE LOOKS LIKE A SUPER MODEL.
HM. I MIGHT HAVE TO FIND AN EXCUSE TO DROP IN TO THE DRAKE HOUSE, TIM.
HE DIDN'T EVEN NOTICE MY BRUISES.
WELL, AT LEAST DANA IS TAKING DAD'S MIND OFF THINKING OF NEW HOBBIES WE CAN SHARE.
JUST IN TIME TOO. I'VE GOT OTHER THINGS TO DO WITH MY NIGHTS.
DOES THAT MEAN THINGS ARE GOING SMOOTHER BETWEEN YOU AND ARIANA?
NOT REALLY.
EVERY TIME I THINK WE'RE FINALLY GETTING ALONG, SOMETHING HAPPENS TO CHANGE ALL THAT.
WELCOME TO THE OPPOSITE SEX, TIM.
LOOK AT YOU WITH THE LAUNDRY. YOU'RE GOING TO MAKE SOME WOMAN HAPPY SOME-DAY.
WELL, IT'S ABOUT TIME YOU LEARNED TO FOLD A TOWEL.
HEY!
I CAN'T DO EVERYTHING AROUND HERE UNTIL ALFRED GETS BACK.

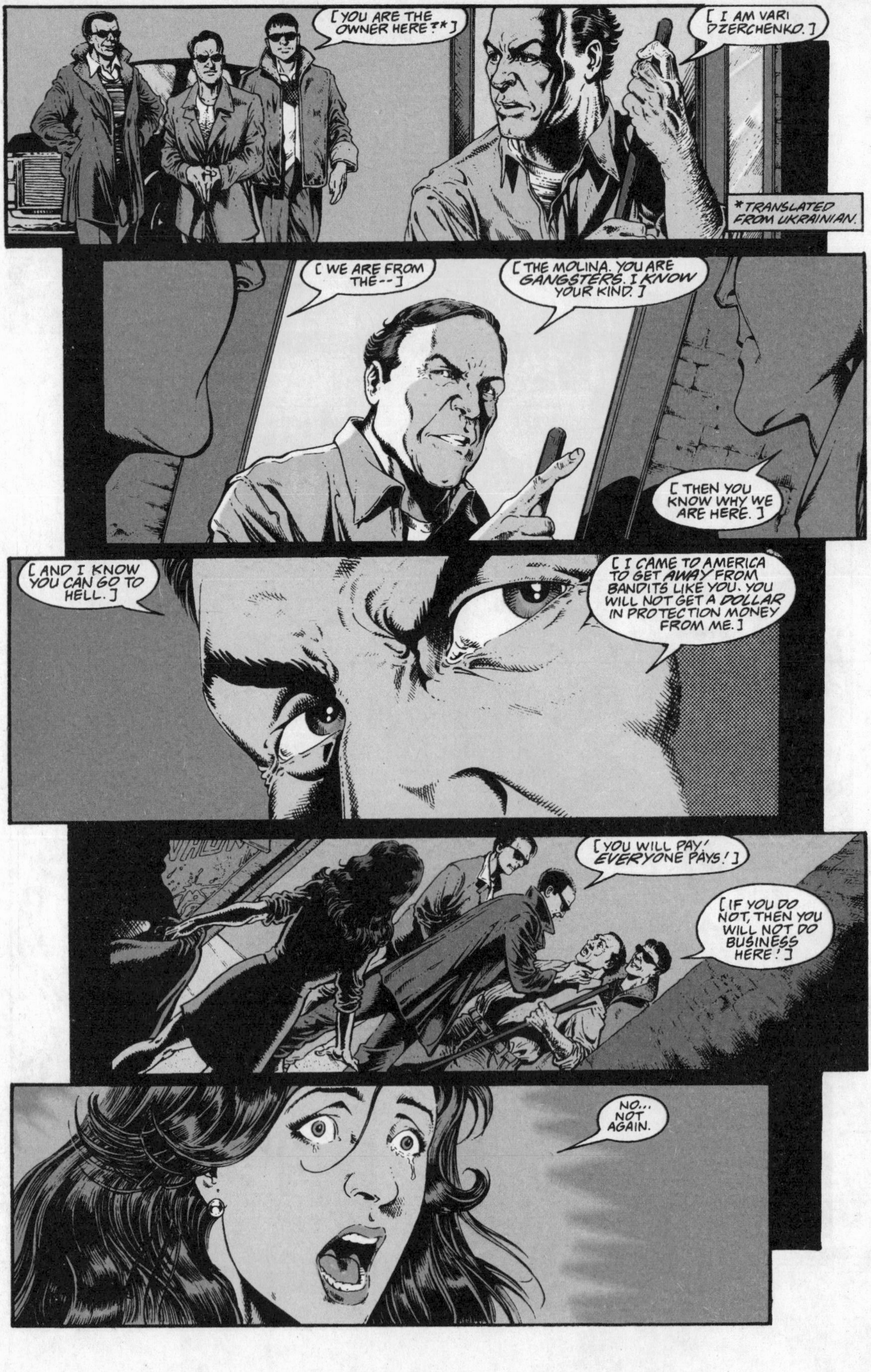
[YOU ARE THE OWNER HERE?*]
[I AM VARI DZERCHENKO.]
*TRANSLATED FROM UKRAINIAN.
[WE ARE FROM THE--]
[THE MOLINA. YOU ARE GANGSTERS. I KNOW YOUR KIND.]
[THEN YOU KNOW WHY WE ARE HERE.]
[AND I KNOW YOU CAN GO TO HELL.]
[I CAME TO AMERICA TO GET AWAY FROM BANDITS LIKE YOU. YOU WILL NOT GET A DOLLAR IN PROTECTION MONEY FROM ME.]
[YOU WILL PAY! EVERYONE PAYS!]
[IF YOU DO NOT, THEN YOU WILL NOT DO BUSINESS HERE!]
NO... NOT AGAIN.

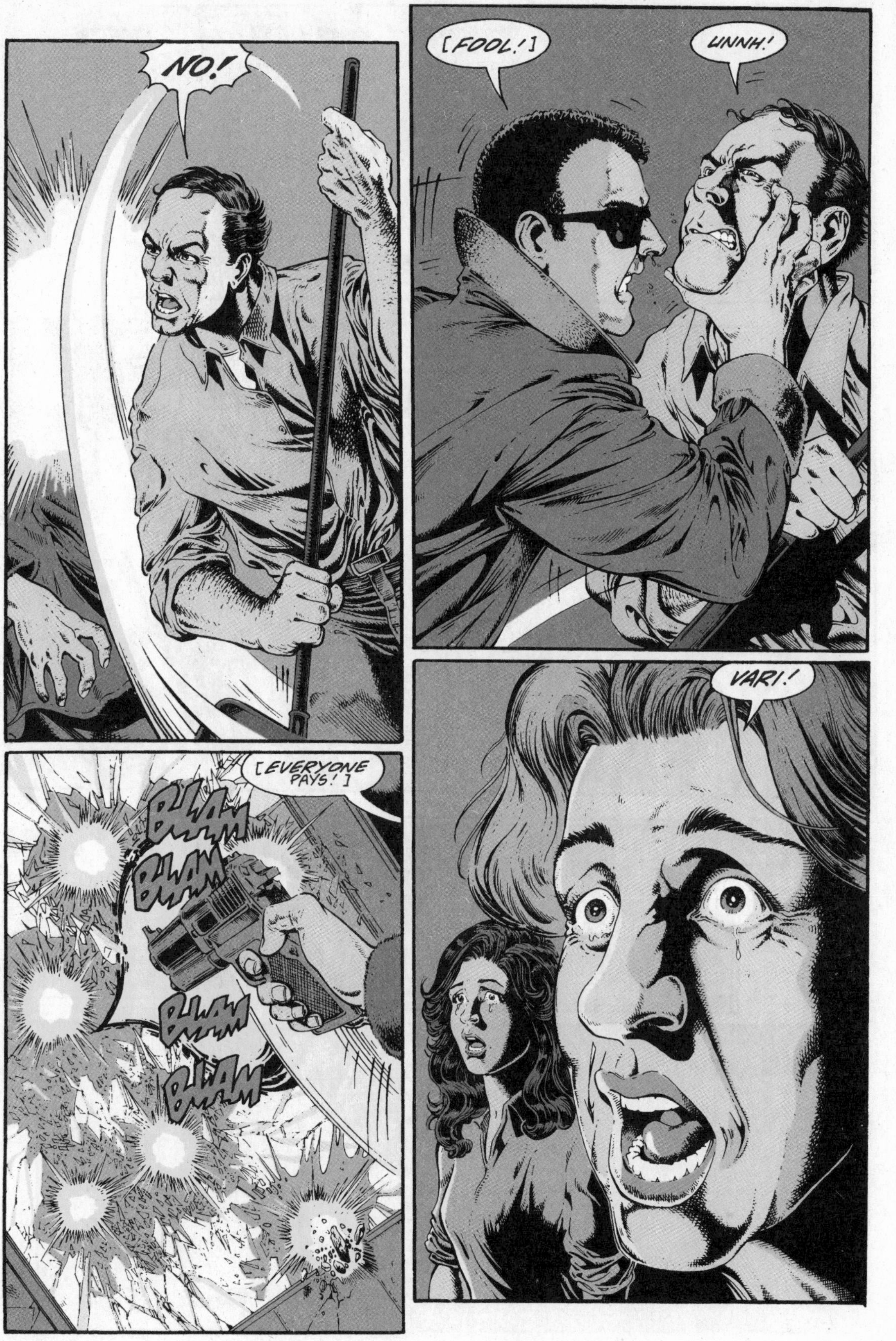
NO!
[FOOL!]
UNNH!
[EVERYONE PAYS!]
BLAM
BLAM
BLAM
BLAM
VARI!

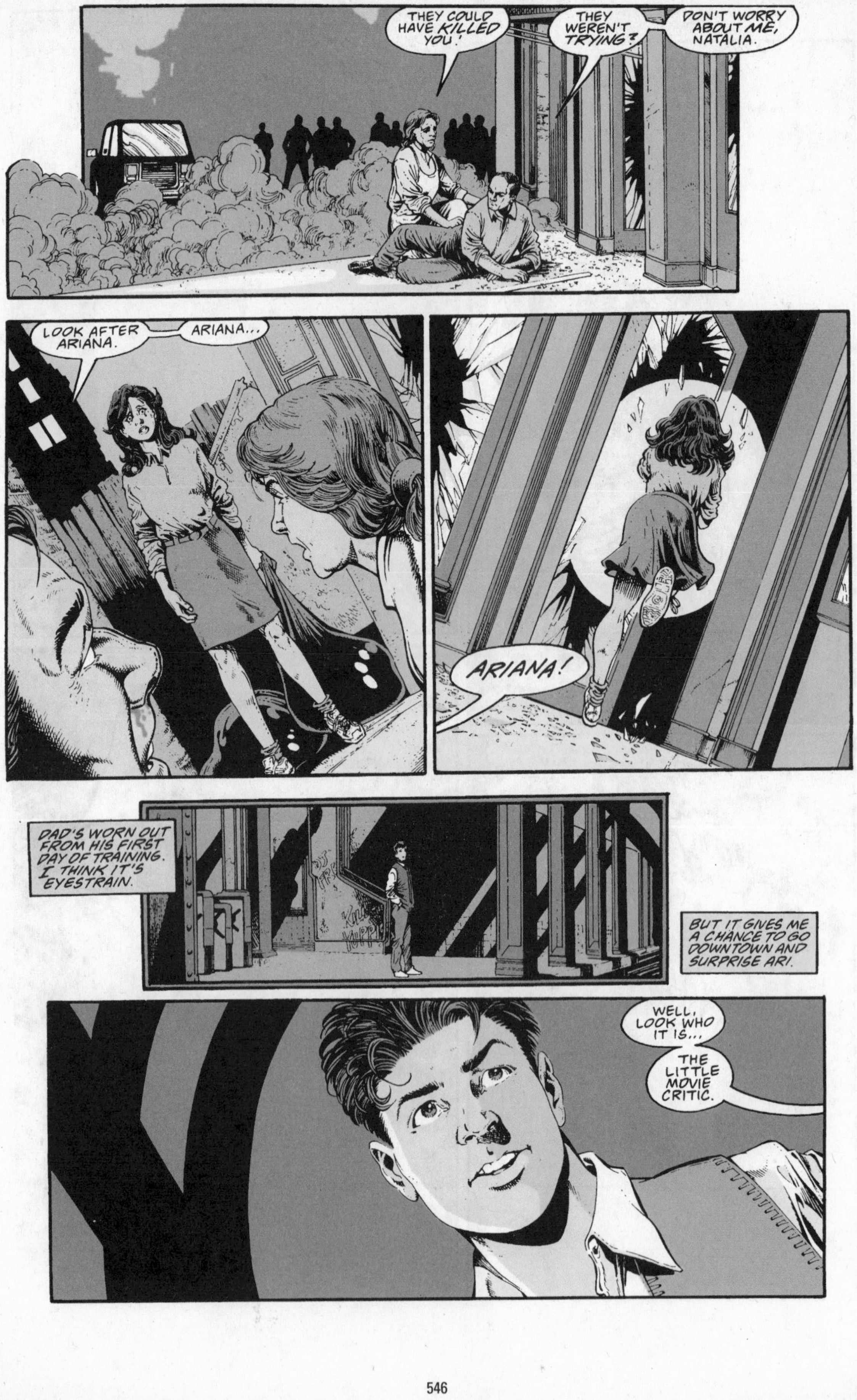
THEY COULD HAVE KILLED YOU!
THEY WEREN'T TRYING?
DON'T WORRY ABOUT ME, NATALIA.
LOOK AFTER ARIANA.
ARIANA...
ARIANA!
DAD'S WORN OUT FROM HIS FIRST DAY OF TRAINING. I THINK IT'S EYESTRAIN.
BUT IT GIVES ME A CHANCE TO GO DOWNTOWN AND SURPRISE ARI.
WELL, LOOK WHO IT IS...
THE LITTLE MOVIE CRITIC.

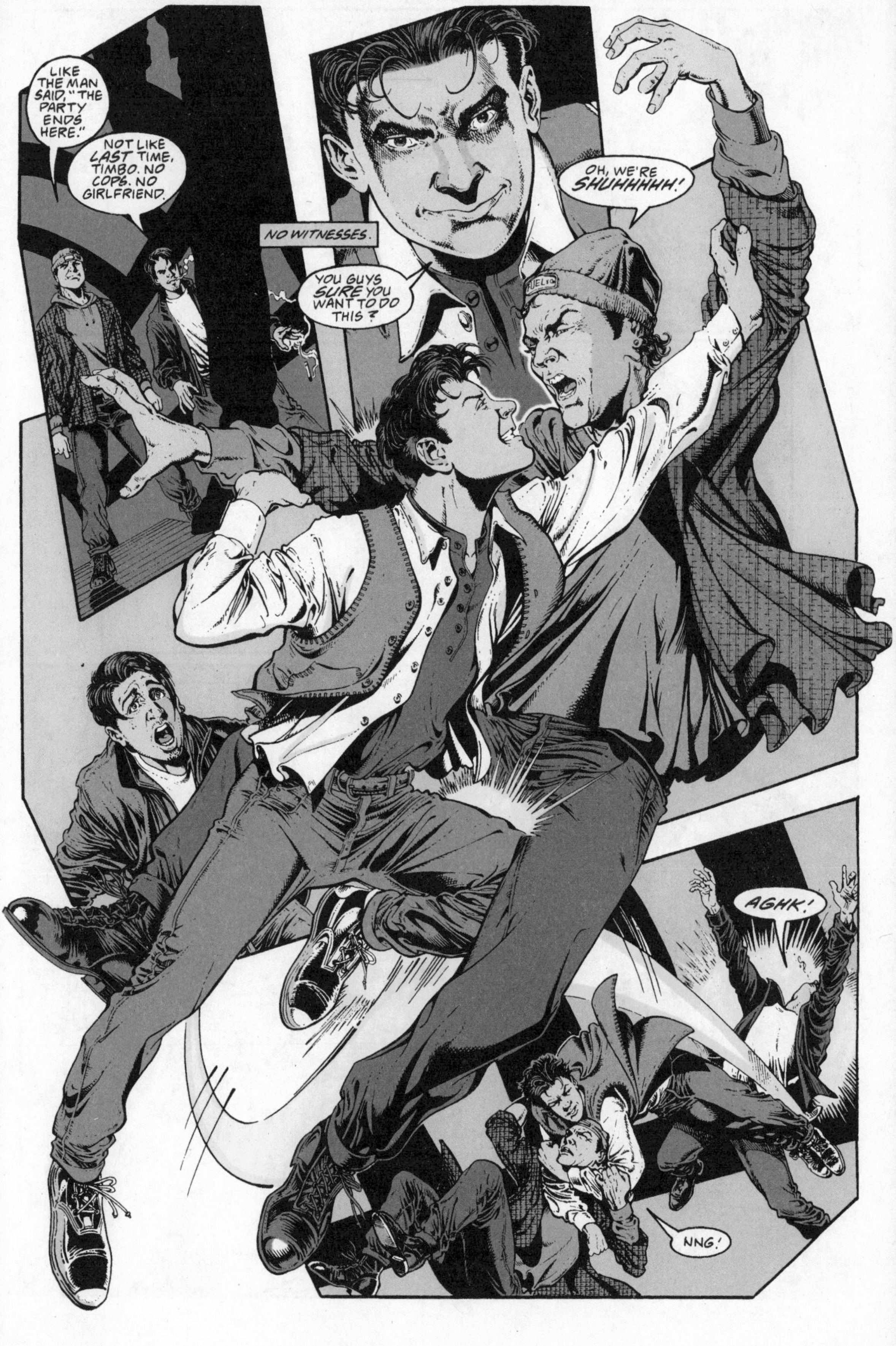

LIKE THE MAN SAID, "THE PARTY ENDS HERE."
NOT LIKE LAST TIME, TIMBO. NO COPS. NO GIRLFRIEND.
NO WITNESSES.
YOU GUYS SURE YOU WANT TO DO THIS?
OH, WE'RE SHUHHHHH!
AGHK!
NNG!

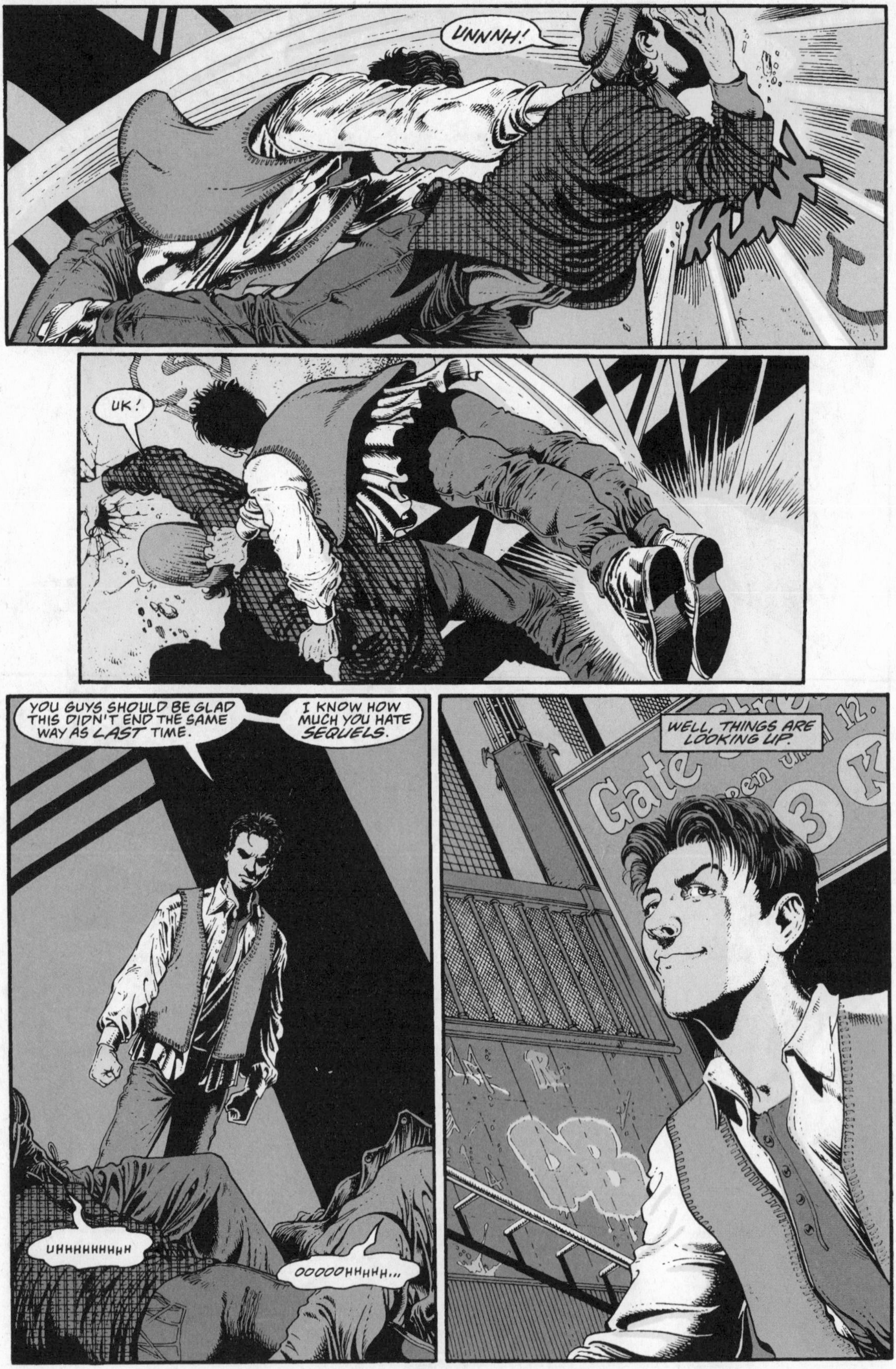
UNNNH!
KLANK
UK!
YOU GUYS SHOULD BE GLAD THIS DIDN'T END THE SAME WAY AS LAST TIME.
I KNOW HOW MUCH YOU HATE SEQUELS.
UHHHHHHHHH
OOOOOHHHHH...
WELL, THINGS ARE LOOKING UP.
Gate
3

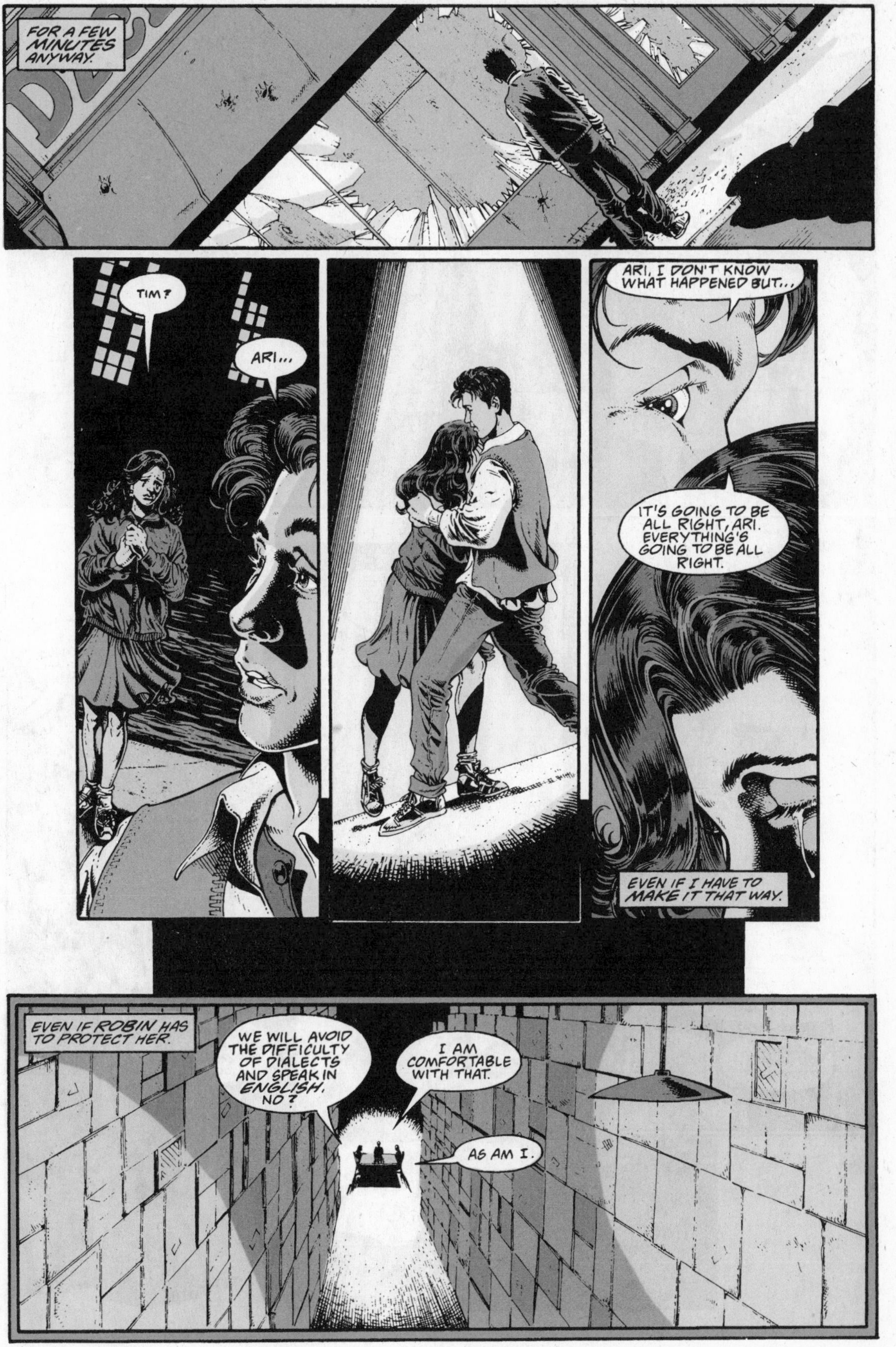
FOR A FEW MINUTES ANYWAY.
TIM?
ARI...
ARI, I DON'T KNOW WHAT HAPPENED BUT...
IT'S GOING TO BE ALL RIGHT, ARI. EVERYTHING'S GOING TO BE ALL RIGHT.
EVEN IF I HAVE TO MAKE IT THAT WAY.
EVEN IF ROBIN HAS TO PROTECT HER.
WE WILL AVOID THE DIFFICULTY OF DIALECTS AND SPEAK IN ENGLISH, NO?
I AM COMFORTABLE WITH THAT.
AS AM I.

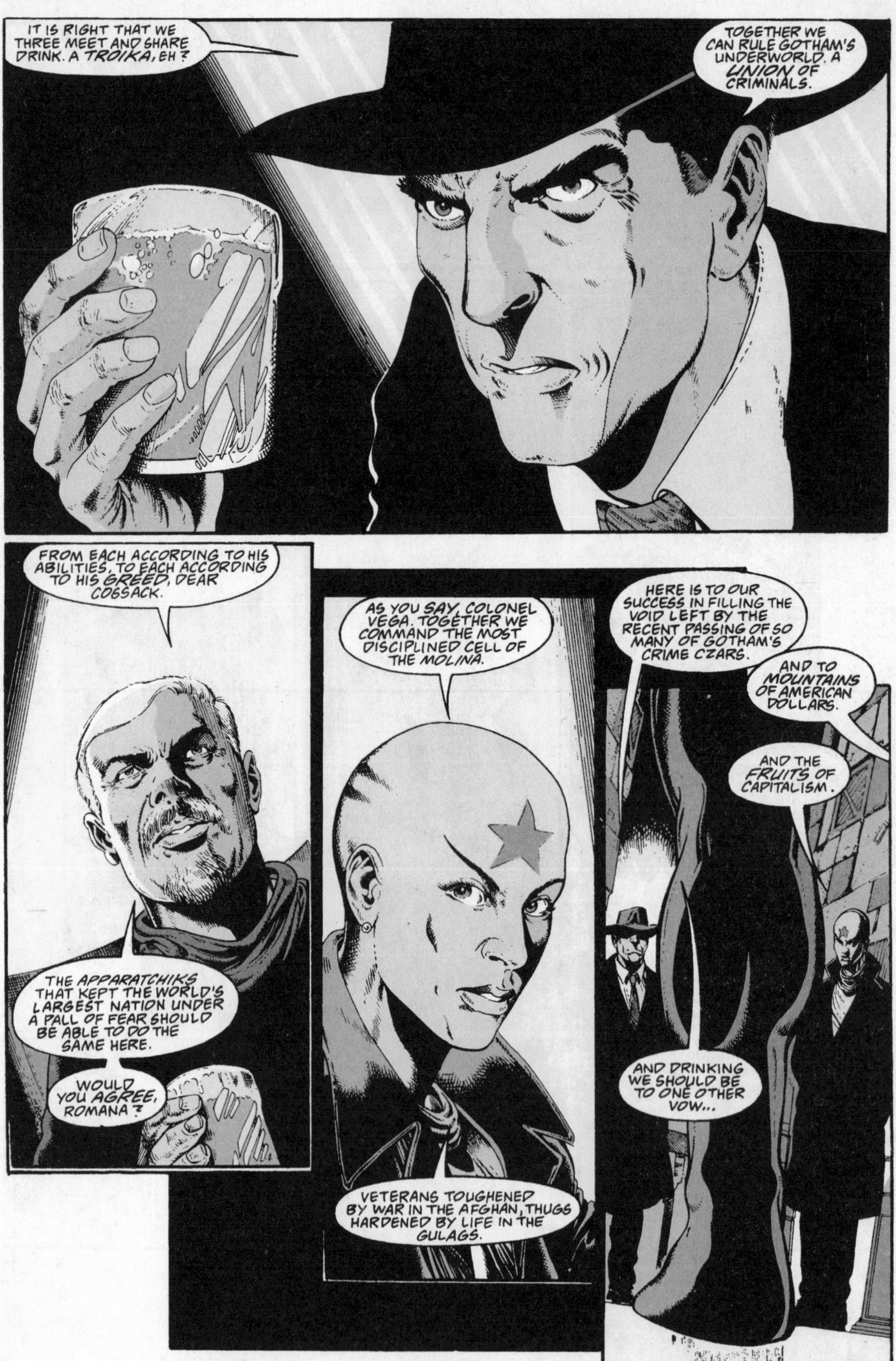
IT IS RIGHT THAT WE THREE MEET AND SHARE DRINK. A TROIKA, EH?
TOGETHER WE CAN RULE GOTHAM'S UNDERWORLD. A UNION OF CRIMINALS.
FROM EACH ACCORDING TO HIS ABILITIES, TO EACH ACCORDING TO HIS GREED, DEAR COSSACK.
THE APPARATCHIKS THAT KEPT THE WORLD'S LARGEST NATION UNDER A PALL OF FEAR SHOULD BE ABLE TO DO THE SAME HERE.
WOULD YOU AGREE, ROMANA?
AS YOU SAY, COLONEL VEGA. TOGETHER WE COMMAND THE MOST DISCIPLINED CELL OF THE MOLINA.
VETERANS TOUGHENED BY WAR IN THE AFGHAN, THUGS HARDENED BY LIFE IN THE GULAGS.
HERE IS TO OUR SUCCESS IN FILLING THE VOID LEFT BY THE RECENT PASSING OF SO MANY OF GOTHAM'S CRIME CZARS.
AND TO MOUNTAINS OF AMERICAN DOLLARS.
AND THE FRUITS OF CAPITALISM.
AND DRINKING WE SHOULD BE TO ONE OTHER VOW...

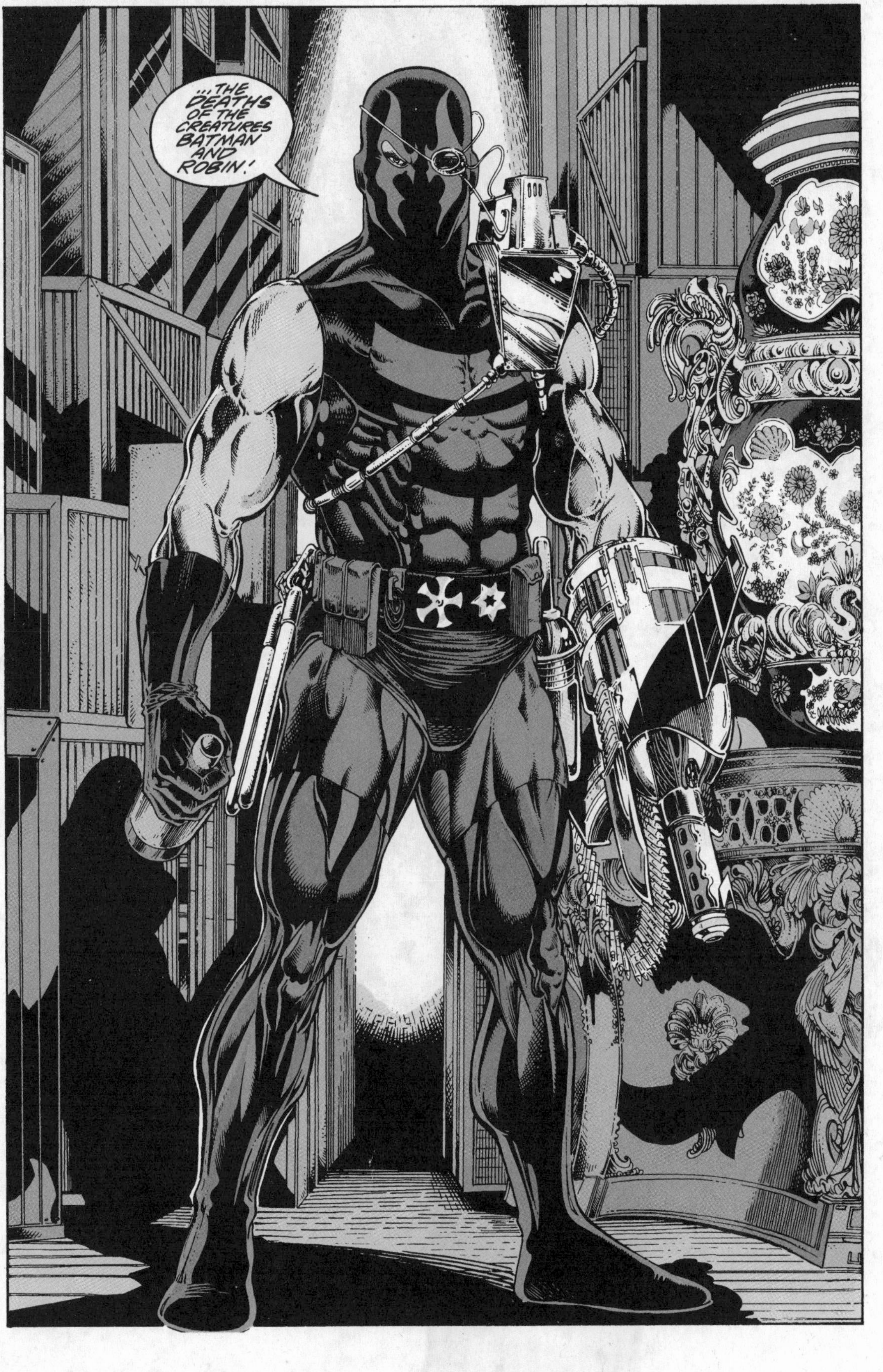
...THE DEATHS OF THE CREATURES BATMAN AND ROBIN!

Cover art by RON WAGNER and JOSEF RUBINSTEIN

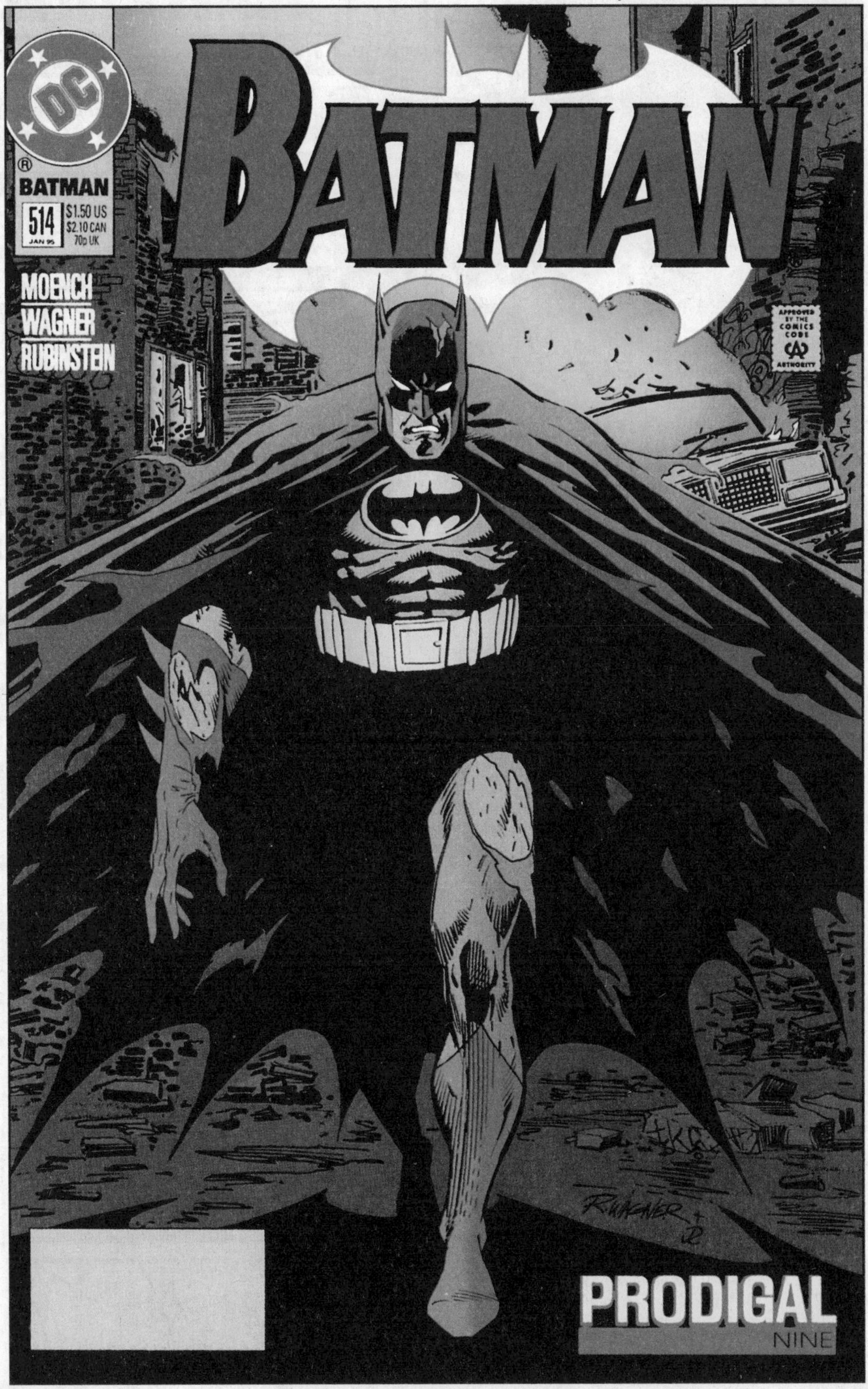
BATMAN
BATMAN
514
JAN 95
$1.50 US
$2.10 CAN
70p UK
MOENCH
WAGNER
RUBINSTEIN
APPROVED BY THE COMICS CODE AUTHORITY
R. WAGNER
PRODIGAL
NINE

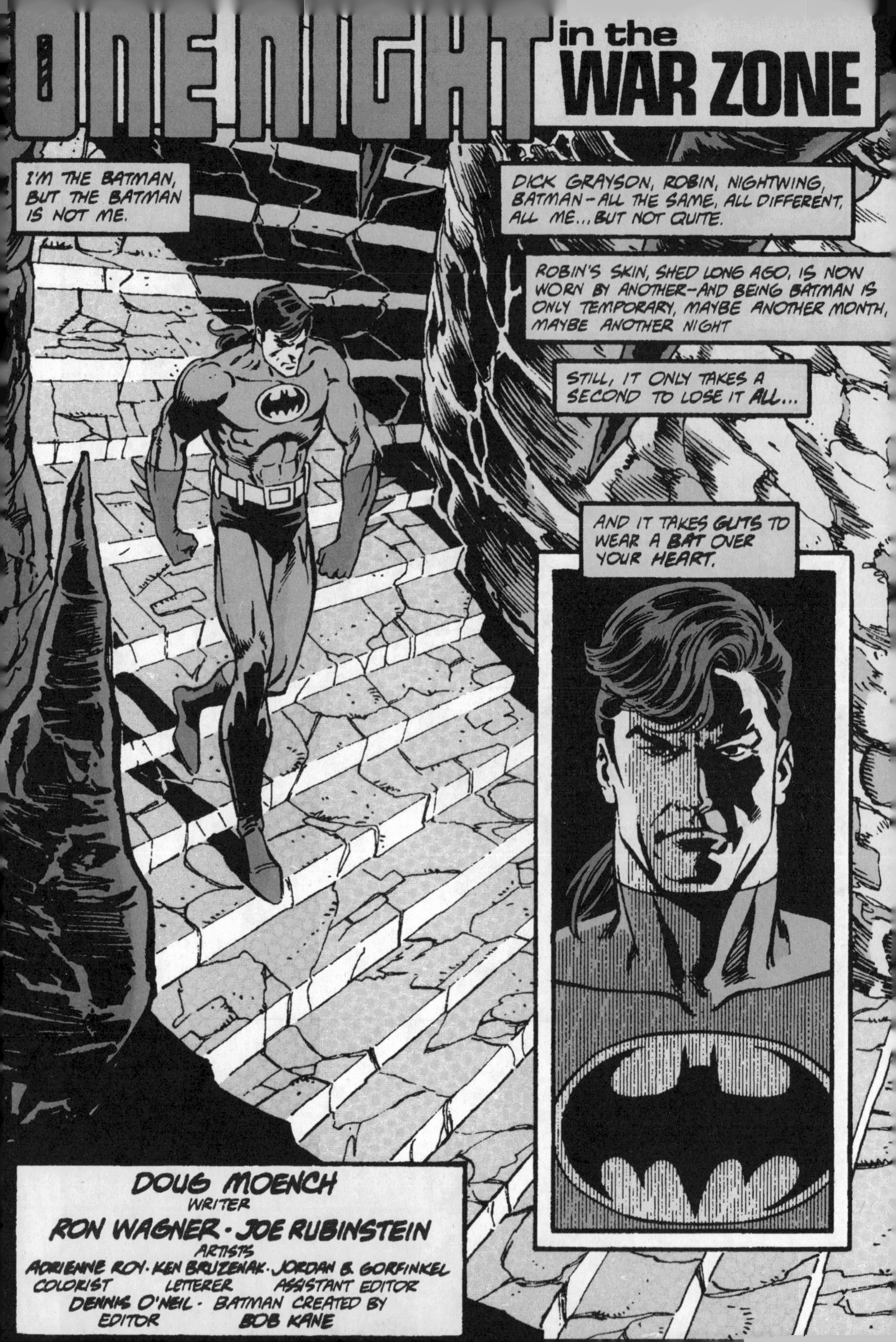
ONE NIGHT in the WAR ZONE
I'M THE BATMAN, BUT THE BATMAN IS NOT ME.
DICK GRAYSON, ROBIN, NIGHTWING, BATMAN—ALL THE SAME, ALL DIFFERENT, ALL ME... BUT NOT QUITE.
ROBIN'S SKIN, SHED LONG AGO, IS NOW WORN BY ANOTHER—AND BEING BATMAN IS ONLY TEMPORARY, MAYBE ANOTHER MONTH, MAYBE ANOTHER NIGHT
STILL, IT ONLY TAKES A SECOND TO LOSE IT ALL...
AND IT TAKES GUTS TO WEAR A BAT OVER YOUR HEART.
DOUG MOENCH WRITER
RON WAGNER · JOE RUBINSTEIN ARTISTS
ADRIENNE ROY · KEN BRUZENAK · JORDAN B. GORFINKEL
COLORIST LETTERER ASSISTANT EDITOR
DENNIS O'NEIL · BATMAN CREATED BY
EDITOR BOB KANE

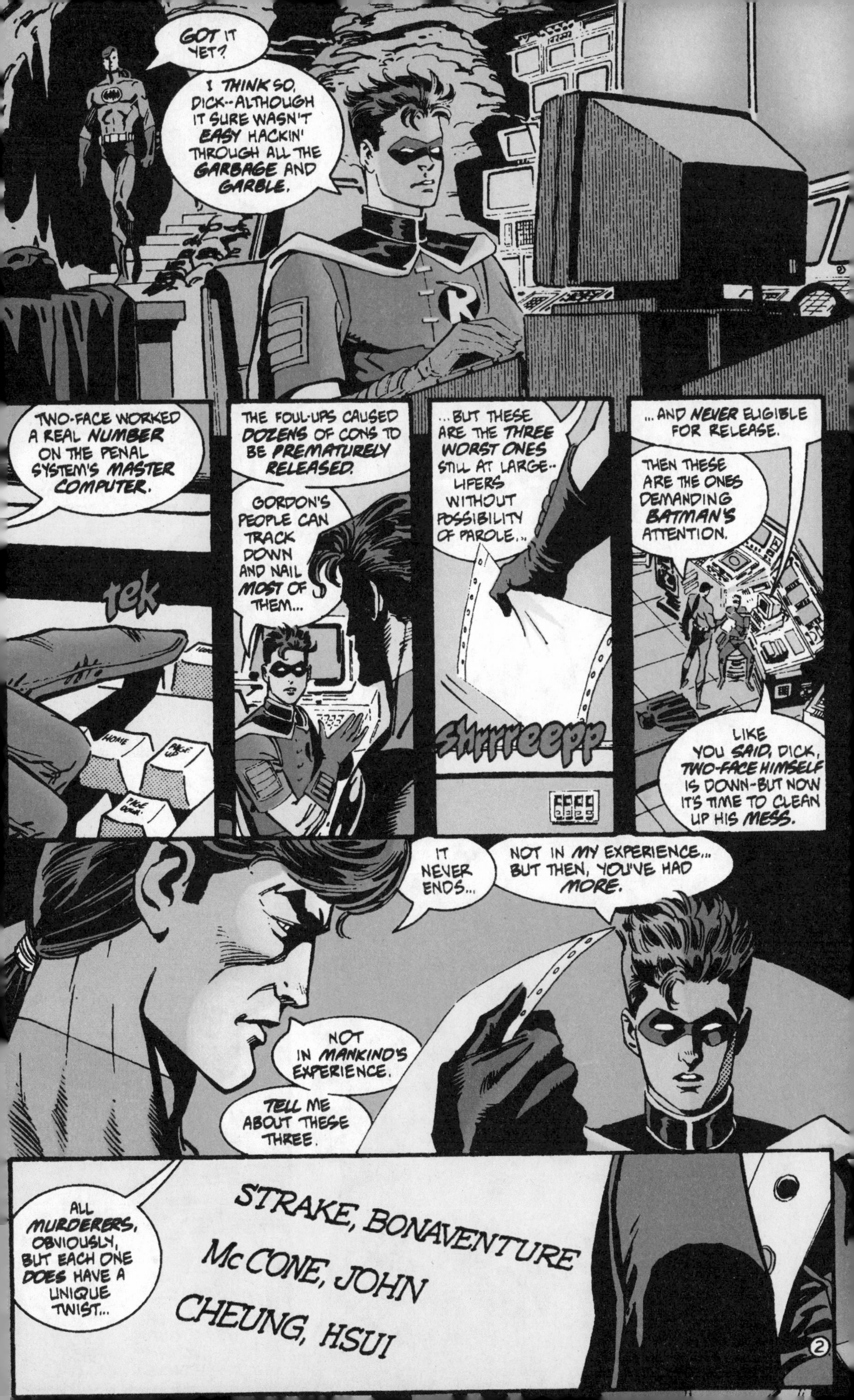
GOT IT YET?
I THINK SO, DICK--ALTHOUGH IT SURE WASN'T EASY HACKIN' THROUGH ALL THE GARBAGE AND GARBLE.
TWO-FACE WORKED A REAL NUMBER ON THE PENAL SYSTEM'S MASTER COMPUTER.
tek
HOME
PAGE UP
PAGE DOWN
THE FOUL-UPS CAUSED DOZENS OF CONS TO BE PREMATURELY RELEASED.
GORDON'S PEOPLE CAN TRACK DOWN AND NAIL MOST OF THEM...
...BUT THESE ARE THE THREE WORST ONES STILL AT LARGE.. LIFERS WITHOUT POSSIBILITY OF PAROLE...
shrrreepp
...AND NEVER ELIGIBLE FOR RELEASE.
THEN THESE ARE THE ONES DEMANDING BATMAN'S ATTENTION.
LIKE YOU SAID, DICK, TWO-FACE HIMSELF IS DOWN--BUT NOW IT'S TIME TO CLEAN UP HIS MESS.
IT NEVER ENDS...
NOT IN MY EXPERIENCE... BUT THEN, YOU'VE HAD MORE.
NOT IN MANKIND'S EXPERIENCE.
TELL ME ABOUT THESE THREE.
ALL MURDERERS, OBVIOUSLY, BUT EACH ONE DOES HAVE A UNIQUE TWIST...
STRAKE, BONAVENTURE
McCONE, JOHN
CHEUNG, HSUI

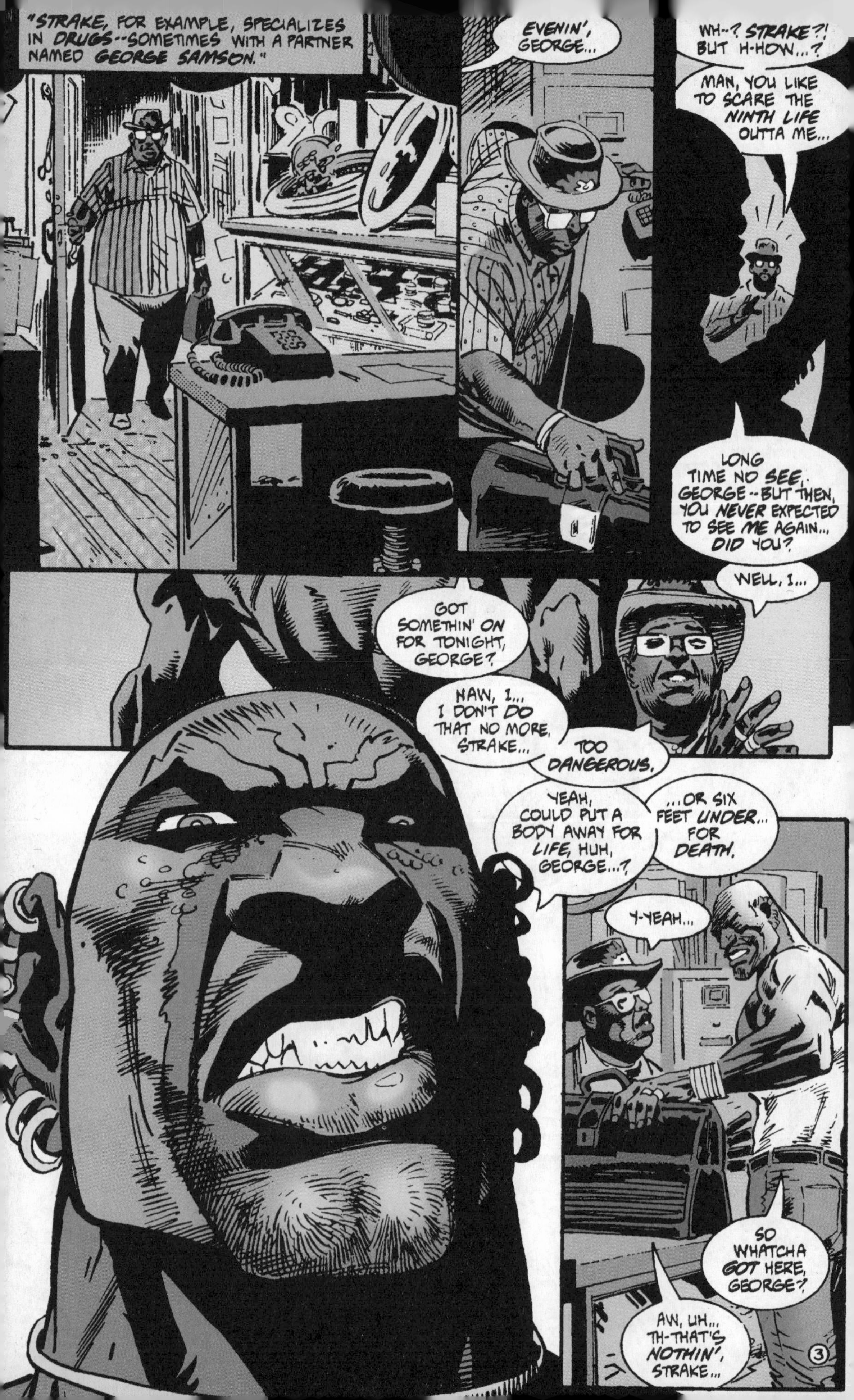
"STRAKE, FOR EXAMPLE, SPECIALIZES IN DRUGS--SOMETIMES WITH A PARTNER NAMED GEORGE SAMSON."
EVENIN', GEORGE...
WH--? STRAKE?! BUT H-HOW...?
MAN, YOU LIKE TO SCARE THE NINTH LIFE OUTTA ME...
LONG TIME NO SEE, GEORGE--BUT THEN, YOU NEVER EXPECTED TO SEE ME AGAIN... DID YOU?
WELL, I...
GOT SOMETHIN' ON FOR TONIGHT, GEORGE?
NAW, I... I DON'T DO THAT NO MORE, STRAKE...
TOO DANGEROUS.
YEAH, COULD PUT A BODY AWAY FOR LIFE, HUH, GEORGE...?
...OR SIX FEET UNDER... FOR DEATH.
Y-YEAH...
SO WHATCHA GOT HERE, GEORGE?
AW, UH... TH-THAT'S NOTHIN', STRAKE...
3

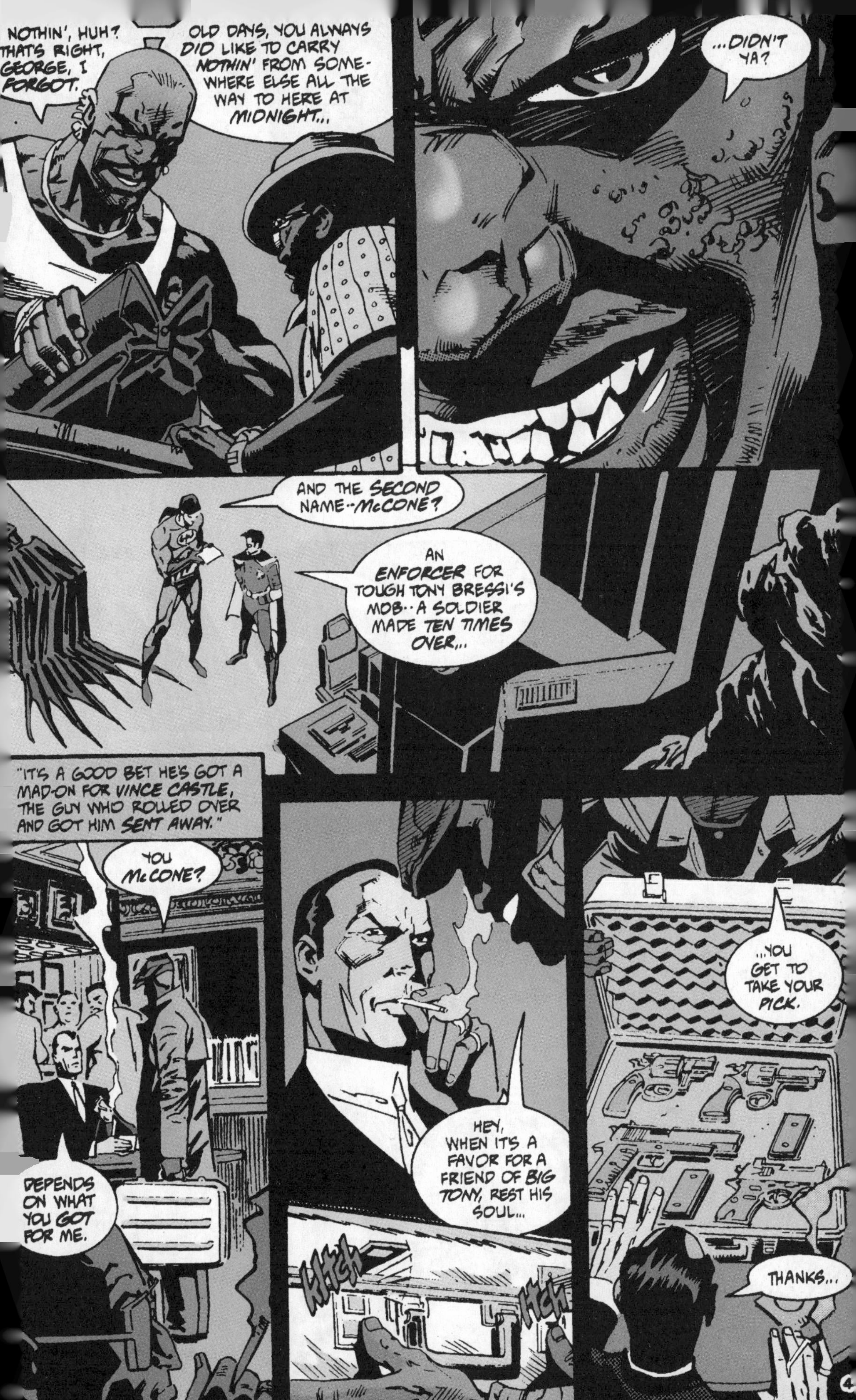

NOTHIN', HUH? THAT'S RIGHT, GEORGE, I FORGOT.
OLD DAYS, YOU ALWAYS DID LIKE TO CARRY NOTHIN' FROM SOMEWHERE ELSE ALL THE WAY TO HERE AT MIDNIGHT...
...DIDN'T YA?
AND THE SECOND NAME--McCONE?
AN ENFORCER FOR TOUGH TONY BRESSI'S MOB--A SOLDIER MADE TEN TIMES OVER...
"IT'S A GOOD BET HE'S GOT A MAD-ON FOR VINCE CASTLE, THE GUY WHO ROLLED OVER AND GOT HIM SENT AWAY."
YOU McCONE?
DEPENDS ON WHAT YOU GOT FOR ME.
HEY, WHEN IT'S A FAVOR FOR A FRIEND OF BIG TONY, REST HIS SOUL...
...YOU GET TO TAKE YOUR PICK.
THANKS...

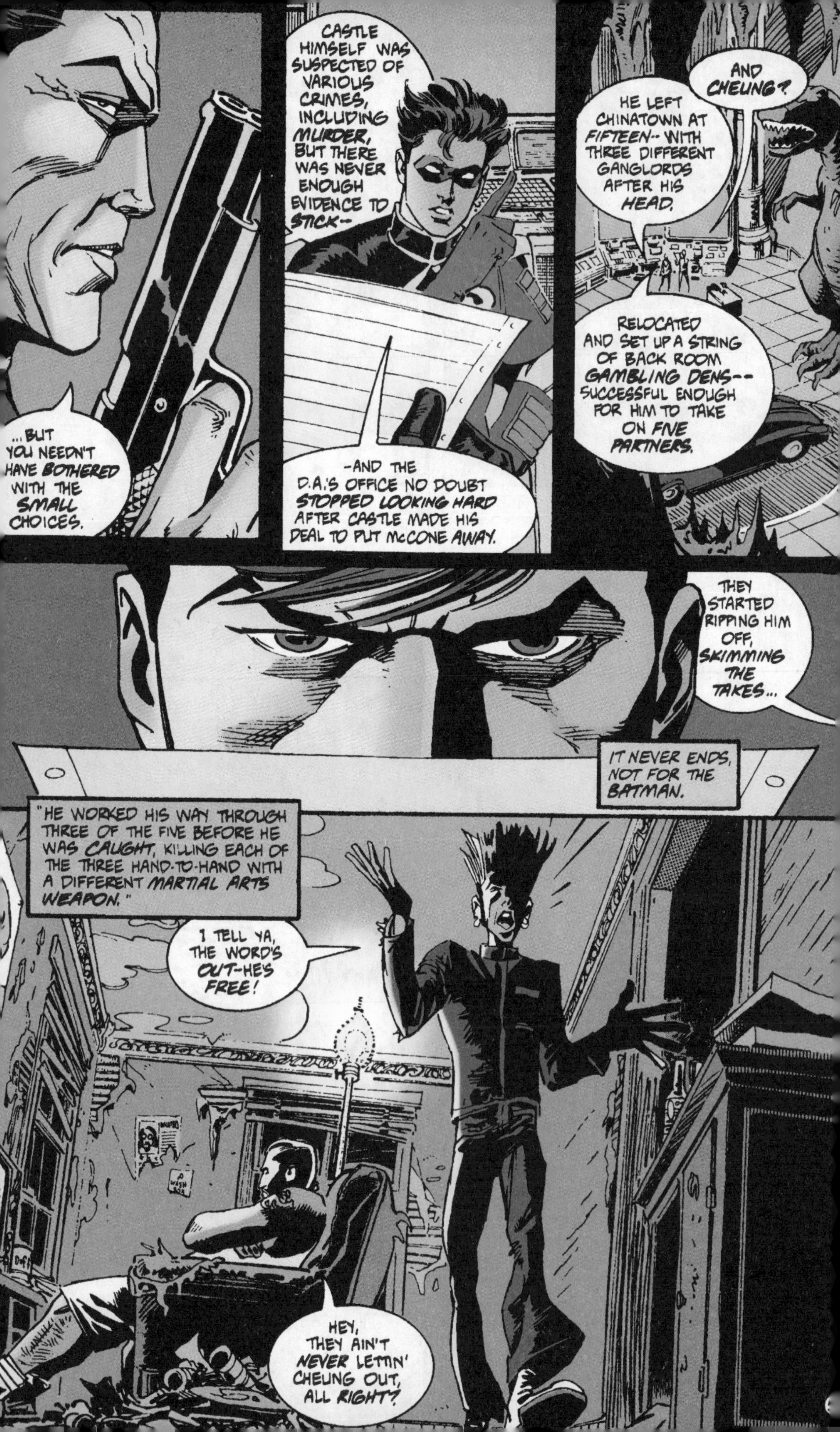
...BUT YOU NEEDN'T HAVE BOTHERED WITH THE SMALL CHOICES.
CASTLE HIMSELF WAS SUSPECTED OF VARIOUS CRIMES, INCLUDING MURDER, BUT THERE WAS NEVER ENOUGH EVIDENCE TO STICK--
-AND THE D.A.'S OFFICE NO DOUBT STOPPED LOOKING HARD AFTER CASTLE MADE HIS DEAL TO PUT McCONE AWAY.
AND CHEUNG?
HE LEFT CHINATOWN AT FIFTEEN-- WITH THREE DIFFERENT GANGLORDS AFTER HIS HEAD.
RELOCATED AND SET UP A STRING OF BACK ROOM GAMBLING DENS-- SUCCESSFUL ENOUGH FOR HIM TO TAKE ON FIVE PARTNERS.
THEY STARTED RIPPING HIM OFF, SKIMMING THE TAKES...
IT NEVER ENDS, NOT FOR THE BATMAN.
"HE WORKED HIS WAY THROUGH THREE OF THE FIVE BEFORE HE WAS CAUGHT, KILLING EACH OF THE THREE HAND-TO-HAND WITH A DIFFERENT MARTIAL ARTS WEAPON."
I TELL YA, THE WORD'S OUT-HE'S FREE!
HEY, THEY AIN'T NEVER LETTIN' CHEUNG OUT, ALL RIGHT?

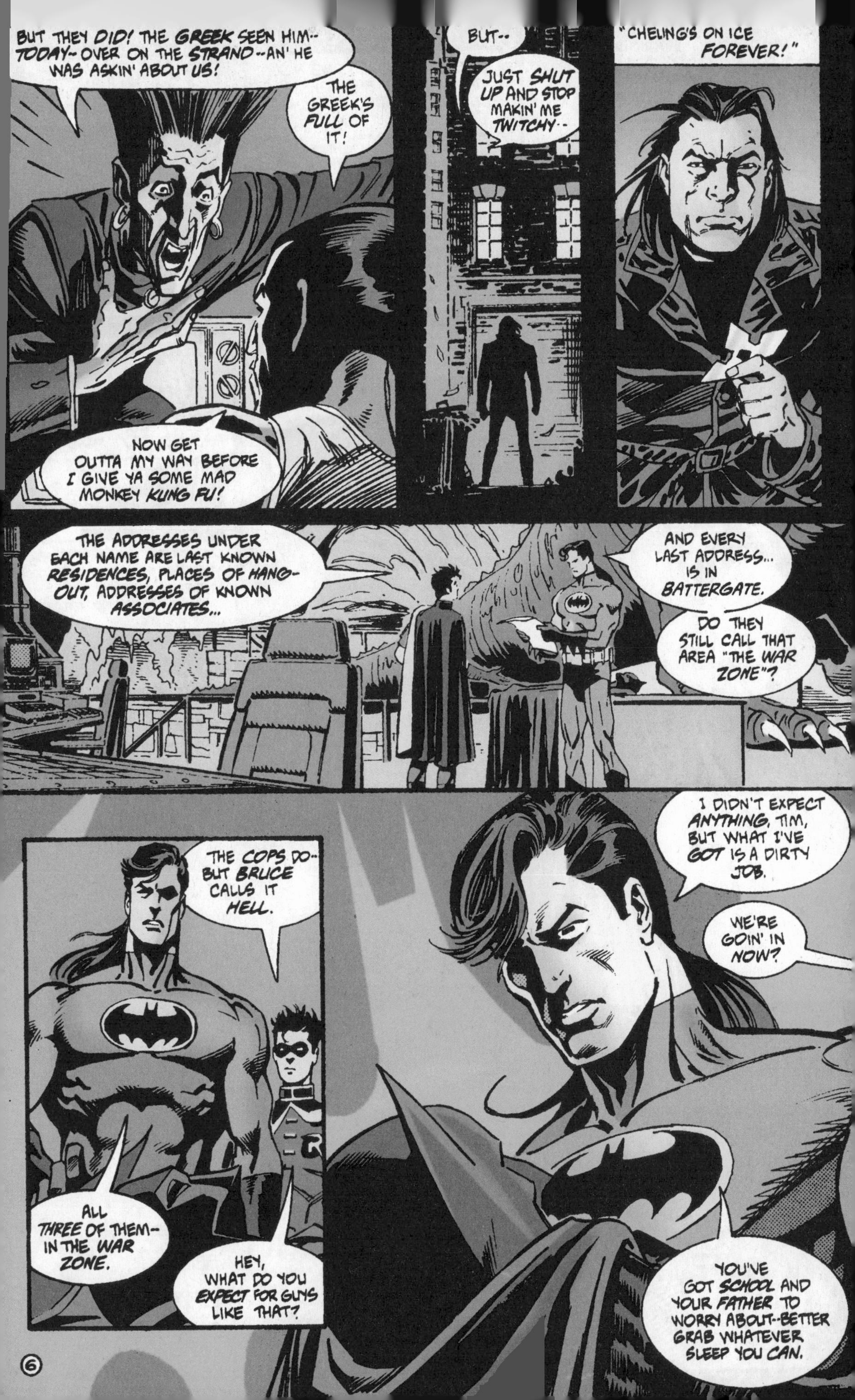
BUT THEY DID! THE GREEK SEEN HIM-- TODAY-- OVER ON THE STRAND--AN' HE WAS ASKIN' ABOUT US!
THE GREEK'S FULL OF IT!
NOW GET OUTTA MY WAY BEFORE I GIVE YA SOME MAD MONKEY KUNG FU!
BUT--
JUST SHUT UP AND STOP MAKIN' ME TWITCHY--
"CHEUNG'S ON ICE FOREVER!"
THE ADDRESSES UNDER EACH NAME ARE LAST KNOWN RESIDENCES, PLACES OF HANG-OUT, ADDRESSES OF KNOWN ASSOCIATES...
AND EVERY LAST ADDRESS... IS IN BATTERGATE.
DO THEY STILL CALL THAT AREA "THE WAR ZONE"?
THE COPS DO-- BUT BRUCE CALLS IT HELL.
ALL THREE OF THEM-- IN THE WAR ZONE.
HEY, WHAT DO YOU EXPECT FOR GUYS LIKE THAT?
I DIDN'T EXPECT ANYTHING, TIM, BUT WHAT I'VE GOT IS A DIRTY JOB.
WE'RE GOIN' IN NOW?
YOU'VE GOT SCHOOL AND YOUR FATHER TO WORRY ABOUT--BETTER GRAB WHATEVER SLEEP YOU CAN.

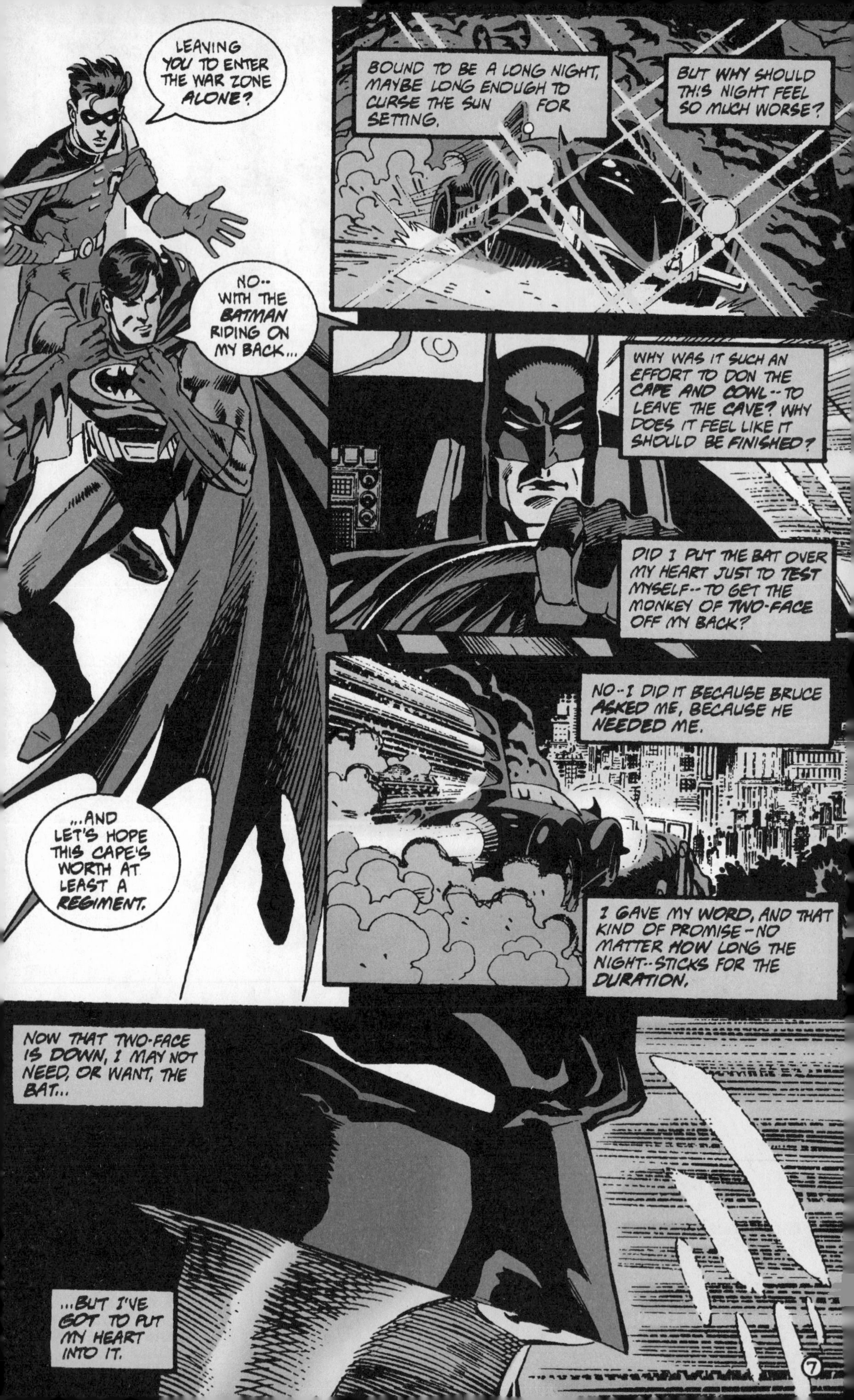

LEAVING YOU TO ENTER THE WAR ZONE ALONE?
NO-- WITH THE BATMAN RIDING ON MY BACK...
...AND LET'S HOPE THIS CAPE'S WORTH AT LEAST A REGIMENT.
BOUND TO BE A LONG NIGHT, MAYBE LONG ENOUGH TO CURSE THE SUN FOR SETTING.
BUT WHY SHOULD THIS NIGHT FEEL SO MUCH WORSE?
WHY WAS IT SUCH AN EFFORT TO DON THE CAPE AND COWL--TO LEAVE THE CAVE? WHY DOES IT FEEL LIKE IT SHOULD BE FINISHED?
DID I PUT THE BAT OVER MY HEART JUST TO TEST MYSELF--TO GET THE MONKEY OF TWO-FACE OFF MY BACK?
NO--I DID IT BECAUSE BRUCE ASKED ME, BECAUSE HE NEEDED ME.
I GAVE MY WORD, AND THAT KIND OF PROMISE--NO MATTER HOW LONG THE NIGHT--STICKS FOR THE DURATION.
NOW THAT TWO-FACE IS DOWN, I MAY NOT NEED, OR WANT, THE BAT...
...BUT I'VE GOT TO PUT MY HEART INTO IT.

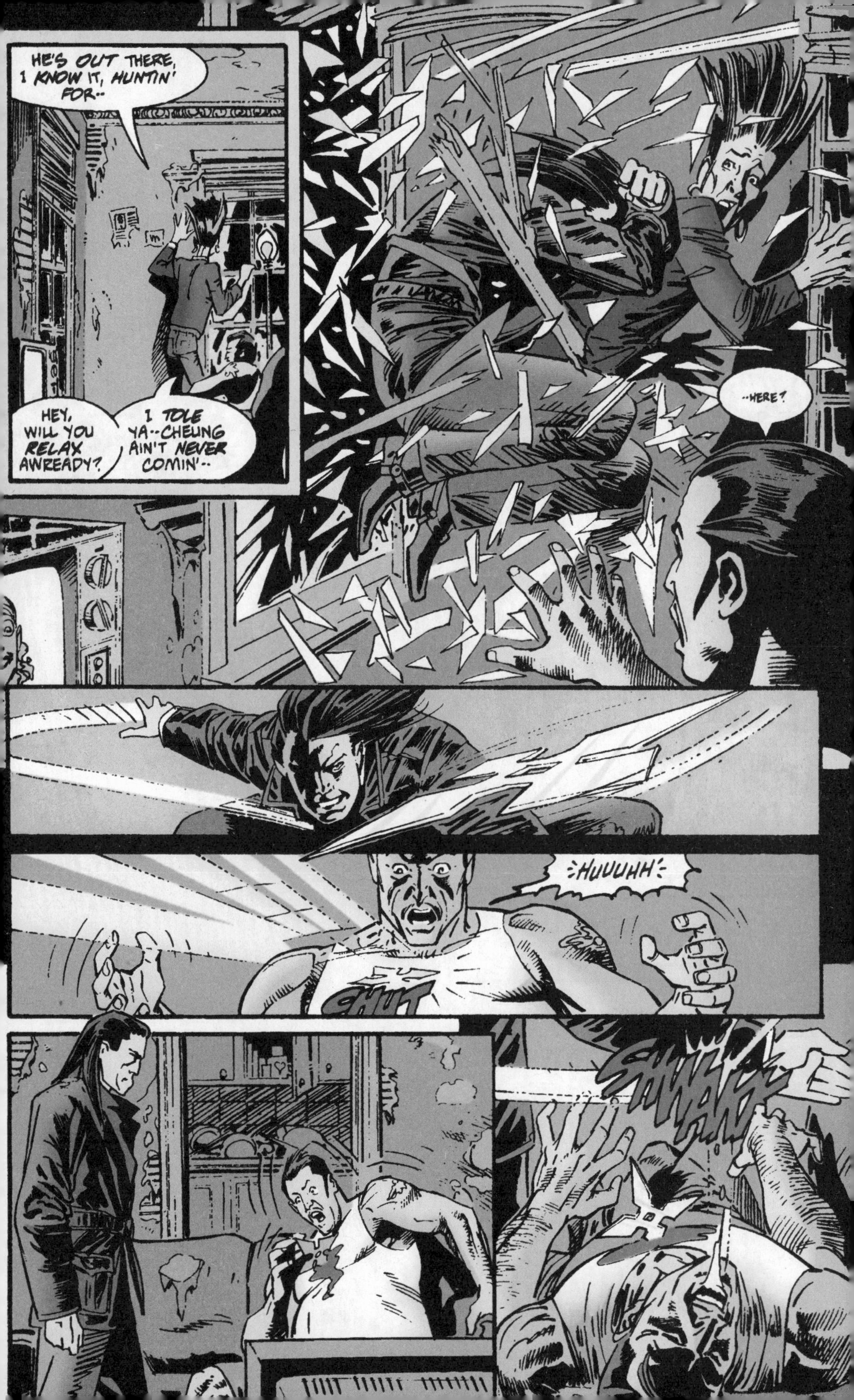

HE'S OUT THERE, I KNOW IT, HUNTIN' FOR--
HEY, WILL YOU RELAX AWREADY?
I TOLE YA--CHEUNG AIN'T NEVER COMIN'--
--HERE?
HUUUHH
CHUT
SHUKK

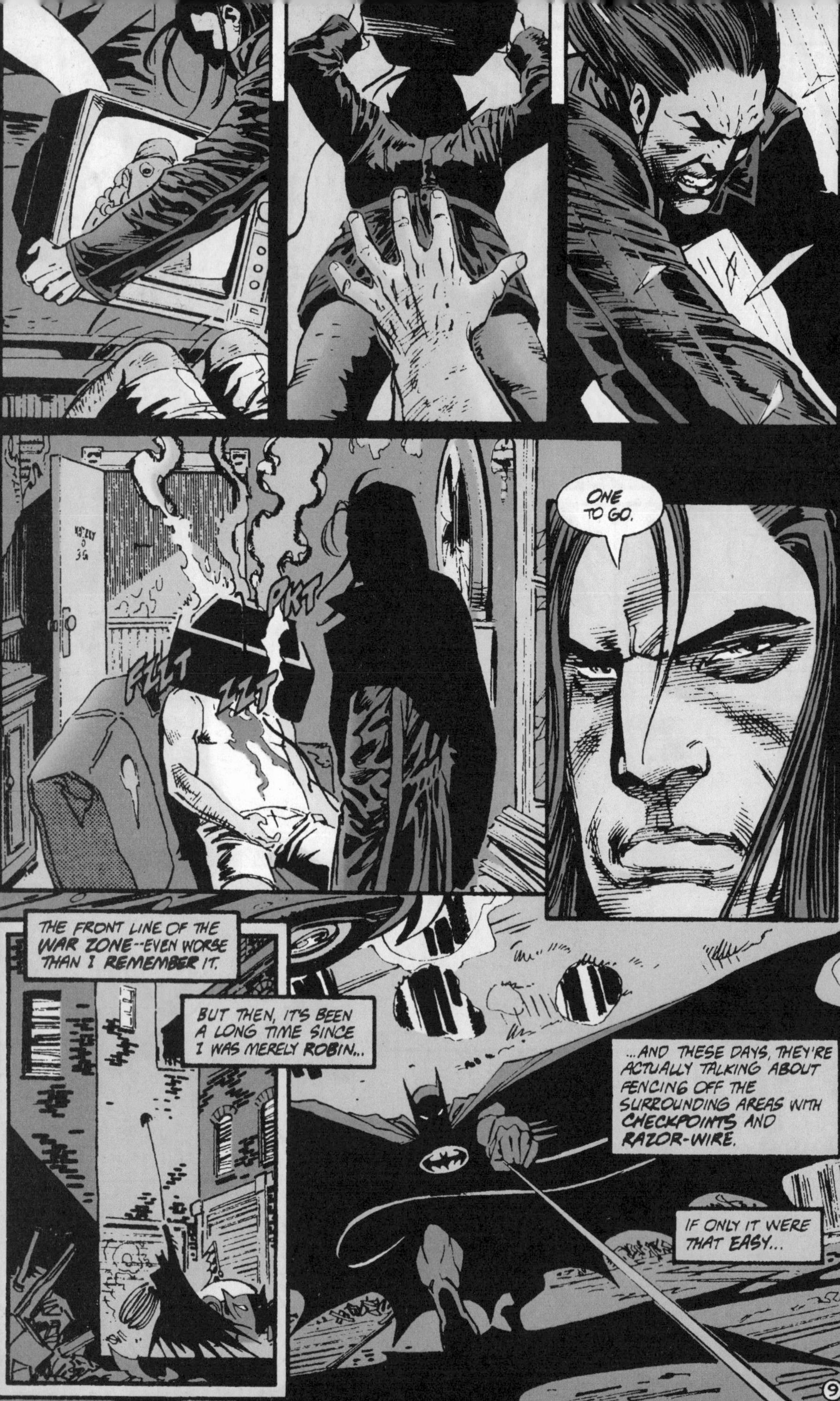
PKT
FZZT
ZZZT
ONE TO GO.
THE FRONT LINE OF THE WAR ZONE--EVEN WORSE THAN I REMEMBER IT.
BUT THEN, IT'S BEEN A LONG TIME SINCE I WAS MERELY ROBIN...
...AND THESE DAYS, THEY'RE ACTUALLY TALKING ABOUT FENCING OFF THE SURROUNDING AREAS WITH CHECKPOINTS AND RAZOR-WIRE.
IF ONLY IT WERE THAT EASY...

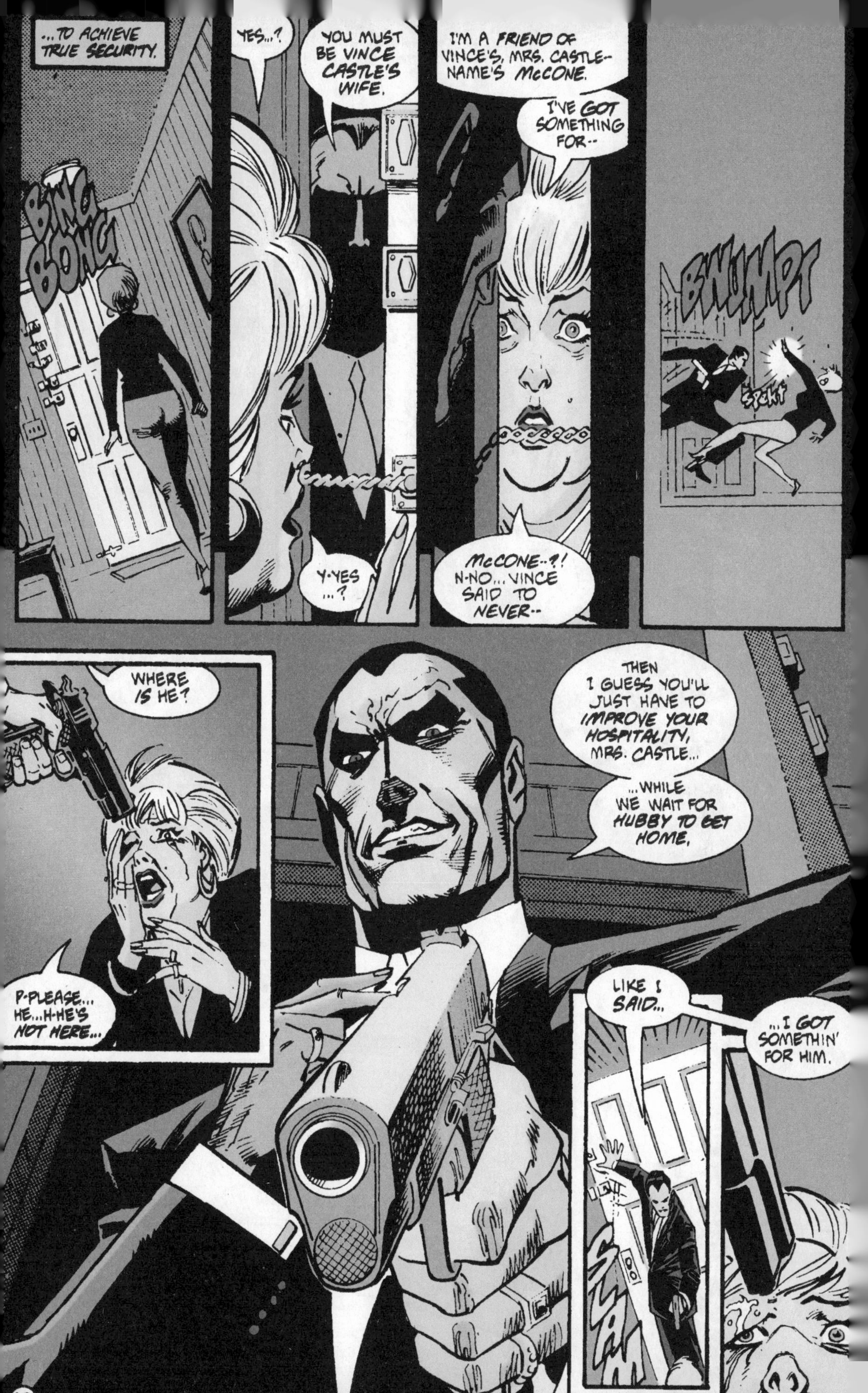

...TO ACHIEVE TRUE SECURITY.
BING BONG
YES...?
YOU MUST BE VINCE CASTLE'S WIFE.
Y-YES ...?
I'M A FRIEND OF VINCE'S, MRS. CASTLE-- NAME'S McCONE.
I'VE GOT SOMETHING FOR--
McCONE--?! N-NO... VINCE SAID TO NEVER--
BHUMPT
SPLKT
WHERE IS HE?
P-PLEASE... HE...H-HE'S NOT HERE...
THEN I GUESS YOU'LL JUST HAVE TO IMPROVE YOUR HOSPITALITY, MRS. CASTLE...
...WHILE WE WAIT FOR HUBBY TO GET HOME.
LIKE I SAID...
...I GOT SOMETHIN' FOR HIM.

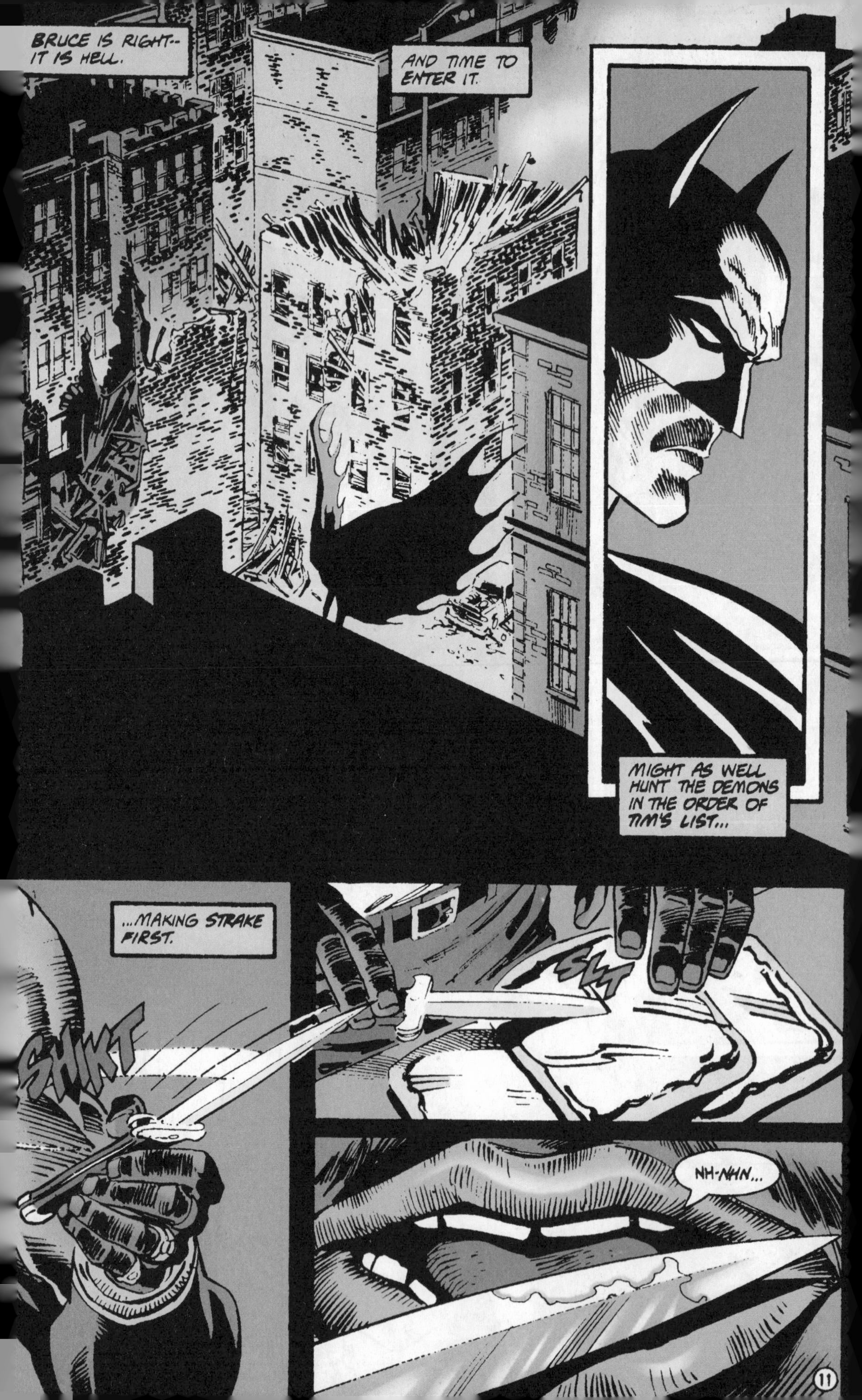
BRUCE IS RIGHT--
IT IS HELL.
AND TIME TO
ENTER IT.
MIGHT AS WELL
HUNT THE DEMONS
IN THE ORDER OF
TIM'S LIST...
...MAKING STRAKE
FIRST.
SHIKT
SLIT
NH-NHN...

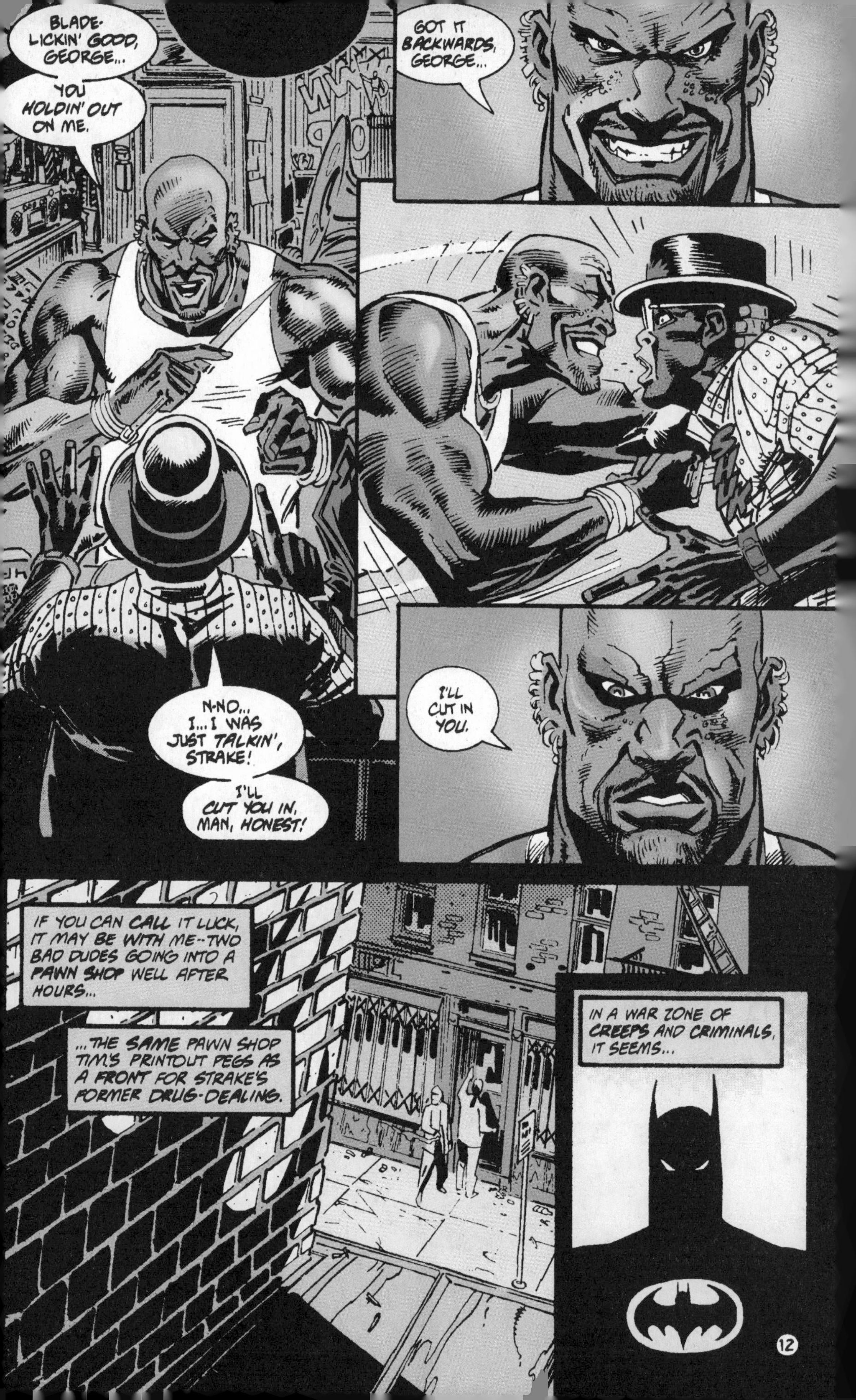
BLADE-LICKIN' GOOD, GEORGE...
YOU HOLDIN' OUT ON ME.
GOT IT BACKWARDS, GEORGE...
N-NO... I... I WAS JUST TALKIN', STRAKE!
I'LL CUT YOU IN, MAN, HONEST!
I'LL CUT IN YOU.
IF YOU CAN CALL IT LUCK, IT MAY BE WITH ME--TWO BAD DUDES GOING INTO A PAWN SHOP WELL AFTER HOURS...
...THE SAME PAWN SHOP TIM'S PRINTOUT PEGS AS A FRONT FOR STRAKE'S FORMER DRUG-DEALING.
IN A WAR ZONE OF CREEPS AND CRIMINALS, IT SEEMS...
12

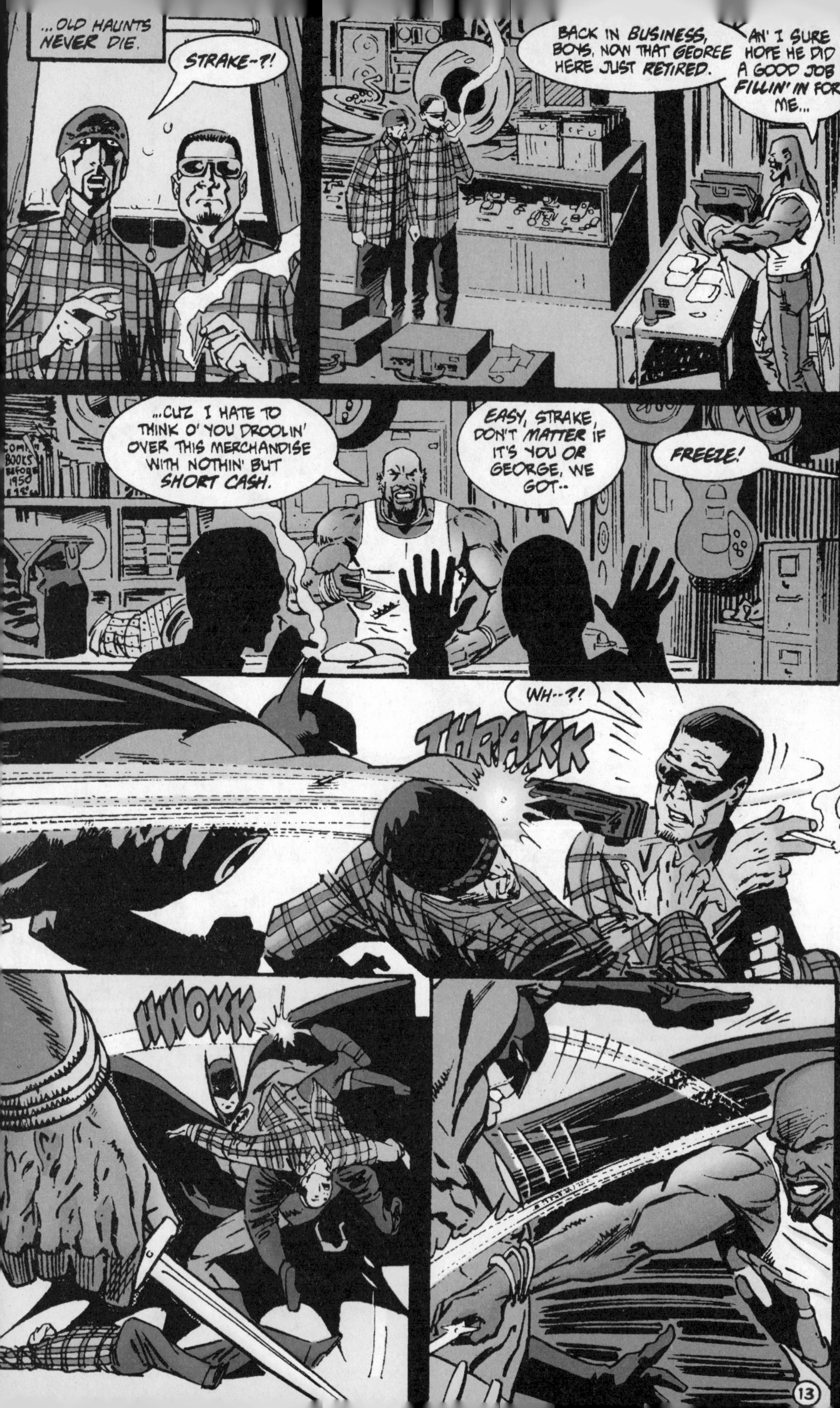
...OLD HAUNTS NEVER DIE.
STRAKE--?!
BACK IN BUSINESS, BOYS, NOW THAT GEORGE HERE JUST RETIRED.
AN' I SURE HOPE HE DID A GOOD JOB FILLIN' IN FOR ME...
...CUZ I HATE TO THINK O' YOU DROOLIN' OVER THIS MERCHANDISE WITH NOTHIN' BUT SHORT CASH.
EASY, STRAKE, DON'T MATTER IF IT'S YOU OR GEORGE, WE GOT--
FREEZE!
WH--?!
THRAKK
HWOKK

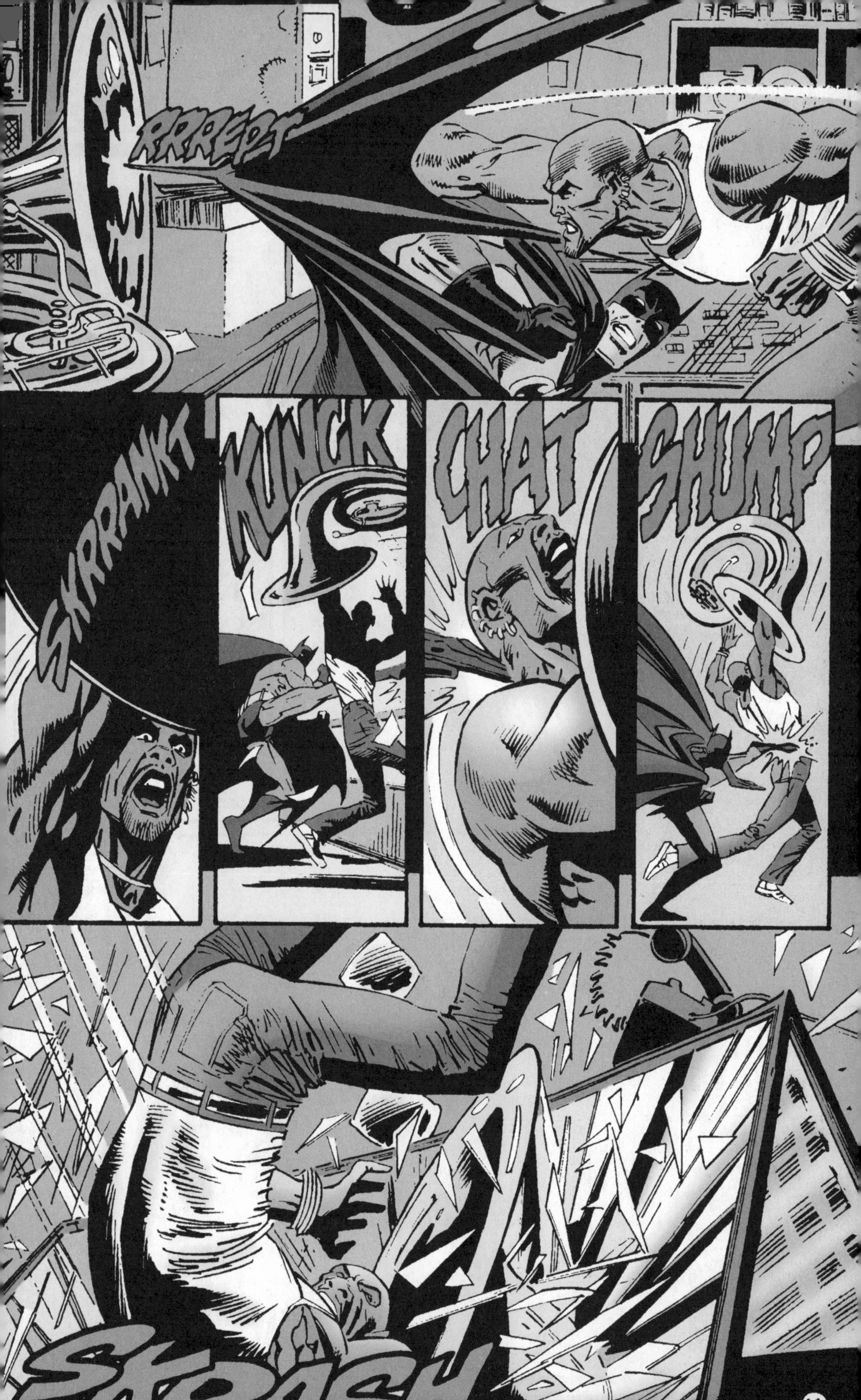
RRREDT
SKRRANKT
KLUNCK
CHAT
SHUMP
SKRASH

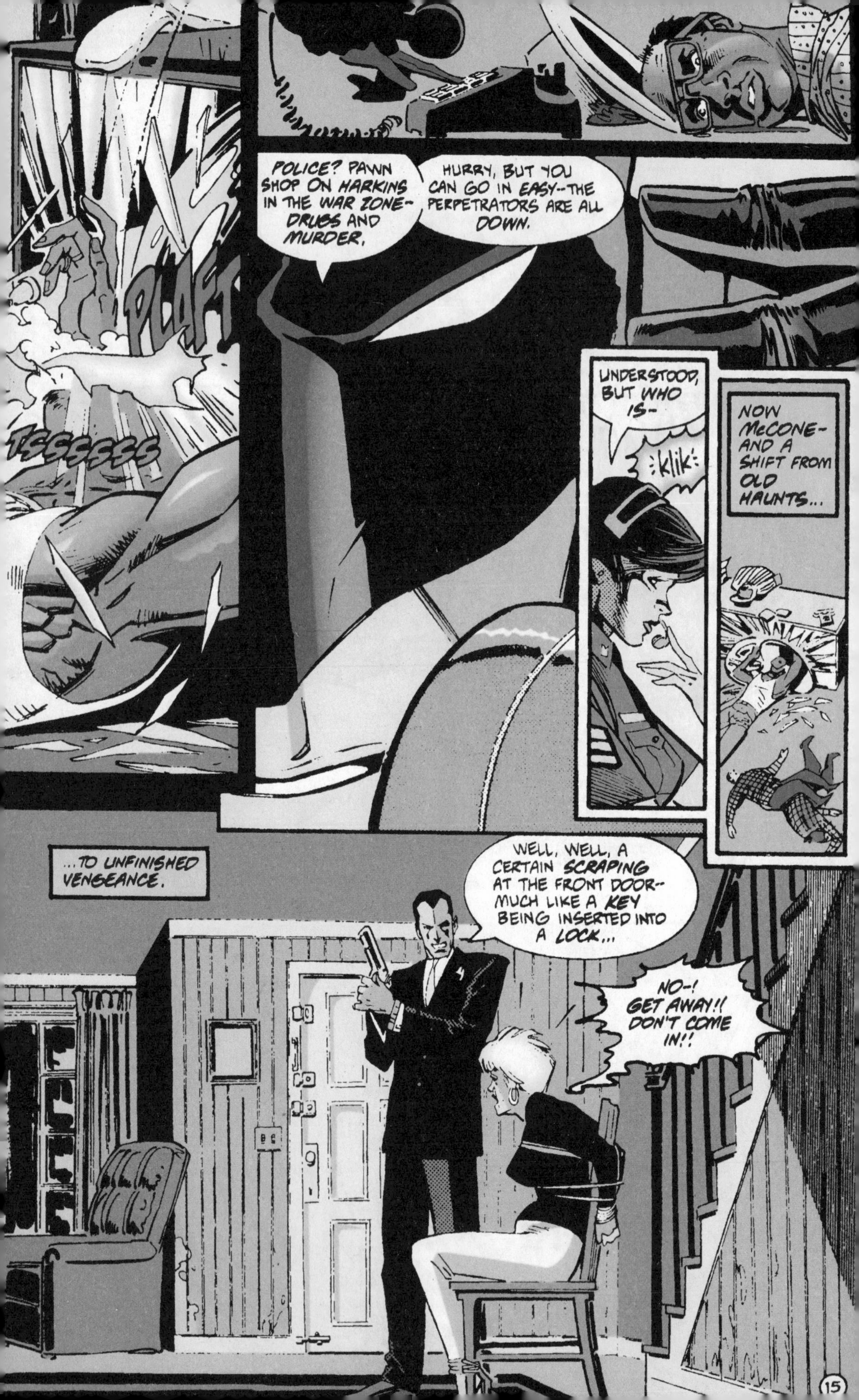
PLAFT
TSSSSSS
POLICE? PAWN SHOP ON HARKINS IN THE WAR ZONE-- DRUGS AND MURDER.
HURRY, BUT YOU CAN GO IN EASY--THE PERPETRATORS ARE ALL DOWN.
UNDERSTOOD, BUT WHO IS--
KLIK
NOW McCONE-- AND A SHIFT FROM OLD HAUNTS...
...TO UNFINISHED VENGEANCE.
WELL, WELL, A CERTAIN SCRAPING AT THE FRONT DOOR-- MUCH LIKE A KEY BEING INSERTED INTO A LOCK...
NO--! GET AWAY!! DON'T COME IN!!

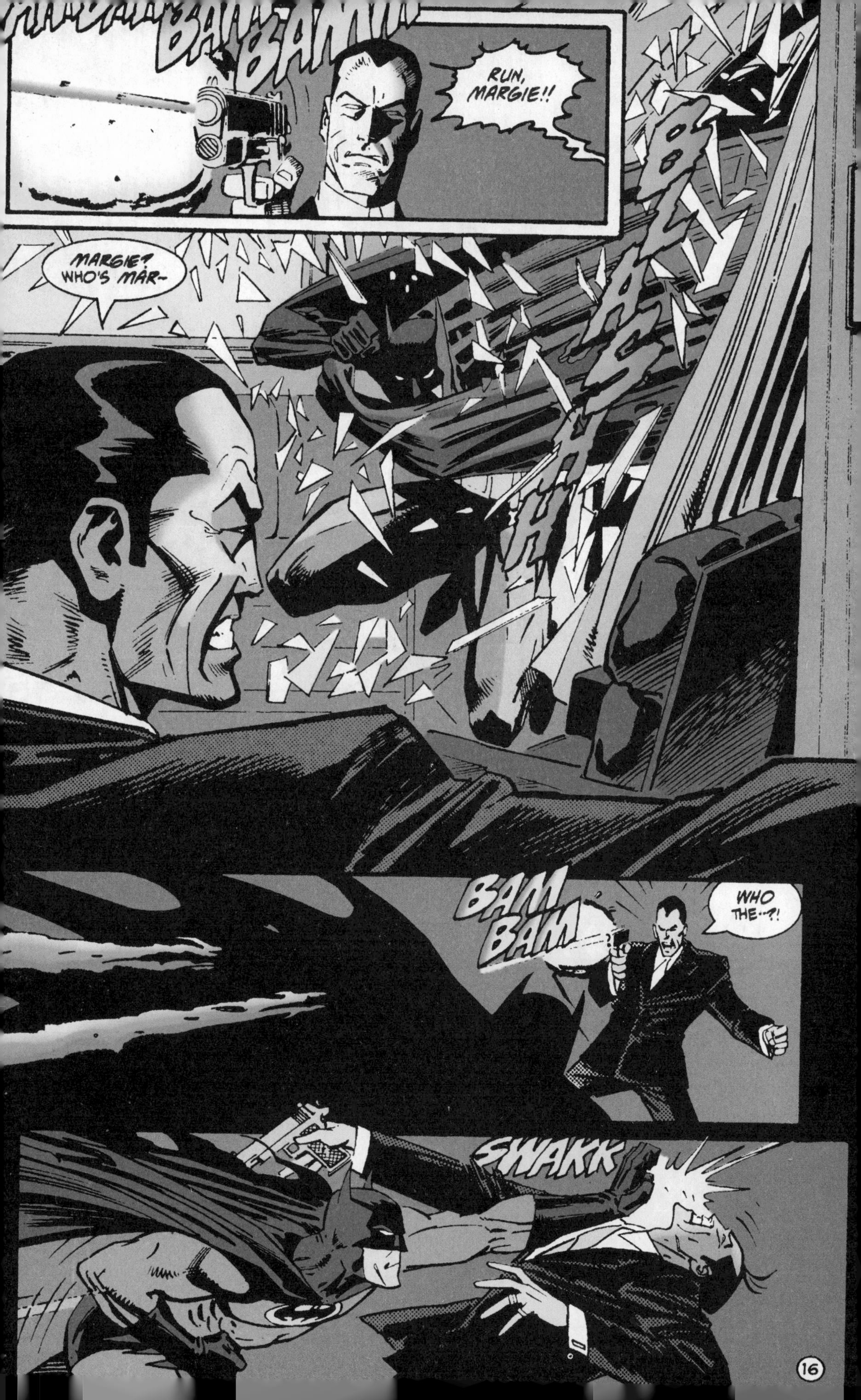
RUN, MARGIE!!
MARGIE? WHO'S MAR–
BAM BAM
WHO THE--?!
SWAKK

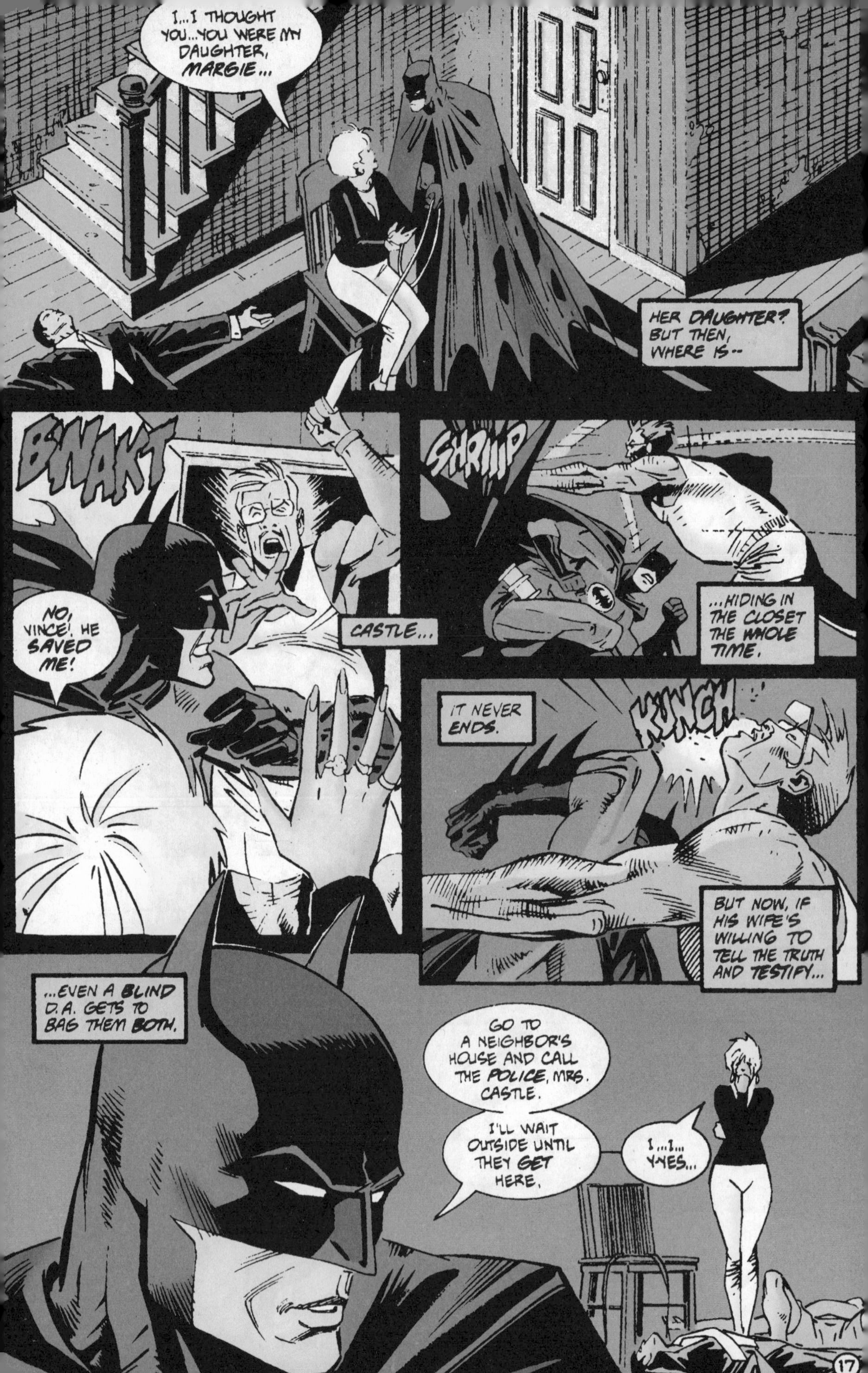
I...I THOUGHT YOU...YOU WERE MY DAUGHTER, MARGIE...
HER DAUGHTER? BUT THEN, WHERE IS--
B'NAKT
CASTLE...
NO, VINCE! HE SAVED ME!
SHRIIIP
...HIDING IN THE CLOSET THE WHOLE TIME.
IT NEVER ENDS.
KUNCH
BUT NOW, IF HIS WIFE'S WILLING TO TELL THE TRUTH AND TESTIFY...
...EVEN A BLIND D.A. GETS TO BAG THEM BOTH.
GO TO A NEIGHBOR'S HOUSE AND CALL THE POLICE, MRS. CASTLE.
I'LL WAIT OUTSIDE UNTIL THEY GET HERE.
I...I... Y-YES...

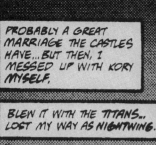

PROBABLY A GREAT MARRIAGE THE CASTLES HAVE... BUT THEN, I MESSED UP WITH KORY MYSELF.

BLEW IT WITH THE TITANS... LOST MY WAY AS NIGHTWING.

I'M TOO OLD TO BE ROBIN...

...AND BEING THE BATMAN ON A GRIM TOUR LIKE THIS CERTAINLY ISN'T ME.

AT LEAST THE CAVALRY'S HERE TO MOP UP THIS SKIRMISH.

BUT WHAT IS? WHAT AM I? --OTHER THAN A RELUCTANT GRUNT IN A FOREIGN WAR ZONE...

TIME FOR CHEUNG... BUT MAN, DO I HATE MARTIAL ARTS GUYS.

THE LAST OF THE THREE ADDRESSES LISTED FOR CHEUNG--AND EVEN LESS PROMISING THAN THE FIRST TWO...

LUCK WAS BOUND TO RUN OUT ON ME-- NO ONE HERE FOR A LONG TIME.

MAYBE THE HEAT'S OFF IN CHINATOWN BY NOW...

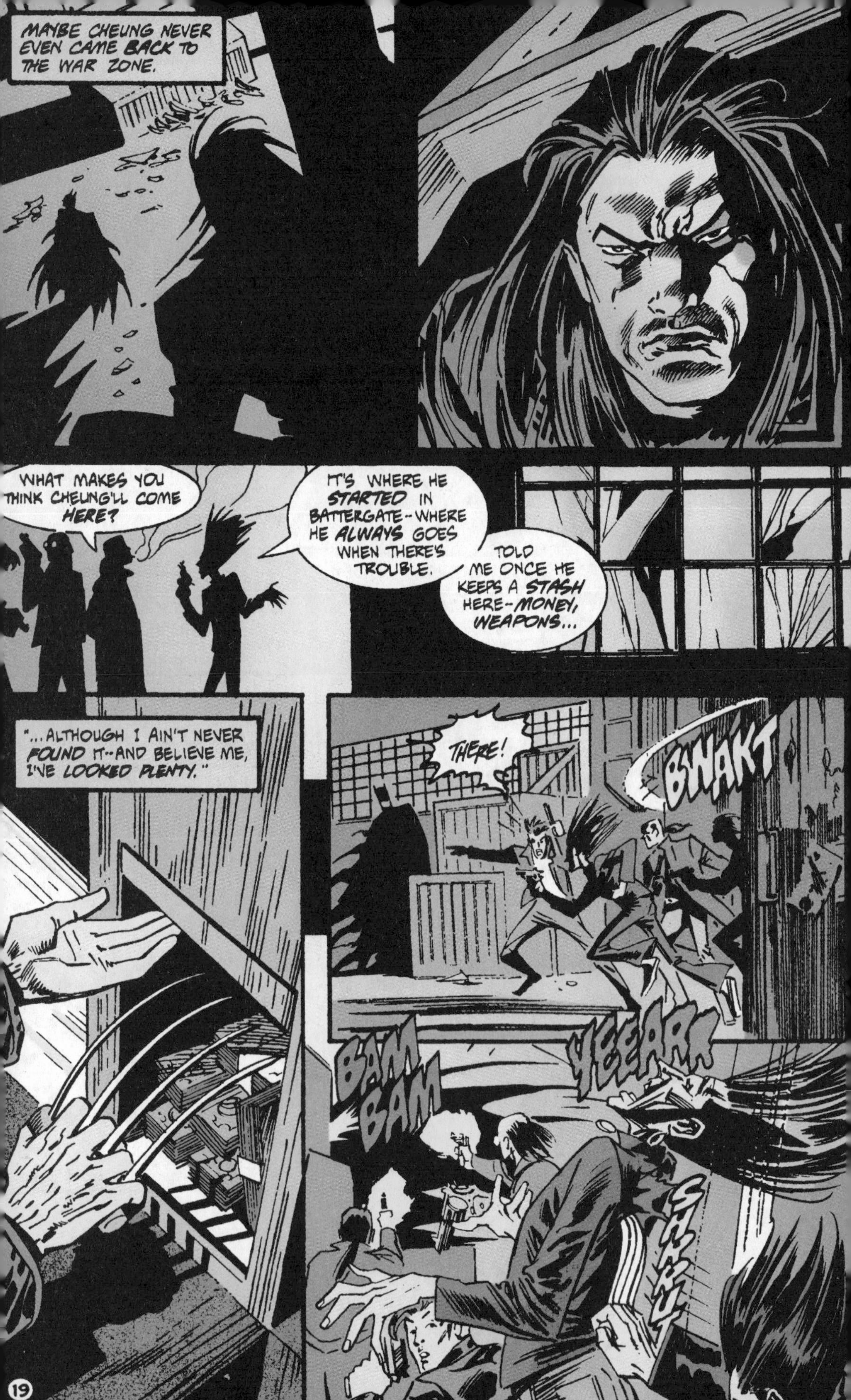
MAYBE CHEUNG NEVER EVEN CAME BACK TO THE WAR ZONE.
WHAT MAKES YOU THINK CHEUNG'LL COME HERE?
IT'S WHERE HE STARTED IN BATTERGATE--WHERE HE ALWAYS GOES WHEN THERE'S TROUBLE.
TOLD ME ONCE HE KEEPS A STASH HERE--MONEY, WEAPONS...
"...ALTHOUGH I AIN'T NEVER FOUND IT--AND BELIEVE ME, I'VE LOOKED PLENTY."
THERE!
B'NAKT
BAM BAM
YEEARK
SHUKK

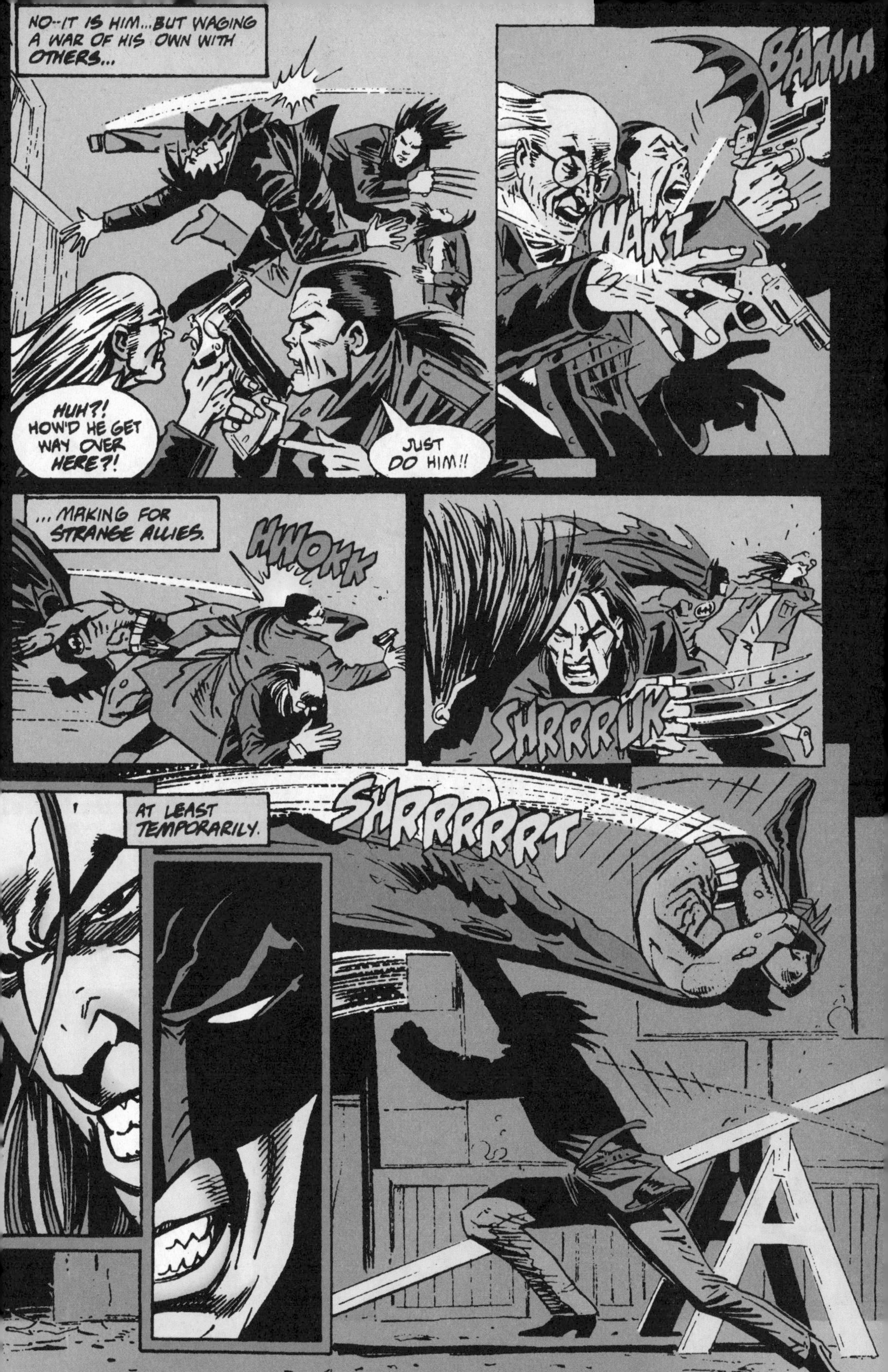
NO--IT IS HIM...BUT WAGING A WAR OF HIS OWN WITH OTHERS...
HUH?! HOW'D HE GET WAY OVER HERE?!
JUST DO HIM!!
BAMM
WAKT
...MAKING FOR STRANGE ALLIES.
HWOKK
SHRRRUK
AT LEAST TEMPORARILY.
SHRRRRRRT

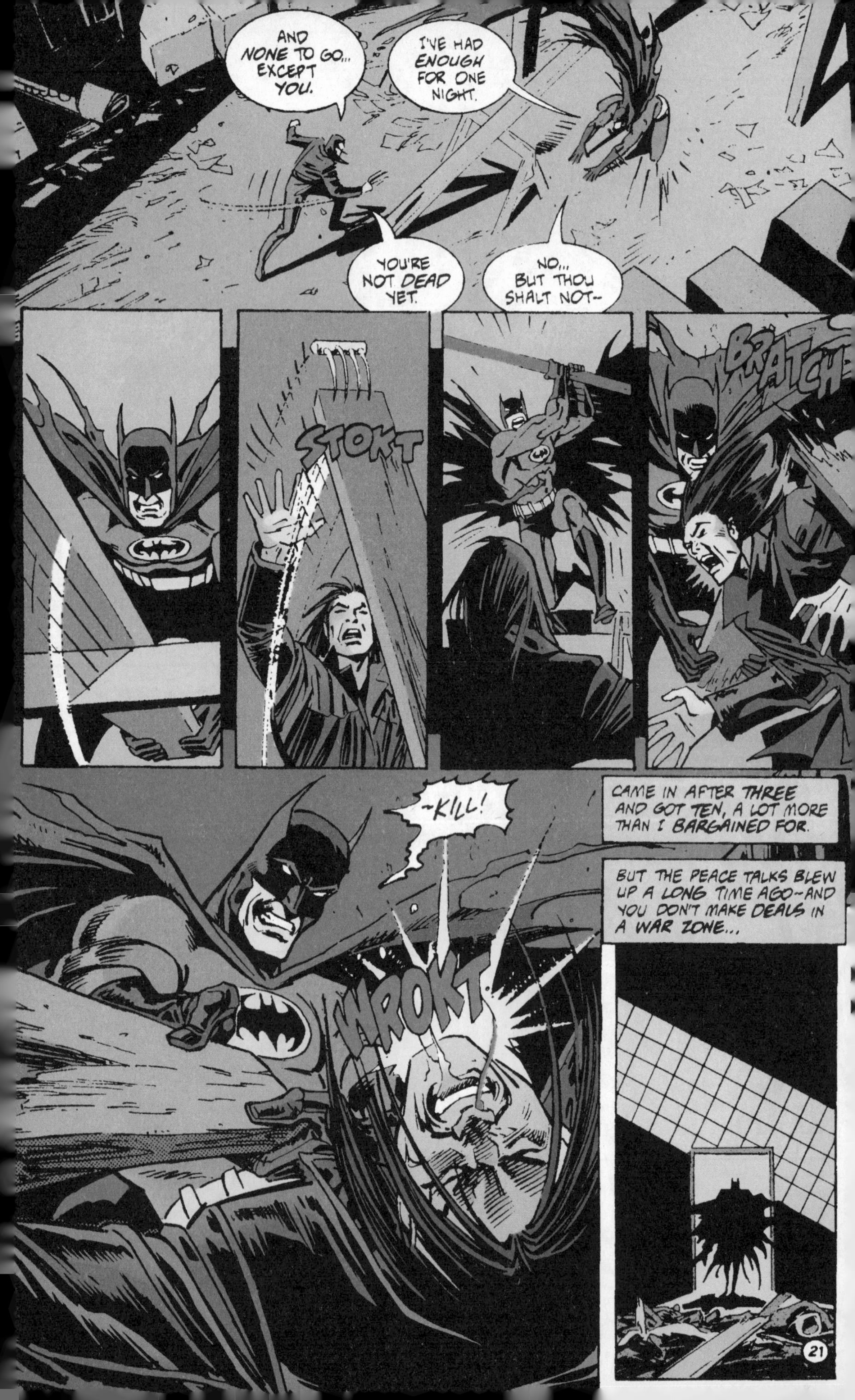
AND NONE TO GO... EXCEPT YOU.
I'VE HAD ENOUGH FOR ONE NIGHT.
YOU'RE NOT DEAD YET.
NO... BUT THOU SHALT NOT--
STOKT
BRATCH
-KILL!
WROKT
CAME IN AFTER THREE AND GOT TEN, A LOT MORE THAN I BARGAINED FOR.
BUT THE PEACE TALKS BLEW UP A LONG TIME AGO--AND YOU DON'T MAKE DEALS IN A WAR ZONE...

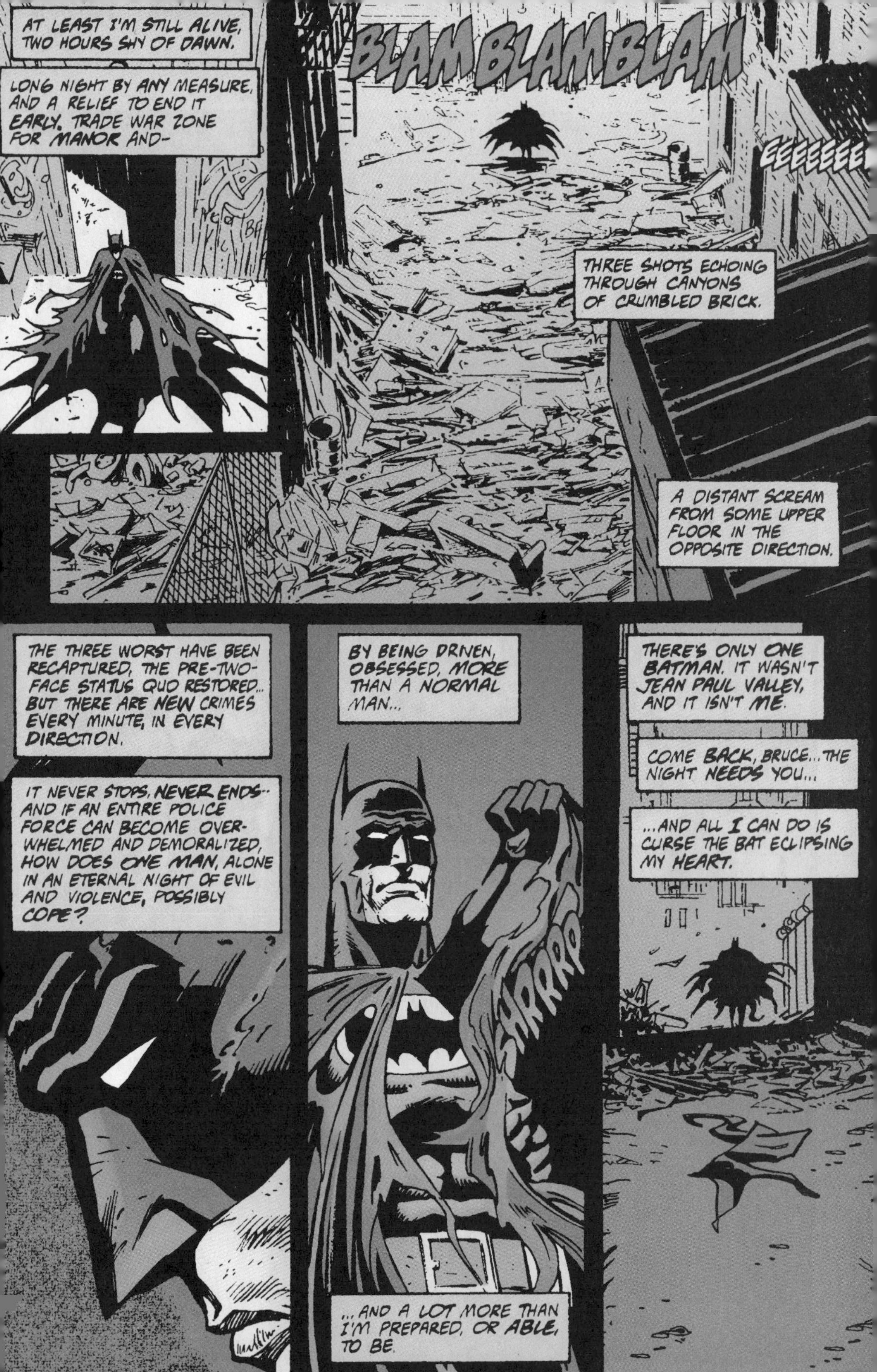
AT LEAST I'M STILL ALIVE, TWO HOURS SHY OF DAWN.
LONG NIGHT BY ANY MEASURE, AND A RELIEF TO END IT EARLY. TRADE WAR ZONE FOR MANOR AND-
BLAM BLAM BLAM
EEEEEEE
THREE SHOTS ECHOING THROUGH CANYONS OF CRUMBLED BRICK.
A DISTANT SCREAM FROM SOME UPPER FLOOR IN THE OPPOSITE DIRECTION.
THE THREE WORST HAVE BEEN RECAPTURED, THE PRE-TWO-FACE STATUS QUO RESTORED... BUT THERE ARE NEW CRIMES EVERY MINUTE, IN EVERY DIRECTION.
IT NEVER STOPS, NEVER ENDS-- AND IF AN ENTIRE POLICE FORCE CAN BECOME OVER-WHELMED AND DEMORALIZED, HOW DOES ONE MAN, ALONE IN AN ETERNAL NIGHT OF EVIL AND VIOLENCE, POSSIBLY COPE?
BY BEING DRIVEN, OBSESSED, MORE THAN A NORMAL MAN...
SHRRRP
...AND A LOT MORE THAN I'M PREPARED, OR ABLE, TO BE.
THERE'S ONLY ONE BATMAN. IT WASN'T JEAN PAUL VALLEY, AND IT ISN'T ME.
COME BACK, BRUCE... THE NIGHT NEEDS YOU...
...AND ALL I CAN DO IS CURSE THE BAT ECLIPSING MY HEART.

Cover art by **BRIAN STELFREEZE**

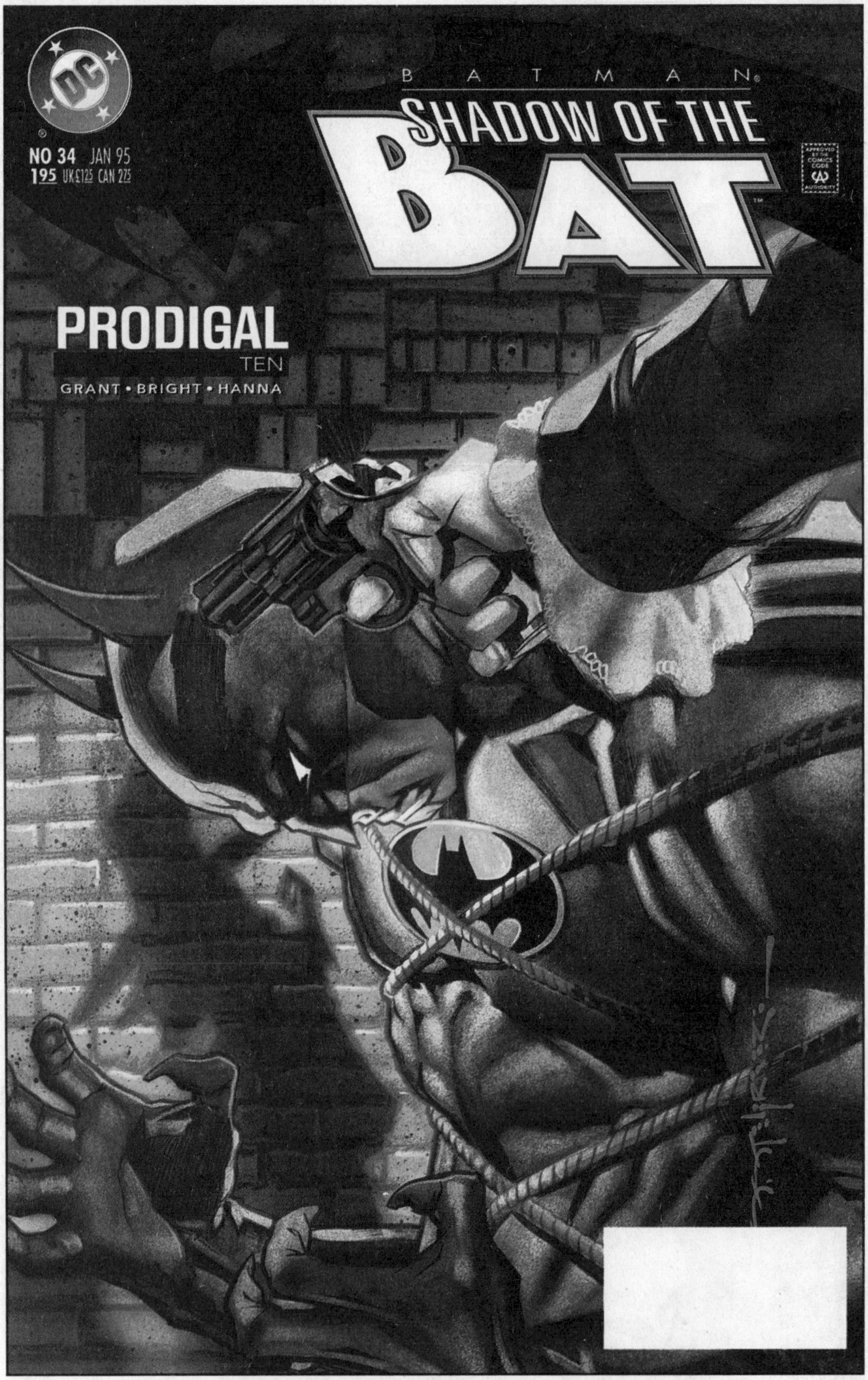
NO 34 JAN 95
195 UK£125 CAN 275
BATMAN
SHADOW OF THE BAT
APPROVED BY THE COMICS CODE AUTHORITY
PRODIGAL
TEN
GRANT • BRIGHT • HANNA

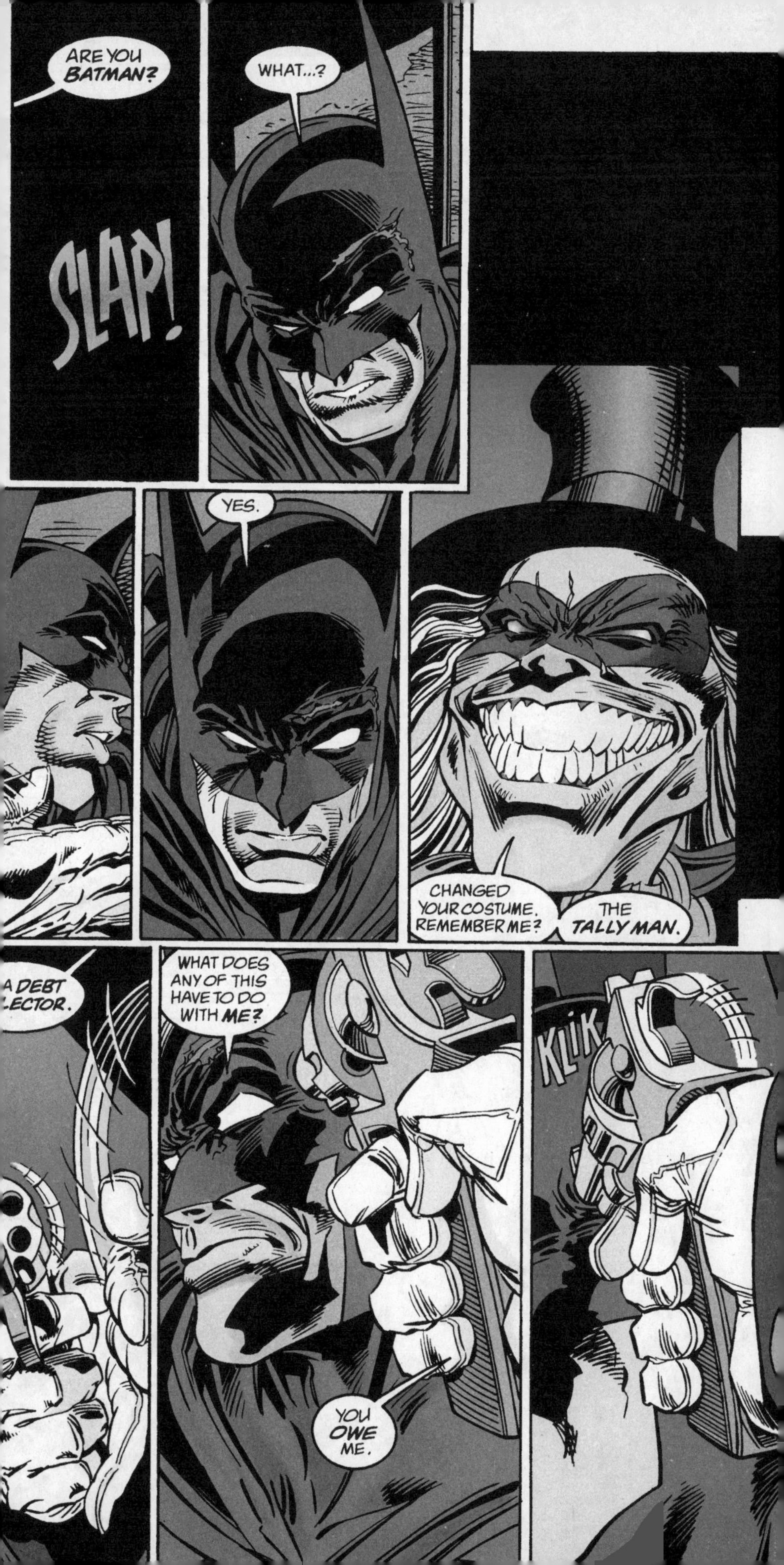
ARE YOU BATMAN?
SLAP!
WHAT...?
YES.
CHANGED YOUR COSTUME. REMEMBER ME?
THE TALLY MAN.
A DEBT
LECTOR.
WHAT DOES ANY OF THIS HAVE TO DO WITH ME?
YOU OWE ME.
KLIK

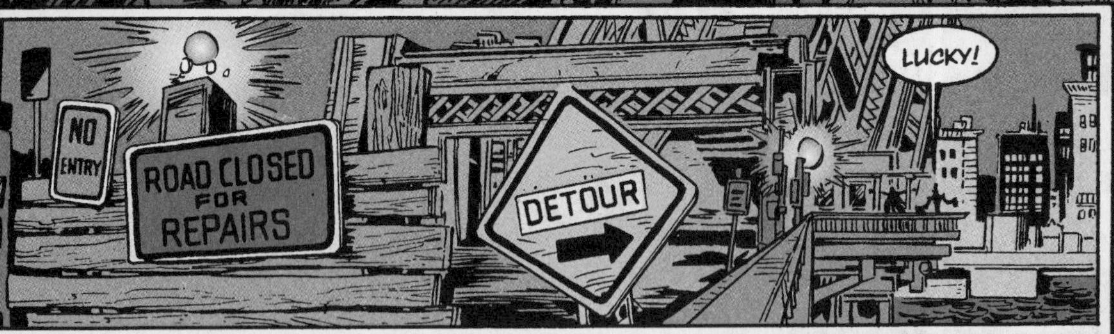
NO ENTRY
ROAD CLOSED FOR REPAIRS
DETOUR
LUCKY!

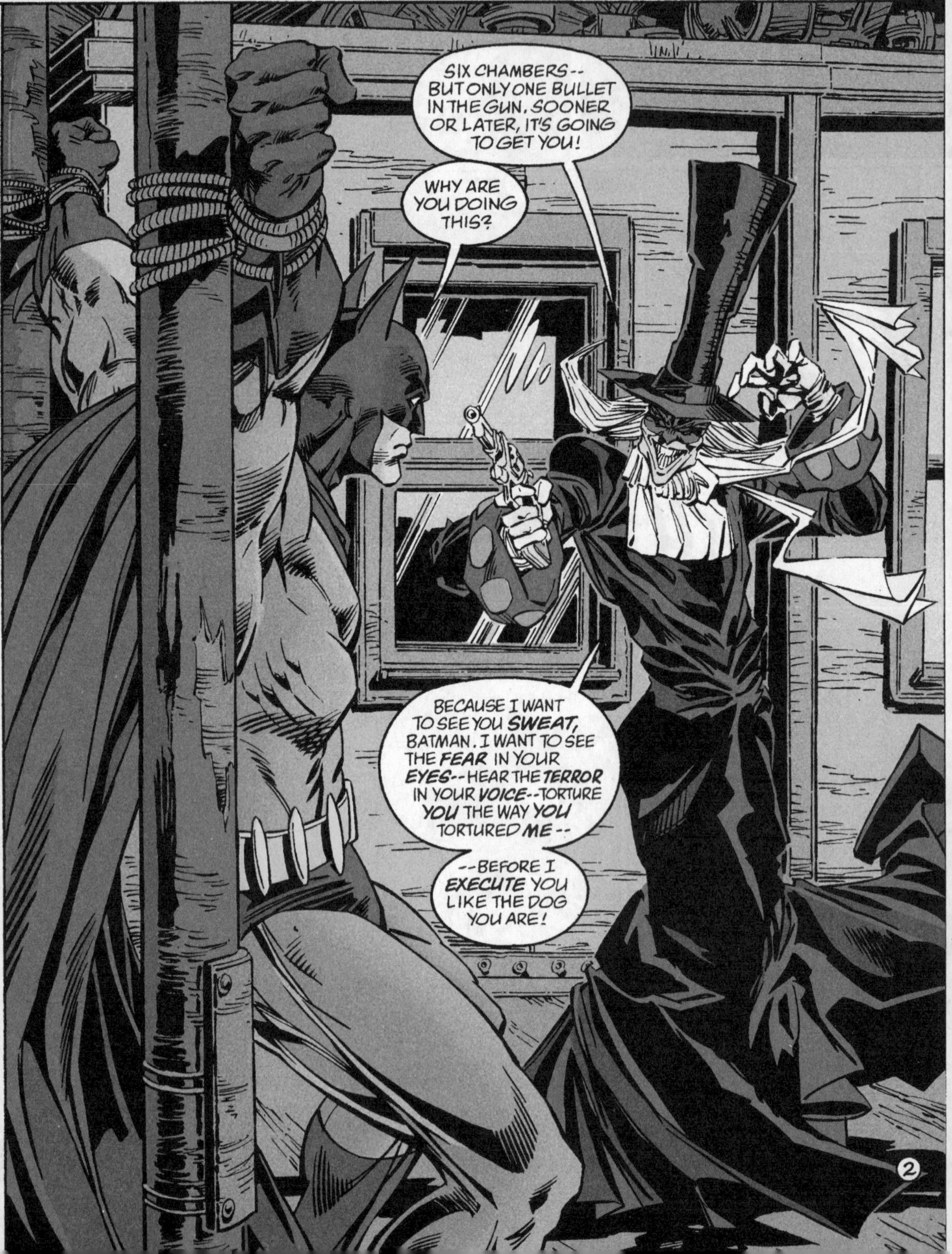
SIX CHAMBERS-- BUT ONLY ONE BULLET IN THE GUN. SOONER OR LATER, IT'S GOING TO GET YOU!
WHY ARE YOU DOING THIS?
BECAUSE I WANT TO SEE YOU SWEAT, BATMAN. I WANT TO SEE THE FEAR IN YOUR EYES--HEAR THE TERROR IN YOUR VOICE--TORTURE YOU THE WAY YOU TORTURED ME--
--BEFORE I EXECUTE YOU LIKE THE DOG YOU ARE!

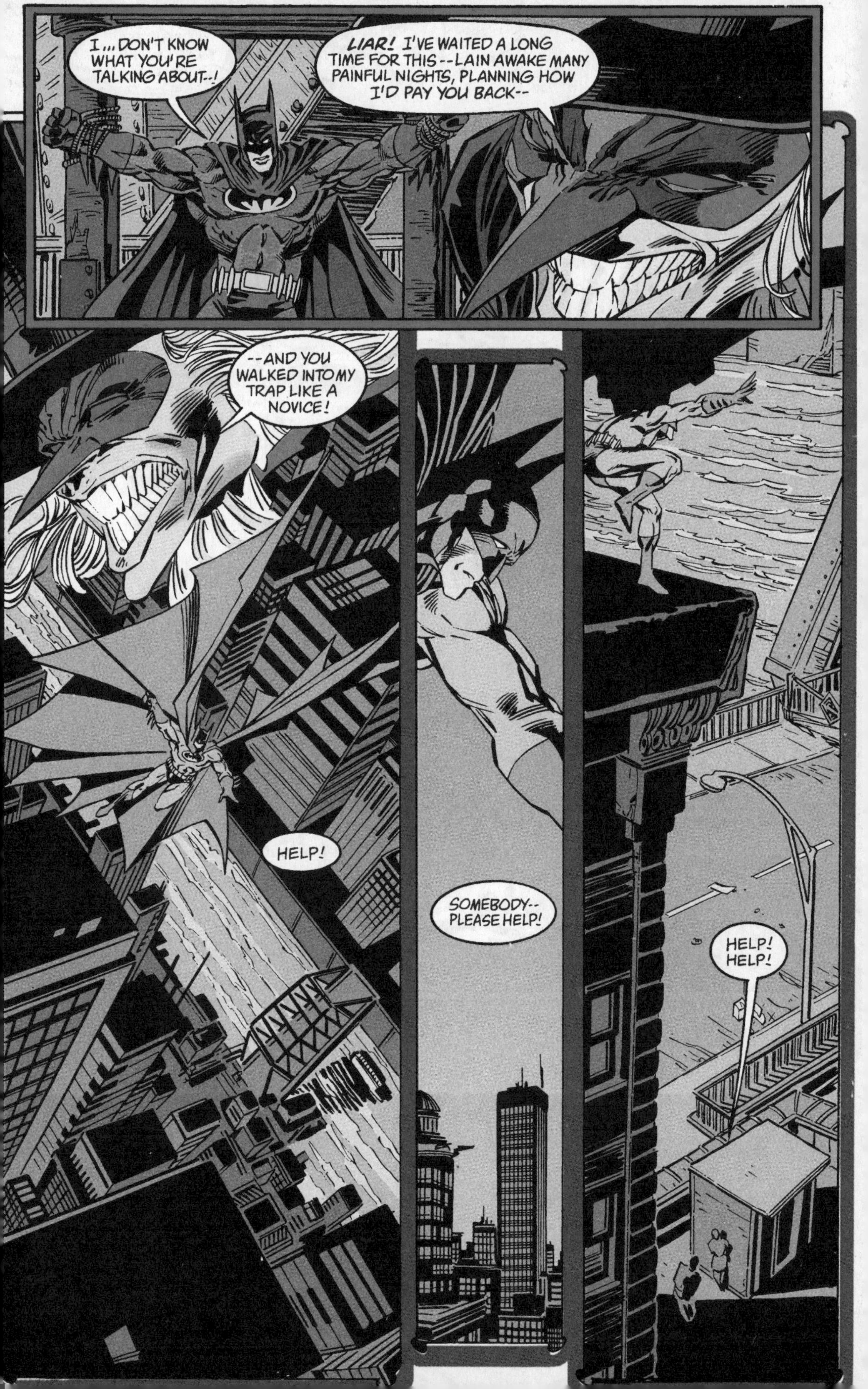
I... DON'T KNOW WHAT YOU'RE TALKING ABOUT--!
LIAR! I'VE WAITED A LONG TIME FOR THIS--LAIN AWAKE MANY PAINFUL NIGHTS, PLANNING HOW I'D PAY YOU BACK--
--AND YOU WALKED INTO MY TRAP LIKE A NOVICE!
HELP!
SOMEBODY--PLEASE HELP!
HELP! HELP!

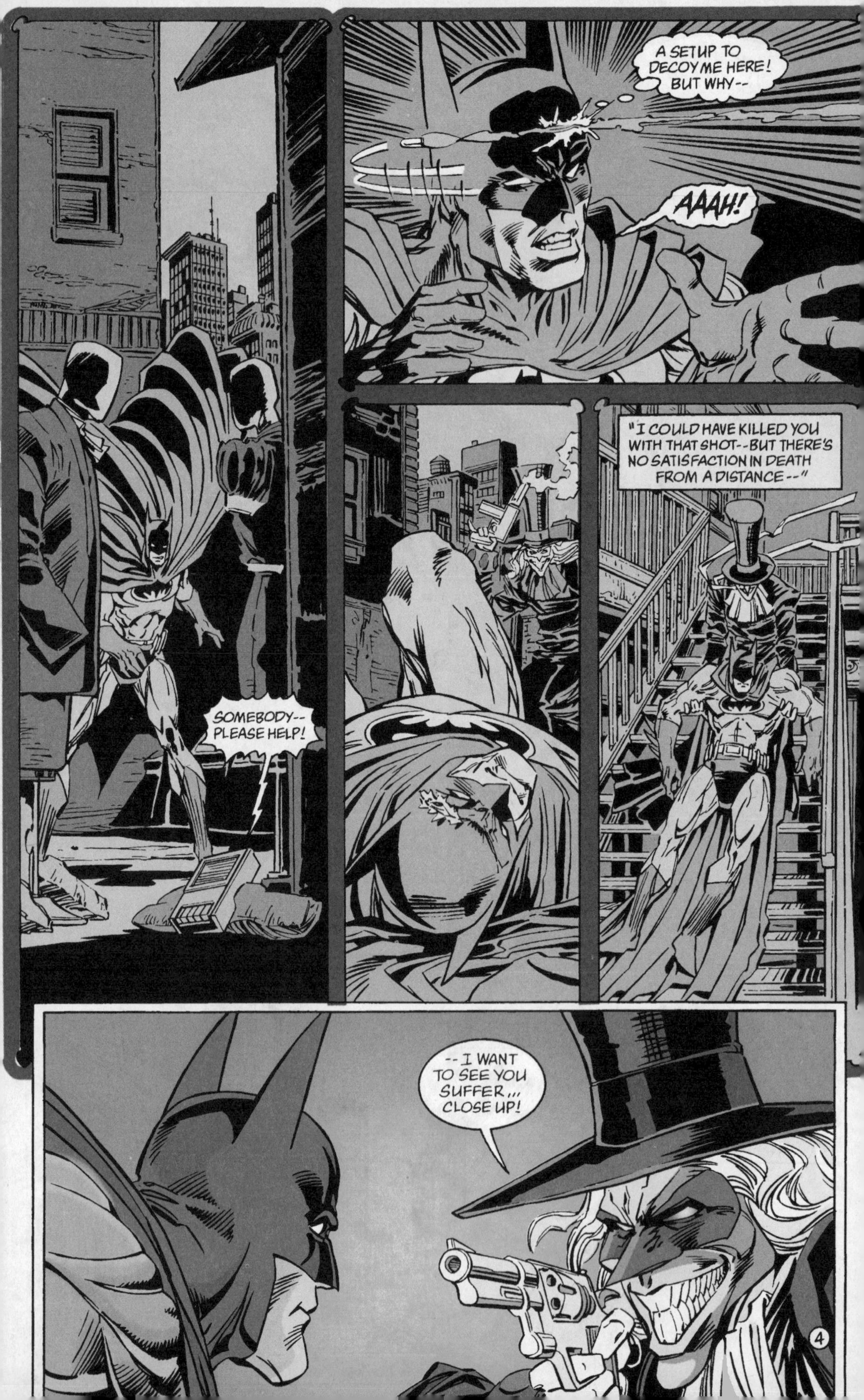
SOMEBODY--
PLEASE HELP!
A SETUP TO
DECOY ME HERE!
BUT WHY--
AAAH!
"I COULD HAVE KILLED YOU
WITH THAT SHOT--BUT THERE'S
NO SATISFACTION IN DEATH
FROM A DISTANCE--"
--I WANT
TO SEE YOU
SUFFER...
CLOSE UP!
4

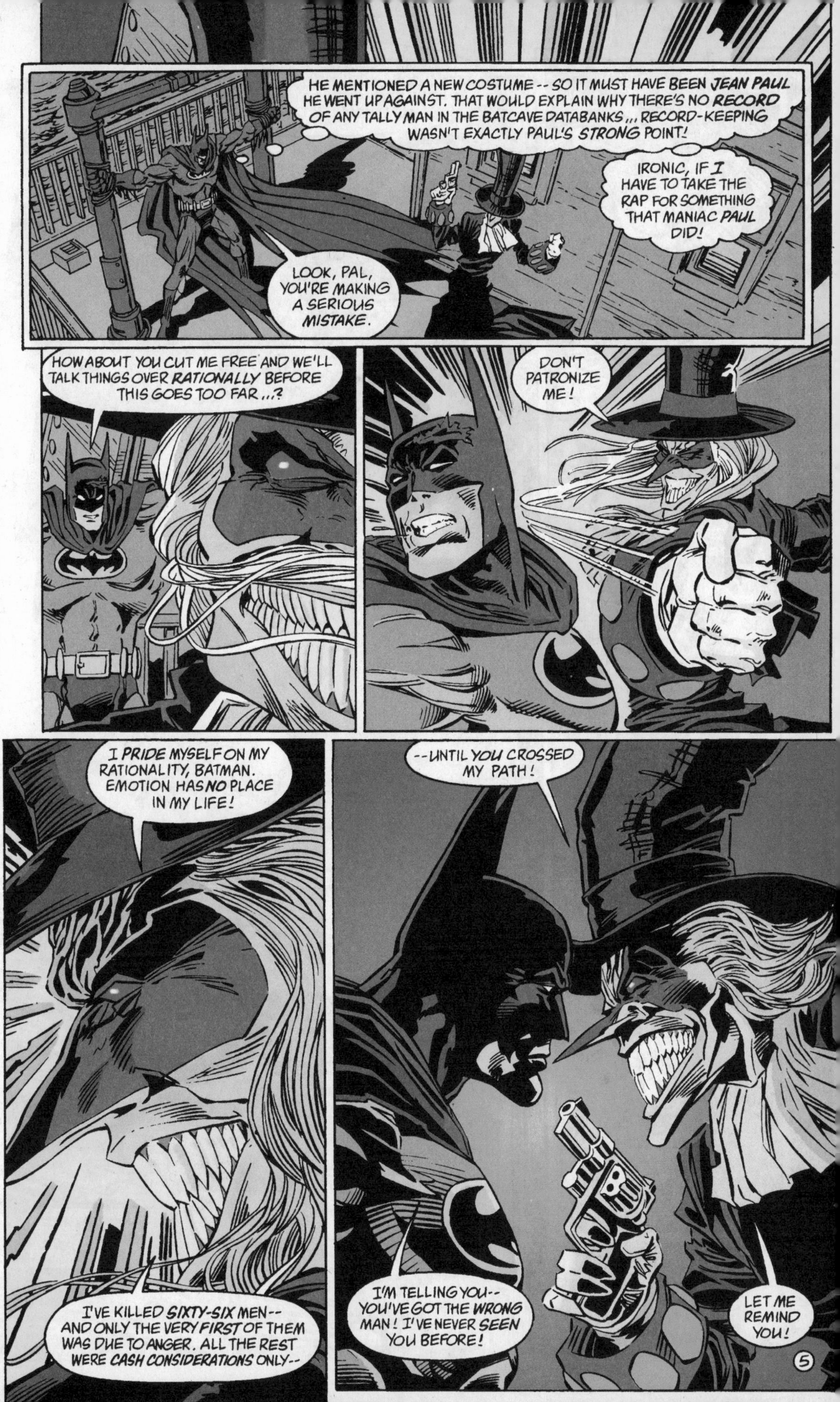
HE MENTIONED A NEW COSTUME -- SO IT MUST HAVE BEEN JEAN PAUL HE WENT UP AGAINST. THAT WOULD EXPLAIN WHY THERE'S NO RECORD OF ANY TALLY MAN IN THE BATCAVE DATABANKS ... RECORD-KEEPING WASN'T EXACTLY PAUL'S STRONG POINT!
IRONIC, IF I HAVE TO TAKE THE RAP FOR SOMETHING THAT MANIAC PAUL DID!
LOOK, PAL, YOU'RE MAKING A SERIOUS MISTAKE.
HOW ABOUT YOU CUT ME FREE AND WE'LL TALK THINGS OVER RATIONALLY BEFORE THIS GOES TOO FAR ...?
DON'T PATRONIZE ME!
I PRIDE MYSELF ON MY RATIONALITY, BATMAN. EMOTION HAS NO PLACE IN MY LIFE!
I'VE KILLED SIXTY-SIX MEN -- AND ONLY THE VERY FIRST OF THEM WAS DUE TO ANGER. ALL THE REST WERE CASH CONSIDERATIONS ONLY --
-- UNTIL YOU CROSSED MY PATH!
I'M TELLING YOU -- YOU'VE GOT THE WRONG MAN! I'VE NEVER SEEN YOU BEFORE!
LET ME REMIND YOU!

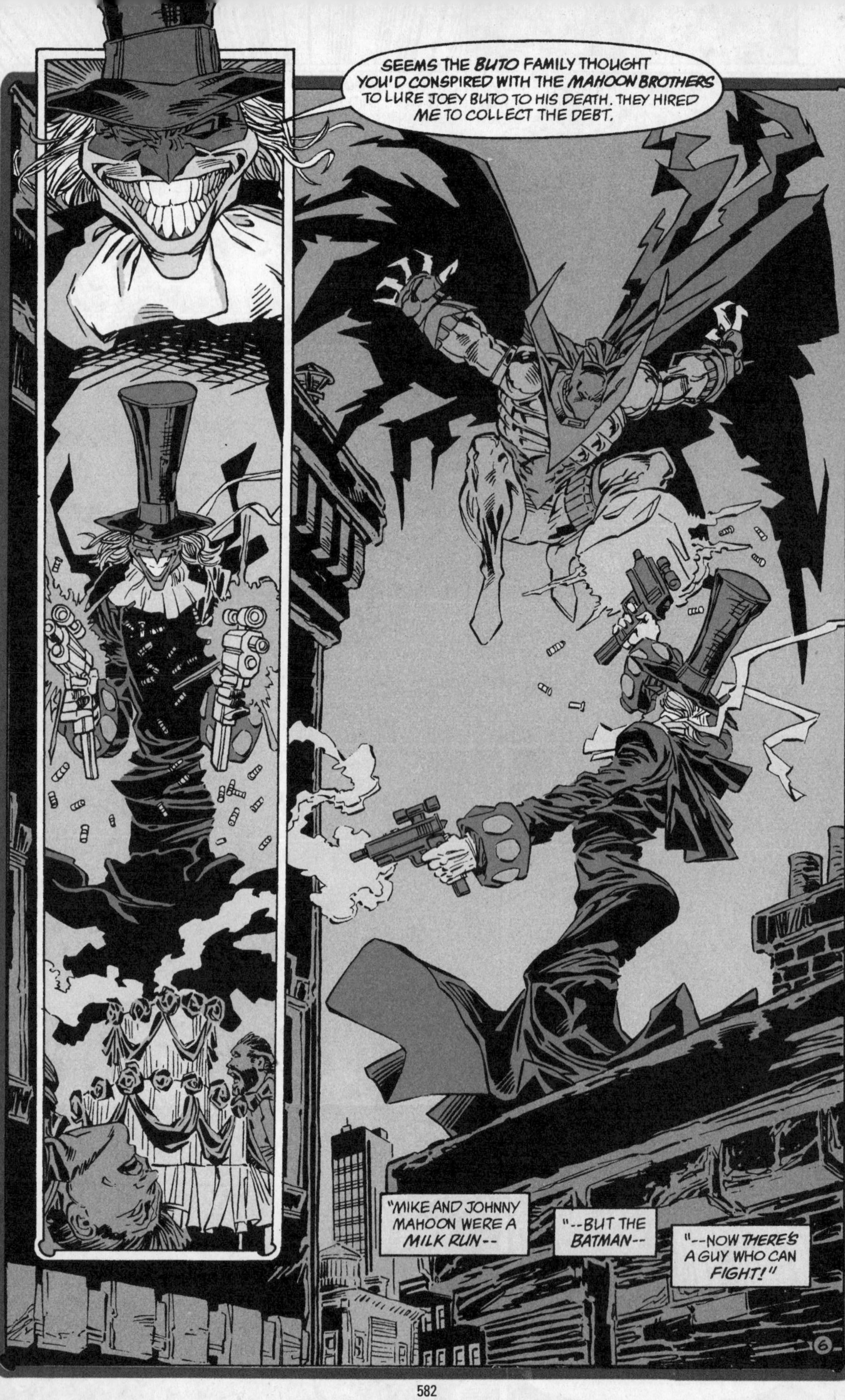

SEEMS THE BUTO FAMILY THOUGHT YOU'D CONSPIRED WITH THE MAHOON BROTHERS TO LURE JOEY BUTO TO HIS DEATH. THEY HIRED ME TO COLLECT THE DEBT.
"MIKE AND JOHNNY MAHOON WERE A MILK RUN--
"--BUT THE BATMAN--
"--NOW THERE'S A GUY WHO CAN FIGHT!"
6

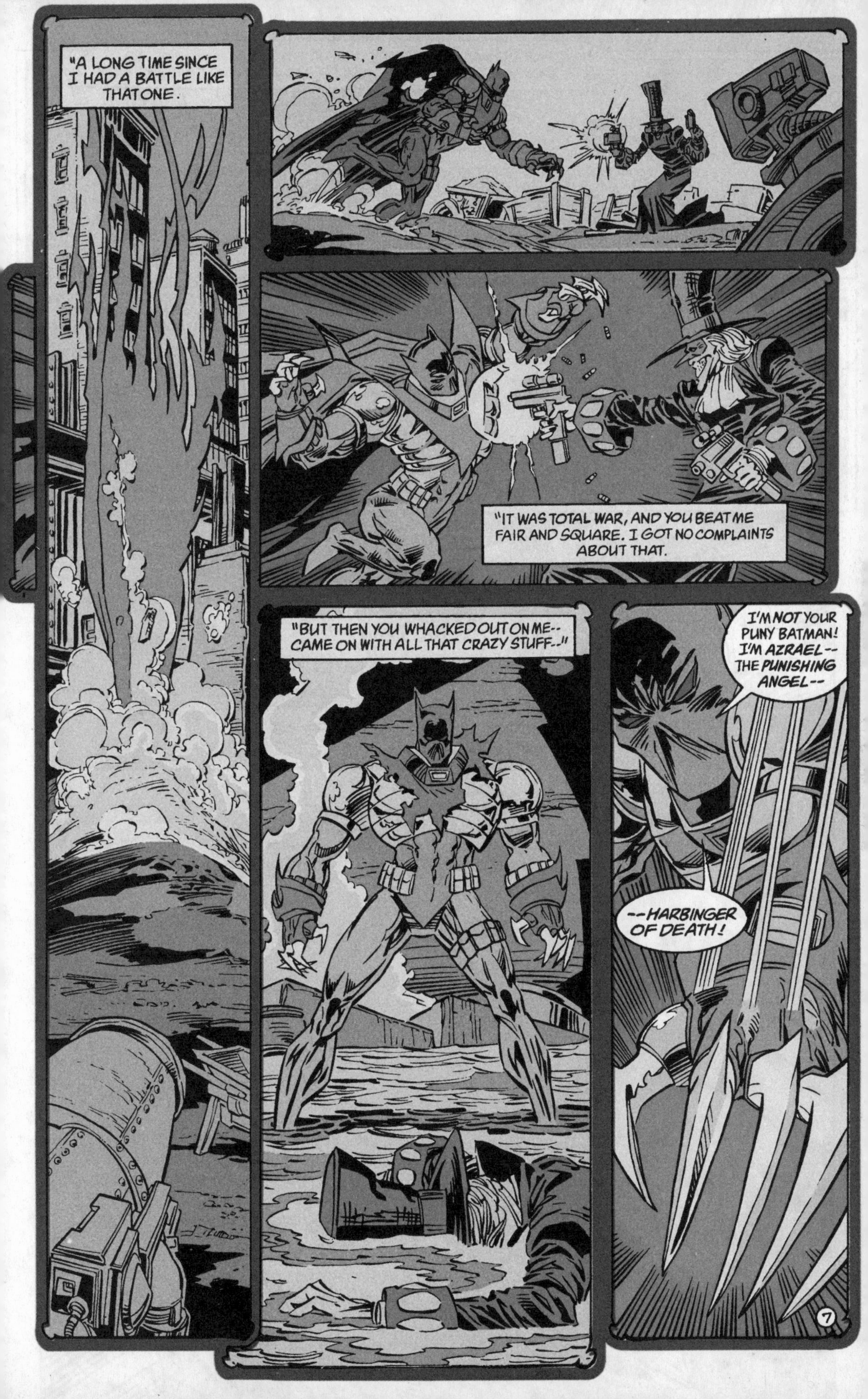
"A LONG TIME SINCE I HAD A BATTLE LIKE THAT ONE.
"IT WAS TOTAL WAR, AND YOU BEAT ME FAIR AND SQUARE. I GOT NO COMPLAINTS ABOUT THAT.
"BUT THEN YOU WHACKED OUT ON ME-- CAME ON WITH ALL THAT CRAZY STUFF--"
I'M NOT YOUR PUNY BATMAN! I'M AZRAEL-- THE PUNISHING ANGEL--
--HARBINGER OF DEATH!
7

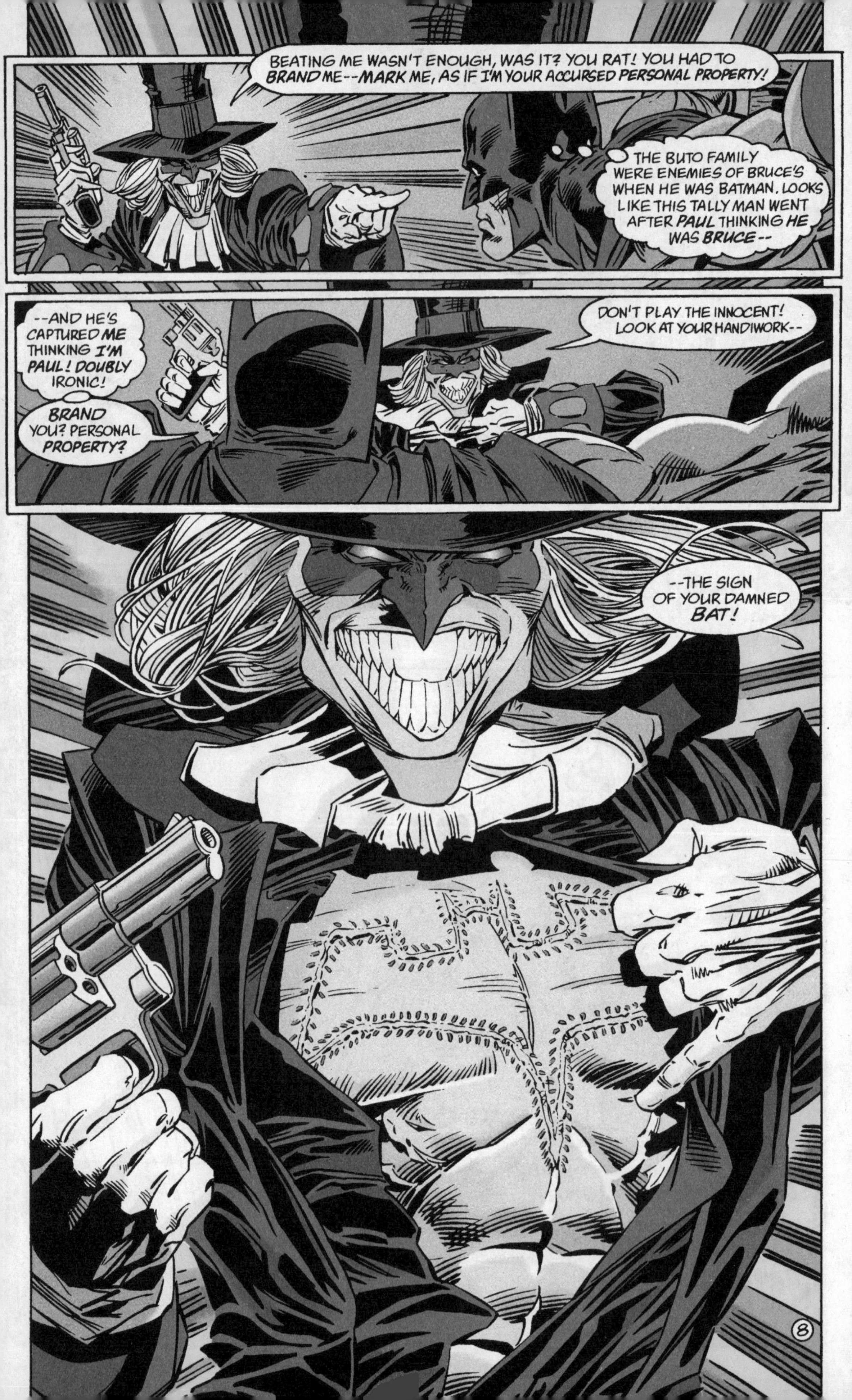

BEATING ME WASN'T ENOUGH, WAS IT? YOU RAT! YOU HAD TO BRAND ME--MARK ME, AS IF I'M YOUR ACCURSED PERSONAL PROPERTY!
THE BUTO FAMILY WERE ENEMIES OF BRUCE'S WHEN HE WAS BATMAN. LOOKS LIKE THIS TALLY MAN WENT AFTER PAUL THINKING HE WAS BRUCE--
--AND HE'S CAPTURED ME THINKING I'M PAUL! DOUBLY IRONIC!
BRAND YOU? PERSONAL PROPERTY?
DON'T PLAY THE INNOCENT! LOOK AT YOUR HANDIWORK--
--THE SIGN OF YOUR DAMNED BAT!
8

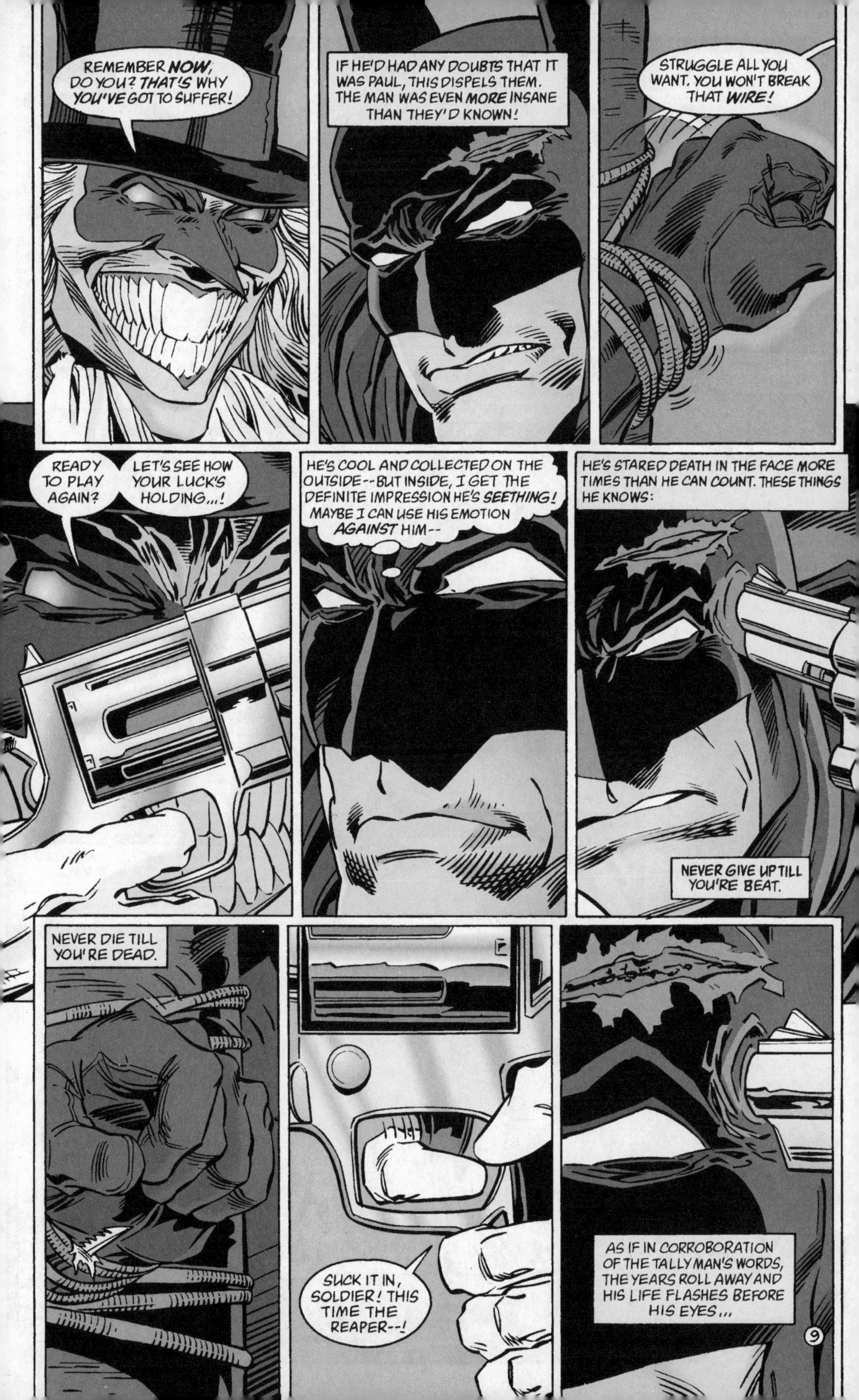

REMEMBER NOW; DO YOU? THAT'S WHY YOU'VE GOT TO SUFFER!
IF HE'D HAD ANY DOUBTS THAT IT WAS PAUL, THIS DISPELS THEM. THE MAN WAS EVEN MORE INSANE THAN THEY'D KNOWN!
STRUGGLE ALL YOU WANT. YOU WON'T BREAK THAT WIRE!
READY TO PLAY AGAIN?
LET'S SEE HOW YOUR LUCK'S HOLDING...!
HE'S COOL AND COLLECTED ON THE OUTSIDE--BUT INSIDE, I GET THE DEFINITE IMPRESSION HE'S SEETHING! MAYBE I CAN USE HIS EMOTION AGAINST HIM--
HE'S STARED DEATH IN THE FACE MORE TIMES THAN HE CAN COUNT. THESE THINGS HE KNOWS:
NEVER GIVE UP TILL YOU'RE BEAT.
NEVER DIE TILL YOU'RE DEAD.
SUCK IT IN, SOLDIER! THIS TIME THE REAPER--!
AS IF IN CORROBORATION OF THE TALLY MAN'S WORDS, THE YEARS ROLL AWAY AND HIS LIFE FLASHES BEFORE HIS EYES...
9

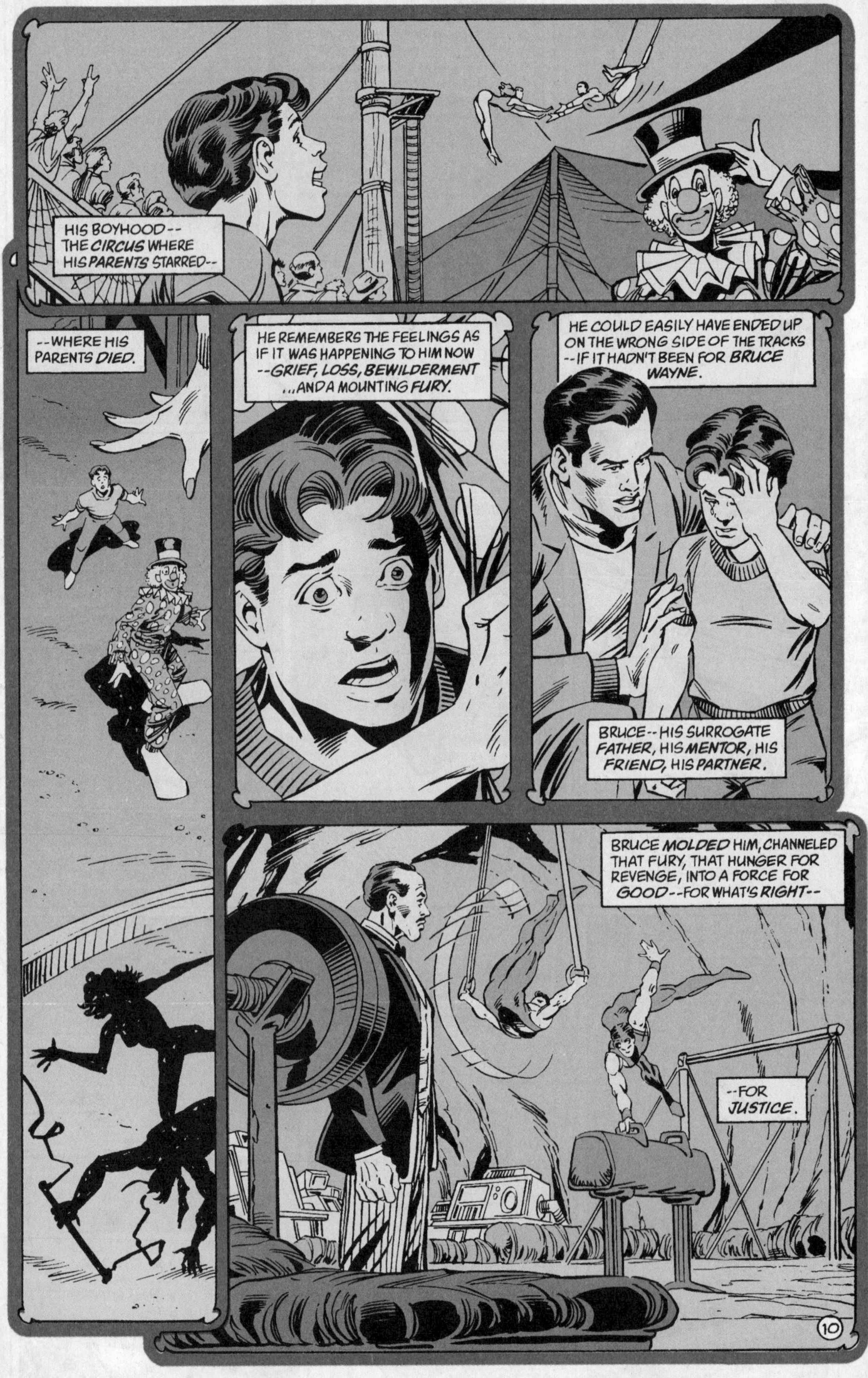

HIS BOYHOOD-- THE CIRCUS WHERE HIS PARENTS STARRED--
--WHERE HIS PARENTS DIED.
HE REMEMBERS THE FEELINGS AS IF IT WAS HAPPENING TO HIM NOW --GRIEF, LOSS, BEWILDERMENT ...AND A MOUNTING FURY.
HE COULD EASILY HAVE ENDED UP ON THE WRONG SIDE OF THE TRACKS --IF IT HADN'T BEEN FOR BRUCE WAYNE.
BRUCE--HIS SURROGATE FATHER, HIS MENTOR, HIS FRIEND, HIS PARTNER.
BRUCE MOLDED HIM, CHANNELED THAT FURY, THAT HUNGER FOR REVENGE, INTO A FORCE FOR GOOD--FOR WHAT'S RIGHT--
--FOR JUSTICE.
10

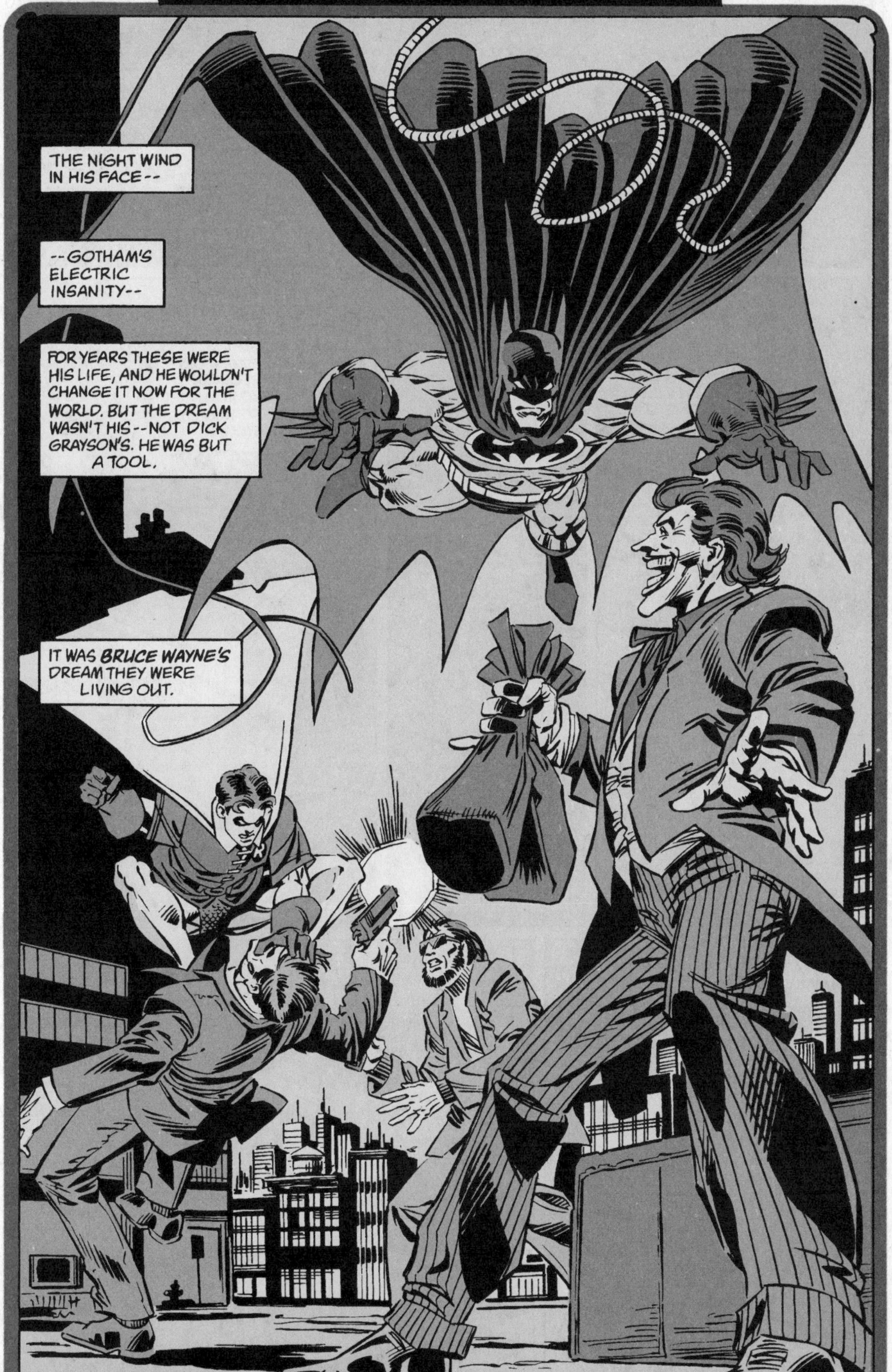
THE NIGHT WIND IN HIS FACE--
--GOTHAM'S ELECTRIC INSANITY--
FOR YEARS THESE WERE HIS LIFE, AND HE WOULDN'T CHANGE IT NOW FOR THE WORLD. BUT THE DREAM WASN'T HIS--NOT DICK GRAYSON'S. HE WAS BUT A TOOL.
IT WAS BRUCE WAYNE'S DREAM THEY WERE LIVING OUT.
11

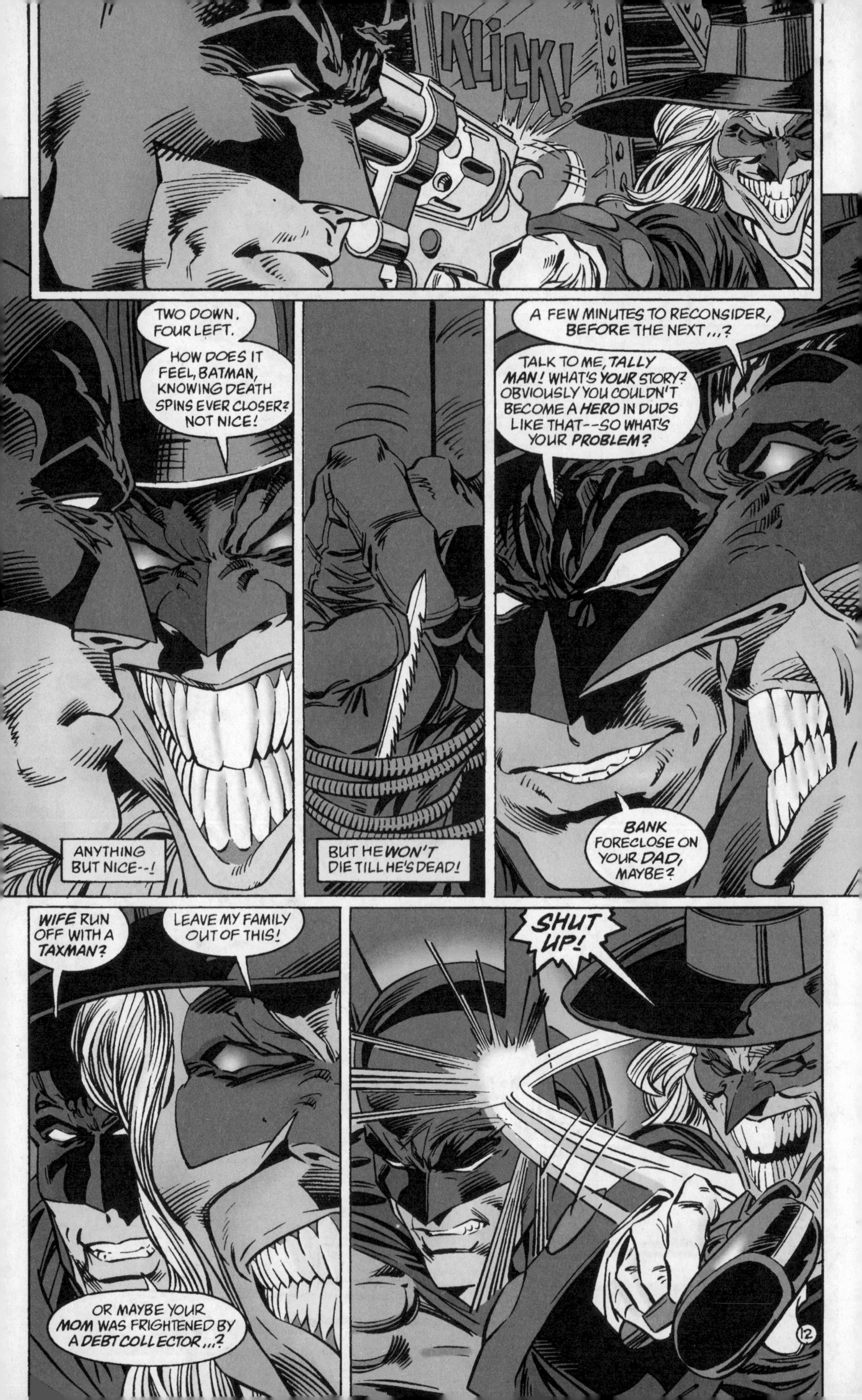
KLICK!
TWO DOWN. FOUR LEFT.
HOW DOES IT FEEL, BATMAN, KNOWING DEATH SPINS EVER CLOSER? NOT NICE!
ANYTHING BUT NICE--!
BUT HE WON'T DIE TILL HE'S DEAD!
A FEW MINUTES TO RECONSIDER, BEFORE THE NEXT...?
TALK TO ME, TALLY MAN! WHAT'S YOUR STORY? OBVIOUSLY YOU COULDN'T BECOME A HERO IN DUDS LIKE THAT--SO WHAT'S YOUR PROBLEM?
BANK FORECLOSE ON YOUR DAD, MAYBE?
WIFE RUN OFF WITH A TAXMAN?
LEAVE MY FAMILY OUT OF THIS!
OR MAYBE YOUR MOM WAS FRIGHTENED BY A DEBT COLLECTOR...?
SHUT UP!
12

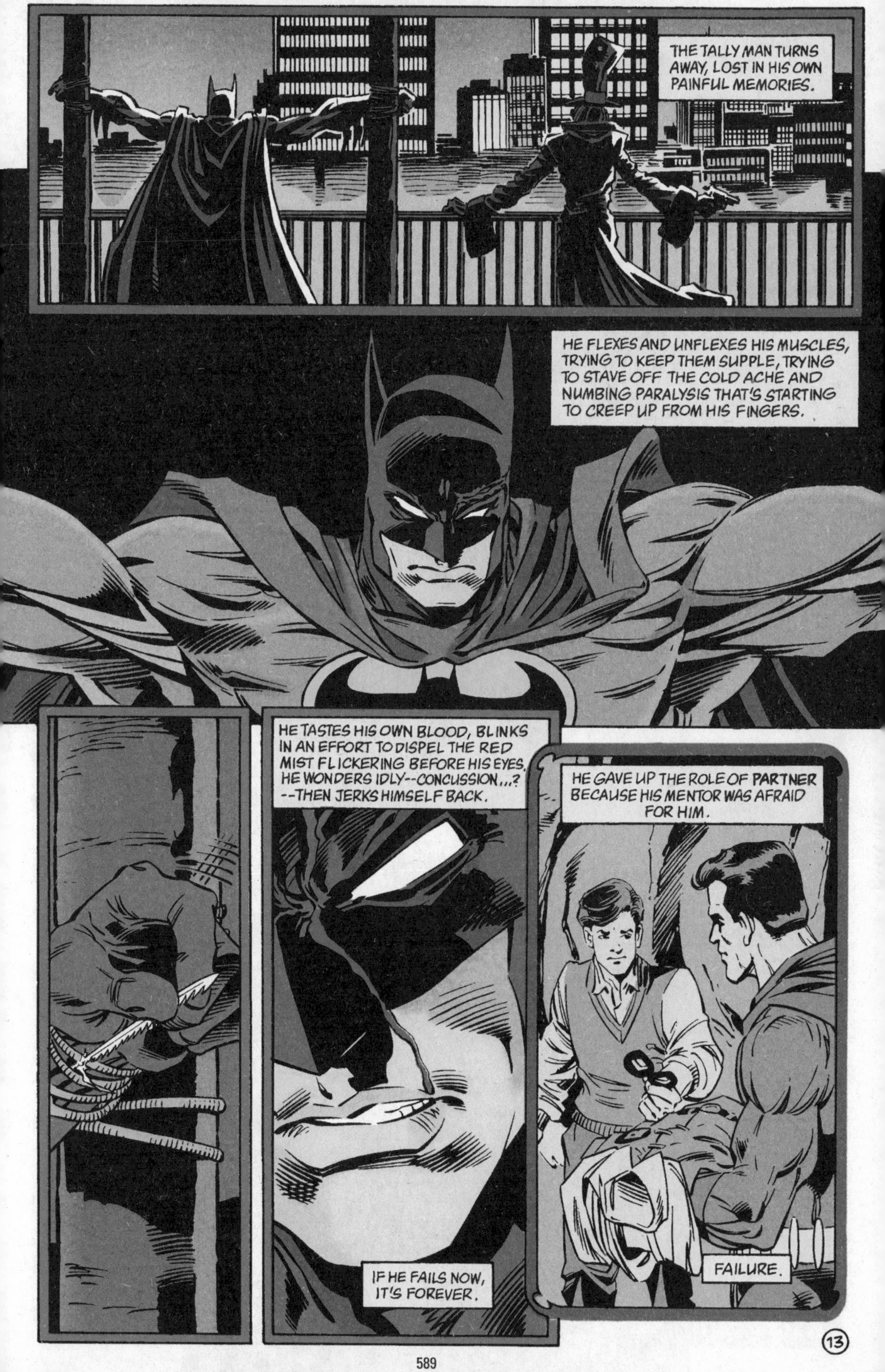
THE TALLY MAN TURNS AWAY, LOST IN HIS OWN PAINFUL MEMORIES.
HE FLEXES AND UNFLEXES HIS MUSCLES, TRYING TO KEEP THEM SUPPLE, TRYING TO STAVE OFF THE COLD ACHE AND NUMBING PARALYSIS THAT'S STARTING TO CREEP UP FROM HIS FINGERS.
HE TASTES HIS OWN BLOOD, BLINKS IN AN EFFORT TO DISPEL THE RED MIST FLICKERING BEFORE HIS EYES. HE WONDERS IDLY--CONCUSSION...? --THEN JERKS HIMSELF BACK.
IF HE FAILS NOW, IT'S FOREVER.
HE GAVE UP THE ROLE OF PARTNER BECAUSE HIS MENTOR WAS AFRAID FOR HIM.
FAILURE.
13

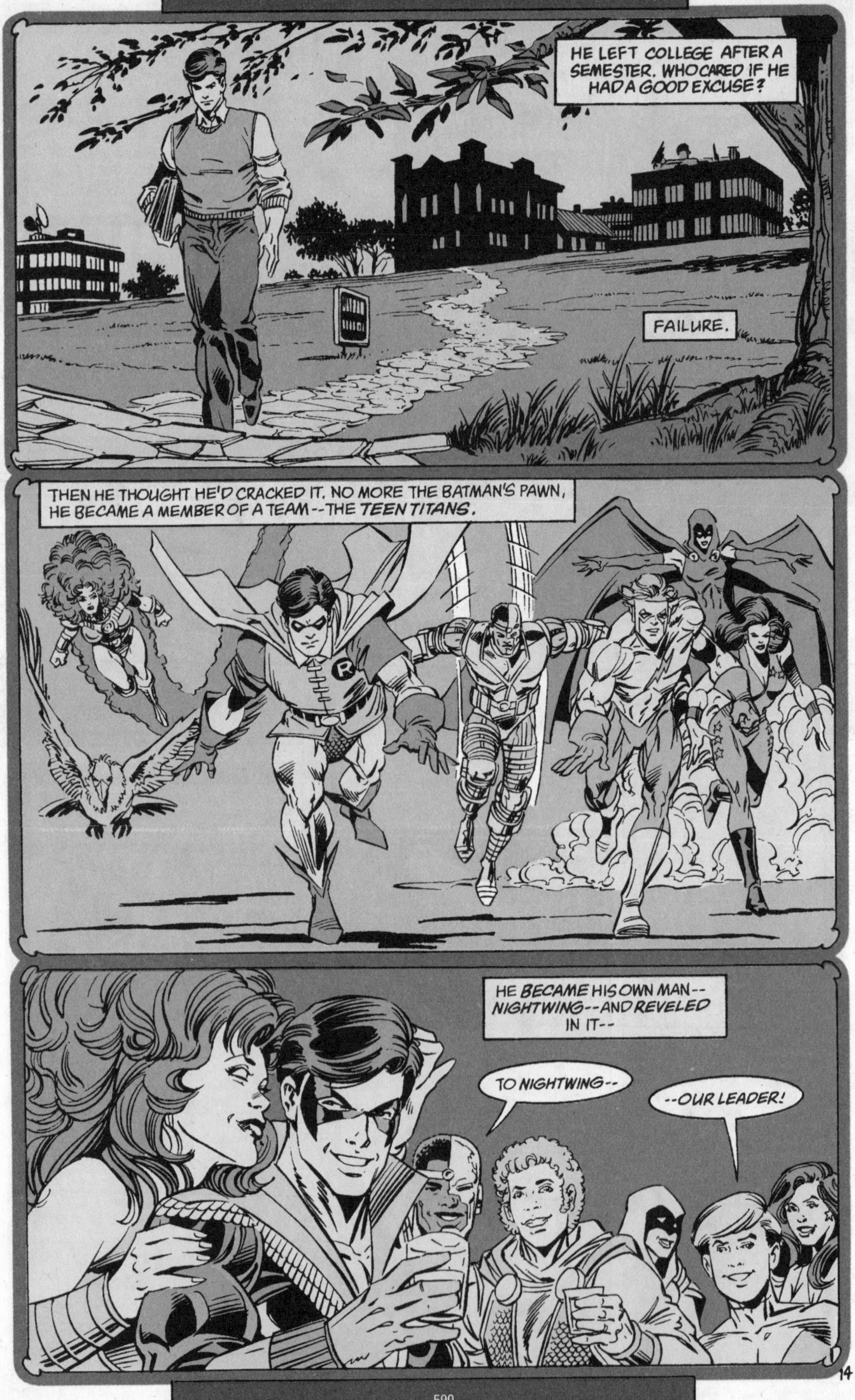
HE LEFT COLLEGE AFTER A SEMESTER. WHO CARED IF HE HAD A GOOD EXCUSE?
FAILURE.
THEN HE THOUGHT HE'D CRACKED IT. NO MORE THE BATMAN'S PAWN, HE BECAME A MEMBER OF A TEAM--THE *TEEN TITANS*.
HE *BECAME* HIS OWN MAN-- *NIGHTWING*--AND *REVELED* IN IT--
TO NIGHTWING--
--OUR LEADER!
14

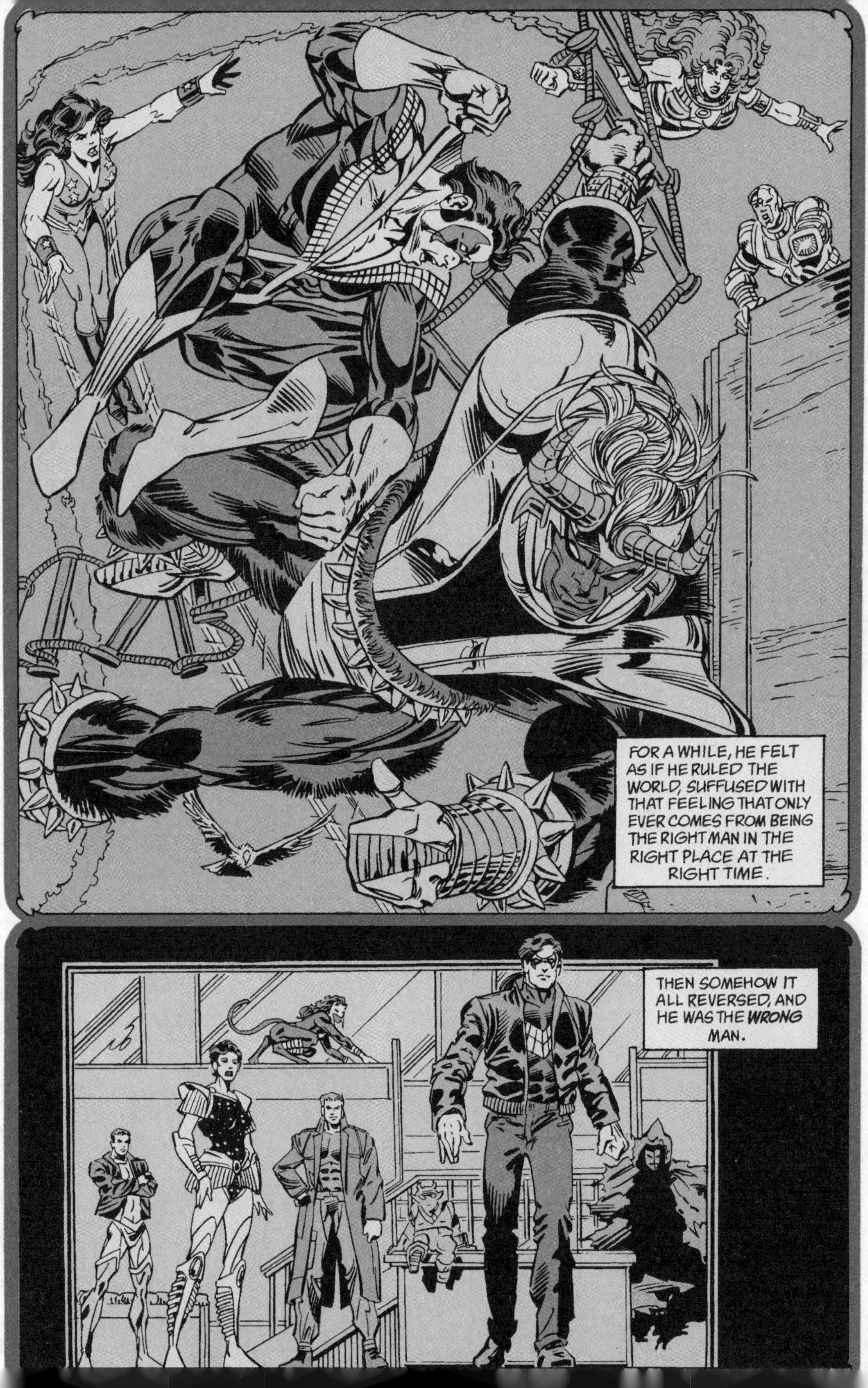
FOR A WHILE, HE FELT AS IF HE RULED THE WORLD, SUFFUSED WITH THAT FEELING THAT ONLY EVER COMES FROM BEING THE RIGHT MAN IN THE RIGHT PLACE AT THE RIGHT TIME.
THEN SOMEHOW IT ALL REVERSED, AND HE WAS THE WRONG MAN.

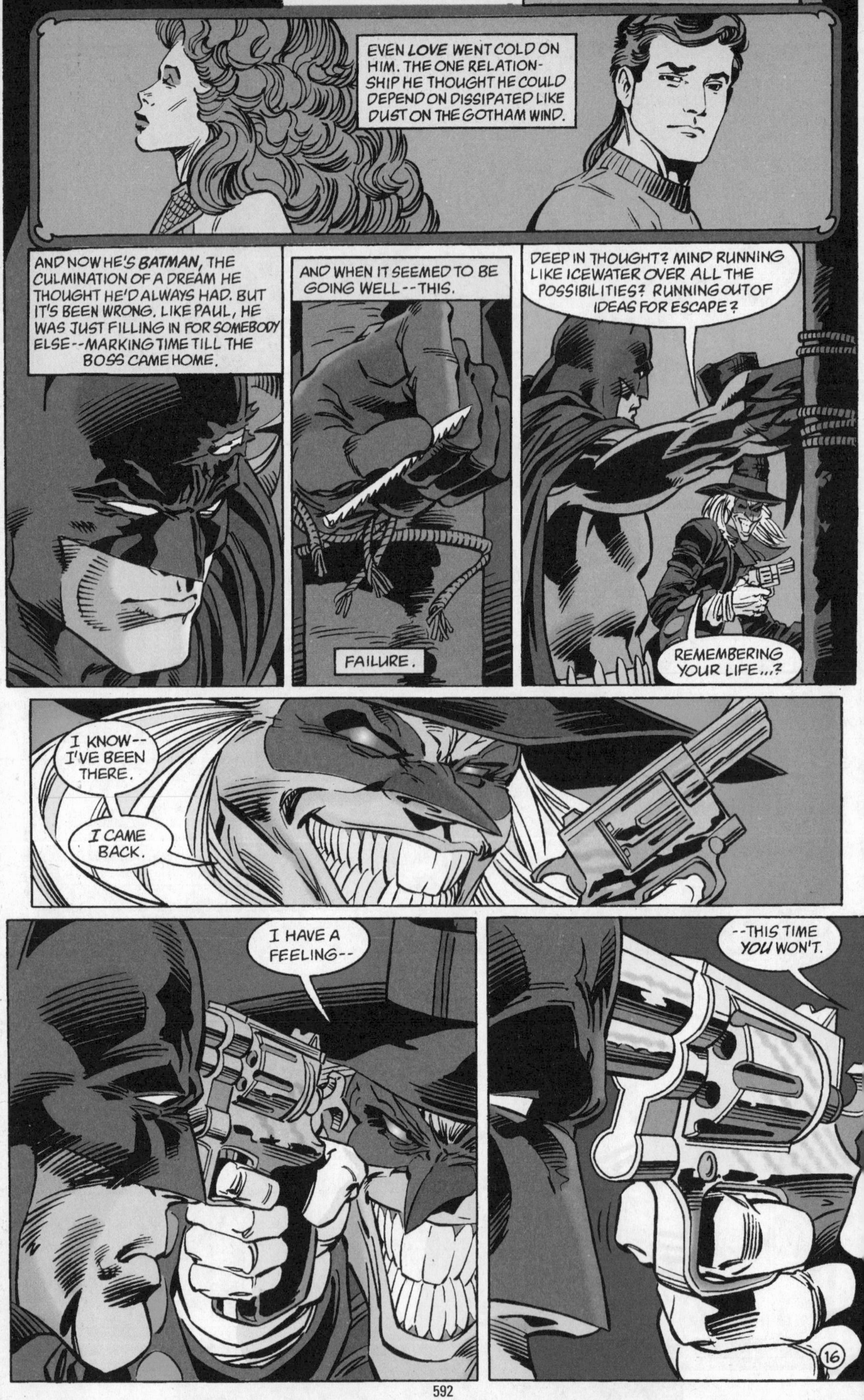
EVEN LOVE WENT COLD ON HIM. THE ONE RELATIONSHIP HE THOUGHT HE COULD DEPEND ON DISSIPATED LIKE DUST ON THE GOTHAM WIND.
AND NOW HE'S BATMAN, THE CULMINATION OF A DREAM HE THOUGHT HE'D ALWAYS HAD. BUT IT'S BEEN WRONG. LIKE PAUL, HE WAS JUST FILLING IN FOR SOMEBODY ELSE--MARKING TIME TILL THE BOSS CAME HOME.
AND WHEN IT SEEMED TO BE GOING WELL--THIS.
FAILURE.
DEEP IN THOUGHT? MIND RUNNING LIKE ICEWATER OVER ALL THE POSSIBILITIES? RUNNING OUT OF IDEAS FOR ESCAPE?
REMEMBERING YOUR LIFE...?
I KNOW--I'VE BEEN THERE.
I CAME BACK.
I HAVE A FEELING--
--THIS TIME YOU WON'T.
16

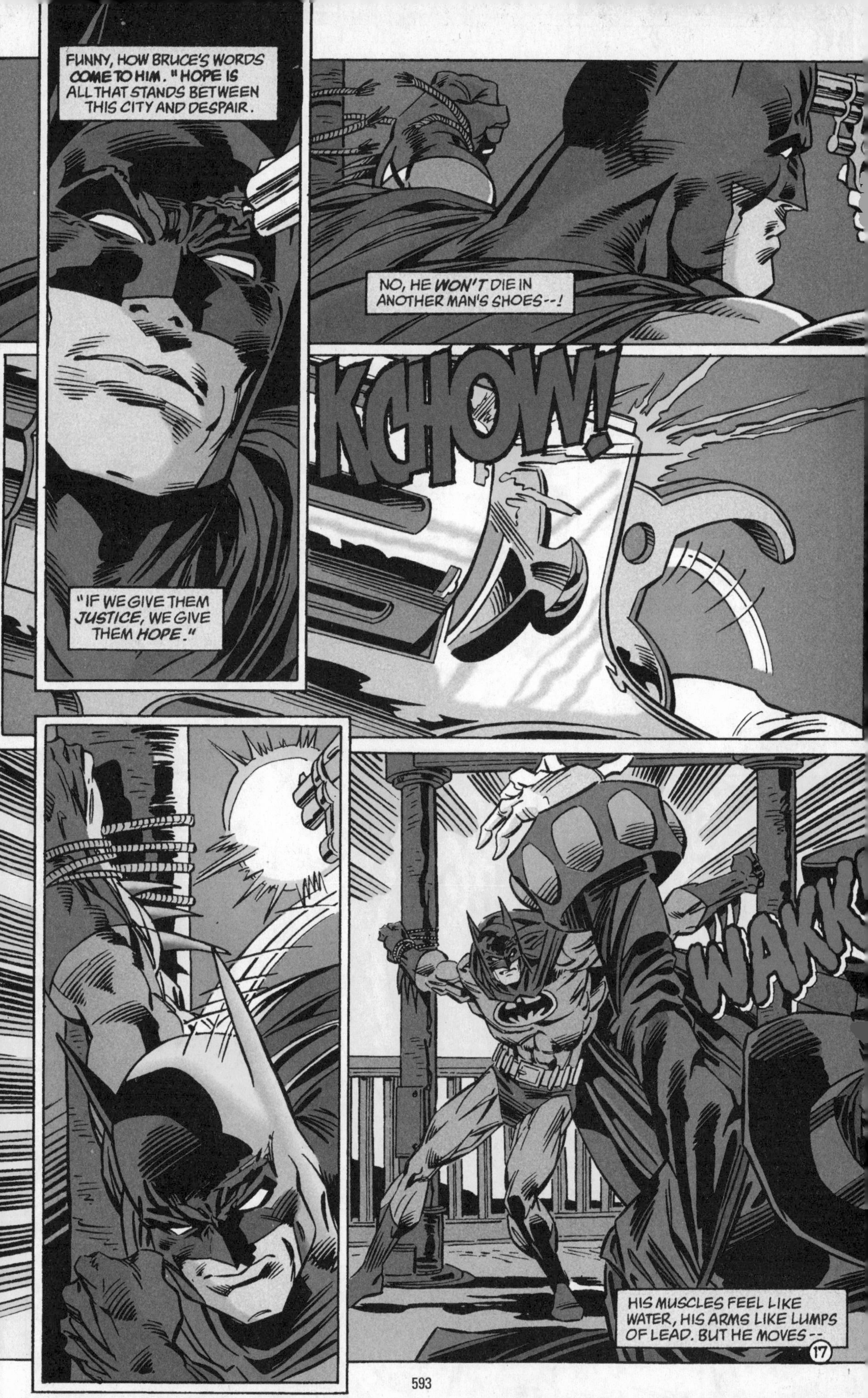
FUNNY, HOW BRUCE'S WORDS COME TO HIM. "HOPE IS ALL THAT STANDS BETWEEN THIS CITY AND DESPAIR.
NO, HE WON'T DIE IN ANOTHER MAN'S SHOES--!
KCHOW!
"IF WE GIVE THEM JUSTICE, WE GIVE THEM HOPE."
WAKK
HIS MUSCLES FEEL LIKE WATER, HIS ARMS LIKE LUMPS OF LEAD. BUT HE MOVES--
17

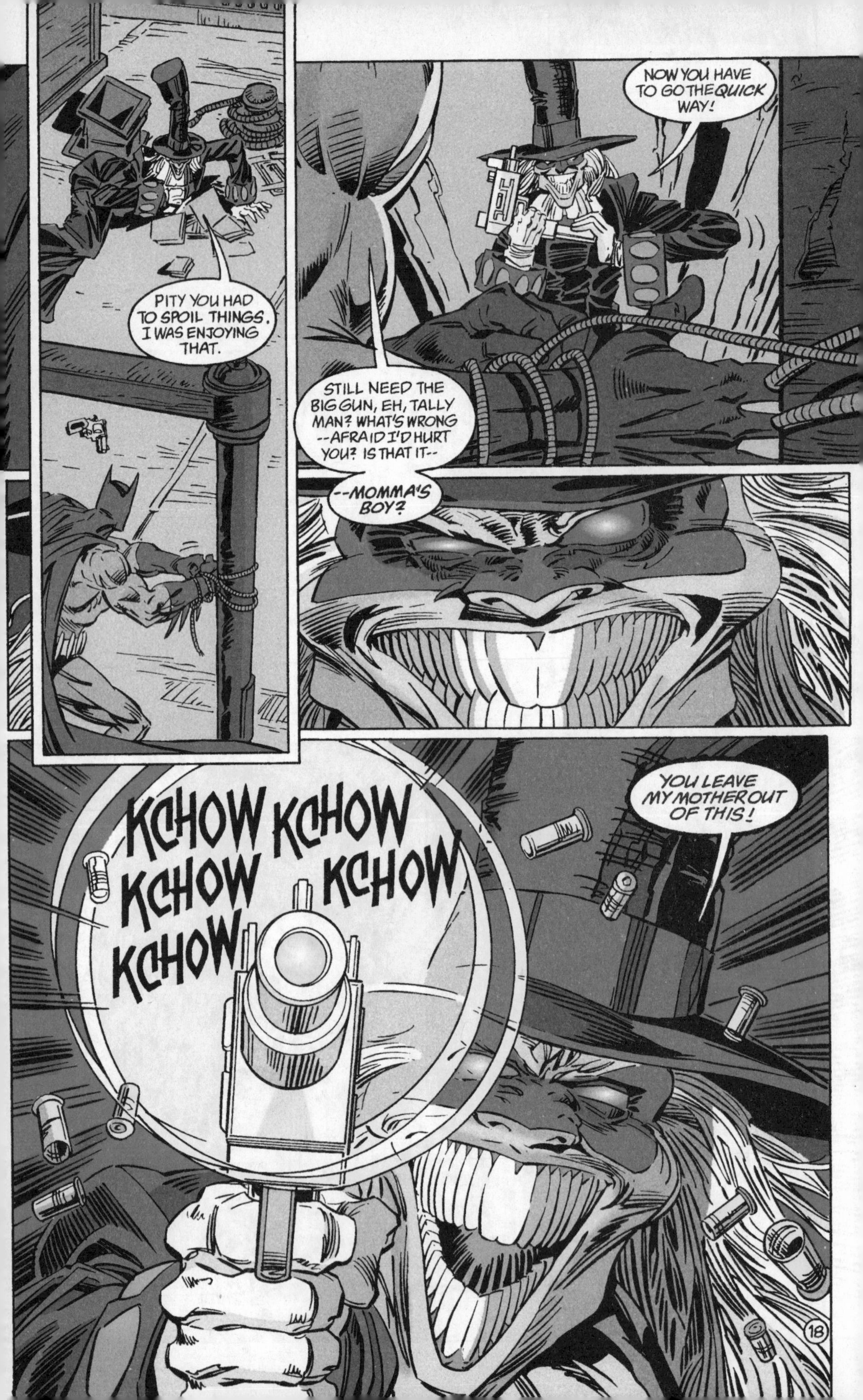
PITY YOU HAD TO SPOIL THINGS. I WAS ENJOYING THAT.
NOW YOU HAVE TO GO THE QUICK WAY!
STILL NEED THE BIG GUN, EH, TALLY MAN? WHAT'S WRONG --AFRAID I'D HURT YOU? IS THAT IT--
--MOMMA'S BOY?
KCHOW KCHOW KCHOW KCHOW KCHOW
YOU LEAVE MY MOTHER OUT OF THIS!
18

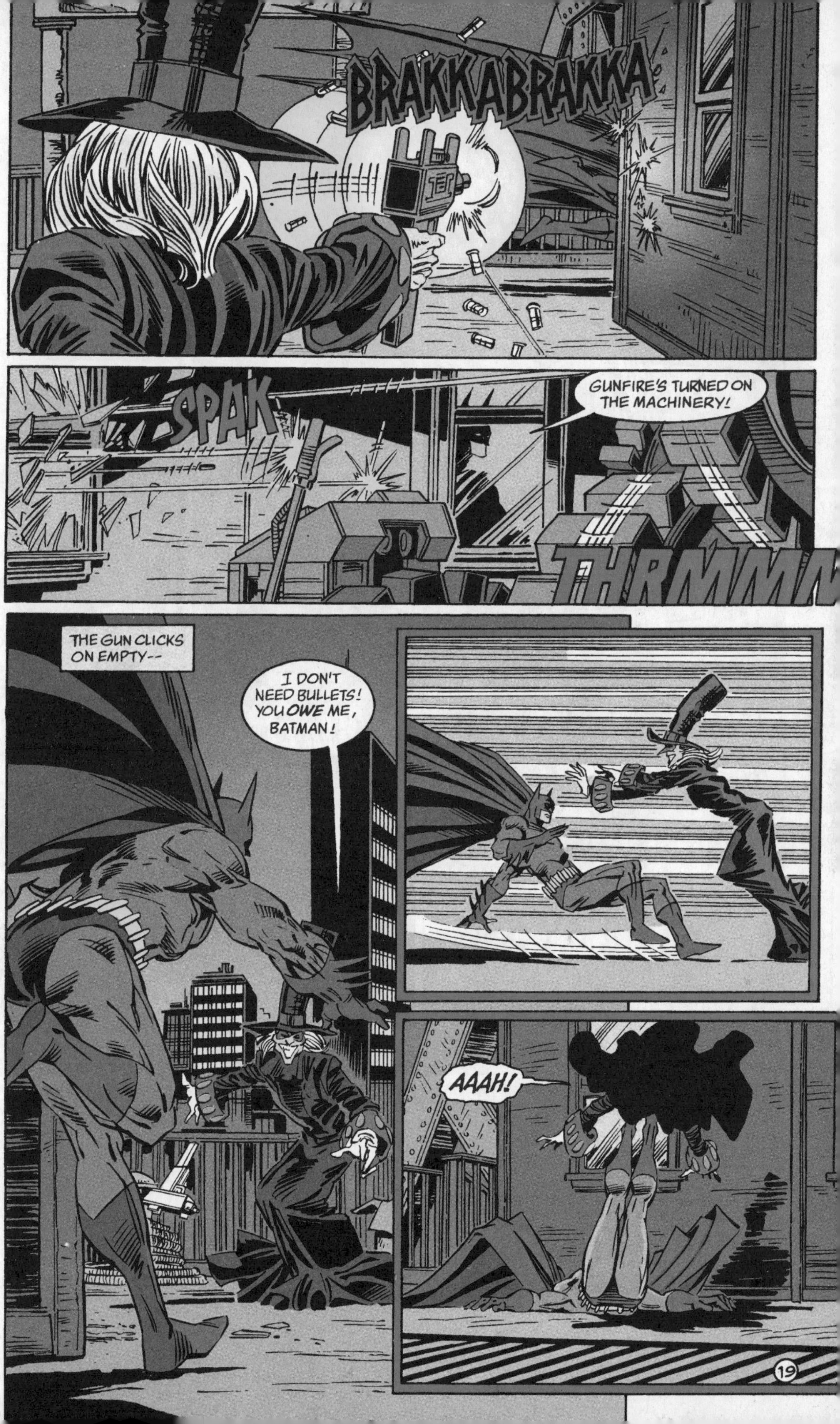
BRAKKABRAKKA
SPAK
GUNFIRE'S TURNED ON THE MACHINERY!
THRMMM
THE GUN CLICKS ON EMPTY--
I DON'T NEED BULLETS! YOU OWE ME, BATMAN!
AAAH!

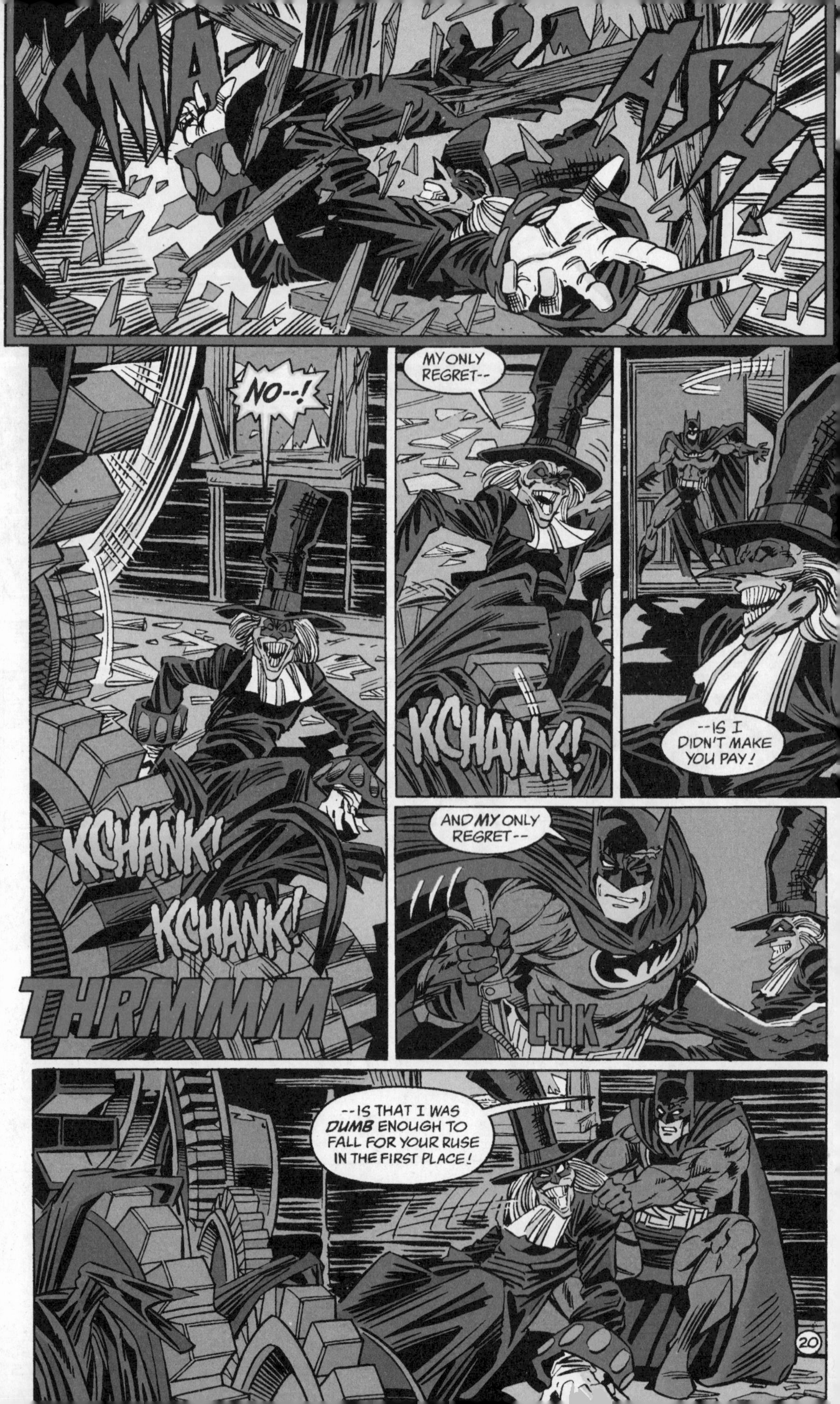

SMAAASH
NO--!
KCHANK!
KCHANK!
THRMMM
MY ONLY REGRET--
KCHANK!
--IS I DIDN'T MAKE YOU PAY!
AND MY ONLY REGRET--
CHK
--IS THAT I WAS DUMB ENOUGH TO FALL FOR YOUR RUSE IN THE FIRST PLACE!
20

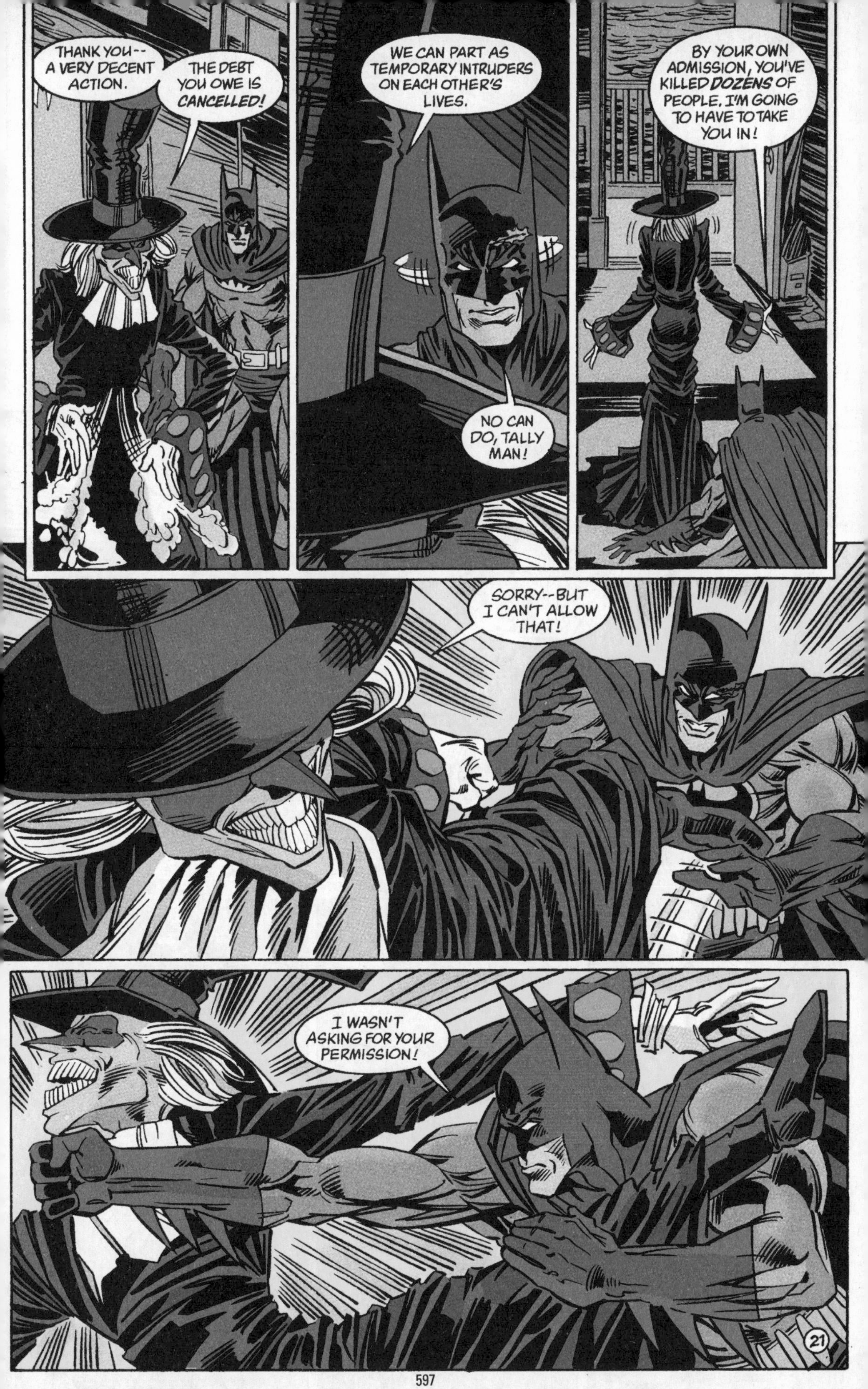
THANK YOU-- A VERY DECENT ACTION.
THE DEBT YOU OWE IS CANCELLED!
WE CAN PART AS TEMPORARY INTRUDERS ON EACH OTHER'S LIVES.
NO CAN DO, TALLY MAN!
BY YOUR OWN ADMISSION, YOU'VE KILLED DOZENS OF PEOPLE. I'M GOING TO HAVE TO TAKE YOU IN!
SORRY--BUT I CAN'T ALLOW THAT!
I WASN'T ASKING FOR YOUR PERMISSION!
21

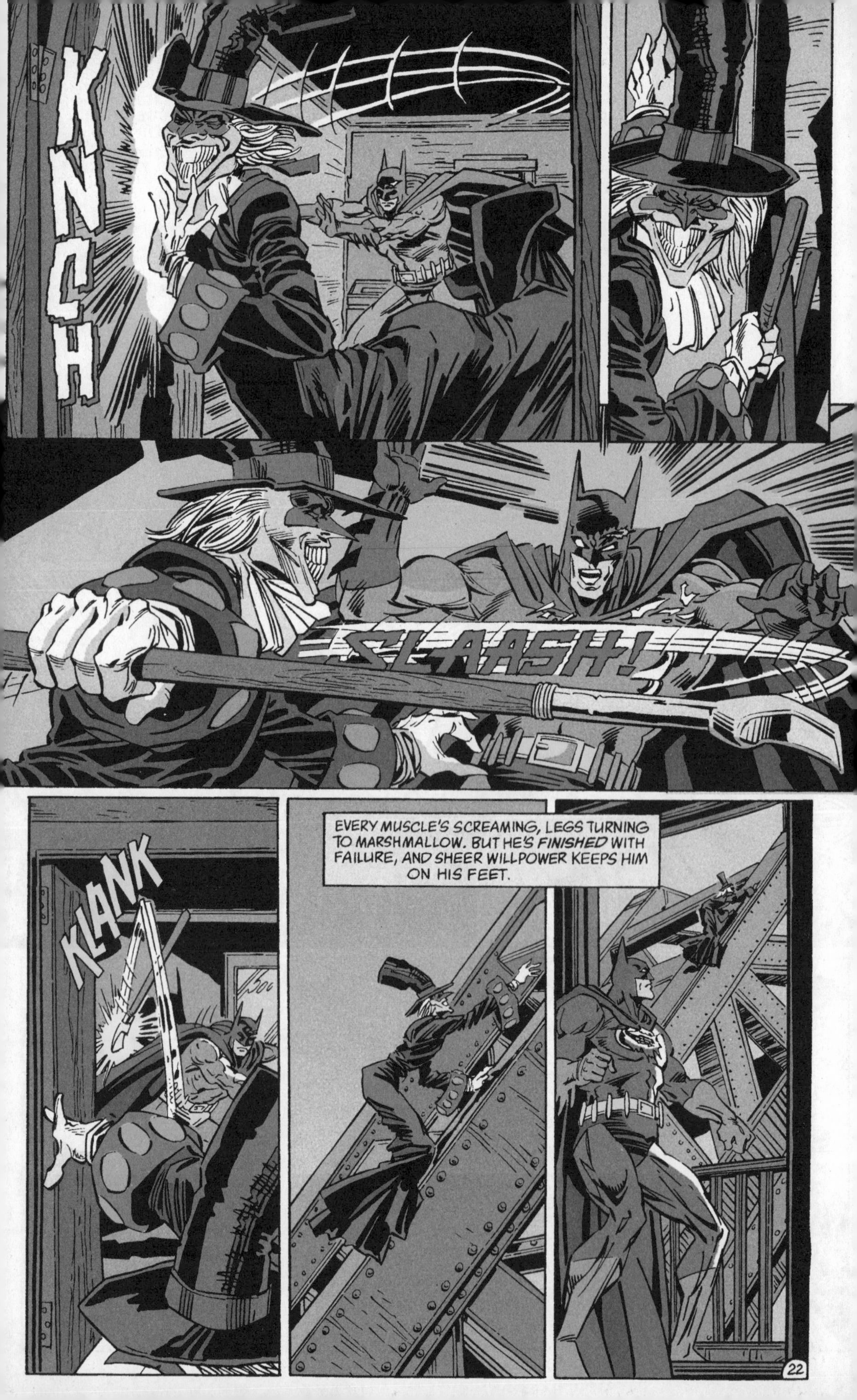
KNCH
SLAASH!
KLANK
EVERY MUSCLE'S SCREAMING, LEGS TURNING TO MARSHMALLOW. BUT HE'S *FINISHED* WITH FAILURE, AND SHEER WILLPOWER KEEPS HIM ON HIS FEET.
22

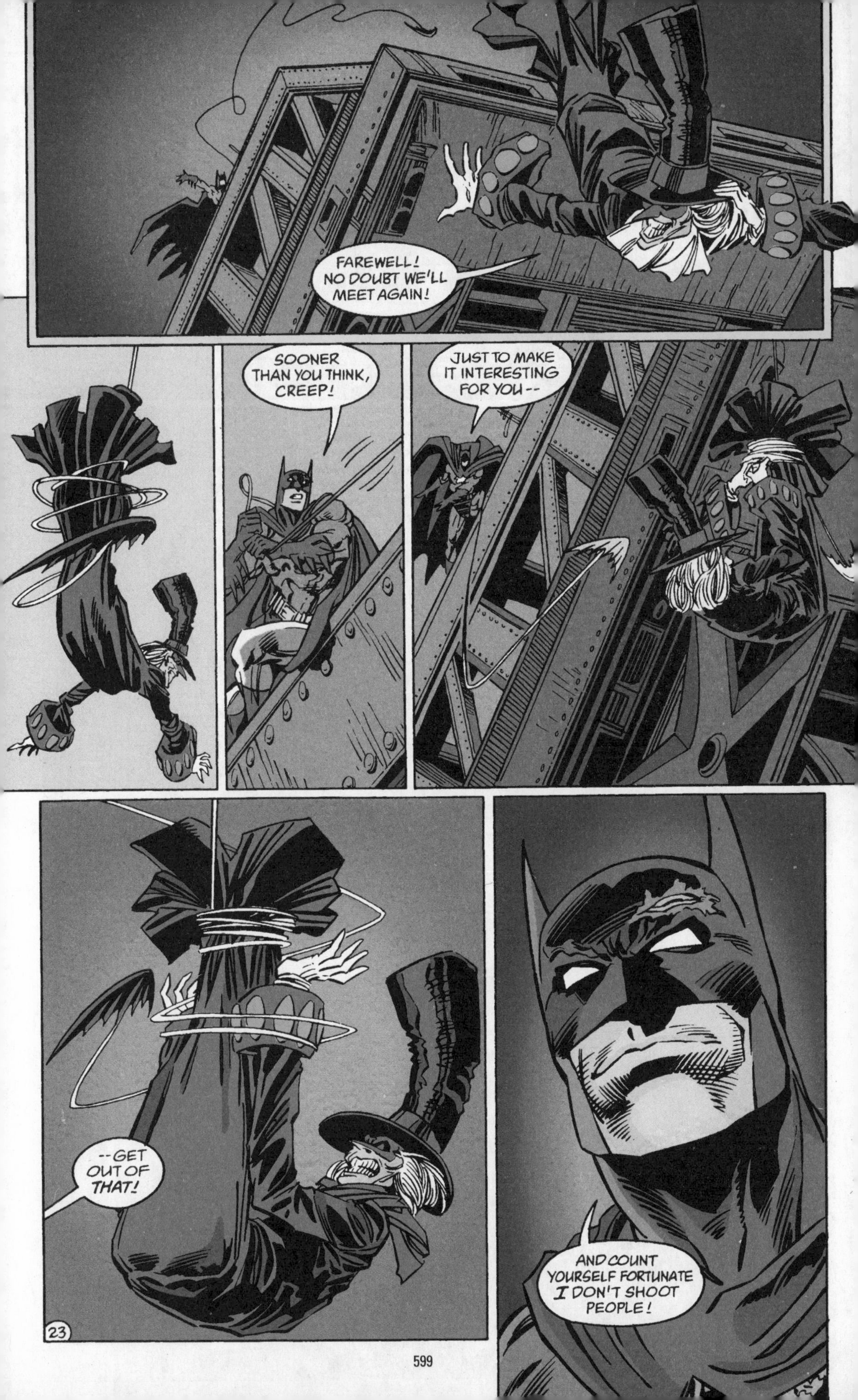
FAREWELL! NO DOUBT WE'LL MEET AGAIN!
SOONER THAN YOU THINK, CREEP!
JUST TO MAKE IT INTERESTING FOR YOU --
-- GET OUT OF THAT!
AND COUNT YOURSELF FORTUNATE I DON'T SHOOT PEOPLE!
23

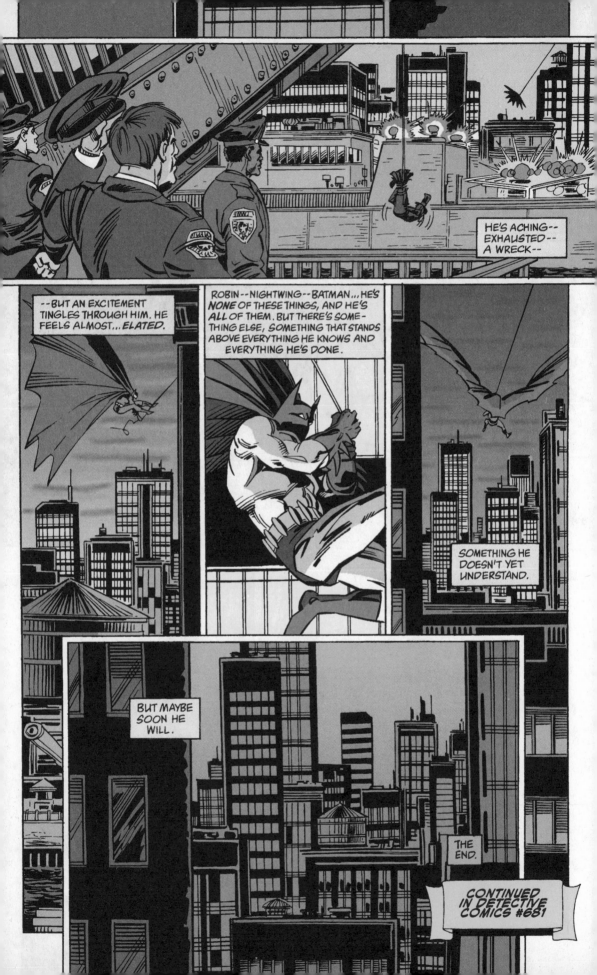

HE'S ACHING--
EXHAUSTED--
A WRECK--

--BUT AN EXCITEMENT TINGLES THROUGH HIM. HE FEELS ALMOST...*ELATED*.

ROBIN--NIGHTWING--BATMAN...HE'S *NONE* OF THESE THINGS, AND HE'S *ALL* OF THEM. BUT THERE'S SOMETHING ELSE, SOMETHING THAT STANDS ABOVE EVERYTHING HE KNOWS AND EVERYTHING HE'S DONE.

SOMETHING HE DOESN'T YET UNDERSTAND.

BUT MAYBE SOON HE WILL.

THE END.

CONTINUED IN DETECTIVE COMICS #681

Cover art by GRAHAM NOLAN

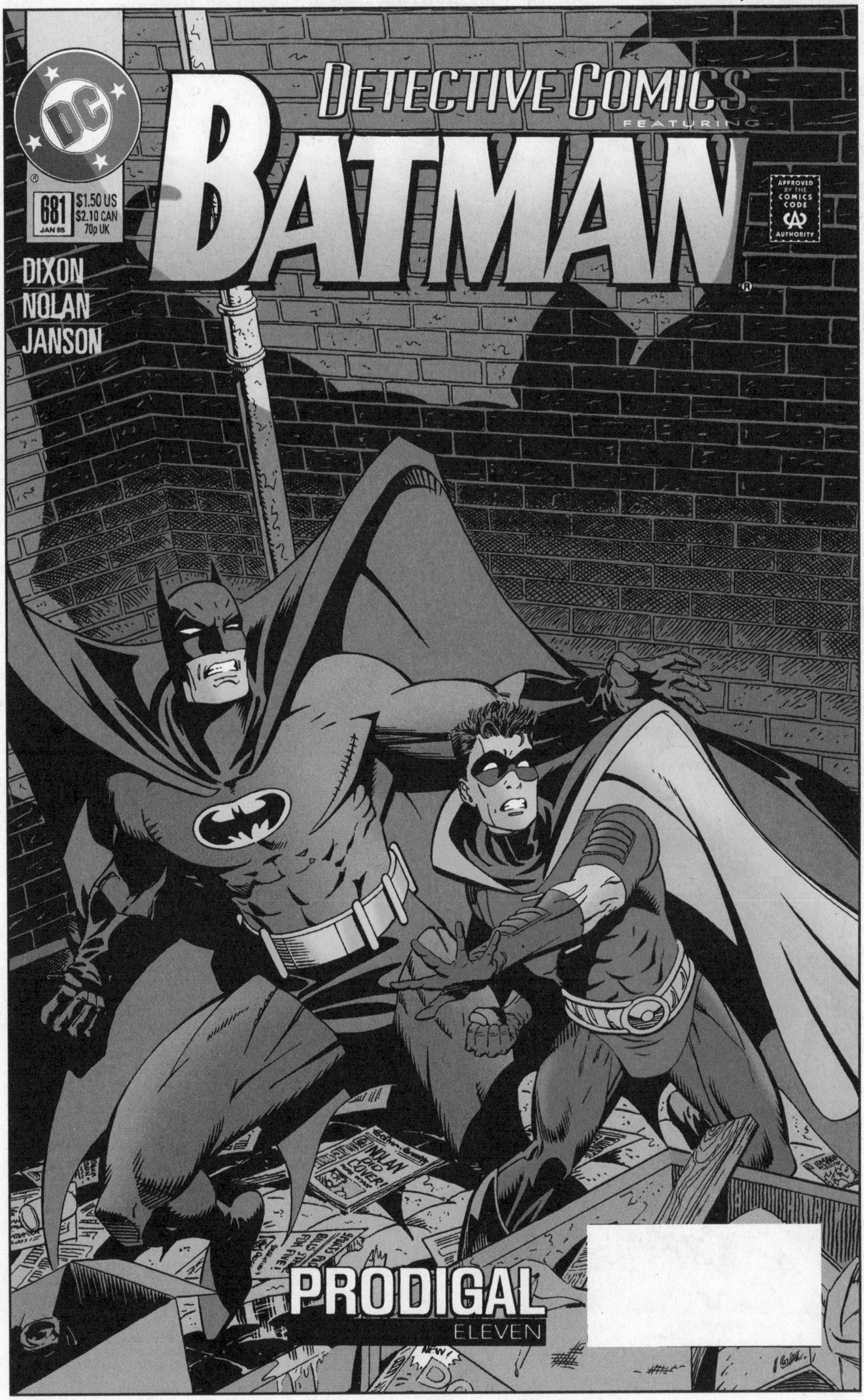
DC
DETECTIVE COMICS
FEATURING
BATMAN
681
$1.50 US
$2.10 CAN
70p UK
JAN 95
APPROVED BY THE COMICS CODE AUTHORITY
DIXON
NOLAN
JANSON
PRODIGAL
ELEVEN

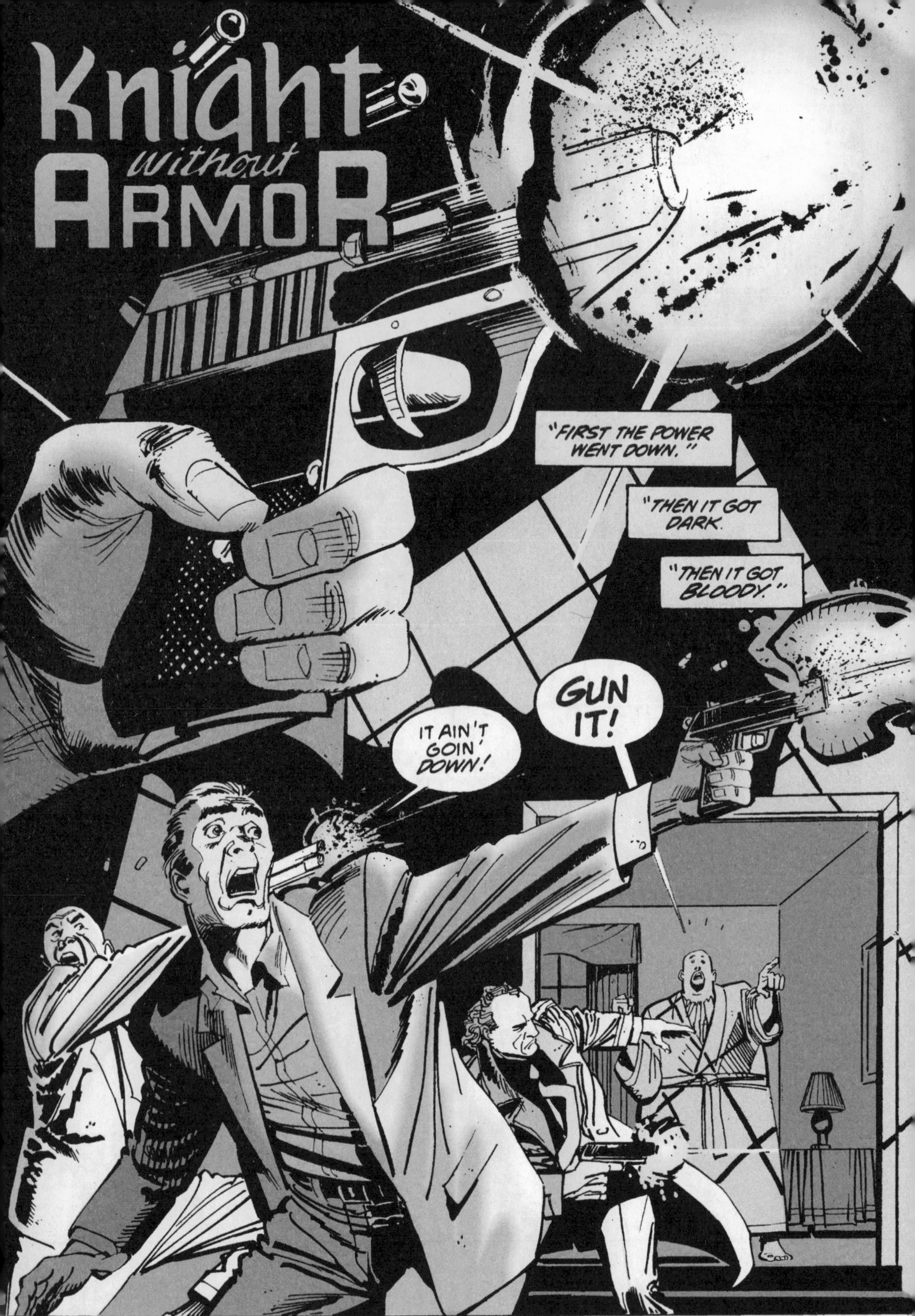
Knight without Armor
"FIRST THE POWER WENT DOWN."
"THEN IT GOT DARK.
"THEN IT GOT BLOODY."
GUN IT!
IT AIN'T GOIN' DOWN!

Chuck Dixon writer • Graham Nolan penciller • Klaus Janson guest inker • Adrienne Roy colorist • John Costanza letterer • Darren Vincenzo assoc. editor • Scott Peterson editor

BATMAN created by BOB KANE

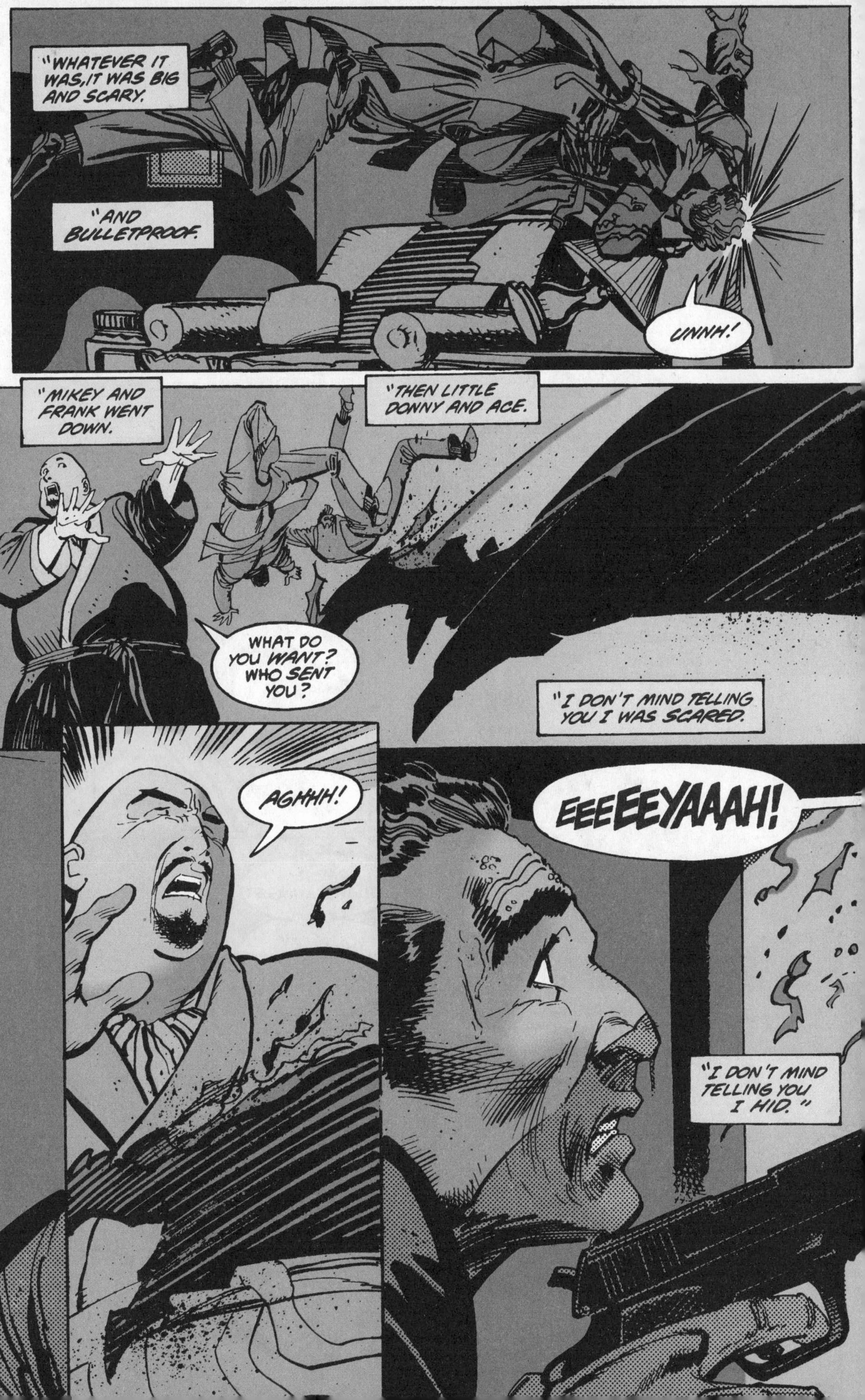
"WHATEVER IT WAS, IT WAS BIG AND SCARY.
"AND BULLETPROOF.
UNNH!
"MIKEY AND FRANK WENT DOWN.
"THEN LITTLE DONNY AND ACE.
WHAT DO YOU WANT? WHO SENT YOU?
"I DON'T MIND TELLING YOU I WAS SCARED.
AGHHH!
EEEEEYAAAH!
"I DON'T MIND TELLING YOU I HID."

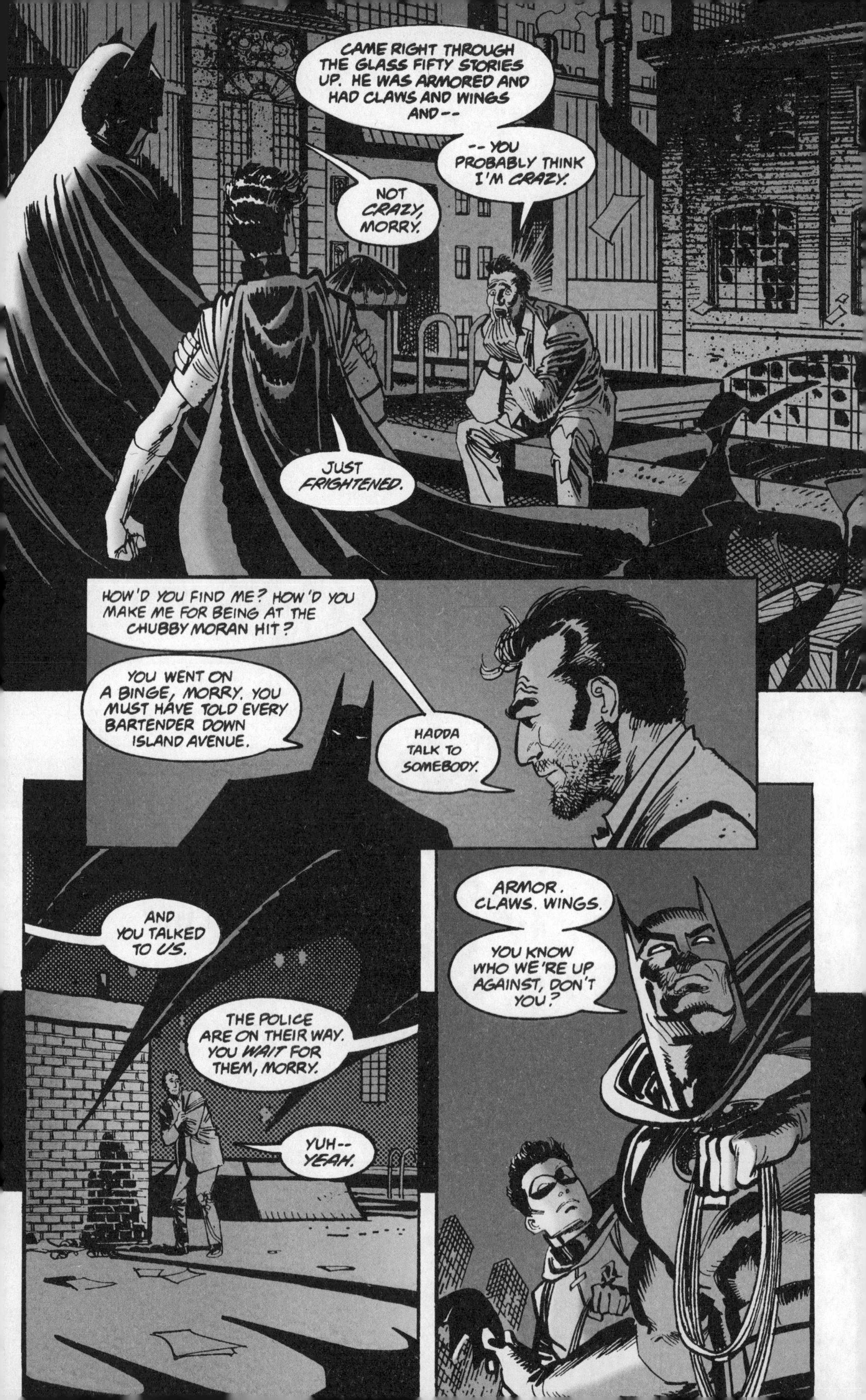
CAME RIGHT THROUGH THE GLASS FIFTY STORIES UP. HE WAS ARMORED AND HAD CLAWS AND WINGS AND--
--YOU PROBABLY THINK I'M CRAZY.
NOT CRAZY, MORRY.
JUST FRIGHTENED.
HOW'D YOU FIND ME? HOW'D YOU MAKE ME FOR BEING AT THE CHUBBY MORAN HIT?
YOU WENT ON A BINGE, MORRY. YOU MUST HAVE TOLD EVERY BARTENDER DOWN ISLAND AVENUE.
HADDA TALK TO SOMEBODY.
AND YOU TALKED TO US.
THE POLICE ARE ON THEIR WAY. YOU WAIT FOR THEM, MORRY.
YUH-- YEAH.
ARMOR. CLAWS. WINGS.
YOU KNOW WHO WE'RE UP AGAINST, DON'T YOU?

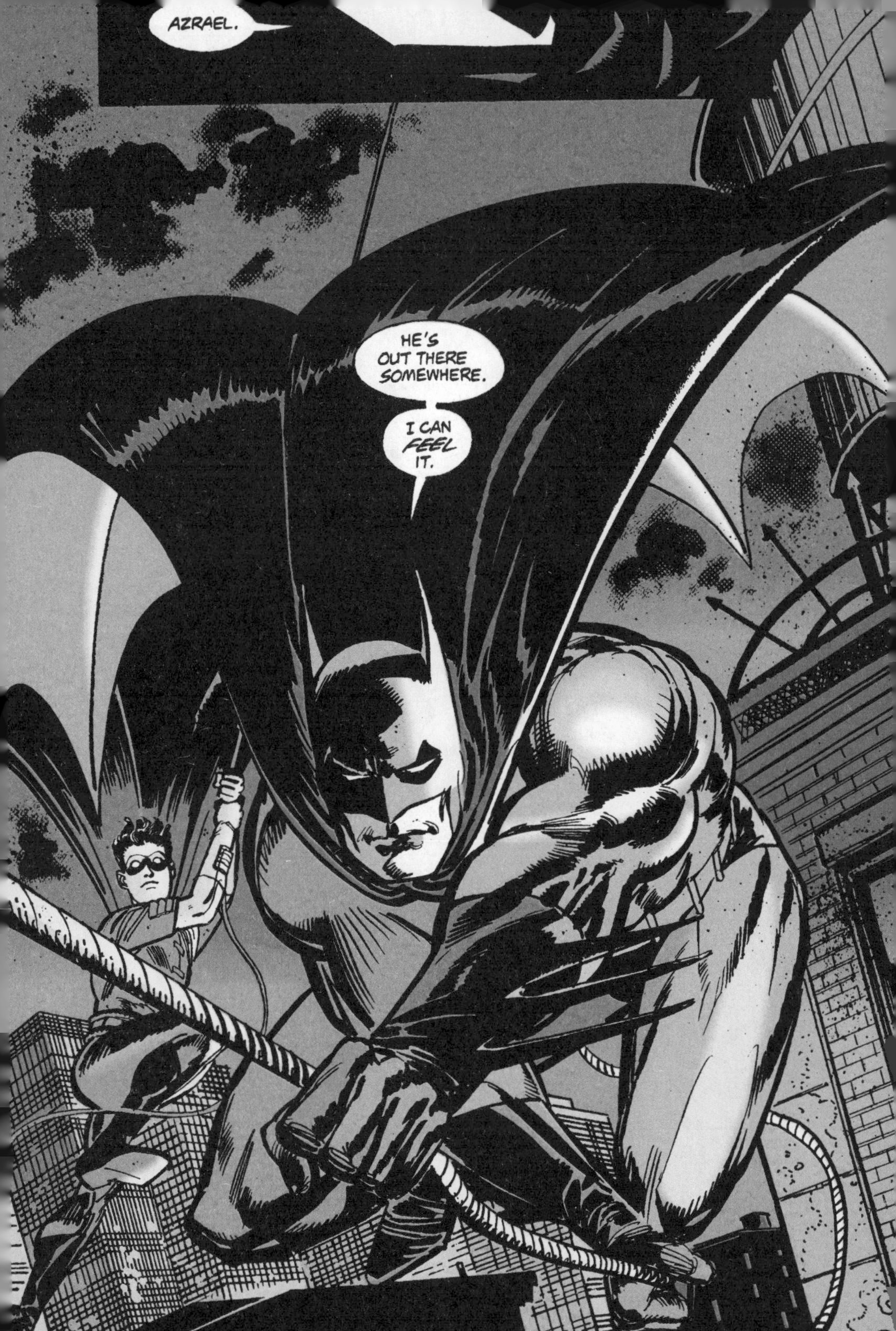
AZRAEL.
HE'S OUT THERE SOMEWHERE.
I CAN FEEL IT.
4

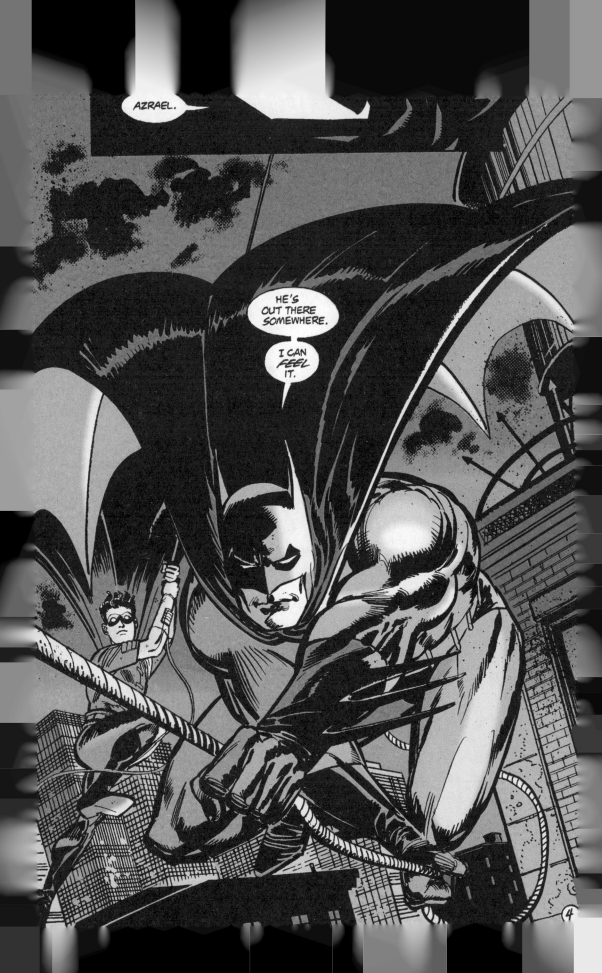

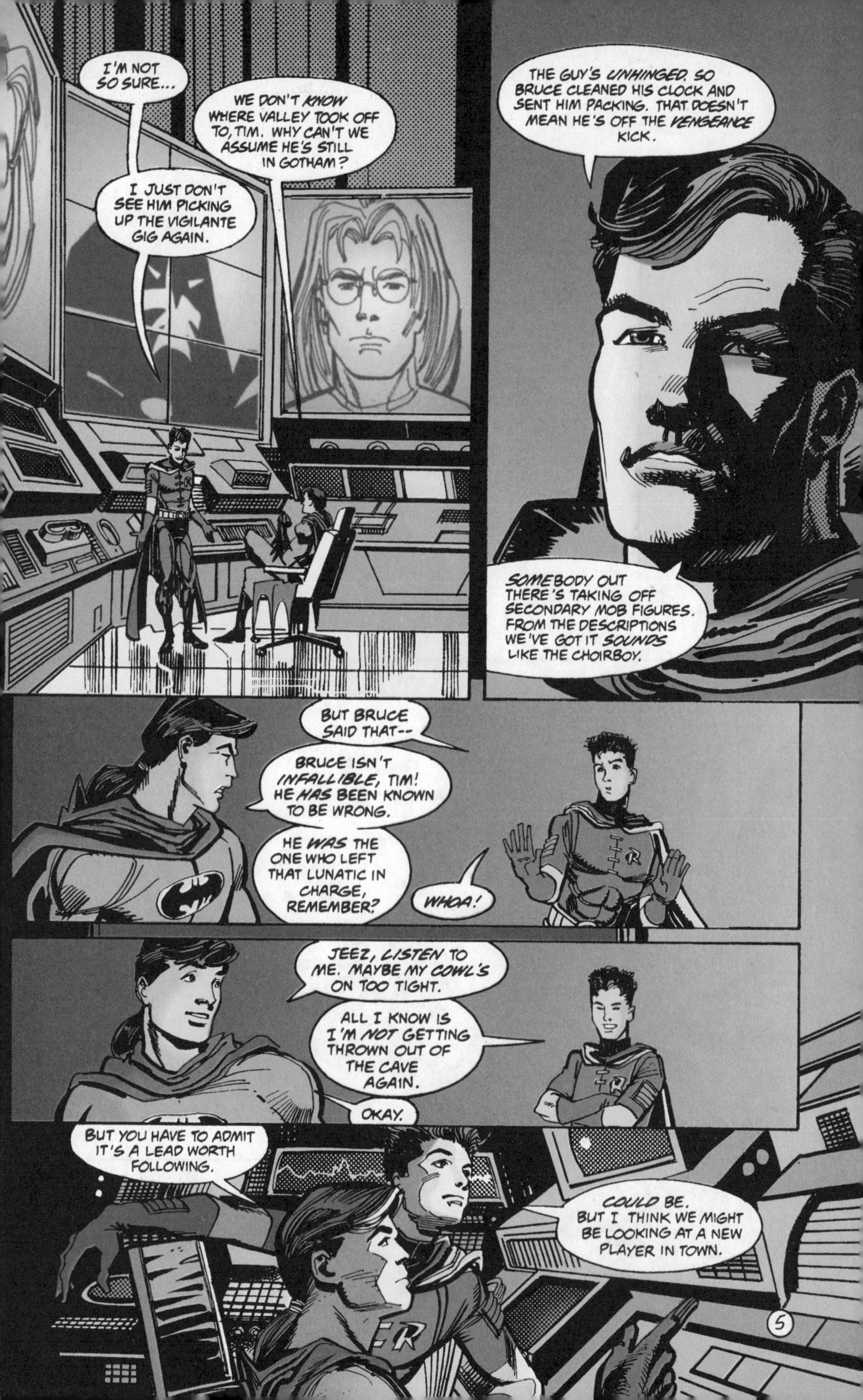
I'M NOT SO SURE...
WE DON'T KNOW WHERE VALLEY TOOK OFF TO, TIM. WHY CAN'T WE ASSUME HE'S STILL IN GOTHAM?
I JUST DON'T SEE HIM PICKING UP THE VIGILANTE GIG AGAIN.
THE GUY'S UNHINGED. SO BRUCE CLEANED HIS CLOCK AND SENT HIM PACKING. THAT DOESN'T MEAN HE'S OFF THE VENGEANCE KICK.
SOMEBODY OUT THERE'S TAKING OFF SECONDARY MOB FIGURES. FROM THE DESCRIPTIONS WE'VE GOT IT SOUNDS LIKE THE CHOIRBOY.
BUT BRUCE SAID THAT--
BRUCE ISN'T INFALLIBLE, TIM! HE HAS BEEN KNOWN TO BE WRONG.
HE WAS THE ONE WHO LEFT THAT LUNATIC IN CHARGE, REMEMBER?
WHOA!
JEEZ, LISTEN TO ME. MAYBE MY COWL'S ON TOO TIGHT.
ALL I KNOW IS I'M NOT GETTING THROWN OUT OF THE CAVE AGAIN.
OKAY.
BUT YOU HAVE TO ADMIT IT'S A LEAD WORTH FOLLOWING.
COULD BE. BUT I THINK WE MIGHT BE LOOKING AT A NEW PLAYER IN TOWN.
5

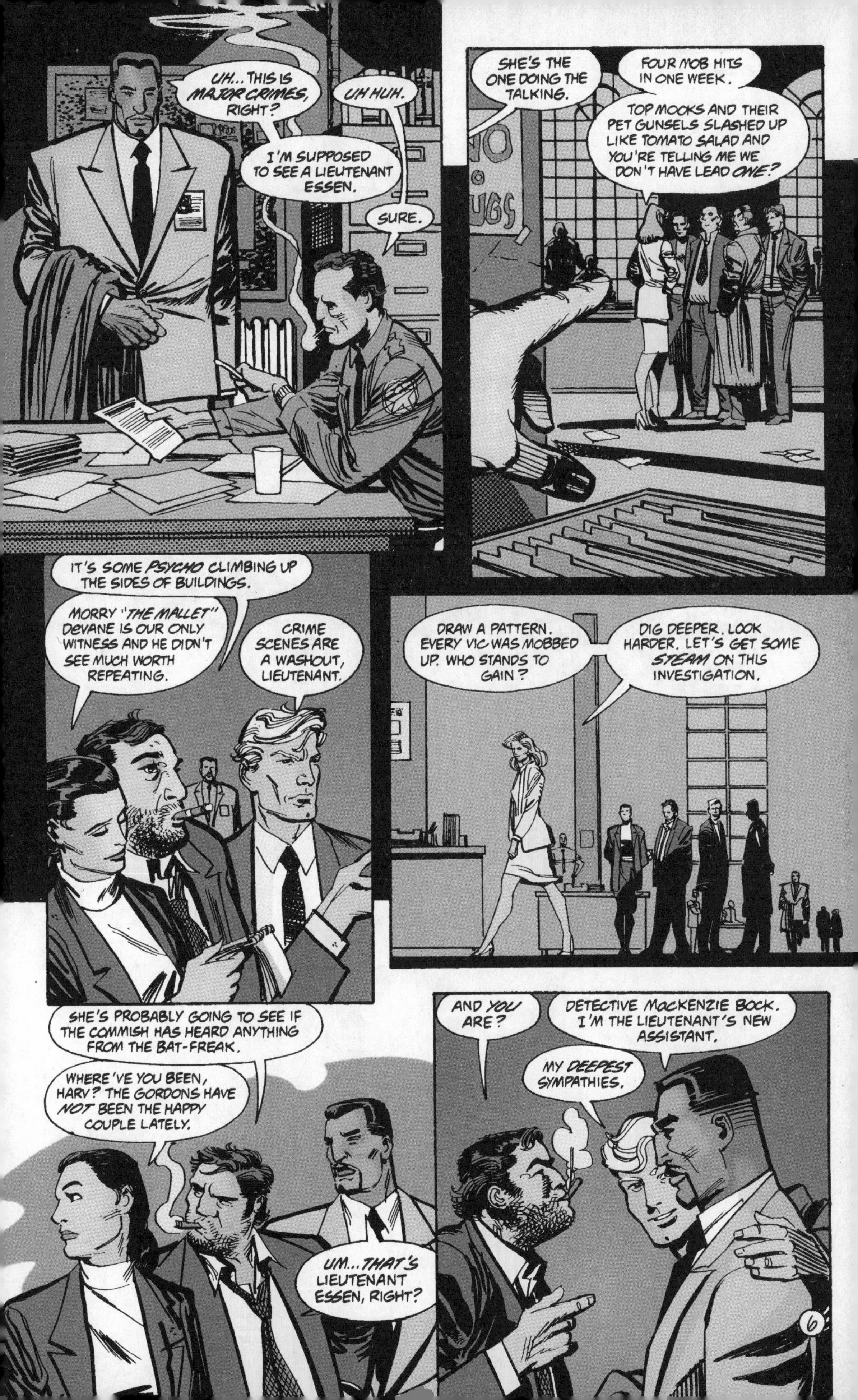

UH... THIS IS MAJOR CRIMES, RIGHT?
UH HUH.
I'M SUPPOSED TO SEE A LIEUTENANT ESSEN.
SURE.
SHE'S THE ONE DOING THE TALKING.
FOUR MOB HITS IN ONE WEEK.
TOP MOOKS AND THEIR PET GUNSELS SLASHED UP LIKE TOMATO SALAD AND YOU'RE TELLING ME WE DON'T HAVE LEAD ONE?
IT'S SOME PSYCHO CLIMBING UP THE SIDES OF BUILDINGS.
MORRY "THE MALLET" DEVANE IS OUR ONLY WITNESS AND HE DIDN'T SEE MUCH WORTH REPEATING.
CRIME SCENES ARE A WASHOUT, LIEUTENANT.
DRAW A PATTERN. EVERY VIC WAS MOBBED UP. WHO STANDS TO GAIN?
DIG DEEPER. LOOK HARDER. LET'S GET SOME STEAM ON THIS INVESTIGATION.
SHE'S PROBABLY GOING TO SEE IF THE COMMISH HAS HEARD ANYTHING FROM THE BAT-FREAK.
WHERE'VE YOU BEEN, HARV? THE GORDONS HAVE NOT BEEN THE HAPPY COUPLE LATELY.
UM... THAT'S LIEUTENANT ESSEN, RIGHT?
AND YOU ARE?
DETECTIVE MacKENZIE BOCK. I'M THE LIEUTENANT'S NEW ASSISTANT.
MY DEEPEST SYMPATHIES.
6

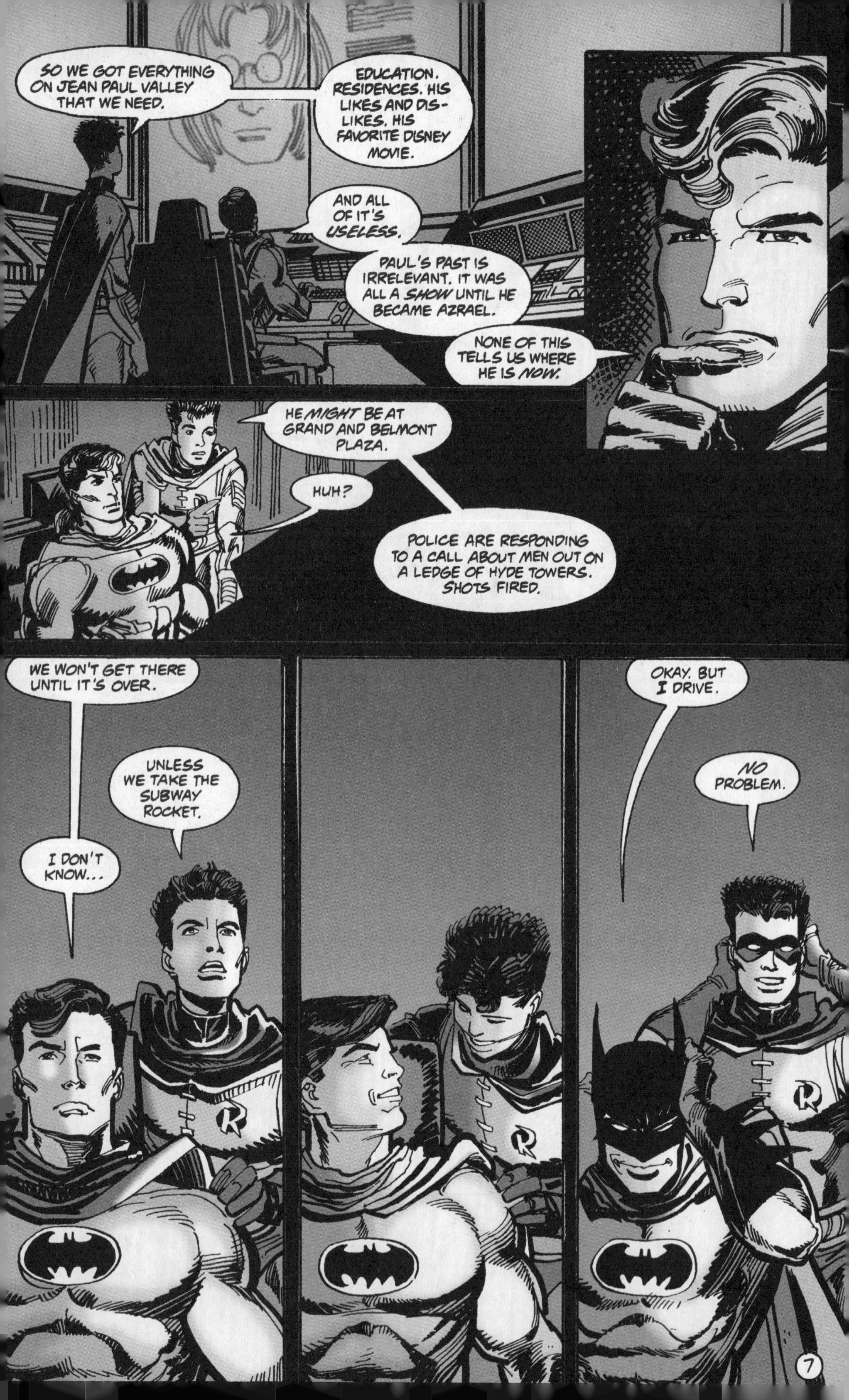
SO WE GOT EVERYTHING ON JEAN PAUL VALLEY THAT WE NEED.
EDUCATION. RESIDENCES. HIS LIKES AND DIS-LIKES. HIS FAVORITE DISNEY MOVIE.
AND ALL OF IT'S USELESS.
PAUL'S PAST IS IRRELEVANT. IT WAS ALL A SHOW UNTIL HE BECAME AZRAEL.
NONE OF THIS TELLS US WHERE HE IS NOW.
HE MIGHT BE AT GRAND AND BELMONT PLAZA.
HUH?
POLICE ARE RESPONDING TO A CALL ABOUT MEN OUT ON A LEDGE OF HYDE TOWERS. SHOTS FIRED.
WE WON'T GET THERE UNTIL IT'S OVER.
UNLESS WE TAKE THE SUBWAY ROCKET.
I DON'T KNOW...
OKAY. BUT I DRIVE.
NO PROBLEM.
7

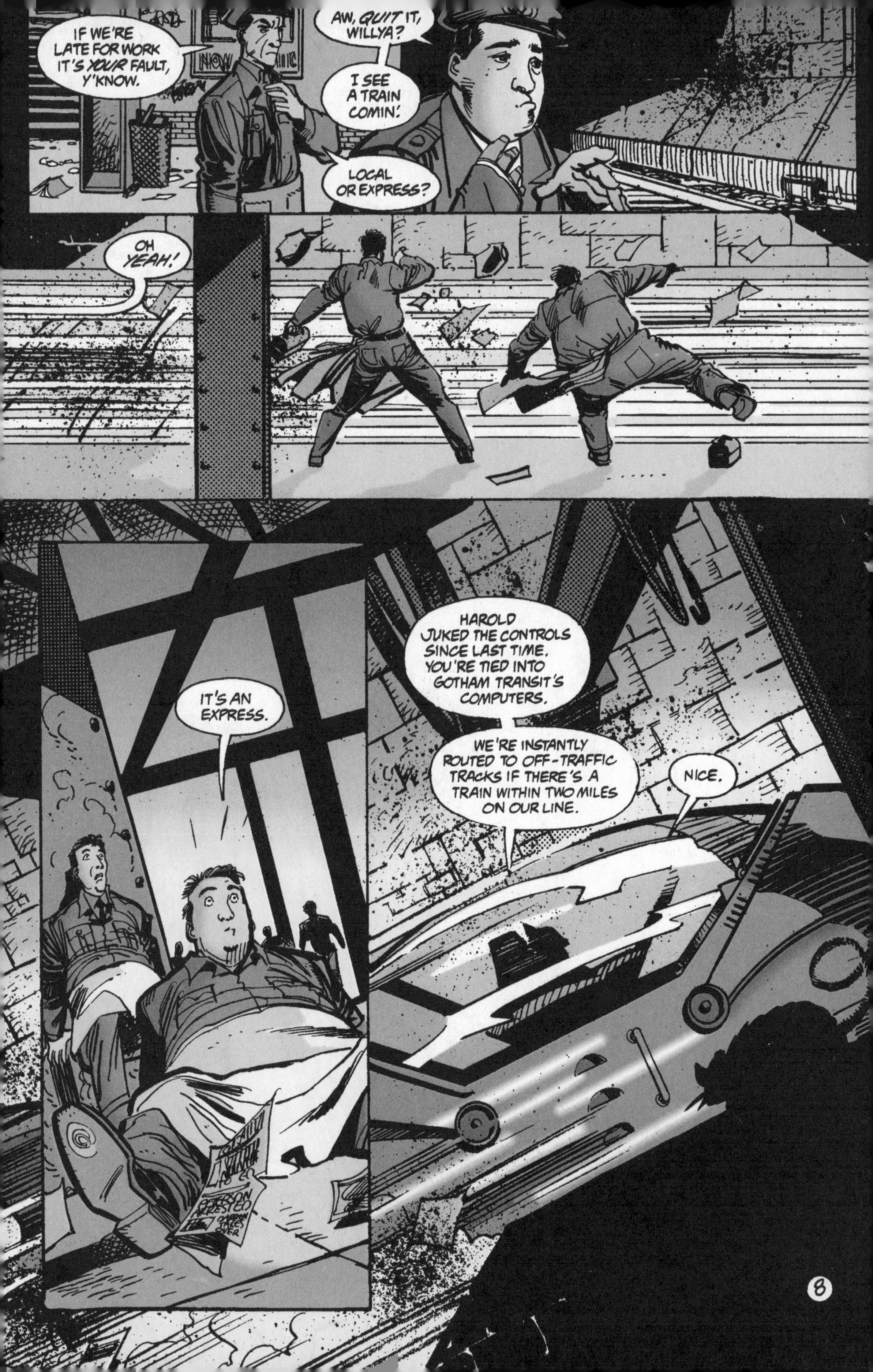
IF WE'RE LATE FOR WORK IT'S YOUR FAULT, Y'KNOW.
AW, QUIT IT, WILLYA?
I SEE A TRAIN COMIN'.
LOCAL OR EXPRESS?
OH YEAH!
IT'S AN EXPRESS.
HAROLD JUKED THE CONTROLS SINCE LAST TIME. YOU'RE TIED INTO GOTHAM TRANSIT'S COMPUTERS.
WE'RE INSTANTLY ROUTED TO OFF-TRAFFIC TRACKS IF THERE'S A TRAIN WITHIN TWO MILES ON OUR LINE.
NICE.

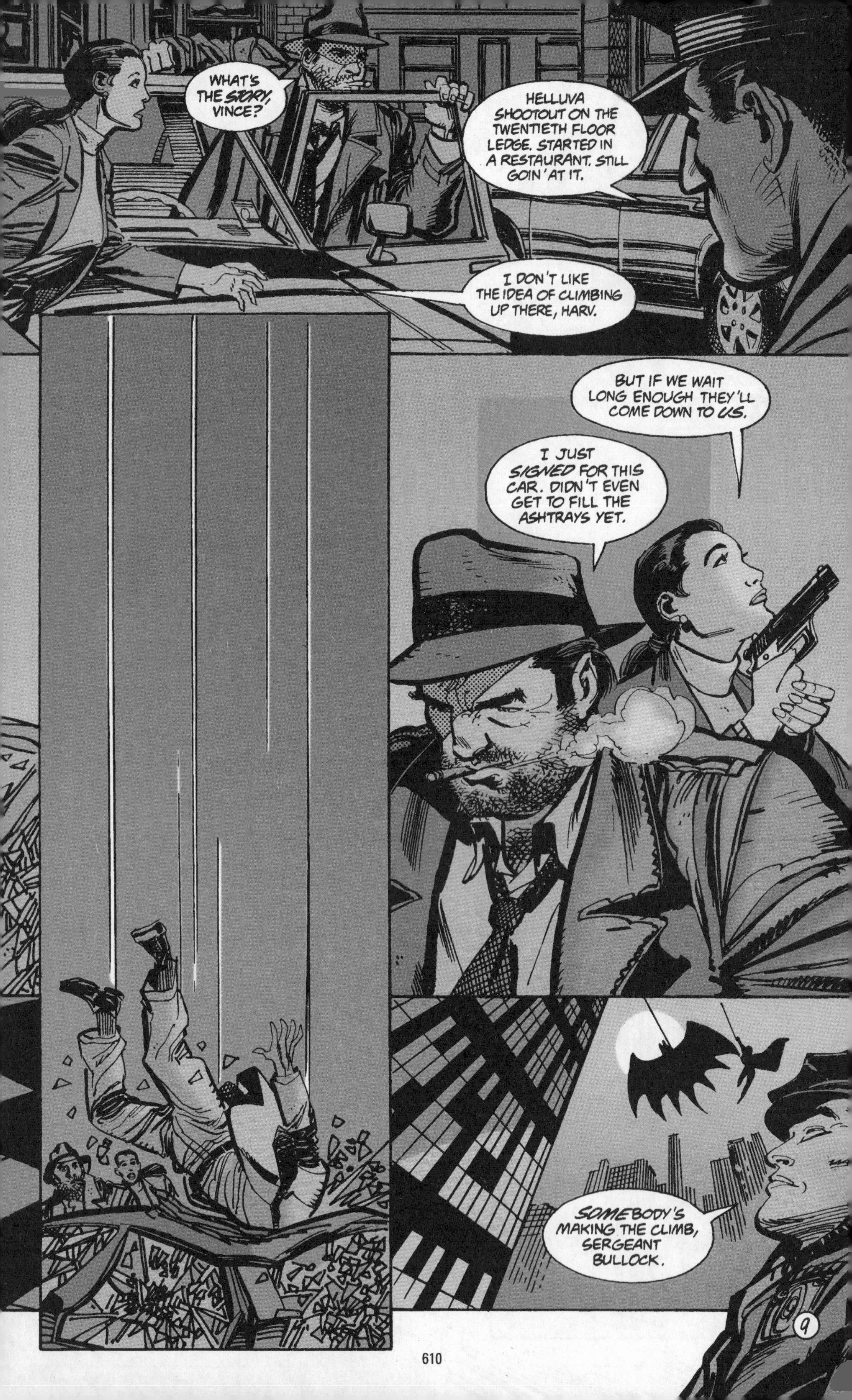
WHAT'S THE STORY, VINCE?
HELLUVA SHOOTOUT ON THE TWENTIETH FLOOR LEDGE. STARTED IN A RESTAURANT. STILL GOIN' AT IT.
I DON'T LIKE THE IDEA OF CLIMBING UP THERE, HARV.
BUT IF WE WAIT LONG ENOUGH THEY'LL COME DOWN TO US.
I JUST SIGNED FOR THIS CAR. DIDN'T EVEN GET TO FILL THE ASHTRAYS YET.
SOMEBODY'S MAKING THE CLIMB, SERGEANT BULLOCK.
9

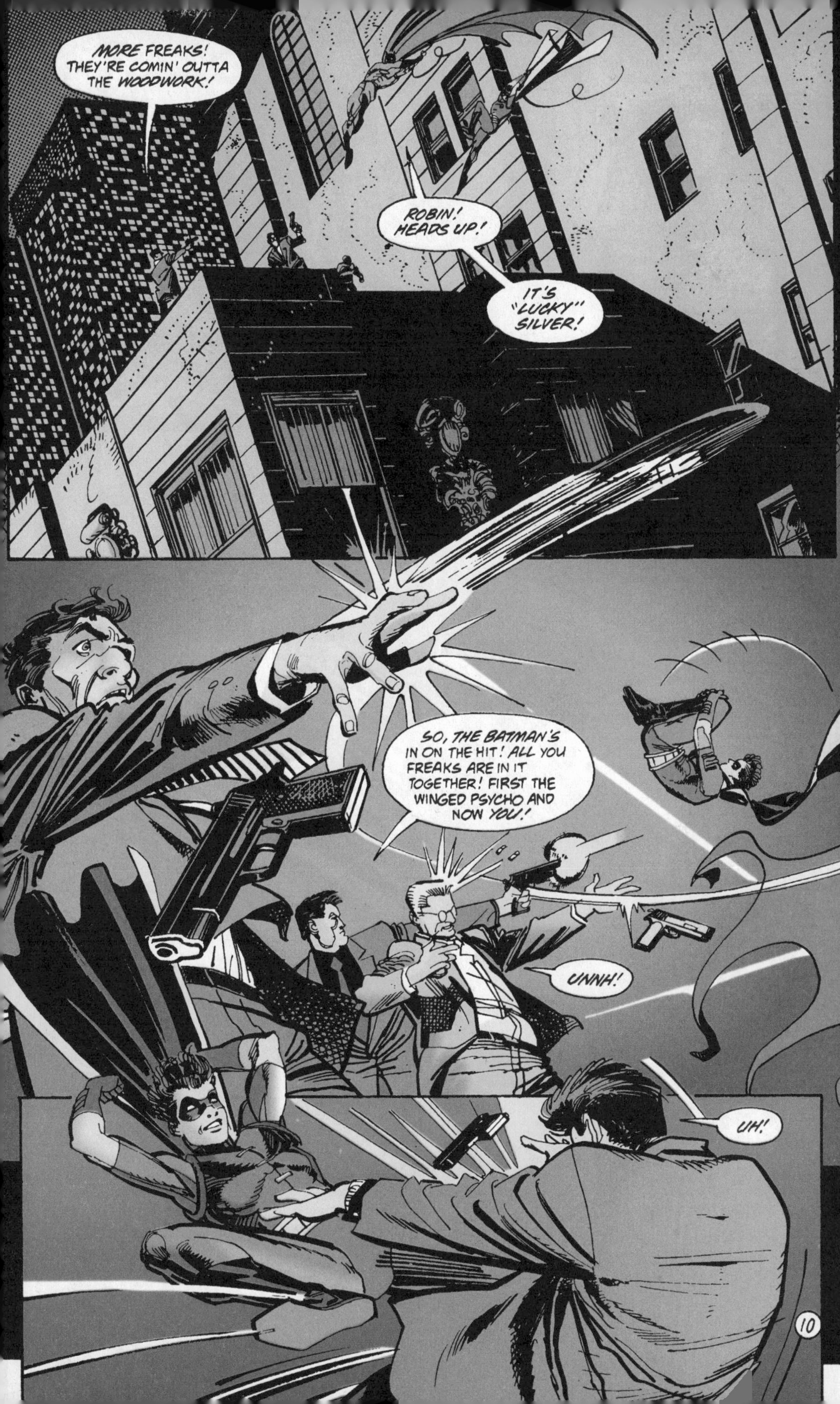
MORE FREAKS! THEY'RE COMIN' OUTTA THE WOODWORK!
ROBIN! HEADS UP!
IT'S "LUCKY" SILVER!
SO, THE BATMAN'S IN ON THE HIT! ALL YOU FREAKS ARE IN IT TOGETHER! FIRST THE WINGED PSYCHO AND NOW YOU!
UNNH!
UH!
10

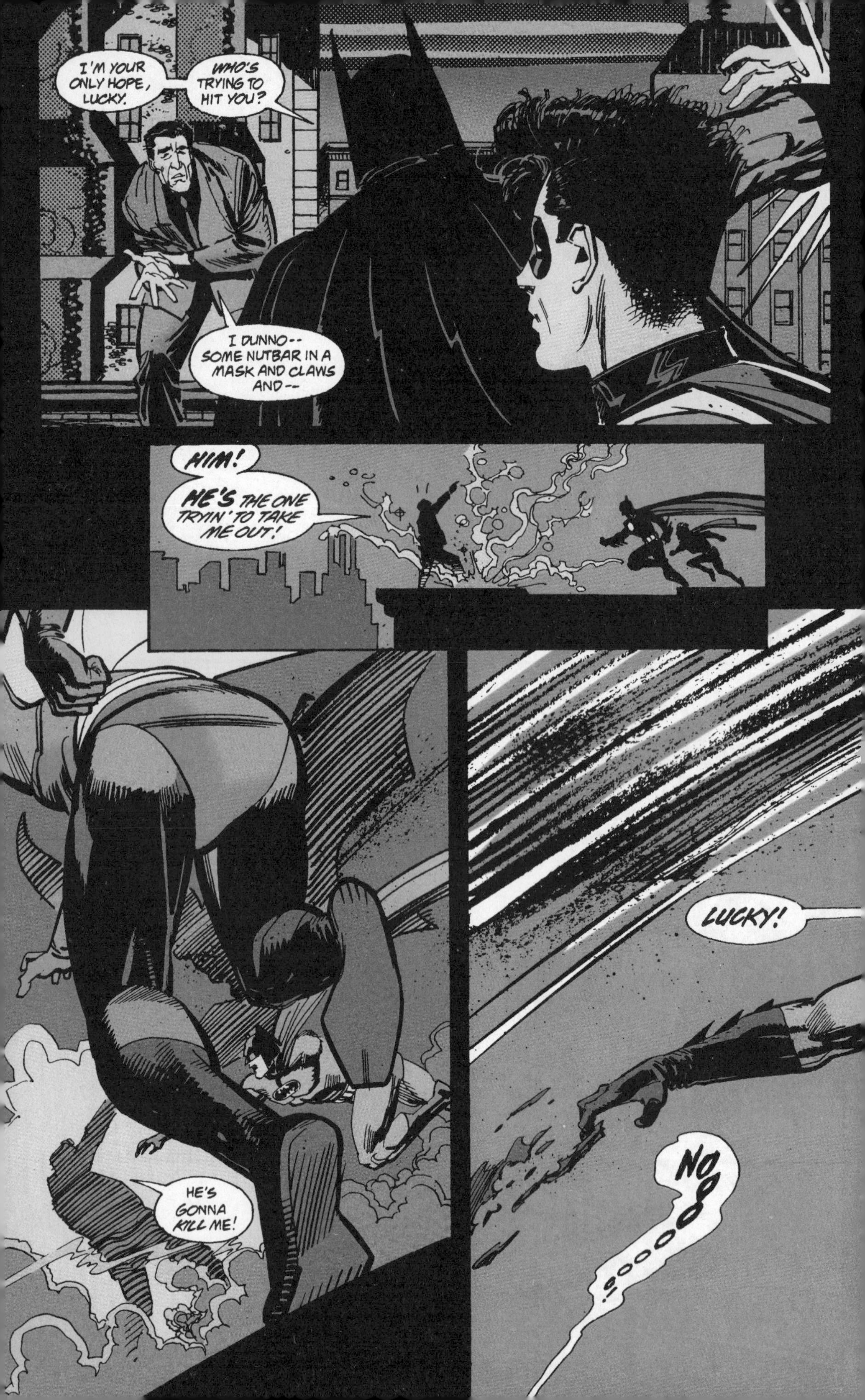
I'M YOUR ONLY HOPE, LUCKY.
WHO'S TRYING TO HIT YOU?
I DUNNO-- SOME NUTBAR IN A MASK AND CLAWS AND--
HIM!
HE'S THE ONE TRYIN' TO TAKE ME OUT!
HE'S GONNA KILL ME!
LUCKY!
NOOOOOO!

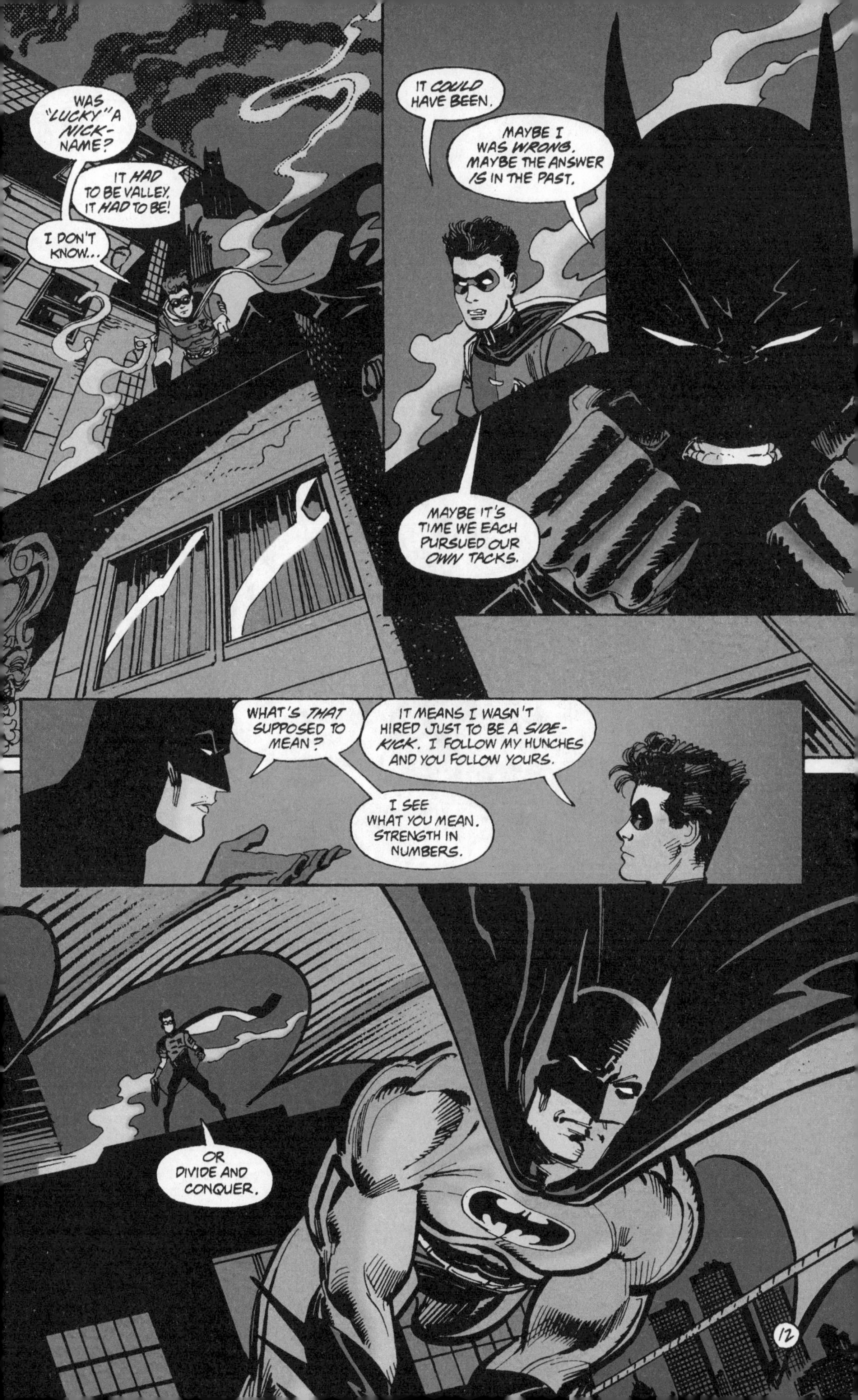

WAS "LUCKY" A NICK-NAME?
IT HAD TO BE VALLEY. IT HAD TO BE!
I DON'T KNOW...
IT COULD HAVE BEEN.
MAYBE I WAS WRONG. MAYBE THE ANSWER IS IN THE PAST.
MAYBE IT'S TIME WE EACH PURSUED OUR OWN TACKS.
WHAT'S THAT SUPPOSED TO MEAN?
IT MEANS I WASN'T HIRED JUST TO BE A SIDE-KICK. I FOLLOW MY HUNCHES AND YOU FOLLOW YOURS.
I SEE WHAT YOU MEAN. STRENGTH IN NUMBERS.
OR DIVIDE AND CONQUER.

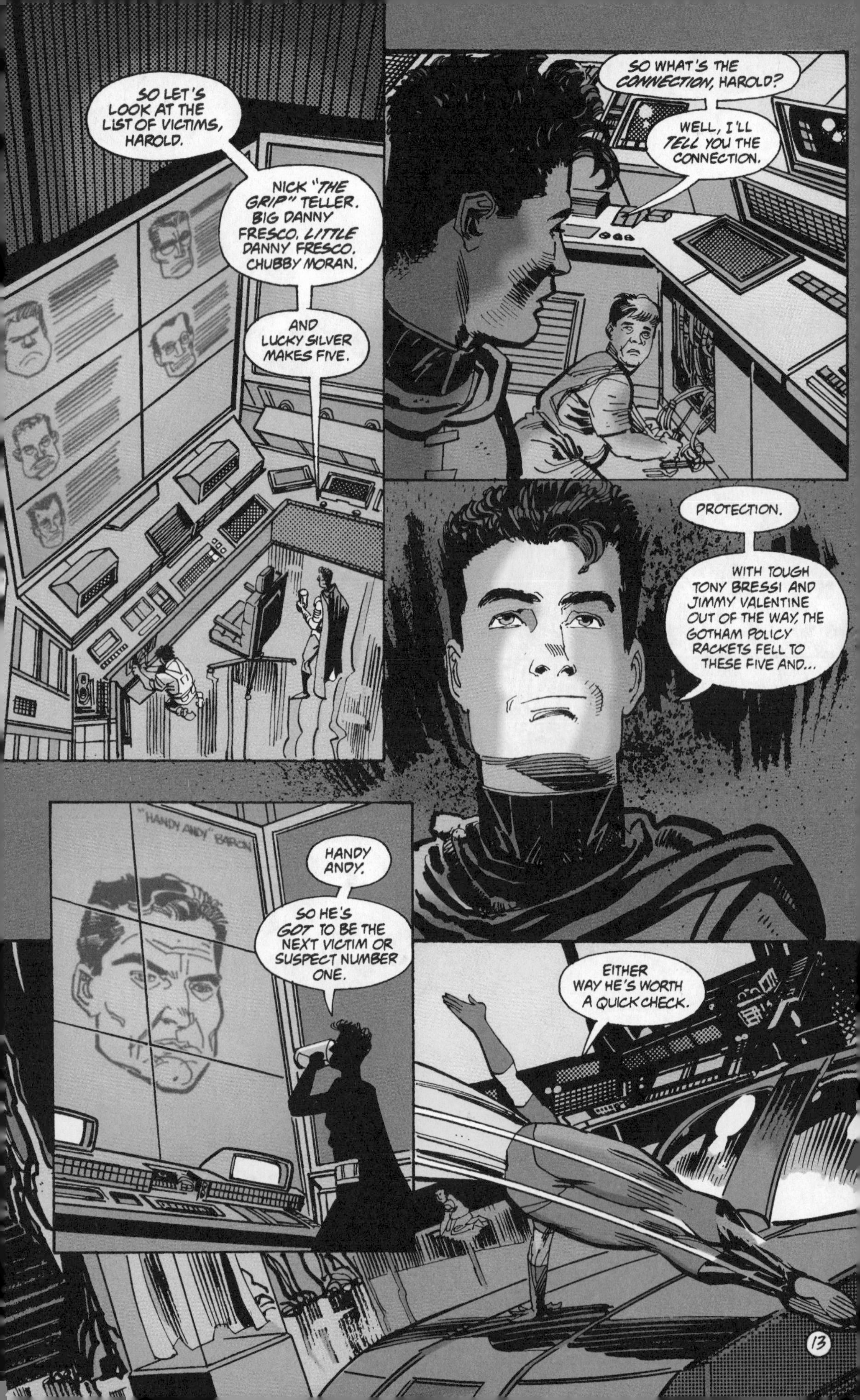
SO LET'S LOOK AT THE LIST OF VICTIMS, HAROLD.
NICK "THE GRIP" TELLER. BIG DANNY FRESCO. LITTLE DANNY FRESCO. CHUBBY MORAN.
AND LUCKY SILVER MAKES FIVE.
SO WHAT'S THE CONNECTION, HAROLD?
WELL, I'LL TELL YOU THE CONNECTION.
PROTECTION.
WITH TOUGH TONY BRESSI AND JIMMY VALENTINE OUT OF THE WAY, THE GOTHAM POLICY RACKETS FELL TO THESE FIVE AND...
"HANDY ANDY" BARON
HANDY ANDY.
SO HE'S GOT TO BE THE NEXT VICTIM OR SUSPECT NUMBER ONE.
EITHER WAY HE'S WORTH A QUICK CHECK.

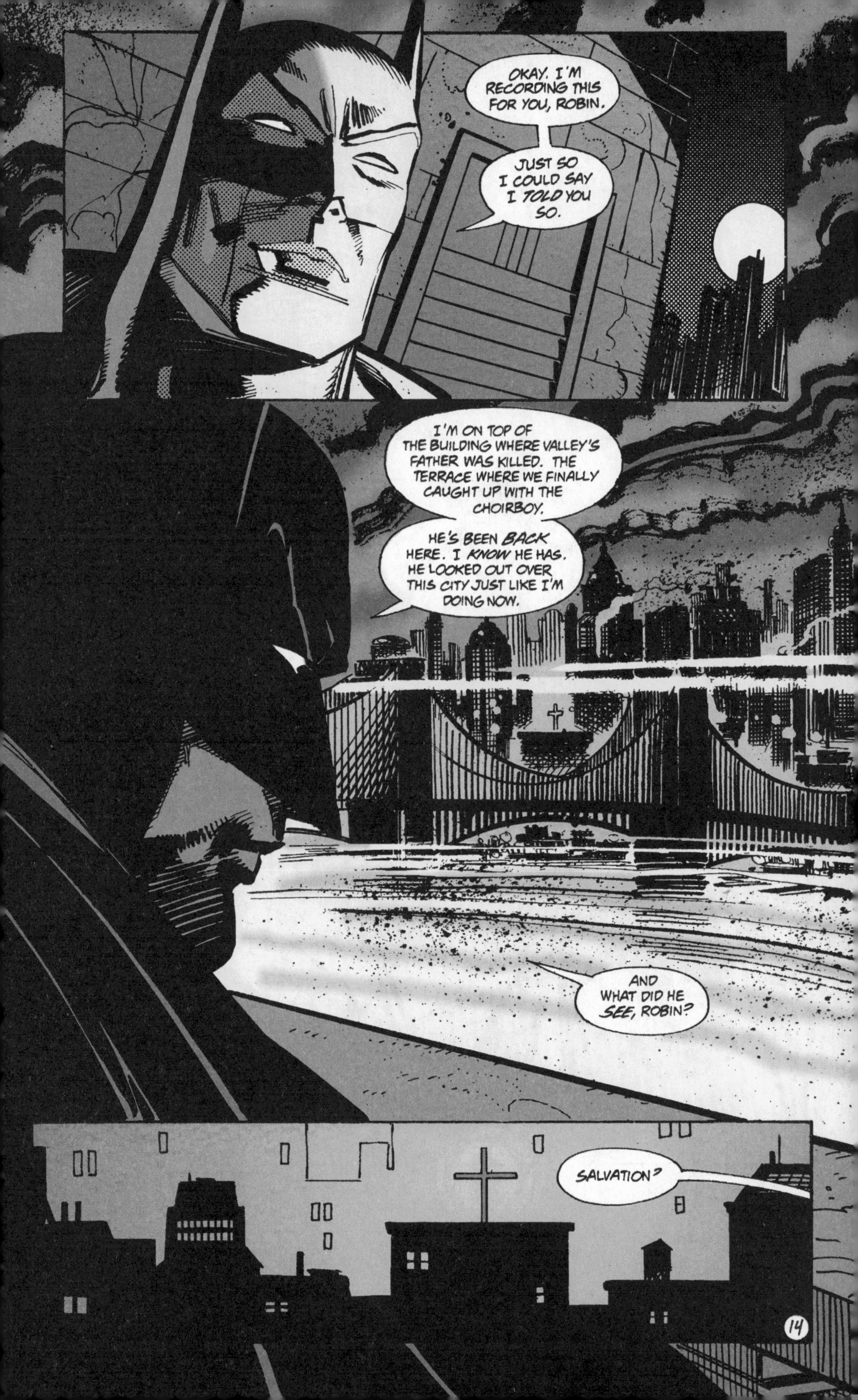
OKAY. I'M RECORDING THIS FOR YOU, ROBIN.
JUST SO I COULD SAY I TOLD YOU SO.
I'M ON TOP OF THE BUILDING WHERE VALLEY'S FATHER WAS KILLED. THE TERRACE WHERE WE FINALLY CAUGHT UP WITH THE CHOIRBOY.
HE'S BEEN BACK HERE. I KNOW HE HAS. HE LOOKED OUT OVER THIS CITY JUST LIKE I'M DOING NOW.
AND WHAT DID HE SEE, ROBIN?
SALVATION?

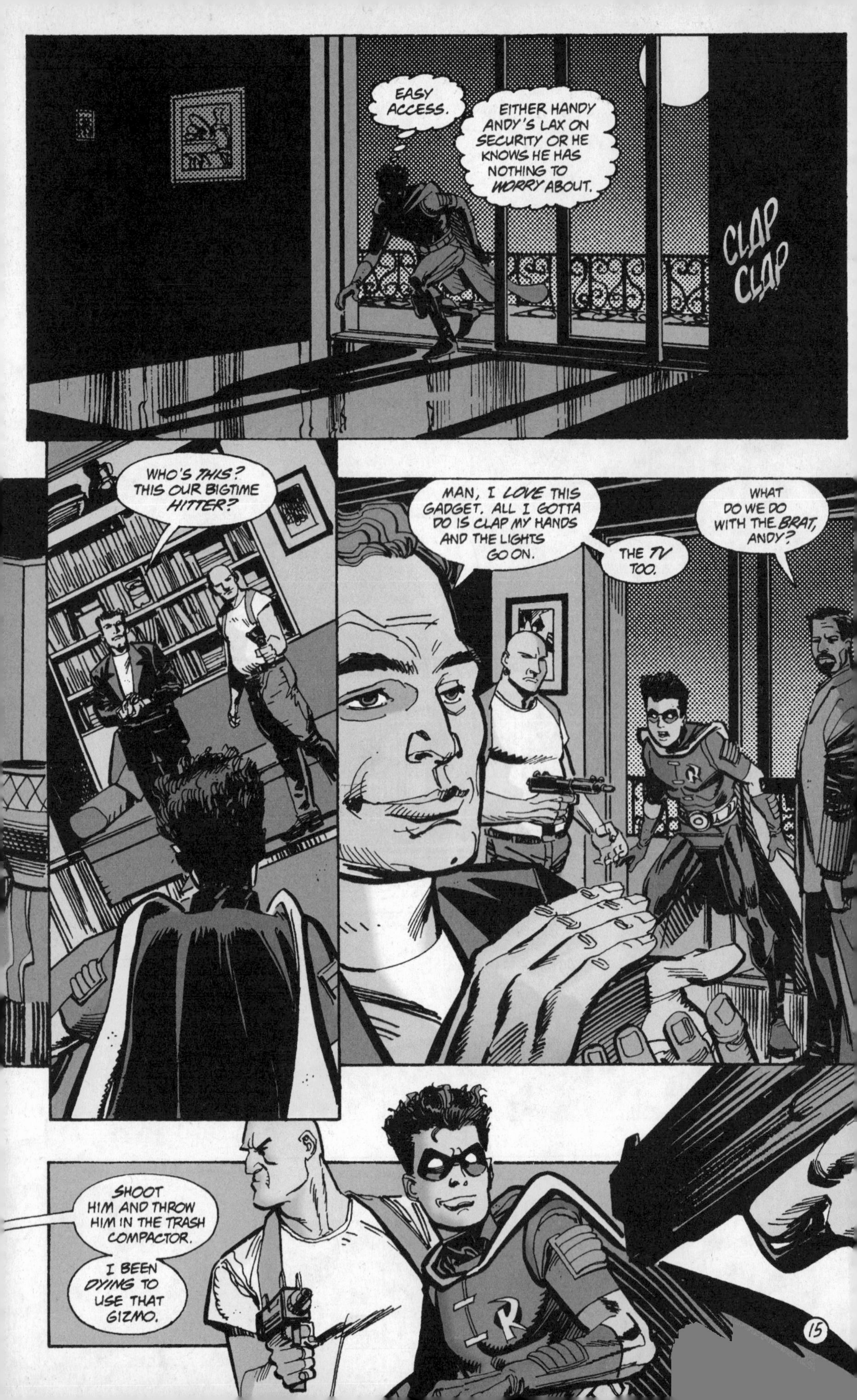
EASY ACCESS.
EITHER HANDY ANDY'S LAX ON SECURITY OR HE KNOWS HE HAS NOTHING TO WORRY ABOUT.
CLAP CLAP
WHO'S THIS? THIS OUR BIGTIME HITTER?
MAN, I LOVE THIS GADGET. ALL I GOTTA DO IS CLAP MY HANDS AND THE LIGHTS GO ON.
THE TV TOO.
WHAT DO WE DO WITH THE BRAT, ANDY?
SHOOT HIM AND THROW HIM IN THE TRASH COMPACTOR.
I BEEN DYING TO USE THAT GIZMO.
15

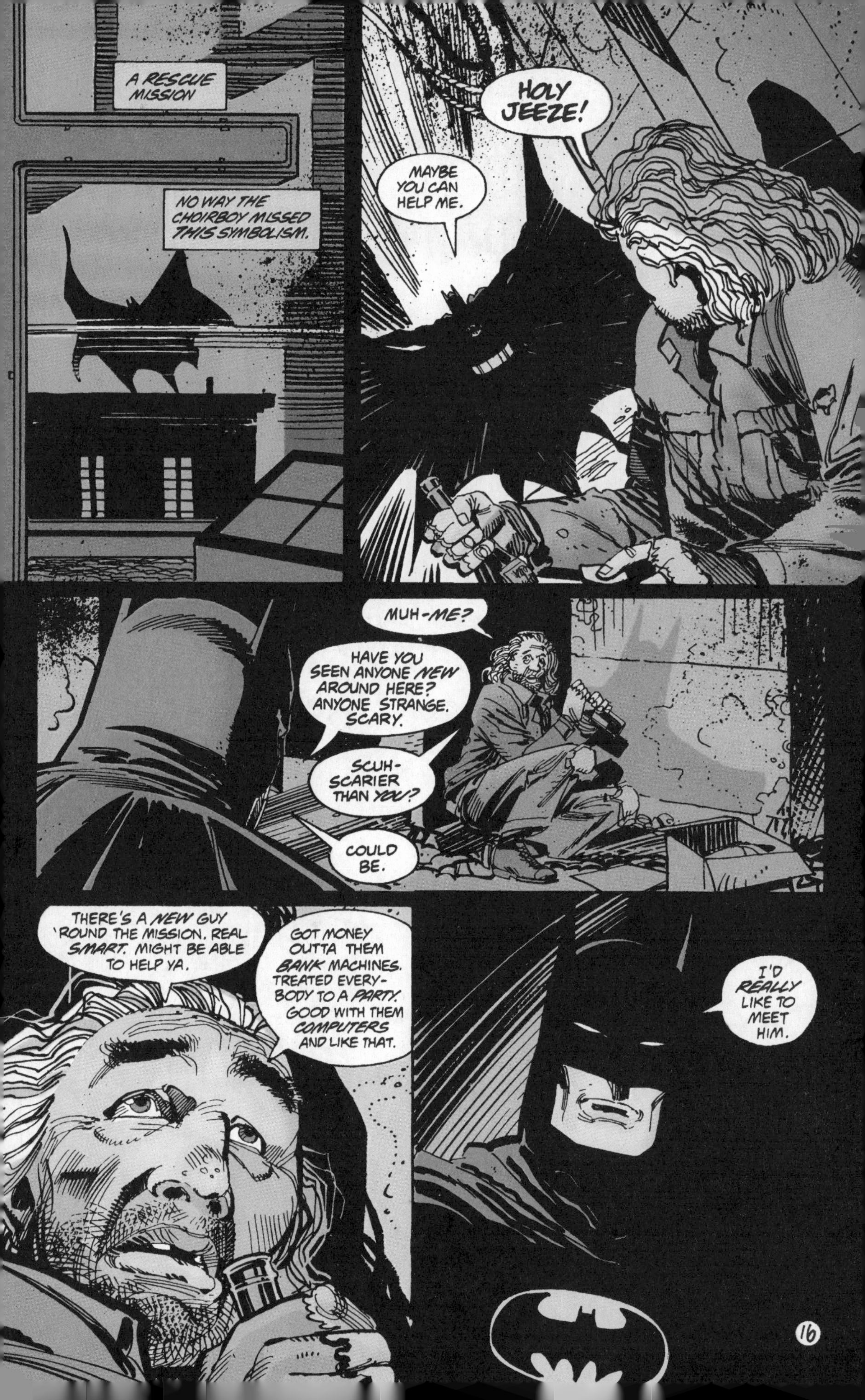
A RESCUE MISSION
NO WAY THE CHOIRBOY MISSED THIS SYMBOLISM.
HOLY JEEZE!
MAYBE YOU CAN HELP ME.
MUH-ME?
HAVE YOU SEEN ANYONE NEW AROUND HERE? ANYONE STRANGE. SCARY.
SCUH-SCARIER THAN YOU?
COULD BE.
THERE'S A NEW GUY 'ROUND THE MISSION. REAL SMART. MIGHT BE ABLE TO HELP YA.
GOT MONEY OUTTA THEM BANK MACHINES. TREATED EVERY-BODY TO A PARTY. GOOD WITH THEM COMPUTERS AND LIKE THAT.
I'D REALLY LIKE TO MEET HIM.
16

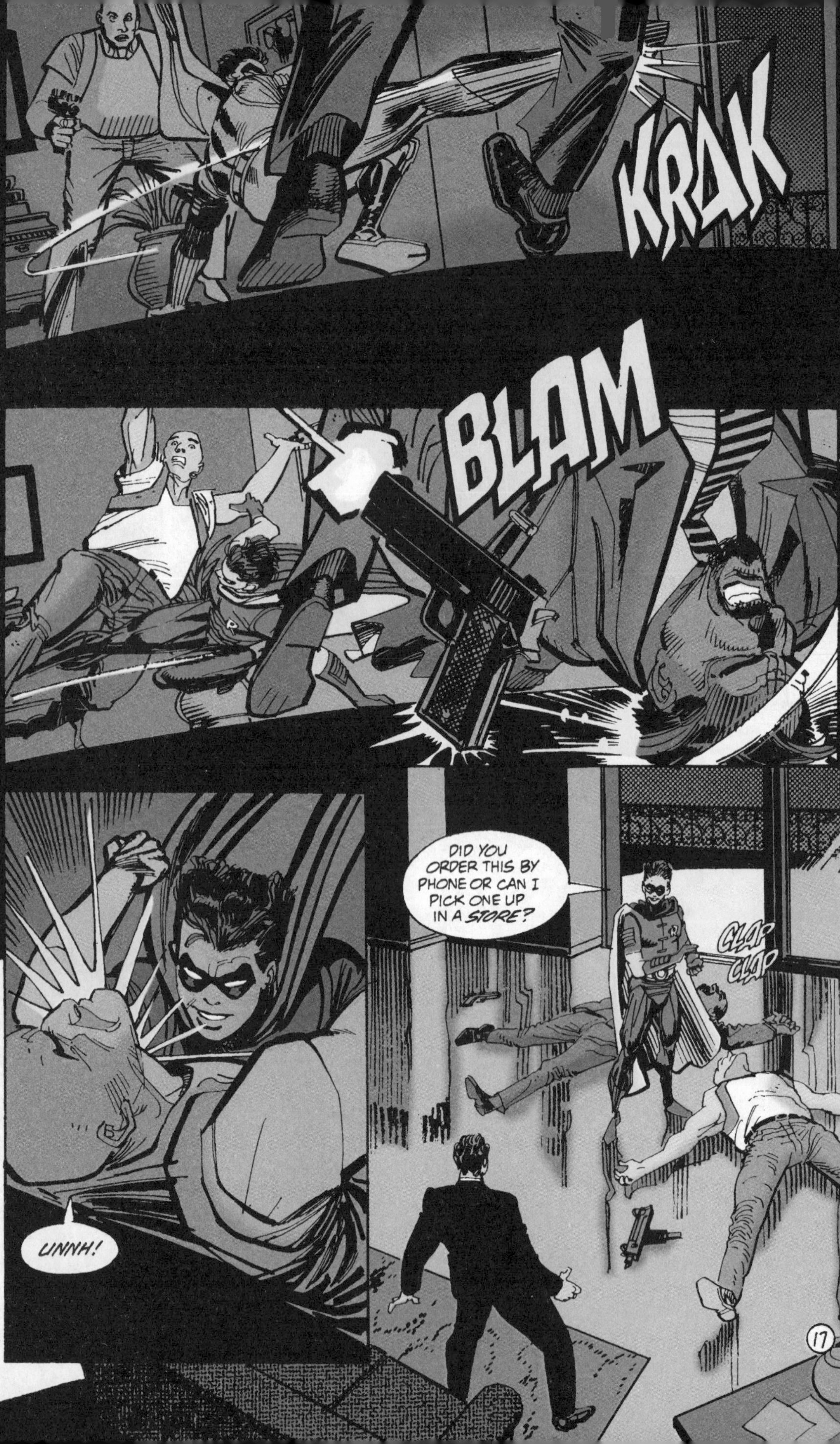
KRAK
BLAM
UNNH!
DID YOU ORDER THIS BY PHONE OR CAN I PICK ONE UP IN A STORE?
CLAP CLAP

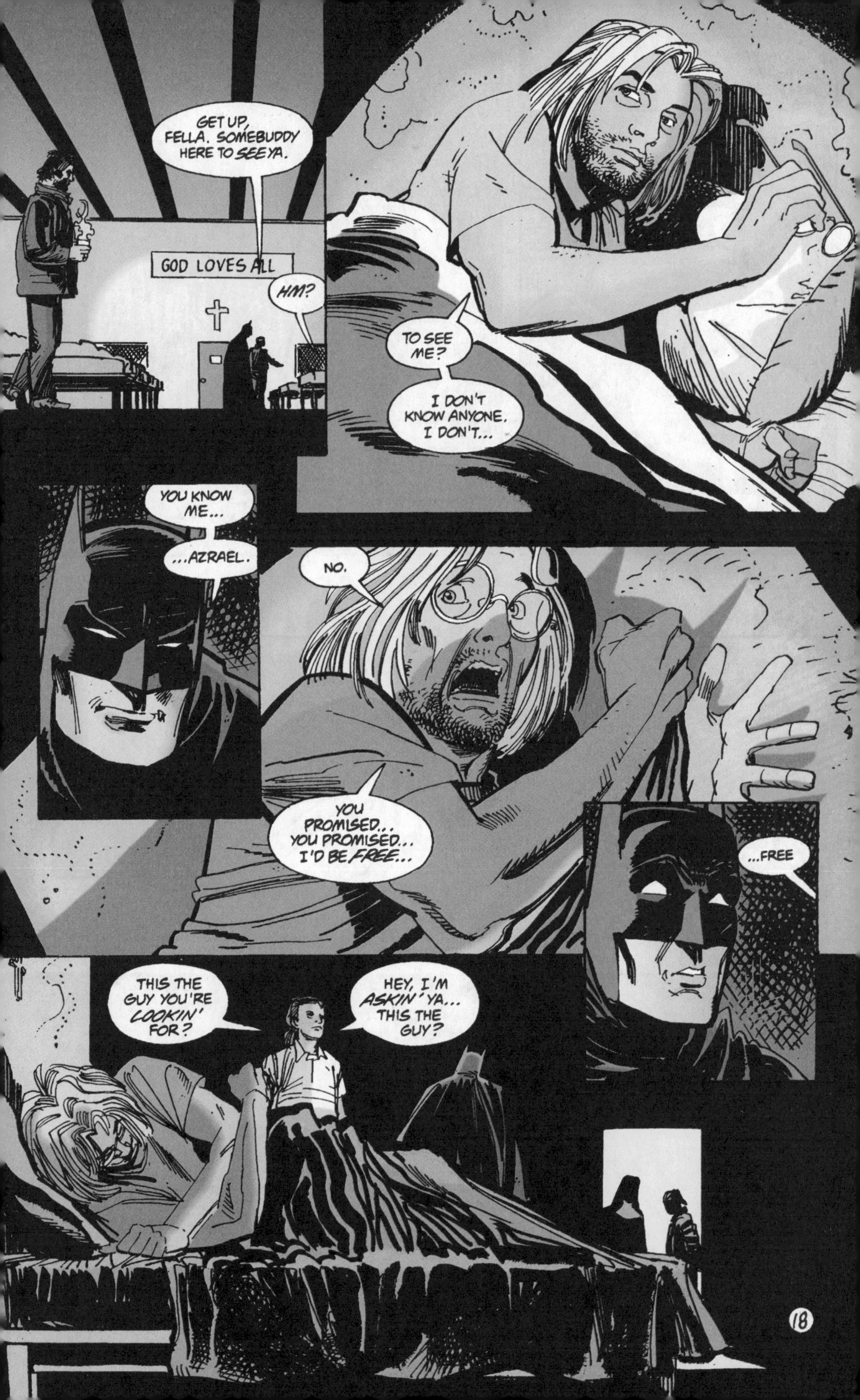
GET UP, FELLA. SOMEBUDDY HERE TO SEE YA.
GOD LOVES ALL
HM?
TO SEE ME?
I DON'T KNOW ANYONE. I DON'T...
YOU KNOW ME...
...AZRAEL.
NO.
YOU PROMISED... YOU PROMISED... I'D BE FREE...
...FREE
THIS THE GUY YOU'RE LOOKIN' FOR?
HEY, I'M ASKIN' YA... THIS THE GUY?
18

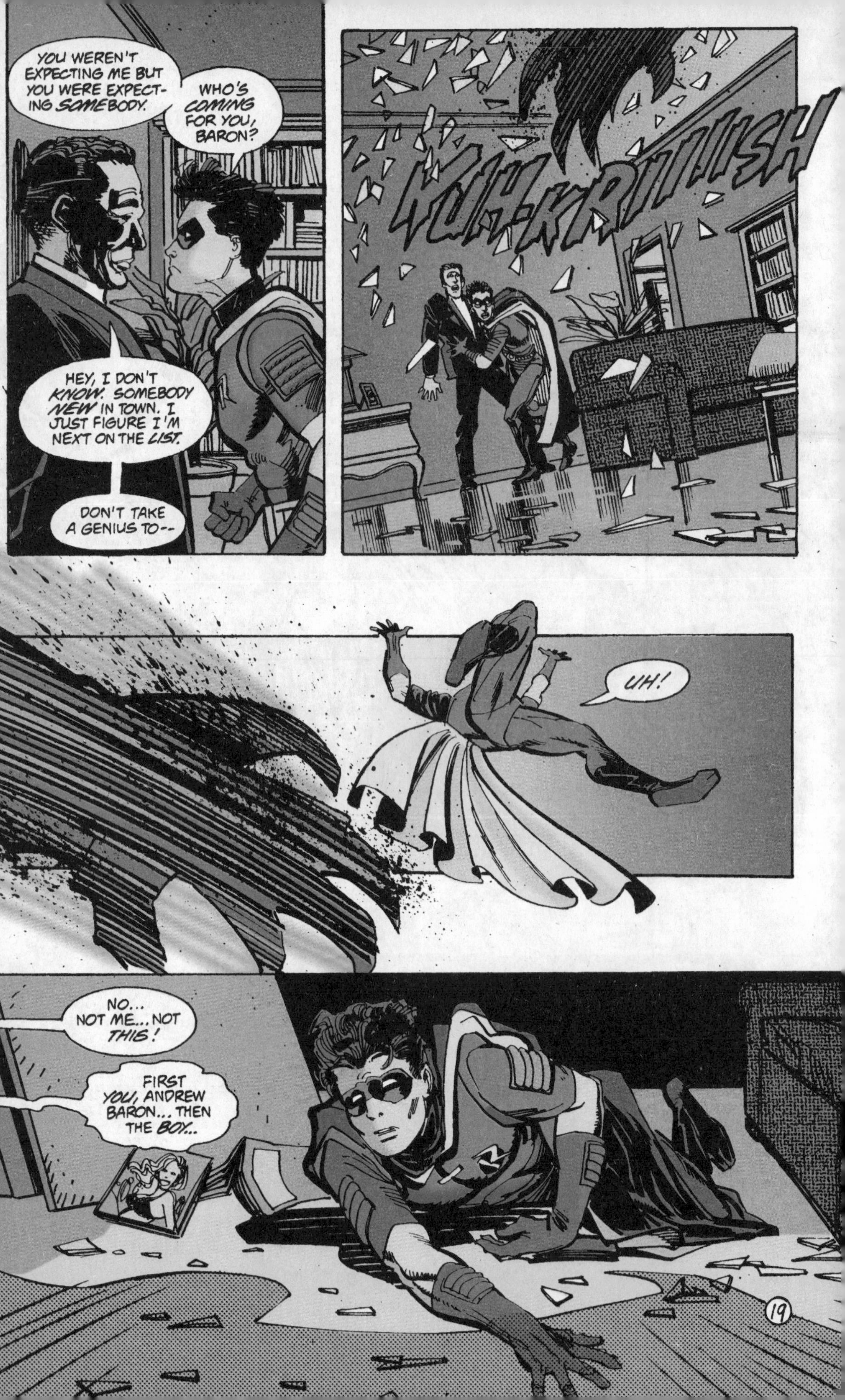
YOU WEREN'T EXPECTING ME BUT YOU WERE EXPECTING SOMEBODY.
WHO'S COMING FOR YOU, BARON?
HEY, I DON'T KNOW. SOMEBODY NEW IN TOWN. I JUST FIGURE I'M NEXT ON THE LIST.
DON'T TAKE A GENIUS TO--
WUH-KRTTTTSH
UH!
NO... NOT ME... NOT THIS!
FIRST YOU, ANDREW BARON... THEN THE BOY...
19

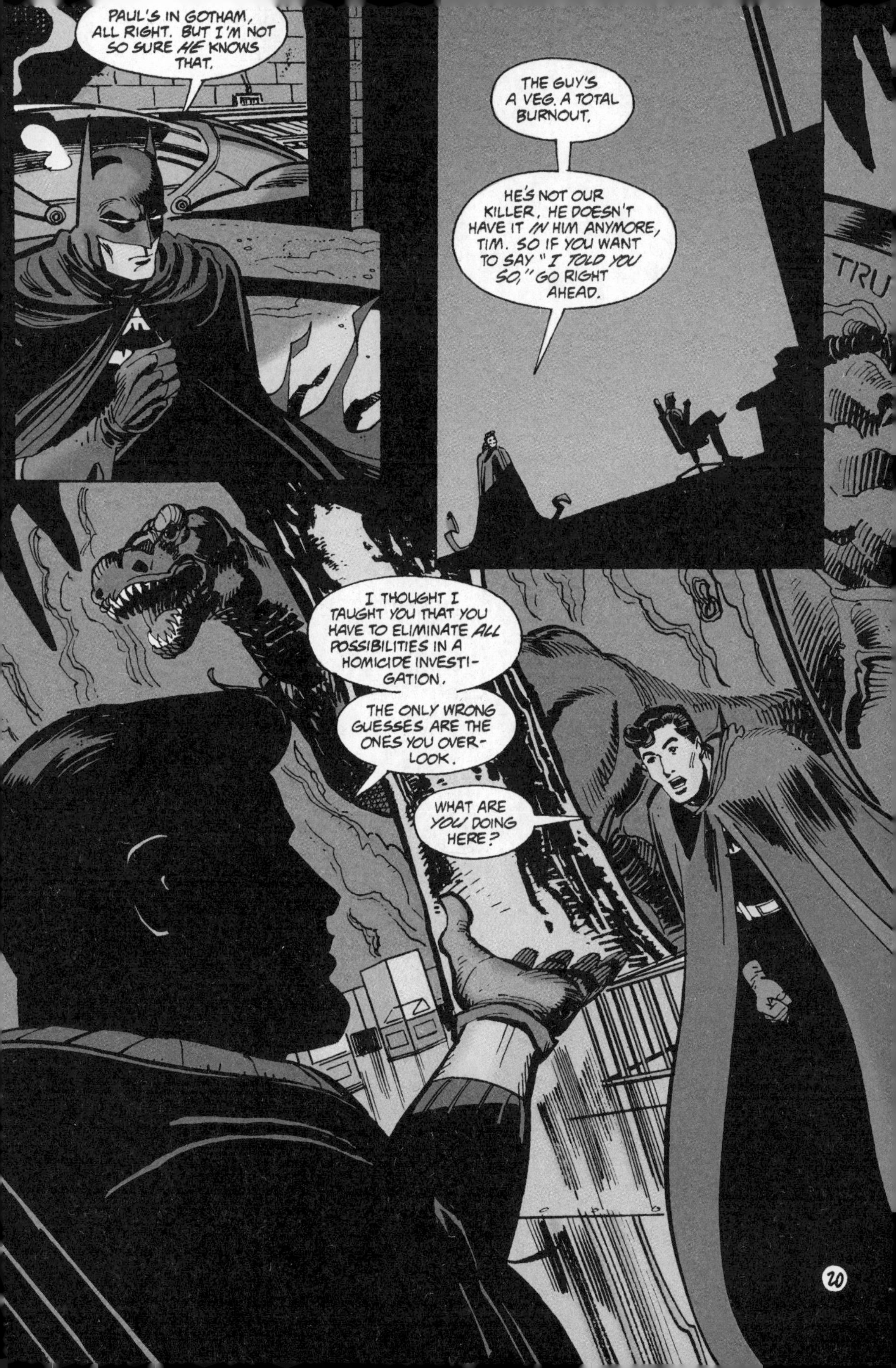
PAUL'S IN GOTHAM, ALL RIGHT. BUT I'M NOT SO SURE HE KNOWS THAT.
THE GUY'S A VEG. A TOTAL BURNOUT.
HE'S NOT OUR KILLER. HE DOESN'T HAVE IT IN HIM ANYMORE, TIM. SO IF YOU WANT TO SAY "I TOLD YOU SO," GO RIGHT AHEAD.
TRU
I THOUGHT I TAUGHT YOU THAT YOU HAVE TO ELIMINATE ALL POSSIBILITIES IN A HOMICIDE INVESTIGATION.
THE ONLY WRONG GUESSES ARE THE ONES YOU OVERLOOK.
WHAT ARE YOU DOING HERE?

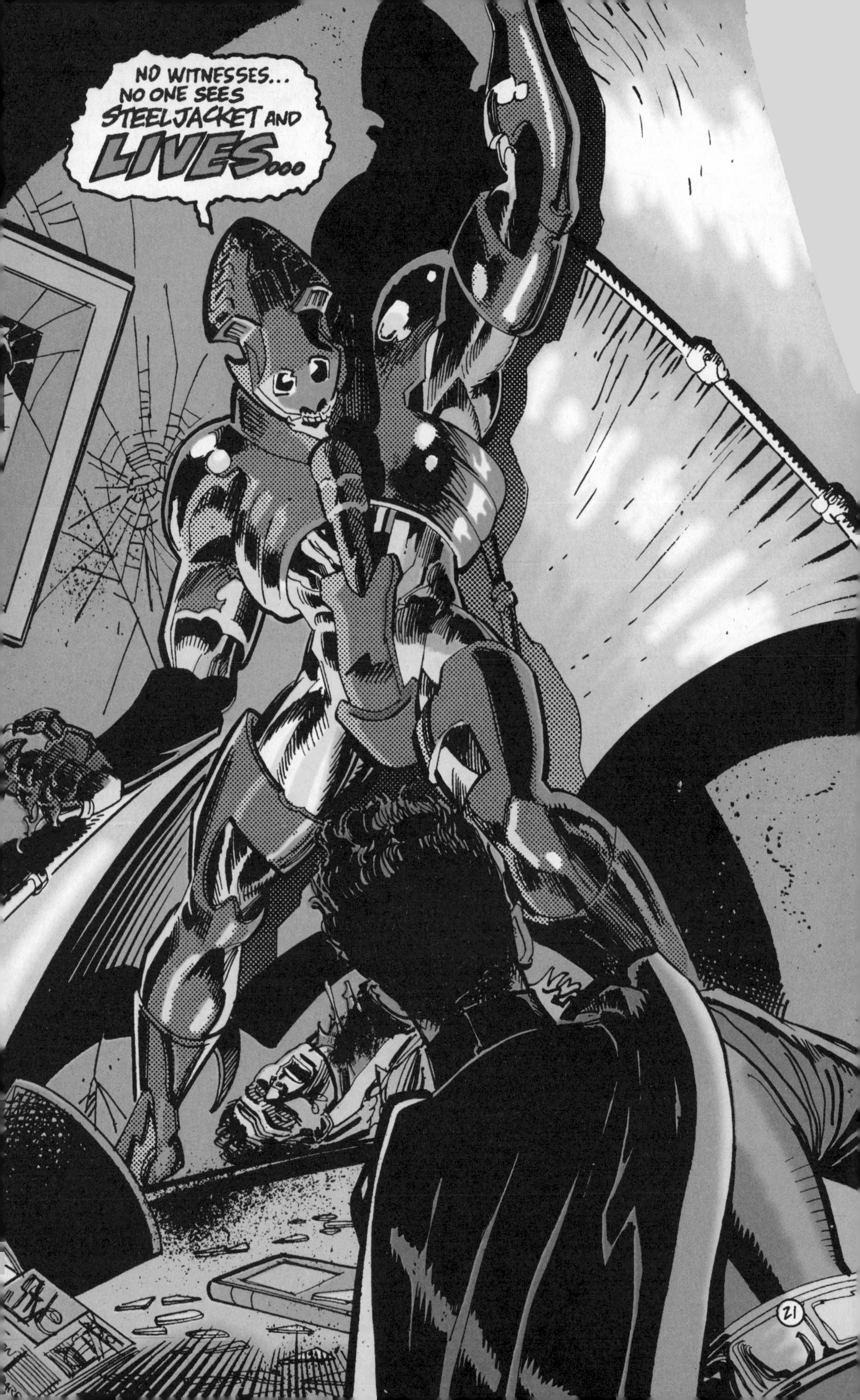
NO WITNESSES... NO ONE SEES STEELJACKET AND LIVES...

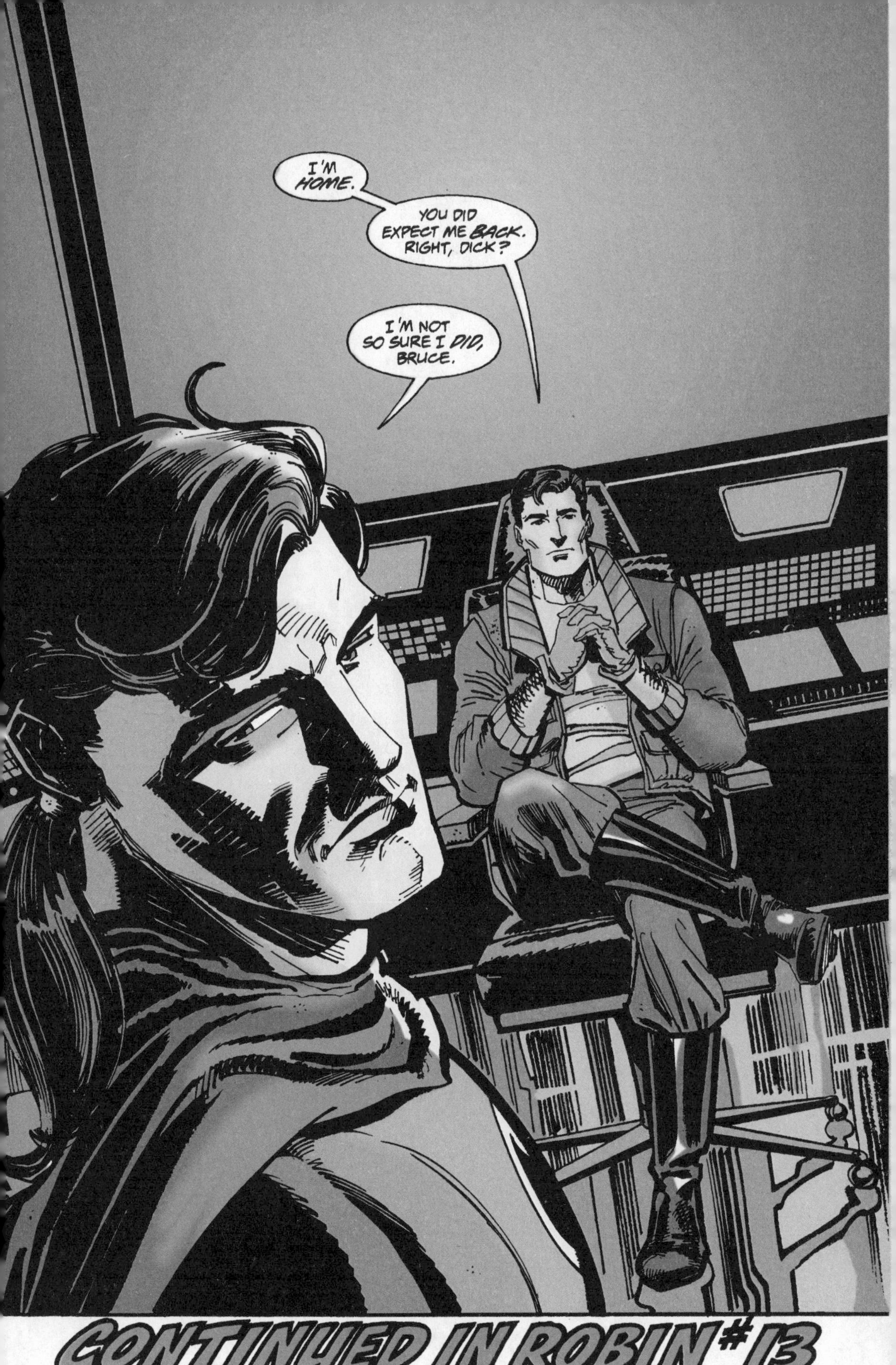
I'M HOME.
YOU DID EXPECT ME BACK. RIGHT, DICK?
I'M NOT SO SURE I DID, BRUCE.

CONTINUED IN ROBIN #13

Cover art by TOM GRUMMETT AND RAY KRYSSING

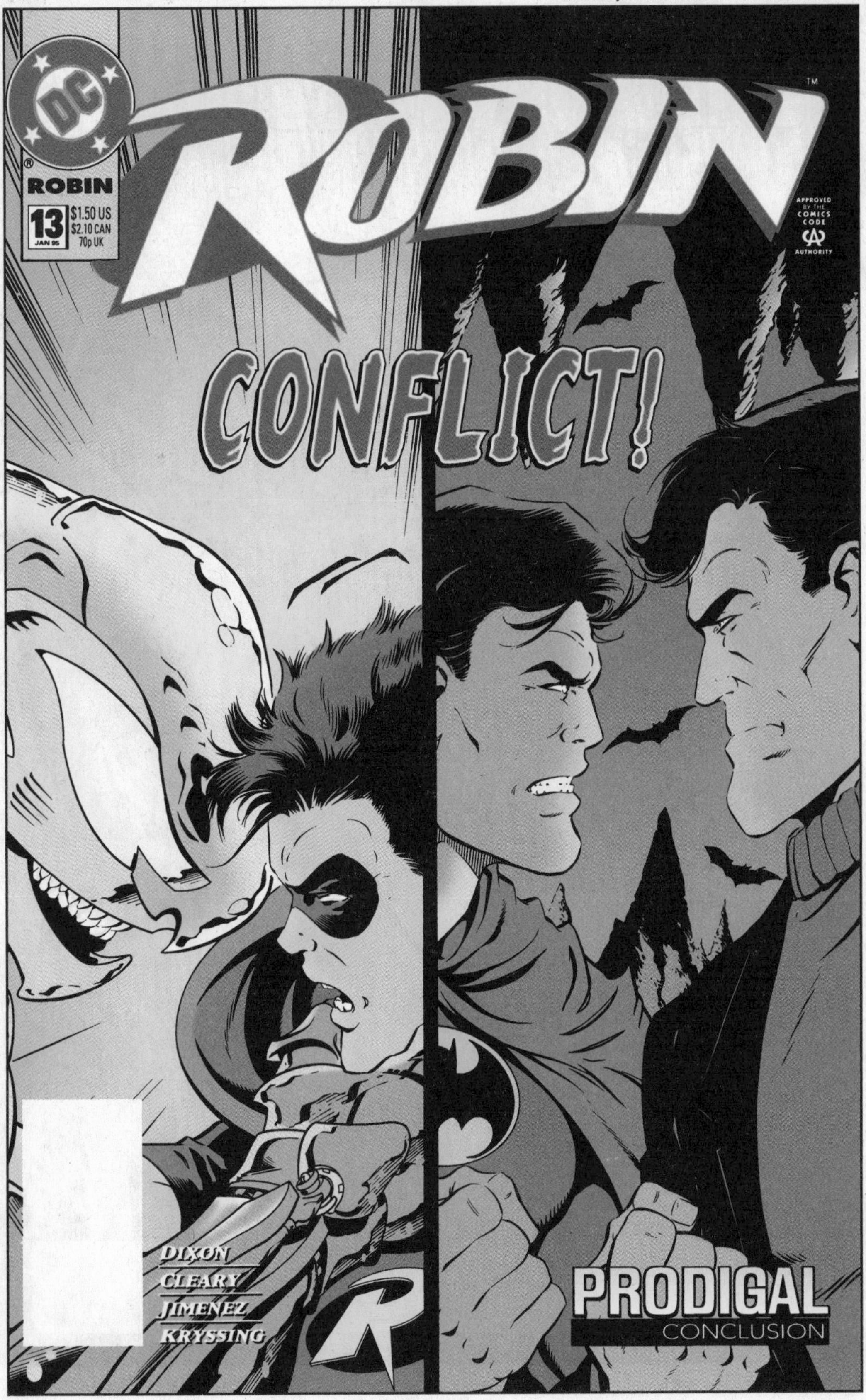

ROBIN
ROBIN
13 JAN 95
$1.50 US $2.10 CAN 70p UK
APPROVED BY THE COMICS CODE AUTHORITY
CONFLICT!
DIXON
CLEARY
JIMENEZ
KRYSSING
PRODIGAL
CONCLUSION

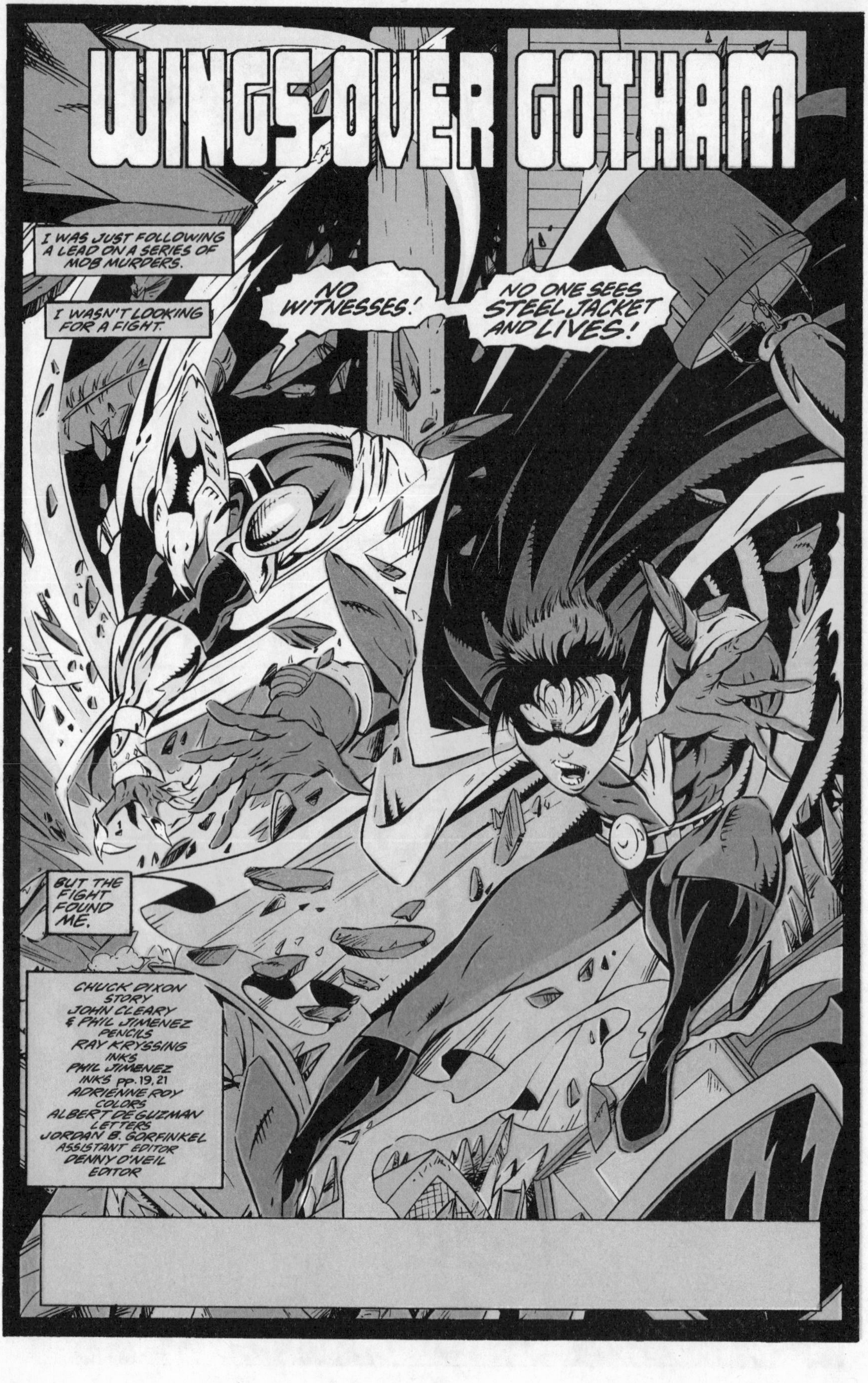
WINGS OVER GOTHAM
I WAS JUST FOLLOWING A LEAD ON A SERIES OF MOB MURDERS.
I WASN'T LOOKING FOR A FIGHT.
NO WITNESSES!
NO ONE SEES STEEL JACKET AND LIVES!
BUT THE FIGHT FOUND ME.
CHUCK DIXON STORY
JOHN CLEARY & PHIL JIMENEZ PENCILS
RAY KRYSSING INKS
PHIL JIMENEZ INKS pp. 19, 21
ADRIENNE ROY COLORS
ALBERT DE GUZMAN LETTERS
JORDAN B. GORFINKEL ASSISTANT EDITOR
DENNY O'NEIL EDITOR

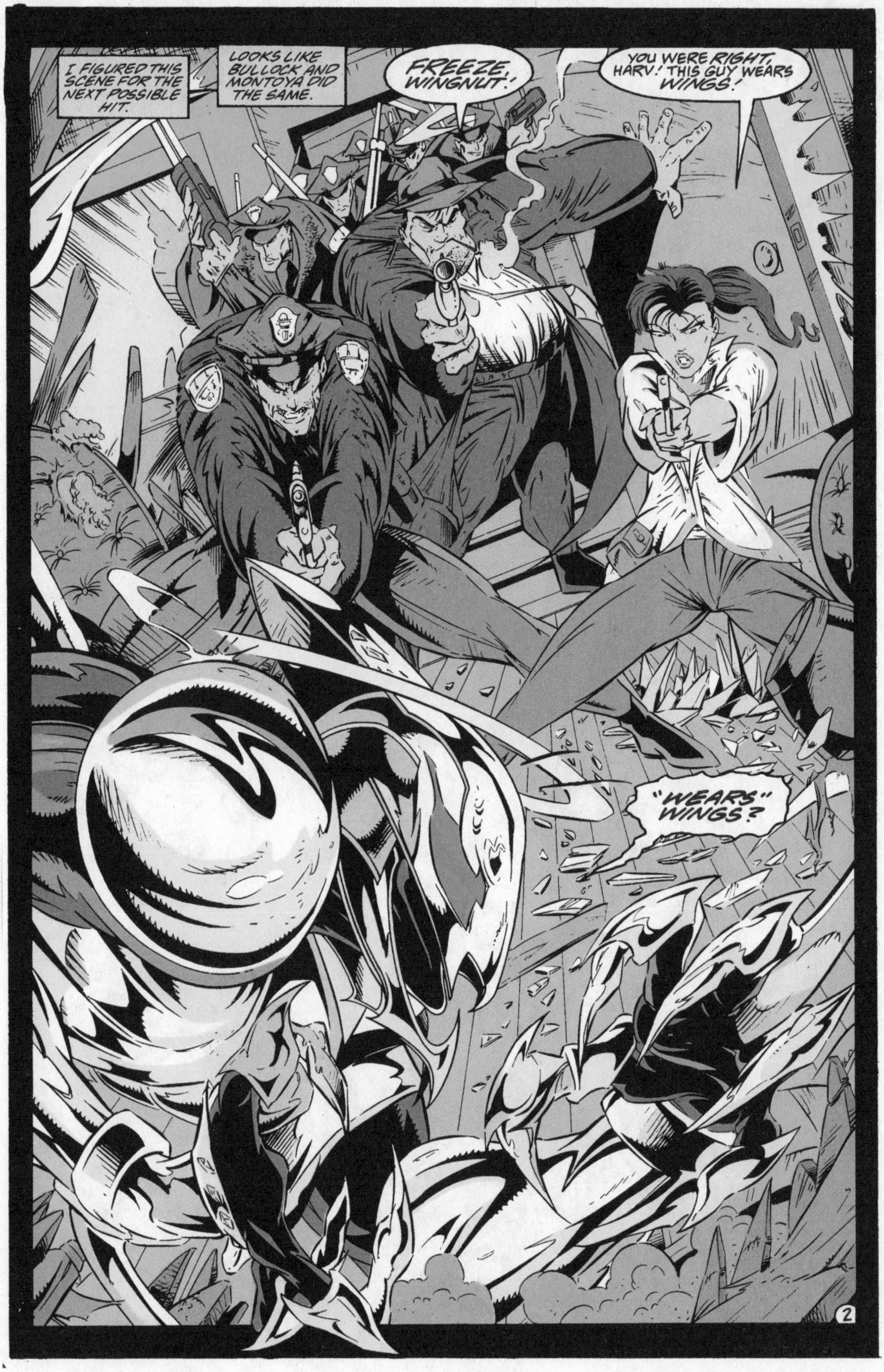
I FIGURED THIS SCENE FOR THE NEXT POSSIBLE HIT.
LOOKS LIKE BULLOCK AND MONTOYA DID THE SAME.
FREEZE, WINGNUT!
YOU WERE RIGHT, HARV! THIS GUY WEARS WINGS!
"WEARS" WINGS?
2

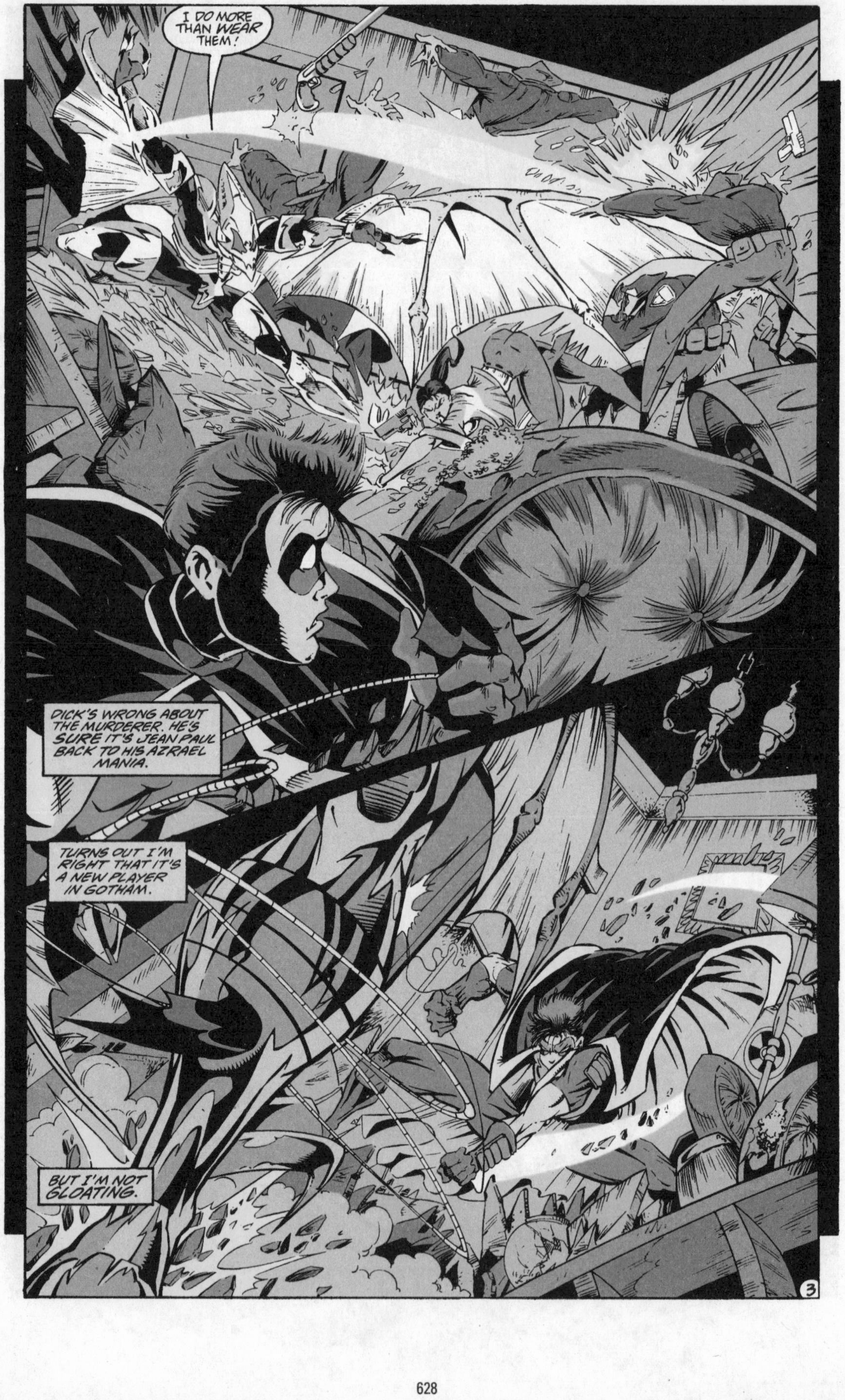
I DO MORE THAN WEAR THEM!
DICK'S WRONG ABOUT THE MURDERER. HE'S SURE IT'S JEAN PAUL BACK TO HIS AZRAEL MANIA.
TURNS OUT I'M RIGHT THAT IT'S A NEW PLAYER IN GOTHAM.
BUT I'M NOT GLOATING.
3

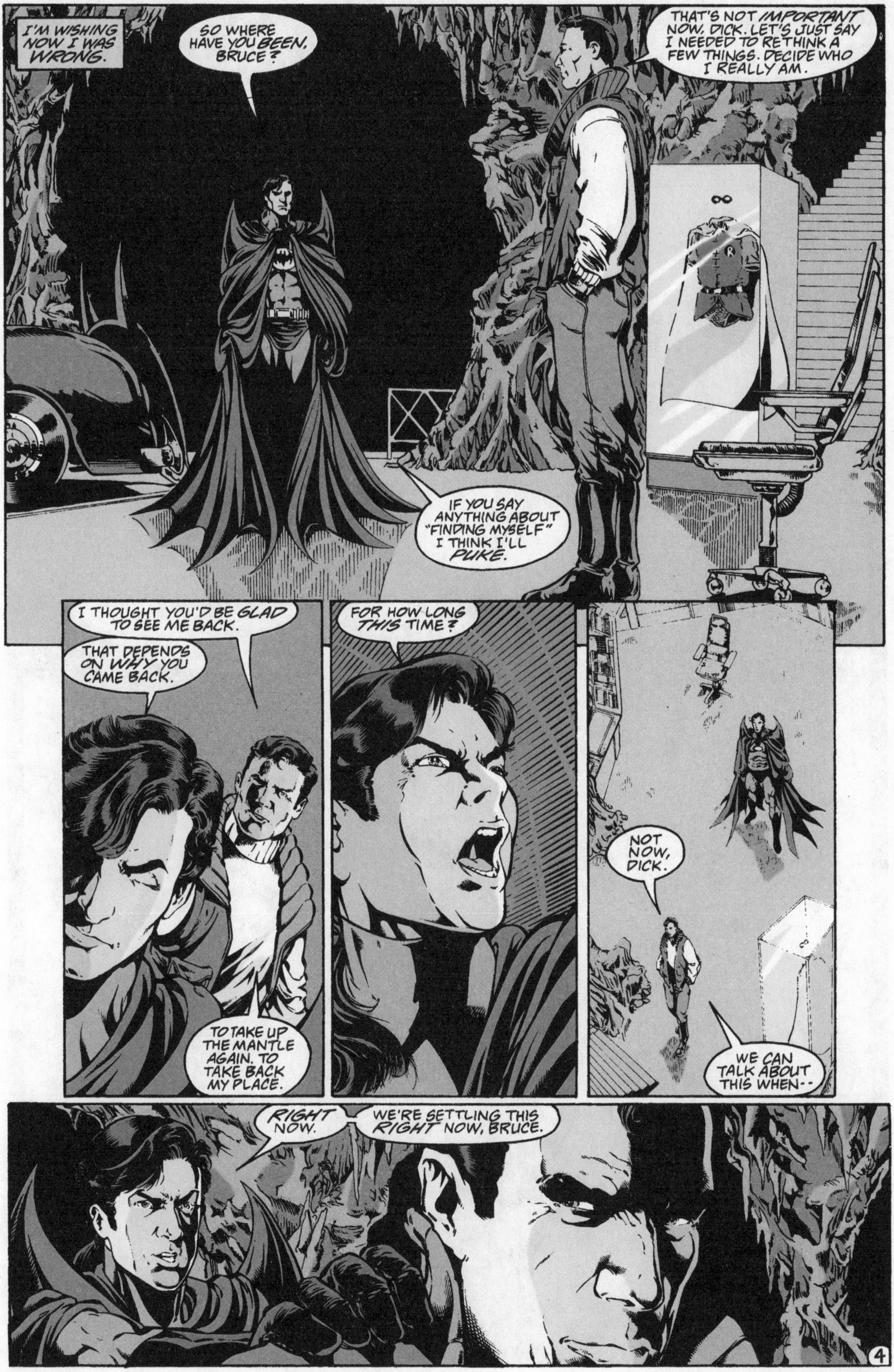
I'M WISHING NOW I WAS WRONG.
SO WHERE HAVE YOU BEEN, BRUCE?
THAT'S NOT IMPORTANT NOW, DICK. LET'S JUST SAY I NEEDED TO RETHINK A FEW THINGS. DECIDE WHO I REALLY AM.
IF YOU SAY ANYTHING ABOUT "FINDING MYSELF" I THINK I'LL PUKE.
I THOUGHT YOU'D BE GLAD TO SEE ME BACK.
THAT DEPENDS ON WHY YOU CAME BACK.
TO TAKE UP THE MANTLE AGAIN. TO TAKE BACK MY PLACE.
FOR HOW LONG THIS TIME?
NOT NOW, DICK.
WE CAN TALK ABOUT THIS WHEN--
RIGHT NOW.
WE'RE SETTLING THIS RIGHT NOW, BRUCE.
4

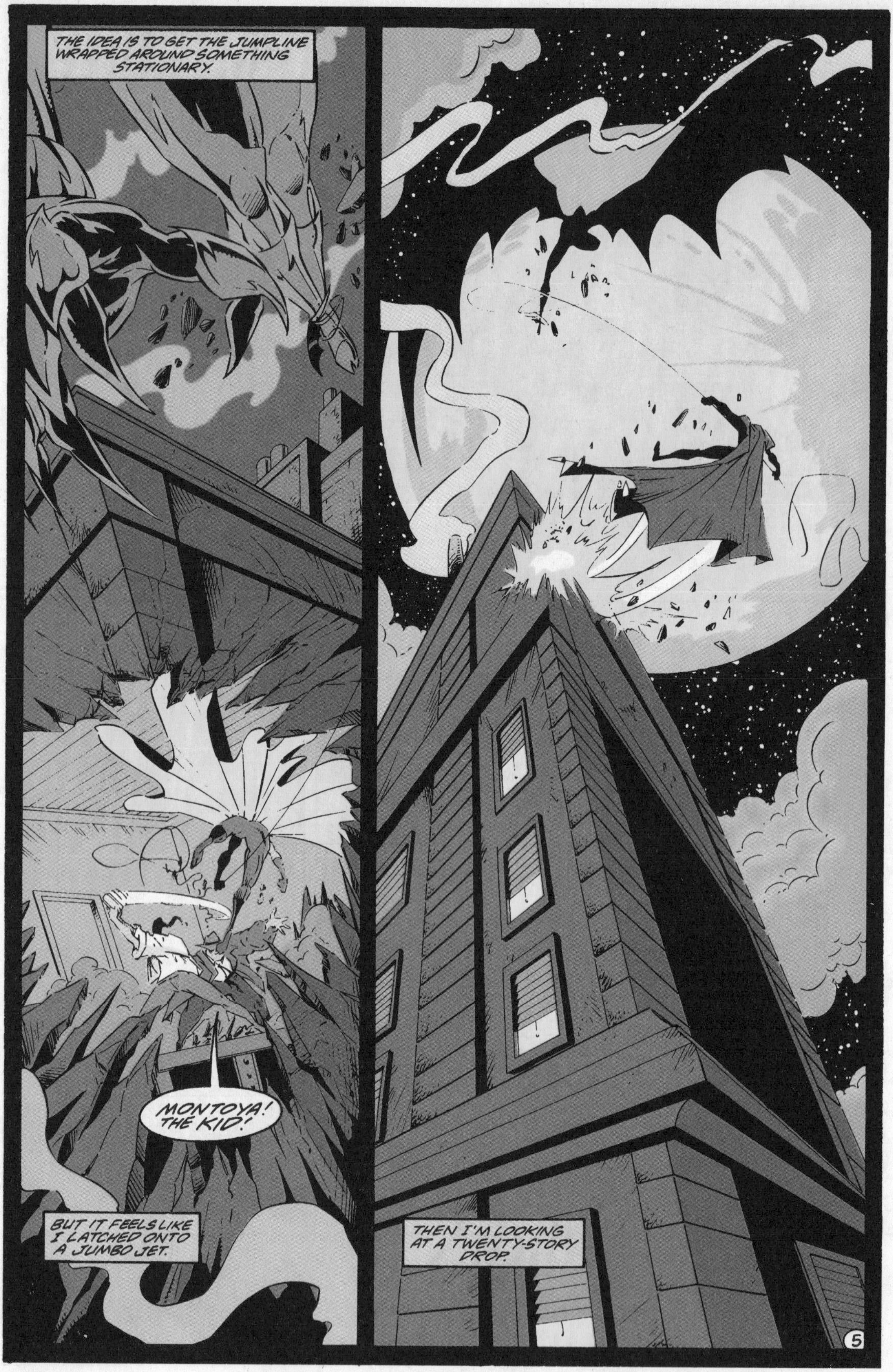
THE IDEA IS TO GET THE JUMPLINE WRAPPED AROUND SOMETHING STATIONARY.
MONTOYA! THE KID!
BUT IT FEELS LIKE I LATCHED ONTO A JUMBO JET.
THEN I'M LOOKING AT A TWENTY-STORY DROP.
5

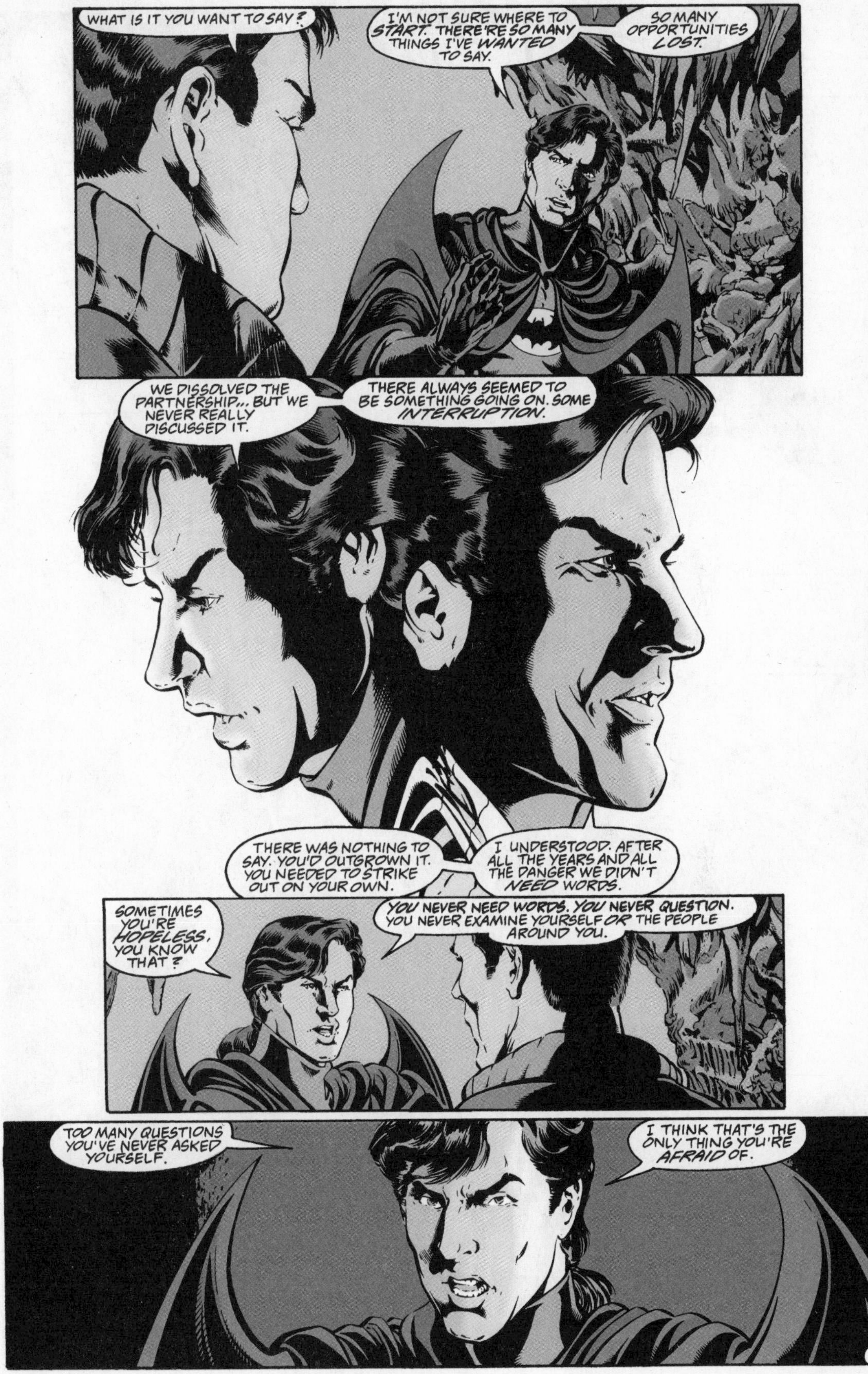
WHAT IS IT YOU WANT TO SAY?
I'M NOT SURE WHERE TO START. THERE'RE SO MANY THINGS I'VE WANTED TO SAY.
SO MANY OPPORTUNITIES LOST.
WE DISSOLVED THE PARTNERSHIP... BUT WE NEVER REALLY DISCUSSED IT.
THERE ALWAYS SEEMED TO BE SOMETHING GOING ON. SOME INTERRUPTION.
THERE WAS NOTHING TO SAY. YOU'D OUTGROWN IT. YOU NEEDED TO STRIKE OUT ON YOUR OWN.
I UNDERSTOOD. AFTER ALL THE YEARS AND ALL THE DANGER WE DIDN'T NEED WORDS.
SOMETIMES YOU'RE HOPELESS, YOU KNOW THAT?
YOU NEVER NEED WORDS. YOU NEVER QUESTION. YOU NEVER EXAMINE YOURSELF OR THE PEOPLE AROUND YOU.
TOO MANY QUESTIONS YOU'VE NEVER ASKED YOURSELF.
I THINK THAT'S THE ONLY THING YOU'RE AFRAID OF.
6

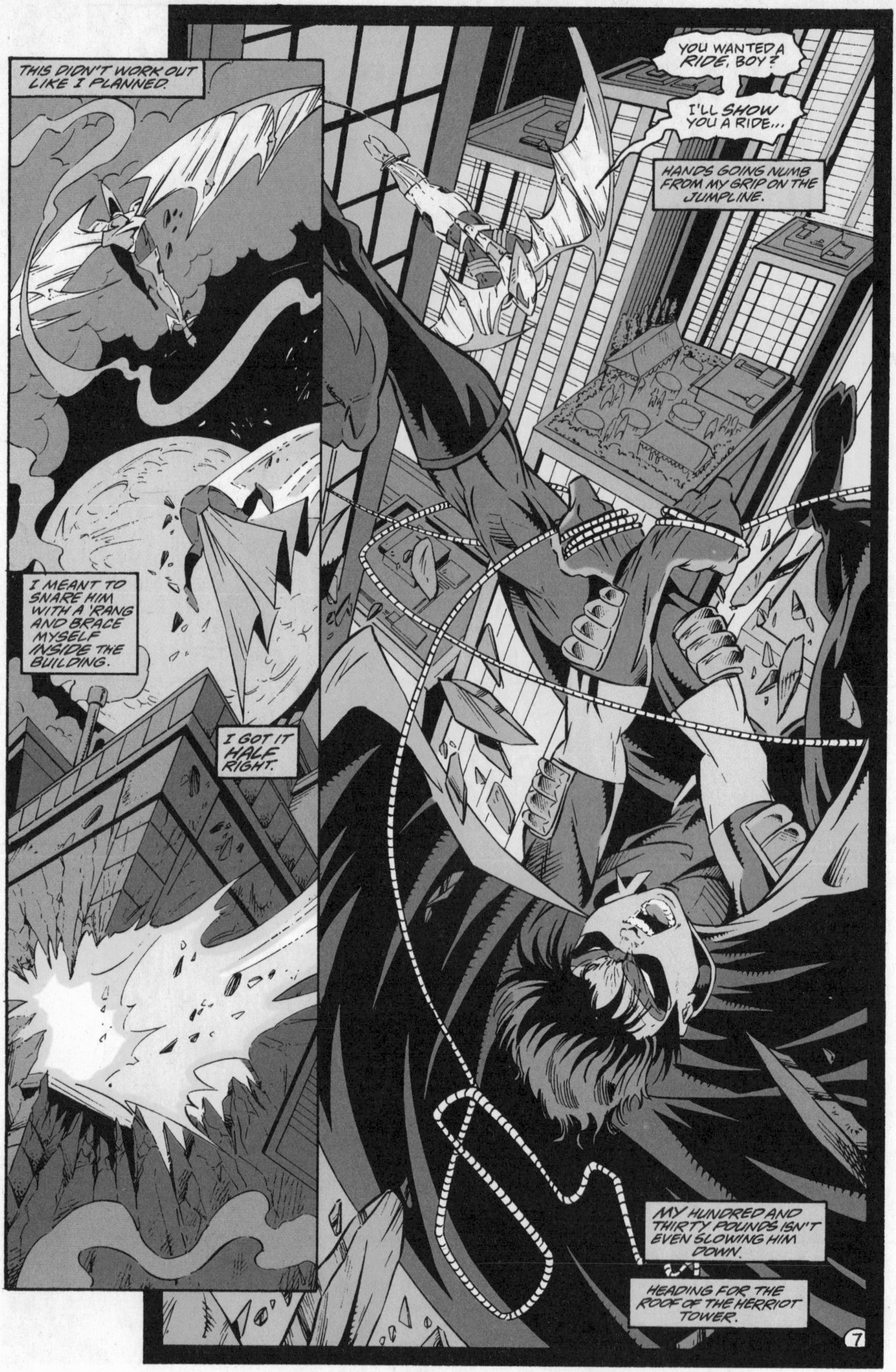

THIS DIDN'T WORK OUT LIKE I PLANNED.
YOU WANTED A RIDE, BOY?
I'LL SHOW YOU A RIDE...
HANDS GOING NUMB FROM MY GRIP ON THE JUMPLINE.
I MEANT TO SNARE HIM WITH A 'RANG AND BRACE MYSELF INSIDE THE BUILDING.
I GOT IT HALF RIGHT.
MY HUNDRED AND THIRTY POUNDS ISN'T EVEN SLOWING HIM DOWN.
HEADING FOR THE ROOF OF THE HERRIOT TOWER.
7

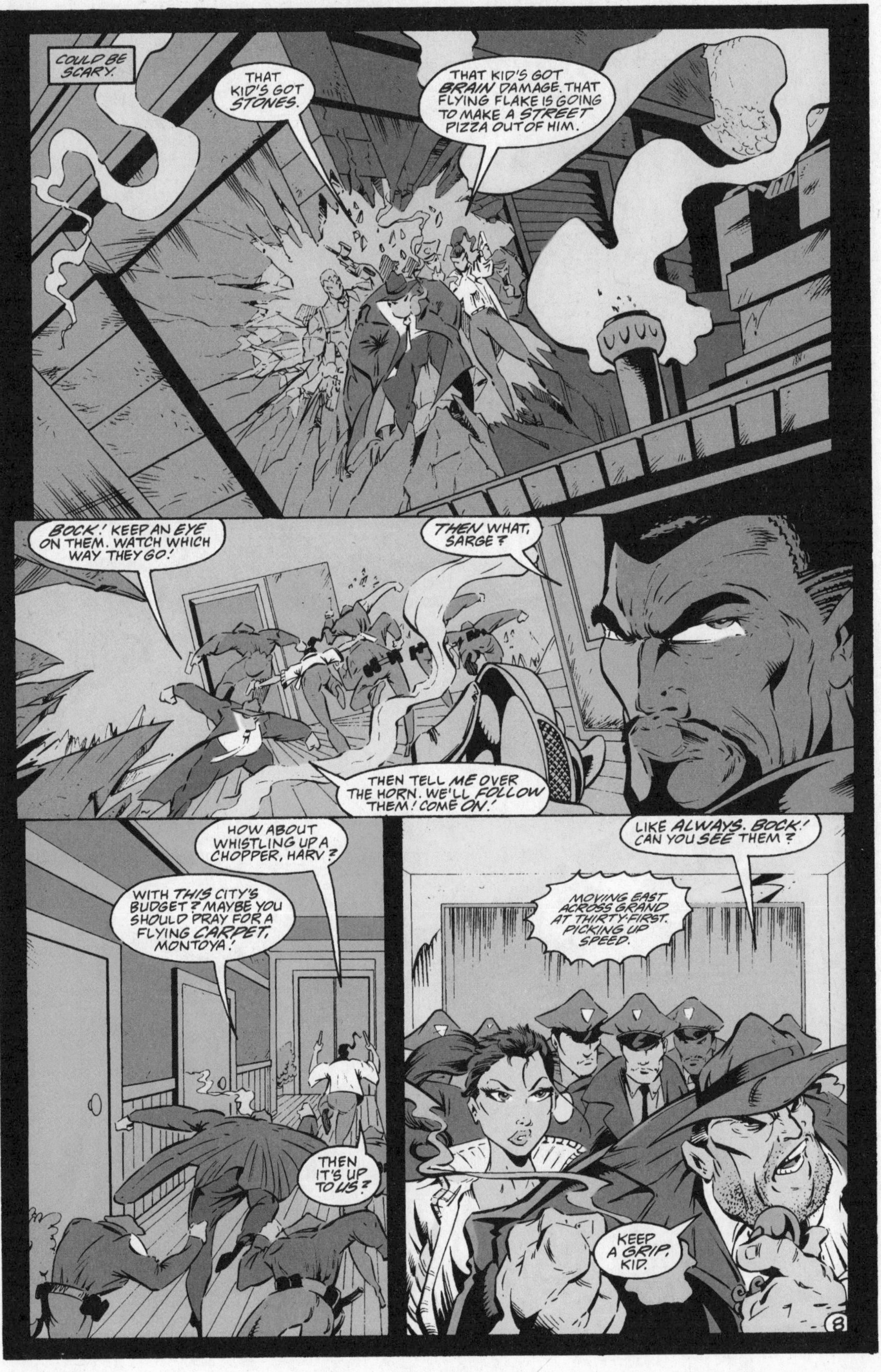
COULD BE SCARY.
THAT KID'S GOT STONES.
THAT KID'S GOT BRAIN DAMAGE. THAT FLYING FLAKE IS GOING TO MAKE A STREET PIZZA OUT OF HIM.
BOCK! KEEP AN EYE ON THEM. WATCH WHICH WAY THEY GO!
THEN WHAT, SARGE?
THEN TELL ME OVER THE HORN. WE'LL FOLLOW THEM! COME ON!
HOW ABOUT WHISTLING UP A CHOPPER, HARV?
WITH THIS CITY'S BUDGET? MAYBE YOU SHOULD PRAY FOR A FLYING CARPET, MONTOYA!
THEN IT'S UP TO US?
LIKE ALWAYS. BOCK! CAN YOU SEE THEM?
MOVING EAST ACROSS GRAND AT THIRTY-FIRST. PICKING UP SPEED.
KEEP A GRIP, KID.
8

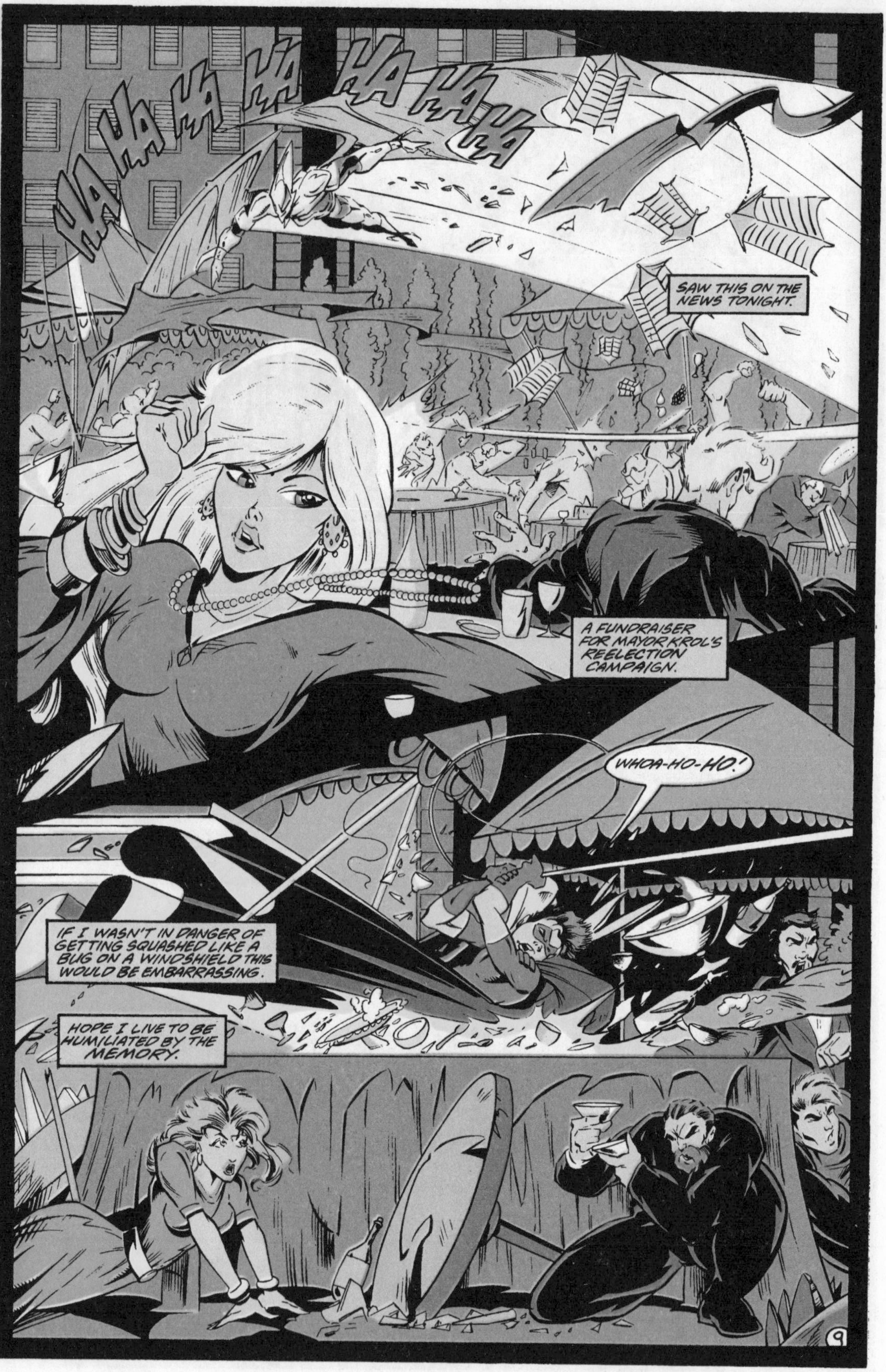
HA HA HA HA HA HA HA HA HA
SAW THIS ON THE NEWS TONIGHT.
A FUNDRAISER FOR MAYOR KROL'S REELECTION CAMPAIGN.
WHOA-HO-HO!
IF I WASN'T IN DANGER OF GETTING SQUASHED LIKE A BUG ON A WINDSHIELD THIS WOULD BE EMBARRASSING.
HOPE I LIVE TO BE HUMILIATED BY THE MEMORY.
9

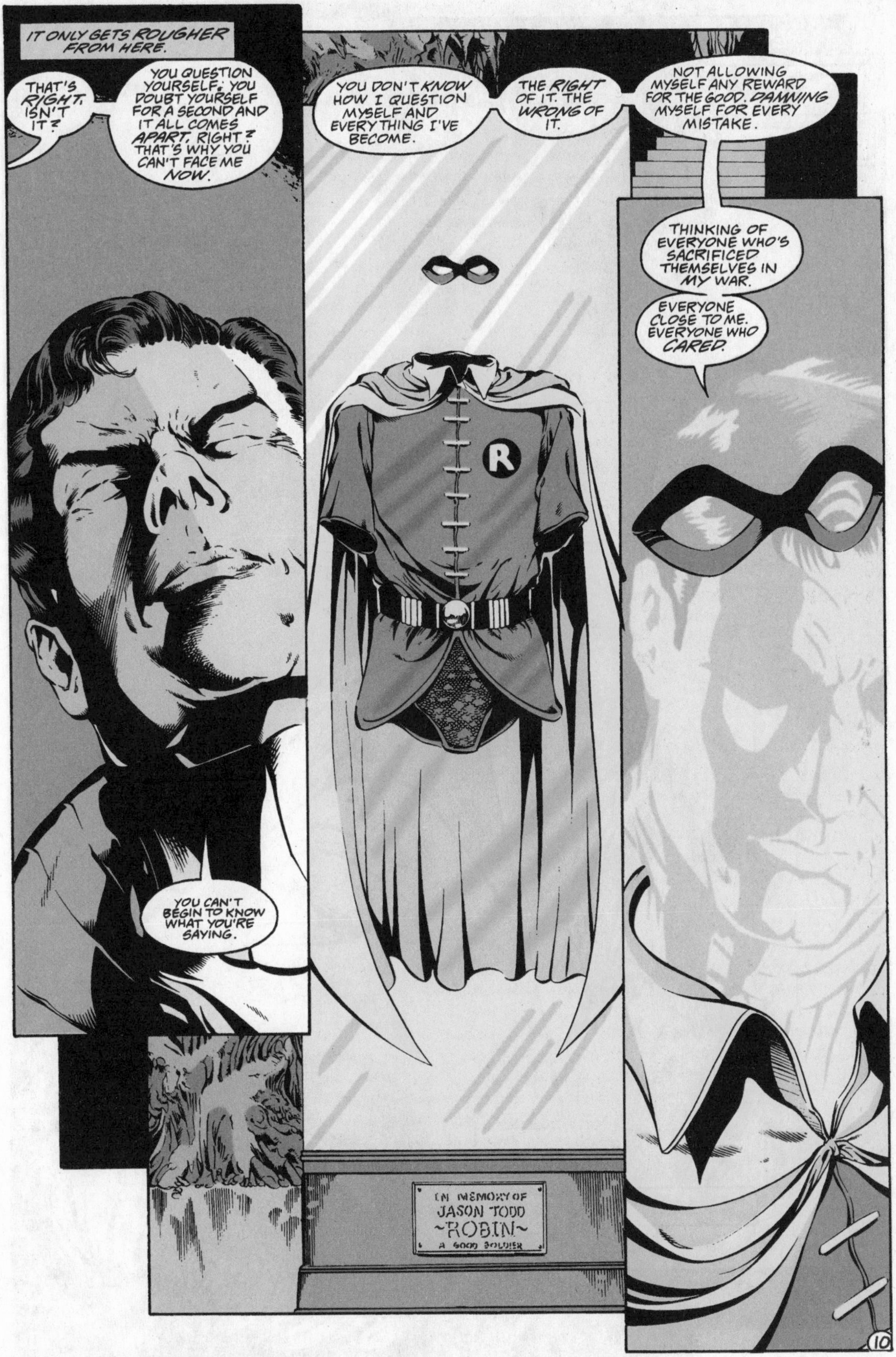
IT ONLY GETS ROUGHER FROM HERE.
THAT'S RIGHT, ISN'T IT?
YOU QUESTION YOURSELF; YOU DOUBT YOURSELF FOR A SECOND AND IT ALL COMES APART, RIGHT? THAT'S WHY YOU CAN'T FACE ME NOW.
YOU DON'T KNOW HOW I QUESTION MYSELF AND EVERYTHING I'VE BECOME.
THE RIGHT OF IT. THE WRONG OF IT.
NOT ALLOWING MYSELF ANY REWARD FOR THE GOOD. DAMNING MYSELF FOR EVERY MISTAKE.
THINKING OF EVERYONE WHO'S SACRIFICED THEMSELVES IN MY WAR.
EVERYONE CLOSE TO ME. EVERYONE WHO CARED.
YOU CAN'T BEGIN TO KNOW WHAT YOU'RE SAYING.
IN MEMORY OF
JASON TODD
~ROBIN~
A GOOD SOLDIER
10

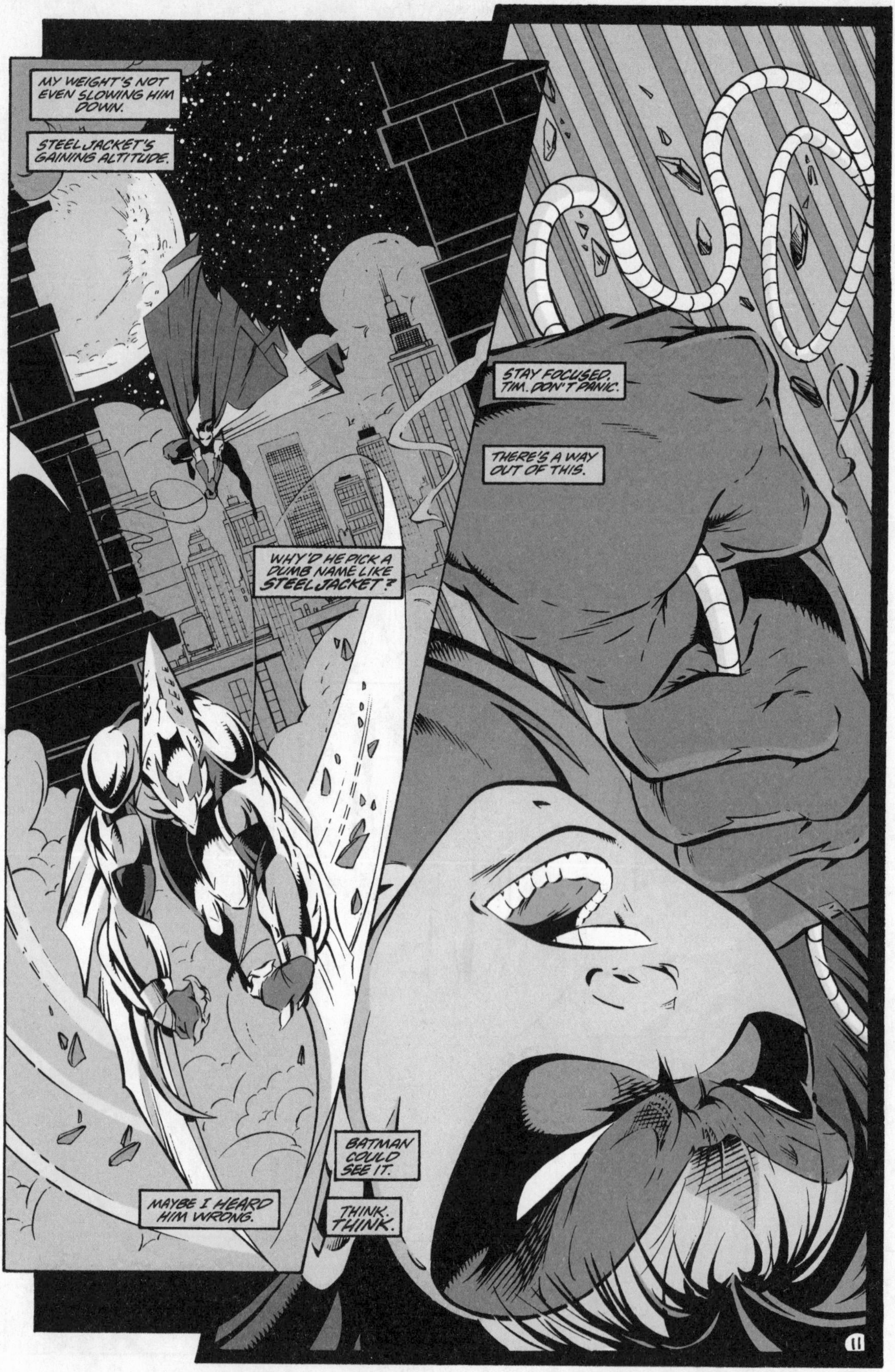
MY WEIGHT'S NOT EVEN SLOWING HIM DOWN.
STEEL JACKET'S GAINING ALTITUDE.
WHY'D HE PICK A DUMB NAME LIKE STEEL JACKET?
MAYBE I HEARD HIM WRONG.
STAY FOCUSED, TIM. DON'T PANIC.
THERE'S A WAY OUT OF THIS.
BATMAN COULD SEE IT.
THINK. THINK.
11

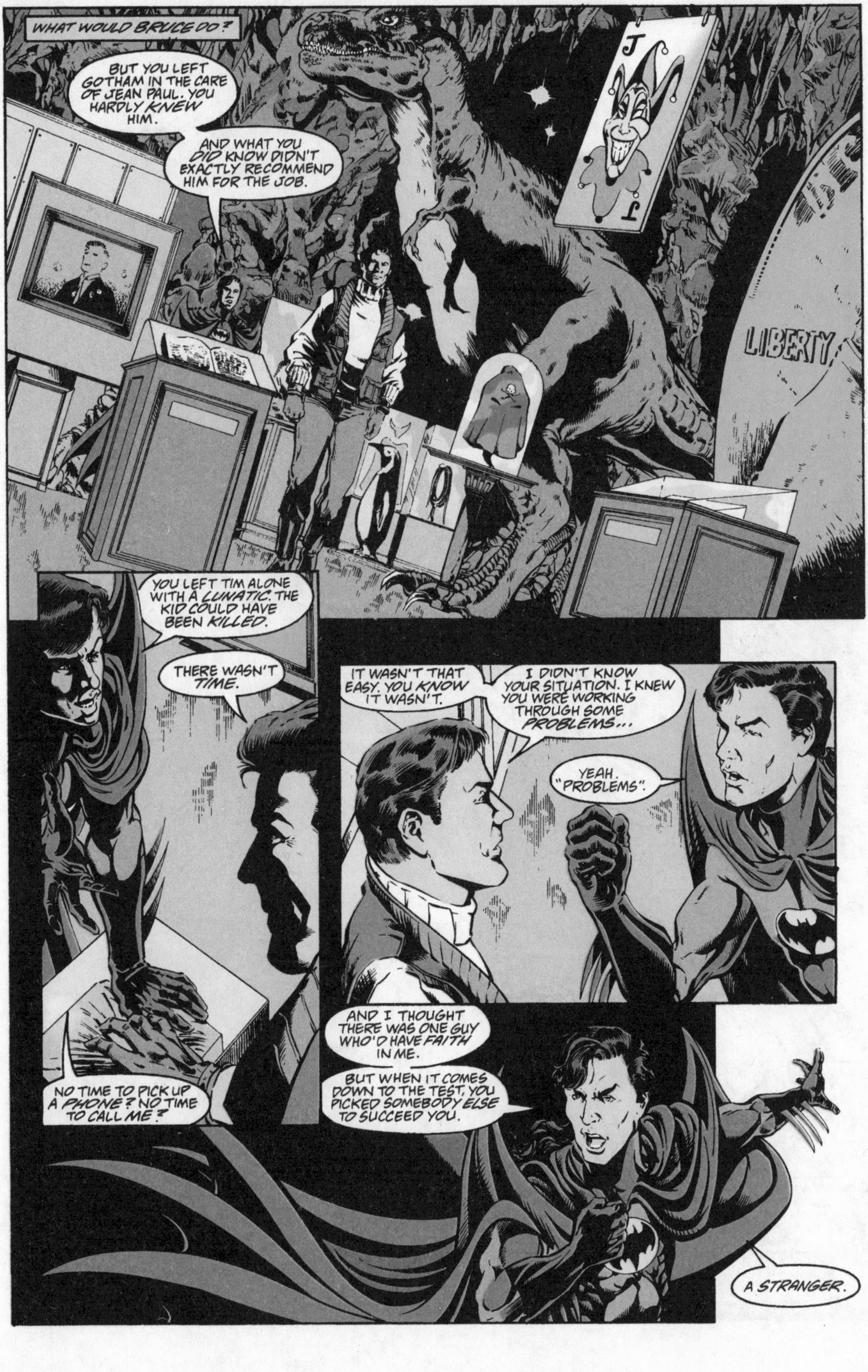
WHAT WOULD BRUCE DO?
BUT YOU LEFT GOTHAM IN THE CARE OF JEAN PAUL. YOU HARDLY KNEW HIM.
AND WHAT YOU DID KNOW DIDN'T EXACTLY RECOMMEND HIM FOR THE JOB.
LIBERTY
YOU LEFT TIM ALONE WITH A LUNATIC. THE KID COULD HAVE BEEN KILLED.
THERE WASN'T TIME.
NO TIME TO PICK UP A PHONE? NO TIME TO CALL ME?
IT WASN'T THAT EASY. YOU KNOW IT WASN'T.
I DIDN'T KNOW YOUR SITUATION. I KNEW YOU WERE WORKING THROUGH SOME PROBLEMS...
YEAH. "PROBLEMS".
AND I THOUGHT THERE WAS ONE GUY WHO'D HAVE FAITH IN ME.
BUT WHEN IT COMES DOWN TO THE TEST, YOU PICKED SOMEBODY ELSE TO SUCCEED YOU.
A STRANGER.

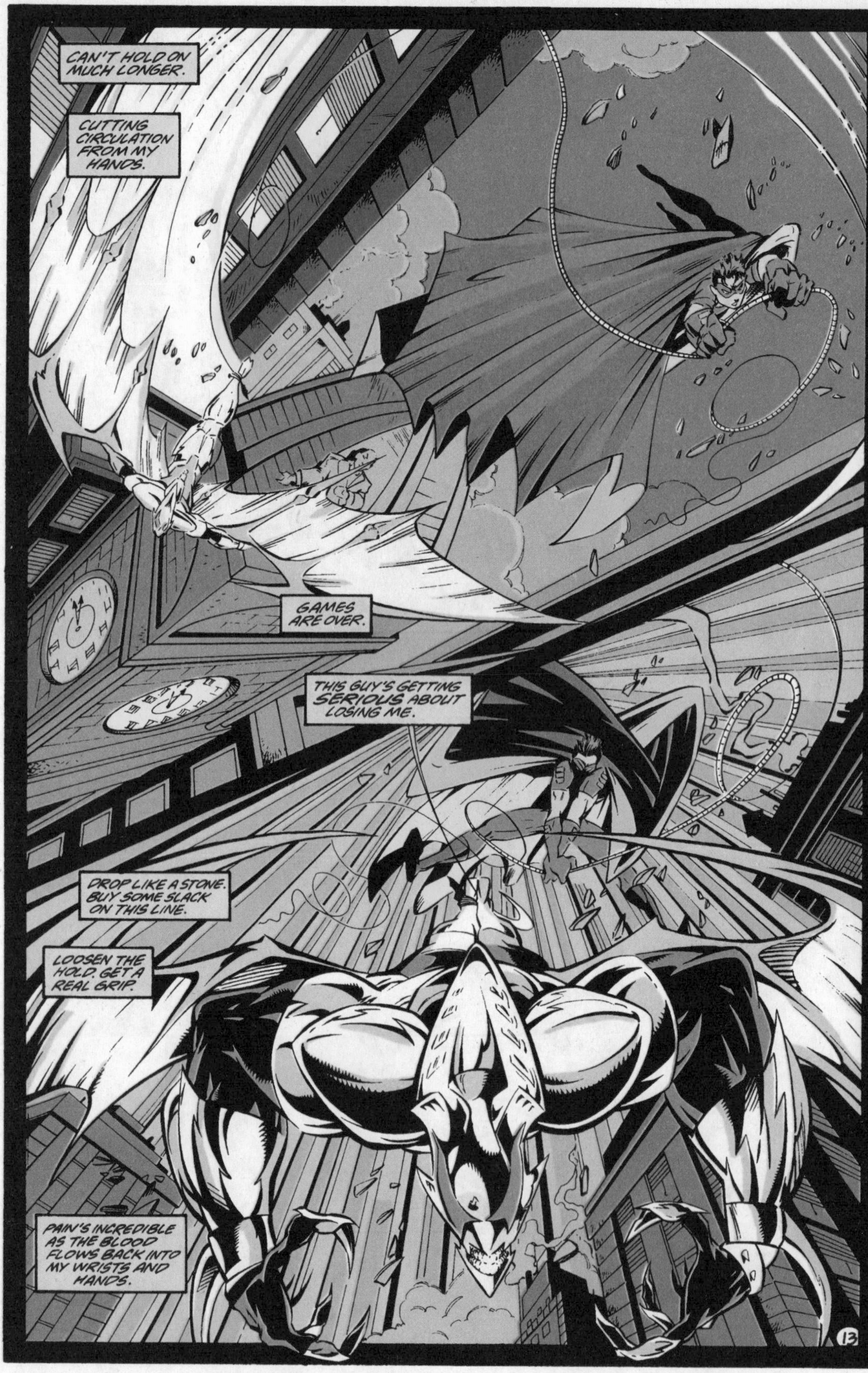
CAN'T HOLD ON MUCH LONGER.
CUTTING CIRCULATION FROM MY HANDS.
GAMES ARE OVER.
THIS GUY'S GETTING SERIOUS ABOUT LOSING ME.
DROP LIKE A STONE. BUY SOME SLACK ON THIS LINE.
LOOSEN THE HOLD. GET A REAL GRIP.
PAIN'S INCREDIBLE AS THE BLOOD FLOWS BACK INTO MY WRISTS AND HANDS.
13

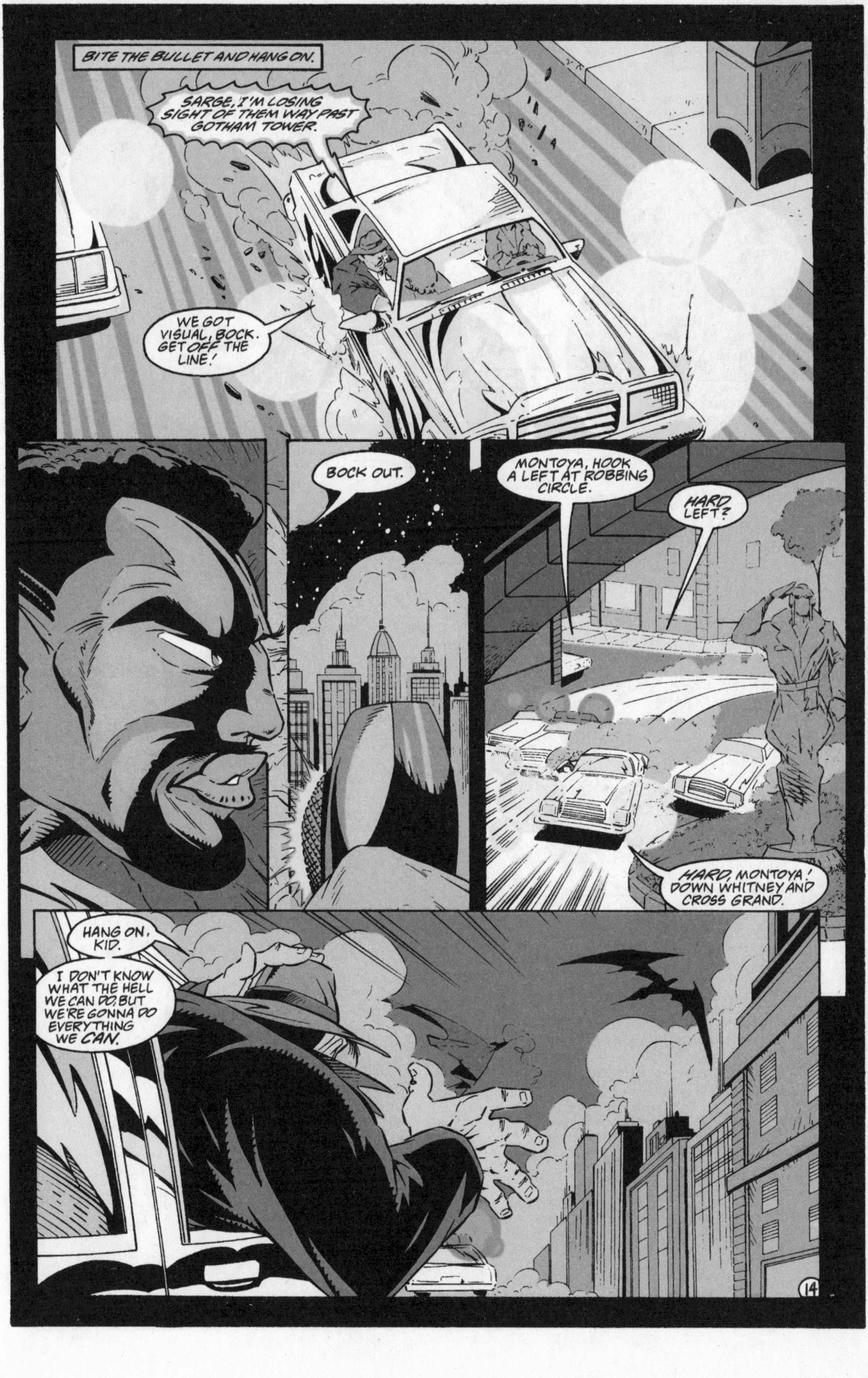
BITE THE BULLET AND HANG ON.
SARGE, I'M LOSING SIGHT OF THEM WAY PAST GOTHAM TOWER.
WE GOT VISUAL, BOCK. GET OFF THE LINE!
BOCK OUT.
MONTOYA, HOOK A LEFT AT ROBBINS CIRCLE.
HARD LEFT?
HARD, MONTOYA! DOWN WHITNEY AND CROSS GRAND.
HANG ON, KID.
I DON'T KNOW WHAT THE HELL WE CAN DO, BUT WE'RE GONNA DO EVERYTHING WE CAN.
14

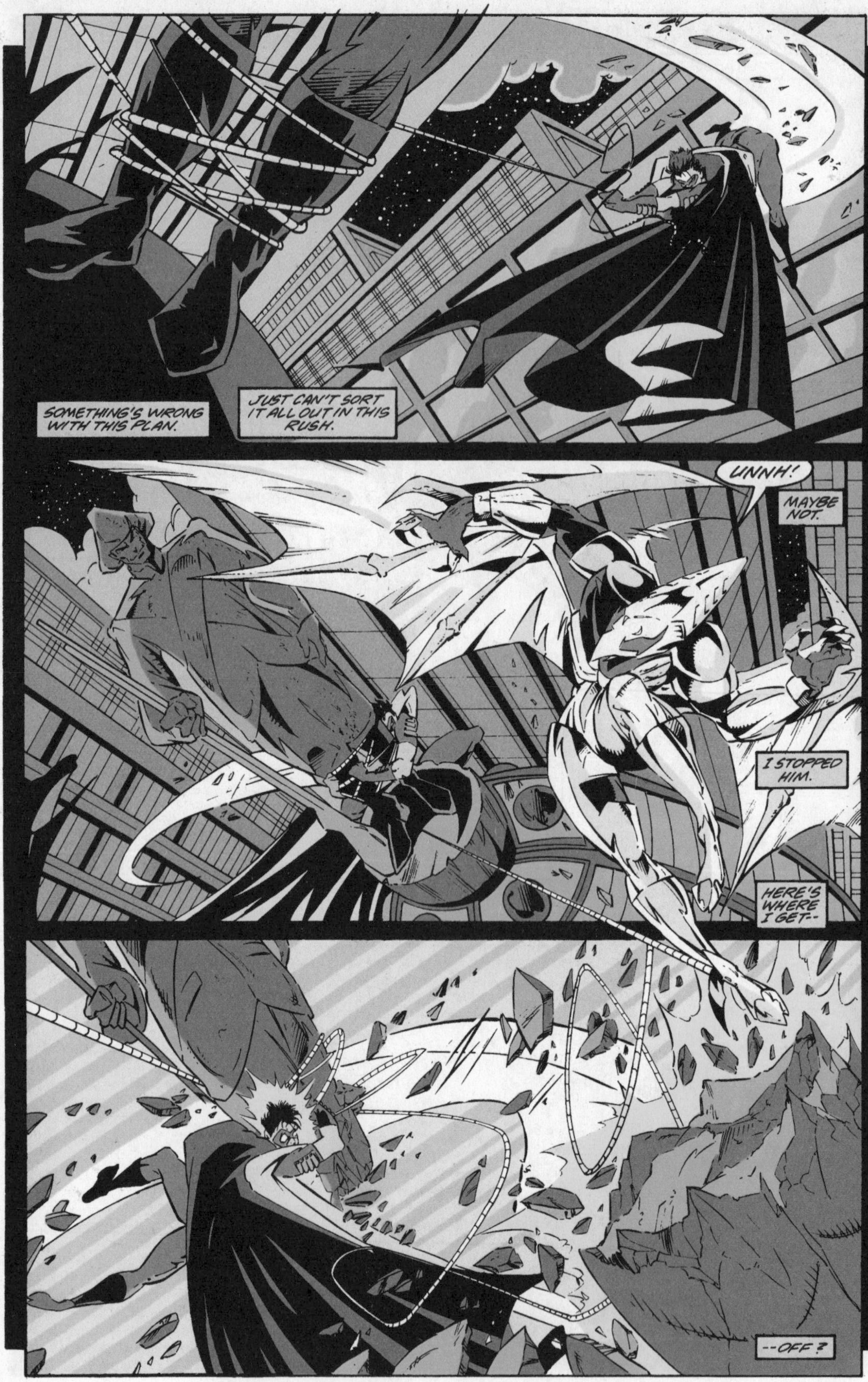
SOMETHING'S WRONG WITH THIS PLAN.
JUST CAN'T SORT IT ALL OUT IN THIS RUSH.
UNNH!
MAYBE NOT.
I STOPPED HIM.
HERE'S WHERE I GET--
--OFF?

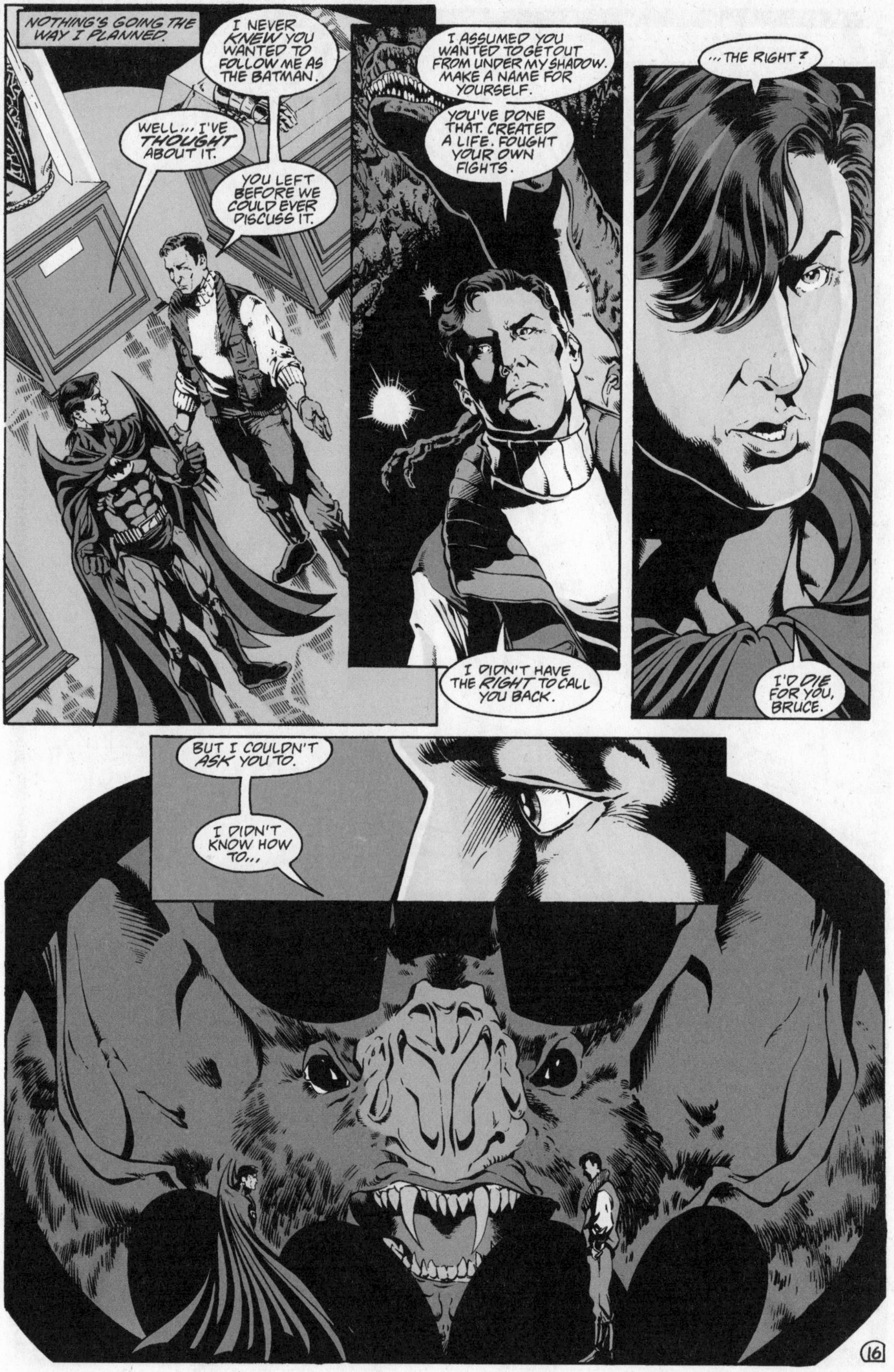
NOTHING'S GOING THE WAY I PLANNED.
I NEVER KNEW YOU WANTED TO FOLLOW ME AS THE BATMAN.
WELL... I'VE THOUGHT ABOUT IT.
YOU LEFT BEFORE WE COULD EVER DISCUSS IT.
I ASSUMED YOU WANTED TO GET OUT FROM UNDER MY SHADOW. MAKE A NAME FOR YOURSELF.
YOU'VE DONE THAT. CREATED A LIFE. FOUGHT YOUR OWN FIGHTS.
I DIDN'T HAVE THE RIGHT TO CALL YOU BACK.
...THE RIGHT?
I'D DIE FOR YOU, BRUCE.
BUT I COULDN'T ASK YOU TO.
I DIDN'T KNOW HOW TO...
16

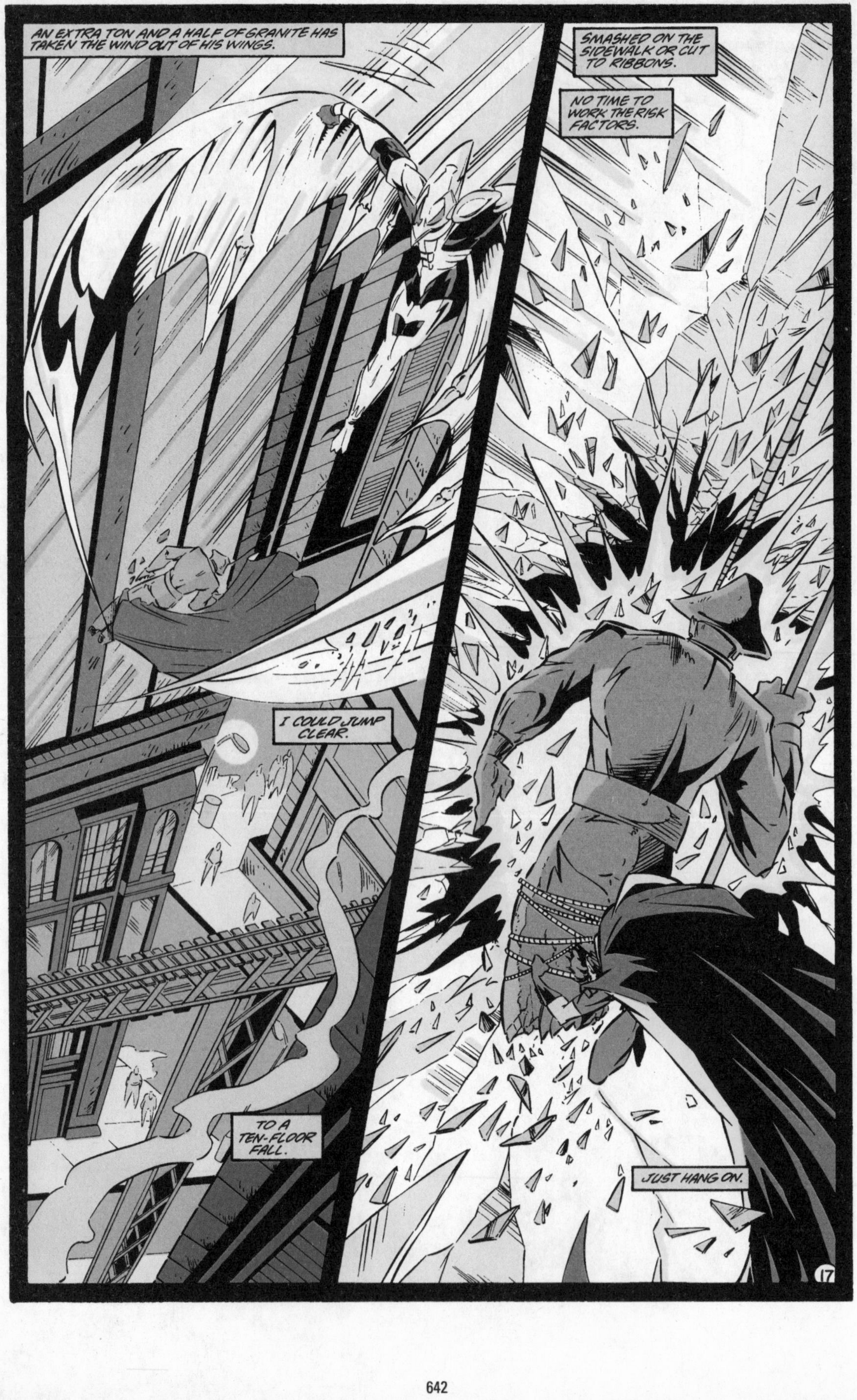
AN EXTRA TON AND A HALF OF GRANITE HAS TAKEN THE WIND OUT OF HIS WINGS.
I COULD JUMP CLEAR.
TO A TEN-FLOOR FALL.
SMASHED ON THE SIDEWALK OR CUT TO RIBBONS.
NO TIME TO WORK THE RISK FACTORS.
JUST HANG ON.
17

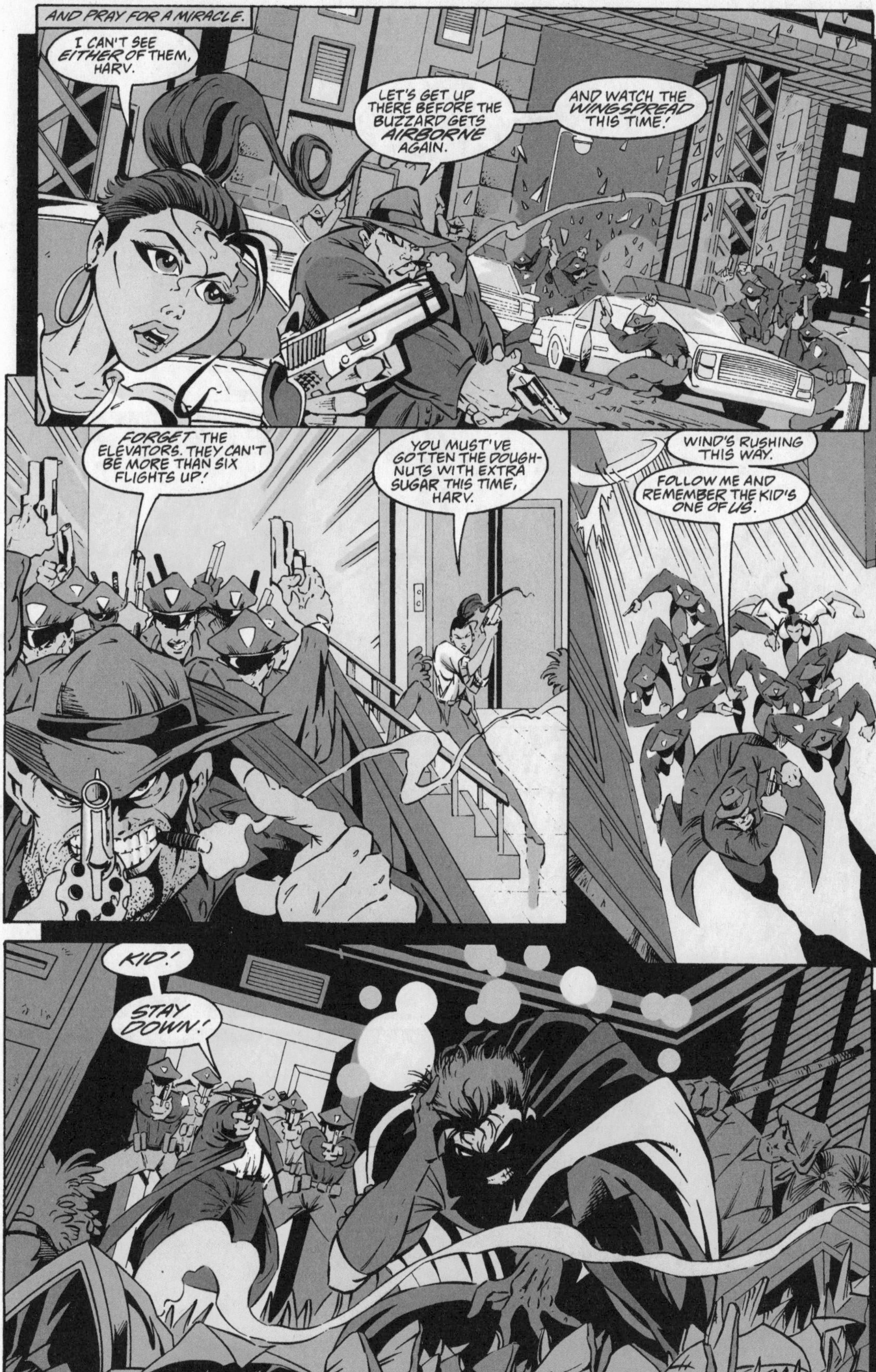
AND PRAY FOR A MIRACLE.
I CAN'T SEE EITHER OF THEM, HARV.
LET'S GET UP THERE BEFORE THE BUZZARD GETS AIRBORNE AGAIN.
AND WATCH THE WINGSPREAD THIS TIME!
FORGET THE ELEVATORS. THEY CAN'T BE MORE THAN SIX FLIGHTS UP!
YOU MUST'VE GOTTEN THE DOUGHNUTS WITH EXTRA SUGAR THIS TIME, HARV.
WIND'S RUSHING THIS WAY.
FOLLOW ME AND REMEMBER THE KID'S ONE OF US.
KID!
STAY DOWN!
18

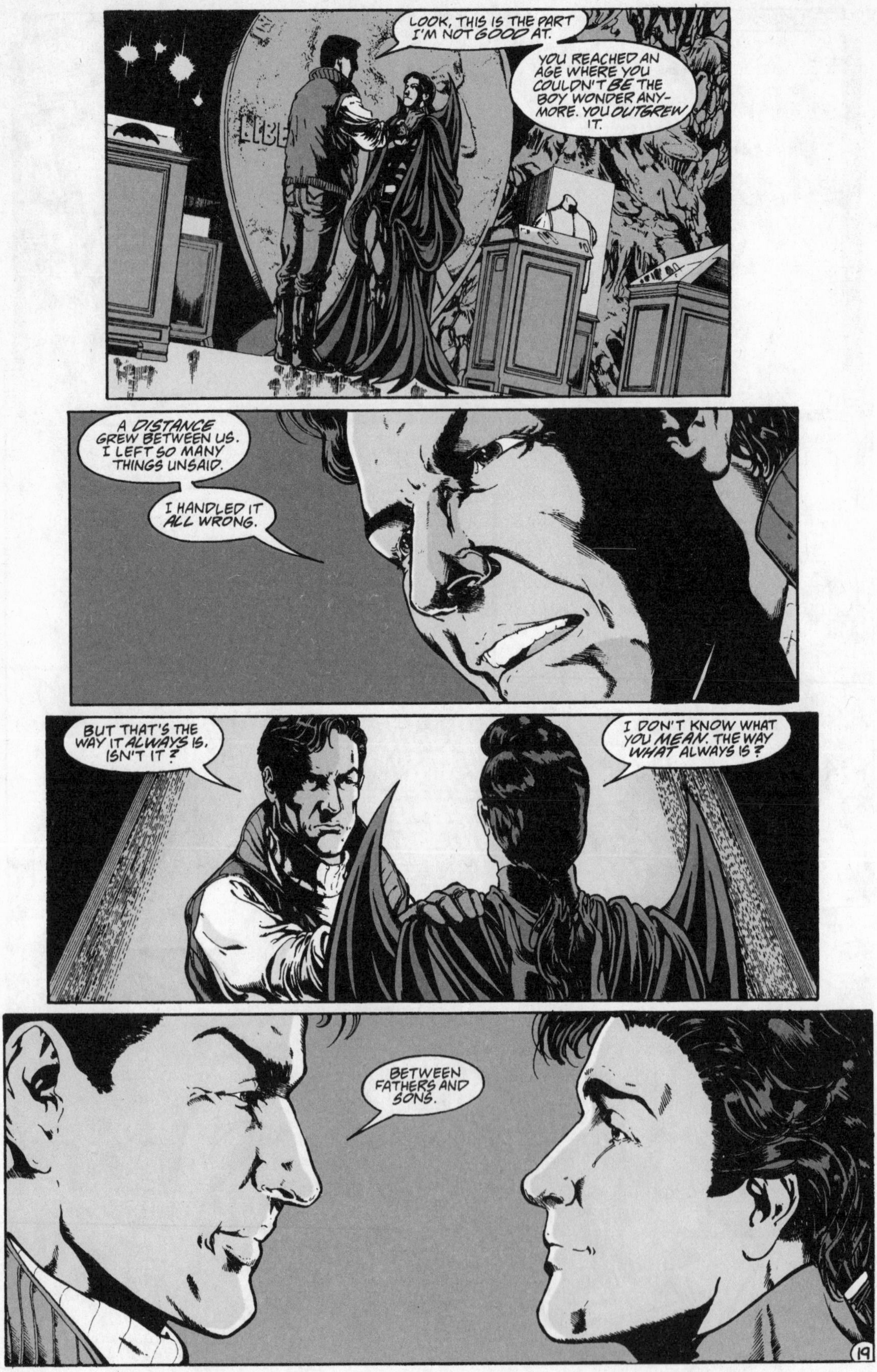
LOOK, THIS IS THE PART I'M NOT GOOD AT.
YOU REACHED AN AGE WHERE YOU COULDN'T BE THE BOY WONDER ANY-MORE. YOU OUTGREW IT.
A DISTANCE GREW BETWEEN US. I LEFT SO MANY THINGS UNSAID.
I HANDLED IT ALL WRONG.
BUT THAT'S THE WAY IT ALWAYS IS, ISN'T IT?
I DON'T KNOW WHAT YOU MEAN. THE WAY WHAT ALWAYS IS?
BETWEEN FATHERS AND SONS.
19

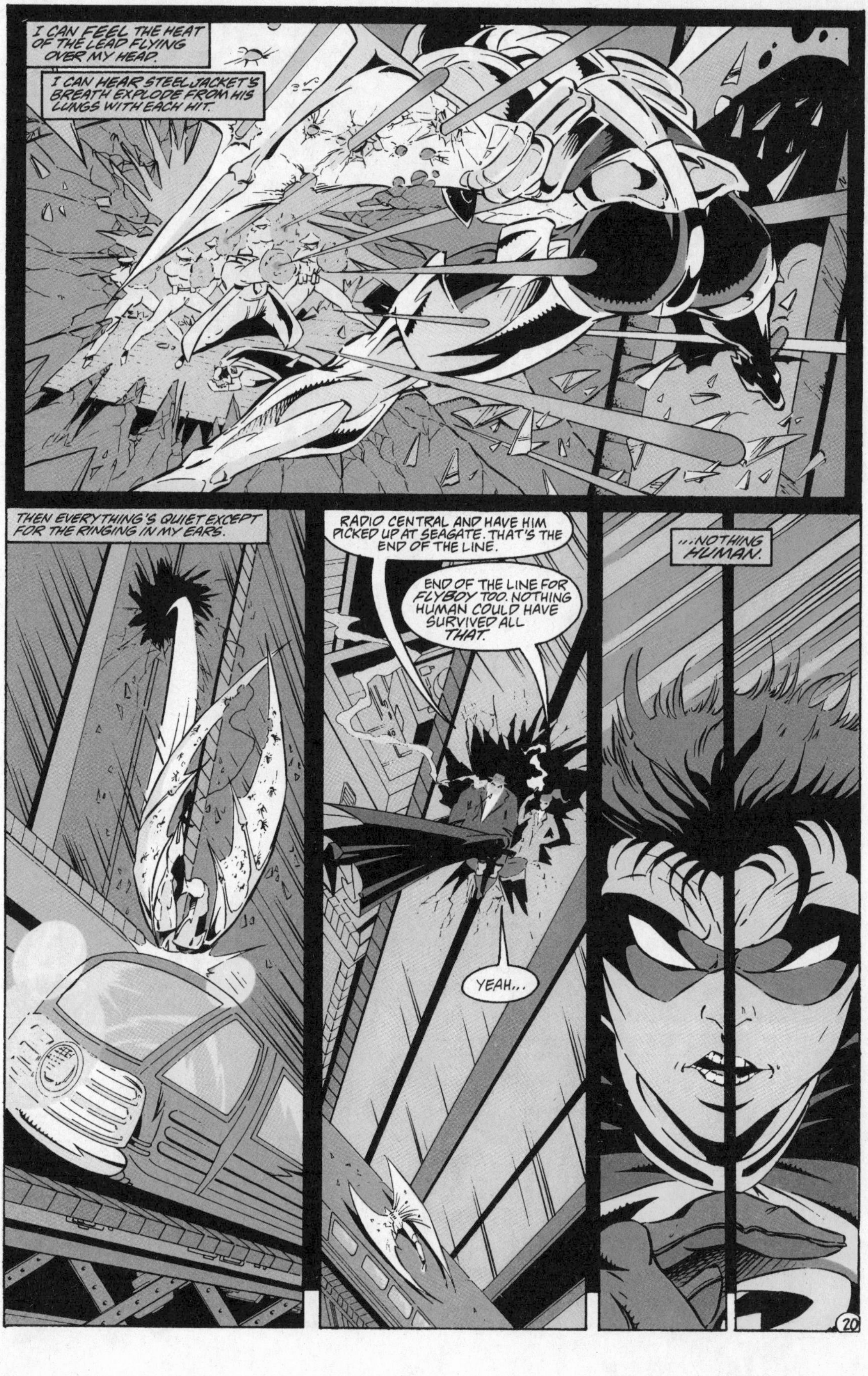
I CAN FEEL THE HEAT OF THE LEAD FLYING OVER MY HEAD.
I CAN HEAR STEELJACKET'S BREATH EXPLODE FROM HIS LUNGS WITH EACH HIT.
THEN EVERYTHING'S QUIET EXCEPT FOR THE RINGING IN MY EARS.
RADIO CENTRAL AND HAVE HIM PICKED UP AT SEAGATE. THAT'S THE END OF THE LINE.
END OF THE LINE FOR FLYBOY TOO. NOTHING HUMAN COULD HAVE SURVIVED ALL THAT.
YEAH...
...NOTHING HUMAN.
20

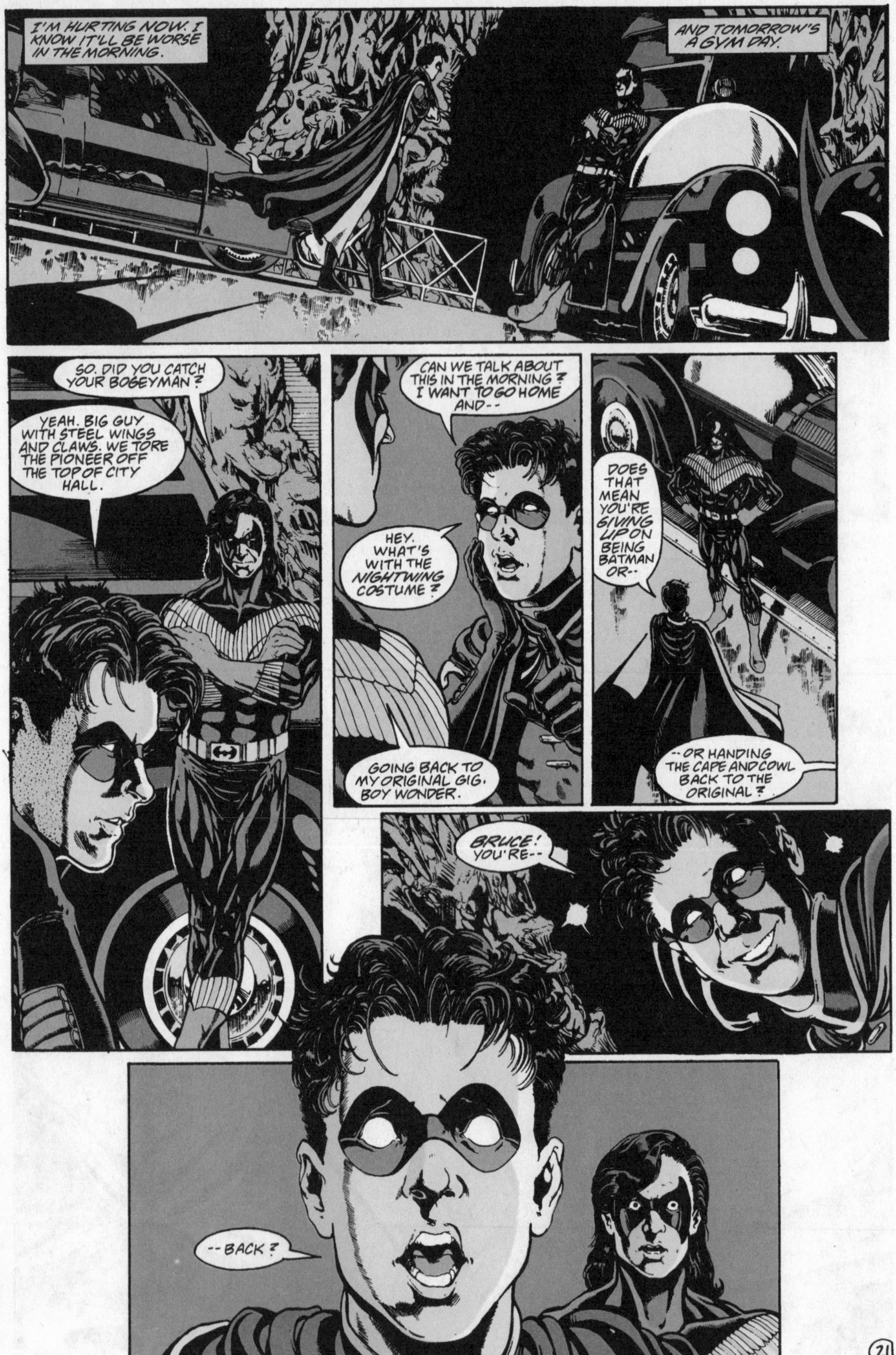
I'M HURTING NOW. I KNOW IT'LL BE WORSE IN THE MORNING.
AND TOMORROW'S A GYM DAY.
SO. DID YOU CATCH YOUR BOGEYMAN?
YEAH. BIG GUY WITH STEEL WINGS AND CLAWS. WE TORE THE PIONEER OFF THE TOP OF CITY HALL.
CAN WE TALK ABOUT THIS IN THE MORNING? I WANT TO GO HOME AND--
HEY. WHAT'S WITH THE NIGHTWING COSTUME?
GOING BACK TO MY ORIGINAL GIG, BOY WONDER.
DOES THAT MEAN YOU'RE GIVING UP ON BEING BATMAN OR--
--OR HANDING THE CAPE AND COWL BACK TO THE ORIGINAL?
BRUCE! YOU'RE--
--BACK?
21

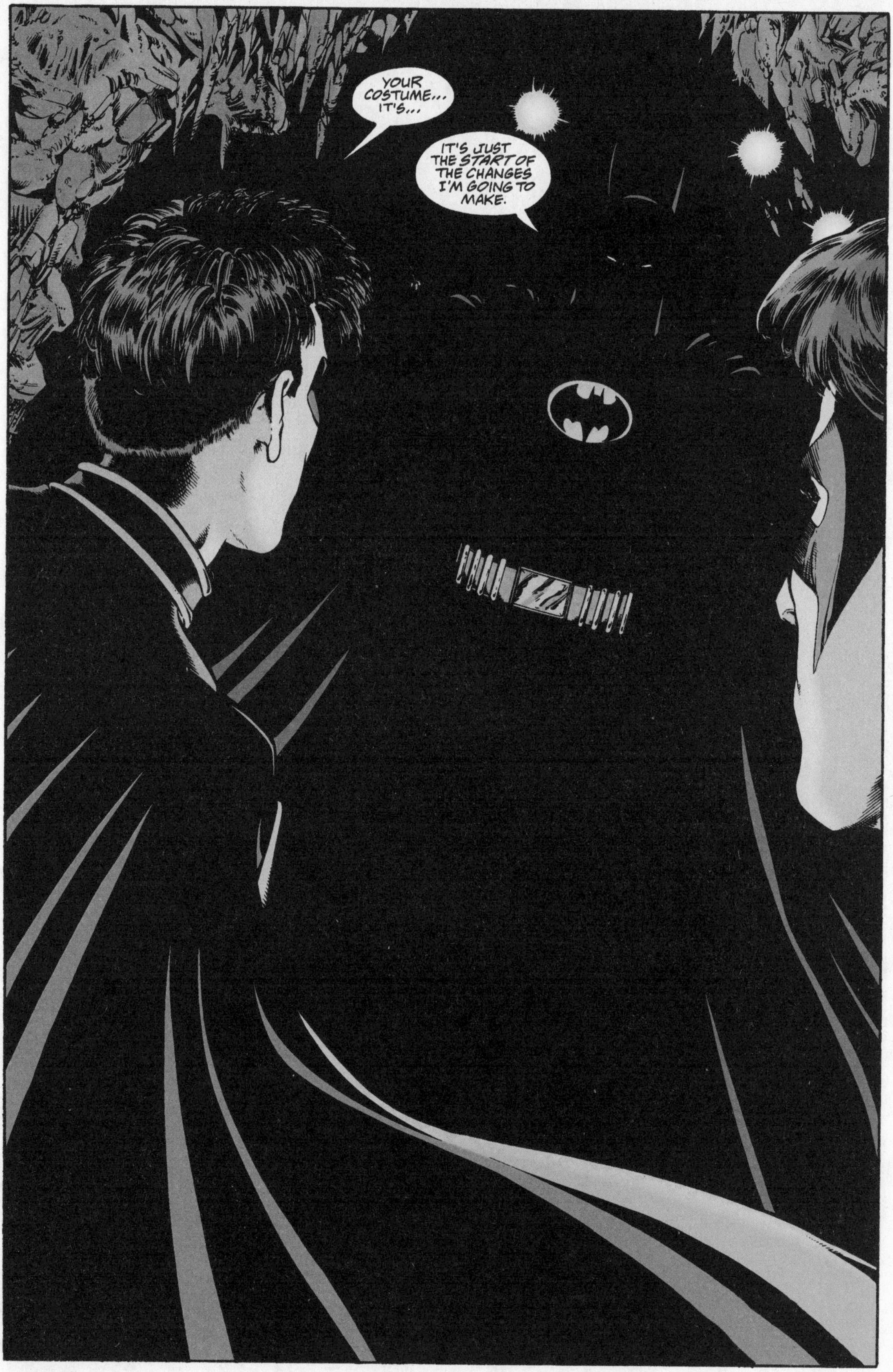
YOUR COSTUME... IT'S...
IT'S JUST THE START OF THE CHANGES I'M GOING TO MAKE.

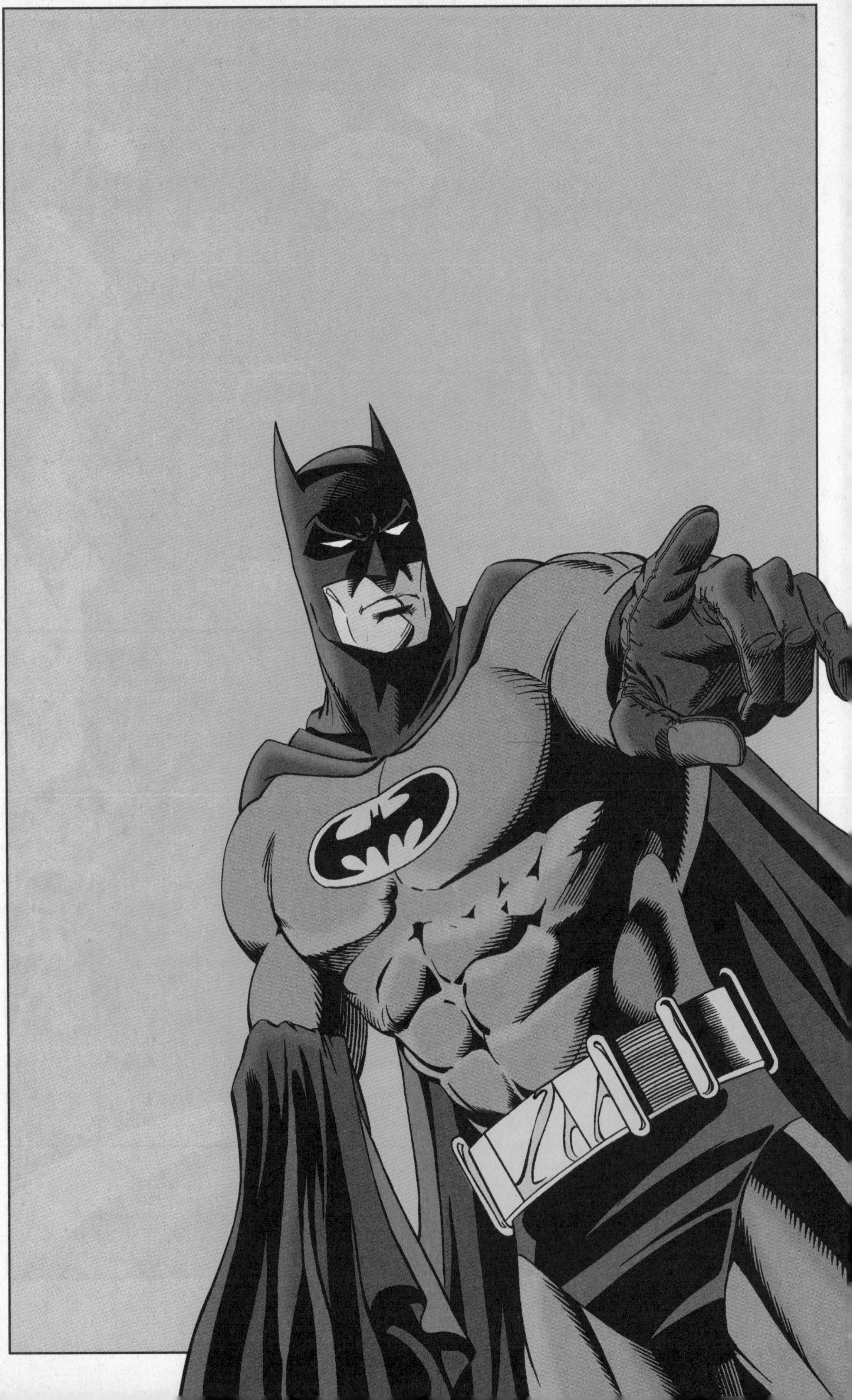

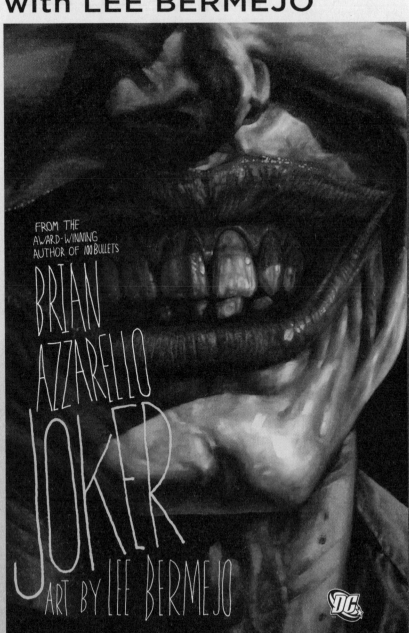

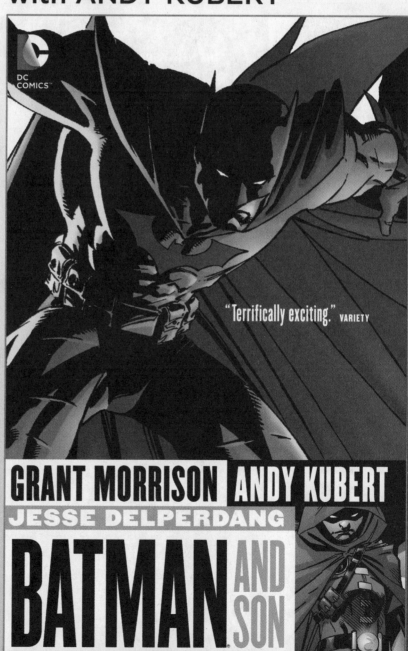

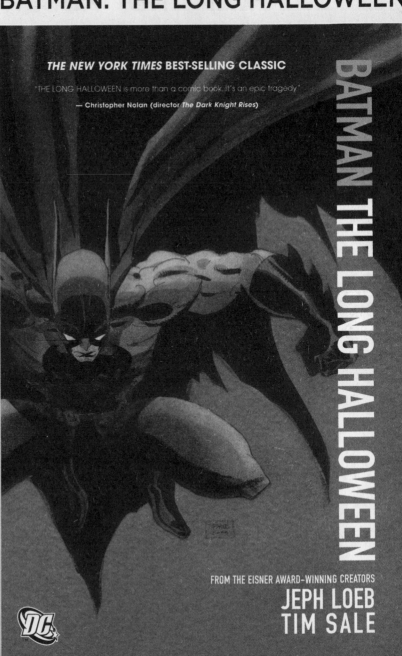